89.50

D0207498

PLACE IN RETURN BOX to remove this checkout from your record.
TO AVOID FINES return on or before date due.

DATE DUE	DATE DUE	DATE DUE
NOV 2 2 2005 / 1 1 0 2 0 5	_____	_____
_____	_____	_____
_____	_____	_____
_____	_____	_____
_____	_____	_____
_____	_____	_____
_____	_____	_____

MSU Is An Affirmative Action/Equal Opportunity Institution

c:\circ\datedue.pm3-p.1

Biographical Dictionary of
American Sports

1992–1995 SUPPLEMENT
FOR
BASEBALL, FOOTBALL, BASKETBALL,
AND OTHER SPORTS

Biographical Dictionary of American Sports

1992–1995 SUPPLEMENT FOR BASEBALL, FOOTBALL, BASKETBALL, AND OTHER SPORTS

Edited by David L. Porter

GREENWOOD PRESS

Westport, Connecticut • London

Library of Congress Cataloging-in-Publication Data

Biographical dictionary of American sports.   1992–1995 supplement for
   baseball, football, basketball, and other sports / edited by David
   L. Porter.
       p.   cm.
    Includes bibliographical references.
    ISBN 0–313–28431–8 (alk. paper)
       1. Athletes—United States—Biography—Dictionaries.   I. Porter,
   David L.
   GV697.A1B494   1995
   796'.092'2—dc20
   [B]   94–27941

British Library Cataloguing in Publication Data is available.

Copyright © 1995 by David L. Porter

All rights reserved. No portion of this book may be
reproduced, by any process or technique, without the
express written consent of the publisher.

Library of Congress Catalog Card Number: 94–27941
ISBN: 0–313–28431–8

First published in 1995

Greenwood Press, 88 Post Road West, Westport, CT 06881
An imprint of Greenwood Publishing Group, Inc.

Printed in the United States of America

The paper used in this book complies with the
Permanent Paper Standard issued by the National
Information Standards Organization (Z39.48–1984).

10 9 8 7 6 5 4 3 2 1

Contents

Preface

The first five volumes of this series were published between 1987 and 1992 and included over 2,700 biographies of notable American sports figures. This volume covers 616 additional distinguished American sports personalities from auto and stock car racing (14), baseball (202), basketball (58), bowling (8), boxing (10), communications (26), football (181), golf (14), horse racing (10), ice hockey (15), shooting (4), skating (6), skiing (4), swimming (10), tennis and other racquet sports (16), track and field (29), wrestling (4), and miscellaneous sports (5), including cycling (2), equestrianism (1), gymnastics (1), and yachting (1). Thirty female athletes, including 6 golfers, 4 skaters, 4 swimmers, 4 tennis or other racquet sports players, 3 bowlers, 3 skiers, 3 track and field participants, 2 basketball coaches, and 1 gymnast, appear in this volume.

The subjects made distinguished achievements as amateur and/or professional sports athletes, managers, coaches, umpires, club officials, league administrators, rules developers, writers, or broadcasters. Entries appear alphabetically by sport and range from 200 to 600 words. The subjects performed since the 1870s, with the vast majority in the 20th century. Most of the individuals are either deceased or retired, but many remain active in athletics as of January 1995.

Nearly every entry met three general criteria. First, he or she either was born in or spent childhood years in the United States. Some foreign-born figures who did not reside in the United States until adulthood but nonetheless played major roles in the development of a particular sport also are included. Second, the subject must have made exceptional career accomplishments in one or more amateur and/or professional sports. Memberships in halls of fame; notable statistical achievements and records; significant honors, awards, or medals won; and participation on championship teams provided the principal measurement standards. Third, the figure must have made a significant impact on at least one major sport. Contemporary athletes who entered American sports after 1985 usually have been excluded but may appear in future volumes. Notable exceptions have been made concerning star American athletes from the 1988 and 1992 Summer Olympic Games and the 1988, 1992, and 1994 Winter Olympic Games.

Selection of the biographical entries proved challenging. Before making final choices, the editor thoroughly researched sports encyclopedias and halls of fame, records, and history books[1] and consulted authorities on particular sports.

1. Many subjects belong to one or more sports halls of fame, including the National Baseball Hall of Fame, National Football Foundation (NFF) College Football Hall of Fame, Pro Football Hall of Fame, Naismith Memorial Basketball Hall of Fame, U.S. Track and Field Hall of Fame, Professional Golfers Association (PGA) World Golf Hall of Fame, Ladies Professional Golfers Association (LPGA) Hall of Fame, International (formerly National Lawn) Tennis Hall of Fame, National Museum of Racing (NMR) Hall of Fame, U.S. Hockey Hall of Fame, Indianapolis Motor Speedway Hall of Fame, International Motorsports Hall of Fame, International Boxing Hall of Fame, American Bowling Congress (AmBC) Hall of Fame, Professional Bowlers Association (PBA) Hall of Fame, Women's International Bowling Congress (WIBC) Hall of Fame, National Wrestling Hall of Fame, U.S. Olympic Hall of Fame, National Sportscasters and Sportswriters (NASS) Hall of Fame, American Sportscasters Association (ASA) Hall of Fame, Helms Athletic Foundation (HAF Citizens Savings Bank) Hall of Fame, or the International Women's Sports (formerly Women's Sports Foundation) Hall of Fame.

2. Many earned major athletic honors, including Most Valuable Player (MVP), Player of the Year, All-American, All-League, or All-Conference, Rookie of the Year, and/or Coach or Manager of the Year, and/or Sportscaster or Sportswriter of the Year. Other accolades include the Cy Young and Gold Glove awards in baseball; the Heisman Trophy and Maxwell, Lombardi, and Outland awards in college football; the John R. Wooden Award in college basketball, the Podoloff Cup in professional basketball; the Vare or Vardon trophies in golf; the Eclipse Award in horse racing; the Calder, Norris, Vezina, and Lady Byng trophies in ice hockey; the U.S. Auto Club (USAC) Award for auto racing; the Winston Cup for National Association for Stock Car Auto Racing (NASCAR); the Edward J. Neil Trophy and James J. Walker Award in boxing; and the Sullivan Memorial Trophy and Hickok Award in various sports.

3. Many excelled in Olympic competition, winning gold, silver, and/or bronze medals in basketball, boxing, cycling, equestrianism, figure skating, gymnastics, ice hockey, shooting, skiing, speed skating, swimming, track and field, or wrestling; and/or represented the United States in international competitions, including the Ryder, Walker, or Curtis cups in golf;

the Davis or Wightman cups in tennis; the World Tournament or Canada Cup in ice hockey; or the Pan-American, Goodwill, or World Games in various sports.

4. Many compiled outstanding statistical achievements, setting records and/or winning major races, tournaments, or championships. In baseball, hitters often compiled impressive lifetime batting averages and/or supplied considerable power. Some demonstrated remarkable fielding and/or running abilities. Pitchers won numerous major league games, achieved outstanding win–loss percentages, and boasted excellent earned run averages. Baseball players frequently appeared in All-Star Games, Championship Series, and/or World Series contests. Football players often accomplished outstanding offensive feats and ranked high in career National Collegiate Athletic Association (NCAA), college conference, and/or professional league rushing, passing, and receiving yardage and touchdowns scored. Some also starred as kickoff, punt, or extra point specialists. Defensively, they excelled in tackles, quarterback sacks, and/or interceptions. A considerable number participated in college bowl or All-Star Games or Pro Bowl, postseason playoff, and Super Bowl games. Basketball players often led their conferences or leagues in scoring, rebounds, assists, and/or blocked shots and performed in NCAA and/or National Invitational Tournament (NIT) postseason events and National Basketball Association (NBA) All-Star Games and playoffs. Ice hockey players frequently starred in NCAA, All-Star Game, or Stanley Cup playoff competitions. Track and field entrants, auto or stock car racers, golfers, skaters, swimmers, bowlers, shooters, or wrestlers established world or U.S. records. Auto or stock car racers won the Indianapolis 500, Daytona 500, or other prestigious events, while thoroughbred trainers prepared Kentucky Derby, Preakness Stakes, and Belmont Stakes winners. Tennis players frequently excelled in the U.S. Open, Wimbledon, and/or other major tournaments, while golfers typically fared well at the Masters, PGA, U.S. Open, British Open, LPGA, U.S. Women's Open, du Maurier, and/or Dinah Shore tournaments. Bowlers scored well in the Bowling Proprietor's Association of America (BPAA) U.S. Men's or Women's Open, Professional Bowlers Association (PBA) Men's or Women's Professional Bowlers Association (WPBA) Tournament of Champions, PBA or WPBA National Championship, American Bowling Congress (AmBC) Masters Tournament, and/or the Women's International Bowling Congress (WIBC) Queens Tournament. NCAA, AAU, and/or TAC titles were earned by some golfers, swimmers, track and field performers, tennis players, and wrestlers.

5. Many of the athletes profoundly influenced the development of their respective sports or were selected to all-time or all-decade lists of greatest performers.

Members of the Society for American Baseball Research (SABR), Pro Football Researchers Association (PFRA), and the North American Society for Sport History (NASSH) helped facilitate the selection process. I am indebted to Bob Carroll and James D. Whalen for helping me immeasurably in determining the professional and college football entries. Roger A. Godin, Adolph H. Grundman, Adam R. Hornbuckle, and Frank V. Phelps provided invaluable assistance in selecting the ice hockey, Amateur Athletic Union (AAU) basketball, track and field, and tennis/racquet sports entries, respectively. Others suggesting biographical subjects included Ronald Crosbie for college basketball, Richard Gonsalves and Edward Pavlick for professional football, James W. Harper for communications, Frederick Ivor-Campbell for baseball, and David DeLorenzo for bowling. Richard Topp of SABR supplied valuable background material on several baseball entries.

Eighty-eight contributors, mostly members of NASSH, SABR, PFRA, the Popular Culture Association, and/or other professional sport history organizations, submitted biographical entries. Numerous contributors are university or college professors, including amateur and/or professional sports authorities teaching courses in American sport history. Public and private school teachers and administrators, writers, publishers, editors, journalists, librarians, consultants, businesspeople, and government employees also participated. Contributors are listed after each entry, then cited alphabetically with occupational affiliation, if known, following the index.

Entries usually indicate the sport subject's (1) full given name at birth; (2) date and place of birth and, when applicable, date and place of death; (3) parental background; (4) formal education; (5) spouse and children, when applicable; and (6) major personal characteristics. Authors searched extensively for this often-elusive data but frequently could not find complete biographical information. Entries feature the subject's sports career through January 1995 and usually include information about his or her (1) entrance into amateur and/or professional sports; (2) career statistical achievements; (3) records set; (4) awards or medals won; and (5) personal impact on a given sport. For figures competing in team sports, entries include the person's (1) positions played; (2) teams performed for, with respective conferences and leagues;[2] (3) All-Star Game appearances and selections; and (4) postseason playoff performances. Biographical and statistical data often proved elusive for Negro League baseball players and other nineteenth- and early twentieth-century athletes. Entries on managers or coaches usually include their (1) teams guided, with inclusive dates; (2) major statistical achievements; (3) career win–loss records, with percentages; (4) premier players coached; and (5) coaching philosophy, strategy, and innovations. Biographies of club executives, league officials, sportswriters, and sportscasters describe their various positions held, notable accomplishments, and impact on their particular sport or sports.

Several additional features are included. First, brief bibliographies list pertinent sources about each biographical subject. Authors frequently benefited from interviews or correspondence with the biographical subject and/or his or her relatives and acquaintances. The National Baseball Hall of Fame, Pro

Football Hall of Fame, NFF College Football Hall of Fame, Naismith Memorial Basketball Hall of Fame, U.S. Hockey Hall of Fame, AmBC Hall of Fame, and other halls of fame; *The Sporting News* (*TSN*); college, university, and public libraries; college and university alumni and athletic offices; athletic associations; the U.S. Olympic Committee (USOC); newspapers and magazines; and radio and television networks provided significant information to essay contributors. Second, whenever an essay cites a subject covered elsewhere in this book, an asterisk follows the person's name. If an individual appears in a previous volume, the work is noted in parentheses as follows: (BB) for Baseball, (FB) for Football, (IS) for Basketball and other Indoor Sports, (OS) for Outdoor Sports, and (S) for the 1989–1992 Supplement. Third, for the sake of consistency, married female athletes usually are listed by their last married name. Fourth, the appendices include (1) an alphabetical listing of biographical entries; (2) entries by particular sport; (3) entries by place of birth; (4) women athletes by sport; (5) maiden names of married women athletes; (6) major sports halls of fame; and (7) locations of Summer and Winter Olympic Games.

The editor deeply appreciates the enormous amount of time, energy, and effort expended by contributors in searching for biographical information. I am particularly indebted to John L. Evers and Adam R. Hornbuckle, who each contributed over 20 entries. Stan W. Carlson, Scott A.G.M. Crawford, Roger A. Godin, Frederick Ivor-Campbell, Brian L. Laughlin, Frank J. Olmsted, Frank V. Phelps, Jim L. Sumner, and James D. Whalen each wrote 10 to 20 entries, while Carl M. Becker, William A. Borst, Robert N. "Bob" Carroll, Larry R. Gerlach, Bill Mallon, Douglas A. Noverr, and Robert B. Van Atta each submitted 9 or 10 entries. Former baseball players John Antonelli, Frank Crosetti, Anthony "Tony" Cuccinello, Linus "Lonny" Frey, Ned Garver, William Jurges, Donald Kessinger, George "Whitey" Kurowski, Hubert "Max" Lanier, Don Larsen, Gilbert McDougald, Donald Money, Wallace "Wally" Moon, Gary Peters, Robert "Bobby" Richardson, George "Birdie" Tebbetts, and John Whitlow Wyatt, football player David Brown, bowler Joseph Norris, and other subjects graciously furnished biographical data. Others supplying invaluable biographical data include Andrew E. Clark III for auto racing, Wayne Patterson for basketball, David DeLorenzo and Charles "Chuck" Pezzano for bowling, James D. Whalen for college football, and Heather Linhart for Olympians. William Penn College librarians Julie Hansen, Jim Hollis, Jim Knutson, and Lauran Lofgren provided considerable assistance, while former William Penn College Academic Dean David Throgmorton and William Penn College faculty members gave encouragement. Cynthia Harris, Susan Badger, and Karen Davis furnished adept guidance and made numerous valuable suggestions in the planning and writing of this volume. My wife, Marilyn, and children, Kevin and Andrea, again demonstrated considerable patience, understanding, and support throughout the project.

NOTES

1. Sources listed in the first five volumes were consulted in preparing this volume. Additional works examined are listed below. Mike Meserole, ed., *The 1994 Information Please Sports Almanac* (Boston, MA, 1994) and *The Sports Illustrated 1994 Sports Almanac* (Boston, MA, 1994) provided invaluable data. Baseball reference sources included *The Baseball Encyclopedia*, 9th ed. (New York, 1993); *The Complete 1994 Baseball Record Book* (St. Louis, MO, 1994); Bill James, *The Baseball Book 1992* (New York, 1992); David Neft and Richard Cohen, eds., *The Sports Encyclopedia: Baseball* (New York, 1993); *1994 American League Red Book* (St. Louis, MO, 1994); *1994 Baseball Almanac* (New York, 1994); *1994 National League Green Book* (St. Louis, MO, 1994); Mike Shatzkin, ed., *The Ballplayers* (New York, 1990); Seymour Siwoff et al., *The 1994 Elias Baseball Analyst* (New York, 1994); *The Sporting News Official Baseball Guide, 1994* (St. Louis, MO, 1994); *The Sporting News Official Baseball Register, 1994* (St. Louis, MO, 1994); and John Thorn and Pete Palmer, eds., *Total Baseball*, 3rd ed. (New York, 1993). For college and professional football, see David S. Neft and Richard M. Cohen, eds., *The Sports Encyclopedia: Pro Football* (New York, 1991); *1993 NCAA Football* (Overland Park, KS, 1992); *The Sporting News Pro Football Guide, 1994* (St. Louis, MO, 1994); *The Sporting News Pro Football Register, 1994* (St. Louis, MO, 1994); and *The Sporting News Super Bowl Book, 1994* (St. Louis, MO, 1994). College and professional basketball reference works included *1994 NCAA Basketball* (New York 1994); David S. Neft and Richard M. Cohen, eds., *Sports Encyclopedia: Pro Basketball*, 5th ed. (New York, 1992); *1993 NCAA Basketball* (New York, 1993); *1993–1994 Basketball Almanac* (New York, 1993); *The Sporting News Official NBA Guide, 1993–1994* (St. Louis, MO, 1993); and *The Sporting News Official NBA Register, 1993–1994* (St. Louis, MO, 1993). Dave Elshoff, ed., *1993 Indy-Car Media Guide* (Bloomfield Hills, MI, 1993); Bob Laycock et al., eds., *1993 Indianapolis 500 Media Fact Book* (Indianapolis, IN, 1993); Ty Norris, ed., *1993 Winston Cup Media Guide* (Winston-Salem, NC, 1993); and Rich Taylor, *Indy: 75 Years of Racing's Greatest Spectacle* (New York, 1991) supplied material on auto and stock car racers, while the American Bowling Congress, *American Bowling Congress Yearbook and Media Guide 1993* (Greendale, WI, 1993); *Bowlers Journal Annual* (Chicago, IL, 1994); Ladies Pro Bowlers Tour, *Ladies Pro Bowlers Tour Guide 1993* (Rockford, IL, 1993); and Professional Bowlers Association, *Professional Bowlers Association Press-Radio-TV Guide 1993* (Akron, OH, 1993) furnished data on bowlers. Golf sources included Gerald Astor, *The PGA World Golf Hall of Fame Book* (New York, 1991); Malcolm Campbell, *The Random House International Encyclopedia of Golf* (New York, 1991); Rhonda Glenn, *The Illustrated History of Women's Golf* (Dallas, TX, 1991); Ladies Professional Golf Association, *LPGA Player Guide 1993* (Daytona Beach, FL, 1993); *1993 Golf Almanac* (New York, 1993); Professional Golfers Association, *Official PGA Tour Book 1993* (Ponte Vedra, FL, 1993); and *Official Senior PGA Tour Book 1993* (Ponte Vedra, FL, 1993). Tennis sources included Pete Alfano et al., eds., *Official ATP Tour Player Guide 1993* (Ponte Vedra Beach, FL, 1993) and United States Tennis Association, *Official USTA Tennis Yearbook 1993* (Lynn, MA, 1993). *The Sporting News Complete Hockey Book, 1993–1994* (St. Louis, MO, 1993) provided invaluable information on ice hockey figures. For horse racing, Breeders Cup Limited, *Breeder's Cup Statistics 1993* (Lexington, KY, 1993); Churchill Downs Public Relations Department, *Kentucky*

Derby Media Guide 1993 (Louisville, KY, 1993); Maryland Jockey Club, *Preakness Press Guide 1993* (Baltimore, MD, 1993); and Thoroughbred Racing Associations of North America, *1993 Directory and Record Book* (Elkton, MD, 1993) furnished important data. Track and field sources consulted included Peter Matthews, *Athletics 1993* (Berkshire, England, 1993) and Roberto Quercetani, *Athletics: A History of Modern Track and Field* (Milan, Italy, 1990), while Olympic sources included William Oscar Johnson, *The Olympics: A History of the Games* (Birmingham, AL, 1992); Bill Mallon, *The Olympic Record Book* (New York, 1988); and David Wallechinsky, *The Complete Book of the Olympics* (Boston, MA, 1992). General biographical reference sources were Ralph Hickok, *The Encyclopedia of North American Sports History* (New York, 1992) and Joseph Vecchione, *The New York Times Book of Sports Legends* (New York, 1991).

2. Professional baseball major leagues represented include the National Association of Professional Baseball Players (1871–1875), National League (1876–), American Association (1882–1891), Union Association of Baseball Clubs (1884), Players League (1890), American League (1901–), Federal League (1914–1915), Negro National League (1920–1931, 1933–1948), Eastern Colored League (1923–1928), and Negro American League (1933–1950). Major college football and/or basketball conferences encompassed the Atlantic Coast, Atlantic Ten, Big East, Big Eight (formerly Missouri Valley, Big Six, Big Seven), Big Ten (formerly Western, Big Nine), Big West, Border, East–West Athletic, Ivy League, Metro, Mid-American, Missouri Valley, Pacific Coast, Pacific Ten (formerly Pacific Eight), Rocky Mountain, Skyline (formerly Mountain States Athletic), Southeastern, Southern, Southwest Athletic, Sun Belt, and Western Athletic Conference. Professional football leagues include the National Football League (1919–), American Football League (1926, 1936–1937, 1940–1941, 1960–1969), All-American Football Conference (1946–1949), World Football League (1974–1975), United States Football League (1984–1985), and World League of American Football (1991–). The National Basketball League (1898–1903), Philadelphia Basketball League (1902–1909), Western Pennsylvania Basketball League (1903–1904, 1912–1913, 1914–1915), Central Basketball League (1906–1912), Eastern League (1909–1918, 1919–1923, 1931–1933), Hudson River League (1909–1912), New York State League (1911–1915, 1916–1917, 1919–1923), Pennsylvania State League (1914–1918, 1919–1921), Interstate League (1915–1917, 1919–1920), Connecticut State League (1917–1919, 1920–1921), Metropolitan Basketball League (1921–1928, 1931–1933), American Basketball League (1925–1931, 1933–1946), National Basketball League (1926–1927, 1929–1930, 1932–1933, 1937–1949), Midwest Basketball Conference (1935–1937), Basketball Association of America (1946–1949), Professional Basketball League of America (1947–1948), National Basketball Association (1949–), and American Basketball Association (1967–1976) compose the main professional basketball leagues. Professional ice hockey leagues include the Pacific Coast Hockey Association, the National Hockey League, the American Hockey League, and the Central Hockey League.

Abbreviations

GENERAL*

AA	American Association
AAU	Amateur Athletic Union
ABA	American Basketball Association
ABC	American Broadcasting Company
ABL	American Basketball League
AC	Athletic Club
ACC	Atlantic Coast Conference
AFL	American Football League
AIAW	Association of Intercollegiate Athletics for Women
AL	American League
AmBC	American Bowling Congress
AMC	America's Cup
AP	Associated Press
AtA	Athletic Association
BBWAA	Baseball Writers Association of America
BC	Border Conference
BEaC	Big East Conference
BEC	Big Eight Conference (also Missouri Valley Intercollegiate Athletic Conference, formerly BSC)
BNC	Big Nine Conference
BSAC	Big Sky Athletic Conference
BSC	Big Six Conference (also Missouri Valley Intercollegiate Athletic Conference)
BTC	Big Ten Conference (also WC, formerly BNC)

*These abbreviations appear in more than one section.

CaCAA	California Collegiate Athletic Association
CBS	Columbia Broadcasting System
CC	Community College
ECAC	Eastern Collegiate Athletic Conference
EL	Eastern League
ESPN	Eastern Sports Network
FBC	Fox Broadcasting Corporation
FCA	Fellowship of Christian Athletes
HAF	Helms Athletic Foundation (Citizens Savings Bank)
H of F	Hall of Fame
IBC	International Boxing Club
IC4A	Intercollegiate Association of Amateur Athletics of America
IL	International League
INS	International News Service
ISL	Interstate League
IvL	Ivy League
JC	Junior College
LPGA	Ladies Professional Golfers Association
LSU	Louisiana State University
MAC	Mid-American Conference
MVC	Missouri Valley Conference
MVP	Most Valuable Player
NAASH	North American Society for Sport History
NAIA	National Association for Intercollegiate Athletics
NBA	National Basketball Association
NBBC	National Baseball Congress
NBC	National Broadcasting Corporation
NCAA	National Collegiate Athletic Association
NEA	Newspaper Enterprise Association
NFL	National Football League
NHL	National Hockey League
NL	National League
NMR	National Museum of Racing
NTF	National Track and Field
NYSL	New York State League
NYT	*New York Times*
NYU	New York University
OlC	Olympic Club
PBA	Professional Bowlers Association
PCC	Pacific Coast Conference
PCL	Pacific Coast League
PEC	Pacific Eight Conference (formerly PCC)
PGA	Professional Golfers Association
PTC	Pacific Ten Conference (formerly PEC)

ROTC	Reserve Officers Training Corps
SA	Southern Association
SC	Southern Conference (now SEC)
SEC	Southeastern Conference (formerly SC)
SI	*Sports Illustrated*
SWC	Southwest Athletic Conference
TAC	Track Athletic Congress
TL	Texas League
TSL	Tri-State League
TSN	*The Sporting News*
UCLA	University of California at Los Angeles
UP	United Press
UPI	United Press International
USOC	United States Olympic Committee
WAC	Western Athletic Conference (formerly CaCAA)
WC	Western Conference (also BTC, BNC)
WIL	Wisconsin-Illinois League
WoC	World Cup
WSF	Women's Sports Foundation
WTC	Washington Touchdown Club

BIBLIOGRAPHY*

AH	*American Health*
ALT	*American Lawn Tennis*
AmM	*America Magazine*
AWN	*Amateur Wrestling News*
BA	*Baseball America*
BD	*Baseball Digest*
BH	*Baseball History*
BI	*Boxing Illustrated*
BM	*Baseball Magazine*
BoD	*Bowling Digest*
BoJ	*Bowlers Journal*
BoM	*Bowling Magazine*
BRJ	*Baseball Research Journal*
BskD	*Basketball Digest*
BW	*Baseball Weekly*
CA	*Contemporary Authors*
CAB	*Cyclopedia of American Biography*
CB	*Current Biography Yearbook*
CFHS	*College Football Historical Society*
CSC	*Canadian Sports Collector*

*These abbreviations are cited in the main text and/or bibliography.

CW	Cycling Weekly
DAB	Dictionary of American Biography
DRF	Daily Racing Form
FA	Football Annual
FD	Football Digest
FN	Football News
GD	Golf Digest
GI	Golf Illustrated
GM	Golf Magazine
GW	Golf World
HD	Hockey Digest
HN	Hockey News
HS	Hockey Stars
IH	Inside Hockey
IS	Inside Sports
JBS	Journal of Baltic Studies
JSH	Journal of Sport History
KOM	KO Magazine
LD	Literary Digest
MT	Morning Telegraph
NCAB	National Cyclopedia of American Biography
NYJ	New York Journal
NYT	New York Times
Ol	The Olympian
PFW	Pro Football Weekly
PUI	Pacemaker Update International
PW	People Weekly
RTV	Rocky Top Views
RW	Running World
SCD	Sports Collectors Digest
SEP	Saturday Evening Post
SH	Sport Heritage
SI	Sports Illustrated
SL	Sport Life
SpL	Sporting Life
SR:B	Sports Review: Basketball
SW	Swimming World
TABR	The American Bloodstock Review
TB	The Backstretch
TBH	The Blood Horse
TCC	The Coffin Corner
TF	Texas Football
TFH	The Florida Horse
TFN	Track and Field News

TNTD	*The National Turf Digest*
TR	*The Ring*
TRq	*The Racquet*
TSN	*The Sporting News*
TT	*Thoroughbred Times*
TTC	*The Thoroughbred of California*
TTR	*The Thoroughbred Record*
TWB	*The Woman Bowler*
USAG	*USA Gymnastics*
USS	*U.S. Swimming*
WS	*Women's Sports*
WSFi	*Women's Sports and Fitness*
WT	*World Tennis*
WUSA	*Wrestling U.S.A.*
WWA	*Who's Who in America*
WWM	*Who's Who in the Midwest*
WWWA	*Who Was Who in America*

AUTO AND STOCK CAR RACING SECTION

AAA	American Automobile Association
AARWB	American Auto Racing Writers and Broadcasters
AuC	Auto Club
GN	Grand National
GoC	Gold Cup
IM	International Motorsports
IMPA	International Motorsports Press Association
IMS	Indianapolis Motor Speedway
ISC	International Speedway Corporation
mph	miles per hour
NASCAR	National Association for Stock Car Auto Racing
NMRPA	National Motor Racing Press Association
SCCA	Sports Car Club of America
USAC	U.S. Auto Club
USRRC	U.S. Road Racing Championship
VC	Vanderbilt Cup
WiC	Winston Cup

BASEBALL SECTION

AlFL	Alabama–Florida League
AmLe	American Legion
ANL	American Negro League
AOA	American Olympic Association

ApL	Appalachian League
ArTL	Arizona-Texas League
ASL	Alaska Summer League
BL	Border League
BPBP	Brotherhood of Professional Baseball Players
BSL	Bi-State League
BStL	Big State League
BUDS	Baseball Umpire Development School
BVL	Blackstone Valley League
CaL	California League
CaPL	Canadian Provincial League
CCSL	Copper Country Soo League
CKAL	Central Kentucky Amateur League
CL	Central League
CML	Connie Mack League
CrL	Carolina League
CSL	Cotton States League
CSSL	California State Semipro League
CtL	Connecticut League
CtSL	Connecticut State League
CUWL	Cuban Winter League
DH	designated hitter
DRWL	Dominican Republic Winter League
EA	Eastern Association
ECA	Eastern Championship Association
ECaL	Eastern Carolina League
ECL	Eastern Colored League
EDL	Eastern Dixie League
ERA	earned run average
ESUTS	Eastern States Umpire Training School
EvL	Evangeline League
EWL	East-West League
FIL	Florida International League
FInL	Florida Instructional League
FL	Federal League
FSL	Florida State League
FWL	Far West League
GCL	Gulf Coast League
GFL	Georgia–Florida League
HRL	Hudson River League
IA	International Association
IOL	Iron and Oil League
JCL	Japanese Central League

JPL	Japanese Pacific League
KL	Kitty League
KOML	Kansas–Oklahoma–Missouri League
LCS	League Championship Series
LL	Longhorn League
MAL	Middle Atlantic League
MEL	Mexican League
MEWL	Mexican Winter League
MkL	Mandak League
ML	Midwest League
MLPA	Major League Players Association
MLUA	Major League Umpires Association
MSA	Massachusetts State Association
MuL	Muny League
MWL	Minnesota–Wisconsin League
NA	National Association
NAL	Negro American League
NAML	National Association of Minor Leagues
NCSL	North Carolina State League
NEL	New England League
NeSL	Nebraska State League
NNL	Negro National League
NoL	Northern League
NSL	Negro Southern League
NWL	Northwestern League
NYPL	New York–Pennsylvania League
NYSL	New York State League
OL	Ohio League
OSL	Ohio State League
PAPBP	Protective Association of Professional Baseball Players
PiL	Piedmont League
PL	Players' League
PNL	Pacific Northwest League
PoL	Pony League
PrL	Pioneer League
PRWL	Puerto Rican Winter League
PSL	Pennsylvania State League
RBIs	runs batted in
SABR	Society for American Baseball Research
SAL	South Atlantic League
SEL	Southeastern League
SL	Southern League
SML	Southern Michigan League

SSL	Sooner State League
3IL	Three I League
TPI	Total Pitcher Index
UA	Union Association
UIL	Utah–Idaho League
VL	Virginia League
VVL	Virginia Valley League
VWL	Venezuelan Winter League
WA	Western Association
WCL	West Carolinas League
WeIL	Western International League
WL	Western League
WSL	Wisconsin State League

BASKETBALL SECTION

ABAUSA	Amateur Basketball Association of the United States of America
BAA	Basketball Association of America
CBA	California Basketball Association
CCL	Chicago Catholic League
CCNY	City College of New York
CIT	Chicago Invitational Tournament
CrC	Carolinas Conference
ECC	Eastern College Conference
LABC	Los Angeles Bicentennial Committee
MBL	Metropolitan Basketball League
MC	Metro Conference
NABC	National Association of Basketball Coaches
NBL	National Basketball League
NIBL	National Industrial Basketball League
NIT	National Invitational Tournament
NYBWA	New York Basketball Writers Association
NYHF	New York Holiday Festival
OSAA	Ohio State Athletic Association
PAIAW	Pennsylvania Association for Intercollegiate Athletics for Women
PSWA	Philadelphia Sports Writers Association
SBC	Sun Belt Conference
SHSSF	Save High School Sport Foundation
SoC	Southland Conference
TAAC	Trans-American Athletic Conference
WBCA	Women's Basketball Coaches Association

WCAC	West Coast Athletic Conference
WCN	World Cup of Nations
WPBL	Women's Professional Basketball League

BOWLING SECTION

ACUI	Association of College Unions International
AmBC	American Bowling Congress
BoWAA	Bowling Writers Association of America
BPAA	Bowling Proprietor's Association of America
ELIBA	Eastern Long Island Bowling Association
HoC	House of Champions
LPBT	Ladies Professional Bowling Tour
NYCBA	New York City Bowling Association
NYSBA	New York State Bowling Association
SCBWA	Southern California Bowling Writers Association
WIBC	Women's International Bowling Congress
WPBA	Women's Professional Bowlers Association

BOXING SECTION

BoC	Boys Club
CYO	Catholic Youth Organization
IBF	International Boxing Federation
ISAC	Illinois State Athletic Commission
NABF	North American Boxing Federation
NSC	National Sporting Club
NSF	National Sports Festival
WBA	World Boxing Association
WBC	World Boxing Council

COMMUNICATIONS SECTION

ASA	American Sportscasters Association
CFWAA	College Football Writers Association of America
GSDSA	Greater San Diego Sports Association
HBO	Home Box Office
HSE	Home Sports Entertainment
MBS	Mutual Broadcasting System
NASS	National Association of Sportscasters and Sportswriters
NFWA	National Football Writers Association
NHC	National Headliner Club
NYBoWA	New York Boxing Writers Association

NYFWA   New York Football Writers Association
NYTWA   New York Track Writers Association
TVS   Television satellite

FOOTBALL SECTION

AAFC   All-America Football Conference
AAGPBL   All-American Girls Professional Baseball League
AAWU   Athletic Association of Western Universities (Big Five)
ACFL   Atlantic Coast Football League
AFC   American Football Conference
AFCA   American Football Coaches Association
AIFRC   American Intercollegiate Football Rules Committee
APFA   American Professional Football Association
ArFL   Arena Football League
BYU   Brigham Young University
CFA   Coaches Football Association
CFL   Canadian Football League
CiL   Citrus League
EASFO   Eastern Association for the Selection of Football Officials
EC   Eastern Conference
EPFC   Eastern Professional Football Conference
FCF   Football Coaches Foundation
FWAA   Football Writers Association of America
GAL   Georgia–Alabama League
GSC   Gulf States Conference
GWC   Gateway Conference
LSC   Lone Star Conference
LSWA   Louisiana Sports Writers Association
MSAC   Mountain States Athletic Conference (also Skyline Confer-
           ence)
MWC   Mid Western Conference
NACDA   National Association of College Directors of Athletics
NAFS   National Association of Football Scouts
NCC   North Central Conference
NeCC   Nebraska College Conference
NFC   National Football Conference
NFF   National Football Foundation
NFLAA   National Football League Alumni Association
NFLPA   National Football League Players Association
NSSAP   National Sportscasters and Sportswriters Association of Penn-
           sylvania
OVC   Ohio Valley Conference
PAT   point(s) after touchdown

PCAA   Pacific Coast Athletic Association
PFRA   Professional Football Researchers Association
PFWAA   Professional Football Writers Association of America
PhCL   Philadelphia Catholic League
RMC   Rocky Mountain Conference
SAC   Southwestern Athletic Conference
SCSBA   Southern California Sports Broadcasters Association
SIAC   Southern Intercollegiate Athletic Conference
SMU   Southern Methodist University
TCU   Texas Christian University
TSC   Tri-State Conference
UIL   University Interscholastic League
USFL   United States Football League
VMI   Virginia Military Institute
WFL   World Football League

GOLF SECTION

CoC   Country Club
FC   Field Club
GC   Golf Club
GWAA   Golf Writers Association of America
MONY   Mutual of New York
USGA   U.S. Golf Association
WPGA   Women's Professional Golf Association

HORSE RACING SECTION

CTBA   California Thoroughbred Breeder's Association
CTC   Calder Turf Club
JG   Jockey's Guild
JoC   Jockey Club
NTWA   National Turf Writers Association
NYRA   New York Racing Association
SaA   Saratoga Association
SDCTC   San Diego County Turf Club

ICE HOCKEY SECTION

AAHA   American Amateur Hockey Association
AHA   Amateur Hockey Association
AHCA   American Hockey Coaches Association
AHL   American Hockey League
AmAA   Amateur Athletic Association

CaC   Campbell Conference
CAL   Canadian-American League
CHL   Central Hockey League
HE   Hockey East
IPHL   International Professional Hockey League
LC   Lake Conference
MHSCA   Minnesota High School Coaches Association
MHSHCA   Minnesota High School Hockey Coaches Association
MSHSL   Minnesota State High School League
NHSS   National High School Sports
OHL   Ontario Hockey League
PCHA   Pacific Coast Hockey Association
PWC   Prince of Wales Conference
USAH   U.S.A. Hockey
USCC   U.S. Canada Cup
WCHA   Western Collegiate Hockey Association
WCHL   Western Canada Hockey League

SHOOTING SECTION

MRRA   Manhattan Rifle and Revolver Association
USRA   U.S. Revolver Association

SKATING SECTION

AAC   Athletic Advisory Council
USFSAIC   U.S. Figure Skating Association International Committee
WSkF   World Skating Federation

SKIING SECTION

FIS   Federation internationale de ski
USSA   U.S. Ski Association

SWIMMING SECTION

SeC   Seacoast Club
SwC   Swim Club

TENNIS AND OTHER RACQUET SPORTS SECTION

ATP   American Tennis Professional
CrC   Cricket Club
RTC   Racquet and Tennis Club

SILCOS	Staten Island Ladies Club for Outdoor Sports
USBA	U.S. Badminton Association
USCTA	U.S. Court Tennis Association
USLTA	U.S. Lawn Tennis Association
USPP	U.S. Public Parks
USTA	U.S. Tennis Association
USTT	U.S. Table Tennis

TRACK AND FIELD SECTION

CiC	City College
FoL	Foothill League
IAAF	Inter-Amateur Athletic Federation
IOC	International Olympic Committee
ITA	International Track Association
ITCA	International Track Coaches Association
NCTCA	National Collegiate Track Coaches Association
NTFCA	National Track and Field Coaches Association
OlC	Olympic Club
OOC	Olympic Organizing Committee
PaCC	Pacific Coast Club
PSAL	Public School Athletic League
TAFWA	Track and Field Writers Association
TrC	Track Club
USTF	U.S. Track and Field
USTFCA	U.S. Track and Field Coaches Association

WRESTLING SECTION

| FILA | Federation internationale de lutters amateur |
| USWF | U.S. Wrestling Federation |

MISCELLANEOUS SPORTS SECTION

IRA	International Racquetball Association
NCU	National Cycle Union
NYYC	New York Yacht Club
USET	U.S. Equestrian Team
USGF	U.S. Gymnastic Federation

Biographical Dictionary of
American Sports

1992–1995 SUPPLEMENT
FOR
BASEBALL, FOOTBALL, BASKETBALL,
AND OTHER SPORTS

AUTO AND STOCK CAR RACING

BAKER, Elzie Wylie Sr. "Buck" (b. March 4, 1919, Richbourg, SC), stock car racer, ranked among the premier NASCAR drivers of the 1950s. The son of Jake Baker and Roxie (Wylie) Baker, he served in the U.S. Navy during World War II. Baker, a versatile driver, excelled in several types of cars during NASCAR's experimental infancy. His first race, held in 1944 at the Charlotte, NC, Fairgrounds, predated the establishment of NASCAR by five years. Baker later competed in the first NASCAR GN race and specialized for several years in the modified class, winning the overall modified championship in 1951. He led Speedway Division drivers in 1952 during the short-lived attempt to use Indy-style cars on NASCAR tracks.

After the failure of the Speedway Division, Baker concentrated on the GN Division. Baker, who won the GN points championship in 1956 and 1957 and finished runner-up in 1955 and 1958, captured 14 victories in 1956 and won the Southern 500 in 1953, 1960, and 1964. Baker reduced his racing schedule after the 1967 season but did not officially retire until the 1977 campaign. He won 46 GN races, his most memorable being the 1964 Southern 500. Although usually regarded as a hard-charger, Baker patiently waited until wrecks or car malfunctions had sidelined the favorites.

Baker, who opened the Buck Baker Racing School in Charlotte, NC, in 1980, has been married three times and has three children. His son Elzie, Jr., nicknamed "Buddy," was born to his first wife, Margaret (Hatchell) Baker, and drives successfully on the NASCAR circuit. Son Randall was born to his second wife, Betsy (Andrews) Baker, while daughter Susan was born to Susan (Painter) Baker, whom he married in 1972. Baker was elected to the IM Hall of Fame (1990) and the North Carolina Sports Hall of Fame.

BIBLIOGRAPHY: Robert Cutter and Bob Fendell, *The Encyclopedia of Auto Racing Greats* (Englewood Cliffs, NJ, 1973); Raleigh (NC) *News and Observer*, 1950–1967; Jim L. Sumner, telephone interview with Elzie Baker, Sr., December 21, 1993.

Jim L. Sumner

CHEVROLET, Louis Joseph (b. December 25, 1878, LaChaux-de-Fonds, Switzerland; d. June 6, 1941, Detroit, MI), auto racing driver and engineer, was the son of Joseph Felicieu Chevrolet, a clock maker. His two youngest brothers, Arthur and Gaston, also became noted race car drivers. The Chevrolets moved to Beaune in Burgundy, France, in 1883.

Chevrolet, self-taught, learned about machinery early in his youth, becoming a technician for the early automobiles. He came to Montreal, Canada, in 1900 and joined the Fiat Agency in New York in 1902. In 1905 Chevrolet married Suzanne Treyvoux. On May 20, 1905, he won his first event, defeating Barney Oldfield (OS) and Walter Christie in a three-mile race with a record speed of 68 mph.

Between 1905 and 1920, he spent most of his time recovering from auto racing accidents. Driving at high speeds and taking risks gave Chevrolet widespread press for his reckless style. One journalist tagged him as "the most audacious driver in the world." Chevrolet won approximately 27 major events during his driving career.

By 1911, Chevrolet's most important contributions came in engineering. William Durant bought the use of the Chevrolet name and contracted Louis to design a car for the newly formed Chevrolet Motor Company. In 1914 Chevrolet split from Durant, losing the chance to become a wealthy man. Chevrolet was also involved with Albert Champion, who founded two spark plug empires. He lost another opportunity to amass a fortune, splitting with Champion over a personal matter.

Chevrolet in 1914 founded the Frontenac Motor Corporation, which built passenger cars and racing cars. By 1919, Frontenac had built cars to race in the Indianapolis 500. Gaston Chevrolet won the 1920 Memorial Day Classic but was killed at a California track in November 1920. Louis quit driving following Gaston's death but designed the 1921 Indianapolis 500 winning car driven by Tommy Milton (OS). Chevrolet had designed two winning cars ("Frontenac Frontys") for Indianapolis in successive years.

The 1922 depression led Chevrolet to another business failure with the Stutz Motorcar Company. Although continuing to enter racing cars at Indianapolis, Chevrolet enjoyed little luck except on the shorter tracks and continued to suffer business reversals. In 1926, Louis and Arthur designed an aircraft engine. The 1929 depression forced them to sell their interest, which later became a part of an aircraft empire. In 1934, a fire destroyed Chevrolet's memorabilia, documents, and engineering drawings of a lifetime. Chevrolet suffered a cerebral hemorrhage, moved to Florida, and remained there until 1941. He died in Detroit, where he and his wife had returned for medical treatment. His brother, Arthur, a boat mechanic, hanged himself in Miami, FL, on April 16, 1946.

Chevrolet was selected in 1952 to the IMS Hall of Fame, and in 1992, to the IM Hall of Fame.

BIBLIOGRAPHY: Robert Cutter and Bob Fendell, *The Encyclopedia of Auto Racing Greats* (Englewood Cliffs, NJ, 1973); Paul Soderberg and Helen Washington, *The Big Book of Halls of Fame in the United States and Canada* (New York, 1977).

John L. Evers

DONOHUE, Mark (b. March 18, 1937, Summit, NJ; d. August 19, 1975, near Graz, Austria), auto racing driver and consultant, was associated with the Roger Penske organization. The son of a well-to-do lawyer, he graduated with a bachelor's degree in Engineering from Brown University in 1959 and began his auto racing career by driving a Corvette to a hill-climb success. By 1961, he had won the SCCA's 'E' production national championship in an Elva Courier.

Until 1966, racing remained an avocation for Donohue. In 1966, place finishes at the Daytona, FL, Continental and Sebring, FL, auto races launched Donohue happily on a committed professional career. The same year, Donohue forged a racing partnership with the Penske Racing Team for the USRRC and the Can-Am series. Donohue won six out of eight races to seize the 1967 USRRC title and finished third on the Can-Am circuit. His domination of the road racing championship continued the next year, as he took the victor's checkered flag in 11 of 16 starts. He codrove a Lola coupe to success in the February 1969 Daytona, FL, 24-hour race.

The Indianapolis 500 remains the Wimbledon, British Open, and Tour de France of auto racing, the unofficial "World Championship." Donohue gravitated to Indy car racing, earning 1969 USAC Rookie of the Year honors, finishing seventh in his first attempt in the Indianapolis 500 race. His training as an engineer paid dividends. At the Indianapolis track, Donohue remarked, "You have to come here and see what the problems are and then go away and decide what you are going to do about them."

One year later, Donohue drove a Penske Sunoco Special Lola-Ford at an average speed of 168.911 mph to a second-place finish and took $86,440 in prize money. His racing successes continued in 1971 with victories at the Pocono 500 and Michigan 200 auto races. The most celebrated triumph of his career came at the Indianapolis 500 race in 1972. Despite only being in third place on the starting grid, he captured the premier prize in auto racing at an average speed of 163.465 mph. The *NYT* lauded Donohue's achievement as "the greatest victory of an illustrious 13 year career." Donohue retired in 1973 and designed the Chesapeake, MD, International Raceway. He lived in Media, PA, and was married with two sons. He came out of retirement in 1974 and sadly was killed on a practice lap while preparing for the 1975 Austrian Grand Prix, a Formula One race. Donohue, who won 57 major titles and over $1 million in prize money, was inducted in 1990 into the Motorsports Hall of Fame of America and the IM Hall of Fame.

BIBLIOGRAPHY: John Arlott, ed., *Oxford Companion to Sports and Games* (New York, 1975); Jack C. Fox, *The Indianapolis 500* (New York, 1967); G. N. Georgano, ed.,

The Encyclopedia of Motor Sport (New York, 1971); Mark Donohue file, courtesy of Bob Laycock, IMS, Indianapolis, IN; John Radosta, "Donohue Sets Record in Winning Indianapolis 500," *NYT*, May 28, 1972.

Scott A.G.M. Crawford

FLOCK, Julius Timothy "Tim" (b. May 11, 1924, Fort Payne, AL), stock car racer, is one of eight children of Carl Lee and Maudie (Williams) Flock. His father, a textile worker, died when Flock was young. Flock's family moved to Atlanta, GA, where he grew up. His older brothers, Robert and Truman Fontell "Fonty," also became successful NASCAR drivers. Along with several other NASCAR pioneers, the Flock family was involved in running moonshine liquor. Flock, however, was too young to drive.

Flock worked as a fireman, bellhop, and parking lot attendant before beginning his racing career in 1947. He captured the GN points title in 1952 and 1955 and won a then-record 18 races in 1955, driving a Chrysler 300. He captured 40 GN races in 189 starts during his 13-year career, the best winning percentage in NASCAR history. He especially succeeded at the Daytona Beach, FL, Race Track.

Flock was regarded as one of the sport's smoothest, most consistent drivers. Although staying away from dramatics on the track, he spent much of the 1950s in a protracted feud with NASCAR czar Bill France, Sr.* He blamed France for reversing several of his victories because of minor rules violations.

Flock, who married Frances Roberts in 1944, has five children, Richard, Donald, Carl, Peggy Ann, and Joy. Since the early 1980s, Flock has worked in promotions for the Charlotte, NC, Motor Speedway. His honors include memberships in the IMPA Hall of Fame, the NMRPA Hall of Fame, and the Georgia Sports Hall of Fame.

BIBLIOGRAPHY: Robert Cutter and Bob Fendell, *The Encyclopedia of Auto Racing Greats* (Englewood Cliffs, NJ, 1973); Jim L. Sumner, telephone interview with Tim Flock, March 16, 1994; Sylvia Wilkinson, *Dirt Tracks to Glory: The Early Days of Stock Car Racing as Told by the Participants* (Chapel Hill, NC, 1983).

Jim L. Sumner

FRANCE, William Henry Getty, Sr. "Bill" (b. September 26, 1909, Washington, DC; d. June 7, 1992, Ormond Beach, FL), stock car race executive, won acclaim as the founding father or patron saint of NASCAR racing. France grew up on a farm and always enjoyed "playing with" cars and motorcycles. At Washington Central High School, he excelled in basketball. Besides being a skilled athlete, the six-foot-five-inch 230-pounder possessed the size to do well in basketball. He married Anne Bledsoe in North Carolina in June 1931 and had two sons, Bill, Jr., and Jim. Both sons have been involved in NASCAR racing and enjoy executive positions in the ISC.

In the fall of 1934, the Frances decided to relocate to Miami, FL. Their car malfunctioned in Daytona Beach, FL, where the France family settled. Eventually, France opened a service station and began experimenting with stock cars. France, not content with being a mechanic, drove a 1935 Ford to a fifth-place finish in the Daytona Beach, FL, race over "the old beach and road course." In 1938, France and a colleague assumed the promotion and organization of the various Daytona Beach–based stock car races. From 1939 to 1945 at the Daytona Beach Boat Works, he constructed motor torpedo boats for hunting down the successful German U-boat submarines.

He resumed stock car racing promotion in 1944 at Daytona Beach. The popularity of the sport spread as France launched stock car races in North Carolina, South Carolina, and Georgia. France became the prime mover in calling together a fascinating, mixed group of stock car enthusiasts, including promoters, drivers, mechanics, sponsors, and community leaders. NASCAR was incorporated in February 1948. The first NASCAR race took place shortly thereafter, while the first GN (WiC) race was launched in 1949. Until the opening of the specialist Daytona International Speedway in 1959, France faced the unenviable task of giving order and structure to the various beach races. France had to determine in advance on what days the tide would be low at the right time to allow races to be held. Handling traffic when the tide was coming in was another tricky problem. Another problem was controlling admissions around a four-mile unfenced race track.

France, as NASCAR president, administered a sport that grew in three decades from erratic car chases on a primitive beach terrain to wonderfully orchestrated, evenly contested, long-distance races on special complexes, including the Alabama International Motor Speedway near Talladega. Observers have described France as the "ruler of a Kingdom built on hairpin curves and free-wheeling weekends." Sportswriter Furman Bisher stated that France and NASCAR had created America's newest class of folk heroes, the stock car racer. France, who shaped and sculpted a whole new spectator sport, "took the car off the streets and turned it into a sport as national as the National Football League." An *SI* profile summed up France's impact: "He made stock-car racing a huge success by building speedways in swamps, keeping corporations guessing and unions at bay. Here is the man who brought you Richard Petty [OS] and bumper-to-bumper competition."

Petty retired in 1993, but France's creation continues to build momentum. Stock car racing has developed into the nation's premier spectator sport with its close edge of competition and narrow margin of victory. The very first France-inspired Daytona race in 1959 took three days to resolve, as NASCAR officials agonized over the photo finish. In 1990, France was inducted into the Motorsports Hall of Fame of America and the IM Hall of Fame.

BIBLIOGRAPHY: Furman Bisher, *Sky* (June 1980); William France, Sr., file, courtesy of Bob Mauk, NASCAR, Daytona Beach, FL; William Neely, *Daytona USA* (Tucson, AZ, 1979); Brock Yates, "He Did It His Way," *SI* 48 (June 26, 1978), pp. 78–82.
                                                                        Scott A.G.M. Crawford

HANKS, Samuel Jr. "Sam" (b. July 13, 1914, Columbus, OH; d. June 27, 1994, Pacific Palisades, CA), auto racer, the son of Samuel Hanks, Sr., was ranked among the busiest, most versatile American race car drivers. Hanks enjoyed victories in three different divisions of the sport in a career spanning over two decades. At high school in Columbus his passion involved machine shop and auto mechanic courses. During the late 1920s, he gained experiences as a "pilot" or race driver. From 1932 to 1935, he raced a Model A Ford and prepared other cars on the Muroc Dry Lake course in California. This course was known as the "Home of the First Drag Racers."

His racing career began in April 1936 on the Los Angeles, CA, area midget racing circuits. By 1938, he had assumed various roles as car owner, driver, and mechanic. Between 1936 and 1941, he won over 80 midget car races. In 1940 he qualified as twelfth fastest for the Indianapolis 500 auto race and finished in thirteenth place. During Hanks's practice run for the 1941 Indianapolis 500, a connecting rod broke and sliced his engine in half. His vehicle somersaulted and tossed him through the air. As Wilbur Shaw (OS) noted in *Gentlemen, Start Your Engines*, "The car looped at the start of the southwest turn and crashed through the inner guard rail." After four days in the hospital, Hanks returned to the track and won the 1941 National Midget Car Championship a month later.

Hanks popularized midget car racing and became the prime mover in seeing the sport featured at the Pasadena, CA, Rose Bowl in 1946. The same year, his first-place finish in the GoC Race at Los Angeles, CA, saw him earn $6,000 from the biggest purse ($28,000) in midget racing history. Hanks raced in the Indianapolis 500 for several years and then returned to the midget car circuit. He retired from midget racing in 1952 as the sport's leading money winner. In both 1952 and 1953, he finished third in the Indianapolis 500 auto race. He also enjoyed remarkable success in the national stock car point standings, finishing second in 1954, fifth in 1956, and third in 1957.

By 1957, Hanks drove a "Belond Exhaust Special with its Offenhauser engine mounted in a horizontal position instead of the conventional vertical manner." He won the 1957 Indianapolis 500, recording a then-average speed of 135.601 mph. The 43-year-old became the oldest driver to win the Indianapolis 500, a record that stood until 1981. No other racer had won more than $100,000 at the IMS, either. "The lean, handsome veteran" announced his retirement from auto racing in Victory Lane after the 1957 race.

Hanks, who directed racing for the Indianapolis Motor Speedway, lived in Pacific Palisades, CA, with his wife Alice. He was inducted into the IMS

Hall of Fame in 1981. Two years later, he was inducted into the Motorsports Hall of Fame of America. His many other honors included the Jimmy Clark Award for outstanding contributions to motor racing from the Indianapolis AuC in 1984.

BIBLIOGRAPHY: Jack C. Fox, *The Indianapolis 500* (New York, 1967); Sam Hanks file, courtesy of Bob Laycock, IMS, Indianapolis, IN; Wilbur Shaw, *Gentlemen, Start Your Engines* (New York, 1955).

Scott A.G.M. Crawford

HARROUN, Raymond "The Little Professor" "The Bedouin" (b. January 12, 1879, Spartansburg, PA; d. January 19, 1968, Anderson, IN), auto racer, won the first Indianapolis 500 auto race in 1911. A fine driver and innovative scientist, he designed auto race cars and variously operated an automobile factory, flew his own airplane, and invented the car bumper or "fender." During the early 1930s, he created the prototype for the eventual "minicar."

Harroun began his auto racing career on the Chicago, IL, Harlem dirt track in 1905. When the IMS was being built, Harroun moved to Indianapolis, IN, and joined the Marmon Company as an engineer and race driver. During the 1910 season, he enjoyed successes on the Playa del Rey board racing track in California. Other victories in Atlanta, GA, and Indianapolis assured him of winning the AAA national driving championship of that year. He announced his retirement before the start of the 1911 season, but the Marmon organization persuaded him to take part in the inaugural Indianapolis 500 auto race. The press nicknamed him "The Little Professor." He created and used one of the first ever rearview automobile mirrors in the 1911 Indianapolis 500 race. His other popular nickname, "The Bedouin," stemmed from his Arabian descent.

Harroun made no secret of why he entered the 1911 Indianapolis 500 race. "It wasn't fame, glory or a burning desire," he admitted. "It was the money! They were offering around $12,500." The *NYT* account of the first Indianapolis 500 remains a classic piece of sports writing, portraying the crowd size and novelty of the occasion. The militia used their guns as clubs to clear a space for the ambulances coming onto the course. "As the race proceeded, however, accidents almost ceased and spectators became hardened to the excitement. Harroun kept in front, earning shouts of encouragement. When he swept into the home stretch on his last lap, the speedway enclosure rang with applause that drowned the loud barking of the seemingly ceaseless motor explosion."

Harroun's victory came by a margin of 1 minute 43 seconds, as he averaged 74.59 mph. The pioneering Harroun was the only race entrant in a single-seater machine, with the standard practice at that time being to have a mechanic "on board." He never raced again following his 1911 Indianapolis 500 victory.

He always maintained close links with the automobile racing world. At the 1961 Indianapolis race, he marked the fiftieth anniversary of his victory by driving an exhibition lap in his original Marmon Wasp. The car remains permanently displayed at the Indianapolis Speedway Museum. He was inducted into the IMS Hall of Fame in 1952 as a charter member.

BIBLIOGRAPHY: Donald Davidson, "Indy Yesterday," courtesy of Bob Laycock, IMS, Indianapolis, IN; G. N. Georgano, ed., *The Encyclopedia of Motor Sport* (New York, 1971); "Marmon Car Wins Death-Marked Race," *NYT*, May 31, 1911; Wilbur Shaw, *Gentlemen, Start Your Engines* (New York, 1955).

Scott A.G.M. Crawford

JARRETT, Ned Miller (b. October 12, 1932, Newton, NC), stock car racer and sportscaster, is the fourth of six children of Homer Jarrett, a farmer and small businessman, and Eoline (Leatherman) Jarrett. He grew up on a farm and learned to drive at age 9. Jarrett, who quit school at age 17 to work in his father's lumber business, first raced in 1952 at nearby Hickory and overcame family opposition to enter racing full-time. He succeeded throughout the 1950s in sportsman racing, winning the overall sportsman championship in 1957 and 1958.

Jarrett committed to the GN circuit in 1959 and became one of the standout racers of the 1960s. He finished first in the GN standings in 1961 while driving Chevrolets and in 1965 while driving Fords. His best year, however, may have been 1964, when he won 15 races with a Ford and narrowly finished second in the GN standings to Richard Petty (OS). In 1965 Jarrett triumphed in 13 races. All but 2 of Jarrett's 50 GN victories came on short tracks. He captured the 1965 Southern 500 at Darlington, SC, silencing critics who claimed he could not triumph on the superspeedways. Jarrett retired after the 1966 season, when Ford withdrew from NASCAR sponsorship.

Subsequently, Jarrett promoted races at Greenville, SC, served as part-owner of a track in Hickory, and sold real estate in his adopted town of Camden, SC. He earned most acclaim, however, as a radio and television announcer. During the 1960s, Jarrett took a Dale Carnegie course on public speaking and became an articulate spokesperson for stock car racing. Since that time, he has been employed as an award-winning sportscaster for CBS, ESPN, and the Nashville Network. In 1978 he started a popular syndicated radio program on NASCAR racing.

Jarrett and his wife, Martha (Bowman) Jarrett, have two sons, Glenn and Dale, and a daughter, Patty. Dale followed his father as a successful NASCAR racing driver. Ned's honors include memberships in the Stock Car Racing Hall of Fame, the NMRPA Hall of Fame, and the North Carolina Sports Hall of Fame.

BIBLIOGRAPHY: Kim Chapin, *Fast as White Lighting: The Story of Stock Car Racing* (New York, 1981); Robert Cutter and Bob Fendell, *The Encyclopedia of Auto Racing*

Greats (Englewood Cliffs, NJ, 1973); NASCAR *Media Guides,* assorted; Sylvia Wilkinson, *Dirt Tracks to Glory: The Early Days of Stock Car Racing as Told by the Participants* (Chapel Hill, NC, 1983).

Jim L. Sumner

JOHNSON, Robert Glenn Jr. "Junior" (b. June 28, 1931, Ingle Hollow, NC),
stock car racer and owner, is the son of Robert Johnson and Lora Bell
(Money) Johnson. His father, nominally a farmer, produced and distributed
moonshine liquor. Junior epitomizes the legendary origins of stock car racing, running his father's moonshine on rural mountain roads in western
North Carolina. Although never caught while driving on the road, he served
a prison term in the middle 1950s after being arrested in front of his father's
still.

Johnson, a dominant racer in the 1950s and 1960s, recorded his first GN
victory in 1955 in Hickory, NC. By his retirement 11 years later, he had
won 50 GN circuit races. His best stock car season came in 1965, when he
captured 13 titles. Johnson, who bridged the gap between dirt tracks and the
superspeedways, was the first driver to win at each of the four original superspeedways: Darlington, SC; Daytona, FL; Charlotte, NC; and Atlanta,
GA. In 1960, Johnson captured both the Daytona 500 and the Coca-Cola
600 at Charlotte.

Johnson, an aggressive driver, followed the motto "Go till you blow." If
he could not win, he did not fight hard for points. This attitude prevented
Johnson from contending for the GN points title but also made him a fan
favorite. Johnson became a successful stock car owner following his retirement from stock car racing. Through 1993, his stock car teams had won
over 130 races and six national championships. He also operated a successful
chicken ranch in Wilkes County, NC.

Johnson belongs to the NMRPA Hall of Fame (1991), the IM Hall of
Fame (1990), and the North Carolina Sports Hall of Fame. He married
Flossie Clark in 1975, but they were divorced in 1992.

BIBLIOGRAPHY: Robert Cutter and Bob Fendell, *The Encyclopedia of Auto Racing
Greats* (Englewood Cliffs, NJ, 1973); Peter Golenbock, *American Zoom* (New York,
1993); Charles Leerhsen, "The King of the Road," *Newsweek* 98 (November 16,
1981), p. 121; Bill Libby, *Heroes of Stock Car Racing* (New York, 1975); Tom Wolfe,
"The Last American Hero Is Junior Johnson," *Esquire* 63 (March 1965), pp. 73–75,
138–157.

Jim L. Sumner

PARSONS, John "Johnnie" (b. July 4, 1918, Los Angeles, CA; d. September
8, 1984, Los Angeles, CA), auto racer, ranked among the premier drivers of
the post–World War II era. His parents worked in the theater business.
Despite his small 5-foot-10 ½-inch, 163-pound stature, Parsons possessed a

dynamic driving style and personal charisma that made him a race track celebrity figure.

Parsons began his racing career in California in 1940, enjoying great success as a midget driver or "pilot." In "big car racing," his first victory came at DuQuion, IL, in 1948. A year later, he won the USAC national driving championship with five first-place finishes. In the 1949 Indianapolis 500 auto race, Parsons, a rookie, drove the red and silver Kurtis-Kraft at an average speed of 119.785 mph to a second-place finish.

At the 1950 Indianapolis 500, Parsons began in fifth place on the starting grid. A crack in the car block made it unlikely that his machine would survive the distance. According to historian Jack Fox, "It was planned for Parsons to go as hard and as long as possible while the engine held together and pick up as much lap money as he could for a sort of consolation prize. When the checkered flag was displayed as he completed his 138th lap [heavy rain stopped the race], Parsons was still in front, the engine performing faultlessly and his closest competitor, Bill Holland, over a lap behind." Parsons's average speed of 124.002 mph broke the record for capturing the Indianapolis 500.

Parsons's victory marked the beginning of the influence and impact on the Indianapolis 500 of drivers from the "Mighty Midget" racing circuit of California. Throughout the 1950s, Parsons remained an entertaining figure as showman and car racer. In 1958, he participated in his tenth Indianapolis 500 race at the IMS and finished in twelfth place. His speed in the Indianapolis 500 race averaged 128.254 mph, while his qualifying time reached an eye-catching 144.683 mph.

Toward the end of his career, Parsons represented the Championship Spark Plug Company and attracted popularity as a speaker at high schools from coast to coast, promoting sensible driving behaviors. Parsons, who was twice married and had three children, Joan, John, and Patty, was inducted into the IMS Hall of Fame in 1986.

BIBLIOGRAPHY: Jack C. Fox, *The Indianapolis 500* (New York, 1967); *The 1959 Speedway Media Book*, courtesy of Bob Laycock, IMS, Indianapolis, IN; Wilbur Shaw, *Gentlemen, Start Your Engines* (New York, 1955).

Scott A.G.M. Crawford

PETTY, Lee Arnold (b. March 3, 1914, Randleman, NC), stock car racer, is the son of Judson E. Petty and Jessie M. Petty, both farmers. He was educated in local schools and worked as a salesman and trucker before pursuing stock car racing shortly after World War II. He participated in the first NASCAR GN races and raced conservatively, preferring consistency to flash. Petty, known for his smooth driving, proved especially dangerous on the short tracks and competed in Oldsmobiles or Plymouths. Petty, who captured GN points titles in 1954, 1958, and 1959 and finished runner-up in 1949 and 1953, was voted the most popular driver in 1953, 1954, and 1955.

Petty's best season came in 1959, when he captured 12 stock car races and won the inaugural Daytona 500 in a pulsating photo finish. The result was so close that it took officials three days to declare Petty the winner. Petty was severely injured in a 1961 crash at Daytona, suffering a broken left leg and a punctured lung. His comeback attempt failed, leaving Petty with a record 54 NASCAR victories. The mark later was exceeded by his son Richard (OS).

Petty, who subsequently headed the successful Petty Enterprises racing team, had married Elizabeth Toomes in 1936. Their sons, Richard and Maurice, became integral parts of NASCAR's most dominant racing team, the former as a driver and the latter as chief mechanic. Lee was elected to the North Carolina Sports Hall of Fame, the NMRPA Hall of Fame, and the IM Hall of Fame.

BIBLIOGRAPHY: Robert Cutter and Bob Fendell, *The Encyclopedia of Auto Racing Greats* (Englewood Cliffs, NJ, 1973); Bill Libby with Richard Petty, *"King Richard": The Richard Petty Story* (Garden City, NY, 1977); Richard Petty with William Neely, *King Richard I* (New York, 1986).

Jim L. Sumner

THOMAS, Herbert Watson "Herb" (b. April 6, 1923, Harnett County, NC), stock car racer, is the son of Alton Thomas, a tobacco farmer and small businessman, and Pearl (Knight) Thomas and graduated from Benhaven High School in Olivia, NC, in 1941. He operated a sawmill business during World War II, supplying lumber to the military.

Thomas began racing locally shortly after World War II, making his NASCAR debut in 1947 and capturing his first GN victory three years later in Martinsville, VA. In 1951, he won stock car races in three different makes of cars, Plymouth, Hudson, and Oldsmobile. Thomas, who triumphed in 12 races in both 1953 and 1954, captured the GN championship in 1951 and 1953 and finished second in 1952, 1954, and 1956. The hard-charging Thomas earned greatest recognition for his success in the prestigious Southern 500, held in Darlington, SC. He won the Southern 500 in 1951, 1954, and 1955, becoming the first stock car driver to take the race three times. His 1954 Southern 500 victory was a dramatic come-from-behind win over Curtis Turner.

In 1955, Thomas broke a leg during a crash in Charlotte, NC, and missed much of the next season. His career abruptly ended on October 23, 1956, when he was involved in a near-fatal crash in a Shelby, NC, stock car race. Thomas made a brief, unsuccessful comeback attempt in 1961, finishing his career with 49 NASCAR victories. Subsequently, he continued to farm and operated a trucking business in Sanford, NC. Thomas, who married Helen Perkins in 1941 and has three children, belongs to the North Carolina Sports Hall of Fame and the NMRPA Hall of Fame.

BIBLIOGRAPHY: Robert Cutter and Bob Fendell, *The Encyclopedia of Auto Racing Greats* (Englewood Cliffs, NJ, 1973); NASCAR *Media Guides*, assorted; Raleigh (NC) *News and Observer*, September 1, 1974.

Jim L. Sumner

VANDERBILT, William Kissam (b. October 26, 1878, New York, NY; d. January 8, 1944, New York, NY), sportsman and auto racer, was the elder son of William K. Vanderbilt and Mrs. O. H. P. Belmont and unsurprisingly grew up with a passion for sport. His father, a member of a victorious syndicate that held on to the AMC in yachting, owned a successful stable of race horses. In 1920, the *NYT* included Vanderbilt senior "among the earliest and most liberal patrons of automobile racing in this country."

William entered Harvard University in 1897 and left college two years later to marry Virginia Fair. They were divorced in 1927, the same year he married Rosamund Warburton. Shortly after his first marriage, he imported a Mercedes racing car, "The Red Devil." He particularly liked Europe, where auto racing was perceived as a legitimate sporting activity. Vanderbilt raced from Monte Carlo, France, to Paris, France, in 17 hours and competed in Vienna, Austria, Madrid, Spain, and other European capital cities. He believed that American auto racing would only come of age with sponsorship and economic support and, therefore, initiated the VC races. Tiffany, the world famous New York jewelers, designed a 10½-gallon cup. American and European drivers took part in the VC races.

A special auto race track was designed on Long Island. The course, a triangular one 30 miles in length, involved a total race distance of 284.4 miles. The inaugural race occurred on October 8, 1904, with Vanderbilt in the spotlight as referee and starter. The notable race was made the featured story in the *NYT*. George Heath drove a French car to victory at an average speed of 52 mph. One driver fatality occurred.

The *NYT* described Vanderbilt as an "early motoring enthusiast" who gave "ardent support to developing faster automobiles." Vanderbilt also predicted that "from motor-car racing would come engineering achievements to equal those already made in Europe." Subsequently, he became a distinguished mariner and had earned a master's certificate by 1927. In a seaplane, he flew around South America and across the Andes in 1927. Vanderbilt, who had two daughters, one son, and two stepchildren, was inducted as a charter member of the IMS Hall of Fame in 1954.

BIBLIOGRAPHY: *DAB*, vol. 19 (New York, 1936), pp. 176–177; *NYT*, July 23, 1920; January 8, 1944; January 21, 1944.

Scott A.G.M. Crawford

WILCOX, Howard "Handsome Howdy" (b. July 24, 1889, Crawfordsville, IN; d. September 4, 1923, Altoona, PA), auto racer, won his first auto race in the five-mile Southern Championships at New Orleans, LA, in November

1909. Wilcox raced when drivers were called "pilots" and when their uniforms, hats, and goggles made them look like World War I aviators rather than automobile drivers. Wilcox, who possessed a cheerful driving personality, became a crowd favorite at the IMS and was nicknamed "Handsome Howdy."

Many of the nation's first car racers, including Wilcox, competed in various races involving different vehicles. In June 1910, Wilcox won a hill climb, 6,000 feet long with a 700-foot rise and a 10 to 22 percent grade, at Wilkes-Barre, PA. The next month, he raced at the IMS and participated in races spanning 10 miles, 15 miles, and 20 miles. Drivers were peripatetic. From the fall of 1910 through spring of 1911, Wilcox raced at Indianapolis, the California Motordome, and the Atlantic-Pablo Beach Races near Jacksonville, FL.

Wilcox's track record at the IMS remained impressive, both in his racing intensity and his ability to handle different racing machines. Between 1911 and 1923, he raced in every Indianapolis 500 except for 1917 and 1918 and competed in National, Pope-Hartford, Stutz, Premier, Peugeot, and Miller cars. In 1915, he won the pole position on the starting grid.

Wilcox's greatest year came in 1919, when he started in second place at the Indianapolis 500. According to Jack Fox in *The Indianapolis 500*, Wilcox "plugged along" to victory. His qualifying speed was 100.01 mph, while his race average speed was 88.05 mph. The race, however, brought tragedy, as accidents killed three racers and critically injured two others.

Wilcox was fatally injured in the inaugural 200-mile race on a new track at Altoona, PA, in September 1923. The *NYT* reported, "Wilcox drove so low on the planking that he was temporarily on the dirt. He swerved to get back on the planking and his wheels struck the oil-soaked boards at the track edge. The car then whirled completely around and rolled over several times." Wilcox, who was survived by his wife and two children, was inducted into the IMS Hall of Fame in 1963.

BIBLIOGRAPHY: Jack C. Fox, *The Indianapolis 500* (New York, 1967); Howard Wilcox file, courtesy of Bob Laycock, IMS, Indianapolis, IN; *NYT*, September 5, 1923.

Scott A.G.M. Crawford

BASEBALL

ALOU, Felipe (Rojas) (b. May 12, 1935, Haina, Dominican Republic), player and manager, is the son of Jose Rojas and Virginia (Alou) Rojas and grew up, with five siblings, in the poverty-stricken environs of Haina. Two of his younger brothers, Mateo* and Jesus, joined Felipe later as major league baseball players. In his youth, Felipe excelled as an all-around athlete and during his senior year of high school set the Dominican record in throwing the javelin. At the University of Santo Domingo, he played on the Dominican baseball squad in the 1955 Pan-American contests. That same year, Horatio Martinez, a university baseball coach and a scout for the New York Giants (NL), signed Alou to a professional baseball contract.

The six-foot, 195-pound Dominican slugger spent the next two years as a minor league outfielder before his debut with the San Francisco Giants (NL) in June 1958. His best year with the Giants came in 1962, when he hit 25 home runs, drove in 98 tallies, and batted .316. His best year overall, however, took place in 1966 during his tenure with the Atlanta Braves (NL). That year, he belted 31 home runs, batted in 74 runs, led the NL with 218 hits and 122 runs scored, and finished second in the batting race with a .327 average. In 1968, the Dominican again led the NL with 210 runs scored. Between 1970 and 1974, Alou performed for the Oakland Athletics (AL), New York Yankees (AL), and Montreal Expos (NL) and concluded his major league career with the Milwaukee Brewers (AL). He finished his playing days with 206 home runs, 852 RBIs, 985 runs scored, and a .286 career batting average.

Alou joined the Expos organization as a minor league manager for the 1975 season and compiled an 844–751 win–loss record in 12 seasons, finishing first three times and winning two minor league championships. On May 22, 1992, he took over the Montreal Expos after manager Tom Runnells was fired. At that point, the Expos were struggling with a 17–20 mark. The crafty rookie manager guided Montreal to an 87–75 second-place finish in the NL Eastern Division. In his second year as manager, the Expos again contended for the title and repeated in second place with a 94–68 record. During the strike-shortened 1994 season, Alou managed the Expos to first place with a 74–40 mark and won AP Major League and BWAA NL Manager of the Year Honors. Alou's youngest son, Moises, has started in the Montreal outfield since 1993.

Alou, currently married to Lucie Gagdon from Canada, has nine children through three previous marriages.

BIBLIOGRAPHY: Felipe Alou with Arnold Hano, "Latin-American Ballplayers Need a Bill of Rights," *Sport* 37 (November 1963), pp. 21, 76–79; Felipe Alou with Herm Weiskopf, *Felipe Alou: My Life and Baseball* (Waco, TX, 1967); Steve Marantz, "The Father and the Son," *TSN*, June 21, 1993, pp. 10–13.

                                                                                          Samuel O. Regalado

ALOU, Mateo (Rojas) "Matty" (b. December 22, 1938, Haina, Dominican Republic), player, is the son of Jose Rojas and Virginia (Alou) Rojas and was the middle of the three Alou brothers who played in the major leagues. Smaller but faster than either Felipe* or Jesus, the five-foot-nine-inch, 160-pound left-handed batting outfielder hit the ball to all fields and also beat out innumerable infield hits.

The San Francisco Giants' (NL) legendary Latin American scout, Horacio Martinez, initially signed Alou. Alou began his professional baseball career in 1957 at Michigan City, IN (ML). His other minor league stops included St. Cloud, MN (NoL), Springfield, MA (EL), and Tacoma, WA (PCL) before he debuted with the San Francisco Giants in 1960. Alou remained with the Giants as a part-time player through the 1965 season and only once batted more than 250 times. Alou, however, made four hits in 12 at bats with one RBI in the 1962 World Series when the New York Yankees (AL) defeated the Giants in seven games.

San Francisco traded Alou to the Pittsburgh Pirates (NL) in October 1965. Alou came into his own as the Bucs' leadoff hitter and center fielder. Pirate manager Harry Walker convinced Alou to switch to a heavier bat and hit to left field. The diminutive Dominican averaged .327 at the plate and scored 434 runs during his five years from 1966 to 1970 with Pittsburgh. In 1966, Alou won the NL batting title with a .342 average. Alou finished second with a .332 batting average in 1968, third behind teammate Roberto Clemente (BB) with a .338 average in 1967, and fourth with a .331 average in 1969. During 1969, the speedy Alou led the NL with 231 hits and 41 doubles and also set a major league record for most at bats in one season with 698. Alou's hitting exploits secured him positions on the NL All-Star team in 1968 and 1969 and the *TSN* All-Star team in 1969.

In January 1971, the Pirates traded Alou to the St. Louis Cardinals (NL) for pitcher Nelson Briles and outfielder Vic Davalillo. After hitting .315 for the Cardinals, he was sent in August 1972 to the Oakland Athletics (AL).

As a late season addition to the A's roster, Alou hit .381 in the 1972 AL Championship Series. He faltered, however, in the World Series against the Cincinnati Reds. Oakland won the World Series for its first championship, but Alou made only one hit in 24 at bats.

In November 1972, the A's traded Alou to the New York Yankees (AL). He played for the St. Louis Cardinals in 1973 and finished his 15 years in the major leagues with the San Diego Padres (NL) in 1974. During his career, Alou appeared in 1,667 games and batted .307 with 1,777 hits. He hit over .300 seven times and made 200 or more hits on two occasions.

The Santo Domingo, Dominican Republic, resident married Theresa Vasquez on October 24, 1962.

BIBLIOGRAPHY: *The Baseball Encyclopedia*, 9th ed. (New York, 1993); Mike Shatzkin, ed., *The Ballplayers* (New York, 1990), p. 16; Bob Smizik, *The Pittsburgh Pirates* (New York, 1990), pp. 81–82.

Frank W. Thackeray

ANTONELLI, John August (b. April 12, 1930, Rochester, NY), player and executive, is the son of August Antonelli, an Italian immigrant railroad contractor, and Josephine (Messore) Antonelli and batted and threw left-handed. The 6-foot-1½-inch, 185-pound Antonelli starred as a baseball pitcher at Jefferson High School in Rochester in 1947 and 1948 and was signed in 1948 out of semiprofessional baseball by the Boston Braves (NL) as one of the first "bonus babies," receiving a reported $75,000. Bonus rules required Antonelli to stay on the major league roster, as the Braves played him sporadically over the next three years. From 1951 through 1952, he was engaged in military service. He joined the Milwaukee Braves (NL) in 1953 and enjoyed his first successful season, winning 12 games with a 3.18 ERA.

In February 1954, Antonelli figured prominently in a multiplayer trade between Milwaukee and the New York Giants (NL). With New York that season, Antonelli enjoyed his greatest success by winning 21 games while losing only 7. He led NL pitchers in winning percentage (.750), shutouts (6), and ERA (2.30). Antonelli added a complete game win and save in the World Series, as the Giants swept the heavily favored Cleveland Indians (AL) in 4 games. His performance earned him third place in the 1954 MVP voting. Antonelli won 20 games in 1956, finishing the season with 11 victories in his last 12 games and triumphs in the final 7 contests. He again led the NL in shutouts (6). In 1959, with the Giants now in San Francisco, Antonelli won 19 games and hurled 4 shutouts to pace the NL for the third time. San Francisco in December 1960 traded Antonelli to the Cleveland Indians (AL). Cleveland sent him to the Milwaukee Braves (NL) in July 1961. After winning only one decision with Milwaukee that year, he was traded in October 1961 to the New York Mets (NL). Antonelli, however, retired from baseball. He pitched in the 1954 and 1956 All-Star Games, gaining a save in the latter, and was selected to the major league BBWAA All-Star team in 1954 and 1959. After retiring from baseball, he entered the tire business in Rochester and served as a director of the Rochester Red Wings (IL). Antonelli married Rosemarie Carbone in October 1951 and has three daughters, Lisa, Donna, and Regina, and one son, John, Jr.

BIBLIOGRAPHY: John August Antonelli file, National Baseball Library, Cooperstown, NY; *The Baseball Encyclopedia*, 9th ed. (New York, 1993); Jack Orr, "Johnny Antonelli's War with San Francisco," *Sport* 28 (December 1959), pp. 18–19, 78–80; Joseph L. Reichler, ed., *The Great All-Time Baseball Record Book* (New York, 1981).

Horace R. Givens

AVILA, Roberto Francisco "Bobby" (b. April 2, 1924, Veracruz, Mexico), player and executive, is the ninth child and fourth son of Jose Avila, a lawyer, and Andrea Avila. He attended Preparatoria School in Veracruz and completed three years at the University of Mexico. After concentrating on soccer, he turned to baseball at the age of 16. He soon progressed to the MEL, where he played for five years. In 1947 he hit a league-leading .347. That year, superscout Cyril C. Slapnicka signed him to a Cleveland Indians (AL) contract. Avila debuted with Class AAA Baltimore (IL) in 1948 before joining the Indians the following season. He batted only 14 times in 1949 but hit .299 the next year in 80 games. He married Elsa Diaz Miron in 1951 and resides in Veracruz with their children, Roberto, Elsa, Patricia, and Jose Alberto.

Avila, the first Mexican to experience real major league success, enjoyed his most productive seasons from 1951 through 1954, hitting .300 or better three times, batting no lower than .286, and leading the AL in triples in 1952. On June 20, 1951, he belted 3 homers, a single, and a double against the Boston Red Sox. On July 1, 1952, he tied an AL record by making 13 assists in a 19-inning game. Twice he scored more than 100 runs. His best season came in 1954, the year the Indians set a record with 111 victories and won the AL pennant. Despite a broken thumb, the right-hander led the AL with a .341 batting average, hit 15 homers and 27 doubles, and scored 112 runs. Defensively, although having a mediocre throwing arm, the 5-foot-10-inch, 175-pound second baseman led the AL in assists. At the All-Star Game in Cleveland, he made hits in all three at bats. Avila's Indians then lost the World Series to the New York Giants in four consecutive games, as he managed only two singles for a .133 average.

Despite vowing to hit .400, Avila never came close to the preceding four-year statistics. In 1955, his batting average slumped to .272, but he hit 13 homers and scored 83 runs. The next season, his batting average plummeted to .224 with only 10 homers and 74 runs scored. Salary disputes had caused dissatisfaction and delayed his spring training appearances. He purchased the Mexico City Reds (MEL) in late 1954, managing and playing second base there. Conceivably, Avila might have overextended himself. Moreover, he suffered an eye infection in the summer of 1955, which probably impaired his vision. Avila, an adept bunter and daring base runner, continued his mediocre play with Cleveland through the 1959 season. One bright spot came in 1957, when he led starting AL second basemen in fielding. He made the All-Star team in 1952 and 1955. In 1960, he closed out his career with Boston (AL), Baltimore (AL), and the Milwaukee Braves (NL). His baseball idol, Ted Williams (BB) of the Red Sox, retired that same year. Avila's career statistics include a .281 batting average, 725 runs scored, and 185 doubles in 1,300 games. Afterward, he returned to Mexico, serving as president of the MEL, a member of the Mexican Congress during the 1960s and 1970s, and mayor of Veracruz from 1976 to 1979.

BIBLIOGRAPHY: Roberto Avila, letter to James N. Giglio, July 2, 1993; Cleveland (OH) *News*, March 20, 1953; April 30, 1953; January 7, 1955; February 3, 1955; July 22, 1955; March 8, 1956; February 28, 1957; April 9, 1958; Cleveland (OH) *Plain Dealer*, October 2, 1954; Gordon Cobbledick, "Viva Avila!," *Sport* 15 (September 1953), pp. 26–27, 83–85; David S. Neft et al., *The Sports Encyclopedia: Baseball*, 1st ed. (New York, 1974); Questionnaire furnished by Richard Topp, former SABR president, October 1992.

James N. Giglio

BANCROFT, Francis Carter "Banny" (b. May 9, 1846, Lancaster, MA; d. March 30, 1921, Cincinnati, OH), manager and executive, was associated with professional baseball for over 40 years. The son of Lorey F. Bancroft and Ann Carter Bancroft, he enlisted with the Union Army, 8th New Hampshire Volunteers, and served 4 years during the Civil War. Bancroft drew upon his amateur playing experience to organize baseball matches among Union regiments. After the war, he settled in New Bedford, MA, and founded a prosperous hotel. Bancroft pursued many business ventures, including theater, opera, ice hockey, and most significantly, baseball.

In 1878 New Bedford entered a team in the IA, baseball's first minor league. Bancroft served as manager, but his duties encompassed all aspects of business and field management. He demonstrated an excellent ability to handle athletes and an innovative business style. He pulled his team from the IA and embarked on a barnstorming tour, playing a record 130 games. Over the winter, he took a team to Cuba and introduced the game there. The next year, he moved to Worcester, MA, and formed a baseball team so good that it was admitted to the NL in 1880.

He managed a still-record seven major league clubs during his nine seasons at the helm. His clubs included the Worcester Ruby Legs (NL) in 1880, the Detroit Wolverines (NL) in 1881–1882, the Cleveland Blues (NL) in 1883, the Providence, RI, Grays (NL) in 1884–1885, the Philadelphia Athletics (AA) in 1887, the Indianapolis Hoosiers (AA) in 1889, and the Cincinnati Reds (NL) in 1902. The 1884 season marked the pinnacle of his career. His Providence Grays won the NL pennant by 10½ games and swept the first World Series from the New York Metropolitans (AA). His lifetime managerial record stands at 375–333–10. Bancroft, an independent, strong-willed sort, often resented ownership involvement in the running of the team. His dissatisfaction with front office interference caused his frequent team changes.

Bancroft joined the front office with which he was so often at odds when he became business manager for the Cincinnati Reds (NL) in 1890. He returned to Cuba with the Reds and also took them to Hawaii. He remained in his post until his death, ranking among the most popular and well-liked executives in the game.

The twice-married Bancroft had at least four children and left his second wife financially well-off.

BIBLIOGRAPHY: Bill Ballou, "Mighty Bancroft Struck Nothing But Goldmines," Worcester (MA) *Sunday Telegram*, October 13, 1985; Frank C. Bancroft, letter to Town Clerk, Lancaster, MA, January 21, 1913; *The Baseball Encyclopedia*, 9th ed. (New York, 1993); Cincinnati (OH) *Commercial Tribune*, March 31, 1921; April 21, 1921; Lew Lipset, *New York Clipper Woodcuts, 1879–1880* (Manhattan, KS, 1984); Robert L. Tiemann and Mark Rucker, eds., *Nineteenth Century Stars* (Kansas City, MO, 1989).

                                                                                                    John R. Husman

BARNHILL, David "Dave" "Impo" "Skinny" (b. October 30, 1914, Greenville, NC; d. January 8, 1983, Miami, FL), player, was a small, hard-throwing strikeout artist with the New York Cubans during the 1940s. Barnhill began his baseball career on the sandlots of North Carolina, where he was discovered by the touring Miami Giants in 1936. Later, the Miami team evolved into the Ethiopian Clowns. Barnhill, pitching under the "Clown name" Impo, remained their star attraction for three seasons until signing with Alejandro Pompez's New York Cubans.

The diminutive hurler also demonstrated his wizardry in Puerto Rico, with a PRWL-leading 193 strikeouts in 1940–1941. He also led the CUWL in strikeouts, wins, and complete games, while compiling a composite three-year win–loss record of 23–19.

Beginning in 1941, he pitched in three consecutive East-West All-Star Games and recorded an aggregate six strikeouts in nine innings. After having been credited with the victory over Satchel Paige (BB) in the 1942 contest, he was selected to start the next season's game against Paige. Managers often paired him opposite Paige in regular season competition, the pair having split two earlier encounters that year in crowd-pleasing matchups at Yankee Stadium.

During his prime, Barnhill in 1942 received a telegram about a tryout with the Pittsburgh Pirates (NL) that would have made him the first black in the major leagues. Although the five-foot-seven-inch, 155-pound right-hander was rated as a "sure fire" prospect, the offer was rescinded, and he stayed on with the Cubans. He helped pitch the Cubans to an NNL pennant in 1947 and tossed a shutout victory over the Cleveland Buckeyes in the ensuing World Series, as the Cubans captured the Negro Championship.

In 1949, the New York Giants (NL) organization signed Barnhill and Ray Dandridge (BB) and assigned them to the Giants' franchise in Minneapolis, MN (AA). Barnhill registered an 11–3 record in 1950 to help the Millers win the AA pennant. He was accused of "cutting" the ball, as opposing managers watched his every move, trying to catch him. When they couldn't find any evidence to support their claim, they accused third baseman Dandridge of doing it for him.

By then, Barnhill's age kept him from appearing in the major leagues. Barnhill played with Miami Beach, FL (FIL), where he finished 13–8 with a 1.19 ERA in 1952 under manager Pepper Martin (BB). He spent the next year with Ft. Lauderdale, FL, in the same league, splitting two decisions in only four games pitched. This marked his last year in baseball. After leaving the diamond, he resided in Miami with his wife and daughter and worked with the Miami Department of Recreation and Parks for 28 years until his retirement in 1981.

BIBLIOGRAPHY: L. Robert Davids, ed., *Insider's Baseball* (New York, 1983); John B. Holway, *Black Diamonds* (Westport, CT, 1989); Robert W. Peterson, *Only the Ball Was White* (Englewood Cliffs, NJ, 1970); James A. Riley, *The All-Time All-Stars of Black Baseball* (Cocoa, FL, 1983); James A. Riley, *The Biographical Encyclopedia of the Negro Baseball Leagues* (New York, 1994); James A. Riley, interviews with former Negro League players, James A. Riley collection, Cocoa, FL; Mike Shatzkin, ed., *The Ballplayers* (New York, 1990), p. 50; Rick Wolff, ed., *The Baseball Encyclopedia*, 9th ed. (New York, 1993).

James A. Riley

BAUER, Henry Albert "Hank" (b. July 31, 1923, East St. Louis, IL), player, manager, and scout, was nicknamed and variously described as "Bauer the Man of the Hour" and the man with a face like a fist. He was employed as an iron worker in 1941, when Oshkosh, WI (WSL) signed him. Bauer, a six-foot, 200-pounder in his prime, spent four years in the minor leagues (1941, 1946–1948), the last two with Kansas City, MO (AA), and four (1942–1946) in the U.S. Marine Corps before making his major league debut in September 1948 with the New York Yankees (AL).

Bauer spent the next 14 years in the major leagues, including 12 with the Yankees. In those seasons in pinstripes, Bauer batted .280 with 158 home runs. These numbers nearly matched those of Yankee teammate Charley "King Kong" Keller (S), a player who Bauer had been favorably compared with by the sons of Larry MacPhail (BB), the Yankees' owners during spring training in 1948. With the Yankees under platoon-happy manager Casey Stengel (BB), Bauer showed a steady but consistent growth as right fielder in his first 6 years. His career batting average had reached .295 in 1954, but his average began to fade thereafter. By retirement, Bauer's lifetime average had dropped to .277. Around 1955, his home run production began to rise. Bauer was never ranked among batting leaders—at least statistically—although sharing the AL lead in triples with nine in 1957. Teammates Harry Simpson and Gil McDougald* also hit nine triples that year. Bauer appeared in three All-Star Games from 1952 to 1954, hitting two singles in seven at bats. The Yankees traded Bauer in December 1959 to the Kansas City Athletics (AL), where he spent his final 2 major league seasons. During 14 major league seasons, Bauer made 1,424 hits, 229 doubles, and 164 home runs, scored 833 runs, and knocked in 703 runs in 1,544 games.

The World Series produced Bauer's most memorable games. Although batting only .245 in 53 games spanning eight fall classics, he set a World Series record by hitting safely in 17 consecutive games. At least twice, his hitting heroics kept the Yankees alive or won the game. In 1955, he batted a superlative .429 against the Brooklyn Dodgers. Three years later, he tied a World Series record with four home runs against the Milwaukee Braves. The strongest World Series image of Bauer came defensively in the ninth inning of the sixth game of the 1951 World Series, when he made a diving, sliding catch of a sinking line drive off the bat of New York Giants' hitter Sal Yvars to preserve a Yankee victory.

Bauer also made his mark in managing, guiding the Baltimore Orioles to their first World Series title in 1966 with a four-game sweep of the favored Los Angeles Dodgers. Three victories came by shutout. In eight managerial seasons, Bauer's teams finished third or higher five times and completed a 594–544 mark for a .522 percentage. Bauer managed the Kansas City Athletics in 1961 and 1962, the Baltimore Orioles from 1964 to 1968, and the Oakland Athletics (AL) in 1969. In 1966 the *TSN* named him Manager of the Year. He later owned a liquor store and scouted for the New York Yankees until July 1987.

Bauer, who married Charlene Friede in October 1949, lives in Overland Park, KS, and has two daughters and two sons. One son, Herman, is named after Bauer's older brother, who was killed in France during World War II.

BIBLIOGRAPHY: Dom Forker, *The Men of Autumn* (Dallas, TX, 1989); Rich Marazzi and Len Fiorito, *Aaron to Zuverink* (New York, 1982); Tom Meany, ed., *The Magnificent Yankees* (New York, 1952); John Thorn and Pete Palmer, eds., *Total Baseball* 3rd ed. (New York, 1993); *TSN Baseball Register*, 1968.

                                                                              Lee E. Scanlon

BECKERT, Glenn Alfred "Bruno" (b. October 12, 1940, Pittsburgh, PA), player, was selected an all-city basketball and baseball player at Pittsburgh's Perry High School and graduated from Allegheny College in 1961. The Boston Red Sox (AL) originally signed him, but the Chicago Cubs (NL) drafted him in 1962. Following three minor league seasons at Waterloo, IA (ML), Wenatchee, WA (NWL), and Salt Lake City, UT (PCL), Beckert became the Cubs' second baseman in 1965. Don Kessinger,* his shortstop partner for the next nine years, also arrived at Chicago that season.

A career .283 hitter, the six-foot-one-inch, 190-pound Beckert led the NL from 1966 through 1969 as the "toughest to strike out." In 1968, he struck out once in every 32.15 trips to the plate. His career 243 strikeouts included 1 every 21.3 at bats. Never a slugger, the right-hander hit only 22 home runs and 196 doubles in his 11-year major league career. He enjoyed two memorable hitting games. When the Cubs defeated the Houston Astros, 9–3, on August 4, 1969, Beckert made 5 hits in 6 at bats. On July 26, 1970, he went 5 for 5, as the Cubs edged the Atlanta Braves, 4–3. Beckert's best hitting year came in 1971 when he averaged .342. He lost the batting crown, however, being sidelined for a month when he injured his right thumb in September.

A smooth-fielding second baseman, he in 1968 won a Gold Glove Award and was named "Chicago Player of the Year." He was selected the All-Star second baseman for four consecutive years, starting in 1968. Injuries began to take their toll on the scrappy Beckert, whose batting average and game appearances dropped steadily after the 1971 season. In November 1973 the Cubs traded him to the San Diego Padres (NL) for Jerry Morales. After playing in only 73 games during the next 2 seasons, Beckert retired. In 11 major league seasons, Beckert had 1,473 hits and knocked in 360 runs. Beckert has two daughters and lives in Palatine, IL.

BIBLIOGRAPHY: Art Ahrens and Eddie Gold, *Day by Day in Chicago Cubs History* (West Point, NY, 1982); *Chicago Cubs Official Roster Book*, 1972, 1973; Eddie Gold and Art Ahrens, *The New Era Cubs* (Chicago, IL, 1985).

Duane A. Smith

BELL, David Russell "Gus" (b. November 15, 1928, Louisville, KY), player, was nicknamed "Gus" by his baseball fan parents, who admired major league catcher Gus Mancuso. The 6-foot-1½-inch, 190-pound power-hitting outfielder, who batted left-handed and threw right-handed, graduated from Flaget High School in 1946 and made his major league debut with the Pittsburgh Pirates (NL) in 1950. Joining future National Baseball Hall of Famer Ralph Kiner (BB) in the Bucs outfield, Bell hit 12 triples in 1951 to lead the NL.

Frequent disagreements with Pittsburgh management prompted the Pirates to trade Bell to the Cincinnati Reds (NL) in October 1952. During his nine years with the Reds, Bell supplied both batting average and power in cozy Crosley Field. In 1953, Bell batted .300 with 30 home runs and 105 RBIs. This performance earned him the first of four (1953, 1954, 1956, 1957) All-Star Game appearances. In 1954, Bell batted a career-high .308

with 101 RBIs. He recorded 104 RBIs the following year and a career-high 115 RBIs in 1959. For the power-rich but pitching-poor Reds, Bell hit 27 home runs in 1955 and 29 round-trippers in 1956. Bell, an accomplished outfielder, held the major league record for most consecutive errorless games by an outfielder (200) and led NL outfielders defensively in 1958 and 1959. In 1961, Bell appeared in his only World Series and went hitless in three pinch hit at bats. The Reds lost the World Series to a mighty New York Yankee team.

In 1957, Bell was selected for the All-Star team. Cincinnati fans stuffed the ballot box, electing Reds to seven of the eight starting positions. Baseball Commissioner Ford Frick (BB), incensed at this perceived injustice, ordered that Bell and teammate Wally Post be removed from the NL starting lineup.

The New York Mets (NL) selected Bell in the 1961 expansion draft. Bell recorded the first base hit in Met history, getting a single on April 11, 1962 against the St. Louis Cardinals. In November 1962, the Mets traded Bell to the Milwaukee Braves (NL) for Frank Thomas (S). Bell finished his major league career in 1964 with Milwaukee. During his 15 years in the major leagues, Bell hit .281 with 206 home runs and 942 RBIs.

Bell married Joyce Sutherland on December 4, 1949 and has five children, Becky, Randy, Timmy, Debby, and Buddy. After his baseball career ended, Bell managed a temporary employment service company in Cincinnati. His son Buddy (S), a former major league infielder, completed an 18-year career in 1989. His grandson, David Bell, plays in the Cleveland Indians (AL) organization, while another grandson, Mike Bell, was selected by the Texas Rangers (AL) in the 1993 free agent draft. If either of Bell's grandchildren reaches the major leagues, they will join the Boones (Ray,* Bob (S), and Bret) as the only three-generation major league family.

BIBLIOGRAPHY: *The Baseball Encyclopedia*, 9th ed. (New York, 1993); Donald Honig, *The Cincinnati Reds* (New York, 1992), pp. 149–164; Mike Shatzkin, ed., *The Ball-players* (New York, 1990), p. 65; Bob Smizik, *The Pittsburgh Pirates* (New York, 1990), pp. 81–82.

Frank W. Thackeray

BELL, George Antonio Mathey (b. October 21, 1959, San Pedro de Macoris, Dominican Republic), player, entered professional baseball in 1978. His brothers include Juan, a major league infielder since 1989, and Rolando, a minor league infielder from 1985 through 1987. Bell, a six-foot-one-inch, 200-pound power hitter outfielder, possesses a strong arm and penchant for committing errors. He has been increasingly used as a designated hitter in recent years and appeared in only 15 games defensively in 1992.

Bell achieved stardom during a nine-season tour with the Toronto Blue Jays (1981, 1983–1990), winning the AL MVP award in 1987. During his MVP campaign, Bell led the major leagues in total bases (369) and the AL in RBIs (134) while hitting a career-high 47 home runs and batting .308. He also started in left field for the AL in the All-Star Game and was named *TSN* Major League Player of the Year. In 1,181 games for the Blue Jays, Bell compiled 202 home runs, drove 740 teammates home, and hit .286. He signed as a free agent with the Chicago Cubs (NL) in 1991 and moved across town to the Chicago White Sox (AL) in 1992.

Bell has also starred in the DRWL, leading the circuit in slugging average, total bases, and doubles in 1983–1984. He helped the 1980–1981 and 1981–1982 Escogido entries win the DRWL title and the 1984–1985 Licey club win the DRWL and Caribbean Series crowns. Bell enjoys a .298 career batting average and a .463 slugging average in the DRWL.

The Spanish-speaking Bell's difficulty expressing himself in English, coupled with an on-the-field confrontation after being hit by a pitch early in his career and disagreement with Toronto manager Jimy Williams over his full-time use as a designated hitter, has been exploited by the press. Newspapers sometimes portray Bell negatively, despite his success as a player.

Bell's AL MVP award marked the first won by either a Dominican Republic native or a member of a Canadian team. His other accomplishments include hitting three home runs on April 4, 1988; tying for the AL lead with 15 game-winning hits in 1986; and leading the AL with 14 sacrifice flies in 1989.

Bell helped Toronto (AL) capture East Division crowns in 1985 and 1989 and Chicago (AL) take a West Division title in 1993 and owns a .271 average in 12 AL Championship Series contests. He has compiled a .278 career batting average with 265 home runs and 1,002 RBIs in 12 major league seasons through 1993. In October 1993, the White Sox released Bell.

Bell married Marie Louisa Beguero on November 11, 1981.

BIBLIOGRAPHY: *Baseball America's 1993 Almanac* (Durham, NC, 1992); *The Baseball Encyclopedia*, 9th ed. (New York, 1993); *Blue Jay Scorebook Magazine* (Toronto, Canada, 1985); *Dominican Baseball Guide* (Santo Domingo, DR, 1986); Rick Matsumoto, "Barfield & Bell," *Street & Smith Baseball Magazine* 47 (1987), pp. 96–97; Michael and Mary Oleksak, *Beisbol* (Grand Rapids, MI, 1991); *TSN Baseball Guide*, 1993; *TSN Baseball Register*, 1993.

Merl F. Kleinknecht

BISHOP, Max Frederick "Tilly" "Camera Eye" (b. September 5, 1899, Waynesboro, PA; d. February 24, 1962, Waynesboro, PA), player, scout, and coach, was the son of Lulu Bishop and spent 12 years in the AL as a slick-fielding second baseman and sharp-eyed leadoff man.

In 1918 the Baltimore Orioles (IL) signed Bishop out of Baltimore City College, a high school for superior students. Bishop remained the Orioles' second sacker until being sold to the Philadelphia Athletics (AL) after the 1923 season. From 1924 through 1933, he proved a mainstay for Connie Mack's (BB) Athletics and teamed with shortstop Joe Boley to form an outstanding double-play combination. Faced with financial problems, Mack in December 1933 sold Bishop, Lefty Grove (BB), and Rube Walberg to the Boston Red Sox (AL) for a reported $125,000 and two players. In Boston, Bishop did not provide the expected strength at second base and shared the position in 1934 and 1935. He completed his playing career with Baltimore (IL) in 1936. After scouting a year for the Detroit Tigers (AL) in 1937, he served as baseball coach at the U.S. Naval Academy from 1938 to 1961. His midshipmen won 306 games and lost only 143.

In 1,338 major league games, Bishop produced 1,216 hits with 236 doubles, 35 triples, and 41 homers. His .271 career batting average included a high of .316 in 1928. He scored 966 runs, batted in 379 runs, and stole 43 bases. In three World Series, he hit only .182 in 18 games. His keen eye at the plate led to his reputation for taking a pitch a quarter inch out of the strike zone. In 1929, he led the AL in walks with 128 and twice drew 8 in a doubleheader. He averaged almost a walk a game, recording 1,153 for 1,338 contests. Defensively, Bishop in 1932 set a record of 53 consecutive errorless games by a second baseman, a mark that stood until 1965. He set a record fielding average for a second baseman (.987) in 1926 and then bettered it in 1932 with a .988 mark.

A longtime resident of Baltimore, Bishop in 1962 returned to his native town of Waynesboro, PA, to attend the funeral of his mother Lulu. While there, he died in his sleep.

BIBLIOGRAPHY: James H. Bready, *The Home Team: Baseball in Baltimore*, 3rd ed. (Baltimore, MD, 1979); Al Hirshberg, *The Red Sox, the Bean and the Cod* (Boston, MA, 1947); Frederick Lieb, *The Boston Red Sox* (New York, 1947); Frederick Lieb, *Connie Mack* (New York, 1945); Connie Mack, *My 66 Years in the Big Leagues* (New York, 1950); *NYT*, February 26, 1962; Father Jerome C. Romanowski (the Baseball Padre), *The Mackmen*, 2nd ed. (Upper Darby, PA, 1979); *TSN*, March 7, 1962.

Ralph S. Graber

BLACKWELL, Ewell "The Whip" (b. October 23, 1922, Fresno, CA), player, batted and threw right-handed with a six-foot-six-inch, 195-pound frame. The son of Flugin Blackwell, he played baseball and basketball at Bonita High School. After attending the University of California and La Verne Teachers College, he worked at Vultee Aircraft Company in Downey, CA. He played semiprofessional baseball in Downey until the Cincinnati Reds (NL) signed him in 1942 and initially assigned him to Ogden, UT (PrL). The same year, Blackwell won 15 games for Syracuse, NY (IL). After being drafted in 1943, he spent three years in the U.S. Army.

Blackwell's return to Cincinnati in 1946 saw him win only 9 games, but he led the NL in shutouts with six. Blackwell enjoyed an exceptional year in 1947, leading the NL in victories (22), strikeouts (193), and complete games (23). He recorded 16 consecutive victories, all complete games. The eighth triumph in the streak featured a no-hitter against the Boston Braves on June 18, 1947. In his next start, Blackwell lasted 8⅓ innings before surrendering two hits to the Brooklyn Dodgers in the ninth inning. Blackwell compiled several good seasons, but several physical problems limited his effectiveness. His health problems included a sore shoulder in 1948, surgery to remove a kidney in 1949, and an emergency appendectomy in 1950, when he still won 17 games and struck out 14 Chicago Cubs in a 10-inning game.

In August 1952 the Reds traded Blackwell to the New York Yankees (AL). He appeared in his only World Series that year, surrendering four earned runs in five innings against the Brooklyn Dodgers. He encountered little success in New York and was voluntarily retired in 1954. He attempted a comeback and was traded in March 1955 to the Kansas City Athletics (AL) but appeared in only 2 games before permanently retiring. During his major league career, Blackwell won 82 games, lost 78 decisions, compiled a 3.30 ERA, and recorded 839 strikeouts. The intimidating pitcher used a sidearm motion and threw with exceptional speed in his early seasons. His fastball, virtually unhittable, seemed to explode at the batter from the third base side of the mound. At Syracuse, Blackwell's teammates refused to take batting practice against him. In 1960, fans elected him to the Cincinnati Baseball Hall of Fame. He was named to the NL All-Star team in 1947 and 1951. Subsequently, Blackwell engaged in retail sales for a large distillery in Tampa, FL, and Columbia, SC, and also worked as a security guard. He resides with his wife, Dottie, in Hendersonville, NC, and has two children.

BIBLIOGRAPHY: *The Baseball Encyclopedia*, 9th ed. (New York, 1993); Ewell Blackwell file, National Baseball Library, Cooperstown, NY; Donald Honig, *Baseball Between the Lines* (New York, 1976); Tom Meany, *Baseball's Greatest Pitchers* (New York, 1951); Joseph L. Reichler, ed., *The Great All-Time Baseball Record Book* (New York, 1981); Rich Westcott, *Diamond Greats* (Westport, CT, 1988).

Horace R. Givens

BOGGS, Wade Anthony (b. June 15, 1958, Omaha, NE), player, was reared in Tampa, FL, by his parents Win Boggs, a U.S. Air Force master sergeant and semiprofessional softball player, and Sue Boggs. Boggs's heavy hitting at Tampa's Plant High School outshone his mediocre fielding and slowness afoot and earned him selection by the Boston Red Sox (AL) in the seventh round of the June 1976 free agent draft. The six-foot-two-inch, 197-pound third baseman rose slowly through Boston's farm system with stops at Class A Elmira, NY (NYPL) in 1976 and Winston-Salem, NC (CrL) in 1977; Class AA Bristol, CT (EL) in 1978–1979; and Class AAA Pawtucket, RI (IL) in 1980–1981. His .335 batting average led the IL in 1981.

After being promoted to Boston in 1982, Boggs became the Red Sox's regular third baseman when Carney Lansford* was injured in late June. Although Boggs recorded too few plate appearances to qualify for the AL batting title, his .349 batting average surpassed official titlist Willie Wilson (BB) by 17 points. Boggs shifted to first base when Lansford returned to the lineup but returned to third base in 1983 after Lansford was traded to the Oakland Athletics.

From 1983 through 1989, Boggs, who bats left-handed and throws right-handed, led the AL five times in batting (1983, 1985–1988, with a career high of .368 in 1985); six times in on base percentage (1983, 1985–1989); twice in doubles (1988, 1989), walks (1986, 1988), and runs scored (1988, 1989); and once in hits (240 in 1985, the most for a major leaguer since 1930). His seven consecutive 200-hit seasons (1983–1989) rank him second only to Willie Keeler's (BB) eight. From 1986 to 1989, Boggs became the first major leaguer ever to record four consecutive seasons with both 200 hits and 100 walks. For six years (1983–1988), Boggs ranked among the four most valuable AL players in Pete Palmer's *Total Baseball* ranking. His rankings included first place in 1987 and second place in 1988.

Boggs attracted the attention of the nonbaseball public in June 1988, when he was sued for breach of contract by California real estate broker Margo Adams. Boggs had broken off a romantic liaison with Adams. Her suit was unsuccessful, but Boggs's celebrity status grew when Adams detailed their affair in *Penthouse* magazine. Boggs and his wife, Deborah Bertercelli, whom he had married in 1976, appeared on network television to affirm the renewed solidity of their marriage.

Boggs's offensive production plummeted to a career low in 1992 partly because of eyesight problems. The Red Sox consequently lost interest in him. In December 1992, the New York Yankees signed free agent Boggs for three years. During the strike-shortened 1994 season, he batted .342 with 11 homeruns and 55 RBIs to help the Yankees capture first place in the AL East Division and won his first Gold Glove award.

Through the 1994 season, Boggs compiled a .335 batting average with 2,392 hits, 467 doubles, and 801 RBIs. He appeared in ten All-Star Games (1985–1994), three AL Championship Series (1986, 1988, 1990), and the 1986 World Series, where he batted .290 against the New York Mets.

The Boggses have one daughter, Meagann, and one son, Brett. Boggs's literary credits include an autobiography, a batting instructional, and *Fowl Tips*, a collection of his mother's and wife's chicken recipes.

BIBLIOGRAPHY: Wade Boggs, *Boggs!* (Chicago, IL, 1986); Wade Boggs and David Brisson, *The Techniques of Modern Hitting* (New York, 1990); *CB* (1990), pp. 66–70; E. M. Swift, "Facing the Music," *SI* 70 (March 6, 1989), pp. 38–40, 45; John Thorn and Pete Palmer, eds., *Total Baseball*, 3rd ed. (New York, 1993), pp. 161, 689.

                                                                                Frederick Ivor-Campbell

BONDS, Barry Lamar (b. July 24, 1964, Riverside, CA), player, is the son of Bobby Bonds (BB), a former major leaguer, and Pat Bonds. The six-foot-one-inch, 190-pound left-handed outfielder graduated from Serra High School in San Mateo, CA, and attended Arizona State University, where he hit .347 with 45 home runs, 175 RBIs, and 57 stolen bases during three seasons. In June 1985, the Pittsburgh Pirates (NL) signed Bonds as their first-round selection in the free agent draft and sixth player taken overall.

After spending only 115 games in the minor leagues, Bonds joined the Pirates in May 1986. During the 1986 season, he led all rookie NL players in home runs (16), RBIs (48), stolen bases (36), and walks (49). Pirate manager Jim Leyland* brought Bonds along slowly. Bonds hit his stride in 1990, when he moved from the leadoff position to the fifth spot in the batting order. Bonds batted .301, with 104 runs scored, 33 home runs, 114 RBIs, and 52 stolen bases, and led the NL with a .565 slugging percentage. His honors included being named NL Player of the Month for July, making his first All-Star appearance, and winning the first of five consecutive Gold Gloves for his play in left field. Bonds, chosen the NL MVP, was selected *TSN* Major League Player of the Year. *TSN* also named him NL Player of the Year in 1991, 1992, and 1993.

Bonds continued his superb play during the 1991 and 1992 seasons. In 1991 he registered 116 RBIs while finishing second to Terry Pendleton* in the NL MVP balloting. In 1992 he garnered his second NL MVP award, hitting .311 with 34 home runs and 103 RBIs. He led the NL in runs scored (109), slugging percentage (.624), walks (127), intentional walks (32), and home run ratio (1 every 13.9 at bats). Bonds, however, did not perform well in the NL Championship Series against the Cincinnati Reds in 1990 and Atlanta Braves in 1991 and 1992. In the three NL Championship Series, he batted only .191 with just 1 home run and 3 RBIs.

After the 1992 season, the San Francisco Giants (NL) signed free agent Bonds to a $43.75 million contract over six years. During the first half of the 1993 season, with his father serving as hitting instructor for the Giants, Bonds led San Francisco to the top of the NL West Division. He was chosen NL Player of the Month for April and was named to the NL All-Star team for the third time. Bonds became the seventh major league player to win the MVP award three times and the first to earn it three times in four seasons. He set career highs for batting average (.336), runs scored (129), RBIs (123), and home runs (46), leading the NL in the latter two categories. The Giants set a franchise record with 103 victories in 1993, being edged on the final day by the Atlanta Braves for the NL West Division title. During the strike-shortened 1994 season, Bonds batted .312 with 37 home runs and 81 RBIs and repeated as an NL All-Star team member. Through 1994, he batted .283 with 276 doubles, 259 home runs, 760 RBIs, and 309 stolen bases in 1,281 games.

Bonds, who resides in Atherton, CA, is separated from his wife Sun and has two children, Nikolai and Shikari.

BIBLIOGRAPHY: *The Baseball Encyclopedia*, 9th ed. (New York, 1993), p. 681; Kevin Cook, "Playboy Interview: Barry Bonds," *Playboy* 40 (July 1993), pp. 59–72, 148; Richard Hoffer, "The Importance of Being Barry," *SI* 78 (May 24, 1993), pp. 13–

21; David A. Kaplan, "The Rising Stock of Bonds," *Newsweek* 121 (May 31, 1993), p. 64; *Pittsburgh Pirates 1991 Record and Information Guide*, pp. 29–31; *San Francisco Giants 1993 Record and Information Guide*, pp. 52–53; Mike Shatzkin, ed., *The Ballplayers* (New York, 1990), p. 90.

Frank W. Thackeray

BONHAM, Ernest Edward "Ernie" "Tiny" (b. August 16, 1913, Ione, CA; d. September 15, 1949, Pittsburgh, PA), player, was the thirteenth of 14 children and grew up on a farm, where he proved as adept at milking cows as he would later be at throwing a baseball. He pitched for Ione High School and later starred for the AmLe Junior Club. Bonham, a logger in northern California, played semiprofessional baseball in Mother Lode Valley. New York Yankee (AL) scout Joe Devine discovered Bonham in 1935. After starting with Modesto, CA (CSSL), he compiled a 14–8 mark in 1936 with Akron, OH (MAL). He finished the 1936 season with Binghamton, NY (NYPL) and compiled a 17–16 mark the next season for the Oakland, CA Oaks (PCL). With Newark, NJ (IL), Bonham in 1938 won 8 of 10 decisions. Later that season, he recorded a 3–4 slate with Kansas City, MO (AA). At Kansas City, former New York Yankee Frank Makosky taught Bonham the forkball, later his most effective pitch in the big leagues. The six-foot-two-inch, 215-pound right-handed Bonham, one of the first to have success with this pitch, stayed with the Blues until the New York Yankees called him up in 1940.

Although Bonham's back still bothered him from a 1939 logging accident, his 1.90 ERA in just 12 games led the AL. Chronic back problems plagued Bonham during his 10-year career. His finest season came in 1942, when he led the AL with a 21–5 record, .808 winning percentage, 22 complete games, and six shutouts. Bonham earned a berth on the AL All-Star team in 1942, his best major league season. The mainstay of the Yankee staff, he won 79 games while losing 50 during his tenure there. Bonham won the fifth and final game of the 1941 World Series against the Brooklyn Dodgers but lost 1 game each to the St. Louis Cardinals (NL) in both 1942 and 1943 World Series.

On October 21, 1946, New York traded the tall, quiet pitcher with a keen wit to the Pittsburgh Pirates (NL) for Cookie Cuccurullo. Bonham compiled winning records in 1947 and 1949 for Pittsburgh. He pitched his last game for the Pirates on August 27, 1949, an 8–2 win over the Philadelphia Phillies (NL) at Shibe Park. On September 6, after weeks of stomach cramps, Bonham entered the hospital. Appendicitis symptoms were discovered. Bonham's wife, Ruth Munsterman, was at his bedside when he succumbed to what doctors later reported as cancer of the colon. The couple had two children, Donna Marie and Ernie, Jr. His composite major league record was 103–72 (.589), with a 3.06 ERA.

BIBLIOGRAPHY: Gene Karst and Martin Jones, Jr., *Who's Who in Professional Baseball* (New Rochelle, NY, 1973); Mike Shatzkin, ed., *The Ball Players* (New York, 1990); *TSN*, September 21, 1949; September 28, 1949.

William A. Borst

BONILLA, Roberto Antonio Jr. "Bobby" "Bobby Bo" (b. February 23, 1963, New York, NY), player, is the son of Roberto Bonilla, Sr., an electrician, and Regina Bonilla. The six-foot-three-inch, 240-pound, switch-hitting Bonilla graduated from Lehman High School in New York. The Pittsburgh Pirates (NL) signed him as a nondrafted free agent in 1981.

After Bonilla experienced an unexceptional minor league career, the Chicago White Sox (AL) drafted him in December 1985. Bonilla debuted as an outfielder for Chicago in April 1986 but was traded back to a woeful Pirate club that July. Bonilla helped lead a baseball renaissance in Pittsburgh that culminated in three consecutive NL East Division titles.

In 1987, the powerful Bonilla played third base and hit .300 for the first time in his career, becoming only the fourth player to belt a fair ball into the upper deck at Three Rivers Stadium. For Bonilla, 1988 marked a banner year. He slugged 24 home runs and drove in 100 runs, tying him with teammate Andy Van Slyke* for third in the NL. His honors included being named NL Player of the Month for both April and May, elected to the NL All-Star team as starting third baseman, and selected for *TSN* Silver Slugger Team. In 1989, Bonilla led the Bucs in home runs (24) and RBIs (86). He also earned his second of four consecutive spots on the NL All-Star team and was tabbed NL Player of the Month for September.

In 1990, Pittsburgh moved Bonilla from third base, where his fielding was barely adequate, to right field. He welcomed the switch, setting career marks for hits (175), RBIs (120), and runs scored (112). His 32 home runs set a season record for a Pirate right fielder. Bonilla led the NL in extra base hits (78) and finished second in RBIs, runs scored, doubles (39), and total bases (324).

Bonilla continued to play well in 1991, hitting .302 with 100 RBIs and an NL-leading 44 doubles. Like the rest of the Pirate sluggers, however, he slumped in the NL Championship Series against the Cincinnati Reds in 1990 and Atlanta Braves in 1991. In the 1990 and 1991 NL Championship Series, Bonilla produced a combined .250 with no home runs and only 2 RBIs.

Following the 1991 season, Bonilla became a free agent and signed a five-year, $29 million contract with the New York Mets (NL). New Yorkers expected Bonilla to lead the Mets to glory, but his production declined in 1992. Despite his career-high 34 home runs in 1993, he received fan and media criticism for the failure of the grossly overrated and overpaid Mets. Through the strike-shortened 1994 season, he has batted .278 with 269 doubles, 189 home runs, and 750 RBIs in 1,293 games.

Bonilla and his wife Millie live in Bradenton, FL, with their daughter Danielle.

BIBLIOGRAPHY: *The Baseball Encyclopedia*, 9th ed. (New York, 1993), p. 681; *New York Mets 1993 Information Guide*, pp. 29–32; *The Official Major League Baseball 1992 Stat Book*, p. 29; *Pittsburgh Pirates 1991 Record and Information Guide*, pp. 31–33; Mike Shatzkin, ed., *The Ballplayers* (New York, 1990), p. 91.

Frank W. Thackeray

BOONE, Raymond Otis "Ray" "Ike" (b. July 27, 1923, San Diego, CA), player and scout, is the son of Donald E. Boone, a lather, and Beulah Boone, a seamstress, of Irish-German ancestry. After graduating from Herbert Hoover High School in San Diego in 1942, he signed with the Cleveland Indians (AL) as a catcher. He played briefly for Wausau, WI (NoL) before beginning a three-year stint in the U.S. Navy. Upon his release, he married Patricia D. Brown, an accomplished synchronized swimmer, in October 1946. They have three children, Robert (S), a renowned major league catcher, Rodney, and Theresa.

After converting to shortstop in the Indians farm system, he joined the Tribe in 1948 as backup for player-manager Lou Boudreau (BB). He requested Class AAA assignment after three weeks of inactivity. He returned from Hollywood, CA (PCL) late in the season to witness the Indians' World Series triumph over the Boston Braves. For the next four seasons, the six-foot, 180-pound Boone played shortstop for the Indians. The high-strung Boone performed in the shadow of the injury-plagued Boudreau, the 1948 AL MVP who departed in 1951. Boone booted balls, which booing fans insisted were routine outs for his predecessor. The right-hander led AL shortstops in errors with 33. He batted .301 in 1950, but his average never exceeded .263 in his other three seasons for Cleveland. In that span, he never hammered more than 12 home runs. The Indians traded him in 1953 to the Detroit Tigers (AL), where he enjoyed his best seasons. Detroit moved Boone to third base, where he performed steadily and hit .312 in 1953 and .308 in 1956. His home run production increased to 26 in 1953 and ranged from 20 to 25 for the next four years. In 1953, he tied an AL standard by hitting four grand-slam homers during the same season. He homered in the 1954 All-Star Game and also made the 1956 AL squad. In 1955 he and Jackie Jensen (S) shared the AL lead in RBIs with 116. From 1953 through 1956, Boone remained Detroit's most consistent power hitter for a perennial second-division team.

Following Boone's move to first base, Detroit traded the slumping infielder to the Chicago White Sox (AL). That season he hit only 13 homers. After batting .273 as a part-time player with Kansas City (AL) in 1959, he closed out his major league career in 1960 with the Milwaukee Braves (NL) and Boston Red Sox (AL). He scouted with the Red Sox organization for the next 33 years. In his 13 major league seasons, Boone hit .275 with 1,260 hits, 151 homers, and 737 RBIs. Defensively, he compiled a .965 mark, tied an AL record for most putouts by a third baseman with 7 on April 24, 1954, and led the AL third basemen in putouts with 170 in 1954.

BIBLIOGRAPHY: Raymond Boone, letter to James N. Giglio, January 9, 1993; Cleveland (OH) *News*, May 14, 1952; March 6, 1953; February 17, 1956; Cleveland (OH) *Plain Dealer*, May 4, 1948; March 6, 1970; February 24, 1974; James N. Giglio, telephone interview with Raymond Boone, June 10, 1993; David S. Neft et al., *The Sports Encyclopedia: Baseball*, 1st ed. (New York, 1974); Questionnaire furnished by Richard Topp, former SABR president, October 1992.

James N. Giglio

BRADLEY, William Joseph "Bill" (b. February 13, 1877, Cleveland, OH; d. March 3, 1954, Cleveland, OH), player, manager, and scout, stood six foot one inch, weighed 190 pounds, and batted and threw right-handed. He received an eight-year parochial school education. In 1905, he married Anna Kellackey. They had two daughters, Anna and Norma, and a son, Norman.

Bradley began his professional baseball career at Utica, NY (NYSL) in 1898, continuing there through most of 1899. In late 1899, the Chicago (NL) team promoted him to play third base, which he did for the Orphans through 1900. In 1901, Bradley jumped to Cleveland in the newly founded AL and enjoyed hometown favorite status as a regular third sacker for the Blues and Naps through 1910. In 1906, he suffered a broken arm when hit by a pitch. This injury and a later typhoid fever attack diminished his playing skills. From 1911 through 1913, he played and managed for Toronto, Canada (EL, then IL). He moved to the rival major league, the FL, as manager of the Brooklyn Tip-Tops in 1914. In 1915 he played intermittently for the Kansas City Packers (FL), where his playing career ended. The Cleveland Indians employed him as a scout from 1928 until his retirement in 1953. Bradley's Cleveland property enabled his family to live comfortably.

Bradley, a good fielder with a strong arm, made many errors, largely a by-product of the small gloves then used. He still shares the AL record for putouts by a third baseman in a nine-inning game (seven), accomplished September 21, 1901, and May 13, 1909. His lifetime fielding average was .934. Prior to his arm injury and typhoid attack, he ranked among the AL's better hitters. In 1902, 1903, and 1904, his name appeared among AL leaders in doubles, triples, home runs, runs scored, RBIs, batting average, slugging percentage, and total bases. In 1902, when foul balls did not count as strikes, he became the first batter to hit home runs in four consecutive games. His 14-year major league career included a .271 batting average, 1,472 hits, 273 doubles, 84 triples, and 552 RBIs.

BIBLIOGRAPHY: Bill Bradley file, National Baseball Library, Cooperstown, NY; *NYT*, March 13, 1954; Rick Wolff, ed., *The Baseball Encyclopedia*, 9th ed. (New York, 1993), p. 706.

Lowell L. Blaisdell

BREWER, Chester Arthur "Chet" (b. January 14, 1907, Leavenworth, KS; d. March 26, 1990, Los Angeles, CA), player, scout, and manager, was the son of William Brewer, a Methodist minister, and Minnie (Davis) Brewer. Brewer studied at the University of Mexico and became fluent in Spanish. The six-foot-four-inch, 185-pound right-handed pitcher was known for his lively fastball and a devastating overhand sinker.

Brewer's professional Negro League career started in 1925 with the Kansas City, MO Monarchs (NNL). In his first full season with the Monarchs in 1926, he compiled a 12–1 win–loss record and hurled eight complete games. Three years later, he led the NNL with 16 wins and 15 complete games and pitched 31 consecutive scoreless innings against the NNL's best. One of his greatest pitching performances came under the lights in 1930 against the Homestead, PA, Grays. Brewer struck out 19 batters, including 10 in a row, but lost, 1–0, in 12 innings. He finished the 1930 season with 30 wins. Brewer won 34 games in 1933 and started the 1934 season with 16 straight victories, en route to 33 triumphs. Brewer spent 14 seasons with the Monarchs and 5 seasons with the Cleveland, OH, Buckeyes (NAL) before retiring in 1948. Brewer also played briefly with the Washington, DC, Pilots (EWL) in 1932, the New York Cubans (NNL) in 1936, the Philadelphia, PA, Stars (NAL) in 1939 and 1941, and the Chicago, IL, American Giants (NAL) in 1946. Brewer claimed his greatest thrills were pitching a no-hitter against Satchel Paige (BB) and the Santa Domingo team, and two no-hitters in the 1939 MEWL.

After retiring as a player, he scouted for the Pittsburgh Pirates (NL) from 1957 to 1974 and managed their rookie team. Later, he worked for the Major League Scouting Bureau, where he discovered Enos Cabell, Willie Crawford, Dock Ellis, Reggie Smith (BB), Bobby Tolan, Ellis Valentine, and Bob Watson.

Brewer married Mary Margaret Davis in 1924. They had two children, Chester Eugene and Marian Louise. In 1973, he married Tina Blanchard. Five years later the Ross Snyder Recreation Center in Los Angeles, CA, was renamed the Chet Brewer Baseball Field to honor his commitment for teaching the mechanics of baseball and the importance of personal behavior to local youths. Brewer epitomized the "classic" man, being a sympathetic manager, a person of principle, a great storyteller, and a superbly conditioned athlete with immense competitive spirits.

BIBLIOGRAPHY: Jack Etkin, *Innings Ago* (Kansas City, MO, 1987); John Holway, *Black Diamonds* (Westport, CT, 1989); Kansas City (MO) *Call*, October 19, 1934;

August 25, 1939; Pittsburgh (PA) *Courier*, August 9, 1930; James A. Riley, *The Biographical Encyclopedia of the Negro Baseball Leagues* (New York, 1994).

Larry Lester

BROWN, Raymond "Ray" (b. February 23, 1908, Ashland Grove, OH; d. 1968, Dayton, OH), player, was the ace pitcher for the Homestead, PA, Grays (NNL) during their dynasty period, when they won nine consecutive pennants from 1937 to 1945. Before turning professional, Brown played high school baseball in Indian Lake, OH, and attended Wilberforce University. He left before graduation to sign with the Homestead Grays. The six-foot-one-inch 195-pounder, a versatile athlete, was an outstanding pitcher and a good hitter with power from both sides of the plate. Early in his career, he played centerfield when not starting on the mound. As the years passed, however, he concentrated more on his pitching. As the son-in-law of Grays' owner Cum Posey (BB), he was thought by some to have a preferred status on the team. Others considered the star hurler temperamental but never questioned his ability and performance. He possessed a very effective knuckleball and curve, complemented with a sinker, slider, and a fine fastball. Most of his 24-year career was spent in the Negro Leagues, but he also pitched in Mexico, Cuba, and Canada.

During Brown's years with the Grays, Homestead played in the first four Negro World Series (1942–1945) held between the NNL and the NAL and won the middle two. In World Series competition, he pitched seven games, posted a combined 3–2 win-loss ledger, and hurled a one-hit shutout of the Birmingham, AL, Black Barons in the 1944 Classic. The workhorse's best pitching gem, however, came in 1945, when he pitched a perfect game in a seven-inning contest against the Chicago American Giants. He also appeared in two East-West All-Star Games (1935, 1940) without a decision.

With the great offensive support generated by the powerful bats in the Grays' lineup, he enjoyed considerable success and ranks high in winning percentage (.762) among all-time Negro League pitchers. Throughout his career, he enjoyed long winning streaks. One stretch in 1936–1937 saw him credited with 28 straight victories. In 1938, the Grays fielded their strongest team during his tenure with the team. Brown finished the season with a 10–0 NNL record and ranked among five players designated by the Pittsburgh *Courier* as certain major league stars. He posted league marks of 18–3 (2.53 ERA) in 1940 and 10–4 (2.72 ERA) in 1941, the same year the big right-hander was credited with 27 straight wins against all levels of opposition. In 1942, he finished 13–6 with the Grays, who notched their sixth straight NNL pennant and lost to the Kansas City, MO, Monarchs in the World Series.

The Cuban favorite won more games in the CUWL than any other black American pitcher and posted a 46–20 record in his five seasons there. In 1936–1937, he led the CUWL in wins with a 21–3 record and hurled a no-hitter among his victories. In 1941–1942, he paced the PRWL in victories with a 12–4 ledger and a 1.82 ERA.

He left the Grays in 1946 and went to the MEL, where he finished 13–9 with a 3.52 ERA. Following a 15–11 mark and a 3.40 ERA in 1949, he left Mexico for the CaPL. He retired after the 1953 season, remarried, and settled in Canada for several years, but later returned to the United States.

BIBLIOGRAPHY: Robert W. Peterson, *Only the Ball Was White* (Englewood Cliffs, NJ, 1970); Pittsburgh (PA) *Courier*, 1935–1946; James A. Riley, *The All-Time All-Stars of Black Baseball* (Cocoa, FL, 1983); James A. Riley, *The Biographical Encyclopedia of the Negro Baseball Leagues* (New York, 1994); James A. Riley, interviews with former Negro League players, James A. Riley collection, Cocoa, FL; Mike Shatzkin, ed., *The Ballplayers* (New York, 1990), p. 125; Rick Wolff, ed., *The Baseball Encyclopedia*, 8th ed. (New York, 1990), p. 2613.

James A. Riley

BRUSH, John Tomlinson Jr. (b. June 15, 1845, Clintonville, NY; d. November 26, 1912, Louisiana, MO), owner and executive, owned the New York Giants (NL) baseball club and designed the baseball rules governing the World Series, still in use.

Brush, the son of John Tomlinson Brush, Sr., and Sarah Farar Brush, was orphaned at age 4 and brought up by his grandfather, Eliphalet Brush. He entered the clothing business at age 17, enlisting in the Civil War in 1863. After the Civil War, he returned to the clothing business and eventually started his own company in Indianapolis, IN. Brush purchased the Indianapolis Hoosiers (NL) franchise in 1886 largely to publicize his clothing stores and became club president a year later.

The NL reduced its membership in 1889, dropping Indianapolis. Brush consented only after retaining his owner's voting rights, being given stock in John B. Day's* troubled New York Giants (NL) and being promised the next open franchise. Brush in 1891 was granted rights to the Cincinnati Reds (NL), which he owned until 1902.

Brush purchased the New York Giants in 1902 and turned the franchise into a winning one, both on and off the field. He hired John McGraw (BB) as field manager, giving him complete control over player dealings. Brush also penned a long-term lease and rebuilt the Polo Grounds, making it baseball's preeminent stadium for years.

Brush's lasting contribution to baseball, however, was creation of the rules organizing the World Series. The Pittsburgh Pirates (NL) met the Boston Pilgrims (AL) franchise in 1903 in a non–league sanctioned championship, which Brush tried to halt in court. Brush's hatred of AL president Ban Johnson (BB) made him oppose any series against the "minor league." His Giants won the 1904 NL pennant but refused a challenge by AL champion Boston.

Brush was criticized harshly by the newspapers and fans and changed his position in 1905. To oversee the World Series, he created several rules.

These "Brush Rules," the majority of which are still used today, required the NL and AL champions to meet in the series. His other rules included the four-out-of-seven series format, a pool of 60 percent of the receipts to be divided between the players (with 70 percent going to the winners and 30 percent to the losers), and allowing only players on the respective clubs prior to September to play. Fittingly, Brush's Giants played in the first league-sanctioned World Series in 1905, defeating Connie Mack's (BB) Philadelphia Athletics, four games to one. Brush's Giants lost two more World Series before his death, the 1911 World Series to Philadelphia and the 1912 Classic to the Boston Red Sox.

Brush's business approach to team administration increased baseball's stature in the early 1900s. He suffered the debilitating effects of rheumatism and locomotor ataxia and died while traveling to California for his health. Brush married Margaret Ewart in 1869 and had a daughter, Eleanor. After his first wife died in 1888, Brush remarried in 1894 to Elsie Boyd and had another daughter, Natalie.

BIBLIOGRAPHY: Gene Karst and Martin J. Jones, *Who's Who in Professional Baseball* (New Rochelle, NY, 1973); *NCAB*, vol. 15 (New York, 1914); *NYT*, November 27, 1912, p. 11; David Pietrusza, *Major Leagues* (Jefferson, NC, 1991); Joseph Reichler, *The World Series* (New York, 1979); Edward Mott Woolley, "Fortunes Made in Baseball," *LD* 45 (July 20, 1912), pp. 119–120.

Brian L. Laughlin

BUSH, Owen Joseph "Donie" (b. October 8, 1887, Indianapolis, IN; d. March 28, 1972, Indianapolis, IN), player, manager, and executive, was the son of Michael Bush and Ellen (Dolphin) Bush and had a sixth-grade education. After playing sandlot and semiprofessional baseball, he turned professional in 1905 as a shortstop with Sault Ste. Marie, MI (CCSL) and spent two seasons in the Class B Central League. He was drafted by the Detroit Tigers (AL) and assigned to Indianapolis, IN (AA), where he enjoyed a splendid season with the pennant-winning Indians.

In 1909 Bush supplanted the veteran shortstop Charley O'Leary and began a 13-year stretch as the linchpin of the Detroit Tiger infield. With the exception of Bobby Wallace (BB), he ranked as the best AL shortstop of his era. He epitomized what later became a well-recognized, affectionately regarded baseball type: the bold, feisty, bear-down, five-foot-six-inch 140-pounder, who always gave 100 percent. A switch-hitter skilled at working pitchers for walks and then for scoring, he usually batted in the leadoff or second spot ahead of Ty Cobb (BB). Afield, he possessed a strong arm and, according to baseball historian Fred Lieb (OS), "covered acres of ground."

His .250 career batting average spanned 16 years and 1,946 games. Primarily a singles hitter, he registered only 186 doubles, 74 triples, and nine homers. The 1,280 runs resulting from his 1,803 hits and 1,158 bases on balls gave him a scoring-effectiveness ratio of .43 percent, a mark achieved by few of the great sluggers. He scored more than 100 runs four times, with his 112 leading the AL in 1917. He stole 403 bases and, despite batting at the top of the order, compiled 436 RBIs. Pitchers struck him out only 346 times.

His .937 career fielding average came in the era of pancake gloves. He tied Hugh Jennings (BB) for most shortstop putouts in a single season (425, 1914) and ranks eleventh for total career putouts with 4,038. His 10,846 total chances place him tenth all-time.

Bush played in only one World Series, batting .261 in the Tigers' seven-game loss to the Pittsburgh Pirates (NL) in 1909. He drove in three runs and stole three bases but fanned five times and committed five errors.

In 1921 the Washington Senators (AL) acquired him on waivers. His playing days ended and his managerial career began in 1923, when he piloted the Senators to a fourth-place finish. Replaced by Stanley Harris (BB), Bush journeyed home to manage the Indianapolis Indians through 1926. Upon returning to the major leagues, he piloted Pittsburgh to a pennant and a crushing four-game defeat by the New York Yankees in the World Series. Hard-nosed as ever, he disciplined great outfielder Kiki Cuyler (BB) after an altercation by benching him for the Series.

Dropped by the Pirates, he moved to the doormat Chicago White Sox (AL) in 1930–1931 and, after winning the 1932 AA pennant with the Minneapolis Millers, ended his major league managing career with the Cincinnati Reds in 1933. Back once more to the AA, he piloted Minneapolis to two pennants in four years (1934–1937) and served as manager and part-owner of the Louisville Colonels (1939–1941). When the Colonels were sold, he rejoined the Indianapolis Indians as part-owner and manager (1942–1943) and served as club president (1952–1968). Subsequently, he scouted for the Boston Red Sox (AL) for three years and was scouting for the Chicago White Sox (AL) when he died, a bachelor, in the house where he was born. Sixty-five years of his life were spent in organized baseball.

BIBLIOGRAPHY: *The Baseball Encyclopedia*, 9th ed. (New York, 1993); Donie Bush file, National Baseball Library, Cooperstown, NY; Pete Cava, Indianapolis, IN, to A. D. Suehsdorf, July 15, 1993; Richard M. Cohen et al., *The World Series* (New York, 1979); J. C. Kofoed, "The Greatest Shortstop in the American League," *BM* 15 (November 1915), pp. 65–67; Frederick G. Lieb, *The Detroit Tigers* (New York, 1946); Dick Mittman, Indianapolis (IN) *News*, family data; Robert Obojski, *Bush League* (New York, 1975); John Thorn et al., *Total Baseball*, 3rd ed. (New York, 1993).

A. D. Suehsdorf

BYRD, William "Bill" "Daddy" (b. July 15, 1907, Canton, GA; d. January 4, 1991, Philadelphia, PA), player, grew up on a farm and was one of the last pitchers to throw a legal "spitter." He learned to throw the spitball as a youngster pitching with the Columbus Blue Birds in 1933 but often only faked the spitter and used it as a psychological weapon. The six-foot-one-inch, 215-pounder joined Tom Wilson's Columbus, OH, Elite Giants (NNL) in 1935 and remained with the team for 16 years, as the franchise was relocated in Washington and finally in Baltimore, MD. During this time, he served as a stabilizing influence on the team and was like a father to the younger players.

The Baltimore Elite Giants' ace proved a gifted ballplayer, whose presence on the mound marked an unflinching dominance. The Elite ace, who once pitched and won a doubleheader, was always available for tough assignments. In addition to his spitball, he used a wide variety of other pitches and possessed excellent control of them all. His repertoire included a slow knuckler, fast knuckler, slider, round-house curve, fastball, and sinker. In Puerto Rico, he was called "El Maestro" and led the PRWL in victories with 15 during the winter season of 1940–1941.

Byrd, almost a perennial member of the East squad in the East-West game, made five pitching appearances between 1936 and 1946 and another as a pinch hitter in 1945. A good hitter from both sides of the plate, he honed his batting skills by hitting rocks with tree branches on the family farm in Canton, GA, and posted season averages of .318 (1936), .286 (1941), .304 (1942), and .344 (1948).

He maintained better than a .600 winning percentage in NNL games from 1932 to 1939 and suffered only one losing season over a 14-year period. In 1936, he was credited with a 20–7 record. After returning from a season in Caracas, Venezuela, he posted NNL marks of 7–3, 10–2, 9–4, 8–7, and 10–6 from 1941 through 1945. After posting his first losing season in 14 years, he added three winning seasons with records of 9–6, 11–6, and 12–3 from 1947 through 1949. His last full year in the NNL in 1949 saw the Elites win their only untainted pennant.

After beginning the 1950 season with the Elites, Byrd quickly retired with a lifetime record of 114–72. Byrd played semiprofessional ball while holding down a regular job at the General Electric Company in Philadelphia, PA, where he worked for 20 years until retiring in 1970. He and his wife, Hazel, had three daughters, Sylvia, Ruth, and Barbara.

BIBLIOGRAPHY: *The Afro-American, 1935–1948*; *Oldtyme Baseball News* (Petoskey, MI, 1989), p. 14; Robert W. Peterson, *Only the Ball Was White* (Englewood Cliffs, NJ, 1970); James A. Riley, *The All-Time All-Stars of Black Baseball* (Cocoa, FL, 1983); James A. Riley, *The Biographical Encyclopedia of the Negro Baseball Leagues* (New York, 1994); James A. Riley, interviews with former Negro League players, James A. Riley collection, Cocoa, FL; Mike Shatzkin, ed., *The Ballplayers* (New York, 1990), p. 143; Rick Wolff, ed., *The Baseball Encyclopedia* (New York, 1993).

James A. Riley

CAMNITZ, Samuel Howard "Howie" (b. August 22, 1881, Covington, KY; d. March 2, 1960, Louisville, KY), player, was the brother of major league baseball pitcher Harry Camnitz. The five-foot-nine-inch, 169-pound Camnitz, who batted and threw right-handed, began his professional baseball career with Greenwood, MS (CSL) in 1902. He moved in 1903 to Vicksburg, MS (CSL) and in 1904 to the Pittsburgh Pirates (NL). After having trouble concealing his pitches, Camnitz spent most of 1904 with Springfield, IL (3IL) and 1905 with Toledo, OH (AA). He returned to the Pittsburgh Pirates in 1906 and stayed there until traded in August 1913 to the Philadelphia Phillies (NL). In 1914, he jumped to the Pittsburgh Rebels (FL). During the 1915 season, Camnitz was released and retired from baseball.

Camnitz, who won 133 major league games and lost 106 decisions, enjoyed his best season in 1909, when his 25–6 record tied Christy Mathewson (BB) for the best NL mark. He also performed well in 1911 with a 20–15 mark and in 1912 with a 22–12 slate and compiled a career 2.75 ERA. He hurled 326 career games, starting 237 contests and completing 137 games. He started the second game of the 1909 World Series against the Detroit Tigers but was replaced in the third inning and took the loss. Camnitz made his first major league start in 1906 with a 1–0 win over the Brooklyn Superbas, the first of seven victories by that score. He possessed outstanding control, averaging only 10.83 base runners per nine innings during his major league career. A careful student of the game, Camnitz studied box scores and related materials to determine which future opponents might give the most trouble. During his first FL season, he compiled a 14–18 record with a poor club. In 1915, he was involved in a fight at a New York City hotel while on a road trip. The Rebels suspended and then released him for violation of rules. Subsequently, Camnitz worked in the auto sales business for 40 years, retiring shortly before his death.

BIBLIOGRAPHY: *The Baseball Encyclopedia*, 9th ed. (New York, 1993); Samuel Howard Camnitz file, National Baseball Library, Cooperstown, NY; Robert Obojski, *Bush League* (New York, 1975); Marc Okkonen, *The Federal League of 1914–1915* (Garrett Park, MD, 1989); Joseph L. Reichler, ed., *The Great All-Time Baseball Record Book* (New York, 1981).

Horace R. Givens

CAMPANERIS, Dagoberto Blanco "Bert" "Campy" (b. March 9, 1942, Pueblo Nuevo, Matanzas, Cuba), player, is one of six children of a Cuban mechanic. Campaneris started to play organized baseball at age 11 and quickly became one of the best players in his region. Following graduation from Jose Tomas High School in Pueblo Nuevo, Campaneris in 1959 played for the Cuban national team in the Pan-American Games in San José, Costa Rica. Shortly thereafter, scout Bobby Delgado of the Kansas City Athletics (AL) signed the youngster to a contract. The young Cuban joined the Athletics' Daytona Beach, FL, farm team in 1962. In an August game that year, Campaneris pitched two innings and threw left-handed to left-handed batters and right-handed to right-handed hitters. The Athletics, however, convinced him to concentrate on his right-handed throwing ability.

After spending two years in the minors with various clubs, the 5-foot-10-

inch, 160-pound Cuban made his major league debut in July 1964 against the Minnesota Twins, hit a home run in his first at bat, and belted another four-bagger later in the game. Only Bob Nieman of the St. Louis Browns had accomplished this feat previously. On September 9, 1965, the talented Cuban became the first major league player in modern baseball history to play all nine positions in a single game. A solid infielder, Campaneris was selected to nine AL All-Star teams (1968–1975, 1977) as a shortstop. The crafty Cuban, equally prolific on the base paths, led the AL in stolen bases six times (1965–1968, 1970, 1972). His most productive offensive campaign occurred in 1968, when he led the AL in hits (177) and stolen bases (62) and batted .276 for the Oakland Athletics (AL). One year later, Campaneris married Norma Fay of Kansas City, MO.

In November 1976, he was traded to the Texas Rangers (AL) and was named as the AL All-Star shortstop. Campaneris joined the California Angels (AL) in a May 1979 trade and ended his major league career with the New York Yankees (AL) in 1983. Nicknamed "Campy," he collected 2,249 career hits, batted .259, and swiped 649 bases. Campaneris ranked eleventh on the all-time major league list in stolen bases upon his retirement. Campaneris also appeared in five AL Championship Series (1971–1975) and three World Series (1972–1974) with the Oakland Athletics. After two games of the 1972 AL Championship Series, Campaneris was suspended for the remainder of the series for flinging his bat at Detroit Tigers pitcher Lerrin La Grow. His most shining postseason performance came in the 1974 World Series, when he batted .353 in five games against the Los Angeles Dodgers.

BIBLIOGRAPHY: Gary Cartwright, "The Bert Campaneris Timetable," *Sport* 42 (May 1966), pp. 69–71; Michael M. Oleksak and Mary Adams Oleksak, *Beisbol: Latin Americans and the Grand Old Game* (Grand Rapids, MI, 1991); John Thorn and Pete Palmer, eds., *Total Baseball*, 3rd ed. (New York, 1993); *TSN*, August 8, 1964; *TSN*, April 25, 1970.

                                                                 Samuel O. Regalado

CANSECO, Jose Jr. (b. July 2, 1964, Havana, Cuba), player, is the son of Jose Canseco, Sr., and the identical twin of Ozzie Canseco, former St. Louis Cardinals (NL) outfielder, and attended Coral Park High School in Miami, FL.

The Oakland Athletics (AL) selected Canseco in the fifteenth round of the free agent draft in June 1982. He played 6 games with Miami, FL (FSL) at third base and 28 contests with Idaho Falls, ID (PrL) at third base and outfield. In 1983, Canseco's stops included Madison, WI (ML) for 34 games and Medford, OR (NWL) for 59 contests. He spent the entire 1984 season with Modesto, CA (CaL), batting .276 and hitting 15 home runs. In 1985, Canseco played 58 games with Huntsville, AL (SL), 60 contests with Tacoma, WA (PCL), and 29 games with the Oakland Athletics (AL), batting .302. The next three seasons saw him with Oakland from 1986 through 1988. After appearing in 9 games with Huntsville, AL (SL) in 1989, he spent full-time with Oakland until traded to the Texas Rangers (AL) for three players and cash in August 1992.

The six-foot-four-inch, 240-pound Canseco, who throws and hits right-handed, was named 1985 *TSN* Minor League Player of the Year. The 1986 season featured him being named AL Rookie Player of the Year by both *TSN* and the BBWAA. Canseco in 1988 batted .307 and led the AL with 42 home runs and 124 RBIs. The *TSN* selected Canseco AL Player of the Year. He made the AL All-Star team in 1988, 1990, and 1991. The same years, he was named outfielder on the AL *TSN* Silver Slugger team. The BBWAA named him 1988 AL MVP. In 1984, Canseco led the CaL outfielders with eight double plays. He hit 3 home runs in one game on July 3, 1988, led the AL with a .569 slugging percentage in 1988, and paced the AL with a career-high 44 home runs in 1991.

From 1988 to 1990, he appeared in three AL Championship Series and three World Series. In the 1989 World Series against the Los Angeles Dodgers, he batted .357 with one home run and three RBIs. Canseco was selected to the AL All-Star team five times but played in only the 1988 and 1990 games. He was chosen in 1986 but did not perform. Although named in 1989 and 1992, he did not play due to injuries. In 1989, Canseco received the then-largest major league raise, a $1.6 million one-year contract. On May 29, 1993, he made his pitching debut and worked the final inning of a 15–1 loss to the Boston Red Sox. He had been a high school pitcher and thrown a few times in the minor leagues. In July 1993, Canseco disclosed he had a torn elbow ligament. The injury probably was related to his pitching stint and sidelined him for the rest of the season. During the strike-shortened 1994 season, he batted .282 with 31 home runs and 90 RBIs and was named AL Comeback Player of the Year.

Canseco's off-season troubles, mainly speeding, caused continual problems for the Oakland Athletics management and led to his being traded. In December 1994, Texas traded him to the Boston Red Sox (AL). Through the 1994 season, he has batted .267 with 276 home runs, 870 RBIs, and 149 stolen bases.

BIBLIOGRAPHY: Stan W. Carlson clipping file, Minneapolis, MN; Patrick Reusse, column, Minneapolis (MN) *Star Tribune*, September 28, 1988; *Texas Rangers Media Guide*, 1994; *TSN Official Baseball Register*, 1994.

                                                                                              Stan W. Carlson

CARROLL, Clay Palmer "Hawk" (b. May 2, 1941, Clanton, AL), player, ranked among the most effective relief hurlers in major league baseball from 1966 through 1976. He grew up in central Alabama, halfway between Birmingham and Montgomery, and worked in a cotton mill with his father when not in school. He left Clanton High School before graduation in 1961 to join spring training with the Milwaukee Braves (NL). Carroll spent three and one-half seasons in the Braves' farm system before being called up to Milwaukee in 1964. A six-foot-one-inch, 188-pound right-hander, he started several games in the next few years. Most of his time, however, was spent working out of the bullpen. In 1966 the Braves' franchise shifted to Atlanta, where he led the NL in games pitched (73) and compiled a 2.38 ERA.

On June 11, 1968, Atlanta traded Carroll to the Cincinnati Reds (NL), where he experienced his most productive seasons as a relief hurler. He also enjoyed a rare batting-pitching highlight on May 30, 1969, when he hit a home run in the tenth inning off Bob Gibson (BB) of the St. Louis Cardinals to give the Reds a 4–3 win. In 1972 he again led the NL in games pitched with 65 and set a new NL record with 37 saves. *TSN* named him the NL Fireman of the Year.

The Reds, managed by Sparky Anderson (BB) and staffed by such batting stars as Johnny Bench (BB), Joe Morgan (BB), Tony Perez (BB), and Pete Rose (BB), dominated the NL in the 1970s. Cincinnati won five NL pennants and 2 World Series. Carroll proved very effective in postseason play. He worked in eight NL championship games, winning two, saving one, and compiling a 1.50 ERA. In 14 World Series games, he triumphed twice, saved one, and had a 1.33 ERA. In the 1970 World Series against the Baltimore Orioles, he recorded the Reds' only victory. In 1975, he won the seventh and deciding game over the Boston Red Sox. In his two-inning stint, he fanned Carlton Fisk (BB). Fisk the night before had hit his dramatic twelfth-inning, game-winning home run off Pat Darcy.

Carroll sought a two-year contract from the Reds after their highly successful championship season in 1975. Cincinnati traded him to the Chicago White Sox (AL), who signed him to a one-year contract around $110,000. He missed one third of the 1976 season because of an injury and was traded to the St. Louis Cardinals (NL) in March 1977. He pitched well for them until traded back to the Chicago White Sox in August 1977. He appeared in only two games for the Pittsburgh Pirates (NL) in 1978 and closed out his career with Vancouver, Canada (PCL) in 1979.

Carroll pitched in 731 major league games, winning 96 decisions, losing 73, and sporting an impressive 2.94 ERA. In 703 relief appearances, he compiled an even better 2.82 ERA and 143 saves. Among the 28 firemen who hurled over 1,000 innings in relief, he recorded the sixth-lowest ERA. He ranks behind Hoyt Wilhelm (BB), Rollie Fingers (BB), Goose Gossage (BB), Dan Quisenberry (BB), and Ron Perranoski (BB).

During and after his pitching career, Carroll resided in Bradenton, FL, and worked in the sporting goods business there. He and his family were victims of a tragic shooting at their home on November 16, 1985. His wife, Frances, and son, Brett, died of wounds, while Carroll, also shot, recovered after hospitalization. Carroll moved to Chattanooga, TN, where he currently resides.

BIBLIOGRAPHY: Clay Carroll, "The Game I'll Never Forget," *BD* 40 (June 1981), pp. 69–73; Clay Carroll file, National Baseball Library, Cooperstown, NY; L. Robert Davids, *Baseball Briefs* (Washington, DC, 1987); John Thorn and Pete Palmer, eds., *Total Baseball*, 3rd ed. (New York, 1993); *TSN Baseball Register*, 1979; *USA Today*, November 18, 1985.

L. Robert Davids

CARTER, Joseph Cris Jr. "Joe" (b. March 7, 1960, Oklahoma City, OK), player, is 1 of 11 children of Joseph Carter, Sr., a service station operator and truck driver, and Athelene Carter, a telephone worker. His brother Fred played outfield in the minor leagues. Carter majored in business administration at Wichita State University, earning *TSN* College All-American baseball team (1980, 1981) and *TSN* College Player of the Year (1981) honors.

The Chicago Cubs (NL) drafted the right-handed outfielder–first baseman as the second overall pick in June 1981 and assigned the six-foot-three-inch, 225-pounder to Midland, TX (TL) and Iowa (AA) from 1981 to 1984. Carter debuted briefly with Chicago in 1983. In June 1984, Chicago traded the easygoing, generous Carter to the Cleveland Indians (AL). His best season came in 1986, when Cleveland secured its first winning season since 1968. Carter led the AL in RBIs (121), reaching career highs in batting average (.302), runs scored (108), hits (200), and triples (9). In 1987, he became only the third major leaguer to attain 100 RBIs, 30 home runs, and 30 stolen bases the same season. Carter belted a career-best 35 round-trippers with 105 RBIs in 1989, tying major league records for most home runs in two consecutive games (5) and most games in a single season with at least three round-trippers (2).

In December 1989, Cleveland traded Carter to the San Diego Padres (NL) for three players. He knocked in 115 runs in 1990, but San Diego sent Carter and Roberto Alomar that December to the Toronto Blue Jays (AL) for Fred McGriff* and Tony Fernandez. The durable Carter in 1991 played every game for the third consecutive season. He batted .273 with 33 home runs, 108 RBIs, and a career-pinnacle 43 doubles, helping the Blue Jays capture the East Division crown. The Minnesota Twins defeated Toronto in the AL Championship Series. The Blue Jays repeated as East Division titlists in 1992, with Carter belting 34 round-trippers and recording 119 RBIs. Toronto vanquished the Oakland A's in the AL Championship Series and the Atlanta Braves in the World Series, as Carter batted .273 with 2 doubles, 2 home runs, and 3 RBIs and became the first player to start three consecutive World Series games at three different positions. In 1991 and 1992, he played in the All-Star Game and made the *TSN* AL All-Star and AL Silver Slugger teams. No major leaguer hit more round-trippers between 1986 and 1993. Carter, an excellent fastball hitter, surpassed 30 home runs in five seasons and 100 RBIs in seven campaigns. He holds the AL career record for most games with at least 3 home runs (5) but has averaged 105 strikeouts since 1986.

In 1993, Carter made the AL All-Star team for the third consecutive season and tied a career high with 121 RBIs, batting .254 and hitting 33 home runs to help the Blue Jays capture a third consecutive East Division crown. Toronto prevailed over the Chicago White Sox in the AL Championship Series and the Philadelphia Phillies, four games to two, in the World Series. Carter belted a dramatic three-run homer in the ninth inning to give Toronto an 8–6 victory in Game 6, the first time a World Series had ended on a round-tripper since 1960 and the only time a Fall Classic had concluded on a home run that rallied the losing team to victory. For the World Series, Carter batted .280 with 2 home runs and 8 RBIs.

In 11 major league seasons, Carter has batted .263 with 322 doubles, 41 triples, 302 home runs, and 1,037 RBIs. Carter set a major league record in 1994 by driving in 31 runs during April, breaking a mark coshared by Ron Cey (BB), Dale Murphy (BB), and Dave Winfield (BB). During the strike-shortened 1994 season, he batted .271 with 27 home runs and 133 RBIs, and again made the AL All-Star team. The Leawood, KS, resident and his wife Diana have three children, Kia, Ebony, and Jordan.

BIBLIOGRAPHY: Ron Fimrite, "Pow! Wow!" *SI* 66 (April 6, 1987), pp. 74–76, 78, 80; Richard Hoffer, "Every Game Is a Home Game," *SI* 72 (April 16, 1990), pp. 78–80; *San Diego Padres 1990 Media Guide; TSN Official Baseball Register*, 1994; Rich Weinberg, "Super Joe," *Sport* 83 (June 1992), pp. 22–23, 26, 28–29.

David L. Porter

CARTY, Ricardo Adolfo Jacobo "Rico" (b. September 1, 1939, San Pedro de Macoris, Dominican Republic), player, grew up in the Dominican professional boxing world. His father worked as a foreman at the local sugar mill, while his mother toiled as a midwife. The elder Carty, however, also trained boxers and prepared his boy for a career in that sport. By age 16, young Carty had won 17 amateur bouts in his native country. Carty then joined various local baseball clubs in his hometown. In 1959, he was invited to join the Dominican Republic national baseball team bound for the Pan-American games in Chicago, IL. The following year, several major league scouts pursued the slugger. Carty mistakenly signed 10 professional baseball contracts. George Trautman NAML president, recognized the error as a matter of Carty's inexperience with contracts. Trautman did not suspend the Dominican but gave the Milwaukee Braves (NL) exclusive rights for Carty's services.

Initially signed as a catcher, Carty spent four years in the Braves minor league system before debuting in the major league on September 15, 1963. In his first full major league season, Carty recorded a banner year with 22 home runs and 88 RBIs and finished second in NL batting with a .330 average. The right-handed slugger remained a steady force with the Braves but was struck with tuberculosis in 1968. After the Braves had moved to

Atlanta, he won the 1970 NL batting title with a .366 average, collected 175 hits, and belted 25 home runs. During that season, Carty hit in 31 straight games for the longest hitting streak by a Latin player and, at that time, the third longest in NL history. He also appeared in his only All-Star contest as the first-ever write-in player. Off the field, Carty experienced problems in 1971, when he was involved in an altercation with Atlanta policemen that led to the suspension of three officers.

Carty split the 1973 season with the Texas Rangers (AL), Chicago Cubs (NL), and Oakland Athletics (AL) and joined the Cleveland Indians (AL) for the 1974 campaign. After four years with Cleveland, the Dominican divided 1978 between the Toronto Blue Jays (AL) and Oakland Athletics (AL). He ended his major league career in 1979 with a second stint for the Toronto Blue Jays. Overall, Carty collected 1,677 hits and batted .299 lifetime. Subsequently, Carty coached several years in the Dominican baseball leagues.

BIBLIOGRAPHY: Atlanta (GA) *Journal*, May 8, 1970, p. 4; "Carty a Born Hitter . . . Can He Reach .400?" *TSN*, July 4, 1970, p. 20; "Carty Kayoes His Hard-Luck Hoodoo," *TSN*, August 28, 1976, p. 3; Michael M. Oleksak and Mary Adams Oleksak, *Beisbol: Latin Americans and the Grand Old Game* (Grand Rapids, MI, 1991); John Thorn and Pete Palmer, eds., *Total Baseball*, 3rd ed. (New York, 1993).

                                                                Samuel O. Regalado

CASE, George Washington Jr. (b. November 11, 1915, Trenton, NJ; d. January 2, 1989, Trenton, NJ), player, coach, and manager, was the son of George Washington Case, a farmer and self-employed businessman, and Clara (McIntyre) Case. His older half brother, William Clifford, encouraged him to participate in basketball and baseball at Trenton Central High School and Peddie School, where he graduated in 1936. A successful tryout with the Philadelphia Athletics (AL) prompted Joe Cambria, Albany, NY (IL) owner and part-time Washington (AL) scout, to sign Case, with Philadelphia's permission, to play in 1936 for the Senators' York, PA (NYPL) farm team. York promptly relocated to Trenton, due largely to Clifford Case's influence. George stole 60 bases and batted .338, only .0002 behind the NYPL leader, for Trenton in 1937 and was named All-NYPL left fielder. The Washington Senators (AL) purchased him in August 1937. He finished the season with Washington, batting .289 in 22 games. During October 1937, he married Helen May Farrell of Trenton. They produced one son, George III, and one daughter, Robin.

An outfielder, Case played regularly 9 seasons for Washington. The Senators traded him in December 1945 to the Cleveland Indians (AL) for 1 disappointing season. Cleveland returned him to Washington in March 1947 for a last part-time performance. A six-foot, 180-pound, right-hand line drive hitter, he seldom homered or struck out as a leadoff batter and batted .282 in 1,226 games during 11 AL seasons. Case scored more than 100 runs in 4 seasons and led the major leagues in stolen bases 5 consecutive seasons

(1939–1943) and the AL in 1946. His highest stolen base production came with 61 in 1943. Unlike later eras, teams then did not attempt steals when significantly ahead or behind. Back disabilities prevented him from sliding properly and disqualified him from military service. Clark Griffith (BB) claimed Case, who stole bases on sheer speed, was the fastest runner in baseball history. Case never lost a match race to another baseball player and barely lost a 100-yard dash in 1946 to sprint-great Jesse Owens (OS) by less than a yard.

Case coached baseball at Rutgers University from 1950 through 1960, the Washington Senators (AL) from 1961 into 1963, and the Minnesota Twins (AL) in 1968. His managerial assignments included Hawaii (PCL) in 1965 and 1966, York, PA (EL) in 1967, and Oneonta, NY (NYPL) from 1969 through 1972. He also scouted for Washington (AL) and the Seattle Mariners (AL) and, being an excellent teacher, served as a minor league batting instructor. The modest, unassuming Case, liked and respected by his peers, enjoyed family life, duck hunting, and fishing. He started in 1939 making color movies of baseball scenes and associates, the best of which are preserved and currently marketed via videotape. Prior to his death from emphysema, he was elected to the Trenton, Washington, and New Jersey Sports Halls of Fame.

BIBLIOGRAPHY: Harrington E. Crissey, Jr., *Teenagers, Graybeards and 4-F's, Volume 2: The American League* (Trenton, NJ, 1982); Frederick G. Lieb, "Raised as Player by His Older Brother, George Case Inherits Speed from His Dad Who Was Noted Sprinter," *TSN*, August 18, 1938, p. 3; Robert Obojski, "George Case: The Stolen Base King of the Golden Era," *CSC* (July 1991), p. 24; Shirley Povich, "1-Run Margin in Game—Case," *TSN*, December 27, 1945, p. 8; Bus Saidt, "Ballplayer George Case Dies at 73," pp. A1, A11; and "Case Will Be Missed By Many," Trenton (NJ) *Times*, January 24, 1989, pp. C1, C9; Rich Westcott, *Diamond Greats* (Westport, CT, 1988).

Frank V. Phelps

CASH, David Jr. "Dave" (b. June 11, 1948, Utica, NY), player and coach, is the son of David Cash, Sr., and enjoyed a solid 12-year major league career with four different NL teams. His major league clubs included the Pittsburgh Pirates (1969–1973), Philadelphia Phillies (1974–1976), Montreal Expos (1977–1979), and San Diego Padres (1980).

The 5-foot-11-inch, 170-pound right-handed hitter began his career in the Pittsburgh organization at Salem, VA (ApL) in 1966. He won the batting title with a .335 average at Gastonia, NC (WCL) the next year. Promoted to the majors in 1969, he was primarily a second baseman and played some games at both shortstop and third base. His impressive lifetime career offensive statistics featured a .283 batting average, 1,571 hits, and 722 runs scored, including a career-high 111 in 1975.

As a leadoff and number-two hitter, Cash averaged over 660 times at bat per season from 1974 through 1978, leading the NL three times. In 1975 he batted a then-record 699 times and struck out just 34 times. During his career, he proved a solid contact hitter and struck out just 309 times in over 5,500 at bats. Cash also led the NL in hits with 213 in 1975 and triples with 12 in 1976.

Cash came into his own in 1974, when Pittsburgh traded him to the Philadelphia Phillies (NL) for pitcher Ken Brett. The team leader's slogan "Yes We Can" galvanized a maturing Phillies team, propelling them into pennant contention for the first time in a decade. With the Phillies, he also ranked among the NL's best second basemen and trailed only Joe Morgan (BB) as an offensive and defensive star. Cash paired with Larry Bowa (BB) to form a solid double play combination. They led the NL three consecutive years in double plays (1974–1976), with Cash leading all second sackers in fielding average in 1976. Cash also was named to the NL All-Star team from 1974 through 1976.

Cash applied for free agency after the 1976 season and signed a three-year pact with the Montreal Expos (NL). He compiled one fine season with Montreal, hitting .289 with 188 hits and 42 doubles in 1977. He sagged badly thereafter and gradually lost his speed around second base, retiring after the 1980 season.

Cash and his wife, Pam, reside in Clearwater, FL, and have two sons and one daughter. Cash has served in the Philadelphia Phillies minor league system since 1988 and coaches with the Phillies' top farm team, the Scranton-Wilkes Barre, PA, Red Barons (IL).

BIBLIOGRAPHY: Frank Bilovsky and Rich Westcott, *The Phillies Encyclopedia* (New York, 1984); *Philadelphia Phillies Media Guide*, 1974–1976.

John P. Rossi

CHAMBERLAIN, Elton P. "Icebox" (b. November 5, 1867, Warsaw, NY; d. September 22, 1929, Baltimore, MD), player, grew up in Warsaw and Buffalo, NY. Before his seventeenth birthday, he played two professional baseball games at third base for Quincy, IL (NWL). The following year, he played for a Hamilton, Canada, club. He spent much of the 1886 season with Macon, GA (SL) as a pitcher with a 13–20 record, and an outfielder. He was signed later that year by the major league Louisville Colonels (AA) club, compiling a 0–3 mark. In 1887, his 18–16 win–loss record established him as a major leaguer at age 19.

Chamberlain began the 1888 season with Louisville, where he compiled a 14–9 win–loss record and 2.53 ERA. His season concluded with the St. Louis Browns (AA), where his brilliant 1.61 ERA and 11–2 record provided the impetus needed to catapult the club to their fourth straight AA pennant. In the World Series against the New York Giants, Chamberlain shut out the NL club in Game 2. He lost the fourth, sixth, and deciding eighth game, however, winning the meaningless tenth game.

The 1889 season proved the busiest and finest for the five-foot-nine-inch, 168-pound right-hander. Despite his chronic laziness (prompting his nickname "Icebox") and a brief suspension late in the 1889 campaign for allegedly careless play, Chamberlain hurled 421⅔ innings and 44 complete games. He won 32 games, sharing third best in the AA, and lost 15 decisions. His 2.97 ERA places fifth among career AA pitchers, while his 4.8 Total Pitcher Index (Pete Palmer's statistic for overall pitcher effectiveness) ranks third. Chamberlain combined with Charles "Silver" King (BB), who compiled a 35–16 record, to keep St. Louis in front of the AA through August. The Browns, however, slipped to second place, two games behind Brooklyn.

In 1890, Chamberlain appeared in just five games with St. Louis, compiling a 3–1 record and high 5.91 ERA. He deserted the Browns, returning home to Buffalo. St. Louis sold his contract to the Columbus, OH, Buckeyes (AA), where he hurled an AA-high six shutouts and finished with a 12–6 record. His season ERA dropped to 2.83, fourth best in the AA.

Chamberlain won 22 games for the Philadelphia Athletics (AA) in 1891, and 19 for the Cincinnati Reds (NL) in 1892, but lost 23 games each season. Although pitching less the next two seasons, he compiled winning records of 16–12 and 10–9. He promised to pitch for the Cleveland Spiders (NL) in 1895 but signed instead with Warren, OH (IOL). He joined Cleveland for the 1896 season but was released in May after two ineffective appearances.

Altogether, Chamberlain won 157 major league games, lost 120 decisions, and compiled a 3.57 ERA in 2,521⅔ innings. He is best remembered, though, for two games: On May 9, 1888, he pitched the final two innings of his 18–6 victory against the Kansas City Cowboys (AA) left-handed. In a Memorial Day 1894 game, he yielded four home runs to Bobby Lowe (BB) of the Boston Beaneaters.

BIBLIOGRAPHY: Al Kermisch, "Elton Chamberlain Another in Ambidextrous Class," *BRJ* 13 (1983), p. 48; Daniel M. Pearson, *Baseball in 1889* (Bowling Green, OH, 1993); John Phillips, *The Spiders: Who Was Who* (Cabin John, MD, 1991); John Thorn and Pete Palmer, eds., *Total Baseball*, 3rd ed. (New York, 1993); Robert L. Tiemann, AA pennant race charts, unpublished; Robert L. Tiemann and Mark Rucker, eds., *Nineteenth Century Stars* (Kansas City, MO, 1989).

Frederick Ivor-Campbell

CHANCE, Wilmer Dean (b. June 1, 1941, Wooster, OH), player, is the son of Wilmer and Florence Chance and preferred his middle name. Of Swiss descent, he grew up on his parents' Ohio farm and rose early in the morning to help his father milk the cows. A star on championship basketball and baseball teams at Northwestern High School, the six-foot-three-inch, 195-pound, right-handed pitcher signed with the Baltimore Orioles (AL) organization.

After spending the 1959–1960 seasons in the Orioles farm system with

Bluefield, WV (ApL) and then Fox Cities, WI (3IL), Chance was selected by the Los Angeles Angels in the AL expansion draft in December 1960. In 1961 he pitched for Dallas–Fort Worth, TX (AA) and joined the Angels late in the season. Chance remained with the Los Angeles (and after 1965, California) Angels through the 1966 season. California traded him to Minnesota (AL), where he pitched for the Twins from 1967 to 1969. Trades followed, as he spent most of the 1970 campaign with the Cleveland Indians (AL). The New York Mets (NL) acquired him in September 1970. In 1971, Chance spent his final season with the Detroit Tigers (AL).

His 11-year major league career was abbreviated by recurrent shoulder problems and squandered potential. Chance pitched 2,147.2 career innings, winning 128 contests and losing 115 games for a .527 winning percentage. During his career, he struck out 1,534 batters, compiled a 2.93 ERA, and registered 33 shutouts. His best season came in 1964, when Chance used his blistering fastball to lead the AL in victories (20), ERA (1.65), complete games (15), innings pitched (278.1), and shutouts (11). Chance suffered only 9 losses to register a .690 winning percentage and recorded 207 strikeouts. The 1964 season made the 23-year-old Chance the then-youngest recipient of the Cy Young Award and the highest salaried player ($41,000) in the brief history of the California Angels. Nonetheless, only in 1967, when his 20–14 win–loss record, which included both a no-hitter and a five-inning (unofficial) perfect game, brought him the AL Comeback Player of the Year honors did Chance ever again approach his early brilliance.

Injuries and dissipation played a significant role in diminishing Chance's career. Early in his career, Chance came under the spell of hedonistic roommate "Bo" Belinsky. Chance's 1961 marriage to Judith Carol Larson, which produced a son, ended in divorce. As an active player, Chance also pursued distracting, failed ventures as a billiards player–promoter and boxing manager–promoter. After the premature end of his baseball career, the Wooster, OH, resident emerged as a midway barker and the peripatetic owner of a few carnival tent show games.

BIBLIOGRAPHY: Myron Cope, "Angel Who Doesn't Fear to Tread," *SEP* 238 (April 10, 1965), pp. 95–99; John Devaney, *Baseball's Youngest Big Leaguers* (New York, 1969); Bill Gallant, "Inside Dean Chance: Baseball's Winningest 'Loser,'" *All-Star Sports* 2 (February 1968), pp. 14–17; Curry Kirkpatrick, "New Dean on List of Great No-Hitters: Dean Chance of Minnesota Twins," *SI* 27 (July 24, 1967), pp. 42–43; Bill Libby, "Chance of a Lifetime," *BD* 23 (December 1964), pp. 41–47.

William M. Simons

CLARK, William Nuschler Jr. "Will" "The Thrill" (b. March 13, 1964, New Orleans, LA), player, is the son of Bill Clark, sales representative for a pest control company, and Letty Clark and made High School Baseball All-America at Jesuit High School in New Orleans, where he broke Rusty Staub's (BB) records. After graduation from high school, he spent three years at Mississippi State University (SEC) and was named a baseball All-America during his sophomore year in 1984. In 1984, he was chosen for the U.S. Olympic Team, which won a silver medal at the Los Angeles, CA, Summer Games. Clark won the Golden Spikes Award as the nation's best collegiate player in 1985. The San Francisco Giants (NL) selected Clark as a first-round draft choice in 1985. Clark played in 65 games at Fresno, CA (CaL), where he batted for a .309 with 10 home runs and 48 RBIs.

In 1986, Clark emerged as the San Francisco Giants first baseman. On opening day, the six-foot, 190-pound left-handed hitter became the fifty-third player to homer in his first major league at bat when he connected on a pitch thrown by Nolan Ryan (BB) of the Houston Astros at the Houston Astrodome. In his rookie season, he hit .287, produced 41 RBIs, and slugged 11 home runs in only 111 games. Any notions of a sophomore jinx in 1987 were dispelled when his statistics improved to a .308 batting average, 91 RBIs, 35 home runs, and a .580 slugging average in 150 games. Since then, he has become one of the game's best players. Known for his consistency and competitiveness, he studies videotapes of his hitting to find ways of improving. Clark has led the NL in RBIs (109) in 1988, bases on balls (100) in 1988, runs scored (104) in 1989, and slugging percentage (.536) in 1991. In 1991, his 303 total bases tied for the NL lead. Starting in 1988, he appeared on five consecutive NL All-Star teams. Although not possessing great range, he furnishes fine defensive play and led NL first basemen in double plays in 1987 (130), 1988 (126), 1990 (118), 1991 (115), and 1992 (130). The sure-handed Clark also topped all others at his position in total chances in 1988 (1,608), 1989 (1,566) and 1990 (1,587). In 1991, he paced all NL first basemen with a .997 fielding percentage and won his first Gold Glove Award.

Clark performed in the 1987 and 1989 NL Championship Series, batting a combined .489 average and earning the 1989 NLCS MVP Award. In the first game, he belted 2 home runs, including a grand slam, and drove in a record 6 RBIs. He also established records for a five-game series with 13 hits, 6 long hits, 8 runs scored, 24 total bases, .650 batting average, and a 1.200 slugging average. Clark played four games in his only World Series appearance in 1989, hitting .250 against the Oakland A's. In December 1993, the Texas Rangers (AL) signed Clark as a free agent. During the strike-shortened 1994 season, he batted .329 with 80 RBIs and made the AL All-Star team. Through 1994, Clark amassed a career .302 batting average, 189 home runs, 789 RBIs, and a .499 slugging average. He remains single and resides in New Orleans, LA.

BIBLIOGRAPHY: William Clark file, National Baseball Library, Cooperstown, NY; *1993 San Francisco Giants Media Guide;* Ray Ratto, "The Thrill of It All," E. M. Swift, "Will Power," *SI* 72 (May 28, 1990), pp. 74–86; Casey Tefertiller, "Clark Figures to Be a Giant Force in the 90's," *Baseball America's Baseball 90,* pp. 126–127;

John Thorn and Pete Palmer, eds., *Total Baseball*, 3rd ed. (New York, 1993), p. 747; *TSN Official Baseball Register*, 1994. *Sport* 81 (July 1990), pp. 24–28.

                                                                       Robert J. Brown

CLEMENS, William Roger "Rocket" (b. August 4, 1962, Dayton, OH), player, ranked among the leading AL pitchers from 1986 through 1992. The youngest of five children of Bill Clemens, a truck driver, and Bess (Wright) Clemens, he moved from Dayton to Vandalia, OH, with his mother after his parents divorced. His mother married Woody Booher, a tool-and-die-maker who died in 1971. After his family moved to Texas in 1977, he attended Dulles High School in Sugar Land as a sophomore and graduated from Spring Woods High School in Houston in 1980. He earned letters in football, basketball, and baseball, compiling a 31–6 pitching record in three seasons. He attended Houston's San Jacinto JC in 1980–1981 and transferred to the University of Texas at Austin. He won 28 games against 7 defeats the next two years and twice pitched the deciding game of the College World Series, losing in 1982 and winning the next year.

Clemens was drafted by the Boston Red Sox (AL) and completed the 1983 season with Winter Haven, FL (FSL) and New Britain, CT (EL), where he clinched the EL playoff title with a three-hit shutout. He began 1984 at Pawtucket, RI (IL) and was promoted on May 11 to Boston. An arm injury ended his season on August 31 with a 9–4 record. The next year, a May shoulder injury worsened and ended his season in mid-August with his record at 7–5. Clemens's shoulder was repaired surgically two weeks later.

"Rocket Roger" burst into stardom at the start of the 1986 season with 14 straight wins, including a record-setting 20–strikeout game against the Seattle Mariners on April 29. He started and won the All-Star Game with three perfect innings and pitched Boston to the AL East title with an AL-high 24 wins against only 4 losses. Clemens's .857 winning percentage, 2.48 ERA, and 5.0 TPI (total pitcher index, Pete Palmer's measure for pitchers' overall effectiveness) also topped the AL, helping earn him both the AL Cy Young and MVP awards. In the AL Championship Series against the California Angels, Clemens lost the opener and won the deciding seventh game. He pitched in two World Series games against the New York Mets without a decision.

Over the next six seasons, Clemens remained at or near the top among AL pitchers. In 1987, he held out through March for more pay and began slowly with a 4–6 record. His 16–3 finish, however, gave him a share of the AL lead with 20 wins and earned him his second Cy Young Award. His .690 winning percentage and seven shutouts also paced the AL. Clemens's record slipped a bit to 18–12 in 1988, but his eight shutouts and 291 strikeouts led the AL and helped Boston win another AL East title. He pitched in one AL Championship Series game with no decision. After finishing 17–11 in 1989, Clemens in 1990 enjoyed perhaps his finest season. His 21–6 record helped

Boston earn its third AL East crown in five years, while his career-best 1.93 ERA and 6.2 TPI led the AL and four shutouts shared the AL lead. Clemens's two AL Championship Series appearances, though, produced a 0–1 record. Umpire Terry Cooney expelled him from Game 4 for swearing.

Clemens continued to top the AL in 1991 and 1992 with 2.62 and 2.41 ERAs, four and five shutouts, and a 5.3 TPI each year. In 1991 he also led the AL with 241 strikeouts and compiled an 18–10 record, earning his third Cy Young Award. In 1992, he posted an 18–11 win–loss record.

A 1993 groin injury that sidelined Clemens for nearly a month in mid-season, late-season elbow pain, and concern over his mother's illness contributed to Clemens's first losing record, an 11–14 mark, and a career-worst 4.46 ERA. During the strike-shortened 1994 season, he compiled a 9–7 mark with a 2.85 ERA. Through his first 11 major league seasons, Clemens hurled 2,393⅓ innings in 326 games, won 172 games, lost only 93 decisions, and compiled a .649 winning percentage. The six-foot-four-inch, 215-pound right-hander spun 36 shutouts and struck out 2,191 batters.

Clemens married Debbie Lynn Godfrey in November 1984 and has two sons, Koby Aaron and Kory.

BIBLIOGRAPHY: *CB Yearbook*, 1987, pp. 115–119; Roger Clemens with Peter Gammons, *Rocket Man: The Roger Clemens Story* (Lexington, MA, 1987); Mike Shalin, "Clemens Goes Home to Texas," Boston (MA) *Herald*, September 23, 1993, pp. 112, 114; John Thorn and Pete Palmer, eds., *Total Baseball*, 3rd ed. (New York, 1993).

Frederick Ivor-Campbell

CLEMENTS, John J. "Jack" (b. July 24, 1864, Philadelphia, PA; d. May 23, 1941, Norristown, PA), player, manager, and umpire, broke into the major leagues in 1884 at age 19 with the Keystone baseball club of Philadelphia (UA). After Keystone dropped out of the UA in August, Clemens moved across town to the Phillies (NL) and played there the next 13 years. A rarity as a left-handed throwing catcher, he lacked outstanding defensive skills. As a left-handed hitter, however, the 5-foot-8½-inch, 204-pound Clements developed into one of the best-*hitting* catchers and one of the better sluggers of the dead ball pre-1920 era. He pioneered in the use of a chest protector in 1884, surviving early laughter to become the first major leaguer to catch 1,000 games.

In 1890 Clements emerged as one of the NL offensive leaders, ranking third in batting average at .315 and second in slugging average with .472. From 1890 through 1896, Clements averaged .317 in batting and .484 in slugging percentage. His 57 home runs in that span placed him among the top 10 major leaguers.

Clements's .310 batting average in 1891 ranked fourth in the NL, while his career-high 17 home runs in 1893 placed second only to teammate Ed Delahanty's (BB) 19. A broken ankle sidelined him much of the following season, but he recovered to hit .394 and compile a .612 slugging average in 1895. Both figures marked personal bests and ranked him third in the NL, as did his 13 home runs.

In 1898 Clements moved on to the St. Louis Cardinals (NL), where he led NL catchers in fielding average for the only time in his career. His major league career wound down with 4 games for the Cleveland Spiders (NL) before his release early in the 1899 season in a cost-cutting move and 16 games with the Boston Beaneaters (NL) in 1900. He finished the 1900 season with Providence, RI (EL) and caught for Worcester, MA (EL) in 1901 and for Springfield, MA (CtSL) in 1902. After his playing days, he worked several years for sporting goods manufacturer A. J. Reach (BB) in Philadelphia. Later he toiled for the Dunbar Furnace Company in Connellsville, PA, and for a baseball manufacturer in Perkasie, PA. A son, John, became a minor league catcher.

Over his 17-year major league career, Clements batted .286, to rank tenth-best all-time among catchers with over 1,000 games. His average of 1.8 home runs per 100 at bats places third among nineteenth-century players and sixth among all dead ball era players. He played in 1,157 major league games, numbering 226 doubles, 60 triples, and 77 home runs among his 1,226 hits. He managed the Phillies for 19 games in Harry Wright's (BB) absence in 1890, compiling a 13–6 record, and served temporarily as an NL umpire during 1892.

BIBLIOGRAPHY: Jack Clements file, National Baseball Library, Cooperstown, NY; John Phillips, *The Spiders: Who Was Who* (Cabin John, MD, 1991); John Thorn and Pete Palmer, eds., *Total Baseball*, 3rd ed. (New York, 1993); Robert L. Tiemann and Mark Rucker, eds., *Nineteenth Century Stars* (Kansas City, MO, 1989).

Frederick Ivor-Campbell

COLLINS, James Anthony "Ripper" (b. March 30, 1904, Altoona, PA; d. April 16, 1970, New Haven, CT), player, coach, manager, scout, and broadcaster, was of Scotch and German descent and received his nickname as a boy. He hit the team's only baseball so hard that when it struck a fence nail, the cover ripped off. He attended Nanty Glo Elementary School in Nanty Glo, PA, through the fifth grade and was employed in the coal mines around Altoona when a minor league scout offered him a contract. The scout, however, refused him a five-dollar bonus, prompting Collins's return to the coal mines.

Collins entered professional baseball in 1923, splitting games between Wilson, VA (VL) and York, PA (NYPL). He quit baseball in 1924 but returned to hit .327 and .313 with Johnstown, PA (MAL) in 1925 and 1926. The switch-hitting Collins batted .388 with 101 RBIs at Danville, IL (3IL) in 1928 and crushed 38 home runs while driving in 134 for Rochester, NY (IL) the next season. The parent St. Louis Cardinals (NL) did not promote him, however, because future Hall of Famer Jim Bottomley (BB) played first base. In 1930 the five-foot-nine-inch, 163-pound Collins forced the Cardinals' hand. At Rochester, he annihilated pitching with 234 hits, 40 home runs, 165 runs scored, 180 RBIs, and a .376 batting average.

In 1931 Collins batted .301 while platooning with Bottomley at first base for the Cardinals. St. Louis traded Bottomley to the Cincinnati Reds (NL) and installed Collins as full-time first baseman. Collins responded with 21 home runs and 91 RBIs in 1932, blending in with other "Gas House Gang" members Dizzy Dean (BB), Paul Dean, Pepper Martin (BB), and Leo Durocher (BB). A noted prankster, he also loved to sing. With Dazzy Vance (BB), Martin, and Dizzy Dean, he formed a quartet who sang on KMOX radio in St. Louis in 1933. He and other Cardinals made newspaper advertisements for Camel cigarettes.

In 1934 Collins enjoyed his finest season. Manager Frankie Frisch (BB) converted him into a disciplined hitter. Collins powered an NL-high 35 home runs, still a Cardinal record for a switch-hitter, and had 200 hits, 128 RBIs, and a .333 batting average. His .367 batting average sparked the Cardinals' seven-game World Series victory over the Detroit Tigers (AL). Collins followed with 23 home runs and 122 RBIs the next season. In 1936 a young, power-hitting first baseman, Johnny Mize (BB), joined the Cardinals. St. Louis traded Collins to the Chicago Cubs (NL) in October 1936.

The Cubs released Collins after the 1938 season. He returned to the minor leagues and collected 402 hits and 239 RBIs in two seasons with the Los Angeles, CA Angels (PCL). The 36-year-old Collins married Jeanne Houser on October 17, 1940. They had three sons and one daughter.

In 1941 he played 49 games for the Pittsburgh Pirates (NL). Collins served as player–manager for Albany, NY (EL) from 1942 to 1946. In 1944 the 40-year-old Collins batted .396, the highest average in professional baseball that year. After managing the San Diego, CA, Padres (PCL) in 1947 and 1948, he spent several years in radio broadcasting and worked in promotions for Wilson Sporting Goods. In 1962 he served as 1 of 10 coaches with the Chicago Cubs in the rotating manager scheme. He then scouted for the St. Louis Cardinals until his death. His major league career totals included 1,084 games, 1,121 hits, 135 home runs, 659 RBIs, and a .296 batting average. Collins's minor league career covered 1,611 games with 1,837 hits, 1,061 runs, 193 home runs, 928 RBIs, and a .331 batting average.

BIBLIOGRAPHY: Bob Broeg, *Redbirds: A Century of Cardinals' Baseball* (St. Louis, MO, 1982); L. Robert Davids, ed., *Minor League Baseball Stars* (Cooperstown, NY, 1978); G. H. Fleming, *The Dizziest Season: The Gashouse Gang Chases the Pennant* (New York, 1984); Gene Karst and Martin Jones, Jr., *Who's Who in Professional Baseball* (New Rochelle, NY, 1973).

Frank J. Olmsted

CONCEPCION, David Ismael (Benitiz) (b. June 17, 1948, Aragua, Venezuela), player, is the son of a truckdriver and attended Agustin Codazzi High School in Aragua. Concepcion considered basketball his favorite sport and did not contemplate a professional baseball career. After his high school graduation, Concepcion's part-time play for the local Aragua team impressed his coach, Wilfredo Calvino, a Cincinnati Reds (NL) scout. Calvino signed Concepcion to a contract in 1967. The frail Venezuelan spent two years in the minor leagues, where Cincinnati focused on his play as a shortstop.

The Reds promoted Concepcion to the parent club in 1970 and made him a full-time starter in 1972. During the decade, he served as a vital member on one of major league baseball's most powerful teams. The media dubbed the Cincinnati club "the Big Red Machine." The Reds named him team captain in 1973. Concepcion contributed 167 hits and 82 RBIs in 1974 and won the Roberto Clemente Award as the top Latin American major league player in 1977. His most productive offensive season came in 1978, when he collected 170 hits and compiled a .301 batting average. No Reds shortstop had batted .300 since Joe Tinker (BB) in 1913.

The Venezuelan's main prowess, however, remained as a fielder. A steady force at shortstop, Concepcion collected five Gold Glove awards during the 1970s and helped the Reds win three NL Championship Series and two World Series. Concepcion, hampered by an injured elbow in 1980, even introduced and perfected the method of bouncing a fielded ball on the artificial turf on throws to first base. His bat at times also made an impact during championship play. In the 1976 World Series triumph against the New York Yankees, the thin shortstop batted an impressive .357. Concepcion also participated in three NL Championship Series and led Cincinnati with a .455 average in 1975. He hit better than .300 three times and was named the Reds' MVP in 1981.

After the 1988 season, the Reds released the nine-time NL All-Star (1973, 1975–1982). In 1989, his attempt to make the California Angels (AL) roster failed. Concepcion returned to his native Venezuela, where he managed his hometown Aragua Tigres. Concepcion concluded his major league career with 2,326 hits, 950 RBIs, and a .267 batting average. He appeared in 2,198 games at shortstop, only 44 games short of the NL record. Concepcion ranks among Reds leaders in doubles (389), games, hits, stolen bases (321), runs, and RBIs. Concepcion and his wife, Delia (Montenegro), have three children, David Alejandro, David Eduardo, and Daneska.

BIBLIOGRAPHY: Stephen Goode, "A New Generation of Latino Athletes," *Nuestro* 9 (September 1985), pp. 26–32; Michael M. Oleksak and Mary Adams Oleksak, *Beisbol: Latin Americans and the Grand Old Game* (Grand Rapids, MI, 1991), "Shortstop: Dave Concepcion: All Decade Team," *BM* 15 (April 1980), p. 19; John Thorn and Pete Palmer, eds., *Total Baseball*, 3rd ed. (New York, 1993).

                                                                    Samuel O. Regalado

COX, Robert Joe "Bobby" (b. May 21, 1941, Tulsa, OK), player and manager, attended high school in Selma, CA, and Reedley JC in California. The Los Angeles Dodgers (NL) signed Cox to a professional baseball contract in 1959. The Chicago Cubs (NL) selected Cox from the Dodgers in the minor league draft in November 1964. In 1966 Cox was acquired by the Atlanta Braves (NL). The six-foot, 185-pound second and third baseman, who threw and batted right-handed, completed his minor league career with stops including Reno, NV (CaL) in 1960; Salem, OR (NWL) and Panama City, FL (AlFL) in 1961; Salem in 1962; Albuquerque, NM (TL) and Great Falls, MT (PrL) in 1963; Albuquerque in 1964; Salt Lake City, UT (PCL) in 1965; Tacoma, WA (PCL) and Austin, TX (TL) in 1966; and Richmond, VA (IL) in 1967.

In December 1967, the Atlanta Braves traded Cox to the New York Yankees (AL) for two players. Cox spent 1970 with Syracuse, NY (IL) and was released by the Yankees in September 1970. Fort Lauderdale, FL (FSL), a Yankee affiliate, signed Cox in July 1971 and released him as a player in August 1971. Cox's only major league experience as a player came with the New York Yankees in 1968 and 1969. He appeared in 135 games in 1968 and 85 contests in 1969, compiling a .225 career major league batting average. He pitched in 3 games for Fort Lauderdale in 1971, losing one decision and boasting a 5.40 ERA.

Cox, a minor league instructor for the New York Yankees organization from October 1970 to March 1971, served as player–manager for Fort Lauderdale in 1971. The following season, he managed West Haven, CT (EL). West Haven won the EL pennant and defeated Three Rivers, Canada, in three straight games in a postseason playoff. From 1972 to 1976, Cox managed Syracuse, NY (IL) to two second-place and two third-place finishes. He became a major league manager in 1978, piloting Atlanta (NL) for four seasons. Atlanta finished sixth his first two years and fourth the next two in the AL West.

The Toronto Blue Jays (AL) hired Cox as manager in 1982. In Cox's first season there, Toronto finished sixth in the AL East. Toronto rose to fourth place in 1983 and second in 1984. In 1985 the Blue Jays came in first in the AL East and lost to the Kansas City Royals in the AL Championship Series. Out of baseball after the 1985 season, Cox returned as manager of the Atlanta Braves (NL) in June 1990 and replaced Russ Nixon with the Braves in sixth place. In 1991, Atlanta finished first in the NL West and defeated the Pittsburgh Pirates for the NL title. Atlanta was defeated by the Minnesota Twins, four games to three, in the World Series.

In 1992, Atlanta repeated as NL West titlist and again defeated Pittsburgh for the NL pennant. The Braves, however, lost to Toronto in Game 6 of the World Series. In 1993, the Braves took the NL West but fell to the Philadelphia Phillies in the six-game NL Championship Series. During the strike-shortened 1994 season, Cox guided the Braves to a 68–46 mark and a second-place NL East Division finish.

In four AL seasons, Cox's teams achieved 355 wins and 292 losses. In eight seasons, his NL teams won 566 games while losing 558. Altogether, Cox's major league managerial totals include 921 wins and 850 losses for a .520 percentage. Cox coached the AL All-Star team in 1985. The BBWAA named him AL Manager of the Year in 1985, while *TSN* designated him Major League Manager of the Year. In 1991 he was chosen NL Manager of the Year by both *TSN* and the BBWAA. Cox is a racing car enthusiast. He and his wife, Pamela, have three children, Kami, Keisha, and Skyla.

BIBLIOGRAPHY: *Atlanta Braves Media Guide*, 1994; *TSN Official Baseball Register*, 1994.

Stan W. Carlson

CRANDALL, Delmar Wesley "Del" (b. March 5, 1930, Ontario, CA), player, manager, and sportscaster, graduated from Fullerton Union High School and broke into professional baseball in 1948 as a catcher with the Leavenworth, KS, club (WA). His .304 batting mark with Leavenworth and .351 average in 38 games the next year with Evansville, IN (3IL) earned him a promotion to the Boston Braves (NL) for the remainder of the 1949 season. The 19-year-old rookie catcher never returned to the minors. In his 16-year major league career, he hit 179 home runs, drove in 657 runs, and compiled a .254 batting average.

The six-foot-1-inch, 180-pound Crandall excelled behind the plate for the Milwaukee Braves, leading NL catchers in assists six times (1953–1954, 1957, 1958–1960); in fielding percentage four times (1956, 1958–1959, 1962); and in putouts three times (1954, 1958, 1960). *TSN* gave him four Gold Glove awards (1958–1960, 1962). Crandall caught three no-hit games, including one each by Jim Wilson, Warren Spahn (BB), and Lew Burdette (BB). Authorities generally regarded him as one of the best catchers of his era, as evidenced by his selection as an NL All-Star in 1953–1956, 1958–1960, and 1962.

He spent most of his career as a member of the Braves organization but also performed brief stints with the San Francisco Giants (NL) in 1964, Pittsburgh Pirates (NL) in 1965, and Cleveland Indians (AL) in 1966. He played on Milwaukee's NL championship teams of 1957 and 1958. The Braves' 1957 World Series triumph over the Yankees ranked as his greatest thrill as a player.

After his playing career ended, he managed at the minor league level beginning with Albuquerque, NM (TL) in 1969. In 1970, his Albuquerque club won the TL championship with a win–loss record of 83–52, an achievement that brought Crandall TL Co-Manager of the Year honors.

After piloting Evansville, IN (AA) in 1971 and briefly the next year, Crandall returned to Milwaukee on May 29, 1972, to take over as the manager of the AL Brewers. In nearly four years as the Brewer skipper, he compiled a record of 271 wins and 338 losses. He also won 93 games and lost 131 as the manager of the Seattle Mariners (AL) in 1983 and 1984. He also worked as a radio broadcaster for the Chicago White Sox (1985–1988) and with the Brewers since then.

Crandall married Frances Sorralls on March 18, 1951, and had six children, including Del, Jr., and Billy. Crandall, a nondrinker and nonsmoker, developed a reputation as the consummate family man and was widely respected for his integrity and character.

BIBLIOGRAPHY: *The Baseball Encyclopedia*, 9th ed. (New York, 1993); Del Crandall file, National Baseball Library, Cooperstown, NY; *Lead Off:* 1992 Milwaukee Brewers official game program, p. 57.

David S. Matz

CRANDALL, James Otis "Doc" (b. October 8, 1877, Wadena, IN; d. August 17, 1951, Bell, CA), player, manager, and coach, performed 24 years as a major and especially a top minor league pitcher. He attended his hometown grammar school. The 5-foot-10½-inch, 180-pound right-hander married Bertha Caldwell in 1905 and was survived by his wife, a son, and a daughter.

Crandall began pitching professionally late in 1906 with Cedar Rapids, IA (3IL) and continued there through 1907. From 1908 through 1913—except for a midseason momentary stop with the St. Louis Cardinals (NL) in the latter year—he mostly relieved for manager John McGraw's (BB) New York Giants (NL). The versatile Crandall also pinch-hit and occasionally played in the infield. When the FL appeared in 1914 and 1915, he pitched and played second base for the St. Louis Terriers. After briefly appearing with the St. Louis Cardinals in 1916, he moved to the West Coast and pitched that year for Oakland, CA (PCL) and then Los Angeles, CA (PCL). With the exception of a brief appearance with the Boston Braves (NL) in the 1918 war year, he pitched for Los Angeles from 1917 through 1926. In 1927–1928, he played and managed at Wichita, KS (WL). Crandall returned to the PCL and performed for Sacramento, CA (PCL) and Los Angeles again in 1928–1929, closing his playing career. He coached for the Pittsburgh Pirates (NL) from 1931 to 1934, Des Moines, IA (WA) in 1935, Seattle, WA (PCL) in 1937, and Sacramento in 1938. In later life, he worked as a security guard.

Crandall, probably the very first clearly demarcated relief pitcher, enjoyed considerable success with the New York Giants. He twice finished second in pitchers' winning percentage, led four times in relief wins, and appeared four times among the (retroactive) relief save leaders. He relieved well in the 1911, 1912, and 1913 World Series, winning one decision and also serving as pinch hitter. With the St. Louis Terriers in 1915, he won 21 games as a starting pitcher. His major league career, approaching 10 years, featured 101 wins, 52 losses, a .620 winning percentage, a 2.92 ERA, and .285 batting average. During his West Coast tenure, Crandall reached stardom as a spitball pitcher, winning 20 or more games five seasons. In the minor leagues, Crandall won 249, lost 163, compiled a .606 winning percentage, enjoyed a 2.96 ERA, and batted .263.

BIBLIOGRAPHY: *The Baseball Encyclopedia*, 9th ed. (New York, 1993); Doc Crandall file, National Baseball Library, Cooperstown, NY; *Minor League Baseball Stars*, Vol. 2 (Manhattan, KS, 1985), p. 136; *NYT*, August 18, 1951.

Lowell L. Blaisdell

CROSETTI, Frank Peter Joseph "Frankie" "The Crow" (b. October 4, 1910, San Francisco, CA), player and coach, is the son of Domenic Crosetti, a stevedore, rancher, and garbage collector, and Rachel (Monteverde) Crosetti and played sandlot baseball and began his professional career as a shortstop with the San Francisco Seals (PCL). The New York Yankees (AL) purchased his contract in 1929. He made the club in 1932 and a key contribution as a rookie, helping the team win its first world championship in 4 seasons. In his 17 seasons with the Bronx Bombers, he performed on nine AL pennant winners and eight World Series champions. He epitomized the typical Yankee star of the 1930s and 1940s, being tough, talented, and dedicated to winning.

From 1932 to 1941 and again in 1943 and 1945, he was the regular Yankee shortstop. Crosetti, who played 62 games at third base in 1941, retired during the 1944 season but returned in 1945. In 1941 and from 1946 to 1948, he was a utility infielder.

In 1938 he led AL shortstops with 352 putouts, 506 assists, and 120 double plays. The following year, he paced AL shortstops in fielding (.968), putouts (323), and double plays (118). The fleet-footed Crosetti led the Yankees in stolen bases for three consecutive seasons (1936–1938) and paced the AL in stolen bases in 1938. He set a major league record for times at bat in a 154-game season with 757. His skills included being adept at the hidden ball play and being one of baseball's best sign stealers.

In 1936 and 1939, Crosetti was selected for the AL All-Star team. As a player and coach, he wore the Yankee pinstripes for a record 23 World Series. The Series appearances involved 8 as a player and 15 as a coach. His only World Series home run was hit off the legendary Dizzy Dean (BB) of the Chicago Cubs in 1938.

From 1949 to 1968, the Yankees employed Crosetti as a third-base coach. Always in great shape, he worked and played for as hard and long as the regulars. In his prime, he remained an underrated player.

In his 17 major league seasons as a Yankee, Crosetti batted .245 in 1,682 games with 1,541 hits and 1,006 runs scored. His extra base hits included

260 doubles, 65 triples, and 98 home runs. In his seven World Series appearances, he played in 29 games.

At rookie and spring training camps, he served as infield instructor. Crosetti was one of the first Yankees that young Mickey Mantle (BB) met in 1951. Mantle possessed an old, beaten-up glove, causing Crosetti to buy him a new one. Crosetti married Norma Devincenzi on October 22, 1938, and had two children, John and Ellen.

BIBLIOGRAPHY: *The Baseball Encyclopedia*, 9th ed. (New York, 1993); Frank Crosetti, letter to Stan W. Carlson, January 1993; *New York Yankee Media Guide*, 1992; John Thorn and Pete Palmer, eds., *Total Baseball*, 3rd ed. (New York, 1993).

Stan W. Carlson

CUCCINELLO, Anthony Francis "Tony" "Chick" (b. November 8, 1907, Long Island City, NY), player, coach, scout, and manager, is the son of Samuel Cuccinello, an engineer with Consolidated Edison, and Amelia (Barberesi) Cuccinello and began his long baseball career in 1926 with Syracuse, NY (IL). After only 4 games, he was sent to Lawrence, MA (NEL) for the remainder of the 1926 season and 1927 campaign. After 127 games at Danville, IL (3IL) in 1928, he was sold to the Cincinnati Reds (NL). Cincinnati optioned him to Columbus, OH (AA) for the rest of the 1928 season and 1929 campaign and recalled him in 1930. Cuccinello enjoyed two outstanding major league seasons while playing several infield positions.

He was traded to the Brooklyn Dodgers (NL) in 1932 during spring training and played there through 1935. In December 1935, Brooklyn sent him to the Boston Bees (NL) in a multiplayer deal. In June 1940, Boston traded him to the New York Giants (NL). In 1941, hobbled by a knee injury, he was assigned to the Giants' farm team in Jersey City, NJ (IL) as player–manager. He agreed to pilot Jersey City again in 1942 but secured his release so that he could join the Boston Braves (NL) as a player–coach. After being let go on July 19, 1943, he was signed the same day by the Chicago White Sox (AL) and played there until unconditionally released on January 5, 1946. After spending a year out of baseball, he returned in 1947 to manage Tampa, FL (FIL) and played in four games.

Known as an intelligent player, Cuccinello then coached for Indianapolis, IN (AA) in 1948; the Cincinnati Reds (NL) from 1949 to 1951; the Cleveland Indians (AL) from 1952 to 1956; the Chicago White Sox (AL) from 1957 to 1966; the Detroit Tigers (AL) in 1967 and 1968; and Chicago (AL) again in 1969. He then scouted for the New York Yankees (AL) until retiring in 1985. He coached on three American League pennant winners, the 1954 Cleveland Indians, the 1960 Chicago White Sox, and the 1968 Detroit Tigers. Detroit won the World Series.

His 1,704 major league games included 1,205 at second base, 468 at third base, and 5 at shortstop. Cuccinello batted .280 with 1,729 hits, recording

334 doubles, 46 triples, and 94 home runs. He drove in 884 runs, scored 730 runs, drew 579 walks, and stole 42 bases. In 1939 he established a major league record for the longest errorless game (23 innings) by a second baseman. He was selected to NL All-Star teams in 1933 and 1938.

Cuccinello's brother, Al, played infield for the New York Giants (NL) in 1935, while his nephew, Sam Mele,* was an AL outfielder and managed the Minnesota Twins (AL). Cuccinello, who married Clara Caroselli in October 1932, lives in Tampa, FL. He has two sons, Anthony, Jr., and Joseph, and one daughter, Darlene Ann.

BIBLIOGRAPHY: Lee Allen, *The Cincinnati Reds* (New York, 1948); Frank Graham, *The Brooklyn Dodgers* (New York, 1945); Harold Kaese, *The Boston Braves* (New York, 1948); Robert L. Tiemann, *Dodger Classics* (St. Louis, MO, 1983); *TSN Official Baseball Register*, 1969; Rich Westcott, *Diamond Greats* (Westport, CT, 1988).

Ralph S. Graber

CULLENBINE, Roy Joseph (b. October 18, 1915, Nashville, TN; d. May 28, 1992, Mt. Clemens, MI), player, was the son of an itinerant tap dancer and a former member of a girls' softball team. The family settled in Detroit, MI, where Cullenbine played football at Eastern High School. He skipped scholastic baseball because a local rule prohibited him from taking part in MuL baseball games if he performed on the high school team. When Cullenbine played in the MuL, he also served as a batboy for the Detroit Tigers (AL) under manager Bucky Harris (BB) in 1930. In 1932 scout "Wish" Eagan saw Cullenbine working out at Navin Field and landed him a job on Harry Heilmann's (BB) All-Stars. Cullenbine signed as an outfielder with Shreveport, LA (EDL) and transferred later that year to Greenwood, MS (EDL). Fort Worth, TX (TL) marked his next stop that season. In 1935 Cullenbine joined Springfield, IL (3IL), where his .338 mark won the six-foot-one-inch, 185-pound switch-hitter a promotion to Beaumont, TX (TL) before the end of the season. He hit .285 in 1936 and joined the Toledo, OH, Mud Hens (AA) in 1937, where he played third base for manager Fred Haney. Cullenbine played in 25 games for the Detroit Tigers before the end of the 1938 season and appeared in 75 games with them in 1939. In a historic decision in 1940, Judge Kenesaw Mountain Landis (BB) decreed that his contract had not been properly handled when he was ascending in the Tiger chain, making Cullenbine a free agent.

The Brooklyn Dodgers (NL) signed him for $25,000, but he did not produce and inspired taunts of "Larry the $25,000 Lemon" in the local press. He was hitting just .180 in late May, when the St. Louis Browns (AL) acquired him in a straight deal for Joe Gallagher. The Browns advised him to cut down on his weight. In 1941, he blossomed into an AL All-Star, hitting .317. He tied an AL record by scoring five runs in the first game on July 31, 1941, and a major league record by tripling and doubling in the fifth inning on June 3, 1941. General manager Bill DeWitt of the Browns quickly tired of Cullenbine and derided his lack of aggressiveness at the plate. During his 10 major league seasons, Cullenbine drew 852 walks to go with his 1,072 hits, an inordinately high percentage. Browns manager Luke Sewell* called him one of the "laziest human beings you ever saw." In June 1942, the Browns shipped Cullenbine and Bill Trotter to the Washington Senators (AL) for Mike Chartak and Steve Sundra, two cogs in the 1944 Browns AL pennant machine. Near the end of the AL season, Washington waived Cullenbine to the New York Yankees (AL). Cullenbine hit .364 in September, enabling him to play in his first World Series, against the St. Louis Cardinals.

The peripatetic infielder was shipped with Buddy Rosar to the Cleveland Indians (AL) for Roy Weatherly and Oscar Grimes in December 1942 and was named to the 1943 AL All-Star team. After Cullenbine played in 8 games in 1945, the Indians returned him to the Tigers for Don Ross and Dutch Meyer. This trade enabled Cullenbine to be on his second pennant winner. He led the AL that season with 112 free passes, batted .335 in 1946, and hit 24 home runs in 1947 for the Tigers. Cullenbine compiled a .276 lifetime batting average in 1,181 games, with 110 homers and 599 RBIs. In 12 World Series games, he batted .244 with 6 RBIs. He married Margaret Bader in February 1938 and later became the divorced father of three children.

BIBLIOGRAPHY: Bill Borst, ed., *Ables to Zoldak*, vol. 1 (St. Louis, MO, 1988); Mike Shatzkin, ed., *The Ball Players* (New York, 1990).

William A. Borst

DALY, Thomas Peter "Tom" "Tido" (b. February 7, 1866, Philadelphia, PA; d. October 29, 1939, Brooklyn, NY), player, manager, and scout, was the brother of Joe Daly, who played briefly in the major leagues from 1890 to 1892. Daly began his baseball career as a catcher with Millville, PA, and the Keystones of Philadelphia in 1884. In 1886 he helped Newark, NJ, to the IL pennant in the IL's first year.

The five-foot-seven-inch, 170-pound catcher made his major league debut with the Chicago White Stockings (NL) in 1887, compiling the best fielding average (.935) among NL catchers. Daly played for the White Stockings two years and accompanied them on an international barnstorming tour in the winter of 1888–1889 but was released on their return. After spending one season with the Washington Senators (NL), he joined the Brooklyn Bridegrooms (NL) in 1890.

The switch-hitting right-hander helped the Bridegrooms capture the NL pennant, batting .243, and participated in his first postseason series. Brooklyn played to a 3–3–draw with the Louisville Cyclones (AA) in the World Series, as Daly made only four hits in 22 at bats. After moving to the infield in 1892, he performed regularly for Brooklyn at second base from 1893 to 1901 except for 1897.

Daly left Brooklyn in 1897 to play for his former catching mate, Connie Mack (BB), who was managing Milwaukee, WI (WL). He returned to Brooklyn in 1898 and helped the club (renamed the Superbas) to the NL pennant again in 1900, hitting .312 for the year. His pinnacle season came in 1901, when he batted .315 and led the NL with 38 doubles.

Daly returned to Chicago in 1902, joining the new White Sox (AL). The following year, he moved at midseason to the Cincinnati Reds (NL) and finished strong with a .293 batting average in 80 games as their regular second baseman. In 16 major league seasons, Daly compiled a .278 batting average with 262 doubles, 103 triples, and 49 home runs. He collected 687 bases on balls, walking an average of once every nine plate appearances. A speedy base runner, he chalked up 385 steals.

He managed Providence, RI (EL) in 1904, Altoona, PA, in 1905 and 1906, and Johnstown, PA, in 1907 and scouted for the Cleveland Naps (AL) in 1911 and 1912 before joining the New York Yankees (AL) scouting staff from 1913 to 1915. Daly resided in Brooklyn until his death from a yearlong illness.

BIBLIOGRAPHY: *The Baseball Encyclopedia*, 9th ed. (New York, 1993); Thomas P. Daly file, National Baseball Library, Cooperstown, NY; Frank Graham, *The Brooklyn Dodgers* (New York, 1945); Mike Shatzkin, ed., *The Ballplayers* (New York, 1990); John Thorn and Pete Palmer, eds., *Total Baseball*, 3rd. ed. (New York, 1993).

Gaymon L. Bennett

DAVIS, Curtis Benton "Curt" "Coonskin" (b. September 7, 1903, Greenfield, MO; d. October 13, 1965, Covina, CA), player, was one of five children of William R. Davis, a real estate broker, and Ida (Brown) Davis. A late starter, he began his professional baseball career in 1928 as a pitcher with Salt Lake City, UT, in the short-lived Class C UIL after working as a lumberjack and playing for two seasons with semiprofessional teams in Vernonia, OR, and Ashland, OR. After enjoying a 16–8 season at Salt Lake as a teammate of pitcher Thornton Lee,* he joined the San Francisco Seals (PCL) in 1929. Not until 1934, however, at age 30, did Davis reach the major leagues with the Philadelphia Phillies (NL).

A six-foot-two-inch, 185-pound right-hander with a sidearm delivery, Davis appeared in an NL-leading 51 games in 1934. He won 19 while losing 17 for a seventh-place club and achieving a 2.95 ERA, the lowest for any Philadelphia starter since 1920. In 1935, the Phillies recorded another seventh-place finish, as Davis took 16 of 30 decisions. During these two years, no other Phillie pitcher garnered more wins than losses.

In May 1936, Philadelphia traded Davis with outfielder Ethan Allen to the Chicago Cubs (NL) for a washed-up Chuck Klein (BB). In 1937 a sore arm sidelined him for half the season, but he returned to compile a 10–5 record. The next spring, Chicago sent Davis, two other players, and

$185,000 to the St. Louis Cardinals (NL) in the famous trade for Dizzy Dean (BB). As the deal turned out, he was the prize. Following a 12–8 season in 1938, he reached his peak with 22 victories to lead the 1939 Cardinals into second place. In June 1940, St. Louis traded a fading Davis and Joe Medwick (BB) to the Brooklyn Dodgers (NL) for $15,000 and three players. Although then age 37, he enjoyed several good, first-division campaigns with the flamboyant Leo Durocher (BB)–era Dodgers. In 1941, his 13–7 record helped the Dodgers take the NL pennant. Davis was bested, 3–2, by Red Ruffing (BB) in the opening game of the World Series, in which the New York Yankees prevailed.

Davis's career ended in 1946 with 158 wins (including 26 in relief), 131 losses, and a 3.42 ERA. His Total Pitcher Index (TPI) rating in *Total Baseball* lists him eighty-second all-time and twenty-first in his era. He was selected an All-Star twice, being hit hard in relief of Carl Hubbell (BB) in the 1936 game and not playing in 1939.

In retirement, he became a real estate salesman. He was married three times: to Lillian Preston in 1935, to Della F. Haggberg in 1954, and to Lennis Hutchison, who survived him, in 1959. He had no children.

BIBLIOGRAPHY: *The Baseball Encyclopedia*, 9th ed. (New York, 1993); Curt Davis file, National Baseball Library, Cooperstown, NY; *TSN*, October 27, 1965; John Thorn and Pete Palmer, eds., *Total Baseball*, 3rd ed. (New York, 1993).

A. D. Suehsdorf

DAVIS, Eric Keith (b. May 29, 1962, Los Angeles, CA), player, is the son of Jimmy Davis and Shirley Davis and grew up in Los Angeles, where he won All-City honors as a shortstop in baseball and as a basketball player at Fremont High School. His close friend Darryl Strawberry* played with him on a CML baseball team. After Davis graduated from high school in 1980, the Cincinnati Reds (NL) signed him as an eighth-round draft choice. Davis declined basketball scholarships from several colleges.

Davis played at Eugene, OR (NWL) in 1980 and 1981, being converted to the outfield. His subsequent minor league stops included Cedar Rapids, IA (ML) in 1982, Waterbury, CT (EL) in 1983, and a brief stint at Indianapolis, IN (AA) in 1983. After starting the 1984 season at Wichita, KS (AA), the six-foot-three-inch, 185-pound hitter displayed midseason statistics of a .314 batting average, 14 home runs, 34 RBIs, and 27 stolen bases. The Reds promoted him and made him the regular center fielder until an injury sidelined him. In 1985, his playing time was split between Cincinnati and Denver, CO (AA).

In his first full season with the Reds in 1986, Davis batted a .277 with 27 home runs, 71 RBIs, and 80 stolen bases. Only Rickey Henderson (BB) previously had hit over 20 home runs while stealing 80 or more bases in a season. The following year appeared to mark the blossoming of a great career. He was named the NL Player of the Month for April and May and set NL records by having 19 home runs through May and hitting three grand slams in May. On August 2, the earliest date of any season, he joined the 30/30 Club with at least 30 or more home runs and stolen bases. The center fielder finished 1987 with a .293 batting average, 37 home runs, 100 RBIs, and 50 stolen bases. Davis, who won Gold Glove awards in 1987, 1988, and 1989, was named to the *TSN* Silver Slugger team in 1987 and 1989 and made the NL All-Star team in 1987 and 1989.

Injuries limited his production, as Davis never played in more than 135 games in a season. He spent considerable time on the disabled list, being sidelined from August 16 to September 1, 1984; May 3 to May 18, 1989; April 25 to May 19, 1990; June 12 to June 27 and July 31 to August 26, 1991; and May 23 to June 19 and August 5 to August 25, 1992. In Game 4 of the 1990 World Series against the Oakland Athletics, he suffered a lacerated right kidney while trying to make a diving catch. Cincinnati traded Davis to the Los Angeles Dodgers (NL) on November 27, 1991. The Dodgers hoped that he would form part of a great offensive combination with his longtime friend and teammate Darryl Strawberry.* Injuries to both, however, prevented that from happening. In August 1993, Los Angeles traded him to the Detroit Tigers (AL). The Tigers released Davis following the 1994 season.

Through the strike-shortened 1994 season, he amassed a .259 batting average, 665 runs scored, 205 home runs, 645 RBIs, and 306 stolen bases. Through 1994, his 306 thefts made him the all-time stolen base percentage leader with 87.4 percent (among those with 300 career attempts). He and his wife Sherrie have two daughters, Erica and Sacha, and reside in Woodland Hills, CA.

BIBLIOGRAPHY: Eric Davis file, National Baseball Library, Cooperstown, NY; Chuck Johnson, "Reds' Davis Gets Results by 'Going on Gut Instincts,'" *USA Today*, April 14, 1989, p. C7; *Los Angeles Dodgers 1993 Media Guide*; Hal McCoy, "Aches, Pains and Superstardom," *TSN*, March 2, 1987, p. 22; Jay Mariotti, "The Ultimate Player—Do Reds Have Him?" *TSN*, June 19, 1987, pp. 10–11; Ron Rapoport, "Eric Davis Soaks It Up," *Sport* 81 (June 1990), pp. 52–54, 56, 60; John Thorn and Pete Palmer, eds., *Total Baseball*, 3rd ed. (New York, 1993), p. 785; *TSN Official Baseball Register*, 1994.

Robert J. Brown

DAY, John B. (b. 1848; d. January 25, 1925, Cliffside, NJ), owner and executive, founded the New York Giants (NL) baseball club and turned it into one of baseball's premier franchises. Day, a lifelong bachelor and successful tobacco merchant in New York City, supported several independent baseball teams. In 1883, Day and Boston sportsman Jim Mutrie formed the Metropolitan Exposition Company and were awarded the Giants NL franchise. They also received the Mets, an AA team, in 1884. Day signed many players from the failed Troy Trojans (NL) franchise and pitcher John Montgomery

Ward (BB) from the Providence Grays (NL) club. The Giants and the Mets both played in the original Polo Grounds until Day sold the Mets in 1885. A canvas fence was raised to separate the two diamonds. After the Mets won the 1884 AA championship, Day funneled off the club's talent to the Giants because the NL charged twice as much for tickets.

The Giants enjoyed success both on and off the field, winning NL pennants in 1888 and 1889 and becoming one of the NL's most valuable franchises. Day, a popular owner with the players, paid some of the best salaries and spared no expense on travel for the team. The onset of the Brotherhood war, however, radically changed Day's fortunes. The BPBP, the players association formed in 1885, began to seek funding for their own teams and started the PL in 1890. Most of Day's Giants squad defected to the BPBP PL. The battle for fans proved especially fierce in New York with five teams, including two NL and three PL competing during the season. Day still fielded a Giants team, but the club failed to remain competitive.

The BPBP war crippled Day financially. To keep the Giants from ruin, Day appealed to the NL for assistance. The NL provided nearly $80,000 in 1891, with several NL owners receiving stock in the troubled club. The NL owners recognized the importance of a New York franchise and loaned Day players to help the Giants. Day sold a share of his Giants club to Edward B. Talcott, owner of a BPBP team, and resigned his club presidency after a disastrous 1892 season. He sold his remaining share of the Giants to Andrew Freedman (BB) in 1895 for $48,000. Day, who never regained his lost fortune, served as director of NL Umpires until his health forced him to resign. In 1916, the NL voted to give Day a pension for life.

BIBLIOGRAPHY: Charles C. Alexander, *Our Game* (New York, 1991); Lee Allen, *The Giants and the Dodgers* (New York, 1964); James M. DiClerico and Barry J. Bavelee, *The Jersey Game* (New Brunswick, NJ, 1991); *NYT*, December 14, 1916, p. 12; January 26, 1925, p. 12; David Pietrusza, *Major Leagues* (Jefferson, NC, 1991); Steven A. Riess, *Touching Base* (Westport, CT, 1980).

Brian L. Laughlin

DEVLIN, Arthur McArthur "Art" (b. October 16, 1879, Washington, DC; d. September 18, 1948, Jersey City, NJ), player and manager, batted and threw right-handed with a six-foot, 175-pound frame. Devlin played football and baseball at Georgetown University in 1900 and 1901 and then signed with New Bern, NC (NCSL). He played in 1903 for Newark, NJ (EL) and in 1904 joined the New York Giants (NL), where he remained until 1911. In December 1911, New York sold him to the Boston Braves (NL). Devlin played with Boston through 1913. After the Braves released him, he signed as playing manager for Oakland, CA (PCL) in 1914, moved to Montreal, Canada (IL) in 1915, and managed Lebanon, PA (PSL) in 1916. Since the PSL closed shortly after opening day, Devlin joined Rochester, NY (IL) for the balance of the 1916 season. His last baseball assignment came in 1917–1918 as manager of Norfolk, VA (VL).

Devlin played most infield positions but was considered the era's finest third baseman. Sportswriter Grantland Rice (OS) named Devlin to his All-Time All-Star team. Devlin batted .269 lifetime with 1,184 base hits and proved a good base runner early in his career, stealing 283 bases. In 1905, he stole 59 bases to share the NL lead. The following year, he stole 54 bases to finish 3 behind NL leader Frank Chance (BB). Leg injuries the latter part of Devlin's career reduced his stolen bases total. He played for the New York Giants in the 1905 World Series against the Philadelphia Athletics, batting .250 with 3 stolen bases. Although not a power hitter, Devlin hit a grand-slam home run in his first major league at bat with the Giants. The NL briefly suspended Devlin in 1910 for fighting with an abusive fan in Brooklyn, NY. In 1906, Devlin married Ilma Wilk, the daughter of Frederick Wilk, a vice-president of the Union Trust Company in Chicago, IL.

BIBLIOGRAPHY: *The Baseball Encyclopedia*, 9th ed. (New York, 1993); Arthur McArthur Devlin file, National Baseball Library, Cooperstown, NY; Joseph L. Reichler, ed., *The Great All-Time Baseball Record Book* (New York, 1981).

Horace R. Givens

DEVLIN, James Alexander "Jim" (b. 1849, Philadelphia, PA; d. October 10, 1883, Philadelphia, PA), player, ranked during his final two major league baseball seasons among the finest pitchers ever. Little is known of the first two thirds of his brief life, but he reportedly played third base at age 22 or 23 for an Easton, PA, club in 1872. The following year, he performed as a reserve infielder for the Philadelphia White Stockings (NA) and batted only .242. With the Chicago White Stockings (NA), though, he played more regularly and boosted his batting average to .291 in 1874 and .292 in 1875. The latter season also marked his pitching debut, as he won 7 games and lost 16 decisions, with an estimated 2.89 ERA.

The newly organized Louisville Grays in 1876 recruited Devlin to play in the NL's inaugural season. Devlin single-handedly carried Louisville to a fifth-place finish, pitching for the NL's weakest offensive team. The 5-foot-11-inch, 175-pound right-hander finished fourth in the NL with 30 wins, while compiling the NL's second-best ERA (1.56). His 35 losses led the NL, but his team scored no runs in 40 percent of those setbacks. Devlin led the NL in the workhorse categories of games (68), complete games (66), and innings pitched (622), topped the NL in strikeouts with 122, and batted .315, outperforming his nearest teammate by 42 points. His NL-leading 7.9 Total Baseball Ranking (an overall performance rating devised by Pete Palmer) for 1876 places him among the top 50 major league single-season performers at all positions and number 21 among pitchers.

The Louisville management fielded a stronger team in 1877. Devlin's effectiveness declined somewhat, partly because he joined some of his team-mates in a gambling conspiracy to lose several games. Nevertheless, his win–loss record improved to 35–25. Louisville led the NL in mid-August, but a suspicious seven-game losing streak dropped the Grays to a second-place finish. Devlin pitched every inning of every game, with his workhorse statistics and 6.3 TBR again leading the NL. He planned to leave Louisville for the St. Louis Browns (NL) in 1878. After the crookedness of the "Louisville Four" was uncovered in October 1877, Devlin admitted his involvement and was expelled from baseball.

Devlin's frequent pleas for reinstatement met with sympathy but firm rejection. Although Devlin found work and respect as a Philadelphia police officer, his wife Kate and son James, Jr., were left "in straitened circumstances" when he died from tuberculosis six years after his expulsion.

In five major league seasons, Devlin batted .288 with 341 hits in 266 games. In three seasons as a pitcher, he hurled 1,405 innings, completed 151 of his 153 starts, and compiled a 72–76 win–loss record.

BIBLIOGRAPHY: James Devlin file, National Baseball Library, Cooperstown, NY; John E. Findling, "The Louisville Grays' Scandal of 1877," *JSH* 3 (Summer 1976), pp. 176–187; Albert G. Spalding, *America's National Game* (New York, 1911); John Thorn and Pete Palmer, eds., *Total Baseball*, 3rd ed. (New York, 1993); Robert L. Tiemann and Mark Rucker, eds., *Nineteenth Century Stars* (Kansas City, MO, 1989).

Frederick Ivor-Campbell

DISMUKES, William "Dizzy" (b. March 14, 1890, Birmingham, AL; d. June 30, 1961, Campbell, OH), player, manager, coach, and executive, was associated with many fine Negro League teams. Dismukes, a product of Stillman College in Alabama, began his professional baseball career as a submarine pitcher with the East St. Louis, IL, Imperials in 1908. The next year, he played with the Kentucky Unions from nearby Lovejoy, IL. The Minneapolis, MN, Keystones signed him in 1910, but he finished the season under legendary manager C. I. Taylor (BB) with the West Badon, IL, Sprudels.

In 1911, the six-foot, 180-pound, right-handed submarine pitcher defeated Howie Camnitz* of the Pittsburgh Pirates (NL), 2–1. The Pirates, playing without shortstop Honus Wagner (BB), were held to four hits and one unearned run. Later that season, a rubber-armed Dismukes won 3 games in two days against the tough Indianapolis, IN, ABCs. One game lasted 12 innings. In 1912, he pitched his first no-hitter, a 1–0 win, against the Chicago, IL, American Giants. Dismukes remained with the Sprudels through the 1913 season. After a brief stay with the Brooklyn, NY, Royal Giants, he joined the Indianapolis, IN, ABCs in 1915. During a 20-game winning streak that season, he pitched his second no-hitter, a 5–0 triumph over the Chicago, IL, Giants.

Upon entering the military in 1918, Dismukes joined the 809 Pioneer Infantry baseball team in Nantes, France. His squad won the championship of southern France. After fulfilling his military obligation, he returned to the Indianapolis ABCs (NNL) and served as player–manager there through part of the 1924 campaign. He pitched briefly with the Birmingham, AL, Black Barons (NNL) in 1924, Memphis, TN, Red Sox (NNL) in 1925, St. Louis, MO, Stars (NNL) in 1926 and 1927, and Columbus, OH, Blue Birds (NNL) in 1933 and managed the powerhouse 1932 Detroit, MI, Wolves in the short-lived EWL.

In 1942, Dismukes became business manager of the Kansas City, MO, Monarchs (NAL). Ten years later, as black players were integrating the major leagues, the New York Yankees (AL) hired him as a scout. After two years in the Yankee organization, he served with the Chicago Cubs (NL) in a similar capacity in 1954 and 1955. His peers often described him as an outstanding manager with a mathematician's mind and great administrative skills. Personally, Dismukes was known for his arbitration abilities with ball players and upper management.

BIBLIOGRAPHY: Indianapolis (IN) *Freeman*, September 16, 1911; May 15, 1915; May 22, 1915; July 31, 1915; Kansas City (MO) *Call*, March 17, 1950; January 23, 1953; Larry Lester, interview with John "Buck" O'Neil, December 6, 1992; James A. Riley, *The Biographical Encyclopedia of the Negro Baseball Leagues* (New York, 1994); Michael Shatzkin, ed., *The Ballplayers* (New York, 1990).

Larry Lester

DONATELLI, August Joseph "Augie" (b. August 22, 1914, Heilwood, PA; d. May 24, 1990, St. Petersburg, FL), player and umpire, was one of eight children born to Italian immigrants Antonio Donatelli, a coal miner, and Vencezna (DiSantis) Donatelli. Upon graduation from high school, he became a coal miner like his father and also played portions of three seasons as an infielder in the lower minor leagues. A B-17 tailgunner during World War II, Donatelli was shot down during the first daylight raid on Berlin, Germany, and spent 15 months as German prisoner of war. He began his umpiring career by officiating softball games in prisoner of war camps. After the war, he used the GI bill to attend Bill McGowan's (BB) Umpiring School and graduated first in his class. A "born" umpire, Donatelli advanced to the major leagues in only fours years. He spent 1946 in the Class C PrL, started 1947 in the Class A SAL, advanced at midseason to the Class AAA IL, and joined the NL in 1950.

Donatelli, one of the most respected and influential major league umpires during his 24-year career, was known for his hustle, unerring judgment, and refusal to tolerate verbal abuse from players or managers. Baseball writers voted him in 1955 as the NL's best base umpire after he had spent only 5 years in the majors. Donatelli's most memorable moment occurred while umpiring home plate. In the fourth game of the 1957 World Series, he resolved a dispute over whether New York Yankees pitcher Tommy Byrne had hit Nippy Jones of the Milwaukee Braves on the foot by a pitch by awarding Jones first base after finding a smudge of black shoe polish on the ball. In 1961, he inadvertently started a style of umpiring balls and strikes that became a standard technique for NL umpires. After finding it necessary to rest on one knee to provide relief from hemorrhoidal pain, he retained the position for the rest of his career because it afforded a better view of low, outside pitches. His most important contribution to the umpiring profession and baseball history was being the principal organizer of the NL umpire's union in 1964. The union, reorganized as the MLUA with the addition of AL arbiters in 1968, brought about greatly improved salaries, benefits, and working conditions for umpires. A crew chief for 14 years, he umpired four All-Star games (1953, 1957, 1961, and 1969), two NL Championship Series (1969, 1972), and five World Series (1955, 1957, 1961, 1967, 1973). In 1973, his fellow arbiters voted him the Al Somers Award as the Outstanding Major League Umpire of the previous year.

Donatelli, who had been on the staff of the Al Somers Umpire School for 30 years, retired after the 1973 season. He became the chief instructor of the ESUTS and then scouted umpiring prospects for the NL. Donatelli, who married Mary Lou Lamont in 1946 and had four children, died in his sleep of a heart attack.

BIBLIOGRAPHY: Harold C. Burr, "Donatelli Drops into Ump Role," *BD* 9 (June 1950), pp. 23–24; Augie Donatelli file, National Baseball Library, Cooperstown, NY; Larry R. Gerlach, "Augie Donatelli: Umpire and Union Organizer," in Peter Levine, ed., *Baseball History: An Annual of Original Baseball Research* (Westport, CT, 1989), pp. 1–11; *TSN*, March 3, 1973; June 4, 1990.

Larry R. Gerlach

DOYLE, John Joseph "Dirty Jack" (b. October 25, 1869, Killorgin, County Kerry, Ireland; d. December 31, 1958, Holyoke, MA), player, manager, umpire, and scout, began his professional baseball career in 1888 as a catcher with the Lynn, MA, team (NEL). In 1889, Doyle signed with Canton, OH (TSL), where he caught 80 games, hit .280, and stole 81 bases. The 19-year-old backstop made his major league debut with Columbus, OH, (AA) in August 1889, playing in 11 games. The next season, he appeared in 77 games, largely in a utility role, with Columbus. In 1891 Doyle, who batted and threw right-handed, played for the Cleveland Spiders (NL), where he batted .276 in 69 games. Early in the 1892 season, Cleveland sent him to the New York Giants (NL), where he appeared in 90 games and raised his average to .298. He stayed with New York through the 1895 season, batting a combined .337. In 1894 the five-foot-nine-inch, 155-pound Doyle found a home at first base, batting a robust .367 with 90 runs scored and 100 RBIs in 99 games. His performance, along with the stellar hitting of George Davis (BB) and George Van Haltren (BB) and superb pitching of Amos Rusie (BB) and Jouett Meekin, sparked New York to an 88–44 record and a second-place finish in the 12-team NL.

During the 1896 and 1897 seasons, Doyle held the regular first baseman's job with the Baltimore Orioles (NL), where he helped manager Ned Hanlon's (S) team win the NL championship in 1896 with a 90–39 record and finish runner-up the next season with a 90–40 mark. In 1896 Doyle recorded career highs in both runs scored (116) and RBIs (101). For the two seasons combined, he averaged 164 hits and 67 stolen bases and batted .346. Doyle moved from one team to another over the next eight seasons. After Doyle played with the Washington Senators (NL) in 1898, the New York Giants (NL) employed him as the team's starting first sacker in 1899 and 1900. He played in 75 games at first base for the Chicago Orphans (NL) in 1901 and saw action with the Washington Senators (AL) and New York Giants (NL) in 1902. The following season, he played 139 games at first base for the Brooklyn Superbas, collecting 164 hits and batting .313. Brooklyn used him briefly in 1904 before sending him to the Philadelphia Phillies (NL). In 1905 he appeared in 1 game for the New York Highlanders (AL).

During his 17 seasons spanning 10 different major league clubs, Doyle remained an accomplished hitter with 1,806 hits and a lifetime .299 batting average. Only 20 major leaguers, including Doyle, have played in at least 100 games at four different positions. Some claim that in an 1892 game he was baseball's first pinch hitter, coming off the bench to single for the Giants. After Doyle finished his playing career, he remained active in professional baseball for the rest of his life. He managed Milwaukee, WI (AA) in 1907 and umpired in the EL in 1910 and the NL and NEL in 1911. After scouting for the Cleveland Naps (AL) in 1913, he umpired in the AA in 1915, the PCL in 1916, and the 3IL in 1919. In 1920 the Chicago Cubs (NL) hired Doyle as the team's New England scout, a position he proudly held until his death 38 years later.

BIBLIOGRAPHY: *The Baseball Encyclopedia*, 9th ed. (New York, 1993); Chicago (IL) *Daily Tribune*, January 1, 1959; January 2, 1959; Craig Carter, ed., *TSN Daguerreotypes*, 8th ed. (St. Louis, MO, 1990), p. 83; John Joseph Doyle file, National Baseball Library, Cooperstown, NY; John Thorn and Pete Palmer, eds., *Total Baseball*, 3rd ed. (New York, 1993).

                                                                        Raymond D. Kush

DYER, Edwin Hawley "Eddie" (b. October 11, 1900, Morgan City, LA; d. April 20, 1964, Houston, TX), player, scout, and manager, was of Scotch and Irish descent. He captained the Morgan City High School football team. Dyer served in the U.S. Army infantry in 1918 and entered Rice University in 1924, returning in 1936 to complete a bachelor of arts degree and coach freshmen football. The 5-foot-11-inch, 175-pound southpaw signed with the St. Louis Cardinals (NL) in 1922 and shuffled between the Cardinals and their farm clubs from 1922 to 1927. After making two relief appearances in 1922, he shut out the Chicago Cubs in his first major league start in 1923. A sore arm caused Dyer to return to the minors and convert to the outfield.

In 69 pitching appearances for St. Louis, he won 15 games and lost 15 decisions with a 4.75 ERA. He played 60 games as a pinch hitter and outfielder. Dyer's career batting average was .223.

On October 6, 1928, Dyer married Geraldine Jennings. They had one son, Edwin, Jr. After Dyer pitched one inning for the Cardinals in 1927, he was hired to manage in the St. Louis farm system. From 1927 to 1942, he piloted Springfield, MO (WA), Houston, TX (TL), and Columbus, OH (AA) and won nine minor league championships. In 1942 *TSN* selected Dyer Minor League Manager of the Year for directing Columbus to an AA pennant. He also scouted for the Cardinals and signed future star hurler Howard Pollet* in 1938. From 1943 to 1945, Dyer supervised the St. Louis farm system.

When Cardinal manager Billy Southworth (BB) left to pilot the Boston Braves, owner Sam Breadon (BB) appointed Dyer. Dyer inherited a St. Louis team that had won NL pennants in three of the preceeding four campaigns. Breadon, however, in 1946 sold star catcher Walker Cooper (S) to the New York Giants in January and first baseman Johnny Hopp to the Boston Braves in February. A month into the season, pitchers Max Lanier* and Fred Martin and second baseman Lou Klein jumped to the MEL. During 1946, Dyer replaced Klein with a youngster named Red Schoendienst (BB), Stan Musial (BB) won another batting title, Enos Slaughter (BB) drove in 130 runs, and Pollet won 21 games and led NL with a 2.10 ERA. The Cardinals finished in a first-place tie with Leo Durocher's (BB) Brooklyn Dodgers with a 96–58 record. In the first-ever NL pennant playoff, Pollet bested the Dodgers, 4–2, in the opener and Murry Dickson (S) finished them off, 8–4, in the second game. Dyer's club then defeated the Boston Red Sox in seven games to earn the World Championship.

Dyer's Cardinals placed second to the Brooklyn Dodgers in 1947 and second to Southworth's Boston Braves in 1948. Dyer's Redbirds entered the final week of the 1949 season ahead of Brooklyn by two games on the loss side but dropped four of the last five contests to finish one game behind the Dodgers. St. Louis posted a 78–75 record in 1950. Dyer was offered a one-year contract but was encouraged to resign by owner Fred Saigh. His managerial record with the Cardinals included 446 wins, 325 losses, and 6 ties. Dyer returned to Houston, TX, and formed Langham, Langston, and Dyer Insurance Counselors. Subsequently, he was joined by his former players Pollet and Jeff Cross in real estate and oil investments.

BIBLIOGRAPHY: Bob Broeg, *Redbirds: A Century of Cardinals' Baseball* (St. Louis, MO, 1981); Edwin Dyer file, National Baseball Library, Cooperstown, NY; Joe Garagiola, *Baseball Is a Funny Game* (New York, 1960); Gene Karst and Martin J. Jones, Jr., *Who's Who in Professional Baseball* (New Rochelle, NY, 1973); Stan Musial and Bob Broeg, *Stan Musial: "The Man's" Own Story* (Garden City, NY, 1964); Mike Shatzkin, ed., *The Ballplayers* (New York, 1990).

Frank J. Olmsted

EASTERLING, Howard (b. November 26, 1911, Mount Olive, MS), player, excelled as a versatile, switch-hitting infielder with the Homestead, PA, Grays (NNL) during the 1940s. A complete ballplayer, he could run, throw, field, hit, and hit with power. The 5-foot-10-inch, 175-pounder, a five-time All-Star during his 14-year career in the Negro Leagues, batted .320 in the East-West classics. He was selected to the West squad as a shortstop in 1937 and to the East squad as a third baseman in 1940, 1943, 1946, and 1949.

A consistent hitter, he began his professional baseball career with the Cincinnati, OH, Tigers (NAL) with batting averages of .326 in 1936 and .386 in 1937. In 1940, the star infielder joined the Homestead Grays (NNL) and generated some offense to help compensate for the loss of Josh Gibson (BB) to the MEL.

In Easterling's first four years with the Grays, Homestead won the NNL pennant each year. Easterling contributed batting averages of .358, .307, .226, and .451 those seasons. Easterling, who usually batted either third in front of the power tandem of Gibson and Buck Leonard (BB) or fifth behind the pair of sluggers, also hit the long ball. The star third sacker made six hits in 10 at bats in a crucial doubleheader during the 1941 LCS victory over the New York Cubans. The first World Series between the NAL and the NNL was played in 1942, with Easterling hitting .332 and slamming a home run. The Grays, however, were swept by the Kansas City, MO, Monarchs. In 1943, Easterling's last season before entering the army in World War II, the Grays defeated the Birmingham, AL, Black Barons in the World Series to reign as champions of black baseball.

After two years of military service, he batted .310 for the Grays in 1946 and closed out his Negro League career with a .302 average for the New York Cubans in 1949. He extended his playing career with Monterrey, Mexico (MEL), batting .323 in 1951 and .379 in 1953. He also played in the VWL, where he topped the circuit in both home runs and doubles.

BIBLIOGRAPHY: Robert W. Peterson, *Only the Ball Was White* (Englewood Cliffs, NJ, 1970); Pittsburgh (PA) *Courier*, 1936–1948; James A. Riley, *The All-Time All-Stars of Black Baseball* (Cocoa, FL, 1983); James A. Riley, interviews with former Negro League players, James A. Riley collection, Cocoa, FL; James A. Riley, *The Biographical Encyclopedia of the Negro Baseball Leagues* (New York, 1994); Mike Shatzkin, ed., *The Ballplayers* (New York, 1990), p. 304; Rick Wolff, ed., *The Baseball Encyclopedia*, 9th ed. (New York, 1993).

James A. Riley

FARRELL, Charles Andrew "Duke" (b. August 31, 1866, Oakdale, MA; d. February 15, 1925, Boston, MA), player, coach, and scout, grew up in Marlborough, MA, where he caught for a strong town team and met his future wife, Julia Bradley. Chicago White Stockings (NL) manager Cap Anson (BB) discovered Farrell in 1887, when he was playing for Salem, MA (NEL). The six-foot-one-inch, 208-pound, right-handed, switch-hitting Farrell began an 18-year major league career the following season with the Chicago White

Stockings. In 1890, he jumped to the Chicago Pirates (PL). When the PL folded after one season, he signed with the Boston Reds (AA). Farrell played the majority of his games at third base, helping lead the Reds to an AA pennant with the finest offensive season of his major league career. His 12 home runs led the AA, while his 110 RBIs shared first and his .474 slugging average ranked third. These marked career highs for Farrell, as did his 108 runs scored.

When the AA was absorbed into the NL after the 1891 season and the Boston club dissolved, Farrell was assigned to the Pittsburgh Pirates. In 1892, he batted a career-low .215. For the only season of his career, he caught no games and played primarily at third base. For the remainder of his career, he principally caught. After a season with the Washington Senators (NL) in 1893, he played 3½ years for the New York Giants (NL). Farrell then returned to the Washington Senators for 2½ seasons, achieving career highs in batting average with .322 in 1897 and .314 in 1898.

Washington sent Farrell in early 1899 to the Brooklyn Superbas (NL), where he remained through 1902. Blood poisoning from a spike wound in 1901 and illness in 1902 limited his playing time, causing Farrell to gain weight and lose much agility. When Brooklyn dropped him after 1902, he signed with the Boston Beaneaters (NL) and lost some excess weight. A broken leg, however, limited Farrell to just 17 games. After a substandard season in 1904, he concluded his major league career with 7 games for Boston in 1905. Subsequently, he worked as a federal marshall and served as battery coach for the New York Highlanders (AL) in 1909, 1911, and 1915–1917. He had scouted and coached two years for the Boston Braves (NL) at the time of his death six weeks after surgery for abdominal trouble. He was survived by a daughter, Grace, and two sisters.

During his major league career, Farrell batted .275 and averaged exactly 1 hit per game. His 1,563 hits included 211 doubles, 123 triples, and 51 home runs. He drove in 912 runs, more than half between 1889 and 1894, when he averaged 81 RBIs per year. His offense ranked about average for catchers of his era, but he excelled defensively. Among major league catchers with 1,000 or more games, Farrell's 1.42 assists per game place second only to Bill Bergen's 1.54, while his 93 fielding runs (a modern measure of a player's overall defensive contribution) rank him eighth on the all-time catchers list. Farrell recorded 2 of the top 10 seasons behind the plate, his 30 fielding runs in 1894 finishing third and his 24 fielding runs in 1890 placing tenth. In three World Series (1894, 1900, 1903), he batted .360 with 9 hits and 4 RBIs in 6 games.

BIBLIOGRAPHY: Charles A. Farrell file, National Baseball Library, Cooperstown, NY; Mike Shatzkin, ed., *The Ballplayers* (New York, 1990); John Thorn and Pete Palmer, eds., *Total Baseball*, 3rd ed. (New York, 1993); Robert L. Tiemann and Mark Rucker, eds., *Nineteenth Century Stars* (Kansas City, MO, 1989).

Frederick Ivor-Campbell

FEHR, Donald Martin (b. July 18, 1948, Marion, IN), executive, is the son of Louis Alvin Fehr and Irene Sylvia (Gullo) Fehr and moved to Prairie Village, MO, where he graduated from Shawnee Mission East High School. Fehr graduated from Indiana University in 1970 with a B.A. degree in history and government and three years later with distinction from the University of Missouri Law School. Married in 1971, Fehr and his wife Stephanie have four children and currently reside in Ryebrook, NY.

As a law school student, Fehr worked for George McGovern's 1972 Democratic Party presidential campaign. Deeply committed to civil rights, the young law student was imbued with "a healthy respect for the individual and skepticism over the nature of big business and monopolies." As a fledgling lawyer, Fehr clerked for two years with U.S. District Court judge Elmo Hunter in Kansas City, MO, and then joined a Kansas City firm that specialized in labor law.

Fehr's involvement with major league baseball came in 1976, when the major league club owners chose the U.S. District Court in Kansas City as the forum for appealing arbitrator Peter Seitz's decision granting pitcher Andy Messersmith's (S) free agency. The MLPA hired Fehr as their local counsel in the case. Fehr persuaded the court to uphold the Seitz decision.

Fehr's adroit handling of this case prompted MLPA executive director Marvin Miller (BB) in 1977 to name him the MLPA's general counsel to replace Dick Moss. In Miller's judgment, Fehr proved to be "a skillful, bright, hard working lawyer who was totally compatible with the players." As Miller's chief lieutenant, Fehr successfully represented the MLPA during the 50-day players' strike of 1981. The following year, Miller retired as executive director of the MLPA. The players fired Miller's successor, Ken Moffett, in November 1983 and named the 35-year-old Fehr its interim director.

As interim executive director, Fehr successfully negotiated a four-year Basic Agreement in 1985. The players retained most of their previous gains while conceding only to raise the time for a player to become eligible for free agency from two to three years.

Fehr contemplated returning to private law practice in 1985 when the players' executive committee offered him a long-term contract as executive director of the MLPA. As director, Fehr continued to consult with Miller, his friend and mentor. Fehr's successful use of arbitration during his first five years won the players an estimated $330 million settlement from the club owners, who were found guilty of collusion against free agent players between 1985 and 1988. In another arbitration action, Fehr blunted the owners' attempt to impose mandatory drug testing on players.

In 1990 an impasse in negotiations prompted the owners to lock out the players from the spring training camps. Fehr, nevertheless, held firm. The resulting Basic Agreement, negotiated by Fehr, fended off owner attempts to impose salary caps and place limits on salary arbitration procedures.

By 1993 the hard-working Fehr's tough-minded approach in labor negotiations had won the respect of major league players and *TSN*, whose
editors ranked him fifth among the 100 most powerful people in professional
sports. Fehr's reputation was further enhanced by the gains scored by organized players under his leadership. Since 1985, players received 40 percent
of the industry's $600 million annual revenues; player salaries averaged above
$1 million a year as of 1993, while the MLPA's annual revenues from li-
censing amounted to $70 million a year. Under Fehr, the MLPA's bargain-
ing strength extended to such issues as deciding on league expansion, league
realignment, rule changes, television contracts, and minor league player development. These issues, along with salaries and pension rights, remained
on the bargaining table in late 1993, when Fehr and the owners met to
hammer out a new Basic Agreement. Since an agreement could not be
reached, the major league players walked out on August 12, 1994. The owners insisted upon establishing a salary cap, a concept the players rejected.
The strike still had not been settled as of press time.

BIBLIOGRAPHY: Michael Knisley, "The TSN 100," *TSN*, January 4, 1993; Lee Low-
enfish and Tony Lupien, *The Imperfect Diamond* (New York, 1991); Steve Mann and
David Pietrusza, "The Business of Baseball," in John Thorn and Pete Palmer, eds.,
Total Baseball, 3rd ed. (New York, 1993); Marvin Miller, *A Whole Different Ball Game;
Sport and the Business of Baseball* (New York, 1991); E. M. Swift, "The Perfect
Square," *SI* 79 (March 8, 1993), pp. 32–35.

David Quentin Voigt

FERGUSON, Robert V. "Bob" "Death to Flying Things" (b. January 31, 1845,
Brooklyn, NY; d. May 3, 1894, Brooklyn, NY), player, executive, captain,
manager, and umpire, began his baseball career in 1864, graduating to the
famous Atlantic Club of Brooklyn in 1866. One of the game's best all-round
players, he specialized as a defensive wizard. His nickname came from his
great range on fly balls. He became the game's premier third baseman but
played every position during his 20-year professional career. At 5 feet 9½
inches and 149 pounds, he threw right-handed and was baseball's first
switch-hitter. He ranked among the first catchers to position himself close
behind the batter.

Ferguson, an established leader, developed distinguished traits. He either
captained or managed every team he played on, beginning in 1869, and
served four years as president of the NA, baseball's first professional league.
Terms like *competitive, absolutely honest, straightforward, quick-tempered, rule-
wise,* and *sterling character* have been used to describe Ferguson. With his
byline being integrity, he did more than anyone else in the fight for honest
baseball and was a constant opponent of gambling.

Ferguson played with the Atlantics (NA) until 1874 with the exception of
spending 1871 with the New York Mutuals (NA). In 1870 Ferguson first
gained national acclaim when his Atlantics team handed the Cincinnati Red

Stockings their first loss in two years. In perhaps the first instance of switch-hitting, he drove in the tying run and later scored the winning tally.

Subsequently, Ferguson played for and captained-managed the Hartford, CT, Dark Blues (NA, NL) 1875 to 1877; Chicago White Stockings (NL), 1878; Springfield, MA (NA), 1879; Troy, NY, Trojans (NL), 1879 to 1882; Philadelphia, PA, Quakers (NL), 1883; and Baltimore, MD, (EL) and Pittsburgh, PA, Alleghenys (AA), 1884. He also managed the New York Metropolitans (AA) in 1886 and 1887, being an outstanding judge and developer of talent.

Ferguson also umpired in the NA from 1871 to 1875, in the NL in 1885, in the AA from 1887 to 1889 and 1891, and in the PL in 1890. As an arbiter, he proved first-class, dictatorial, and impeccably honest. His understanding and interpretation of the game remained so basic and logical that many of his decisions influenced rules.

He suffered from partial paralysis that may have been caused by excessive smoking and died as a result of an attack of apoplexy. He proved wise in financial investments and was well-off at his death.

Ferguson was involved in our national game for 28 straight seasons, usually serving in several capacities at once. The much-respected, very prominent baseball personality wielded a major influence on how the game developed.

BIBLIOGRAPHY: Sam Crane, *NYJ*, December 23, 1911; David Pietrusza, *Major Leagues* (Jefferson, NC, 1991); Mike Shatzkin, ed., *The Ballplayers* (New York, 1990); *SpL*, May 12, 1894; John Thorn and Pete Palmer, eds., *Total Baseball*, 3rd ed. (New York, 1993); Robert L. Tiemann and Mark Rucker, eds., *Nineteenth Century Stars* (Kansas City, MO, 1989).

                                                                    John R. Husman

FIELDER, Cecil Grant "The Big Man" (b. September 21, 1963, Los Angeles, CA), player, dazzled Detroit Tiger (AL) and AL fans with his home run slugging in the early 1990s. He is the son of Tina Fielder, a business manager, and graduated from Nogales High School in La Puenta, CA, where he made All-State in baseball, football, and basketball. Although basketball was his best sport, he attended the University of Nevada at Las Vegas on a baseball scholarship. The Baltimore Orioles (AL) drafted him in the thirty-first round in June 1981, but the Kansas City Royals (AL) took him in the fourth round of the 1982 secondary draft and traded the right-handed batting and throwing first baseman to the Toronto Blue Jays (AL) the following year. The six-foot-three-inch, 250-pound Fielder made it to the major leagues by 1985 but never exceeded 175 at bats with the Blue Jays through 1988. In December 1988, Toronto sold Fielder to the Hanshin Tigers (JCL), where he ranked among the JCL leaders in most offensive categories in 1989 with a .302 batting average, 38 home runs, and 81 RBIs in 106 games.

The Detroit Tigers in January 1990 signed Fielder, who set Motown agog by clubbing a major league–leading 51 homers—including a 520-foot tape measure blast—and leading the major leagues with 132 RBIs. His final two round trippers came dramatically at Yankee Stadium on October 3, the last day of the 1990 season, against the New York Yankees. Fielder also led the AL in total bases (339), slugging average (.592), and strikeouts (112). In 1991, his 44 home runs tied for the AL lead, while his 133 RBIs topped the major leagues again. A major league–leading 124 RBIs in 1992 made Cecil (pronounced Sessil) the first slugger since Babe Ruth (BB) to lead the major leagues in RBIs three consecutive years. Fielder made the AL All-Star team in 1990, 1991, and 1993 and finished runner-up in the MVP voting in 1990 and 1991. A 1990 *USA Today* survey of AL players revealed Fielder to be the overwhelming choice for MVP among his peers. He was named *TSN* AL Player of the Year in 1990 and *TSN* All-Star team member and *TSN* Silver Slugger member in 1990 and 1991. In his first four years with the Tigers, Fielder *averaged* over 125 RBIs per season. Through the strike-shortened 1994 season, he had compiled a .259 career batting average, 219 home runs, 680 RBIs, 863 strikeouts, and no stolen bases. Fielder, who proved particularly effective in night games and against left-handed pitching, became one of the few players to homer over the roof in Tiger Stadium and the first to power a fair ball out of Milwaukee's County Stadium.

A fan favorite in Motown, Fielder is admired for his prodigious slugging, affability, modesty, and devotion to his family. He is married to Stacey (Granger) and has one son, Prince, his costar in a widely seen TV commercial, and a daughter, Cecilyn.

BIBLIOGRAPHY: Barbara Corlisle Bigelow, *Contemporary Black Biography*, vol. 2 (Detroit, MI, 1992), pp. 75–78; *Detroit Tiger Yearbooks*, 1991–1994; Gary Gillette, *The Great American Baseball Statbook* (New York, 1993); *USA Today; TSN Official Baseball Register*, 1994; *WWA*, 48th ed., (1994), p. 1087.

Sheldon L. Appleton

FORD, Russell William "Russ" (b. April 25, 1883, Brandon, Manitoba, Canada; d. January 24, 1960, Rockingham, NC), player, was credited with inventing the "emery ball," a delivery that allowed him to rank among the game's best pitchers in 1910 and 1911. His father, a native of Scotland who farmed and played cricket, encouraged his sons to play baseball. The elder Ford moved his family from Nova Scotia to Manitoba the year before Russell's birth and by 1900 had moved south to Minneapolis, MN.

Two of Ford's brothers played professionally. Eugene, the eldest, the first to reach the majors, played briefly with the Detroit Tigers (AL) in 1905. Ford's successful pitching for semiprofessional teams in Enderline, ND, and Lisbon, SD, led Minneapolis, MN (AA) to sign him to his first professional contract in 1904. After failing to make an impression that year, Ford pitched for Cedar Rapids, IA (3IL) in 1905 and 1906. In the latter year, Ford's 22 victories led Cedar Rapids to the 3IL pennant and earned him a promotion to Atlanta, GA (SA). He enjoyed two solid years there, with 18 and 16 wins. The New York Highlanders (AL) drafted Ford but quickly sold him to Jersey City, NJ (EL).

A misshapen thumb and a crushed third finger on his right hand enabled Ford to develop unusual movement on his pitches. With Atlanta, he added the spitball to his repertoire. At Jersey City, he discovered that a ball scuffed with emery paper moved in unusual ways and sewed pieces of emery paper to his glove. After Ford's 13 wins at Jersey City in 1909, New York reacquired him.

Ford's trick pitches made him almost unhittable his first two seasons in the majors. In 1910 he won 26 games, the second highest in the AL, while losing only six decisions, compiling a 1.65 ERA, and allowing only 5.8 hits per nine innings. In 1911, Ford posted his second straight 20-win season with a 21–11 mark. In 1912, the Highlanders plummeted to last place, with Ford's record reflecting the fortune of the team. His 13 wins led the club in both 1912 and (renamed the Yankees) 1913, but his 21 losses topped all AL pitchers in 1912.

When the FL began operation in 1914, the Buffalo Buffeds inked Ford to a $24,000 four-year contract. In its inaugural season, Ford led the FL in ERA and win–loss percentage with a 20–6 record. For the 1915 season, however, the FL banned the emery ball. With his main pitch no longer legal, Ford slipped to a dismal 4–16 record for the Blues with a 4.52 ERA. His major league career ended with the demise of the FL. He won 98 major league games against 71 losses, with a lifetime 2.59 ERA. Ford pitched effectively (16–9) for Denver, CO (WL) in 1916 and ineffectively (1–2) for Toledo, OH (AA) in 1917.

After his baseball career, he was employed as a structural engineer for the Submarine Boat Corporation in Newark, NJ. In 1922, he moved with his two daughters, Mary and Jean, and his wife, Mary Hunter (Bethel) Ford, to Mary's hometown in Rockingham, NC, and became a bank cashier. The depression saw the Fords move north, where Russell worked as a draftsman in New York City. After his wife's death in 1957, he returned to North Carolina to live with a daughter and died there of a heart attack.

BIBLIOGRAPHY: Mark and Neill Gallagher, *Baseball's Great Dynasties: The Yankees* (New York, 1990); Dan Gutman, *It Ain't Cheatin' If You Don't Get Caught* (New York, 1990); Tommy Holmes, "Baseball's Inventive Ford," *BD* 4 (September 1945), pp. 37–39; Frederick G. Lieb, "Russell Ford," *BM* 7 (August 1911), pp. 36–42; Marc Okkonen, *The Federal League of 1914–1915* (Garrett Park, MD, 1989).

William E. Akin

FORSCH, Robert Herbert "Bob" "Forschie" (b. January 13, 1950, Sacramento, CA), player, is the son of Herbert Forsch, a semiprofessional baseball player in the San Joaquin Valley, CA, League during the 1940s and owner of an electric motor repair shop, and the brother of Ken Forsch, a pitcher for 16 years with the Houston Astros (NL) and California Angels (AL). The St. Louis Cardinals (NL) selected Forsch in the thirty-eighth round of the 1968 free agent draft from Sacramento City College as a third baseman.

Forsch struggled for four years with Cardinal farm clubs before converting to a pitcher at Cedar Rapids, IA (ML) in 1971. There, the six-foot-three-inch, 212-pound right-hander met and married Mollie Kneen. They have two daughters, Amy Lynn and Kristin Rae. Forsch pitched no-hitters for Arkansas (TL) in 1972 and Tulsa, OK (AA) in 1973 before joining the Cardinals during the 1974 season and fashioning a 7–4 win–loss record with a 2.97 ERA. From 1975 to 1988, he led Cardinal pitchers in victories six times and enjoyed his best season in 1977 with a 20–7 mark.

Forsch hurled a 5–0 no-hitter against the Philadelphia Phillies on April 16, 1978, and became the only Cardinal pitcher in history to toss more than one no-hitter, when he silenced Montreal Expo bats, 3–0, September 26, 1983. Bob and Ken Forsch remain the only brothers in major league history to pitch no-hitters. Forsch began as a power pitcher but developed pinpoint control. The fine fielder and fierce competitor was an outstanding hitting pitcher. He batted .308 in 1975 and won *TSN* Silver Slugger awards in 1980 and 1987. On August 10, 1986, Forsch smashed a grand-slam home run off the Pittsburgh Pirates' Mike Bielecki.

On August 31, 1988, St. Louis traded the popular Forsch to the Houston Astros (NL) for infielder Denny Walling. Although Forsch never was named to an All-Star team, the Cardinals honored him at Busch Stadium in St. Louis on May 29, 1989, at Bob Forsch Appreciation Day. Only Hall of Famers Bob Gibson (BB) and Jesse Haines (BB) pitched more innings and won more games for the Cardinals than Forsch. Forsch's career totals included 2,795 innings pitched, 168 wins, 136 losses, 1,133 strikeouts, and a 3.76 ERA in 498 games. He pitched in the 1982, 1985, and 1987 World Series for St. Louis, winning one of four decisions.

Forsch declined offers to come to spring training or coach in 1990, opting to spend time with his family and build a new home in Chesterfield, MO. He enjoys golf and bass fishing.

BIBLIOGRAPHY: Kevin Horrigan, "Forsch Adrift After 15 Years of Cards Stability," St. Louis (MO) *Post-Dispatch*, September 2, 1988, pp. F1–F2; Rich Hummel, "Forsch Locks Self Out for Summer," St. Louis (MO) *Post-Dispatch*, March 5, 1990, p. C5; John Sonderegger, "Finesse: Variety Adds Spice to Forsch Deliveries," St. Louis (MO) *Post-Dispatch*, August 10, 1986, pp. F1, F15; John Sonderegger, "Forsch-ful," St. Louis (MO) *Post-Dispatch*, August 11, 1986, pp. 1–2; Marybeth Sullivan, ed., *The Scouting Report: 1986* (New York, 1986); Tom Wheatley, "Complete Game: Bob Forsch Enjoys Retirement with No Regrets," St. Louis (MO) *Post-Dispatch*, August 23, 1990, pp. C1, C4; Tom Wheatley, "Forsches Wisely Heeded Pa's Pitch," St. Louis (MO) *Post-Dispatch*, July 7, 1987, pp. C1, C4.

Frank J. Olmsted

FRANCO, Julio Cesar (b. August 23, 1961, San Pedro de Macoris, Dominican Republic), player, attended Divine Providence High School in San Pedro de Macoris and was signed as a free agent by the Philadelphia Phillies (NL) in June 1978. His minor league stops included Butte (PrL) that season, Central Oregon (NWL) in 1979, and Peninsula (CrL) in 1980. He played with Reading, PA (EL) in 1981 and with Oklahoma City, OK (AA) and the Philadelphia Phillies (NL) in 1982, batting .276 in 16 games with the major league club. In five minor league seasons, Franco batted .300 or better every campaign. He hit 53 home runs, including 21 in 1982. His highest RBI season came in 1980 with 99 for Peninsula.

The six-foot-one-inch, 190-pound second baseman–shortstop bats and throws right-handed. Philadelphia traded Franco in December 1982 to the Cleveland Indians (AL), for whom he played six seasons and batted over .300 three seasons. In his first season with Cleveland, Franco played shortstop in 149 games and hit .273 with 80 RBIs. He played 160 games at shortstop in 1984, hitting .286 with 79 RBIs. He split duties between second base and shortstop from 1985 to 1987 and played second base from 1988 to 1991. In 1985 he performed in 160 games, batting .287 with 90 RBIs. He hit .306 in 1986, providing 74 RBIs in 149 games. In 1987, he batted .319 with 52 RBIs in 128 games. His final year with Cleveland featured him batting .303 and attaining 54 RBIs.

In December 1988, Cleveland traded Franco to the Texas Rangers (AL). During his first season with the Rangers in 1989, he batted .316 with 92 RBIs in 150 games. The next season, he hit .296 in 157 games with 69 RBIs. In 1991 he played in 146 games, led the NL in hitting with .341, and produced 78 RBIs. Injuries in 1992 limited Franco to only 35 games at second base and outfield. His batting average fell to .234 with only 8 RBIs. Franco rebounded the following season to bat .289 and knock in 84 runs. During the strike-shortened 1994 season, he batted .319 with 20 home runs and 98 RBIs for the Chicago White Sox (AL). In December 1994, the Chiba Lotte Marines (JCL) signed Franco to a $3.5 million, one-year contract.

Franco was selected on the AL All-Star team from 1989 through 1991, hitting .333 in the first two games. He was named CrL MVP in 1980, second baseman on the *TSN* AL Silver Slugger team in 1988 and 1991, and second baseman on the *TSN* AL All-Star team from 1989 to 1991. In 1979 he led the NWL with 153 total bases and paced shortstops with 45 double plays. He also paced the CrL shortstops with 73 double plays in 1980. Through 1994, he has batted .301 with 1,922 hits, 861 RBIs, and 237 stolen bases.

Franco and his wife, Rose Trueba Franco, have one son, Joshua.

BIBLIOGRAPHY: *Texas Ranger Media Guide*, 1994; *TSN Official Baseball Register*, 1994.
Stan W. Carlson

FREEMAN, John Frank "Buck" "Bucky" (b. November 30, 1871, Catasauqua, PA; d. June 25, 1949, Wilkes-Barre, PA), player, manager, umpire, and scout,

made his major league debut on June 27, 1891, with the Washington Statesmen (AA) as a pitcher. He compiled a 3–2 win–loss record with a 3.89 ERA
and batted .222 in five games. The five-foot-nine-inch, 160-pounder, who
threw and batted left-handed, spent the next six seasons in the minor leagues
and was converted to the outfield. In 1894 for Haverhill, MA (NEL), he hit
.390 with 31 home runs, 27 doubles, and 29 stolen bases. During one game
on July 5, he accumulated 20 total bases on 4 home runs and a double in
five at bats. He joined the Washington Senators (NL) in 1898 and the next
year belted 25 home runs to establish the major league record, which stood
until Babe Ruth's (BB) 29 in 1919.

The Boston Beaneaters (NL) purchased Freeman in 1900, but he jumped
to the Pilgrims (later Red Sox) when the AL was formed in 1901. He ranked
second in the AL in home runs (12) in 1901 and led the AL in RBIs (121)
in 1902, again finishing second in round-trippers (11). He paced the AL in
both RBIs (104) and home runs (13) in 1903, becoming the first batter to
lead both the NL and AL in home runs. Slugger Sam Crawford (BB) remains
the only other player to achieve that feat. The Pilgrims captured the first
AL pennant in 1903. Freeman hit three triples, helping Boston defeat the
Pittsburgh Pirates, 5–3, in the first World Series. The Pilgrims won the AL
pennant the following season but did not play a postseason series because
New York Giants manager John McGraw (BB) refused to meet the AL
champions.

Freeman led the AL with 19 triples in 1904 and remained a popular player
with Boston fans, but the cost-cutting owners released him early in the 1907
season. He joined Minneapolis, MN (AA), finishing the season with a .335
batting average and leading all minor leaguers with 18 homers in 142 games.
He completed his playing career in the minor leagues, serving his final season with Scranton, PA (NYSL) in 1912 as player–manager. He owned a
popular pool hall in Wilkes-Barre, PA, and remained active in baseball, umpiring in the minor leagues from 1913 to 1925, scouting for the St. Louis
Browns (AL) from 1926 to 1933, and managing Bloomsburg, PA, in 1934
and 1935.

In his 11-year major league career, Freeman batted .293 with 199 doubles,
131 triples, 82 home runs, and 92 stolen bases. As an outfielder, he possessed
speed and a strong arm. Several attempts have been made, most notably in
1958 and 1976, to influence the National Baseball Hall of Fame Committee
on Veterans to induct the first "Home Run King." Freeman died after a
brief illness, being survived by four sons and a sister. He was preceded in
death by his wife Annie (Kane) Freeman.

BIBLIOGRAPHY: *The Baseball Encyclopedia*, 9th ed. (New York, 1993); John F. Freeman
file, National Baseball Library, Cooperstown, NY; Gene Karst and Martin J. Jones,
Jr., eds., *Who's Who in Professional Baseball* (New Rochelle, NY, 1973); Frederick G.
Lieb, *The Boston Red Sox* (New York, 1947); Shirley Povich, *The Washington Senators*

(New York, 1954); Mike Shatzkin, ed., *The Ballplayers* (New York, 1990); John Thorn and Pete Palmer, eds., *Total Baseball*, 3rd ed. (New York, 1993).

                                                                      Gaymon L. Bennett

FREY, Linus Reinhard "Lonny" "Junior" (b. August 23, 1912, St. Louis, MO), player, is the son of Frank B. Frey, a salesman, and Louise (Scherer) Frey and grew up in St. Louis, where he worked in a factory after graduating from grammar school. An amateur baseball player, he pursued the sport professionally after losing a factory job in St. Louis in 1931. He played for Montgomery, AL (SEL) and York, PA (NYPL) in 1932 and for Nashville, TN (SL) in 1933. The Brooklyn Dodgers (NL) promoted Frey in August 1933 because of injuries to their infielders. Frey made his major league debut at shortstop on August 29, 1933. He started at shortstop for the Dodgers from 1934 to 1936 and was dealt to the Chicago Cubs (NL) in December 1936 for Roy Henshaw and Elwood "Woody" English. After Frey played one season with the Cubs, Chicago sent him to the Cincinnati Reds (NL) for cash in February 1938. Frey played six seasons at second base for the Reds before joining the U.S. Army in late 1943. After his discharge, he played for Cincinnati in 1946 and split the 1947 season between the Chicago Cubs and the New York Yankees (AL).

Frey, a rather ordinary hitter, compiled a career .269 batting average with just 61 home runs. He possessed some speed, leading the NL in stolen bases with 22 in 1940. His best year came in 1939, when he batted .291, scored 95 runs, and hit a career-high 11 home runs. Defensively, he played significantly better at second base than shortstop. He led all shortstops in errors in 1935 and 1936, making a remarkable 62 miscues in 131 games in 1936. But he led NL second basemen in fielding in 1941 and 1943, in putouts and assists in 1940, and in double plays from 1940 to 1943.

Frey, voted the starting second baseman on the 1939 NL All-Star team, also made the 1941 and 1943 teams and batted .333 in All-Star play. He also played in the 1939 and 1940 World Series with the Cincinnati Reds and in the 1947 World Series with the New York Yankees but made no hits and walked just once in 20 trips to the plate. A broken toe limited him to pinch-hitting duty in the 1940 World Series.

Frey married Mary Albrecht in October 1935 and had three children. Contemporaries described him as a "good, fast, smart" ballplayer, known for his "tricky and spectacular hook slide" and his ability to tag runners trying to reach second base. Following his retirement from baseball, he and his family moved to the Pacific Northwest, where he lives quietly in Snohomish, WA, and enjoys bow hunting.

BIBLIOGRAPHY: Lonny Frey file, National Baseball Library, Cooperstown, NY; Lonny Frey file, *TSN*, St. Louis, MO; *NYT*, August 27, 1933; October 1, 1940; October 2, 1940; December 12, 1943; Mike Shatzkin, ed., *The Ballplayers* (New York,

1990), p. 363; John Thorn and Pete Palmer, *Total Baseball*, 3rd ed. (New York, 1993); Rick Wolff, ed., *The Baseball Encyclopedia*, 9th ed. (New York, 1993).

John E. Findling

GAETTI, Gary Joseph (b. August 19, 1958, Centralia, IL), player, is the youngest of two children born to Bill Gaetti and Jackie Gaetti and excelled in football and baseball at Centralia High School. Following graduation in 1976, Gaetti continued his baseball career while attending Lakeland JC in Matton, IL, in 1977 and Northwest Missouri State University in Maryville, MO, in 1978. The Chicago White Sox (AL) and the St. Louis Cardinals (NL) selected him in separate amateur drafts in 1978. After spending one more year at Northwest Missouri, Gaetti signed as a third baseman with the Minnesota Twins (AL) in June 1979 and played for Elizabethton, TN (ApL). The Twins promoted Gaetti to Wisconsin Rapids, WI (ML) in 1980 and Orlando, FL (SL) in 1981.

The six-foot, 200-pound Gaetti joined the Twins in September 1981 and hit a home run in his first major league at bat. With Minnesota from 1981 to 1990, the right-handed-hitting Gaetti ranked among the rising AL stars. As a Twin, he batted .256 in 1,361 games, powered 201 home runs, and produced 758 RBIs. He won four consecutive Gold Gloves from 1986 to 1989 and enjoyed the unique experience of participating in two triple plays in one game against the Boston Red Sox in 1990. Gaetti performed in the 1988 and 1989 All-Star games. In the 1987 AL Championship Series against the Detroit Tigers, he batted .300, became the first player to hit home runs in his first two at bats in a league Championship Series contest, and was named its MVP. Gaetti played in the 1987 World Series against the St. Louis Cardinals, helping Minnesota win in 7 games.

Following the 1990 season, free agent Gaetti signed a four-year contract with the California Angels (AL). For the Angels, Gaetti divided his time between third base and first base. In June 1993, California released him unconditionally. The Kansas City Royals (AL) signed him the same month as a utility infielder/designated hitter. In 14 major league seasons, Gaetti has a career .254 batting average with 257 home runs and 979 RBIs.

Gaetti and his wife Debbie have two sons, Joseph and Jacob, and reside in Raleigh, NC.

BIBLIOGRAPHY: *The Baseball Encyclopedia*, 9th ed. (New York, 1993); Hank Hersch, "The Gospel and Gaetti," *SI* 71 (August 21, 1989), pp. 42–44; *Minnesota Twins Yearbook*, 1990; James E. Welch, telephone conversation with Randy List, sports editor, Centralia (IL) *Sentinel*, July 2, 1993.

James E. Welch

GARVER, Ned Franklin (b. December 25, 1925, Ney, OH), player, is the son of Arl H. Garver, a farmer, and Susie L. (Connelly) Garver and started playing baseball at age 14 on the sandlots of Ney, a rural hamlet of 300 people in northwestern Ohio. He starred in baseball and basketball at Washington Township School, where he graduated in 1943. Garver married his high school sweetheart, Dorothy Sims, on June 4, 1943. The couple have two children, Donnie and Cheryl.

His professional career began in 1944 with Newark, OH (OSL), where he compiled a 21–8 win–loss record as a pitcher and hit .407. He pitched at Elmira, NY (EL) and Toledo, OH (IL) in 1945 and San Antonio, TX (TL) in 1946 and 1947 before joining the St. Louis Browns (AL).

The boyish-looking 5-foot-10-inch, 190-pound right-hander fast became a mainstay of the Browns' staff. A 7-game winner in his rookie 1948 season, Garver led the AL in losses with 17 the following season. In 1950, he finished 13–18 and led the AL for the first time with 22 complete games. In June 1950, Garver won the final game of a 3-game series, 10–5, at Fenway Park in Boston, MA, after the Boston Red Sox had trounced the Browns, 20–4 and 29–4. Garver's 20–12 record in 1951 made him the only twentieth-century pitcher to win 20 games for a team that lost at least 100 and finished in last place. Garver, whose 24 complete games led the AL, also pitched in the All-Star Game that year. His outstanding skill with a bat kept him in so many games. In 1951 he compiled the highest average on the Browns with a .305 mark in 95 at bats and occasionally batted sixth. He lost his zest for hitting after Early Wynn (BB) beaned him midway through his career and finished with a lifetime .218 batting average.

Later known as the "Mayor of Ney," Garver signed a $25,000 contract in 1952. The contract amount tied him with immortal George Sisler (BB) as the highest paid player in Browns history. In August 1952, owner–president Bill Veeck (BB) traded him to the Detroit Tigers (AL) in a multiplayer deal. Garver endured three straight fifth-place finishes with the Tigers from 1952 to 1956. Detroit shipped him to the Kansas City Athletics (AL), where he suffered through three straight seventh-place finishes between 1957 and 1959. In 1960, Garver's dream of playing for a winner faded, as the A's finished last. As a member of the eighth-place expansion Los Angeles Angels (AL), Garver finished his 14-year major league career. Besides having the unique career statistic of 881 walks and 881 strikeouts, he compiled a composite record of 129–157. He pitched in 2,477.1 innings with a 3.73 ERA and 18 shutouts.

He subsequently worked as personnel and industrial relations director for a food company in his native Ney. A cerebral player who still likes to discuss his philosophy of pitching, Garver was inducted into the St. Louis Browns Hall of Fame in 1985.

BIBLIOGRAPHY: Bill Borst, ed., *Ables to Zoldak*, vol. 1 (St. Louis, MO, 1988); Bill Borst, ed., *The Brown Stockings*, vol. 1 (St. Louis, MO, 1986); Bill Borst, *Still Last in the American League* (West Bloomfield, MI, 1992); Arthur Doranzo, Detroit (MI) *Free Press*, January, 18, 1953, p. 12; Gene Karst and Martin Jones, Jr., *Who's Who in*

Professional Baseball (New Rochelle, NY, 1973); Mike Shatzkin, ed., *The Ballplayers* (New York, 1990).

William A. Borst

GILLIAM, James William "Junior" "Jim" (b. October 17, 1928, Nashville, TN; d. October 8, 1978, Inglewood, CA), player and coach, joined the Baltimore Elite Giants (NNL) upon graduation from Pearl High School in 1946. Teammates nicknamed him "Junior" because at age 17 he was the youngest player on the team. From 1947 to 1950, he and shortstop Tom "Pee Wee" Butts formed one of the best double play combinations in the Negro Leagues. Besides having fine defensive skills, the 5-foot-11-inch, 175-pound Gilliam proved a good switch-hitter and base stealer and was named to the NNL East All-Star team each year from 1948 to 1950.

In 1951, the Brooklyn Dodgers (NL) tried to buy the contract of pitcher Leroy Farrell from the Baltimore Elite Giants. Baltimore asked $10,000, which the Dodgers thought too high. Brooklyn agreed to the price when the Elite Giants included Gilliam and pitcher Joe Black. Gilliam reported to the Montreal, Canada, Royals (IL), batting .287 in 1951 and .301 in 1952. He led the IL in runs scored both seasons with 117 and 111 and second basemen in fielding average with a .987 in 1952.

In 1953, the Dodgers moved Jackie Robinson (BB) to the outfield and third base and installed Gilliam at second base. Gilliam responded with a rookie record 100 bases on balls. He led the NL in triples (17) and scored 125 runs, winning the NL Rookie of the Year honors. Gilliam scored more than 100 runs per season from 1953 to 1956 and batted .300 in 1956. Writer Roger Kahn (S) described Gilliam as "a black deer, lovely to behold as he turned the bases." Gilliam drew over 90 walks in a season five times, being the toughest Dodger in history to strike out. He teamed with shortstops Pee Wee Reese (BB) and Maury Wills (BB) to anchor the Dodgers' middle infield for more than a decade. Don Drysdale (BB) claimed that Wills became such a great base stealer because Gilliam batted behind him. On July 21, 1956, Gilliam set a major league record, making 12 assists in a game. In 1957, he led NL second basemen in putouts (416) and fielding average (.987).

In his only All-Star Game, Gilliam homered for the NL in 1959. He batted .211 in seven World Series with the Brooklyn and Los Angeles Dodgers. The Dodgers named Gilliam coach after the 1964 season, but he came out of retirement in 1965 and 1966 to play third base. He returned to coaching full-time for the Dodgers from 1967 until his death. He died of a cerebral hemorrhage two days before the Dodgers entered the 1978 World Series. Los Angeles retired his uniform number 19. Dodger coach and manager Tommy Lasorda (S) called Gilliam "one of the greatest human beings I could ever come across."

Gilliam, an avid billiards players, married Gloria White in 1949. After their divorce, he married Edwina Fields in April 1959. His career totals included 1,956 games, 1,163 runs, 1,889 hits, 65 home runs, 558 RBIs, 203 stolen bases, and a .265 batting average.

BIBLIOGRAPHY: Stanley Cohen, *Dodgers! The First 100 Years* (New York, 1992); Don Drysdale with Bob Verdi, *Once a Bum, Always a Dodger* (New York, 1990); James Gilliam file, National Baseball Library, Cooperstown, NY; Peter Golenbock, *Bums: An Oral History of the Brooklyn Dodgers* (New York, 1984); Roger Kahn, *The Boys of Summer* (New York, 1973); Gene Karst and Martin J. Jones, Jr., *Who's Who in Professional Baseball* (New Rochelle, NY, 1973); Dan Riley, ed., *The Dodgers Reader* (New York, 1992); James A. Riley, *The Biographical Encyclopedia of the Negro Baseball Leagues* (New York, 1994); Richard Whittingham, *The Los Angeles Dodgers: An Illustrated History* (New York, 1982).

                                                                                    Frank J. Olmsted

GOODEN, Dwight Eugene "Doc" "Doctor K" (b. November 16, 1964, Tampa, FL), player, is the youngest of six children of Dan Gooden and Ella Mae Gooden. Upon encouragement from his parents, he began pitching baseball at age 12 and starred as a senior hurler for Hillsboro High School. His professional baseball career began in 1982, when the New York Mets (NL) signed him for $600 a month plus an $85,000 bonus. After spending 1982 in the lower minor leagues, he compiled an outstanding 19–4 record and 300 strikeouts in just 191 innings for Little Falls, NY (NYPL) in 1983.

The rangy, six-foot-three-inch, 190-pound moundsman with a fluid pitching motion joined the New York Mets in 1984 and became an instant sensation. His great poise, crackling 95-mph fastball, and good curveball enabled the 19-year-old Gooden to win 17 games and lead the NL with 276 strikeouts in just 218 innings. Gooden's ratio of 11.39 strikeouts per 9 innings marked the best in major league history to that point for a starter. Gooden, an excellent batsman, won NL Rookie of the Year honors and became the youngest player to appear in an All-Star Game. In 1985, NL batters found him almost unhittable, as he led the senior circuit in wins (24), strikeouts (268), and ERA (1.53). The unanimous NL Cy Young Award selection seemed ready to dominate the game, but the 1986 campaign marked a different story. Although Gooden helped the Mets reach the World Series with a 17–6 record, his performance dropped off noticeably. He began to experience off-the-field problems, including a bout with drugs. Gooden no longer dominated games, as his fastball lost much of its natural movement, his strikeouts declined, and his ERA ballooned. Subsequent seasons saw him frequently on the disabled list. Nevertheless, Gooden maintained winning records and in 1991 signed a three-year contract with the Mets for $15.45 million.

From 1992 through 1994, Gooden lost more games than he won. The erosion of the Mets as a team and the possible overuse of his pitching arm at too young an age may have contributed to his declining performance. In

June 1994, Gooden was suspended for substance abuse. The suspension was extended to include the entire 1995 season. Nevertheless, the 30-year-old Gooden maintains an outstanding 157–85 mark, a .649 winning percentage, and 1,875 strikeouts and only 651 walks in 2,169.2 innings. He has compiled a 0–1 record and 2.04 ERA in the 1986 and 1988 NL Championship Series and a 0–2 mark and 8.00 ERA in the 1986 World Series against the Boston Red Sox. Despite his recent decline, the tall, handsome flamethrower remains a formidable presence in the game.

Gooden married Monica Colleen Harris in November 1987 and has three children, Dwight, Jr., Ashley, and Ariel.

BIBLIOGRAPHY: Tom Callahan, "Doctor K Is King of the Hill," *Time* 127 (April 7, 1986), pp. 54–58+; *CB* (1986), pp. 177–180; Barry Jacobs, "Baseball's Youngest Legend," *SEP* 258 (July–August 1986), pp. 54–55; Mike Lupica, "Fear Strikes Out Again," *Esquire* 113 (May 1990), pp. 71–73; Craig Neff, "Doctor K: Awesome and Then Some," *SI* 63 (September 2, 1985), pp. 14–19; E. M. Swift, "So Good, So Young," *SI* 62 (April 15, 1985), pp. 28–32+; Tom Verducci, "From Phenom to Phantom," *SI* 78 (March 22, 1993), pp. 34–37; Ralph Wiley, "Doc and Darryl," *SI* 69 (July 11, 1988), pp. 70–74+; Steve Wulf, "A Crash Landing for an Ace," *SI* 66 (April 13, 1987), pp. 32–34.

Frank P. Bowles

GREENWELL, Michael Lewis "Mike" (b. July 18, 1963, Louisville, KY), player, graduated in 1982 from North Fort Myers, FL, High School, where he starred in baseball. The Boston Red Sox (AL) drafted Greenwell in the third round in June 1982 and assigned the six-foot, 205-pound infielder to Elmira, NY (NYPL). Greenwell, who bats left-handed and throws right-handed, played the outfield at Winston-Salem, NC (CrL) in 1983 and 1984 and spent the next two seasons at Pawtucket, RI (IL), with two brief stints at Boston. His first three major league hits were home runs, the initial blast winning a 13-inning September 1985 game against the Toronto Blue Jays. Boston used Greenwell as a pinch hitter against the California Angels in the 1986 AL Championship Series and the New York Mets in the World Series.

Greenwell, among baseball's best hitters, swings smoothly like George Brett (BB) and exhibits patience, seldom striking out. In 1987 he finished third in the AL Rookie of the Year balloting, batting a career-best .328 with 31 doubles, 19 round-trippers, and 89 RBIs. He replaced left fielder Jim Rice (BB) in 1988, hitting .325 and attaining career highs in hits (192), doubles (39), triples (8), home runs (22), RBIs (119), walks (87), and stolen bases (16). Boston captured the AL East Division crown, as Greenwell led the AL with 23 game-winning RBIs and made the first of two consecutive AL All-Star appearances. The Oakland A's defeated the Red Sox in the AL Championship Series, limiting Greenwell to 1 home run and 3 RBIs. Greenwell's postseason honors included making the *TSN* AL All-Star and Silver Slugger teams. In 1989, he batted .308 with 14 home runs and 95 RBIs.

Greenwell's power production declined thereafter because a foot injury forced him to stop using his rear foot as a springboard during his swing. In 1990 his .297 batting average, 14 round-trippers, and 73 RBIs helped Boston garner another AL East Division title. The Oakland A's held Greenwell hitless in the AL Championship Series. Greenwell hit .300 with 83 RBIs in 1991 but belted only 9 home runs. Elbow and knee surgery sidelined him much of 1992, but Greenwell batted .315 with 38 doubles, 13 home runs, and 72 RBIs in 1993.

In ten major league seasons, Greenwell has batted .304 with 230 doubles, 108 home runs, and 605 RBIs. He has struck out in only seven percent of his at bats but possesses a weak arm and lacks speed. He and his wife Tracy have one son, Bo, and reside in Cape Coral, FL.

BIBLIOGRAPHY: John Hough, *A Player for a Moment: Notes from Fenway Park* (San Diego, CA, 1988); *1994 Baseball Almanac*; Mike Shatzkin, ed., *The Ballplayers* (New York, 1990); Dan Shaughnessy, *The Curse of the Bambino* (New York, 1990); Dan Shaughnessy, *One Strike Away: The Story of the 1986 Red Sox* (New York, 1987); *TSN Official Baseball Register*, 1994.

David L. Porter

GUERRERO, Pedro "Pete" (b. June 29, 1956, San Pedro de Macoris, Dominican Republic), player, is the son of Francisco Sanchez and M. Guerrero. His brother Luis played minor league baseball in 1977. Major leaguers Joaquin Andujar, George Bell,* Mariano Duncan, Tony Fernandez, Julio Franco,* and Juan Samuel also came from San Pedro de Macoris. The Cleveland Indians (AL) signed Guerrero in January 1973 at age 16 after he led the entire Dominican Republic Legion with a .438 batting average. Guerrero played third base and shortstop for the Sarasota, FL, Indians (GCL) before being traded to the Los Angeles Dodgers (NL) for pitcher Bruce Ellingsen. Guerrero batted .327 in six seasons with the Dodgers' farm system and led the PCL in RBIs at Albuquerque, NM, with 116 in 1978 and 103 in 1979. His best position, first base, was occupied by perennial All-Star first baseman Steve Garvey (BB).

From 1980 to 1987, the six-foot, 195-pound Guerrero compiled a .310 batting average and exceeded 30 home runs three times while dividing time between third base and left field. In June 1985, the right-handed power hitter was selected NL Player of the Month, tying the major league record for home runs in June with 15. He batted .196 in three NL Championship Series with Los Angeles but was named co-MVP in the Dodgers' 1981 World Championship over the New York Yankees (AL) when he batted .333, belted 2 home runs, and drove in seven tallies.

On August 16, 1988, Los Angeles traded Guerrero to the St. Louis Cardinals (NL) for pitcher John Tudor.* In 1989 Guerrero enjoyed his finest overall season. After moving to first base, he played every game, batted .311, drove in a career-high 117 runs, and led the NL with 42 doubles. Guerrero hit .406 with runners in scoring position and drove in 1 of every 5 Cardinal runs.

Guerrero was hounded by injuries much of his career, suffering back spasms, a pinched nerve in the neck, pulled hamstrings, strained wrists, a fractured leg, and knee surgery. After spending most of 1992 on the disabled list, Guerrero was granted free agency. He played for the Jalisco, Mexico, Charros (MEL) in 1993 but was released in June. His 15-year major league career included 1,536 games, 1,618 hits, 267 doubles, 215 home runs, 898 RBIs, and a .300 batting average.

Guerrero married Denise Chavez in 1980 and has a daughter, Ashley Maria. They reside in Rio Rancho, NM, but return often to the Dominican Republic. Guerrero enjoys playing the drums, Latin music, and fishing.

BIBLIOGRAPHY: Brian Bartow and Jeff Wehling, *St. Louis Cardinals 1991 Media Guide* (St. Louis, MO, 1991); John Dewan, ed., *The Scouting Report: 1990* (New York, 1990); Rick Hummell, "At Age 36, Guerrero Looks for Another Job as Hitter," St. Louis (MO) *Post-Dispatch*, June 13, 1993, p. F3; Richard Justice, "Pedro Guerrero: Making the Grade to Stardom," *BD* 42 (November 1983), pp. 46–48; Dan Schlossberg, *Baseball Stars: 1986* (Chicago, IL, 1986); Larry Whiteside, "How Pedro Guerrero Joined the Majors' Home Run Elite," *BD* 44 (October 1985), pp. 65–66.

Frank J. Olmsted

GWYNN, Anthony Keith "Tony" (b. May 9, 1960, Los Angeles, CA), player, is the second of three sons of Charles A. Gwynn and Vandella (Douglas) Gwynn and grew up with two baseball-playing brothers. Charles, Jr., was drafted by the Cleveland Indians (AL), while Chris was selected number one by the Los Angeles Dodgers (NL) in 1985. Tony starred in both baseball and basketball at Long Beach, CA, Poly High School and attended San Diego State University on a basketball scholarship. After being requested to play baseball in his sophomore year, he hit .301, .423, and .416 in his last three seasons for the Aztecs. The San Diego Padres (NL) selected the 5-foot-11-inch, 200-pound outfielder in the third round of the June 1981 free agent draft. The San Diego Clippers (NBA) drafted him the same day.

In 1981, Gwynn, who bats and throws left-handed, led Class A Walla Walla, WA (NWL) with a .331 batting average in 42 games and finished the season with Class AA Amarillo, TX (TL). The next season, he hit .328 against Class AAA pitching in 93 games at Hawaii (PCL). San Diego promoted him in July 1982, and he finished the season with a .289 batting average. After the first 17 games of the 1983 season at Class AAA Las Vegas, NV (PCL), he completed the campaign with the Padres, batting .309 in 86 games.

Gwynn led the NL in both batting average (.351) and hits (213) in 1984, his first full season. He again led the NL in hits (218) in 1986, as well as in runs scored (107). His .370 batting average led both major leagues in 1987, while his 218 hits topped the NL. A .313 average the next season enabled him to repeat as NL champion, and he led the NL again in both batting average (.336) and hits (203) in 1989. Gwynn believes that conflict with a few teammates hampered his performance in 1990, but he still batted .309 and tallied 177 hits. He batted a superlative .358 in 1993, trailing only Andres Galarraga of the expansion Colorado Rockies. In the strike-shortened 1994 season, Gwynn batted a career-high .394 with 165 hits and 64 RBIs.

Since 1983, his season average has not fallen below .300, and he holds the Padres record for hits (2,204), accomplished with a 32½ inch, 31-ounce bat, one of the smallest in the majors. Through 1994, he has compiled a career .333 batting average with 351 doubles, 79 triples, and 78 home runs. In 6,609 at bats, he has struck out only 329 times. With above-average speed, he has stolen 268 bases.

Gwynn, admired for his work ethic, has combined video technology with hours of extra drill, to transform his natural batting talent into consistent efficiency at the plate and his suspect fielding ability into above-average skill. He has received Gold Glove honors 5 times in the past 9 seasons and has also been named to the NL All-Star team 10 times in the past 12 years.

In the 1984 NL Championship Series, Gwynn batted .368 and made key hits in the final two games to help the Padres defeat the Chicago Cubs. He hit .263 against the Detroit Tigers, as the Padres lost the World Series, four games to one.

Although playing on an inconsistent, unstable team, Gwynn remains a model of consistency and stability and ranks among the game's most complete players. He lives in Poway, CA, northeast of San Diego, with his wife Alicea and their two children, Anthony II and Anisha.

BIBLIOGRAPHY: *The Baseball Encyclopedia*, 9th ed. (New York, 1993); Ron Fimrite, "Small Stick, Tall Stats," *SI* 64 (April 14, 1986), pp. 50–52; Bill Gutman, *Baseball's Hot New Stars* (New York, 1988); Kevin Kernan, "The Sport Q & A: Tony Gwynn," *Sport* 82 (July 1991), pp. 34–38; Danny Knobler, "Pssst . . . Heard About Tony Gwynn?" *Newsweek* 80 (August 1989), pp. 22–28; Tim Kurkjian, "Beginning Again," *SI* 74 (March 11, 1991), pp. 44–47; Ivan Maisel, "He's a Hefty Problem for Pitchers," *SI* 60 (May 14, 1984), pp. 70–71; Malcolm Moran, "Gwynn Finds Camera Doesn't Lie," *NYT Biographical Service* 15 (May 1984), p. 660; Mike Shatzkin, ed., *The Ballplayers* (New York, 1990); Samantha Stevenson, "Tony Gwynn: A Portrait of the Scientist in the Batter's Box," *NYT Biographical Service* 22 (June 1991), pp. 616–617; John Thorn and Pete Palmer, eds., *Total Baseball*, 3rd ed. (New York, 1993); George Vecsey, "Tony Gwynn: Just Arriving," *NYT Biographical Service* 15 (October 1984), pp. 1323–1324.

Gaymon L. Bennett

HAYES, Frank Whitman "Blimp" (b. October 13, 1915, Jamesburg, NJ; d. June 22, 1955, Point Pleasant, NJ), player, impressed umpire Frankie Marshall officiating games of Pennington Prep High. The umpire sent the six-foot, 190-pound Hayes to Philadelphia Athletics (AL) manager Connie Mack

(BB). After noting his size, the fatherly Mack advised Hayes to catch and optioned him to Albany, NY (IL) and Buffalo, NY (IL) for seasoning in 1933. Although still a rookie, Hayes joined Babe Ruth (BB) and other major league All-Stars on their 1934 trip to the Orient. His first full season with the Athletics in 1936 saw Hayes catch 144 games and hit .271. Hayes developed a reputation for durability. He tied a major league mark by hitting four homers in 1 game on July 25, 1936, always batting right-handed.

Hayes, well liked for his work habits, exhibited some defensive weaknesses, especially on pop fouls. Coach Russell "Lena" Blackburne successfully drilled Hayes hard on improving his defensive skills. Hayes enjoyed his best year in 1940, batting .308 and being compared with Bill Dickey (BB). Hayes's trade in June 1942 to the St. Louis Browns (AL) caused his career to take a downturn. Rick Ferrell (BB), the regular Browns catcher, prevented Hayes from getting enough work. Fortunately, the Athletics reacquired Hayes in February 1944. Hayes caught all 155 games for Philadelphia during the 1944 season. Short of playing talent during wartime baseball, Connie Mack asked Hayes to catch as many games as he could. Hayes replied, "That is all right with me." His 312 consecutive game streak set a major league record for catchers covering the 1943–1946 seasons. During that span, Hayes caught for the St. Louis Browns, Philadelphia Athletics, and Cleveland Indians (AL). After the Indians acquired Hayes in May 1945, the streak ended in bitterness on April 21, 1946. Cleveland manager Lou Boudreau (BB) removed Hayes from the starting lineup without telling him, causing the catcher to react angrily. Hayes caught Bob Feller's (BB) no-hitter later that spring, winning the game, 1–0, on his solo homer. Nevertheless, the estrangement between manager Boudreau and Hayes remained irreparable. In July 1946, the Indians sold Hayes to the Chicago White Sox (AL) for the waiver price. Ironically, the news leaked out the day of the 1946 All-Star Game, for which Hayes was the starting AL catcher! An All-Star being sold for the $7,500 waiver price seemed strange. Hayes also had performed in the 1940, 1941, and 1944 All-Star Games and had been chosen for the 1939 team but did not play. His major league career ended in 1947 after 5 games with the Boston Red Sox (AL). In 14 major league seasons, he batted .259 with 119 home runs and 628 RBIs.

Hayes, who married Helen Morton in February 1942, earned the respect of many baseball authorities. Sportswriter Frank Gibbons called Hayes "a good fellow, proud of his ability . . . and record," while sportswriter Franklin Lewis praised "his courage . . . strength, and . . . steadiness [as] . . . a real big leaguer." Hayes remained the true professional.

BIBLIOGRAPHY: Stan Baumgartner, "A Durable Hayes Ready to Take Up Where 'Iron Man' Mueller Left Off," *TSN*, March 22, 1945; Ed Burns, "What Will People Say? Chisox Get All-Star Hayes on Waivers," *TSN*, July 17, 1946; Frank Gibbons, "The Hayes Misunderstanding," *BD* 5 (November 1946); Franklin Lewis, "Rain in Philly Led to Hayes Deal, New Champ Hailed," Cleveland (OH) *Press*, June 29,

1945; Red Smith, "Prodigal Pappy: Frankie Hayes," *BD* 3 (May 1944); John Thorn and Pete Palmer, eds., *Total Baseball*, 3rd ed. (New York, 1993); Rick Wolff, ed., *The Baseball Encyclopedia*, 9th ed. (New York, 1993).

William J. Miller

HEATH, John Geoffrey "Jeff" (b. April 1, 1915, Ft. William, Ontario, Canada; d. December 9, 1975, Seattle, WA), player and sportscaster, recorded more major league hits, doubles, triples, home runs, and RBIs than any Canadian-born player.

Heath's father, Harold, moved the family to Seattle, WA, during the Great Depression. Heath starred in football and baseball at Garfield High School, where he graduated in 1934. His professional career began in 1936 when he set the Class C MAL record by knocking in 187 runs for Zanesville, OH. He also batted .383 with 28 home runs. For Milwaukee, WI (AA) in 1937, he hit a resounding .367.

In 1938, the sturdy 5-foot-11-inch, 185-pound Heath played left field for the Cleveland Indians (AL), leading the AL with 18 triples, belting 21 home runs, driving in 112 runs, and batting .343. After Heath's outstanding rookie season, his batting average slipped to .292 in 1939 and .219 in 1940.

Heath enjoyed his finest major league year in 1941, when he batted .340, drove in 123 runs, and hit 32 doubles, 20 triples, and 24 home runs. His feat of becoming the first major league player to collect more than 20 doubles, triples, and homers in one season went unnoticed. The same season, he became the first player to hit a home run into the upper deck of Cleveland's Municipal Stadium.

By the end of World War II, he had worn out his welcome in Cleveland. The press labeled him a "trouble-maker" and "Peck's Bad Boy," with Heath later admitting to being "temperamental, a cry baby and hard to handle." Cleveland dealt him to the Washington Senators (AL) in 1946 for George Case.* In 1947, the Senators traded Heath to the St. Louis Browns (AL) for Joe Grace.

Sold to Boston (NL) after batting only .251 in 1947, Heath helped the Braves capture the 1948 NL pennant. Heath batted .319 and finished second on the Braves in home runs (20) and RBIs (76). Tragically, Heath broke his ankle sliding into home shortly before the 1948 season ended and lost his only chance to play in a World Series. He saw limited service with Boston in 1949, but an injured leg and advancing age forced him to retire. In 14 major league seasons, he batted .293 with 279 doubles, 102 triples, 194 home runs, and 887 RBIs.

Heath continued to reside in Seattle, where he had attended the University of Washington in off-seasons. A broadcaster in Seattle, he did color commentary for baseball games and made commercials. He and his wife, Theabelle Callard, had two daughters and a son. His death came from a heart attack in 1975.

BIBLIOGRAPHY: Gordon Cobbledick, "Heath Hustles—In His Own Way!" *BD* 2 (October 1943), pp. 60–63; Stan Grosshandler, "Heroes of the Middle Atlantic League," *BRJ* 2 (1973), pp. 56–58; John G. "Jeff" Heath, "I Did It the Wrong Way," *BD* 12 (January 1953), pp. 5–8; Franklin Lewis, *The Cleveland Indians* (New York, 1949).

William E. Akin

HERSHISER, Orel Leonard IV "Bulldog" (b. September 16, 1958, Buffalo, NY), player, is the first of four children of Orel Leonard Hershiser III and Mildred Hershiser. Small for his age, he did not make the varsity baseball team at Cherry Hills, NJ, East High School until his junior year.

In 1976, he received a partial baseball scholarship from Bowling Green, OH, State University (MAC), where he compiled a 6–2 record in his third season. The Los Angeles Dodgers (NL) selected the six-foot-three-inch, 192-pound right-hander in the seventeenth round of the 1979 free agent draft and signed him for a $10,000 bonus. The Dodgers assigned him to Class A Clinton, IA (ML) in 1979, Class AA San Antonio, TX (TL) in 1980 and 1981, and Class AAA Albuquerque, NM (PCL) the next two seasons before he made his major league debut in September 1983.

His pitching success began in 1984 after Dodger manager Tom Lasorda (S) dubbed him "Bulldog" to inspire aggressiveness. Shortly afterward, Hershiser compiled a season-best 33-inning scoreless streak. In 1985, he won 19 of 22 decisions to lead the NL with an .864 winning percentage. From 1984 to 1987, he tallied 60 wins, 9 more than Don Sutton (BB) and Don Drysdale (BB), the Dodgers' all-time victory leaders, won in their first four major league seasons. His success depends on a full arsenal of pitches, including an outstanding sinking fastball, all delivered with deadly accuracy. He studies opposing batters carefully, recording their performance on a personal computer and pitching them accordingly.

Hershiser's finest season came in 1988, when he led the NL in wins (23), innings pitched (267), and shutouts (8) and shared the lead in complete games (15). He surpassed Drysdale's record of 58 consecutive scoreless innings in his final regular season start, shutting out the San Diego Padres for 10 innings to raise his total to 59.

He appeared in four of the seven 1988 NL Championship Series games, recording a win and a save. He shut out the Oakland Athletics in the second game of the World Series and clinched the series for the underrated Dodgers in the fifth contest, going the distance for a 4–2 victory. Hershiser, who enjoys batting, tied a World Series record in Game 2 with three hits in three at bats. He hit two doubles and a single, as many hits and more total bases than he allowed. In 1993, Hershiser batted .356, making 26 hits.

In 1988, he was honored as the MVP in both the NL Championship Series and the World Series, received the NL Cy Young Award, and was named the *SI* Sportsman of the Year, *TSN* Major League Player of the Year, and AP Male Athlete of the Year. After the season, Hershiser signed a three-year, $7.9 million contract, the highest at the time in major league baseball.

Shoulder surgery forced him to miss most of the 1990 season, diminishing his pitching effectiveness. The Dodgers released him following the 1994 season. Through the strike-shortened 1994 season, he has compiled a 134–102 win–loss record with 1,443 strikeouts, 24 shutouts, and a 3.00 ERA. He was named to the NL All-Star team in 1987, 1988, and 1989.

An outspoken Christian and model family man, Hershiser resides in Pasadena, CA, with his wife Jamie and two sons. He enjoys golf and baseball card collecting.

BIBLIOGRAPHY: *The Baseball Encyclopedia*, 9th ed. (New York, 1993); *CB* (1990), pp. 297–301; Peter Gammons, "A Case of Orel Surgery," *SI* 69 (October 31, 1988), pp. 36–37; Orel Hershiser with Jerry B. Jenkins, *Out of the Blue* (Brentwood, TN, 1989); Ross Newhan, "King of the Hill," *Sport* 79 (September 1988), pp. 51–56; Bruce Newman, "A Big-Name Pitcher," *SI* 64 (May 5, 1986), pp. 36–42; Joseph Nocera, "The Man with the Golden Arm," *Newsweek* 113 (April 10, 1989), pp. 42–48; Scott Ostler, "Orel in Wonderland," *Sport* 80 (March 1989), pp. 32–34; Mike Shatzkin, ed., *The Ballplayers* (New York, 1990); John Thorn and Pete Palmer, eds., *Total Baseball*, 3rd ed. (New York, 1993); Steve Wulf, "Destiny's Boys," *SI* 69 (October 31, 1988), pp. 32–36; Steve Wulf, "Sportsman of the Year," *SI* 69 (December 19, 1988), pp. 60–76.

Gaymon L. Bennett

HILLER, John Frederick (b. April 8, 1943, Toronto, Ontario, Canada), player, achieved one of the most memorable comebacks in major league baseball history. The oldest of two sons of Donald Hiller, a car collision shop owner, and Ethel (Cassis) Hiller, he attended David and Mary Thompson High School in Toronto before being signed by the Detroit Tigers (AL) as a free agent in 1962. The six-foot-one-inch, 190-pound right-handed-hitting southpaw spent most of 4½ years in the minor leagues, interrupted by brief stints with the Tigers in 1965 and 1966. Partway through the 1967 season, Hiller joined the parent club and became an effective reliever and spot starter in the Tigers' "near miss" drive for the 1967 AL pennant and on their 1968 world championship team. Hiller, who compiled nine wins, five saves, and a 2.39 ERA in 1968, saw action in two World Series games against the St. Louis Cardinals.

After experiencing mediocre performances in 1969 and 1970, Hiller suffered a heart attack in 1971 and underwent bypass surgery. Hiller retired, with his baseball career seemingly over. Hiller, however, made excellent progress, being resigned as a Tiger batting practice pitcher in June 1972 and as an active player in July. He pitched in 24 games with a 2.05 ERA that season and hurled 3⅓ scoreless innings in 3 games of the 1972 AL Championship Series against the Oakland A's, winning Game 4 in extra innings. Over the next four years, Hiller established himself as one of the premier major league closers. He led the AL in games pitched (65) in 1973 and established a since-eclipsed major league record for saves (38), winning 10 games, losing 5, and sporting a 1.44 ERA! That year, he was named *TSN* Comeback Player of the Year, *TSN* Fireman of the Year, and Fred Hutchinson Award recipient. The following year, his 17 wins and 14 losses both tied AL records for relief pitchers. He also was selected an AL All-Star.

In 15 major league seasons through 1980, Hiller pitched in 545 games, still a Tiger record, with 125 saves, 1,036 strikeouts, and a 2.84 ERA. Several peers, surveyed in the mid-1980s, cited Hiller as having the best "change up" they had ever seen.

Hiller married Janis Baldwin and had three children, Wendy, Joseph, and Danielle, and a stepson, Joseph Sabatini. After retiring in 1980, he lived in Iron Mountain, MI, and married his second wife, Linette Lynn LaChapelle, on March 23, 1985.

BIBLIOGRAPHY: *Detroit Tigers Media Guides; TSN Official Baseball Register,* 1981; John Hiller, letter to Sheldon Appleton, January 1993; Eugene and Roger McCaffrey, *Players' Choice* (New York, 1987); John Thorn and Pete Palmer, eds., *Total Baseball,* 3rd ed. (New York, 1993).

Sheldon L. Appleton

HISLE, Larry Eugene (b. May 5, 1947, Portsmouth, OH), player and coach, was orphaned and brought up by relatives. At Portsmouth High School, he excelled in basketball, baseball, and academics. Hisle, a high school All-America basketball player, belonged to the National Honor Society. Hisle spent one weekend touring the University of Michigan campus with basketball stars Lew Alcindor (Kareem Abdul-Jabbar) (IS) and Cazzie Russell (IS) but accepted a basketball scholarship at Ohio State University (BTC). Before Hisle attended Ohio State, however, the Philadelphia Phillies (NL) selected him in the second round of the June 1965 free agent draft and gave him a $40,000 bonus. In 1966, he was assigned to Huron, MI (NoL), where he batted .433, knocked in 13 runs, and belted 3 home runs in 21 games. The following year found Hisle in Tidewater (CrL) with a .302 batting average, 23 home runs, and 74 RBIs in 136 games. He spent the majority of the 1968 season with San Diego, CA (PCL), hitting .303 in 69 games. In September 1968, Hisle batted .364 in 7 games for the Philadelphia Phillies.

Hisle spent the 1969 and 1970 full seasons and part of the 1971 campaign with the Phillies. His best year with Philadelphia came in 1969, when he hit .286 and stroked 20 home runs. He finished the 1971 season with Eugene, OR (PCL) and batted .325 with 91 RBIs and 23 home runs for Albuquerque, NM (PCL) in 1972. Following the 1972 season, Hisle changed clubs three times within 40 days. On October 22, he was traded to the Los Angeles Dodgers (NL) for first baseman Tommy Hutton. Four days later, the Dodgers sent him to the St. Louis Cardinals (NL) for pitchers Rudy Arroyo and

Greg Millikan. The following month, St. Louis shipped him with pitcher John Cumberland to the Minnesota Twins (AL) for pitcher Wayne Granger. Hisle played five seasons from 1973 to 1977 with the Twins and enjoyed his best performance there in 1977, when he led the AL with 119 RBIs, batted .302, slammed 28 home runs, and played in the All-Star Game at New York's Yankee Stadium. Minnesota granted him free agency following the 1977 season. Hisle signed that November with the Milwaukee Brewers (AL), where he played from 1978 until his retirement in 1982. His best Brewer performance occurred in 1978 with a .290 batting average, 115 RBIs, 34 home runs, and an All-Star Game appearance at San Diego, CA. During 14 major league seasons, Hisle hit .273 with 193 doubles, 166 home runs, and 674 RBIs.

From 1983 to 1984, Hisle served as an outfield instructor in Milwaukee's minor league system. In 1989, the Houston Astros (NL) appointed him minor league hitting instructor. The next two years, he held the same title with the Toronto Blue Jays (AL). Since 1992, Toronto has utilized Hisle as Blue Jay hitting coach and won World Series Championships in 1992 and 1993. Hisle lives in Mequon, WI, with his wife Shelia and their son, Larry, Jr.

BIBLIOGRAPHY: *The Baseball Encyclopedia*, 9th ed. (New York, 1993); Mark Mulvoy, "Money in the Phillies' Bank," *SI* 28 (April 22, 1968), p. 55; *TSN Official Baseball Register*, 1983; James E. Welch, telephone conversation with Toronto Blue Jays Public Relations Office, Toronto, Canada, April 28, 1994.

James E. Welch

HOLLIDAY, James Wear "Bug" (b. February 8, 1867, St. Louis, MO; d. February 15, 1910, Cincinnati, OH), player, grew up in St. Louis and began playing with local amateur teams in 1881. In 1885, using the name "Hall," he played right field for the Chicago White Stockings (NL) for four games in the World Series against the St. Louis Brown Stockings in St. Louis. In 1886, he played professionally, still under the name of Hall, for St. Joseph, MO (WL). In 1887, performing under his own name, he starred for Topeka, KS (WL) and helped that team win the pennant. Holliday moved to Des Moines, IA, of the new WA in 1888, and his .311 batting average helped that team win the league championship. Holliday played for the Cincinnati Red Stockings (AA) in 1889 and batted .343 as a rookie. From 1890 to 1898, he played with the Cincinnati Reds (NL) and compiled a career .316 batting average. A power hitter in his era, he stroked 65 home runs among his 1,155 hits and led the AA in round-trippers with 19 in 1889 and the NL with 13 in 1892. His best all-around season came in 1894, when he batted .383 with 13 home runs and 119 RBIs.

Almost exclusively an outfielder, Holliday started as Cincinnati's center fielder from 1889 through 1894. During his career, he also appeared in 18 games as an infielder and 2 as a pitcher. His career fielding average was .934.

After his playing career, Holliday umpired in the NL in 1903 and later in the AA. He worked in a Cincinnati poolroom and also covered horse racing for a local newspaper. Holliday had contracted rheumatism by 1907 and died in 1910 after a long bout with locomotor ataxia, a convulsive affliction brought on by syphilis. The right-handed five-foot-seven-inch, 165-pound Holliday hit from a crouched stance and reputedly possessed the quickest swing of his time. His obituary in the St. Louis (MO) *Post-Dispatch* called him "once one of the best known and most popular of ballplayers."

BIBLIOGRAPHY: *The Baseball Encyclopedia*, 9th ed. (New York, 1993); Peter C. Bjarkman, "Cincinnati Reds," in Peter C. Bjarkman, ed., *Encyclopedia of Major League Baseball Team Histories: National League* (Westport, CT, 1991); New York *Clipper*, September 22, 1889; St. Louis (MO) *Post-Dispatch*, February 15, 1910; St. Louis (MO) *Republican*, October 18, 1885; Mike Shatzkin, ed., *The Ballplayers* (New York, 1990); John Thorn and Pete Palmer, eds., *Total Baseball*, 3rd ed. (New York, 1993); *TSN*, March 17, 1886.

John E. Findling

HOWSER, Richard Dalton "Dick" (b. May 14, 1937, Miami, FL; d. June 17, 1987, Kansas City, MO), player, coach, scout, and manager, was of German descent. He graduated from Palm Beach, FL, High School and earned a bachelor of science degree in education from Florida State University, garnering All-American honors at shortstop in 1957 and 1958. The five-foot-nine-inch, 155-pound Howser received a $21,000 bonus to sign with the Kansas City Athletics (AL) in 1958. He played shortstop at Winona, MN (3IL) in 1958 and Sioux City, IA (3IL) in 1959 and 1960 and batted .338 over the final half of the 1960 campaign for Shreveport, LA (SL).

The right-handed Howser played 157 games at shortstop for Kansas City in 1961, batting .280, scoring 108 runs, stealing 37 bases, leading AL shortstops in putouts, playing in the All-Star Game, and being voted AL Rookie of the Year. Injuries shortened Howser's 1962 campaign to 83 games, and Kansas City traded him with catcher Joe Azcue to the Cleveland Indians (AL) for catcher Elston Howard (BB) and $100,000 in May 1963. In 1964, Howser tied the AL record for games played at shortstop in a season by starting all 162 games. He scored 101 runs and reached a career-high 52 RBIs. He split shortstop duties with Larry Brown in 1965 and 1966 before the Indians traded Howser to the New York Yankees (AL) in December 1966. He served as a utility infielder with the Yankees in 1967 and 1968. Howser's career included 789 games, 617 hits, 398 runs, 16 home runs, 165 RBIs, 105 stolen bases, and a .248 batting average.

The Yankees retained Howser as third base coach from 1969 to 1978. He served as head baseball coach at Florida State University in 1979, leading the Seminoles to 43 wins, 17 losses, and 1 tie. Owner George Steinbrenner* hired Howser to manage the Yankees in 1980. Howser led New York to an AL East title with 103 victories, but the Yankees lost 3 straight in the best of 5 AL Championship Series to the Kansas City Royals (AL). Steinbrenner ordered Howser to fire third base coach Mike Ferraro as a scapegoat for failing to win the AL pennant. Howser quietly refused, however, and was dismissed with Ferraro.

The Kansas City Royals hired Howser to replace Jim Frey as manager in August 1981. The Royals won 20 of 33 games under Howser to win the second-half title in the split season, but then lost 3 consecutive contests to the Oakland Athletics in the AL West playoff. The Royals finished second under Howser in 1982 and 1983. Howser directed the Royals to the AL West title in 1984, but Kansas City lost the AL pennant to the Detroit Tigers in 3 games in the Championship Series. Kansas City in 1985 fielded virtually the same team, which many considered mediocre. Howser, nonetheless, won the AL West, came back from a 3 games to 1 deficit to defeat the Toronto Blue Jays for the AL pennant, and again overcame a 3 games to 1 disadvantage to win the World Series over the St. Louis Cardinals (NL).

In 1986, Howser managed the AL All-Star team but forgot the names of several players and seemed detached from the game. A week later on July 22, surgeons operated on Howser to remove a cancerous brain tumor. Royals coach Mike Ferraro, who had recovered from cancer of the kidney, was named interim manager. On December 5, 1986, Howser underwent experimental brain surgery called immunotherapy. He and his wife, Nancy, who had two daughters, Jan and Jill, received over 10,000 cards and bouquets from well-wishers. Howser tried to resume managerial duties with Kansas City in the spring of 1987 but retired after two days because of physical weakness. His teams won 507 games and lost 424.

Players, managers, and umpires respected Howser for his loyalty, integrity, and warm personality. For him, the players were family and the fans were extended family. Baseball writer Thomas Boswell (S) paid tribute to Howser, "In another 20 years of managing he probably would have won more pennants. But he could not have proved anything new about himself. All the best was already on display." Today the Dick Howser Trophy is awarded through the *BW* coaches' poll to the nation's outstanding college player.

BIBLIOGRAPHY: Thomas Boswell, *The Heart of the Order* (New York, 1989); Richard Howser file, National Baseball Library, Cooperstown, NY; Kansas City Royals, "Blending Talent Is Howser's Recipe for Success," *Grandslam* (1982); Bob Nightengale, "Biggest Game for K.C.'s Howser," *TSN*, July 28, 1986, p. 20; Bob Nightengale, "Experimental Surgery for Royals' Howser," *TSN*, December 15, 1986, p. 51; Bob Nightengale, "Royals Stadium: Empty Chair," *TSN*, August 4, 1986, p. 24.

Frank J. Olmsted

HRBEK, Kent Alan (b. May 21, 1960, Minneapolis, MN), player, is the oldest of two children born to Ed Hrbek and Justina Hrbek and played first base and pitched in baseball at Kennedy High School in Bloomington, MN. His baseball talents, however, escaped professional scouts, including those of the

Cincinnati Reds (NL) and Los Angeles Dodgers (NL) observing him at tryout camps. His playing abilities caught the attention of the Minnesota Twins (AL) through discussions that started in the concessions department and worked their way up to owner Calvin Griffith (BB). Griffith sent Twins scout Angelo Giuliani to see Hrbek play. The Twins signed Hrbek in the summer of 1978 and sent him to Elizabethton, TN (ApL) for 17 games. The 1980 season found Hrbek at Wisconsin Rapids, WI (ML), where he was named to the ML All-Star team. In 1981, Kent was promoted to Visalia, CA (CaL) and was selected to the CaL's All-Star squad.

The six-foot-four-inch, 252-pound Hrbek joined the Twins in September 1981, the fifteenth Minnesotan to play there. In his first major league game, he belted a twelfth-inning, game-winning home run off New York Yankee reliever George Frazier. With the Twins from 1981 to 1994, the left-handed-hitting, right-handed-throwing first baseman ranked among the best all-around AL players. In 14 major league seasons, Hrbek batted .282 with 1,749 hits, 293 round-trippers, and 1,086 RBIs. During this span, he made only 82 errors in 13,226 total chances for a .994 fielding percentage. Hrbek played in the 1982 All-Star Game, two AL Championship Series against the Detroit Tigers in 1987 and Toronto Blue Jays in 1991, and two World Series against the St. Louis Cardinals (NL) in 1987 and the Atlanta Braves (NL) in 1991. The Twins won both 7-game World Series. In 24 postseason games, Hrbek batted .154, with three home runs, and 12 RBIs.

Hrbek, who retired in August 1994, resides in Bloomington, MN, with his wife, Jeanie (Burns) Hrbek, and one daughter, Heidi.

BIBLIOGRAPHY: *The Baseball Encyclopedia*, 9th ed. (New York, 1993); *Minnesota Twins Media Guide*, 1994; Steve Wulf, "Local Boy Makes Good, Local Team Makes Bad," *SI* 57 (July 5, 1982), pp. 24–27.

James E. Welch

HUGHSON, Cecil Carleton "Tex" (b. February 9, 1916, Kyle, TX; d. August 6, 1993, San Marcos, TX), player, attended the University of Texas and began his professional baseball career with Moultrie, GA (GFL) in 1937. The following season, Hughson led the Canton, OH, Terriers (MAL) pitchers, winning 22 games and losing just 7 decisions. He pitched for Scranton, PA (EL) in 1939 before joining Louisville, KY (AA) in 1940. With Louisville, Hughson's career received a great boost from Boston Red Sox (AL) pitcher "Broadway" Charlie Wagner. Wagner spent some time in Louisville in 1940 and saw Hughson pitch in the sweltering heat. When Boston manager Joe Cronin (BB) asked Wagner about Louisville's best pitchers, the latter recommended Hughson.

After compiling a 7–1 win–loss record in 1941 with Louisville, Hughson joined the Boston Red Sox and finished with a 5–3 mark. The six-foot-three-inch, 198-pound right-hander, who usually wore high-heel boots and spurs that jingled and dangled, probably ranked as the AL's best pitcher in 1942, when he compiled a 22–6 mark and led the AL in wins, complete games (22), innings (281), and strikeouts (113). He was named to the AL All-Star team for the first of three straight times and pitched 2 innings during the Summer Classic. In April 1943, he set a record by defeating the New York Yankees for the sixth consecutive time, a streak extending back to July 1942. Hughson enjoyed a tremendous season in 1944 with an 18–5 mark before entering military service. His .783 winning percentage led the AL hurlers.

The tall Texan spent the 1945 season pitching for military service teams and returned to the Red Sox in 1946 with a 20–11 record, leading Boston to the AL pennant. In the World Series against the St. Louis Cardinals, Hughson triumphed in the opening game and lost Game 4. Cardinal star Stan Musial (BB) claimed that Hughson had shown him the best stuff for Boston during the classic, which St. Louis won on Enos Slaughter's (BB) tally from first base in the eighth inning of the seventh game.

Recurring arm problems plagued Hughson the remainder of his career. He won 12 of 23 decisions in 1947, including four 1–0 victories and 3 of 4 decisions in 1948. The Red Sox in June 1948 sent Hughson to the Austin, TX, Pioneers (BSL), where he wore the number 13 on his uniform. Hughson returned to the major leagues with Boston in 1949, recording a 4–2 mark. Boston traded Hughson to the New York Giants (NL) in 1950, but he was released before the season started. During his eight-year major league career, Hughson compiled a 96–54 record with a 2.94 ERA. Hughson, who married Roena Moore in May 1937, retired to his farm in Kyle, TX, and later resided in San Marcos, TX. The Hughsons had one son, Stanley, and two daughters, Dixie and Jane.

BIBLIOGRAPHY: John Drohan, "Tex Won Spurs After Broadway Boosting," *TSN*, June 26, 1946, p. 9; Weldon Hart, "Hughson Story Makes Unique Baseball History," Austin (TX) *Statesman*, June 2, 1948; Ed Rummil, " 'Hold That Locker, I'll Be Back,' Says Tex on Departure," *TSN*, May 29, 1948; Mike Shatzkin, ed., *The Ballplayers* (New York, 1990).

William A. Borst

HURST, Bruce Vee (b. March 24, 1958, St. George, UT), player, is the son of John T. Hurst and Elizabeth (Bruhn) Hurst and attended Dixie JC, helping his basketball team win the National JC tournament. The Boston Red Sox (AL) selected the six-foot-three-inch, 219-pound Mormon left-handed pitcher in the first round of the 1976 draft and assigned him to Elmira, NY (NYPL) in 1976, Winter Haven, FL (FSL) in 1977 and 1979, Bristol, CT (EL) in 1978 and 1979, and Pawtucket, RI (IL) in 1980 and 1981.

Hurst briefly pitched with Boston in 1980 and 1981 and started there from 1982 to 1988, compiling an 88–73 overall win–loss mark. He led the Red Sox staff with 15 pickoffs in 1984 and 189 strikeouts the following season.

In 1986 Hurst helped Boston capture the AL pennant with a 13–8 overall mark and 2.99 ERA, averaging nearly 1 strikeout per inning. He recorded a 1–0 mark in his two AL Championship Series starts against the California Angels and defeated the New York Mets twice in the World Series. Hurst won the opening game, 1–0, surrendering four hits and striking out eight batters. He went the distance in a 4–2 Boston triumph in Game 5 and also started Game 7 on just three days' rest. In 1987 Hurst triumphed 15 times, was selected to the AL All-Star team, and established a career-best 190 strikeouts, the most ever by a Boston left-hander. His career-high 18 victories the next season helped the Red Sox win the AL East title. He became the second-winningest southpaw in Fenway Park history and compiled 11 victories following Boston losses, but the Oakland A's defeated him twice in the AL Championship Series.

In December 1988, the San Diego Padres (NL) signed Hurst as a free agent. In 1989, Hurst enjoyed a 15–11 slate and career-best 2.69 ERA. He shared the NL lead in complete games (10) and recorded 179 strikeouts, second best in Padre history. The Atlanta Braves made only one hit against him on April 10, as 13 batters struck out. The following season, Hurst shared the NL lead in shutouts (4) and hurled 27 straight scoreless innings. He posted at least 11 victories 10 consecutive seasons from 1983 to 1992. In July 1993, San Diego traded Hurst and Greg Harris to the Colorado Rockies (NL). The Texas Rangers (AL) signed Hurst in December 1993. Hurst boasts a 145–113 mark and 3.92 ERA with 1,689 strikeouts, 63 pickoffs, and 23 shutouts in 13 major league campaigns.

He and his wife Holly have two sons, Ryan and Kyle, and one daughter, Jordan, and reside in St. George, UT.

BIBLIOGRAPHY: *San Diego Padres 1993 Media Guide*; Mike Shatzkin, ed., *The Ballplayers* (New York, 1990); Dan Shaughnessy, *The Curse of the Bambino* (New York, 1990); *TSN Official Baseball Register*, 1994.

David L. Porter

HUTCHINSON, Frederick Charles "Fred" "Big Bear" "Hutch" (b. August 12, 1919, Seattle, WA; d. November 12, 1964, Bradenton, FL), player and manager, was the son of Dr. J. L. Hutchinson, a physician. Uncertainty about Hutchinson's fastball kept him from getting a contract with a major league baseball organization despite an impressive amateur pitching record. In 1938, he signed with Seattle, WA (PCL), winning 25 games. *TSN* named him Minor League Player of the Year. The Detroit Tigers (AL), who could have signed him right out of high school, purchased his contract for $50,000 and four players. Hutchinson did not enjoy immediate success, however, shuttling between the Tigers and affiliates in Buffalo, NY (IL) and Toledo, OH (AA) the next three seasons. He remained with the Tigers long enough in both 1939 and 1940 to win 3 games and pitched an inning against the Cincinnati Reds in the 1940 World Series. In 1941 he appeared in just 2 games with the Tigers, both as a pinch hitter, but won 26 games for Buffalo. Hutchinson then enlisted in the U.S. Navy, where he directed athletics and instructed recruits in rifle marksmanship. Hutchinson, who was discharged with the rank of lieutenant commander, married Patricia Finley in 1943 and had four children, including Rick, Jack, and Patty.

After World War II, Hutchinson, a six-foot-two-inch, 210-pound right-hander, used his control and assortment of off-speed pitches to win 10 or more games with the Tigers six consecutive seasons. He peaked with 18 victories in 1947 and 17 in 1950 and pitched in the 1951 All-Star Game. Arm trouble plagued Hutchinson in 1952. He replaced "Red" Rolfe (S) in midseason as manager of the Tigers, then mired in last place. He ended his pitching career the following season with a 95–71 career win–loss record and 3.73 ERA. As manager, he made progress in rebuilding the Tigers by adding youngsters Harvey Kuenn (BB) and Al Kaline (BB) to the lineup. The Tigers, however, did not climb above fifth place. Hutchinson resigned as pilot after the 1954 campaign, when Detroit refused to give him more than a one-year contract. After managing Seattle, WA (PCL) in 1955, he took over the St. Louis Cardinals' (NL) helm. Hutchinson led the Cardinals to first-division finishes in 1956 and 1957 and was named NL Manager of the Year in 1957. The Cardinals fired him when the club slumped in 1958.

On July 9, 1959, Hutchinson was named manager of the seventh-place Cincinnati Reds (NL). By season's end, the Reds, led by slugger Frank Robinson (BB), had risen to fifth place. Hutchinson enjoyed great success with Cincinnati. An outstanding handler of pitchers, Hutchinson demanded that his players work hard and insisted that "sweat is a ballplayer's only salvation." A fiery temper led him to smash lightbulbs and clubhouse furniture on several occasions, but he exhibited patience in handling personnel. Players knew that he would treat them fairly, recalled Gordon Coleman, who played first base for Hutchinson in Cincinnati. Hutchinson guided the Reds to an NL pennant in 1961, the club's first title since 1940. The New York Yankees, however, defeated Cincinnati in the World Series. The Reds improved with 98 wins the following year, yet trailed both the Los Angeles Dodgers and San Francisco Giants in the standings. Cincinnati slumped in 1963, but Hutchinson added Pete Rose (BB) to the lineup at second base and developed Jim Maloney (S) into a top pitcher. The Reds contended in 1964 before chest cancer forced Hutchinson to take a leave of absence on August 13. He died three months later. Hutchinson compiled an 830–827 win–loss record in 12 years as a major league manager.

BIBLIOGRAPHY: "Angry Boss of the Reds," *Look* 27 (August 27, 1963), pp. 67–69; Cincinnati Reds Public Relations Department, Cincinnati, OH; Lloyd Graybar, phone interview with Gordon Coleman, February 1, 1993; *NYT*, November 13, 1964.

Lloyd J. Graybar

HUTCHINSON, William Forrest "Wild Bill" (b. December 17, 1859, New Haven, CT; d. March 19, 1926, Kansas City, MO), player, starred for Yale University in baseball as a shortstop and batter, graduating in 1880. Hutchinson, whose father served as a Yale University professor, did postgraduate work before moving to Kansas City, MO, to go into the railroad and lumber business. Spurning professional offers, he played amateur baseball until pitching for Des Moines (IA) in 1887 and 1888. Reportedly his $3,800 salary was the highest in the minor leagues. In 1889, the 29-year-old rookie was sold to the Chicago White Stockings (NL). Definitely one of the earliest major leaguers to be a college graduate, Hutchinson was possibly the first such in White Stockings history. Hutchinson won 16 games and lost 17 his 1889 rookie year while striking out 136 batters.

The following three years with the Colts, this workhorse led the NL in victories (42, 43, and 37), games (including a high of 77), and innings pitched. Hutchinson averaged over 60 complete games per year. His 627 innings pitched in 1892 remains a Chicago record. On May 30, 1890, he won both games of a doubleheader, giving up only 3 earned runs. His fastball proved his best pitch, as he led the NL with 316 strikeouts in 1892. He had trouble controlling the pitch, however, and averaged over 170 walks per season from 1890 through 1893. Hutchinson also relieved, winning 7 games and saving 1 in 1891, his best season. A better-than-average hitter for a pitcher, he batted .309 in 1894 and recorded a lifetime .215 mark. He belted 12 career home runs, 1 of which on May 8, 1890, hit a horse and carriage in center field, helping Chicago rally to win, 18–9.

In 1893, the pitching distance was increased to 60 feet 6 inches from 50 feet. Hutchinson, among other pitchers, found it difficult to adjust. He never again recorded a winning record and saw his control problems worsen, with his bases on balls total nearly doubling his strikeouts. Hutchinson, released after a 13–21 season in 1895, failed in a comeback two years later with the St. Louis Browns (NL). The lifelong bachelor worked for many years with the Kansas Southern Railroad. His eight-year career in the major leagues resulted in a 182–158 record with a 3.59 ERA.

BIBLIOGRAPHY: Art Ahrens and Eddie Gold, *Day by Day in Chicago Cubs History* (West Point, NY, 1982); Eddie Gold and Art Ahrens, *The Golden Era Cubs* (Chicago, IL, 1985); Robert L. Tiemann and Mark Rucker, eds., *Nineteenth Century Stars* (Kansas City, MO, 1989).

Duane A. Smith

JANSEN, Lawrence Joseph "Larry" (b. July 16, 1920, Verboort, OR), player and coach, is one of eight children of Albert Jansen, a farmer, and Dora (Van Dyke) Jansen. Jansen, who grew up on a farm, usually played shortstop in high school and sandlot ball but impressed scouts as a natural pitcher. Jansen declined to sign with the San Francisco, CA, Seals (PCL) in 1939 but inked a contract with the Boston Red Sox (AL). Commissioner Kenesaw Mountain Landis (BB) invalidated his contract when the Red Sox failed to assign Jansen to a minor league team as the 1940 season neared. Jansen then signed with the San Francisco Seals and was sent to Salt Lake City, UT (PrL), where he won 20 games. He pitched for the Seals the next two years but remained out of organized baseball in 1943 and 1944 to work on the family farm during World War II. After returning to the Seals late in the 1945 campaign, he won 30 games in 1946.

The six-foot-two-inch, 190-pound right-hander joined the New York Giants in 1947, winning 21 games. The Giants tied the major league home run record but proved weak on the mound. As the Giants rebuilt to feature speed and defense, Jansen remained a stellar pitcher. He relied on an outstanding curve and superb control that enabled him to spot the ball on the corners of the plate. The highlight of his career came in the 1950 All-Star Game, which the National League won in an extra-inning thriller. Jansen hurled five innings, yielding only one hit and striking out six batters. In 1951, he won the final game of the regular season to clinch a first-place tie and relieved the third, deciding playoff game with the Brooklyn Dodgers. He pitched a scoreless ninth inning and was credited with the victory on Bobby Thomson's (S) dramatic home run. Jansen pitched well but lost the second game of the World Series against the New York Yankees. The Yankees shelled him in a fifth-game start.

Jansen began to lose his effectiveness by 1952 and did not play a significant role when the Giants won the World Series in 1954. He served as a pitcher–coach for the Seattle, WA, Rainiers (PCL) in 1955 and returned to the major leagues the following year, when he won two games for the Cincinnati Reds (NL). After four seasons in the PCL as a pitcher and coach for Seattle and Portland, OR, Jansen coached for the San Francisco Giants from 1961 through 1971 and tutored Juan Marichal (BB) and Gaylord Perry (BB) at the start of their splendid careers. He spent the 1972 and 1973 seasons as a pitching coach with the Chicago Cubs before retiring to spend more time with his family. Jansen, who married Eileen Vandehey in August 1939, has 10 children.

In nine major league seasons, Jansen won 122 games, lost 89 decisions, compiled a 3.58 ERA, and hurled 17 shutouts. His best years were 1951 when he tied teammate Sal Maglie (S) for the NL lead in wins and 1950 when he hurled 5 shutouts to lead the NL.

BIBLIOGRAPHY: Brent Kelley, "Larry Jansen," *SCD* 18 (November 1, 1991), pp. 170–172; Thomas Kiernan, *The Miracle at Coogan's Bluff* (New York, 1974); Tom Meany, *Baseball's Greatest Pitchers* (New York, 1951); Joe Reichler, "Larry Jansen, The Giants Giant-Killer," in Joe Reichler, ed., *Inside the Majors* (New York, 1952), pp. 120–122.

Lloyd J. Graybar

JOHNSON, Howard Michael "Hojo" (b. November 29, 1960, Clearwater, FL), player, attended St. Petersburg JC in St. Petersburg, FL. A selection in the twenty-third round of the 1978 free agent draft, he started his professional baseball career with Lakeland, FL (FSL) in 1979. He first joined the Detroit Tigers (AL) in 1982 after ascending through the parent chain with Birmingham, AL (SL) in 1980 and 1981 and Evansville, IN (AA) in 1982. He hit .316 in 54 games for the Tigers but started the 1983 season with Evansville. Injuries sidelined him most of the 1983 season, as he appeared in only 27 games for Detroit.

Johnson's first full major league season came in 1984, when the 5-foot-11-inch, 195-pound switch-hitter hit 12 homers and knocked in 50 runs. His lack of aggressiveness at the plate caused manager Sparky Anderson (BB) to trade him to the New York Mets (NL) in December 1984 for pitcher Walt Terrell. In New York his situation did not improve, as he was platooned with Ray Knight at third base. The Tigers had defeated the San Diego Padres (NL) in the 1984 World Series, while the Mets triumphed over the Boston Red Sox (AL) in the 1986 World Series. Johnson became just the twenty-seventh major leaguer to play for a World Series champion in both leagues.

New York traded Knight after the 1986 World Series, enabling Johnson to play regularly. Johnson came into his own in 1987, when he and Darryl Strawberry* became the first teammates to join the exclusive 30–30 home run, stolen base club. Johnson's season included 36 homers, a record for switch-hitters, 32 stolen bases, and 99 RBIs. Whitey Herzog (S) and other NL managers checked his bats for cork, but Mets manager Davey Johnson (S) suggested they check his arms.

Although the Mets won an NL East Division title in 1988, Johnson produced just 24 homers to rank fifth in the NL in an injury-marred season. The following season, he enjoyed the best year of his career with 101 RBIs (tied for fourth in the NL), 41 steals (tied for third), a .287 batting average, and 36 home runs (second best in the NL). He became only the third player to produce two 30–30 seasons. Johnson was selected to the *TSN* All-Star team and his first All-Star Game. His 41 doubles marked a Mets record, while his 41 stolen bases tied for fourth in the NL. Johnson's .559 slugging average was ranked second in the NL. Although having an injury-plagued 1990 season, he hit at least 1 homer in the first seven positions in the batting order. After having off-season arthroscopic shoulder surgery, Johnson in 1991 enjoyed career highs, Mets records, and NL highs with 117 RBIs, 38 homers, and a career-high 108 runs scored.

Johnson, nicknamed "Hojo," demonstrated his versatility in the field and willingness to help the team in 1992, when Mets manager Jeff Torborg made him opening day center fielder after finishing 1991 in right field. The experiment led to disastrous results for both Johnson and the Mets. Several nagging injuries, including a broken wrist that effectively ended his season in August, limited him to just seven home runs, the lowest output of his career. In November 1993, the Colorado Rockies (NL) signed Johnson as a free agent. He was released following the 1994 season.

Johnson, a quiet, nearly shy individual, used to get free ice cream at Howard Johnson Restaurants as a youngster. A dead fastball hitter, Johnson always experienced trouble with the off-speed deliveries. He has engaged reliever Todd Worrell of the San Diego Padres in several duels over the years, with Johnson homering on several occasions. Johnson, who has failed to hit in six World Series at bats, and his wife Kim have two daughters, Shannon Leigh and Kayla Mae, and one son, Glen. His 12-year career includes a .251 batting average, 221 home runs, 738 RBIs, and 230 stolen bases.

BIBLIOGRAPHY: Duncan Bock and John Jordan, *The Complete Year-by-Year N.Y. Mets Fan's Almanac* (New York, 1992); Mike Shatzkin, ed., *The Ballplayers* (New York, 1990).

William A. Borst

JURGES, William Frederick "Billy" (b. May 9, 1908, Bronx, NY), player, coach, manager, and scout, is the son of Frederick Jurges, a shipping clerk, and Anna (Horstman) Jurges and grew up in Brooklyn, NY, where he attended Richmond High School. In 1927, he entered professional baseball with Manchester, NH (NEL). The good fielding, wide-ranging shortstop attracted the attention of the Chicago Cubs (NL), who signed him after he batted .322 in 1928. Jurges spent two years with Reading, PA (IL) before Chicago brought him to the major leagues in 1931. Despite being shot by a spurned showgirl during the 1932 season, Jurges returned to bat .364 against the New York Yankees in the World Series. The scrappy 5-foot-11-inch, 175-pound Jurges teamed with second baseman Billy Herman (BB) to become one of the famous Cubs' double play duos. For the next six seasons, the right-handed Jurges anchored the Cub infield. Few NL infields were better in that era. He led NL shortstops in double plays in 1935 and four times paced NL shortstops in fielding percentage.

The Cubs finished no lower than third during this span, winning the NL pennant twice. His best hitting year came in 1937, when he batted .298 with 18 doubles and 10 triples. His .258 career batting average included 1,613 hits. Never a power hitter, Jurges hit only 43 home runs during his 17-year major league career and knocked in 656 runs.

The Cubs offered him the manager position in 1938, but he suggested Gabby Hartnett (BB) instead. Hartnett led the Cubs to the pennant, only again to lose the World Series to the New York Yankees. After the season, the Cubs traded Jurges to the New York Giants (NL). Chicago later came to regret the trade. Jurges had given them stability at shortstop, if not an outstanding bat. His best year with the Giants came in 1941, when he batted .293. After the 1943 season, his last as a regular, Jurges played third base and some shortstop. He later returned to the Cubs in 1946 as a utility player, staying two more seasons before retiring. Jurges then became a scout and minor league manager with Cedar Rapids, IA (3IL) in 1950 and Hagerstown, MD (PiL) in 1953. He returned to the majors as a coach with the Washington Senators (AL) from 1956 through July 1959. He landed a managerial job with the Boston Red Sox (AL) midway through the 1959 season, only to be fired a year later with a 78–83 composite record. Under Jurges, infielder Pumpsie Green ended the Red Sox status as the only major league team without an African-American player. Jurges, who married Mary Huyette in June 1933 and has one daughter, Suzanne, scouted for the Cubs until 1982 and resides in Largo, FL.

BIBLIOGRAPHY: Art Ahrens and Eddie Gold, *Day by Day in Chicago Cubs History* (West Point, NY, 1982); *The Baseball Encyclopedia*, 9th ed. (New York, 1993); Eddie Gold and Art Ahrens, *The Golden Era Cubs* (Chicago, IL, 1985); Rich Westcott, *Diamond Greats* (Westport, CT, 1988).

Duane A. Smith

KAUFF, Benjamin Michael "Benny" (b. January 5, 1890, Pomeroy, OH; d. November 17, 1961, Columbus, OH), player, led the FL in batting and stolen bases in both years of its operation. Only one other major league baseball player, Honus Wagner (BB), won back-to-back batting and stolen base titles. Later, baseball commissioner Kenesaw Mountain Landis (BB) banned Kauff from professional baseball in a highly autocratic, arbitrary decision.

The son of a Slavic coal miner, William Kauff, he dropped out of school at age 11 to work as a breaker boy at the coal mines around Middletown, OH. Although only five feet eight inches and 157 pounds, he developed thick, powerful legs and a barrel chest from the mine work. Foot speed, self-confidence, and a drive to escape the mines helped the left-handed hitter star on local teams, the amateur Keystone club in 1908, and the Middleport, OH, semiprofessional team in 1909.

Kauff turned professional in 1910 with Parkersburg, WV (VVL), where he led organized baseball with a .417 batting average and also stole 87 bases. In 1911 at Bridgeport, CT (CtL), he hit a solid .294. The New York Highlanders (AL) purchased him before the 1912 season but shipped him to Rochester, NY (IL) after only five games. Rochester sold him to Brockton, MA (NEL), where his poor .208 batting average led again to his sale to Hartford, CT (CtL). There, he regained his batting stroke, hitting .321 for the remainder of 1912 and leading the EA in 1913 with a .345 batting average.

Kauff achieved his greatest fame as the outstanding player of the upstart

FL. When the FL declared itself to be a major league, Kauff signed with the Indianapolis, IN, Hoosiers. In 1914, he led the FL in batting (.370), stolen bases (75), hits (211), doubles (44), and runs scored (120) and was lauded as "the Ty Cobb of the Federal League." Shifted to the Brooklyn Tip-Tops (FL) in 1915, Kauff again led the FL in batting (.342) and stolen bases (55). New York Giants (NL) manager John McGraw (BB) attempted to sign Kauff in 1915, but the deal was voided by the NL president. When the FL disbanded, McGraw's Giants purchased Kauff's contract from the Brooklyn Tip-Tops for $35,000. Kauff refused to report to the Giants until they agreed to pay him a $5,000 settlement.

Kauff developed the image of a "dandy" or "sport." When Kauff arrived for spring training in 1916, a reporter wrote: "He wore a loudly-striped silk shirt, an expensive blue suit, patent leather shoes, a fur-collared overcoat and a derby hat . . . a huge diamond stick-pin and a gold watch encrusted with diamonds."

Despite Kauff's foppish attire and rather disappointing playing statistics with the Giants, McGraw admired his hustle and aggressive playing style. To the fiery manager, Kauff was "a player of the old school. He thinks and lives baseball. . . . There aren't many players like that today." After hitting only .264 in 1916, Kauff raised his batting average to .308 in 1917 to help the Giants win the NL pennant. He batted a weak .160 in the Giants' World Series loss to the Chicago White Sox.

Kauff's fast living led to his banishment. He was rumored to have been involved in, or at least to have known about, the famous White Sox fix of the 1919 World Series. At the 1920 grand jury hearings in Chicago, Kauff testified that his 1919 teammates Hal Chase (BB) and Heinie Zimmerman (S) had offered him bribes to throw games. As a result of Kauff's testimony, Zimmerman was suspended from baseball. In February 1920, Kauff was indicted in New York for auto theft. When his trial date was postponed, Kauff played in 1920. In July 1920, however, the Giants traded him to Toronto, Canada (IL) for Vernon Spencer. Commissioner Landis suspended Kauff from baseball before the 1921 season pending the outcome of his trial. The original charge of grand larceny was reduced to receiving stolen property, and character testimony from McGraw and former NL president John K. Tener (BB) helped Kauff gain acquittal.

Despite the jury's verdict, Landis in August 1921 refused to lift Kauff's suspension. Kauff went to court to seek his return to baseball. At the trial, Landis labeled Kauff's earlier acquittal "one of the worst miscarriages of justice" and charged that Kauff's "mere presence in the line-up would inevitably burden patrons of the game with grave apprehensions as to its integrity." The New York Supreme Court ruled against Kauff. Thereafter, Kauff maintained, "I never did anything wrong." After 1921, he worked as a salesman in Columbus, OH, for the John Lymann Company. In parts of eight major league seasons, he batted .311 with 49 home runs, 454 RBIs, and 234 stolen bases in 859 games. He died of a cerebral hemorrhage in Columbus, OH, still hoping a new commissioner would absolve him.

BIBLIOGRAPHY: Charles C. Alexander, *John McGraw* (New York, 1988); Frank Graham, "There Was Only One Benny Kauff," *BD* 21 (February 1962), p. 81; Bob Lemke, "The Bleacher Bum: The Benny Kauff Story," *SCD* 20 (April 2–30, 1993); Marc Okkonen, *The Federal League of 1914–1915* (Garrett Park, MD, 1989); J. G. Taylor Spink, *Judge Landis and Twenty-Five Years of Baseball* (New York, 1947).

William E. Akin

KELLY, Jay Thomas "Tom" (b. August 15, 1950, Graceville, MN), player and manager, graduated from St. Mary's High School in South Amboy, NJ, and attended Mesa, AZ, CC and Monmouth College in New Jersey. He was selected by the Seattle Pilots (AL) franchise, which moved to Milwaukee in 1970 as the Brewers, in the eighth round of the free agent draft in June 1968. Kelly played outfield with Newark, NJ (NYPL) in 1968, Clinton, IA (ML) in 1969, and Jacksonville, FL (SL) in 1970 but remained on the inactive list most of that season. Jacksonville released him in April 1971, but he signed with Charlotte, FL (FSL) of the Minnesota Twins (AL) organization the same month. From 1972 through 1975, he alternated as an outfielder–first baseman for Tacoma, WA (PCL) and spent 49 games with the Minnesota Twins (AL). Tacoma loaned Kelly to Rochester, NY (IL) for the 1976 season. Kelly rounded out his minor league career with Tacoma, WA (PCL) in 1977, Toledo, OH (IL) in 1978, and Visalia, CA (CaL) in 1979.

Kelly began his managing career as a player–manager with Tacoma in June 1972, piloting the PCL club for the remainder of the season. In 1978, he served as a player–coach at Toledo, OH (IL). After managing at Visalia in 1979 and 1980, he spent the next two seasons piloting Orlando, FL (SL). From 1983 until September 1986, Kelly coached with the Minnesota Twins (AL).

Kelly replaced Ray Miller as manager of the Minnesota Twins on September 12, 1986, with the club mired in seventh place with 59 wins and 80 losses. For the balance of the 1986 season under Kelly, the Twins won 12 games and lost 11. In his first full season as Twins manager, Kelly piloted the 1987 Twins to first place in the AL West. Minnesota defeated the Detroit Tigers for the AL pennant and the St. Louis Cardinals, 4 games to 3, in the World Series. Kelly guided the 1988 Twins to second place with 91 wins and 71 losses. Minnesota dropped to fifth place in 1989 with 80 wins and 82 losses and seventh place in 1990 with 74 wins and 88 losses.

With 95 victories and 67 defeats in 1991, the Twins rose to first place in the AL West. Minnesota defeated the Toronto Blue Jays for the AL championship and the Atlanta Braves in the World Series, 4 games to 3. Under Kelly, Minnesota finished with a 90–72 mark in 1992, a 71–91 slate in 1993, and a 53–60 record in the strike-shortened 1994 season.

In his first eight years as a major league manager, all with the Minnesota

Twins, his teams won 651 games while losing 619 for a .513 percentage. Kelly was named CaL Manager of the Year in 1980. His other honors included being named SL Manager of the Year in 1981 by both the *TSN* and the BBWAA and coaching the AL All-Star team in 1991.

BIBLIOGRAPHY: Stan Carlson, Newspaper Clipping file, Minneapolis, MN; Tom Kelly, letter to Stan W. Carlson, November 1993; *Minnesota Twins Media Guide*, 1994; *TSN Official Baseball Register*, 1994.

Stan W. Carlson

KESSINGER, Donald Eulon "Don" "Kess" (b. July 17, 1942, Forrest City, AK), player and manager, is the son of Howard M. Kessinger, a grocery store owner, and Ida (Bannister) Kessinger and was selected as an All-SEC baseball and basketball star at the University of Mississippi. He signed with the Chicago Cubs (NL) after his graduation in 1964. The lanky six-foot-one-inch, 175-pound Kessinger made a token appearance with Chicago at the end of the year but was assigned to Dallas–Fort Worth, TX (TL) for more experience. The Cubs, desperate for a good fielding shortstop, rushed Kessinger back to the major leagues partway through the next season. He participated in three triple plays in 1965 but batted .201 and drove in only 14 runs.

The next season, Kessinger improved dramatically. His batting average soared to .271, as he joined with Ron Santo (BB), Glenn Beckert,* and Ernie Banks (BB) to form one of the greatest infields in Cub history. Kessinger's fielding and defensive skills remained his strengths. The 1967 season amply displayed his talents, as he led the NL in assists, double plays, and most chances per game. For the first time in 22 years, the Cubs led the NL in fielding. In 1969, he led the NL in every defensive department and set a record of playing 54 consecutive errorless games. Kessinger won Gold Glove awards in 1969 and 1970 and was selected for the NL All-Star team 5 consecutive years from 1968 to 1972. Chicago traded Kessinger, who established a Cub record of 1,618 games at shortstop, to the St. Louis Cardinals (NL) following the 1975 season.

Never a high percentage hitter, he compiled a .252 career average with 14 home runs. Kessinger's best year came in 1972, when he hit .274. In 1971, he collected six hits on June 17, as the Cubs edged St. Louis, 7–6. When the Cubs defeated the Montreal Expos on August 31, he went five for six. Kessinger enjoyed no success as a pinch hitter, making no hits in 33 tries. He played one and one-half years with the Cardinals before being traded in August 1977 to the Chicago White Sox (AL). Late in his career, he played some at second base and third base. In 1979 he served as player–manager for the White Sox, leading them to a 46–60 win–loss record before resigning. Simultaneously, he also retired as a player, ending a 16-year major league career. After a decade in the securities business, Kessinger has been baseball coach for the University of Mississippi since 1990. Kessinger, who married Carolyn Crawley and has two sons, R. Keith and Kevin M., lives in Oxford, MS.

BIBLIOGRAPHY: *The Baseball Encyclopedia*, 9th ed. (New York, 1993); *Chicago Cubs Official Roster Book*, 1970, 1974, 1975; *Chicago Cubs Vineline* (February 1993); Eddie Gold and Art Ahrens, *The New Era Cubs* (Chicago, IL, 1985).

Duane A. Smith

KILLEN, Frank Bissell (b. November 30, 1870, Pittsburgh, PA; d. December 3, 1939, Pittsburgh, PA), player and umpire, twice led the NL in wins while pitching for his hometown Pirates. The six-foot-one-inch, 200-pound left-hander drew notice in his youth as a baseball catcher before converting to pitching in his late teens. After turning professional at age 19, he compiled a 30–8 win–loss record for three minor league clubs in 1890. Killen recorded 21 wins and 15 losses by August 1891 for Minneapolis, MN (WA), when the club disbanded. The Milwaukee Brewers, another WA club, moved to the major league AA and signed Killen. Killen's 7–4 record for Milwaukee included a one-hitter against the pennant-bound Boston Reds.

When the AA folded after the 1891 season, Killen was assigned to the Washington Senators (NL). In 1892 he won 29 games while losing 26 for a tenth-place team in the 12-team NL. When Killen held out for more money in 1893, Washington traded him to the Pittsburgh Pirates. Some pitchers could not handle the lengthening of the pitching distance from 51 feet to 60 feet 6 inches that year. Killen, however, enjoyed his finest season, winning an NL-high 36 games while losing only 14 and leading the Pirates to a strong second-place finish. A line drive broke his arm in July 1894, when his record stood at 14–11. Blood poisoning from an infected spike wound sidelined him in June 1895 with a 5–5 season record. He came back in 1896 to tie Kid Nichols (BB) for the NL lead, recording 30 wins against 18 losses and amassing NL and personal highs in complete games (44) and innings pitched (432⅓). He logged lackluster marks of 17–23 in 1897 and 10–11 through the following July, when Pittsburgh released him. The Washington Senators signed Killen, who finished 1898 winning just 6 of 15 decisions. The Senators dropped Killen after he lost his first two starts the next April. The Boston Beaneaters signed him in May 1899 but released him two months later with a 7–5 record.

Killen's major league career ended in June 1900 with a 3–3 mark for the Chicago Orphans (NL). He lost one game for the Chicago White Stockings in the then-minor AL in 1900 and finished his pitching career with minor league seasons at Wheeling, WV (WA) in 1901, Indianapolis, IN (AA) in 1902 and part of 1903, and Atlanta (SL) the remainder of 1903.

During his major league career, Killen won 164 games and suffered 131 losses in 321 games. He completed 253 of 300 starts and compiled a 3.78

ERA, striking out 725 batters, yielding 2,730 hits, and issuing 822 walks. Following his playing career, Killen umpired a few seasons in the AA, CL, and SL and operated a bar in Pittsburgh until his death.

BIBLIOGRAPHY: Frank Killen file, National Baseball Library, Cooperstown, NY; John Thorn and Pete Palmer, eds., *Total Baseball*, 3rd ed. (New York, 1993); Robert L. Tiemann and Mark Rucker, eds., *Nineteenth Century Stars* (Kansas City, MO, 1989).

                                                        Frederick Ivor-Campbell

KINDER, Ellis Raymond "Old Folks" (b. July 24, 1914, Atkins, AK; d. October 16, 1968, Jackson, TN), player, quit a $175-a-month job driving a bulldozer to sign a professional baseball contract with Jackson, TN (KL) for $75 a month in 1938. The right-hander, who had only an eighth-grade education, attracted little attention until compiling a 21–9 win–loss record for Jackson in 1940, striking out 307 batters in just 276 innings. Kinder married Hazel McCabe on March 31, 1934. The couple had three children, Charles, Betty, and Jimmy. After their divorce, he married Ruth in 1951.

The New York Yankees (AL) purchased Kinder's contract conditionally in 1941 for $5,000 but returned him after he failed his short trial at Binghamton, NY (EL). Kinder pitched for Memphis, TN (SL) in 1942 and left baseball in 1943 for his off-season job as a pipefitter for the Illinois Railroad in Jackson.

The six-foot, 215-pounder returned to the Memphis club in 1944, finishing 19–6 as a teammate of Pete Gray. The St. Louis Browns (AL) purchased his contract, but Kinder joined the Seabees before starting his major league career with St. Louis in 1946 at age 31. In December 1947, after having two mediocre seasons, Kinder was traded to the Boston Red Sox (AL). Kinder enjoyed the best season of his major league career in 1949, leading the AL with a 23–6 win–loss record for a .793 winning percentage and with six shutouts. His record stood at 4–4 in June. Kinder won 19 of his next 20 decisions before losing on the last day of the season to the New York Yankees with the AL pennant at stake. The defeat severely disturbed Kinder for the remainder of his life. With Boston losing 1–0, manager Joe McCarthy (BB) lifted him for a pinch hitter in the eighth inning. The Yankees tagged successors Mel Parnell (BB) and Tex Hughson* for four runs. The Red Sox rallied but lost the game and the AL pennant, 5–3. Kinder claimed, "The Yankees wouldn't have gotten any more runs off me."

Kinder developed into one of the premier AL relief pitchers after switching to the bullpen in 1950. Owner Tom Yawkey (BB) suggested that manager Steve O'Neill (S) put Kinder in the bullpen, starting him on a new career. The 1951 campaign saw him lead the AL with 63 appearances and 14 saves. In 1953, the right-handed Kinder broke Ed Walsh's (BB) AL record by appearing in 69 games for the Red Sox with 27 saves. Kinder advised younger pitchers, "The main thing is to keep throwing each day, whether you pitched yesterday or not."

The Red Sox in December 1955 sold Kinder to the St. Louis Cardinals (NL), who waived him in July 1956 to the Chicago White Sox (AL). The White Sox released him in May 1957, two months before his forty-third birthday. The wiry Tennesseean, who possessed a great curveball, pitched for San Diego, CA (PCL) before retiring. His major league career ended with a 102–71 mark and a 3.43 ERA in 484 games. Kinder, who gained notoriety for his late-night carousing, died of complications from open heart surgery.

BIBLIOGRAPHY: Bill Borst, ed., *Ables to Zoldak*, vol. 2 (St. Louis, MO, 1989); Bill Borst, *Still Last in the American League* (West Bloomfield, MI, 1992); Gene Karst and Martin Jones, Jr., *Who's Who In Professional Baseball* (New Rochelle, NY, 1973); Steve O'Leary, "Wonder-Kid Kinder, 'Just Starting' at 35," *TSN*, September 28, 1949; *TSN*, March 16, 1955, p. 5; *TSN*, November 2, 1968, p. 44.

William A. Borst

KUROWSKI, George John "Whitey" (b. April 19, 1918, Reading, PA), player and manager, is the son of Anthony F. Kurowski, a steel mill worker, and Victoria (Swiecicka) Kurowski and developed osteomyelitis at age eight, the result of an accident and blood infection. Two operations left the right-hander's throwing arm three inches shorter than the left arm. He played three years of high school baseball in Reading and attended Wyomissing Poly two years. Caruthersville, MO (KOML) manager Harrison Wickel, a Reading native, needed an infielder in 1937 and signed the 18-year-old Kurowski for $70 per month. In 1938, the 5-foot-11-inch, 192-pound Kurowski led the MAL with a .386 batting average at Portsmouth, OH. Kurowski played in the St. Louis (NL) farm system until he and Stan Musial (BB) were promoted from Rochester, NY (IL) to the Cardinals in September 1941. Amid his baseball success, Kurowski experienced personal tragedy. As he prepared for his first professional baseball assignment in 1937, his brother Frank was killed in a mining mishap. Kurowski's father collapsed from a fatal heart attack while the infielder tried to win a position on the Cardinals during spring training in 1942.

From 1942 to 1947, Kurowski started at third base for St. Louis and remained a paradigm of consistency. He crowded home plate and used a 33-ounce, 34½-inch bat, hitting .323 in 1945, .301 in 1946, and .310 in 1947. Kurowski, who enjoyed a 22-game hitting streak in 1943, recorded career highs of 27 home runs, 104 RBIs, and 108 runs scored in 1947. Walker Cooper (S), Kurowski, and Danny Litwhiler belted consecutive home runs in a 1944 contest. Kurowski possessed decent speed despite a stocky build. Musial noted that it seemed that whenever a pitcher brushed back or knocked down Kurowski, he would hit the next pitch over the fence. Kurowski annihilated left-handed pitching.

Kurowski teamed with Musial, Red Schoendienst (BB), Marty Marion (BB), Enos Slaughter (BB), and Cooper to give the Cardinals one of the most imposing batting orders of the 1940s. In 1942, the Cardinals won a franchise-high 106 games and the NL pennant. Kurowski's greatest thrill came against the New York Yankees in the fifth game of the 1942 World Series, when his two-run home run off Red Ruffing (BB) won the game and the World Championship. Kurowski's winner's share of $6,192 surpassed what he made the entire regular season. In the 1943 fall classic, Kurowski hit .222, and the Yankees dropped the Cardinals in five games. He experienced his second World Championship in 1944, when the Cardinals defeated the St. Louis Browns in six games. Kurowski played a central role in the Cardinals' two-game sweep of the Brooklyn Dodgers in the first-ever major league playoff in 1946. He drove in the tying run and scored the winning run in the first game and plated two runs in the second game. Kurowski batted .296 with five RBIs against the Boston Red Sox (AL) in the 1946 World Series, which the Cardinals won, 4–3.

An increasingly painful right arm limited Kurowski to 77 games and a .214 batting average in 1948. Thirteen operations on his arm and elbow had taken a heavy toll, forcing Kurowski to retire after playing 10 games in 1949. Kurowski enjoyed his nine years with St. Louis because the Cardinals finished first four times and second five times. He made 925 hits in 916 games, scored 518 runs, hit 106 home runs, tallied 529 RBIs, and batted .286. He led NL third basemen three times in assists and twice in putouts.

For the rest of the 1949 season, Kurowski managed the Cardinal farm club in Lynchburg, VA (PiL). He discovered talent and enjoyed managing, piloting St. Louis farm teams through the 1962 season in Allentown, PA (ISL), Peoria, IL (3IL), Billings, MT (PrL), Denver, CO (WL), Winnipeg, Canada (NoL), and Tulsa, OK (TL). Kurowski managed the New York Mets' (NL) top farm club at Buffalo, NY (IL) in 1964 and took the reins at Reading, PA (EL), a Cleveland Indian (AL) affiliate, in 1965. He later worked as an inspector of weights and measures for Berk County, PA. He married Joan Setley in November 1941 and lives near Reading in Shillington, PA, where he enjoys visits with his four children, George, Jr., Joanne, James, and Georgeann, and plays golf twice a week.

BIBLIOGRAPHY: David Craft and Tom Owens, *Redbirds Revisited* (Chicago, IL, 1990); Stan Musial and Bob Broeg, *Stan Musial "The Man's" Own Story* (Garden City, NY, 1964); Michael Shatzkin, ed., *The Ballplayers* (New York, 1990); Rich Westcott, *Diamond Greats* (Westport, CT, 1988).

Frank J. Olmsted

LANE, Ferdinand Cole "F.C." (b. October 25, 1885, near Moorehead, MN; d. April 20, 1984, Hyannis, MA), writer, was the fourth child of Alpheus Ferdinand Lane and the third (and youngest) child of Alpheus's second wife,

Mary (Cole) Lane. Born on a wheat farm, Lane moved with his family to Minneapolis, MN, Akron, OH, Canton, OH, and Lowell, MA, before settling at age seven in Truro, MA, on Cape Cod. Six years later the Lanes moved to Marion, MA, where Ferdinand completed his secondary education at Tabor Academy. He attended Boston University for seven years, receiving a B.A. degree in 1907. Lane worked during graduate school as an assistant biologist for Boston University and the Massachusetts Commission of Fisheries and Game.

After spending half a year in a log cabin in Alberta to strengthen his weak lungs, Lane found employment writing for *BM* in Boston, MA, and later in New York. He soon was named editor. Under his leadership, *BM* became the game's premier monthly and devoted extensive and detailed analysis to baseball's personnel, events, and styles of play. Besides writing several hundred articles for *BM*, Lane performed ghostwriting and syndicate work. His 1925 instructional book *Batting* featured advice from the great hitters of the era.

After 27 years with *BM*, Lane tired of sportswriting and returned to Cape Cod in the latter 1930s. Despite frequent absence, he regarded Cape Cod as home for the remainder of his life. From 1941 to 1943, he headed the Department of History at Piedmont College in Demorest, GA, and established a journalism program there. Piedmont awarded him an honorary Doctor of Humanities degree in 1941.

A wanderlust first drew Lane to the Mediterranean during his college years. He and his wife Emma, whom he had married in her Brooklyn, NY, home in June 1914, made numerous overseas voyages, traveling around the world six times. In the 1940s and 1950s, Lane wrote several books on geography and nature for adults and youth. In 1958 he published *On Old Cape Cod*, a collection of his poems.

The Lanes lived the final years of their nearly 70-year marriage in a Cape Cod nursing home, where Emma survived Ferdinand by 10 months.

BIBLIOGRAPHY: *BM*, 1910–1937; Stanley J. Kunitz, ed., *Twentieth Century Authors*, 1st supp. (New York, 1955); F. C. Lane, *Batting* (New York, 1925); Ferdinand C. Lane file, National Baseball Library, Cooperstown, NY; Piedmont College Archives, Demorest, GA.

Frederick Ivor-Campbell

LANIER, Hubert Max (b. August 18, 1915, Denton, NC), player, coach, scout, and manager, is the son of Stephen Ashley Lanier, a farmer and carpenter, and Remetta (Morris) Lanier, of Irish, English, and French descent, and graduated from Denton High School. He threw right-handed as a child, but a broken arm forced him to switch to left-handed. Although winning an athletic scholarship to Duke University, he signed with the St. Louis Cardinals (NL) in 1934 and joined the Class B Greensboro, NC (PiL) club.

He left after a week to play semiprofessional baseball in North Carolina. Lanier accepted assignment to the Cardinals' top farm club in Columbus, OH (IL) in 1937, winning 10 of 14 decisions. He compiled 2 victories and 4 defeats in trials with St. Louis in 1938 and 1939. From 1940 to 1942, Cardinal skipper Billy Southworth (BB) used Lanier as a spot starter and reliever with excellent results. Lanier posted a 20–14 record while starting and a 12–6 record from the bullpen. In 1943, he won 15 decisions and lost 7 with a 1.90 ERA. In 1944, he followed with 17 wins and a career-high 141 strikeouts. Lanier pitched for the Cardinals in three straight World Series from 1942 to 1944, winning 2 of 3 decisions and recording a 1.71 ERA in 31.2 innings.

The 5-foot-11-inch, 180-pound southpaw entered the U.S. Army in 1945 at Ft. Bragg, NC, and played on the army baseball team to entertain troops. By spring training 1946, Lanier returned to a Cardinal uniform. After winning his first six starts, Lanier accepted a $125,000 contract from Jorge Pasquel and Bernardo Pasquel to play five years in their MEL. He had made only $11,000 the year before. Lanier, therefore, joined Cardinal second baseman Lou Klein and reliever Fred Martin in jumping to Veracruz, Mexico (MEL). After the 1947 season, the Pasquels broke their contract with Lanier. The major leagues banned Lanier for five years, causing him to play semiprofessional ball in Canada in 1948. Lanier and Martin then brought a $2.5 million lawsuit against major league baseball. The case settled out of court, with Lanier, Martin, and Klein being reinstated by Commissioner Happy Chandler (BB). Lanier and Martin rejoined the Cardinals in 1949. Lanier struggled to get back in shape, winning 5 and losing 4 in 15 starts and taking 11 of 20 decisions each of the next two seasons. St. Louis traded Lanier to the New York Giants (NL) in December 1951 for Eddie Stanky (S), who was named Cardinal manager. Released by the Giants following the 1952 season, Lanier pitched in 10 games and lost his only decision for the St. Louis Browns (AL) in 1953. His major league record included 327 games, 1,618 innings, 108 wins, 82 losses, 17 saves, and 821 strikeouts.

Lanier's first wife, Lillie Belle Lanier, died in an automobile accident. Their son, Hal, played infield in the major leagues for 10 years, coached for the St. Louis Cardinals, and managed the Houston Astros (NL). Lanier and his second wife, Evelyn Jane, were married on August 29, 1948. Lanier worked as a representative of A. G. Edwards Investments and owned a restaurant in St. Petersburg, FL, for several years. He scouted for the San Francisco Giants in 1961 and 1962 and managed the Lexington, NC, Giants (WCL) from 1963 to 1966 and the Batavia, NY, Trojans (NYPL) in 1967. Lanier, who suffered a heart attack in 1968, is retired and lives in Dunnellon, FL.

BIBLIOGRAPHY: Bob Broeg, *Redbirds: A Century of Cardinals' Baseball* (St. Louis, MO, 1981); David Croft and Tom Owens, *Redbirds Revisited* (Chicago, IL, 1990); Max

Lanier file, National Baseball Library, Cooperstown, NY; Stan Musial and Bob Broeg, *Stan Musial, "The Man's" Own Story* (Garden City, NY, 1964).

Frank J. Olmsted

LANSFORD, Carney Ray (b. February 7, 1957, San Jose, CA), player, is the son of Tony Ray Lansford and Bobbye (Wells) Lansford. Two brothers followed Carney into professional baseball. Phil was selected number one by the Cleveland Indians (AL) in 1978, while Joe was chosen first by the San Diego Padres (NL) the following year.

The California Angels (AL) drafted the six-foot-two-inch, 195-pound third baseman out of Wilcox High School in San Jose in the third round of the 1975 free agent draft. The Angels assigned Lansford to Idaho Falls, ID (PrL) in 1975 and Class A Quad Cities (ML) in 1976. For Class AA El Paso, TX (TL) in 1977, he batted .332 and led TL third basemen in every major defensive category.

Lansford, who batted and threw right-handed, began the 1978 season with California (AL) and was named Angels Rookie of the Year, finishing third in the AL balloting. After pacing the AL in putouts (135) and fielding average (.983) in 1979, he repeated in 1980 as putout leader (151) and led the AL in sacrifice flies (11). The Angels traded Lansford to the Boston Red Sox (AL) in December 1980. He led the AL in hitting with a .336 batting average in 1981, the first right-hander to win the title in a decade. To make room for hitting star Wade Boggs,* the Red Sox traded Lansford in December 1982 to the Oakland Athletics (AL).

Known for his bat control and clutch hitting, he ranks among the leaders in most of the Athletics' offensive categories. He hit .300 or higher three times with Oakland, finishing second in the AL with a .336 batting average in 1989 and making his only All-Star Game appearance in 1988. Lansford played in five AL Championship Series, appearing with California in 1979 and with Oakland from 1988 to 1990 and in 1992. In 1989, he paced all Athletics hitters in the AL Championship Series, batting .455 against the Toronto Blue Jays to help the Athletics prevail, 4–1. He made seven hits and batted .438, as Oakland swept the San Francisco Giants in the earthquake-delayed World Series.

An injury in a 1991 snowmobile accident limited Lansford to only five games. He retired at the end of the 1992 season with a 15-year .290 batting average, a .411 slugging percentage, and 2,074 hits, including 332 doubles, 40 triples, and 151 home runs. A sure-handed fielder, he led the AL four times in fielding average and finished tenth all-time among third basemen with a career .966 average.

Lansford resides in Baker City, OR, with his wife Debbie and their two sons and enjoys hunting and other outdoor sports with former teammate Joe Rudi.

BIBLIOGRAPHY: *The Baseball Encyclopedia*, 9th ed. (New York, 1993); Peter Gammons, "Carney Lansford: A Batting Champion Without FanFare," *BD* 41 (January 1982), pp. 42–45; Robert E. Kelly, *Baseball's Best: Hall of Fame Pretenders Active in the Eighties* (Jefferson, NC, 1988); Carrie Seidman, "Carney Lansford: He'll Be One of the Stars of the '80s!" *BD* 39 (February 1980), pp. 63–65; Mike Shatzkin, ed., *The Ballplayers* (New York, 1990); John Thorn and Pete Palmer, eds., *Total Baseball*, 3rd ed. (New York, 1993); *TSN Official Baseball Register*, 1986.

Gaymon L. Bennett

LARKIN, Henry E. "Ted" (b. January 12, 1863, Reading, PA; d. January 31, 1942, Reading, PA), player and manager, began his professional baseball career in 1883 as an outfielder for his hometown Reading, PA, team (ISL) and made his major league debut in May 1884 with the Philadelphia Athletics (AA). With the Athletics, Larkin played the outfield from 1884 through 1887 and the next season moved to first base, the position he played for the rest of his career. In 1885 and 1886, Larkin led the AA in doubles, helping Philadelphia record two consecutive third-place finishes. Larkin, who batted and threw right-handed, enjoyed his best season in 1886, when he hit .319, collected 180 hits, and scored 133 runs. In six years with Philadelphia, he compiled an impressive .325 batting average and scored more than 100 runs on four occasions.

Unhappy in the AA, the 5-foot-10-inch, 175-pound Larkin jumped to the fledgling PL in 1890, joining well-known infielders Ed Delahanty (BB) and Patsy Tebeau (S) on the Cleveland Infants club. Larkin hit a personal-high .332 that season and piloted Cleveland to a 27–33 record as one of the three managers the team employed that year. In 1891 Larkin returned to his former Philadelphia Athletics (AA) team, where he hit .279 and slammed a career-high 10 home runs. The next year, Larkin signed with the Washington Senators of the newly expanded 12-team NL. The lowly Senators finished in tenth place in 1892 and twelfth place in 1893, as Larkin hit .295 and averaged 115 hits for those two seasons. During his 10-year career, Larkin batted a respectable .303 and collected 1,430 hits in 1,184 games. On June 7, 1892, against Cincinnati in the nation's capital, he collected 6 base hits to become only the fifteenth major league player to accomplish that feat.

BIBLIOGRAPHY: *The Baseball Encyclopedia*, 9th ed. (New York, 1993); Craig Carter, ed., *TSN Complete Baseball Record Book*, 1994 ed. (St. Louis, MO, 1994); Craig Carter, ed., *TSN Daguerreotypes*, 8th ed. (St. Louis, MO, 1990); Chicago (IL) *Tribune*, June 8, 1892; Henry E. Larkin file, National Baseball Library, Cooperstown, NY; John Thorn and Pete Palmer, eds., *Total Baseball*, 3rd ed. (New York, 1993); Robert L. Tiemann and Mark Rucker, *Nineteenth Century Stars* (Kansas City, MO, 1989).

Raymond D. Kush

LARSEN, Don James "Gooneybird" (b. August 7, 1929, Michigan City, IN), player, enjoyed a legendary career. His 2–0 perfect game on October 8, 1956, against the Brooklyn Dodgers (NL) in the fifth game of the World Series at Yankee Stadium remains one of the greatest pitching feats in all of baseball history. Pitching without a windup, he struck out pinch hitter Loren Dale Mitchell* with umpire Babe Pinelli* behind the plate for his twenty-seventh straight out. The final out came on only his ninety-seventh pitch of the contest, played before 64,519 fans.

The six-foot-four-inch, 230-pound right-hander is the son of James Henry Larsen, a jeweler, and Charlotte Gimple (Brown) Larsen, and broke into professional baseball with Aberdeen, SD (NoL) in 1947. Two seasons later, he pitched for Springfield, IL (3IL), and Globe-Miami, AZ (ArTL). He split the 1950 season with Wichita, KS (WL) and Wichita Falls, TX (BStL). The St. Louis Browns (AL) assigned him to their San Antonio, TX (TL) roster for the 1951–1952 seasons, but Larsen spent those campaigns in military service. After an undistinguished minor league career in which his best season was his 17–11 record with Aberdeen in 1948, Larsen joined the St. Louis Browns in 1953 without ever pitching an inning for San Antonio.

Larsen compiled a 7–12 win–loss mark his first season with the Browns. When the Browns moved to Baltimore in 1954, Larsen became the mainstay of the Orioles' pitching staff with a 3–21 mark. Two of his 3 wins came against the New York Yankees, who had won 103 games but still lost the AL pennant to the Cleveland Indians. The Yankees acquired Larsen in November 1954 in an 18-player deal, which included Larsen's soulmate "Bullet Bob" Turley. Yankee general manager George Weiss (BB) believed that Larsen possessed more potential than Turley. Larsen had shown great promise with the Browns but had driven manager Marty Marion (BB) to distraction with his curfew violations. Larsen married his first wife, Vivian, a telephone operator, in April 1955.

The New York Yankees sent Larsen in 1955 to the Denver, CO, Bears (AA), where he compiled a 9–1 mark for manager Ralph Houk (S). The same season saw Larsen finish 9–2 with the Yankees. Although compiling an 11–5 record in 1956, Larsen had gotten off to a bad start during spring training. He wrapped his car around a telephone pole after falling asleep at the wheel at 5:00 A.M. in St. Petersburg, FL, prompting manager Casey Stengel (BB) to quip, "He was probably out mailing a letter."

After Larsen slipped to 6–7 in 1959, the Yankees traded him to the Kansas City Athletics (AL). Larsen struggled with a 1–10 mark there. Called "Gooneybird," which is how he addressed everyone else, Larsen improved to a 7–2 mark for the Chicago White Sox (AL) in 1961. He pitched for the San Francisco Giants (NL) from 1962 to 1964 and the Houston Colt-.45's-Astros (NL) in 1964 and 1965 before returning to Baltimore for his last hurrah in 1965. The last active member of the St. Louis Browns, Larsen appeared in his final three major league games with the Chicago Cubs (NL) in 1967. He then pitched in the minor leagues until he was nearly 40.

Larsen pitched 1,548 innings, compiling an 81–91 win–loss mark with a

3.78 ERA, 44 complete games, 11 shutouts, 725 walks, and 849 strikeouts. Larsen was credited with a World Series win for San Francisco over the New York Yankees, giving him a composite 4–2 mark and a 2.75 ERA in five classics. Larsen, who pinch-hit 66 times, batted .242 lifetime. Larsen set a major league record for pitchers with 7 straight hits for St. Louis in 1953. Four of his 14 career homers came in 1958, when he hit .306 for New York. Larsen's .371 career slugging average ranks tenth highest among twentieth-century pitchers. He lives in Hayden Lake, ID, with his second wife, Corrine (Bruess) Larsen, after retiring as a salesman with the Blake, Moffet, and Thomas Paper Company in San Jose, CA, and has one son, Don Scott.

BIBLIOGRAPHY: Bill Borst, ed., *Ables to Zoldak*, vol. 2 (St. Louis, MO, 1989); Peter Golenbock, *Dynasty: The New York Yankees, 1949–1964* (New York, 1975); Gene Karst and Martin Jones, Jr., *Who's Who in Professional Baseball* (New Rochelle, NY, 1973); John Schulian, *TSN*, October 31, 1981, p. 16; Mike Shatzkin, ed., *The Ballplayers* (New York, 1990); Art Spander, "Fans Won't Let Larsen Forget His Perfecto," *TSN*, October 23, 1976, p. 11; Rich Westcott, *Diamond Greats* (Westport, CT, 1988).

William A. Borst

LARY, Frank Strong "Mule" "Yankee Killer" (b. April 10, 1931, Northport, AL), player, is the son of J. Milton "Mitt" Lary, a farmer, and Margaret Lary. Lary, one of seven boys, grew up on a farm about five miles from Northport. "Mitt" Lary, a former semiprofessional pitcher, encouraged his sons to pitch after farm chores. Five of the seven Lary boys lettered in baseball for the University of Alabama. Frank, a 5-foot-11-inch, 180-pound right-hander and the smallest of the brothers, proved the most competitive and ultimately the most successful. Although the top punter in Alabama high school competition, Lary gave up football to concentrate on pitching for the University of Alabama team under manager Joe Sewell (BB). After his sophomore year at Alabama, Lary signed with the Detroit Tigers (AL) in 1950 for a modest bonus of about $15,000.

Lary split his first professional baseball season between Tiger farm teams in Thomasville, GA (GFL) and Jamestown, NY (PoL) and then was drafted for military service. Discharged in time for the 1953 season, Lary won 17 games for Buffalo, NY (IL) and spent spring training with the Detroit Tigers in 1954. "He just couldn't get the ball over the plate," complained Tigers manager Fred Hutchinson.* Detroit sent Lary back to Buffalo, where he again pitched well. He finished the 1954 campaign with Detroit and made the Tigers rotation in 1955, winning 14 games. Mixing a fastball, curve, sinker, and occasional knuckler, Lary became a mainstay with the Tigers. "Once the fellow learned the knuckler," slugger Ted Williams (BB) remarked, "he was able to keep you guessing. You never know what he's going to throw, and he's got the guts to fight you all the way." Lary started more than 30 games for seven consecutive seasons and led the AL in innings pitched and complete games three times. In 1962, arm problems caused him to struggle, relegating him to a spot starter role. The Tigers released him in 1964. Lary pitched briefly for the Milwaukee Braves (NL), New York Mets (NL), and Chicago White Sox (AL), retiring in the 1965 season.

Lary, who made the AL All-Star team in both 1960 and 1961, won 21 games in 1956 and 23 decisions in 1961. He closed his major league career with 128 victories, 116 losses, and a 3.49 ERA. Lary married Emma Lou Barton in July 1951 and operates a carpet cleaning business with his brother Al in Northport, AL.

BIBLIOGRAPHY: Furman Bisher, "How Frank Lary Learned to Pitch," *Sport* 16 (August 1961), pp. 28–29, 58–59; Gene Karst and Martin J. Jones, *Who's Who in Professional Baseball* (New Rochelle, NY, 1973), p. 550.

Lloyd J. Graybar

LATHAM, Walter Arlington "Arlie" "The Freshest Man on Earth" (b. March 15, 1860, West Lebanon, NH; d. November 29, 1952, Garden City, NY), player, umpire, manager, coach, executive, and press box attendant, enjoyed a baseball career that spanned an incredible 76 years. The renowned free spirit earned his nickname from a song written for him as one of baseball's unique personalities. He led baseball in enthusiasm, alternating as a fierce competitor, cheerleader, clown, and merciless heckler.

A diminutive, five-foot-eight-inch 150-pounder, the stellar third baseman batted and threw right-handed and began his professional baseball career in 1875 at age 16. Latham played eight years in various cities before joining the St. Louis Browns (AA) and was the spark plug of Chris Von der Ahe's (BB) highly successful teams, winners of four consecutive AA pennants. He played part of the 1890 season with the Chicago Pirates (PL) but moved to the Cincinnati Reds (NL) later in the year. After spending five seasons there, Latham found his playing days essentially over. He made several subsequent token appearances, the last coming at age 50. Latham stole a base, probably making him the oldest player to do so. He managed two games while still a player and then piloted in minor leagues. He umpired in the NL in 1899, 1900, and 1902 and became baseball's first full-time and paid coach for the 1909 New York Giants, teaching players the art of base stealing. The 1911 Giants stole a record 347 bases on their way to the NL pennant.

Latham's popularity carried over to the theater, where he performed during a short stage career. He began acting while still in baseball. After World War I, he lived 17 years in England and served as administrator (commissioner) of baseball. Latham mingled with British royalty, becoming a close friend of the Prince of Wales. Upon returning to the United States, he spent his last 16 years working for the New York clubs. Latham served as custodian of the New York Yankees (AL) press box when he died at age 92.

Latham batted over .300 three times in his 17 major league seasons and stole over 100 bases twice. He led his league in defensive statistics numerous times and possessed one of the strongest arms in the game. He remains in the record books as a career standout at his position, ranking eighth in assists, twelfth in putouts, and sixth in total chances. In addition, he ranks seventh on the all-time list in runs scored per game. For his career, he played in 1,627 games, batted .269, stole 739 bases, and scored 1,478 runs.

Latham was married and the father of three daughters, Mrs. James Tait, Mrs. Frank Wakeman, and Mrs. Claude Sanford, and one son, Walter, Jr.

BIBLIOGRAPHY: Garden City (NY) *News*, December 4, 1952; John R. Husman, interview with Robert A. Latham, November 8, 1993, St. Petersburg, FL; Robert A. Latham, letter to John R. Husman, November 9, 1993; John Thorn and Pete Palmer, eds., *Total Baseball*, 3rd ed. (New York, 1993); Robert L. Tiemann and Mark Rucker, eds., *Nineteenth Century Stars* (Kansas City, MO, 1989); Toledo (OH) *Blade*, May 18, 1897.

John R. Husman

LAU, Charles Richard "Charlie" (b. April 12, 1933, Romulus, MI; d. March 18, 1984, Key Colony Beach, FL), player and coach, signed as a catcher with the Detroit Tigers (AL) in 1952 and enjoyed immediate success at Jamestown, NY (NYPL), batting .332 with 58 RBIs in 92 games. Lau spent two years in the U.S. Army but returned to professional baseball in 1955 at Durham, NC (CrL) and belted 18 home runs with a .293 batting average. He married Barbara McCommins on September 16, 1955. From 1956 to 1959, the six-foot, 185-pound, right-handed-throwing, left-handed-hitting receiver played for Charleston, WV (AA). The Tigers briefly called him up in 1956, 1958, and 1959 and on October 15, 1959, traded him to the Milwaukee Braves (NL). After the Braves released Lau during the 1961 season, the Baltimore Orioles (AL) signed him. Lau batted .294 in 81 games for the Orioles in 1962, hitting four doubles in a game on July 13. Baltimore traded Lau to the Kansas City Athletics (AL) on July 1, 1963, and then reacquired him from Kansas City on June 15, 1964. On June 24, 1964, Lau made two pinch hits in one inning. He recorded a .295 batting average in 1965 with the Orioles, but surgery on his right elbow in 1966 limited him to pinch hitting with Baltimore and the Atlanta Braves (NL) in 1967. Lau's major league career included 527 games, 298 hits, 105 runs, 16 home runs, 140 RBIs, and a .255 batting average.

Lau managed Shreveport, LA (TL) to a second-place finish in 1968 before returning to the Baltimore Orioles as hitting coach for the 1969 campaign. The Orioles, however, did not renew his contract when he demanded $40,000 a year, double what most coaches then earned. He served as hitting coach for the Oakland Athletics (AL) in 1970, the Kansas City Royals (AL) from 1971 to 1978, the New York Yankees (AL) from 1979 to 1981, and the Chicago White Sox (AL) from 1982 until his death.

Lau, regarded as one of the best hitting instructors in baseball, had carefully observed the mechanics of hitters as a catcher. He questioned age-old maxims of good hitting, spending countless hours analyzing videotapes of hitters until he could identify what he thought were the mechanics of the best hitters. He developed his "absolutes for hitting," the basis for his two highly acclaimed books, *The Art of Hitting .300* and *The Winning Hitter.*

Lau established four precepts of hitting: "Use the entire field, always keep your head down, rock back before moving forward in your swing, and hit through the ball." One of Lau's greatest pupils, the Royals' George Brett (BB), reviewed the precepts every time he stood in the on-deck circle. Lau understood that most players lacked power but could learn to knock line drives up the middle and poke hard ground balls into the gaps. Lau, recognized as an excellent teacher, said, "Knowing what I do about players, I almost think I'd rather err by praising them too much than by not doing it enough."

During the 1983 season, Lau voluntarily resigned his coaching position so that Chicago White Sox scout Loren Babe, who was suffering from lung cancer, could gain enough time to qualify for a 10-year major league pension. Babe died in February 1984, just one month before Lau succumbed to colon cancer.

BIBLIOGRAPHY: Richie Ashburn, "Hitting According to the Gospel of Charlie Lau," *BD* 42 (June 1983), pp. 48–49; Del Black, "Royals Retain Herzog, Drop Lau as Coach," *TSN*, November 4, 1978, p. 46; *TSN Official Baseball Register*, 1967; Charlie Lau with Alfred Glossbrenner, *The Art of Hitting .300* (New York, 1980); Charlie Lau with Alfred Glossbrenner, *The Winning Hitter* (New York, 1984); Daniel Okrent, *Nine Innings* (New York, 1985); Michael Shatzkin, ed., *The Ballplayers* (New York, 1990).

Frank J. Olmsted

LAW, Vernon Sanders "Vern" "Deacon" (b. March 12, 1930, Meridian, ID), player and coach, is the father of professional baseball player Vance Law. He is the second of three children of Jesse Law, a farmer, machinist, and mechanic of English descent, and Melva (Sanders) Law, of Swedish descent. He grew up in Meridian, winning 12 high school varsity letters and leading his baseball and football teams to state championships. He attended Boise JC and then signed with the Pittsburgh Pirates (NL) as a pitcher in 1948, partly through the efforts of Idaho Senator Herman Welker and singer Bing Crosby. Pittsburgh assigned him to Santa Rosa, CA (FWL) in 1948, to Davenport, IA (3IL) in 1949, and to New Orleans, LA (SA) in 1950 before calling him up to the Pirates.

Law served in the U.S. Army during the 1952 and 1953 seasons and then joined Bob Friend (BB) as one of the mainstays of the Pirates' pitching staff, helping them rise to respectability. In 1955 he pitched 18 innings in a game and then pitched 13 more innings four days later. He finished with a 14–12 mark in 1958 and an 18–9 record in 1959. Law then produced a Cy Young

Award–winning season in 1960, making the NL All-Star team and compiling a 20–9 slate with an NL-leading 18 complete games. That fall in the World Series he won 2 games against the New York Yankees and pitched well in the decisive seventh game, contributing significantly to the Pirates' upset victory. An injured ankle led to a rotator cuff injury in 1961, as his record fell to 3–4. But by 1964 he resumed his workhorse status, pitching 192 innings and winning 12 games. His best overall season may have been 1965, when he won 17 of 26 decisions with a 2.15 ERA. He received the Lou Gehrig Memorial Award as Comeback Player of the Year. His performance then declined again. He retired after a 2–6 performance in 1967. Overall, in 16 major league years, the six-foot-two-inch, 195-pound right-hander won 162 games, lost 147 decisions, and hurled 2,672 innings with a 3.77 ERA.

Subsequently, Law coached for the Pirates in 1968 and 1969, for 10 years at Brigham Young University, and for 2 years in Japan. After coaching at Denver, CO (AA) in 1982–1983, he left baseball to pursue business in Provo, UT.

Law married his high school sweetheart, VaNita Cora McGuire, on March 3, 1950. They have six children, Veldon, Veryl, Vaughn, Varlin, VaLynda, and Vance. He is an ordained minister of the Church of Jesus Christ of Latter Day Saints.

A rugged and durable performer, Law won acclaim mainly for his leadership of the 1960 World Champions.

BIBLIOGRAPHY: Richard L. Burtt, *The Pittsburgh Pirates: A Pictorial History* (Virginia Beach, VA, 1977); *CB* (1961), pp. 255–256; Dick Groat and Bill Surface, *The World Champion Pittsburgh Pirates* (New York, 1961); Vernon Law file, National Baseball Library, Cooperstown, NY; Bob Smizik, *The Pittsburgh Pirates: An Illustrated History* (New York, 1990); Luther Spoehr, interview with Vernon Law, July 8, 1993.

Luther W. Spoehr

LEE, Thornton Starr "Lefty" (b. September 13, 1906, Sonoma, CA), player, was one of four children of Starr Lee, a railroad worker, and Celia (Steinhoff) Lee. The six-foot-three-inch, 205-pound left-hander, an impressive figure on the mound, threw a deceptively sinking fastball. It took him a decade, however, to establish himself as a major league pitcher. He spent six seasons with seven minor league clubs and four disappointing campaigns with the Cleveland Indians (AL) before starring with Jimmy Dykes's (BB) Chicago White Sox (AL) in 1937.

He graduated from high school and spent a year at California Polytechnic Institute before signing with the San Francisco, CA, Seals (PCL). San Francisco optioned him in 1928 to Salt Lake City, UT (UIL), where he shared pitching duties with rookie Curt Davis.* With fifth-place Toledo, OH (AA) in 1933, he compiled a 13–11 record in 220 innings pitched and was purchased by the Cleveland Indians. Under managers Walter Johnson (BB), a notoriously poor handler of pitchers, and Steve O'Neill (S), Lee struggled to a 12–17 mark between 1933 and 1936.

The Indians traded Lee to the Chicago White Sox in a three-way exchange of pitchers that sent Chicago's Jack Salveson to the Washington Senators (AL) and Washington's Earl Whitehill (BB) to Cleveland. Lee quickly became one of the AL's premier left-handers, largely owing to the guidance of pitching coach Herold "Muddy" Ruel. Lee attained his peak in 1941, when he pitched 300 innings while winning 22 and losing 11 decisions. His 2.37 ERA and 30 complete games led the AL, although the White Sox played only .500 baseball in achieving third place. His opponents' .286 on-base percentage was the lowest allowed by any AL pitcher, while their combined .232 batting average was ranked the third lowest. As the first White Sox hurler to win more than 20 games since Ted Lyons's (BB) 22 in 1930, Lee received a $2,500 bonus.

Bone chips and a fracture in Lee's throwing arm sidelined him for the next three seasons. He recovered to post a 15–12 record in 1945, but the White Sox released him after two more minimal seasons. His baseball career ended with the New York Giants (NL) at age 42. In 16 major league seasons, he won 117 games and lost 124 with a 3.56 ERA. Subsequently, he worked as a cost analyst for an engineering firm and resided in Tucson, AZ.

He and his wife, Esther Hill, whom he married in 1929, had one son, Donald, a right-hander who compiled a 40–44 record with seven teams in a nine-year major league career from 1957 to 1966. Ted Williams (BB) hit home runs off both Thornton and Don, the only instance in baseball history of one hitter victimizing both father and son.

BIBLIOGRAPHY: *The Baseball Encyclopedia*, 9th ed. (New York, 1993); Thornton Lee file, National Baseball Library, Cooperstown, NY; A. D. Suehsdorf, telephone interviews with Don Lee, December 29, 1992, and May 19, 1993; John Thorn and Pete Palmer, *Total Baseball*, 3rd ed. (New York, 1993).

A. D. Suehsdorf

LEMON, Chester Earl "Chet" (b. December 2, 1955, Jackson, MS), player, performed 16 AL seasons with the Chicago White Sox and Detroit Tigers. He graduated from Fremont High School in Los Angeles, noted for the athletes it has produced in several sports. The six-foot, 190-pound Lemon attended Cerritos College and Pepperdine University. A 1972 Oakland A's (AL) first-round draft selection, he played third base and shortstop in several minor league cities until traded in June 1975 to the Chicago White Sox. In September 1975, after gaining some outfield experience, Lemon was brought up to the major leagues to stay. By 1976, the White Sox made him the regular center fielder. In 1977, Lemon set AL records for most putouts (512) and chances (524) by an outfielder. He eventually set the AL record for most years (5) with 400 or more outfield putouts. Lemon batted .300, .318, .292, and .302 for the White Sox between 1978 and 1981 and played in the 1978 and 1979 All-Star Games.

Chicago traded Lemon to the Detroit Tigers in November 1981. He belted 24 round-trippers in 1983. The right-hand-batting and -throwing Lemon, an important cog in the 1984 "wire-to-wire" world championship juggernaut, played outstanding defense while batting .287 with 20 home runs and 11 game-winning hits. An AL All-Star again, he went hitless in the AL Championship Series against the Kansas City Royals and batted .294 in the World Series against the San Diego Padres. Lemon, an important part of the 1987 Tiger AL East champions, hit .277 with 20 home runs in the regular season and batted .294 with 2 home runs in the 5-game AL Championship Series. The Tigers, however, lost the AL Championship Series to the Minnesota Twins.

By the close of his 16-year major league career in 1990, Lemon sported a .275 career batting average with 1,875 hits, 215 home runs, and 884 RBIs. His 2.59 career average for outfield putouts per game ranked him among the top 10 in major league history. With his crowd-the-plate batting stance, he was hit by 151 pitches to rank fifth on the all-time list. The speedy, hustling, but erratic base runner frequently slid headfirst into first base and stole 58 career bases.

Lemon married Valerie Jones and had four children, Geneva, Chester, Jr., David, and Marcus Devon. After retiring in 1991, he founded Chet Lemon's School of Baseball in Orlando, FL, and resides in Lakeland, FL.

BIBLIOGRAPHY: *Detroit Tiger Yearbooks and Media Guides,* 1982–1990; *The Official Major League Baseball 1991 Statbook* (New York, 1991); Seymour Siwoff et al., *The 1991 Elias Baseball Analyst* (New York, 1991); *TSN Official Baseball Register,* 1991.

Sheldon L. Appleton

LEONARD, Hubert Benjamin "Hub" "Dutch" (b. April 16, 1892, Birmingham, OH; d. July 11, 1952, Fresno, CA), player, enjoyed a very successful major league career as a pitcher for much of the period from 1913 through 1925. The 5-foot-10-inch, 185-pounder threw and batted left-handed.

Leonard entered professional baseball off the Santa Clara, CA, College campus in 1912 and spent only a year in the minor leagues at Denver (WL), where he won 22 and lost 9. He pitched for the Boston Red Sox (AL) from 1913 through 1918 and with the Detroit Tigers (AL) from 1919 to 1921 and in 1924 and 1925. A rara avis, Leonard starred as a left-handed spitball pitcher and likewise possessed an excellent fastball. Several indicators attest to his unusual ability. Leonard still holds the one-year major league ERA record at 1.01, set in 1914. In four different years, he ranked among the first five AL pitchers in winning percentage, strikeouts, shutouts, wins, complete games, ERA, and (retroactive) saves. Leonard pitched no-hit games on August 30, 1916, against the St. Louis Browns and on June 3, 1918, against the Detroit Tigers. He defeated the great Grover Cleveland Alexander (BB) of the Philadelphia Phillies (NL), 2–1, in the 1915 World Series and Rube Marquard (BB) of the Brooklyn Robins (NL), 6–2, in the 1916 World Series. Leonard's career featured 138 wins, 113 losses, a .550 winning percentage, a 3.25 ERA, 1,150 strikeouts in 2,190 innings, and 32 shutouts.

Leonard did not pitch many years or achieve career statistics of National Baseball Hall of Fame proportions because of his obstreperous, vain, suspicious, and defiant personality. He repeatedly disputed with baseball authorities, engaged in salary disputes, and more than once quit his team. In 1926, he accused superstars Tris Speaker (BB) and Ty Cobb (BB) of knowingly participating in Cleveland's alleged deliberate loss to Detroit on September 25, 1919. A careful review of the circumstantial evidence indicates that Leonard and two other players bet on the game but that Cleveland's loss was not prearranged. Cobb's and Speaker's exoneration by Commissioner Kenesaw Mountain Landis (BB) was justified. Leonard probably sought revenge against Detroit manager Cobb for releasing him in 1925 after a successful but incomplete half season of service.

Leonard married actress Sybil Hitt in 1917 and was divorced in 1932. His second wife, Viola, survived him. Leonard enjoyed outstanding success in California viniculture, leaving to his widow and brothers an estate worth more than $2 million.

BIBLIOGRAPHY: *The Baseball Encyclopedia*, 9th ed. (New York, 1993); Tyrus R. Cobb, *My Life in Baseball, the True Record* (New York, 1961); Dutch Leonard file, National Baseball Library, Cooperstown, NY; *NYT*, December 21–31, 1926; January 6, 1927; January 10–15, 1927; January 24, 1927; January 25, 1927; January 28, 1927; January 29, 1927; July 12, 1952.

Lowell L. Blaisdell

LEWIS, John Kelly Jr. "Buddy" (b. August 10, 1916, Gastonia, NC), player and coach, is a six-foot-six-inch 175-pounder from a small-town environment. His parents were John Kelly Lewis, Sr., and Ada Mae Lewis. Lewis, talented in several sports, played football one year for Wake Forest College but did not graduate. Junior Legion baseball, however, primarily attracted him. Although virtually ignored at a New York Giants (NL) tryout camp at age 18, Lewis persevered and played third base for the Chattanooga, TN (SA) club in 1934. After Lewis spent just two years in the minors, the parent Washington Senators (AL) promoted him in September 1935. Lewis, however, hit only .107 in just eight games. Nonetheless, he played so impressively the following spring that Ossie Bluege (BB), veteran third-sacker for the club, admitted, "That skinny kid is my successor." Opening day presented Lewis a problem with President Franklin D. Roosevelt and a crowd of 34,000 in attendance. An obviously tense Lewis asked manager "Bucky" Harris (BB) to delete him from the lineup, admitting, "I'm just plain scared." Harris commended Lewis for his honesty and saw him hit .291 for his rookie

1936 season. He led the AL in at bats (668) in 1937 and triples (16) in 1939. Lewis was chosen for the AL All-Star team in 1939 and 1947. Around 1940 he began switching to the outfield, but he surely had become an established performer.

Flying became Lewis's second interest. During spring training in 1940, he took flying lessons at an Orlando, FL, airport without President Clark Griffith's (BB) knowledge. He joined the U.S. Army Air Corps in 1942 during World War II and put a transport plane into a dive as a farewell over Griffith Stadium in Washington while his teammates waved from their dugout. Subsequently, he served 15 months overseas in the China-Burma-India Theater, flying some 369 missions in a C-47. For the Burma invasion in 1944, he flew a dual-glider tow over the "Hump." *Yank* commended Lewis's achievement, remarking that it was "done with the same . . . split-second timing" as on the ball field. The Distinguished Flying Cross was awarded him. When Lewis fought overseas, Clark Griffith kept his framed picture on his desk. Lewis named his plane *Old Fox* after his boss.

Lewis resumed his baseball career as an outfielder in 1945, but his crash into a fence severely injured his hip and forced his retirement by 1949. In 11 major league seasons, he batted .297 with 1,563 hits, 71 home runs, and 607 RBIs. He returned to Gastonia, operating his automobile business for the next 30 years, and coaching AmLe teams. He married Frances Oates and had three children. His town named a street after him. He kept flying until 1990, when he sold his Cessna 182, but still retained his commercial license. "He's a real gentleman," one neighbor said, and the baseball world respected him highly as well.

BIBLIOGRAPHY: *The Baseball Encyclopedia*, 9th ed. (New York, 1993); "Buddy Lewis of Senators Hangs Up Spikes at 33," *TSN*, March 8, 1950; "Buddy Lewis Would Pilot Team on Tour," *TSN*, July 26, 1945; Shirley Povich, "Can Buddy Lewis Come Back?" *BD* 8 (May 1949); Shirley Povich, "John 'Buddy' Lewis, a Boy Who Does a Man Size Job," *TSN*, July 23, 1936; Shirley Povich, "Lewis Spikes Capital Tale He'll Doff Spikes Again," *TSN*, November 9, 1949; Shirley Povich, "This Morning," Washington *Post*, February 17, 1944; Jack Smith, "Bud Lewis—Ace of Giant Discards," New York (NY) *Daily News*, August 14, 1938; John Thorn and Pete Palmer, eds., *Total Baseball*, 3rd ed. (New York, 1993).

William J. Miller

LEYLAND, James Richard "Jim" (b. December 15, 1944, Toledo, OH), player and manager, grew up in Perrysburg, OH, as one of seven children of James Leyland, a Libbey-Owens-Ford glass factory foreman, and Veronica Leyland. He played football, basketball, and baseball at Perrysburg High School, graduating in 1963, and then signed as a catcher with the Detroit Tigers (AL). After playing six minor league seasons, he coached with Montgomery, AL (SL) in 1970 and managed Bristol, VA (ApL), Clinton, IA (ML), Montgomery, AL, and Lakeland, FL (FSL), and Evansville, IN (AA), the Tigers' top farm team. He led his minor league teams to postseason play six times in 11 years, three times being named Manager of the Year. From 1982 through 1985, he coached at third base for the Chicago White Sox (AL) under manager Tony LaRussa (S).

Before the 1986 season, Leyland became manager of the Pittsburgh Pirates (NL), a team that had lost 104 games the previous year. The Pirates improved steadily under Leyland for three years, slumped in 1989, then won three consecutive NL East titles. They lost in the NL Championship Series in 1990 to the Cincinnati Reds and to the Atlanta Braves in 1991 and 1992. After the 1992 season, financial pressures forced the virtual dismantling of the team. Expensive stars, such as Barry Bonds,* Doug Drabek, and Jose Lind, were lost to free agency or traded for less distinguished players. The Pirates struggled to a 75–87 mark and a fifth-place finish in 1993, and a 53–61 slate and a third place Central Division finish in the strike-shortened 1994 season.

By the end of 1994, Leyland's 721 victories (against 689 losses) made him the third-winningest manager in Pirates history. He was named NL Manager of the Year by the BBWAA and the *TSN* managers' poll in 1990, finished runner-up for the BBWAA Award in 1991, and shared the *TSN* Award with Tommy Lasorda (S) in 1988. In 1990 he also won the Dapper Dan Man-of-the-Year Award.

Leyland, who resides in Pittsburgh with his second wife, Katie, and their son, Patrick, is active in the Arthritis and Epilepsy foundations and enjoys hunting in the off-season. Generally considered one of the best managers in contemporary baseball, Leyland helped to rebuild a franchise in disarray and then saw his team taken apart by economic forces beyond the club's control. His energy and empathy for players are being tested anew as Pittsburgh again tries to rebuild.

BIBLIOGRAPHY: Jim Leyland file, National Baseball Library, Cooperstown, NY; Peter Pascarelli, *The Toughest Job in Baseball* (New York, 1993); Steve Rushin, "Glad to Be in the Game," *SI* 78 (January 25, 1993), pp. 42–46.

Luther W. Spoehr

LOGAN, John Theodore Jr. "Johnny" "Yachta" (b. March 23, 1927, Endicott, NY), player, performed for the Milwaukee Braves (NL) as a key supporting player on their 1957 World Championship team and 1958 NL pennant winners. He is the son of John Logan, Sr., a Russian-born machinist in the Endicott forging works, and Helen Logan and made All-State in football, baseball, and basketball at Union-Endicott High School. Logan declined several college athletic scholarships and was drafted into the U.S. Army in 1945. He was signed by the Boston Braves (NL) and spent several seasons in the minor leagues as a shortstop. Logan attended Harpur College for 1 year. After beginning his major league career with the Boston Braves in 1951, the scrappy, 5-foot-11-inch, 175-pound shortstop moved with the team to Milwaukee in 1953 and remained there through the 1956–1959 "glory years." The Braves in June 1961 traded Logan to the Pittsburgh Pirates (NL), where he finished his 13-year major league career in 1963.

Logan batted a career-high .297 in 1955, when he led the NL in doubles (37). In 1956, the Braves lost the NL pennant to the Brooklyn Dodgers on the last day of the season. Milwaukee won the 1957 NL flag and defeated the New York Yankees in a seven-game series, featuring three wins by pitcher Lew Burdette (BB). Although Logan hit only .185 for the World Series, his solo home run in the second game contributed to Burdette's 4–2 first victory. In 1958 the Braves topped the NL again but this time lost to the New York Yankees in seven games. Logan batted only .120 in the 1958 fall classic. The following year, Milwaukee tied the Los Angeles Dodgers for first place during the regular season, only to lose two straight contests in a playoff. Logan enjoyed one of his best years in 1959, hitting .291 with 13 home runs.

With the Braves, the right-handed-batting and -throwing Logan was overshadowed by future National Baseball Hall of Famers Henry Aaron (BB), Eddie Mathews (BB), Warren Spahn (BB), and Red Schoendienst (BB) and stars Burdette and Joe Adcock (BB). Usually batting in the second slot between Schoendienst or Billy Bruton (BB) and Mathews, Logan combined steady hitting (.268 lifetime average) with outstanding defensive play at the key shortstop position. His play proved critical to the Braves' success and was recognized by knowledgeable observers. John Thorn and Pete Palmer rate him as the top major league defensive player at any position in 1953 and among the top five in the NL in 1954 and 1957. He made the 1955 and 1958 All-Star teams and received MVP votes four of the five years from 1953 through 1957. In 1,503 games, Logan hit 93 home runs and knocked in 547 runs. He married Dorothy Ahlmeyer in October 1953 and has a stepson, Bruce. They reside in Milwaukee, WI, where Logan sells advertising novelties.

BIBLIOGRAPHY: Red Gleason, "Johnny Logan's A Fighter," *Sport* 21 (June 1956), pp. 42–44, 92–93; Rich Marazzi and Lew Fiorito, *Aaron to Zuverink* (New York, 1982); John Thorn and Pete Palmer, eds., *Total Baseball*, 3rd ed. (New York, 1993).
                                                              Sheldon L. Appleton

LUCAS, Henry Van Noye (b. September 5, 1857, St. Louis, MO; d. November 15, 1910, St. Louis, MO), owner and executive, was a St. Louis businessman and avid baseball enthusiast. He used a million-dollar inheritance from his father, James H. Lucas, to buy his own team and essentially his own league. After being denied an NL franchise, he organized the UA, which competed on a major league level with the NL and the AA in 1884. Lucas was elected UA president because of his baseball and business knowledge and personal wealth, being the fledgling league's driving force and its principal source of enthusiasm, ideas, and capital. He once declared, "I am the Union Association." Many players jumped to the UA from the other leagues, as Lucas made public his disdain for the reserve rule. The UA promised a newer, more exciting, and high-scoring game because of a lively ball.

Lucas owned the St. Louis Maroons (UA) franchise, resplendent in their silk stockings and lamb's wool sweaters, and built for them a spectacular park on his suburban estate. The Palace Park of America seated 10,000 spectators and contained many features, including caged canaries. The Maroons made a shambles of the pennant race with a 94–19 win–loss mark, the all-time best major league record. But his team's enormous success helped kill spectator interest in the UA, which folded after only one season. Lucas lost more than $250,000 in the venture.

In exchange for dropping the UA and reversing his stance on the reserve rule, Lucas was granted an NL franchise for the St. Louis Maroons in 1885. His championship team of the previous year finished in last place in 1885, however, and improved only to sixth place in 1886. The Maroons could not compete with the crosstown St. Louis Browns (AA), who sold beer, played on Sundays, halved ticket prices, and won AA pennants both years.

Lucas left baseball permanently after the 1886 season, his NL experience having cost him over $100,000 in losses. Soon he suffered more business failures and saw his entire fortune disappear. After separating from his wife, Louise (Espenscheid) Lucas, he worked as a railway clerk and later tried other unsuccessful ventures. Upon his death, he was earning only $75 a month as an employee of the St. Louis Street Department.

BIBLIOGRAPHY: Charles C. Alexander, *Our Game* (New York, 1991); *The Baseball Encyclopedia*, 9th ed. (New York, 1993); Harvey Frommer, *Primitive Baseball* (New York, 1988); David Pietrusza, *Major Leagues* (Jefferson, NC, 1991); *SpL*, November 26, 1910; Robert L. Tiemann and Mark Rucker, eds., *Nineteenth Century Stars* (Kansas City, MO, 1989); David Quentin Voigt, *American Baseball*, vol. 1 (Norman, OK, 1966).

John R. Husman

LUDERUS, Frederick William "Fred" "Ludy" (b. September 12, 1885, Milwaukee, WI; d. January 5, 1961, Three Lakes, WI), player, was the youngest of five children of Peter Luderus, a laborer, and Johanna (Bliese) Luderus. Luderus, who batted left-handed but threw right-handed, played four years of minor league baseball. The Chicago Cubs (NL) bought him for $2,200 in 1909, after he led the Class D WIL with a .321 batting average for cellar-dwelling Freeport, IL. Luderus replaced ailing first baseman Frank Chance (BB) for a few games, but the Cubs traded him to the Philadelphia Phillies (NL) in July 1910 for Bill Foxen, a journeyman pitcher.

In 1911, Philadelphia manager "Red" Dooin replaced the elegant, aging Kitty Bransfield at first base with the burly 5-foot-11½-inch, 185-pound Luderus, who batted .301 with 16 homers, 99 RBIs, and 260 total bases in

146 games. Through 1919, Luderus proved a consistent, reliable, yet un-derrated performer. Teammate Gavvy Cravath (BB) overshadowed him as a hitter, while pitchers believed Luderus could not hit curveballs. Luderus, slow afield and on the bases, never led the NL league statistically in anything. Yet his impressive home run production included 16 in 1911, the NL's sec-ond-best total, and 18 in 1913, trailing Cravath by 1. His 56 round-trippers between 1911 and 1914 marked the most ever in a four-year span to that time. Luderus, the first player to blast 2 home runs over the Baker Bowl fence in 1 game, was never lifted for a pinch hitter in a 1,346-game career.

In 1915 he was named team captain and enjoyed his best season at the plate, hitting .315 to help Philadelphia win its first NL pennant and becom-ing the only Phillie able to solve Boston Red Sox pitching in the losing World Series. He pounded the ball for a .438 average and batted in 6 of Philadelphia's 10 runs. In 12 major league seasons, he batted .277, with 251 doubles, 81 home runs, and 647 RBIs. Although leading NL first basemen in errors four times, he compiled a respectable .986 lifetime fielding average and tied a major league record with seven assists in 1 game. Luderus, an "Iron Man," played 533 consecutive games between 1915 and 1919 to set a then–major league record.

After the Phillies released him in 1920, he signed with Toledo, OH (AA) and began a successful eight-year career as a minor league playing manager.

He and his wife Emmy had five children. During retirement, he rebuilt his Wisconsin home with the help of architect Fred "Cy" Williams (BB), the longtime NL outfielder, Phillie teammate, and Three Lakes neighbor.

BIBLIOGRAPHY: *The Baseball Encyclopedia*, 9th ed. (New York, 1993), pp. 182, 217, 1159; J. C. Kofoed, "A Much Under-rated Star," *BM* 11 (July 1915), pp. 33–36; Fred Luderus file, National Baseball Library, Cooperstown, NY; *NYT*, January 6, 1961; *Phillies Report*, August 16, 1990; *TSN*, n.d., 1947; Vital Records, Madison, WI.

                                                                    A. D. Suehsdorf

McBRIDE, James Dickson "Dick" (b. 1845, Philadelphia, PA; d. 1916, Phil-adelphia, PA), player and manager, enjoyed a 16-year career with the Phil-adelphia Athletics. He joined the club at its inception in 1860 as an outfielder but served also as catcher and shortstop and emerged as one of the great pitchers of the decade before the NL's formation.

The five-foot-nine-inch, 150-pound right-hander was noted for a hot tem-per, a sharp tongue, and an inclination to argue with umpires. By 1864, a year after his pitching debut, he was the Athletics' premier hurler. Throwing underhand from a level pitcher's box 50 feet distant from the plate, he was described by the sporting newspaper *New York Clipper*, as "an . . . effective player . . . possessing command of the ball, great speed, considerable powers of endurance, and plenty of pluck withal."

In 1871, when the NA structured itself as a professional league, the Athletics were its first champions and McBride its leading pitcher. To the A's 21–7 record, he contributed 25 complete games, 18 wins, and five losses. He served as team captain or on-field manager and was elected to its board of directors.

He finished 30–14 in 1872, pitching the A's entire schedule for a fourth-place club. In 1873, as the team slipped to fifth, his 24–19 record included a two-hit shutout at Boston, the first "whitewash" ever for the powerful Red Stockings. The *New York Clipper* awarded him "the palm of [pitching] supremacy" for the season, picking him even over the great Albert Spalding (BB). In 1874 McBride again provided all of Philadelphia's 33 wins and 22 losses, all complete games, and compiled a 2.55 ERA.

In midseason, the Athletics and Boston sailed to England for a series of exhibition baseball games and occasional cricket matches against British sides. Head to head, the A's won 8 of 13 games, including a McBride triumph over Spalding. The two pitchers also combined as bowlers to win a cricket match.

Home again, the A's finished third. The *New York Clipper* saw signs of dissension: "Blundering" directors did not permit Captain McBride to "place his men as he wanted them," while the team suffered from "jealousies and weaknesses."

In 1875 McBride achieved his peak performance with 44 wins, 14 losses, 59 complete games, and a 1.97 ERA. The A's once more trailed Boston. But McBride's final game for Philadelphia was a humiliating one. After being hit hard, he was removed by the board of directors and deposed as captain in favor of first baseman Adrian Anson (BB).

A nucleus of the Athletics stayed with the Philadelphia entry in the new NL in 1876, but McBride joined the Boston Red Caps and compiled a 0–4 record that ended his career. Overall, in his six seasons of organized baseball, he recorded 149 wins and 74 losses. Of his 233 starts, 224 were complete games and 10 were shutouts. In 2,048 innings, his ERA was 2.56.

BIBLIOGRAPHY: *Baseball Encyclopedia*, 9th ed. (New York, 1993); New York (NY) *Clipper*, 1864–1873; Preston Orem, *Baseball (1845–1881) from the Newspaper Accounts* (Altadena, CA, 1961), p. 237; Philadelphia, PA *Record*, 1871–1876; Philadelphia, PA *Times*, 1871–1876; William J. Ryczek, *Blackguards and Redstockings* (Jefferson, NC, 1992), p. 28; John Thorn and Pete Palmer, eds., *Total Baseball*, 3rd ed. (New York, 1993), pp. 1644, 1882–1887, 2195; Robert L. Tiemann, "Dick McBride," *More Nineteenth Century Stars* (Cleveland, OH, 1993).

A. D. Suehsdorf

McDOUGALD, Gilbert James "Gil" "Smash" (b. May 19, 1928, San Francisco, CA), player, is the son of William J. McDougald, a U.S. Post Office supervisor, and Ella (McGuire) McDougald and attended Stanford University one year. He began his professional baseball career in the New York Yankees (AL) organization in 1948 at Twin Falls, ID (PrL), where he hit .340 in 101 games. The next year at Victoria, Canada (WeIL), he batted .344 with 13 home runs and 116 RBIs. In 1950 as a second baseman under manager Rogers Hornsby (BB), he enjoyed another tremendous year at Beaumont, TX (TL) with 13 home runs, 115 RBIs, and a .336 batting average. His honors included being named the All-Star second baseman and the TL MVP.

McDougald, a six-footer weighing 180 pounds who threw and batted right-handed, joined the New York Yankees (AL) in 1951. His ability and attitude impressed manager Casey Stengel (BB) and a month before his twenty-third birthday, the Yankees made him the regular third baseman. In July 1951 regular second baseman Jerry Coleman was benched and McDougald was switched there. Altogether, he played 82 games at third base and 55 games at second base. His .306 batting average led the Yankees, helping him become the AL Rookie of the Year. A versatile infielder, McDougald remains the only player in Yankee history to excel at third base (1952, 1953, 1960), second base (1954, 1955, 1958), and shortstop (1956, 1957).

The confident, gutsy McDougald ranked among the most versatile infielders in major league baseball history. This was shown especially in 1959, when he played 53 games at second base, 52 at shortstop, and 25 at third base and consistently performed the best at any infield position he played. Three times, he led the AL in making double plays at three different positions.

McDougald hit for both average and power, twice batting higher than .300. Only seven right-handed Yankee batters surpassed his 112 home runs. On May 3, 1951, he knocked in 6 runs in the ninth inning against the St. Louis Browns (AL) to tie the AL record for most RBIs in one inning. The 1950's Yankee "Murderers Row" included McDougald, Mickey Mantle (BB), Yogi Berra (BB), and Bill Skowron (BB), among others.

On May 7, 1957, McDougald hit a wicked liner up the middle that struck Cleveland Indians (AL) pitcher Herb Score (S) near the right eye. Three bones were broken in Score's face. Score recovered but never regained his outstanding form.

During 10 Yankee seasons, McDougald proved a vital cog in eight AL titles and five World Series victories. In 1956, he finished second in the AL MVP voting and hit .311. Mantle won the triple crown that year while being voted AL MVP. McDougald made the AL All-Star team five seasons (1952, 1956–1959) and was an All-Star starter at third base, second base, and shortstop. He retired in 1960, but the Los Angeles Angels (AL) selected him in the expansion draft of that year. Despite a large contract offer, he decided to remain retired while on top.

McDougald, who married Lucille Tochlin on April 8, 1948, batted .276 lifetime with 1,291 hits, 113 home runs, and 576 RBIs. The McDougalds have four children, Christina, Gilbert, Jr., Todd, and Denise. He owns Yankee Maintenance Company in Spring Lake, NJ, and coached baseball at Fordham University for several years.

BIBLIOGRAPHY: *The Baseball Encyclopedia*, 9th ed. (New York, 1993); Gil McDougald, letter to Stan Carlson, December 1992; *New York Yankees Media Guide, 1994*; John Thorn and Pete Palmer, eds., *Total Baseball*, 3rd ed. (New York, 1993).

Stan W. Carlson

McGEE, Willie Dean (b. November 2, 1958, San Francisco, CA), player, is the son of Hurdice McGee, a machinist in the Oakland Naval Yards, and Jessie Mae (Jennings) McGee. He graduated from Harry Ellis High School in Richmond, CA, and completed one year at Diablo Valley CC in Pleasant Hill, CA. The New York Yankees (AL) drafted him in January 1977. After McGee spent five seasons in the farm system, the Yankees traded him to the St. Louis Cardinals (NL) for pitcher Bob Sykes in October 1981.

McGee, an instant success and fan favorite with St. Louis, was installed by Redbird manager Whitey Herzog (S) in center field. He batted .296, utilizing his great speed to swipe 24 bases and cover the spacious reaches of Busch Stadium as a rookie. The six-foot-one-inch, 176-pound McGee said, "The best way to judge whether a player is doing his job is if his team gets into the World Series." By that criterion, McGee performed his job very well. The Cardinals appeared in the World Series three of McGee's first six years, making the 1982, 1985, and 1987 fall classics. On June 23, 1984, McGee hit for the cycle and drove in 6 runs against the Chicago Cubs. McGee was named NL MVP for 1985, when he led the NL in hits (216), triples (18), and batting average (.353) and established the NL record for highest season batting average for a switch-hitter. Two years later, McGee reached personal highs in doubles (37), home runs (11), and RBIs (105).

In 1990 McGee became the only player in history to win a batting title while finishing the season in the other league. He batted .335 for St. Louis before being dealt to the AL pennant–bound Oakland Athletics for outfielder Felix Jose and third baseman Stan Royer on August 29. The San Francisco Giants (NL) signed McGee as a free agent following the 1990 season. He batted .312 in 1991, .297 in 1992, .301 in 1993, and .282 in the strike-shortened 1994 season for San Francisco.

McGee, notorious for swinging at pitches high and inside and breaking balls in the dirt, struck out at least 80 times eight seasons and never drew more than 38 bases on balls in a season. He hit pitches thrown just about anywhere, owning a .298 career batting average through 1994. McGee, who won a 1985 *TSN* Silver Slugger Award and *TSN* Gold Gloves in 1983, 1985, and 1986, played on four NL All-Star teams. He has played in 1,637 games, has 1,876 hits and 845 runs scored, and has pilfered 320 bases.

McGee, a quiet, hardworking, deeply religious player who does not complain, remains very modest about his many accomplishments. McGee's father, a deacon in the Pentecostal church, anoints his hands and feet with holy oil each season that they may be spared from injury. McGee and his wife, Vivian (Manyweather) McGee, have two children and reside in Hercules, CA.

BIBLIOGRAPHY: Peter Alfano, "Willie McGee: The Cardinals' Man of Many Talents," *BD* 45 (January 1986), pp. 26–28; John Dewan, ed., *The Scouting Report: 1990* (New York, 1990); Jeff Gordon, "St. Louis Will Ever Remember a Cardinal Named Willie," *BD* 50 (January 1991), pp. 37–41; Zander Hollander, ed., *The 1991 Complete Handbook of Baseball* (New York, 1991); Kip Ingle and Jim Toomey, *St. Louis Cardinals 1986 Media Guide* (St. Louis, MO, 1986); Willie McGee and George Vass, "The Game I'll Never Forget," *BD* 46 (April 1988), pp. 79–81; Mark Whicker, "Willie McGee: The Cardinals' Self-Made Star," *BD* 44 (December 1985), pp. 29–32.

Frank J. Olmsted

McGRIFF, Frederick Stanley "Fred" (b. October 31, 1963, Tampa, FL), player, is the youngest of five children of Earl McGriff, a television repair shop owner–operator, and Eliza McGriff, an elementary school teacher, and starred in baseball as a junior and senior at Jefferson High School in Tampa. The New York Yankees (AL) drafted McGriff in the ninth round in June 1981 and assigned him to Bradenton, FL (GCL).

In December 1982, the Yankees traded the patient, easygoing, six-foot-three-inch, 215-pound left-hander to the Toronto Blue Jays (AL). His minor league stops from 1983 through 1986 included Florence, SC (SAL), Kinston, NC (CrL), Knoxville, TN (SL), and Syracuse, NY (IL). Toronto promoted McGriff briefly in 1986 and named him designated hitter in 1987, when he broke Jesse Barfield's rookie club record for round-trippers (20). Although striking out frequently, McGriff walked often, recorded high on-base and slugging percentages, and belted tape measure home runs. No major leaguer matched his 106 round-trippers from 1988 to 1990. In 1988, he led AL first basemen in fielding (.997) and finished second in home runs (34), slugging percentage (.552), and extra base hits (73). McGriff, who belted the Skydome's first round-tripper, paced the AL with 36 home runs, knocked in 92 runs, and established a club record with 119 walks in 1989, helping the Blue Jays take the AL East title. McGriff's honors included making the *TSN* Silver Slugger and All-Star teams. In 1990, he batted .300, slammed 35 home runs, and ranked second in on-base percentage (.400).

In a blockbuster December 1990 trade, Toronto sent McGriff and Tony Fernandez to the San Diego Padres (NL) for Roberto Alomar and Joe Carter.* McGriff knocked in a career-pinnacle 106 runs and led the NL in intentional walks (26) in 1991. He tied a major league record in August, belting grand-slam home runs in consecutive games against the Houston Astros. In June 1992, the NL suspended McGriff four games for charging the mound and fighting San Francisco Giants pitcher Trevor Wilson. He still plated 104 runs and became the first Padre to pace the NL in home runs (35). No other player has led both major leagues in round-trippers. McGriff made two hits in his first All-Star Game and received *TSN* NL All-

Star and Silver Slugger team honors. McGriff also helped newly acquired third baseman Gary Sheffield enjoy a superlative season.

In July 1993, the Padres traded McGriff to the Atlanta Braves (NL) for three minor leaguers. The Braves possessed the NL's best pitching staff but floundered at the plate until McGriff arrived. Subsequently, Atlanta averaged nearly 6 runs a game, compiled a 54–19 record the second half of the season to overtake the San Francisco Giants for the NL West crown, and set a franchise record with 104 victories. McGriff finished the 1993 season with a .291 batting average, a career-high 37 home runs (including 19 with the Braves), and 101 RBIs. The Philadelphia Phillies upset Atlanta in the NL Championship Series, as McGriff batted .435 with 1 home run and 4 RBIs. During the strike-shortened 1994 season, he batted a career-best .318 with 34 home runs and 94 RBIs. His dramatic game-tying home run for the 1994 NL All-Stars in the ninth inning earned him MVP honors, enabling the NL ultimately to end a six-game losing streak to the AL All-Stars. In 1994 he became only the ninth player in major league history to belt at least 30 round trippers seven consecutive seasons.

In nine major league seasons, the Tampa, FL, resident has batted .285 with 202 doubles, 262 home runs, and 710 RBIs in 2,147 games. Forty-two percent of his 1,136 hits have been for extra bases. He and his wife, Veronica, married in October 1988 and have two children, Erick and Ericka.

BIBLIOGRAPHY: "The Quiet Man," *TSN 1994 Baseball Yearbook*, pp. 138–139; *San Diego Padres 1991 Media Guide;* Mike Shatzkin, ed., *The Ballplayers* (New York, 1990); *TSN Official Baseball Register*, 1994; Ralph Wiley, "Hit It a Mile," *SI* 70 (May 8, 1989), pp. 34–36.

David L. Porter

McGWIRE, Mark David (b. October 1, 1963, Pomona, CA), player, is the son of a dentist, attended Damien High School in Claremont, CA, and played three years of college baseball at the University of Southern California, holding the PTC record for home runs in a season with 32. His brother Dan, quarterback for the Seattle Seahawks (NFL), was that club's number-one selection in the 1991 NFL draft. The six-foot-five-inch, 225-pound first baseman, who throws and bats right-handed, was selected by the Montreal Expos (NL) in the eighth round of the free agent draft in June 1981.

McGwire enrolled at Southern California as a promising pitcher, rated by coach Rod Dedeaux (BB) as having major league ability on the mound. His future changed when, after his freshman season, he led the ASL in hitting. As a freshman pitcher, he won four decisions and lost four games with a 3.04 ERA. He was switched to first base as a sophomore, hitting .319 with 19 home runs. His junior year saw him bat .387 with 32 home runs.

McGwire played on the Pan-American and U.S. Olympic teams in 1984. Selected by the Oakland Athletics (AL) in the first round of the June 1984 free agent draft (tenth overall pick), he played 16 games with Modesto, CA (CaL) in 1984. He spent a full season there in 1985, hitting 24 home runs, producing 106 RBIs, and batting .274. In 1986, he played 55 games at Huntsville, AL (SL), 78 games at Tacoma, WA (PCL), and 18 games with Oakland (AL) at third base. He made 41 errors in 1986, trying to master third base.

Fourteen games into the 1987 season, McGwire became the regular Oakland first baseman. In 1987, he established a major league record for most home runs by a rookie with 49 and also set a mark for extra bases on long hits (183). His honors included being named AL Rookie of the Year by the *TSN* and the BBWAA. From 1987 through 1994, McGwire's major league production included 834 hits, 238 home runs, 657 RBIs, and a .250 batting average. The good clutch hitter gained free agent status in October 1992 but resigned with Oakland on December 24, 1992. McGwire shares the major league record for most home runs in two consecutive games (5), hitting 3 on June 27 and 2 more on June 28, 1987. He holds the AL rookie season record for highest slugging percentage, attaining .618 in 1987.

In four AL Championship Series (1988–1990, 1992), McGwire batted .258 with three home runs and 11 RBIs. In three World Series (1988–1990), he batted an anemic .188 with a single home run. He was selected on the AL All-Star team six consecutive times from 1987 to 1992 but was injured in 1991 and did not play. In 1984, McGwire was named *TSN* College Player of the Year and first baseman on the *TSN* College All-America team. Besides being AL Gold Glove first baseman, he, in 1992, was named first baseman on the *TSN* AL All-Star and Silver Slugger teams. In 1985, he led CaL third basemen with 239 assists and 354 total chances. McGwire paced all AL first basemen in 1990 with 1,429 total chances. He appeared on the disabled list from April 11 to 26, 1989, August 22 to September 11, 1992, and much of the 1993 season. He resides in Pomona, CA, plays golf for a hobby, and has one son, Matthew.

BIBLIOGRAPHY: Dennis Bracken, "Mr. Nice Guy," Minneapolis (MN) *Star Tribune*, July 31, 1987, pp. 1, 70; Stan Carlson, Clipping file 1987–1990, Minneapolis, MN; *Oakland Media Guide*, 1994; *TSN Official Baseball Register*, 1994.

Stan W. Carlson

MADDOX, Garry Lee (b. September 1, 1949, Cincinnati, OH), player and sportscaster, was called "the Secretary of Defense" of the great Philadelphia Phillies (NL) teams of the 1975–1983 era and enjoyed a distinguished 15-year major league career. After growing up in California, Maddox attended Harbor College in Wilmington, CA, and spent 2 years in Vietnam from 1968 to 1970.

The six-foot-three-inch, 205-pound right-hander came up to the San Francisco Giants (NL) in 1972 after only two years in the minor leagues, as

the successor in center field to Willie Mays (BB). Maddox played three seasons with the Giants before being traded to the Philadelphia Phillies (NL)
in May 1975 for first baseman Willie Montanez. Maddox achieved stardom
with the Phillies as the premier center fielder of his era. He won eight Gold
Gloves, averaging over 400 putouts for five straight years from 1976 to 1980.

Maddox's career .285 batting average included two .300 seasons. His stellar .330 batting mark in 1976 ranked him third in the NL. He also tied for
third in doubles with 37 that season. During his career, he recorded 1,802
hits, 337 doubles, 117 home runs, and 754 RBIs. He also stole 248 bases,
establishing season highs of 42 in 1975 and 1976.

Maddox, essentially a gap and line drive hitter, proved a vital cog, as the
Phillies won five NL East Division titles, two NL pennants, and one World
Series title during his tenure there. The high point of his career came in
Game 5 of the dramatic 1980 NL Championship Series with Houston, when
he doubled to score Del Unser and give the Phillies their first NL pennant
in 30 years. Back injuries forced him to retire in May 1986.

Maddox and his wife Sondra have two sons and reside in the Philadelphia,
PA, area. He works in the Phillies' Community Relations Department and
serves as a color commentator for the Phillies' cable TV games. He also
remains active in charitable organizations including the Philadelphia Child
Guidance Center, where he has served on the board of directors.

BIBLIOGRAPHY: Frank Bilvosky and Rich Westcott, *The Phillies Encyclopedia* (New
York, 1984); *Philadelphia Phillies Media Guide*, 1976–1986.

John P. Rossi

MATTINGLY, Donald Arthur "Don" (b. April 20, 1961, Evansville, IN),
player, is the New York Yankees' (AL) finest first baseman since Lou Gehrig
(BB) and, through his first 11 seasons, the greatest Yankee never to play in
a World Series. He is the youngest of five children born to Bill Mattingly,
a postman, and Mary Mattingly. A brother, Jerry, was killed in a highway
construction accident at age 23. Don, who was only 7 at the time, wears the
number 23 in Jerry's memory.

At Evansville Memorial High School, Mattingly played basketball, foot-
ball, and baseball. Most teams expected Mattingly to attend Indiana State
University, and as a result, he was not selected until the nineteenth round
of the 1979 draft. The New York Yankees signed him for a $25,000 bonus.
Mattingly, who played in the minor leagues from 1979 to 1983, became the
Yankees' regular first baseman in June 1983.

In 1984, his first full major league season, Mattingly hit .343 and became
the Yankees' first AL batting champion since Mickey Mantle (BB) in 1956.
Early in 1985, Mattingly underwent arthroscopic knee surgery. He enjoyed
a great year, leading the AL in six offensive categories, winning MVP honors, and becoming the Yankees' first AL RBI league leader (145) since Roger
Maris (BB) in 1961.

In a 1986 poll of major leaguers, Mattingly was selected as baseball's best player. He hit .352 and finished second in the AL MVP balloting. Mattingly topped Gehrig's team record for doubles (53) and broke a Yankee record for hits (238), set by Earle Combs (BB). His .352 batting average made him the eighth Yankee to crack the .350 mark. In 1987, a disc problem in his back ended his 335 consecutive game-playing streak. Nevertheless, his six grand slams set a major league mark. During a hot streak in July, Mattingly homered in eight straight games to tie a major league record.

Mattingly batted .311 in 1988 and .303 in 1989, becoming the sixth player in Yankee history and the first since Joe DiMaggio (BB) in 1942 to hit .300 or better for six consecutive years. In 1990, disabled by back problems from late July through mid-September, he slipped to .256. Mattingly, named team captain for 1991, rebounded to hit .288, although his homer total dropped to 9. In mid-August, he was benched in a dispute over the length of his hair. Mattingly proved the Yankees' most productive hitter in 1992, batting .288 with 86 RBIs. In 1993, Mattingly was involved in his first real AL pennant race, and helped keep the Yankees in contention. He finished with a .291 batting average, 17 homers, and 86 RBIs. In the strike-shortened 1994 season, he hit .304 with 51 RBIs to help the Yankees win the AL East. Through 1994, he has batted .309 with 410 doubles, 215 home runs, and 1,050 RBIs. He has not yet played in a postseason game. The six-time AL All-Star (1984–1989) also won eight career Gold Glove awards, the most by any Yankee, one ahead of George Scott (S) for most among AL first basemen.

Mattingly married Kim Sexton on September 8, 1979, and has three children, Taylor Patrick, Preston Michael, and Jordon William.

BIBLIOGRAPHY: Don Burke, "The Missing Link," *Yankees Magazine* 14 (June 8, 1993), pp. 12–16; Pete Cava, telephone interview with Thelma Halvorson, general manager, Mattingly's 23 Restaurant, Evansville, IN, October 26, 1993; Jack Curry, "Different Mattingly Still Gains Respect," Indianapolis (IN) *News*, April 14, 1993, p. B4; Moss Klein, "At Last, Mattingly May Find a Happy Ending," Newark (NJ) *Star-Ledger*, August 6, 1993, p. 73; Sean McAdam, "Mattingly the Most Disappointed of All Yankees After Late Swoon," Indianapolis (IN) *Star*, September 29, 1993, p. C6; *1992 New York Yankees Team Media Guide*, pp. 172–180; Steve Rushin, "First-Rate," *SI* 79 (August 30, 1993), pp. 14–17; Allan Simpson, *The Baseball Draft: The First 25 Years, 1965–1989* (Durham, NC, 1990), p. 180; *TSN Official Baseball Register*, 1994; Tom Weir, "Mattingly Finally Gets Satisfaction," *USA Today*, September 30, 1993, p. C3.

                                                                                                      Peter Cava

MELE, Sabath Anthony "Sam" (b. January 21, 1923, Astoria, NY), player, scout, coach, and manager, spent nine major league seasons with six different teams including five AL clubs and one NL team. Despite his many trades and moves, Mele remained a remarkably consistent player both defensively and offensively. He attended NYU, where he starred in basketball for the

Violets in 1943. One of his best games came when NYU defeated Temple University for their eleventh consecutive victory. Mele scored 17 points to lead both teams in scoring. Mele then served in the U.S. Marines and was stationed at Pearl Harbor.

His professional baseball career began in 1946 with Louisville, KY (AA) and then Scranton, PA (EL), where he hit a career-high .342. He opened the 1947 season in right field for the Boston Red Sox (AL) and hit .302, his best major league season. The 1947 season marked the first year of Rookie of the Year voting. Jackie Robinson (BB), who hit .297, won the award. Over the next two seasons, Mele's batting average dropped to the .230s. Boston traded Mele to the Washington Senators (AL) in June 1949. During his four years with the Senators, Mele batted in the .270 range and ranked second in 1950 and then first in 1951 in the clutch-hitting index. In 1951, he shared the AL lead in doubles at 36 with George Kell (BB) and teammate Eddie Yost (BB) and netted a career-high 94 RBIs.

Mele bounced around over the next four years with the Chicago White Sox (AL) from May 1952 to February 1954, the Baltimore Orioles (AL) until July 1954, Boston (AL) through June 1955, and the Cincinnati Reds (NL) until January 1956, ending his major league playing career with the Cleveland Indians (AL). In the fourth inning on June 10, 1952, Mele tied a major league record for most RBIs (6) and long hits (2) in an inning with a three-run homer and bases loaded triple against the Philadelphia Athletics. He played two more minor league seasons with Indianapolis, IN (AA) and Buffalo, NY (IL), retiring after the 1958 season. Mele fielded well, never making more than five errors in any of his 10-year major league seasons and finishing with a .985 career fielding average. In 1,046 games, he batted .267 with 80 home runs and 544 RBIs.

The Washington Senators (AL) hired Mele as a scout in 1959 and coach from July 1959 through 1960. After the Senators moved to Minnesota in 1961, Mele replaced Cookie Lavagetto as manager on June 23. He managed the Twins through 1967, guiding them to second-place finishes in 1962 and 1966 and an AL pennant in 1965. In seven managerial seasons, Mele piloted the Twins to a 518–427 win–loss mark. The Twins featured slugger Harmon Killebrew (BB), outfielder Tony Oliva (S), and pitchers Jim Kaat (BB) and Camilo Pascual.* The Twins lost the 1965 World Series in seven games to the Los Angeles Dodgers. *TSN* named Mele Major League Manager of the Year in 1965. Mele, who married Constance Mary Clemens in January 1949, has scouted for the Boston Red Sox since 1967. During off-seasons, he wrote a sports column for the Quincy (MA) *Ledger*.

BIBLIOGRAPHY: Jack Lauter, *Fenway Voices* (Camden, ME, 1990); *NYT*, 1943; Mike Shatzkin, ed., *The Ballplayers* (New York, 1990); John Thorn and Pete Palmer, eds., *Total Baseball*, 3rd ed. (New York, 1993); *TSN Baseball Register*, 1967.

Lee E. Scanlon

MERKLE, Frederick Charles "Fred" (b. December 20, 1888, Watertown, WI; d. March 2, 1956, Daytona Beach, FL), player, was born of German parentage and grew up in Toledo, OH. The six-foot-one-inch, 190-pound first baseman played semiprofessional baseball in Toledo in 1905 and 1906 before signing his first professional contract with Tecumseh, MI (SML). His success with the Tecumseh team in 1907 motivated manager John McGraw (BB) of the New York Giants (NL) to purchase him for $2,500. Merkle made 47 plate appearances that year with the Giants, hitting .255.

The following year, the 19-year-old rookie was involved in one of the most controversial plays in baseball history. On September 23, the Giants met the Chicago Cubs at the Polo Grounds in New York. Both teams, along with the Pittsburgh Pirates, were involved in a tight race for the NL championship. Fred Tenney (BB), the Giants' regular first baseman, was out of the lineup with an injury, thus thrusting Merkle into his first start of the season.

The game entered the bottom of the ninth inning tied at 1–1. With two men out, Harry "Moose" McCormick singled. Merkle followed with a single, sending McCormick to third base. Shortstop Al Bridwell then lined a shot to center field, scoring McCormick with the putative winning run. Merkle, assuming that the game had ended, sprinted to the locker room without touching second base. After some confusion, Cubs second baseman Johnny Evers (BB) got the ball and tagged second base.

A heated argument arose, with umpires Hank O'Day (BB) and Bob Emslie finally agreeing with the Cubs that Merkle was the third out, that McCormick's run did not count, and that the game was still tied. Since the spectators had swarmed onto the field, extra innings were an impossibility. Ultimately, the NL office backed the umpires and declared that the game would have to be replayed at season's end, if necessary. The Cubs and the Giants finished the regular season with identical records of 98 wins, 55 losses, as the Cubs captured the playoff.

Sportswriters and fans endlessly excoriated Merkle for his rookie mistake. The *NYT*, for example, began its account of the game with the words "censurable stupidity by player Merkle." Merkle's teammates and McGraw stood by him, however, and within a few years, he had become the Giants' regular first baseman.

Merkle enjoyed a solid 16-year major league career with the Giants, Brooklyn Robins (NL), New York Yankees (AL), and ironically, the Cubs, compiling a .273 lifetime batting average. He made 1,579 base hits, including 289 doubles and 733 RBIs, and also stole 271 bases. He appeared in 27 World Series games (1911–1913, 1916, 1918), hitting .239. But baseball authorities forever remembered him for one "bonehead" play on the afternoon of September 23, 1908. He was survived by three daughters, Mrs. L. J. Robinson, Mrs. John Kasbaum, and Jeannette.

BIBLIOGRAPHY: *The Baseball Encyclopedia*, 9th ed. (New York, 1993); Frederick Merkle file, National Baseball Library, Cooperstown, NY; Lawrence Ritter, *The Glory of Their Times* (New York, 1966).

David S. Matz

MILLS, Abraham Gilbert "The Bismarck of Baseball" (b. March 12, 1844, New York, NY; d. August 26, 1929, Falmouth, MA), counsel, executive, maintained a lifelong interest in sports and baseball in particular. After growing up in New York City, Mills enlisted with the 5th New York Volunteers in 1862 and served in the Civil War. He was commissioned a second lieutenant in 1864 and later held the honorary rank of colonel. As a soldier, he always carried a bat and baseball in his field gear and spread the gospel of baseball.

Mills graduated from Columbian (now George Washington University) Law School in 1869 but never practiced. His first involvement in the baseball business came in 1876, when he published an article attacking baseball clubs for breaking up opposing teams by hiring away their players. That same year, he became associated with William Hulbert (BB) as counsel to the future NL president. After Hulbert's death, Mills was elected NL president. Mills staunchly supported the reserve rule as "The Father of the National Agreement." The Tripartite National Agreement constituted a milestone pact between the NL, AA, and NWL, in which Mills awarded major league status to the AA and high minor league status to the NWL. The parties agreed to pay players at least $1,000 per season and, most important, to respect each others' reserve lists. Players were prohibited from dealing with other teams between April 1 and October 20. Exclusive territorial rights were also defined.

Mills's termination as NL president oddly resulted from the failure of the competing UA in 1884. Players, who had jumped to the rival UA, were allowed to return to the NL by the NL owners, while former UA president Henry Lucas* was given a franchise. Due to his opposition to these moves, Mills was removed from office in November 1884. Mills returned to the baseball scene in 1905 with a six-man group, the Mills Commission, charged to determine the origins of baseball. The Mills Commission, influenced by Albert Spalding (BB), who wanted a purely American basis for the National Pastime, adopted the grossly inaccurate immaculate conception theory that the game was the brainchild of Abner Doubleday.

Mills worked with the Otis Elevator Company for over 50 years, serving as its senior vice president of sales from 1898 until his death. He married Mary Chester Steele in 1872 and had three daughters. He continued his involvement in sports, organizing the AOA, participating in the AAU, and serving as president of the New York AC.

BIBLIOGRAPHY: Charles C. Alexander, *Our Game* (New York, 1991); Harvey Frommer, *Primitive Baseball* (New York, 1988); John R. Husman, interview with James

Mallinson, Floral Park, NY, December 8, 1993; *NYT*, August 28, 1929, p. 25; Obituary, September 5, 1929, National Baseball Library, Cooperstown, NY; *Otis Bulletin* (April–May 1949); David Pietrusza, *Major Leagues* (Jefferson, NC, 1991); David Quentin Voigt, *American Baseball*, vol. 1 (Norman, OK, 1966).

John R. Husman

MITCHELL, Kevin Darrell (b. January 13, 1962, San Diego, CA), player, grew up in San Diego. His parents separated when he was two years old. He was brought up primarily by his paternal grandmother, Josie Whitfield, and lived in a very tough neighborhood, being shot three times as a teenager. Participation in sports, including baseball, was encouraged by his grandmother. After graduation from Claremont High School, Mitchell played in a baseball league in San Diego and was signed by the New York Mets (NL) as an undrafted free agent in 1980. Mitchell began his minor league career at Kingsport, TN (ApL) in 1981 and performed stints at Lynchburg, VA (CrL) in 1982, Jackson, TX (TL) in 1983, and Tidewater, VA (IL) in 1984 and 1985. The right-handed hitter compiled minor league batting averages of .335, .318, .299, .243, and .290. During most of his stay in the minor leagues, he played third base and the outfield. Tidewater, however, also used him at first base.

In his rookie season with the New York Mets in 1986, he hit .277 with 43 RBIs and 12 home runs. Mitchell played six different positions including first base, third base, shortstop, left field, center field, and right field and finished third in the balloting for the NL Rookie of the Year. In December 1986, New York traded Mitchell to the San Diego Padres (NL). Subsequent trades sent him to the San Francisco Giants (NL) in July 1987, Seattle Mariners (AL) in December 1991, and Cincinnati Reds (NL) in November 1992. The 5-foot-11-inch, 210-pound muscular Mitchell emerged as one of the game's most feared sluggers in 1989. Besides hitting .291, he led the NL in home runs (47), RBIs (125), total bases (345), slugging percentage (.635), and extra base hits (87). He set a major league record for a right-handed hitter by receiving 32 intentional walks. His honors for the 1989 season included the NL MVP Award, *TSN* Major League Player of the Year Award, and selection to *TSN* All-Star and Silver Slugger teams. Mitchell batted a career-high .341 in 1993 and .326 with 30 home runs and 77 RBIs in the strike-shortened 1994 season, but was released following the 1994 campaign. Cincinnati finished first in the NL Central Division with a 66–48 mark in 1994. In February 1995, the Daiei Hawks (JPL) signed Mitchell. Mitchell, a member of the 1989 and 1990 NL All-Star teams, batted .291 in three NL Championship Series (1986, 1987, 1989) and .280 in two World Series against the 1986 Boston Red Sox and the 1989 Oakland A's. Through the 1994 season, his career totals include a .286 batting average, a .529 slugging average, 220 home runs, and 689 RBIs. He is single and lives in Chula Vista, CA.

BIBLIOGRAPHY: Barry M. Bloom, "Hope Dies by Degrees," *USA Today Baseball Weekly*, May 19–25, 1993, p. 23; Kevin Mitchell file, National Baseball Library,

Cooperstown, NY; *1993 Cincinnati Reds Media Guide*; Nick Peters, "A New Image for Giants Mitchell," *TSN*, May 8, 1989, p. 16; Mark Purdy, "Earth to Mitchell," *TSN 1990 Baseball Yearbook*, pp. 4–8, 10, 12; Rob Rains, "Mitchell Suffering Guilt by Association," *USA Baseball Today Weekly*, May 19–25, 1993, pp. 22–23; *TSN Official Baseball Register*, 1994; John Thorn and Pete Palmer, eds., *Total Baseball*, 3rd ed. (New York, 1993), p. 1080.

Robert J. Brown

MITCHELL, Loren Dale (b. August 23, 1921, Colony, OK; d. January 5, 1987, Tulsa, OK), player, was involved in one of major league baseball's most dramatic moments. The tall, slender left-hander strode forward, and then held back his swing as umpire Babe Pinelli* raised his arm in the classic strike pose. The called strike three marked the third and final out of Don Larsen's* historic no-hit gem for the New York Yankees in Game 5 of the 1956 World Series. To his dying day, Mitchell of the Brooklyn Dodgers (NL) thought the pitch was off the plate for a ball. The memory remains unfair to Mitchell, who played 11 major league seasons and never saw his career batting average dip below its final .312 mark. He ranks sixty-eighth on the all-time batting average list, ahead of stars Willie Mays (BB), Harvey Kuenn (BB), Pete Rose (BB), Mel Ott (BB), Hank Aaron (BB), and George Brett (BB).

The six-foot-1-inch, 195-pound Mitchell began his professional baseball career in 1946 with Oklahoma City, OK (TL), leading the TL with a sparkling .337 batting average. He made his major league debut with the Cleveland Indians (AL) in September 1946, hitting .432 in 11 games. The performance impressed player–manager Lou Boudreau (BB), who named Mitchell his starting center fielder in spring training the following year. Mitchell played for the Indians until sold to the Brooklyn Dodgers in July 1956. In Cleveland's championship 1948 season, he hit .336 to rank third in the AL behind Boudreau (.355) and batting champion Ted Williams (BB) (.369). Mitchell also finished second in the AL in hits with 204 and fourth in stolen bases with 13. In 1949, Mitchell led the AL in hits (203) and triples (23) and ranked fourth in batting (.317) and total bases (274). He finished second in the AL batting race in 1952 with .323, four points behind Ferris Fain's (S) .327.

Mitchell played in the 1948, 1954, and 1956 World Series, making four hits in 29 at bats and batting only .139. All four of his World Series hits came in the 1948 Series, when the Indians defeated the Boston Braves in six games. The New York Giants swept favored Cleveland in the 1954 World Series. Mitchell appeared in the 1949 and 1952 All-Star Games and was selected for the 1951 contest, knocking in one run with a double as a late-inning substitute for Ted Williams in 1949. During 11 major league seasons, he struck out only 119 times in 3,984 at bats. An outstanding defensive outfielder, he led outfielders in fielding percentage in 1948 (.991) and 1949

(.994). Mitchell married Margaret Emerson on May 26, 1942, and worked as a manager for an oil company in Tulsa, OK.

BIBLIOGRAPHY: Mike Shatzkin, ed., *The Ballplayers* (New York, 1990); John Thorn and Pete Palmer, eds., *Total Baseball*, 3rd ed. (New York, 1993); *TSN Daguerreotypes of Great Stars of Baseball*, 1968.

Lee E. Scanlon

MONEY, Donald Wayne "Don" (b. July 6, 1947, Washington, DC), player, is the son of Robert J. Money, Jr., a carpenter, and Frances (Greenfield) Money and performed 16 years in the major leagues with the Philadelphia Phillies (NL) from 1968 to 1972 and the Milwaukee Brewers (AL) from 1973 to 1983. The highly touted infielder was signed by Syd Thrift and Joe Consoli and began his career at Salem, VA (ApL) in the Pittsburgh Pirates (NL) organization in 1965. Along with Woodie Fryman, Bill Laxton, and Harold Clem, Money was traded to the Phillies in December 1967 for pitcher Jim Bunning (BB). Money's brief trial with the Phillies in 1968 was followed by his joining the team full-time in 1969. On opening day of 1969, he hit two home runs against the Chicago Cubs. Money started as a short-stop but was moved to third base when the Phillies brought up Larry Bowa (BB) in 1970.

The six-foot-one-inch, 190-pound right-hander enjoyed his best of four seasons with the Phillies in 1970. He batted over .300 most of the season and fielded his position brilliantly. He hit .295, committed just 15 errors, and fielded .961, placing him second in the NL behind Doug Rader of the Houston Astros. After Money hit in the .220s the next two seasons, the Phillies traded Money and two others to the Milwaukee Brewers (AL) in October 1972 for Ken Brett, Jim Lonborg, and two other pitchers.

At age 25, Money came into his own with Milwaukee and developed into a solid all-around player. The third baseman, nicknamed "Brooks" for his defensive skills, began serving as a designated hitter in 1977 when the Brewers got Sal Bando (S) from the Oakland A's to play third base. Money experienced his best years between 1973 and 1978, averaging around .280 at the plate for that span. Money was selected to the AL All-Star teams in 1974 and from 1976 through 1978.

In 1977 he hit 25 homers and drove in 83 runs, both career highs. The next season, he scored a career-high 88 runs. Money's career featured a .261 batting average with 1,623 hits, 302 doubles, 176 homers, and 729 RBIs. Among Brewers, he ranks among the top five or six in every career offensive category. The high point of Money's career came in 1982, when he served as designated hitter for the Brewers in the AL Championship Series against the California Angels and in the World Series against the St. Louis Cardinals. He hit .231 in that World Series.

Money retired from baseball after the 1983 season. He played briefly in

Japan in 1984 and returned to his Vinland, NJ, home after that season. He coached high school baseball in the Vinland area for five years before his retirement and lives with his wife, Sharon Ann, in Vinland. They have two sons.

BIBLIOGRAPHY: Frank Bilovsky and Rich Westcott, *The Phillies Encyclopedia* (New York, 1984); John P. Rossi, interview with Donald Money, January 1993; Bert Randolph Sugar, *Baseballistics* (New York, 1990).

John P. Rossi

MOON, Wallace Wade "Wally" (b. April 3, 1930, Bay, AR), player and coach, is the son of Henry A. Moon, a farmer–laborer, and Margie (Vernon) Moon, is of Scotch and Irish heritage, and graduated from Bay High School. He earned a Bachelor of Science degree in physical education and a Master of Education degree in administrative education from Texas A & M University. The six-foot, 175-pound, right-handed, athletically built Moon received a $6,000 signing bonus from the St. Louis Cardinals (NL) in 1950. From 1950 to 1952, the Cardinals allowed Moon to report late to Omaha, NE (WL) after his college semesters were completed. Moon, who batted .307 in 131 games at Rochester, NY (IL) in 1953, was booed in St. Louis at his first major league game in 1954. To make room for him, the Cardinals had traded popular outfielder Enos Slaughter (BB) to the New York Yankees (AL) the day before. The jeers turned quickly to cheers, as Moon smashed a home run in his first major league at bat. He compiled a .304 batting average with 12 home runs, 106 runs, and 76 RBIs, edging out Henry Aaron (BB) to become the first Cardinal to win the NL Rookie of the Year Award. From 1954 to 1957, Moon remained a paradigm of consistency in the St. Louis lineup, never batting below .295. In 1957, he belted a career-high 24 home runs and enjoyed a 24-game hitting streak. Moon played first base 51 games in 1955 and 52 games in 1956 on days when regular first baseman Stan Musial (BB) moved to the outfield.

Cardinal general manager Bing Devine, however, wanted to improve the outfield defensively after the 1958 season. Moon did not have a strong arm and just had completed an injury-marred season, batting only .238. On December 4, 1958, St. Louis traded him to the Los Angeles Dodgers (NL) for outfielder Gino Cimoli.

In the Los Angeles Coliseum, the left field wall stood only 251 feet away from home plate and was topped with a 40-foot screen. Moon developed an inside-out swing to loft opposite field home runs. In 1959, he belted 14 of his 19 home runs, or "Moon shots," over the left field screen, batting third in the Dodger lineup ahead of Duke Snider (BB). Moon, who also led the NL in triples with 11 and batted .302, hit .261 in the 1959 World Series, helping the Dodgers defeat the Chicago White Sox (AL) in six games. Moon batted .299 and won a Gold Glove in 1960 while compiling a career-high

.328 batting average the following season. In the early 1960s, the Dodgers developed young outfielders Tommy Davis (BB), Willie Davis (BB), and Frank Howard (BB). They gradually pushed Moon into a utility, pinch-hitting role from 1962 until his retirement after the 1965 season. His major league record included 1,457 games, 737 runs, 1,399 hits, 212 doubles, 142 home runs, 661 RBIs, and a .289 batting average.

Moon married Bettye Lewis Knowles on December 21, 1951, and has five children, Wallace Joseph, Zola, Elizabeth, Mary, and Larhesa. He served as athletic director at John Brown University from 1967 to 1977 and coached baseball until the program was discontinued. Moon presides over Triangle Financial Corporation in Bryan, TX, and lives in College Station.

BIBLIOGRAPHY: Bob Broeg, *Redbirds: A Century of Cardinals' Baseball* (St. Louis, MO, 1981); Henry L. Freund, Jr., "Change of Allegiance Inspired by a New Hero," *BRJ* 14 (1985), pp. 33–34; Gene Karst and Martin J. Jones, Jr., *Who's Who in Professional Baseball* (New Rochelle, NY, 1973); Wallace W. Moon file, National Baseball Library, Cooperstown, NY; Stan Musial and Bob Broeg, *Stan Musial: "The Man's" Own Story* (Garden City, NY, 1964).

                                                                                        Frank J. Olmsted

MOORE, Walter "Dobie" (b. January 1891, Fayetteville, GA; d. between 1938 and 1942, Detroit, MI), player, starred for the Kansas City Monarchs (NNL) from 1920 through 1926. Moore lived in Georgia with grandparents by 1900. He joined the U.S. Army as a young adult and helped the powerful Philippines-based 25th Infantry black team gain acclaim as the armed forces' top baseball club in 1911. In 1915, Moore starred as the Hawaii baseball twenty-fifth squad gained their Post's Championship. His final military assignment came at Fort Huachuca, AZ, where he still played baseball for the 25th Infantry. In 1919, the Monarchs signed Moore and teammates Wilbur Rogan (BB), Lemuel Hawkins, and Oscar Johnson.

During Moore's seven-year NNL stint, he became recognized as the circuit's outstanding shortstop. The stout right-handed batter with power stood 5 foot 11 inches and weighed over 200 pounds. Moore attained a .365 career batting average as a Monarch, including an NNL-leading .453 in 1924. Moore also led the NNL in 1924 with 139 hits and 26 doubles while posting a .694 slugging average. A loop leading 12 triples followed in 1925.

Moore continued to pound the ball, with a .381 batting average, when tragedy struck in May 1926. The married Moore suffered multiple leg fractures from gun shots fired by a local female acquaintance, with whom he had a questionable relationship. Moore vowed annually to make a comeback even into the 1930s, but the wounds ended his baseball career.

During Moore's brief, illustrious sojourn in professional baseball, he also proved an outstanding base runner and defensive shortstop. His play drew raves from major leaguers John McGraw (BB) and Casey Stengel (BB) as well as teammates and opponents in the U.S. Army and the NNL.

The Kansas City Monarchs claimed consecutive NNL pennants from 1923 through 1925 and won the 1924 Black World Series, with Moore at shortstop. Moore hit .323 in 16 World Series contests during the 1924 and 1925 classics.

Moore, who married Frances Davis, probably spent his final years in Detroit.

BIBLIOGRAPHY: *The Baseball Encyclopedia*, 9th ed. (New York, 1993); Chicago (IL) *Defender*, 1924–1925; Phil Dixon, *The Negro Baseball Leagues* (Mattituck, NY, 1992); John B. Holway, *Blackball Stars* (Westport, CT, 1988); Larry Lester, Negro Leagues Baseball Museum, Kansas City, MO, letter to Merl F. Kleinknecht, December 12, 1992; Robert W. Peterson, *Only the Ball Was White* (Englewood Cliffs, NJ, 1970); Philadelphia (PA) *Tribune*, 1924–1925; Pittsburgh (PA) *Courier*, 1924–1925; James A. Riley, *The Biographical Encyclopedia of the Negro Baseball Leagues* (New York, 1994).

Merl F. Kleinknecht

MORRIS, Edward "Cannonball" (b. September 29, 1862, Brooklyn, NY; d. April 12, 1937, Pittsburgh, PA), player, ranked among the best major league pitchers for four seasons in the 1880s before injuries and strong drink prematurely ended his playing career. Morris grew up in San Francisco, playing for the National and Mystic clubs there from 1880 to 1882 and then came East to catch for Philadelphia, PA (ECA). With Reading, PA (ISL) in 1883, the 165-pound switch-hitting left-hander became a pitcher and compiled a 16–6 win–loss record.

For the major league Columbus, OH, Buckeyes (AA) in 1884, Morris won 34 games, lost only 13 decisions, hurled a no-hitter in May against the Pittsburgh Alleghenys, and compiled an AA-high .723 winning percentage. His pitching helped propel Columbus to a second-place finish from sixth the previous year. The AA dropped Columbus when it shrunk from 12 clubs to 8, sending Morris and nine of his teammates to revive the struggling Alleghenys. The Alleghenys improved from tenth place in 1884 to third in 1885, as Morris won 39 games, 1 less than the AA leader. He led the AA with 63 complete games, 581 innings pitched, 298 strikeouts, and 7 shutouts. In 1886, the Alleghenys rose to second place. Morris tied Dave Foutz (BB) of the St. Louis Browns for the AA lead with 41 wins, again pacing the AA with 12 shutouts. Both figures remain Pittsburgh club records. Morris incredibly completed all his 126 games started in 1885 and 1886. Ralph Horton's Relative Performance System rates Morris the top pitcher in the AA for both seasons.

The Alleghenys moved from the AA to the NL in 1887, finishing sixth. Morris, plagued by a sore arm, a new pitching rule that curbed his leaping delivery, a suspension for refusing to pitch in a game, and fines for drunkenness, appeared in only 38 games and compiled a 14–22 win–loss record. In the off-season, Morris mastered the pitching restriction. Although the Alleghenys again finished sixth in 1888, Morris regained much of his former effectiveness. He led the NL with 54 complete games, winning 29 and losing 23. A sore arm and stomach muscle injury limited Morris to 21 games and a subpar 6–13 record in 1889. He jumped to the Pittsburgh Burghers (PL) club for 1890, his final major league year. Morris missed part of the season under expulsion for heavy drinking and pitched in only 18 games, compiling an 8–7 record. In seven major league seasons, Morris won 171 games and lost 122. He struck out 1,217 batters, yielded 2,468 hits in 2,678 innings, and compiled a 2.82 ERA. He completed 297 of his 307 starts and hurled 29 shutouts.

Morris remained in Pittsburgh after his playing career, building and operating a hotel near the ball park. He four years later opened another nearby hotel, which he operated until 1902. He also helped operate a pool hall and earned extra money providing legal assistance "as an attorney in fact." From 1907 to 1912, he formed a wholesale liquor business. In 1912 he was appointed as night captain at Rockview Penitentiary. Morris was hired in 1916 by former major league pitcher Ad Gumbert, who had been elected an Allegheny County commissioner, as a highway department foreman and worked for the county until complications of a toe infection brought on his final illness.

BIBLIOGRAPHY: Ralph L. Horton, *Baseball's Best Pitchers 1876–1992* (St. Louis, MO, 1993); Ed Morris file, National Baseball Library, Cooperstown, NY; John Thorn and Pete Palmer, eds., *Total Baseball*, 3rd ed. (New York, 1993); Robert L. Tiemann and Mark Rucker, eds., *Nineteenth Century Stars* (Kansas City, MO, 1989).

Frederick Ivor-Campbell

MOSTIL, John Anthony "Johnny" "Bananas" (b. June 1, 1896, Chicago, IL; d. December 10, 1970, Midlothian, IL), player, manager, and scout, was a fast and wide-ranging outfielder for the Chicago White Sox (AL) who might have been ranked among the greats of the 1920s except for a bizarre suicide attempt that ruined his career. A lifelong Chicagoan, Mostil was the son of Casper Mostil of suburban Whiting, IN. The White Sox signed him as a second baseman off the sandlots in 1918. He played 10 major league games before the end of the 1918 season but was optioned to Milwaukee (AA) for two years. Having Eddie Collins (BB) at second base, the White Sox encouraged Mostil's conversion to the outfield. After returning in 1921, Mostil peaked in the middle of the decade. He scored 135 runs in 1925—a team record that still stands—and batted a career-high .328 in 1926. He led the AL in stolen bases in both years but was considered shy, withdrawn, and neurasthenic.

The five-foot-eight-inch, 169-pound right-hander joined the team for spring training for 1927 in the Youree Hotel in Shreveport, LA. On March 8, after a reportedly amicable conversation with pitcher Red Faber (BB) and Mrs. Faber, Mostil rushed impulsively to the room of Pat Prouty, a fan who had accompanied the team. Mostil gashed himself with a razor blade and pocketknife 13 places on his neck, torso, legs, and left arm. Mostil hemorrhaged so severely that he was given the last rites of the Roman Catholic Church. The press reported that the suicide attempt stemmed from despondency at the spread of neuralgia. Rumors quickly arose that the meeting with Faber and his wife had actually been a violent confrontation in which Faber accused Mostil of an adulterous affair with Mrs. Faber. The episode broke Mostil's engagement to Margaret Carroll of Hammond, IN.

Mostil survived the ordeal but never married and was not expected to resume baseball because of damage to ligaments in his left wrist. He recovered enough to rejoin the White Sox for 13 games at the end of the season, but his ability was clearly diminished. He played regularly in 1928, batting .270, but appeared in only 12 games in 1929 because of a broken ankle. The White Sox released him to Toledo, OH (AA) in January 1930. He participated in spring training with the New York Giants (NL) that year but failed to make the team. He played for Toledo in 1930 and 1931 and Little Rock (SA) in 1932 and then became a successful minor league manager, mainly in the NoL.

Mostil became a White Sox career employee, serving as scout, instructor, and manager in their farm system until two years before his death. In 972 major league games, he batted .301 with 1,054 hits and 336 stolen bases.

BIBLIOGRAPHY: Richard Lindberg, "Johnny Mostil," in Mike Shatzkin, ed., *The Ballplayers* (New York, 1990), p. 766; John Mostil file, National Baseball Library, Cooperstown, NY; Obituaries, Chicago (IL) *Tribune* and Chicago (IL) *Sun-Times*, December 11, 1970, and *TSN*, December 26, 1970; *TSN Baseball Register*, 1952, pp. 296–297; Larry Woltz, "Mostil, Sox Star, Cuts Throat," Chicago (IL) *Herald & Examiner*, March 9, 1927, p. 1.

George W. Hilton

MUNGO, Van Lingle (b. June 8, 1911, Pageland, SC; d. February 12, 1985, Pageland, SC), player and manager, was a colorful right-handed pitcher with a fastball said to be as swift as Bob Feller's (BB). His lilting name, deriving from his Dutch ancestry (Lingle was his mother's maiden name) became the title of a popular song by Dave Frishberg in 1970.

Mungo signed in 1929 as an outfielder with Charlotte, NC (PiL). Mungo, because of his powerful arm, was switched to pitching and spent most of the year at Fayetteville, NC (ECaL). He moved up in 1930 to Winston-Salem, NC (PiL) and in 1931 to Hartford, CT (EL). His 15–5 win–loss record there led to his being acquired in September 1931 by the Brooklyn Dodgers (NL).

One of the top NL pitchers, Mungo remained with Brooklyn until spring 1941. Brooklyn demoted Mungo to the Montreal, Canada (IL) farm team because of arm problems and his off-field behavior. During spring training with Brooklyn in Havana, Cuba, in 1941, he was hastily sent back to the

United States when he became involved, according to one account, with a former bullfighter and his girlfriend and, to another, in a fight with a Cuban dance team. By his own admission, Mungo paid $15,000 in fines during his career and was suspended by managers several times.

Mungo's pitching and pinch hitting helped Montreal win the IL playoffs in 1941. After a fracas with top officials of the Montreal team, however, he was traded to Minneapolis, MN (AA). His record there in 1942 led to his being acquired by the New York Giants (NL) late that year. He left New York to enter the U.S. Army in February 1944. After his discharge, he rejoined the New York Giants in 1945. He retired as a player in spring 1946 and finished the year as manager of Clinton, NC (TSL). He later coached the Pageland AmLe team, operated a movie theater, a dry-goods store, and a trucking business in Pageland.

In his 14-year major league career, Mungo appeared in 364 games, pitched 2,113 innings, and won 120 and lost 115 with 1,242 strikeouts, 868 walks, and a 3.47 ERA. He led the NL in 1934 in innings pitched (315.1) and in 1936 in strikeouts (238) and was selected to the NL All-Star team in 1934 and 1937. After injuring his arm in the latter game, he developed an illegal slippery elm pitch to compensate for the loss of his great fastball and sharp curve. A good hitter for a pitcher, he batted .345 in 1939.

Mungo married Eloise Camp on December 10, 1932, and had two sons, Van Lingle, Jr., and Ernest. A 2.5 mile boulevard in Pageland was named for him in 1983. In addition to the popular "Van Lingle Mungo" song, a tempera painting by Richard Merkin, "Van Lingle Mungo's Havana" (1973), and a poem, "Van Lingle Mungo" (1985), by Paul Parker kept his name alive.

BIBLIOGRAPHY: Frank Graham, *The Brooklyn Dodgers* (New York, 1945); Paul Green, "An Interview with Van Lingle Mungo," *SCD* 11 (December 7, 1984), pp. 142–170; Kirby Higbe and Martin Quigley, *The High Hard One* (New York, 1967); Gene Karst and Martin J. Jones, Jr., *Who's Who in Professional Baseball* (New Rochelle, NY, 1973); *NYT*, February 14, 1985, Sec. II, p. 12; Robert L. Tiemann, *Dodger Classics* (St. Louis, MO, 1983).

                                                                                              Ralph S. Graber

MURPHY, Daniel Francis "Danny" "Old Reliable" (b. August 11, 1876, Philadelphia, PA; d. November 22, 1955, Jersey City, NJ), player, manager, scout, and coach, began his professional baseball career as a second baseman with Worcester, MA (NEL) in 1894. He remained there until 1899, when an independent North Attleboro, MA, team secured his services. In 1900, he joined the Norwich, CT, club (CtL). His performance impressed the New York Giants (NL), who purchased him that September. Murphy debuted with the Giants on September 17 and stayed there the first part of the 1901 season but then was returned to Norwich. His sensational play with Norwich in 1902 featured a .462 batting average in 49 games. Manager

Connie Mack's (BB) Philadelphia Athletics (AL), who had failed to retain the services of star Nap Lajoie (BB), purchased Murphy in July 1902.

Murphy's 1902 debut as the Athletics' second baseman remains surely one of the most auspicious in major league history. Arriving late in Boston on July 8, he did not enter the game with the Pilgrims until the second inning. Murphy then made six hits, including a grand-slam home run, in six times at bat. Defensively, he handled 14 chances for five putouts, seven assists, and two errors as the A's defeated Boston, 22–9. The five-foot-nine-inch, 175-pound right-hand-hitting infielder finished the season with a .313 batting average, helping Mack win his first AL pennant. Philadelphia captured four more AL crowns during Murphy's tenure there.

Murphy played with Philadelphia the next 11 seasons, batting .319 in his last four years with the Mackmen. He performed at second base until the middle of the 1908 season, when Mack switched him to right field to make room for future National Baseball Hall of Famer Eddie Collins (BB). Murphy appeared in the 1905, 1910, and 1911 World Series with the Athletics. His timely hitting against the Chicago Cubs (NL) in 1910 and the New York Giants (NL) in 1911 accounted for 10 runs and keyed Philadelphia championships. Murphy batted .350 in the 1910 and .304 in the 1911 fall classics. The excellent sign stealer was well liked by his teammates, Mack, and the Quaker City fans. The quiet, retiring, but quick-thinking Murphy captained the Athletics in 1911. A knee injury sidelined him for much of the 1912 and 1913 seasons.

Philadelphia released Murphy to the Baltimore, MD, Orioles (IL) before the 1914 season. Murphy, however, jumped to the Brooklyn Tip Tops of the newly formed FL. Advancing age and injuries limited his play the following two seasons, but management designated him as an unofficial adviser, coach, and scout. His major league career ended with the demise of the Brooklyn club and the FL following the 1915 season. In his 16-year major league career spanning 1,518 games in the "dead ball" era, Murphy scored 710 runs, recorded 708 RBIs, and compiled a .288 batting average. His .977 fielding average led AL outfielders in 1909. He finished with a .953 career fielding average.

Murphy managed two EL clubs, New Haven, CT, from 1916 to 1918 and Hartford, CT, in 1919, and scouted and coached with Mack's Philadelphia Athletics from 1921 to 1924. Murphy concluded his baseball career in 1927, when former A's teammate and newly appointed manager Stuffy McInnis (BB) appointed him as a coach with the Philadelphia Phillies (NL).

Subsequently, Murphy became a hardware dealer in Jersey City, NJ, and was employed by Hudson County, NJ, at the County Institutions in Laurel Hill. He married Catherine Moriarity in 1902 and had no children.

BIBLIOGRAPHY: *The Baseball Encyclopedia*, 9th ed. (New York, 1993); Frederick G. Lieb, *Connie Mack: Grand Old Man of Baseball* (New York, 1945); Danny Murphy file, National Baseball Library, Cooperstown, NY; Daniel Okrent and Harris Lewine, eds., *The Ultimate Baseball Book* (Boston, MA, 1979); Joe Reichler, ed., *Ronald Encyclopedia of Baseball* (New York, 1962); John Thorn and Pete Palmer, eds., *Total Baseball*, 3rd ed. (New York, 1993).

Jack C. Braun

O'NEIL, John Jordan Jr. "Buck" (b. November 13, 1911, Carabelle, FL), player, manager, and scout, is the son of John O'Neil, Sr., a sawmiller, and Luella (Taswell) O'Neil, a restaurant cook and part-time teacher. He married Ira Lee Owen from Memphis, TN, in 1946 and had no children.

O'Neil's initial baseball preparation came from hard-nosed coach "Ox" Clemons at Edward G. Waters College in Jacksonville, FL. O'Neil then played with several semiprofessional teams, including the Tampa, FL, Smokers in 1931, Miami, FL, Giants from 1932 to 1934, and the Shreveport, LA, Acme Giants in 1935 and 1936. His first professional team was the Memphis, TN, Red Sox (NAL) in 1937. The following season, O'Neil, a first baseman, joined the Kansas City, MO, Monarchs (NAL). A two-year tour with the U.S. Navy in 1944 and 1945 interrupted his baseball career.

The six-foot-two-inch, 190-pound right-hander played in three East-West All-Star Games (1942, 1943, 1949) and demonstrated his leadership abilities as manager of the West squad from 1951 through 1955. In 1942, O'Neil batted a World Series high .353, in the Monarchs' four-game sweep of the powerful Homestead, PA, Grays. In 1946, he won the NAL batting crown with a fantastic .350 average. That season, the Monarchs met the Newark, NJ, Eagles for the Black World Series championship. He hit .333 against the Eagles with two home runs (including one grand slam), but the Monarchs lost in seven games. O'Neil's lifetime batting average came to exactly .300.

O'Neil became manager of the Monarchs in 1948 and sent more than three dozen players into major league organizations. His noteworthy players included George Altman, Gene Baker, Willard Brown (BB), Elston Howard (S), Connie Johnson, Lou Johnson, Satchel Paige (BB), Hank Thompson, and Bob Thurman. In 1955, the Chicago Cubs (NL) signed O'Neil as a scout. His notable finds included star players Ernie Banks (BB), Lou Brock (BB), and Joe Carter.* Perhaps, O'Neil's greatest personal accomplishment came in 1962, when the Cubs named him as the first African-American coach in major league baseball. Since 1988, O'Neil has scouted for the Kansas City Royals (AL). He also serves on the Veterans' Committee for the National Baseball Hall of Fame and is chairman of the board for the Negro Leagues Baseball Museum in Kansas City, MO. O'Neil provided commentary on the Negro Leagues for the 1994 documentary film *Baseball* by Ken Burns.

BIBLIOGRAPHY: Larry Lester Collection, Kansas City, MO; Larry Lester interviews with John O'Neil, December 1991, January 1992; James A. Riley, *The Biographical Encyclopedia of the Negro Baseball Leagues* (New York, 1994).

Larry Lester

O'NEILL, James Edward "Tip" (b. May 25, 1858, Springfield, Ontario, Canada; d. December 31, 1915, Montreal, Quebec, Canada), player and executive, ranks as the greatest Canadian-born hitter. O'Neill, among his era's most popular players, starred on the St. Louis Brown Stockings (AA) dynasty of the 1880s.

He grew up in an Irish-Canadian family in Woodstock, Ontario. His father, who owned and operated O'Neill House, the town's hotel, brought up four sons and three daughters.

Young O'Neill grew to six feet, 167 pounds and began pitching for the local amateur clubs, including the Harriston Browns and the Young Canadians of Woodstock, the Canadian amateur champions in 1880. He left home in 1881 to play for the barnstorming Hiawatha Grays, a Detroit-based professional team. The following year, he signed with the original New York Metropolitans, the top U.S. independent professional team. In 1883, the Mets' owner, John B. Day,* gained an AA franchise for the Metropolitans and an NL club, the Gothams. Day shifted O'Neill to the Gothams, where the young right-hander won only 5 of 17 games and batted an anemic .179.

In 1884, O'Neill joined the St. Louis Browns, the AA's best and most colorful team. Day attempted to return O'Neill to the Mets, but Canadian-born St. Louis sportswriters Alfred and Billy Spink convinced O'Neill to sign with the Browns. O'Neill posted a good (11–4, 2.68 ERA) pitching record but experienced arm trouble. Before the 1884 season ended, he became the club's left fielder.

With O'Neill established as their leading hitter as third batter in the order, the Browns from 1885 through 1888 became the first and only nineteenth-century team to capture four straight pennants. During that span, O'Neill batted .350 in 1885, .339 in 1886, a monster .435 in 1887, and an AA-leading .332 in 1888. In the era's loosely organized World Series, the Browns tied the Chicago White Stockings (NL) in the disputed 1885 fall classic. St. Louis won in 1886 against Chicago, as O'Neill batted .400. The Browns lost badly to the Detroit Wolverines in 1887 and dropped a heartbreaking 11-game series, 6–5, to the New York Giants in 1888. In the 1886 fall classic, he became the first player to hit two home runs in a World Series game.

O'Neill became a crowd favorite, especially with Irish-Americans. Clean shaven in an era of facial hair, he cut a handsome figure. Browns' center fielder Curt Welsh nicknamed O'Neill "Tip," short for Tipperary, an obvious reference to his Irish heritage.

O'Neill enjoyed a phenomenal season in 1887, when he dominated his league as no player before or since. He swept all offensive categories, leading or sharing the AA lead in base hits (225), doubles (52), triples (14), home runs (14), total bases (357), batting average (.435), slugging average (.691), and runs scored (167). He probably topped the AA in RBIs, although accurate records were not kept. He set new major league records for hits, batting average, doubles, runs, total bases, and slugging average, a record that stood until broken by Babe Ruth (BB). His .435 batting average marks the highest achieved prior to the 60-feet pitching distance.

O'Neill's statistics slipped in 1888, but he still led the AA in batting and in base hits. Both O'Neill and the Browns slipped a notch in 1889, although his .335 batting average and the Browns ranked second best. O'Neill followed with two more .300 seasons, batting .302 with the Chicago Pirates (PL) in 1890 and .321 with the St. Louis Browns (AA) in 1891. His final season came in 1892 with the Cincinnati Reds (NL). In 10 major league seasons, the lifetime bachelor batted .326 with 222 doubles, 92 triples, and 52 home runs.

When his father died, Tip, his mother, three brothers, and a sister moved to Montreal and acquired Hoffman Cafe on Notre Dame Street. He served as president of Montreal's EL club when the city acquired a franchise in 1897. After his brother George died in 1909, O'Neill operated the saloon and restaurant until his death.

BIBLIOGRAPHY: Harvey Frommer, *Primitive Baseball: The First Quarter Century of the National Pastime* (New York, 1988); William Humber, *Cheering for the Home Team: The Story of Baseball in Canada* (Erin, Canada, 1983); Jerry Lansche, *Glory Fades Away: The Nineteenth Century World Series Rediscovered* (Dallas, TX, 1991); Robert L. Tiemann and Mark Rucker, eds., *Nineteenth Century Stars* (Kansas City, MO, 1989).

                                                                    William E. Akin

PALERMO, Stephen Michael "Stevie" "Steve" (b. October 9, 1949, Worcester, MA), umpire, is the son of Vincent Palermo, a school principal, and Angela (Gentile) Palermo. Palermo began umpiring Little League games at age 13 in Oxford, MA, and left Norwich University in Northfield, VT, to attend the BUDS in 1972. Upon graduating, he skipped the normal rookie league assignment and signed with the Class A NYPL. He began 1973 with the Class A CrL but advanced to the Class AA EL by season's end. In the off-season, he umpired in the FInL, DRWL, and PRWL and from 1973 to 1976 was a BUDS instructor. He reached Class AAA in 1975 and was promoted to the AL in September 1976.

As suggested by his rapid rise to the majors in only five years, Palermo proved to be a gifted arbiter with natural umpiring instincts and confidence that bordered on cockiness. He quickly established himself as one of the premier AL ball-strike arbiters without employing the ball-strike indicator used by all other umpires. After the strike-induced split season of 1981, Palermo umpired the AL West Division playoffs between the Oakland Athletics and Kansas City Royals. He also umpired three AL Championship Series (1980, 1982, and 1989), the 1983 World Series, and the 1986 All-Star Game. Palermo, who recovered from a serious case of mononucleosis that sidelined him for most of 1988, easily topped a 1990 poll of general managers as the AL's best umpire.

His career was suddenly interrupted on July 7, 1991, when he was shot while attempting to apprehend muggers who had assaulted two waitresses outside a Dallas, TX, restaurant. Palermo, paralyzed from the waist down by a bullet that hit his spinal column, challenged the medical prognosis that he probably would never walk again by undertaking tortuous therapy. With the aid of crutches and full leg braces, he threw out the first ball of the 1991 World Series. Over the next two years, he increased his mobility to a point where he needed only canes to walk. In November 1993, he risked permanent, total paralysis by undergoing high-risk surgery. The successful surgery might permit further rehabilitation and thus keep alive his dream of returning to umpiring.

A 1975 marriage ended in divorce seven years later. He married Debbie Aaron in February 1991, five months before being shot. He has no children. In recognition of his heroism, Palermo was inducted in 1992 as an honorary member of the Texas Baseball Hall of Fame.

BIBLIOGRAPHY: "Interview: Steve Palermo," *Referee* 14 (October 1989), pp. 20–23; Kansas City (MO) *Star*, November 14, 1993; Bruce Newman, "Pain and Progress," *SI* 76 (July 6, 1992), pp. 28–33; Steve Palermo file, National Baseball Library, Cooperstown, NY; *TSN*, October 28, 1991; December 23, 1991; *USA Today Baseball Weekly*, November 11, 1993.

Larry R. Gerlach

PAOLINELLI, Rinaldo Angelo. *See* Ralph Arthur Pinelli.

PARRISH, Lance Michael (b. June 15, 1956, Clairton, PA), player, starred as the outstanding major league catcher in the mid-1980s. A football All-America and star baseball third baseman at Walnut High School in California, the right-handed-batting and -throwing Parrish declined a UCLA football scholarship. The Detroit Tigers (AL) selected him in the first round of the June 1974 draft and signed Parrish. After spending a season with Bristol, VA (ApL), he switched to catching with Lakeland, FL (FSL) in 1975 and led the SL in 1976 and AA in 1977 in assists and fielding average. An All-Star with Evansville, IN (AA) in 1977, he was promoted to the Detroit Tigers in September.

The six-foot-three-inch, 210-pound Parrish remained with the Tigers through 1986, winning three Gold Gloves (1983–1985) and six AL All-Star selections (1980, 1982–1986). From 1982 through 1985, he averaged 30 homers and 99 RBIs per year. Parrish, one of the keys to the Tigers' 1984 world championship, blasted home runs in the first game of their AL Championship Series sweep of Kansas City and in the decisive fifth game of their World Series triumph against the San Diego Padres. During these years, his on-the-field performance and bulging biceps made him a special favorite of women Tiger fans.

Parrish, however, in 1986 suffered a back injury, which dogged him for the rest of his career. Since the Tigers were unwilling to assume the risk of the long-term contract that free agent Parrish wanted, he signed with the Philadelphia Phillies (NL) in March 1987. He endured two subpar seasons there and was traded to the California Angels (AL) in October 1988. Parrish regained his earlier form in 1990, when he batted .268 with 24 home runs and led AL catchers in percentage of runners caught stealing. He finished the 1992 season with the Seattle Mariners (AL) and split the 1993 season between Albuquerque, NM (PCL) and the Cleveland Indians (AL). In February 1994, the Detroit Tigers signed Parrish to a minor league contract. Parrish finished the strike-shortened 1994 season with the Pittsburgh Pirates (NL) but then was released. His 17-year major league career has featured a .253 batting average, 320 home runs, 1,048 RBIs, and eight All-Star selections (1980, 1982–1986, 1988, 1990).

The Yorba Linda, CA, resident, who married Arlyne Nolan, has three children, David, Matthew, and Ashley Lyne.

BIBLIOGRAPHY: *Detroit Tiger Media Guides*, 1978–1986; John Thorn and Pete Palmer, eds., *Total Baseball*, 3rd ed. (New York, 1993); *TSN Official Baseball Register*, 1994.

Sheldon L. Appleton

PASCUAL, Camilo Alberto y Lus "Little Potato" (b. January 20, 1934, Havana, Cuba), player and scout, is one of three children born to Camilo Pascual and Maria Pascual and started playing organized baseball at age 12 as a shortstop and pitcher. In 1951, the Washington Senators (AL) signed him to a professional baseball contract as a pitcher. In his first season, Pascual divided his time between Geneva, NY (BL), Big Springs, TX (LL), and Chickasha, OK (SSL). He appeared in 16 games, compiling a record of 5 wins and 4 losses. The 1952 campaign found the right-hander beginning the year in Havana, Cuba (FIL), but a midseason trade sent him to Tampa, FL (FIL). He pitched in 24 games, finishing the 1952 season with 8 wins and 6 losses. Pascual returned in 1953 to Havana, Cuba (FIL), where he recorded 10 wins and 6 losses in 25 games.

The 5-foot-11-inch, 175-pound curveballer joined the Washington Senators (AL) in 1954, the first of 18 consecutive major league seasons. From 1954 to 1960, Pascual compiled a 57–84 win–loss record with 10 saves in 248 games. He pitched 1,180.2 innings during that span, striking out 891 batters, completing 47 games, and hurling 13 shutouts. He led the AL in complete games (17) and shutouts (6) in 1959.

In 1961, the Washington Senators became the Minnesota Twins (AL). For the next six seasons, Pascual anchored the Twins' starting rotation. Over this period, he took the mound in 184 games, pitched in 1,284.2 innings, completed 72 contests, hurled 18 shutouts, struck out 994 batters, and walked only 431. Pascual led the AL in strikeouts in 1961 (221), 1962 (206), and 1963 (202) and in complete games in 1961 (8) and 1962 (5). His best season came in 1963, when he finished 21–9 with a 2.46 ERA. In 248.1 innings that season, he struck out 202 batters while walking only 81, completed 18 of 31 starts, and shut out opponents 3 times. In the 1965 World Series against the Los Angeles Dodgers, Pascual lost his only start. He made four All-Star teams (1961, 1962 twice, 1964), losing the first 1962 contest at Washington.

His last five major league seasons were spent with four different clubs, including the Washington Senators (AL) from 1967 to 1969, Cincinnati Reds (NL) in 1969, Los Angeles Dodgers (NL) in 1970, and Cleveland Indians (AL) in 1971. During 18 major league seasons, Pascual won 174 games, lost 170, and produced 36 shutouts with a career 3.63 ERA. In 2,930 innings, he struck out 2,167 batters while walking 1,069. At the plate, Pascual batted .205 in 967 plate appearances with five home runs. Although considered one of the best fielding pitchers, he was overshadowed by Gold Glove teammate Jim Kaat (BB).

Pascual scouts in Latin America for the Los Angeles Dodgers and lives in Miami, FL, with his wife Rachel. They have two sons and two daughters.

BIBLIOGRAPHY: *The Baseball Encyclopedia*, 9th ed. (New York, 1993); *Minnesota Twins Yearbooks*, 1961–1966; James E. Welch, phone conversation with Camilo Pascual, January 1993; Rich Westcott, *Diamond Greats* (Westport, CT, 1988).

James E. Welch

PEÑA, Antonio Francisco "Tony" (b. June 4, 1957, Monte Christi, Dominican Republic), player, is the son of Octaviano Peña and Rosalio Padilla. His brother Arturo played in the Pittsburgh Pirates (NL) farm system, while Ramon pitched for the Detroit Tigers (AL) in 1989. Peña attended Liceo-Marti High School in Monte Christi and learned baseball from his mother, an outstanding softball player. As a child, Peña idolized major league catchers Manny Sanguillen and Johnny Bench (BB). The Pittsburgh Pirates (NL) signed Peña as a free agent and used him as a catcher in their minor league system from 1976 to 1978, but he struggled at the plate. Peña, however, slugged 34 home runs and batted .313 at Buffalo, NY (EL) in 1979 and followed with a .327 batting average at Portland, OR (PCL) the next season.

Peña shared catching chores with Pirate Steve Nicosia in 1981, but his .300 batting average and strong defense won him full-time duties behind the plate. From 1982 to 1986, Peña batted .285, hit at least 10 home runs each year, and demonstrated good speed on the bases. His catching position of almost sitting with one leg thrust out enabled him to block the plate very effectively. Despite the unusual receiving stance, Peña threw out even the best base stealers with his quick release and rifle arm.

St. Louis Cardinals (NL) manager Whitey Herzog (S) believed he could win an NL pennant in 1987 if he could acquire a solid catcher. In April 1987, the Redbirds traded center fielder Andy Van Slyke,* catcher Mike

LaValliere, and pitcher Mike Dunne to the Pirates for Peña. A few games into the 1987 season, Peña broke his thumb and spent six weeks on the disabled list. Although hitting only .214 for the campaign, he started wearing glasses late in the season and batted .381 in the NL Championship Series against the San Francisco Giants and .409 in the World Series versus the Minnesota Twins (AL). Peña led the NL in fielding average in 1988 and 1989. The Redbirds did not resign the five-time NL All-Star in 1990 because youthful catchers Todd Zeile and Tom Pagnozzi were ready for the major leagues.

Peña signed a $6.4 million, three-year contract with the Boston Red Sox (AL). After a productive offensive 1990 season, he batted only .231 in 1991 and .241 in 1992. He won a fourth Gold Glove in 1991, however, and remained a good handler of pitchers. Peña signed a one-year, $2.5 million contract to stay in Boston for 1993 but batted only .181 that year. The Red Sox released him following the 1993 season. In February 1994, the Cleveland Indians (AL) signed Peña, who batted .295 in 40 games. In 15 major league seasons, he has batted .263 with 101 home runs and 643 RBIs.

Peña married Amaris Garcia on January 7, 1976. They have two children, Tony, Jr., and Jennifer, and reside in Santiago, Dominican Republic, where his family has a farm.

BIBLIOGRAPHY: John Dewan, ed., *The Scouting Report: 1990* (New York, 1990); Zander Hollander, ed., *The Complete Book of Baseball 1994* (New York, 1994); Kip Ingle and Brian Bartow, *The St. Louis Cardinals Media Guide 1988* (St. Louis, MO, 1988); Antonio Peña file, National Baseball Library, Cooperstown, NY; George Vass, "Major Leagues Facing a Crisis in Catching," *BD* 49 (July 1990), pp. 20–24.

                                                                    Frank J. Olmsted

PENDLETON, Terry Lee (b. July 16, 1960, Los Angeles, CA), player, graduated from Channel Island High School in Oxnard, CA, where he lettered in baseball, football, and basketball. He majored in physical education at Oxnard College and Fresno State College. As a senior at Fresno State, Pendleton played the outfield, batted .397, and collected 65 RBIs. The St. Louis Cardinals (NL) selected Pendleton in the seventh round of the June 1982 draft. The five-foot-nine-inch, 193-pound, right-handed Pendleton played second base at Johnson City, TN (ApL) and St. Petersburg, FL (FSL) in 1982. In 1983, a fractured wrist limited him to 48 games at Arkansas (TL). The switch-hitting Pendleton moved to third base at Louisville, KY (AA) in 1984 and batted .297 in 91 games before St. Louis purchased his contract. Pendleton made 65 consecutive starts at third base for the Cardinals, enjoying 24 multiple hit games and batting .324. In 1985, Pendleton played every day and hit just .240 with only 24 extra base hits. He batted .208 in the triumphant NL Championship Series against the Los Angeles Dodgers and

.261 in the World Series, which the Cardinals lost in 7 games to the Kansas City Royals (AL).

Pendleton's 1986 season proved a carbon copy of the 1985 campaign. Pitchers knew Pendleton swung freely and pitched him out of the strike zone. His .239 batting average included only one home run in 159 games. Despite a short, stocky physique, Pendleton showed tremendous range at third base and worked hard to improve his glove work. In 1985 and 1986, Pendleton came to the ball park every afternoon to field 100 extra ground balls. From 1986 to 1992, Pendleton led NL third basemen five times in assists and twice in putouts and earned three Gold Gloves. His over-the-shoulder catches while running away from home plate were remarkable.

Pendleton's best season with the Cardinals came in 1987, when he batted .286 with 12 home runs and 96 RBIs. He collected four hits against the San Francisco Giants in the NL Championship Series, but a pulled ribcage muscle limited him to 3 games as a pinch hitter and designated hitter in the World Series. St. Louis lost the fall classic in 7 games to the Minnesota Twins. Hamstring and knee injuries limited Pendleton's 1988 campaign to 110 games and a .253 batting average. He rebounded in 1989 to play 162 games and hit .264. Pendleton never got on track in 1990, as St. Louis tried catcher Todd Zeile at third base. Pendleton rode the bench in September, finishing with a .230 batting average.

The Atlanta Braves (NL) signed Pendleton in December 1990 to a four-year deal worth $10.2 million. Few players have made more dramatic turn-arounds. In 1991, Pendleton led the NL with 187 hits and a .319 batting average, solidifying the Braves infield and being named NL MVP and Comeback Player of the Year. Although Pendleton batted only .167 in the NL Championship Series against the Pittsburgh Pirates, he hit .367 with two home runs in the World Series. The Braves, however, lost the fall classic in seven games to the Minnesota Twins. In 1992, Pendleton reached personal highs of 98 runs scored, 105 RBIs, and 199 hits, batted .311, and played in his first All-Star Game. The Braves won the NL West, again defeating the Pittsburgh Pirates for the NL pennant. Pendleton batted only .240 in the World Series, which the Toronto Blue Jays garnered in six games.

In 1993, Pendleton, who general manager John Schuerholz calls "the cornerstone of the club," joined teammates in coming alive at midseason. Pendleton finished 1993 with a .272 batting average, 17 home runs, and 84 RBIs, helping Atlanta win a third consecutive NL West title. Pendleton was denied a fifth World Series appearance, though, when the Philadelphia Phillies overcame the Braves in the NL Championship Series. The Braves released Pendleton following the 1994 season. Through the strike-shortened 1994 campaign, Pendleton had played in 1,478 games, collected 1,524 hits, 702 runs, 111 home runs, 747 RBIs, and 121 stolen bases, and compiled a .272 batting average.

Pendleton married Catherine Grindulo Marguez in October 1984 and lives in Oxnard, CA.

BIBLIOGRAPHY: John Dewan, ed., *The Scouting Report: 1990* (New York, 1990); David Faulkner, *Nine Sides of the Diamond: Baseball's Great Glove Men on the Fine Art of Defense* (New York, 1990); Zander Hollander, ed., *The Complete Handbook of Baseball 1994* (New York, 1994); Rob Rains, "Pendleton's Attitude Keeps Braves Sharp," *USA Today Baseball Weekly*, September 16–22, 1993, p. 8; *St. Louis Cardinals 1990 Media Guide;* John Sonderegger, "Cardinals' Terry Pendleton Comes of Age as a Hitter," *BD* 46 (October 1987), pp. 42–45.

Frank J. Olmsted

PETERS, Gary Charles (b. April 21, 1937, Grove City, PA), player, grew up in the northwestern Pennsylvania town of Mercer and is the son of Thomas Peters, a gas heater plant foreman, and Elizabeth (Rowe) Peters. An All-State interscholastic basketball player, Peters starred as a hoopster at Grove City College. Neither his high school nor college fielded a baseball team, but Peters played sandlot and AmLe ball, winning recognition as a hard-hitting first baseman–outfielder. The Chicago White Sox (AL) signed Peters in 1952 and converted him to a pitcher on the recommendation of coach Ray Berres. His first season of professional baseball at Holdredge, NE, saw Peters lead the NeSL in strikeouts and innings pitched. He married Jean A. Jackal on January 31, 1958, and has two daughters.

Although never winning more than 13 games in a minor league season, Peters impressed Chicago management and won steady promotions. Peters pitched briefly for the White Sox from 1959 through 1962, but inconsistency plagued him. The White Sox, who had used up Peters's options, finally kept him on their roster in 1963. Manager Al Lopez (BB) needed an additional starter in May and turned to Peters, who soon settled into the rotation and became AL Rookie of the Year. A six-foot-two-inch, 200-pound southpaw, Peters batted left-handed and was used frequently as a pinch hitter in most of his major league campaigns. With the exception of 1968, when he won only 4 games for a ninth-place team, Peters recorded 10 or more victories for the White Sox each season through 1969. His best years saw him rely on a slider and especially on a sinking fastball that he had first learned to throw properly in PRWL ball. No longer a dominant pitcher, Peters was traded to the Boston Red Sox (AL) in a four-player deal in December 1969. Peters stayed in Boston three years and was released after the 1972 campaign. He retired the following spring after failing to win a spot with the Kansas City Royals (AL).

During his major league career, Peters won 124 games and lost 103 decisions with a 3.25 ERA and 23 shutouts. He led the AL in ERA with 2.33 in 1963 and 1.98 in 1966 and won 20 games in 1964. He triumphed 19 times in 1963 and recorded 16 victories for the White Sox in 1967 and the Red Sox in 1970. In 1959, he pitched a no-hitter against the Minneapolis, MN,

Millers (AA). Peters resides in Sarasota, FL, and works as a construction company foreman.

BIBLIOGRAPHY: "For Peters' Sake," *Senior Scholastic* (April 10, 1964), p. 84; Jerome Holtzman, "Prize Rookie Pitcher Polishes Hill Weapons," *TSN*, December 28, 1963, p. 7; Gene Karst and Martin J. Jones, *Who's Who in Professional Baseball* (New Rochelle, NY, 1973), p. 756.

Lloyd J. Graybar

PETROCELLI, Americo Peter "Rico" (b. June 27, 1943, Brooklyn, NY), player and manager, is the youngest of seven children of Attilio Petrocelli, a foundry worker, and Louise Petrocelli, both Italian immigrants, and graduated from high school in Brooklyn. The Boston Red Sox (AL) signed him in 1961 to a bonus contract eventually worth $60,000. Petrocelli, a six-foot, 188-pound right-handed shortstop, gained minor league experience with Winston-Salem, NC (CrL) in 1962, Reading, PA (EL) in 1963, and Seattle, WA (PCL) in 1964. The moody, sensitive Petrocelli often clashed with managers but gradually matured.

Petrocelli played shortstop with Boston from 1965 through 1970. The resurgent Red Sox captured the 1967 AL pennant, as Petrocelli, an AL All-Star team selection, batted .259 with 17 home runs and 66 RBIs. Petrocelli caught Rich Rollins's short fly to clinch the AL pennant against the Minnesota Twins. Boston lost a seven-game World Series to the St. Louis Cardinals, but Petrocelli belted 2 home runs in Game 6 at Fenway Park. In the fourth inning, Carl Yastrzemski (BB), Reggie Smith (BB), and Petrocelli set a World Series record by slugging home runs in the same stanza.

Petrocelli's best season came in 1969, when he batted a career-best .297 with 97 RBIs and made the AL All-Star team for the second time. He established an AL mark for most home runs by a shortstop (40), led AL shortstops defensively for the second consecutive year, and tied an AL standard for fewest single-season errors (14) at his position. The Red Sox shifted Petrocelli to third base in 1971 upon acquiring shortstop Luis Aparicio (BB). Petrocelli adjusted well, pacing third basemen in fielding that year. The powerful Petrocelli belted 29 home runs with a career-high 103 RBIs in 1970 and 28 home runs with 89 RBIs in 1971. Injuries diminished his offensive production thereafter. Boston won the AL pennant in 1975, but Petrocelli slumped offensively. The Cincinnati Reds defeated the Red Sox in a seven-game World Series, as Petrocelli batted .308 with 8 hits and 4 RBIs. During 13 major league seasons through 1976, Petrocelli batted .251 with 1,352 hits, 237 doubles, 210 home runs, and 773 RBIs.

The Lynnfield, MA, resident, who managed Pawtucket, RI (IL) in 1992 and served as hitting and infield instructor for New Britain, CT (EL) in 1994, married Elsie Jensen in March 1965 and has four children.

BIBLIOGRAPHY: Ross Forman, " '67 Red Sox Rehash the Impossible Dream," *SCD* 19 (November 6, 1992), pp. 140–142; Al Hirshberg, "How Rico Put 'Pop' in His Game," *Sport* 44 (September 1967), pp. 26–27, 29, 83–84; Barry McDermott, "Petrocelli Pulls Up His Sox," *SI* 36 (April 3, 1972), pp. 67, 70; Mike Shatzkin, ed., *The Ballplayers* (New York, 1990), p. 680; *TSN Baseball Register*, 1976, p. 281.

David L. Porter

PFEFFER, Edward Joseph "Jeff" "Hassen" (b. March 4, 1888, Seymour, IL; d. August 15, 1972, Chicago, IL), player, pitched in major league baseball between 1911 and 1924, compiling a lifetime 158–112 win–loss mark and a 2.77 ERA. The six-foot-three-inch, 220-pound right-handed hurler, the younger brother of pitcher Francis Xavier "Big Jeff" Pfeffer, began his professional baseball career in 1909 with LaCrosse, WI (MWL), winning 18 games. In the fall of 1909, his contract was purchased by Fort Wayne, IN (CL). Pfeffer pitched for Fort Wayne in 1910 and 1911, triumphing in 29 games over the two seasons. His work in Fort Wayne attracted the attention of the St. Louis Browns (AL), who gave him a brief, undistinguished trial in September 1911.

After pitching for Grand Rapids, MI (CL) the next two seasons and winning 25 games in 1913, Pfeffer returned to the major leagues in September 1913 with the Brooklyn Dodgers (NL). He pitched for Brooklyn from 1914 until June 1921, serving in the U.S. Navy Reserves in 1918 and attaining 67 victories from 1914 to 1916. In June 1921, Brooklyn traded Pfeffer to the St. Louis Cardinals (NL) for pitcher Ferdie Schupp and utility infielder Hal Janvrin. He won 19 games in 1923 for St. Louis and closed out his major league career in 1924 with the Pittsburgh Pirates (NL). Pfeffer later hurled for San Francisco, CA (PCL) in 1925 and Toledo, OH (AA) in 1926 and 1927. Pfeffer also pitched in two World Series with Brooklyn, appearing in 1916 against the Boston Red Sox and 1920 against the Cleveland Indians. His only decision, a 4–1 setback, came in the fifth and decisive game of the 1916 fall classic.

An amusing story about a card game involving Pfeffer occurred during one of the St. Louis Cardinals' railroad trips. Left-handed pitcher Bill Bailey criticized a play Pfeffer made in the game, whereupon Pfeffer commented in an uncomplimentary fashion about the intelligence of southpaws. Bailey retorted, "Well, you never saw one of them digging a ditch, did you?" "No," replied Pfeffer, "but that's because they want the ditches straight."

BIBLIOGRAPHY: *The Baseball Encyclopedia*, 9th ed. (New York, 1993); Edward Joseph Pfeffer file, National Baseball Library, Cooperstown, NY.

David S. Matz

PIERSALL, James Anthony "Jimmy" (b. November 14, 1929, Waterbury, CT), player, starred in basketball at Waterbury High School before attracting the attention of baseball scouts. Piersall broke into professional baseball as an outfielder with Scranton, PA (EL) in 1948 and then played for Louisville, KY (AA) in 1949 and 1950. In 1950 the Boston Red Sox promoted the six-foot, 175-pound outfielder to the parent club. He spent the 1951 season shuffling between Louisville and Birmingham, AL (SL), finishing with a .346 batting mark for Birmingham. The following season, he was hospitalized for a nervous breakdown. His breakdown was poignantly recounted in a book and then a baseball film, aptly entitled *Fear Strikes Out.*

On June 10, 1953, in the first game of a doubleheader against the St. Louis Browns (AL), Piersall made six hits in six trips to the plate for Boston, tying an AL record. The performance marked his comeback and his new philosophy for dealing with the taunts of unruly fans who rode him unmercifully. Piersall replaced Dom DiMaggio (S) as the regular Red Sox center fielder the following season and was named an AL All-Star in 1954 and 1956. Piersall's career was characterized by numerous bizarre and zany antics, including a celebrated fight with New York Yankee ruffian Billy Martin (BB).

In December 1958, Boston traded Piersall to the Cleveland Indians (AL) for Vic Wertz (S) and Gary Geiger. The six-foot, 184-pound right-handed Piersall played a very shallow center field but won Gold Gloves in 1958 and 1961. His best offensive production included his AL-leading 40 doubles in 1956, 19 home runs and 103 runs scored in 1957, and a career-high 18 steals for the Cleveland Indians in 1960, fifth best in the AL. The best average of his major league career, a .322 mark for the 1961 Indians, placed him fourth in the AL. Manager Casey Stengel (BB) once said of him, "He's great, but you got to play him in a cage."

Piersall in 1961 earned $45,000, his highest salary. He was traded to the expansion Washington Senators (AL) in October 1961 and to the New York Mets (NL) in May 1963 for first baseman Gil Hodges (BB), who became the Washington manager. Piersall's running the bases backwards after hitting his one hundredth major league home run epitomized his zany approach to the game. The home run came on July 26, 1963, off Dallas Green of the Philadelphia Phillies (NL) at the Polo Grounds.

Manager Casey Stengel released him the next day, saying, "There's room for just one clown on this team!" Piersall trekked down from the Polo Grounds to Yankee Stadium, where the Los Angeles Angels (AL) were playing the New York Yankees (AL) and asked old friend and manager Bill Rigney for a job. He hit .314 for the Angels in 1964 as a part-timer, being voted the Comeback Player of the Year.

After retiring as a player in 1967, Piersall spent two years as the general manager of the Roanoke, VA, Buckskins (ACFL). In 1973, he managed the Orangeburg, SC, Cardinals (WCL). The high-strung, volatile Piersall carried his combative nature to the broadcast booth, where he announced for the Chicago White Sox (AL) before being fired for criticizing management.

During his 17-year career, Piersall compiled a lifetime .272 batting average in 1,734 major league games. He made 1,604 hits with 256 doubles, 52 triples, 104 homers, and 591 RBIs. Piersall married Mary Teevan on October 22, 1949, and had nine children, including Eileen, Doreen, Claire, and Jimmy. Since their divorce, he has married two other times.

BIBLIOGRAPHY: Gene Karst and Martin Jones, Jr., eds., *Who's Who in Professional Baseball* (New Rochelle, NY, 1973); Jimmy Piersall and Al Hirshberg, *Fear Strikes Out* (New York, 1956); Jimmy Piersall with Richard Whittingham, *The Truth Hurts* (Chicago, IL, 1984); Mike Shatzkin, ed., *The Ballplayers* (New York, 1990); George Sullivan, *Baseball's Wacky Players* (New York, 1984).

William A. Borst

PINELLI, Ralph Arthur "Babe" "The Soft Thumb" (b. Rinaldo Angelo Paolinelli, October 18, 1895, San Francisco, CA; d. October 2, 1984, Daly City, CA), player and umpire, was the son of Italian immigrants Rafael Paolinelli, a grocer, and Ermida (Silvestri) Paolinelli. He left school at age 10 to help support the family after his father died in the San Francisco, CA, earthquake of 1906. A tough street kid, he gained local prominence as an amateur boxer and a scrappy infielder in semiprofessional leagues. He signed with Portland, OR (PCL) in 1917 and adopted an Anglicized version of his name at the request of a sportswriter. Pinelli joined the Chicago White Sox (AL) as a wartime replacement at the end of the 1918 season but returned to Sacramento, CA (PCL) for 1919. After a trial with the Detroit Tigers (AL) in 1920 and an outstanding year with Oakland, CA (PCL) in 1921, Pinelli took over as the regular third baseman of the Cincinnati Reds (NL) in 1922. He proved a solid contact hitter with little power in six years with the Reds. Besides hitting over .300 in two of his first three seasons, he posted a career .276 batting average with only five home runs. A "smart" player and master of the "hidden-ball trick," he performed sparingly the last two years because of defensive shortcomings. Pinelli, released during the 1927 season, returned to the PCL, where he averaged over .300 in five seasons with San Francisco and Oakland and once hit two grand-slam homers in a single game.

Pinelli started as a PCL umpire in 1933, using personal contacts to overcome his lack of experience, and joined the NL two years later. His understanding of the game and affable personality made him a popular, highly respected arbiter. Although a fiery umpire-baiter during his playing days, Pinelli earned the nickname, "The Soft Thumb" for his reluctance to eject players and managers. He worked four All-Star Games (1937, 1941, 1950, and 1956) and six World Series (1939, 1941, 1947, 1948, 1952, and 1956). He also umpired the first night game in major league history on May 24, 1935, at Cincinnati between the Philadelphia Phillies and the Reds. Pinelli's finest hour occurred at the end of his career. The plate umpire for the fifth game of the 1956 World Series between the New York Yankees (AL) and the Brooklyn Dodgers (NL), he called a game-ending third strike on Brooklyn Dodger pinch-hitter Dale Mitchell* to preserve the first perfect game in World Series by Don Larsen* of the New York Yankees. Some claimed that the pitch was low and outside by a few inches, but the veteran Pinelli never hesitated in calling a strike and thereby enforced baseball's unwritten code requiring a batter to swing at a close pitch in that situation.

Pinelli, who claimed never to have missed a game during 22 major league seasons, retired after the 1956 campaign. He married Mable McKee in December 1916 and had two children.

BIBLIOGRAPHY: Stephen Jay Gould, "The Strike That Was Low and Outside," *NYT*, November 10, 1984; Babe Pinelli as told to Joe King, *Mr. Ump* (Philadelphia, PA, 1953); Babe Pinelli file, National Baseball Library, Cooperstown, NY; San Francisco (CA) *Examiner*, October 23–25, 1984; Herbert Simons, "The Babe in Blue," *BM* 68 (February 1942), pp. 401–402; *TSN*, November 5, 1984.

Larry R. Gerlach

PIPP, Walter Clement "Wally" (b. February 17, 1893, Chicago, IL; d. January 11, 1965, Grand Rapids, MI), player, grew up in Grand Rapids and attended Catholic University. He signed with Kalamazoo, MI (SML) in 1912 and played first base with Providence, RI (IL) and Scranton, PA (NYSL) in 1913, debuting in the major leagues in September 1913 with the Detroit Tigers (AL). After having a good season at Rochester, NY (IL) in 1914, he was sold in January 1915 to the New York Yankees (AL).

Pipp's name has become part of the legend and lore of baseball history. To "Pipp" is to be replaced due to injury or illness and never regain one's position. On June 1, 1925, Pipp begged out of a Yankee game, due to a headache. He was replaced in the lineup by Lou Gehrig (BB), who had started his 2,130 consecutive playing game streak the previous day as a pinch hitter. Miller Huggins's (BB) famous last words to Pipp were, "The kid can replace you and you can take the day off." Pipp later was beaned in practice during the 1925 season by Yankee rookie pitcher Charlie Caldwell (FB), later Princeton University football coach. The pitch fractured his skull, causing him to spend two weeks in the hospital. When he had recovered, his regular position with the Yankees was gone permanently.

Pipp showed considerable power during the dead ball era, leading the AL in 1916 in home runs with 12 and RBIs with 99. The following season, the left-handed hitter repeated as home run champion with 9. The six-foot-one-inch, 180-pound Pipp enjoyed his best seasons as the Yankees won their first three AL pennants from 1921 through 1923. Pipp compiled batting averages of .296, .329, and .304 during this period.

Pipp's career was always deeply intertwined with that of Gehrig. Pipp scouted Gehrig at the suggestion of William C. Smith, the owner of the Indianapolis, IN, club (AA) and offered him $500 to sign. Gehrig refused because the New York Yankees and New York Giants (NL) had offered him more money. Gehrig was not the only replacement the oft-injured Pipp had. After Pipp sprained his ankle on September 27, 1923, the Yankees called up Gehrig from Hartford, CT (EL) for the World Series against the New York

Giants. The Giants, however, refused to approve this replacement, causing the Yankees to play Babe Ruth (BB) at first base the rest of the season. Pipp answered the bell for the World Series with his ankle heavily taped. He reinjured the ankle, sliding in the third game. Ruth replaced him for the remainder of that contest, but Pipp returned the next day to complete the series.

In February 1926 the Yankees sold the sure-handed first baseman to the Cincinnati Reds (NL), where he played three seasons. Pipp finished his major league career with 1,870 games, a .281 batting average, 1,939 hits, 90 homers, and 996 RBIs. In three World Series, Pipp batted .224 with 15 hits. His last professional role as a player came in 1930 with Newark, NJ (IL), where he hit .312.

Following his playing career, Pipp worked in publishing, aired a pregame show, and even wrote scripts for a Detroit announcer. He later worked as a manufacturer's representative in the automotive supply business, selling screws and bolts. Pipp spent his last days in a rest home after suffering several debilitating strokes. He was survived by his wife, Nora Powers, and their three sons, Tom, Ben, and Walter, Jr., and a daughter, Mrs. William Bibler.

BIBLIOGRAPHY: Paul Dickson, *The Dickson Baseball Dictionary* (New York, 1989); Ernie Harwell, "Pipp Picks Out Highlights of His Career at Gateway," *TSN*, December 20, 1961, p. 17; Gene Karst and Martin Jones, Jr., eds., *Who's Who in Professional Baseball* (New Rochelle, NY, 1973); Obituary, *TSN*, January 23, 1965, p. 26; Mike Shatzkin, ed., *The Ballplayers* (New York, 1990).

William A. Borst

POLLET, Howard Joseph "Howie" (b. June 26, 1921, New Orleans, LA; d. August 8, 1974, Houston, TX), player and coach, was of French ancestry and attended Jesuit Prep High School and Fourtier High School in New Orleans. St. Louis Cardinals (NL) scout Eddie Dyer* signed Pollet, who joined New Iberia, LA (EvL) in 1939. The 6-foot-½-inch, 175-pound southpaw won 20 games for Houston, TX (TL) in 1940 and 1941. Cardinals general manager Branch Rickey (BB) promoted Pollet in September 1941, provided he sign a contract for 1942 at $600 per month. After signing reluctantly, Pollet in September hurled 6 complete games, won five contests, and pitched two shutouts. Pollet married Virginia Clark on October 18, 1941, and had seven children, including Roberta, Howard, Jr., Shirley, Christopher, and John. He divided time in 1942 between the bullpen and starting rotation, winning 7 of 12 decisions. Pollet retired the only batter he faced in the fourth game of the 1942 World Series, in which St. Louis defeated the New York Yankees in 5 games.

In 1943, Pollet hurled three consecutive shutouts and raised his record to eight wins and four losses before entering the U.S. Army Air Corps on July 11. He was attached to the 58th Bomb Wing, 20th Air Force in the Pacific theater. With fellow players Enos Slaughter (BB), Billy Hitchcock, Birdie Tebbetts,* Joe Gordon (S), and Tex Hughson,* Pollet said his purpose was "to provide recreation and entertainment for the men over there. We accomplished our mission in excellent fashion as any G.I. who witnessed the games will agree." He was discharged in November 1945, missing the St. Louis NL pennants in 1943 and 1944.

Pollet returned in 1946 to enjoy the finest season of his major league career, leading the NL with 21 victories, 266 innings pitched, and a 2.10 ERA. Manager Dyer's Cardinals defeated Leo Durocher's (BB) Brooklyn Dodgers twice in the second-ever major league playoff to win the NL pennant. Pollet pitched 10 innings in the first game of the World Series against the Boston Red Sox (AL) but lost, 3–2, when Rudy York (S) belted a change-up over the fence. Pollet started Game 5 with pain in his arm and could not make it through the first inning. St. Louis won the World Championship in 7 games. After arm surgery, he won only 9 of 20 decisions in 1947. Pollet recovered to win 13 of 21 decisions in 1948. He used a moving fastball, straight change-up, and slow curveball to win 20 games, hurl five shutouts, and record a 2.77 ERA in 1949, but the Cardinals fell 1 game short of the NL pennant-winning Brooklyn Dodgers. Teammate Stan Musial (BB) described Pollet as "a class pitcher, a stylist with pitching rhythm, and a student of the game."

Pollet, who was often bothered by a bad back, won 14 contests and lost 13 games in 1950. After Pollet dropped his first 3 decisions in 1951, the Cardinals in June traded him with catcher Joe Garagiola (BB) to the Pittsburgh Pirates (NL). Pollet lost 10 of 16 decisions for the Pirates in 1951 and stumbled to a 7–16 record in 1952. On June 4, 1953, Pittsburgh sent Pollet as part of a 10-player deal to the Chicago Cubs (NL). In three seasons with the Cubs, he won 17 contests and lost 19 games. He divided the 1956 campaign between the Chicago White Sox (AL) and the Pittsburgh Pirates, compiling a 3–5 record. Pollet's major league career included 403 games, 2,107.1 innings, 131 victories, and 116 defeats with 20 saves and 934 strikeouts.

Pollet pursued the insurance business during the off-season with Eddie Dyer in Houston, TX, and served as St. Louis Cardinals pitching coach from 1959 to 1964, being credited with developing Ernie Broglio, Bob Gibson (BB), and Ray Sadecki. He held the same position with the Houston Astros (NL) in 1965.

BIBLIOGRAPHY: Bob Broeg, *Redbirds: A Century of Cardinals' Baseball* (St. Louis, MO, 1981); Gene Karst and Martin Jones, Jr., *Who's Who in Professional Baseball* (New Rochelle, NY, 1973); Stan Musial and Bob Broeg, *Stan Musial, "The Man's" Own Story* (Garden City, NY, 1964); Howard Pollet file, National Baseball Library, Cooperstown, NY; *St. Louis Cardinals' Yearbook, 1962.*

Frank J. Olmsted

PORTER, Darrell Ray (b. January 17, 1952, Joplin, MO), player, is the son of Raymond Porter, a driver for United Transport Company, and Twila Mae (Conley) Porter, a high school cafeteria manager, and was the second of five children. Porter, the MVP in football, basketball, and baseball at Southeast High School in Oklahoma City, OK, was selected an All-State Catcher in Oklahoma for 1968 and 1969. After Porter signed a football letter of intent to attend the University of Oklahoma, the Milwaukee Brewers (AL) made him the fourth player picked in the 1970 major league baseball draft. The six-foot-one-inch, 200-pound Porter signed a $70,000 plus incentives contract with Milwaukee and reported to Clinton, IA (ML).

A 24–home run outburst at Danville, IL (ML) in 1971 earned the left-handed-batting Porter a trial with the Brewers. After more seasoning at Evansville, IN (AA), Porter started as Milwaukee's catcher in 1973. He showed promise with the Brewers but blossomed after being dealt to the Kansas City Royals (AL). Two fine seasons with the Royals were followed by his best year in 1979 with 20 home runs, as Porter became only the second catcher in history to exceed 100 walks, runs scored, and RBIs in a season. Royals skipper Whitey Herzog (S) argued Porter should have been AL MVP.

Although Porter enjoyed success on the field, his personal life was collapsing. He married Teri Brown on June 2, 1972, but they divorced in 1976. They had no children. While playing winter ball in 1970, Porter was introduced to marijuana. The next few years saw him start taking quaaludes, amphetamines, and finally cocaine. During spring training in 1980, Porter sought help from former Brooklyn Dodger (NL) great Don Newcombe (BB) and entered a rehabilitation program. Porter, who credited his deep Christian faith in helping him through, returned to the Kansas City Royals six weeks later. He hit .249 with seven home runs, batted only .100 in the AL Championship Series, and hit .143 in the World Series, lost to the Philadelphia Phillies (NL).

Over the Thanksgiving holiday in 1980, Porter married Deanne Gaulter and agreed to a five-year deal worth $3.5 million with Herzog, now general manager of the St. Louis Cardinals (NL).

Porter endured three months on the disabled list in 1981 and criticism of St. Louis fans, who lamented the departure of his popular predecessor Ted Simmons (BB). However, 1982 marked a new beginning for Porter. A daughter, Lindsey, was born in March. An excellent handler of pitchers, Porter was named NL Championship Series MVP as the Cardinals defeated the Atlanta Braves and World Series MVP when the Redbirds downed the Milwaukee Brewers in seven games. Porter sparkled defensively and at bat in both series. He returned to postseason play a fifth time in 1985, when St. Louis defeated the Los Angeles Dodgers for the NL pennant. The Cardinals, however, lost the World Series in seven games to Porter's old teammates, the Kansas City Royals.

The Texas Rangers (AL) in 1986 signed Porter, who experienced two productive seasons as occasional designated hitter and backup receiver. He retired with 1,369 hits, 188 home runs, 765 runs scored, 826 RBIs, and .247 batting average and played on the AL All-Star team in 1978, 1979, and 1980. Porter resides in Lee's Summit, MO, where he oversees his investments and enjoys fishing.

BIBLIOGRAPHY: Whitey Herzog and Kevin Horrigan, *White Rat: A Life in Baseball* (New York, 1987); Arnold Irish, "He Has a Talent for Guiding Pitchers," *BD* 42 (August 1983), pp. 80–82; Kansas City Royals, *Grandslam* (Kansas City, MO, 1980); Darrell Porter with William Deerfield, *Snap Me Perfect: The Darrell Porter Story* (Nashville, TN, 1984).

Frank J. Olmsted

PUCKETT, Kirby (b. March 14, 1961, Chicago, IL), player, is the youngest of nine children born to William Puckett and Catherine Puckett and started playing baseball in the south Chicago projects of Robert Taylor Homes, just one mile south of Comiskey Park. At Chicago's Calumet High School, he starred as a third baseman and earned All-America honors. Following graduation in 1979, however, Puckett received no baseball offers and worked at a Ford plant. Bradley University coach Dewey Kalmer, who spotted Puckett at a Kansas City Royals (AL) free agent tryout in the summer of 1980, offered him a baseball scholarship and moved him to center field. Following his father's death in 1981, Puckett left the Peoria, IL, campus to live closer to his mother and enrolled at Triton CC in River Grove, IL. In his one season for Triton CC in 1982, he hit .472, belted 16 home runs, stole 42 bases, and was named 1982 Region IV Player of the Year. In 1993, Puckett was inducted into the Triton Hall of Fame.

The Minnesota Twins (AL) made the right-handed-hitting and -throwing outfielder their first selection and third overall pick in the January 1982 free agent draft and assigned him to Elizabethton, TN (ApL), where he led the ApL in batting (.382), at bats (275), runs scored (65), hits (105), total bases (135), and stolen bases (43). Puckett was named to the ApL All-Star team and ApL Player of the Year by *BA*. Minnesota assigned him in 1983 to Visalia, CA (CaL), where he led the CaL in at bats (548), finished second in doubles (29), fourth in triples (7), and sixth in batting (.314), and was named to the CaL All-Star team and CaL Player of the Year.

Puckett's 1984 season began with Toledo, OH (IL), but on May 8 Minnesota promoted him to the major league club for a game with the California Angels. Puckett, only the ninth major league player to get 4 hits in his initial game, made the Topps' Major League All-Rookie Team and finished third to Alvin Davis of the Seattle Mariners in the AL Rookie of the Year balloting. Since 1985, Puckett has been considered the heart and soul of the Twins with a .321 batting average, 164 home runs, 843 RBIs, and 156 games per year average. Puckett has appeared in nine consecutive All-Star Games (1986–1994), starting in 1986, 1989, 1992, 1993, and 1994. In All-Star contests, he has batted .318 and was named 1993 MVP with a double, home run, and 2 RBIs. Puckett played in the AL Championship Series against the Detroit Tigers in 1987 and Toronto Blue Jays in 1991. The Twins won both series in 5 games. In 10 AL Championship Series games, the 1991 Series MVP batted .311 with 3 home runs and 9 RBIs. Puckett appeared in the World Series against the St. Louis Cardinals in 1987 and Atlanta Braves in 1991, helping the Twins win both 7-game series. Puckett's World Series statistics include a .308 batting average, 16 hits, 2 home runs, and 7 RBIs. In 1991, he became the ninth player to end a World Series game with a home run, belting an eleventh inning round-tripper in Game 6 against Charlie Liebrandt.

From 1984 to 1994, the five-foot-nine-inch, 215-pound Puckett has batted .318 with 2,135 hits (the most by any major leaguer during that span), 184 home runs, 988 runs scored, and 986 RBIs. Puckett's best offensive year came in 1988, when he batted .356 with 234 hits, 24 home runs, 109 runs scored, and 121 RBIs. In 1989, Puckett won his only AL batting title with a .339 average. During his career, he has won six *TSN* Gold Glove (1986–1989, 1991–1992) and six Silver Slugger (1986–1989, 1992, 1994) awards. Puckett resides in Edina, MN, with his wife, Tonya (Hudson) Puckett, one daughter, Catherine, and one son, Kirby, Jr.

BIBLIOGRAPHY: Henry Hecht, "Cal Can Bring 'em Up Right," *SI* 61 (July 23, 1984), pp. 56–57; *Minnesota Twins Media Guide*, 1994; Rick Telander, "Minny's Mighty Mite," *SI* 66 (June 15, 1987), pp. 46–49.

James E. Welch

RADCLIFFE, Alexander "Alec" (b. July 26, 1905, Mobile, AL; d. July 18, 1983, Chicago, IL), player, performed in the Negro Leagues from 1932 to 1947 and was one of eight children born to James Radcliffe, a construction worker, and Mary (Marsh) Radcliffe. His older brother, Ted,* was an East-West All-Star pitcher and catcher. His first wife, Narlean, had three children, while his second wife, Gladys, had four children.

The six-foot-two-inch, 210-pound Radcliffe, a rangy third baseman with speed, mobility, and an accurate arm, was quick for his size and once stole home plate against Satchel Paige (BB) in a 1944 contest to win the game. He also hit for power, capturing the NAL home run titles in 1944 and 1945.

Radcliffe began his professional baseball career with Cole's American Giants (NSL) in 1932. The majority of his career was spent with the Chicago, IL, American Giants (NAL) from 1933 to 1939 and from 1941 to 1944. Brief stints came with the New York Cubans (NNL) in 1936, Memphis, TN, Red Sox (NAL) in 1940 and 1946, and the Indianapolis, IN, Clowns (NAL) from 1943 to 1945. His exemplary career was ended with the semiprofessional Detroit Senators in 1947.

In his first pro season with Cole's American Giants, Radcliffe hit a home run off his brother Ted to defeat the Pittsburgh Crawfords, 1–0. In 1934, he made his first appearance at the East-West All-Star summer game en route to 7 consecutive selections. Altogether, the right-handed hitter made 11 game appearances in East-West All-Star competition, hitting .341 in 44 at bats. Radcliffe led All-Star players in hits (15) and ranked second in runs scored (7) and RBIs (10).

Dave Malarcher (BB), Richard Lundy (BB), Ray Dandridge (BB), Judy Johnson (BB), and Radcliffe were considered the elite Negro League third basemen.

BIBLIOGRAPHY: *The Baseball Encyclopedia*, 9th ed. (New York, 1993); Larry Lester, interviews with Ted Radcliffe, December 1992 and January 1993; Larry Lester, interview with Margaret Hedgepath, February 1993; James A. Riley, *The Biographical Encyclopedia of the Negro Baseball Leagues* (New York, 1994); Michael Shatzkin, ed., *The Ballplayers* (New York, 1990).

                                                                          Larry Lester

RADCLIFFE, Theodore Roosevelt "Ted," "Double Duty" (b. July 7, 1902, Mobile, AL), player and manager, participated in the Negro Leagues from 1928 to 1950 and was one of eight children born to James Radcliffe, a construction contractor, and Mary (Marsh) Radcliffe. His brother Alec* was an East-West All-Star third baseman. He married Alberta Robinson and had one daughter, Shirley, who died in 1927 during childbirth. His nickname, "Double Duty," was given to him by New York sportswriter Damon Runyon (OS), who saw Radcliffe catch Satchel Paige (BB) in one game and pitch a shutout in the nightcap of a 1932 doubleheader.

The chunky, 5-foot-9½-inch, 210-pound catcher started his 23-year professional career with the Detroit, MI, Stars (NNL) in 1928. His much-traveled career included stops with the St. Louis, MO, Stars (NNL) in 1930, Homestead, PA, Grays (NNL) in 1931, 1933, and 1946, Pittsburgh, PA, Crawfords (EWL) in 1932, Columbus, OH, Blue Birds (NNL) in 1933, Brooklyn, NY, Eagles (NNL) in 1935, Cincinnati, OH, Tigers (NAL) in 1937, Memphis, TN, Red Sox (NAL) in 1938 and 1939, Chicago, IL, American Giants (NAL) in 1941, 1943, and 1949–1950, Birmingham, AL, Black Barons (NAL) in 1942, 1944–1945, Kansas City, MO, Monarchs (NAL) in 1945, and several nonleague teams like the New York Black Yankees in 1933 and the Harlem Globetrotters in 1945.

Radcliffe appeared in six East-West All-Star Games (1937–1939, 1941, 1943–1944), with three as a catcher and three as a pitcher. He hit .308 in 13 at bats, including one home run, and recorded an All-Star victory in 1939. Against major league competition in nine exhibition games, he hit .376 in 29 at bats. Radcliffe's lifetime batting average is listed at .282, with his win–loss pitching record at 53–33. In 1943, he was named the team's MVP as player–manager of the Chicago American Giants. Radcliffe's biggest thrill came in the 1944 East-West All-Star classic, when he hit a home run in the presence of his mother. In 1952, he was selected to the Pittsburgh, PA, *Courier*'s all-time, all-star team as fourth team pitcher and third team catcher.

BIBLIOGRAPHY: *The Baseball Encyclopedia*, 9th ed. (New York, 1993); Larry Lester, interview with Ted Radcliffe, December 1992 and January 1993; James A. Riley, *The Biographical Encyclopedia of the Negro Baseball Leagues* (New York, 1994); Mike Shatzkin, ed., *The Ballplayers* (New York, 1990).

Larry Lester

RANDOLPH, William Larry Jr. "Willie" (b. July 6, 1954, Holly Hill, SC), player, coach, and executive, is the son of Willie Randolph, Sr., a construction worker, and Minnie Randolph and moved to Brooklyn, NY, with his family as an infant. As a youth, he played stickball in the streets and baseball at Tilden High School. Several major league baseball teams scouted the infield prospect, who graduated in 1972 and was signed by the Pittsburgh Pirates (NL) in the seventh round of the June 1972 free agent draft. Assigned to Bradenton, FL (GCL) in 1972, Randolph spent subsequent minor league seasons at Charleston, SC (WCL) in 1973, Thetford, Canada, Mines (EL) in 1974, and Charleston, WV (IL) in 1975. Upon joining the Pirates in July 1975, he led the IL in hitting. Pittsburgh traded the 5-foot-11-inch, 170-pound, right-handed-hitting second baseman to the New York Yankees (AL) in December 1975.

In his 1976 rookie season, Randolph hit .267, stole 37 bases, and quickly became known as a very smooth second baseman with a good arm and good range. His ability to turn the double play proved excellent. His career 1,547 double plays at second base was exceeded in major league history only by Nellie Fox (BB, 1,619) and Bill Mazeroski (BB, 1,706). Randolph in 1992 became the all-time leader in games played for a Yankee second baseman with 1,689 and shares the all-time single-game record for assists by a second baseman with 13, accomplished on August 25, 1976, in 19 innings against the Minnesota Twins. During that same game, he also established an AL single-game record for most chances accepted by a second baseman with 20. During his career, he led the AL in several categories. In 1979, Randolph topped AL second basemen with 846 total chances, 355 putouts, 478 assists, and 128 double plays. He also led the AL in 1984 with 112 double plays and 119 walks in 1980. Contemporaries respected Randolph as a student of the game. In 1986, Randolph and Ron Guidry (BB) were named cocaptains of the New York Yankees. Often, he was mentioned as a possible future manager.

The Los Angeles Dodgers (NL) signed Randolph as a free agent in December 1988. In May 1990, the Oakland Athletics (AL) acquired him in a trade. The Milwaukee Brewers (AL) signed him as a free agent in April 1991, while the New York Mets (NL) obtained him as a free agent in December 1991. Six times, Randolph made his leagues' All-Star team. In 1976, he became the first rookie listed on an All-Star ballot. He was selected but could not play due to injury. His other All-Star team designations included the 1977, 1980, 1981, and 1987 AL All-Star squads and the 1989 NL aggregate. *TSN* chose him for second base on its 1977, 1980, and 1987 All-Star teams and 1980 AL Silver Slugger team.

Randolph's playing career ended after the 1992 season. He compiled a lifetime .276 batting average with 1,239 runs scored, 2,210 hits, 54 home runs, 687 RBIs, 271 stolen bases, and a .979 fielding average. He hit .271 in NL and AL Championship Series play after appearing in the 1976, 1977, 1980, 1981, and 1990 AL Championship Series and the 1975 NL Championship Series. His 1976, 1977, 1981, and 1990 World Series appearances led to a combined .181 batting average. In 1993, he became an assistant general manager for the New York Yankees (AL). The following year, the Yankees made him a coach. Randolph and his wife Gretchen have four children, Taniesha, Chantre, Ciara, and Andre.

BIBLIOGRAPHY: John Dewan and Don Zminda, ed., *The Scouting Report: 1993* (New York, 1993), p. 552; Jon Heyman, "Willie's Back," *Newsday*, April 14, 1993, pp. 132, 138; *Los Angeles Dodgers 1989 Media Guide; New York Mets 1992 Media Guide; New York Yankees 1988 Media Guide*; Phil Pepe, "Willie Randolph on the Way to Greatness," *BD* 39 (September 1980), pp. 60–61; Willie Randolph file, National Baseball Library, Cooperstown, NY; Seymour Siwoff, ed., *The 1993 Elias Baseball Analyst* (New York, 1993), p. 204; John Thorn and Pete Palmer, eds., *Total Baseball*, 3rd ed. (New York, 1993), pp. 1162–1163; *TSN Official Baseball Register*, 1993.

Robert J. Brown

REARDON, Jeffrey James "Jeff" "The Terminator" (b. October 1, 1955, Pittsfield, MA), player, is one of six children of John T. Reardon, a security guard, and Marion (Stevens) Reardon and grew up in Dalton, MA, and majored in history at the University of Massachusetts. The New York Mets (NL) signed the six-foot, 205-pound right-hander in June 1977 and assigned the starting pitcher to Lynchburg, VA (CrL) in 1977 and Jackson, TX (TL) in 1978. New York converted him to a reliever at Tidewater (IL) in 1979. Reardon split relief responsibilities for the New York Mets with Neil Allen from 1979 to 1981.

Montreal (NL) in May 1981 acquired Reardon, who compiled a career-best 2.06 ERA with 26 saves in 1982 and saved 44 games the next two seasons. Manager Buck Rodgers designated Reardon the exclusive closer in 1985, when the bearded fastball pitcher led the major leagues with 41 saves, made the NL All-Star team, and was named *TSN* NL Fireman of the Year. Mitch Melnick, the Montreal announcer, nicknamed him "The Terminator." In 1986, he saved 35 contests and repeated as an NL All-Star selection.

In February 1987, Montreal traded Reardon to the Minnesota Twins (AL). Reardon helped Minnesota capture the 1987 AL pennant with 31 saves, striking out 83 batters in 80.1 innings. His honors included winning the Twins' MVP Award and sharing AL Fireman of the Year accolades. Reardon saved 2 games and split two decisions in the AL Championship Series against the Detroit Tigers. Minnesota defeated the St. Louis Cardinals in the 7-game World Series, as Reardon hurled 4.2 scoreless innings and saved the decisive seventh game. Reardon in 1988 saved a career-high 42 games with a 2.47 ERA, making the AL All-Star team.

After Reardon saved 31 games in 1989, the Boston Red Sox (AL) signed him as a free agent that December. Reardon relied more on his curveball and accurate control. His best season with Boston came in 1991, when he saved 40 games and was selected to the AL All-Star team. Reardon in 1992 surpassed Rollie Fingers (BB) as the all-time save leader with 342. In August 1992, the Red Sox traded Reardon to the Atlanta Braves (NL). Reardon compiled a 3–0 record and a 1.15 ERA with 3 saves, helping Atlanta garner the NL West Division title. He recorded 1 win and 1 save in the NL Championship Series when the Braves defeated the Pittsburgh Pirates to take the NL pennant. Reardon struggled in the World Series, blowing 2 save opportunities against the Toronto Blue Jays. The Cincinnati Reds (NL) signed him as a free agent in January 1993 and used him primarily as a setup reliever. Reardon signed with the New York Yankees (AL) before the 1994 season, but appeared in only 11 games.

The quiet, unemotional Reardon, who seldom relieves for more than one inning, ranks second to Lee Smith (S) in career saves with 365. In 880 major league games spanning 16 seasons, he has 73 wins, 77 losses, a 3.16 ERA, and 877 strikeouts in 1,132 innings. From 1982 to 1992, no other major league reliever recorded at least 20 saves each season.

He and his wife Phebe have two sons, Jeffrey and Shane, and reside in Palm Beach Gardens, FL.

BIBLIOGRAPHY: Jim Kaplan, "Saving Face in Montreal," *SI* 62 (June 24, 1985), pp. 58, 60; Steve Rushin, "The Pen Ultimate," *SI* 76 (June 8, 1992), pp. 54–57; Mike Shatzkin, ed., *The Ballplayers* (New York, 1990); *TSN Official Baseball Register*, 1994.

David L. Porter

REISER, Harold Patrick "Pete" "Pistol Pete" (b. March 17, 1919, St. Louis, MO; d. October 25, 1981, Palm Springs, CA), player, coach, scout, and manager, had German and Irish roots and came from a family of 12 children. He attended Beaumont High School in St. Louis for 2 years. St. Louis Cardinal (NL) scouts began watching Reiser when he was only 12 years old. In 1934, 15-year-old Reiser lied about his age to attend a Cardinal tryout camp. St. Louis scout Charley Barrett signed him for $50 a month in 1937 and sent him to New Iberia, LA (EvL) to play shortstop. St. Louis general manager Branch Rickey (BB) administered 50 farm teams, holding over 1,000 players under contract. In 1938, baseball commissioner Kenesaw Mountain Landis (BB) declared 100 Cardinal minor league players free agents. Rickey, who did not want to lose Reiser, asked longtime friend Larry MacPhail (BB), general manager of the Brooklyn Dodgers (NL), to sign Reiser, hide him in his farm system for a few years, and then trade him back to St. Louis. MacPhail initially agreed, but when Reiser batted over .300 at Superior, WI (NoL) in 1938 and Elmira, NY (EL) in 1939 and 1940, he reneged on the agreement. MacPhail promoted Reiser to the Dodgers, where he batted .293 in 58 games over the last half of the 1940 season.

Reiser's first full season with the Dodgers remains legendary. Manager Leo Durocher (BB) moved him from shortstop to the outfield. Reiser led the NL with 117 runs scored, 17 triples, and a .343 batting average and belted 14 home runs and 39 doubles. The 22-year-old was the youngest player to win a major league batting crown. Reiser, unfortunately, played with reckless abandon, shortening his career. In 1942, the switch-hitting Reiser batted .310 but fractured his skull when he crashed into a wall trying to catch St. Louis Cardinal outfielder Enos Slaughter's (BB) drive. After serving in the U.S. Army cavalry from 1943 to 1945, the 5-foot-10½-inch, 185-pound Reiser batted .277 in 1946 and .309 in 1947 for the Dodgers. In 1946, he stole home seven times, establishing an NL record. Reiser was carried off the field nine times after slamming into walls, resulting in seven fractures or dislocations. One pitch hit him on the head, causing a cerebral blood clot. Nevertheless, he always maintained a joyful, optimistic disposition. Leo Durocher recalled, "Willie Mays [BB] had everything. Pete Reiser had everything but luck." Sportswriter Red Smith (OS) noted, "There never was a ballpark big enough to contain his effort."

After Reiser played only 64 games in 1948, the Dodgers traded him to the Boston Braves (NL) that December. Reiser served as a reserve outfielder for the Braves in 1949 and 1950, signed with the Pittsburgh Pirates (NL) in 1951, and finished his major league career with the Cleveland Indians (AL) in 1952. Reiser also played for the NL squad in the 1941, 1942, and 1946 All-Star contests. He batted .214 in the 1941 and 1947 World Series against the New York Yankees. His 10-year major league career included 861 games, 786 hits, 473 runs, 55 home runs, 368 RBIs, and a .295 batting average.

Reiser compiled a record of 366 victories and 348 defeats managing Thomasville, GA (GFL), Kokomo, IN (ML), Green Bay, WI (3IL), Spokane, WA (PCL), and Dallas–Ft. Worth, TX (TL) from 1955 to 1959, 1965, and 1966. He served as a coach with the Los Angeles Dodgers (NL) from 1960 to 1964; the Chicago Cubs, where he rejoined manager Leo Durocher from 1966 to 1969 and 1972 to 1973; and the California Angels (AL) in 1970 and 1971.

Reiser, who married Patricia T. Hurst on March 29, 1942, and had two daughters, Sally and Shirley, enjoyed woodworking, cooking, ice skating, and golf. He recovered from a 1965 heart attack but died 16 years later of respiratory problems.

BIBLIOGRAPHY: Stanley Cohen, *Dodgers! The First 100 Years* (New York, 1990); Peter Golenbock, *Bums: An Oral History of the Brooklyn Dodgers* (New York, 1984); Rich Koster, "Pete Reiser: He Was the Original Mr. Hustle," *BD* 41 (April 1982), pp. 53–56; Kevin Nelson, *Greatest Stories Ever Told About Baseball Players* (New York, 1986); Danny Peary, ed., *Cult Baseball Players: The Greats, the Flakes, the Weird, and the Wonderful* (New York, 1990); Harold Reiser file, National Baseball Library, Cooperstown, NY.

Frank J. Olmsted

RENNERT, Laurence Henry Jr. "Dutch" (b. June 12, 1934, Oshkosh, WI), umpire, is the son of Laurence Rennert, Sr., and Viola Rennert and received his nickname not because of his German heritage but in honor of major league pitcher Emil "Dutch" Leonard (BB). A three-sport athlete in high school, Rennert briefly played semiprofessional baseball and football before attending the Al Somers Umpire School in 1957. He began his professional umpiring career in the Class D AlFL and advanced to the Class C PrL in 1958, Class B 3IL in 1959, Class AA SA in 1961, and Class AA TL in 1962. Although signing a major league contract after the 1964 season, he umpired in the Class AAA PCL from 1965 until being called up to the NL in September 1973.

Despite exemplary umpiring ability, Rennert found his promotion to the major leagues blocked by the prevailing preference for umpires at least 6 feet tall and 200 pounds. After 17 years in the minor leagues, the 5-foot-8-inch, 176-pound Rennert finally reached the majors when 5-foot-10-inch Al Barlick (BB) became supervisor of NL umpires. A fan favorite, Rennert became the most colorful NL arbiter and used a booming voice and exaggerated motions, especially when calling strikes, to compensate for his relatively small stature. He also enjoyed the respect of the players, who, in a 1983 *NYT* poll, named him the best all-around NL umpire. In 19 full major league seasons, he umpired two All-Star Games (1979, 1984), six NL Championship Series (1977, 1981, 1982, 1986, 1988, 1990), and three World Series (1980, 1983, 1989).

Rennert, who suffered from an astigmatism and damaged knee cartilage, retired in January 1993 after 37 years of professional umpiring. "I always said," he explained, "if I didn't feel I was doing a 100 percent job, if I started slipping, that would be it for me." Rennert married Shirley Malchow in 1964 and has four children.

BIBLIOGRAPHY: "Interview: Laurence 'Dutch' Rennert," *Referee* 15 (April 1990), pp. 20–23; *Referee* 18 (April 1993), p. 16; Dutch Rennert file, National Baseball Library, Cooperstown, NY; *USA Today*, January 11, 1993.

Larry R. Gerlach

RHODEN, Richard Alan "Rick" (b. May 16, 1953, Boynton Beach, FL), player, overcame a serious childhood illness to become a successful major league pitcher. Rhoden suffered from osteomyelitis, a bone disease that caused him to wear a leg brace and necessitated the removal of part of his left knee. Nevertheless, the six-foot-three-inch, 195-pound right-hander developed into a fine athlete. The Los Angeles Dodgers (NL) selected Rhoden as their first-round (twentieth player taken overall) draft pick in the 1971 free agent draft.

After pitching in the minor leagues at Daytona Beach, FL (FSL), El Paso, TX (TL), and Albuquerque, NM (PCL), Rhoden debuted for the Los Angeles Dodgers in 1974. In 1976, Rhoden posted a 12–3 win–loss record with a 2.98 ERA and was named to the NL All-Star squad. The following year, he won a career-high 16 games, a figure he matched in 1987 while pitching for the New York Yankees (AL). Rhoden played in two NL Championship Series with the Dodgers (1977, 1978) without any decisions. He pitched in the 1977 World Series, where he was charged with 1 loss in two appearances against the New York Yankees. Working chiefly as a starting pitcher for the Dodgers, Rhoden won 42 games and lost 24. In April 1979, Los Angeles traded Rhoden to the Pittsburgh Pirates (NL) for pitcher Jerry Reuss (S).

Rhoden's career with the Pirates began inauspiciously when shoulder surgery forced him to miss almost the entire 1979 season and the first part of the 1980 season. Rhoden returned as the mainstay of the Pirate staff in 1981 and started 193 games over six years for a talent-poor Pirate club that was further demoralized by a sensational drug scandal. He led the Pirates in wins with 9 in 1981, fourteen in 1984, and 15 in 1986, being named to the 1986 All-Star team.

The Pirates in November 1986 traded Rhoden to the New York Yankees for several players including Doug Drabek, the 1990 NL Cy Young Award winner. Rhoden won 16 games for the Yankees in 1987 but believed that he was denied a place on that year's AL All-Star team because of frequent accusations that he scuffed the ball. The Yankees traded Rhoden to the Houston Astros (NL) in January 1989. Rhoden completed his 16-year major league career in 1989.

Rhoden compiled a career record of 151 wins and 125 losses for a .547 winning percentage and 3.60 ERA. Rhoden, quite an accomplished hitter, batted .238 with 181 hits and nine home runs. Between 1984 and 1986, he won three NL Silver Slugger awards for pitchers.

An avid golfer and fisherman, Rhoden won the $22,500 1993 Celebrity Golf Classic at Brampton, Ontario, with a 2-under-par score of 214. Rhoden and his wife Leslie reside in Canoga Park, CA, with their son Tanner.

BIBLIOGRAPHY: *The Baseball Encyclopedia*, 9th ed. (New York, 1993), p. 2192; *1981, 1985, 1986 Pittsburgh Pirates Yearbook;* Mike Shatzkin, ed., *The Ballplayers* (New York, 1990), p. 905.

Frank W. Thackeray

RICHARDSON, Robert Clinton Jr. "Bobby" (b. August 19, 1935, Sumter, SC), player and coach, is the son of Robert Clinton Richardson, Sr., who owned and operated a marble and granite company, and Willie (Owens) Richardson. Although small for his age, Richardson acquired a love of baseball from his father and as a youth played for a team sponsored by the Salvation Army. By the time he began high school, he had won the second base position on his AmLe team by performing better than boys three or four years older. As a sophomore, he started at second base for his high school nine.

The five-foot-nine-inch, 160-pound Richardson did not hit with power but, as he related, "walked, bunted, and depended on my legs to get on base and keep moving." Scouts from a dozen major league teams followed him by his senior year. Within a few hours after his high school graduation in 1953, he signed with the New York Yankees (AL). He started his minor league career with Norfolk, VA (Class B PiL) but was sent down to Olean, NY (PoL) in Class D and hit .412 there. He starred for Binghamton, NY (EL) in 1954 and Denver, CO (AA) the following year. He played briefly with the Yankees in 1955 and 1956 but did not stay in the major leagues until 1957. After spending two years in a reserve role, Richardson became the Yankees' regular second baseman in 1959 and won raves for his ability to cover ground, sure hands, and deft pivot play on double play balls. He also proved a timely hitter. The devout Baptist had begun to think of retirement before his thirtieth birthday to spend time working with children in Sumter, SC, where he maintained his off-season residence. He retired after the 1966 season and subsequently coached baseball at the University of South Carolina, Coastal Carolina CC, and Liberty University in Lynchburg, VA. In 1976, he was defeated in a bid for a seat in the U.S. House of Representatives. Richardson, who married Alice Elizabeth Dobson on June 8, 1956, and has five children, has been involved with FCA and serves as president of Baseball Chapel in Asheville, NC.

Richardson spent 10 full years with the New York Yankees, batting over .300 in 1959 and in 1962. In 1962, he led the AL in hits with 209 and finished second to teammate Mickey Mantle (BB) in the MVP balloting. In the major leagues, Richardson had a .266 career batting average with 1,432 hits. He played in seven World Series, winning acclaim in 1960 by batting .367 with 12 RBIs against the Pittsburgh Pirates and again in 1964 by getting 13 base hits against the St. Louis Cardinals. In 1961, he tied a World Series record with 9 hits against the Cincinnati Reds in a five-game series.

BIBLIOGRAPHY: *CB* (1966), pp. 330–332; Dom Forker, *Sweet Seasons: Recollections of the 1955–64 New York Yankees* (Dallas, TX, 1990); Gene Karst and Martin J. Jones, *Who's Who in Professional Baseball* (New Rochelle, NY, 1973), p. 788; Bob McCormick, "Bobby Richardson and Tom Tresh," in Jack Orr, ed., *Baseball's Greatest Players Today* (New York, 1963); Bobby Richardson, *The Bobby Richardson Story* (Westwood, NJ, 1965).

Lloyd J. Graybar

RICHMOND, J. Lee (b. May 5, 1857, Sheffield, OH; d. September 30, 1929, Toledo, OH), player, was the son of Cyrus R. Richmond, a Baptist minister, and Eliza (Tinan) Richmond and first played baseball as a left-handed pitcher with Oberlin College of Ohio from 1873 to 1876. He enrolled at Brown University in 1876, performing the fall season as an outfielder. Richmond was elected class president, played on the school's first football team, and spent the next two seasons as a baseball outfielder and pitcher for Brown. Richmond labored in Brown's gymnasium the winter of 1878–1879, developing several curved deliveries. His devastating curves broke up and down rather than in and out and combined well with his rare left-hand delivery. Richmond, slight in stature at 5 feet 10 inches and 142 pounds, did not overpower hitters and consequently allied his unusual pitches with cunning, deception (including a change of pace), and strategy. He studied hitters and kept a book on them.

Richmond burst upon the baseball scene in 1879, leading his Brown University nine to the college championship and pitching a no-hitter in his professional debut. His composite record for the 1879 season included 47 wins and an above-.350 batting average. He pitched a second no-hitter later in the season and made his major league debut with the Boston Red Caps (NL).

Richmond signed with the Worcester Ruby Legs (NL) for a record $2,400 for the 1880 season, perhaps making him sports' first "franchise player." He pitched the entire three-year history of the Worcester franchise, accounting for 80 percent of the club's wins. He played for the Providence Grays (NL) in 1883 and briefly for the Cincinnati Red Stockings (AA) in 1886.

Richmond accounted for many "firsts" during his short major league career and hurled baseball's first perfect game, a 1–0 win over the Cleveland Blues on June 12, 1880. Since he played concurrently as an amateur and professional, baseball established the first rules barring professionals from participating with amateurs. These rules continue with virtually all sports worldwide. He struck out a record five consecutive batters in his first major league game and gave up the first grand-slam home run. Besides being the first hurler to win 20 games for a last-place team, he became the first pitcher to relieve and be relieved for an opposite-side hurler. His portside delivery led to the first platooning and popularized switch-hitting, strategies integral to every game today.

Richmond used baseball to finance his education and earned bachelor's and master's degrees from Brown and his medical degree from the University of the City of New York (now NYU) while still in the game. For seven years, he played baseball in the summer and attended school in the winter. He ranked among the first collegians to play major league baseball and marked the first physician to do so.

After retiring from baseball in 1883, he returned to northeastern Ohio to practice medicine. He later gave up medicine for an education career spanning 40 years in Toledo, OH. He served as a teacher, orchestra leader, coach, and principal at Toledo high schools. At age 65, he "retired" to the University of Toledo to serve as Dean of Men. Richmond, a lifelong baseball fan and scratch golfer, married Mary Naomi Chapin and had three daughters.

BIBLIOGRAPHY: *The Baseball Encyclopedia*, 9th ed. (New York, 1993); *BH* (1986); John Richmond Husman, "J. Lee Richmond's Remarkable 1879 Season," *The National Pastime* 4 (Winter 1985), pp. 65–70; Martin Kaufman, ed., *Historical Journal of Massachusetts*, vol. 19 (Westfield, CT, 1991); Ronald A. Mayer, *Perfect!* (Jefferson, NC, 1991); Ronald A. Smith, *Sports & Freedom* (New York, 1988); Robert L. Tiemann and Mark Rucker, eds., *Nineteenth Century Stars* (Kansas City, MO, 1989).

                                                                          John R. Husman

RIPKEN, Calvin Edwin Jr. "Cal" (b. August 24, 1960, Havre de Grace, MD), player, is the second of four children of Calvin Ripken, Sr., and Viola Ripken and graduated in 1978 from Aberdeen High School, starring for its State Championship baseball team. His father, who played and managed minor league baseball, coached for (1976–1986, 1988–1992) and piloted (1987– 1988) the Baltimore Orioles (AL), while his brother Billy performed at second base for Baltimore (1987–1992). Baltimore drafted the six-foot-four-inch, 220-pound Ripken in the second round in June 1978 and assigned the generous, competitive infielder to Bluefield, WV (ApL), Miami, FL (FSL), Charlotte, NC (SL), and Rochester, NY (IL) between 1978 and 1981. Ripken joined the Orioles in August 1981 and began 1982 at third base. Manager Earl Weaver shrewdly switched the excellent fielder to shortstop, where he played every inning from June 1982 to September 1987. Ripken earned AL Rookie of the Year honors in 1982, batting .264 with 28 home runs and 93 RBIs. Baltimore lost the AL East title to the Milwaukee Brewers in the season finale.

Ripken garnered AL MVP and Major League Player of the Year accolades in 1983, helping the Orioles dominate the AL East. He led the AL in runs scored (121), hits (211), and doubles (42), batting .318 with 27 round-trippers and 102 RBIs and topping AL shortstops in assists, total chances, and double plays. Baltimore defeated the Chicago White Sox in the AL Championship Series, as Ripken hit .400, and nearly swept the Philadelphia Phillies in the World Series. The Orioles struggled from 1984 through 1988. Ripken batted .304 with 27 home runs and 86 RBIs in 1984, hitting for the cycle against the Texas Rangers on May 6 and establishing a record for most assists by an AL shortstop (583). Ripken's 110 RBIs in 1985 marked his second-highest run production. Baltimore barely lost the 1989 East Division title to the Toronto Blue Jays, as Ripken became the first AL shortstop to register eight consecutive 20–home run campaigns. On June 12, 1990, he played his 1,308th straight game, attaining second on the all-time list and breaking Everett Scott's record for most successive games at one position.

He led AL shortstops in fielding percentage (.996) in 1990, setting major league shortstop marks for fewest errors (3) and most consecutive contests (95) without a miscue.

Ripken garnered a second AL MVP Award in 1991, the third player ever designated from a losing team. Ripken, the Major League Player of the Year and All-Star Game MVP, belted a three-run homer that sparked a 4–2 AL victory. He ranked second in home runs (34), hits (210), doubles (46), and slugging percentage (.556), fourth in RBIs (114), and sixth in batting average (.323). His 368 total bases and 85 extra base hits led the major leagues. Ripken earned his first Gold Glove, pacing AL shortstops in fielding percentage (.986), putouts, assists, total chances, and double plays. He also won the Gold Glove in 1992, but his offensive production plummeted. During the strike-shortened 1994 season, he batted .315 with 13 home runs and 75 RBIs. On August 1, 1994, Ripken appeared in his 2,000th major league game.

The 12-time AL All-Star may break Lou Gehrig's (BB) all-time record of 2,130 consecutive games and holds the major league record for most career home runs by a shortstop with 302, 25 more than Ernie Banks (BB). Through 1994, he has batted .277 with 2,227 hits, 414 doubles, 312 home runs, and 1,179 RBIs in 2,074 games, holds the AL record for most seasons leading shortstops in putouts (6), and has paced AL shortstops in assists and double plays six times, total chances four times, and fielding percentage twice. *TSN* honored him as AL All-Star team shortstop six times (1983–1985, 1989, 1991, 1994) and as AL Silver Slugger team member seven times (1983–1986, 1989, 1991, 1994). The Reistertown, MD, resident married Kelly Greer in 1987 and has one daughter, Rachel.

BIBLIOGRAPHY: "Cal's 2,000," Baltimore *Sun*, July 31, 1994, pp. 1C, 12C, 13C; *CB* (1992), pp. 470–474; Ron Fimrite, "He's Done His Daddy Proud," *SI* 60 (April 2, 1984), pp. 34–36; Hank Hersch, "One Big Rip-Roaring Family Affair," *SI* 66 (March 9, 1987), pp. 26–28; Tim Kurkjian, "Rip on a Tear," *SI* 75 (July 29, 1991), pp. 24–26; Lois Nicholson, *Cal Ripken, Jr., A Quiet Hero* (Centreville, MD, 1993); Peter Schmuck, "A Matter of Record," *Sport* 83 (May 1992), pp. 22–24, 26–27; *TSN Official Baseball Register*, 1994; Ralph Wiley, "A Monumental Streak," *SI* 72 (June 18, 1990), pp. 70–74; *WWA*, 47th ed. (1992–1993), p. 2827.

David L. Porter

RITCHEY, Claude Cassius "Little All Right" (b. October 5, 1873, Emlenton, PA; d. November 8, 1951, Emlenton, PA), player, was the son of Lucretia Anita Ritchey, a schoolteacher. He began his professional baseball career as an infielder with Franklin, PA, in 1894, moving in 1895 to the Warren, OH, Wonders (IOL) and 1896 to Buffalo, NY (EL). As a result of his excellent play, he was drafted by the major league Brooklyn Bridegrooms (NL) for the 1897 season. Brooklyn sold him to the Cincinnati Reds (NL) as a replacement for a player who had failed to report to that club. As a substitute infielder–outfielder, Ritchey played three positions with Cincinnati. The Louisville, KY, Colonels (NL) acquired him in 1898 to play shortstop and switched him in midseason to second base, where he remained a fixture thereafter. As the starting second baseman for Louisville in 1899, he hit .300 for the highest batting average of his major league career. After the Louisville franchise was transferred to Pittsburgh (NL), Ritchey batted .292 in 1900, .296 in 1901, .277 in 1902, and .287 in 1903 for the Pirates. His average steadily declined after that until he hit only .172 in 30 games in 1909, his final major league season. He finished with a 13-year .273 career batting average, 1,618 hits, and 673 RBIs.

Ritchey's deft, quick play at second base, however, ranked him among the era's most valuable major league players. He and future National Baseball Hall of Fame shortstop Honus Wagner (BB) provided a brilliant keystone combination, enabling the Pittsburgh Pirates to win three consecutive NL pennants from 1901 to 1903. The 5-foot-6½-inch, 167-pound Ritchey led or tied NL second basemen in fielding average from 1902 to 1907. With the exception of Nap Lajoie (BB), he compiled the highest major league fielding average (.960) at that position during the first decade of the twentieth century. The rugged Ritchey also performed more games at second base (1,262) than any other player during this period and led NL second basemen in assists in 1903. Ritchey appeared in the first modern World Series that year against the Boston Pilgrims, establishing one-game fall classic records for most chances and assists at second base. His records endured for many years. He finished his major league career with a .957 fielding average.

Ritchey remained with the Pirates until December 1906, when he was traded with Ginger Beaumont (BB) and Pat Flaherty to the Boston Doves (NL) for second baseman Ed Abbaticchio. After playing 30 games with Boston in 1909, he was released to Providence, RI (EL) and refused to report there. Louisville (AA) signed Ritchey in 1910, but he played only two weeks there. A broken arm, suffered while sliding into second base, ended his baseball career.

Subsequently, Ritchey was employed for many years as a laborer with the Quaker State Oil Refining Company in Emlenton. He was married twice, first to Sophia Augusta Bayer in 1902. Following their divorce in 1917, he wed Kathryn Ruth Kunselman in 1924. He had a daughter, Eleanor, by his first marriage, and three children, Jack, Lois, and Marian, by his second marriage.

BIBLIOGRAPHY: *The Baseball Encyclopedia*, 9th ed. (New York, 1993); Jack C. Braun, telephone interview with Jack Ritchey, October 4, 1993; Richard L. Burt, *The Pittsburgh Pirates, a Pictorial History: A Century Old Baseball Tradition* (Virginia Beach, VA, 1977); Frederick G. Lieb, *The Pittsburgh Pirates* (New York, 1948); David Nemac and Pete Palmer, *1001 Fascinating Baseball Facts: Records, Anecdotes, Quotes, Lore, and More!* (Stamford, CT, 1993); Claude Ritchey file, National Baseball Library, Cooperstown, NY; John Thorn and Pete Palmer, eds., *Total Baseball*, 3rd ed. (New York, 1993).

Jack C. Braun

ROGERS, Stephen Douglas "Steve" (b. October 26, 1949, Jefferson City, MO), player, graduated from Glendale High School in Springfield, MO, in 1967 and attended the University of Tulsa. At Tulsa, he pitched splendidly with a four-year college record of 31 wins and 5 losses and won the 1971 Jack Charvat Award as the top amateur athlete in the American Southwest. Rogers, who was selected to the College World Series All-Star team in 1971, earned a Bachelor of Science degree in petroleum engineering.

The six-foot-one-inch, 175-pound right-handed pitcher, who batted right-handed, was selected by the New York Yankees (AL) in the sixtieth round of the free agent draft in June 1967 and by the Montreal Expos (NL) in the secondary phase of the free agent draft in June 1971. In 1971, he pitched in 15 games for Winnipeg, Canada (IL), working 102 innings, winning only 2 games, and losing 10 decisions. The following year, he pitched in 13 games for Peninsula (IL), winning 2 games and losing 6.

He appeared in 17 games for the Montreal Expos (NL) in 1973 after spending the early part of that season with Quebec City, Canada (EL) and Peninsula. With Montreal, he compiled 10 wins and 5 losses in 1973. His entire major league career was spent with Montreal, where he won 15 of 22 decisions in 1974 and 11 of 23 in 1975 with a 3.29 ERA. He triumphed only 7 times while dropping 17 in 1976. In 1977, he pitched 302 innings in 40 games, winning 17 games and losing 16. He struck out 206 batters while boasting a 3.10 ERA. In 1978, he appeared in 30 games and 219 innings, won 13 decisions and lost 10, and compiled a 2.47 ERA. He again recorded 13 victories while dropping 12 in 1979 and won 16 times while losing 11 with a 2.98 ERA in 1980, appearing in 37 games both seasons.

After winning 12 and losing 8 decisions in 22 games in 1981, he pitched in 35 games in 1982, triumphing 19 times, with 8 setbacks and a 2.40 ERA. In 1983 he hurled in 36 games, winning 17, losing 12, and recording 146 strikeouts with a 3.22 ERA. He struggled in his final season, taking only 2 of 8 decisions in 1985. In 13 seasons with Montreal through 1985, he pitched in 399 games, won 158 contests, and lost 152 decisions with a career 3.17 ERA and 1,621 strikeouts.

Rogers led the NL in sacrifice hits (20) in 1983, shutouts (5) in 1983, and complete games (14) in 1980 and shared the NL lead in shutouts (5) in 1979. He was selected *TSN* NL Rookie Pitcher of the Year in 1973 and right-handed pitcher on the *TSN* NL All-Star team in 1982. In the NL East Division playoff series with the Philadelphia Phillies in 1981, Rogers won 2 games and lost none with a 9.51 ERA. In the NL Championship Series that year against the Los Angeles Dodgers, he split 2 decisions with a 1.80 ERA.

Rogers pitched in three All-Star Games (1978, 1979, 1982), winning the 1982 contest and compiling an impressive 1.29 ERA. He was named to NL All-Star teams in 1974 and 1983 but did not play.

Rogers married Barbara Boduarchuk of Winnipeg, Canada, on September 16, 1972, and has three children, Colleen, Stephen Jason, and Geoffrey Douglas. For hobbies, he collects coins and Indian arrowheads, plays golf, and enjoys working crossword puzzles.

BIBLIOGRAPHY: Stan W. Carlson, letter to Montreal Expos Public Relations, October 1993; *Montreal Expos Media Guide*, 1985; *TSN Baseball Register*, 1986.

Stan W. Carlson

ROWLAND, Clarence Henry "Pants" (b. February 12, 1879, Platteville, WI; d. May 17, 1969, Chicago, IL), player, manager, umpire, scout, owner, and executive, grew up in Dubuque, IA. As a youngster, he worked as a hotel bellhop and first came into contact with the professional baseball players for Dubuque's (3IL) team. One of these players, upon learning Rowland's first name, thought it inappropriate and started calling him "Pants." The nickname remained.

His professional baseball career began in 1903 as a catcher with the Dubuque (3IL) club. After being injured or ill much of the 1904–1906 seasons, he returned to catch for and manage Dubuque in 1907 and 1908. Following brief stints with Aberdeen, SD (NoL), Jacksonville, IL (Ind), and Winnipeg, Canada (NoL) over the next two seasons, he returned to Dubuque as the owner–manager from 1911 to 1913. In 1914, he managed Peoria, IL (3IL), transforming a losing team into a contender. His work at Peoria led 3IL president Al Tierney to recommend Rowland to owner–president Charles Comiskey (BB) for the vacant Chicago White Sox (AL) managerial post. Accordingly, in December 1914, Rowland was appointed to the job. Critics sneered at Comiskey for "digging a manager out of the bushes," but Rowland soon proved his mettle.

Rowland guided the White Sox from 1915 to 1918, winning 339 games and losing 247. Chicago finished third in 1915 and second in 1916 before winning the AL pennant in 1917. His 1917 White Sox prevailed in the World Series, defeating manager John McGraw's (BB) New York Giants, 4–2. A sixth-place finish in 1918 cost Rowland his job. He was replaced for the turbulent, scandal-ridden 1919 season by "Kid" Gleason (S).

Rowland's exit from the baseball scene remained brief. He managed the Milwaukee, WI, club (AA) in 1919 and moved on to Columbus, OH (AA) for a three-year stint as pilot from 1920 to 1922. In 1923, his career took an unusual twist. Rowland became an AL umpire, a post he held for five years. He later managed the Nashville, TN, club (SA), scouted for the Chicago Cubs (NL), and presided over the PCL from 1944 to 1954. He eased into his twilight years as executive vice president of the Cubs and ended his long, colorful baseball career with that club as an honorary vice president, the title that he held at his death.

BIBLIOGRAPHY: *The Baseball Encyclopedia*, 9th ed. (New York, 1993); Clarence Rowland file, National Baseball Library, Cooperstown, NY.

David S. Matz

RUCKER, George Napoleon "Nap" (b. September 30, 1894, Crabtree, GA; d. December 19, 1970, Alphabetta, GA), player, was a successful baseball pitcher during the pre-1920 "dead ball" era. His parents were John Rucker, a farmer, and Sara (Embree) Rucker. Rucker, who obtained an eighth-grade grammar school education, married Edith Wood on October 1, 1911, and had a daughter, Anne. Rucker stood 5 feet 10 inches, weighed 190 pounds, threw left-handed, and batted right-handed.

Rucker began baseball professionally with Atlanta, GA (SL) in 1904 and pitched for Augusta, GA (SAL) in 1905 and 1906. His major league career lasted exactly a decade, from 1907 to 1916, entirely with the weak-hitting Brooklyn Superbas-Dodgers-Robins (NL). Rucker pitched very well and remains a classic example from the pre–free agent age of how restriction to an inferior team could mar a hurler's record. In Rucker's first eight years with Brooklyn, the Superbas-Dodgers-Robins did not once finish in the first division or reach a .500 winning percentage and averaged a sixth-place finish. In his career, Rucker exactly split 268 decisions and compiled an individual winning percentage 58 points above his team. He possessed an outstanding fastball until 1913, when he hurt his arm. In his last three years with the Robins-Dodgers, he pitched cleverly but less effectively with a slower ball. Charles Ebbets (BB), the club owner, admired Rucker for his cooperative attitude and friendly disposition.

Despite his lowly teams, Rucker finished five seasons among the NL's pitching leaders in various pitching categories. He led the NL in innings pitched (320) in 1910 and won 22 in 1911. On September 5, 1908, he pitched a no-hit game against the Boston Doves, striking out 14 batters and allowing no bases on balls. On July 14, 1909, he permitted only two hits, struck out 16 batters, and walked three. He achieved an admirable 2.42 career ERA, struck out 1,217 batters in 2,375 innings, and hurled 38 shutouts. Brooklyn won the NL pennant in Rucker's last year, when his arm had given out. He made a token 2 inning appearance in one game of the 1916 World Series against the Boston Red Sox (AL), not permitting a run.

Rucker scouted for the Brooklyn Robins-Dodgers from 1919 to 1934 and 1939 to 1940. Subsequently, back in Georgia, he farmed, operated a wheat and corn mill, and served as mayor of Roswell, water commissioner, and umpire of local baseball games.

BIBLIOGRAPHY: *The Baseball Encyclopedia*, 9th ed. (New York, 1993); *DAB*, Supp. 8 (New York, 1988), pp. 558–559; *NYT*, December 21, 1970; Nap Rucker file, National Baseball Library, Cooperstown, NY.

Lowell L. Blaisdell

SABERHAGEN, Bret William (b. April 11, 1964, Chicago Heights, IL), player, is the son of Robert Saberhagen. The six-foot-one-inch, 190-pound pitcher bats and throws right-handed and attended Cleveland High School in Reseda, CA. Saberhagen, selected by the Kansas City Royals (AL) in the nineteenth round of the free agent draft in June 1982, pitched in 1983 for Fort Myers, FL (FSL), winning 10 games and losing 5 decisions. He finished the 1983 season with Jacksonville, FL (SL), producing a 6–2 win–loss record.

In 1984, Saberhagen began an eight-season stint with the Kansas City Royals (AL), recording 10 victories and 11 setbacks. He won 20 games and lost only 6 in 1985. After winning only 7 contests and dropping 12 in 1986, he compiled 18 victories against only 10 losses in the next season. In 1988, his record slipped to 14 triumphs and 16 losses. Saberhagen enjoyed his best season in 1989, winning 23 games against only 6 setbacks. He led the AL in victories, complete games (12), ERA (2.16), and innings pitched (212⅓). In 1990, he triumphed only 5 times while dropping 9. The 1991 campaign saw him win 13 games and lose only 8. On December 11, 1991, Kansas City traded him to the New York Mets (NL). With the Mets, he took only 3 games and dropped 5 decisions in 1992, being on the disabled list from May 16 to July 18 and again from August 2 to September 7. He compiled a 7–7 record and 3.29 ERA for the last-place Mets in 1993 and a superb 14–4 mark and 2.74 ERA during the strike-shortened 1994 season.

Saberhagen, *TSN* AL Pitcher of the Year in 1985 and 1989, was named right-handed pitcher on the *TSN* All-Star team in 1985 and 1989. The BBWAA voted him the AL Cy Young Award, the top pitching honor, in both 1985 and 1989, while *TSN* named him the Comeback Player of the Year in 1987 and the AL Gold Glove recipient as a pitcher in 1989. On August 26, 1991, Saberhagen pitched a 7–0, no-hit victory against the Chicago White Sox. He hurled in the AL Championship Series in 1984 and 1985 without any decisions. Saberhagen pitched in the 1987 and 1990 All-Star Games and was credited with the AL victory in 1990. He won two games for victorious Kansas City against the St. Louis Cardinals in the 1985 World Series.

In eight AL seasons, Saberhagen won 110 games and lost 78 contests for a 3.21 ERA. In three NL seasons he won 24 of 40 games. His major league career included 1,410 strikeouts and a 3.19 ERA with 134 victories and 94 losses. Saberhagen and his wife Janeane have three children, Drew, Daulton William, and Brittany. His hobbies are golf and boating.

BIBLIOGRAPHY: *New York Mets Media Guide*, 1994; *TSN Official Baseball Register*, 1994.

Stan W. Carlson

SANDBERG, Ryne Dee "Ryno" (b. September 18, 1959, Spokane, WA), player, excelled as an all-around sports star at Spokane's North Central High School. He earned All-City honors in basketball and baseball and was selected All-State in football. Drafted by the Philadelphia Phillies (NL) in 1978, Sandberg played four years in their farm system before appearing in 13 major league games at the end of the 1981 season. The Phillies traded Larry Bowa (BB) and Sandberg to the Chicago Cubs (NL) for Ivan DeJesus in January 1982. This marked one of the great trades in Chicago Cubs history.

Despite making only one hit in his first 32 at bats in his rookie year, Sandberg ended the 1982 season with a .271 batting average and a club record of 103 runs scored. His 32 stolen bases established a Cub record for third basemen. The Cubs switched him to second base in 1983, resulting in his emergence as a premier NL player and a Cub favorite. A smooth-fielding, power-hitting player, the six-foot, 185-pound, right-handed Sandberg established many records in the following decade. He became the first second baseman in major league history to win nine Gold Glove awards and holds the major league record for 123 consecutive errorless games from June 21, 1989, to May 17, 1990, at his position, involving 584 chances. During his major league career, he enjoyed 15 streaks of at least 30 errorless games. The modest Sandberg commented, "I've worked at it. It hasn't come easy." He holds the major league career record of highest fielding percentage by a second baseman with .990.

Sandberg in 1990 became the first second baseman since Rogers Hornsby (BB) in 1925 to lead the NL in home runs, hitting 40 round-trippers. The same season, he became only the third player in major league history to hit 40 home runs and steal 25 bases. No other second baseman in major league history previously had reached the 30 home run plateau in consecutive seasons. His .309 batting average in 1993 marked the fifth time in his Cub career that he surpassed .300. From 1984 to 1993, Sandberg appeared in 10 consecutive All-Star Games.

He helped lead the Cubs to two NL East titles. The first came in 1984, when he achieved his best all-around batting average with .314 and played 61 consecutive games without an error. Sandberg's efforts won him the 1984 NL MVP Award. Sandberg retired in June 1994 after slumping to a career-low .238 batting mark. With the Cubs 13 years, Sandberg ranked among the team's top 10 in many categories. These included stolen bases (325), home runs (245), total bases (3,361), hits (2,133), and RBIs (905). He has a

.289 career batting average. Sandberg, who married Cindy White and has two children, lives in Phoenix, AZ.

BIBLIOGRAPHY: *1994 Chicago Cubs Information Guide; Chicago Cubs Vineline* (December 1990, May 1991, December 1992); *TSN Official Baseball Register,* 1994.

Duane A. Smith

SEWELL, James Luther "Luke" (b. January 5, 1901, Titus, AL; d. May 14, 1987, Akron, OH), player, coach, and manager, was the brother of baseball players Joe Sewell (BB) and Tommy Sewell. The five-foot-nine-inch, 160-pound Sewell, who batted and threw right-handed, originally signed with the Cleveland Indians (AL) after his 1921 graduation from the University of Alabama, where he had starred in football and baseball. After performing brief periods with Columbus, OH (AA) and Indianapolis, IN (AA), he then stayed in the major leagues. He played with Cleveland through 1932, primarily as a catcher. In January 1933, Cleveland traded him to the Washington Senators (AL) for Roy Spencer. Sewell appeared in all 5 games of the 1933 World Series against the victorious New York Giants (NL). Washington traded Sewell to the St. Louis Browns (AL) in January 1935. The same day, St. Louis sold him to the Chicago White Sox (AL). Chicago sent him to Cleveland in December 1938, where his playing career ended in 1939 (except for token appearances with the 1942 St. Louis Browns). Sewell played 1,630 major league games, 1,561 behind the plate. He compiled a .259 lifetime batting average and batted in 696 runs on 1,393 hits, mostly singles. A good, alert, defensive catcher, Sewell once made a double play at second base by trapping two base runners in a rundown. He caught no-hit games by Wes Ferrell (BB), Vern Kennedy, and Bill Dietrich.

Sewell's most noteworthy achievements came as a manager. In May 1941, Sewell replaced Fred Haney as St. Louis Browns manager. He guided the 1942 team to a third-place finish and the 1944 Browns to their only AL pennant, edging the Detroit Tigers and the New York Yankees on the last day of the season. After leading two games to one, the Browns lost the 1944 World Series in six games to the rival St. Louis Cardinals. The Browns finished third in 1945 and then dropped to seventh place in 1946, causing Sewell's dismissal. After spending 2 years in business, he was hired as a coach by the Cincinnati Reds (NL) in 1949 and replaced manager Bucky Walters (BB) for the final three games. He managed the Reds to sixth-place finishes in 1950 and 1951 and a seventh-place in 1952. In 10 years as a major league manager, Sewell compiled a 606–644 mark for a .485 win–loss percentage. From 1953 to 1955, he managed the Toronto, Canada, Maple Leafs (IL). Sewell joined an unsuccessful group in Seattle, WA, seeking a major league franchise. Sewell left baseball permanently and pursued business interests in the Akron, OH, area. He married Edna Ridge on August 14, 1926.

BIBLIOGRAPHY: *The Baseball Encyclopedia,* 9th ed. (New York, 1993); Robert Obojski, *Bush League* (New York, 1975); Joseph L. Reichler, ed., *The Great All-Time Baseball*

Record Book (New York, 1981); James Luther Sewell file, National Baseball Library, Cooperstown, NY.

Horace R. Givens

SEYBOLD, Ralph Orlando "Socks" (b. November 13, 1870, Washingtonville, OH; d. December 22, 1921, Greensburg, PA), player, held the AL season home run record for 17 years until slugger George H. "Babe" Ruth (BB) hit 29 round-trippers in 1919. Seybold, originally from extreme eastern Ohio, came to Jeannette, PA, a glass manufacturing town, where he started his baseball career in 1890 with the Grays. After playing locally, he began his professional career with Easton, PA, in 1894 and played his first major league game with the Cincinnati Reds (NL) on August 20, 1899. From 1901 until a broken leg ended his career in 1908, the 5-foot-11-inch, 175-pound right-handed outfielder and occasional first baseman played for manager Connie Mack's (BB) Philadelphia Athletics (AL). Mack had brought Seybold, whom he described as "the sturdiest and most serviceable of players," with him from the WA.

Seybold's major league career included 997 games, 1,085 hits, 218 doubles, 54 triples, 57 home runs, 556 RBIs, and a .294 batting average. His 16 home runs in 1902, the second AL season, also led the major leagues. He also led the major leagues with 45 doubles in 1903 and attained his highest batting average with .334 in 1901. In the 1905 World Series against the New York Giants, he hit only .125 in 5 games. Seybold batted safely in 27 consecutive games in 1901 and three times surpassed both a .300 batting average and 90 RBIs. He finished second in the AL in RBIs in 1907 and fourth in 1902. Although not considered adept defensively, he made two unassisted double plays from the outfield in 1907.

Seybold returned to his home town of Jeannette, PA, after his baseball career and managed an industrial semiprofessional baseball team. He was serving as the steward at the Jeannette Eagles Club at the time of his death, which resulted from a broken neck when his car went over a bank along the Lincoln Highway near Greensburg, PA.

BIBLIOGRAPHY: Greensburg (PA) *Morning Review*, December 23, 1921; *History of Jeannette* (Jeannette, PA, 1976); Mike Shatzkin, ed., *The Ballplayers* (New York, 1990); John Thorn and Pete Palmer, eds., *Total Baseball*, 3rd ed. (New York, 1993).

Robert B. Van Atta

SIEBERT, Wilfred Charles III "Sonny" (b. January 14, 1937, St. Marys, MO), player and coach, is the son of Wilfred Siebert, Jr., a National Lead Company worker, and Fern Rose (Gross) Siebert. Siebert, who received the nickname "Sonny" from his parents, grew up in St. Louis, MO, and graduated from Bayless High School. He attended the University of Missouri in Columbia for three years, starring in basketball with an 18-point per game average. Siebert also played shortstop and first base at Missouri and signed after his junior year with the Cleveland Indians (AL) for a $35,000 bonus. The six-foot-three-inch, 200-pound Siebert played right field at Burlington, NC (CrL) and Batavia, NY (NYPL) in 1958 and at Minot, ND (NoL) in 1959 before the St. Louis Hawks (NBA) basketball club drafted him. Siebert, however, decided to remain in baseball.

In 1960, Siebert returned to Burlington as a pitcher and won 8 of 15 decisions. He hurled for Salt Lake City, UT (PCL) and Reading, PA (EL) in 1961. The right-hander blossomed at Charleston, WV (IL) in 1962, winning 15 games and losing 8. After spending another year of seasoning at Jacksonville, FL (IL) in 1963, Siebert won 7 and lost 9 decisions for the Cleveland Indians (AL) in 1964. His record included a respectable 3.23 ERA and 144 strikeouts in 156 innings. In 1965 and 1966, he produced 16–8 records for the Indians. The hard-throwing Siebert in 1965 struck out a career-high 191 batters, including 15 Washington Senators in 1 game. In his next start against Washington on June 10, 1966, he hurled a 2–0 no-hitter in outdueling Phil Ortega. Siebert pitched two perfect innings in the 1966 All-Star Game.

Despite winning only 10 of 22 decisions in 1967, Siebert recorded a career-best 2.38 ERA. On September 13, 1967, he matched the Chicago White Sox's Gary Peters* with 11 innings of shutout pitching and allowed only four base runners. The Indians finally won, 1–0, in 17 innings. Siebert hurled 23 consecutive scoreless innings over three starts. In 1968, he surrendered only 145 hits in 206 innings and compiled a 2.98 ERA but won only a dozen games.

In April 1969 Cleveland dealt Siebert to the Boston Red Sox (AL). Siebert immediately became a mainstay of their rotation, winning 14 in 1969, 15 in 1970, and 16 in 1971. In 1971, he batted .266 and belted six home runs. On September 2, 1972, he pitched a 3–0 shutout over the Baltimore Orioles and smashed solo and two-run home runs off Pat Dobson. He recalled "missing a third home run when my drive tailed foul by a few feet." Siebert remains the last AL pitcher to hit two home runs in a game.

In May 1973 Boston sold Siebert's contract to the Texas Rangers (AL). After a difficult 7–12 campaign, Siebert returned to his St. Louis hometown in 1974 and split 16 decisions with the Cardinals (NL). On September 11, 1974, Siebert won the second-longest game in major league history, holding the New York Mets (NL) scoreless in the twenty-third, twenty-fourth, and twenty-fifth innings. The Cardinals scratched out a 4–3 victory, after which Siebert went "out with Cards' announcer Jack Buck [OS] and several players for New York cheesecake at 5 or 6 AM." Siebert divided the 1975 season between the San Diego Padres (NL) and Oakland Athletics (AL), winning 7 and losing 6. The power pitcher, who relied on a 90-mph-plus fastball, said, "My best success came against the power hitters and I had the most trouble with the punch and judy hitters." His career included 399 games,

140 wins, 114 losses, 16 saves, 1,512 strikeouts, and 21 shutouts. In 2,152.2 innings, Siebert yielded only 1,919 hits. He also hit 12 home runs.

Siebert subsequently attended Northeast Missouri State University in Kirksville and Southern Illinois University at Edwardsville, serving the latter as pitching coach. Siebert owned a Baskin-Robbins ice cream parlor and St. Louis, MO, *Post-Dispatch* and *Suburban Journal* newspaper routes. From 1984 to 1993, Siebert served as a pitching instructor throughout the San Diego Padres (NL) farm system. In November 1993, the Padres appointed him pitching coach.

Siebert married Carol Ann Buckner on June 28, 1958, and has four children, Scott, Steve, a former middle infielder in the San Diego Padres and Chicago White Sox (AL) farm systems, Sherri, and Sandi. He still makes St. Louis his home.

BIBLIOGRAPHY: Rich Marazzi and Len Fiorito, *Aaron to Zipfel* (New York, 1985); Jeff Miller, *Down to the Wire* (Dallas, TX, 1992); Frank J. Olmsted interview with Sonny Siebert, October 24, 1993; Mike Shatzkin, ed., *The Ballplayers* (New York, 1990); Sonny Siebert file, National Baseball Library, Cooperstown, NY; Rick Spiritosanto, "Sonny Siebert Recalls When He Put End to Marathon Game," *BD* 45 (August 1987), pp. 31–32.

Frank J. Olmsted

SMITH, Elmer Ellsworth "Mike" (b. March 23, 1868, Pittsburgh, PA; d. November 5, 1945, Pittsburgh, PA), player, began his professional baseball career in 1886 as a pitcher with the minor league Nashville, TN, club (SL). After Smith played only 10 games there, the Cincinnati Red Stockings (AA) promoted the 5-foot-11-inch, 178-pound southpaw, who finished the campaign with a mediocre 4–5 record. The next season, 19-year-old Smith posted an astounding 34–17 record and completed 49 games. The young fastballer, along with veteran hurler Tony Mullane (BB), who compiled a 31–17 mark, helped pace Cincinnati to a strong second-place finish. In 1888, Smith's record fell to 22–17 due largely to a recurring sore shoulder. Throughout the next season, the ailment limited Smith to only 29 games and a disappointing 9–12 record.

Cincinnati, fearing that Smith's pitching career was finished, released him in October 1889. Smith went back to the minor leagues for the 1890 and 1891 seasons and hit a composite .320 as an outfielder and occasional pitcher for Kansas City, MO (WA). In 1892, Smith returned to the major leagues, signing with the hometown Pittsburgh Pirates (NL). He remained the team's regular left fielder through the 1897 season, averaging .325 and 160 hits per year. His best season came in 1893, when he batted .346 with 179 hits, 121 runs, and 103 RBIs. His strong performance, coupled with the hitting of Jake Beckley (BB) and Jake Stenzel (S), helped the Pirates to an impressive 81–48 record and a second-place finish in the 12-team NL. After the 1897 season, Pittsburgh traded Smith to Cincinnati. In 1898, his solid .342 batting average helped Buck Ewing's (BB) Reds finish in third place with a 92–60 mark. Smith was sold in June 1900 to the New York Giants (NL), where he played the rest of the season, and then split duty between the Pittsburgh Pirates (NL) and Boston Beaneaters (NL) in the 1901 campaign. For the next five seasons, Smith bounced around the minor leagues with Kansas City, MO (AA) in 1902, Minneapolis, MN (AA) in 1903, Kansas City, MO (AA) and Ilion, NY (NYSL) in 1904, Scranton, PA (NYSL) in 1905, and Binghamton, NY (NYSL) in 1906.

During his 14-year major league career, Smith compiled a .311 batting average and 137 triples among his 1,462 hits. On the mound, he won 74 of 133 decisions for a .554 winning percentage and completed 123 of 137 games started. In 1887, he led all AA hurlers with a 2.94 ERA. He resided his entire life in Pittsburgh and worked in the iron and steel mills. His wife died of tuberculosis in 1889.

BIBLIOGRAPHY: *The Baseball Encyclopedia*, 9th ed. (New York, 1993); Craig Carter, ed., *TSN Daguerreotypes*, 8th ed. (St. Louis, MO, 1990), p. 268; Elmer Ellsworth Smith file, National Baseball Library, Cooperstown, NY; John Thorn and Pete Palmer, eds., *Total Baseball*, 3rd ed. (New York, 1993); Robert L. Tiemann and Mark Rucker, *Nineteenth Century Stars* (Kansas City, MO, 1989).

Raymond D. Kush

SODEN, Arthur Henry (b. April 23, 1843, Framingham, MA; d. August 13, 1925, Lake Sunapee, NH), owner and executive, was one of the original owners of the Boston Red Caps (NL) franchise and originated baseball's reserve clause. Soden, the son of Samuel Soden, a book publisher, and Ferona Soden, grew up and was educated in rural Massachusetts, where he began playing baseball. Soden, who served in the Civil War and married Mary Simpson, started his own roofing business in Boston, MA, in 1867 and operated the company for 50 years. In 1874, Soden accompanied a Boston baseball team on a tour of England, the first international tour by an American baseball club.

In 1876, Soden purchased shares in the Boston baseball club in the newly formed NL and expressed immediate interest in club affairs. Two years later, Soden obtained a controlling interest in the Boston team and became club president. The club lost money for five seasons despite finishing in second place, causing Soden to assume tight control over club finances. He cut players' salaries, made players work the turnstiles before games, booked the team into third-rate hotels to cut travel expenses, charged players' wives full ticket prices, and removed the press box to accommodate more seats for fans. Soden's response to baseball's falling economy typified club owners' views on overpaid and pampered players.

Despite his tight-fisted reign, Soden's team excelled on the field, especially in the 1890s. His clubs won eight NL championships, including five in the 1890s, and finished second four times from 1876 to 1900. His teams featured stellar managers Frank Selee (BB) and Harry Wright (BB) and National Baseball Hall of Famers Jimmy Collins (BB), Hugh Duffy (BB), and Tom McCarthy (BB).

Soden's lasting influence on baseball remained his proposal for a "reserve clause." The NL adopted the clause in 1879 to prevent bidding wars for players, allowing NL clubs to keep control of players and prevent other teams from signing them. The NL clubs also agreed not to play games with any teams or leagues violating this rule. Although the clause was ruled illegal in 1974 and paved the way for free agency, players initially viewed the clause as a status symbol. Soden resigned from baseball in 1906 but retained his stock in the Boston club and managed his roofing business until 1917.

BIBLIOGRAPHY: Charles Alexander, *Our Game* (New York, 1991); *CAB* Supp., vol. 11 (New York, 1928); Paul Dickson, *The Dickson Baseball Dictionary* (New York, 1989); *NYT*, August 15, 1925, p. 7; Harold Seymour, *Baseball: The Early Years* (New York, 1960).

Brian L. Laughlin

SPENCE, Stanley Orvil "Stan" (b. March 20, 1915, South Portsmouth, KY; d. January 9, 1983, Kinston, NC), player, was a 5-foot-10½-inch 180-pounder who played baseball for the CKAL. Boston Red Sox (AL) scout Fred Hunter walked onto the field during a game delay to persuade Spence to sign professionally. Hunter brought the contract to the garage where Spence worked and saw him lifting the front end of a car so blocks could be set. Hunter declared, "He was as strong as a bull." Spence, however, spent the 1940–1941 seasons on the Boston bench because Ted Williams (BB), Dom DiMaggio (S), and Lou Finney held the outfield jobs. "I'm as good a center-fielder," Spence insisted, "as Dom DiMaggio." In December 1941, Boston traded Spence to the Washington Senators (AL). Bucky Harris (BB), Senators' manager, said, "He always looks like a .300 hitter to me, whatever his average."

Spence performed better in Washington than at Boston. He enjoyed his best major league season in 1942, hitting .323 in 149 games and leading the AL with 15 triples. His defensive ability, however, drew more notice, as the left-handed-throwing Spence owned "the most feared arm in the league." Spence made the 1942, 1944, 1946, and 1947 All-Star teams, playing in the last three. The high, hard pitch did not intimidate him at bat. "Those battles at the plate," Spence remarked, "are a lot of fun." Spence made life miserable for the St. Louis Browns (AL) especially. In a 7-game series with St. Louis from August 22 through 25, 1943, he made 14 hits in 27 at bats with 6 homers. On June 1, 1944, Spence produced hits in all 6 at bats. He ended with 11 for 21 for the entire series at Sportsman's Park, where "I just feel at home." He spent 1945 with the U.S. Navy.

Upon returning to the Senators, Spence hit .292 in 152 games in 1946 and then fell to .279 in 1947. Washington returned him to Boston for a disappointing 1948 season. He batted just .235 and then was traded in May 1949 to his "favorite" team, the St. Louis Browns. Spence's final major league season resulted in a .240 average. The Browns sent him to the minor leagues, selling him to the Los Angeles, CA (PCL) club. Spence protested the deal, calling it "raw" because it deprived him of a tenth major league season and a lifetime pension. In nine seasons, he batted .282 with 95 home runs and 575 RBIs.

Spence married Mildred Virginia Harper on October 15, 1938. In retirement, he owned and operated the Southern Equipment Company in Kinston, NC. During the final game of the 1949 season, this writer witnessed Spence's last major league at bat, ironically in Sportsman's Park. Spence lined a pinch single on the first pitch, a solid hit from a solid performer.

BIBLIOGRAPHY: *The Baseball Encyclopedia*, 9th ed. (New York, 1993); Tommy Fitzgerald, "Signed Between Putouts," *BD* 6 (August 1947); "Hats Off," *TSN*, September 2, 1943; Frank O'Brien, "Spence on Sit-Down over Sale to Angels," *TSN*, February 15, 1950; John B. Old, "Spence Misses a Game on Phony Phone Call," *TSN*, May 10, 1950; Frank "Buck" O'Neill, "Hitting 'Em Where They Can't Get 'Em, Spence's Explanation for St. Louis Streak," *TSN*, June 8, 1944; Shirley Povich, "The Spence Is Terrific," *BD* 3 (October 1944); Shirley Povich, "This Morning," Washington *Post*, August 23, 1944; John Thorn and Pete Palmer, eds., *Total Baseball*, 3rd ed. (New York, 1993).

                                                                              William J. Miller

STAHL, Charles Sylvester "Chick" (b. January 10, 1873, Avila, IN; d. March 28, 1907, West Baden, IN), player and manager, was the sixth of nine children of Reuben Stahl, a carpenter, and Barbara (Stadtmiller) Stahl. Player–manager Garland "Jake" Stahl was not related. Nicknamed "Chick," Stahl was meagerly educated at Fort Wayne, IN, schools and concentrated early on baseball. A left-handed 5-foot-10-inch 160-pounder, he pitched for the local semiprofessional Pilseners and moved to the outfield because of his formidable hitting skills. His swift progress included stops at Roanoke, VA (VL) in 1895, Buffalo, NY (EL), where he hit .337 in 122 games in 1896, and the powerful Boston Beaneaters (NL) in 1897. The right fielder became a Boston fan favorite, batting .354 and .308 in the NL pennant-winning 1897 and 1898 seasons, .351 in 1899, and .295 in 1900.

Stahl joined his close friend Jimmy Collins (BB) in jumping to the Boston Pilgrims of the newly formed AL in 1901. The Pilgrims switched him to center field, where he resumed his stout hitting with a .309 mark in 1901 and a .323 average in 1902. Injuries limited Stahl to 77 games with a .274 batting average in 1903, but his .303 led all Pilgrim hitters to help Boston down the Pittsburgh Pirates in the first-ever World Series. The Pilgrims again finished first in 1904, as Stahl hit a solid .295 and led the AL in triples with 19. This gave him a unique record as the only performer ever to play twice for Boston pennant winners in two leagues.

After slipping to fourth in 1905, the Pilgrims plummeted to the cellar in 1906. Stahl batted .286 and assumed managerial duties for the final 40 games after Boston owner John I. Taylor, exasperated by the Pilgrims' collapse, suspended Collins.

In November 1906, Stahl married Julia Harmon, thereby removing himself from prominence as one of baseball's eligible bachelors. During the winter, he tried unsuccessfully to persuade Taylor to reinstate Collins. He pleaded a lack of managerial temperament and ambition but took the team—now named the Red Sox—to spring training in 1907. In late March he resigned abruptly as manager but agreed to serve as field captain. Three days later, in a West Baden, IN, hotel room prior to an exhibition game, he drank a fatal dose of carbolic acid. Shocked speculation persisted as to the reason for Stahl's aberrant death, although longtime Indiana friends were not surprised. Throughout his life, Stahl was plagued by bouts of depression, and more than once had threatened suicide.

In 1,304 major league games spanning a decade, Stahl batted .306, with 1,552 hits, 219 doubles, 117 triples, and 623 RBIs. His .961 fielding average included 159 outfield assists.

BIBLIOGRAPHY: *The Baseball Encyclopedia*, 9th ed. (New York, 1993); Cincinnati (OH) *Enquirer*, March 29, 1907; Fort Wayne (IN) *Journal Gazette*, December 22, 1906; March 29–31, 1907; Charles Stahl file, National Baseball Library, Cooperstown, NY; Glenn Stout, "The Manager's Endgame," *Boston Magazine*, November 1987, p. 134; Dick Thompson, "And in an Unrelated Development...The 'Brothers' Stahl Weren't," *The Fan*, November 1987; *TSN*, April 6, 1907.

A. D. Suehsdorf and Dick Thompson

STEINBRENNER, George Michael III (b. July 4, 1930, Rocky River, OH), sports owner, executive, and football coach, is the son of Henry G. Steinbrenner II, a rigid German disciplinarian, fierce business and sports competitor, and owner of the Kinsman Marine Transit Company, and Rita (Haley) Steinbrenner. He succeeded his father as head of Kinsman and later merged it with his own American Ship Company.

At Culver Military Academy in Indiana, Steinbrenner excelled as a multisports athlete and was selected to the Culver Athletic Hall of Fame. His later athletic accomplishments were limited to serving as assistant football coach at Northwestern University in 1955 and Purdue University from 1956 to 1967, both BTC schools.

Steinbrenner graduated from Williams College with a bachelor's degree in English in 1952 and participated as a hurdler on the school's track and field team. He pursued a master's degree in physical education at Ohio State University in 1954 and 1955 and met his wife, Elizabeth Joan Zieg, whom he married in May 1956. They have four children, Henry III, Jennifer, Jessica, and Harold.

In 1960, he acquired the Cleveland Pipers (ABL) against his family's wishes. The Pipers went bankrupt two years later.

Steinbrenner led a group of unsuccessful investors seeking to buy the Cleveland Indians (AL). The New York Yankees (AL), owned by CBS, became available for sale. On January 3, 1973, Steinbrenner appeared at a press conference in the Bronx to announce that he was coleader of a syndicate buying the Yankees for $10 million. The franchise is now valued at from $200 to $250 million. Steinbrenner did not plan to be active in the day-to-day operations of the club.

On August 30, 1974, Steinbrenner pleaded guilty to making illegal campaign contributions to Richard Nixon's presidential election campaign and was fined $15,000. President Ronald Reagan later pardoned him. Three months later, baseball commissioner Bowie Kuhn (BB) suspended him from the Yankees for 15 months for conduct "not in the best interests of baseball." During this exile, others close to the game suspected him of still running the team.

After the suspension, he in 1975 hired Billy Martin (BB) to manage the Yankees. The appointment marked the first of five tours by Martin as pilot of the New York club. Since 1975, Steinbrenner has changed New York managers 19 times. The Yankees finished first in the AL East 6 times and won the World Series over the Los Angeles Dodgers in 1977 and 1978. New York also appeared in the 1981 World Series, losing to the Los Angeles Dodgers.

Steinbrenner remains heavily involved in civic and community causes and holds four honorary doctoral degrees. He founded the Silver Shield Foundation, which provides college education for children of New York City policemen and fire-fighters who died in the line of duty. He chaired the U.S. Olympic program. Since February 1989, he has served as vice president of USOC.

Steinbrenner also owns the Tampa Bay Lightning, a new NHL franchise. Steinbrenner's controversies with several Yankee players have caused him to be called the "most hated man in baseball."

BIBLIOGRAPHY: *Baseball Encyclopedia*, 9th ed. (New York 1993); *New York Yankees 1994 Information Guide*; George Steinbrenner, letter to Stan W. Carlson, December 10, 1992; John Thorn and Pete Palmer, eds., *Total Baseball*, 3rd ed. (New York, 1993); George Will, "The Most Hated Man in Baseball," *Newsweek* 116 (August 6, 1990), pp. 52–59; *WWA*, 47th ed. (1992–1993) p. 3332.

                                                         Stan W. Carlson

STEWART, David Keith (b. February 19, 1957, Oakland, CA), player, is of African-American descent and the son of David Stewart, Jr., and Nathalie Helen (Dixon) Stewart. He grew up within walking distance of the Oakland

Coliseum and starred in three sports at Oakland's St. Elizabeth High School. Stewart also attended Merritt College in Oakland and California State University at Hayward.

His professional baseball career was launched at Bellingham, WA (NWL) in 1975 and included stints with the Los Angeles Dodgers (NL) in 1978 and 1981 to 1983, Texas Rangers (AL) from 1983 to 1985, and the Philadelphia Phillies (NL) in 1985 and 1986 prior to his achieving stardom with the Oakland Athletics (AL). The Athletics signed Stewart, the Phillies having released him in the spring of 1986 with a mediocre 30–35 major league record.

Stewart's dedication, self-confidence, and hard work finally paid dividends when he became an outstanding pitcher for Oakland (AL). He helped spur the Athletics' drive to three consecutive AL pennants from 1988 through 1990 and their 1989 World Series triumph over the San Francisco Giants.

From 1987 through 1990, Stewart proved baseball's outstanding pitcher. He topped the AL in games started each season while earning 20, 21, 21, and 22 victories. His 20 triumphs paced the AL in 1987. He also led the major leagues in innings pitched in 1988 and 1990, hurling the most shutouts the latter season. No other major league pitcher won 20 games three times during the 1980s.

The talented six-foot-two-inch, 200-pound right-hander possesses an overpowering fastball and outstanding forkball among his repertoire of pitches. Stewart has proven especially dominant in the spring and during postseason play. His early season accomplishments included four straight opening day triumphs (1988–1991) and a 16–0 mark in April from 1988 through 1990. He holds the record for most wins in league Championship Series competition with a perfect 8–0 log.

Stewart participated on the Dodgers' 1981 World Series winner, the Athletics' 1989 World's Champions, 1988 and 1990 AL pennant winners, 1992 AL West titlist, and the Toronto Blue Jays 1993 World Series Champions. His honors included being named to the 1988 *TSN* AL All-Star team and selected MVP of the 1989 World Series and 1990 and 1993 AL Championship Series. Stewart's greatest honor may have come in 1993 when the Baseball Assistance Team awarded him the Bart Giamatti Award for exceptional community service.

Stewart, who won 116 games while losing 71 contests for Oakland from 1986 to 1992, married Vanessa McKinney on July 8, 1977, and has a daughter. Stewart signed an $8.5 million contract with the Toronto Blue Jays (AL) for 1993 and 1994. His 12–8 mark in 1993 and 7–8 slate in 1994 brought his major league record to 165–122 with a 3.86 ERA. Toronto released Stewart following the 1994 season.

BIBLIOGRAPHY: Dwight Chapin, "Throwing Smoke," *Street & Smith Baseball Magazine* 51 (1991), pp. 30, 40; National Baseball Hall of Fame, questionnaire completed by David Stewart, 1981; *The 1994 Information Please Sports Almanac* (Boston, MA, 1993); *TSN Baseball Guides*, 1988–1994; *TSN Official Baseball Register*, 1993; *USA*

Today, January 27, 1993; *USA Today Baseball Weekly*, January 27, 1993; February 9, 1993.

Merl F. Kleinknecht

STOVEY, George Washington (b. 1866, Williamsport, PA; d. March 22, 1936, Williamsport, PA), player and umpire, was of mixed parentage with a white father and a black mother, whose names and backgrounds are unknown. He stood approximately six feet tall, weighed about 165 pounds, and threw left-handed. He played amateur baseball in the early 1880's until joining the all-black Cuban Giants of Trenton, NJ in 1886. After pitching just 1 game, he jumped to Jersey City, NJ (IL) in a "daring midnight raid." In 31 games for Jersey City that season, Stovey held opposing batters to an unbelievably low .167 batting average. In a heartbreaking loss against Bridgeport, CT, he struck out 22 batters.

Stovey's fine career was marred by racial controversy. At the end of the 1886 season, the New York Giants (NL) almost signed Stovey. Since virulent racist, highly influential Cap Anson of the Chicago White Stockings (NL) vigorously opposed Stovey's signing, the Giants bowed to Anson's wishes. Stovey enjoyed his best season in 1887 while pitching for Newark. He dominated the IL with a 34–14 win–loss record, a victory mark unlikely to be broken. He also participated in a historic first that season when he and catcher Fleet Walker formed organized baseball's first all-African-American battery. Stovey became a cause célèbre in July 1887, when his Newark team was scheduled to play an exhibition with Anson's Chicago White Stockings. Anson refused to let his White Stockings play Newark if Stovey pitched against them. This incident may have led to the erection of organized baseball's color line. Stovey's contract with Newark was not renewed for the following year. Stovey played for Worcester, MA (NEL), Troy, NY (NYSL), and in 1891 for one of the all-time great black teams, the Big Gorhams of New York. His career ended with the Cuban Giants in 1893.

At the height of Stovey's career, a Binghamton, NY, newspaper described him as "the fellow with the sinister fin who has such a knack of tossing up balls that they appear as large as an alderman's opinion of himself, but you can't hit with a cellar door."

Stovey returned to his native Williamsport, working as a laborer in a sawmill, possibly as a barber, and in other odd jobs. Stovey kept involved in baseball, playing intermittently with local amateur teams until his early fifties. He also umpired frequently, his judgment being respected. Williamsport's African-American community highly respected Stovey and his athletic accomplishments in his youth. Most baseball historians regard Stovey as the greatest African-American pitcher of the nineteenth century. Stovey, a bachelor, died destitute at the age of 70.

BIBLIOGRAPHY: Binghamton (NY) *Leader*, quoted in the Newark (NJ) *Journal*, July 29, 1887; Cleveland (OH) *Gazette*, May 13, 1892; *SpL*, February 23, 1887; Trenton (NJ) *True American*, February 23, 1887; Williamsport (PA) *The Grit*, March 29, 1936.
                                                                    Louis E. Hunsinger, Jr.

STRAWBERRY, Darryl Eugene "Straw" (b. March 12, 1962, Los Angeles, CA), player, is the son of Henry Strawberry, a post office employee, and Ruby Strawberry and grew up in Los Angeles. He played basketball and baseball at Crenshaw High School, from which he graduated in 1980. In his senior year, he ranked among the most scouted baseball prospects in the nation. The New York Mets (NL), who had the first overall pick in the June 1980 major league draft, selected Strawberry and signed him for a $200,000 bonus. The six-foot-six-inch, 215-pound left-handed-hitting outfielder was assigned to Kingsport, TN (ApL) in 1980. After spending the 1981 season at Lynchburg, VA (CrL), he batted .283 for Jackson, TX (TL) in 1982 with a TL-leading 34 home runs, .602 slugging average, and 100 bases on balls. Strawberry was named the TL MVP and played for a Caracas, Venezuela, team in the winter of 1982.

After playing 16 games in 1983 for Tidewater (IL), he was promoted to the New York Mets and compiled a .257 batting average with 74 RBIs, 26 home runs, and a .512 slugging average. He was named NL Rookie of the Year and *TSN* NL Rookie Player of the Year. Strawberry, blessed with tremendous power, hit at least 26 home runs every year in his first nine NL seasons. During this period, he belted a major league–leading 280 home runs. Good speed enabled him to join the 30/30 Club with at least 30 home runs and 30 stolen bases in 1987, when he hit 39 home runs and stole 36 bases. Teammate Howard Johnson* also accomplished the same feat in 1987, making them the first pair of 30/30 teammates in major league history. In 1988, Strawberry led the NL with 39 home runs and a .545 slugging percentage. The glare of the spotlight constantly focused on Strawberry, who had been dubbed "The Black Ted Williams" since high school. He found that his actions on and off the field were carefully scrutinized. Spectators in the stands frequently chanted "Darryl" in unison.

The Los Angeles Dodgers (NL) signed Strawberry as a free agent in November 1990. After appearing in 139 games in 1991, he played in only 43 games in 1992 and 32 games in 1993. A herniated disk eventually required an operation. The San Francisco Giants (NL) signed Strawberry in June 1994 after the Dodgers released him because of substance abuse problems. From 1984 to 1991, he made eight straight NL All-Star teams. *TSN* selected him for its NL All-Star teams in 1988 and 1990 and as an outfielder on its NL Silver Slugger team in 1988 and 1990. Strawberry shares two NL Championship Series records, recording the most strikeouts (12, 1986) and most at bats (30, 1988). In these two appearances, he hit a combined .269 with three home runs and 11 RBIs. During his only World Series, he hit .208 with 1 home run and 1 RBI for the 1986 World Championship Mets against the Boston Red Sox.

Through the strike-shortened 1994 season, Strawberry has batted .259 with 294 home runs, 886 RBIs, 1,232 hits, .513 slugging average, and 205 stolen bases. Darryl is divorced and has two children, Darryl, Jr., and Diamond. In December 1994, he was indicted for not reporting over $500,000 in income from sports autograph shows. In February 1995, he was suspended for 60 days for violating major league baseball's drug policy and the terms of his aftercare program. The Giants released him the next day.

BIBLIOGRAPHY: *Los Angeles Dodgers 1994 Media Guide;* William Nack, "The Perils of Darryl," *SI* 60 (April 23, 1984), pp. 32–39; Seymour Siwoff, ed., *The 1992 Elias Baseball Analyst* (New York, 1992), p. 210; Darryl Strawberry, *Darryl* (New York, 1992); Darryl Strawberry file, National Baseball Library, Cooperstown, NY; John Thorn and Pete Palmer, eds., *Total Baseball,* 3rd ed. (New York, 1993), p. 1259; *TSN Official Baseball Register,* 1994.

Robert J. Brown

STRONG, T. R. "Ted" (b. January 2, 1917, South Bend, IN; d. 1951, Chicago, IL), player, excelled as a versatile athlete by starring in baseball with the Kansas City Monarchs (NAL) and performing for basketball's original Globetrotters. The six-foot-six-inch 210-pounder, an ideal baseball player, possessed all the tools required for stardom and proved outstanding in all phases of the game. Defensively, he was an accomplished fielder with an exceptionally strong arm. Offensively, the switch-hitter demonstrated good power from both sides of the plate.

The talented Strong was selected to five East-West All-Star teams during a six-year interval from 1937 to 1942, missing only the 1940 season when playing in Mexico. He started at three different positions (shortstop, first base, and outfield) and compiled a career .313 All-Star batting average. His first two All-Star appearances came as a member of the NAL's Indianapolis, IN, ABCs ball club, while all other appearances were with the Kansas City Monarchs.

In his last two All-Star seasons, Strong batted .319 in 1941 and .345 in 1942 with good power. The latter year marked the Monarchs' fourth consecutive NAL pennant since Strong joined the team and the initiation of World Series play between the NNL and the NAL. The Monarchs swept the Homestead Grays, as Strong hit .316 with a home run.

Following the 1942 World Series, he entered military service for three years and returned to help the Monarchs capture the 1946 NAL pennant. A pull-hitter, he led the NAL in both home runs (seven) and RBIs (45) while batting .287. He and Satchel Paige (BB) missed the last two games of the World Series against the Newark Eagles, under circumstances that are unclear.

During the 1940 season, he played with Nuevo Laredo (MEL) and batted .332 with a .603 slugging percentage. After leaving the Monarchs, he played with the Indianapolis, IN, Clowns (NAL) in 1948, Minot, ND (MkL) in 1950, and the Chicago American Giants (NAL) in 1951.

BIBLIOGRAPHY: Janet Bruce, *The Kansas City Monarchs* (Lawrence, KS, 1985); Chicago (IL) *Defender*, 1937–1948; Robert W. Peterson, *Only the Ball Was White* (Englewood Cliffs, NJ, 1970); James A. Riley, *The All-Time All-Stars of Black Baseball* (Cocoa, FL, 1983); James A. Riley, *The Biographical Encyclopedia of the Negro Baseball Leagues* (New York, 1994); James A. Riley, interviews with former Negro League players, James A. Riley collection, Cocoa, FL; Mike Shatzkin, ed., *The Ballplayers* (New York, 1990), p. 1056.

James A. Riley

SUMMERS, William Reed "Bill" (b. November 10, 1895, Harrison, NJ; d. September 12, 1966, Upton, MA), umpire, was the son of Scottish immigrants John Summers and Jenny (Reed) Summers. He grew up in Woonsocket, RI, and quit school in the seventh grade to work with his father in a textile mill to help support the family. Since boxing was his favorite sport, he fought professionally as a 135-pound lightweight under the names of Marty Winters and Marty Summers. He quit the ring in April 1917 after marrying Mary Ellen Van Riper, with whom he had eight children. His umpiring career began in 1913, when he was called from the stands to officiate a high school game after the regular umpire failed to appear. Summers, initially relying upon his reputation as a fighter to control the game, quickly earned a reputation for accurate, authoritative decisions and for the next 8 years umpired local amateur and industrial league games. He became a professional umpire upon losing his job as a policeman following the famous 1919 Boston, MA, police strike. After a season in the independent BVL, he joined the EL in 1921 and spent 10 years in that Class A circuit before advancing to the AA IL during the 1931 season. In 1933 Summers finally reached the major leagues at the relatively advanced age of 37.

A protégé of Bill McGowan (BB), Summers quickly emerged as one of the AL's finest umpires and was assigned in 1936 to both the All-Star Game and World Series in only his fourth year. Indicative of his reputation as an arbiter, he was selected in 1948 to umpire the one-game AL playoff between the Boston Red Sox and the Cleveland Indians. In 1950 he was appointed to represent AL umpires on the committee that rewrote and recodified the rule book. Summers, especially adept at calling balls and strikes, earned the respect of players and managers for his levelheaded, even-tempered style of umpiring and experienced far fewer on-field confrontations than most umpires. Summers ranks near the top in career service for major league umpires, his 27 seasons exceeded by only 12 arbiters. He and Al Barlick (BB) worked the most All-Star Games at seven (1936, 1941, 1946, 1949, 1952, 1955, and 1959). Only 3 umpires surpassed his eight World Series assignments (1936, 1939, 1942, 1945, 1948, 1951, 1955, and 1959).

Summers, a popular after-dinner speaker, retired after the 1959 season.

He worked for AL president Joe Cronin (BB) as a goodwill ambassador for baseball, giving lectures and conducting clinics at American military bases around the globe.

BIBLIOGRAPHY: *NYT*, September 13, 1966; *TSN*, September 24, 1966; Bill Summers file, National Baseball Library, Cooperstown, NY; Bill Summers with Tim Cohane, "Baseball Boors I Have Known," *Look* 24 (July 5, 1960), pp. 65–69, 71.

Larry R. Gerlach

SUTTON, Ezra Ballou (b. September 17, 1850, Palmyra, NY; d. June 20, 1907, Braintree, MA), player, played amateur baseball in Rochester, NY, and began his 20-year professional baseball career in 1870 at age 19 as third baseman for Forest City of Cleveland. He remained with the Forest City club when it joined the NA, baseball's first professional league, in its inaugural 1871 season. After Forest City folded in August 1872, Sutton signed with the Athletics of Philadelphia (NA, NL) and played there 4 years. The Chicago White Stockings signed him for the first NL season in 1876, but he broke the contract and remained in Philadelphia when the Athletics offered him more money than Chicago. After the 1876 season, Sutton signed with the Boston Red Stockings (NL) and played his final 12 major league years for Boston.

Although primarily a third baseman, he also played shortstop and the other infield and outfield positions. The 5-foot-8½-inch, 153-pound right-hander possessed a strong, accurate throwing arm, although statistics show him somewhat below average as a fielder. He batted cross-handed early in his career and switched to a standard grip as the quality of major league pitching improved. After hitting .311 over his first six major league seasons from 1871 through 1876, he dropped to a .255 batting average in his first five years with Boston and then rebounded from 1883 through 1885 with his three finest seasons. In 1883 he hit .324 and ranked among the top four NL hitters in hits, triples, runs, slugging average, and RBIs. Boston surprised forecasters by winning the 1883 NL pennant. Sutton's 162 hits tied for the NL lead in 1884, while his .346 batting average ranked third. His .313 batting average in 1885 dropped him out of the upper echelons, but his 143 hits shared fourth in the NL.

Sutton batted .277 for Boston in 1886 and .304 in 1887. After hitting only .218 in 28 games in 1888, he finished the season with minor league Rochester, NY (IA). After playing a year with minor league Milwaukee, WI (WA) in 1889, Sutton retired from the game. With his baseball earnings, he had bought an interest in a Palmyra, NY, concern (variously identified as an ice plant, grist mill, or sawmill) in 1886. The business, however, failed in 1890, the same year Sutton experienced the onset of locomotor ataxia, a gradual paralysis that incapacitated him by 1902. His wife Susie, whom he had married in 1871, died in January 1906 of burns suffered six weeks earlier. A lamp had exploded, igniting her dress in front of the helpless Sutton. Sutton was hospitalized in Rochester, NY, that April and was later moved to hospitals in Boston and Braintree, MA, to be closer to his baseball friends. Two children predeceased him. He was survived by a daughter, Georgia, and two elder brothers. In 1,263 major league games, Sutton batted .294. His 1,575 hits included 229 doubles, 97 triples, and 26 home runs.

BIBLIOGRAPHY: William J. Ryczek, *Blackguards and Red Stockings: A History of Baseball's National Association, 1871–1875* (Jefferson, NC, 1992); Ezra Sutton file, National Baseball Library, Cooperstown, NY; John Thorn and Pete Palmer, eds., *Total Baseball*, 3rd ed. (New York, 1993); Robert L. Tiemann and Mark Rucker, eds., *Nineteenth Century Stars* (Kansas City, MO, 1989).

Frederick Ivor-Campbell

TAYLOR, John W. "Jack" (b. September 13, 1873, Straightville, OH; d. March 4, 1938, Columbus, OH), player, starred as an early twentieth-century major league pitcher. The 5-foot-10-inch, 170-pound Taylor threw and batted right-handed.

Taylor first pitched professionally for Milwaukee, WI (WL) in 1897 and most of 1898. He advanced to the Chicago Orphans (NL) in late 1898 and pitched for the Chicago Orphans-Cubs through 1903. Chicago traded Taylor to the St. Louis Cardinals (NL), for whom he hurled in 1904, 1905, and the first half of 1906. Taylor returned to the Chicago Cubs (NL) for the remainder of that season and 1907, thus ending his decade-long major league career.

In that era, clubs carried small pitching staffs. Pitchers were expected to complete what they started. With a 97 percent ratio in completing 278 of 286 major league starts, Taylor retains the highest complete game ratio of all long-term starting pitchers. He ranked as one of the NL's better pitchers, tying for the NL lead in complete games (39) in 1902 and finishing among the leaders several other years. He also remained high in innings pitched different seasons. He led the NL retroactively in ERA in 1902 with a low 1.33 and won 20 or more games four times. Taylor holds a unique record of having completed every game he started for four straight years from 1902 to 1905, hurling 139 consecutive complete games. This streak included an 18-inning, 2–1 loss on June 24, 1904. For his career, he won 150 games, lost 139 decisions, and compiled a 2.66 ERA with 657 strikeouts in 2,617 innings and 20 shutouts.

Taylor's rash personality, a penchant for alcohol, and a tendency to gamble aroused suspicions of his honesty and probably prevented him from realizing a longer, more eminent career. Some suspected him of losing games deliberately in the first Chicago City Series in 1903 between the Chicago White Sox (AL) and his own club and, at the instigation of gamblers, dropping a contest to the Pittsburgh Pirates (NL) on July 30, 1904. At hearings, Taylor effectively refuted both charges. Backing came from fellow players and St. Louis Cardinal owner Frank D. Robison, who regarded him as unfairly maligned. By contrast, Chicago owner James S. Hart disliked Taylor and had planned to trade him well before he grew suspicious of his pitching in the 1903 City Series. Aside from being fined for pitching while inebriated in the Pittsburgh game, Taylor was fully exonerated. His serious threat to sue baseball ownership probably contributed to his acquittal.

BIBLIOGRAPHY: *The Baseball Encyclopedia*, 9th ed. (New York, 1993); New York *Tribune*, January 18, 1905; February 14–15, 1905; *NYT*, June 25, 1904; July 30, 1904; January 10, 1905; February 14–16, 1905; St. Louis (MO) *Post-Dispatch*, January 6, 1905; January 11, 1905; January 13, 1905; February 14, 1905; February 16, 1905; Jack Taylor file, National Baseball Library, Cooperstown, NY.

Lowell L. Blaisdell

TEBBETTS, George Robert "Bird" "Birdie" (b. November 10, 1911, Burlington, VT), player, manager, executive, and scout, is the son of Charles Tebbetts, a salesman, and Elizabeth (Ryan) Tebbetts. An aunt nicknamed him, "Bird," remarking that he had "lips just like a bird!" After influenza killed his father, Tebbetts moved with his mother, sister, and brother to Nashua, NH, in 1917. At Nashua High School, Tebbetts made All-State in football and starred in basketball and baseball. The Detroit Tigers (AL) signed the catcher and paid him $200 a month while he attended Providence College on a baseball scholarship. After earning a bachelor's degree in philosophy in 1934, Tebbetts played for Bedford, MA (NEL), Springfield, IL (3IL), and Beaumont, TX (TL).

Tebbetts caught for the Detroit Tigers from September 1936 to 1947 except for U.S. Army service from 1943 to 1945. The 5-foot-11-inch, 200-pound right-hander, one of the smartest, most dedicated catchers, handled pitchers astutely and intimidated opponents with his high-pitched shriek. The witty, scrappy Tebbetts led AL catchers in assists (1939–1941) and made the AL All-Star team in 1941 and 1942. He batted .296 in 1940, as the Tigers won the AL pennant and lost the World Series to the Cincinnati Reds. In May 1947 Detroit traded Tebbetts to the Boston Red Sox (AL), where he batted .280 in 1948 and a career-high .310 in 1950. Boston nearly won AL pennants in 1948 and 1949, seasons that Tebbetts made the AL All-Star team. The Red Sox in December 1950 sent Tebbetts, who sold insurance during the off-season, to the Cleveland Indians (AL) after he publicly criticized teammates. Tebbetts retired following the 1952 campaign, having batted .270 with 1,000 hits and 469 RBIs in 14 major league campaigns.

Tebbetts, an excellent teacher, managed Indianapolis, IN (AA) in 1953 and the Cincinnati Reds (NL) from 1954 through 1958. The 1956 Reds, featuring sluggers Frank Robinson (BB), Ted Kluszewski (BB), and Wally Post, finished only two games behind the Brooklyn Dodgers, as *TSN* named Tebbetts NL Manager of the Year. Tebbetts, vice president of the Milwaukee Braves (NL) from 1959 until September 1961, piloted Milwaukee through 1962 and the Cleveland Indians (AL) from 1963 through 1966. Tebbetts's clubs compiled a 748–705 win–loss record over 11 seasons. Scouting assignments followed with the New York Yankees (AL) from 1975 to 1982, Cleveland Indians (AL) from 1983 to 1988, Baltimore Orioles (AL) from 1989 to 1992, and Florida Marlins (NL) in 1993.

Tebbetts married Mary Hartnett in October 1950 and has three daughters, Susan, Elizabeth, and Patricia. Boston fans in 1969 voted the Anna Maria, FL, resident the Red Sox all-time catcher. Tebbetts served on the Veterans Committee of the National Baseball Hall of Fame.

BIBLIOGRAPHY: "A Game of Inches," *Time* 70 (July 8, 1957), pp. 42–44, 47; Robert Creamer, "The Three Worlds of Birdie Tebbetts," *SI* 6 (February 25, 1957), pp. 60–66; Al Hirshberg, *Baseball's Greatest Catchers* (New York, 1966); Ed Linn, "The Man in the Dugout," *Sport* 17 (September 1954), pp. 50–60; Harry T. Paxton, "Can He Lift the Redlegs Out of the Rut?" *SEP* 226 (May 22, 1954), p. 31; Birdie Tebbetts, "I'd Rather Catch," *Atlantic* 184 (September 1949), pp. 45–48; Birdie Tebbetts, letter to David L. Porter, August 11, 1993; *TSN Official Baseball Register*, 1963.

David L. Porter

THORNTON, Andre "Andy" "Thor" "Thunder" (b. August 13, 1949, Tuskegee, AL), player, is the son of Harold Thornton and Arcola (Williams) Thornton and played baseball at Phoenixville, PA, High School, where he led his team to the Middle Atlantic title and a berth in the 1965 Babe Ruth World Series. The Philadelphia Phillies (NL) in 1967 signed Thornton, who made his professional debut with Huron, MI (NoL). During the next four and one-half seasons (interrupted by brief stints in the National Guard), he played first base, third base, and the outfield for several Philadelphia minor league teams. His stops included Eugene, OR (NWL) in 1968, Spartanburg, SC (WCL) in 1969, Peninsula (CrL) in 1970, Reading, PA (EL) in 1971, and Eugene, OR (PCL) in 1972. In June 1972, the Atlanta Braves (NL) acquired him in a trade and assigned him to Richmond, VA (IL), where he played until May 1973. The Braves traded Thornton to the Chicago Cubs (NL) for Joe Pepitone and cash. The Cubs sent Thornton to their Wichita, KS (AA) affiliate. He made his major league debut with Chicago in July 1973.

The six-foot-three-inch, 200-pound Thornton, who hit and threw right-handed, played in 106 games for the Cubs in 1974. The next season, he fractured his right wrist in spring training and missed the first month. Nevertheless, he still managed to hit .293 and belt 18 home runs. Chicago traded Thornton in May 1976 to the Montreal Expos (NL), which dealt him, in turn, to the Cleveland Indians (AL) that December. As the Indians' regular first baseman from 1977 through 1979, he posted impressive slugging figures and averaged 29 homers and 89 RBIs. In June 1979 Thornton was presented with the ninth annual Roberto Clemente (BB) Award, given to the player who best exemplifies the game through his playing ability, sportsmanship, character, and community involvement. During spring training in 1980, Thornton suffered torn knee ligaments and cartilage and was sidelined for the entire season. The next year saw him limited to only 69 games, as a broken hand and a badly sprained thumb twice put him on the disabled list.

In 1982, Thornton rebounded with a "career year," in which he batted .273 with 32 home runs and 116 RBIs in 161 games and won the *TSN* 1982 AL Comeback Player of the Year Award. For the 1983 and 1984 seasons, he continued as the Indians' regular first baseman. In 1984, he walloped a career-high 33 home runs and earned a spot on the *TSN* AL Silver Slugger team. Granted free agency after the 1984 season, he re-signed with Cleveland. Thornton became the team's designated hitter during the 1985 and 1986 seasons, averaging nearly 20 home runs and 77 RBIs in the 2-year span. Thornton retired after the 1987 season to devote his time and energy to the Board of Christian Family Outreach, Incorporated, and other business interests. In his 14-year major league career, Thornton played in 1,565 games, hit .254, and collected 253 home runs and 895 RBIs. He participated in the 1982 and 1984 All-Star Games but never played in a league Championship Series or World Series.

Thornton attended Cheyney State College and Nyack College. He and his wife Gertrude were married in 1970 and had two children, Andre, Jr., and Theresa. In 1977, Thornton's wife and daughter were killed in an automobile accident on the Pennsylvania Turnpike. He later married Gail Jones, with whom he had two sons, Jonathan and Andy.

BIBLIOGRAPHY: *Chicago Cubs Official Press, Radio, and TV Roster Book*, 1974, 1975, 1976; Craig Carter, ed., *TSN Daguerreotypes*, 8th ed. (St. Louis, MO, 1990), p. 283; Eddie Gold and Art Ahrens, *The New Era Cubs 1941–1985* (Chicago, IL, 1985); John Thorn and Pete Palmer, eds., *Total Baseball*, 3rd ed. (New York, 1993); Andre Thornton file, National Baseball Library, Cooperstown, NY; *TSN Baseball Guide*, 1981, 1982; *TSN Official Baseball Register*, 1988, pp. 488–489.

Raymond D. Kush

TORGESON, Clifford Earl "The Earl of Snohomish" (b. January 1, 1924, Snohomish, WA; d. November 8, 1990, Everett, WA), player, was known as a "walking man" and idolized baseball star Earl Averill (BB) as a youth. Torgeson, the son of a carpenter, signed out of high school and began his professional baseball career with Wenatchee, WA (WIL) in 1942 and served from 1943 to 1945 in the armed forces. In his major league rookie 1947 season, the left-handed-hitting and -throwing first baseman batted .281 for the Boston Braves (NL) with 16 home runs, 11 stolen bases (fifth highest in the NL), and a .403 on-base percentage. On May 30, 1947, he tied a major league record for first basemen by playing the entire game without a putout.

In 1948, the Braves captured the NL flag. Torgeson, who played mostly against right-hand pitching, tied for fourth in the NL in walks and ranked fifth in stolen bases. He led all batters in the Braves' six-game World Series loss to the Cleveland Indians with a superlative .389 average. Torgeson missed most of 1949 with a shoulder injury but rebounded in 1950 with his best year. He batted .290 with 23 home runs, an NL-leading 120 runs scored, 119 walks (third), 15 stolen bases (fourth), and a .412 on-base percentage. In 1951, he again finished among NL leaders in walks (102) and stolen bases (20).

After spending the 1952 campaign with the Braves, the six-foot-three-inch, 180-pound Torgeson was traded to the Philadelphia Phillies (NL) in February 1953, sold to the Detroit Tigers (AL) in June 1955, and sent to the Chicago White Sox (AL) in June 1957. Torgeson started the 1959 season as the regular first baseman for the AL champion "Go Sox" and drew 62 walks in only 277 official at bats but was replaced in August by newly acquired Ted Kluszewski (BB). Torgeson made only 1 official at bat (plus a walk, of course) in the White Sox's World Series loss to the Los Angeles Dodgers. Torgeson continued with Chicago as a reserve player in 1960 and early 1961 and ended his major league career with a brief stint on the mighty 1961 New York Yankees (AL).

Although Torgeson's batting average over his five-team, 15-year career was just .265, he proved a good clutch hitter and fine base runner. Torgeson literally walked his way into the record books. His .387 major league on-base percentage ranked among the hundred highest ever achieved and tied that of Honus Wagner (BB) and Willie Mays (BB). His ratio of 16.47 walks per 100 at bats ranks the thirteenth highest in major league history.

Torgeson, who married Norma Syverson in March 1946 and had one daughter, Christine, and one son, Andy, enjoyed basketball, golf, and bowling. He worked as a lumber company salesman and supervisor of logging operations in Everett, WA, following his retirement from baseball.

BIBLIOGRAPHY: Harold Kaese, "It's Now or Never for Torgeson," *Sport* 12 (May 1952), pp. 34–35, 93–95; Rich Marazzi and Len Fiorito, *Aaron to Zuverink* (New York, 1982); David Neft et al., *The Sports Encyclopedia: Baseball* (New York, 1993); John Thorn and Pete Palmer, eds., *Total Baseball*, 3rd ed. (New York, 1993); *TSN Official Baseball Register*, 1961.

Sheldon L. Appleton

TRENT, Theodore "Ted" "Highpockets" "Big Florida" (b. December 17, 1905, Jacksonville, FL; d. January 10, 1944, Chicago, IL), player, performed in the Negro Leagues from 1927 to 1939. Trent, the ace pitcher for the champion St. Louis, MO, Stars (NNL), led the Stars to championships in 1928, 1930, and 1931. The long-legged pitcher relied on his roundhouse curveball and nasty slider. Trent's best year came in 1928, when he compiled a 21–4 win-loss record and led the Stars in innings pitched, strikeouts, complete games, and shutouts. The six-foot-three-inch, 185-pound Trent appeared in four East-West All-Star Games from 1934 to 1937 and started for the West squad in 1934 and 1937 with no decisions.

After leading the St. Louis Stars to a 1931 NNL championship, Trent defeated an All-Star major league team composed of "Babe" Herman (BB), Bill Terry (BB), Hack Wilson (BB), and brothers Paul Waner (BB) and Lloyd Waner (BB). National Baseball Hall of Famer Terry, who had batted over .400 the previous year, struck out three times against the tall right-hander. Trent defeated the major leaguers, 8–6, striking out 16 batters.

Trent's career included appearances with the Detroit, MI, Wolves (EWL) in 1932, Washington, DC, Pilots (EWL) in 1932, Kansas City, MO, Monarchs (NSL) in 1932, New York Black Yankees in 1933 and 1934, and Chicago, IL, American Giants (NAL) from 1933 to 1939. Overall, Trent compiled a 94–49 win-loss record, triumphing in 66 percent of his decisions over 13 years.

BIBLIOGRAPHY: Chicago (IL) *Defender*, July 28, 1934; John B. Holway, *Blackball Stars* (Westport, CT, 1988); James A. Riley, *The Biographical Encyclopedia of the Negro Baseball Leagues* (New York, 1994); Michael Shatzkin, ed., *The Ballplayers* (New York, 1990).

Larry Lester

TROUPPE, Quincy Thomas (b. December 25, 1912, Dublin, GA; d. August 10, 1993, St. Louis, MO), player, manager, and scout, was the youngest of 10 children born to Charles Trouppe, a Georgia sharecropper, and Mary Trouppe. The Trouppes moved when Quincy was a youngster to Compton Hill in south St. Louis, MO, where Charles was employed by the American Car Foundry. Quincy attended Vashon High School, located across from the home park of the St. Louis Stars (NNL). He served as the Stars' batboy while playing for the Tom Powell AmLe Post 77 and later enrolled at Lincoln University of Missouri.

A six-foot-three-inch, 200-pound catcher, Trouppe began nearly a quarter century in professional baseball in 1931 with the NNL Champion St. Louis Stars. He also played for the Detroit, MI, Wolves–Homestead, PA, Grays (EWL) in 1932 and the racially mixed Bismarck, ND, Cubs (Independent) from 1933 to 1936, catching for Satchel Paige (BB) and Hilton Smith (BB). Injuries sidelined Trouppe for the 1937 season, but he returned with the Indianapolis, IN, ABCs (NAL) in 1938 and spent six years in the MEL from 1939 to 1944. In 1936, Trouppe also won an amateur boxing championship.

Trouppe excelled as an All-Star player and Championship manager in the Negro Leagues, MEL, and Latin American Winter Leagues. His Negro League play led to five East-West All-Star Game appearances (1938, 1945–1948) and a .299 career batting average, including a pinnacle .352 mark with the 1947 Cleveland, OH, Buckeyes (NAL). During a three-year stint with the Buckeyes, Trouppe managed Cleveland to NAL championships in 1945 and 1947 and the 1945 Black World Series crown. The 1947 titlists fielded future major leaguers Vibert Clarke, Sam Jethroe (BB), Sam Jones, Al Smith, and Trouppe. Trouppe played for the Chicago, IL, American Giants (NAL) in 1948 and posted a .342 average with 10 home runs in 52 games. He hit .282 for Drummondville, Canada (CaPL) in 1949 prior to returning to the MEL for the 1950 and 1951 schedules. His eight MEL campaigns produced a .304 batting mark and three MEL All-Star Game appearances (1943, 1944, 1950). He managed Jalisco, Mexico (MEL) to the top regular season record with a 50–34 win–loss mark and the 1950 second half title, before losing in the MEL Championship Series. He also played winter ball in Colombia, Cuba, Puerto Rico, and Venezuela. Trouppe topped the 1941–1942 PRWL with 57 RBIs and managed Caguas, Puerto Rico, to the 1947–1948 PRWL championship. He made the Negro Leagues All-Star team, along with Roy Campanella (BB), Jethroe (BB), and Jackie Robinson (BB), which performed in Caracas, Venezuela, following the 1945 regular season.

The switch-batting Trouppe performed in eight leagues in seven nations prior to getting the opportunity to play in recognized organized baseball at age 39 with the Cleveland Indians (AL) organization. During the 1952 season, he appeared in six contests with Cleveland and in 84 games with their Class AAA farm club at Indianapolis, IN (AA).

Trouppe married Dorothy Smith in 1938, but they divorced in 1943. He wed Myralin Donaldson in 1952, with another divorce resulting in 1957. The first marriage produced two sons, while the second produced one daughter. Trouppe, who moved to Los Angeles, CA, married Bessie Cullen in 1962 and owned and operated a restaurant there. He also scouted for the St. Louis Cardinals (NL) and resided in St. Louis, MO, at his death. His autobiography, *20 Years Too Soon*, was published in 1977.

BIBLIOGRAPHY: *The Baseball Encyclopedia*, 9th ed. (New York, 1993); Pedro Treto Cisneros, *Enciclopedia del beisbol Mexicano* (Mexico, 1992); Cleveland (OH) *Call & Post*, 1945–1947; Merritt Clifton, *Disorganized Baseball* (Brigham, Quebec, 1982); Rafael Costas, *Enciclopedia beisbol Ponce Leons 1938–1987* (Santo Domingo, Dominican Republic, 1989); G. B. Mijares and E. D. Rangel, *El beisbol en Caracas* (Caracas, Venezuela, 1967); *Official Negro American League Statistics*, 1945–1948; James A. Riley, *The Biographical Encyclopedia of the Negro Baseball Leagues* (New York, 1994); Pepe Seda, *Don Q Baseball Cues* (Ponce, Puerto Rico, 1970); Quincy Trouppe, *20 Years Too Soon* (Los Angeles, CA, 1977).

Merl F. Kleinknecht

TUCKER, Thomas Joseph "Tommy" "Foghorn" "Noisy Tom" (b. October 28, 1863, Holyoke, MA; d. October 22, 1935, Montague, MA), player and coach, began his professional baseball career in 1884 with the nearby minor league Springfield, MA, team (MSA) and played for the Newark, NJ, club (EL) in 1885 and 1886. A switch-hitting first baseman throughout his career, Tucker made his major league debut with the original Baltimore Orioles

(AA) in 1887 and compiled a .275 batting average with 85 stolen bases and an AA-leading 1,346 putouts. After raising his batting average to .287 the next season, he enjoyed his finest year in 1889 and led the AA in both hits (196) and batting average. His .372 mark that season remains the highest ever for a switch-hitter. In three seasons with the Orioles, he batted a composite .311 and averaged 175 hits.

The 5-foot-11-inch, 165-pound Tucker played from 1890 through 1896 with Boston (NL), managed by Frank Selee (BB), and helped the Beaneaters win three consecutive NL pennants from 1891 through 1893. During his 7 years in Boston, Tucker averaged 146 hits and 92 runs scored and batted a respectable .288. Boston sold Tucker early in the 1897 season to the Washington Senators (NL) club, where he hit .338 in 93 games. Tucker split duty between the Brooklyn Bridegrooms (NL) and St. Louis Cardinals (NL) in 1898 and finished his major league career in 1899 with the hapless Cleveland Spiders (NL), who lost a record 120 games. Returning to his native New England, Tucker played minor league baseball for Springfield, MA (EL) in 1900, New London, CT (CtSL) in 1901, and Meriden, CT (CtSL) in 1902. Nicknamed for his boisterous and flamboyant style as a base coach, he was once assaulted by Philadelphia fans after leading his Boston teammates in game-stalling tactics in hopes of a rainout. In his 13-year major league career, Tucker, who threw right-handed, batted .290 with 1,882 hits, 1,084 runs, and 352 stolen bases. He scored more than 100 runs in five seasons and led his league in being hit by pitched balls on five occasions. Tucker tied a major league record with four doubles in a July 22, 1893, contest. On July 15, 1897, he collected 6 hits in six at bats for Washington in a game against the Cincinnati Reds. A flashy first baseman, he made dazzling one-handed scoops with his small glove at a time when using two hands was the conventional method.

BIBLIOGRAPHY: *The Baseball Encyclopedia*, 9th ed. (New York, 1993); Boston (MA) *Evening Transcript*, October 22, 1935; Craig Carter, ed., *TSN Complete Baseball Record Book*, 1992 ed. (St. Louis, MO, 1992); J. Thomas Hetrick, *Misfits! The Cleveland Spiders in 1899* (Jefferson, NC, 1991); John Thorn and Pete Palmer, eds., *Total Baseball*, 3rd ed. (New York, 1993); Robert L. Tiemann and Mark Rucker, eds., *Nineteenth Century Stars* (Kansas City, MO, 1989); Thomas Joseph Tucker file, National Baseball Library, Cooperstown, NY.

Raymond D. Kush

TUDOR, John Thomas "Tute" (b. February 2, 1954, Schenectady, NY), player and coach, is the son of Metton Tudor and the grandson of George Robinson, a minor league baseball player. He graduated from Peabody, MA, Veterans Memorial High School. Tudor, the MVP in baseball at North Shore CC in Beverly, MA, in 1973, received a bachelor's degree in criminal justice at Georgia Southern College in Statesboro, GA, in 1978. The Boston Red Sox (AL) signed Tudor in January 1976. The six-foot, 185-pound left-

hander pitched for Winston-Salem, NC (CrL), Bristol, CT (EL), and Pawtucket, RI (IL) from 1976 to 1980, winning 33 and losing 28 while allowing
only 507 hits in 543 innings.

After being called up in September 1979, Tudor returned to the Boston
Red Sox at midseason in 1980 and posted 8 wins and 5 losses with a 3.03
ERA in 16 games. He won 13 games each in 1982 and 1983. On December
6, 1983, Tudor was traded to the Pittsburgh Pirates (NL) for outfielder Mike
Easler. In 1984, he captured 12 of 23 decisions for the last-place Pirates. In
December 1984, Pittsburgh swapped Tudor to the St. Louis Cardinals (NL)
for outfielder George Hendrick and catcher Steve Barnard.

The 1985 season began in a disappointing manner, as Tudor dropped 7
of 8 decisions. Dave Bettencourt, Tudor's high school catcher, watched a
televised Cardinals game, however, and noticed a flaw in the southpaw's
motion. He phoned his old friend, who immediately corrected it and built
one of the finest pitching stretches in baseball history. From June through
season's end, Tudor won 20 of 21 decisions. He hurled 10 shutouts, a record
for Redbird southpaws. Tudor's four-month streak included a one-hitter, a
two-hitter, and two three-hitters. He opened September with 3 straight shutouts and 31 consecutive scoreless innings. Tudor finished the season with a
1.93 ERA, being named to the *TSN*, UPI, and AP All-Star teams. Dwight
Gooden,* however, edged him out for the NL Cy Young Award. He defeated the Los Angeles Dodgers in an NL Championship Series game and
triumphed twice over the Kansas City Royals (AL) in the World Series,
before yielding five runs in the Cardinals' seventh-game loss.

After enjoying a 13–7 season in 1986, he missed half of the 1987 campaign
when New York Mets catcher Barry Lyons fell into the St. Louis dugout
chasing a foul ball and broke Tudor's knee. Tudor returned in August 1987,
ending with 10 wins and 2 losses. Tudor began the 1988 campaign on the
disabled list with a sore elbow. St. Louis traded Tudor to the Los Angeles
Dodgers (NL) on August 16, 1988, for outfielder Pedro Guerrero.* Tudor
underwent surgery on his left elbow during the off-season and pitched in
only six games in 1989. He made one appearance with the Dodgers in the
1988 NL Championship Series against the New York Mets and one in the
1988 World Series against the Oakland Athletics.

Tudor returned to St. Louis as a free agent in 1990, winning 12, losing
4, and compiling a 2.40 ERA despite spending time on the disabled list. His
62–26 win–loss record with the Cardinals produced a .705 winning percentage, the highest in team history for a hurler with at least 50 decisions.
He was employed as a minor league pitching instructor for the St. Louis
Cardinals in 1991 and 1992, the Philadelphia Phillies (NL) in 1993 and 1994,
and the Texas Rangers (AL) in 1995.

Tudor, who married Gail Norgard on November 12, 1988, and resides in
Peabody, MA, enjoys playing ice hockey and scuba diving.

216   BASEBALL

BIBLIOGRAPHY: Peter Gammons, "John Tudor: His Competitive Fire Burned Brightly in '85," *BD* 45 (January 1986), pp. 65–67; Joe Henderson, "John Tudor: The Man and the Image," *BD* 45 (August 1986), pp. 48–55; Kip Ingle and Brian Bartow, *St. Louis Cardinals 1990 Media Guide* (St. Louis, MO, 1990); Dan Schlossberg, *Baseball Stars: 1986* (Chicago, IL, 1986); Michael Shatzkin, ed., *The Ballplayers* (New York, 1990); John Tudor file, National Baseball Library, Cooperstown, NY.

Frank J. Olmsted

TURNER, James Riley "Jim" "Milkman Jim" (b. August 6, 1903, Antioch, TN), player, coach, and manager, is a six-foot, 185-pound pitcher who attended Antioch High School and played amateur and semiprofessional baseball. His parents were Charles Gray Turner and Hattie Mae Turner. His nickname came from his off-season dairy business. Turner, dedicated to hard work and eager to learn, signed professionally with Paris, TN (KL) in 1923 and began a slow climb to the major leagues as a right-handed pitcher. Scouts, looking for the live arm and great fastball, often passed him over. Turner relied on control and intelligence, advancing slowly. Turner admitted, "I was in the minors 14 years . . . a long, hard haul." General manager Bob Quinn (BB) of the Boston Bees (NL) club purchased Turner in 1936 from Indianapolis, IN (AA).

Nonetheless, the 34-year-old Turner astounded everyone in 1937 with a 20–11 mark and an NL league–leading 2.38 ERA, being the first freshman hurler to win 20 games since Grover Cleveland Alexander (BB) in 1911. Without overpowering speed, Turner "cut corners" and threw the batter off stride, forcing a hitter "to bite at bad ones." He pitched for the NL in the 1938 All-Star Game. A subpar season followed, however, causing him to be traded in December 1939 to the Cincinnati Reds (NL). Turner helped the Reds win an NL pennant and World Series against the Detroit Tigers in 1940 with a 14–7 mark and 2.89 ERA. After being traded to the New York Yankees (AL) in July 1942, he appeared in the World Series that year against the St. Louis Cardinals. A relief pitcher through 1945, he mastered the art of pitching low balls to make the batter hit grounders and threw strikes. He won 287 games altogether, including a 69–60 record and 3.22 ERA in the major leagues.

After managing two minor league clubs, Turner returned to the New York Yankees as pitching coach in 1949. Manager Casey Stengel (BB), who had piloted Turner in Boston, recalled the latter's dedication and intelligence. The Yankees' skipper relied considerably on Turner, stating, "I've got to talk to Jim." Turner's supervision of their staff paid off with five consecutive World Series titles from 1949 to 1953. He left the Yankees after 11 seasons following 1959 and became pitching coach for the Cincinnati Reds from 1961 to 1965 under manager Fred Hutchinson.* His career climaxed in a final term with the Yankees from 1966 to 1973 under manager Ralph Houk (BB).

Young pitchers appreciated Turner's realistic approach and ability to communicate. Turner stressed "condition and control." During spring training, he considered running essential to strengthen arms and legs and believed that an athlete could not really play himself into shape. As for control, Turner remarked, "You keep on throwing until you get it." He believed only hard work would suffice and deemed mastery of the fastball, curve, and change-up was necessary. "Jim always talks sense," Houk observed.

Turner married Annie Pauline Sanford on October 2, 1926, and had two daughters. He was elected to the Tennessee Sports Hall of Fame, regularly attended New York Yankees' and Cincinnati Reds' old-timer's games and Nashville, TN, Sounds (SA) baseball club contests. Turner remained grateful to baseball for his 51 consecutive seasons to which he contributed his dedication, intelligence, and compatibility.

BIBLIOGRAPHY: *The Baseball Encyclopedia*, 9th ed. (New York, 1993); Bill Corum, "Turner: Yankee Man Behind the Scenes," New York *Journal-American*, March 13, 1952; L. H. Gregory, "A Pitcher's Face Tells the Story," *BD* 7 (July 1948); Joe King, "Turner's Success Speeds Trend to Pitching Coaches," *TSN*, July 9, 1958; Ed Rumill, "A Turn with Turner," *BM* 41 (September 1945); Fred Russell, "Milkman Jim Starts 48th Season over Same Route," *TSN*, February 28, 1970; Paul Shannon, "Jim Turner, 20 Game Winner for the Bees," *TSN*, March 10, 1938; Joseph M. Sheehan, "Sophomore Pitchers Help Yankee Flag Drive," *NYT*, August 31, 1956; J. G. Taylor Spink, "Milkman Puts Cream in Marse Joe's Coffee," *TSN*, June 14, 1945; J. G. Taylor Spink, "Professor Turner's Tips on Twirling," *TSN*, April 7, 1954; John Thorn and Pete Palmer, eds., *Total Baseball*, 3rd ed. (New York, 1993); Joe Trimble, "Fireman Jim Turner Rescues Yankees," New York *Daily News*, June 10, 1945.

William J. Miller

VALENZUELA, Fernando (Anguamea) (b. November 1, 1960, Navoja, Sonora, Mexico), player, is the youngest of nine children born to farmers Avelino Valenzuela and Hemeregilda Valenzuela and grew up in the small Mexican village of Etchohuaquila in the state of Sonora. Valenzuela, at age 13, began to play organized baseball with his seven brothers on the local town club. In 1976, his professional career commenced in the rugged MEL. He played with numerous clubs, most prominently the Los Mayos de Navojoa team. Los Angeles Dodgers (NL) scout Mike Brito in 1978 signed Valenzuela, who ascended through the Dodgers minor league chain the next two years. Valenzuela eventually debuted with the Los Angeles Dodgers on September 15, 1980, in Atlanta against the Braves. The Mexican lefty dazzled hitters with his screwball and did not allow an earned run in 17⅔ innings pitched that year.

Valenzuela captured the national spotlight in 1980, when the rookie opened that campaign with eight consecutive victories. During that remarkable streak, he tossed 7 complete games, hurled 5 shutouts, and boasted a 0.50 ERA. The young left-hander also became a folk hero, particularly to the large Mexican American community in the Los Angeles area. In June 1981, President Ronald Reagan invited him to a White House luncheon during a visit by Mexican president Jose Lopez de Portillo. Valenzuela on December 28, 1981, married Linda Burgos, a Merido, Mexico, school-teacher. They have three children, Ricardo, Fernando, Jr., and Linda. The southpaw completed his strike-shortened 1981 "dream season" as the NL leader in complete games (11), shutouts (8), innings pitched (192), and strike-outs (180). For his efforts, he won both the Cy Young and NL Rookie of the Year awards. No major leaguer prior to that time had ever accomplished such a feat.

Valenzuela continued to pitch quality baseball throughout the 1980s. He led the NL in games won (21) and complete games (20) in 1986 and again paced the NL in complete games (12) in 1987. Valenzuela's durability also became his trademark, as the screwball artist averaged 255 innings pitched per season between 1981 and 1987. He also appeared in six consecutive All-Star Games from 1981 to 1986. Valenzuela, beset with arm troubles, was released by the Dodgers in 1990 and joined the California Angels (AL) but lasted only a few games. After a year's MEL stint, however, Valenzuela re-emerged in the major leagues for the 1993 season with the Baltimore Ori-oles. That year the left-hander finished with an 8–10 win–loss record, struck out 78 batters, threw 2 shutouts, pitched 5 complete games, and compiled a 4.94 ERA. In 1994, Valenzuela returned to the MEL. He compiled a 10–3 record with the Jalisco Cowboys before the Philadelphia Phillies (NL) signed him in June. Philadelphia released him following the 1994 season. His over-all career major league statistics include a 150–130 win–loss record, 31 shut-outs, 1,861 strikeouts, and a 3.44 ERA.

BIBLIOGRAPHY: Tony Castro, "Something Screwy Going on Here," *SI* 63 (July 8, 1985), pp. 31–37; Robert Heuer, "Ethohuaquila: Tracing Fernando's Roots," *TSN*, June 13, 1981; Mike Littwin, *Fernando* (Los Angeles, CA, 1981); Eddie Rivera, "In America, Only in the Land of Opportunity . . . Could a Kid from Anywhere Go to Sleep a Pauper and Wake Up a Millionaire," *IS* 9 (June 1987), pp. 45–47, 50–52.

Samuel O. Regalado

VAN SLYKE, Andrew James "Andy" "Slick" (b. December 21, 1960, Utica, NY), player, starred as an All-American in baseball at New Hartford High School, where his father, Jim, served as principal. The St. Louis Cardinals (NL) selected the six-foot-two-inch, 195-pound outfielder in the first round (the sixth player taken overall) of the June 1979 free agent draft. Van Slyke, who bats left-handed and throws right-handed, debuted for the Cardinals in June 1983 and was named the Cardinal Rookie of the Year by the St. Louis BBWAA chapter. In 1986, Van Slyke led the Cardinals in home runs (13) and total bases (189) and shared the team lead in RBIs (61).

The following year, St. Louis traded Van Slyke to the Pittsburgh Pirates (NL), where he blossomed. A fixture in center field, the witty, talkative Van Slyke utilized his speed and a strong, accurate arm to win five consecutive

Rawlings Gold Glove awards from 1988 to 1992. Van Slyke's offensive skills also impressed the baseball world. In 1988, Van Slyke hit .288 with 101 runs scored, 25 home runs, 100 RBIs, 30 stolen bases, and an NL-leading 15 triples. Van Slyke was named to his first All-Star team, while *TSN* selected him NL Player of the Year and also placed him on its Silver Slugger team.

Van Slyke sparked a Pirate team that won three consecutive NL East titles from 1990 to 1992. In 1992, Van Slyke led the major leagues in multihit games (65) and the NL in doubles (45), shared the NL lead in hits (199), finished second in the NL batting race (.324), and ranked third in the NL in runs scored (103), total bases (310), and triples (12). He made both the 1992 and the 1993 All-Star teams and batted .310 in his injury-shortened 1993 season. Despite these impressive statistics, Van Slyke performed poorly in four NL Championship Series, hitting only .202 with one home run and 10 RBIs. He appeared in the NL Championship Series against the Los Angeles Dodgers in 1985, Cincinnati Reds in 1990, and Atlanta Braves in 1991 and 1992. In the 1985 World Series against the Kansas City Royals, Van Slyke made only 1 hit.

Van Slyke, who married Lauri Griffiths in 1983, has three sons, A. J., Scott, and Jared, and lives in Chesterfield, MO. In 1987, 1988, and 1992, the popular Van Slyke won the Roberto Clemente Award, an award presented annually by the Pittsburgh BBWAA chapter to the Pirate who best exemplifies the standard of excellence established by the late Pittsburgh star. Pittsburgh released him following the 1994 season. Through 1994, Van Slyke has batted .276 with 282 doubles, 89 triples, 158 home runs, and 768 RBIs in 1,578 games.

BIBLIOGRAPHY: *The Baseball Encyclopedia*, 9th ed. (New York, 1993), p. 1569; *The Official Major League Baseball 1992 Stat Book*, p. 228; *Pittsburgh Pirates 1994 Record and Information Guide*; Steven Rushin, "Playing for Laughs," *SI* 77 (September 21, 1992), pp. 56–64; Mike Shatzkin, ed., *The Ballplayers* (New York, 1990), p. 1114.

Frank W. Thackeray

VEALE, Robert Andrew Jr. "Bob" (b. October 28, 1935, Birmingham, AL), player and coach, is the second of 14 children of Robert Andrew Veale, Sr., a workman for Tennessee Coal and Iron Company who pitched briefly for the Homestead, PA, Grays (NNL), and Olie Belle (Ushry) Veale, of African-American descent. Veale graduated from Holy Family High School in Birmingham, where he participated in baseball and basketball, and attended St. Benedict's College in Atchison, KS, for three years, also playing basketball and baseball there. He served in the U.S. Marine Corps Reserve from 1959 to 1962 and then received a medical discharge for a knee injury.

The Pittsburgh Pirates (NL) signed Veale in 1958 and assigned the pitcher in 1958 to Las Vegas, NV (CaL), in 1959 to Wilson, NC (CrL), and in 1960 and 1961 to Columbus, OH (IL). After starting the 1962 season with Columbus, he was called up to the Pirates in April. From 1964 through

1970, he was the mainstay of the Pirates' staff and never pitched less than 200 innings a year. The imposing six-foot-six-inch, 212-pound bespectacled left-hander proved an imposing figure on the mound. He consistently ranked among the NL's leaders in both strikeouts and walks, leading the NL in both categories in 1964 and in walks in 1965, 1967, and 1968. Veale won 16 or more games four times, with 18 victories in 1964 marking his personal best. Despite finishing under .500 at 13–14 in 1967, he compiled a 2.05 ERA. Pittsburgh sold Veale in September 1972 to the Boston Red Sox (AL), where he served as a relief pitcher until his retirement following the 1974 season. Overall, Veale won 120 games (116 with Pittsburgh) and lost 95 (91 with Pittsburgh) with a 3.08 ERA. In 1,925.2 major league innings, he surrendered 1,684 hits, struck out 1,703 batters, and walked 858. His 7.96 strikeouts per 9 innings ranks sixth on the all-time list.

After retiring as an active player, Veale worked as a pitching coach in the Atlanta Braves (NL) farm system for 10 years and for another year in the New York Yankees (AL) system. He lives in Birmingham, AL, with his wife Eredean and has one daughter. Veale and Sandy Koufax (BB) were the hardest-throwing left-handers of the 1960s. With Koufax, Don Drysdale (BB), Bob Gibson (BB), Juan Marichal (BB), and others, Veale excelled in the "Age of the Pitcher."

BIBLIOGRAPHY: Richard L. Burtt, *The Pittsburgh Pirates: A Pictorial History* (Virginia Beach, VA, 1977); Bob Smizik, *The Pittsburgh Pirates: An Illustrated History* (New York, 1990); Luther Spoehr, interview with Bob Veale, August 17, 1993; Bob Veale file, National Baseball Library, Cooperstown, NY; Rich Westcott, *Diamond Greats* (Westport, CT, 1988).

                                                                    Luther W. Spoehr

VINCENT, Francis Thomas Jr. "Fay" (b. May 29, 1938, Waterbury, CT), executive, grew up in Waterbury as the son of Francis T. Vincent, Sr., and Alice (Lynch) Vincent. After graduating from the Hotchkiss School, he entered Williams College and sustained there a serious spinal injury that permanently restricted his mobility. Vincent graduated with a Bachelor of Arts degree from Williams College in 1960 and earned a law degree from Yale University in 1963. In July 1965, he married Valerie McMahon. They have three children.

Vincent specialized in securities law, spending 15 years with New York and Washington firms and a brief stint with the Securities and Exchange Commission. In 1978 Columbia Pictures appointed him president. When Columbia Pictures was acquired by the Coca-Cola Company in 198?, Vincent headed its entertainment division. He held this post until 1987, when the division's declining earnings prompted his resignation.

The affluent Vincent had resumed his legal career when his friend A. Bartlett Giamatti (S), the newly appointed commissioner of major league baseball, persuaded him to become the sport's first deputy commissioner.

During Giamatti's brief six-month incumbency in 1989, Vincent drafted the agreement that banned player Pete Rose (BB) from the game. Upon Giamatti's death in September 1989, Vincent was officially elected commissioner and was contracted to serve the remaining years of Giamatti's five-year term.

Vincent's three stormy years as commissioner were marked by steadily eroding relations with his club owner employers. His early decision to delay the 1989 World Series for 10 days, owing to the earthquake that disrupted play between the San Francisco Giants and Oakland Athletics, was generally applauded. Vincent's subsequent efforts to function as an activist commissioner, however, evoked increasing resentment from some owners.

In March 1990, Vincent angered several owners by seeking to end the labor dispute, which involved the owners locking the players out of spring training camps. Vincent persuaded the owners to reopen the camps, but his role in negotiating the Basic Agreement that followed was criticized by some owners and by the MLPA. The MLPA faulted him for refusing to discipline owners after an arbitrator found the latter guilty of collusion against free agent players during the 1985–1989 period. In 1991, owners criticized Vincent's negotiations, which ended a brief umpires' strike, for conceding too much to the umpires. The owners in 1992 named Richard Ravitch to be their chief negotiator and paid him a higher salary than that of Vincent.

In 1992 Vincent's rulings sought to make the game a more cohesive industry, but widened the rift with the owners. After the NL owners voted to expand by admitting the Colorado Rockies and Florida Marlins clubs, Vincent in June ended the owners' impasse over the division of entry fees and the stocking of new teams with players. He ruled that both major leagues must supply players and must share in the division of the $190 million entry fees paid by the new clubs. Vincent's preemptory ruling angered owners in both leagues. Soon afterward, his decision to allow a Japanese corporation to become the principal owner of the Seattle Mariners (AL) club angered those AL owners who wanted the franchise moved to another city. Vincent, acting on the advice of some NL owners, ordered the NL to realign its two divisions on more logical geographical lines. The Chicago Cubs, however, in August won a federal court injunction against his ruling.

Vincent's decision on the realignment issue precipitated the owners' action to oust him from his post. On September 7, 1992, a two-thirds majority of major league owners voted no confidence in him and demanded his resignation. Although insisting that his contract prevented his dismissal until the 1994 expiration of his contract, Vincent resigned in September 1992.

Following Vincent's resignation, the owners assumed full control of the game. For over two years, an executive council of owners took control. Bud Selig, the principal owner of the Milwaukee Brewers (AL), functioned as interim commissioner. An owners' search committee continued to ponder the choice of a new commissioner, while the ousted Vincent wrote a book on 15 people he was privileged to meet during his lifetime. Vincent serves on the board of directors of the New York Mets (NL).

BIBLIOGRAPHY: Roger Cohn, "Nothing But Curve Balls," *NYT Magazine*, June 3, 1990, pp. 34, 56–58; John Funstein, *Play Ball: The Life and Troubled Times of Major League Baseball* (New York, 1993); Michael Knisley, "Friends or Foes?" *TSN*, September 21, 1993, pp. 11–12; Richard Sandomir, "Twists of Fate," *Sports Inc.*, February 27, 1989; A. D. Suehsdorf, "Baseball Commissioners," in John Thorn and Pete Palmer, eds., *Total Baseball*, 3rd ed. (New York, 1993); George Vecsey, "Fay Vincent Speaks from Exile," *NYT*, June 23, 1993; Tom Verducci, "Have You Seen This Man?" *SI* 79 (July 5, 1993), pp. 38–41.

David Quentin Voigt

VIOLA, Frank John Jr. (b. April 19, 1960, East Meadow, NY), player, is the son of Frank Viola, Sr., a radio station comptroller, and Helen (Weindler) Viola, graduated from East Meadow High School, and attended St. John's University of New York, where he pitched the Redmen to the 1980 College World Series and a 1981 NCAA appearance. In the 1981 NCAA Northeast regional tournament, he bested Ron Darling of Yale University, 1–0, in 12 innings.

The Minnesota Twins (AL) drafted the six-foot-four-inch, 210-pound Viola in the second round in June 1981 and assigned the meticulous, tempestuous left-hander to Orlando, FL (SL) in 1981 and Toledo, OH (IL) in 1982. Viola debuted with Minnesota in 1982 and struggled through two consecutive losing seasons. He won 18 games in 1984 and 1985 and 16 contests in 1986, leading the AL in games started (37). The Twins suffered losing seasons from 1982 through 1986 before capturing the West Division title in 1987. After developing among the best change-ups in the AL, Viola in 1987 compiled a 17–10 record and 2.90 ERA and did not lose a game at the Metrodome after May 22. Minnesota upset the Detroit Tigers in the AL Championship Series, as Viola won Game 4. The Twins defeated the St. Louis Cardinals in the World Series, with Viola garnering MVP honors. Viola took Game 1, 10–1, lost Game 4, 7–2, and triumphed in Game 7, 4–2, striking out 16 batters in 19.1 innings.

In 1988 Viola enjoyed his best major league season, earning AL Cy Young Award and *TSN* AL Pitcher of the Year honors. He led the AL in victories (24) and winning percentage (.774), while losing only 6 decisions. Viola, who finished third in the AL with 193 strikeouts and a career-best 2.64 ERA, hurled 2 innings to earn credit for the victory in the All-Star Game. His 93 victories from 1984 through 1988 paced all major league pitchers. In July 1989, Minnesota traded Viola to the New York Mets for five players. Viola won 20 of 32 decisions with a 2.67 ERA in 1990, leading the NL in starts (35) and innings pitched (249.2) and being named *TSN* NL All-Star left-hander. Viola, a consistent control artist, made the NL All-Star team in 1990 and 1991. In January 1992, the Boston Red Sox (AL) signed him as a free agent. Viola was released after the 1994 season. In 13 major league seasons, he has recorded 175 victories, 146 losses, a 3.67 ERA, 16 shutouts, and 1,822 strikeouts in 2791.2 innings.

The Longwood, FL, resident married Kathy Daltas of Roseville, MN, and has two children, Frankie and Brittany.

BIBLIOGRAPHY: Peter Gammons, "Concerto for Viola and Twins," *SI* 67 (November 2, 1987), pp. 32–33; Peter Gammons, "Near Perfect Pitch," *SI* 69 (August 22, 1988), pp. 44–46, 56, 58–59; Mike Shatzkin, ed., *The Ballplayers* (New York, 1990); *TSN Official Baseball Register*, 1994.

David L. Porter

WELCH, Robert Lynn "Bob" (b. November 3, 1956, Detroit, MI), player, is the youngest of three children of Rupert Welch and Loraine (Mungle) Welch and grew up in the Detroit suburb of Ferndale, MI. The three-sport athlete at Hazel Park High School pitched for Eastern Michigan University and, as a freshman, helped the Hurons make the 1975 College World Series.

The number-one draft choice of the Los Angeles Dodgers (NL) in 1977, Welch signed for a $55,000 bonus and pitched for Class AA San Antonio, TX (TL) in 1977. He started the 1978 season at Albuquerque, NM (PCL) but joined the Dodgers on June 20. Welch capped his rookie 7–4 season by earning a win in the NL Championship Series against the Philadelphia Phillies (NL) and striking out Yankee slugger Reggie Jackson (BB) to save the second game in the World Series. The Yankees won the World Series, 4–2.

The six-foot-three-inch, 190-pound right-hander battled problems with alcohol and his pitching arm in 1979, slipping to a 5–6 record. He pioneered major league baseball's drug and alcohol treatment efforts by committing himself to The Meadows, a rehabilitation facility in Wickenburg, AZ, during the off-season. He posted a 14–9 win-loss record with a 3.29 ERA and earned All-Star recognition in 1980, becoming the Dodgers' steadiest pitcher over the next seven seasons. He in 1983 recorded the NL third-best ERA (2.65) and in 1985 finished with a 14–4 record and a 2.31 ERA. In his last season with the Dodgers, he compiled a 15–9 record with a 3.22 ERA and led the NL with four shutouts.

The Dodgers traded Welch to the Oakland Athletics (AL) in December 1987. He developed a split-finger pitch to complement his fastball and curve, compiling 17–9 and 17–8 records the next two seasons. His career season came in 1990, when his 27–6 (.818) record paced the major leagues and his 238 innings placed third in the AL. Besides pitching in his second All-Star Game, he won the AL Cy Young Award and led the Athletics to the World Series. Oakland lost the fall classic to the Cincinnati Reds in four games. The Athletics released him after the 1994 season.

Welch has appeared in eight league Championship Series, four each for Los Angeles and Oakland, and five World Series, two for the Dodgers and three for the Athletics. Through the strike-shortened 1994 season, he has compiled an overall 211–146 win–loss record for a .591 winning percentage and 3.47 ERA. He has struck out 1,969 batters while walking only 1,034 for nearly a 2:1 strikeouts-to-walks ratio. As a National Leaguer, he batted .151 with a high of .243 in 1980.

Welch resides in San Francisco with his wife Mary Ellen and their two sons.

BIBLIOGRAPHY: *The Baseball Encyclopedia*, 9th ed. (New York, 1993); Ron Fimrite, "One Pitch at a Time," *SI* 73 (September 17, 1990), pp. 58–63; Robert E. Kelly, *Baseball's Best: Hall of Fame Pretenders Active in the Eighties* (Jefferson, NC, 1980); Joe McDonnell, "Bob Welch Sets Goals for '84 Season," *BD* 43 (May 1984), pp. 48–53; Mike Shatzkin, ed., *The Ballplayers* (New York, 1990); John Thorn and Pete Palmer, eds., *Total Baseball*, 3rd ed. (New York, 1993); George Vecsey, "Bob Welch: Young, Talented and an Alcoholic," *NYT Biographical Service* 11 (April 1980), pp. 626–628; Bob Welch and George Vecsey, *Five O'Clock Comes Early: A Young Man's Battle with Alcoholism* (New York, 1982).

Gaymon L. Bennett

WHITE, Roy Hilton (b. December 27, 1943, Los Angeles, CA), player, performed for the New York Yankees (AL) from 1965 through 1979. White, the son of Marcus White, an artist and sculptor, and Margaret White, grew up in Compton, CA, and attended Centennial High School and Compton JC.

White began his professional baseball career in the New York Yankee farm system with Greensboro, NC (CrL) in 1962 as a second baseman. In 1963 he proved his offensive abilities by posting a .309 batting average and leading the CrL in runs scored (117) and games played (146). Defensively, he paced second basemen in errors (33). White culminated two Columbus, GA (SL) campaigns in 1965 with the circuit best in at bats (560), runs scored (103), hits (168), total bases (279), and triples (14). His defensive woes continued, however, as he topped the circuit's keystoners with 27 errors. A composite minor league .956 fielding average in four seasons as a second sacker prompted the Yankees to find a defensive post better suited to his abilities. The New York Yankees (AL) promoted White for parts of the 1965 season. He batted a career-high .343 in 84 games with Spokane, WA (PCL) in 1967 before returning permanently to the Yankees. After being given trials as a third baseman, White became a sure-handed, full-time outfielder for New York in 1968.

His gentlemanly demeanor and consistent play brought a touch of dignity to the once-powerful Yankees, as the club struggled in the late 1960s. White, ever the consummate team player, set an AL standard with 17 sacrifice flies in 1971. He played the full slate of 162 games in 1970 and 1973, achieving a circuit-high 639 at bats the latter season. White posted a perfect 1.000 fielding average in 1971 and paced the AL in bases on balls (99) in 1972 and runs scored (104) in 1976.

White proved instrumental in the Yankees' return to glory, helping them to three consecutive AL pennants from 1976 to 1978 and World Series triumphs over the Los Angeles Dodgers (NL) the latter two seasons. He hit .316 in 14 AL Championship Series contests and .244 in 12 World Series encounters.

White, one of many successful switch-batters to don the Bronx pinstripes, posted a .271 batting average with 300 doubles, 160 home runs, and 758 RBIs in 15 years and made the 1969 and 1970 AL All-Star squads. The 5-foot-10-inch 170-pounder achieved his best major league batting average as a regular with .296 in 1970 and belted 22 home runs.

White married Linda Hoxie on December 12, 1966, and has two children, Loreena and Reade. Since retiring from the Yankees, White has been enshrined in the NJ Sports Hall of Fame. He resides in Oradell, NJ, and operates his own baseball camps and clinics.

BIBLIOGRAPHY: *The Baseball Encyclopedia*, 9th ed. (New York, 1993); *1978 New York Yankees Yearbook*; Questionnaire completed by Roy White, 1993; *TSN Official Baseball Register, 1980.*

Merl F. Kleinknecht

WHITNEY, Arthur Carter "Pinky" (b. January 2, 1905, San Antonio, TX; d. September 1, 1987, Center, TX), player, began his professional baseball career with the Cleveland Indians (AL) organization in 1925. Before Whitney appeared in a major league game, Cleveland optioned him to Decatur, IL (3IL). After spending the 1926 season at Decatur, Whitney was traded to New Orleans, LA (SA). His .339 average there in 1927 inspired the Philadelphia Phillies (NL) to draft him. In 1928 he won the starting position as the Phillies' third baseman and became one of the NL top players at that spot. He batted .301 his first season and recorded 200 hits for the 1929 Phillies, the only team in NL history to have four players reach 200 or more hits in a season. In 1930 he enjoyed his best major league season with 207 hits and a .342 batting average. On June 17, 1933, the financially strapped Phillies traded Whitney and Hal Lee to the Boston Braves (NL) for two players and cash. The Braves made Whitney unhappy by playing him at second base frequently and shortstop occasionally. Whitney consequently welcomed the trade that returned him to the Philadelphia Phillies in April 1936. Whitney retired after the 1939 season and returned to the San Antonio, TX, area, where he operated bowling alleys and later worked as a public relations representative of Lone Star Brewery. He was named to the South Texas Sports Hall of Fame.

In 1,539 major league games, Whitney batted .295, with 1,701 hits, 303 doubles, 56 triples, 93 homers, and 927 RBIs. He hit .300 or better four times, recording a high of .342 in 1930. He hit 26 or more doubles six times, drove in 100 or more runs four seasons, scored 696 runs, and drew 400 walks. He was selected for one All-Star Game (1936) and hit .333 in that contest.

Although playing all the infield positions, Whitney saw action mainly at third base with 1,394 games. He led NL third sackers in putouts three times, in assists four years, and in double plays and fielding average three times.

Whitney was survived by his wife Harriet, one son, and one daughter.

BIBLIOGRAPHY: Frank Bilovsky and Rich Westcott, *The Phillies Encyclopedia* (West Point, NY, 1963); Harold Kaese, *The Boston Braves* (New York, 1948); Allen Lewis, *The Philadelphia Phillies: A Pictorial History* (Virginia Beach, VA, 1981); Frederick Lieb and Stan Baumgartner, *The Philadelphia Phillies* (New York, 1953); San Antonio (TX) *Express-News*, September 2, 1987; *TSN*, September 21, 1987.

Ralph S. Graber

WHITNEY, James Evans "Grasshopper Jim" (b. November 10, 1857, Conklin, NY; d. May 21, 1891, Binghamton, NY), player, was reared in Binghamton, NY, and played with his brother Charlie for independent professional baseball clubs in the mid-1870s. Nicknamed "Grasshopper Jim" for his distinctive walk, he entered organized baseball with Binghamton, NY (IA) in 1878 and played for Omaha, NE (NWL) in 1879 and the Knickerbockers of San Francisco, CA (CaL) in 1880.

In his first major league season with the 1881 Boston Red Stockings (NL), he led NL pitchers in innings pitched (552⅓) and shared the NL lead in wins (31) and complete games (57). His 33 losses for the weak-hitting Red Stockings also led the NL. In 1882, the six-foot-two-inch, 172-pound left-handed batter and right-handed hurler ranked among NL leaders both in hitting and pitching. His .323 batting average placed fifth in the NL, while his .382 on base percentage and .510 slugging average ranked third. Pete Palmer's statistical assessment in *Total Baseball* rates Whitney's 1882 batting performance the third best ever by a major league pitcher. Whitney also posted a winning 24–21 record as pitcher, finishing among the NL's top five in innings pitched, complete games, and strikeouts.

In 1883 Whitney married a Miss Haddock and enjoyed his finest season. Missing only two of Boston's games, he performed in the outfield when not pitching. Whitney batted .281 and compiled a career-best .638 winning percentage with a 37–21 pitching record, propelling Boston to the NL pennant. His personal-best 345 strikeouts, along with his average 6.04 strikeouts per nine innings, led the NL. The fastballer's accuracy also gave him the first of five straight NL titles in fewest walks per nine innings. Only one other major league pitcher, Walter Johnson (BB) of the 1920 Washington Senators, led his league in most strikeouts and fewest walks per nine innings the same season.

Whitney enjoyed another winning season with a 23–14 mark in 1884, although illness limited him to 66 games altogether and 38 as pitcher. His 1885 record fell to 18–32, an NL high in losses. He was signed for 1886 by the new Kansas City Cowboys (NL) franchise. He endured his worst season there, again losing 32 games while winning only 12. His ERA ballooned to 4.49, 2 full points above his average for first five major league seasons.

When Kansas City was dropped from the NL after just one year, Whitney signed with the Washington Senators (NL) and compiled an impressive 24–21 record for the seventh-place club in 1887. The next year, however, he slipped to an 18–21 mark. The 1889 season found him with the Indianapolis, IN, Hoosiers (NL). After a 2–7 start with Indianapolis, he finished the season with minor league Buffalo, NY (IA). Whitney returned to the major leagues with Philadelphia's Athletics (AA) in 1890, pitching in only six games and compiling a 2–2 record. The tuberculosis, which killed him a year later, already had begun to damage his health.

In 10 major league seasons, Whitney posted a 191–204 win–loss record and 2.97 ERA in 3,496.1 innings. His 550 games included 413 pitching appearances and 377 complete games in 396 starts.

BIBLIOGRAPHY: Harold Kaese, *The Boston Braves* (New York, 1948); Paul Mac-Farlane, ed., *Daguerreotypes of Great Stars of Baseball* (St. Louis, MO, 1981); John Thorn and Pete Palmer, eds., *Total Baseball*, 3rd ed. (New York, 1993); Robert L. Tiemann and Mark Rucker, eds., *Nineteenth Century Stars* (Kansas City, MO, 1989).

Frederick Ivor-Campbell

WICKWARE, Frank "Red Ant" (b. 1888, Coffeyville, KS; d. November 2, 1967, Schenectady, NY), player, ranked among the premier players in the preleague days of Negro baseball. Wickware, a right-handed pitcher, was known for his blazing fastball and his propensity for winning clutch games. His baseball career began in 1910 with the Rube Foster's (BB) Chicago, IL, Leland Giants. Wickware joined legends Frank "Pete" Duncan, Pat Dougherty, Pete Hill (BB), Grant "Home Run" Johnson (BB), John Henry Lloyd (BB), Andrew "Jap" Payne, and Bruce Petway. The Leland Giants, called by Foster his greatest team ever, compiled an incredible 123–6 win–loss record that season.

After spending three seasons with the Giants, he moved to the Mohawk Giants of Schenectady, NY. The semiprofessional team, owned by Bill Wernecke, a General Electric factory worker and former semiprofessional outfielder, arranged a game against the All-Americans, led by future National Baseball Hall of Fame pitcher Walter "Big Train" Johnson (BB). Wernecke selected Wickware to pitch the October 1913 contest, despite having legends Walter Ball and "Smokey Joe" Williams (BB) on his pitching staff. After five and one-half innings, the game was called on account of darkness. Wickware outdueled Johnson, 1–0. Wickware faced Johnson twice more, splitting the decisions. In 1912 he enjoyed one of the finest seasons in the CUWL, leading the CUWL with 10 wins against four losses and hurling 11 complete games. His team, Fe, won only 14 games.

Wickware's barnstorming career included stays with the Chicago, IL,

American Giants (1911–1912, 1914–1920), Brooklyn, NY, Royal Giants (1913), Louisville, KY, White Sox (1914), Indianapolis, IN, ABCs (1916), Detroit, MI, Stars (1919), and Chicago, IL, Giants (NNL) in 1921.

In 1925, police charged Wickware with the homicide of 27-year-old Ben Adair of New York City. Wickware, however, was cleared of all charges due to lack of evidence. His overall greatness was recognized in a 1952 poll by the Pittsburgh (PA) *Courier*, which selected him to their fourth all-time, all-star team for Negro League players.

BIBLIOGRAPHY: Chicago (IL) *Defender*, May 23, 1925; Frank Keetz, "When 'The Big Train' Met 'The Red Ant,'" *BRJ* 20 (1991), pp. 63–65; James A. Riley, *The Biographical Encyclopedia of the Negro Baseball Leagues* (New York, 1994); Michael Shatzkin, ed., *The Ballplayers* (New York, 1990).

Larry Lester

WILLIAMS, James Thomas "Jimmy" "Buttons" "Home Run" (b. December 20, 1876, St. Louis, MO; d. January 16, 1965, St. Petersburg, FL), player and scout, was a five-foot-nine-inch, 175-pound infielder associated with baseball for 40 years. He started in baseball primarily as a third baseman with Pueblo, CO, in 1895–1896, Leadville, CO, and Albuquerque, NM, in 1896, and finally Kansas City, MO, in 1897. Kansas City sold him to the Pittsburgh Pirates (NL) in 1899 as a third baseman under managers Bill Watkins and Patsy Donovan (BB), who led the Pirates to a seventh-place finish with a 76–73 win–loss record. Williams excelled that year with a .355 batting average, the highest of his major league career, and led the NL in triples (27) and putouts (251). Nicknamed "Home Run," he belted a career-high nine round-trippers as a rookie. Under a new manager, Fred Clarke (BB), however, his batting average dropped to just .264 in 1900. The 1900 season, Williams's last as a full-time third sacker, saw the Pirates rise to second place. Williams shifted permanently to second base with the Baltimore Orioles in the new AL in 1901, batting a healthy .317 and leading the new circuit with 21 triples under distinguished manager John McGraw (BB). Now established at his new position, he hit .313 the next year, again paced the junior circuit in three baggers with 21, and made six hits in the August 25 game. The Orioles in 1903 shifted their Baltimore franchise to New York as the Highlanders, managed by the "Old Fox," Clark Griffith (BB).

Williams was stationed at second base regularly. His batting suffered with New York, ranging from .267 in 1903 to .277 in 1906, while his home run production there peaked at 6 in 1905. The Highlanders traded Williams in February 1908 to the St. Louis Browns (AL), managed by Jim McAleer. Williams, infielder Hobe Ferris, and outfielder Danny Hoffman were sent to the "Mound City" for pitcher Fred Glade and outfielder Charlie Hemphill. Williams spent his last two major league seasons with the Browns, hitting .236 in 1908 and just .195 the following year. Defensively, he proved a steady, far-ranging second baseman most of his career. For his 11 major league seasons, he compiled a .275 batting average with 1,507 hits, 49 homers, and 794 RBIs.

The Browns sold Williams to the minor league Minneapolis Millers (AA), where he played from 1910 through 1916. Although never a star, Williams, nevertheless, epitomized the dedicated professional. After remaining out of baseball until 1930, he scouted for the Cincinnati Reds (NL) from 1930 through 1935. Williams married Nan M. Smith on December 5, 1900.

BIBLIOGRAPHY: *The Baseball Encyclopedia*, 9th ed. (New York, 1993); "James Thomas Williams," *TSN* card file, St. Louis, MO; Obituary, "James Thomas ('Home Run') Williams, 88," *TSN*, January 31, 1965; Mike Shatzkin, ed., *The Ballplayers* (New York, 1990); John Thorn and Pete Palmer, eds., *Total Baseball*, 3rd ed. (New York, 1993).

William J. Miller

WILLIAMSON, Edward Nagle "Ned" (b. October 24, 1857, Philadelphia, PA; d. March 3, 1894, Hot Springs, AR), player, is rated as the finest third baseman of the 1880s. The son of a middle-class awning manufacturer, the lifetime Episcopalian enjoyed a more respectable reputation than most players, even though liking a drink and cards. A sportswriter described the 5-foot-11-inch 170-pounder as a "perfect physical machine." In 1875 he started the season with the amateur Shibe Club in Philadelphia, joined a semiprofessional club in Burlington, NJ, and caught for Braddock, PA. The following summer, he caught and played third baseman for the independent professional Neshannock Club of New Castle, PA, and concluded the season with the Aetnas of Detroit. He hit poorly with the Allegheny Club of Pittsburgh (IL) in 1877 but fielded well enough for the Indianapolis Hoosiers (NL) to sign him for 1878.

The Chicago White Stockings (NL) established baseball's first real dynasty, capturing no less than five NL titles in the 1880s. Williamson joined Chicago in 1879 and remained an integral part of the White Stockings and Colts until his retirement in 1891. He teamed with Adrian "Cap" Anson (BB), Fred Pfeffer (S), and Tommy Burns to form the famous "Stonewall Infield," the finest of the nineteenth century. Williamson played third base through 1885, being rated the best of his era at that position. He possessed a powerful, accurate arm, perhaps the strongest in baseball. In 1886 he switched positions with shortstop Burns. Chicago repeated as NL champion in 1886 but did not win again with Williamson at shortstop.

Williamson's most lasting fame came as a hitter. A right-handed batter with power to the opposite field, he was perfectly suited for Lakefront Park in Chicago. In 1883 the right field fence there was moved in to only 200 feet from home plate. Due to the short dimension, balls hit over this fence were declared ground-ruled doubles. The same year, Williamson belted an NL record 49 doubles. In 1884, the ground rules were changed to allow balls hit over the short fence to count as home runs. Williamson continued to drive balls over the fence, hitting 25 before the season ended. Away from Lakefront Park, he hit only 2 homers. Williamson's 27 round-trippers stood as a major league record until Babe Ruth (BB) slammed 29 in 1919.

An injury Williamson received on A. G. Spalding's (BB) "Around the World Tour" in the spring of 1889 shortened his career. He injured his leg badly playing in Paris, France, and blood poisoning complicated his recovery. In limited playing time in 1889, Williamson hit only .237. The following year, his batting average dropped to a feeble .195. Despite Williamson's disappointing ending, Chicago manager Anson remembered Williamson as "the greatest all-around ball player the country ever saw."

Subsequently, Williamson opened a saloon in Chicago. He and his wife, Nettie Jean, appeared comfortable and respectable. His health declined, however, and doctors diagnosed his illness as dropsy. He traveled to Hot Springs, AR, in January 1894, hoping that the mineral baths would improve his condition. He died there at age 36.

BIBLIOGRAPHY: Adrian C. Anson, *A Ball Player's Career* (Chicago, IL, 1900); Dennis Goldstein, "Edward Nagle Williamson," in Robert L. Tiemann and Mark Rucker, eds., *Nineteenth Century Stars* (Kansas City, MO, 1989); Jerry Lansche, *Glory Fades Away: The Nineteenth Century World Series Rediscovered* (Dallas, TX, 1991); John J. O'Malley, "The Great Pennant Race of 1885," *BRJ* 6 (1977), pp. 81–87.

William E. Akin

WILSON, Arthur Lee "Artie" (b. October 28, 1920, Springville, AL), player, excelled as a defensive shortstop for the Birmingham, AL, Black Barons (NAL) during the 1940s. A master of the double play, he also won batting titles in 1947 and 1948 with .370 and .402 averages. The ideal left-handed leadoff batter demonstrated speed on the bases and hit the ball to the opposite field, compiling a high batting average. He notched batting averages of .346 in 1944 and .374 in 1945, finishing second to Sam Jethroe (BB) each time. The 5-foot-10-inch, 160-pound speedster also ranked among the NAL leaders in stolen bases each season.

In his five NAL seasons from 1944 to 1948, he appeared in four East-West All-Star Games, missed only the 1945 classic, and helped the Black Barons win NAL pennants in 1943, 1944, and 1948. Unfortunately, the Black Barons lost the World Series to the NNL's Homestead, PA, Grays in each instance.

After the color line was eradicated, Wilson made the transition to the major leagues with the New York Giants (NL). Initially, he became the center of a controversy between the New York Yankees (AL) and the Cleveland Indians (AL), with both teams claiming him. Commissioner "Happy" Chandler (BB) resolved the disagreement by ruling in favor of the Yankees. Wilson entered Organized Baseball in 1949 and enjoyed two PCL seasons with the Oakland, CA, Oaks, batting .348 and .312 and earning a place on the New York Giants' (NL) roster in 1951. Opponents used a shift on him like he was a right-handed pull-hitter, but he just could not pull the ball to overcome the shift. Wilson, used sparingly, hit .182 in only 22 major league at bats. The Giants promoted Willie Mays (BB) later in the season, farming out Wilson to Minneapolis, MN (AA) and Oakland, CA, for the remainder of the season. Despite starring in the PCL, he never received another look at the major leagues.

Wilson settled in the PCL, compiling batting averages of .316, .332, .336, .307, .293, and .263 from 1952 through 1957. He led the PCL in hits in 1952 and in triples in 1953 and 1954. His best years came with Seattle, WA, but he also played with Portland, OR, Oakland, CA, and Sacramento, CA. After four years away from baseball, he returned to Portland in 1962. The layoff proved too much to overcome, as he finished the season with Kennewick, WA (NWL). Wilson retired with a .312 minor league batting average and opened a car dealership in Portland, OR.

BIBLIOGRAPHY: *The Baseball Encyclopedia*, 9th ed. (New York, 1993); Chicago (IL) *Defender*, 1944–1948; Robert W. Peterson, *Only the Ball Was White* (Englewood Cliffs, NJ, 1970); James A. Riley, *The All-Time All-Stars of Black Baseball* (Cocoa, FL, 1983); James A. Riley, *The Biographical Encyclopedia of the Negro Baseball Leagues* (New York, 1994); James A. Riley, interviews with former Negro League players, James A. Riley collection, Cocoa, FL; Mike Shatzkin, ed., *The Ballplayers* (New York, 1990), p. 1184.

James A. Riley

WOODLING, Eugene Richard "Gene" "Old Faithful" (b. August 16, 1922, Akron, OH), player and scout, is one of four sons of Harvey Woodling and Alvada Woodling and graduated in 1940 from Akron East High School, where he participated in swimming, baseball, basketball, and football. One of his brothers won a swimming championship at Ohio State University.

Woodling's professional baseball career began when in 1940 he was signed by Cleveland Indians (AL) scout Bill Bradley* and assigned to Mansfield, OH (OSL). He played with three other minor league teams before the Indians brought him up in September 1943. He spent 1944–1945 in the military and returned to Cleveland for 61 games in 1946, batting an uninspiring .188. In December 1946, Cleveland traded him to the Pittsburgh Pirates (NL) for catcher Al Lopez (BB). His 1 season with Pittsburgh saw him hit .266 in only 22 games. Woodling's next two years were spent in the minors with Newark, NJ (IL) and San Francisco, CA (PCL). He feasted on PCL pitching at a .385 batting clip in 1949 and joined the New York Yankees (AL) for the next five years. His best years in New York came when he hit .309 in 1952 and .306 in 1953. When he left the Yankees for the Baltimore Orioles (AL) in a record 17-player trade in December 1954, his career batting average stood at .280. Upon retiring eight years later, his career batting average had improved to .284. The 5-foot-10-inch, 195-pound Woodling, who batted left-handed and threw right-handed, hit .300 or better in 6 of his 17 seasons. Woodling played from June 1955 until April 1958 with the Cleveland Indians and from April 1958 through 1961 with the Baltimore Orioles. His .321 batting average with Cleveland in 1957 placed him third among AL hitters that year. From 1957 to 1960, Woodling frequently ranked among the top five hitters in production, total average, on-base percentage, and clutch-hitting index. His major league career ended in 1962, when he hit .274 for the expansion New York Mets (NL) and the Washington Senators (AL).

The outspoken Woodling appeared in 5 consecutive World Series from 1949 to 1953, compiling a .318 batting average for the triumphant New York Yankees. He scored 21 runs and walked 19 times in 26 World Series games. He is proudest of his hitting feats with the 1959 Baltimore Orioles, with his RBIs winning several contests. In 1,796 major league games spanning 17 seasons, he made 1,585 hits with 257 doubles, 147 home runs, 830 RBIs, and 921 walks.

Woodling, who worked for the Eaton Corporation and scouted part-time for the Cleveland Indians, raises horses and enjoys fishing and traveling. He married Betty Nicely in October 1942, resides in Medina, OH, and has three children, Pamela, Gene, and Kimberly.

BIBLIOGRAPHY: Dom Forker, *The Men of Autumn* (New York, 1989); Rich Marazzi and Len Fiorito, *Aaron to Zuverink* (New York, 1982); Tom Meany, ed., *The Magnificent Yankees* (New York, 1952); Mike Shatzkin, ed., *The Ballplayers* (New York, 1990); John Thorn and Pete Palmer, eds., *Total Baseball*, 3rd ed. (New York, 1993); *TSN Official Baseball Register*, 1962; Rich Westcott, *Diamond Greats* (Westport, CT, 1988); Gene Woodling, letter to Lee Scanlon, 1994.

Lee E. Scanlon

WRIGHT, Burnis "Bill" "Wild Bill" (b. June 6, 1914, Milan, TN), player and coach, excelled as a big, strong, swift outfielder with the Elite Giants' (NNL) franchise in Nashville, TN (1932–1934), Columbus, OH (1935), Washington, DC (1936–1937), and Baltimore, MD (1938–1939, 1942, 1945). One of the league's fastest players, he batted fourth and hit the long ball when needed. The switch-hitter performed best in the clutch, exhibiting a compact swing and making good contact. Wright hit better from the left side. He was selected seven times to the East-West All-Star squad, including five consecutive appearances from 1935 to 1939 and others in 1942 and 1945. He batted .318 in All-Star competition.

His nickname "Wild Bill" came as a teenaged pitcher, who lacked control for a local team, the Milan Buffalos, in 1931. The next year, Nashville owner Tom Wilson's Elite Giants gave him a tryout, but he hurt his arm by throwing too hard in the cold weather and was switched to the outfield. With Wilson's club for 12 seasons, he was credited with batting averages of .300, .244, .300, .244, .293, .410, .316, and .488 for his first 8 seasons from 1932 through 1939. The 1939 season marked the highlight for both the Elite Giants and Wright. The Elite Giants defeated the Homestead, PA, Grays in a postseason playoff, as Wright copped the NNL batting title with his extraordinary .488 average.

Wright succumbed to the lure of Mexico in 1940 and remained in the MEL for the balance of his career except for two seasons during World War II, when he returned to Baltimore due to his draft status. In these last two Negro League seasons, he batted .303 in 1942 and .371 in 1945 and registered a .517 slugging percentage the latter season. He finished with a lifetime .361 batting average in the Negro Leagues. In the MEL, he quickly became one of Mexico's most productive and most popular players, registering batting averages of .360, .390, .366, .335, .301, .305, .326, .282, .299, and .362 while playing primarily with the Mexico City, Mexico, Reds. Wright led the MEL in several categories during his career there, tying for the lead in doubles while ranking fifth in batting average in 1940. In 1941 he led the MEL in both stolen bases and batting average. Wright's ultimate accomplishment came in 1943, when he won the triple crown and missed the stolen base crown by only a single theft. The six-foot-four-inch 220-pounder circled the bases in 13.2 seconds and proved a skilled drag bunter, a combination enabling him to avoid a prolonged batting slump.

After a baseball career that spanned a quarter of a century as a player from 1931 to 1956 and an additional three seasons as a coach, he made Mexico his permanent home. The popular outfielder opened a restaurant, Bill Wright's Dugout, in Aquascalientes, Mexico. During his long career, he attained legendary status on the Mexican baseball diamonds and was elected to the Mexican Hall of Fame.

BIBLIOGRAPHY: *The Afro-American*, 1935–1948; *The Baseball Encyclopedia*, 9th ed. (New York, 1993); Robert W. Peterson, *Only the Ball Was White* (Englewood Cliffs, NJ, 1970); James A. Riley, *The All-Time All-Stars of Black Baseball* (Cocoa, FL, 1983); James A. Riley, *The Biographical Encyclopedia of the Negro Baseball Leagues* (New York, 1994); James A. Riley, interviews with former Negro League players, James A. Riley collection, Cocoa, FL; James A. Riley, "Wild Bill Wright: A Mexican League Legend Comes Home," *Oldtyme Baseball News* (1991), p. 17; Mike Shatzkin, ed., *The Ballplayers* (New York, 1990), p. 1202.

James A. Riley

WYATT, John Whitlow "Whit" (b. September 27, 1907, Kensington, GA), player, coach, and manager, is the son of James Colquit Wyatt, a railroad engineer, and Leila (Whitlow) Wyatt and was a right-handed pitcher known for his outstanding slider, beginning his professional baseball career in 1928 with Evansville, IN (3IL). After Wyatt compiled a 22–6 win–loss record there in 1929, the Detroit Tigers (AL) purchased him at the end of the season. He spent 1930 with Detroit and was optioned to Beaumont, TX (TL) in 1931. After being recalled in 1932, he pitched for Detroit until May

1933. Detroit then traded Wyatt to the Chicago White Sox (AL). He remained with Chicago until the spring of 1936, when he was acquired by Kansas City, MO (AA). The Cleveland Indians (AL) purchased Wyatt, but he enjoyed little success there in 1937 and was sent to Milwaukee, WI (AA) in 1938. Wyatt's 23–7 record there prompted the Brooklyn Dodgers (NL) to purchase his contract. He became the mainstay of the Brooklyn pitching staff from 1939 to 1944, dropping to a 2–6 win–loss record the last year. In March 1945, Brooklyn sold him to the Philadelphia Blue Jays (NL). After Wyatt's 0–7 record that year, Philadelphia unconditionally released him in February 1946.

In 16 major league seasons, Wyatt appeared in 360 games, won 106 and lost 95 with 872 strikeouts and 642 walks in 1,762 innings, and compiled a 3.78 ERA. His best year came in 1941, when he posted a 22–10 record to lead the NL in victories. He was selected to the NL All-Star teams from 1939 through 1942 but participated only in the 1940 and 1941 games. He pitched 2 innings in each, allowing only one hit. Wyatt started for Brooklyn against the New York Yankees in the 1941 World Series, compiling a 2.50 ERA, winning the second game, and losing the fifth contest. Wyatt encountered mediocre success as a pitcher until learning to control a sharp-breaking slider and to pitch inside and high to batters. His brushback pitches as a Dodger led to beanball battles, particularly with the Boston Braves and Chicago Cubs.

Wyatt remained out of organized baseball from 1946 until 1950, when the Atlanta, GA, Crackers (SA) signed him as a coach. Wyatt remained there as a coach through 1953 and pitched in one game in 1951. Atlanta named him manager in 1954. That year, the Crackers won the SA pennant, the SA playoff championship, and the Dixie Series against the TL winner. Wyatt then coached for the Philadelphia Phillies (NL) from 1955 through 1957 and for the Milwaukee Braves (NL) from 1958 to 1965. He remained with the Braves when they moved to Atlanta in 1966 and then retired at the end of the season.

Wyatt, who married Edna Carle White on February 4, 1933, has one son and one daughter. He lives on his farm in Buchanan, GA, and enjoys hunting.

BIBLIOGRAPHY: Furman Bisher, *Miracle in Atlanta* (Cleveland, OH, 1966); Frank Graham, *The Brooklyn Dodgers* (New York, 1945); Paul Green, "An Interview with Whitlow Wyatt," *SCD* 13 (March 28, 1986), pp. 172–220; Robert L. Tiemann, *Dodger Classics* (St. Louis, MO, 1983); *TSN Official Baseball Register*, 1966.

Ralph S. Graber

ZACHARY, Jonathan Thompson Walton "Tom" "Ol' Tom" (b. May 7, 1896, Graham, NC; d. January 24, 1969, Graham, NC), player, was a left-handed pitcher perhaps best known for surrendering Babe Ruth's (BB) sixtieth home run on September 30, 1927. The six-foot-one-inch 187-pounder pitched 19 major league seasons, compiling a record of 185 wins, 191 losses, and a 3.72 ERA. He also won three World Series games without a loss, including a 2–0 mark for the victorious Washington Senators against the New York Giants in the 1924 fall classic.

Zachary attended Guilford College and spent the summer of 1918 in Philadelphia, awaiting an overseas assignment with a Red Cross unit. He approached manager Connie Mack (BB) about playing for the Philadelphia Athletics (AL). Mack agreed but insisted that Zachary should play under the name of "Zach Walton."

From 1919 to 1926, Zachary pitched for the Washington Senators (AL) under his real name. Later, he hurled for the St. Louis Browns (AL), New York Yankees (AL), Boston Braves (NL), and Brooklyn Dodgers (NL) before finishing his career in 1936 with the Philadelphia Phillies (NL). Zachary later recalled, "I always said if I ever got stuck in that Baker Bowl it would be time to quit."

Ruth's renowned sixtieth home run of the 1927 season was hit down the right field line. Zachary argued vehemently with umpire Bill Dinneen (S) to no avail that the ball was foul. When the two rivals met in Yankee Stadium at a 1947 Old-Timers gathering, Ruth remarked to Zachary, "You crooked-arm sonofabitch, are you still claiming that ball was foul?"

Zachary's most remarkable season came in 1929, when he won 12 games without a loss as both a starter and reliever, ironically, for the Yankees. Zachary retired to Graham, NC, where he worked in real estate and land development. He and his wife Etta had two children, Sally and Tom, Jr.

BIBLIOGRAPHY: *The Baseball Encyclopedia*, 9th ed. (New York, 1993); Robert W. Creamer, *Babe: The Legend Comes to Life* (New York, 1974); Jonathan Thompson Walton Zachary file, National Baseball Library, Cooperstown, NY.

David S. Matz

ZIMMER, Charles Louis "Chief" (b. November 23, 1860, Marietta, OH; d. August 22, 1949, Cleveland, OH), player, manager, and umpire, began his professional baseball career with Ironton, OH (OL) in 1884. As captain of the Poughkeepsie, NY, Indians (HRL) in 1886, he batted .409 and acquired the nickname "Chief." Zimmer was given brief major league trials with the Detroit Wolverines (NL) in 1884 and New York Metropolitans (AA) in 1886. He played most of 1887 with Rochester, NY (IL) and joined the Cleveland Blues (AA), where he became one of the finest catchers of his era.

Authorities credit Zimmer with being the first catcher to position himself close behind the batter for every pitch. Earlier, catchers moved up only with men on base. The quiet, six-foot, 190-pound right-hander shared catching duties with Charles "Pop" Snyder in 1888 and became Cleveland's principal catcher in 1889, when the club transferred from the AA to the NL. After the season, he signed with Cleveland's entry in the short-lived PL. Unlike most of his teammates, who remained in the PL, Zimmer returned to Cleveland's NL club, now known as the Spiders, before the 1890 season. He became rookie pitcher Cy Young's (BB) battery mate, catching a career-high 125 games and 111 in a row, both major league records. Zimmer, a carpenter apprenticed with a cabinet maker, built the furniture and the house in which he, his wife, and three daughters lived in Cleveland.

In 1898, Lou Criger replaced Zimmer as Young's primary catcher. When the next season opened, Zimmer was one of only two Cleveland players remaining from the 1898 Spiders roster. Most team members had been sent to strengthen the St. Louis Browns (NL). But Cleveland considered Zimmer too expensive for its failing club and released him in June. Zimmer signed with the Louisville Colonels (NL) for the rest of the 1899 season and joined the Pittsburgh Pirates with many teammates in 1900, when Louisville was dropped from the NL.

In June 1900, Zimmer was elected president of the newly formed PAPBP. He created a loophole through which NL players could jump to the renegade AL in 1901 without losing the PAPBP-negotiated rights. Zimmer remained in the NL until Pittsburgh released him during the 1902 season. He signed with Tacoma, WA (PNL) but was released and returned to Pittsburgh (NL) for the remainder of the season. He managed the Philadelphia Phillies (NL) to seventh place in 1903 while catching part-time. Zimmer umpired in the NL in 1904 and the EL in 1905. After serving as part owner–manager of Little Rock, AR (SA) in 1906 and an SA umpire in 1907, Zimmer retired from baseball.

Zimmer batted over .300 four times and compiled a .269 career batting average, with 1,224 hits in 1,280 games. Fielding, however, marked his forte. He led NL catchers several seasons in putouts, assists, double plays, and fielding average. His 1,580 career assists rank fifth all-time among major league catchers, as do his 105 fielding runs (a statistic devised by Pete Palmer to evaluate players' overall fielding effectiveness). In four World Series (1892, 1895, 1896, 1900), Zimmer batted .250 with 16 hits and seven RBIs. Aficionados of baseball board games regard his colorful Zimmer's Base Ball Game (1893) as the most beautiful ever produced.

BIBLIOGRAPHY: John Phillips, *The Spiders: Who Was Who* (Cabin John, MD, 1991); Harold Seymour, *Baseball: The Early Years* (New York, rpt., 1989); Mike Shatzkin, ed., *The Ballplayers* (New York, 1990); John Thorn and Pete Palmer, eds., *Total Baseball*, 3rd ed. (New York, 1993); Charles Zimmer file, National Baseball Library, Cooperstown, NY.

                                                                                        Frederick Ivor-Campbell

ZISK, Richard Walter "Richie" (b. February 6, 1949, Brooklyn, NY), player and coach, is the older of two sons of Walter Zisk, a production supervisor at a chemical plant and semiprofessional baseball player, and Veronica (Murowski) Zisk, both of Polish descent. His family resided in Livingston, NJ, until he was age 14 and then moved to Parsippany, NJ. Zisk graduated from Parsippany High School, where he played baseball and was named All-State twice, and attended Seton Hall University for two years. The Pittsburgh Pirates (NL) selected him in the third round in the 1967 free agent draft. He hit .307 with Salem, VA (ApL) in 1967 and then played at Gastonia, NC (WCL) in 1968 and Salem, VA (CrL) in 1969. In 1970 at Waterbury, CT (EL), he led the EL with 34 home runs. With Charleston, WV (IL), he paced the IL in RBIs (109) in 1971 and homers (26) in 1972. He received brief trials with the Pittsburgh Pirates in 1971 and 1972 and then came up to stay in 1973. Over the next four years, he averaged .299, 17 home runs, and 80 RBIs per season. Pittsburgh traded Zisk to the Chicago White Sox (AL) in December 1976. The Texas Rangers (AL) signed him as a free agent in November 1977. Recurring knee injuries increasingly limited his range in the outfield, making him spend more time as a designated hitter. In December 1980, he was traded to the Seattle Mariners (AL). He hit .311 in 94 games in 1981, being named *TSN* Comeback Player of the Year and *TSN* and UPI DH of the Year. His knee problems became increasingly severe, however, and forced his retirement before the 1984 season.

A right-handed, line drive hitter, the six-foot-one-inch, 200-pound Zisk sprayed the ball well to all fields. In 1,453 major league games, he hit .287 with 207 home runs and 245 doubles. Defensively, he possessed a strong arm. Although lacking mobility, he made an All-Star fielding team at the Class AAA level.

Zisk married Barbara Louise Boice on May 27, 1969, and has three children. After retiring as a player, he completed a college degree in communications. Since 1987, he has served as the minor league hitting instructor for the Chicago Cubs (NL). He lives in Florida with his family.

BIBLIOGRAPHY: *The Baseball Encyclopedia*, 9th ed. (New York, 1993); Luther W. Spoehr, interview with Richie Zisk, February 9, 1994; Richie Zisk file, National Baseball Library, Cooperstown, NY.

Luther W. Spoehr

BASKETBALL

ANDREAS, Lewis Peter "Lew" (b. February 25, 1895, Sterling, IL; d. June 18, 1983, Syracuse, NY), college athlete, coach, and executive, served as basketball coach 25 years and as athletic director 22 years at Syracuse University. The son of Harry G. Andreas and Jenny (Young) Andreas, he was introduced to sports in the Sterling public schools. After graduation, Andreas enrolled at the University of Illinois (WC) in 1916 and played freshman basketball and baseball there. With the American entry into World War I, he left Illinois to enlist in the U.S. Army. The private was assigned to Camp Crane in Allentown, PA, and starred on its 21–0 basketball team. Andreas drove an ambulance in France but was gassed at Soissons, France. He was discharged from the U.S. Army in May 1919 as a top sergeant.

Andreas subsequently attended Syracuse University, played end on the football team, and caught for the baseball team, among the Orangemen's best teams to date. After graduation, he taught and coached football, basketball, and baseball at Norwich, NY, High School. In his second year at Norwich, he also became the school's principal. In 1925, Andreas returned to Syracuse University as a physical education instructor, director of freshman athletics, and head basketball coach. He coached basketball 25 years, from 1925 to 1943 and 1945 to 1950, producing a 364–145 record and .715 winning percentage. Only three of his quintets suffered losing records. Despite the lack of an organized championship in the 1920s, Andreas's teams uncharacteristically played a truly national schedule. During his second year in 1926, his Orangemen were named HAF National Champions. The Orangemen finished 19–1, led by three-time All-America Vic Hanson (IS). Andreas also served terms as president of the NABC and ECAC and as a charter member of the NCAA Basketball Tournament Committee.

From 1927 to 1929, Andreas also coached the Syracuse football team to a 15–10–3 mark. His football teams did not excel, but Andreas consistently scheduled the nation's finest teams, including the University of Notre Dame, Georgia Tech, University of Illinois, University of Nebraska, and University of Pittsburgh. His greatest contribution to football may have been as Syracuse's athletic director for 27 years from 1937 until 1964. During his tenure, the basketball team continued its success, a new field house was constructed, and Archbold Stadium was expanded to 40,000 seats. Andreas also fostered the development of a nationally prominent football program, featuring stars Jim Brown (FB) and Ernie Davis (FB).

Andreas was lauded upon retirement by several coaches and athletic directors, President Lyndon Johnson, and New York Governor Nelson Rockefeller. Andreas married Annetta Smith in 1925 and had one daughter, Elizabeth.

BIBLIOGRAPHY: Lewis Andreas clipping file, Syracuse University Archives, Syracuse, NY; Ronald L. Mendell, *Who's Who in Basketball* (New Rochelle, NY, 1973); *NYT*, May 11, 1963, p. 19; June 19, 1983, sec. 1, p. 32.

Brian L. Laughlin

BANKS, David "Davey" "Flash" "Fatty" "Pretzel" (b. 1901, New York, NY; d. August 24, 1952, Troy, NY), professional player and coach, was the son of Samuel Banks. The five-foot-eight-inch 155-pounder, nicknamed "Flash," "Fatty," and "Pretzel," played professional basketball from 1921 to 1935 and resided in Mineola, NY, until his death.

An offensive player and top shooter, Banks played for several teams (including Springfield, MA, Holyoke, MA, Toledo, OH (ABL), and Troy, NY) during his professional basketball career. His career began with the Assumption Crowns (MBL) and Visitation Triangles (MBL), both Brooklyn, NY–based teams. Banks also spent time with the Philadelphia SPHAS (EL) before joining the Original New York Celtics (ABL) in 1927.

The Original Celtics, organized by Jim Furey in 1918 after World War I, proved the dominant professional basketball squad of the 1920s. The Celtics entered the ABL in 1926 and easily won the ABL title in 1927 and 1928. After playing 10 games in the 1928–1929 season, though, the Celtics encountered financial problems due to the high salaries paid by Furey and were disbanded. Banks then joined the New York Hakoah's, a new team he helped organize in the ABL. When Furey reorganized the Celtics for the 1929–1930 season, he reunited only Banks and two other previous Celtic players. Since the Celtics once again faced financial problems, the team was turned over to the ABL. The Fort Wayne, IN, Hoosiers paid the ABL $3,100 for Banks's services for the remainder of the 1928–1929 season. Banks then played for the Toledo, OH, Redmen (ABL) in the 1929–1930 campaign. The Celtics regrouped again in 1931 and barnstormed as independents for the next six years. The rest of the basketball world quickly caught up, however, to the underpaid, aging Celtic players.

From 1927 to 1931, Banks ranked in the top eight in ABL scoring. In 1927–1928, he tied for top honors in points per game (8.4) and ranked second in field goals (170) and total points (412). In the 1930–1931 season, although his Toledo team finished last in the NBL, Banks earned second-place honors in field goals (94), free throws (66), and total points (254).

In 1946, Banks coached the Troy, NY, Celtics (ABL). He was killed in an automobile accident during which time he apparently was negotiating with the University of Notre Dame about becoming the assistant basketball coach for the 1952–1953 season.

BIBLIOGRAPHY: Glenn Dickey, *The History of Professional Basketball Since 1896* (New York, 1982); Bill Himmelman, telephone conversation with Susan J. Rayl, Norwood, NJ, October 1993; Zander Hollander, ed., *The Modern Encyclopedia of Basketball* (New York, 1973); David S. Neft and Richard M. Cohen, *The Sports Encyclopedia: Pro Basketball*, 5th ed. (New York, 1992); *NYT*, August 25, 1952, pp. 17, 25; Robert W. Peterson, *From Cages to Jump Shots* (New York, 1990); Troy (NY) *Record*, August 25, 1952, pp. 1, 7.

Susan J. Rayl

BARKSDALE, Don Angelo (b. March 31, 1923, Oakland, CA; d. March 8, 1993, Oakland, CA), college, amateur, and professional player and scout, ranks among the pioneer African-American basketball players. Barksdale graduated from Berkeley High School, where he was cut from the basketball team. At UCLA, he became the first African-American to earn All-America basketball honors. The HAF and *True* magazine both placed him on their All-America basketball teams.

From 1947 to 1951, Barksdale played AAU basketball for the Oakland Bittners and Oakland Blue 'n Gold. During the 1947–1948 season with the Bittners, the six-foot-six-inch, 200-pound Barksdale led the ABL in scoring with a 16.7 scoring average and finished well ahead of Vince Boryla* and Bob Kurland (IS). Barksdale remained the only African-American ABL player. A major interesting issue raised that ABL season revolved around whether Barksdale would be allowed to play in games scheduled against the Phillips 66ers in Bartlesville, OK, and Oklahoma City, OK. Oklahoma, then a segregated state, fought efforts to desegregate its schools. No African-American had played in an integrated athletic contest in the state's history. Barksdale not only performed but scored 17 points in the first game in leading the Bittners to a 45–41 victory over the Phillips 66ers. Phillips had compiled a 36-game winning streak entering the contest. Newspapers from the Midwest to California praised Barksdale as an "ambassador of goodwill for his race" and compared his performance favorably to Jackie Robinson (BB), who had integrated major league baseball the previous year.

Since 1948 marked an Olympic year, the National AAU tournament at Denver, CO, assumed special meaning. The top three AAU teams earned the right to enter the Olympic tournament at Madison Square Garden in

New York. Barksdale led the Bittners to a third-place finish. The USOC named Barksdale to the 1948 U.S. Olympic team following the tournament, making him the first African-American to win this honor. Barksdale joined mostly Phillips 66ers and University of Kentucky Wildcats at the London, England, Summer Olympic Games and helped the United States win its second gold medal in basketball.

For the next three years, Barksdale remained a dominant AAU basketball player. At the 1949 National AAU tournament, he scored 17 points to pace the Bittners to a 55–51 victory over Phillips 66 and break Phillips' string of six consecutive National AAU championships. In 1950, Barksdale led the Oakland Blue 'n Gold to the AAU tournament finals before losing to Phillips. The Oakland Blue 'n Gold joined the NIBL during Barksdale's last year there in 1950–1951. Barksdale topped the NIBL in scoring and was named NIBL MVP. Although injured during the National AAU tournament, Barksdale was selected to the AAU All-America squad for the fourth successive year. Jack Carberry, the dean of Denver's sportwriters, lauded Barksdale as "the best basketball player in the amateur ranks today."

In 1951 the Baltimore Bullets (NBA) made Barksdale the fourth black NBA player. During his third NBA season, Barksdale joined the Boston Celtics (NBA) and on January 13, 1953, became the first African-American player to perform in an NBA All-Star Game. Barksdale, who retired after the 1954–1955 season, scored 2,895 points and averaged 11 points per game in four NBA seasons.

Subsequently, Barksdale owned several Oakland, CA, night clubs, hosted a television show, scouted for the Golden State Warriors (NBA) basketball club, and worked as a disc jockey at several black radio stations. In 1982 Barksdale created the SHSSF to fund financially strapped athletic programs in the San Francisco Bay Area. By his death, the SHSSF had raised over $1 million to help high school sports. The Barksdales had two sons, Donald and Derek.

BIBLIOGRAPHY: Denver (CO) *Post*, 1947–1951; Zander Hollander and Alex Sachare, eds., *The Official NBA Basketball Encyclopedia* (New York, 1989); Bill Mallon and Ian Buchanan, *Quest for Gold: The Encyclopedia of American Olympians* (New York, 1984); David S. Neft and Richard M. Cohen, *The Sports Encyclopedia: Pro Basketball*, 5th ed. (New York, 1992); *USA Today*, February 19, 1993; Alexander Weyand, *The Cavalcade of Basketball* (New York, 1960).

Adolph H. Grundman

BLACKMAN, Rolando Antonio "Ro" (b. February 26, 1959, Panama City, Panama), college and professional player, acquired a reputation as a consummate, if unflashy, professional for the expansion Dallas Mavericks (NBA). At age eight, Rolando Blackman and his sister Angela left their native Panama in 1967 to live with their grandmother in East Flatbush, Brooklyn, NY. Their parents, John Blackman, a computer programmer for the U.S. government, and Gloria Blackman, followed three years later but separated soon thereafter. Blackman, who grew up in Brooklyn, preferred soccer but switched to basketball at the Ditmas neighborhood playground. The switch proved difficult because Blackman was cut from his seventh-, eighth-, and ninth-grade basketball teams at Meyer Levin Junior High School. Blackman was not deterred, however, spending his summers working out at 6 A.M. with the inspirational playground coach, Teddy Gustus, instead of the ever-present Tomahawks and the Jolly Stompers gangs.

For safety reasons, Blackman enrolled in William E. Grady Vocational School on Coney Island, NY. Under coach Fred Moscowitz, Blackman blossomed and prepared for collegiate basketball. Six times a month, he also watched his idols, Earl Monroe (IS), Walt Frazier (IS), and Bill Bradley (IS), play for the New York Knicks (NBA) at the fabled Madison Square Garden in New York.

The heavily recruited six-foot-six-inch, 206-pound Blackman spurned big-name schools for Kansas State University (BEC), where he was coached by Jack Hartman, who served as a second father. Blackman became a team leader as a sophomore, earning First-Team All-BEC conference honors. Three times, he was selected the BEC Defensive Player of the Year. In 1981, *TSN* named him First Team All-America. For 121 college games, Blackman shot 51.7 percent, scored 1,844 points, and averaged 15.2 points a game.

Although still a Panamanian citizen in 1980, Blackman won a spot on the U.S. Olympic team that year. President Jimmy Carter, however, barred American teams from competition in the Moscow, Russia, Summer Olympic Games in retaliation for the Soviet invasion of Afghanistan. Blackman became a U.S. citizen in 1986.

Blackman, the ninth player selected in the 1981 NBA draft, joined the Dallas Mavericks. With volatile forward Mark Aguirre (IS) and steady backcourt mate Derek Harper, Blackman quickly became a mainstay of coach Dick Motta's (IS) team. He was named team captain in 1983 and was voted six times Most Popular Maverick by the Dallas fans. The Mavs reached the playoffs six times from 1984 to 1990, as Blackman improved his performance to 21.6 points a game. He was known for both his uncanny ability to sink the clutch shot at the buzzer to win games and his smothering defense against the NBA's best guards. The four-time NBA All-Star (1985–1987, 1990) scored 17.8 points a game.

The Mavericks' team performance declined disastrously in the wake of poor personnel decisions, causing the front office to rebuild for the future. In June 1992, Dallas traded Blackman to the New York Knicks, where he joined Patrick Ewing (IS) in contending for the NBA championship. But Blackman did not keep John Starks from the starting guard position. The Knicks reached the NBA playoffs in 1993 and the NBA finals in 1994, losing to the Houston Rockets in seven games. Blackman remains the Mavericks' career leader in game starts (781), minutes played (29,684), points (16,643, a 19.2-point scoring average), field goals made (6,487), and free throws made (3,501). In July 1994, the Knicks released him. Through the 1993–1994 season, he tallied 17,623 points (18.0-point average), grabbed 3,278 rebounds, and dished out 2,981 assists in 980 games.

Others laud Blackman for his straight-arrow lifestyle and tireless charitable actions. He and his wife Tamara have four children, Valarie, Brittany, Briana, and Vernell. His community activities include Big Brothers and Big Sisters, the Special Olympics, the Muscular Dystrophy Association, and the American Cancer Society. He has also worked to renovate the Ditmas playground on which he grew up. After his NBA career ends, Blackman aspires to become a television news anchorman like his favorite Peter Jennings of ABC News. Consequently, he has taken classes at Columbia School of Journalism, hosted his own weekly radio program in Dallas, TX, and interned at several television stations.

BIBLIOGRAPHY: Dan Baldwin, "Honor Guards," *D Magazine* 18 (October 1991), pp. 27–29; Curtis Bunn, "A Ro Model for Starks," New York *Daily News*, February 4, 1994, p. 73; Dallas Mavericks press release, 1994; Cecil Harris, "Rolando Blackman: Living the Dream," *City Sun*, January 17–23, 1990, pp. 39–40; Rafael Hermoso, "Blackman: Mavs' Loss City's Gain," New York *Newsday*, June 25, 1992, p. 127; New York Knicks press release, 1994; Ian O'Connor, "The Real Ro," New York *Daily News*, August 23, 1992, pp. 74–75; Bill Reel, "Rolando, the Man," Brooklyn Sunday *Newsday*, August 30, 1992; Steve Serby, "Roland's Return Great for Apple," New York *Post*, June 25, 1992, pp. 46, 67; Mark Zeske, "The Go-To Guy," *Beckett Basketball Monthly* 2 (November 1991), pp. 41–42.

Bruce J. Dierenfield

BOONE, Ronald Bruce "Ron" (b. September 6, 1946, Oklahoma City, OK), college and professional player and sportscaster, is the son of Herman Boone and Olivia (Wilson) Boone. After starring in several sports at Omaha Tech, he played basketball one year at Iowa Western CC before transferring to Idaho State University (BSAC), where he averaged 20 points per game and was twice named All-BSAC. Drafted in 1968 by the Phoenix Suns (NBA) in the eleventh round (one hundred and forty-seventh pick overall) and the Dallas Chaparrals (ABA) in the eighth round, Boone progressed from a long-shot to an All-Star during eight ABA and five NBA seasons.

The six-foot-two-inch, 200-pound guard, named to the 1969 ABA All-Rookie Team after averaging 18.9 points per game with the Chaparrals, was traded in January 1971 to the Utah Stars (ABA). Boone enjoyed his finest professional seasons with the Stars, sparking Utah to an ABA championship in 1971 and four consecutive Western Division titles from 1971 to 1974. Besides being elected to the ABA All-Star team four times (1971, 1974–1976), he was named All-ABA Second Team in 1974 and First Team in 1975. When Utah folded in December 1975, Boone was sold to the Spirits of St. Louis (ABA). Kansas City (NBA) selected Boone in the August 1976 dispersal draft following the demise of the ABA. Boone promptly led the Kings in scoring with a 22.2-point average. After playing in 1978–1979 with the Los Angeles Lakers (NBA), Boone was traded to the Utah Jazz (NBA) in October 1979 and ended his career there in 1981.

Boone, an unselfish, all-around player, ranked either first or second on his team nine times in assists and six times in scoring during his first 10 seasons and led Kansas City in both categories in 1977–1978. Over a 13-year career, he averaged 3.7 assists and 4.2 rebounds per game and scored in double figures in 11 seasons. Boone finished with 17,437 points for a 16.8 average (18.4 in the ABA and 13.9 in the NBA). A career .837 free throw shooter, the remarkably durable performer never missed a game in 13 seasons and holds the professional basketball record for the most consecutive games played with 1,041 (662, ABA; 379, NBA).

Boone, who serves as the color commentator for Utah Jazz radio and television broadcasts and cohost of a radio sports talk show in Salt Lake City, UT, married Jacqueline Cotton in 1971 and has two children. In 1992, his son Jaron entered the University of Nebraska (BEC) with a basketball scholarship.

BIBLIOGRAPHY: Larry R. Gerlach, interview with Ronald Boone, December 7, 1993; David S. Neft and Richard M. Cohen, *The Sports Encyclopedia: Pro Basketball*, 5th ed. (New York, 1992); Martin Taragano, *Basketball Biographies . . . 1891–1990* (Jefferson, NC, 1991); *TSN Official NBA Register*, 1993–1994.

Larry R. Gerlach

BORYLA, Vincent Joseph "Vince" (b. March 11, 1927, Hammond, IN), college and professional player, coach, scout, and executive, is the son of Vincent Stanley Boryla and Phyllis (Tiliczuk) Boryla and possessed one of the greatest hook shots in basketball history. Boryla, a six-foot-five-inch, 200-pound forward, played for several colleges, but his career was interrupted by military service during World War II. After graduating from East Chicago, IN, High School, Boryla began his college basketball career at the University of Notre Dame in the summer of 1944. As a freshman, Boryla broke Notre Dame records for most points scored in one season (322) and one game (31, against the University of Detroit). After one season there, Boryla transferred to the U.S. Naval Academy. He already had spent a few months in the U.S. Navy at the Great Lakes Naval Training Station. He reenrolled at Notre Dame after spending some time at Annapolis but left South Bend, IN, in 1946 to enlist in the U.S. Army. The U.S. Army assigned Boryla to Denver, CO, where he played for two seasons with the Denver Nuggets (AAU) and twice was named AAU All-America. In 1948, Boryla made the U.S. Olympic team and helped the United States to win a gold medal in basketball at the London, England, games.

After the Olympics, the peripatetic Boryla was discharged from the U.S.

Army and enrolled at the University of Denver. Boryla made First-Team All-America in his only season (1948–1949) at Denver and then turned professional. After leaving college, he played in the NBA from 1949 to 1954 with the New York Knicks. With the Knicks from 1949 to 1954, Boryla tallied 3,187 career points with an 11.2 points per game average and primarily used the hook shot. The Knicks won regular season Eastern Division titles in 1952–1953 and 1953–1954, losing in the NBA finals to the Rochester Royals in 1950–1951 and the Minneapolis Lakers in the next two seasons. Boryla played in the NBA's first All-Star Game in 1951 in Boston, MA. Boryla coached the Knicks from the middle of the 1955–1956 season through the 1957–1958 season, ending with a career NBA coaching record of 80 wins and 85 losses. Boryla served as the Knicks general manager for five years following his coaching career. He then scouted for the Knicks but continued to pursue business and real estate interests in the Denver area. In 1970, Boryla helped negotiate the purchase of the Los Angeles Stars (ABA) and moved the franchise to Salt Lake City, UT. The club became the Utah Stars and in 1971 won the first ABA championship. From 1984 through October 1987, he served as president of the Denver Nuggets (NBA). Boryla in 1948 wed Catherine Brogan of Denver, by whom he had one daughter and four sons.

BIBLIOGRAPHY: Zander Hollander and Alex Sachare, eds., *The Official NBA Basketball Encyclopedia* (New York, 1989); Bill Mallon, telephone interviews with Vincent Boryla, May 9, 1993, June 1, 1993; Bill Mallon and Ian Buchanan, *Quest for Gold: The Encyclopedia of American Olympians* (New York, 1983); Martin Taragano, *Basketball Biographies . . . 1891–1990* (Jefferson, NC, 1991); University of Notre Dame Sports Information, Vincent Boryla file, Notre Dame, IN.

Bill Mallon

BOUSHKA, Richard J. "Dick" (b. July 29, 1934, St. Louis, MO), college and amateur player, is the son of Richard Boushka and Mildred (Eberle) Boushka and graduated from Champion Jesuit High School in Prairie du Chain, WI. During his senior year, Boushka set the single-game scoring record for the Wisconsin High School basketball tournament with 42 points and made the All-State basketball team. Boushka played basketball at St. Louis University, where he made the All-MVC team for three consecutive years and the 1954–1955 All-America squad his senior year. His 1,440 points and 20.1-point average established a St. Louis University scoring mark.

In 1955–1956, Boushka joined the Wichita, KS, Vickers (NIBL) and made the All-Star basketball team his rookie year. The Seattle, WA, Buchan Bakers, the 1956 National AAU tournament champion, added Boushka for the U.S. Olympic tournament at Kansas City, MO. After this tournament, the USOC selected Boushka to join the 1956 U.S. Olympic team. The U.S. basketball squad won the gold medal at the Melbourne, Australia, Summer Games. In the 1956–1957 season, Boushka played for Kirkland, WA, Air

Force Base. Kirkland won the National Air Force basketball championship, as Boushka was named the tournament MVP. Boushka then joined an Air Force All-Star team, which breezed to the 1957 National AAU basketball tournament title. Boushka, named to the AAU All-America basketball squad, was selected the tournament's MVP.

Boushka returned to the Wichita Vickers in 1957 for three more seasons and led the Vickers to a share of the NIBL 1957–1958 title. In the 1958–1959 campaign, Boushka led the NIBL in scoring with a 25.2-point average and directed the Vickers to their only AAU basketball championship. The Vickers pummeled the Phillips 66ers, 105–83. For a second time, Boushka was named to the AAU All-America basketball team and the tournament's MVP. In 1959, Boushka also played on the successful U.S. team at the Pan-American games in Chicago, IL. Boushka once again made the NIBL All-Star basketball team in 1959–1960, as he led the NIBL in scoring with a 27.7-point scoring average, the highest in NIBL history. Although the Vickers fell in the quarter-final round of the 1960 National AAU basketball tournament, Boushka joined the Akron Goodyears for the Olympic tournament in Denver, CO, and was named an alternate member of the U.S. Olympic team.

After the 1959–1960 season, Boushka retired from AAU basketball. Boushka, a member of the HAF Hall of Fame, St. Louis University Sports Hall of Fame, and Missouri Sports Hall of Fame, presided over the Naismith Memorial Basketball Hall of Fame. Boushka served as an executive in the oil business until 1980 and now presides over Boushka Properties. He and his wife Joan live in Wichita, KS, and have five children, Richard, Michael, James, Patrick, and John.

BIBLIOGRAPHY: Dick Boushka scrapbooks, in possession of Dick Boushka, Wichita, KS; Bill Mallon and Ian Buchanan, *Quest for Gold: The Encyclopedia of American Olympians* (New York, 1984); Alexander Weyand, *The Cavalcade of Basketball* (New York, 1960).

Adolph H. Grundman

BRIAN, Frank Sands "Flash" "Frankie" (b. May 1, 1923, Zachary, LA), college and professional player, graduated from Zachary High School and played basketball at guard for Louisiana State University (SEC) in 1942–1943, 1945–1946, and 1946–1947, serving from 1943 to 1945 in the armed forces. During Brian's sophomore year, LSU compiled an 18–4 record under coach Dale Morey in 1942–1943. The popular Brian helped coach Harry Rabenhorst's Tigers to an 18–3 mark and second-place SEC finish in 1945–1946 and a 17–4 slate in 1946–1947.

In 1947, the Anderson, IN, Duffy Packers (NBL) drafted the six-foot-one-inch, 180-pound Brian. As a rookie starting guard, Brian led the 42–18 Packers in scoring with 651 points (11-point average) in 1947–1948 and made the All-NBL Second Team. Anderson finished second in the Eastern Division and reached the NBL semifinals. Brian attained All-NBL First Team honors in 1948–1949, helping the 49–15 Packers dominate the NBL. He paced Anderson in scoring with 633 points (9.9 points average) and the NBL in foul shooting percentage (78.5 percent). The Packers defeated the Oshkosh, WI, All-Stars to take the NBL championship, with Brian scoring 79 points (11.3-point average). Anderson joined the NBA in 1949–1950, finishing second in the Western Division. Brian, a Second Team All-NBA selection, ranked third among NBA scorers with 1,138 points for a career-best 17.8-point average and fifth with an 82.4 foul shooting percentage. He tallied nearly 12 points a game during the playoffs, but the Minneapolis Lakers eliminated Anderson in the semifinals. When the Packers' franchise folded, the Chicago Stags (NBA) assumed Brian's contract and sent him to the Tri-Cities Blackhawks (NBA) for rookie guard Bob Cousy (IS). During the 1950–1951 season for the struggling Blackhawks, Brian attained career highs in points (1,144), rebounds (244), and assists (266). Besides repeating as an All-NBA Second Team member, he scored 14 points in the first NBA All-Star Game. Tri-Cities traded Brian to the Fort Wayne Pistons (NBA) before the 1951–1952 campaign.

Brian completed his NBA career with the Pistons, retiring after the 1955–1956 season. Although Fort Wayne struggled in 1951–1952, Brian ranked sixth in NBA scoring with 1,051 points (15.9-point average) and fourth in foul shooting (84.8 percentage) and appeared in his second consecutive All-Star Game. Subsequent acquisitions of veteran guards Andy Phillip (IS), Fred Scolari, and Max Zaslofsky (IS) gradually diminished Brian's playing time. Nevertheless, Brian ranked second in NBA foul shooting in 1954–1955 with a career-high 85.1 percentage. Fort Wayne won Western Division titles in 1954–1955 and 1955–1956 and lost the 7-game 1955 NBA finals to the Syracuse Nationals, as Brian averaged nearly 10 points a game. During his NBL–NBA career, the Hanna, LA, resident scored 6,663 points (11.9-point average), converted 81.2 percent of his foul shots, grabbed 903 rebounds, and dished out 1,138 assists in 561 games. In 56 NBL-NBA playoff games, he scored 520 points (9.3-point average), converted 81.2 percent of his foul shots, and made 93 assists.

BIBLIOGRAPHY: Zander Hollander, ed., *The Modern Encyclopedia of Basketball* (New York, 1973); David S. Neft and Richard M. Cohen, eds., *The Sports Encyclopedia: Pro Basketball*, 5th ed. (New York, 1992); *TSN NBA Register*, 1994–1995.

David L. Porter

BUBAS, Victor Albert "Vic" (b. January 28, 1927, Gary, IN), college player and coach, was the third child of Joseph Bubas and Katharine Bubas. His father owned and operated a Gary hardware store. Bubas graduated from Gary's Lew Wallace High School in 1944 and served in the U.S. Army after graduation. Following his discharge, he was discovered playing AAU basketball by North Carolina State University (SC/ACC) coach Everett Case (IS). Bubas attended North Carolina State from 1947 until his graduation in 1951. A defensive-oriented, playmaking guard, Bubas averaged 6.3 points per game and played on four SC championship teams. His senior year saw him named 1 of 12 members of Golden Chain, a leadership and scholarship fraternity.

Bubas remained at North Carolina State as freshman coach from 1952 through 1955, compiling a 64–10 record. From 1956 through the 1959 season, he served as varsity assistant to Case. In May 1959, Bubas was named head basketball coach at nearby Duke University (ACC). He enjoyed immediate success, coaching a mediocre Blue Devil club to an ACC championship in the 1960 postseason tournament and Duke's first two victories in the NCAA tournament. The Blue Devils also won the ACC title in 1963, 1964, and 1966 and finished first during the regular season in 1963, 1964, 1965, and 1966. Duke advanced to the Final Four in 1963, 1964, and 1966, finishing second in 1964 and third the other two seasons. The Blue Devils were invited to the NIT in 1967 and 1968 and finished in the final AP top 10 from 1961 to 1966 and in 1968. Bubas's five All-Americas included Art Heyman (S), consensus National Player of the Year in 1963, Jeff Mullins, Jack Marin, Bob Verga, and Mike Lewis. His 10-year 213–67 mark at Duke included a 22–6 record in the ACC tournament and an 11–4 slate in the NCAA tournament. The ACC named Bubas Coach of the Year in 1963, 1964, and 1966. Bubas, who resigned from coaching after the 1969 season to become director of public relations at Duke, was vice president of community relations at the school from 1974 until 1976. In 1976 he became the first SBC commissioner, a position he held until his retirement in 1990. During his tenure, the SBC obtained an automatic berth in the NCAA basketball tournament.

The soft-spoken Bubas proved a highly organized recruiter and an astute judge of talent. His assistant coaches at Duke included future NBA coaches Chuck Daly* and Hubie Brown. Bubas married Tootie Boldt in 1949 and has three daughters, Sandy, Vikki, and Karen. He is a member of the North Carolina and Duke University Sports Halls of Fame.

BIBLIOGRAPHY: Smith Barrier, *On Tobacco Road: Basketball in North Carolina* (New York, 1983); Bill Brill, *Duke Basketball: An Illustrated History* (Dallas, TX, 1986); Vic Bubas file, Sports Information Department, Duke University, Durham, NC; Ron Morris, *ACC Basketball: An Illustrated History* (Chapel Hill, NC, 1988).

Jim L. Sumner

CARPENTER, Gordon "Shorty" (b. September 24, 1919, Ash Flat, AR; d. March 8, 1988, Denver, CO), college and amateur player, coach, and official, is the son of Odus Carpenter and Virgie (Wadley) Carpenter and ranks among the finest basketball players in Arkansas history. Carpenter's basketball career began in Ash Flat, a tiny hamlet of 300 people in the Ozarks. Nicknamed "Shorty," he perfected his game on outdoor courts and a gymnasium built by the Works Progress Administration during the depression. In 1939, his senior year, he led Ash Flat to victories over Little Rock, AR, and Pine Bluff, AR, to win the state championship. The six-foot-six-inch 200-pounder possessed excellent speed and a fierce competitive attitude. Upon graduation, Carpenter played basketball at the University of Arkansas (SWC) for two years under Glen Rose and his senior year under Eugene Lambert. Carpenter started as a sophomore for the Razorbacks, who performed a perfect 12–0 slate in SWC play and lost in the championship game of the NCAA regional at Kansas City, MO, to Washington State University. Arkansas shared the SWC title in Carpenter's junior year. As a senior, Carpenter made the All-SWC squad.

After completing his 1943 season at Arkansas, Carpenter joined the powerful Phillips 66 basketball team of Bartlesville, OK, in time to enter his first AAU tournament in March. Several businesses employed basketball players, who performed a regular schedule and participated in a weeklong national tournament at Denver, CO. This tournament featured some of the nation's best players and teams. Between 1943 and 1948, Phillips 66 won the national championship a record six consecutive times. Carpenter made the AAU All-America team each year from 1943 to 1947. He scored 2,366 points, ranking as the fifth leading scorer in Phillips history. The 66ers, coached by Bud Browning, featured Bob Kurland (IS), Jesse "Cab" Renick, and Carpenter. In March 1948, Phillips 66 defeated Adolph Rupp's (IS) University of Kentucky Wildcats, 53–49, in the finals of the Olympic tournament at Madison Square Garden in New York. The starting five for Phillips 66 consequently made up part of the 1948 U.S. Olympic team, coached by Browning and Rupp. The United States won the gold medal at London, England, in 1948, barely defeating a scrappy Argentine team, 59–47. With four minutes left in the game and the United States trailing by 6 points, Browning inserted Carpenter into the game. Carpenter responded by scoring 10 points in two minutes to help secure the victory.

After 1948, Carpenter moved to Denver, CO, with his wife, Mildred, and played and coached three years for the Denver Chevrolets (AAU). In 1950, he made the AAU All-America team for the sixth and last time. Carpenter, who left basketball from 1951 until 1954, returned as an official and eventually worked games in the BSAC and BEC. He and his wife had four children, David, Mark, Craig, and Carol. Carpenter, inducted into the HAF Hall of Fame in 1960 and the Arkansas Sports Hall of Fame in 1965, worked for Chevrolet until retiring in 1987.

BIBLIOGRAPHY: Gordon Carpenter scrapbooks, in possession of Mildred Carpenter, Denver, CO.

Adolph H. Grundman

CHAMBERS, Thomas Doane "Tom" (b. June 21, 1959, Ogden, UT), college and professional player, spent his formative years in Boulder, CO, and played basketball at Fairview High School, where he earned All-America honors while averaging 27.6 points and 17.3 rebounds per game as a senior. Chambers attended the University of Utah (WAC), where he made the All-WAC Second Team as a sophomore and junior. During his senior season, he led Utah to a 25–5 record and paced the Redskins in scoring with 18.6 points per game. His honors included making the All-WAC First Team and earning Honorable Mention All-America. Chambers completed his collegiate career as Utah's sixth all-time leading scorer and second all-time leading rebounder.

The San Diego Clippers (NBA) selected the 6-foot-10-inch, 230-pound Chambers in the first round in 1981. As a rookie, Chambers led the Clippers in scoring with a 17.2-point average and pulled down 6.9 rebounds per game. He provided one of the few bright spots in an otherwise dismal season for San Diego. His second pro season also proved solid, as he scored 17.6 points per game.

In August 1983, San Diego traded Chambers to the Seattle SuperSonics (NBA). He averaged 18.1 points per game in his first year with Seattle and saw his first playoff action. He played five seasons with the SuperSonics and enjoyed his best season in 1986–1987, averaging 23.3 points per game. He also appeared in his first All-Star Game, replacing the injured Ralph Sampson (IS). Before his hometown Seattle crowd, Chambers scored 34 points and was named the game's MVP.

In July 1988, Chambers signed with the Phoenix Suns (NBA) as the first unrestricted free agent in NBA history. In his first year with Phoenix, he set career highs in nearly all offensive statistical categories. His season featured a 25.7-point scoring average and a team-leading 8.4 rebounds per game. He and Kevin Johnson* helped the Suns improve by 27 wins to 55 victories and a trip to the WC finals. The 1989–1990 season saw Chambers fare even better, as he finished fourth in the NBA in scoring with 27.2 points per game and attained a career-high and team-record 60 points in a March game against Seattle.

A painful back limited Chambers the following two seasons, as his scoring average declined to 19.9 points per game in 1990–1991 and 16.6 points per game in 1991–1992. In June 1992, Phoenix traded for All-Star forward Charles Barkley (S) and moved Chambers to the bench. Although no longer the primary focus of the Phoenix offense, Chambers adapted well to his new reserve role. He recorded career lows in minutes played and scoring, but his valuable experience and clutch substitute play helped the Suns post a 62–20 record. In August 1993, the Utah Jazz (NBA) signed Chambers as a free agent. His point production declined further, but he played a valuable supportive role.

One of the most fluid, versatile players to play in the NBA, Chambers excelled at both the forward and center positions. He has used his quickness against centers or strong forwards and his size to his advantage against small forwards. He has played in 13 NBA seasons through 1993–1994, scored 19,521 points for a 19.3 points per game average, and has grabbed 6,474 rebounds (6.4 average). A four-time All-Star Game performer (1987, 1989, 1990, 1991), he has compiled an impressive 19.3 scoring average in those contests. Chambers, who made Second Team All-NBA as a forward in 1989 and 1990, has two daughters, Erika and Megen, and one son, Skyler.

BIBLIOGRAPHY: *Fast Break* 3 (December 1991); *Phoenix Suns Media Guide*, 1992–1993; Martin Taragano, *Basketball Biographies . . . 1891–1990* (Jefferson, NC, 1991); *TSN Official NBA Guide*, 1994–1995; *TSN Official NBA Register*, 1994–1995.

Curtice R. Mang

CONRADT, Jody (b. May 13, 1941, Goldthwaite, TX), college player, coach, and athletic administrator, grew up in a small farming and ranching community about 100 miles northwest of Austin, the daughter of an athletic-minded family. In Texas, six-player girls' basketball provided the best opportunity for females to compete athletically at that time. Conradt averaged 40 points per game in high school and played basketball at Baylor University (SWC), where she obtained a bachelor's degree in physical education in 1963. She accepted a teaching job at Waco Midway High School, but coaching became the focus of her life. Conradt never married.

After developing some coaching ideas at the high school level, she in 1969 was appointed women's coach for basketball, volleyball, and track and field at Sam Houston State University, on a $600 annual budget. Four years later, Conradt became coordinator of women's athletics at the University of Texas at Arlington, in suburban Dallas. She created a women's basketball program that attracted the attention of other schools when her teams upset more powerful opponents. Her teams used a tough man-to-man defense, developed from reading an outline of coach Dean Smith's (IS) run and jump defense. In 1976, the University of Texas at Austin (SWC) hired Conradt to build its program to national prominence. Her first team finished 36–10. The Lady Longhorns, the dominant women's basketball team of the 1980s, ranked in the AP top ten 11 of 12 years between the 1979 and 1990 seasons. Texas won the national championship in 1986 and was ranked number one nationally 4 consecutive years. The 34–0 championship Longhorn team, sparked by Clarissa Davis, Andrea Lloyd, and Kamie Ethridge, defeated the Cheryl Miller (IS)–led University of Southern California squad, 97–81, for the 1986 NCCA title in Lexington, KY. Conradt in 1993 became the first women's coach to record 600 wins, having recorded over 500 victories at the University of Texas. She has compiled a 642–162 record for a .799 winning percentage, in 25 years of college coaching. One of her biggest accomplishments, a SWC record 183-game victory streak, lasted from January 1978 to January 1990. Another accomplishment of lasting satisfaction involved attracting new fans. Texas led the nation in women's home basketball attendance from 1986 to 1991, including an NCCA record average of 8,481 spectators for one season. "We proved to a skeptical audience," Conradt stated, "that women's basketball was appealing. It was fun. We did our part to legitimize the sport and change the face of women's basketball." In 1992, Texas appointed Conradt women's athletic director, reducing the opportunities for her favorite hobby of playing golf.

Conradt, named national Coach of the Year three times (1980, 1984, 1986) and SWC Coach of the Year four times, received the WBCA Carol Eckman Award in 1987 and was inducted into the Texas Women's Hall of Fame in 1986. Many of her former Longhorn players coach sports throughout the Southwest.

BIBLIOGRAPHY: Rick Cantu, "Conradt Refused to Let Ego Get Inflated," Austin (TX) *American Statesman*, December 13, 1992, pp. C1+; Skip Hollandsworth, "She's Stealing the Heart of Texas," *WSFi* 9 (February 1987), pp. 49–51, 72; Ivy McLemore, "600: Conradt Charters Club," Houston (TX) *Post*, December 12, 1992, pp. C1, C8; Steve Richardson, "599 and Counting: UT's Jody Conradt on Verge of Another Milestone," Dallas (TX) *Morning News*, December 13, 1992, pp. C1–C3.

Dennis S. Clark

DALY, Charles Joseph "Chuck" (b. July 20, 1930, Kane, PA), college and professional player, coach, and sportscaster, has enjoyed a basketball career characterized by his hard drive and skillful use of people. Daly, born to traveling salesman Earl Daly and Geraldine Daly in a western Pennsylvania coal mining town during the Great Depression, captured the sports fever of that region. He soon developed an aggressive defensive style, the eventual hallmark of all his teams.

Daly's scrappy high school hoop performance won a basketball scholarship to St. Bonaventure University in New York. The six-foot-two-inch, 180-pound Daly, however, left that powerhouse program after one year, realizing that he stood little chance of playing regularly. In 1949, he transferred to small Bloomsburg State College in Pennsylvania. During his two collegiate basketball seasons as a forward, he scored 418 points in 32 games for a 13.1-point average in the 1950–1951 and 1951–1952 campaigns.

Despite his undistinguished playing career, Daly made basketball coaching his life work. Like most ambitious, successful coaches, he continually sought better positions. After a two-year military hitch, Daly began his coaching career at Punxsutawney, PA, High School in 1955. Daly, frustrated at his low pay and anonymity, wrote a letter to Duke University basketball coach Vic Bubas* asking for a job. He surprisingly was offered a spot as an assistant basketball coach at Duke University (ACC) from 1963 to 1969 before advancing to the head coaching job at Boston College from 1969 to 1971. Daly's teams, laboring in the shadow of the previous coach, NBA legend

Bob Cousy (IS), finished 26–24 over two seasons. When the University of Pennsylvania (IvL) head coaching job became available, Daly accepted that assignment. From 1971 to 1977, he led the Quakers to a .767 winning percentage and four IvL titles and NCAA berths, more than any other coach in the Quakers' history. His star performers included Kevin McDonald, Bob Morse, Corky Calhoun, Phil Hankinson, Ron Haigler, and Edward Stefanski. Daly also earned a master's degree in educational administration at Pennsylvania State University in 1958.

Daly, who chafed under IvL recruiting restrictions, jumped from the collegiate ranks in 1978 to become an assistant coach of the Philadelphia 76ers (NBA). Working under Billy Cunningham (IS), Daly helped the 76ers win two Atlantic Division titles and place second twice during his four-year tenure there. Philadelphia made the playoffs each of his seasons there.

Daly, nonetheless, yearned for an NBA head coaching job and earned a chance in 1981 with the lowly Cleveland Cavaliers (NBA). Unfortunately, Daly's team won only 9 of its first 41 games, resulting in his midyear dismissal. Daly finally got his break, when he moved to the equally inept Detroit Pistons (NBA) the next season. The Pistons featured a talented backcourt in Isiah Thomas (IS) and Joe Dumars and an aggressive frontcourt of "Bad Boys" including Bill Laimbeer, Dennis Rodman, and Rick Mahorn. Daly never experienced a losing record in the Motor City and was known as a "players' coach." Daly's Pistons won three Eastern Conference titles and three Central Division titles, registered five consecutive 50-plus win seasons, and garnered NBA championships in 1989 and 1990, only the third time in NBA history that the same team won consecutive titles. Red Auerbach's (IS) Boston Celtics and Pat Riley's (IS) Los Angeles Lakers also accomplished the feat. Daly's winning percentage with the Pistons reached .633, as the Pistons made the playoffs all his nine years there.

Having conquered the NBA and grown weary of team infighting, Daly resigned from the Pistons in 1992. He then assumed the challenge of coaching the U.S. Olympic basketball team in the 1992 Barcelona, Spain, Summer Olympic Games. With NBA players being permitted for the first time, Daly's team marked perhaps the greatest ever assembled in any venue. Michael Jordan (IS), Magic Johnson (IS), and Larry Bird (IS) predictably decimated their international competition by the greatest margins in Olympic basketball history, capturing a gold medal for the United States.

Daly's desire to continue NBA coaching led him to decline a lucrative television analyst's position and accept the helm of the New Jersey Nets (NBA). In 1992–1993, the Nets, led by Derrick Coleman, Drazen Petrovic, and Kenny Anderson, compiled a 43–39 record for third place in the Atlantic Division. Despite the tragic death of Petrovic, New Jersey repeated in third place in 1993–1994 with a 45–37 mark. Daly retired following the 1993–1994 season, having achieved an overall NBA coaching record of 564–379 for a .598 winning percentage. In 1994, he was elected to the Naismith Memorial Basketball Hall of Fame and joined the Turner Network as a basketball analyst.

Daly, an avid golfer, enjoys fine clothes, crooners Frank Sinatra and Bobby Short, and mystery novels. He and his wife Terry have one daughter, Cydney.

BIBLIOGRAPHY: "Chuck Daly," *CB* (1991), pp. 172–175; Chuck Daly, letter to Bruce Dierenfield, March 1994; Jack McCallum, "A Perfect Fit," *SI* 71 (December 18, 1989), pp. 52–58; New Jersey Nets press release, 1994; Cameron Stauth, *Franchise* (New York, 1990).

Bruce J. Dierenfield

DAVIES, Charles Robinson "Chick" (b. 1900, New Castle, PA; d. April 15, 1985, Pittsburgh, PA), college player and coach, was the son of a steel worker and grew up in Homestead, PA. Davies quit public school at age 14 to work in the steel mills and enlisted in the U.S. Navy in 1910. After becoming head basketball coach at Duquesne in 1924, he earned his high school diploma, B.A., and Master's degrees from Duquesne. He coached both intercollegiate and interscholastic basketball in the Pittsburgh area for 31 years, with a combined record of 505 victories against 143 defeats. He served as head basketball coach at Duquesne University until 1948, compiling a 314–106 record and ranking eleventh on the NCAA all-time list at the time of his death.

Under Davies, the Iron Dukes gained national prominence by the late 1930s. His most famous teams, the 1939–1940 and 1940–1941 squads, used only six players in most games. The 1939–1940 team played in both the NCAA and then more prestigious NIT postseason tournaments, ending with a 20–3 record. The following season, Duquesne lost to the University of Colorado in the NIT championship game and posted a 17–3 record. Davies coached All-Americas Paul Birch in 1935, Herb Bonn in 1936, and Moe Becker in 1941. Dudey Moore, one of his former players, succeeded Davies as head coach and maintained the Iron Dukes' winning tradition.

After leaving Duquesne, Davies coached at Homestead, PA, High School, near Pittsburgh, for 10 years. He enjoyed seven winning seasons there, guiding Homestead to the 1950 Pennsylvania State scholastic championship.

His coaching emphasized a disciplined control game and adept ball-handling, outfinessed the opposition, worked for open high-percentage shots, and employed strong defense. His salary as head coach at Duquesne University started at only $300 yearly and reached $3,500 his final year there. Survivors included one son, Charles R., Jr., and one daughter, Elizabeth Ann.

BIBLIOGRAPHY: Paul Demilio, Archives, Duquesne University Library, Pittsburgh, PA, fax letter to David L. Porter, September 8, 1994; *Duquesne University Basketball Media Guides;* Chet Smith and Marty Wolfson, *Greater Pittsburgh History of Sports*

(Pittsburgh, PA, 1969); *TSN*, April 29, 1985, p. 48; Robert Van Atta, interview with Lou Kasperik, 1939–1941 player, Derry, PA, 1993.

Robert B. Van Atta

DEE, John F. "Johnny" (b. September 12, 1923, Cedar Rapids, IA), college player and amateur coach, is the son of John F. Dee and Melinda (Dieterlie) Dee and began his athletic career at Loyola Academy in Chicago, IL, where he competed in basketball, football, and track and field. Dee, however, learned basketball from coach Leonard Sachs (IS), who produced some outstanding teams at Loyola University. As a youngster, Dee served as a waterboy and scoreboard keeper for Sachs. Although Dee expected to play for Sachs at Loyola, the latter's untimely death from a heart attack in 1942 and World War II sidetracked Dee's plans. After spending a semester at Loyola, Dee joined the U.S. Coast Guard for two years. Dee was discharged in 1944 and enrolled at the University of Notre Dame, where he played for two seasons. Although only five foot eight inches, the very strong, extremely aggressive Dee possessed a deadly two-handed set shot. In 41 games with the Irish, Dee averaged 10 points per game. During his first season, he tied the existing Chicago Stadium scoring record with 27 points. After two successful years at Notre Dame, Dee returned to Loyola University in 1946 for his senior year. When Dee scored 23 points in a 60–53 Loyola victory over Indiana University, Branch McCracken (IS), the Hoosier coach, described the shooting exhibition as the best he had seen in a college or professional game.

Dee launched his coaching career in 1947 at St. Mel's High School in the CCL. For the 1951–1952 season, Dee returned to Notre Dame as assistant basketball coach under John Jordan. The University of Alabama (SEC) in 1952 made him head basketball and assistant football coach. In four years at Alabama, Dee's basketball squads compiled a 68–25 record. His 1955–1956 Crimson Tide finished a perfect 14–0 to become the first basketball team outside of Adolph Rupp's (IS) University of Kentucky Wildcats to enjoy a perfect SEC season record. Since the SEC had allowed freshmen to play varsity basketball, Dee's starting five was ineligible for the NCAA tournament. The NCAA tournament limited competition to players with no more than three years of eligibility. Dee, shut out of the NCAA tournament, took his seniors to the 1956 AAU tournament in Denver, CO, where they played as the ADA Oilers. Bud Adams, later the owner of the Houston Oilers (NFL), sponsored the ADA Oilers. In the AAU semifinals, the powerful Phillips 66ers defeated Dee's team, 71–69. A victory would have given Dee's club an opportunity to participate in the Olympic tournament.

The 1956 AAU tournament altered the direction of Dee's career. George Kolowich, president of the Denver-Chicago Trucking Company, offered Dee the head coaching position of Denver's D-C Truckers and entry in the powerful NIBL. In five seasons, Dee guided the D-C Truckers to one NIBL title and two AAU finals. More important, Dee revived basketball enthusiasm in Denver, pouring his enormous energy into ticket sales and promotions. As the NIBL faded, Dee joined the ABL for the 1962–1963 season with the Kansas City Steers. The Steers compiled a 25–9 record before the ABL collapsed. In 1964, Notre Dame hired Dee as head coach to revive its basketball program. In seven years, Dee's Notre Dame teams won 116 against 80 losses. His Irish squad compiled four consecutive 20-win seasons, made four NCAA tournament appearances, and participated in one NIT tournament. His best player, Austin Carr (IS), was selected first in the 1971 NBA draft. Dee's most memorable victory came in 1971, when the Irish triumphed, 89–82, over coach John Wooden's (IS) undefeated UCLA Bruins.

Dee never coached again after the 1970–1971 season, despite his impressive 346–191 overall coaching record. He returned to Denver and pursued a career in law and politics, serving between 1975 and 1979 as Denver's city auditor. He and his wife Katherine have three children, Melinda, Dennis, and John III.

BIBLIOGRAPHY: John Dee scrapbooks, in possession of John Dee, Denver, CO; Alexander Weyand, *The Cavalcade of Basketball* (New York, 1960).

Adolph H. Grundman

DREXLER, Clyde Austin (b. June 22, 1962, New Orleans, LA), college and professional player, is one of five siblings and the son of Eunice (Scott) Drexler, a single parent who stressed education as the first priority to her children. Drexler's family moved to Houston, TX, when he was four years old. Drexler did not begin playing basketball until his junior year in high school but started two years at Sterling High School. His honors included being named Sterling's MVP and an All-Houston Independent School District selection as a senior.

Drexler, recruited by only three colleges, attended the local University of Houston (SWC). The Cougars, led by Drexler and Hakeem Olajuwon,* became known as "Phi Slama Jama" for their above-the-rim acrobatics. Houston made two consecutive trips to the NCAA Final Four, including reaching the championship game against North Carolina State University in 1983. Drexler, a tremendous leaper, scored and rebounded in double figures in 45 games during his college career and became the first Houston player to score more than 1,000 points, grab over 900 rebounds, and earn 300 assists in a career. As a junior, he was named the SWC Player of the Year.

The six-foot-seven-inch, 222-pound Drexler skipped his senior season, becoming eligible for the 1983 NBA draft. The Portland Trail Blazers (NBA) chose Drexler in the first round. In his rookie season with Portland, he averaged 7.7 points per game and joined two other Trail Blazers appearing in all 82 games. The next season, Portland moved him into the starting lineup. Drexler responded with a 17.2-point scoring average and finished second on the Trail Blazers in assists. Drexler's offensive production steadily increased each season. In 1985–1986, he scored 18.5 points per game and appeared in his first All-Star Game, tallying 10 points in 15 minutes. He averaged 27.0 points per game in 1987–1988 and a career-high 27.2 points per contest in 1988–1989. Although Drexler had become one of the NBA premier players, the Trail Blazers encountered trouble advancing beyond the first round of the playoffs. In June 1989, Portland obtained power forward Buck Williams from the New Jersey Nets (NBA) to help solidify the Trail Blazers. Although Drexler's scoring average dipped to 23.4 points per game, Portland won 20 more games than the previous season and reached the NBA finals before falling to the Detroit Pistons.

Portland posted the best NBA record with 63–19 the next season, but the Los Angeles Lakers (NBA) upset them in the Western Conference finals. Drexler's scoring average fell for the second consecutive season, as he scored 21.5 points per game. The Trail Blazers returned to the NBA finals in the 1991–1992 season, losing 4–2 to the Chicago Bulls (NBA). Drexler started for the WC All-Stars, garnering 22 points, nine rebounds, and six assists. He recorded a 25.0-point scoring average, was named to the All-NBA First Team, and played on the U.S. "Dream Team" that won the Olympic gold medal at the 1992 Barcelona, Spain, Summer Olympic Games. Knee and hamstring injuries limited Drexler to just 49 games during the 1992–1993 season and kept his season average below 20 points per game for the first time in seven seasons. He started his second consecutive All-Star Game, but Portland was eliminated in the first round of the playoffs. The following season, he placed second on the Trail Blazers in scoring and helped Portland again reach the playoffs. In February 1995, Portland traded Drexler to the Houston Rockets (NBA) for Otis Thorpe.

Drexler has compiled 17,136 points (20.7-point average) in 826 games through 1993–1994, finishing among the top 10 in steals five different seasons. He ranks eighth on the all-time steals list and remains Portland's all-time leader in games played, points scored, and steals. His size, quickness, and agility have enabled him to play effectively at both forward and guard throughout his career. He has appeared in eight All-Star Games. Drexler and his wife Gaynell have a son, Austin, and a daughter, Elise.

BIBLIOGRAPHY: *Great Athletes—The Twentieth Century*, vol. 5 (Pasadena, CA, 1992); *Portland Trail Blazers Media Guide*, 1993–1994; *TSN Official NBA Guide*, 1994–1995; *TSN Official NBA Register*, 1994–1995.

Curtice R. Mang

DUKES, Walter (b. June 23, 1930, Youngstown, OH), college and professional player, is the son of a factory operator and a tailor and moved to Rochester, NY, at age 10. He starred at Rochester East High School in basketball, football, baseball, and track and field and graduated in 1949 from Seton Hall Prep School, where he participated in cross-country and track and field. In 1949, his team won the mile relay at the Penn Relay Carnival in Philadelphia, PA.

Dukes, who planned to become a lawyer, enrolled in 1949 at Seton Hall University and earned a "B" academic average in economics. The coordinated, mobile, seven-foot 220-pounder impressed classmates as good-natured, friendly, conscientious, and modest. John "Honey" Russell (IS) lauded Dukes, who performed four varsity basketball seasons, as the best player he had ever coached. The agile and graceful Dukes shot equally well with both hands, converting nearly 50 percent of his baskets and over 70 percent of his foul shots. Defensively, his height and cat-quick reflexes enabled him to seize rebounds and start the fast break.

During 89 career basketball games for the Pirates, Dukes scored 1,779 points (20-point average) and converted an NCAA record 611 foul shots. A broken leg sidelined him most of his freshman basketball season, but he competed that spring in the 440-yard run and the 880-yard run. As a sophomore in 1950–1951, Dukes scored 404 points and guided 24–7 Seton Hall to the NIT semifinals. Seton Hall lost the semifinals to Brigham Young University. Dukes earned Second Team All-America honors in 1951–1952 for 25–2 Seton Hall and scored a school record 524 points (20.2-point average). His 19.7 rebounds per game ranked second nationally. Three-point losses to Siena University and Loyola University marred a perfect regular season. La Salle University eliminated the Pirates in the NIT first round.

In 1952–1953, Dukes enjoyed one of the best seasons in NCAA history. Dukes, a First Team All-America, combined with guard Richie Regan to lead 31–2 Seton Hall. Besides scoring 861 points (26.1-point average), he snared 734 rebounds. The Pirates won 27 consecutive games and averaged around 80 points a game. At the NIT, Seton Hall conquered St. John's University, 58–46, in the finals before a record Madison Square Garden crowd of 18,496. Dukes, a superlative defender, scored 21 points against St. John's and tallied 70 points in three NIT games to earn MVP honors. Seton Hall ranked second to Indiana University in the final AP poll.

After spending two seasons with the Harlem Globetrotters, Dukes performed in the NBA for losing teams from 1955–1956 through 1962–1963. His NBA career included stints with the New York Knickerbockers in 1955–1956, Minneapolis Lakers in 1956–1957, and Detroit Pistons from 1957–1958 through 1962–1963. Dukes's best offensive production came in 1959–1960, when he scored 1,004 points (15.2-point average). Dukes ranked among NBA leaders five seasons in personal fouls and rebounds, grabbing a career-high 1,028 rebounds in 1960–1961. During eight NBA seasons, he tallied 5,765 points (10.4-point average), made 6,223 rebounds (11.3 rebound average), and committed 2,260 personal fouls in 553 games. His 121 game disqualifications rank second in NBA history. Dukes appeared in 35 playoff games, scoring 447 points (12.8-point average) and making 432 rebounds

(12.3 rebound average). He started at center for the West All-Stars in 1960 and appeared as a reserve the following year.

BIBLIOGRAPHY: Zander Hollander, "The Pros Can't Wait for Dukes," *Sport* 14 (April 1953), 46–47, 77–78; Zander Hollander, ed., *The Modern Encyclopedia of Basketball*, rev. ed. (New York, 1973); Neil D. Isaacs, *All the Moves: A History of College Basketball* (Philadelphia, PA, 1975); John D. McCallum, *College Basketball U.S.A. Since 1892* (New York, 1978); *NCAA Official Collegiate Basketball Record Book*, 1955; David S. Neft and Richard M. Cohen, eds., *The Sports Encyclopedia: Pro Basketball*, 5th ed. (New York, 1992); "Reluctant Hero," *Newsweek* 41 (January 26, 1953), pp. 96–97; "Taskmaster & Pupil," *Time* 61 (February 15, 1953), pp. 76–78; Alexander Weyand, *The Cavalcade of Basketball* (New York, 1960).

David L. Porter

EMBRY, Wayne Richard (b. March 26, 1937, Springfield, OH), college and professional player and executive, is the son of Floyd Embry and Anna Elizabeth (Gardner) Embry and graduated with a B.S. degree from Miami University of Ohio in 1958. The six-foot-eight-inch, 255-pound center starred for coach Bill Rohr, helping Miami (MAC) to a 14–9 record as a sophomore in 1955–1956. Embry paced the 1956–1957 Indians to a 12–8 mark, MAC title, and a first-round NCAA Mideast Regional tournament appearance. Embry's scoring and rebounding helped Miami repeat as MAC champion in 1957–1958 and reach the semifinal round of the NCAA Mideast Regional tournament.

The Cincinnati Royals (NBA) chose Embry in the 1958 draft. Embry starred with Cincinnati from the 1958–1959 through 1965–1966 seasons, being selected for the 1961 through 1965 All-Star Games. He started at center as a rookie, averaging 11.4 points a game. Cincinnati struggled Embry's first three seasons but recorded winning marks and made the NBA playoffs the next five seasons. In 1961–1962, Embry recorded career highs in points scored (1,484), scoring average (19.8), field goal percentage (69), rebounds (977), and rebound average (13). NBA statistics listed Embry seventh in rebounds and ninth in field goal percentage. Embry enjoyed his second-best season in 1962–1963, scoring 1,411 points, averaging 18.6 points per game, and ranking sixth among NBA rebounders with 936. Cincinnati, led by brilliant guard Oscar Robertson (IS), set a franchise record with 55 victories in 1963–1964. Embry averaged 17.8 points per game, placed tenth among NBA rebounders with 925, and led the NBA in personal fouls. His offensive production declined the next two seasons. The Royals traded Embry in September 1966 to the Boston Celtics (NBA), where he played a reserve role for two campaigns. In May 1968, the Milwaukee Bucks (NBA) selected Embry in the expansion draft. Embry ended his NBA playing career in 1968–1969, tallying over 13 points per game for the struggling franchise.

During 11 NBA seasons, Embry scored 10,380 points (12.5-point average) and made 7,544 rebounds in 831 games. He appeared in 56 NBA playoff games from 1961–1962 through 1967–1968, scoring 566 points (10.1-point average) and grabbing 448 rebounds. Cincinnati reached the NBA semifinals in 1962–1963 and 1963–1964, while Boston followed suit in 1966–1967. Embry's lone NBA championship came as a reserve with the 1967–1968 Celtics, who defeated the Los Angeles Lakers in the six-game NBA finals. Embry scored 32 points in four All-Star Games, missing the 1963 contest with an injury.

Embry, a trustee of the Naismith Memorial Basketball Hall of Fame, married Theresa Jackson on June 6, 1959, and has three children, Deborah, Jill, and Wayne. After serving as director of recreation for Boston, MA, in 1969–1970, he rejoined the Milwaukee Bucks as general manager from 1972 to 1977 and vice president and consultant from 1977 to 1985. Milwaukee made the NBA finals in 1973–1974 and the Eastern Conference finals in 1982–1983 and 1983–1984. Embry served as vice president and consultant for the Indiana Pacers (NBA) in 1985–1986 and as vice president and general manager of the Cleveland Cavaliers (NBA) since 1986. Cleveland appeared in the Eastern Conference finals in 1991–1992.

BIBLIOGRAPHY: Zander Hollander, ed., *The Modern Encyclopedia of Basketball*, rev. ed. (New York, 1973); Zander Hollander and Alex Sachare, eds., *The Official NBA Basketball Encyclopedia* (New York, 1989); David S. Neft and Richard M. Cohen, eds., *The Sports Encyclopedia: Pro Basketball*, 5th ed. (New York, 1992); *TSN Official NBA Guide*, 1969–1970, 1994–1995; *WWA*, 47th ed. (1992–1993), p. 992.

David L. Porter

FEERICK, Robert Joseph "Bob" (b. January 2, 1920, San Francisco, CA; d. June 8, 1976, Oakland, CA), college and professional player and coach, graduated from Santa Clara University. At Santa Clara from 1937 to 1941, the six-foot-three-inch, 190-pound Feerick was selected an All-Coast performer in basketball in 1940 and 1941 and belonged to the Magicians of Maplewood. He was elected a member of the Santa Clara Hall of Fame.

Upon returning from the military service, Feerick scored 198 points in 21 games with Oshkosh, WI (NBL) during the 1945–1946 season. He joined the Washington Capitols (BAA) in 1946 and starred there four seasons, tallying 2,936 in 221 games for a 13.3-point average. Feerick, who ranked among the top BAA scorers in 1946–1947 and 1947–1948, led the BAA in field goal percentage (.401) in 1946–1947, paced the BAA in free throw percentage (.859) in 1948–1949, and appeared in nine playoff games, averaging 11.2 points per game. In the 1949–1950 season, Feerick served as player–coach for the 32–36 Capitols.

In 1950, Feerick returned to Santa Clara University (CBA) as basketball coach and athletic director. In his 12 seasons as basketball coach, Santa Clara compiled a 193–118 record, won four CBA titles, and made four trips to the NCAA West Regionals. His 1951–1952 quintet advanced to the NCAA Final Four.

In 1962 the San Francisco Warriors (NBA) appointed Feerick as head coach. He coached the Warriors in 1962–1963 to a 31–49 mark and served as the club's general manager from 1963 through 1974. Prior to his death, he served as director of player personnel for the Warriors. Feerick married Eleanor Rogus on September 5, 1941, and had four children, Robert, Jr., Richard, Dee (deceased), and Charles.

BIBLIOGRAPHY: Zander Hollander and Alex Sachare, eds., *The Official NBA Basketball Encyclopedia* (New York, 1989); David Neft and Richard M. Cohen, eds., *The Sports Encyclopedia: Pro Basketball*, 5th ed. (New York, 1992); *NYT*, June 8, 1976; Santa Clara University Sports Information Department, Santa Clara, CA.

Allan Hall

FITZSIMMONS, Lowell Cotton (b. October 7, 1931, Hannibal, MO), college and professional player and coach, executive, and sportscaster, is the son of Clancy Fitzsimmons and Zelda Curry (Gibbs) Fitzsimmons and attended Bowling Green High School in Missouri. He matriculated at Hannibal-LaGrange College as a freshman before transferring to Midwestern State University in Wichita Falls, TX. His collegiate varsity basketball scoring average came to 13.3 points per game.

His basketball coaching career began at Moberly JC in 1958. In nine years there, he compiled a 223–59 win–loss record and guided his teams to at least 24 victories in each of his final seven seasons. In 1966 and 1967, Moberly won the National JC basketball title. Fitzsimmons was named JC Coach of the Year both seasons. Kansas State University (BEC) named him basketball coach in 1968. Fitzsimmons compiled a 34–20 record in his two seasons there, being selected as the BEC Coach of the Year in 1970.

Fitzsimmons experienced a well-traveled career as an NBA coach. In 1970, he began his NBA career as head coach of the Phoenix Suns. In his first season, the Suns finished with a 48–34 record. Phoenix produced a 49–33 record the next season. Although amassing among the top NBA records both seasons, Phoenix finished third in the Midwest Division behind strong Milwaukee Bucks and Chicago Bulls teams.

For the 1972–1973 season, Fitzsimmons moved to the Atlanta Hawks (NBA) as head basketball coach and guided the Hawks to a 46–36 regular season record and playoff berth. The Hawks did not finish above the .500 mark in any of the next three seasons, however, and failed to make the playoffs. Atlanta fired Fitzsimmons near the end of the 1975–1976 season. After a year away from basketball, Fitzsimmons joined the Buffalo Braves (NBA) as head coach. The Braves lacked talent, finishing with a 27–55 record.

The next season, he guided the Kansas City Kings (NBA) to a 48–34 record and first-place finish in the Midwest Division. Fitzsimmons earned his first NBA Coach of the Year Award. Although unable to match his first-year record, he led the Kings five more seasons and performed one of his best coaching jobs in the 1980–1981 season. The Kings struggled to a 40–42 record through the regular season but placed second in their division and earned a playoff berth. Kansas City upset the Portland Trail Blazers in the first playoff round and used a slowed-down offensive scheme to defeat the heavily favored Phoenix Suns in the next round. The Houston Rockets ousted Kansas City in the WC finals.

Fitzsimmons coached the San Antonio Spurs (NBA) from 1984 through 1986, compiling a 76–88 record and two more playoff appearances. In 1987, Phoenix named him the Suns' director of player personnel. He largely engineered a blockbuster multiplayer trade, sending Larry Nance to the Cleveland Cavaliers (NBA) in exchange for Kevin Johnson.*

The following year, Fitzsimmons began his second stint as head coach of the Suns. With Johnson and newly acquired Tom Chambers* leading the way, Phoenix compiled a 55–27 record for a 27-victory improvement over the previous season. The Suns appeared in the WC finals for the first time since 1984, with Fitzsimmons being selected as the NBA Coach of the Year a second time. Fitzsimmons coached the Suns to three more 50-win seasons and one more trip to the WC finals before retiring as coach in 1992. He currently serves as senior executive vice president and television commentator for the Suns.

During his 19-year NBA coaching career, Fitzsimmons amassed an 805–745 record to rank as the sixth all-time winningest coach in NBA history. His best seasons as an NBA mentor came in Phoenix, where he compiled a very impressive 314–178 record over six seasons. The Missouri Basketball Hall of Fame enshrined him in 1988, while the National JC Hall of Fame inducted him in 1985. He married JoAnn D'Andrea in 1978, but they are divorced. His son Gary serves as the director of player personnel for the Cleveland Cavaliers (NBA).

BIBLIOGRAPHY: *Phoenix Suns Media Guide*, 1989–1990; Martin Taragano, *Basketball Biographies . . . 1891–1990* (Jefferson, NC, 1991); *TSN Official NBA Guide*, 1994–1995; *TSN Official NBA Register*, 1994–1995.

Curtice R. Mang

FORTE, Fulvio Chester Jr. "Chet" "Chet the Jet" (b. August 7, 1935, Hackensack, NJ), college player and television producer–director, is the only son of Fulvio Chester Forte, Sr., a pediatrician, and graduated from Hackensack High School, where he starred in basketball. Columbia University (IvL) basketball coach Lou Rossini recruited the five-foot-nine-inch, 145-pound set shot artist to play guard. As a sophomore in 1954–1955, Forte became the first Lion hoopster to score over 500 points in a season. He tallied 559 points (22.4-point average) in 25 games and converted 84 percent of his foul shots, fourth best nationally. Forte helped Columbia share the IvL title and led IvL scorers, making the All-IvL and NYBWA All-Metropolitan teams.

Forte played the first half of the 1955–1956 season, scoring 358 points (22.4-point average) in 16 games and battling Johnny Lee of Yale University for the IvL scoring title. Forte, a great dribbler and remarkable shooter, made 42.4 percent of his field goals as a repeat All-IvL and NYBWA All-Metropolitan team member. Defenders moved in tight, preventing speedy, feisty Forte from set shooting, forcing him to drive to the basket for layups or take jump shots. Failure in an organic chemistry course made Forte academically ineligible for second semester.

In 1956–1957, Forte garnered consensus First Team All-America and All-IvL honors and earned UPI and NYBWA Metropolitan College Basketball Player of the Year accolades. Forte scored 693 points (28.9-point average) for 18–6 Columbia and ranked fifth nationally in scoring. Columbia shared third place in the IvL, as Forte shattered the IvL single-season scoring mark with 403 points (28.8-point average). At Columbia, he scored 1,610 career points (24.8-point average) in 65 games.

The Cincinnati Royals (NBA) drafted Forte in 1957, but he played basketball weekends for the Williamsport, PA, Billies (EL). After graduating with a B.A. degree in premedicine in 1958, Forte barnstormed with the Harlem Globetrotters. He joined CBS-TV Sports in New York City as an associate producer and was promoted to producer. In 1963, ABC-Sports President Roone Arledge (OS) hired Forte as a producer and director. Arledge, cognizant of the growing American obsession with sports, wanted to make ABC-Television the major network for sports programming. Forte remained at ABC-Sports until 1987, receiving nine Emmys for outstanding sports production and direction. The perfectionist became the best sports television producer–director, helping build ABC into the top sports television network. After handling NBA games and "Wide World of Sports," he produced and directed "Monday Night Football" from 1970 to 1986 and melded field action, technology, and celebrity into a tight, compelling package. Forte supervised placement of cameras and picked his own crews, searching the sidelines and crowds for action shots. His diverse producer–director sports assignments included the Summer Olympic Games from 1960 to 1984; AFL, NCAA, College Bowl, and Super Bowl football; All-Star, League Championship Series, and World Series baseball; Kentucky Derby, Preakness, and Belmont Stakes horse racing; and Indianapolis 500 Auto Race, Grand Prix, Daytona 500, and NASCAR races. When Capital Cities acquired ABC-TV in 1986, Forte clashed with Dennis Swanson, new ABC-Sports president, and negotiated a buyout of his contract. From 1989 to 1991, he served as an independent producer and director for sports programs on NBC, ESPN, and other networks. Forte married Patricia Ann Richey on January 27, 1977, and has one daughter, Jacqueline.

Forte became a compulsive gambler by the 1980s and owed over $1.5 million to banks, Atlantic City, NJ, casinos, and personal debtors. He gambled with funds from Starkives, a talent agency, using investor's money to pay gambling debts. In April 1990, a federal grand jury in Camden, NJ, indicted Forte on nine charges of fraud and failure to file income tax returns. After pleading guilty to three counts, he was sentenced in March 1992 to five years' probation. Since May 1991, the San Diego, CA, resident has enjoyed cohosting a popular afternoon sports talk show on XTRA-Radio.

BIBLIOGRAPHY: *Dell Basketball Annuals*, 1956, 1957, 1958; Chet Forte, Biographical Sheets, 1993; Zander Hollander, ed., *The Modern Encyclopedia of Basketball*, rev. ed. (New York, 1973); Geoffrey Norman, "After the Fall," *SI* 74 (May 20, 1991), pp. 72–76+; *NYT*, March 7, 1957, p. 36; March 14, 1957, p. 37; March 18, 1957, p. 24; March 13, 1992, p. B14; March 14, 1992, p. 37; *NYT Biographical Service*, May 1990, pp. 422–424; *WWA*, 41st ed. (1980–1981), p. 1128.

David L. Porter

FRANCIS, Clarence "Bevo" (b. September 5, 1932, Hammondsville, OH), college and professional player, is the son of a clay miner. After missing two years of school because of chronic anemia as a child, he played pick-up basketball games on weekends in a barn. Francis attended Irondale High School in 1948–1949 but played no basketball. His family moved to Wellsville in 1949 amid reports that alumni and boosters exerted undue influence. The OSAA declared Francis ineligible for basketball during the 1949–1950 and 1950–1951 seasons. In 1951–1952, Francis led Ohio in scoring with 776 points (31.0-point average) in 25 games and tallied 57 points against Alliance High School. Francis outscored the entire opposing team six different times, once by 21 points. His honors included making All-Ohio and receiving an HAF citation. After participating in the North-South classic at Murray, KY, Francis garnered Third Team All-America accolades. He secretly married Mary Chrislip of Wellsville his sophomore year and has one son, Frank.

Although not receiving his high school diploma until January 1953, Francis received 63 college basketball scholarship offers and enrolled at tiny Rio Grande College of Ohio in September 1952. Newt Oliver, his fiery high school basketball coach, became Rio Grande hoop mentor in 1952 and made the six-foot-nine-inch center the nation's most publicized, prolific scoring collegiate basketball player. The carefree, shy, unassuming Francis led Rio Grande to a 39–0 record. Several teams triple teamed Francis in 1952–1953, but he still broke all existing college scoring records with 1,954 points (50.1-point average) in 39 games and helped Rio Grande tally over 100 points a game. In a 150–85 victory over Ashland, KY, JC, he shattered all single-game scoring records with 116 points. Fifty-five of those points came in the 10-minute last quarter. His other offensive outbursts included 76 points against Lees JC, 72 against California, PA, State Teacher's College, 69 against Wilberforce University, and 68 against Mountain State College. The NCAA did not share the fans' admiration for Francis's fabulous exploits and refused to recognize any of his records set against non-four-year colleges. Rio Grande had drawn numerous spectators against JC and armed forces teams, profiting considerably on its basketball program. Francis probably rescued the 92-student college from closing for financial reasons. Rio Grande was eliminated in the second round of the NAIA tournament.

In 1953–1954, Oliver's team scheduled only 27 games and played more formidable opponents in larger arenas. Francis even performed before 13,800 fans at Madison Square Garden in New York. Rio Grande earned up to $35,000 a game and compiled a 20–7 mark, averaging 91.3 points per game. Francis easily led collegiate scorers with 1,255 points, averaging 46.5 points per contest. His 444 field goals made, 510 free throw attempts, 367 free throws converted, 1,255 points, and 46.5-point average all set NCAA official single-season records. Rio Grande scored 2,465 points, making Francis the only NCAA player to score over half of his team's points in a season. He tallied 113 points against Hillsdale College on February 2, establishing official NCAA records for points, field goals (38), free throws (37), and free throw attempts (45). Other scoring outbursts produced 84, 82, 72, 69, and 61 points. Against Alliance College, he made a record 71 field goal attempts. During two seasons, he scored 1,176 field goals, 898 free throws, and 3,250 career points (50.1-point average). Francis, who made Second Team All-America both years, relinquished his final two years of eligibility and joined for the Boston Whirlwinds on professional tours against the Harlem Globetrotters. He played minor league basketball until 1962 and later was employed in construction and trucking.

BIBLIOGRAPHY: Ken Davis, "Is Bevo Big League?" *Sport* 16 (January 1954), pp. 26–27, 72–74; *The Lincoln Library of Sports Champions*, vol. 5 (Columbus, OH, 1974), pp. 8–11; Bill Mokray, "Bevo of Rio Grande," *SR: B* 14 (1954), pp. 22–24; *NCAA Official Collegiate Basketball Record Book*, 1955; Wayne Patterson and Lisa Fisher, *100 Greatest Basketball Players* (New York, 1989); Reference Librarian, J. A. Davis Library, University of Rio Grande, Rio Grande, OH, letter to David L. Porter, April 5, 1994.

David L. Porter

FREE, Lloyd. *See* World B. Free.

FREE, World B. (b. Lloyd Free, December 9, 1953, Atlanta, GA), college and professional player, is the son of Charles Free and Earlene Free and grew up in Brooklyn, NY, where his father worked as a longshoreman. Although born Lloyd Free, he changed his name legally to World B. Free.

Free played college basketball at Guilford College (CrC) in Greensboro, NC. As a freshman, the six-foot-two-inch, 180-pound guard teamed with M. L. Carr to lead Guilford to the 1973 NAIA championship. Free, who was named MVP of the tournament, the only freshman so honored, was selected First Team All-NAIA All-America in 1974 and 1975. In the summer of 1974, he was chosen MVP of an NAIA team that won a silver medal in the WCN Tournament in Bogotá, Colombia. His honors also included being named in 1987 to the NAIA Golden Anniversary Team. Free scored 2,006 points in three seasons at Guilford, averaging 23.3 points per game.

Free turned professional after the 1975 season. The Philadelphia 76ers (NBA) made him a second-round draft pick. Free spent three campaigns in Philadelphia before being traded to the San Diego Clippers (NBA), where he played two seasons. He played with the Golden State Warriors (NBA) until the middle of the 1983 season, when he was traded to the Cleveland Cavaliers (NBA). He returned to Philadelphia in 1987 and finished his career the following season with the Houston Rockets (NBA). Free scored 17,955 NBA points, averaging 20.3 points per game and compiling 3,319 assists. Free averaged 28.8 points per game in 1979 and 30.2 in 1980, finishing behind only George Gervin (IS) in the NBA scoring race each of those seasons. Besides placing in the top 10 in scoring in 1981, 1982, 1983, and 1986, he was named Second Team All-NBA in 1979 and scored 14 points in the 1980 NBA All-Star Game.

The well-traveled Free proved an exciting if erratic player, famous for his creative shot selection. Coaches may have held their objections, but fans loved his daring style. Free has not married.

BIBLIOGRAPHY: Herb Appenzeller, *Pride in the Past: Guilford College Athletics, 1837– 1987* (Greensboro, NC, 1987); World Free file, Guilford College Sports Information Department, Greensboro, NC; Zander Hollander and Alex Sachare, eds., *The Official NBA Basketball Encyclopedia* (New York, 1989).

Jim L. Sumner

GRIFFITH, Darrell Steven "Griff" "Golden Griff" "Dr. Dunkenstein" (b. June 16, 1958, Louisville, KY), college and professional player, is the son of Monroe Griffith, Sr., a welder and steelworker, and Maxine Griffith. One of five children, the six-foot-four-inch, 190-pound Griffith led Male High School of Louisville to the Kentucky State basketball championship in 1975.

Griffith enrolled at the University of Louisville (MC). During his four-year career there from 1977 to 1980, he sparked the Cardinals to a composite record of 101 wins and 25 losses and their first NCAA national championship in 1980. Griffith, who played guard for Louisville and recorded a 48-inch vertical leap, led Louisville to regular season MC titles in 1977, 1978, and 1980, MC tournament championships in 1978 and 1980, and four straight NCAA tournament appearances.

In 1980, Griffith paced the Denny Crum (IS)–coached Cardinals to a season record of 33 wins and 3 losses. In the NCAA tournament semifinal against the University of Iowa, Griffith scored 34 points. During the championship game versus UCLA, he tallied a game-high 23 points. UCLA coach Larry Brown (IS) called Griffith, named the tournament's MVP, "the greatest player in the country."

Griffith, who received a bachelor's degree in mass communications, closed his career at Louisville as the Cardinals' all-time basketball scorer with 2,333 points and the single-season scoring leader with 825 points in 1980. In 1980, the *TSN* named Griffith its Player of the Year, while the *TSN*, AP, and UPI placed him on their First-Team All-America teams. His other honors also included the John Wooden Award as college basketball's Player of the Year and the MC Player of the Year. The University of Louisville retired his jersey at the end of the 1980 season.

The Utah Jazz (NBA) drafted Griffith in the first round as the second pick overall in 1980. Griffith was named NBA Rookie of the Year, compiling a 20.6 points per game scoring average. During the 1984–1985 season, Griffith set the NBA single-season mark for 3-pointers made with 92 and also averaged a career-high 22.6 points per game. Griffith spent his entire NBA career from 1980 to 1991 with the Jazz, finishing with 12,391 points for a 16.2 points per game average. Griffith, the Jazz all-time leader in 3-point goals (530), ranks second in games played (802) and third in points scored and steals. When the Jazz retired Griffith's number in December 1993, Frank Layden, the team's president, commented, "Griff is the guy who changed the way people thought about basketball in Salt Lake City. . . . He is the guy who taught us about winning."

Griffith returned to Louisville after his career with the Jazz and resides there with his wife Kathy and their children. The popular, articulate Griffith has invested in several Louisville business ventures and does promotional and advertising work.

BIBLIOGRAPHY: *Deseret News*, October 25, 1993; October 26, 1993; Darrell Griffith file, University of Louisville, Louisville, KY; Zander Hollander and Alex Sachare, eds., *The Official NBA Basketball Encyclopedia* (New York, 1989); Curry Kirkpatrick, "A Big Hand for the Cards," *SI 52* (March 30, 1980), pp. 10–13; Louisville (KY) *Courier Journal*, December 4, 1993; *TSN*, March 22, 1980; *University of Louisville 1993–1994 Basketball Information Guide; Utah Jazz Media Guide*, 1987–1988.

Frank W. Thackeray

HALDORSON, Burdette Eliele "Burdie" (b. January 12, 1934, Freeborn County, MN), college and amateur player, is the son of Dorothy Haldorson, a public school teacher, and began his basketball career in Austin, MN, where he made the All-State High School basketball team in 1951. He enrolled at the University of Colorado (BSC) in 1951 and played four varsity basketball seasons for coach Bebe Lee. In 1953–1954 and 1954–1955, Haldorson led the Buffaloes to BSC titles and NCAA basketball tournament appearances. Colorado reached the 1954–1955 NCAA Final Four, losing to the University of San Francisco Dons, 75–54, in the semifinal round. In Haldorson's junior and senior years at Colorado, he won the BSC basketball scoring championship.

One week after the Final Four tournament, Haldorson embarked upon a remarkable AAU basketball career. In March 1955, Haldorson and six Colorado Buffalo teammates entered the National AAU basketball tournament as the Luckett-Nix Clippers. The Clippers, a Boulder, CO, team, was sponsored by Phillips 66 Petroleum Company jobber Hap Luckett and University of Colorado barber Ed Nix. The Denver fans immediately rallied behind the Clippers, the tournament's Cinderella team and a local favorite, who did not disappoint them. After recording two relatively easy victories, Luckett-Nix stunned the Peoria, IL, Caterpillars, winners of the three previous AAU tournaments, 70–67. Haldorson scored 33 points, prompting a Denver (CO) *Post* writer to describe him as "a high-flying Eagle, soaring all alone above the rest of the flock." The following night, the Clippers defeated the Quantico, VA, Marines, led by future NBA star Richie Guerin (IS), in overtime, 63–56. Haldorson scored 24 points in the AAU championship game, but the Phillips 66ers captured the national title, 66–64, on a last-second shot.

In 1955, Haldorson joined the Phillips 66ers primarily because he wanted an opportunity to play on the U.S. 1956 Olympic basketball team. Haldorson's 21.5 scoring average his first season led all NIBL scorers, helping Phillips 66 win the NIBL crown. Phillips 66 lost the AAU championship game to the Seattle, WA, Buchan Bakers, 59–57, but the second-place finish earned Haldorson an invitation to the U.S. Olympic tournament in Kansas City, MO. Phillips won this tournament, as five 66ers, including Haldorson, made the 1956 U.S. Olympic team. The U.S. squad won the gold medal at the Melbourne, Australia, Summer Games.

In his next four seasons with the 66ers, Haldorson led Phillips to two NIBL titles and one shared crown. Haldorson won the NIBL scoring title in 1957–1958 with a 26.7-point scoring average. During that season and the 1958–1959 campaign, Haldorson's opponents selected him the NIBL's MVP. In 1958, Haldorson performed on the first U.S. athletic team to play in the Soviet Union. He played on the triumphant U.S. basketball team at the 1959 Pan-American Games in Chicago, IL. Haldorson's final season, the 1959–1960 campaign, also marked an Olympic year. By taking the NIBL title, Phillips earned a place in the Olympic tournament held at Denver, CO. After the tournament, the USOC placed Haldorson on the U.S. Olympic basketball team for the second time.

After winning his second Olympic gold medal in basketball at the Rome, Italy, Summer Games, Haldorson retired. During his amateur basketball career, Haldorson won AAU All-America honors four times and was voted to five consecutive NIBL All-Star teams. He holds almost every Phillips scoring record, including most career points (4,472), highest career point scoring average (19.5), and most points in a game (53). Haldorson, a member of the Colorado, Minnesota, and Olympic Halls of Fame, worked for the Phillips 66 Oil Company for 10 years and then started his own business, Bonded Petroleum Company, in Colorado Springs, CO. He and his wife Kaye have three children, Linda, Brian, and Kari.

BIBLIOGRAPHY: George Durham, "He's a High Flying Burd!" *SR: B* (1959), pp. 70–72; Bill Mallon and Ian Buchanan, *Quest for Gold: The Encyclopedia of American Olympians* (New York, 1984); *Philnews*, a Phillips 66 monthly magazine, Phillips 66 Archives, Bartlesville, OK; Alexander Weyand, *The Cavalcade of Basketball* (New York, 1960).

Adoph H. Grundman

HASKINS, Donald Lee "Don" "The Bear" "H" (b. March 31, 1930, Enid, OK), college player and coach, is the son of Paul Haskins, a truck driver, and Opal (Richey) Haskins and was nicknamed "H" at Enid High School, where he pitched and played third base on the baseball team and gained All-State honors as a baseball pitcher and basketball player in 1948. Haskins attended Oklahoma A & M (renamed Oklahoma State) University (MVC) and played guard and forward for the fabled Hank Iba (IS) on basketball teams that twice won MVC titles and NCAA tournament trips. Haskins was named Second Team All-MVC as a senior, helped Oklahoma A & M to a 23–7 record in 1952–1953, and played for the Artesia REA Travelers (NIBL) from 1953 to 1955.

Haskins in 1955 became basketball coach at Benjamin, TX, High School, drove a school bus, and coached six-man football and girls basketball. His boys basketball team compiled a 21–10 record. Haskins spent the next four years at Hedley, TX, High School, guiding his teams to three district titles, a regional crown, and the school's first trip to the state tournament while achieving an overall 114–24 mark. In 1960–1961, his 25–7 Dumas, TX, High School squad won the district and regional championships and a state tournament bid. Haskins's six-year 160–41 record and postseason success led to his only college coaching job.

In his first year at Texas Western College (renamed the University of Texas at El Paso), Haskins's 18–6 squad recorded the most victories in the Miners' history. The Miners steadily improved the next two years. After boosting a 16–9 mark in Haskins's fourth year, Texas Western enjoyed a brilliant 28–1 campaign in 1965–1966. The season produced an NCAA championship, as the Miners defeated the University of Kentucky, 72–65, in the title game. This game marked the first national crown of any kind for a Miners team. Even more notable, no team with an all-black starting lineup previously had taken the national basketball crown. Texas—El Paso joined the WAC in 1970 and won the WAC title repeatedly. Haskins's only assistant coaching job came in the 1972 Munich, Germany, Summer Olympic Games, when he helped Iba for the U.S. team. His players included All-Americas Jim Barnes, Bobby Joe Hill, and Nate Archibald (IS) and highly successful college coach Nolan Richardson.* Haskins was inducted into the Texas Sports Hall of Fame in 1987.

In 33 years at Texas—El Paso through 1993–1994, Haskins compiled a 641–288 win–loss mark. From the outset, "The Bear" stressed defense and rebounding. Nationally, his 1963–1964 Miners team ranked third for fewest points allowed per game and first for highest rebound average. Subsequent teams consistently finished among the national leaders in these statistics. Haskins married Mary Gorman on March 14, 1951, and has four sons, Mark, Brent, Steve, and David. Haskins's hobbies are fishing and hunting.

BIBLIOGRAPHY: Frank Deford, "The Champions Get After It," *SI* 25 (December 12, 1966), pp. 26–28, 31; Frank Deford, "Go-Go with Bobby Joe," *SI* 24 (March 28, 1966), pp. 26–29, 60–61; Frank Deford, "Now There Are Four," *SI* 24 (March 21, 1966), pp. 22–24; Joe Gergen, *The Final Four* (St. Louis, MO, 1987); Eddie Mullens, ed., *The Man They Call the Bear* (El Paso, TX, 1990).

Thomas P. Wolf

HUNDLEY, Rodney Clark "Hot Rod" (b. October 26, 1934, Charleston, WV), college and professional player and sportscaster, is the son of a pool shark and gambling father and a mother who reportedly worked as a madam at a brothel. His parents divorced and left West Virginia when Hundley was very young. Hundley was brought up by several different people around the Charleston area and found a home on the playgrounds, developing the skills that would make him the first real basketball hero from West Virginia.

Over 100 schools tried to recruit Hundley, with Everett Case (IS), head coach at North Carolina State University, displaying particular persistence. Hundley had planned on enrolling at North Carolina State (ACC) in 1954, but that same year the ACC and NCAA announced sanctions against the Wolfpack for recruiting violations. Case advised Hundley to attend West Virginia University (SC) instead. Red Brown, the new athletic director at West Virginia, signed Hundley and even became his legal guardian.

Hundley's freshman year did little to sharpen his basketball skills, as the Mountaineers played against weak competition. He spiced up blowout games by taking shots from his knees and behind his back and spinning the ball on his fingertips. Hundley averaged 35 points per game for the freshman team, even though not shooting in six games. As a sophomore, he helped lead West Virginia to 19 wins and their first SC title. He paced the Mountaineers in scoring with 711 points, establishing a new national scoring record for sophomores and being named the MVP of the SC tournament.

Hundley improved his junior year, scoring 798 points. West Virginia won the SC title for the second consecutive year, as Hundley again was named the SC tournament MVP. Hundley's final collegiate season saw him score less but enjoy it more. West Virginia finished with a 25–5 record and clinched the SC title for the third straight year, as Hundley finally won All-America honors. Many scouts and sportswriters considered him the best college player ever.

The six-foot-four-inch, 185-pound Hundley was selected in the first round of the 1957 NBA draft by the Minneapolis Lakers. His NBA career, however, never matched his college accomplishments. In six seasons with the

Minneapolis Lakers and Los Angeles Lakers (NBA), he averaged only 8.4 points per game. His best year came during the 1959–1960 campaign, when he averaged 12.8 points per game and finished eighth in the NBA in assists with a 4.6 assists per game average.

Hundley retired from the Lakers in 1964 and moved to the broadcast booth. He broadcast Los Angeles Lakers (NBA) games for two years before joining the Phoenix Suns (NBA) announcing team in 1969. In 1974, he became the announcer for the expansion New Orleans Jazz (NBA). He moved with the Jazz when it relocated to Utah and has remained its play-by-play broadcaster ever since. He also spent five years broadcasting the CBS NBA "Game of the Week."

As his nickname denotes, "Hot Rod" was known more as an entertainer than as a player. Hundley, who appeared in NBA All-Star Games in 1960 and 1961, was named to the NCAA Silver Anniversary All-America team in 1982 and was selected to the West Virginia Sports Hall of Fame. He was recently inducted into the West Virginia University Hall of Fame. Hundley has three daughters, Kimberly, Jackie, and Jennifer, and resides in Salt Lake City, UT.

BIBLIOGRAPHY: Neil D. Isaacs, *All the Moves* (Philadelphia, PA, 1975); Bruce Nash and Allan Zullo, *Basketball Hall of Shame* (New York, 1991); Terry Pluto, *Tall Tales* (New York, 1992); *TSN Official NBA Guide*, 1961–1962; *Utah Jazz Media Guide*, 1992–1993; Alexander M. Weyand, *Cavalcade of Basketball* (New York, 1960).

Curtice R. Mang

JOHNSON, Kevin Maurice (b. March 4, 1966, Sacramento, CA), college and professional player, grew up with his mother, Georgia West, and grandparents, George and Georgia Peat, and attended Sacramento High School, where he led the state in basketball scoring as a senior with a 32.5-point average. His final season included a game in which he scored 56 points.

Johnson stayed close to home, attending the University of California at Berkeley (PTC). The lightning-quick basketball guard became California's all-time leader in scoring with 1,655 points, assists with 521, and steals with 155. He posted the first recorded triple double in PTC history, making 22 points, 10 rebounds, and 12 assists against the University of Arizona. His junior and senior seasons saw him named to the All-PTC First Team. The Oakland Athletics (AL) selected Johnson, an excellent baseball player, in the 1986 draft, but basketball remained his primary focus.

The six-foot-one-inch, 190-pound Johnson was chosen seventh in 1987 by the Cleveland Cavaliers (NBA). He remained with Cleveland for only part of his rookie season before being sent in a February 1988 multiplayer trade to the Phoenix Suns (NBA) in exchange for Larry Nance. He started 25 of 28 games after the trade and finished his first NBA season with a 9.2 scoring average. Both Johnson and the Suns flourished in his first full season in Phoenix. Johnson averaged 20.4 points per game and set a Suns record with 991 assists, as he and Tom Chambers* led Phoenix to a 55–27 mark. He became only the fifth player in NBA history to average over 20 points and 10 assists per game, being selected as the NBA's Most Improved Player.

Johnson, the prototypical point guard, not only directed the offense but also provided a major scoring threat. He continued scoring over 20 points per game and dishing out over 10 assists per game for the 1989–1990 and 1990–1991 seasons. The following season saw Johnson's scoring average fall below 20 points per game for the first time since his rookie season, but he finished second in the NBA in assists with a 10.7 average.

Injuries limited Johnson's 1992–1993 season to only 49 games. Both his scoring and assist averages dropped, while his role changed. Johnson no longer served as the focal point of the Phoenix offense because the Suns acquired Charles Barkley (S) in June 1992. With Johnson concentrating more on defense, the Suns finished the season with the best NBA record at 62–20. Johnson ranked fifth among NBA leaders with 637 assists (9.5-point average) in 1993–1994, helping 56–26 Phoenix compile the third-best WC record. Through the 1993–1994 season, he has scored 9,424 points (18.4-point average), recorded 4,912 assists (9.7 average), and made 822 steals.

One of his dreams came true in 1992, when his St. Hope Academy officially opened in Sacramento. This organization, founded by Johnson, targeted inner-city youth at risk by providing them opportunities for educational, spiritual, and social edification. The unmarried Johnson devotes most of his time to this organization during the off-season.

Johnson has appeared in three All-Star Games, starting for the West in 1991. An All-NBA Second Team selection in 1989, 1990, 1991, and 1994 and a Third Team selection in 1992, he received the J. Walter Kennedy Citizenship Award in 1991. Johnson played on Dream Team II, which won the gold medal in the 1994 World Championship of Basketball in Toronto, Canada.

BIBLIOGRAPHY: *Fast Break* 3 (November 1991); *Phoenix Suns Media Guide*, 1994–1995; *TSN Official NBA Guide*, 1994–1995; *TSN Official NBA Register*, 1994–1995.

Curtice R. Mang

KAFTAN, George A. "The Golden Greek" (b. February 22, 1928, New York, NY), college and professional player and coach, led Holy Cross College to the 1947 NCAA basketball title, garnering All-America and NCAA tournament MVP honors. His parents were Greek immigrants, Angelo Kaftan, a restauranteur, and Esther Kaftan. Born premature, Kaftan was given little chance of surviving and did not begin playing basketball until his sophomore year at Xavier High School in Manhattan. As a senior, he led Xavier to a 25–4 record and captured the New York City scoring title with 435 points.

Kaftan attended Holy Cross College, where he played for Alvin "Doggie" Julian (IS). The six-foot-three-inch, 200-pound Kaftan made his mark quickly, setting the single-season scoring record as a freshman with 237 points. Kaftan's sophomore season in 1946–1947, however, marked his most memorable. He broke his season scoring record with 468 points, lifting the Crusaders to a 27–3 record. In the 1947 NCAA tournament, Holy Cross defeated the U.S. Naval Academy and CCNY en route to the championship game and triumphed, 58–47, over the University of Oklahoma for the title. The 19-year-old Kaftan was named NCAA tournament MVP, leading in nearly all offensive categories. He scored 63 points in three games, including 30 points against CCNY, and fell 1 point shy of the NCAA record. He scored 41 points in three games against the University of Michigan, University of Kentucky, and Kansas State University, leading the Crusaders to a third-place finish in the 1948 NCAA tournament.

From 1946 to 1949, Kaftan totaled 1,177 career points and was twice named an HAF and Converse All-America. He broke nearly every individual record at Holy Cross, while Julian's squads shattered every team record. By his junior year, Kaftan was considered the college's greatest basketball player. Many of his accomplishments, however, soon were surpassed by teammate Bob Cousy (IS).

Kaftan graduated in February 1949 after playing only 14 games that season for the Crusaders. He promptly signed with the struggling Boston Celtics (NBA) and averaged 14.5 points in 21 games his rookie 1948–1949 season, the most prolific of his NBA career. Kaftan spent another year with Boston and two seasons with the New York Knicks (NBA) as a low-scoring role-player. The Knicks, however, finished runner-up for the NBA crown both seasons Kaftan played there. He completed his basketball career with the Baltimore Bullets (NBA), contributing nearly 6 points per game in 1952–1953. For his NBA career, Kaftan scored 1,594 points in 212 games and averaged 7.5 points per game.

After retiring from professional basketball, Kaftan practiced dentistry on Long Island and taught biology and coached men's basketball at C. W. Post College. Kaftan coached 15 years there from 1958 through 1972, compiling a 188–101 record and .651 winning percentage, and served on the NIT Selection Committee. Kaftan and his wife reside in Long Island, NY, and have three daughters.

BIBLIOGRAPHY: Zander Hollander and Alex Sachare, eds., *The Official NBA Basketball Encyclopedia* (New York, 1989); *Holy Cross Basketball Media Guide*, 1947–1948, 1948–1949, 1949–1950; George Kaftan clipping file, College of Holy Cross Archives, Worcester, MA; Ronald L. Mendell, *Who's Who in Basketball* (New Rochelle, NY, 1973).

                                                                                    Brian L. Laughlin

LAETTNER, Christian Donald (b. August 17, 1969, Buffalo, NY), college and professional player, is the son of George Laettner, a newspaper printer, and Bonnie Laettner, a schoolteacher, and was selected a High School All-America at Nichols Academy, from where he graduated in 1988.

Laettner matriculated at Duke University (ACC), leading the Blue Devils to the 1991 and 1992 NCAA championships and becoming one of the most celebrated college players ever. Under the tutelage of head coach Mike Krzyzewski (S), the 6-foot-11-inch, 230-pound forward/center was named Second Team All-ACC in 1990 and First-Team All-ACC in 1991 and 1992. His honors included being voted ACC Player of the Year in 1992 and winning the McKelvin Award as the ACC's top athlete in 1991 and 1992. Laettner, named Second Team AP All-America in 1991, made every All-America First Team in 1992 and captured every major Player of the Year award, including the Wooden Award, Naismith Award, Eastman Award, and Rupp Award. He led Duke in rebounding in 1990, 1991, and 1992 and in scoring in 1991 and 1992. Laettner ended his college career with 2,460 points, 1,149 rebounds, a .574 field goal percentage, and an .806 free throw percentage. Duke retired his number 32. Laettner, who played on both the 1990 U.S. National team and the 1991 U.S. Pan-American team, was the only collegian selected to participate on the 1992 U.S. Olympic team at the Barcelona, Spain, Summer Games.

Laettner enjoyed exceptional success in the NCAA tournament and started in every Final Four from 1989 through 1992, becoming the first player to start in four Final Fours. His 407 points set an NCAA tournament career scoring record. Laettner was named to the All-Eastern Regional team in 1989, 1990, and 1992 and the All-Midwest Regional squad in 1991. His last-second baskets gave Duke 1-point victories in the 1990 and 1992 Eastern Regional finals, with Laettner being voted Eastern Regional MVP in both of those seasons. He was selected to the All–Final Four team in 1990, 1991, and 1992, earning Final Four MVP honors in 1991. Laettner's two free throws gave Duke a 79–77 victory over defending national champion University of Nevada at Las Vegas in the 1991 Final Four. He led all scorers in the 1991 and 1992 national title games.

Laettner's aggressiveness made him a controversial player. Some applauded his intensity and desire to win, while others criticized him as immature. Laettner, a matinee idol, received attention from various non–sports media outlets.

The Minnesota Timberwolves (NBA) made Laettner the number-three pick in the 1992 NBA draft. Laettner immediately starred with Minnesota, scoring 1,472 points for an average of 18.2 points per game and snaring 708 rebounds for an average of 8.7 rebounds per game in 1992–1993. In 1993–1994, he led the Timberwolves in scoring with 1,173 points (16.8-point average) and 602 rebounds. Altogether, he has tallied 2,645 points (17.5-point average) and grabbed 1,310 rebounds (8.7 average). He also continued to generate as much publicity for his personality as for his basketball abilities.

BIBLIOGRAPHY: Bill Brill with Mike Krzyzewski, *A Season Is a Lifetime* (New York, 1993); Mike Cragg and Mike Sobb, *Back to Back: The Story of Duke's 1992 NCAA Basketball Championship* (Durham, NC, 1992); Mike Cragg and Mike Sobb, *Crowning Glory: The Story of Duke's 1991 Championship Season* (Durham, NC, 1991); Curry Kirkpatrick, "Devilishly Different," *SI* 75 (November 25, 1991), pp. 62–73; Christian Laettner files, Duke Sports Information Department, Duke University, Durham, NC; Alexander Wolff, "The Man Couldn't Miss," *SI* 76 (April 6, 1992), pp. 16–17; Alexander Wolff, "The Shot Heard Round the World," *SI* 77 (December 28, 1992), pp. 32–42.

Jim L. Sumner

LEMONS, A. E. Jr. "Abe" (b. November 21, 1922, Walters, OK), college player, coach, and administrator, coached Oklahoma City University, Pan-American University of Texas, and the University of Texas basketball teams to a 597–344 composite record over 34 years. His teams made eight NCAA tournament trips and earned two NIT berths.

Lemons's parents did not name him, giving him the initials A. E. after his father. Lemons failed eighth grade and subsequently spent an extra year in public school. At age 19, he began playing high school basketball. The season's performance earned Lemons a scholarship at Southwestern Oklahoma University, where he stayed one year. Since he needed a full first name to enlist with the armed forces, Lemons placed a "B" between the "A" and "E" on his birth certificate and joined the U.S. Merchant Marine in 1942 for World War II service. After World War II, the 24-year-old Lemons entered Oklahoma City University and became the school's career leading scorer with a 7.1 points per game average. Upon graduation in 1949, he was named assistant basketball coach under Doyle Parrack.

Parrack led Oklahoma City to four straight NCAA tournaments from 1952 to 1955. Lemons kept up the winning tradition upon being named head coach in 1956. His 1956 and 1957 teams finished Regional runner-up, the first two of his seven tournament entries at Oklahoma City. Between 1956 and 1973, Oklahoma City won 308 games, lost 179 contests, led the nation in scoring three times, played twice in the NIT, and produced seven All-America players.

Lemons moved to Pan-American University as head basketball coach and athletic director in 1974, doubling his earlier $14,000 salary. Lemons coached only three years at Pan-American, producing a 55–16 record. In 1976, Pan-American boasted the nation's leading scorer in Marshall Rogers.

University of Texas (SWC) athletic director and former football coach Darrell Royal (FB), who hoped to raise Longhorn basketball to the level of its football and baseball programs, hired Lemons as head basketball coach in 1977. In six years, Lemons produced a 110–63 record at Texas. His Longhorns won the NIT title in 1978, when he was named NABC Coach of the Year. Lemons's 1979 squad reached the NCAA tournament. In 1982, however, new Texas athletic director Delodd Doss wanted different leadership and fired Lemons as coach. Lemons continued to serve as assistant athletic director until Oklahoma City rehired him for the 1984 season. Lemons produced a 123–84 record in seven more years at Oklahoma City. Oklahoma City switched from the NCAA to the NAIA in 1986. In 1987, Lemons's team finished 34–1 and was seeded first in the NAIA tournament. He retired after the 1990 season, having compiled a 597–344 record for 34 seasons.

Lemons, often called the funniest man in basketball, became widely known for his exciting, high-scoring teams and colorful players. He and his wife Betty Jo have two daughters.

BIBLIOGRAPHY: Frank Deford, "Abe Lemons and His Poor Ol' Hongry Farm Boys," *SI* 22 (January 4, 1965), pp. 46–47; *NCAA Basketball's Finest* (Overland Park, KS, 1991); *NYT*, March 11, 1982, sec. 2, p. 17; April 10, 1983, sec. 5, p. 5; Edwin Shrake, "A Shot of Lemons to Cure the Blues," *SI* 46 (January 17, 1977), pp. 32–39.

Brian L. Laughlin

LEONARD, Christopher Michael "Archie" "Chick" "The Dog" "Chris" (b. 1891, New York, NY; d. May 11, 1957, Manhasset, NY), college and professional player, was the son of Michael Leonard, manager of a piano-moving company in New York. Leonard, who married Agatha Taylor and had one sister, attended Manhattan College and played basketball there from 1909 to 1912.

Leonard began his professional basketball career in 1912 and played for several teams, including the Philadelphia, PA, Jasper Jewels (EL), Bridgeport, CT, Blue Ribbons (ISL), Paterson, NJ, Crescents (ISL), Newark, NJ, Turners (ISL), Hazelton, PA, Mountaineers (PSL), and Glens Falls, NY (NYSL). After serving as an infantryman in World War I, Leonard resumed his professional basketball career. He starred for the Germantown, PA, Hessians (PSL), Albany, NY, Senators (NYSL) and the New York Whirlwinds, a team organized by promoter Tex Rickard (IS). Jim Furey spotted Leonard and teammate Nat Holman (IS) in a 1921 New York Celtic–Whirlwind matchup and signed them to contracts with the Original Celtics in 1922. Furey and his brother Tom had organized the Original Celtics in 1918.

Leonard, one of the best-known Celtic players, ranked among the best shooters and team players of the 1920s. The Celtics originally used the above-six-foot 190-pounder at center but shifted him to guard in 1923, when Joe Lapchick (IS) joined the team as a center. Leonard's teammates referred to him as "The Dog" because of his tenacious play on the court but also nicknamed him "Archie," "Chick," and "Chris."

The Original Celtics dominated professional basketball in the 1920s, averaging wins in five of every six games. Most of their games took place on the road in old barns, armories, and dance halls. The Celtics, who made famous the pivot play, the switching defense, and the give-and-go offense, joined the ABL in 1927 and easily won the ABL Championship in 1927 and 1928.

Leonard retired from professional basketball in 1927 when the Original Celtics disbanded for the first time. He owned the Leonard Delivery and Warehouse Corporation in the Bronx from 1933 until his death and also served until about 1952 as an assistant coach for high school basketball teams in Great Neck, NY, and Manhasset, NY.

BIBLIOGRAPHY: Glenn Dickey, *The History of Professional Basketball Since 1896* (New York, 1982); Bill Himmelman, telephone conversation with Susan J. Rayl, Norwood, NJ, October 1993; Zander Hollander, ed. *the Modern Encyclopedia of Basketball* (New York, 1973); Christopher Leonard file, Manhattan College Sports Information Department, New York, NY; *NYT*, May 13, 1957, p. 31; Robert W. Peterson, *From Cages to Jump Shots* (New York, 1990).

Susan J. Rayl

LUBIN, Frank John (b. January 7, 1910, East Los Angeles, CA), college and amateur player and coach, is the son of Konstantin Lubin and Antoinina (Vausokaite) Lubin and participated in three sports at Lincoln High School in Los Angeles. After high school graduation, Lubin enrolled at UCLA in 1927 and started three years on the basketball team. Upon graduation in 1931, Lubin abandoned dreams of law school and worked as a laborer with Universal Studios because the United States had sunk into the Great Depression. This job enabled him to play on Universal's AAU basketball team. Lubin's first distinction in AAU basketball came in 1936, when his Universal team played in the Olympic basketball tournament in New York. Universal had finished in second place at the national AAU tournament in Denver, CO, and won the Olympic tournament by edging the AAU champions, the McPherson Globe Oilers, 44–43.

The victory secured a place for Lubin on the first U.S. Olympic basketball team. Lubin captained the 1936 Olympic squad. After winning a gold medal in the Berlin, Germany, Summer Olympic Games, Lubin, whose parents were Lithuanian, received an invitation from the Lithuanian government to visit that nation. This marked the beginning of a three-year odyssey in which Lubin became a Lithuanian citizen and played on and coached Lithuania's national team. He played under his Lithuanian name, Pranas Lubinas, becoming "The Godfather of Lithuanian Basketball." He scored the winning basket against Latvia, enabling Lithuania to win the 1939 European championship, 36–35. Lubin also coached Lithuania's women's team, which included his wife, Mary Agnes, whom he met in Wichita, KS.

Upon returning to the United States in 1939, he moved over to Twentieth Century Fox to work as a stagehand and continued his basketball career. Before playing in Lithuania, Lubin had been named an AAU All-America. Besides exhibiting excellent basketball skills, Lubin also proved a popular showman. One of his favorite routines involved dressing up as Frankenstein and mingling with the crowd. Lubin, who made the AAU All-America team in 1941, 1942, and 1945, played in his last AAU tournament in 1951 and scored 37 points in a tournament game at age 41.

In 1981, the LABC chose Lubin as 1 of the 20 best basketball players from southern California. When the Soviet Union's basketball team defeated the United States and won the gold medal at the 1988 Seoul, South Korea, Summer Olympics, four of its players came from Lithuania. The Soviet team was coached by Lubin's students. In 1988, Lithuania invited Lubin to celebrate the fiftieth anniversary of its European Cup. After retiring from Twentieth Century Fox, Lubin joined the Spirit Team, a group of past Olympians working with young people. He and his wife live in Glendale, CA, and have two children, Joan and John.

BIBLIOGRAPHY: Bill Mallon and Ian Buchanan, *Quest for Gold: The Encyclopedia of American Olympians* (New York, 1984); Alfred Erich Senn, "American Lithuanians and the Politics of Basketball in Lithuania, 1935–1939," *JBS* (Summer 1988), pp. 146–156; Andy Wodka, "The Godfather," *Ol* (February 1990), pp. 28–30.

Adolph H. Grundman

McKINNEY, Horace Albert "Bones" (b. January 1, 1919, Lowland, NC), college and professional player, coach, and sportscaster, was the youngest of four children of Martin Van Buren McKinney and Julia B. McKinney. His father, a farmer, died when McKinney was two. In 1924, his mother moved to Durham, NC, to work in a mill.

The restless McKinney dropped out of Durham High School for two years but returned to lead that school to 69 consecutive basketball wins and three consecutive state championships. He graduated in 1940 and subsequently entered North Carolina State College (SC), leading the SC in scoring in 1941–1942. The U.S. Army drafted him in 1942. After his discharge, he enrolled at the University of North Carolina (SC). A six-foot-six-inch, 187-pound stringbean, McKinney sparked the Tar Heels to a 29–5 win–loss mark and a second-place finish in the 1946 NCAA tournament.

McKinney dropped out of North Carolina after the 1946 season to support his family. He played for the Washington Capitols (BAA, NBA) from 1946 until that club folded in January 1951. He completed that season and the 1951–1952 campaign with the Boston Celtics (NBA). His honors included being named First Team All-BAA in 1947 and Second Team All-NBA in 1949. McKinney tallied 2,994 points and averaged 9.4 points per game in his six pro seasons and served as a player–coach for Washington in 1950–1951, when they compiled a 10–25 mark.

McKinney in 1952 entered Southeastern Baptist Seminary in Wake Forest, NC, where he became an ordained Baptist minister and preached part-time in a Raleigh, NC, church. He served as an assistant coach at Wake Forest University (ACC) until March 1957, when he became head coach. Wake Forest enjoyed its greatest successes under McKinney, recording a third-place finish in the 1962 NCAA tournament and ACC titles in 1961 and 1962. McKinney compiled a 122–94 mark in eight seasons at Wake Forest.

McKinney left Wake Forest after the 1965 season but returned to the sidelines to coach the Carolina Cougars (ABA) to a 42–42 mark in 1969–1970. His retirement came in the middle of the following season with a 17–25 mark. After leaving coaching, McKinney broadcast basketball games and engaged in business in Hickory, NC.

McKinney, a colorful and highly animated player and coach, once wore a seatbelt on the bench in an unsuccessful attempt to stay seated. He married Edna Ruth Stell in 1941, has six children, and is a member of the North Carolina Sports Hall of Fame.

BIBLIOGRAPHY: Smith Barrier, *On Tobacco Road: Basketball in North Carolina* (New York, 1983), pp. 93–104; Horace McKinney file, Wake Forest University Sports Information Department, Winston-Salem, NC; Bones McKinney with Garland Atkins, *Bones: Honk Your Horn If You Love Basketball* (Gastonia, NC, 1988); Ron Morris, *ACC Basketball: An Illustrated History* (Chapel Hill, NC, 1988).

Jim L. Sumner

MALONE, Karl Anthony "The Mailman" (b. July 24, 1963, Summerfield, LA), player, is the son of P. J. Malone and Shirley Ann Jackson. His father abandoned the family when Karl was three, and his mother five years later married Ed Turner. He was named three-time All-SoC First Team at Louisiana Tech University, where he earned the nickname "The Mailman" because he always delivered in the clutch. The Utah Jazz (NBA) chose Malone as the thirteenth pick in the first round of the 1985 NBA draft. The six-foot-nine-inch, 256-pound Malone was named to the 1986 All-Rookie Team and quickly developed into one of the NBA's premier power forwards.

Malone's development from raw rookie to superstar reflected his dedication to improving his skills and commitment to weight lifting to increase his strength and endurance. Malone, considered the NBA's strongest player, possesses unusual speed and agility for his size. One of the most durable players in NBA history, he missed only four games in his first nine seasons and remains the only active player to have logged over 3,000 minutes for seven consecutive seasons from 1988 to 1994.

The leading rebounder in Jazz history, he has paced Utah in rebounding in each of his nine seasons and seven times has ranked among the NBA's top 10 rebounders. Malone, however, is best known as a multidimensional offensive force. With outside jump shots, powerful low-post moves, and thunderous dunks at the end of fast breaks, the consistent and profilic scorer has averaged between 24 and 31 points per game from 1988 to 1994. He has led the Jazz in scoring each of the last eight seasons from 1987 to 1994 and ranked among the top NBA scorers, finishing second four straight years from 1989 to 1992, third in 1993, and fifth in 1994. Upon entering the

1994–1995 season, the Jazz's all-time leading scorer has tallied 19,050 points and ranked eighth in NBA history with a career season scoring average of 26.0 points per game. He has recorded 8,058 rebounds in 734 games, averaging nearly 11 per contest.

After being selected Second-Team All-NBA in 1988, Malone made the first team selection the next six years from 1989 to 1994. He was elected to the All-Star team eight consecutive years from 1988 to 1995, being named the MVP of the 1989 game and co-MVP in 1993 with Jazz teammate John Stockton.* His 21.0-point scoring average ranks second to Michael Jordan's (IS) 22.0 in All-Star history. A member of the "Dream Team," which captured the gold medal in basketball for the United States in the 1992 Summer Olympics at Barcelona, Spain, Malone tied for team honors in rebounding.

With business interests extending beyond the basketball court, Malone has fulfilled his childhood dreams of being a cowboy and truck driver as the owner of several cattle ranches and a long-haul trucking company. He married Kay Ann Kinsey, former Miss Idaho USA, in 1990 and has two children.

BIBLIOGRAPHY: *CB* (1993), pp. 37–41; Chuck Daly with Alex Sachare, *America's Dream Team: The Quest for Olympic Gold* (Atlanta, GA, 1992); Phil Elderkin, "Karl Malone Makes Hard Work Pay Off," *BskD* 16 (June–July 1989), pp. 72–74; Larry R. Gerlach, interview with Karl Malone, December 7, 1993; Kurt Kragthorpe, "Karl Malone: Utah's Jazzy Young Leader," *BskD* 15 (January 1988), pp. 16–22; Clay Latimer, "This Mailman Only Rings Once," *BskD* 18 (April 1991), pp. 38–41; Jack McCallum, "Big Wheel," *SI* 76 (April 27, 1992), pp. 62–74; Craig Neff, "The Mailman Does Deliver," *SI* 62 (January 14, 1985), pp. 88, 90, 94; *Salt Lake* (UT) Tribune, January 31, 1993; February 20, 1993; October 17, 1993; *TSN*, November 8, 1993; *TSN Official NBA Guide*, 1994–1995; *TSN Official NBA Register*, 1994–1995; *Utah Jazz 1994–95 Media Guide*; Ralph Wiley, "Does He Ever Deliver!" *SI* 69 (November 7, 1988), pp. 72–77.

Larry R. Gerlach

MEARS, Ramon B. "Ray" (b. November 8, 1926, Dover, OH), college player, coach, and administrator, was the son of a working-class family in a northwestern Ohio steel town. He aspired to be a great athlete but tested positive for tuberculosis in eleventh grade and was encouraged to quit sports. In order to keep close to basketball, Mears directed a sixth-grade team to a league championship in his first coaching experience. He worked in local steel mills to save money to attend Miami University of Ohio, where he also played basketball in the late 1940s. Mears, who earned a master's degree from Kent State University, married Dana Davis and has three sons, Steven, Michael, and Matthew.

Mears coached high school basketball at Cadiz, OH, and Cleveland's West Tech before becoming head coach of Wittenberg University, a small Lutheran school in Springfield, OH. In six seasons from 1957 to 1962, the Wittenberg Tigers won 121 games and lost only 23 contests. Wittenberg led the nation in scoring defense his last three years, holding opponents to 46.8, 43.8, and 41.9 points per game, and won an NCAA College Division tournament championship in 1961. His coaching philosophy was strongly influenced by acquaintance with Clair Bee (IS), who advocated playing zone defenses, taking the high percentage shot, and keeping errors to a minimum. The University of Tennessee in 1963 hired Mears to build a winning tradition in the University of Kentucky–dominated SEC. Mears compiled a 278–112 win–loss mark in 15 years, recording seven 20-win seasons, winning the 1967 SEC championship, sharing the 1972 and 1977 titles, and making six postseason tournament appearances. Tennessee also rejected another NIT bid. Mears's last three squads featured future NBA players Ernie Grunfeld and Bernard King (IS), who combined to average 50 points per game and brought Tennessee much national attention. Mears's coaching career was terminated in 1978 by a "nervous problem," later identified as bipolar disorder (manic depression). Mears never experienced a losing season, compiling a 399–135 career coaching record. His .747 winning percentage still ranks among the best in college basketball history. He served as athletic director at the University of Tennessee—Martin from 1980 to 1989.

Mears, selected SEC Coach of the Year in 1967 and 1977, was elected to the Miami of Ohio and Tennessee Sports Halls of Fame and the Wittenberg University Athletic Hall of Honor. Although a premier coach, he may be remembered longer for masterful promotion of basketball at both Wittenberg and Tennessee. His promotions included having players introduced by spotlights or crashing through a paper tiger's head, using special uniforms and player chairs, employing orange and white basketballs, conducting spectacular pregame ball-handling drills, using basketball-juggling unicycle riders, adopting catchy program slogans (TNT—Tennessee's Nuclear Tempered Offense, "Big Orange Country"), engaging in pregame walks that incited opponents, wearing Laurel and Hardy ties, and creating special big-game strategies. Mears orchestrated exciting basketball events.

BIBLIOGRAPHY: Ben Byrd, *The Basketball Vols: University of Tennessee Basketball* (Huntsville, AL, 1974); Barry McDermott, "It's the Bernie and Ernie Show," *SI* 44 (February 9, 1976), pp. 18–25; Ronald L. Mendell, *Who's Who in Basketball* (New Rochelle, NY, 1973); Jim Steele, "Ray Mears: The Master Promoter Who Made Tennessee Big Orange Country," *RTV*, October 16, 1991, pp. 8–9; Martin West, "Ray Mears Era (1962–78) Ends at Tennessee," Knoxville (TN) *News-Sentinel*, March 7, 1978, pp. 12–13.

Dennis S. Clark

MOIR, John (b. May 22, 1917, Rutherglen, Scotland; d. November 15, 1975, Carlisle, PA), college and professional player, was selected a three-time All-America and HAF Player of the Year in 1936 under coach George Keogan (IS) at the University of Notre Dame. The son of John Moir, a carpenter, and Elizabeth Moir, he was one of three children and immigrated with his family to Niagara Falls, NY, in 1923. Moir stood only five feet two inches when he entered Niagara Falls High School and did not play basketball. Upon graduation, Moir enrolled in Trott Vocational School. He enjoyed his first chance to play organized basketball and grew to six feet two inches and 184 pounds. After finishing his vocational education, Moir worked as a bookkeeper for American Sales Book Company and performed on the company's industrial league team. Moir's job performance garnered him offers to attend college, something he had not previously considered.

Moir chose Notre Dame and played basketball there under Keogan. In his first season of eligibility as a sophomore, Moir paced the 22–2–1 Fighting Irish to the 1936 HAF national championship and was named HAF Player of the Year. Moir led Notre Dame in scoring during each of his three seasons, averaging 11.3, 13.2, and 10.5 points per game. He also broke all Notre Dame scoring records of Ed "Moose" Krause (IS), a three-time All-America. Teammate Paul Nowak (IS) joined Moir as three-time HAF and Converse All-Americas, 2 of only 18 consensus All-Americas in college basketball history. His outstanding teammates also included Naismith Memorial Basketball Hall of Fame coach Ray Meyer (IS) of DePaul University and George Ireland, longtime mentor of Loyola, IL, University.

Moir and Nowak both played with the Akron, OH, Firestones (NBL) upon graduation and helped the Firestones garner NBL championships in 1938–1939 and 1939–1940. Moir averaged 7 points per game over the two seasons and led the 1940 playoffs in scoring with an 11-point average. Moir spent the 1940–1941 campaign with Akron and joined the independent Rochester, NY, Seagrams in 1941, the predecessor of the NBA's Rochester Royals. The Seagrams disbanded during World War II. After World War II, Moir ended his basketball career with the Cleveland Allmen Transfers (NBL) in 1945–1946. In four NBL seasons, he scored 562 points in 89 games and averaged 6.5 points per game. Moir, who subsequently worked for the Carlisle Tire & Rubber Company, and his wife Marjorie had two daughters and one son.

BIBLIOGRAPHY: Ronald L. Mendell, *Who's Who in Basketball* (New Rochelle, NY, 1973); David S. Neft and Richard M. Cohen, eds., *The Sports Encyclopedia: Pro Basketball*, 5th ed. (New York, 1992); *1991–92 Notre Dame Basketball Guide*; South Bend (IN) *Tribune*, November 18, 1975; C. H. Welsh scrapbook, Archives of the University of Notre Dame, Notre Dame, IN.

Brian L. Laughlin

O'BRIEN, John Thomas "Johnny" (b. December 11, 1930, South Amboy, NJ), college athlete and professional baseball player, is the son of Edward J. O'Brien, a marine foreman for the Pennsylvania Railroad, and the twin brother of Edward, a Seattle University basketball player and Pittsburgh Pirates (NL) baseball player. O'Brien graduated in 1948 from St. Mary's High School, where he starred in baseball and made All-State for the state titlist basketball team. He originally planned to play college basketball near home, but major universities considered him too small. O'Brien played shortstop for South Amboy at the 1949 Semi-Pro Baseball Tournament in Wichita, KS.

Al Brightman, Seattle University head basketball coach, recruited the five-foot-nine-inch, 170-pound O'Brien for his relatively small Jesuit school. O'Brien performed B-plus academic work and graduated from Seattle University with a bachelor's degree in business in 1956. The fearless, friendly, popular, humorous guard made Seattle a nationally known basketball program. His natural instincts, speed, incredible spring, catlike quickness, and accurate hook, jump, and bank shots placed him among the sport's biggest showmen. As a sophomore guard, he scored 766 points for the 32–5 Chieftains in 1950–1951. The NCAA officially credited O'Brien with 248 baskets and 187 free throws for 683 points (20.7-point average) in 33 games. Seattle reached the third round of the 1951 National Catholic tournament and then upset the Harlem Globetrotters, 84–81, as O'Brien tallied 43 points. He in February 1952 broke the NCAA season scoring record of 967 points, held by George King of Morris Harvey College. Altogether, he scored 1,051 points for the 29–8 Chieftains and set a national season record with 361 free throws. The NCAA officially listed O'Brien with 314 baskets and 342 free throws for 970 points (27.7-point average) in 35 games. In the NIT, Seattle lost to powerful Holy Cross College, 77–72. The Second Team All-America made only 3 baskets but broke a Madison Square Garden record with 15 foul shots.

O'Brien earned unanimous First Team All-America honors as a senior, leading the nation with 884 points (28.5-point average) on 276 baskets and 332 free throws and ranking among the top five in field goal accuracy. Seattle showcased his talents in Eastern doubleheaders before enormous crowds. In December 1952, the Chieftains capitalized on 62 points by the O'Brien twins to upset NYU, 102–101. A week later, O'Brien shattered a Boston Garden scoring record with 41 points in a 99–86 triumph over Boston College. The 29–4 Seattle quintet reached the second round of the NCAA Far West Regional. According to the NCAA, he established career scoring records with 838 field goals and 861 free throws for 2,537 points (25.6-point average). Nate DeLong of River Falls State University held the previous NCAA scoring record with 2,445 career points. O'Brien also played shortstop in baseball for the Chieftains, batting over .430 in 1953.

The Pittsburgh Pirates (NL) signed the O'Brien twins to $40,000 bonus baseball contracts, employing them as a double play combination in 1953. O'Brien batted .247 in 89 games that season, mostly as a second baseman. The twins were drafted into the U.S. Army in September 1953 and played professional basketball for Lancaster, PA (EL). Johnny married Jean Kumhera in the fall of 1954 and returned to Pittsburgh in June 1955, batting .299 in 84 games. Bill Mazeroski (BB) replaced O'Brien as regular second baseman in 1956, causing the latter to become a part-time pitcher. O'Brien divided the 1958 campaign between Pittsburgh, the St. Louis Cardinals (NL), and Rochester, NY (IL), split the 1959 season with the Milwaukee Braves (NL) and Rochester, and ended his baseball career in 1960 with Seattle, WA. In six major league seasons, O'Brien batted .250 with four home runs and 59 RBIs and compiled a 1–3 record with a 5.61 ERA. The Seattle, WA, resident served as a King County commissioner and headed security at the Kingdome, home of the Mariners (AL) and Seahawks (NFL).

BIBLIOGRAPHY: *The Baseball Encyclopedia*, 9th ed. (New York, 1993); Larry Fox, *Little Men in Sports* (New York, 1963); Zander Hollander, ed., *The Modern Encyclopedia of Basketball*, rev. ed. (New York, 1973); Rich Marazzi and Len Fiorito, *Aaron to Zuverink* (New York, 1982); Boyd Smith, "Deadeye Johnny O'Brien," *Sport* 14 (February 1953), pp. 38–39, 82–83; Emmett Watson, "The Clan O'Brien Sticks Together," *Sport* 21 (February 1956), pp. 30–33, 95.

David L. Porter

OLAJUWON, Hakeem Abdul "The Dream" (b. January 21, 1963, Lagos, Nigeria), college and professional player, made a most improbable journey to NBA stardom. His parents, Salaam Olajuwon and Abike Olajuwon, operated a profitable cement business in Lagos, Nigeria, and encouraged him to play sports, but basketball was regarded as a minor sport then. Consequently, Hakeem, whose name means "wise one" in Arabic, excelled at soccer, team handball, field hockey, and the high jump at the Moslem Teacher's College in Lagos. His introduction to competitive basketball came in 1978, when his college asked him to play in a basketball tournament.

In 1980, Olajuwon emigrated to Houston, TX, as an imported 6-foot-10-inch Goliath from Nigeria. Twice he led coach Guy Lewis's (IS) University of Houston basketball team to SWC championships, as the Cougars compiled an 88–16 record. A panel of media and coaches selected the catlike Olajuwon SWC Player of the Decade for the 1980s. Three times he led his Houston team to the Final Four as a member of the dunking Phi Slamma Jamma. In 1983, Olajuwon came within one basket of helping the University of Houston win an NCAA national championship. He watched futilely, however, as North Carolina State University snatched victory on a miraculous, last-second shot.

During his collegiate career, Olajuwon collected 1,067 rebounds and 1,332 points for a 13.3-point average. In 1983–1984, he led the nation with a 67.5 percent field goal accuracy and a 13.5 rebounding average per game, only the third player in Division I history to lead the nation in at least two categories.

After Olajuwon completed his collegiate basketball apprenticeship, the Houston Rockets (NBA) bet their franchise on his continued improvement. Although the Rockets often produced disappointing results, Olajuwon performed extraordinarily and quickly won numerous awards. In 1984, he was

selected First Team All-Rookie and finished runner-up to Michael Jordan
(IS). His other honors included being named NBA Defensive Player of the
Year (1993, 1994), making the All-NBA First Team (1987–1989, 1993, 1994)
and First Team All-Defense (1987–1988, 1990, 1993, 1994), and earning
Player of the Month four times and Player of the Week six times. Although
given the IBM Award for overall statistical contributions to the Rockets in
1993, Olajuwon finished second that year to Charles Barkley (IS) of the
Phoenix Suns in the NBA's MVP voting. Olajuwon, the only center in NBA
history besides Kareem Abdul-Jabbar (IS) selected First Team All-NBA and
All-Defense in the same season, remains only the third player in NBA history to have 2,000 points, 1,000 rebounds, and 300 blocked shots in the
same campaign and the third player in NBA history to record at least 10,000
points, 5,000 rebounds, and 1,000 steals, assists, and blocks.

Through the 1993–1994 NBA season, Olajuwon has compiled 17,902
points (23.7-point average), 9,464 rebounds (12.5 average), 2,741 blocks,
1,830 assists, and 1,448 steals. Olajuwon has also rewritten the Houston
Rockets' record book as the team's career leader in rebounds, steals, blocked
shots, and free throw attempts and ranks second behind guard Calvin Murphy (IS) on the all-time scoring list. Following the 1993–1994 season, Olajuwon was selected NBA MVP for the first time, named NBA Defensive
Player of the Year for the second consecutive year, and made the NBA All-
Defensive First Team for the fifth time. No foreign-born player previously
had garnered NBA MVP honors. Olajuwon also was named MVP of the
1994 NBA playoffs, helping the Houston Rockets win their first NBA title.
The Rockets defeated the New York Knicks in the seven-game NBA finals.

Olajuwon concentrates on developing his overall condition off the court,
especially after enduring problems with phlebitis, a shattered right eye
socket, a rapid heartbeat, and a hamstring pull. His regimen includes practicing Islam, a strict diet, and quiet time at home. In his spare time, he
operates an export sporting goods business to Nigeria. Olajuwon, who has
gradually adjusted to life in the United States, speaks English, French, and
four Nigerian dialects. Although he sees his five-year-old daughter, Abby,
infrequently because she lives in Los Angeles, CA, Olajuwon still finds family
in south Texas. Three brothers and a nephew live nearby and join him for
family meals, including an appetizing stew called *fufu* that Olajuwon makes
himself. He became an American citizen in 1993.

BIBLIOGRAPHY: John Capouya, "Beers with Akeem Olajuwon," *Sport* 79 (April
1988), pp. 21–23; Robert Falkoff, "MVP Talk Must Include Olajuwon," Houston
(TX) *Post*, February 21, 1993, pp. B1–B2; Lianne Hart, "With 'Twin Towers' Ralph
Sampson and Akeem Olajuwon, Houston Rockets to the Top of the NBA," *People
Weekly* 22 (December 17, 1984), pp. 144–146; Richard Hoffer, " 'H' as in Hot," *SI*
74 (April 8, 1991), pp. 54–59; *Houston Rockets Media Guide*, 1994; Charles Leerhsen,
"Rampaging Rookies," *Newsweek* 104 (November 26, 1984), pp. 121–122; Jack
McCallum, "Double Trouble, Houston Style," *SI* 61 (November 5, 1984), pp. 18–

21; Jack McCallum, "A Dream Come True," *SI* 76 (March 22, 1993), pp. 16–21; Jackie MacMullan, "Dream Season," Boston (MA) *Globe*, January 12, 1994, pp. 49, 53; Renee D. Turner, "The House Akeem Olajuwon Helped Design," *Ebony* 47 (March 1991), pp. 46–48, 50.

Bruce J. Dierenfield

O'NEAL, Shaquille Rashaun "Shaq" (b. March 6, 1972, Newark, NJ), college and professional player, is the son of Philip Harrison, a U.S. Army sergeant, and Lucille O'Neal and was born two years before his parents married. O'Neal, whose first name means "little warrior," attended grade schools in Newark, NJ, and on military bases in Bayonne, NJ, Eatontown, NJ, Fort Stewart, GA, and Germany. His first exposure to basketball came in Germany. O'Neal graduated in 1989 from Cole High School in San Antonio, TX, where he averaged 30 points, 22 rebounds, and six assists a game as a senior. In one game alone, he scored 27 points, grabbed 36 rebounds, and blocked 26 shots.

LSU (SEC) coach Dale Brown won the recruiting battle for the seven-foot-one-inch, 301-pound O'Neal's services. In 1989–1990, O'Neal gave the 23–9 Tigers a powerful inside game, while All-America guard Chris Jackson connected well from the outside. As a freshman, O'Neal scored 445 points (13.9-point average), ranked sixth nationally with 115 blocked shots (3.6 average), and placed ninth with 385 rebounds (12-rebound average). LSU shared second place in the SEC and made the second round of the NCAA tournament. In 1990–1991, O'Neal earned AP and UPI Player of the Year honors, made consensus All-America, and gave the Tigers a powerful inside game and share of the SEC title. He led the nation with 411 rebounds (14.7 per game), ranked third with 140 blocked shots (5 per game), and placed seventh with 774 points (27.6-point average). The 20–10 Tigers lacked an outside game, however, and were eliminated in the first round of the NCAA tournament. In 1991–1992, LSU compiled a 21–10 record, placed second in the SEC, and reached the second round of the NCAA tournament. O'Neal repeated as an All-America, pacing the nation with 157 blocked shots (5.2 per game), ranking second with 421 rebounds (14.0 average), and scoring 722 points (24.1-point average). David Robinson (IS) of the U.S. Naval Academy recorded the only higher season blocked shot figure in NCAA history. During his three-year LSU career, O'Neal scored 1,941 points (21.6-point average), converted 61 percent of his field goals, made 1,217 rebounds (13.5 average), and blocked 412 shots (4.6 average) in 90 games. O'Neal ranks second to Robinson in NCAA career blocked shots average and fifth in career rebound average.

In 1992, the Orlando Magic (NBA) made O'Neal the first player selected in the draft. O'Neal paid immediate dividends for Orlando, garnering NBA Rookie of the Year and NBA All-Rookie First Team honors. In 1992–1993, he ranked eighth in scoring with 1,893 points (23.4-point average), fourth in field goal percentage (56.2 percent), and second in rebounds with 1,122 (13.9 average) and blocked shots with 286 (3.53 per game) in 81 games. Orlando finished with a 41–41 record, fourth in the Atlantic Division. O'Neal scored a season-high 46 points against the Detroit Pistons on February 16 and destroyed the entire hydraulic basket support system in a nationally televised game on February 7 against the Phoenix Suns. He dunked a follow shot with such force that the basket collapsed, delaying the game 35 minutes. David Robinson of the San Antonio Spurs edged O'Neal for the 1993–1994 NBA scoring title, tallying 71 points on the final night. For that season, O'Neal tallied 2,377 points (29.3-point average), led the NBA in field goal percentage (59.9 percent), placed second in rebounds with 1,072 (17.3 average), and sixth in blocked shots with 231 (2.9 average). He established NBA season highs with 15 blocked shots against the New Jersey Nets on November 20 and 14 offensive rebounds against the Boston Celtics on February 15. Orlando finished second in the Atlantic Division and made the NBA playoffs for the first time, boasting a 50–32 record. O'Neal starred on Dream Team II, which won the gold medal in the 1994 World Championship of Basketball in Toronto, Canada. Through the 1993–1994 season, O'Neal has tallied 4,270 points (26.4-point average), converted 58.2 percent of his field goals, grabbed 2,194 rebounds (13.5 average), and blocked 517 shots (3.2 average). He appeared in the 1993, 1994, and 1995 NBA All-Star Games and was named 1994 USOC Basketball Male Athlete of the year.

O'Neal, who remains single and wears a size 20 shoe, possesses enormous crowd appeal as perhaps the NBA's marquee player since the retirement of Michael Jordan (IS). He has signed a $40 million contract with Orlando and negotiated another $30 million in endorsement deals, including his own signature ball, own line of clothing, a basketball shoe, and toy action figure. In 1993, he coauthored *Shaq Attaq!* with Jack McCallum and released rap albums, *Shaq Diesel* and *Shaquille O'Neal: Larger than Life.* He also costarred in a 1994 movie, *Blue Chips,* with Nick Nolte.

BIBLIOGRAPHY: Mike Meserole, ed., *The 1994 Information Please Sports Almanac* (Boston, MA, 1993); Shaquille O'Neal, "The Real Shaquille," *USA Weekend* (October 1–3, 1993), pp. 6–8; Shaquille O'Neal and Jack McCallum, *Shaq Attaq!* (New York, 1993); *Street & Smith College and Prep Basketball Yearbook,* 1989–1993; *TSN College Basketball Yearbook,* 1990–1993; *TSN Official NBA Guide,* 1994–1995; *TSN Official NBA Register,* 1994–1995; *USA Today,* February 18, 1993, pp. A1–A2.

David L. Porter

PARISH, Robert Lee "Chief" (b. August 30, 1953, Shreveport, LA), college and professional player, attended Woodlawn High School in Shreveport, where he played four years of prep basketball. Parish enrolled at Centenary College, being named to the *TSN* All-America First Team in 1976 and participating for the gold medal winners in the 1975 World University games. In four years at Centenary, he averaged 21.6 points per contest in 108 collegiate games. The 7-foot-½-inch, 230-pound hoopster scored 50 points against the University of Southern Mississippi and once grabbed 33 rebounds in a game.

The Golden State Warriors (NBA) selected Parish in the first round of the 1976 draft as the eighth pick overall. He played his first four NBA seasons in Oakland and in June 1980 was involved in a blockbuster trade. Golden State sent him to the Boston Celtics (NBA) along with first-round pick Kevin McHale (S). With the sudden retirement of Dave Cowens (IS), Parish became the Boston starting center. Parish, who has appeared in nine All-Star Games (1981–1987, 1990–1991), finished runner-up to Larry Bird (IS) in the 1982 All–Star MVP balloting. The durable Parish produced a streak of 116 straight playoff appearances and played in 99 of 100 games in the 1985–1986 season.

For seven NBA seasons from 1985–1986 through 1991–1992 campaigns, he placed among the NBA's top 10 in field goal accuracy each year. He scored the ten-thousandth point of his career on February 26, 1984, against the Phoenix Suns and grabbed his ten-thousandth rebound on February 22, 1989, against the Philadelphia 76ers.

The 1991–1992 season saw Parish setting many NBA milestones. In his sixteenth NBA season, he tallied his twenty-thousandth point on January 17, 1992, against Philadelphia. An exceptionally conditioned athlete, he missed few games in his long professional career. The often underrated, very steady performer was overshadowed by teammates Bird and McHale. In July 1994, the Charlotte Hornets (NBA) signed Parish as a free agent. Parish, the oldest NBA player, has tallied 22,494 career points (15.9-point average) and 13,883 rebounds (9.8 average) through 1993–1994. Parish and Kareem Abdul-Jabbar (IS) alone have compiled NBA career marks of 22,000 points, 13,000 rebounds, 2,200 blocks, and 1,400 games.

Parish and his wife Nancy have one son, Justin. Parish resides in the Boston area, where his recreational pleasures include judo, racquetball, backgammon, jazz music, boxing, reading, and horror films. He lists Boston's 1981 NBA championship over the Houston Rockets as his most memorable basketball experience.

BIBLIOGRAPHY: *Boston Celtics Pre-season Media Guide*, 1993; *Complete Handbook of Pro Basketball* (New York, 1993); Zander Hollander, ed., *Official NBA Basketball Encyclopedia* (New York, 1993); Robert Parish, letter to Stan W. Carlson, December 1992.
Stan W. Carlson

PITINO, Richard "Rick" (b. September 18, 1952, New York, NY), college and professional player and coach, graduated from St. Dominic's High School in Oyster Bay, NY, in 1970. The six-foot, 165-pound Pitino attended the University of Massachusetts and played guard in basketball between 1970 and 1974. His best season with the Minutemen came as a freshman in 1970–1971, when he scored 306 points (16.1-point average). His scoring production dropped to 115 points (4.3-point average) in 1972–1973 and rose slightly to 136 points (5.2-point average) in 1973–1974. His coaching apprenticeship came as an assistant at the University of Hawaii in 1975–1976 and Syracuse University from 1976 to 1978. For the next five seasons, Pitino served as head coach at Boston University. The Terriers enjoyed winning marks of 17–9 in 1978–1979 and 21–9 in 1979–1980. After struggling to a 13–14 record in 1980–1981, Boston University rebounded with 19–9 in 1981–1982 and 21–10 in 1982–1983.

The New York Knickerbockers (NBA) hired Pitino as an assistant basketball coach from 1983 to 1985. After the Knicks plunged to a last-place Atlantic Division finish in 1984–1985, Pitino returned to the collegiate ranks as head coach at Providence College. Under Pitino, the Friars attained a 17–14 mark in 1985–1986 and boasted a stellar 25–8 record in 1986–1987. *TSN* and NABC named Pitino 1987 College Coach of the Year for unexpectedly guiding Providence to the NCAA Final Four, where the Friars lost the semifinals, 77–63, to Syracuse University. In 1987, Pitino rejoined the New York Knickerbockers (NBA) as head coach. The Knicks shared second place in the Atlantic Division with a lackluster 38–44 mark in 1987–1988 and lost to the Boston Celtics in the first round of the NBA playoffs. Under Pitino, New York won the Atlantic Division with a 52–30 record in 1988–1989. Center Patrick Ewing (IS) ranked among NBA leaders in scoring, field goal percentage, and blocked shots. The Knicks ousted the Philadelphia 76ers in the first playoff round, but the Chicago Bulls eliminated them in the Eastern Conference semifinals. During two NBA seasons, he compiled a 90–74 overall mark.

Pitino landed among the nation's most prestigious collegiate jobs, taking over a beleaguered University of Kentucky program from Eddie Sutton.* The Wildcats overachieved Pitino's first year with a 14–14 overall record, winning all nine SEC home games and breaking seven NCAA 3-point records. Pitino recruited forward Jamal Mashburn, one of the nation's best and most versatile players. Kentucky improved to a 22–6 mark in 1990–1991, using a full-court press and making 3-pointers. During the 1991–1992 season, the Wildcats won the SEC title and ranked second nationally with a 29–7 mark. Mashburn averaged 21.8 points and 7.8 rebounds, led the Wildcats with 65 steals, and shot 56.7 percent from the field. Pitino's club came within a miracle shot by Christian Laettner* of Duke University of being the first SEC team since 1986 to reach the Final Four. In 1992–1993, Kentucky ranked second nationally with a 30–4 record and second in the SEC East with a 13–3 mark. Mashburn made First Team All-America and helped Kentucky reach the Final Four, but the Wildcats bowed, 81–70, to the University of Michigan. Kentucky recorded a 27–7 mark in 1993–1994, but Marquette University upset the Wildcats in the second round of the NCAA tournament. Pitino's club set an NCAA record in 1994 by rallying from a 31-point deficit to defeat LSU. Pitino, noted for building winning teams, has compiled a 122–38 mark in four Kentucky campaigns and a 255–112 mark in 11 collegiate seasons. He and his wife have four children.

BIBLIOGRAPHY: *TSN College Basketball Yearbooks*, 1990–1991, 1993–1994; *TSN Official NBA Register*, 1988–1989; *WWA*, 48th ed. (1994), p. 2728.

David L. Porter

QUIGLEY, Ernest Cosmas "Ernie" (b. March 22, 1880, New Castle, New Brunswick, Canada; d. December 10, 1960, Lawrence, KS), sports official and athletics administrator, was the son of Lawrence B. Quigley and Mary J. (Wier) Quigley. He graduated from Concordia, KS, High School in 1900 and entered the University of Kansas, where he quarterbacked the football team, participated in track and field, and played basketball for James Naismith (IS). Quigley left Kansas in 1902 to become football coach at Central Missouri State University in Warrensburg, MO, and then moved to St. Mary's College of Kansas, where he served as athletics director and football, basketball, baseball, and track and field coach from 1903 to 1914.

Quigley began officiating sports events to supplement his income, but it soon became a year-round activity. He refereed college football for 40 years from 1904 to 1943, working classics including the Army-Navy and Yale University–Harvard University series, three Rose Bowls, and one Cotton Bowl, then the Dixie Classic. He also officiated college and AAU basketball for 37 years from 1906 to 1942, refereeing NCAA and NIBL tournaments, 19 consecutive AAU national championships, and the U.S. Olympic basketball finals in 1936. Quigley began umpiring baseball in 1910 after breaking his hand playing in the minor leagues, spending two seasons in the WIL and working the NYSL in 1912. He started the 1913 season in the IL but advanced to the NL in June. During 24 years, he ranked among the NL's most respected arbiters and umpired six World Series (1916, 1919, 1921, 1924, 1927, and 1935). He served as the NL's supervisor of umpires in 1936 and public relations director from 1937 to 1944.

From 1944 to 1950, Quigley was the athletics director at the University of Kansas (BSC). He quickly retired the department's large debt and reinvigorated the Jayhawks athletics programs, hiring outstanding football, basketball, and track and field coaches. In 1958, Kansas named its baseball facility Quigley Field in his honor.

The greatest all-around sports official in history, Quigley estimated that during 40 years he traveled 100,000 miles a year and officiated some 5,400 baseball games, 1,500 basketball games, and 400 football games. The NBBC in 1957 established an award in his name to be given annually to the nation's top amateur umpire. Quigley was inducted in 1956 into the NAIA Hall of Fame and in 1961 became the second referee elected to the Naismith Memorial Basketball Hall of Fame. He married Margaret Darlington and had two sons, Ernest, Jr., and Henry.

BIBLIOGRAPHY: Mike Fisher, *Deaner: Fifty Years of University of Kansas Athletics* (Kansas City, MO, 1986); Ronald L. Mendell, *Who's Who in Basketball* (New Rochelle, NY, 1973); Sandy Padwe, *Basketball's Hall of Fame* (Englewood Cliffs, NJ, 1970); Ernest Quigley file, Naismith Memorial Basketball Hall of Fame, Springfield, MA; Ernest Quigley file, National Baseball Hall of Fame, Cooperstown, NY; Ernest Quigley file, University Archives, Kansas University, Lawrence, KS; *TSN*, December 21, 1960.

Larry R. Gerlach

REIFF, Joseph "Joe" (b. June 6, 1911, Muskogee, OK), college and amateur player and referee, graduated in 1929 from Crane Technical High School and with a bachelor's degree in 1933 from Northwestern University (WC), where he starred in basketball three years from 1930–1931 through 1932–1933. Dutch Lonborg (IS) coached Northwestern to its first WC basketball title in 1930–1931 with an 11–1 record. Lonborg employed the sensational six-foot-three-inch Reiff at center with forwards Bert Riel and Robert McCarnes and guards Frank Marshall and Arthur Smith. Reiff led the WC in scoring with 123 points (10.0-point average) in 12 games and performed as the center pivot on set plays. Northwestern finished 16–1 overall, losing 34–28 to the University of Illinois. Besides sweeping all other WC rivals, the Wildcats defeated the University of Notre Dame twice and the University of Alabama and Bradley University once each. The HAF named Reiff to its First Team All-America and designated Northwestern as National Champions.

The Wildcats shared second place in the WC with the University of Minnesota in 1931–1932, trailing HAF National Champion Purdue University. Guard John Wooden (IS) of Purdue led the WC in scoring, denying the slender, indefatigable Reiff a second consecutive title. Reiff again paced Northwestern, finishing second in the WC scoring race and making Third Team All-America as a forward. In 1932–1933, the Wildcats tied Ohio State University for the WC title with 10–2 records. Reiff tallied 168 points (14.0-point average) in 12 games to lead the WC in scoring for a second time, followed by teammate Elmer Johnson with 109 points. Don Brewer, Nelson Culver, Al Kawal, and Eggs Manske played valuable supporting roles. Northwestern finished 15–4 overall, splitting series with Purdue, Illinois, Notre Dame, and Marquette University. Reiff earned First Team All-America honors as a forward.

After the 1933 season, Reiff starred at forward for Rosenberg-Arvey of Chicago in the national AAU basketball tournament and made the All-AAU team. Rosenberg-Arvey lost the AAU championship game, 25–23, to the undefeated Diamond D-X Oilers of Tulsa, OK. Reiff, who practiced as an attorney, married Clarisse Livingston and has two sons, Joseph and Philip. From 1937 to 1947, he refereed WC basketball games.

BIBLIOGRAPHY: *NCAA Official Collegiate Basketball Record Book*, 1955; Wayne Patterson, Naismith Memorial Basketball Hall of Fame, Springfield, MA, letter to David

L. Porter, February 8, 1994; Alexander M. Weyand, *The Cavalcade of Basketball* (New York, 1960); Kenneth Wilson and Jerry Brondfield, *The Big Ten* (Englewood Cliffs, NJ, 1967).

David L. Porter

RICHARDSON, Nolan Jr. (b. December 27, 1941, El Paso, TX), college player and coach, was hired as University of Arkansas (SWC) head basketball coach after similar positions at Western Texas JC and the University of Tulsa (MVC). Richardson enjoys a 17-year combined 439–125 record through 1993–1994, boasting a national JC championship, an NIT title, and an NCAA crown in 10 tournament trips.

Richardson was brought up from age 3 by Rose Richardson, his paternal grandmother. His mother died when he was 3, while his father, Nolan, Sr., died when he reached age 12. Richardson, the first black to attend El Paso Bowie High School in 1955, earned All-District honors in baseball, basketball, and football. Richardson played baseball at Eastern Arizona JC in Thatcher, AZ, being selected an All-America first baseman. The Houston Astros (NL) drafted him in 1960, but he did not sign. Richardson returned to El Paso and enrolled at Texas Western University, which had no baseball team. He joined its basketball team, one of the first blacks to do so. Richardson averaged nearly 20 points per game as a sophomore, while new coach Don Haskins* transformed him from a scorer to a defensive star in 1962. Haskins greatly influenced Richardson's future coaching style.

After graduating from Texas Western in 1964, Richardson tried out with the San Diego Chargers (NFL) and Dallas Chaparrals (ABA). A recurring hamstring injury, however, kept him off both teams. He returned to Bowie High School in El Paso as the first black coach at a desegregated Texas high school and was named Coach of the Year three times in 10 seasons. Western Texas JC appointed Richardson head basketball coach in 1978, making him the first black coach at an integrated Texas JC. In three seasons at Western Texas, Richardson's clubs finished 100–13 and won the 1980 JC national championship with star guard Paul Pressey.

Richardson was hired to head the University of Tulsa basketball program in 1981, becoming the first black coach at a major Oklahoma university. Tulsa produced a 119–37 record in his five seasons there and earned post-season tournament bids every season. Tulsa played in two NIT tournaments, winning the 1981 title, and the 1982, 1984, and 1985 NCAA tournaments.

In 1986 the University of Arkansas selected Richardson as head basketball coach to replace Eddie Sutton,* making him the first black head coach in SWC history. Richardson struggled his first two years, beset by team drug problems and his daughter Yvonne's fight against and death from leukemia. In his first nine seasons at Arkansas, Richardson has produced a 220–75 record with seven NCAA tournament appearances. His 1989–1990 squad shared third in the NCAA tournament, while his 1990–1991 team finished regional runner-up. He guided the 31–3 1993–1994 Razorbacks to the school's first national hoop title, making him the second African-American coach with John Thompson (IS) of Georgetown University to garner an NCAA Division I basketball crown. Arkansas started five underclassmen during the 1993–1994 campaign and rallied from a 10-point deficit in the final 17 minutes to defeat Duke University, 76–72, in the championship game. Versatile Scotty Thurman arced a dramatic three-point shot with just 50 seconds left to break a 70–70 tie and propel the Razorbacks to victory. Guard Corey Beck and forward Corliss Williamson also sparked Richardson's squad.

Richardson serves as chairman of Easter Seals and on the board of directors of the American Red Cross. He has three children, Madalyn, Bradley, and Nolan III, from his first marriage. He and his second wife, Rose (Davila) Richardson, have two children, Yvonne and Sylvia.

BIBLIOGRAPHY: Frank Deford, "Got to Do Some Coaching," *SI* 68 (March 7, 1988), pp. 94–106; Des Moines (IA) *Register*, April 5, 1994, pp. 15, 35; *NCAA Basketball's Finest* (Overland Park, KS, 1991); *Official NCAA Final Four* (Overland Park, KS, 1993); Gene Wojciechowski, "College Basketball Report," *TSN*, September 21, 1992, p. 55.

                                                                  Brian L. Laughlin

RISEN, Arnold Denny "Arnie" "Stilts" (b. October 9, 1924, Williamstown, KY), college and professional player, is the eldest of four children of John D. Risen, Sr., a railway mail clerk, and Alvira (Scroggins) Risen and graduated from Williamstown High School in 1942. After attending Kentucky State University in 1942–1943, he starred in basketball at Ohio State University (BTC) from 1943–1944 to 1945–1946. In 1943–1944, he led the 14–7 Buckeyes to the NCAA tournament semifinals, where Dartmouth College ousted Ohio State, 60–43. The six-foot-nine-inch, 210-pound Risen, among the first outstanding slim, mobile, modern basketball centers, made Third Team All-America in 1944–1945. The 15–5 Buckeyes, coached by Harold Olsen (IS), won the BTC title and again reached the NCAA semifinals before being eliminated by NYU, 70–65. In 1945–1946, Risen paced the 16–5 Buckeyes to a third-place finish at the NCAA tournament. The University of North Carolina defeated Ohio State, 60–57, in the NCAA semifinals.

Risen joined the Indianapolis Kautskys (NBL) in 1945–1946 and performed there until January 1948, scoring 1,606 points and averaging 13.1 points per game in 123 regular season games. In 1946–1947, he led Indianapolis in scoring with 582 points (13.2-point average). In January 1948, the Rochester Royals (NBL) purchased Risen. Risen in 1948 led the 44–16 Royals to first place in the Eastern Division with a 14.5-point scoring average. A broken jaw sidelined Risen from the NBL finals against the victorious Minneapolis Lakers. Rochester, featuring fast-breaking guards Bob

Davies (IS) and Bobby Wanzer (IS), jumped to the rival BAA before the 1948–1949 season and edged the Lakers for the Western Division regular season title. Risen paced the BAA in field goal percentage (42.3 percent) and ranked fourth in scoring with 995 points. Minneapolis eliminated Rochester in the BAA semifinals. The Royals, relying on Risen's mobility and Davies's and Wanzer's ballhandling, shared the NBA Central Division crown with 51–17 Minneapolis in 1949–1950.

Risen enjoyed his best NBA season in 1950–1951, ranking fourth among NBA rebounders with 795 (12.0 per game) and ninth in scoring with a career-high 1,077 points (16.3-point average). He also led the NBA playoffs in scoring with 273 points (19.5-point average) and 196 rebounds, helping Rochester defeat the New York Knickerbockers in the seven-game NBA finals. In 1951–1952, Rochester edged the Lakers for the Western Division title with an NBA-best 41–25 record. Risen again placed fourth in rebounds with a career-high 841 rebounds (12.7 average) and ninth in scoring with 1,032 points (15.6-point average). Rochester lost to Minneapolis in the 1951–1952 NBA semifinals. Risen's offensive production declined steadily the next two seasons.

Risen spent his final three NBA campaigns with the Boston Celtics, who won the NBA title against the St. Louis Hawks in 1956–1957 and the Eastern Division crown in 1957–1958. During 11 NBA seasons, he tallied 7,633 points (12.0-point average) and grabbed 5,011 rebounds in 637 regular season games and recorded 790 points (13.0-point average) and made 561 rebounds in 61 playoff games. Risen, who married and had one son, Dennis, and one daughter, Barbara, performed in the 1952–1954 NBA All-Star Games and made the All-BAA Second Team in 1948–1949. The Cleveland Heights, OH, resident helped build a subdivision in Webster, NY, following his NBA career and enjoys bowling, golfing, horse racing, and playing cards.

BIBLIOGRAPHY: Zander Hollander, ed., *The Modern Encyclopedia of Basketball* (New York, 1973); Zander Hollander and Alex Sachare, eds., *The Official NBA Basketball Encyclopedia* (New York, 1989); Leonard Koppett, *24 Seconds to Shoot: An Informal History of the National Basketball Association* (New York, 1968); David S. Neft and Richard M. Cohen, eds., *The Sports Encyclopedia: Pro Basketball*, 5th ed. (New York, 1992); Elizabeth L. Schneider, Director of Grant County Public Library, Williamstown, KY, letter to David L. Porter, March 16, 1994.

David L. Porter

SADOWSKI, Edward A. "Big Ed" (b. July 11, 1916, Johnstown, PA; d. September 18, 1990, Wall, NJ), college and professional player, was a strong, six-foot-five-inch, 265-pound center and led North High School of Akron, OH, to the state basketball championship in 1935, being named All-State. Sadowski matriculated at Seton Hall University, where coach John "Honey" Russell lauded him as one of his greatest players. Sadowski scored 757 career points for Seton Hall, making the All-Eastern squad as a sophomore in 1938 and receiving All-America mention in 1940. He led Seton Hall to a 19–0 record in 1939–1940, the only undefeated season in the Pirates' history, and played professional basketball for a Syracuse team under an assumed name. He played in the first college All-Star Game in Chicago, IL, in 1941.

Sadowski declined a football contract with the New York Giants (NFL). The Detroit Eagles (NBL) drafted Sadowski, who averaged 10.7 points per game in 1940–1941. He played 24 games before entering the U.S. Army. After performing with the Wilmington, DE, Blue Bombers (ABL), he played with the Fort Wayne, IN, Zollners (NBL) in 1944–1945 and 1945–1946. Sadowski scored 592 points in 59 NBL games for a 10 points per game average.

With the formation of BAA, Sadowski split the 1946–1947 season between the Toronto, Canada, Huskies and the Cleveland Rebels. He led the Rebels with 877 points (16.5 points per game) and finished second among BAA scorers. In the 1947–1948 season, Sadowski joined the Boston Celtics (BAA) and scored 910 points in 47 contests for a career best 19.4-point average to place third among BAA scorers.

Sadowski, selected to the All-BAA First Team in 1947–1948, spent the 1948–1949 season with the Philadelphia Warriors (NBA) and split the following year between Philadelphia and the Washington Bullets (NBA). In 229 BAA–NBA games, he scored 3,579 points (15.6-point average) and tallied 152 points in eight playoff games.

Sadowski retired from professional basketball in 1950, worked as a labor negotiator for the Cities Service Oil Company and was employed by a beverage distributor. Sadowski, who married Charlotte K. O'Maro on February 2, 1942, and had two sons, Charles and Edward, resided in Wall, NJ.

BIBLIOGRAPHY: Akron (OH) *Beacon Journal*, September 19, 1990; Zander Hollander and Alex Sachare, eds., *The Official NBA Basketball Encyclopedia* (New York, 1989); David S. Neft and Richard M. Cohen, eds., *The Sports Encyclopedia: Pro Basketball*, 5th ed. (New York, 1992); *NYT*, September 19, 1990; Robert Sadowski, brother, letter to Allan Hall, January 20, 1994; Seton Hall University Sports Information Department, South Orange, NJ; *TSN*, October 1, 1990, p. 49; Robert White, high school coach, letter to Allan Hall, January 7, 1994.

                                                                                          Allan Hall

SAILORS, Kenneth Lloyd "Kenny" (b. January 14, 1921, Bushnel, NE), college, amateur, and professional player, is the son of Edward Sailors and Corabell (Houtz) Sailors and ranks among the greatest players in Wyoming basketball history. Sailors grew up on a ranch in Hillsdale, WY, and played basketball at Laramie High School, where he twice made the All-State team. At the Hillsdale ranch, Sailors developed a one-handed jump shot to become one of the real innovators in basketball history. According to Sailors, he developed the shot to compete against his oldest brother, Bud, a six-foot-five-inch basketball All-Stater. The Sailors duo played one-on-one and used a hoop nailed to a windmill on their ranch.

Sailors in 1939 enrolled at the University of Wyoming (BSAC), where he made two-time basketball All-America under coach Ev Shelton (IS). His most memorable season came in 1942–1943, when the Cowboys won the NCAA title by defeating Georgetown University, 46–34, at Madison Square Garden in New York. Sailors led all players that game with 16 points. The NIT then still shared the college basketball spotlight with the NCAA as a test of college basketball excellence. Consequently, two nights after vanquishing Georgetown, the Cowboys returned to Madison Square Garden and edged NIT champion St. John's University in overtime, 52–47, in a benefit game for the American Red Cross.

During their championship 1942–1943 season, the Cowboys compiled a 31–2 record. Sailors averaged 15 points per game and directed Wyoming on the floor. His style of play attracted the attention of fans and sportswriters. Although players possessed a limited offensive repertoire, Sailors employed a unique jump shot. Coaches marveled when Sailors dribbled the ball at a faster pace than most other players could run. Although the 195-pound Sailors stood only 5 foot 10 inches tall, he possessed, as one commentator wrote, "wide shoulders and the biceps and long arms of a heavyweight-wrestler." In close games, he delighted his fans by freezing the ball. Joe Commisky, sports editor of New York's *PM*, recalled this wizardry after the Georgetown game. "This Sailors," Commisky wrote, "can do everything with a basketball but tie a seaman's knot." Sailors began picking up recognition in 1943, when he was named First Team All-BSAC. To prepare for the NCAA tournament, the Cowboys entered the annual AAU basketball tournament in Denver, CO, in mid-March. Wyoming lost to the Denver Legion in the semifinals but defeated the University of Denver for third place. Sailors, a First Team AAU All-America, was selected the most promising youngster of the tournament. In the regional basketball tournament at Kansas City, MO, the Cowboys overcame a 9-point deficit to edge University of Oklahoma, 53–50, and a 13-point deficit to defeat the University of Texas, 58–54. After defeating Georgetown University in the NCAA final, Sailors won various All-America accolades and the Chuck Taylor Medal as the outstanding College Player of the Year.

Within a month, Sailors enlisted in the U.S. Marines. After two years in military service, Sailors returned to the University of Wyoming for his last year of eligibility. He made the *True* magazine's First Team All-America in 1946 and played in the fledgling BAA-NBA for five seasons. He made the All-Rookie Team in 1946–1947 with the Cleveland Rebels (BAA), averaging 9 points a game. His 1947–1948 BAA campaign was split between the Chicago Stags, Philadelphia Warriors, and Providence Steamrollers. He made the All-BAA Second Team in 1948–1949, when he averaged 15.8 points a game with Providence. He enjoyed his best year in 1949–1950, when he finished fourth in scoring while averaging 17.3 points per game for the Denver Nuggets (NBA). He completed his NBA career in 1950–1951 with the Boston Celtics and Baltimore Bullets. He scored 3,480 points altogether and averaged 12.6 points per game for his BAA-NBA career.

After retiring from professional basketball, Sailors operated a dude ranch in Wyoming and pursued a career in politics. In 1965 he moved to Alaska and became a master guide for big game hunters and fishermen. He and his wife Marilynne have two children, Dan and Linda, and divide their time between Alaska and Phoenix, AZ. Sailors was selected among the initial inductees to the Wyoming Athletics Hall of Fame.

BIBLIOGRAPHY: Zander Hollander and Alex Sachare, eds., *The Official NBA Basketball Encyclopedia* (New York, 1989); Kenneth Sailors file, University of Wyoming Department of Athletics, Laramie, WY; Alexander Weyand, *The Cavalcade of Basketball* (New York, 1960).

Adolph H. Grundman

SAITCH, Eyre "Ayers" "Bruiser" (b. February 22, 1902, New York, NY; d. November 28, 1985, Englewood, NJ), athlete, graduated in January 1921 from DeWitt Clinton High School in New York, where he starred in basketball. Saitch began playing professional basketball for the all-black New York Renaissance, during the 1925–1926 season, when manager–coach Bob Douglas (IS) acquired him.

Known for his outside shooting ability, Saitch played guard in professional basketball from 1926 to 1941. He participated on the seven-member 1932–1933 New York Renaissance team, winners of 88 consecutive basketball games. The 1932–1933 team was inducted into the Naismith Memorial Basketball Hall of Fame in 1963 and included teammates Tarzan Cooper (IS), William Smith,* Fats Jenkins (IS), Pappy Ricks, Casey Holt, and Bill Yancey (IS). Saitch also helped the 1939 Renaissance team defeat the Oshkosh, WI, All-Stars (NBL) to win the first-ever Professional Tournament in Chicago, IL. He was acknowledged as the player whom women came to see because of his handsome profile.

Saitch also excelled as a nationally ranked tennis player in the 1920s and 1930s. His several singles tennis titles included the 1928 and 1929 New York State championships and the 1930 New England Tennis Tournament. Saitch, equally impressive in doubles play, teamed with Dr. Sylvester Smith of New York to win the 1929 National Colored Doubles title and the 1930 New England Tennis championship. During the late 1920s and early 1930s, Saitch ranked among the best African-American tennis players in the United States. Although Saitch performed against white players on the basketball court, discrimination prevented him from playing against white athletes in tennis. Upon his death, Saitch resided in Englewood, NJ.

BIBLIOGRAPHY: Ocania Chalk, *Pioneers of Black Sport* (New York, 1975); Glenn Dickey, *The History of Professional Basketball Since 1896* (New York, 1982); Zander

Hollander, ed., *The Modern Encyclopedia of Basketball* (New York, 1993); New York *Amsterdam News*, August 31, 1929, p. 9; July 9, 1930, p. 13; Wayne Patterson, Naismith Basketball Hall of Fame, Springfield, MA; Robert W. Peterson, *From Cages to Jump Shots* (New York, 1990); Susan J. Rayl, telephone conversation with Bill Himmelman, Norwood, NJ, October 1993.

Susan J. Rayl

SEYMOUR, Paul Norman (b. January 30, 1928, Toledo, OH), college and professional player and coach, graduated from Woodward High School in Toledo in 1945 and lettered in basketball for the 20–7 University of Toledo in 1945–1946. During the 1946–1947 season, the six-foot-two-inch, 180-pound guard began his professional basketball career with the Toledo, OH, Jeeps (NBL). He split the 1947–1948 campaign between the Baltimore Bullets (BAA) and Syracuse Nationals (NBL) and remained a reserve through the 1950–1951 season. Syracuse, the 1949–1950 Eastern Division titlists with a 51–13 mark, lost the NBA finals in six games to the Minneapolis Lakers. Seymour started with rookie George King in 1951–1952, helping the 40–26 Eastern Division champions reach the NBA semifinals. Coach Al Cervi (IS) employed a tenacious defense and disciplined offense.

Seymour's best NBA seasons came between 1952 and 1955, when he blossomed into a potent scorer. He unveiled an accurate two-handed set shot to accompany his one-handers, nearly doubling his scoring production average. Seymour, an aggressive, hard-driving, scrappy defensive guard who collaborated effectively with star forward Dolph Schayes (IS), made the All-NBA Second Team in 1953–1954 and 1954–1955 and participated in the All-Star Game from 1953 through 1955. He averaged 14.2 points per game during 1952–1953, ranking fifth in NBA assists (294, 4.4 per game) and seventh in foul shooting percentage (81.7 percent). Syracuse shared second place in the Eastern Division in 1953–1954, as Seymour finished fourth in NBA free throw percentage (81.3 percent) and assists (364). The Minneapolis Lakers defeated the Nationals in the seven-game NBA finals, but Seymour tallied 14.9 points per game and shared the playoff lead in assists (60). Syracuse captured the Eastern Division crown with a 43–29 record in 1954–1955. Seymour attained career highs in points (1,050), scoring average (14.6 points), and assists (483), ranking second in NBA minutes played (2,950), fourth in assists (6.7 average), and eighth in free throw percentage (81.1). The Nationals garnered their only NBA championship, defeating the Ft. Wayne Pistons in seven games. Seymour, who contributed 137 points (12.5-point average) and 75 assists in the playoffs, remained with Syracuse through the 1959–1960 campaign. During his NBL-NBA career, he scored 6,450 points (8.6-point average), converted 78.2 percent of his foul shots, and recorded 2,341 assists in 748 regular season games and tallied 740 points (9.3-point average) and recorded 257 assists in 80 playoff games.

In November 1956, Syracuse appointed Seymour to replace Cervi as head coach. Under Seymour, the Nationals recorded second-place Eastern Division finishes in 1956–1957 and 1957–1958 and reached the NBA semifinals against the Boston Celtics in 1956–1957 and 1958–1959. Syracuse posted its best mark under Seymour in 1959–1960 at 45–30 but did not survive the first playoff round. The St. Louis Hawks (NBA) named Seymour in 1960 to replace head coach Ed Macauley (IS). Seymour employed a running game, which vaulted St. Louis to a franchise record 51–28 mark and Western Division crown, but the Boston Celtics defeated the Hawks in the five-game NBA finals. In December 1961, owner Ben Kerner fired Seymour over strategy differences. Seymour briefly coached the Baltimore Bullets (NBA) to a franchise record second-place finish in 1965–1966 and the Detroit Pistons (NBA) to a 22–38 mark in 1968–1969. Altogether, Seymour compiled a 271–241 regular season coaching record in eight seasons and a 14–21 playoff mark.

Seymour, who married Doris Ann Hansen and has two sons, Shaun and Paul F., resided in Toledo, OH, and worked in the retail business from 1954 to 1990.

BIBLIOGRAPHY: Zander Hollander and Alex Sachare, eds., *The Official NBA Basketball Encyclopedia* (New York, 1989); Leonard Koppett, *24 Seconds to Shoot: An Informal History of the National Basketball Association* (New York, 1968); David S. Neft and Richard M. Cohen, eds., *The Sports Encyclopedia: Pro Basketball*, 5th ed. (New York, 1992); Wayne Patterson, Naismith Memorial Basketball Hall of Fame, Springfield, MA, letter to David L. Porter, February 8, 1994.

David L. Porter

SMITH, William T. "Wee Willie" "Slim Green" (b. April 22, 1911, Montgomery, AL; d. March 14, 1992, Cleveland, OH), professional player, was the son of Isaac Smith and Mary Smith. The six-foot-five-inch, 235-pound Smith married Estelle Taylor in 1937 and had three children, James, Faith, and June.

Nicknamed "Wee Willie" due to his large frame and also "Slim Green," he played professional basketball in the 1930s and 1940s. Smith performed for Cleveland's Slaughter Brothers team prior to 1932, when he was spotted by New York Renaissance club owner Bob Douglas (IS). Douglas signed Smith to play center for the New York Renaissance team from 1932 through the 1941–1942 season. Smith became known for his defensive and rebounding skills and strong, aggressive play on the court. As an inside shooter, he ranked among the era's top players and starred on the superlative 1932–1933 Renaissance team. The Renaissance won 88 consecutive basketball games, breaking the professional record of 44 set by the Original Celtics. The Renaissance, consisting of just seven players, was elected to the Naismith Memorial Basketball Hall of Fame in 1963. Teammates included Tarzan Cooper (IS), Fats Jenkins (IS), Pappy Ricks, Eyre Saitch,* Casey Holt, and Bill Yancey (IS).

Smith also helped the Renaissance team win the first-ever Professional

Tournament, held at Chicago, IL, in March 1939. Smith and his teammates frequently experienced discrimination and prejudice on the road and on one occasion became involved in a fight. The Renaissance team had to be escorted by police to leave town safely. After his tenure with the Renaissance, Smith played for the Allmen Transfers (NBL) and the Chase Brass (NBL) teams in Cleveland, OH, in the early 1940s.

Following his basketball career, Smith worked for the Cleveland, OH, Public Transit System and the board of education. He was inducted into the Cleveland Sports Hall of Fame in the 1970s and resided in Cleveland, OH, until his death.

BIBLIOGRAPHY: Ocania Chalk, *Pioneers of Black Sport* (New York, 1975); Glenn Dickey, *The History of Professional Basketball Since 1896* (New York, 1982); Nelson George, *Elevating the Game: Black Men and Basketball* (New York, 1992); Zander Hollander ed., *The Modern Encyclopedia of Basketball* (New York, 1973); Wayne Patterson, Naismith Basketball Hall of Fame, Springfield, MA; Robert W. Peterson, *From Cages to Jump Shots* (New York, 1990); Susan J. Rayl, telephone conversation with Bill Himmelman, Norwood, NJ, October 1993; Susan J. Rayl, telephone conversation with Faith Foster (daughter of William Smith), Cleveland Heights, OH, December 1993.

Susan J. Rayl

STOCKTON, John Houston III (b. March 26, 1962, Spokane, WA), college and professional player, is the son of John H. Stockton, Jr., a tavern owner, and Clementine (Frey) Stockton and was a surprise first-round selection (sixteenth pick overall) by the Utah Jazz in the 1984 NBA draft. The six-foot-one-inch, 175-pound Stockton, who was twice All-WCAC and WCAC MVP at Gonzaga University, combined uncanny "floor sense" and passing ability with hard-nosed competitiveness to become one of the top point guards in NBA history.

At the start of the 1994–1995 season, Stockton ranked third in NBA history in career assists (9,383) and first in average assists per game for both career (11.5) and season (14.5). In February 1995 he recorded his 9,922nd assist to break Magic Johnson's (IS) career assist mark. The NBA leader in assists seven consecutive seasons (1988–1994), he ranked second to Naismith Memorial Basketball Hall of Famer Bob Cousy (IS) in most seasons (8) and most consecutive seasons (8), pacing the NBA. The only NBA player to compile over 1,000 assists in more than one season, Stockton has accomplished the feat seven times (1988–1994) and holds the NBA record for the most assists in a single season (1,164). In 1993 and 1994, he won the first Bausch & Lomb NBA Court Vision Awards as the NBA's assist leader. Stockton made 28 assists on January 15, 1991, against the San Antonio Spurs and 10 steals on December 9, 1993, against the Washington Bullets. The extremely accurate shooter, who consistently scores in double figures, began the 1994–1995 season with 10,870 career points (13.3 point scoring average) and .512 field goal and .822 free throw percentage marks. The tenacious Stockton, also an outstanding defensive player, led the NBA in steals twice (1989, 1992), ranks third in career steals (2,031), and was named three times to the NBA's All-Defensive Second Team (1989, 1991, 1992).

In recognition of his all-around abilities, he was voted five times Second Team All-NBA (1988–1990, 1992–1993), once First Team All-NBA (1994), and once Third Team All-NBA (1991). He was also elected to seven consecutive All-Star teams (1989–1995) and was named co-MVP of the 1993 All-Star Game with teammate Karl Malone.* The member of "Dream Team I," which won the gold medal at the 1992 Summer Olympics in Barcelona, Spain, missed the four preliminary games because of a hairline fracture of the right fibula, suffered during practice, and played sparingly in medal-round games. Stockton also played on Dream Team II, which won the gold medal in the 1994 World Championship of Basketball in Toronto, Canada.

New York Knickerbockers coach Pat Riley (IS) stated Stockton's "ball-handling skills are second to none, his decision-making and running of the offense are flawless, and he [is] a productive shooter." Utah Jazz president Frank Layden asserts, "Many people say Magic [Johnson] was a point guard and a better player than John. But as for a pure point guard, I defy anyone to say there has been anyone better than John Stockton." Stockton, a private person who avoids the spotlight, married Nada Stepovich in 1986 and has four children.

BIBLIOGRAPHY: Chuck Daly and Alex Sachare, *America's Dream Team: The Quest for Olympic Gold* (Atlanta, GA, 1992); *Deseret News*, November 4, 1993; Larry R. Gerlach, interview with John Stockton, December 7, 1993; Kurt Kragthorpe, "John Stockton's Stock Keeps Rising," *BskD* 15 (March 1988), pp. 44–46; Jack McCallum, "The Assist Man," *SI* 76 (February 17, 1992), p. 77; Brad Rock, "Jazz Maestro Stockton Plays a Quiet Tune," *BskD* 20 (March 1993), pp. 44–48; Steve Rushin, "City of Stars," *SI* 77 (July 27, 1992), pp. 62–74; *TSN Official NBA Guide*, 1994–1995; *TSN News NBA Register*, 1994–1995; *Utah Jazz 1994–1995 Media Guide*.

Larry R. Gerlach

STOKES, Maurice "Mo" (b. June 17, 1933, Pittsburgh, PA; d. April 6, 1970, Cincinnati, OH), college and professional player, enjoyed a spectacular basketball career that prematurely ended after three NBA years with a disabling form of encephalitis, manifested by a heart attack from rehabilitative strain that actually took his life. The son of Tero Stokes from Pittsburgh's Homewood section, he launched his outstanding performances as a basketball player with Pittsburgh's Westinghouse High School and starred at tiny St. Francis College in Loretto, PA. He established numerous Frankies' game, season, and career records, as he led the team in scoring and rebounding all four years. He combined speed and agility with size and strength to rank him among the greatest all-around players of his era. As a freshman, he averaged 16.7 points a game. He compiled 2,282 career points, including 760 his senior year in 1954–1955, and 1,819 career rebounds (25.3 per game average), with 733 in 1954–1955. His best individual single-game perform-ances included 43 points against the University of Dayton in the March 1955 NIT and 35 rebounds versus John Carroll College in 1954–1955.

Walter McLaughlin, NIT Selection Committee chairman, called Stokes's effort against Dayton, in which he snared 19 rebounds, "the greatest per-formance I have ever seen." Stokes, the NIT MVP, nearly led St. Francis to the NIT finals, dropping an overtime semifinal game to Dayton, 79–73. His small-school anonymity mitigated against All-America recognition, with the NIT visibility coming too late.

The six-foot-seven-inch, 240-pound, broad-shouldered center, who re-jected an offer from the Harlem Globetrotters, was drafted by the Rochester Royals (NBA) in 1955 and quickly became one of the NBA's top performers. He ranked among the top three in rebounds and assists and averaged 16.3 points per game, compiling a 202-game career total of 1,251 field goals and 813 free throws for 3,315 points. His soft shooting touch and strength on the boards awed scouts and garnered him NBA Rookie of the Year honors in 1955–56. He appeared in the All-Star Game and made Second Team All-NBA all three NBA seasons.

The Rochester franchise was moved to Cincinnati for the 1957–1958 sea-son. In his brief NBA tenure, he became a friend of teammate Jack Twyman (IS). The friendship lasted the rest of the crippled player's life as Twyman, a great humanitarian, became his guardian. Following the 1957–1958 season, Stokes collapsed and spent several months in a coma. Encephalitis, a crip-pling brain disease, made him an invalid. Stokes began a long and painful period of rehabilitation but died at age 36 after a courageous battle.

BIBLIOGRAPHY: Zander Hollander, ed., *The Modern Encyclopedia of Basketball* (New York, 1973); Zander Hollander and Alex Sachare, eds., *The Official NBA Basketball Encyclopedia* (New York, 1989); *St. Francis College Basketball Media Guides;* Chet Smith and Marty Wolfson, *Greater Pittsburgh History of Sports* (Pittsburgh, PA, 1969).

                                                        Robert B. Van Atta

STONER, C. Vivian. *See* C. Vivian Stoner Stringer.

STRINGER, C. Vivian Stoner (b. March 16, 1945, Edenborn, PA), college player and coach, is the daughter of Charles H. Stoner, a coal miner and musician, and Thelma Stoner. Stoner graduated in 1966 from German Township High School and in 1970 with a B.S. degree in health and physical education from Slippery Rock College, where she played for the nationally ranked basketball, tennis, field hockey, and softball teams. In 1974, she earned an M.S. degree in physical education from Slippery Rock.

In 1971 Cheyney, PA, State College hired her as assistant professor of recreation, health, and physical education and head women's basketball coach. Stringer remained at Cheyney State 11 seasons, producing a 251–51 win–loss record. Her 28–3 1981–1982 squad, led by All-America Valerie

Walker, made the first-ever NCAA Women's Final Four, losing the championship game, 76–62, to Louisiana Tech University. In 1982, Stringer was named Stayfree NCAA Division I Basketball Coach of the Year. Her other honors included being chosen Women's Basketball Coach of the Year by the PSWA twice and PAIAW once. *Ebony* in 1980 ranked her among the Outstanding Black Women in Sports.

In 1983 the University of Iowa (BTC) named her head women's basketball coach to revive its program. Through the 1993–1994 season, she compiled a 258–67 record for the Hawkeyes. Iowa finished 29–2 in 1987–1988, winning its first outright BTC title and ranking first nationally for eight consecutive weeks. Michelle Edwards was selected WBCA Player of the Year and Iowa's initial First Team All-America. The Hawkeyes fared 21–9 in 1990–1991, 27–4 in 1992–1993, and 21–7 in 1993–1994, ranking third nationally and sharing the BTC crown with Ohio State University in 1992–1993. Iowa reached the 1993 NCAA Final Four, losing the semifinals to Ohio State. BTC Player of the Year awards were earned by Hawkeye stars Franthea Price in 1990 and Toni Foster in 1993. Stringer was named WBCA Basketball Coach of the Year in 1988 and 1993 and BTC Women's Basketball Coach of the Year in 1991 and 1993. In 1993 she received *SI* Women's Basketball Coach of the Year honors and the WBCA Carol Eckman Award for her coaching spirit, integrity, and courage. Stringer made women's basketball more exciting, boosting home attendance. In 1988, 22,157 spectators attended the Iowa–Ohio State game at Carver-Hawkeye Arena, shattering the single-game national women's basketball attendance record.

Altogether, Stringer compiled a 509–118 record through 1993–1994. Her .812 winning percentage ranks as the nation's third best and highest for coaches with over 400 victories. Only four active women's basketball coaches have recorded more victories. In January 1994, Stringer became only the third woman to achieve 500 career victories. No other NCAA Division I women's basketball coach has taken two different teams to the NCAA Final Four. Stringer has promoted the development of women's basketball internationally and organizationally. She coached U.S. teams touring the People's Republic of China in 1981, at the 1985 World University Games, and at the 1989 World Championship zone qualifications. Her team won a bronze medal at the 1991 Pan-American Games in Havana, Cuba. Besides helping start the WBCA, she participates on the Kodak All-America Selection Committee and serves on the Advisory Board of the WSF, ABAUSA, and Nike Shoes.

She married William D. Stringer, an exercise physiologist, in 1971 and has three children, David, Janine (who has meningitis), and Justin. Stringer took a five-week leave of absence from coaching following her husband's sudden death of a heart attack at age 47 in November 1992. Her careful analysis of opposition game plans, meticulously planned practices, brilliant game plans, 97 percent player graduation rate, devotion to charitable organizations, and role as mother best exemplify her.

BIBLIOGRAPHY: Arthur R. Ashe, *A Hard Road to Glory: A History of the African-American Athlete Since 1946* (New York, 1988); Janice A. Beran, letter to David L. Porter, February 15, 1994; Des Moines (IA) *Register*, March 23, 1988, pp. S1, S4; November 28, 1992, pp. S1, S4; March 30, 1993, p. S1; April 3, 1993, pp. S1–S2; January 21, 1994, p. S1; January 29, 1994, p. S1; Cheryl Levitt, Iowa Intercollegiate Athletics, Iowa City, IA, memorandum to David L. Porter, April 13, 1994; *Street & Smith's College Basketball Yearbooks*, 1982–1994.

David L. Porter

SUTTON, Eddie (b. March 12, 1936, Bucklin, KS), college player and coach, graduated from Bucklin High School in 1954 and from Oklahoma State University (BSC), where he earned both the bachelor's (1958) and master's (1959) degrees. Sutton played guard for the legendary Hank Iba (IS), averaging 6.6 points per game in his three-year varsity career.

Sutton's basketball coaching career began as a graduate assistant at Oklahoma State, followed by a 119–51 record as head coach at Tulsa, OK, Central High School from 1960 to 1966. He then coached basketball at Southern Idaho JC, just starting its basketball program. His 83–14 record from 1967 to 1969 there led to his selection as Creighton University (MVC) basketball coach. Sutton's five years at Creighton featured an 82–50 overall record and 2–1 mark in the NCAA tournament. The University of Arkansas (SWC) hired Sutton, who took over a mediocre basketball program averaging under 10 wins a year the previous decade. Sutton made Arkansas a consistent winner, guiding nine NCAA appearances in 11 years and compiling a 260–75 overall mark and 10–9 NCAA record. By nearly tripling attendance to a 9,000 average, Sutton turned Arkansas' home court, Barnhill Arena, into one of the toughest places for visitors to play. His Razorbacks lost only eight games there. During this period, he was named SWC Coach of the Year four times and won that honor twice nationally. Ten Razorbacks, including Sidney Moncrief (IS), made the NBA. Sutton completed his tenure at Arkansas with the highest winning percentage in SWC history.

Unlike the Creighton and Arkansas jobs, Sutton assumed one of the most successful college basketball programs when he joined the University of Kentucky (SEC) as head coach for the 1985–1986 season. He had followed the distinguished Kentucky program by radio as a lad. Kentucky's preeminence was created by fellow Kansan Adolph Rupp (IS). Rupp's successor, Joe B. Hall, continued Kentucky's winning tradition and garnered an NCAA title in 1978. At one of the most demanding posts in college basketball, Sutton enjoyed immediate success with a 32–4 mark his first year. The Wildcats won the SEC regular season and tournament crowns and reached the NCAA Final Eight before losing to LSU. He was named both SEC and national 1986 Coach of the Year. Sutton coached four more years at Kentucky, winning both the 1988 SEC regular season and tournament and resigning in 1989. Sutton's overall 88–39 Kentucky record included his first losing season in 1988–1989 and a 5–3 NCAA tournament mark.

After a one-year absence from basketball coaching, Sutton returned to his alma mater at Oklahoma State. In Sutton's first year, the Cowboys won the 1991 BEC title. Sutton, the first coach to take teams from four different universities to the NCAA tournament, compiled a 526–199 mark in 26 collegiate seasons through the 1993–1994 season. The Cowboys, led by center Bryant Reeves, finished with a 24–10 mark but were upset by the University of Tulsa in the second round of the NCAA tournament.

He married Patsy Wright and has three sons, Steve, Sean, and Scott. Scott played for his father at Oklahoma State, while Sean started for his father at Kentucky.

BIBLIOGRAPHY: Russell Rice, *Kentucky Basketball's Big Blue Machine* (Huntsville, AL, 1987); Alexander Wolff, "For Now He's the Cat's Meow," *SI* 63 (December 16, 1985), pp. 30–32, 36.

Thomas P. Wolf

VAN BREDA KOLFF, Willem Hendrick "Bill" "Butch" (b. October 28, 1922, Glen Ridge, NJ), college and professional player and coach, coached Princeton University (IvL) to the 1965 NCAA basketball Final Four and the Los Angeles Lakers to the NBA finals in 1968 and 1969. Van Breda Kolff has produced a 474–252 college record through 1992–1993 and a 308–354 record in 10 NBA campaigns.

Van Breda Kolff, the son of former Dutch Olympic soccer player and stockbroker Jan Van Breda Kolff, began playing basketball at home in Montclair, NJ. Van Breda Kolff played soccer and basketball in 1941 at Princeton University before flunking out as a sophomore. He served 42 months in the U.S. Marines during World War II and returned to Princeton. Van Breda Kolff captained the 1946 Princeton basketball team and was named All-America in soccer before flunking out a second time. He finished his bachelor's degree at NYU while playing guard for the New York Knicks (NBA). In four seasons from 1946 through 1950 under coach Joe Lapchick (IS), Van Breda Kolff played in 175 games and averaged 4.7 points per game for New York.

Van Breda Kolff began coaching basketball at Lafayette College in 1951 and produced a 68–34 record in four seasons there, earning an NIT berth. He coached basketball at Hofstra University from 1955 to 1962, compiling a 136–43 mark. His greatest success as a college basketball coach, however, came at Princeton University, where he won 103 games and four IvL titles in five years. His 1965 squad, featuring star Bill Bradley (IS), finished third in the NCAA tournament. Van Breda Kolff's 17-year 307–109 cumulative record made him the third winningest active college basketball coach behind Adolph Rupp (IS) and John Wooden (IS).

Van Breda Kolff in 1968 joined the Los Angeles Lakers (NBA), winners of only 36 games the previous year, as head basketball coach. Van Breda Kolff's Lakers captured consecutive WC titles, triumphing in 52 and 55 games, respectively, but lost in the NBA finals both seasons to the Boston Celtics. With the Lakers, he coached stars Jerry West (IS), Elgin Baylor (IS), and Wilt Chamberlain (IS).

Friction with Chamberlain forced Van Breda Kolff to accept a head basketball coaching assignment with the Detroit Pistons (NBA) in 1969. He coached the Pistons two seasons, producing a franchise-best 45–37 mark his second season, but left Detroit 12 games into the 1971 season. The Phoenix Suns (NBA) hired him in 1972 and quickly fired him 8 games into that campaign. Van Breda Kolff coached the Memphis Tams (ABA) in 1973 and moved to the New Orleans Jazz (NBA) the following year. He produced a 93–135 record in three seasons with New Orleans until being fired in 1977. Star Pete Maravich (IS) played under Van Breda Kolff at New Orleans.

After leaving the NBA ranks, Van Breda Kolff spent two years as basketball coach and athletic director at the University of New Orleans and two seasons as basketball coach with the New Orleans Pride (WPBL). He held several jobs out of basketball and coached high school basketball before returning to coach basketball at Lafayette College (ECC) in 1985. In 1989, Van Breda Kolff returned to coach basketball at Hofstra University (ECC) and retired after the 1993–1994 season. Upon returning to college coaching, Van Breda Kolff compiled a 119–107 record at New Orleans, Lafayette, and Hofstra through 1993–1994. He and his wife, Florence (Smith) Van Breda Kolff, have four children, Jan, who coaches basketball at Vanderbilt University, and daughters Kaatje, Karen, and Kristina.

BIBLIOGRAPHY: Ronald L. Mendell, *Who's Who in Basketball* (New Rochelle, NY, 1973); William Nack, "I Made My Own Bed, I've Got to Lie in it," *SI* 60 (February 20, 1984), pp. 60–76; David S. Neft and Richard M. Cohen, eds., *The Sports Encyclopedia: Pro Basketball*, 4th ed. (New York, 1991); *1994 NCAA Basketball;* Gary Nuhn, "ECC," *Street and Smith's College and Prep Basketball*, 1993–1994; Jack Olsen, "The Hedonist Prophet of the Spartan Game," *SI* 29 (September 23, 1968), pp. 28–39.

Brian L. Laughlin

WILKES, Glenn Newton (b. November 28, 1928, Mansfield, GA), college player and coach, served as basketball coach at Stetson University for 36 years and authored several books on basketball coaching. Wilkes compiled a career 551–436 record at Stetson from 1958 to 1993.

Wilkes, the son of Homer Wilkes and Dorothy Wilkes, attended Mansfield, GA, public schools and played basketball at Mercer University in Macon, GA, where he graduated with a Bachelor of Arts in physical education in 1950.

Wilkes coached basketball at Brewton-Parker College in Mt. Vernon, GA, in 1950 and 1951 and served in the U.S. Army from 1951 to 1953, attaining the rank of sergeant. After leaving the U.S. Army, Wilkes coached basketball at Baker County High School in Newton, GA, for one season. Wilkes returned to Brewton-Parker College as basketball coach in 1954 and remained there until 1957 while completing his M.A. degree at Peabody College. In 1957, Stetson University in DeLand, FL, hired Wilkes as head basketball coach. Wilkes married his wife Jan in 1957 and has five children.

Wilkes served 36 seasons as head basketball coach at Stetson from 1957 to 1993. As of 1993, his 551 wins ranked him twenty-third on the list of most major college basketball coaching victories. During the mid-1960s, Wilkes earned his Ph.D. in physical education from Stetson. He served as athletic director from 1965 to 1985. His teams competed in the NAIA until 1966, joined the NCAA Division II in 1966, and entered the NCAA Division I in 1973. Wilkes's first Division I squad, his single best team, produced a 22–4 record. Wilkes's clubs remained independent until joining the TAAC in 1987. Wilkes has produced two NAIA All-Americas, Joel Hancock and Lamar Deaver, and one NCAA Division II All-America, Earnest Killum. His teams reached the NAIA championship tournament five times (1953, 1957, 1960, 1962, 1963), made the NCAA Division II tournament in 1967 and 1970, and captured third place in 1971.

Wilkes's longevity has earned him numerous distinctions among college basketball coaches. He coached 987 games, twelfth highest in college basketball history. One dozen mentors have coached more years, but only 9, including Adolph Rupp (IS), Ray Meyer (IS), and Henry Iba (IS), have remained as many or more years at one school. Only 40 coaches spanning all college classifications have surpassed Wilkes in career victories.

Wilkes wrote several books on basketball coaching, his first being *Winning Basketball Strategy* (1959). His third book, *Men's Basketball*, published in 1969, appeared in five editions. He also authored *The Basketball Coach's Complete Handbook* (1962) and *Fundamentals of Coaching Basketball* (1982). Besides writing several books and articles, Wilkes has produced motivational tapes for coaches and athletes. Wilkes still teaches physical education at Stetson and helps arrange exhibition games between college and foreign basketball teams.

BIBLIOGRAPHY: *CA* 17 (1986), p. 483; Brian L. Laughlin, interview with Jim Jordan, Stetson University, January 4, 1994; *Official 1994 NCAA Basketball; Stetson University 1993–94 Basketball Media Guide; Who's Who in the South and Southwest*, 1980.

Brian L. Laughlin

WOOLPERT, Philipp D. "Phil" "The Thin Man of the Hilltop" (b. December 19, 1915, Danville, KY; d. May 5, 1987, Sequim, WA), college and professional player and coach, graduated from Manual Arts High School in Los Angeles, CA, in 1933 and earned a bachelor's degree in 1940 from Loyola University of Los Angeles, where he played basketball as a forward-center under coach James Needles. Woolpert's teammates included later coaching rivals Pete Newell (IS) and Scotty McDonald. Loyola combined a tight, aggressive defense with a disciplined, patterned offense. Woolpert, a tall, thin, nervous, serious-minded intellectual, coached basketball at St. Ignatius Prep School in San Francisco, CA, from 1940 to 1950.

In 1950 the University of San Francisco, a Jesuit school, named Woolpert to replace Newell as head basketball coach. The Dons did not have a full-time assistant coach or their own gymnasium, practicing at St. Ignatius and playing home games at the Cow Palace. Woolpert, an introverted defensive genius, employed a tight, aggressive press, disdaining frills, showmanship, and racehorse basketball. San Francisco struggled to a 30–41 mark during Woolpert's first three seasons. Woolpert recruited several local African-American prospects, who could play pressure defense and perform well academically. Minimal budgets mandated that players be recruited from the San Francisco area, not noted for its prep basketball. African-American recruits included Bill Russell (IS), a tall, lanky center who had not started at McClymonds High School in Oakland, K. C. Jones, a football star at Commerce High School in San Francisco, and Hal Perry. Woolpert taught Russell how to rebound and block shots, Jones how to renew his confidence after a ruptured appendix, and Perry how to play tough defense. Woolpert produced his first winning season with a 14–7 mark in 1953–1954, Russell's sophomore campaign.

After losing the third game of the 1954–1955 season to UCLA, 47–40, San Francisco charged through their remaining 26 games without defeat. The 28–1 Dons won the CBA title and led the nation in defense for the second consecutive year. Russell tallied 622 points, grabbed 594 rebounds, and blocked many shots, vaulting San Francisco to first place AP and UP national rankings. In the 1955 NCAA finals at Kansas City, MO, the Dons triumphed over La Salle University, 77–63. Russell, the tournament MVP, scored 118 points in 5 games and earned First Team All-America honors, while Jones sparkled defensively.

San Francisco repeated as NCAA champions in 1955–1956 with a 29–0 record, capturing the CIT and NYHF and overwhelming all CBA rivals. San Francisco defeated all opponents by at least 7 points, leading the nation in scoring (87.3 points per game average) and ranking second defensively (55.5-point average). Russell grabbed 607 rebounds, blocked many shots, and scored 597 points, while Jones and Perry played stellar defense. San Francisco defeated the University of Iowa, 83–71, to take the NCAA crown again at Evanston, IL, as Russell scored 26 points and snared 27 rebounds. The Dons had attained 55 consecutive victories, retaining first place AP and UP national rankings. "I can't imagine a better team," Woolpert acknowledged. "We had fine balance, excellent shooting, and tremendous defense." Russell and Jones, both First Team All-Americas, made the victorious 1956 U.S. Olympic team.

Woolpert guided San Francisco to a 21–7 mark in 1956–1957. The University of Illinois snapped the Dons' winning streak at 60 games, but San Francisco repeated as CBA titlists and reached the NCAA semifinals at Kansas City. Led by All-America Mike Farmer, the 24–4 Dons won another CBA title in 1957–1958, led the nation defensively, and ranked among the top four. San Francisco slumped to a 6–20 mark in 1958–1959, causing Woolpert to resign as head coach. The pressures of coaching, big-time recruiting, noisy crowds, ticket hustlers, alumni, and zone defenses, along with a back injury, discouraged him.

Woolpert had guided the Dons to a 153–78 record, three NCAA Final Four appearances, and two NCAA championships in nine seasons. The Dons' 60-game consecutive winning streak stood until UCLA broke it in the 1970s. Woolpert, UP Coach of the Year in 1955 and 1956 and NABC president, dared to start black players when other coaches demurred. His innovative defense and textbook press were adopted successfully by Newell at the University of California and John Wooden (IS) at UCLA.

After coaching the San Francisco Saints of the short-lived ABL in 1961–1962, Woolpert coached the University of San Diego to a 90–90 record from 1962 to 1968. Woolpert, who boasted a 243–168 composite coaching record, served as athletic director at San Francisco from 1951 to 1959 and San Diego from 1962 to 1972. Woolpert and his wife Mary had three daughters, Mary Ann, Teresa, and Lorraine, and settled in Sequim, WA, where he grew vegetables and drove a local school bus. In 1992, the Naismith Memorial Basketball Hall of Fame posthumously enshrined him. Woolpert also was inducted into the University of San Francisco and University of San Diego Halls of Fame.

BIBLIOGRAPHY: Zander Hollander, *The Modern Encyclopedia of Basketball* (New York, 1973); Neil D. Isaacs, *All the Moves: A History of College Basketball* (Philadelphia, PA, 1975); John D. McCallum, *College Basketball, U.S.A.* (New York, 1978); Jim Scott, "Success Story at U.S.F.," *Sport* 25 (March 1958), pp. 28–29, 64–67; *TSN*, May 18, 1987, p. 51; Alexander M. Weyand, *The Cavalcade of Basketball* (New York, 1960).

David L. Porter

BOWLING

ADAMEK, Donna (b. February 1, 1957, Apple Valley, CA), bowler, began her road to professional bowling in 1975, when she was listed as a "Star of Tomorrow" by the ACUI, sponsors of intercollegiate bowling tournaments. Adamek has won 19 titles and earned $473,984 since 1975, ranking as the fifth leading money winner on the WPBA and LPBT all-time leaders list in 1992. She joins Patty Costello* and Lisa Wagner* as the only women to have captured more than 18 career titles. The BoWAA membership honored Adamek as Woman Bowler of the Year in 1978, 1979, 1980, and 1981. She took the BPAA U.S. Open tournament championship in 1978 and 1981, WIBC Queens title in 1979 and 1980, and WIBC Open Division Doubles championship in 1981 and 1982, making the top team in 1981 and 1987. Adamek stands among three women to have won the WPBA and LPBT crowns three times, accomplishing it consecutively from 1978 through 1980, and claimed the Sam's Town Invitational title in 1988. After competing in this tournament in 1989, however, she was advised to take some time off to recuperate from nagging back trouble.

Her back grew stronger as she participated in the LPBT 1991 fall tour. Adamek placed second at the Ebonite Fall Classic and won the Columbia 300 Delaware Open. That year, she recorded the second-highest average among the LPBT, averaging 211.4785 for 769 games. Adamek was edged out by another right-hander, Leanne Barrette, who averaged 211.4787. They both made the 1991 *TWB* magazine All-America team. On the LPBT 1992 Spring–Summer tour, she finished second at the New Orleans Classic. Adamek was recently appointed manager of AMF Rocket Bowl, a 32-lane facility in Chatsworth, CA, and still plans to compete in tournaments at her own pace while expanding her career into management.

BIBLIOGRAPHY: *AmBC Yearbook & Media Guide*, 1993; Karen Sytsma, "Bowling's Fab Five," *TWB* 56 (February 1992), pp. 15–18; *WIBC Media Guide*, 1992.

Charlene E. Agne-Traub

AULBY, Mike (b. March 25, 1960, Indianapolis, IN), bowler, is a superb left-handed professional and currently serves as PBA president. The PBA tour veteran since 1978 was elected by his peers to the presidential office, where he represents the PBA at regional, national, and senior-level tours. The position also gives him the opportunity to attend many charitable functions in communities across the United States. He and his wife Tami have one child, Chris. His many professional honors include 22 PBA championships and a fourth-place ranking in lifetime earnings with $1,404,710. Only ten PBA bowlers have become millionaires in career earnings.

Aulby's professional career began just seven months after his 1978 graduation from Franklin Central High School in Indianapolis. His early success produced PBA Rookie of the Year honors for 1979. Aulby won the PBA national championship tournament in 1979 and 1985, joining four other professionals to have triumphed two or more times. He achieved the top PBA earnings for 1985 and 1989, taking BoWAA Male Bowler of the Year accolades. *BoM* named Aulby to their All-America First Team for 1980, 1984, 1985, and 1989 and their Second Team in 1987. To no surprise, he was chosen 1980's Bowler of the Decade by this same publication. He frequently contributes instructional articles to the *BoM* to help league bowlers improve their game. He concluded that decade by winning both the AmBC Masters tournament and BPAA U.S. Open in 1989.

He continues bowling on the PBA tour in the 1990s, making approximately 35 tournament appearances a year while performing his public relations and liaison duties as PBA president.

BIBLIOGRAPHY: *AmBC Yearbook & Media Guide*, 1993; Jeff Clarkson, "An Early Vintage," *BoD* 7 (January–February 1993), pp. 36–38, 40; Dick Denny, "Mike Aulby's Amazing Comeback," *BoD* 8 (July–August 1989), pp. 42–44; Matt Fiorito, "Mike Aulby: Men's Pro Bowler of the Year," *BoD* 11 (March–April 1990), pp. 16–18.

Charlene E. Agne-Traub

COSTELLO, Patty (b. May 8, 1947, Scranton, PA), bowler, remains one of only four women professional bowlers to have won more than 18 career titles. Through 1992, this fine left-hander has captured 25 titles and ranks fifteenth in career earnings on the LPBT with $242,321. The BoWAA members honored her as Woman Bowler of the Year in 1972 and 1976, while the October 1976 issue of *TWB* magazine named her to the 1975–1976 All-America team. In 1976, Costello won the BPAA U.S. Open tournament, capturing the $2,000 first-place prize. She stands as the only three-time champion of the WPBA national tournament, triumphing in 1971, 1972, and 1976, and led the WPBA in earnings in 1970, 1972, and 1976, garnering

$9,317 in 1970, $11,350 in 1972, and $39,585 in 1976. Costello won the WIBC Open Division team title in 1970 and 1972. The LPBT named her Player of the Year in 1985, the same year she won the LPBT Tournament of Champions, now called the Sam's Town Tournament of Champions. In 1993 she placed second at the WIBC Queens tournament.

Costello received the ultimate honor for any professional sports performer, being inducted into the National Bowling Hall of Fame's WIBC Superior Performance Hall in 1989. Many visitors view her photo and accomplishments at the National Bowling Hall of Fame and Museum in St. Louis, MO. This national museum honors both women and men who have made a significant impact on bowling. Costello well deserves her place of honor in this fine landmark to bowling history.

BIBLIOGRAPHY: *AmBC Yearbook & Media Guide*, 1993; "It's Patty Again in Miami Classic," *TWB* 40 (October 1976), p. 42; *WIBC Media Guide*, 1992.

                                                          Charlene E. Agne-Traub

HOLMAN, Marshall "The Medford Meteor" (b. September 29, 1954, San Francisco, CA), bowler, is the son of Phil Holman, a Jewish disc jockey, and has lived in Medford, OR, since 1959. Holman, who graduated from Medford High School, began competing in junior bowling leagues at age 12 and joined his first adult league four years later, averaging 190. The next year his bowling average jumped dramatically to 220.

The brash, cocky, short-tempered Holman, among the most animated, controversial professional bowlers in history, joined the PBA tour in 1974 and won the Fresno Open the next year. In 1976, the 21-year-old became the youngest kegler to capture the Firestone Tournament of Champions. "Winning that tournament," Holman recalled, "was unreal. Nobody expected me to make the TV show, much less win." His most exciting victory came in the 1977 Brunswick World Open, where he threw three consecutive strikes to edge Pete Couture by a pin. He won four titles in 1979, trailing only Mark Roth (IS) in earnings and becoming only the third bowler to ever earn $100,000 in a single year. Holman and Roth both capitalized on hooking the ball back from the right side. The 1980s brought Holman Bowler of the Decade honors and 10 more victories, including the 1981 and 1986 BPAA U.S. Open tournaments and 1986 Firestone Tournament of Champions crown. The latter triumph vaulted his career earnings above $1 million, a figure only bowlers Earl Anthony (IS) and Roth had achieved. Holman, who also enjoys golf, won the 1987 Bowler of the Year award and ranks as the PBA's all-time leading money winner with over $1.6 million through 1993. Besides enjoying eight $100,000 seasons, he placed second five times in annual earnings. Through 1990, he finished among the top five 109 times with 21 victories, 32 seconds, 16 thirds, 21 fourths, and 19 fifths.

Holman consistently has ranked among the top 10 in bowling averages and has posted the high average on three different occasions, bowling 215 or better for more than 1,000 competitive games each time. He leaps, clenches his fists, waves his arms and legs in various ways, and yells and gestures at the pins when he bowls. Many bowling fans find his emotional displays entertaining, but others dislike his antics. In 1980, PBA officials suspended him 10 weeks for his antics. The five-foot-nine-inch, 155-pound right-hander, who rolls one of the strongest balls on the PBA tour and possesses a strong mental drive to succeed, has excelled in specialty television shows, winning $169,000 in the 1988 and 1989 shootouts. The 12-time *BoM* All-America selection was elected to the PBA Hall of Fame in his first year of eligibility in 1990 and to the Jewish Sports Hall of Fame. His goal remains to win the PBA National Championship, the one major bowling title that has eluded him. He and his longtime girlfriend, Terry Chouinard, reside in Medford.

BIBLIOGRAPHY: Mark Baker, "Friend to Friend," *BoJ* 78 (July 1990), pp. 38, 40, 42–44, 46; Marshall Holman file, NaBC Hall of Fame, Greendale, WI; Joe LoVerde, "Mr. Nice Guy?" *BoJ* 80 (July 1992), pp. 84–86; Mark Miller, "Marshall Holman . . . Not Ready for Social Security Just Yet," *Bowling* 58 (April–May 1991), pp. 35–37; Chuck Pezzano, letter to David L. Porter, February 12, 1994; "What, Me Slump?" *BoJ* 77 (August 1989), pp. 50, 52, 54, 56–57, 60–61.

David L. Porter

NORRIS, Joseph John "Joe" (b. February 10, 1908, Springfield, IL), bowler, is the son of Anton Norris, a coal miner and food store operator, and Margaret Norris and grew up in Schenectady, NY, and Detroit, MI. He graduated from Cass Tech High School in Detroit in 1924, around the time his parents separated, and studied architecture nights for two semesters at Wayne State University. The 5-foot-11½-inch, 180-pound Norris worked as a pin boy at the Fairview Recreation bowling lanes, meat market sales clerk, and production clerk for Fisher Body auto parts in Detroit. From 1927 to 1946, he supervised assembly lines at Briggs Body auto parts.

Norris finished fourth in the all-events at the 1927 AmBC Tournament and helped the Palace Recreation team finish third at the 1931 AmBC Tournament. At the 1932 AmBC Tournament, he attained seventh in singles and helped the Chene-Trombly team place fifth. In 1933, his Young's Coca-Cola team finished sixth at the AmBC Tournament. Norris, among the greatest all-time bowling team captains, organized the Stroh's Bohemian Beer team in 1933. Under his captaincy through 1946, Stroh's won the 1934 AmBC Tournament championship, placed eighth in the 1937 AmBC Tournament championship and ninth in the 1946 AmBC Tournament championship, and captured five other national team titles between 1934 and 1945. Stroh's in 1936 became the first team to wear white uniforms and carry white bowling bags and made extensive exhibition tours. Stroh's won numerous national and sectional titles, inspiring other nationally sponsored teams.

Norris moved in 1946 to Chicago, IL, as assistant service manager for the Brunswick Company in AmBC Tournament lane installation and served as general service manager from 1950 to 1963. His company popularized bowling nationally by installing and servicing well-lighted alleys with automatic pin-spotters. Norris captained the Brunswick Mineralites and bowled for the Tri-Par Radio, Fox Deluxe Beer, and Hamm's Beer teams. At AmBC Tournaments, he finished fifth in all events in 1947 and ninth in singles in 1948. In 1954, Tri-Par captured both the team and team all-events titles at AmBC Tournaments. Eight years later, Hamm's placed eighth in the Classic team event at AmBC Tournaments. Since 1963, he has performed numerous exhibitions and clinics and served as an international goodwill bowling ambassador.

The superbly conditioned, dedicated Norris bowls three times a week and carries a 194 average for 62 AmBC Tournaments, averaging 197 the last decade. Norris, who has a Masters 100-game average of 194, on March 12, 1986, became the third bowler in AmBC Tournament history to knock down 100,000 pins and on March 10, 1992, set the record for all-time pinfall with 111,117. He was elected in 1954 to the AmBC Hall of Fame and also belongs to the Michigan Amateur Sports Hall of Fame (1973), Detroit Sports Hall of Fame (1958), San Diego Sports Hall of Fame (1985), Southern California Sports Hall of Fame (1990), and National Senior Sports Hall of Fame. *BoM* named him to its Second Team, All-America, Pre-1950, while *BoJ* designated him First Team, All-America from 1939 to 1946. His other honors included the HoC Sportsman Award in 1964, John O. Martino Award in 1983, SCBWA Merle Matthews Memorial Award in 1985, and Raymon Kowalski Memorial Award in 1989. Norris, who has bowled one 300 game and a 799 series in AmBC Tournaments, served as president of the AmBC Hall of Fame Board from 1971 to 1973. He married Wilda "Billie" Haynie, a dancer and photographer, on June 6, 1933. They have resided in San Diego, CA, since 1963 and have no children. Norris initially met his wife when his car crashed into her mother's back car bumper. When Billie yelled at him, he replied, "But, honey, I can see you're beautiful."

BIBLIOGRAPHY: *AmBC Yearbook & Media Guide*, 1993; Dan Harbst, "Just Color Him An Ordinary Joe," *BoJ* 78 (December 1990), pp. 74–76; Joseph Norris, letter to David L. Porter, March 8, 1994; Joseph Norris file, AmBC Hall of Fame, Greendale, WI; Chuck Pezzano, letter to David L. Porter, February 11, 1994; Bruce Pluckhahn, "Not Your Average Joe," *BoJ* 80 (December 1992), pp. 57–60; Don Snyder, "Give This Man a Hand," *Bowling* 59 (February–March 1992), pp. 20–25.

David L. Porter

RATHGEBER, Lisa. *See* Lisa Rathgeber Wagner.

SALVINO, Carmen Mario "Spook" (b. November 23, 1933, Chicago, IL), bowler, is the son of Mike Salvino and Theresa (DeVito) Salvino and attended Chicago public schools. He has participated in professional bowling for 42 years and remains involved both on and off the lanes. Salvino, who performs in regular and senior tournaments when his bowling research and development business permits, proved instrumental in obtaining a patent in 1982 on the dynamic balance of a ball and licensed his technology to Ebonite. Consequently, he helped design Ebonite's "Thunderbolt" and "Thunderbolt D/B" balls. In 1982, he also joined an elite group of bowling professionals who have earned more than $500,000 in their careers.

Salvino's bowling career began in 1949 in a Chicago high school league, where he held a 203 average at age 16. He won his first AmBC title in 1954 and had accumulated 19 PBA titles from 1961 through 1988. Salvino set a record by competing in more than 700 PBA tournaments and still fares well. Salvino in 1980 broke the PBA record for 16 games, compiling a 251 average (4,015 pins). Salvino's phenomenal feat, accomplished at age 46, remains the record. His achievements are noted in the National Bowling Hall of Fame Register in St. Louis. He has been enshrined in the PBA (1976), AmBC, Illinois (1974), Chicago, and National Italian-American Sports Hall of Fame. *BoM* named him to their All-America First Team in 1975 and 1976 and their Second Team in 1963, 1967, and 1973. Salvino, a PBA charter member, also has served as its president. His AmBC tournament average for the past 30 years is 200, 4 pins below his 100-game Masters average. Salvino has rolled seven 300 games, with his highest series being 846. Salvino's most memorable match came in his 846 series, bowled on television against Tony Lindemann. This highest series ever bowled on television remains part of a tape, "Bowling Stars."

Salvino shows no signs of slowing down and provides model leadership for league participants, who know bowling is a lifetime sport for all age groups. Numerous articles delineate this energetic personality. He hopes to keep bowling well into his eighties, patterning after the renowned Andy Varipapa.* Salvino married Virginia Morelli in May 1955 and has one daughter, Corinne. Salvino's love for them is matched by his devotion to bowling.

BIBLIOGRAPHY: *AmBC Yearbook & Media Guide*, 1993; Joe LoVerde, "Carmen Salvino: The Match I'll Never Forget," *BoD* 8 (July–August 1990), pp. 46–48; Carmen Salvino, "Carmen on Carmen: Keeping the Ball Rolling," *BoD* 11 (March–April 1993), pp. 46–48; *WWA*, 40th ed. (1978–1979), p. 2829.

                                                            Charlene E. Agne-Traub

VARIPAPA, Andrew "Andy" (b. March 31, 1891, Carfizzi, Italy; d. August 25, 1984, Hempstead, NY), bowler, was the son of Frank Varipapa, a wealthy farmer who died in 1894, and Concetta Varipapa and emigrated at age 11 with his mother, stepfather Frank, and brother Joseph to Brooklyn, NY. He played semiprofessional baseball, boxed briefly, and began bowling in 1907.

Varipapa worked as an errand boy and in a butcher shop and sold insurance for John Hancock Company, attending night school at Pratt Institute. After serving as a toolmaker in the Brooklyn Navy Yard from 1917 to 1920, Varipapa owned the Empire Billiard Academy in Brooklyn from 1920 to 1926 and managed a bowling alley at the Schubert Theatre Building in Brooklyn from 1926 to 1931. He won the 1928 Long Island Singles bowling championship and joined Dwyer's Major League in New York City in 1929. Varipapa first attracted national attention in 1930, when he teamed with world champion Joe Falcaro in a doubles match against AmBC champion Charles Riley and Philadelphia titleholder Jim Murgie in New York and Philadelphia, PA. Varipapa averaged 234 for 42 games.

The five-foot-five-inch, 157-pound Varipapa, the greatest showman in bowling history, developed and popularized trick shot bowling and starred in the first bowling film, *Strikes and Spares*, in 1934. Besides making numerous films and being a prominent bowling instructor, he staged bowling exhibitions, rolled countless match games, and pioneered successful nationwide tours. Varipapa's trick shooting often overshadowed his almost legendary achievements on the lanes. He participated in his first bowling tournament in 1932, averaging 210 in 128 games in eight cities. From 1938 to 1947, he led the nation with a 204.72 bowling average for 10 consecutive AmBC tournaments. Varipapa won the 1946 and 1947 All-Star/U.S. Open tournaments in Chicago, IL, at ages 55 and 56, becoming the first bowler to capture that most prestigious title consecutive years. In 1948, he narrowly missed winning a third successive All-Star/U.S. Open tournament. He and AmBC Hall of Famer Lou Campi took the BPAA doubles crown in 1947 and 1948. Varipapa's Brunswick Mineralites team placed second in AmBC tournaments in 1947, the same year he ranked sixth in singles (717 average) and tenth in doubles with Graz Castellano in AmBC tournaments. In 1952, he finished second in Bud Light Masters AmBC tournaments, compiling a 32-game 198.8 average.

Varipapa, a loquacious, smiling, friendly, prideful kegler who bowled one AmBC-sanctioned 300 game and over 80 perfect games altogether, carried a 184 average for 38 years in AmBC tournaments and compiled a Masters 54-game 190 average. He popularized bowling on national television, rolling nine consecutive strikes to break the Phillies Jackpot in 1959. The quotable Varipapa, who often boasted, "I am the greatest," also enhanced bowling purses and conducted international bowling clinics. At age 78, he developed painful wrist and arm problems that prevented his bowling right-handed. He learned to bowl left-handed, averaging 180 within 18 months. In 1981, the "That's Incredible" television show featured Varipapa's incredible control of a bowling ball and appealing, witty chatter.

"Varipapa amazed, astounded, amused, and instructed the bowling world for more than 70 years." The 1948 BWAA Bowler of the Year was elected in 1957 to the AmBC Hall of Fame and in 1980 became the first bowler enshrined in the Italian-American Sports Hall of Fame. He also belonged to the NYSBA Hall of Fame, NYCBA Hall of Fame (1951), and ELIBA Hall of Fame (1973). *BoM* named him to its First Team All-America, Pre-1950. His other achievements included the BPAA All-Star Award of Merit (1963), BWAA John O. Martino Award in 1977, and the Brunswick Memorial World Open Award in 1981. He married his wife, Alice, on June 17, 1917, and had three children, Constance, Frank, and Lorraine.

BIBLIOGRAPHY: *AmBC Yearbook and Media Guide*, 1993; "Andy the Great Proves That He Is," *Life* 23 (December 29, 1947), pp. 62–63; "Bowling's Varipapa Dies," *Bowling* 51 (October 1984), p. 36; Bob Cherin, "Varipapa the Magnificent," *BoJ* 69 (December 1981), pp. 54–55, 57–59; "Greatest Bowler," *Time* 49 (May 5, 1947), p. 79; *The Lincoln Library of Sports Champions*, vol. 13 (Columbus, OH, 1974); *NYT*, December 15, 1947, p. 38; August 31, 1948, p. 20; August 27, 1984, p. A16; Chuck Pezzano, "Andy Varipapa," *Bowling* 49 (December 1982), pp. 20–23; Chuck Pezzano, letter to David L. Porter, February 11, 1994; Andrew Varipapa file, AmBC Hall of Fame, Greendale, WI; John Walter, "Andy Varipapa," *BoM* (June 1951), pp. 6–7, 26.

David L. Porter

WAGNER, Lisa Rathgeber (b. May 19, 1961, Palmetto, FL), bowler, was named 1980's Bowler of the Decade by *TWB, BoJ*, and *Bowling* magazine. Her successful bowling career began in an outstanding junior program, coached by her parents. Her first year as a professional came in 1980, when she earned LPBT and WPBA Rookie of the Year honors. In 1988, she became the first woman bowler to earn $100,000 in a single year and captured the women's BPAA U.S. Open championship. Wagner's honors included being named BoWAA Bowler of the Year in 1983, 1986, and 1988 and LPBT Player of the Year in 1983, 1985, and 1988. During the 1980s, *TWB* magazine named Wagner an All-America team member seven times.

Wagner, a fine right-hander, earned WIBC Championship Tournament titles in doubles in 1982 and in all-events in 1988 and garnered the LPBT tour championship for 1983, 1988, and 1989. Wagner joined Donna Adamek* and Patty Costello* as the only women to have earned more than 18 career titles. In November 1993, Wagner captured the Hammer Midwest Open for her twenty-eighth professional title in just 14 LPBT seasons. Wagner's twenty-eighth victory enabled her to become the first female bowler to have earned over $500,000 altogether with $543,277.

She married Kent Wagner, a successful professional bowler, in 1984. She possesses excellent form, demonstrating consistency in rolling the ball on line, and emphasizes rhythm instead of muscle power to ensure consistency in hitting shots on any lane condition. Her style provides a worthwhile example for the average bowler to emulate.

BIBLIOGRAPHY: "Recap Sheet," *TWB* 57 (May–June 1993), p. 54; Karen Sytsma, "What Everyone Should Know About the System of Bowling," *TWB* 55 (May–June 1991), pp. 34–39; Lisa Wagner, "Let Tempo Generate a Powerful Shot," *BoD* 7 (January–February 1990), pp. 22–24; *WIBC Media Guide*, 1992.

Charlene E. Agne-Traub

BOXING

BARRY, Jimmy "Chicago's Little Tiger" (b. March 7, 1870, Chicago, IL; d. April 4, 1943, Chicago, IL), boxer, was one of the true little giants of the ring in the 1890s. The diminutive, five-foot-two-inch Barry, who never weighed more than 113 pounds, possessed power rare in boxers of his stature. His knockout abilities earned him two world titles but ultimately stifled his career.

His first-round knockout victory over Fred Larson in Chicago in 1891 began his undefeated ring career. In his first year as a professional boxer, Barry recorded 15 straight victories. Twelve more wins followed in 1892, with another 10 in 1893. Barry's final triumph of 1893, a December 5 knockout of Jack Levy in 17 rounds at Roby, IN, enabled him to capture the world 100-pound championship, then the flyweight limit.

Barry's unchallenged successes continued throughout 1894, as he recorded seven more wins. His most severe test came against Italian-American fan favorite Casper Leon on September 15. In a fiercely fought bout, Barry emerged the winner by a twenty-eighth-round knockout. During Barry's glory days, the world titles in the lighter weight classifications were not highly regarded and carried no real monetary value. Barry consequently never defended his 100-pound crown but continued to record victories. Barry fought Walter Croot, a master defensive boxer from England, on December 6, 1897, to take the world bantamweight title, vacated by George Dixon.

In a tremendous 20-round contest at London's NSC, Croot used his technical skills to keep Barry at bay. Until the final round, Barry trailed the British fighter by a large margin. In a surprise move, Croot opened round 20 by physically slugging it out with Barry. The strategy proved costly, as Barry landed a ferocious right cross that knocked the Englishman cold. Tragically, Croot died later that night from head injuries. Barry was charged with manslaughter but was exonerated by the magistrate.

Croot's death deeply affected Barry, who never again fought with such fury. Although engaging in nine more fights in 1899, Barry fought passively to eight draws. Until his death, Barry remained haunted by the death of Croot, his greatest opponent.

Barry's overall record included 59 wins, nine draws, and two no-decisions in 70 bouts. Thirty-nine of his wins came by knockout. Although the draws on his record tarnish his accomplishments, Barry ranks among a select few world champions never to lose a professional bout.

BIBLIOGRAPHY: Sam Andre and Nat Fleischer, *A Pictorial History of Boxing* (New York, 1975); Herbert G. Goldman, *1986–87 Ring Record Book and Boxing Encyclopedia* (New York, 1987); Gilbert Odd, *The Encyclopedia of Boxing* (Secaucus, NJ, 1989); Bert Randolph Sugar, *The 100 Greatest Boxers of All Time* (New York, 1984).

John Robertson

BENITEZ, Wilfred "The Dragon" (b. September 12, 1958, Bronx, NY), boxer, was the youngest fighter ever to win a professional championship title. Benitez, encouraged to box by his enthusiastic father, Gregorio, turned professional just after his fifteenth birthday. In his professional debut, Benitez scored a first-round knockout over Hiram Santiago in San Juan, Puerto Rico, on November 22, 1973. Benitez, of Puerto Rican ancestry, fought often in the San Juan vicinity and quickly became a fan favorite among his people. Benitez's cagy defensive style frustrated many opponents, who found it difficult to land meaningful blows.

Benitez remained undefeated through 1975 with 25 consecutive victories, earning a world title fight against defending WBA junior welterweight champion Antonio Cervantes. Despite being just 17 years old, Benitez easily outboxed Cervantes, a talented tactician, to win his first championship on March 6, 1976, in San Juan. To date, no professional boxer has claimed a title at a younger age. From 1976 to 1978, Benitez successfully defended his junior welterweight title three times and defeated top-ranking welterweights Harold Weston, Randy Shields, and Bruce Curry. On January 14, 1979, Benitez won his second world title by easily outboxing defending WBC welterweight champion Carlos Palomino in San Juan.

After a successful title defense against Harold Weston in March, Benitez lost his WBC welterweight title in a thrilling bout against Sugar Ray Leonard (IS) on November 30, 1979. Benitez, who frequently avoided training, later admitted he had only spent nine days in the gymnasium preparing for the skilled Leonard. Nevertheless, it took Leonard until round 15 to stop Benitez. Benitez subsequently scored three straight comeback wins and then knocked out England's Maurice Hope on May 23, 1981, in Las Vegas, NV, to win his third title, the WBC superwelterweight crown. Successful defenses followed against Carlos Santos and Roberto Duran. Benitez lost his WBC superwelterweight title to Thomas Hearns (S) in New Orleans, LA, on December 3, 1982. Hearns clearly outboxed Benitez, signaling the end of Benitez's once-masterful ring skills.

From 1983 to 1986, Benitez engaged in 11 bouts and lost all four times he faced quality opponents. After stopping Benitez in two rounds in 1984, Davey Moore accurately noted that 25-year-old Benitez was "a young man but an old fighter." By the end of 1986, Benitez had won 51 of 58 career fights and was clearly declining. Financial problems forced Benitez to remain active into the 1990s, when his losses became more frequent. It is a sad legacy to a boxer, whose skills once inspired *TR*'s Bert Sugar to write, "If boxing is chess played on bodies instead of boards, then Wilfred Benitez is its Capablanca, its Spassky, its Fischer."

BIBLIOGRAPHY: Richard Baker, "Clinging to Yesterday: The Sad Saga of Wilfred Benitez," *TR* 70 (April 1991), pp. 32–33; Gregorio Benitez, "Why Benitez Won't Win," *TR* 58 (November 1979), p. 22; Steven Farhood, "International Report," *KOM* (December 1984), p. 22; Herbert G. Goldman, *1986–87 Ring Record Book and Boxing Encyclopedia* (New York, 1987); Mario Rivera Martino, "Benitez Takes Jr. Welter Title from Cervantes," *TR* 55 (June 1976), pp. 13–17; William Nack, "On Top of the World," *SI* 51 (December 10, 1979), pp. 26–29; Pat Putnam, "It Was All Over Before the End," *SI* 50 (January 22, 1979), pp. 16–17; Bert Randolph Sugar, *The 100 Greatest Boxers of All Time* (New York, 1984); Bert Randolph Sugar, "Ringside Reports," *TR* 62 (February 1983), pp. 46–47.

John Robertson

DOUGLAS, James "Buster" (b. April 7, 1960, Columbus, OH), boxer, scored one of the greatest upsets in sports history by defeating Mike Tyson (S) in February 1990 to capture the undisputed world heavyweight championship. The son of Billy "Dynamite" Douglas, former middleweight and light heavyweight boxing contender, and Lula Pearl Douglas, he encountered an erratic career that made his ascension to the heavyweight title even more remarkable.

Douglas began his professional boxing career on May 31, 1981, by stopping Dan Banks in three rounds. Four more wins resulted that year before the more experienced David Bey stopped him in two rounds. Thirteen straight victories in 1982 and 1983 were recorded by Douglas, who then inexplicably was knocked out by mediocre journeyman Mike White in December 1983. The loss came largely from poor conditioning, causing boxing enthusiasts to doubt Douglas's commitment to the sport.

From 1984 to 1987, Douglas's career was checkered with many unpredictable outcomes. A solid win over Randall Cobb was followed by an embarrassing loss to Jesse Ferguson. A fine performance in decisioning Greg Page preceded a dismal tenth-round technical knockout loss to Tony Tucker for the vacant IBF heavyweight title. Douglas, however, rebounded by scoring six consecutive victories to earn a world title heavyweight fight with 23-year-old champion Tyson, considered virtually invincible at the time.

On February 10, 1990, in Tokyo, Japan, Douglas, a huge 42–1 underdog, startled the entire sports world by rallying from a knockdown to score a dramatic tenth-round technical knockout victory over Tyson. Douglas was inspired by the death of his mother, who succumbed to a stroke three weeks before the fight. His title reign lasted only eight months, as Evander Holyfield* took the heavyweight crown in Douglas's first title defense on October 25, 1990, at Las Vegas, NV. Douglas looked contented with his past achievements and came into the Holyfield bout badly out of shape. Holyfield dispatched Douglas with an impressive third-round knockout.

Douglas, financially secure, announced his retirement after losing his heavyweight title, having recorded 31 wins (21 knockouts), five losses, and one no-contest. Douglas remains an enigma to boxing fans, scoring unexpected wins while sometimes displaying an apparent lack of enthusiasm against lesser opponents. He has two children, Lamar and Cardae, and resides in Westerville, OH.

BIBLIOGRAPHY: Robert Cassidy, "The Heart of the Matter: Who Will Survive the Douglas-Holyfield War?" *KOM* (December 1990), pp. 32–59; Herbert G. Goldman, *1986–87 Ring Record Book and Boxing Encyclopedia* (New York, 1987); Richard Hoffer, "The Fight," *SI* 72 (February 19, 1990), pp. 12–29; Pat Putnam, "Busted," *SI* 73 (November 5, 1990), pp. 76–85; Jeff Ryan, "KO Closeup: Buster Douglas," *KOM* (August 1990), pp. 35–38.

John Robertson

FLOWERS, Theodore "The Georgia Deacon" "Tiger" (b. August 5, 1895, Camilla, GA; d. November 16, 1927, New York, NY), boxer, was the first black fighter to hold the world middleweight championship. His professional boxing career began at the relatively advanced age of 23 in 1918. Nicknamed "The Georgia Deacon" because of his staunch religious beliefs, Flowers mainly boxed other black fighters in the American South early in his professional career. Flowers, predominantly left-handed, exhibited a peculiar fighting style, featuring flailing arms and relentless attacking. Flowers's blows seldom overpowered, but their frequency kept opponents off balance. A resourceful tactician, Flowers often used mauling tactics to stifle more skillful foes.

Flowers's early professional boxing record remains sketchy. By 1924, under manager Walk Miller, he fought main events in the Northeast. His most impressive early victory came on December 9, 1924, when he stopped former middleweight titlist Johnny Wilson in 3 rounds in New York City. In 1923, Flowers lost just 3 of 31 professional bouts. Two losses came against future light heavyweight champion Jack Delaney (IS), while the other loss involved a disputed decision to Mike McTigue. On February 26, 1926, Flowers scored a significant upset in New York City by winning a 15-round decision over reigning world middleweight champion Harry Greb (IS). Flowers's style resembled that of Greb, who could not cope with the rough tactics employed by Flowers.

Flowers engaged in six nontitle fights in 1926 before granting Greb a rematch on August 19 in New York City. In a repetition of his title-winning effort, Flowers decisioned Greb in a fight marred by considerable wrestling and holding. Three more nontitle fights followed before Flowers defended the middleweight crown against former welterweight champion Mickey Walker (IS) on December 3, 1926, at Chicago, IL. In a hotly disputed decision, referee Benny Yanger, the sole arbiter, declared Walker the victor after 10 rounds. Suspicions linger that Yanger's verdict may have smacked of racism because some reporters scored 8 of the furiously fought rounds in favor of Flowers.

Flowers was never given an opportunity for a rematch. Nevertheless, he maintained a busy schedule in 1927 and lost just 1 of 18 contests. After knocking out Leo Gates in New York City on November 12, 1927, Flowers entered a private hospital for surgery to remove excess facial scar tissue. The routine operation turned tragic, as Flowers died in his sleep shortly after the surgery. Before his death, Flowers had been promised a rematch by champion Walker. Flowers, elected to *TR*'s Boxing Hall of Fame in 1971 and the International Boxing Hall of Fame in 1993, won 133 bouts (52 by knockout), lost 15 contests, drew 7 times, and fought 1 bout ruled a no-contest.

BIBLIOGRAPHY: Sam Andre and Nat Fleischer, *A Pictorial History of Boxing* (New York, 1975); Herbert G. Goldman, ed., *1986–87 Ring Record Book* (New York, 1987); Nat Loubet, "Graziano, Saddler, Berlenbach, Clark, Flowers, Elected," *TR* 51 (April 1972), pp. 12–37; Bert Randolph Sugar, *The 100 Greatest Boxers of All Time* (New York, 1984).

John Robertson

GRAHAM, William "Billy" (b. September 9, 1922, New York, NY; d. January 22, 1992, West Islip, NY), boxer and referee, was a five-foot-seven-inch, 149-pound welterweight and was the son of Irish-American parents, who operated a bar. Graham, who did not complete his second year of high school, spent all his time at the local gymnasium. After turning professional in 1941, he won his first 58 bouts. He did not possess the knockout punch, relying instead on quick footwork, fast-moving hands, and stylish, subtle moves. As Graham expressed it, "A punch is something you're born with. Either you have it or you don't." From 1941 to 1955, he recorded 102 victories, 15 losses, and 9 draws, earning most of his wins by decision. The clean-living, hard-working, dedicated Graham trained intensely, often at Greenwood Lake, NY. "You've got to drive yourself," Graham recalled. "Camp is a place for work." Graham, who usually was "nervous but not scared before fights," drank and smoked sparingly.

His career included wins over the best welterweights, including Kid Gavilan, Carmen Basilio (IS), Terry Young, and Art Aragon. Nicknamed "Billy," he was managed jointly by Jack Reilly, Billy Cohan, and Irving Cohan. Graham met hard times financially because the really big boxing prize money went to the heavyweights. A 1952 *Sport* article revealed that Graham held only about $10,000 in the bank and owned a modest home and car. He married Lorraine Hansen in October 1948 at St. Patrick's Cathedral in New York and had three children. Graham usually cleared under $20,000 a year after paying his managers, plus stipends for his sparring partners and trainers. Yet the role of sports celebrity gave him much compensation, for his fans' enthusiasm made Billy a headline Madison Square Garden attraction.

Failure to win the welterweight championship, however, marked Graham's most bitter disappointment in his 15-year ring career. He nearly captured the title several times, especially in his second bout with the spirited Cuban Kid Gavilan. Graham lost both that November 17, 1950, bout by split decision and a rematch the following August. A sympathetic press called Graham "the champ without the crown." Graham acknowledged, "The title means everything—the big percentage, extra TV money, an above-average guarantee when you hit the road." He had promised his wife Lorraine a mink stole if he won the welterweight championship, but fortune did not smile on him.

Some consolation came with his victory over middleweight Joey Giardello at Madison Square Garden on March 6, 1953, a bout witnessed by the author. The previous December, Giardello had decisioned Graham. New York State Boxing Commissioner Bob Christenberry had overruled a judge and awarded the verdict to Graham. The state Supreme Court, however, denied the commissioner's ruling in a tangled legal hassle. The press referred to Graham as the "split-decision kid," but he gained a clear victory on points over the middleweight after 12 rounds before an enthusiastic Madison Square Garden crowd of 8,638. As H. C. Heinz summarized, "By the middle of the fight it was a pro working on a kid." After the bout, one writer observed that Graham had never been knocked down.

Following his retirement from boxing in 1955, Graham used his father's connections to work for several liquor companies and was employed by Seagram's for 25 years. He also often served as a boxing judge and referee. Graham, who reached a most praiseworthy level of integrity to his many associates in the boxing world, died of cancer. To the great majority of sportswriters, he will always remain "the uncrowned welterweight champion."

BIBLIOGRAPHY: "Champ with the Crown," *Time* 60 (October 15, 1952), p. 48; Nat Fleischer, ed., *The Ring Magazine's Annual on TV Fights* (1954), p. 83; Billy Graham, "You Don't Get Rich Fighting," *Sport* 13 (August 1952), pp. 22–23, 86–87; W. C. Heinz, "Punching Out a Living," *Collier's* 131 (May 2, 1953), pp. 40–45; Barney Nagler, "The Kid from Camaguey," *Sport* 15 (September 1953), pp. 18–21, 85–87; Joseph C. Nichols, "Graham 8–5 Choice to Beat Giardello," *NYT*, March 6, 1953,

p. 31; Joseph C. Nichols, "Graham Gains Unanimous Verdict over Giardello; Outcome Reverses Reversal by Court," *NYT*, March 7, 1953, p. 19; Obituary, "Billy
Graham 70: Welterweight Boxer," *NYT*, January 22, 1992, p. A19.

William J. Miller

HOLYFIELD, Evander (b. October 19, 1962, Atmore, AL), boxer, was arguably the most successful graduate of the 1984 U.S. Olympic boxing team.
The youngest of eight children, Holyfield moved with his family at age three
to Atlanta, GA. He first became interested in boxing at age eight, when he
won a peewee tournament at the Warren BoC in Atlanta.

Holyfield's amateur career flourished during his teenage years. In 1983,
he captured the gold medal in the NSF and the silver medal at the Pan-
American Games. Holyfield was ranked the solid favorite to win a gold medal
at the 1984 Los Angeles, CA, Summer Olympic Games in the light heavyweight division after winning the 1984 National Golden Gloves title by
scoring five straight knockouts. Holyfield's quest for the Olympic championship was derailed, however, by a controversial referee's decision in his
semifinal bout against New Zealander Kevin Barry. Barry fouled Holyfield
several times, but the Georgian thoroughly dominated the fight. The Yu-
goslavian referee, Gligorije Novicic, was calling for a break to penalize Barry
for another infraction, when Holyfield landed a solid left hook, which
floored the New Zealander. To the amazement of the spectators, Novicic
disqualified Holyfield, leaving him with the bronze medal. Ironically, the
furor generated by Holyfield's bronze medal overshadowed the nine gold
medals won by other American boxers.

Authorities considered Holyfield a solid professional prospect. Holyfield
won his first professional fight on November 15, 1984, a decision over tough
journeyman Lionel Byram. Ten more victories during the next 18 months
earned Holyfield a world title fight with WBA junior heavyweight champion
Dwight Muhammad Qawi on July 12, 1986. Holyfield emerged the winner
by decision after 15 highly competitive rounds. After successfully defending
his title several times (including a rematch victory over Qawi), Holyfield
jumped into the more lucrative heavyweight division. The move paid dividends, as Holyfield defeated several serious contenders to earn a chance at
the world heavyweight title, held by James "Buster" Douglas.*

On October 25, 1990, Holyfield reached the pinnacle of his sport by
knocking out Douglas in 3 rounds to win the undisputed world heavyweight
crown. Douglas entered the fight in woeful physical condition and did not
match Holyfield, who always trains zealously for every bout. Although Holyfield held the title, boxing fans often charged that the champion's defenses
came against fighters having little chance of defeating him. A tough decision
victory over 42-year-old George Foreman (IS), a narrow triumph versus
mediocre Bert Cooper, and a lackluster outing with Larry Holmes (IS) aug-
mented the criticism. Holyfield's initial tenure as heavyweight titlist ended

on November 13, 1992, when he lost a thrilling bout to Riddick Bowe by a unanimous 12-round decision at Las Vegas, NV. Holyfield, who has earned more than $90 million in the ring, initially announced his retirement following his first defeat but then won a unanimous decision over Alex Stewart on June 26, 1993, in Atlantic City, NJ.

In November 1993, Holyfield regained the heavyweight crown in a 12-round decision over Riddick Bowe at Caesar's Palace in Las Vegas, NV. Two judges voted for Holyfield, while a third judge ruled the bout a draw. During the seventh round, a skydiver crashed into the ring ropes and halted the fisticuffs for 21 minutes. In April 1994, Holyfield lost the IBF and WBA heavyweight crowns to undefeated Michael Moorer in a 12-round decision at Las Vegas, NV. Upon the advice of doctors, he retired from the ring four days later due to a heart condition. Doctors later cleared him to fight again.

Holyfield's professional record in 1994 stood at 31–2 with 22 knockouts. His style resembles that of a boxer–puncher, who patiently waits to exploit his opponent's tactical errors. Holyfield has brought a tremendous sense of dignity to the title, reminiscent of the legendary Joe Louis (IS).

BIBLIOGRAPHY: Steve Farhood, "Holmes vs. Foreman: The Fight Evander Holyfield Should Have Prevented," *KOM* (November 1992), pp. 28–31; Herbert G. Goldman, *1986–87 Ring Record Book and Boxing Encyclopedia* (New York, 1987); Peter King, "KO Closeup: Evander Holyfield," *KOM* (January 1987), pp. 35–38; Ed Maloney and Steve Farhood, "Evander Holyfield's Title Reign: A Reason to Hide or a Reason for Pride," *KOM* (July 1992), pp. 28–31; Pat Putnam, "Let's Get Ready to . . . Rummmble," *SI* 77 (November 23, 1992), pp. 16–29.

John Robertson

McFARLAND, Patrick Francis "Packy" (b. November 1, 1888, Chicago, IL; d. September 23, 1936, Joliet, IL), boxer, was born into a large Irish family in the tough stockyards district of Chicago. He attended St. Anne's elementary school but began working in sewer construction at age 14. At age 15, he embarked on a new career as a professional prizefighter and earned $3 in his first bout. The sum was split with his mother. After losing an early bout, McFarland honed his defensive technique and eschewed the street-brawling skills that had produced six knockouts against local opponents in 1904. McFarland then challenged top contenders nationally, never losing over the next decade. Authorities considered him one of the best defensive fighters of all time. McFarland's speed and intelligence, however, prevented any champion from granting him a title fight.

In 1908, McFarland knocked out Jimmy Britt, the former lightweight champion. He then hounded Battling Nelson (IS) for a title fight without success. A 1910 bout for the lightweight championship against Ad Wolgast (IS) was stopped by a Milwaukee, WI, sheriff as an illegal prizefight. McFarland fought three memorable contests against Freddie Welsh, the British and future world lightweight champ. McFarland won the first bout, while the next two were declared draws. He defeated Cyclone Johnny Thompson, claimant to the middleweight crown, and battled Jack Britton (IS), future welterweight champ, to three draws and two no-decisions. He fought a final no-decision bout on November 9, 1915, against Mike Gibbons (IS), a claimant to the middleweight title, and earned $40,000. His 97 consecutive bouts without a loss stood as a record.

With American entry into World War I, McFarland joined the U.S. Army as a boxing and physical training instructor at Camp Taylor, KY. After the war, he retired with a sizable fortune to Joliet, IL. McFarland, married since 1911 to Margaret Loughran, started a paving company, rose to vice president of his father-in-law's bank, and assisted in his brewery business. The financial collapse of his businesses during the depression cost McFarland two thirds of his $750,000.

In 1931 McFarland became a boxing instructor for the CYO. Two years later, he was selected as a member of the ISAC. He also chaired the Will County Democratic Committee before influenza and a lingering streptococcal infection brought his death. His wife, three daughters, and a son survived.

BIBLIOGRAPHY: Peter Arnold, *Illustrated History of World Boxing* (New York, 1989); Chicago (IL) *Tribune*, September 23, 1936, p. 26; September 24, 1936, pp. 25, 29; Nat Fleischer and Sam Andre, *A Pictorial History of Boxing* (New York, 1987); John D. McCallum, *The Encyclopedia of World Boxing Champions Since 1882* (Radnor, PA, 1975); Bert Randolph Sugar, *The 100 Greatest Boxers of All Time* (New York, 1984); Arch Ward, ed., *The Greatest Sports Stories from the Chicago Tribune* (New York, 1953).

Gerald R. Gems

MANCINI, Raymond Michael "Ray" "Boom Boom" (b. March 4, 1961, Youngstown, OH), boxer, is the son of Lenny Mancini, a lightweight boxer, and Ellen Mancini and fought with a direct, energetic, and hard-slugging style. His twin boxing goals included winning the world title that his father could not achieve because of World War II injuries and making his family financially secure. The 5-foot-6½ inch, 134- to 140-pound contender, managed by David Wolf, reached both goals soon after beginning his professional career in October 1979.

On May 16, 1981, Mancini defeated Jorge Morales at the Concord Resort Hotel in Kiamesha Lake, NY, to win the NABF lightweight title. In July 1981, Mancini vanquished José Ramirez of Mexico to retain the NABF title. Alexis Arguello of Nicaragua kept the WBC lightweight title in October 1981 at Atlantic City, NJ, stopping Mancini with a fourteenth-round technical knockout. On May 8, 1982, Mancini captured the WBA title in 2 minutes 34 seconds of the first round against American Arturo Frias at Las Vegas, NV. Mancini defended the title on July 4, 1982, in Warren, OH, against Ernesto España of Venezuela in six rounds.

Mancini already had become a marketable commodity with an earnest, voluble personality and clean morals. His star lost some of its luster after a

Las Vegas, NV, bout on November 13, 1982, against Duk-Koo Kim. After a grueling battle on both sides, Mancini knocked out Kim in 14 rounds. The Korean fighter died five days later from a brain hemorrhage, never having regained consciousness. Mancini withdrew for a few months before resuming his livelihood. He soon became depressed, having achieved wealth and fame so quickly and having virtually nothing else to strive for. Mancini, however, recovered his self-esteem with the assistance of his family priest.

Mancini defeated Orlando Romero of Peru in New York City in 9 rounds in September 1983 and stopped American Bobby Chacon in 3 rounds in Reno, NV, in January 1984. In June 1984 at Buffalo, NY, Livingston Bramble of the United States defeated Mancini in the fourteenth round and took the WBA lightweight title. The return bout at Reno, NV, in February 1985 featured Mancini losing again to Bramble in a 15-round decision.

Mancini already had made over $6 million in his boxing-related career. A television movie, *I Walk in His Shadow*, produced by Sylvester Stallone, was based on Mancini's adoring relationship with his father. Another television movie, *Heart of a Champion: The Ray Mancini Story*, was produced by Robert Papazian and directed by Richard Michaels. Mancini made an exercise video, owned a management company, and appeared in situation comedies, including his friend Tony Danza's "Who's the Boss?" Commercial endorsement offers did not follow, but he popularized the lightweight boxing division.

Mancini retired from the ring at age 24 after the Bramble rematch, although American Hector Camacho lured him out again in March 1989. Mancini sought to increase his profile as an actor/director with the Camacho contest. On March 6, 1989, Camacho won on a split decision victory in Reno, NV, to become WBA junior welterweight champion. Both Camacho and his trainers agreed, however, that the controversial decision might well have gone to Mancini. Mancini retired again from the ring with 29 wins and 4 losses in his professional career. Since 1991, Mancini has settled down with his wife and two children and pursued an acting career on the New York stage. Mancini sees stage acting, unlike television acting, as more akin to boxing—both have live action and live audiences.

BIBLIOGRAPHY: Nat Fleischer and Sam Andre, *Pictorial History of Boxing* (New York, 1981); *NYT*, November 14–15, 1982; February 17, 1985; March 6–7, 1989; November 8, 1991; Gilbert Odd, *Encyclopedia of Boxing* (New York, 1983); *The Ring . . . Record Book and Boxing Encyclopedia* (New York, 1985); *USA Today*, November 24, 1982; December 21, 1982; January 3, 1984; January 12, 1984; August 27, 1984; January 3, 1985; February 14, 1985; February 18, 1985; January 6, 1989; March 6, 1989; March 8, 1989; Washington (DC) *Post*, May 17, 1981; July 20, 1981; October 4, 1981; September 15–17, 1983; January 14–16, 1984; June 2, 1984; February 16–17, 1985; Washington (DC) *Times*, March 31, 1986.

Frederick J. Augustyn, Jr.

MOORE, Davey (b. November 1, 1933, Lexington, KY; d. March 23, 1963, Los Angeles, CA), boxer, ranked among the most talented fighters in the lower-weight classifications that the United States has ever produced. Moore enjoyed a fine amateur boxing career and first gained national attention by winning the 1952 National AAU bantamweight title. During his first year as a professional boxer, Moore in 1953 won seven of eight bouts.

From 1954 to 1958, Moore traveled widely to advance his boxing career. The cities where he showcased his talents included Montreal, Canada, Havana, Cuba, Mexico City, Mexico, and Colón, Panama. During that time, Moore lost just 4 of 33 bouts. Thirteen straight victories in 1957 and 1958 earned Moore a bout with Hogan "Kid" Bassey of Nigeria for the world featherweight championship. On March 18, 1959, Moore scored a decisive 13-round knockout over Bassey in Los Angeles, CA, to win the featherweight title. Five months later, Moore defended his crown by stopping Bassey in round 11 of their rematch at Los Angeles.

Moore only defended his title once more in the next 18 months but participated in many nontitle bouts ranging from Caracas, Venezuela, to Tokyo, Japan. Moore retained his crown with a 15-round decision over Kazuo Takayama on August 29, 1960, in Tokyo, Japan. Two successful defenses followed in 1961, an easy first-round knockout of Danny Valdez in Los Angeles and another decision over Takayama in Tokyo. Moore also recorded seven other victories that year. Moore won all four 1962 bouts, including a second-round knockout of Olli Maeki on August 17 while defending his title at Helsinki, Finland.

Tragically, Moore's next defense of his featherweight crown cost him his title and his life. On March 21, 1963, at Los Angeles, Moore was knocked out in the tenth round of a spirited contest by Cuba's Ultiminio "Sugar" Ramos. Ramos knocked him down twice in the final round, having battered the latter when referee George Latka stopped the contest. An hour later, Moore collapsed and went into a coma. He died within two days, never regaining consciousness. Moore's death, along with a similar ring tragedy involving welterweight champion Benny Paret in 1962, aroused public opinion against boxing. Televised bouts, very common during the 1950s, became rare. Over a decade elapsed before professional boxing regained its status as a regular part of network sports programming. Moore's career record included 59 wins (30 by knockout), seven losses, and one draw.

BIBLIOGRAPHY: Sam Andre and Nat Fleischer, *A Pictorial History of Boxing* (New York, 1975); Alan Clevens, "Rings Around the World," *BI* 3 (October 1961), p. 60; Herbert G. Goldman, *1986–87 Ring Record Book and Boxing Encyclopedia* (New York, 1987); Gilbert Odd, *The Encyclopedia of Boxing* (Secaucus, NJ, 1989); Robert J. Thornton, "Rings Around the World," *BI* 2 (October 1960), p. 13.

John Robertson

NORTON, Kenneth Howard Sr. "Ken" (b. August 9, 1945, Jacksonville, IL), boxer, is the son of John Norton and Ruth Norton and played football fullback in high school and for Northeastern Missouri State University. Norton served in the U.S. Marine Corps from 1963 to 1967, winning three All-Marine boxing titles. As an amateur, Norton won the Pan-American Games trials and finished runner-up for the AAU boxing title in 1967. The six-foot-three-inch, 210-pound Norton turned professional on November 14, 1967, knocking out Grady Brazell, an ex–Golden Gloves champion. A former Joe Frazier (IS) sparring partner, Norton was considered a journeyman heavyweight until his March 31, 1973, heavyweight title fight with Muhammad Ali (IS). Norton decisively defeated Ali in a 15-round decision, breaking the latter's jaw in the process.

Thereafter, Norton was known for his losses. Aside from his brutal second-round knockout by George Foreman (IS) for the heavyweight title in Caracas, Venezuela, in March 1974, Norton's setbacks came by close margins. Norton lost twice in rematches with Ali, including a September 1973 reprise for the NABF heavyweight title in Los Angeles, CA, and a razor-thin 15-round loss for the world heavyweight crown at Yankee Stadium in New York on September 28, 1976. Norton was proclaimed heavyweight champion by the WBC in 1978 but lost his first defense to Larry Holmes (IS) in a close 15-round decision at Las Vegas, NV, in June 1978. Knockout defeats by Earnie Shavers in 1979 and Gerry Cooney in 1981 caused Norton to retire.

Norton's other careers included acting leads in *Mandingo* in 1974 and *Drums* in 1975, television sports commentating, and print-advertising modeling. A 1986 automobile accident left Norton with traumatic injuries, including a shattered jaw and fractured skull. During his recovery, he lost 43 pounds. Norton had one son, Ken, Jr., a professional football player, from his brief first marriage. Norton married Jackie Halton in 1977 and has three children, Brandon, Kenisha, and Kene Jon. Norton's professional boxing record comprised 42 wins (33 by knockout), seven losses, and one draw.

BIBLIOGRAPHY: Dave Anderson, "The Nortons: So Close and Yet So Far Apart," *NYT*, January 28, 1993, p. B9; *NYT*, 1973–1992; Ralph Wiley, "Like Father, Like Son," *SI* 67 (October 12, 1987), pp. 74–78; *WWA*, 42nd ed. (1982–1983), p. 2488.

John H. Ziegler

COMMUNICATIONS

ABRAMSON, Jesse Peter "The Book" (b. March 10, 1904, Mountaindale, NY; d. June 11, 1979, Mount Vernon, NY), sportswriter and track and field meet director, ranked among America's finest journalists and gained the reputation of being one of the most knowledgeable and precise track and field correspondents. The Abramson family moved to New York City, where Jesse graduated from high school. The New York *Herald* hired Abramson as a sportswriter and paid him $8 a column, one each daily for both the morning and the evening editions. Often the New York *Herald* paid him for both columns, although only one was published daily. Abramson earned up to $120 a week before the newspaper placed him on the salaried writing staff at $40 a week. In 1924, the New York *Herald* became the *Herald-Tribune*. In that year, Abramson rewrote the cable dispatches of Grantland Rice (OS) from the Summer Olympic Games at Paris, France. He subsequently attended every Summer Olympiad from 1928 through 1976 and reported on the Olympic games for the *Herald-Tribune* until the newspaper folded in 1966. Abramson served as foreign press liaison for the 1968 Mexico City, Mexico, Summer Olympic Games, covered the 1972 Munich, Germany, Summer Olympic Games for the *International Herald-Tribune*, and served as press liaison at the 1976 Montreal, Canada, Summer Olympic Games. Abramson, who became the director of the USOC Olympic Invitational track and field meet in 1969, served as the publicist for the Millrose Games and other meets held at Madison Square Garden in New York.

Abramson's knowledge of track and field was punctuated by an unparalleled memory for detail and a penchant for debate. In 1965, he corrected James L. Reid, a Maine judge, about his time in winning the IC4A two-mile in 1929. According to Reid, his time was 9 minutes 20 seconds. Abramson, however, insisted that the time was 2 seconds slower. To settle the dispute, the judge sent an aide to his chambers for his scrapbook that confirmed

Abramson was indeed correct. A member of the NTF Hall of Fame (1981), Abramson received numerous honors, including the Grantland Rice Award of the Sportsmanship Brotherhood, the James J. Walker Award for service to boxing, and the NYTWA Award for distinguished service. Abramson, for whom the NYTWA's annual award to the outstanding male indoor athlete is named, founded and was longtime president of the association. He also served as the president of the NYFWA and vice president of the NYBoWA. Abramson, who died after a long bout with cancer, was the father of a son and a daughter.

BIBLIOGRAPHY: Bob Hersh, "Jesse Abramson," *TFN* 32 (August 1979), p. 75; Red Smith, "Jesse P. Abramson, Sportswriter for Herald Tribune, Dead at 75," *NYT*, June 12, 1979, p. D16.

Adam R. Hornbuckle

ALBERT, Marvin Philip "Marv" (b. Marvin Philip Aufrichtig, June 12, 1943, New York, NY), sportscaster and director, is the son of Max Aufrichtig, a grocer, and Alida (Kahn) Aufrichtig and grew up in Brooklyn, NY, with an early enthusiasm for sports broadcasting. With his younger brothers, Al and Steve, Marv made phantom broadcasts of family sporting contests on a tape recorder, simulating the styles of local sportscasters Marty Glickman* and Ken Keiter. Albert attended Syracuse University from 1960 to 1963, when he gained his first live radio experience as a disc jockey and newscaster on small local stations. His first big break in sportscasting came with Syracuse, NY, radio station WFBL, for whom Albert broadcast the games of the Syracuse Chiefs (IL) minor league baseball team. During Marv's time at Syracuse, his father changed the family name from *Aufrichtig* to *Albert* out of consideration for his oldest son's career aspirations.

The turning point in Albert's early career came in late 1963, when he was hired as an office boy at radio station WHN in New York City. He transferred from Syracuse University to NYU, graduating with a bachelor's degree in journalism in 1964. After only three years at WHN, Albert served as sports director there from 1967 to 1973. In January 1963, Albert received his big early break when he served as a last-minute stand-in for Glickman in a television broadcast of the New York Knicks–Boston Celtics NBA game at Boston, MA. In 1967, he also began announcing for both the New York Knicks (NBA) and New York Rangers (NHL). In 1974, WNBC-TV hired Albert as sports director. Three years later, he began his role as an NBC-Sports Network announcer of basketball, football, and boxing. As one of the most visible NBC sports announcers, Albert developed a unique style that conveyed energy, enthusiasm, careful preparation, an ability to create effective byplay with his analysts and color men, and a frequent, witty irreverence. Albert's speciality remains play-by-play; he is noted for his versatility and personal style. As sports director for WNBC-TV since 1974 and earlier, he interviewed athletes by relying on often tough, direct questioning, an ability to adjust quickly by listening carefully to the responses to his questions, and shrewd awareness of the personalities of his interview subjects. His trademarks include his wit, humor, and candid honesty. He was regularly recognized for his interviewing and announcing skills as the Sportscaster of the Year, an award NASS gave him from 1971 to 1986. He has developed a style particularly well suited to the high visibility of the New York City media market. His two younger brothers, Al and Steve, also broadcast sports, both becoming nationally recognized for their work in professional basketball and boxing. Albert published three books, *Krazy About the Knicks* (1970), *Marv Albert's Quiz Book* (1976), and *Yesss! Marv Albert on Sportcasting*, written with veteran AP sportswriter Hal Bock (1979).

On August 15, 1965, Albert married Benita Caress. They have two sons, Kenneth and Brian, and two daughters, Denise and Jackie. Albert belongs to the B'nai B'rith Lodge in New York City. His oldest son, Kenny, started his career in sportscasting by handling play-by-play for the Washington Capitals (NHL) in the 1992–1993 season. Albert played himself in *The Fish That Saved Pittsburgh*, a 1979 film about a fictional NBA franchise, and has frequently appeared on the "Late Night with David Letterman" show.

BIBLIOGRAPHY: Marv Albert with Hal Bock, *Yesss! Marv Albert on Sportcasting* (New York, 1979); Melissa Ludtke, "From the Basement to the Booth," *SI* 78 (February 6, 1978), p. 40; Richard Sandomir, "Suiting Up in the N.B.A.: Finding the Right Fits," *NYT*, November 6, 1992; Steve Wulf, "Born to the Booth," *SI* 77 (November 2, 1992), pp. 75–85; *WWA*, 45th ed. (1988–1989), p. 32.

Douglas A. Noverr

AUFRICHTIG, Marvin Philip. *See* Marvin Philip Albert.

BERMAN, Christopher "Chris" "Boomer" (b. May 10, 1955, New York, NY), sportscaster and anchor, is the son of James K. Berman, a mechanical contractor, and Peggy T. Berman, a *Time* magazine researcher, and grew up in Rye, NY, and Tarrytown, NY. At Hackley School in Tarrytown, Berman played varsity soccer, basketball, and tennis and worked on the student newspaper and radio station. A history major at Brown University, Berman served as sports director for WBRU, the campus radio station, and broadcast for the Bruins sports teams. He also reported sports for the Brown *Daily Herald* and administered the campus intramural programs for a year. After graduating from Brown with a bachelor's degree in 1977, he joined radio station WERI-AM-FM as a general announcer. His first big break came when WNVR, a radio station in Waterbury, CT, hired him as a sports talk show host in 1978. The next year, Berman also anchored weekend sports for WVIT-TV in Hartford, CT.

Chet Simmons, the first president of the ESPN-Network, hired Berman as a sports anchor in 1979 and assigned him as host of the nightly "Sports

Center" sports news program and the weekly NFL highlights show. Berman quickly distinguished himself as a sportscaster with zest, quick wit, a pell-mell delivery, and enthusiasm. His colleagues affectionately refer to him as "Boomer." Berman's style suited well a developing cable television network with a more experimental approach and open format and that hoped to develop broadcast personalities who could attract audience allegiance. Berman's repertoire expanded to include his now-trademark knack for instantly developing unusual nicknames for athletes through the technique of combining their names with puns, catchy phrases, references to rock n' roll music and films, foods or products, or anything he can blend in before, in the middle of, or after their first and last names. In 1985 an ESPN producer prohibited Berman's name making, but an outpouring of fan mail restored his signature nicknaming style. Another Berman trademark remains his bravura performance of the NFL Sunday game highlights, billed as the "fastest three minutes in sports." Berman's success and national popularity rest on his enthusiastic involvement in his material and his irrepressible good humor and sense of fun in delivering his material as entertainment and news. He admires Jack Whitaker, whom Berman describes as a "great wordsmith," and Brent Musberger (S), whom Berman describes as "the BEST studio host."

In 1989, NBC engaged in a bidding war for Berman's services, but ESPN signed him to a five-year contract worth nearly $3 million. His assignments include a play-by-play role in broadcasting baseball games, the key anchor role of the "Baseball Tonight" highlights show, where he has worked smoothly with Peter Gammons (S) and Ray Knight, and the "NFL Game Day" show with Tom Jackson and Robin Roberts. Berman also anchors ESPN specials, such as the NFL player drafts and the Super Bowl. In 1989 and in 1990, NASS voted Berman Sportscaster of the Year, reflecting his popularity and recognition and ESPN's prominent position in television sportscasting. The Academy of Television Arts and Sciences awarded the "NFL Game Day" studio show Emmy awards in 1988 and 1991, with "Sports Center" receiving an Emmy in 1990. In 1994 *TSN* ranked him among the 100 most powerful people in sports. Berman and his wife Katherine were married in 1983 and have two children, Meredith and Douglas.

BIBLIOGRAPHY: Chris Berman, letter to Douglas A. Noverr, July 22, 1993; Franz Lidz, "Yabba-Dabba-Doo!: Chris Berman, ESPN's Answer to Fred Flintstone Has Struck Pay Dirt in the Cable-TV Quarry," *SI* 72 (March 26, 1990), pp. 38–41; Steven H. Scheuer, ed., *Who's Who in Television and Cable* (New York, 1983); Alexander Wolff, "Late-Night Score Wars: It's CNN's Hick 'n' Nick vs. ESPN's Baby Boomers," *SI* 70 (June 26, 1989), p. 74.

Douglas A. Noverr

BURICK, Simon "Si" (b. June 14, 1909, Dayton, OH; d. December 10, 1986, Dayton, OH), sportswriter, is the only member of the Writers Section of the National Baseball Hall of Fame from a city with no major league team.

A popular dean of American sports reporting, he was the firstborn of Samuel and Lillian Burick's six children. Burick's father, a Polish-Russian immigrant, served as a rabbi at a Dayton synagogue. During his junior year at Dayton's Stivers High School, Burick became a correspondent for the Dayton *Daily News*. His first byline appeared on August 26, 1925. Burick continued to work for the *Daily News* while attending the University of Dayton. He left school, intending to earn enough money to return to his studies. In November 1928, the publisher of the *Daily News* offered Burick the sports editor's post. Burick, then just 19 years old, had accumulated only 18 months of full-time newspaper experience.

During his 61 years with the *Daily News*, Burick covered various sports, including baseball (his first love), boxing, horse racing, basketball, football, ice hockey, and tennis. He attended high school, college, and professional events and reported from four Olympics. Other midwestern sports reporters followed Burick's lead in making the world his beat.

Burick, Ohio's Sportswriter of the Year 18 times, was enshrined in the writer's wing of the National Baseball Hall of Fame in 1983. Two years later, the NASS Hall of Fame inducted him. In June 1986, he became the sixth recipient of the Red Smith Award. Burick received the Governor's Award in 1955 for his contributions to Ohio.

Burick married Rachel Siegal, a schoolteacher from New York, on June 28, 1935, and had two daughters, Lenore and Marcia. Burick suffered from heart and blood ailments in his later years and died following a massive stroke.

Burick authored three books, *Alston and the Dodgers* (1966); *The Main Spark*, about Sparky Anderson (BB) (1978); and *Byline*, a collection of his columns (1982).

BIBLIOGRAPHY: Si Burick obituary, *TSN Official Baseball Guide*, 1987; "Sports Editor Si Burick Dies at Age 77," Dayton (OH) *Daily News*, December 11, 1986, p. 1.

Peter Cava

CANNON, Jimmy (b. April 10, 1909, Brooklyn, NY; d. December 5, 1973, New York, NY), sportswriter, was the son of Thomas J. Cannon, a minor Tammany Hall politician, and Loretta (Monahan) Cannon. He grew up in New York City but left high school after one year. A lifelong bachelor, Cannon served as Third Army correspondent for *Stars and Stripes* during World War II and worked as a war correspondent during the Korean conflict.

Cannon, who began as a copy boy for the New York *Daily News* from 1927 to 1930, reported for the New York *Daily Telegram* from 1930 to 1934 and served as a feature writer for INS from 1935 to 1936. His coverage of the Charles Lindbergh kidnapping drew praise from Damon Runyon (OS), who encouraged Cannon to follow sportswriting. Cannon wrote columns on sports and national events for the New York *Journal-American* from 1936 through 1939. After World War II, he joined the New York *Post* from 1946 to 1950. Cannon returned in 1952 to the *Journal-American*, where he worked until the eve of his death.

By 1949 Cannon arguably ranked as New York's leading sportswriter. A street-smart reporter who socialized with Joe DiMaggio (BB) and novelist Ernest Hemingway, he always expected the best table and free drinks at the restaurant of his good friend Toots Shor. Cannon was the prototypical hard-drinking reporter, caught in movies such as *Deadline USA*. His adoring, mostly blue-collar New York *Post* readers were baseball fanatics. That sport remained Cannon's first love, but he also wrote engagingly about football, boxing, and horse racing.

Cannon praised heroes but condemned frauds and greed. He took the bromide that Joe Louis (IS) was a credit to his race and sharpened it into "Joe Louis is a credit to his race—I mean the human race." Using Louis's example, Cannon in 1946 denounced baseball on ABC-Radio for its segregation, charging that the game "was run by a group of bigoted men with Jim Crow as an umpire." When Jackie Robinson (BB) broke the color line with the Brooklyn Dodgers (NL) in 1947, Cannon sympathized with his struggle, declaring, "He is the loneliest man I have ever seen in sports."

Sportswriter Red Smith (OS) envied Cannon's sharpness with a phrase, defining a knuckleball as "a curve that doesn't give a damn." Of baseball stars Roy Campanella (BB) and Stan Musial (BB), Cannon commented, "If they had a Hall of Fame for people, they would make that too." Cannon wrote two books, *The Sergeant Says* (1942), which recounted his war correspondent experiences, and *Nobody Asked Me* (1950), which drew from his columns. His brothers issued an expanded anthology of his work, also entitled *Nobody Asked Me* in 1978. Cannon received the E. P. Dutton Award for sportswriting three times and was elected to the NASS Hall of Fame in 1986.

BIBLIOGRAPHY: Tommy Cannon and Jack Cannon, eds., *Nobody Asked Me, But: The World of Jimmy Cannon* (New York, 1978); Paul Dickson, *Baseball's Greatest Quotations* (New York, 1991); David Halberstam, *Summer of 49* (New York, 1989); Chris Mead, *Champion: Joe Louis, Black Hero in White America* (New York, 1986); *NYT*, December 6–7, 1973; July 2, 1978; Jules Tygiel, *Baseball's Great Experiment* (New York, 1983); *WWA*, 37th ed. (1972–1973), p. 489.

James W. Harper

CARMICHAEL, John Peerless (b. October 16, 1902, Madison, WI; d. June 6, 1986, Chicago, IL), sportswriter, was the son of George J. Carmichael and Margaret (Mooney) Carmichael, married Marie Bannon on January 29, 1929, and had two children, John, Jr., and Joan Marie. After his wife died in June 1953, he wed Kay Haughton on December 27, 1956. Carmichael studied at Campion College in Prairie de Chien, WI, and finished his college education at the University of Wisconsin, Madison. He began his newspaper career as a reporter on the Milwaukee (WI) *Journal* and reporter and columnist with the Milwaukee *Leader*.

Carmichael became a sports reporter for the Chicago (IL) *Herald-Examiner*, working under Warren Brown. He joined the now defunct Chicago *Daily News* in 1932 and worked nearly 40 years there, serving as sports editor from 1943 to 1971. In 1934, Carmichael originated a syndicated column, "The Barber Shop." His column led others to describe him as one of the nation's most respected sports columnists. Upon his retirement in 1972, he was honored at a testimonial banquet organized by the sports editors of the Chicago *News, Tribune, Sun-Times*, and *Chicago Today*.

In 1975, Carmichael was inducted into the writer's section of the National Baseball Hall of Fame. Five years later, he was selected for the Chicago Press Club's new Journalism Hall of Fame. Carmichael was included in the *Best Sports Stories of 1952* with his article "That Blow on Coogan's Bluff." He was known as one of the nation's most mobile sports editors, traveling to where the sports news was being made. In 1994, the NASS Hall of Fame inducted Carmichael.

Carmichael authored the book *My Greatest Day in Baseball* (1945) and, with Marshall B. Cutler, edited *Who's Who in the Major Leagues* annually. A Catholic, he belonged to the Knights of Columbus. Carmichael suffered a stroke several years prior to his death and remained in failing health through his twilight years.

BIBLIOGRAPHY: *CA*, 119 (1987), p. 50; Irving T. Marsh and Edward Ehre, eds., *Best Sports Stories* (New York, 1952); *NYT*, June 8, 1986, p. 44; *WWA*, 34th ed. (1966–1967), p. 169; *WWM*, 6th ed. (1958), p. 340.

Stan W. Carlson

COHANE, Timothy Sylvester "Tim" (b. February 7, 1912, New Haven, CT; d. January 22, 1989, Nashua, NH), sportswriter, was the son of Sylvester T. Cohane and Margaret (Hogan) Cohane, grew up in New Haven, and graduated from Fordham University in 1935. Due to Cohane's success as sports editor for the student newspaper, Fordham hired him as director of athletic publicity from 1935 to 1940. Cohane coined the phrase "The Seven Blocks of Granite" to describe the famous 1937 Fordham football line that held its eight opponents to just 16 points.

In 1940, Cohane joined the staff of the New York *World-Telegram*, covering the Brooklyn Dodgers (NL), college football, and college basketball. His "Frothy Facts" sports column was syndicated nationally. Cohane became the sports editor of *Look* magazine in 1944 and served 21 years in this influential role. Besides writing over 500 articles on numerous sports, he made his annual preseason predictions and rankings of college football teams and inaugurated the Grantland Rice Award, presented yearly to the college football champions chosen by national football writers. Cohane resigned from

Look before its demise in 1965 and served as editor of *Sunrise*, a New England regional sports magazine that failed financially and ceased publication in 1967.

Cohane the next year began teaching newswriting in the School of Public Communication at Boston University, retiring as professor emeritus in 1978. In 1975, he created the "East Indies," a weekly evaluation of the major Eastern college football independents, and was inducted into the Fordham Sports Hall of Fame. Between 1948 and 1974, Cohane published three important college football histories: *Gridiron Grenadiers: The Story of West Point Football* (1948), *The Yale Football Story* (1951), and *Great College Football Coaches of the Twenties and Thirties* (1974), an indispensable biographical reference source on the lives and careers of 43 coaching greats from these decades. He also helped write Earl H. "Red" Blaik's (FB) autobiography entitled *You Have to Pay the Price* (1960). His own reminiscences, drawn partly from his *Look* articles, were published as *Bypaths of Glory: A Sportswriter Looks Back* (1963). In all his sports writings, Cohane sought to identify and characterize the human elements and personal resources that accounted for success and greatness, using telling anecdotes, unknown "inside" stories, wit, and humor.

Cohane, who married Margaret U. Hill on December 29, 1936, had two sons and five daughters. In the 1980s, Cohane designed and taught Corporate Communications Seminars for businesspeople, sharing his wealth of experience as a sportswriter and professor of communications. Cohane, who retired in Derry, NH, suffered a paralytic stroke in January 1987. In June 1987, the CFWAA honored him with the McGrane Award, which was accepted by his wife and son Timothy, Jr.

BIBLIOGRAPHY: *CA*, 1st rev., 9–12 (1974), pp. 175–176; "Tim Cohane, 76, Sports Editor at Look," *NYT*, January 24, 1989; "Timothy S. Cohane, 76: Author and Former Sports Editor of Look," Boston (MA) *Globe*, January 24, 1989; *WWA*, 41st ed. (1980–1981), p. 658.

                                                                    Douglas A. Noverr

CONSIDINE, Robert Bernard "Bob" (b. November 4, 1906, Washington, DC; d. September 1, 1975, New York, NY), tennis player, sportswriter, and author, was the son of James William Considine and Sophie (Small) Considine and attended Gonzaga High School in the nation's capital. He won the National Public Parks tennis doubles championship in 1929, District of Columbia tennis singles title in 1930, and about 50 other state and regional tennis titles. Considine's early enthusiasm for tennis led to his newspaper career. In 1927, a Washington newspaper misspelled his name in an account of a tennis match. He visited the paper as an indignant subscriber to have his name corrected and talked the sports editor into letting him submit occasional tennis news. In 1923, he entered federal government service as a messenger in the U.S. Census Bureau. He transferred to the U.S. Bureau of

Public Health and then became a typist in the U.S. Treasury Department. In 1927, he joined the U.S. State Department as a clerk.

To achieve his ambition of becoming a writer, he enrolled in evening courses in journalism and short story writing at George Washington University for four years. In 1929, Considine began writing a weekly tennis column for the Washington *Post* at $5 a week. A year later, the *Post* offered Considine a full-time position in the sports department. Considine passed up consular work in the U.S. State Department against the advice of his mother and accepted the newspaper job at a lower salary. He stayed at the *Post* for three years. In 1933, the Washington *Herald* (later *Times-Herald*) offered Considine a sports staff position at twice his previous salary. He briefly became the *Herald*'s sports editor, but his superiors wanted him to concentrate on writing. Subsequently, he covered the Washington Senators (AL) baseball team, wrote editorials, and prepared daily stories about U.S. government clerks, entitled "Uncle Sam's Children." During that time, his syndicated column, "On The Line," first appeared. Considine, a six-foot-one-inch, 180-pound Roman Catholic, married Mildred (Millie) Anderson, a buxom blonde columnist, on July 21, 1931, and had four children, two being adopted.

In 1937, publisher William Randolph Hearst brought Considine to New York with a five-year contract to write for the New York *American* (later *Journal-American*). Considine succeeded Damon Runyan (OS) as sports columnist and expanded the column to include varied subjects. After working as a correspondent during World War II, he roamed the world as a Hearst correspondent. Considine wrote or coauthored over 25 books, notably *Thirty Seconds over Tokyo*, with Ted W. Lawson (1943), and *General Wainwright's Story*, with Jonathan M. Wainwright (1946), both best-sellers. His other books included *MacArthur the Magnificent* (1942); *Where's Sammy*, with Sammy Schulman (1943); *The Babe Ruth Story*, with Babe Ruth (1948); *Innocents at Home* (1950); *Panama Canal* (1951); *Man Against Fire* (1955); *Ripley: The Modern Marco Polo* (1961), and a biography and movie script about baseball star Lou Gehrig (BB), *Pride of the Yankees.* He also appeared as a commentator on radio and TV news programs. Considine, a member of the National Press Club and Artists and Writers Club, was elected president of the Overseas Press Club in 1947. In 1980, he was enshrined in the NASS Hall of Fame.

BIBLIOGRAPHY: *CB* (1947) p. 131; *Celebrity Register* (1973); *NYT*, September 26, 1975, p. 40; *Readers Encyclopedia of American Literature* (New York, 1972); WWA, 24th ed. (1946–1947).

Stan W. Carlson

COSTAS, Robert Quinlan "Bob" (b. March 22, 1952, Queens, NY), sportscaster and talk show host, is the son of John George Costas, an electrical engineer, and Jayne (Quinlan) Costas and grew up in Commack, NY. Costas loved playing sandlot baseball and listening to the play-by-play radio coverage of major league baseball by announcers Mel Allen (OS), Red Barber (OS), Lindsay Nelson (OS), and Vin Scully (OS). Young Costas was drawn to the mystique of baseball broadcasting and to the romance of the airwaves. His Greek-American father, who died in 1970, taught him to revere the New York Yankees (AL) and idolize Mickey Mantle (BB).

After graduating from Commack High School in 1970, Costas majored in communications at Syracuse University, known for its broadcasting curriculum and successful graduates like Marty Glickman* and Marv Albert.* Costas worked for four years at the WAER-FM campus radio station, learning to smooth out his voice and lose his pronounced New York accent. In his senior year, Costas broadcast the Syracuse Blazers minor league hockey games. After his graduation in 1974, he worked for six months in Syracuse for WXYR-TV and Radio as a weekend sportscaster, substitute weatherman, and host of a "Bowling for Dollars" local television show.

Costas's first big break came in late 1974, when he sent radio station KMOX-AM in St. Louis a tape of game highlights for the Syracuse University basketball games he had broadcast. At age 22, he was selected to broadcast the basketball contests of the St. Louis Spirits (ABA). When the Spirits franchise folded in 1976 after just two seasons, Costas started working freelance, broadcasting regional college and professional football and basketball games on the weekends for CBS-Sports. He also worked his regular assignments for KMOX-AM, which included announcing the University of Missouri basketball games.

By 1980, Costas had gained six years of play-by-play experience and joined NBC-Sports. He covered regional college football games and early rounds of the NCAA basketball tournament and, in fall 1982, joined Bob Trumpy (S) in doing NFL telecasts. In 1983, he began teaming with Tony Kubek (S) in handling the Saturday afternoon major league backup broadcast. Costas became the television studio host of the "NFL '84" show, a demanding role that involved updates on games, contest summaries, interviews, background information, and pregame, halftime, and postgame shows for all the NBC NFL games. Costas adeptly mastered a constant flow of information, quickly shifting contexts and coordinating smoothly the roles of others in his anchor position. Costas also hosted the NFL Monday night game on NBC-Radio, conducted two syndicated radio shows, *"TSN Report"* and "Sports Flashback," and hosted a weekly call-in program on KMOX-FM in St. Louis. He also became well known through his guest appearances and zany sportscaster routines on "Late Night with David Letterman."

Costas's rich array of media talents has taken him beyond his play-by-play and studio host roles, as he has become one of media's best interviewers. Since August 1988, he has hosted "Later with Bob Costas," a four-day-a-week, half-hour interview show that followed David Letterman's "Late

Night" show. These personal interviews reveal Costas's solid preparation, ability to ask questions that elicit substantial and personal responses, incredible memory and familiarity with pop music and film, and curiosity about the creative process in all fields. He also hosts "Costas Coast to Coast," a live Sunday night radio sports conversation show that features past and present sports figures, allowing Costas to pursue his deep interest in sports history. He has also hosted some prime-time interview specials for NBC. Costas often interjects some skeptical humor and occasional silliness into his interviews to keep them from becoming too serious.

During the 1988 Summer Olympics in Seoul, South Korea, Costas served as a secondary anchorman. For the 1992 Summer Olympic Games in Barcelona, Spain, he anchored NBC's coverage, spending 5 hours a day on the air and working another 8 to 10 hours. His performance received high praise for his excellent mix of news, human drama, social perspective and history, and the lighter side. Costas's amazing success as a sportscaster and studio host has been based on his ability to tell the stories of sporting events at many levels in a flowing, natural narrative without hyping the event or sports figures and without trying to create stories or to push stories into controversies.

In a national network career of less than 15 years, Costas has received a constant flow of awards. NASS named him Sportscaster of the Year in 1985, 1987, 1988, 1991, and 1992, while the ASA designated him Sportscaster of the Year in 1989, 1991, 1992, and 1993. He also has won four National Emmy awards.

Costas married Carole Randall Krumemacher, an elementary school teacher, on June 24, 1983, and has a son, Keith, and a daughter, Taylor. Costas keeps an apartment in New York City for his work there, but the family lives in suburban St. Louis.

BIBLIOGRAPHY: *CB* (1993), pp. 10–14; David Ellis, "America's Host," *Time* 140 (August 3, 1992), p. 64; Glen Macnow, "Bob Costas," *Contemporary Newsmakers 1986 Cumulation* (Detroit, MI, 1987), pp. 76–78; Mike Meserole, ed., *The 1994 Information Please Sports Almanac* (Boston, MA, 1993); Curt Smith, *Voices of the Game* (South Bend, IN, 1987); William Taffe, "The Voices from Syracuse," *SI* 60 (March 12, 1984), p. 65; *WWA*, 46th ed. (1990–1991), p. 681.

Douglas A. Noverr

DREES, John Henry "Jack" (b. February 8, 1917, Chicago, IL; d. July 27, 1988, Dallas, TX), sportscaster, was the son of Frank Drees and Rena (Nelvick) Drees and starred in basketball at Chicago's Anston High School. The six-foot-six-inch Drees made All-BTC center at the University of Iowa. Drees's 47-year sportscasting career began in May 1938 for Chicago, IL, radio station WJJD, which hired him as a backup announcer. He started out broadcasting baseball and then switched to horse racing. For CBS-Radio, he conducted a weekend sports commentary show. This top-rated network radio show made his voice and his insights on sport nationally known. World War II interrupted his career, as he served as a lieutenant in the U.S. Navy from 1942 to 1945. In the late 1940s, he covered the Wednesday night televised fights. Dr. Joyce Brothers, a psychologist with an uncanny degree of boxing knowledge, assisted Drees. Drees covered the television broadcast of the Sonny Liston (IS)–Floyd Patterson (IS) heavyweight rematch title fight in 1963 and announced the first Super Bowl game in 1967 between the Green Bay Packers and the Kansas City Chiefs. As a freelance sportscaster, he also reported the Kentucky Derby, Masters golf tournament, and NCAA basketball tournament.

Drees's association with WGN-TV, an important part of his career, made him a prominent Chicago sports fixture. He broadcast the Chicago White Sox (AL) games on WGN-TV from 1968 to 1972, conducted a sports show called "Sports Unlimited," and handled the play-by-play for the Illinois state high school tournaments in the 1960s. He also hosted a sports radio show on WBKB in Chicago. Drees and James C. Mullen in 1974 published *Where Is He Now? Sports Heroes of Yesterday—Revisited*, which featured revealing updated portraits of 39 sports figures. Drees used a straightforward, direct sportscasting style that relied on precise accuracy and a sense of factual immediacy. His generation of sportscasters, grounded in radio, made a successful transition to television due to their versatility, professionalism, and established reputations. Drees spent the last nine years of his broadcasting career from 1977 to 1985 with WKRG-TV in Mobile, AL, and then retired in Dallas, TX. Drees and his wife Mary were married on August 16, 1939, and had three children, Brian, a sports commentator for KMGH-TV in Denver; Barry, a Dallas attorney; and Marilyn, a Washington, DC attorney.

BIBLIOGRAPHY: "Jack Drees, Retired Sports Announcer, Dead at 71," Chicago (IL) *Tribune*, July 28, 1988; Mary Drees, telephone interview with Douglas A. Noverr, May 24, 1993.

Douglas A. Noverr

ELLIOT, Irwin "Win" (b. May 7, 1915, Chelsea, MA), athlete, sportscaster, and analyst, is the son of I. Michael Elliot and Susan Miriam (Shalek) Elliot and participated in varsity ice hockey and track and field at the University of Michigan. After graduating with a Bachelor of Science degree in zoology in 1937, Elliot announced for radio station WMEX in Boston, MA, until 1939. His assignments included covering the Boston Red Sox baseball club (AL) and the Boston Bruins (NHL) hockey club. During the next two years, he broadcast the news and served as a sports editor for radio station WFBR in Baltimore, MD. Elliot was affiliated with NBC- and ABC-Radio during 1940 in Washington, DC. Elliot's first big break came after 1941, when he became a freelance sports emcee, sports commentator, and announcer for all the radio networks. The versatile, gifted Elliot possessed an ability to set the scene and background of major sporting events and became one of radio's most recognizable voices and talents.

After being with the U.S. Maritime Service from 1939 to 1941, Elliot moved to New York City and expanded his broadcasting career beyond sports to include hosting radio and television quiz shows. He worked primarily for CBS-Radio, gaining national recognition as one of the most knowledgeable broadcasters of thoroughbred horse racing with his annual coverage of the Triple Crown races and the All-American Futurity. He also hosted weekly and weekend sports shows and sports specials connected with the World Series, Super Bowl, Kentucky Derby, and Stanley Cup. In his numerous roles, he became a truly national sportscasting figure heard in many time slots and on major occasions in a wide variety of sports. With an encyclopedic memory and a personal knowledge and familiarity with those involved in sports, Elliot added a human sense of drama to sporting events and gave them a behind-the-scenes meaning. He shared his extensive information in an unpretentious, direct way, always reporting in an observant, informed manner without intruding his personality. In 1971 and 1976, he received the Eclipse Award for excellence in thoroughbred racing reporting.

Elliot married Rita A. Barry on November 3, 1951, and has six sons and four daughters. The Westport, CT, resident served as a member and representative of the Town Meeting and made significant contributions as a local citizen.

BIBLIOGRAPHY: Maury Allen, *Voices of Sport* (New York, 1971); *WWA*, 42nd ed. (1982–1983), p. 944.

Douglas A. Noverr

GLICKMAN, Martin "Marty" (b. 1917, East Bronx, New York City, NY), athlete and sportscaster, is the son of Harry Glickman, a salesman and delivery man, and Molly Glickman and grew up in Brooklyn, NY. Glickman's Jewish Rumanian immigrant parents sent their son to the Hebrew school. At James Madison High School in Brooklyn, Glickman starred in track and field and football and won the national schoolboy sprint championship in 1934. He succeeded Jesse Owens (OS), who had run a record 9.4 seconds in the 100 yards for Cleveland East Tech High School in 1933.

Glickman enrolled at Syracuse University without an athletic scholarship but earned one starting his sophomore year due to his outstanding freshman year performance on the track and field team. In July 1936, he earned a place on the U.S. Olympic track and field team, placing fifth in the 100-meter run Olympic trials. Although scheduled to compete in the 400-meter relay race in the 1936 Berlin, Germany, Summer Olympics, Glickman and Sam Stoller, another American Jewish athlete, were replaced on the day of the trials by Owens and Ralph Metcalfe (OS). The controversial decision, made by Lawson Robertson, head coach of the U.S. Olympic track team, and Dean Cromwell (OS), assistant coach, was questioned and criticized by the American Jewish press. Glickman claimed that the decision to replace Stoller and him was due to the anti-Semitism of Avery Brundage (OS), USOC head, and Cromwell's favoritism for Metcalfe.

After his bitter disappointment over the Berlin Olympics, Glickman competed in several European track meets. He returned to Syracuse University, playing tailback and defensive back on the football team. During the 1937 season, he scored two touchdowns for the Orangemen in an upset over Cornell University. The next day, he began his broadcasting career by hosting a 15-minute radio sports show on WAER, the Syracuse campus station. Glickman continued to earn $15 a broadcast until graduating from Syracuse in 1939. After graduation, Glickman played semiprofessional basketball in Syracuse and football for the Jersey City, NJ, Giants (AA). Glickman also worked in New York City as a salesman at Gimbel's and an unpaid errand boy at Radio Station WHN, where he eventually handled his own sports highlights and summary program.

During World War II, Glickman served as a lieutenant in the U.S. Marine Corps. His first big break as a sportscaster came in 1945–1946, when he began announcing the Madison Square Garden basketball doubleheaders and thus originated basketball play-by-play. From 1947 to 1967, he broadcast New York Knickerbockers (NBA) basketball games. He also started announcing games for the New York Giants (NFL) in 1949 and covered New York Jets (AFL) games starting in 1960. As a local independent sportscaster with no national network affiliation, Glickman covered various New York City sporting events ranging from high school sports to professional wrestling. For 17 years, he served as the track announcer at the Yonkers Raceway.

Glickman was hired by HBO in 1972 and developed its sports programming and broadcasting. He pioneered cable broadcasting, doing a Little League game on Manhattan Cable in 1966 and the first HBO sports telecast in 1972, an NHL game broadcast to 365 subscribers in Wilkes-Barre, PA. In 1983, Mike Weisman of NBC-Sports hired Glickman as television's first broadcasting coach and mentor. Until 1990, Glickman offered his expert analysis and advice to such sportscasters as Marv Albert,* Bob Griese (FB), John Brodie (FB), Merlin Olsen (FB), Bob Trumpy (S), and Mary Lou Retton (IS). Glickman's distinguished sportscasting career lasted for over 50 years, as he participated in and played a key role in the development of play-by-play sportscasting. Glickman, the eighth sportscaster inducted into the NASS Hall of Fame in 1992, became a member of the ASA Hall of Fame in 1993.

BIBLIOGRAPHY: Peter Levine, *Ellis Island to Ebbets Field: Sport and the American Jewish Experience* (New York, 1992); Rudy Martzke, "Glickman: NBC's Costas' Best Ever," *USA Today*, December 2, 1993; William Taaffe, "The Players Finally Get a Coach,"

SI 59 (October 10, 1993), p. 62; William Taaffe, "The Voices from Syracuse," *SI* 60 (March 12, 1984), p. 65.

Douglas A. Noverr

HARMON, Merle Reid Sr. (b. June 21, 1927, Orchardville, IL), sportscaster, is the son of Herschel Harmon and Oda Ethel (Holler) Harmon. Following U.S. Navy service from 1944 to 1946, Harmon received his Associate of Arts degree from Graceland College in 1947 and Bachelor of Arts degree from the University of Denver in 1949. He married Jeanette Kinner on December 31, 1947, and has five children, Reid, Keith, Kyle, Bruce, and Kira.

Harmon began his broadcasting career as a sportscaster in Topeka, KS, in 1949 and worked for the University of Kansas Radio Network in Lawrence, KS, from 1952 until 1954. From 1954 through 1961, Harmon served as the radio voice of the Kansas City Athletics baseball club (AL) and started his rise to prominence as a baseball announcer. His sportscasting career included stints with the Milwaukee Braves (NL) in 1964 and 1965, Minnesota Twins (AL) from 1967 to 1969, and Milwaukee Brewers (AL) from 1970 to 1979. He combined his baseball assignments with broadcasting work for ABC-TV from 1961 to 1973 and NBC-TV from 1979 until 1987, handling baseball and football. From 1987 until 1991, he covered play-by-play for Texas Rangers (AL) baseball games on HSE. His wide-ranging assignments also included covering the New York Jets (NFL) from 1964 to 1972, the World University Games in Moscow, Russia, for TVS in 1973, and BTC basketball from 1974 until 1980.

Listeners respected Harmon for his enthusiasm, skillful play-by-play, and clear, perceptive commentary. His career touched many turning points in televised baseball. In Kansas City, he educated a new region to the games of the transplanted Philadelphia Athletics (AL). With the Milwaukee Braves, he possessed the distinct displeasure of broadcasting sparsely attended games for a team that had announced its intentions to leave that city for Atlanta, GA. At Minnesota, Harmon participated in pioneering regional team telecasts. His service with ABC and NBC took place at a critical period in the history of national Games of the Week, while his last tour with HSE in Texas coincided with the rise of local team cable. Harmon blended smoothly with many partners, including Keith Jackson (OS), Chris Schenkel,* and Joe Garagiola (OS). The accessible, unassuming Harmon helped start the career of two famous television personalities. Milwaukee partner Bob Uecker credits Harmon for persuading him to audition for ABC-TV, while ex-umpire Ron Luciano acknowledged his great debt to Harmon for encouraging him to audition for NBC and shepherding him through his first year as a broadcaster.

A NASS Hall of Fame member, Harmon was recognized for his work by his undergraduate college and the NAIA. He also participated in civic affairs and the Church of Jesus Christ of the Latter Day Saints. In 1977, Harmon branched into the sporting apparel business by creating Merle Harmon's Fan Fare, a chain of stores mostly in shopping malls. These stores specialized in sports clothing and featured team logos, getting an early start and significant part of what became a $3 billion business by 1988.

BIBLIOGRAPHY: Ron Luciano and David Fisher, *The Umpire Strikes Back* (New York, 1982); Curt Smith, *Voices of the Game* (South Bend, IN, 1987); "Sports Merchandise," *Venture* (September 1988), pp. 76, 80; Bob Uecker and Mickey Herskowitz, *Catcher in the Wry* (New York, 1982); *WWA*, 46th ed. (1990–1991), p. 1394.

James W. Harper

McCARTHY, Charles Louis "Clem" (b. September 9, 1882, East Bloomfield, NY; d. June 5, 1962, New York, NY), sportscaster, began his life with close links to the horse world. His Irish-born father worked as a horse dealer and auctioneer and took him as a youth to race tracks and horse fairs all over the United States. His peripatetic education involved study as a teenager at various schools in many different cities.

McCarthy initially desired to be a jockey, but experts correctly warned him that he would grow too tall and weigh too much. McCarthy's enthusiasm for the racing world remained undiminished, however, as he found employment as a horse racing sports writer in southern California in the 1920s. In 1927, he discovered what would make him a sportscasting legend. At Arlington Park in Chicago, IL, a public address system was installed in 1927. McCarthy soon became the most celebrated of horse racing commentators, as his voice and persona enabled his broadcasts to create layers of excitement around an athletic event. McCarthy's magical descriptions transformed athletic contests into a form of social theater, where listeners became energized by the cadences of McCarthy's staccato chatter. He broadcast the legendary Joe Louis (IS)–Max Schmeling boxing rematch at Yankee Stadium in New York in 1938. His first position came with radio station KYW in Chicago, IL, in 1928. A year later, he signed with NBC-Radio and covered horse racing and other significant sports contests. He attracted tremendous popular appeal via his broadcasts for WMCA-Radio in New York.

He pioneered the technique of "race calling." With binoculars in one hand and microphone in the other, he correctly called thousands of races. His only gaffe, a major one, came when he named the 1947 Preakness winner as Jet Pilot rather than Faultless. The *NYT* described the scene, " 'Ladies and gentlemen,' he [McCarthy] rasped on the air, 'I have made a horrible mistake. Babe Ruth [BB] struck out. Today I did the same. I am in distinguished company.' " McCarthy covered every Kentucky Derby from 1928 to 1950 and became a household name with his opening of "R-r-r-racing fans, this is Clem McCarthy."

He married Vina Smith, a vaudeville actress, in 1929 and had no children. In 1954, his wife died of cancer. Three years later, he was seriously injured in an automobile accident. McCarthy's last tragic years found him battle the ravages of Parkinson's disease and the despair of poverty. At McCarthy's funeral in New York, distinguished sportscaster Red Barber (OS) delivered the eulogy. The organ played "My Old Kentucky Home," the "national anthem" of the most famous of the Churchill Downs races, the Kentucky Derby. McCarthy had made his voice an inherent part of that equestrian, social celebration from 1928 to 1950. In 1962, Ed Sullivan and NBC shared the expenses in producing a long-playing record entitled "Clem McCarthy, the Voice of American Sports." He was enshrined in the NASS Hall of Fame (1970) and the ASA Hall of Fame (1987).

BIBLIOGRAPHY: *CB* (1941), pp. 542–543; "Clem McCarthy Is Dead at 79," *NYT*, June 5, 1962; Frank G. Menke, ed., *The Encyclopedia of Sports* (New York, 1975); "Sportscaster Gives Eulogy at Rites for Clem McCarthy," *NYT*, June 8, 1962.

Scott A.G.M. Crawford

MEANY, Thomas William "Tom" (b. September 21, 1903, Brooklyn, NY; d. September 11, 1964, New York, NY), sportswriter, author, and executive, attended St. John's Prep School, where he played football and baseball. He managed the 1921–1922 prep basketball team, winners of the state championship, and later graduated from St. John's University.

Meany was employed as a timekeeper for the Brooklyn-Manhattan subway system, when the New York *Journal* decided to publish a Brooklyn edition in 1922. Garry Schumacher was named sports editor and hired Meany as a space writer. Meany's byline appeared for the first time in 1923, when he joined the Brooklyn *Daily Times* and was assigned to cover the Brooklyn Dodgers (NL) baseball club. In 1929, Meany left the *Daily Times* to write for the New York *Telegram* (later the *World-Telegram*) and began covering the New York Giants (NL) baseball club. In June 1932, he gained one of his most famous scoops when he journeyed to the Polo Grounds on a rainy day and revealed the greatest baseball story of the decade. Pinned to the New York Giants manager's door was a typed announcement that pilot John J. McGraw (BB) had resigned after 30 years at the helm.

Meany worked for *PM* from 1940 until that paper folded in 1948 and then was employed by the New York *Star*. After the *Star* ceased publication, he served as a columnist for *The Morning Telegraph* for a year and then became sports editor for *Collier's* magazine. He remained there until *Collier's* ceased publication in December 1956. Since he worked for two newspapers and a magazine that folded, Meany called himself "the journalistic kiss of death." He then spent two years as a freelance writer, producing numerous articles for *SEP*, *Look*, and many other publications.

In 1958, Meany was hired by the New York Yankees (AL) baseball club to work on special promotion projects. With the formation of the New York Mets (NL) baseball club in 1962, he was named the new club's publicity director. He later became promotional director of the Mets and served in that post until his death.

Meany, a noted after-dinner speaker, authored 21 baseball books, including analytical volumes on the game's greatest hitters and greatest pitchers along with histories of various teams. He "ghosted" two books for New York Yankee slugger Joe DiMaggio (BB) and became known as one of the nation's better sportswriters. Meany's books included *Babe Ruth* (1947), *Baseball's Greatest Teams* (1949), *Baseball's Greatest Hitters* (1950), *Baseball's Greatest Pitchers* (1951), *The Magnificent Yankees* (1952), *Baseball's Greatest Players* (1953), *The Artful Dodgers* (1953), *Milwaukee's Miracle Braves* (1954), *Collier's Greatest Sports Stories* (1955), *The Incredible Giants* (1955), *The Boston Red Sox* (1956), *Mostly Baseball* (1958), *The Yankee Story* (1960), *There've Been Some Changes in the World of Sports* (1962), *How to Bat* (with Harry Walker, 1963), *Baseball's Best* (with Tommy Holmes, 1964), *Kings of the Diamond* (with Lee Allen, 1965), and biographies of Joe DiMaggio (BB), Ted Williams (BB), Stan Musial (BB), and Ralph Kiner (BB), all published in 1951 in the Barnes All-Star Library.

Meany was voted the J. G. Taylor Spink Award for 1975 by the BBWAA for meritorious contributions to baseball writing, giving him membership in the writers wing of the National Baseball Hall of Fame. During the 1950s, Meany wrote a widely acclaimed annual preview of the major league baseball pennant races for *Collier's*. He predicted the order of finish in both leagues, the batting champions, Rookie of the Year, and possible 20-game winners. A Roman Catholic, Meany married Clara M. Maxwell in 1932 and had no children.

BIBLIOGRAPHY: Bob Broeg, column, St. Louis (MO) *Post-Dispatch*, December 13, 1975; *BBWAA Scorebook No. 4* (New York 1965); Clippings, 1938, 1964, 1975, National Baseball Hall of Fame Library, Cooperstown, NY; *Collier's Magazine Baseball Previews*, February 28, 1953; March 5, 1954; March 30, 1956; Carl Lundquist, column, New York, April 18, 1964; Murray Robinson, Column, New York *Journal-American*, undated.

Stan W. Carlson

MURPHY, Jack Raymond Jr. (b. February 5, 1933, Tulsa, OK; d. September 25, 1980, San Diego, CA), sportswriter, was the son of James Raymond Murphy and Eula (Wholf) Murphy. After receiving primary and secondary education in Tulsa Roman Catholic schools, he worked as a reporter for the Tulsa *World* from 1940 to 1942 and attended the University of Tulsa from 1942 to 1943 and Southwestern Louisiana Institute in 1943. During World War II, he served with the U.S. Marines from 1943 to 1945. On May 17, 1947, he married Hester Ahniwake Aston. The couple had a daughter, Robin (Mrs. William George), and a son, John Patrick.

A second tour followed at the Tulsa *World* in 1946 and 1947. Murphy reported for the Fort Worth (TX) *Star-Telegram* from 1947 to 1949 and the Oklahoma City (OK) *Daily Oklahoman* from 1949 to 1951. Murphy began a 30-year career as a sportswriter for the San Diego (CA) *Union* in 1951 and held that position for the rest of his life. During the 1960s, he gained national prominence for his magazine articles in the *NYT Magazine, The New Yorker, Time,* and *Newsweek.*

A pipe-smoking, gentle writer with a superb sense of humor, Murphy covered all sports from boxing to horse racing and devoted considerable space to probing personalities. During the 1960s, he became a regular drinking buddy and traveling companion of Red Smith (OS). They covered the Kentucky Derby, the 1960 Winter Olympics at Lake Placid, NY, and the Super Bowl, comparing and judging each other's stories on these major events. Smith indicated that whenever they wrote a piece together, Murphy deserved 70 percent of the credit. Smith and many others claimed that Murphy wrote best about hunting and fishing, and the outdoors of southern California, but his interest ranged to team sports and boxing. The politically active Democrat, a longtime member of the GSDSA, served as its president in 1967–1968. Murphy's significant role in the efforts to secure professional football and baseball franchises for San Diego led to the stadium being named in his honor.

Murphy, who presided over the NFWA in 1965, earned the NHC's Headliners Award in 1954, Bill Corum Thoroughbred Racing Association Award in 1965, and E. P. Dutton & Company Award in 1961. He wrote a book, *Abe and Me,* in 1977 and died after a three-month battle with cancer of the spine. In 1988, he was elected to the NASS Hall of Fame.

BIBLIOGRAPHY: Ira Berkow, *Red: A Biography of Red Smith* (New York, 1986); Jack Murphy, "Champ Behind the Mask," *NYT Magazine* (July 21, 1963), pp. 18ff; *NYT,* September 26, 1980, p. A28; "Open Locker," *Time* 47 (January 15, 1965) p. 23; "Profiles," *New Yorker* 37 (November 11, 1961), pp. 61–62ff; *WWA,* 40th ed. (1978–1979), p. 2345.

James W. Harper

PARKER, Daniel Francis "Dan" (b. July 1, 1893, Waterbury, CT; d. May 20, 1967, Waterbury, CT), sportswriter, was the son of Robert Parker and Catherine (Scanlan) Parker and attended Crosby High School in Waterbury. Parker married Marjorie Barry on October 14, 1928, and had two children, Daniel Thomas and Barry Noel, before the marriage ended in divorce. His second marriage to Norma Murray on February 29, 1940, produced a daughter, Norma. After Norma's death in July 1958, Parker married Alice McLoughlin in December 1961.

Parker's newspaper career started with his hometown Waterbury *Republican* in 1912 and 1913. He became a reporter for the Waterbury *American* from 1913 to 1920 and served as a sergeant in the American Expeditionary

Force during World War I. Parker moved to New York in 1920 and joined the New York *Daily Mirror* as a staff writer from 1920 to 1924. He became sports editor and a regular columnist at the *Daily Mirror* in 1926, remaining there until that paper folded in 1963. Thereafter, he wrote for the New York *Journal-American* until his death.

The six-foot-four-inch 240-pounder, with a moustache and receding hairline, proved a sharp reporter and crusaded against commercialism and shoddy practices in sport. His criticisms of corruption in boxing and wrestling led to state investigations. Damon Runyon (OS) quickly noticed his work and promoted his articles, praising Parker as "the most consistently brilliant of all sportswriters."

Parker, among boxer Joe Louis's (OS) strongest supporters, was one of few writers to praise "The Brown Bomber" before his June 1938 bout with Max Schmeling. Afterward, Parker declared, "Louis has finally come into his full estate as a great world champion. If anyone doubts his greatness after his masterful job last night, he's plain plumb prejudiced." He advocated ending the color line in organized baseball in 1946 but doubted Brooklyn Dodgers (NL) president Branch Rickey's commitment. Parker wrote, "Any resemblance between Branch Rickey and Abraham Lincoln is purely coincidental." Yet Parker praised the integration effort, lauding Atlanta, GA, for resisting efforts to bar Jackie Robinson (BB) from a 1947 exhibition game. He declared, "When the liberal forces in Atlanta, the stronghold of the Ku Klux Klan, defeated the white shirters who wanted to bar Robinson, a powerful blow was struck against the color line."

Parker, who covered all sports, penned the humorous poem "Leave Us Go Root for the Dodgers, Rogers" and in 1947 wrote a book entitled *The ABC's of Horseracing*. Despite his crusading, Parker held a light view of sportswriters. He suggested that the best sportswriters "remain perpetually juvenile" and reflected that "a facetious sort of cynicism is the favorite pose of the profession." Parker also wrote humorously about eccentrics and peppered his column with Yiddish and Italian phrases. In 1958, he quipped, "The reason that the Yankees never lay an egg is because they don't operate on chicken feed."

His honors included the NHC's Headliners Sports Writing Award and the Newspaper Guild's Page One Award three times (1951, 1956, 1961). He received Long Island University's Polk Memorial Award in 1954 and garnered the NASS Award in 1960. Red Smith (OS) listed Parker, who was elected in 1975 to the NASS Hall of Fame, as one of the best sportswriters between the 1920s and the 1970s.

BIBLIOGRAPHY: Ira Berkow, *Red: A Biography of Red Smith* (New York, 1986); Paul Dickson, *Baseball's Greatest Quotations* (New York, 1991); David Halberstam, *Summer of 49* (New York, 1989); Chris Mead, *Champion: Joe Louis* (New York, 1986); *NYT*,

May 21, 1967, p. 86; June 17, 1967; Jules Tygiel, *Baseball's Great Experiment* (New York, 1983); *WWA*, 34th ed. (1966–1967), p. 1630.

James W. Harper

POVICH, Shirley Lewis (b. July 15, 1905, Bar Harbor, ME), sportswriter, is the son of Nathan Povich and Rosa (Orlovich) Povich and grew up in Maine. Povich arrived in Washington, DC to attend Georgetown University from 1922 to 1924. He married Ethyl Friedman on February 21, 1932, and had three children, David, Lynn, and Maurice. Maury became a well-known talk show host and television personality.

The opportunity to report sports for the Washington *Post* between 1922 and 1926 lured Shirley from a law career. He served as sports editor of the paper from 1926 to 1933 and became a featured columnist thereafter. Povich spent three years as a correspondent during World War II in the South Pacific, receiving a commendation "for outstanding service" from Secretary of the Navy James Forrestal.

Upon returning to the *Post* in 1946, Povich became one of the nation's premier sportswriters. He was given the NHC's National Headliners Sports Writing Award in 1947 and served as BBWAA president in 1955. Povich was elected to the writers wing of the National Baseball Hall of Fame in 1976 and the NASS Hall of Fame in 1984. He wrote two books, *The Washington Senators: An Informal History* in 1954 and an autobiographical *All These Mornings* in 1969, and authored articles in *SEP* and other magazines.

Povich recognized the broader implications of boxer Joe Louis's (OS) June 1938 championship fight with Max Schmeling for race relations. "He was a credit both to his sport and to his people," Povich said, "and since both of these are part of America, he was a credit to all of us." Povich also called for the integration of organized baseball in 1941. "There's a couple of million dollars worth of baseball talent on the loose," he wrote, "ready for the big leagues, yet unsigned by any major league team. Only one thing is keeping them out of the big leagues—the color of their skin." In 1954, he criticized Washington Senators (AL) owner Clark Griffith (BB) for his slowness to integrate, charging Griffith "would give Washington players from other lands, but never an American Negro." When outfielder Larry Doby (BB) of the Chicago White Sox (AL) decked pitcher Art Ditmar of the New York Yankees (AL) in 1957 after being hit by a pitch, Povich declared that the incident "marked the complete emancipation of the American Negro in America's national game" as the first time "a Negro had thrown the first punch in a player argument."

The longtime columnist was highly regarded by fellow sportswriters, fans, and players. Pitcher Bob Feller (BB) of the Cleveland Indians (AL) called Povich "one of the best baseball writers in history." Others especially praised Povich for his commitment and enthusiastic pen. Typical was his commentary after Don Larsen* of the New York Yankees (AL) hurled a perfect game against the Brooklyn Dodgers (NL) in the 1956 World Series: "The million to one shot came in. Hell froze over. A month of Sundays hit the calendar. Don Larsen today pitched a no-hit, no-run, no-man-reach-first game in a World Series."

Povich has served as adjunct professor of communications at American University since 1976 and holds his sports columnist title for the *Post* in 1995 at age 89.

BIBLIOGRAPHY: Paul Dickson, *Baseball's Greatest Quotations* (New York, 1991); Bob Feller with Bill Gilbert, *Now Pitching Bob Feller* (New York, 1990); Chris Mead, *Champion: Joe Louis, Black Hero in White America* (New York, 1985); Shirley Povich, "Littlest Big Leaguer," *SEP* 231 (May 15, 1959), p. 34; Shirley Povich, *The Washington Senators* (New York, 1954); Jules Tygiel, *Baseball's Great Experiment* (New York, 1983); *WWA*, 42nd ed. (1982–1983), p. 2694; *WWA*, 47th ed. (1992–1993), p. 2707.

James W. Harper

RICHTER, Francis Charles "Frank" (b. January 26, 1854, Philadelphia, PA; d. February 12, 1926, Philadelphia, PA), sportswriter, was the son of Gottlieb Richter, a boilermaker, and Johanna Richter, emigrants from Germany. Richter apprenticed to a shirtmaker in youth, played amateur baseball and in 1872 became a newspaper reporter with the Philadelphia *Day*. He in 1875 married Helen "Nellie" Dwyer and had 10 children, including sons Thomas, Francis, and Chandler, all sportswriters at times. His daughters included Helen, Edith, Florence, May, Beatrice Olive, who married noted radio newscaster Boake Carter, Gladys, and 1 child who died young.

Richter advanced to managing editor before Philadelphia *Day* dissolved in 1880 and next reported baseball for the Philadelphia *Sunday World*. Richter soon switched to the Philadelphia *Public Ledger*, where, according to his son Thomas, he "started the first sporting department ever included in any newspaper." The innovator joined Thomas Stotesbury Dando and August Rudolph in founding *SpL*, a weekly periodical specializing in presenting baseball and other competitive sports news. It commenced at Philadelphia on April 14, 1883, three years before the debut of its chief competitor, *TSN*. The famous baseball journalists from other cities, whose reports appeared regularly in *SpL*, included Ed Bang (Cleveland, OH), John B. Foster (Brooklyn, NY), Jake Morse (Boston, MA), Ren Mulford (Cincinnati, OH), and Bill Phelan (Chicago, IL). Henry Chadwick (BB) also contributed articles frequently. Richter continued to publish and edit the paper until 1917, when wartime shortages of personnel and material supplies forced him to sell his interest.

Richter, acknowledged as a facile writer with a trenchant pen, excellent speaker, expert analyst, and authority on baseball, was respected for his accuracy, integrity, and steadfast devotion. Frequently, his views on baseball politics opposed those of executives who controlled the sport. Reputedly, he helped create the AA in 1882 and the National Agreement in 1883, place the Philadelphia clubs in the AA in 1882 and the NL in 1883, and assimilate the AA into the NL in 1891. Aggressive promotion of his "Millennium Plan," proposed in 1887, resulted in the major leagues granting the minor leagues a player reservation privilege in 1888 and a draft system in 1891. He served as an official scorer at World Series games for many years and declined the presidency in 1907, as he had other baseball administrative positions previously.

After authoring *A Brief History of Baseball* in 1909, he expanded the book five years later into a major work, *Richter's History and Records of Baseball*, a "concise, yet complete," highly valued reference. He also wrote "The Press and Sport" in *Athletic Sports in America, England and Australia* (1889) and two booklets, *The Millennium Plan* (1888) and *How the White Sox Won the World's Championship* (1907). Richter edited the *Sporting Life's Official Base Ball Guide and Hand-Book of the National Game* (1891) and *The Reach Official American League Base Ball Guide* from 1902 through 1926. The 1926 edition manuscript was completed the day before Richter's sudden death from bronchial pneumonia.

BIBLIOGRAPHY: John B. Foster, "To the Memory of Francis C. Richter," *TSN*, February 25, 1926, p. 6; Philadelphia (PA) *Inquirer*, February 13, 1926; Philadelphia (PA) *Public Ledger*, February 13, 1926; Thomas D. Richter, "Obituary of Francis C. Richter," *Reach Official American League Base Ball Guide*, 1926, p. 244; *SpL*, March 14, 1908, 25th anniv. issue; *TSN*, February 18, 1926, pp. 2–3.

Frank V. Phelps

SCHENKEL, Christopher Eugene "Chris" (b. August 21, 1923, Bippus, IN), sportscaster, grew up in a family of six children in a rural Indiana farm community with an early love of sports broadcasting on radio and a desire to announce like the famed Ted Husing (OS). As a student at Purdue University, Schenkel began announcing for a radio station in Muncie, IN, in 1942. After graduating from Purdue with a bachelor's degree in radio broadcasting in 1943, he served in the U.S. Army from 1943 to 1946. Upon returning to the Midwest, he resumed his sportscasting career. He worked at a radio station in Providence, RI, while serving as a horse race caller at Narragansett Park.

Dumont Television hired Schenkel as the radio broadcast voice of the New York Giants (NFL) in 1949. Schenkel spent 13 seasons broadcasting their games, calling the famous December 1958 championship sudden-death overtime classic between the Giants and Baltimore Colts. Schenkel originally worked for CBS-TV, but his long connection with ABC-TV brought him national recognition. He served as the principal voice of ABC's coverage of college football, working with Red Grange (FB), Paul Christman (FB), Bud Wilkinson (FB), Bill Flemming, and Keith Jackson (OS) as his partners. Jackson replaced Schenkel on the primary games starting with the 1974 season. Schenkel anchored the coverage of the 1968 Mexico City, Mexico, Summer Olympics, the tragedy-marred 1972 Munich, Germany, Olympics, and seven other Summer and Winter Olympics. His ABC-Sports assignments have included doing segments for "Wide World of Sports" on boxing, motor racing, figure skating, horse racing, and golf. He also covered professional basketball, working with Jack Twyman (IS) and Bill Russell (IS), and professional football, teaming with Johnny Lujack (FB) and Pat Summerall (FB). His lone experience with broadcasting baseball came in 1965, when he worked on ABC's "Game of the Week" with Merle Harmon,* Keith Jackson, and Howard Cosell (OS). Disastrously low ratings caused ABC to drop the "Game of the Week" after only 1 season.

Others have sharply criticized Schenkel for his homey style, mannerisms, and unwillingness to criticize or offend anyone, but his low-key personality and unapologetic self-image have served him well in the high-pressure world of sportscasting. He has always believed that the announcer should not upstage the sporting event, that the color man and analyst compose an equal part of a sportscasting team, and that filling a broadcast with talk is unnecessary. Schenkel's longest-running, most successful job as sports commentator has been with the PBA tour, continuous since 1962. This role has earned him election in 1976 to the PBA Hall of Fame and in 1978 to the AmBC Hall of Fame as well as numerous awards for his contributions to bowling. He hosted the Championship Bowling film series in 1954 and 1955 and narrated numerous films for all segments of the bowling industry.

Schenkel's other awards and recognition have included being named Sportscaster of the Year by the NASS in 1963, 1964, 1967, and 1970, being inducted into the NASS Hall of Fame in 1981, receiving the Pete Rozelle/ Pro Football Hall of Fame Radio-Television Award in 1992, and earning a Sports Emmy Life Achievement Award in 1993.

Schenkel married Fran Paige, a former professional dancer, in 1955 and has three children, Christina, Ted, and John. Schenkel has appeared in five feature films, including a role in *Maurie* (1973), a biographical film of NBA star Maurice Stokes.* He narrated many PGA films and has received honorary doctorates from Purdue University and Ball State University.

BIBLIOGRAPHY: Maury Allen, *Voices of Sport* (New York, 1971); John Battle, "Golden Voice of Television: ABC Commentator Enters His 32nd Year with Pro Tour," Lansing (MI) *State Journal*, December 6, 1992; Jack Olsen, "Virtue Is Its Own Reward," *SI* 73 (January 22, 1973), pp. 64–74; Richard Sandomir, "With Words to Spare, Schenkel Strikes a Chord," *NYT*, April 13, 1993; Curt Smith, *Voices of the Game* (South Bend, IN, 1987); Bert Randolph Sugar, *"The Thrill of Victory": The Inside Story of ABC Sports* (New York, 1978); *WWA*, 42nd ed. (1982–1983).

                                                                                    Douglas A. Noverr

SCOTT, Raymond "Ray" (b. 1918, Johnstown, PA), sportscaster, began his broadcasting career in his hometown at age 19, working for small local radio station WJAC as copywriter, announcer, and advertising salesman. He also developed and hosted a regular sports show and, during World War II, served four years in the U.S. Army. He returned to Pennsylvania after the war, working for radio station WCAE in Pittsburgh. He broadcast college football games for Carnegie Tech and the University of Pittsburgh and basketball games for Duquesne University, also being employed by a local advertising agency. The WDTV DuMont Television Network affiliate in Pittsburgh hired Scott in 1952 and assigned him in 1953 and 1954 to broadcast a weekly Saturday night NFL game on a coast-to-coast hookup. Scott's work for the DuMont Network also involved covering two national political conventions and working with noted political correspondent Bob Trout.

The dramatic turning point in Scott's career came on January 1, 1956, when he broadcast the Sugar Bowl for ABC-TV and took over when a drug overdose prevented Bill Stern (OS) from performing. This exposure, along with his effective handling of the situation, caused CBS-TV to hire him to handle television broadcasts for the Green Bay Packers (NFL) starting in the 1956 season. Scott's timely association with the Packers lasted from 1956 through 1968, enabling him to call nine NFL title games and four Super Bowls and bringing him national recognition as a skillful, seasoned play-by-play announcer. His distinctive voice and straightforward, factual style put the game directly before the fans and let the circumstances and developments of the game provide their own drama. His trademark style included concise and economical commentary and a reliance on the range, pauses, and intonations of his voice. Scott became close personal friends with Green Bay coach Vince Lombardi (FB) and the most recognized voice of the NFL during its time of growth and success as a televised sport. For CBS, he broadcast golf and various other sports. The NASS named Scott Sportscaster of the Year in 1968 and 1971 and inducted him into the NASS Hall of Fame in 1982.

From 1961 through 1967, Scott covered radio and television broadcasts of the Minnesota Twins (AL) games. In 1965, Scott broadcast the World Series, working with Vin Scully (OS). After leaving baseball announcing for a year, he returned to call the Washington Senators (AL) games in 1969–1970, the Twins' television contests in 1973 and 1975, and the Milwaukee Brewers' (AL) television package in 1976. His distinguished NFL broadcasting career for CBS ended in 1974 with some disillusionment and bitterness when the networks turned away from his traditional style and mode of broadcasting to the announcer as personality and to ex-athletes. After 1974, Scott worked for the Hughes Sports and Mizlou television sports syndicate networks. During the 1988 Seoul, South Korea, Summer Olympics, NBC hired Scott as one of the replacements for network sportscasters on assignment in South Korea. Following a lapse of 14 years, he broadcast NFL games once again as a stand-in announcer.

In 1989, Scott began broadcasting Arizona State University (PTC) football games, handled play-by-play for the Phoenix Cardinals (NFL) preseason games, and appeared on daily sports segments on station KTVK in Phoenix. He returned to Minneapolis, conducting a daily sports talk show on a radio station and covering the St. John's University football games in Collegeville, MN. He and his wife Edna have five children.

BIBLIOGRAPHY: Maury Allen, ed., *Voices of Sport* (New York, 1971); Ron Fimrite, "Ray Scott Redux: Return of a Golden Oldie," *SI* 69 (September 12, 1988), pp. 10–11; Steve Nidetz, "2 Voices of a Golden Era Are Heard Again," Chicago (IL) *Tribune*, February 9, 1992; Curt Smith, *Voices of the Game* (South Bend, IN, 1987).

Douglas A. Noverr

SIMPSON, James Shores "Jim" (b. December 20, 1927, Washington, DC), sportscaster, is the son of Elmer Orem Simpson and Elizabeth Louise (Shores) Simpson and grew up in the Washington, DC area, where he attended George Washington University in 1945 and 1946. His broadcasting career began in 1950 with WTOP-TV in Washington, DC and continued in 1952 with WRC-TV. Simpson won three local Emmy awards for his work at these two stations. From 1951 through 1953, Simpson served with the U.S. Naval Reserve. In 1955, he was hired as a sportscaster for NBC-TV in Washington, DC. His early national exposure came through his football play-by-play for ABC (1960–1962), CBS (1962–1964), and NBC (after 1964). At ABC, Simpson worked with Jim McKay (OS) on "Wide World of Sports." With NBC, the versatile Simpson covered NFL games, major league baseball, Wimbledon Open tennis, and NCAA basketball championships. He broadcast the 1968, 1969, 1971, and 1972 World Series and, during the regular season, handled the backup "Game of the Week" with Tony Kubek (S), Sandy Koufax (BB), and Maury Wills (BB). Simpson, known for his formal and economical announcing style, reported the facts and situations with few anecdotes or personal observations. He demonstrated considerable mentoring abilities and understanding patience with new sportscasters, giving important help to Kubek in baseball and Len Dawson (FB) in football. Simpson has covered nine Olympiads, beginning with the 1952 Helsinki, Finland, Summer Olympics. During the 1972 Sapporo, Japan, Winter Olympics, Simpson pioneered as the first television announcer to broadcast live via satellite from Japan while working with Curt Gowdy (OS).

In 1979, Simpson joined ESPN as a play-by-play announcer and talk show host, providing the new cable sports channel with a recognizable talent and veteran experience. He primarily covers the early rounds of the U.S. Open, British Open, LPGA tournaments, Seniors PGA tour, and other golf events.

Simpson, who married Sara Catherine Kanaga on August 12, 1950, has five children, Bret, Kim, Sherry, Susanne, and Barbara. He holds memberships in the Touchdown Club and the National Press Club.

BIBLIOGRAPHY: *Les Brown's Encyclopedia of Television*, 3rd ed. (Detroit, MI, 1992), p. 508; Steven H. Scheuer, ed., *Who's Who in Television and Cable* (New York, 1982),

p. 449; Curt Smith, *Voices of the Game* (South Bend, IN, 1987); *WWA*, 41st ed. (1980–1981), p. 3048.

Douglas A. Noverr

STOCKTON, Dick (b. Dick Stokovis, November 22, 1942, Philadelphia, PA), sportscaster, is the son of Joseph William Stokovis and Beatrice Stokovis, grew up in Queens, NY, and graduated from Syracuse University with a B.S. degree in communications in 1964. He began his broadcasting career in Philadelphia as a newscaster with radio station KYW-AM from 1965 to 1967 and a television sportscaster with KYW-TV in 1966 and 1967. Stockton served as sports director for KDKA-TV in Pittsburgh, PA, from 1967 to 1971 and for WBZ-TV in Boston, MA, from 1971 to 1973. He handled play-by-play basketball telecasts for the Boston Celtics (NBA) from 1972 to 1975 and New York Knicks (NBA) in 1975 and 1976. Stockton replaced Ken Coleman as a television play-by-play voice for Boston Red Sox (AL) games in 1975 and 1976 and joined Curt Gowdy (OS) as the local guest announcer during 1975 NBC World Series coverage. Stockton's exposure to a 125 million audience in what came to be regarded as one of the best fall classics greatly enhanced his reputation. Stockton began his association with CBS, handling an NFL postgame radio show from 1967 through 1973 and pregame radio commentary after 1980. In 1980 Stockton became a regular CBS sports commentator after hosting "The CBS Sports Spectacular," from 1978 to 1980. He broadcast play-by-play of college and professional basketball and handled radio and television coverage of baseball. His career grew with the rising popularity of college basketball.

Audiences praised Stockton for his witty and easygoing manner. He attracted critical support and considerable exposure for his play-by-play skill, especially of basketball contests. Early in his career, he showed a remarkable ability to team with other announcers. These partners ranged from the widely acclaimed voices of Gowdy and Brent Musberger (OS) to his often-criticized partners Billy Packer and Ken Harrelson. One critic noted, "Harrelson is doing for instant replays what the Boston strangler did for door to door salesmen." Stockton's greatest skill seemed his ability to focus on the action without letting his personality or opinions overshadow the sporting event being covered.

Stockton's celebrity status was enhanced in 1983 when he married Lesley Visser, one of the first female network sports reporters. The pair, called "the first couple of TV sports," had met in 1975 at the Boston *Globe*, where she was interning. Visser recalled, "It seemed to me as if he was a million years old, but he's the only man I know who can name every starter on every [college basketball] Final Four and play Gershwin on the piano." The conversation topic on one of their first dates had been his detailed account of the thrilling 1951 NL baseball pennant race. The couple both worked for

CBS-TV by the 1990s and sometimes covered the same events, with the husband doing play-by-play and the wife handling feature reporting. In 1994 Stockton joined the FBC.

BIBLIOGRAPHY: Ira Berkow, *Red: A Biography of Red Smith* (New York, 1986); Shirley Levitt and Mary Huzinec, "They're Truly a Pair for All Seasons," *People* 38 (November 16, 1992), pp. 133–134; "Love and the Polo Grounds," *Newsday*, October 18, 1987; Curt Smith, *Voices of the Game* (South Bend, IN, 1987); *WWA*, 42nd ed. (1982–1983), p. 3224.

James W. Harper

STOKOVIS, Dick. *See* Dick Stockton.

WIND, Herbert Warren (b. August 11, 1916, Brockton MA), sportswriter, is the son of Max Wind and Dora Wind and earned a B.A. degree from Yale University in 1937 and an M.A. degree from Cambridge University in England in 1939. From a family of ardent golf fans, he started to play at age 10 on the city's four courses and soon met golf immortals Francis Ouimet (OS), Walter Hagen (OS), and Gene Sarazen (OS). He first wrote on golf for his freshman thesis at Yale. After serving with the U.S. Army Air Force in the Pacific from 1942 to 1946, he served as a staff writer for *The New Yorker* from 1947 to 1954 and as an *SI* editor and golf writer from 1954 to 1960. He returned to *The New Yorker* in 1962, authoring the column "Sporting Scene" through 1990.

Wind, a golf consultant, writer, and associate producer of the television series "Shell's Wonderful World of Golf" in 1961 and 1962, taught a seminar on the literature of sports at Yale University in 1973 and soon became the nation's most perceptive and brilliant golf writer. He authored, edited, or compiled *The Story of American Golf* (1948); *Tips from the Top* (1955); *Golf Tips from the Top Professionals* (1958); with Peter Schwed, *Great Stories from the World of Sport* (1958); *On Tour with Harry Sprague* (1960); *The Gilded Age of Sport* (1961); *The Complete Golfer* (1964); *The Realm of Sport* (1966) [considered his seminal work]; *Golf Book* (1971); with Donald Steel and Pete Ryde, *The Encyclopedia of Golf* (1975); with Jack Nicklaus (OS), *The Greatest Game of All* (1969); *Game, Set, and Match: The Tennis Boom of the 1960's and 70's* (1979); *The World of P. G. Wodehouse* (1971); *Golf Quiz* (1980); *Following Through* (1985); with Ben Hogan (OS), *Five Lessons: The Modern Fundamentals of Golf* (1957, 1985); and with Gene Sarazen, *Thirty Years of Championship Golf: The Life and Times of Gene Sarazen* (1950, 1990).

Wind, a bachelor, played golf with a handicap of four and performed on every continent except Africa and Antarctica. Golf immortal Bobby Jones (OS) called Wind "a fine, sensitive writer on the game whose works range from essays of the most accurately appreciative kind to some of the finest golf reporting I have ever read."

BIBLIOGRAPHY: *Almanac of Famous People*, 1989; *CA*, vol. 6, new rev. ed. (1982), p. 556; Donald Steel et al., eds., *The Encyclopedia of Golf* (New York, 1975); Herbert Warren Wind, *The Gilded Age of Sport* (New York, 1961); *WWA*, 42nd ed. (1982–1983), p. 3600; *WWA*, 47th ed. (1992–1993), p. 3601.

Frederick J. Augustyn, Jr.

WISMER, Harry (b. June 30, 1913, Port Huron, MI; d. December 4, 1967, New York, NY), sportscaster and professional football owner, was the son of Fred Wismer and Blanche (Mitchell) Wismer and studied at St. John's Military Academy in Delafield, WI, from 1929 to 1932, the University of Florida from 1932 to 1933, and Michigan State College from 1933 to 1936. On May 11, 1941, he married Mary Elizabeth Bryant. Before their divorce, they had two children, Henry Richards and Wendy Wright.

Wismer began his broadcasting career as sports director of the Michigan State College radio station WKAR in Lansing, MI, in 1934. From 1935 to 1940, he served as sports announcer, featured announcer, and sports director at radio station WJR, Detroit, MI. In 1940, he became a sports announcer at radio station WXYZ in Detroit. From 1941 to 1943, he announced sports on the NBC Blue Network in New York City. For the next nine years, from 1943 to 1952, he was sports director for ABC, New York City. Wismer in 1952 was appointed general executive of General Tel-Radio, New York, which included MBS, WOR, Yankee Radio Network, Don Lee Network, and General Tire and Rubber interests, and also served as vice president of Bert L. Coleman Associates.

Wismer founded and chaired the AFL from 1960 to 1963, owning the New York Titans (AFL) franchise. The Titans struggled, causing Wismer to sell the team for $1 million to Sonny Werblin (OS). Werblin changed the Titans' name to the New York Jets.

In 1946, the Junior Chamber of Commerce named Wismer as one of America's 10 outstanding young men. He belonged to the President's Council on Youth Fitness and served as a director of the Rural Research Institute, a trustee on the attorney general's Board for Prevention of Juvenile Delinquency, and a member of the Cancer Fund and the Crusade for Children, a relief project. His many prestigious awards included the U.S. Marine Corps citation for outstanding contributions through sports (1949), American Legion Award (1950), Veterans of Foreign Wars Certificate of Merit Award (1948), HAF Highest Merit Award (1949), National Conference of Christians and Jews citation (1949), Ernie Pyle Plaque (1947), and other sports broadcasting awards.

Wismer belonged to many broadcasting associations and country clubs, the Washington Board of Commerce, and the Touchdown Club of Washington, DC. He was inducted into the writer's section of the National Baseball Hall of Fame in 1975. In 1965, he authored *The Public Calls It Sport*. In

December 1967, a skull fracture suffered when he fell down a flight of stairs in a New York restaurant proved fatal.

BIBLIOGRAPHY: "Milestones," *Time* 90 (December 15, 1967), p. 104; *NYT*, December 5, 1967, p. 29; "Transitions," *Newsweek* 70 (December 18, 1967), p. 70; *WWWA*, vol. 4 (1961–1968), p. 1071.

Stan W. Carlson

WOODWARD, Rufus Stanley "Stan" (b. June 5, 1895, Worcester, MA; d. November 29, 1965, White Plains, NY), college football player, sportswriter, and sportscaster, was the son of Rufus Stanley Woodward and Stella (Brooks) Woodward and graduated in 1917 from Amherst College, where he played tackle in football. Woodward, who served in the U.S. Merchant Marines in World War I, began his journalistic career as a reporter for the Worcester (MA) *Gazette* in 1920 and rose to city editor by 1922. He moved to the Boston (MA) *Herald* that same year as makeup man, becoming sports editor by 1925.

In 1930, Woodward joined the New York *Herald-Tribune*, the paper with which his name grew synonymous. Woodward filled many roles at the *Herald-Tribune*, serving as sportswriter from 1930 to 1938, sports editor from 1938 to 1941 and 1946 to 1948, and war correspondent from 1944 to 1946. As the last named Woodward, whose vision was terrible and depended on correction glasses, he jumped with the 101st Airborne at Arnhem, the Netherlands. He served aboard the *Hornet* and *Enterprise* in the Pacific and covered the invasions of Iwo Jima and Guam. Woodward's argument with *Herald-Tribune* owner Helen Rogers Reid about covering a woman's golf tournament in Westchester, NY, caused his dismissal in 1948. Woodward did not think the event worth covering and bluntly told her so.

Until being rehired by the *Herald-Tribune* in 1959, Woodward worked as editor of the "old" *SI* in 1948, columnist for the New York *Daily Compass* in 1949 and 1950, sports editor of the Miami (FL) *News* from 1950 through 1955, and writer for Newhouse newspapers from 1955 to 1958. In 1962, Woodward retired from the *Herald-Tribune* as sports editor emeritus. Woodward's greatest accomplishment as *Herald-Tribune* sports editor may have been upgrading its sports section to the level of the archrival *NYT*, whose building Woodward could see from his office window. Until his death, Woodward remained active as occasional contributor to the *Herald-Tribune* and radio sports commentator from his Brookfield Center, CT, home.

Woodward seemed intimidating physically and intellectually as a six-foot-two-inch 230-pounder. Subordinates adored Woodward for his kindness and encouragement, but he acted waspish with superiors and any sportswriters who did not share his purist approach to language. Woodward, who coined the phrase "Ivy League" and recruited sportswriter Red Smith (IS) to work at the *Herald-Tribune*, remained close friends with college football coaches

Jock Sutherland (FB), Dick Harlow (FB), Red Blaik (FB), and Tuss Mc-Laughry. Woodward authored *Sports Page* in 1949 and *Paper Tiger* in 1964. Woodward married Esther Rice on February 20, 1932, and had two daughters, Ellen and Mary.

BIBLIOGRAPHY: Ira Berkow, *Red: A Biography of Red Smith* (New York, 1986); Arthur Daley, "Stanley Woodward," *NYT*, November 30, 1965, p. 51; "Stanley Woodward Dead at 71; Sports Editor Was the Coach," *NYT*, November 30, 1965, p. 41; *WWA*, 32nd ed. (1962–1963), p. 3454.

John H. Ziegler

FOOTBALL

ALZADO, Lyle Martin (b. April 3, 1949, Brooklyn, NY; d. May 14, 1992, Lake Oswego, OR), college and professional player, was the son of Maurice Alzado and Martha (Sokolow) Alzado and moved with his family at age 10 to Long Island, NY. At Lawrence High School, Alzado lettered in track and field and started for four years at defensive end in football, achieving All-America, All-State, and All-League honors in his senior year. Alzado, an aggressive personality, also competed in Golden Gloves competition, becoming regional heavyweight champion and reaching the national semifinals. In 1967, Alzado entered tiny Yankton College in South Dakota, earning two-time All-TSC defensive lineman and Little All-America honors in football. Alzado graduated with a bachelor's degree in special education in 1971. Four years later, he married Sharon Pike. They had one son, Justin. Following their divorce, Alzado married Kathy Davis in 1991.

The Denver Broncos (NFL) selected the six-foot-three-inch, 270-pound defensive tackle in the fourth round of the 1971 NFL draft as the seventy-ninth pick overall. With Denver's "Orange Crush" defense, the intense, moody Alzado played in 66 of 68 games from 1971 until sidelined with a leg injury in 1976. In 1977, Alzado was named NFL Defensive Lineman of the Year and All-Pro, helping the Broncos capture their first AFC Western Division crown. After defeating the Oakland Raiders, 20–17, for the AFC championship, Denver lost to the Dallas Cowboys, 27–10, in Super Bowl XII. Alzado also received the 1977 NFLPA Byron "Whizzer" White (FB) Award for community service. In 1978, Alzado again made All-Pro, as the Broncos repeated as Western Division champions. The Pittsburgh Steelers defeated Denver, 33–10, for the AFC title.

Following a salary dispute, Denver traded Alzado in August 1979 to the Cleveland Browns (NFL) for three draft picks. With the Browns three seasons, Alzado played both defensive end and tackle. He achieved All-AFC status in 1979 and 1980 and All-Pro in 1980 and in 1981 led the Browns in sacks and tackles among defensive linemen. In 1980, Cleveland won the AFC Central Division championship, losing to Oakland, 14–12, in the playoffs.

The Browns, believing Alzado had lost his effectiveness, traded him in April 1982 to the Los Angeles Raiders for an eighth-round pick. With his pride hurt by his low trade value and encouraged by the Raiders' "naturally aggressive" style, Alzado saw his career revived in Los Angeles. Named *PFW*'s 1982 Comeback Player of the Year, Alzado made eight quarterback sacks in the strike-shortened 9-game season. The Raiders eventually lost to the New York Jets, 17–14, in the AFC playoffs. In 1983, Alzado recorded seven sacks as the Raiders, AFC Western Division titlists, defeated the Seattle Seahawks, 31–14, for the AFC crown, and the Washington Redskins, 38–9, in Super Bowl XVII. In 1984, Alzado made 63 tackles, including eight sacks, and ranked among five finalists for NFL Man of the Year in recognition of Alzado's charitable work with hospitalized children. Alzado was placed on injured reserve after 11 games of the 1985 season, as Los Angeles, AFC Western Division champions, lost in the playoffs, 27–20, to the New England Patriots. Alzado retired after the 1985 campaign. In 196 games spanning 15 seasons, Alzado recovered 19 fumbles and recorded two safeties.

Subsequently, Alzado appeared in television and feature films. In 1990 at age 41, Alzado attempted a comeback with the Raiders, but training camp injuries ended his quest. Diagnosed with brain cancer in 1991, Alzado moved to Oregon to be near his wife's family. Alzado attributed his disease to his lifetime use of steroids and human growth hormone, a practice begun in college and, at times, costing $30,000 per year. Alzado campaigned the last 15 months of his life warning others of the dangers of steroid use.

BIBLIOGRAPHY: Lyle Alzado with Paul Zimmerman, *Mile High: The Story of Lyle Alzado and the Amazing Denver Broncos* (New York, 1978); Los Angeles (CA) *Times,* May 15, 1992; *Los Angeles Raiders Media Guide,* 1990; *TSN Pro Football Register,* 1985.
David Bernstein

AMES, Knowlton Lyman "Snake" (b. May 27, 1868, Chicago, IL; d. December 23, 1931, Chicago, IL), college athlete, was selected a football All-America at Princeton University in 1889 and starred four seasons from 1886 to 1889 at fullback for the Tigers, which compiled a combined 35–3–1 win–loss record. Ames, who was elected in 1969 to the NFF College Football Hall of Fame, amassed an incredible 730 career points with 62 touchdowns, 176 conversions, and 26 field goals, worth 4, 2, and 5 points, respectively, under existing rules.

Ames attended Lawrenceville, NJ, Preparatory School, where he excelled in football, baseball, tennis, track and field, and gymnastics before graduating in 1886. He helped Princeton tie Yale University for the intercollegiate championship in 1886. The Tigers held the Elis to a disputed scoreless tie called because of darkness, with Yale leading, 4–0. Ames, an exceptional open field runner, slithered through opponents to earn the nickname "Snake." A sure tackler and catcher of punts, he excelled at dropkicking field goals and conversions and used the spiral punt. Ames starred in 1889 on Princeton's championship 11, which finished 10–0–0. He scored three touchdowns and 10 conversions in a 72–4 humbling of the University of Pennsylvania and produced a touchdown, field goal, 2 conversions, and runs of 70 and 105 yards during a 41–15 comeback victory over Harvard University. He also booted a conversion from a difficult angle to help the Tigers triumph, 10–0, over Yale, recording their first victory over the Elis in four years and ending the Bulldogs' 48-game undefeated string.

The 150-pound Ames performed with other Princeton greats, including tackle Hector Cowan (FB), quarterback Edgar Allen Poe (FB), halfback Roscoe Channing, and center Bill George. Amos Alonzo Stagg (FB) boasted, "He [Ames] was one of the shiftiest backs I ever met." Ames, an excellent baseball pitcher, helped the Tigers defeat Yale, Harvard, Pennsylvania, and the New York Giants (NL). Following graduation from Princeton in 1890, he guided Purdue University to a 12–0 record over two football seasons. Ames joined the coal and gas business, served as president of Booth Fisheries Company, and owned *The Journal of Commerce* and the Chicago (IL) *Evening Post* newspapers. He married Adelaide Schroeder of Brooklyn, NY, in 1893 and had two sons and two daughters. Ames, one of Chicago's leading golfers, became disconsolate over ill health and financial matters and shot himself while in his limousine at Lincoln Park.

BIBLIOGRAPHY: Jay Dunn, *The Tigers of Princeton* (Huntsville, AL, 1977); E. K. Hall, ed., *Spalding's Football Guide* (New York, 1932); Ralph Hickok, *Who Was Who in American Sports* (New York, 1971); Ronald L. Mendell and Timothy B. Phares, *Who's Who in Football* (New Rochelle, NY, 1974); Frank Presbrey and James Moffatt, *Athletics at Princeton* (New York, 1901); Seeley G. Mudd Manuscript Library, Princeton University, letter to James Whalen, April 3, 1993.

James D. Whalen

ANGSMAN, Elmer Joseph Jr. "Bud" (b. December 11, 1925, Chicago, IL), college and professional player, participated in the famed "Dream Backfield" that led the Chicago Cardinals to the NFL Championship. Angsman attended Mt. Carmel High School in Chicago and then matriculated at the University of Notre Dame, where he earned a B.A. degree in journalism. He played fullback and left and right halfback for the 1943–1945 Notre Dame football teams. In 1943, Notre Dame won the national championship with a 9–1 mark. As a junior, Angsman rushed for 273 yards on 58 attempts and scored three touchdowns for the 8–2 Fighting Irish. In his senior season, he led 7–2–1 Notre Dame in scoring with seven touchdowns and in rushing with 616 yards on 87 carries for a 7.1-yard average. He played in the 1946

College All-Star Game at Chicago, IL, and was selected on the third round by the Chicago Cardinals in the annual NFL player draft.

The Cardinals, long NFL doormats, had carefully improved their roster during World War II with intelligent drafting. As a rookie in 1946, the 5-foot-11-inch, 200-pound Angsman joined a backfield that included former All-Americas Paul Christman (FB) at quarterback, Marshall Goldberg (FB) at halfback, and Marlin "Pat" Harder (FB) at fullback. Angsman rushed for 328 yards, as the Cardinals finished 6–5–0 for their first winning record in 11 years. When the Cardinals signed the University of Georgia's Charlie Trippi (FB) for 1947, the term "Dream Backfield" was at first applied to what was expected to be a starting four of All-Americas with Angsman in reserve. Coach Jimmy Conzelman (FB), however, used Goldberg on defense and started Angsman at right halfback on offense, making him the fourth "Dream Backfielder."

Angsman led the Cardinals in rushing in 1947 with 412 yards and scored eight touchdowns, as Chicago won the NFL's Western Division with a 9–3–0 record. The championship game against the Philadelphia Eagles was played at Comiskey Park in Chicago on a frozen field. Angsman broke two 7–yard touchdown runs, sparking a 28–21 victory. At the time, his 159 rushing yards set an NFL Championship game record.

The 1948 Cardinals compiled an 11–1–0 regular season record, as Angsman rushed for 638 yards and scored nine touchdowns. The NFL Championship game at Philadelphia, PA, was played in the midst of a blizzard, making offense impossible. The Eagles won, 7–0, recovering a fumble by the Cardinals' quarterback Christman deep in the Chicago territory late in the fourth quarter.

Angsman, the first NFL player to wear contact lenses on the field, rushed for 674 yards in 1949 and was chosen to the 1950 Pro Bowl. The Cardinals, however, slumped, as age caught up with many of their stars. Angsman retired to enter business in Chicago after the 1952 season. At the time, he ranked as the Cardinals' all-time leader in rushing with 2,908 yards on 683 attempts for 27 touchdowns. He also caught 41 passes for 654 yards (16-yard average) and 5 touchdowns.

BIBLIOGRAPHY: *Chicago Cardinals 1952 Media Guide;* Richard M. Cohen et al., *The Notre Dame Football Scrapbook* (New York, 1977); David S. Neft et al., eds., *The Football Encyclopedia* (New York, 1994); Beau Riffenburgh, *The Official NFL Encyclopedia,* 4th ed. (New York, 1986); Howard Roberts, *The Pro Football Story* (New York, 1953); *TSN Football Register,* 1966.

Robert N. "Bob" Carroll

APPLETON, Gordon Scott (b. February 20, 1942, Brady, TX; d. March 2, 1992, Austin, TX), college and professional player, is the son of Alberda Appleton and attended Brady High School, where he became a star lineman on the football team. The six-foot-three-inch, 260-pound Appleton enrolled at the University of Texas (SWC) and became a star defensive tackle there.

After playing on an undefeated freshman team, he joined the varsity for the next three years. Appleton dominated the defense, as the Longhorns lost only three games and won three SWC titles, two Cotton Bowls, and their first national title in 1963. Individual honors came to Appleton, as he was selected All-SWC twice, unanimous All-America in 1963, Best Lineman of the Year in 1963 by both the AP and UPI, and winner of the 1963 Outland Trophy. His brilliant career ended in the 1964 Cotton Bowl, as Texas dominated the Navy, 28–6. Appleton played an outstanding game.

Like other star college players of the early 1960s, Appleton became the center of a tug of war between the NFL and AFL. He was the first draft pick of both the Dallas Cowboys (NFL) and the Houston Oilers (AFL). Dallas eventually traded their pick to the Pittsburgh Steelers. The bidding war was finally won by the Oilers. Appleton played for Houston from 1964 through 1966 and was traded to the San Diego Chargers (AFL) prior to the 1967 season. He played with the Chargers in 1967 and 1968. He intercepted two passes in 1964 and scored a touchdown on a fumble recovery in 1967.

After his professional football career, Appleton struggled with alcoholism and eventually became a minister. He died of heart disease, leaving a daughter, Taunya.

BIBLIOGRAPHY: Richard M. Cohen et al., *Scrap Book History of Football* (Indianapolis, IN, 1979); David S. Neft et al., eds., *The Football Encyclopedia*, 2nd ed. (New York, 1994); *NYT*, March 5, 1992, p. B15; *Official 1992 NCAA Football*; Beau Riffenburgh, *The Official NFL Encyclopedia*, 4th ed. (New York, 1986).

Stanley Grosshandler

ARNETT, Jon Dwayne "Jaguar Jon" (b. April 20, 1935, Los Angeles, CA), college and professional player, is the son of Marc Arnett and Dorothy Arnett. As a gymnast at Manual Arts High School in Los Angeles, Arnett had developed a keen sense of balance that helped to make him a great open field runner. Arnett excelled as a broad jumper on the track and field team and a football halfback at the University of Southern California (PCC) from 1954 to 1956. After starring in the Rose Bowl as a sophomore, he won All-America recognition from *Look* magazine and the UP in 1955 and ranked second nationally in scoring with 108 points. UCLA coach Red Sanders (FB) claimed, "He's the greatest football animal I've ever seen." Involved in PCC payoff scandals, Arnett was restricted to only five games as a senior.

The Los Angeles Rams made Arnett their first—and the NFL's fourth— draft choice in 1957. During his rookie season, Arnett gained 347 yards rushing as a reserve halfback and led the NFL in kickoff returns, averaging 28.0 yards per return. In 1958, Rams' head coach Sid Gillman (FB) inserted Arnett into the starting backfield. That season, Arnett experienced his biggest NFL day by accumulating 298 total yards (including runs from scrimmage of 52 and 38 yards, a 72-yard pass reception, and punt returns of 58, 36, and 24 yards) against the Chicago Bears. Arnett finished the 1958 season by leading the Rams in rushing with 683 yards, fifth best in the NFL. He also led the NFL in punt returns with a 12.4 yards per return average. For his 1958 efforts, Arnett was named to the All-Pro team and made his first of five consecutive appearances in the Pro Bowl. Arnett scored the winning touchdowns for the WC in both the 1961 and 1962 Pro Bowls.

Arnett, although unable to match his 1958 performance, led the Rams in rushing in 1960 (436 yards) and 1961 (609 yards). He remained a topflight kickoff and punt returner through 1961, when he averaged 26.1 yards per kickoff return. Arnett's role was diminished in 1962 and 1963, as the Rams attempted to rebuild under new coach Harland Svare.

In 1964, Los Angeles traded Arnett to George Halas's (FB) Chicago Bears (NFL). Chicago used Arnett more frequently. Arnett responded to the challenge, leading the Bears in rushing (400 yards) and punt returns (9.9 average) in 1964. Although still a major contributor in 1965, he was overshadowed by rookie Gale Sayers (FB). Nonetheless, Arnett still gained 363 yards rushing, helping to make Chicago the third best NFL rushing team. After an unproductive 1966 season, Arnett retired.

Arnett finished his NFL career with 3,833 yards rushing on 964 attempts (4.0 yards per attempt average) and 26 touchdowns. He caught 222 passes for 2,290 yards and 10 touchdowns; returned 120 punts for 981 yards (8.2 yards per return average) and 1 touchdown; and returned 126 kickoffs for 3,110 yards (24.7 yards per return average) and 2 touchdowns. Arnett has since worked as a stock broker and is married to Yvonne Flint.

BIBLIOGRAPHY: Steve Bisheff, *Los Angeles Rams* (New York, 1973); Harold Claassen and Steve Boda, Jr., eds., *Ronald Encyclopedia of Football* (New York, 1963); Ronald L. Mendell and Timothy B. Phares, *Who's Who in Football* (New Rochelle, NY, 1974); David S. Neft et al., *The Football Encyclopedia*, 2nd ed. (New York, 1994); Murray Olderman, *The Running Backs* (Englewood Cliffs, NJ, 1969); Beau Riffenburgh, *The Official NFL Encyclopedia*, 4th ed. (New York, 1986); Fred Russell and Leonard George, *Big Bowl Football: The Great Post-Season Classics* (New York, 1963); Al Stump, "Resourceful Ram," *Sport* 28 (December 1959), pp. 28–29, 81–83; *Who's Best in Sports 1959.*

Marc S. Maltby

BARRAGAR, Nathan "Nate" (b. 1907, KS; d. August 10, 1985, Los Angeles, CA), college and professional player, starred at the University of Southern California (PCC) from 1927 to 1929 on teams that won or shared three PCC titles and one national championship. Barragar, a two-time All-PCC center and guard, captained the Trojans his final season and was named All-America guard by football authorities Walter Eckersall (FB) and Tom

Thorp. He performed on the 1931 Green Bay Packers' NFL Championship team and made All-Pro at center a year later.

Barragar moved with his family to San Fernando, CA, at age seven and starred as a fullback at San Fernando High School. He continued at fullback on Southern California's 1926 freshman team, but Trojan coach Howard Jones (FB) converted him to center and linebacker the following season. The six-foot, 182-pound Barragar won the starting job in the fourth game of 1927 after enjoying an outstanding performance in a 13–13 tie with PCC cochampion Stanford University. The Trojans finished 9–0–1 in 1928 and shared the national championship, triumphing over Stanford and the University of Notre Dame. Southern California played a famous scoreless duel with the University of California, suspected of hosing down the field at Berkeley, CA.

Jones needed the talented, flexible Barragar at running guard in 1929 but kept him at linebacker on defense. Southern California destroyed the undefeated University of Pittsburgh, 47–14, in the 1930 Rose Bowl, with the Panthers boasting four bona fide All-Americas. Barragar observed, "His [Jones's] teams had more straight power than deception. There was nothing fancy. We'd actually tell the other team where we were going to run the ball." Outstanding Trojan teammates Morley Drury (FB), Jess Hibbs, Erny Pinckert (FB), and Gus Shaver helped Southern California compile a combined 27–3–2 record.

Barragar's early NFL career in 1930 and part of 1931 was sidetracked when the Minneapolis Red Jackets' and Frankford, PA, Yellow Jackets' franchises disbanded. He performed at center with the Green Bay Packers (NFL) the balance of 1931 and in 1932, 1934, and 1935 with Arnie Herber (FB), Clarke Hinkle (FB), Johnny "Blood" McNally (FB), and Don Hutson (FB). Green Bay won the NFL title with a 12–2 record in 1931. Barragar performed in minor acting roles in Hollywood, CA, but preferred working behind the camera, producing films including *The Greatest Story Ever Told*, several John Wayne pictures, and a Bob Hope spectacular for television. He returned to Green Bay annually for Packers' homecoming games.

BIBLIOGRAPHY: Jody Brown, *The Best Little Rivalry in Town* (West Point, NY, 1982); Braven Dyer, *Ten Top Trojan Football Thrillers* (Los Angeles, CA, 1949); Ken Rappoport, *The Trojans* (Huntsville, AL, 1974); Beau Riffenburgh, *The Official NFL Encyclopedia*, 4th ed. (New York, 1986); USC–Pittsburgh Rose Bowl Football Game Program, January 1, 1930.

James D. Whalen

BARRETT, Charles "Chuck" (b. November 3, 1893, Bellevue, PA; d. May 21, 1924, Tucson, AZ), college player and coach, was selected a football All-America quarterback in 1914 and 1915 at Cornell University (IvL) and was elected to the NFF College Football Hall of Fame in 1958. A three-year starting quarterback, he starred on Big Red clubs that compiled a combined

22–6–1 record. Barrett, who captained the Big Red in 1915, led Cornell to a 9–0–0 finish and a national championship.

Barrett attended University School in Cleveland, OH, and starred on the gridiron before graduating in 1912. In 1912 he enrolled at Cornell and played on the freshman football team. The following year, Barrett helped Coach Al Sharpe turn around the Big Red's 3–7–0 record of the previous year and guided them to 5–4–1 in 1913. Cornell's four losses were inflicted by strong opponents with only four combined setbacks among them. The Big Red improved to 8–2–0 in 1914, winning its last seven games in succession while defeating the Carlisle Indians, University of Michigan, and University of Pennsylvania.

Cornell halted Harvard University's 33-game undefeated streak in 1915, garnering a 10–0 triumph and spoiling the Crimson's otherwise perfect season. Barrett scored the only touchdown before leaving the game with an injury. He helped Cornell overwhelm Michigan, 34–7, and scored all of the Big Red's points in a come-from-behind 24–9 triumph over Pennsylvania. Barrett shared All-America honors with four teammates, including fullback Fritz Shiverick, ends John O'Hearn and Murray Shelton, and center Gib Cool. Walter Camp (FB) wrote, "Barrett and [Harvard's] Mahan [FB] are so strong and powerful that they could pound the line to pieces as well as running the ends. At quarter, Barrett of Cornell is preeminent in the position, although he could play halfback or fullback equally well. In fact, he is a star performer all around." Barrett returned several punts and kickoffs for touchdowns and dropkicked field goals and conversions. Barrett's outstanding play selection blended well with his inspiring leadership.

Barrett, who served as president of the student body and belonged to Delta Kappa Epsilon fraternity and Sphinx Head, graduated from Cornell in 1916 with a bachelor's degree in mechanical engineering. Barrett volunteered for military service with the U.S. Navy during World War I, becoming an ensign assigned to the U.S.S. *Brooklyn* of the Asiatic Fleet. He was severely injured in an explosion aboard ship in Yokohama, Japan, harbor and never fully recovered. Barrett married Edna Stevens of San Francisco, CA, in 1919 and coached football in California secondary schools for a short period. He developed tuberculosis and moved to Tucson, AZ, to recuperate but eventually succumbed to the disease. A tablet erected in Cornell's Schoellkopf Memorial Hall by his teammates, friends, and the 1915 Pennsylvania football team notes, "As a tribute to his splendid loyalty and leadership and as an homage to a most worthy gridiron adversary, we respectfully dedicate this tablet."

BIBLIOGRAPHY: L. H. Baker, *Football: Facts and Figures* (New York, 1945); Carl A. Kroch Library, Rare and Manuscript Collections, Cornell University, Ithaca, NY, letter to James D. Whalen, November 11, 1993; Cornell-Brown Football Game Program, Ithaca, NY, October 24, 1914; Allison Danzig, *The History of American Football* (Englewood Cliffs, NJ, 1956); Ralph Hickok, *Who Was Who in American Sports* (New

York, 1971); John D. McCallum and Charles H. Pearson, *College Football U.S.A. 1869–1972* (New York, 1972).

James D. Whalen

BECHTOL, Hubert "Hub" (b. April 20, 1926, Amarillo, TX), college and professional player, exhibited a true skill for catching passes as a junior high player. At Lubbock High School, he captained the football and basketball teams and also lettered in track and field.

Bechtol wanted to remain with his family in Lubbock so he entered Texas Tech University (BC). A six-foot-three-inch 202-pounder, he lettered in both football and basketball as a freshman. The following year he spent at the University of Texas (SWC) as a V-12 trainee.

An end for the Longhorns from 1944 through the 1946 season, he ranked among the top wingmen in the nation and was named to several All-America teams each year. He led the Longhorns in receptions his first two seasons, and in 1946, he teamed with the fabled quarterback Bobby Layne (FB) to become one of the best passing duos the SWC has ever seen. In the 1946 Cotton Bowl, he caught nine passes for 138 yards to help Texas crush the University of Missouri, 40–27. Prior to Bechtol's senior year, Texas Tech tried to lure him back. He became the center of a tug of war between Texas Tech and Texas, finally deciding at the last moment to return to Texas.

Following his graduation, Bechtol was drafted by the Miami Seahawks (AAFC) and the Pittsburgh Steelers (NFL). He eventually played three seasons for the Baltimore Colts (AAFC). He caught 17 passes for one touchdown in 1947 but had only two receptions in 1948. Bechtol's final season in 1949 saw him confined to playing defensive end.

He married Elizabeth Robinson while in college and had one son, Roy. Following his professional career, he worked in real estate. In 1991, Bechtol was inducted into the NFF College Football Hall of Fame.

BIBLIOGRAPHY: Allison Danzig, *The History of American Football* (New York, 1956); Bernie McCarty, *All-Americans 1889–1945* (University Park, IL, 1991); David S. Neft et al., eds., *The Football Encyclopedia*, 2nd ed. (New York, 1994); *1992 NCAA Football*; Beau Riffenburgh, *The Official NFL Encyclopedia*, 4th ed. (New York, 1986); George White, "Big Boy Bechtol of Texas," *Sport* 1 (November 1946), pp. 18–20.

Stanley Grosshandler

BEHMAN, Russell K. "Bull" "Bully" (b. January 15, 1900, Steelton, PA; d. March 24, 1950, Harrisburg, PA), college and professional player and coach, was the youngest of seven children of Jacob H. Behman and Elizabeth (Kissinger) Behman and excelled as lineman in the NFL's first decade of existence. Although not large by today's standards, the 5-foot-10-inch, 210- to 225-pound Behman was described by contemporaries and historians alike as "monstrous," "a rock of Gibraltar," and "agile as a cat." He was "almost impossible to block, so many extra blockers being assigned to stop him that plays came apart." After starring for Steelton High School in 1916 and 1917, Behman played football at Lebanon Valley College in Annville, PA, in 1920 and 1921 and Dickinson College in Carlisle, PA, in 1922 and 1923. Behman captained the 1923 Red Devils 11. Coach Glenn Killinger called him "one of the greatest college linemen in the country."

In 1924, the 60-minute tackle-guard-center joined the Frankford Yellow Jackets (NFL), a suburban Philadelphia veteran professional team in its first year in the still-fledgling NFL. Behman helped lead Frankford to an 11–2–1 record and a third-place NFL finish. As captain of the 1925 squad, the rugged lineman proved instrumental in winning several crucial games for the Yellow Jackets in a 13–7 season record. Offensively, he emerged as a formidable place kicker while converting on 12 PATs and five field goals, two of the latter providing victories. His defensive play sparkled, as he scored touchdowns on a blocked kick and a pass interception in one game. Ironically, Frankford won its only NFL Championship in 1926, when Behman played with the Philadelphia Quakers of the newly formed rival AFL. The captain, nicknamed "Bull," led the Quakers to an 8–2 record and the AFL title with two decisive late-season triumphs over "Red" Grange's (FB) New York Yankees. The AFL collapsed after only one season, with Behman rejoining the Yellow Jackets in 1927. The young, immature Frankford team managed only a 6–9–3 season that year, but the Behman-inspired Yellow Jackets almost took the NFL title in 1928 with an 11–3–2 mark.

In 1929 Behman became player–coach, handling most of the Yellow Jackets' punting duties. Frankford compiled a respectable 9–4–5 record, finishing third. The collapse of the nation's economy in 1930, however, brought financial difficulties for the Yellow Jacket sponsors and the loss of several veteran players. Although continuing to play, Behman resigned as coach in midseason. The Yellow Jackets finished 1930 with a dismal 4–13–1 record. Behman returned as the Yellow Jackets' aging player–coach in 1931, but economic problems still plagued the Frankford management. The club moved home games to Baker Field in Philadelphia, losing much fan support. The Yellow Jackets, mired in a miserable 1–6–1 record, folded during the 1931 season, ending one of the NFL's most successful franchises (65–45–14) and the career of one of its early great unsung warriors.

During the 1930s, Behman worked as a labor organizer in the Hershey, PA, area. He was a guard with the Dauphin County Prison system in Harrisburg, PA, at the time of his death from a heart attack, being survived by his wife Ada and a stepdaughter, Georgia Ann.

Official All-Pro football teams were not selected in the 1920s, but two newspapers chose annual All-Pro teams. In 1926, Wilfred Smith of the Chicago (IL) *Tribune* drew selections from both the NFL and AFL, placing Behman at tackle on his All-Pro Second Team. The Green Bay (WI) *Press-Gazette*, perhaps the newspaper giving the most NFL coverage, selected Behman as tackle on its 1928 and 1929 NFL All-Pro First Team. In 1929, Rud

Rennie of the New York *Herald-Tribune* and Coach Leroy Andrews of the New York Giants (NFL), whose selections appeared in the New York *Post* and New York *World*, placed Behman on their First Team.

BIBLIOGRAPHY: Howard Lee Barnes, *A Documentary Scrap Book of Football in Frankford* (Philadelphia, PA, 1985); Russell Behman file, Pro Football Hall of Fame, Canton, OH; Frankford Yellow Jackets file, Pro Football Hall of Fame, Canton, OH; John Hogrogian, "All Pros of the Early NFL," *TCC* 4 (November 1982), pp. 3–7; John Hogrogian, "All Pros of 1926," *TCC* 5 (June 1983), p. 7; John Hogrogian, "All Pros of 1929," *TCC* 5 (May 1983), p. 5; Al Meyers, " 'Bull' Behman and the Jackets," *TCC* 5 (August 1983), pp. 3–4; David S. Neft et al., eds., *The Football Encyclopedia*, 2nd ed. (New York, 1994); Richard Pagano and C. C. Staph, "The Frankford Yellow Jackets; Part 2: The Good Years," *TCC* 9 (1987), pp. 5–8.

Jack C. Braun

BELL, Ricky Lynn (b. April 8, 1955, Houston TX; d. November 28, 1984, Inglewood, CA), college and professional player, was the son of Ruth Bell and the fifth of seven brothers. After moving to Los Angeles, Bell attended Fremont High School and achieved All–Los Angeles City selection as a senior linebacker and blocking back. In 1973, Bell entered the University of Southern California. Trojan coach John McKay (FB) switched Bell from defense to offense, where the latter became a fullback and blocker for tailback Anthony Davis* in Southern California's famous Power I formation. Bell moved to tailback in his junior year, leading the nation in rushing with 1,875 yards on 385 carries. He broke O. J. Simpson's (FB) PEC and Trojan records for yardage and carries, finishing third in the Heisman Trophy balloting. A midseason leg injury limited Bell's senior year total yardage to 1,433, as he finished second to Tony Dorsett (FB) for the Heisman Trophy. At Southern California, Bell rushed for 3,689 yards (5.2 yards per carry) and scored 28 touchdowns. In 1979, Bell received his bachelor's degree in speech and communications.

The Tampa Bay Buccaneers (NFL) selected the six-foot-two-inch, 215-pound halfback as the first pick in the first round of the 1977 NFL draft. Coach McKay made Bell the focus of the offense, but the latter operated behind an inexperienced offensive line. In 1977 and 1978, Bell accumulated 1,115 yards on 333 carries for a 3.35-yard average. Bell led the Buccaneers in 1979 to the NFC Central Division title by rushing for 1,263 yards, fourth in the NFL, on 283 attempts for a 4.5-yard average and seven touchdowns. Two other scores came through the air, as Bell caught 25 passes for 248 yards. Tampa Bay defeated the Philadelphia Eagles in the NFC playoffs, as Bell set an NFL playoff record for most rushing attempts (38), gained 142 yards, and scored two touchdowns. In the 9–0 loss to the Los Angeles Rams for the NFL Championship, Bell rushed for 59 yards on 20 carries.

Bell's career in 1980 began a downward slide, punctuated by nagging injuries and slow recoveries, the result, apparently, of the disease that tragically shortened his life. Bell missed part of five games with a bruised knee, carrying the ball 174 times for 599 yards and two touchdowns and making 38 catches for 292 yards and one touchdown. A chip fracture of the shoulder limited Bell to seven games in 1981, as he ran for 80 yards on 30 attempts and snagged eight passes for 92 yards. Bell, frustrated by his diminished numbers, requested a trade. In March 1982, Tampa Bay dealt Bell to the San Diego Chargers (NFL) for a fourth-round draft choice.

Severe pain, swelling of the joints, and a dramatic weight loss from 225 pounds to 198 pounds reduced Bell's 1982 Charger campaign to just 4 games and 6 rushing yards on two carries. Bell was placed on inactive reserve with a nonfootball injury in December 1982 and retired before the 1983 season. During a six-year NFL career, Bell played in 64 games, rushed 822 times for 3,063 yards (3.7-yard average), and caught 97 passes for 842 yards. He scored 114 points with 16 rushing touchdowns and 3 tallies via passes. He lived in the Scripps Ranch area of San Diego, CA, with his wife Natalie and daughter Noelle. An older son, Ricky, Jr., lived in Los Angeles. Extensive tests identified Bell's medical condition as dermatomyositis, an inflammation of the skin and muscles, and cardiomyopathy, a severe muscular disease of the heart. Bell died of cardiac arrest. Coach McKay noted, "[Bell] was one of the finest football players I ever had the pleasure of coaching and even a finer man. I don't know anyone who didn't like Ricky Bell."

BIBLIOGRAPHY: Mal Florence, *The Trojan Heritage* (Virginia Beach, VA, 1980); Los Angeles (CA) *Times*, November 29, 1984; *San Diego Chargers, Media Guide*, 1983; *TSN Pro Football Register*, 1983.

David Bernstein

BENNETT, Cornelius O'Landa "Biscuit" (b. August 25, 1966, Birmingham, AL), college and professional player, is the son of Lino Bennett, a retired steelworker, and Lillie Bennett and grew up in the Ensley section of Birmingham. Bennett, the state's top football prospect as a senior at Ensley High School in 1982, ran for 1,099 yards as a fullback and caught 12 touchdown passes as a tight end the same year.

Bennett attended the University of Alabama (SEC), where he studied social work and became one of the greatest defensive football players in Crimson Tide history. His honors included being named to numerous All-America and All-SEC teams three consecutive years from 1984 through 1986. Bennett finished his Alabama career with 287 tackles, 16 sacks, six forced fumbles, two interceptions, 15 knocked down passes, and three fumble recoveries. The six-foot-two-inch, 237-pound Bennett in 1986 became the first linebacker to win the Vince Lombardi Trophy, given to the nation's top lineman. Under coach Ray Perkins, Bennett led the Crimson Tide to three Bowl victories. These triumphs included a 27–7 decision over SMU in the 1983 Sun Bowl, a 24–3 win over the University of Southern California in the 1985 Aloha Bowl, and a 28–6 victory over the University of Washington in the 1986 Sun Bowl. Bennett was chosen as the MVP in the latter two Bowl contests.

The Indianapolis Colts (NFL) selected Bennett in the first round of the 1987 draft as the second pick overall. Bennett was placed on the reserve/unsigned list when he did not report to the Colts camp and remained a holdout for six months. In October 1987, Indianapolis traded him to the Buffalo Bills (NFL) in exchange for the Bills' first-round pick in the 1988 draft, first- and second-round selections in the 1989 draft, and running back Greg Bell. Since his arrival at Buffalo, Bennett has developed into one of the premier NFL linebackers. Bennett started the final seven games of the 1987 season, being named on several All-Rookie teams and *SI* Rookie of the Year. An All-Pro choice in 1988, he placed second among Bills tacklers with 103 and second in sacks with 9.5. Bennett missed five games in 1989 due to a knee injury but recorded his two hundredth career tackle in only his second full season. Following the 1989 season, he was awarded the SingTon Trophy as the outstanding professional Male Athlete of the Year in Alabama. During the 1990 campaign, Bennett led Buffalo in quarterback pressures with 18 and scored his first NFL touchdown on an 80-yard return of a blocked field goal. He became the first figure in NFL history to be named Player of the Week in successive weeks. An All-Pro First Team selection in 1991, Bennett played five different positions and led the Bills in sacks, quarterback pressures, and forced fumbles. Against the Miami Dolphins, Bennett tackled quarterback Dan Marino (FB), forcing him to fumble, picked up the ball, and ran for his second career touchdown.

Through the 1994 season, Bennett's records in 115 regular season games included over 500 tackles, 50.5 sacks, 5 interceptions, 21 forced fumbles, and 17 fumble recoveries. His honors have been being AFC Co-Defensive Player of the Year and AFC Linebacker of the Year in 1988, AFC Defensive Player of the Year in 1991, and Pro Bowl selection following the 1988, 1990, 1991, 1992, and 1993 seasons. He played in four consecutive Super Bowl games, with the Bills losing to the New York Giants, 20–19, in Super Bowl XXV, to the Washington Redskins, 37–24, in Super Bowl XXVI, and to the Dallas Cowboys, 52–17, in Super Bowl XXVII and 30–13, in Super Bowl XXVIII.

Bennett and his wife Tracey reside in Orchard Park, NY.

BIBLIOGRAPHY: *Buffalo Bills Media Guide*, 1994; *Buffalo Bills Postseason Guide*, 1993; Dan Herbeck, "Buffalo Soldier," *Sport* 79 (October 1988), pp. 33–34; *TSN Pro Football Register*, 1994.

John L. Evers

BINGAMAN, Lester "Les" (b. February 3, 1926, MacKenzie, TN; d. November 20, 1970, Miami, FL), college and professional player and coach, attended Lew Wallace High School in Gary, IN, and the University of Illinois, where he earned three letters in football as a guard and anchor of the defensive line. With Bingaman in the middle, Illinois took the WC title in 1946 and a 45–14 Rose Bowl victory over UCLA in January 1947.

The Detroit Lions (NFL) drafted Bingaman as their number-three pick in 1948. Bingaman enjoyed a stellar career as a defensive star over the next seven seasons. His mammoth six-foot-three-inch, 335-pound frame presaged the era of the agile big lineman in professional football. Bingaman's agility, strength, and toughness made him a fan favorite. In only his second NFL year, Bingaman was chosen a team cocaptain, an honor repeated in 1953. With Bingaman's help, the Lions captured three NFC titles in 1951, 1952, and 1953 and two NFL Championships. He recovered a fumble on the Cleveland Browns' 13-yard line in the 1953 NFL title game to set up the Lions' first touchdown in their 17–16 triumph. Bingaman, named to the All-NFL team from 1951 to 1954, played in the 1952 and 1954 Pro Bowl games.

Authorities considered Bingaman the best middle guard of his time. Bingaman retired after the 1954 season but returned as an assistant coach for the Detroit Lions from 1960 to 1964. In 1965, he became an original member of the Miami Dolphins (AFL) coaching staff, serving as a special assistant and player personnel director. As defensive line coach four years later, Bingaman collapsed on the sidelines during a game. An irregular heartbeat was detected as the cause. Heart trouble brought Bingaman's once-massive size down to 225 pounds. Nevertheless, he suffered a heart attack and died in his sleep. He was survived by his wife Betty and a son, Lester III.

BIBLIOGRAPHY: Les Bingaman file, Pro Football Hall of Fame, Canton, OH; Chicago (IL) *Tribune*, November 21, 1970, p. B4; Miami (FL) *News*, November 20, 1970; Roger Treat, ed., *Encyclopedia of Football*, 16th rev. ed. (New York, 1979).

Gerald R. Gems

BOSWORTH, Brian Keith "The Boz" (b. March 9, 1965, Oklahoma City, OK), college and professional player, is the son of Foster Bosworth, a retired factory worker, and Kathy Bosworth. He began playing football at age six and participated in football and basketball at MacArthur High School in Irving, TX, where he was a 1983 graduate and an honor student.

At the University of Oklahoma (BEC) from 1984 to 1986, Bosworth excelled as college football's most noted linebacker. Known for his defiant style of play, he was selected a Second Team All-America in 1984 and a unanimous choice the next two seasons. He finished fourth in the 1986 Heisman Trophy voting. In 1985 and 1986, he won the Dick Butkus Award as the nation's outstanding collegiate linebacker. Bosworth, a three-time All-BEC selection, was named BEC Defensive Player of the Year in 1985 and 1986. He was chosen First Team Academic All-America in 1986 and became the first player in Oklahoma history to start 36 consecutive games over three seasons. During that time, the Sooners compiled a 31–4–1 win–loss record, captured three BEC titles, appeared in three Orange Bowls, and won the National Championship after the 1985 season with a 25–10 triumph over Pennsylvania State University. Bosworth led the Sooners in tackles each of his three years, totaling 395. He recorded 39 tackles for losses, 12 sacks, and a career-high 136 tackles in 1986.

At the close of the 1986 season, Bosworth was ruled ineligible to play in the Orange Bowl because testing indicated he had used anabolic steroids. Although dropped from the football team for his senior year, he graduated in 1987 with a 3.3 grade-point average in business. The Seattle Seahawks made Bosworth the first pick in the June 1987 NFL supplemental draft, signing him to a 10-year, $11 million contract. He played in 12 games as a rookie and ranked second on the team in tackles, being selected on the All-NFL Rookie team. Shoulder injuries limited his playing time to only half of the Seahawks' 48 games over three seasons and forced him into retirement during the summer of 1990.

Besides coauthoring *The Boz*, Bosworth, who is single, also operates a business, "44" Boz, Incorporated, that sells clothing apparel. Since his retirement from football, he has pursued an acting career and starred in his first movie, *Stone Cold*.

BIBLIOGRAPHY: Brian Bosworth and Rick Reilly, *The Boz* (New York, 1988); *Seattle Seahawks Media Guide*, 1989; Craig Tomashoff, "No Tackling Dummy," *People Weekly* 22 (June 10, 1991), pp. 97–98.

John L. Evers

BOYDSTON, Max Ray (b. January 22, 1932, Ardmore, OK), college and professional player and scout, is the son of John Boydston, a mechanical engineer, and Wanda Mae Boydston and moved to Muskogee, OK, following eighth grade. Boydston, an end and fullback, joined other future University of Oklahoma (BSC) Sooners Kurt Burris, Robert Burris, and Bo Bolinger in leading Muskogee Central High School to the Oklahoma State football championship in 1948 and 1950. Boydston also starred on Muskogee's 1951 State runner-up basketball team.

Boydston enrolled at the University of Oklahoma during the "Golden Age of Sooner Football." Sooner head coach Bud Wilkinson (FB) won three straight BSC championships from 1952 to 1954 and achieved a 27–2–2 overall record. The AP ranked the Sooners third nationally in 1952 and 1953 and second in 1954. Due to a BSC rule prohibiting consecutive Bowl appearances, Boydston's only postseason appearance came in a 7–0 victory over the University of Maryland in the 1954 Orange Bowl. During three varsity seasons, Boydston caught 28 passes for 698 yards and six touchdowns. The speedy Boydston often ran the end around play, averaging 10.6 yards per carry in 1953.

The six-foot-two-inch, 210-pound Boydston was named All-BSC end three straight years from 1952 to 1954, All-America in 1953, and consensus All-America in 1954. The Washington, DC Touchdown Club selected him College Lineman of the Year in 1955.

The Chicago Cardinals (NFL) drafted Boydston as their number-one pick in 1955 and used him four seasons at both end and slot back. Boydston caught 27 passes for three touchdowns from 1955 to 1958. After the Cardinals released him due to a shoulder injury, Boydston played the 1959 season for the Hamilton, Canada, Tiger-Cats (CFL). The Dallas Texans (AFL) signed him in 1960. Boydston experienced more success in the pass-oriented AFL, catching 29 passes for three touchdowns in 1960 and 12 aerials for one touchdown in 1961. Dallas traded Boydston to the Oakland Raiders (AFL) in the off-season. Boydston enjoyed his most productive year as a professional in 1962, catching 30 passes for 374 yards.

After retiring from professional football in 1963, Boydston coached high school football and taught history and computing for 29 years at Southlake Carroll, TX, Stratford, TX, Garland, TX, Sherman, TX, and Talequah, OK. He also scouted one year for the Kansas City Chiefs (NFL) and spent several years in private business.

Boydston, who married Kay Cheatham on July 1, 1965, is retired, lives in Checotah, OK, and has two sons, Stanley and Brady.

BIBLIOGRAPHY: "He's the End!," *Senior Scholastic* (November 3, 1954), p. 34; John Hillman, telephone interview with Max Boydston, July 24, 1993; John D. McCallum, *Big Eight Football* (New York, 1979); David S. Neft et al., eds., *The Football Encyclopedia*, 2nd ed. (New York, 1994); Don Schiffer, ed., *1959 Pro Football Handbook* (New York, 1959); University of Oklahoma, *Oklahoma Football—1988* (Norman, OK, 1988); Jim Weeks, "The 'B' Boys," *Sooners Illustrated* (September 15, 1990), pp. 12–16.

John Hillman

BRAY, Raymond Robert Sr. "Ray" "Muscles" (b. February 1, 1917, Caspian, MI; d. December 26, 1993, Mesa, AZ), college and professional player, attended Vulcan High School and then enrolled at Western Michigan University, where he lettered three years in football and track and field. He was selected Little All-America in football as a senior and was later named to the Western Michigan University Hall of Fame. During Bray's intercollegiate career, Western Michigan compiled marks of 2–5 in 1936, 5–3 in 1937, and 4–3 in 1938. Bray earned a bachelor's degree in physical education at Western Michigan and a master's degree in education at the University of Michigan. He and his wife Juanita had four children.

In 1939 the Chicago Bears (NFL) selected Bray, a six-foot, 235-pound guard, on the seventh round. Bray started for the 8–3 1940 NFL Championship team but missed the historic 73–0 Bear victory over the Washington Redskins in the title game because of a knee injury. He played on a second championship Bears team with a 10–1 mark in 1941 and on the 1942 Western Division–winning 11–0 squad, upset by Washington in the title game. During World War II, he spent three years in military service. He served as a physical fitness instructor for U.S. Navy preflight and starred for the Jacksonville, FL, Navy service team. He returned to the Bears in 1946 and performed on his third NFL Championship team, which boasted an 8–2–1 mark. Although playing both offense and defense most of his career, Bray specialized on defense in his last seasons. His most memorable play came against the Los Angeles Rams in 1951, while he was standing on the sidelines. When a Ram player intercepted a pass, Bray stepped in bounds and tackled him without being penalized for illegal participation. In 1952, Chicago traded Bray to the Green Bay Packers (NFL) for his eleventh and final professional season.

Bray, one of the NFL's strongest players during his day, captured arm wrestling championships and did 50 one-arm pushups. He became one of the first professional players seriously to pursue weight lifting. Although overshadowed in his early years by established Bears All-Pro lineman Danny Fortmann (FB) and Joe Stydahar (FB), he finally gained recognition as one of the NFL's top guards after World War II. Besides being selected All-NFL in 1946, 1948, 1949, and 1950, he was chosen to the Pro Bowl following the 1950 and 1951 seasons. Only Fortmann and Stan Jones (FB), both members of the Pro Football Hall of Fame, have been more honored among Bear guards. After leaving professional football, he worked in the sales division of Cadillac Motors in Chicago and retired to the Phoenix, AZ, area in 1973.

BIBLIOGRAPHY: "Bears, Then and Now," *Pro*, August 16, 1978; *Chicago Bears Media Guide* 1951; Bob McGinn, "Where Are You Now Ray Bray?" Green Bay (WI) *Press-Gazette*, December 27, 1981; David S. Neft et al., eds., *The Football Encyclopedia*, 2nd ed. (New York, 1994); Beau Riffenburgh, *The Official NFL Encyclopedia*, 4th ed. (New York, 1986).

Robert N. "Bob" Carroll

BRITO, Gene Herman (b. October 23, 1925, Los Angeles, CA; d. June 8, 1965, Los Angeles, CA), college and professional player, played defensive end with the Washington Redskins (NFL) and the Los Angeles Rams (NFL) during the 1950s and early 1960s. He was the son of Gene Joseph Brito, a professional boxer, and had two sisters.

Brito graduated from Lincoln High School in Los Angeles and then entered the military service. After three years' duty as a paratrooper in the Philippines, Brito starred in football, baseball, basketball, and track and field at Loyola University of Los Angeles from 1947 to 1951. He started every football game for Loyola during his four years there and made the Independent College All-Coast team in 1950. During Brito's senior year in 1950, Loyola compiled an 8–1 record under coach Jordan Olivar. In 1951, he earned a bachelor's degree and planned to teach.

The Washington Redskins (NFL) selected the six-foot-two-inch 230-pounder in the seventeenth round of the 1951 draft. Brito played offensive and defensive end with the Redskins. His career pass catching record included 47 receptions for 618 yards and two touchdowns. His best offensive season came his rookie year, when he caught 24 passes for 313 yards. Brito was selected to play in the Pro Bowl four times. His other honors included being named the Outstanding Lineman of the 1957 Pro Bowl game, winning the MVP Pro Award from the Washington Touchdown Club in 1957, being named to the AP All-NFL team from 1955 through 1957, and being voted to the UPI All-NFL team in 1955, 1956, and 1958.

With Washington, Brito never missed a game and played in 84 consecutive contests. The streak was interrupted during the 1954 season when Brito jumped to the Calgary, Canada, Stampeders (CFL). He returned to the Washington Redskins in 1955. In the winter of 1958, Washington traded Brito to the Los Angeles Rams (NFL) for linebacker Larry Morris.* Brito played with the Rams until 1962, when he became ill with muscular dystrophy during training camp. He never regained his health and died three years later, leaving his wife, June (DeLaura) Brito, and two daughters.

BIBLIOGRAPHY: Robert L. Cannon, interview with June Brolin, widow of Gene Brito, December 27, 1992; *Los Angeles Rams Media Guide*, 1960; *NYT*, Obituary, June 9, 1965; Washington (DC) *Evening Star*, Obituary, June 9, 1965; Washington Redskins Program, December 14, 1958.

                                                                Robert L. Cannon

BROOKE, George Haycock (b. July 9, 1874, Brookville, MD; d. November 16, 1938, Tucson, AZ), athlete, starred as a football All-America at the University of Pennsylvania from 1893 to 1895, later served as head football coach at Stanford University, Swarthmore College, and his alma mater, and won a national squash racquets championship. He was the son of Walter H. Brooke and Caroline (Leggett) Brooke. After attending prep school, he starred at Swarthmore College in baseball, captained the football team in 1892, and received a B.S. degree in 1893. He then enrolled at the University of Pennsylvania, earning a degree from Wharton School in 1895 and a law degree in 1898.

The University of Pennsylvania (IvL) at that time used varsity athletes such as Brooke, who had previously played at other institutions, to develop outstanding football teams. The Quakers' NFF College Football Hall of Fame coach George Woodruff (S) developed a unique "guards back" offensive system in which the two guards moved into the backfield to provide moving interference for the running backs. He also used the punt and drop-kick as offensive weapons.

The five-foot-nine-inch, 175-pound Brooke fit well into this new system. Running from the halfback or fullback position, he first attracted attention in 1893 with his skill in the open field, rushes up the center, dropkicking, kick returns, and play as safety on defense. But he gained most attention for his punting and is credited with coining the phrase "coffin-corner" to describe the long punts he placed out of bounds deep in his opponent's territory.

By fall 1894, Brooke was regarded as one of the best collegiate fullbacks and a prolific scorer. Pennsylvania finished 12–0 that year, outscoring opponents, 366–20, and posting important victories over Princeton University and Harvard University. Three Pennsylvania stars, including Brooke, made the 1894 All-America team. Pennsylvania returned most of its veteran players in 1895, again finishing undefeated, 14–0–0, outscoring opponents, 480–24, and being regarded as the national champion. Brooke suffered from various injuries that season, but his strong kicking and running again earned him All-America honors.

By then, Brooke had played seven seasons of intercollegiate football. Speculation abounded that he might return and captain the 1896 Pennsylvania team. But he concentrated instead on completing his legal studies, although never actually practicing law.

He compiled a 4–1 mark as football coach at Stanford University in 1897 before enlisting the following spring in the first Pennsylvania unit mustered in the Spanish-American War. After brief service in the Puerto Rican campaign, he was discharged later that year. He then served as football coach at Swarthmore from 1898 to 1911 and compiled a 13–7–1 mark at Pennsylvania in 1912 and 1913 before entering the insurance business.

Brooke, an outstanding squash racquets player, won the national singles championship in 1904 and doubles championship in 1917. That same year, he also captured the Pennsylvania lawn tennis doubles championship. He was well known in various athletic clubs in the Philadelphia area and helped found the Penn AC. He suffered from a serious heart ailment and spent his final years on the West Coast. Brooke and his wife Marie had no children.

BIBLIOGRAPHY: L. H. Baker, *Football: Facts and Figures* (New York, 1945); Edward R. Bushnell, *The History of Athletics at Pennsylvania* (Philadelphia, PA, 1909); Allison Danzig, *Oh, How They Played the Game* (New York, 1971); John D. McCallum and Charles H. Pearson, *College Football U.S.A., 1869–1973* (New York, 1973); *1991 NCAA Football*; *NYT*, November 3, 1893, p. 9; November 11, 1894, p. 3; October 28, 1895, p. 3; November 24, 1895, p. 3; November 29, 1895, p. 2; November 17, 1938, p. 25; Tom Perrin, *Football: A College History* (Jefferson, NC, 1987); University of Pennsylvania Archives, Philadelphia, PA; Alexander M. Weyand, *The Saga of American Football* (New York, 1955).

Daniel R. Gilbert

BROOKS, James Robert (b. December 28, 1958, Warner Robbins, GA), college and professional player, is the son of John Brooks and Eura Lee Brooks, a public school custodian, and was brought up mainly by his mother. Brooks graduated from Warner Robbins High School and attended Auburn University (SEC). Primarily a running back, Brooks spent three years from 1981 to 1983 with the San Diego Chargers (NFL) and eight campaigns from 1984 to 1991 with the Cincinnati Bengals (NFL). Brooks, who holds several Bengals team records, was claimed as a free agent by the Cleveland Browns (NFL) in March 1992. Brooks retired after performing with Cleveland and the Tampa Bay Buccaneers (NFL) during the 1992 season.

After being chosen a football All-America at Warner Robbins High School, Brooks played football four years at Auburn from 1977 to 1980. Brooks set an Auburn career rushing record (3,523 yards) that stood until broken by Bo Jackson (FB) and was chosen an All-America his senior year. In his four years at Auburn, the Tigers finished with 25 wins, 18 losses, and one tie.

The San Diego Chargers selected Brooks in the first round of the 1981 draft and quickly used him as an all-purpose offensive threat. Brooks gained 949 yards on kickoff returns his rookie season. In the strike-shortened 1982 season, he led the NFL in kickoff return yardage with 749 yards in nine games. San Diego also employed him as a punt returner. The Chargers made the AFC playoffs after Brooks's rookie season and defeated the Miami Dolphins, 41–38, in the first round, as Brooks caught two touchdown passes. Following the 1982 season, Brooks ran for an 18-yard touchdown to help the Chargers defeat the Pittsburgh Steelers, 31–28, in the first round of the AFC playoffs.

San Diego traded Brooks to Cincinnati for running back Pete Johnson in May 1984. The Bengals used Brooks mainly as a running back, but he remained a threat as a receiver out of the backfield and combined for over 1,000 total yards rushing and receiving five different seasons. Brooks was selected to the Pro Bowl after the 1986 season, when he rushed for 1,087 yards and led the NFL with 5.3 yards per carry. He also made the Pro Bowl three consecutive years following the 1988 through 1990 seasons. Brooks rushed for just 24 yards and added only 20 yards receiving in the Bengals' 20–16 loss to the San Francisco 49ers in Super Bowl XXIII following the 1988 season. He set the Bengals' record for rushing yardage in a single season with 1,239 in 1989 and a team mark by rushing for 201 yards against the Houston Oilers in 1990. Brooks, the Bengals' all-time leading rusher with 6,447 yards, rushed for 7,962 yards (4.7 yards average) and 49 touchdowns and caught 383 passes for 3,621 yards and 30 touchdowns. His 565 punt return yards and 2,762 kickoff return yards gave Brooks 14,910 combined net yards, ranking him among NFL career leaders.

Brooks and wife Simone have one child and reside in Villa Hills, KY.

BIBLIOGRAPHY: *Cincinnati Bengals Media Guide*, 1991; David S. Neft et al., eds., *The Football Encyclopedia*, 2nd ed. (New York, 1994); *TSN Pro Football Register*, 1992.

                                                                                          Brian S. Butler

BROOKSHIER, Thomas J. "Tom" (b. December 16, 1931, Roswell, NM), college athlete and coach, professional football player, and sportscaster, is the son of Orville Brookshier and Dola (Thorton) Brookshier and the youngest of five children. He attended Roswell High School, where he played basketball, baseball, and football. Brookshier never got the recognition he deserved as a 145-pound football halfback but earned a baseball scholarship as a pitcher to the University of Colorado. In his first year at Colorado (BEC), he transformed from a 145-pound baseball pitcher to a 175-pound football player. After Brookshier graduated from the University of Colorado in 1953, the Philadelphia Eagles (NFL) drafted him in the tenth round.

In his 1953 rookie season, he earned the starting job as a defensive back for Philadelphia and never lost it. His rookie season featured eight interceptions. The 1954 and 1955 seasons saw him at the U.S. Air Force Academy, where he served as an assistant football coach. After his two-year absence from football, he returned to the Philadelphia Eagles. His honors included being named to the NFL Pro Bowl team following the 1959 and 1960 seasons. He participated in the 1960 NFL Championship team, which defeated the Green Bay Packers, 17–13, at Franklin Field in Philadelphia, PA. During his NFL career, he proved an agile, smart, sure tackler and intercepted 20 passes. His playing career ended in 1961, when he suffered a compound fracture of his right leg.

The next day, CBS hired him as a radio sports broadcaster. From his hospital bed, Brookshier began his broadcasting career the following day on WCAU-AM, a CBS-owned radio station in Philadelphia.

After Jack Whitaker left WCAU-AM in 1964, Brookshier started his television career. Later, he developed a personal friendship with Pat Summerall (FB), forming CBS's first team on the NFL telecasts. His CBS career lasted for 24 years. He not only covered NFL football but handled boxing on the "CBS Sports Spectacular." His most memorable moments in doing boxing included covering the championship fights of Muhammad Ali (IS).

The Eagles retired Brookshier's jersey number 40. In 1989, he was inducted into the Philadelphia Eagles Honor Roll. The NSSAP named him Sportscaster of the Year, while the Pennsylvania Junior Chamber of Commerce selected him as Man of the Year.

Brookshier, who is involved in many charity organizations, remains one of Philadelphia's leading citizens. He and his wife Barbara have three children, Linda, Tommy, Jr., and Betsy, and live in Bryn Mawr, PA. Brookshier philosophizes, "My life to me has always been one big challenge. It's like pushing a big rock up a hill. I know I can do it, and I will succeed."

BIBLIOGRAPHY: Ray Fetters, personal interview with Tom Brookshier, October 21, 1992; Jim Gallager, Philadelphia Eagles Public Relations Department, Philadelphia,

PA; Gene Quinn, "Talk, a Conversation with Tom Brookshier," *Game Day Magazine* (September 1989), pp. 15–16.

Raymond C. Fetters

BROWN, David Steven "Dave" (b. January 16, 1953, Akron, OH), college and professional player and coach, is the son of Asa C. Brown, a Goodyear Tire and Rubber Company employee, and Lillian Tommie (Jones) Brown and attended Garfield High School in Akron, where he played football and basketball. The six-foot-one-inch, 197-pound Brown started three years at safety and returned kicks for the University of Michigan (BTC) during the 1972, 1973, and 1974 seasons. Under coach Glenn "Bo" Schembechler (FB) during these three campaigns, the Wolverines posted a 30–2–1 win–loss record and shared three BTC championships. An All-BTC choice and an All-America in 1973 and 1974, Brown cocaptained the Wolverines in 1974 and played in the East-West Shrine, Hula Bowl, Coaches All-America, and College All-Star Games following his senior season. He was named in 1983 to Michigan's All-Time Half-Century football team. Brown graduated as a speech, radio, and television major.

The Pittsburgh Steelers (NFL) selected Brown in the first round of the 1975 draft as the twenty-sixth player overall. Brown played in 13 regular season games for the Steelers, being used primarily on punt returns and returning 22 kicks for 217 yards. Brown also returned three punts for 14 yards in Super Bowl X as the Steelers triumphed, 21–17, over the Dallas Cowboys. On March 30, 1976, the Seattle Seahawks selected Brown in the NFL expansion draft and used him at cornerback 11 seasons from 1976 through 1986. Brown, who led the Seahawks in interceptions four times (1976, 1979, 1980, 1986) and finished second four times, served as defensive captain between 1983 and 1986. He registered five touchdowns with Seattle on interception returns, including 90-yard and 58-yard returns against the Kansas City Chiefs on November 4, 1984, to equal an NFL single-game record. The Seahawks made four interception returns for touchdowns that day against the Chiefs, setting an NFL mark. Brown holds the Seattle record for most career interceptions (50) and most career interception return yardage (643). He was voted to the Pro Bowl after the 1984 season, earning First Team All-NFL and All-AFC honors.

Seattle traded Brown to the Green Bay Packers (NFL) in August 1987 for an eleventh-round 1988 draft choice. Brown played for the Packers from 1987 through 1989 but missed the 1990 season because of an Achilles tendon injury and retired prior to the 1991 season. Brown started all his 44 games with Green Bay and captained their defensive unit in 1988, leading the Packers with 12 interceptions in three seasons. He played in 216 NFL games, starting 203. Brown finished his career with 62 interceptions, sharing fifth place in NFL history.

Seattle employed Brown as an assistant defensive coach from 1992 through

1994. Brown, an excellent raquetball player, was named the 1982 Seattle NFL Man of the Year for his community work. He and his wife Rhonda have two sons, Aaron and Sterling.

BIBLIOGRAPHY: David Brown, letter to David L. Porter, November 20, 1993; Will Perry, *The Wolverines: A Story of Michigan Football* (Huntsville, AL, 1979); *Seattle Seahawks Media Guide*, 1987; *Seattle Seahawks Media Guide*, 1994; *TSN Pro Football Register*, 1987.

John L. Evers

BROWN, Hardy "Butcher Boy" "The Hump" "Thumper" (b. May 8, 1924, Childress, TX; d. November 8, 1991, Stockton, CA), college and professional player, excelled as one of the toughest football players of any size in NFL history. His father was murdered when Hardy was only four years old. His mother sent him the next year to the Masonic Home Orphanage in Fort Worth, TX. Brown later starred as a high school football player on the orphanage team.

He attended SMU (SWC) in 1941 but became a U.S. Marine paratrooper at the outbreak of World War II. Brown enrolled at the University of Tulsa (MVC), where he was named a three-time All-MVC choice as a blocking fullback and vicious linebacker from 1945 to 1947.

The six-foot-one-inch, 193-pound Brown, best known as a hard-hitting middle linebacker in professional football, often dropped his shoulder and then exploded up into the face of his opponent. Opponents often suffered broken noses or jaws, knocking them out of games. Brown developed extraordinary strength in his shoulders. He did not tackle low intentionally with his arms and hands but met ball carriers with the crack of his shoulders. From 1948 through 1950, Brown played linebacker with the Brooklyn Dodgers (AAFC), Chicago Hornets (AAFC), Baltimore Colts (NFL), and Washington Redskins (NFL). His best playing years, however, came from 1951 to 1956 with the San Francisco 49ers (NFL).

Although never an All-Pro or Pro Bowl selection, Brown remained legendary among NFL players. He was credited with knocking 21 opposition NFL players out of games during the 1951 season by using his shoulder. "Not big, but the toughest linebacker I ever saw," commented 49er quarterback Y. A. Tittle (FB). Pro Football Hall of Fame halfback Doak Walker (FB) remarked, "Brown had more career knockouts than Joe Louis [IS]." Brown spent the 1956 season with the Chicago Cardinals (NFL). After leaving football for the next three seasons, he returned at age 36 with the new Denver Broncos (AFL) in 1960. After being released by the Broncos, he held numerous labor jobs. Brown's heavy drinking problems and marital problems with his wife Betty caused him in 1986 to be institutionalized, where he spent his last five years.

BIBLIOGRAPHY: Hardy Brown, Clipping file, Pro Football Hall of Fame, Canton, OH; Bob Carroll and Bob Barnett, "Black Hats in a Golden Age," *SH* 1 (January–

February 1989), pp. 43–53; Dwight Chapin, "The Toughest 49er Ever," *TCC* (Winter 1993), pp. 9–10, 23; Ray Didinger, "Hardy was Not a Softy," Philadelphia (PA) *Daily News*, November 13, 1991; Dan McGuire, *San Francisco 49ers* (New York, 1960); David Neft et al., eds., *The Football Encyclopedia*, 2nd ed. (New York, 1994); Murray Olderman, *The Defenders* (Englewood Cliffs, NJ, 1973).

C. Robert Barnett

BROWN, Johnny Mack "Dothan Antelope" (b. September 1, 1904, Dothan, AL; d. November 14, 1974, Woodland Hills, CA), college player and coach, lettered as a football halfback at the University of Alabama (SC) from 1923 to 1925 and starred on coach Wallace Wade's (FB) undefeated 1925 team. Brown, one of four brothers to play for the Crimson Tide, possessed a marvelous open field running style resembling a moving antelope. Coach Wade devised low-cut football shoes for Brown, among the nation's quickest running backs, and tailored the Alabama offense to utilize his fine pass catching skills. As a sophomore, Brown scored a touchdown against the University of Mississippi for the 7–2–1 Crimson Tide.

Alabama compiled an 8–1 record in 1924, as Brown scored three touchdowns against Union College, caught a 37-yard touchdown pass in a 14–0 upset over Georgia Institute of Technology, and returned a 65-yard pass interception for a score in a resounding 33–0 triumph over the favored University of Georgia. Alabama won its first SC title, but a stunning 17–0 loss to Centre College denied the Crimson Tide an undefeated season and possible Rose Bowl invitation. In 1925, the 10–0 Crimson Tide outscored opponents, 277–7, to garner the HAF and *FA* national titles. Alabama used Brown as a wingback and tailback to showcase his running and pass catching abilities and exhibit the outstanding running and passing skills of Pooley Hubert. Alabama triumphed 7–0 over previously undefeated Georgia Tech, as Brown scored the only touchdown on a twisting, 55-yard punt return.

On New Year's Day in 1926, Alabama, the first Southern Rose Bowl participant, edged the University of Washington, 20–19. The 180-pound Brown helped show that southern teams could play energetically. Until then, "national" football powers usually did not include southern teams. According to Brown, the Crimson Tide played for the reputation of the whole South, not just Alabama. During one of the most exciting Rose Bowls ever, the Crimson Tide exploded for all of their 20 points in a seven-minute span in the third quarter to preserve their undefeated season. Brown earned HAF Citizens Savings Rose Bowl Player of the Year honors after helping Alabama upset Washington in what the AP called "one of the ten greatest football contests ever." Brown scored two touchdowns on passes of 59 yards from Grant Gillis and 30 yards from Hubert. He was elected to the NFF College Football Hall of Fame in 1957.

Brown married his college sweetheart, Cornelia, shortly after graduation and had four children. George Fawcett, a character actor, remembered

Brown from the 1926 Rose Bowl. When Brown returned to California in 1927 as an Alabama assistant football coach, he visited Fawcett. Fawcett introduced the young coach to the director Erich von Stroheim, who gave him a screen test. Brown made his film debut in *The Bugle Call* (1926). Brown's early screen career matched him with formidable female stars Greta Garbo in *A Woman of Affairs* (1928), Joan Crawford in *Our Dancing Daughters* (1928), and Mary Pickford in her first talkie, *Coquette* (1929). Brown switched genres in 1930, appearing in his first western, *Billy the Kid*, costarring with Wallace Beery.

Brown ultimately appeared in over 300 pictures, mostly B-grade westerns and serials, and often was paired with his horse Reno. Between 1940 and 1950, Brown ranked among the top 10 money-making western stars. He retired in the 1950s to host and manage a San Fernando Valley restaurant, often playing polo, golf, and tennis for recreation. Brown made a brief film comeback in 1965 with *The Bounty Killer* and *Apache Uprising* and died of kidney failure.

BIBLIOGRAPHY: Clyde Bolton, *The Crimson Tide* (Huntsville, AL, 1972); Clyde Bolton, *Unforgettable Days in Southern Football* (Huntsville, AL, 1974); Jack Clary, *College Football's Greatest Dynasties* (New York, 1991); Leslie Halliwell, *The Filmgoer's Companion* (New York, 1971); Herb Michelson and Dave Newhouse, *Rose Bowl Football Since 1902* (New York, 1977); *NYT*, November 16, 1974, p. 34; David Ragan, *Who's Who in Hollywood* (New York, 1992); Christy Walsh, comp. and ed., *College Football and All America Review* (Culver City, CA, 1949); Washington (DC) *Post*, November 16, 1974, p. E6.

Frederick J. Augustyn, Jr.

BRUCE, Earle Dunseth Jr. (b. March 8, 1931, Pittsburgh, PA), college player and coach, is the son of Earle Dunseth Bruce, Sr., a fire safety engineer, and Mildred Bruce. An All-State halfback at Cumberland, MD, High School, Bruce also held state interscholastic records in the 100- and 220-yard dashes. He enrolled at Ohio State University (BTC) in September 1949, but a knee injury ended his playing career. After graduating from Ohio State with a bachelor's degree in 1953, Bruce accepted his first football coaching job the same year as an assistant at Mansfield, OH, High School. His first head coaching football assignment came at Salem, OH, High School, where he compiled a 28–9 win–loss record between 1956 and 1959. A four-year stint at Sandusky, OH, High School (34–3–3 record) and a two-year stop at Massilon, OH, High School (20–0 record) followed. Both of his Massilon teams won Ohio State championships. Bruce's high school coaching career produced a phenomenal 82–12–3 composite record for an .861 winning percentage. He was named Ohio High School Football Coach of the Year three times, finishing his high school coaching career with a 42–game winning streak.

Bruce began his college career as an assistant football coach at Ohio State

University from 1966 to 1971 under Woody Hayes (FB). In 1972, he served as head football coach at the University of Tampa, compiling a 10–2 record and a 21–18 Tangerine Bowl victory over Kent State University. Iowa State University (BEC) selected Bruce head football coach the following season. Bruce compiled a 36–32 record with the Cyclones between 1973 and 1978 and enjoyed winning seasons his last 3 years, the first time Iowa State had accomplished that feat in 54 years. Bruce was named BEC Football Coach of the Year two times and directed the Cyclones to the 1977 Peach Bowl against North Carolina State University and the 1978 Hall of Fame Classic against Texas A & M University.

Upon returning to Ohio State University as head football coach in 1979, Bruce led the Buckeyes to a BTC championship and an 11–1 record. The AFCA and FWAA named Bruce Football Coach of the Year. In 9 years at Ohio State from 1979 through 1987, Bruce compiled an impressive 81–26–1 record and four BTC championships and led the Buckeyes to eight consecutive Bowl games. His Bowl teams boasted a 5–3 record. In spite of his excellent winning percentage, Ohio State dismissed him in 1988. Bruce moved to Northern Iowa University (GWC), guiding the Panthers to five victories. Following the 1988 season, Colorado State University (WAC) named him head football coach. In 1990, Bruce led the Rams to a 9–4 season, tying the all-time Rams record for most victories. The season ended with a thrilling 32–31 victory over the University of Oregon in the Freedom Bowl, the Rams' first postseason appearance in 42 years. Bruce became 1 of only 3 intercollegiate coaches to guide four different schools to Bowl games, joining the University of Notre Dame's Lou Holtz (S) and Indiana University's Bill Mallory.* Colorado State released Bruce following the 1992 season, with the latter having amassed a 22–24–1 record there. Bruce's 154–90–2 record spanning 21 seasons ranked him among the top 10 contemporary coaches in winning percentage and among the top 12 in victories. He coached the Cleveland Thunderbolts (ArFL) to a 2–10 record in 1994. In October 1994, the expansion St. Louis Stampede (ArFL) named Bruce as head coach. Bruce and his wife Jean have four daughters, Lynn, Michele, Aimee, and Noel.

BIBLIOGRAPHY: *Colorado State Football Media Guide*, 1992; *Ohio State Football Media Guide*, 1987; Oskaloosa (IA) *Herald*, January 12, 1979.

John L. Evers

BUDDE, Edward Leon "Ed" (b. November 2, 1940, Highland Park, MI), college and professional player, is the son of Max Budde and Agnes Budde and first demonstrated his athletic prowess at Detroit's Derby High School, where he starred at tackle, end, and halfback on the football squad. Budde enrolled at Michigan State University (BTC) in 1959. Under the tutelage of celebrated Spartan football coach Duffy Daugherty (FB) during the winning 1960, 1961, and 1962 seasons, Budde emerged as one of the greatest linemen in collegiate history at both the guard and tackle positions. In these years, the Spartans compiled 18 victories, 8 losses, and one tie. In the last era of "two platoon" football, Budde played 209 minutes in 1960, mostly at defensive tackle. The Spartans used him primarily as an offensive guard in 1961, when he performed 221 minutes. In 1962, he again played mostly as a defensive tackle, registering 276 minutes. Budde was named to *Time's* 1962 All-America team and in 1969 to the All-Spartan team. In 1963, he played in the Senior Bowl and captained the College All-Star team, which upset the Green Bay Packers, 20–17.

The six-foot-five-inch, 260-pound Budde enjoyed a magnificent professional career as an All-Pro left guard (1966, 1969) for the Kansas City Chiefs (AFL-NFL) from 1963 to 1976. His highlights included participation in the Super Bowl I 35–10 loss in 1967 to the Green Bay Packers and the Super Bowl IV 23–7 upset victory in 1970 over the Minnesota Vikings. He played in the Pro Bowl in 1971 and 1972. A Hall of Fame Selection Committee named Budde as a guard on the All-Time AFL team. He also was inducted as a member of the Chiefs' Hall of Fame in 1983.

Budde still resides in the Kansas City area, where he works as an account manager for Coca-Cola. He graduated from Michigan State University with a bachelor's degree in physical education in 1965. Budde married his high school sweetheart, Carolyn, in 1958. One son, Brad, later played for the Kansas City Chiefs in the 1980s, while another son, John, performed for the Spartans in the later 1980s. Budde also has one daughter, Tionne. A superior blocker and tackler, Budde remains the model for the qualities a powerful lineman must possess. These qualities include quick intelligence, a broad knowledge of the game, and unparalleled leadership skills.

BIBLIOGRAPHY: Edward Budde, telephone interviews, January 10, 1994, February 1, 1994; Duffy Daugherty with Dave Diles, *Duffy: An Autobiography* (Garden City, NY, 1974); *Michigan State University Football Media Guide*, 1992; Michigan State University, Sports Information Office, East Lansing, MI; David Neft et al., eds., *The Football Encyclopedia*, 2nd ed. (New York, 1994); Bob Pille, "How MSU Hides Giant Tackle," Detroit (MI) *Free Press*, October 30, 1962; Fred Stabley, *The Spartans: Michigan State Football* (Tomball, TX, 1988); Roger Treat, *The Encyclopedia of Football*, 16th rev. ed. (New York, 1979); *TSN Pro Football Register*, 1976.

Erik S. Lunde

BURK, Adrian Matthew (b. December 14, 1927, Mexia, TX), college athlete and professional football player and official, starred as a six-foot two-inch, 190-pound quarterback for Baylor University (SWC) in 1948 and 1949 under coach Bob Woodruff. In 1948, he directed the Bears to a 5–3–2 record, a third-place SWC tie, and a 20–7 victory over Wake Forest College in the Dixie Bowl, the school's first postseason appearance. Burk led the nation in passing in 1949, completing 110 of 191 passes (57 percent) for 1,428 yards and 14 touchdowns and throwing only 6 interceptions. Baylor won its first six games before losing, 20–0, to the University of Texas. In the 35–26 victory over SMU the next week, Burk tossed an 80–yard touchdown pass and 2 other touchdown aerials. Baylor finished the season with an 8–2 mark for second place in the SWC, outscoring opponents 232–120. During two seasons, Burk completed 172 of 312 passes (55.1 percent) for 2,024 yards and 20 touchdowns with only 13 interceptions. He also punted 113 times for 4,025 yards (35.6-yard average).

The Baltimore Colts (NFL) selected Burk in the first round of the 1950 NFL draft. After the Baltimore franchise dissolved in 1951, Burk joined the Philadelphia Eagles (NFL). Burk responded well to his new team, completing 92 passes in 218 attempts for 14 touchdowns. Utilizing excellent receivers Pete Pihos (FB) and Bobby Walston (FB), Burk enjoyed a banner 1954 campaign with 123 completions in 231 attempts for 23 touchdowns, all career highs. On October 17 against the Washington Redskins, he tossed 7 touchdowns to tie the NFL record for most scoring strikes in a game. Sid Luckman (FB) of the Chicago Bears had set the mark 11 years earlier.

Burk played two more years with the Eagles, retiring after the 1956 season. In seven NFL seasons, he completed 500 of 1,079 passes for 7,001 yards and 61 touchdowns. He played in the Pro Bowl following the 1955 and 1956 seasons. During his six-year tenure with Philadelphia, Burk shared quarterback duties with Bobby Thomason. Nevertheless, his 55 career touchdown passes and 23 touchdown aerials in 1954 rank him second among Eagles quarterbacks.

Burk also excelled as a punter. During his first NFL season, he led the NFL with 81 punts for Baltimore (40-yard average). Burk topped the NFL again in 1952 with 83 punts, in 1954 with 73 punts, and in 1956 with 68 punts. His 1952 figure remains the second highest for an NFL season. The same year, Burk tied an NFL mark for most punts in a game with 12 against the Green Bay Packers. His best NFL kicking performance came in 1953, when he punted 41 times for a 43-yard average. In 1955, he unleashed a 75-yarder for the longest punt of his NFL career. Overall, Burk punted 474 times for a 40.8-yard average.

Burk studied law during the latter part of his NFL career and became a licensed attorney in 1957. With the Houston Oilers of the fledgling AFL in the early 1960s, he served as assistant to the president and general counsel. From 1965 to 1976, Burk worked as an NFL back judge to become the only person in NFL history to combine as a player, game official, and front office executive. He and his wife Neva have been married 44 years, reside in Massachusetts, and have one son, Robert.

BIBLIOGRAPHY: Denne H. Freeman, *That Good Old Baylor Line* (Huntsville, AL, 1975); Rick Gonsalves, interview with Adrian Burk, March 11, 1994; *Philadelphia Eagles Press Guide*, 1957; *TSN Pro Football Register*, 1957; James D. Whalen, letter to David L. Porter, March 21, 1994.

Richard Gonsalves

BYNER, Earnest Alexander (b. September 15, 1962, Milledgeville, GA), college and professional player, is the son of Bernice Bailey and was brought up by his grandmother, Evelyn Reeves. He graduated from Baldwin High School in Milledgeville and attended East Carolina University. A football running back, the 5-foot-10-inch, 218-pound Byner was drafted in the tenth round in 1984 by the Cleveland Browns (NFL). He spent five seasons with the Browns before being traded to the Washington Redskins (NFL) in April 1989. In May 1994, the Cleveland Browns signed him as a free agent.

Byner, who attended East Carolina University after his high school retired his jersey, started three years from 1981 to 1983 at fullback in football for East Carolina. He majored in physical education but did not earn a degree. His 2,049 career yards rank Byner among the top 10 rushers in Pirate history.

In five NFL years with the Cleveland Browns, Byner proved a hard-nosed fullback. His good hands also made him a fine receiver. Following the 1985 season, Byner broke Jim Brown's (FB) postseason team record by rushing for 161 yards in a losing playoff game effort against the Miami Dolphins. His 66-yard touchdown run in the third quarter broke Leroy Kelly's (FB) team mark for the longest postseason touchdown run. Although placed on injured reserve for an ankle injury midway through the 1986 season, Byner played in the AFC championship game. The Browns lost in overtime to the Denver Broncos, 23–20, as Byner caught one pass for 4 yards. Denver again defeated the Browns in the AFC championship following the 1987 season, but Byner rushed for 67 yards and gained 120 yards receiving.

Byner, having proved his value as an all-purpose back, became a free agent following the 1988 season. Although the Browns re-signed Byner on draft day, Cleveland traded him in April 1989 to the Washington Redskins (NFL) for running back Mike Oliphant. In 5 seasons with the Redskins, Byner proved a durable, dependable runner. In 1990, he led the NFL with 297 rushing attempts. His 1,219 rushing yards in 1990 remain the Redskins' third best single-season mark. He was voted to the Pro Bowl following the 1990 and 1991 seasons, rushing for 1,048 yards in the latter. After the 1991 season, Byner rushed for 49 yards and gained 24 yards receiving, including a 10-yard touchdown reception, to help the Redskins defeat the Buffalo Bills, 37–24, in Super Bowl XXVI. Six times in 11 NFL seasons, Byner has combined for more than 1,000 yards rushing and receiving. Through the 1994 season, he has rushed 6,872 yards (4-yard average) for 50 touchdowns and caught 400 passes for 3,713 yards (9.3-yard average) and 12 touchdowns.

Byner and his wife Tina reside in Centreville, GA, and have four children.

BIBLIOGRAPHY: David S. Neft et al., eds., *The Football Encyclopedia*, 2nd ed. (New York, 1994); *TSN Pro Football Register*, 1994; *Washington Redskins Media Guide*, 1993.

Brian S. Butler

CAFEGO, George "Bad News" (b. August 30, 1915, Whipple, WV), college and professional player and coach, was born into a poor coal mining family near Scarbro, WV. An orphan, he lived with various relatives during his youth. Cafego first played football in junior high school and starred in football and baseball at Oak Hill High School in Scarbro from 1933 to 1936.

Cafego enrolled at the University of Tennessee (SEC), where he played football for legendary coach Robert Neyland (FB). From 1937 to 1939, Cafego excelled as a tailback on offense, starred at defensive back and punter, and became known for his hard-hitting, aggressive style. The six-foot-one-inch 174-pounder rushed for 1,589 yards in his Tennessee career, averaged 6.1 yards per carry, and passed for an additional 550 yards. Cafego intercepted five passes and averaged 38 yards per punt. His success helped propel the University of Tennessee to national football prominence, where the program has remained.

The 1938 SEC Player of the Year, Cafego earned All-America honors following the 1938 and 1939 seasons. During his career, Tennessee compiled a 27–4–1 win–loss record. This record included a 17–0 Tennessee victory over Oklahoma in the 1939 Orange Bowl and a 14–0 loss to the University of Southern California in the 1940 Rose Bowl. Cafego led a history-making 1939 squad not yielding a point in 10 regular season games, the last major college team to accomplish the feat. Cafego injured his knee that season and did not play in the Rose Bowl. The University of Southern California defeated Tennessee, handing the Volunteers their lone loss.

In 1940, the Chicago Cardinals made Cafego the first player selected in the NFL draft and then traded him to the Brooklyn Dodgers (NFL). Cafego served in the U.S. Army in 1942 and 1943 and played briefly with the Washington Redskins (NFL) and Boston Yanks (NFL) in 1943. Bad knees ended his professional football career.

From 1944 to 1948, Cafego returned home and worked in private business in Scarbro. Cafego's football coaching career began in 1948 as an assistant coach at Furman University (SC). He served as an assistant coach at the University of Wyoming (BSAC) from 1949 to 1952, the University of Arkansas (SWC) in 1953 and 1954, and the University of Tennessee (SEC) from 1955 until 1984. In 1954, Cafego married Maxine Fullington and had two children, Rosalie and Gary.

Coaching also brought recognition to Cafego, a renowned kicking instructor. Several of his former pupils enjoyed outstanding careers, including Johnny Majors (S), Herman Weaver, Neal Clabo, and Fuad Reveiz. After retiring from the University of Tennessee, Cafego continued to coach beyond age 70 for the Denver Broncos (NFL) and Minnesota Vikings (NFL) in 1986 and 1987.

Cafego is a member of the Tennessee and West Virginia Halls of Fame. The crowning achievement of his career came in 1969 with his selection to the NFF College Football Hall of Fame.

BIBLIOGRAPHY: Russ Bebb, *The Big Orange: A Story of Tennessee Football* (Huntsville, AL, 1973); George Cafego file, Sports Information Office, University of Tennessee, Knoxville, TN; Bud Fields and Bob Bertucci, *Big Orange: A Pictorial History of University of Tennessee Football* (West Point, NY, 1982); Tom Siler, *The Volunteers* (Knoxville, TN, 1950); Mike Siroky and Bob Bertucci, *Orange Lightning: Inside University of Tennessee Football* (West Point, NY, 1982).

Robert T. Epling

CARSON, Harry Donald (b. November 26, 1953, Florence, SC), college and professional player, is the youngest of six children born to Edgar Carson and Gladys Carson and attended McClenaghan High School, where he became a star defensive lineman. At all-black South Carolina State College, he played defensive end, served as team captain for two years, and scored 30 quarterback sacks his senior year. Twice named MVP in his conference, Carson was also awarded honors for academic achievement. In 1993, he was named to the Black College Football one hundredth year All-Time team as linebacker.

Carson launched his career in professional football in 1976 by signing as middle linebacker for the New York Giants (NFL). The same year, he was selected for the All-NFL Rookie team. The son of a railroad worker and a domestic, Carson yearned for the West Coast team rather than the losing Giants squad. Turnaround came slowly, as Carson in 1980 was chosen NFC Linebacker of the Year by the NFLPA. The Giants in 1981 made the playoffs for the first time in many years. Knee surgery sidelined Carson in 1983.

The Giants' improved record enhanced Carson's standing among the nation's premier athletes. Emotionally close to his daughter Aja, he settled into a pattern of disciplined play and mature team leadership that led New York to an NFC championship in 1986 and a Super Bowl victory over the Denver Broncos in 1987. The Giants' linebackers were again the most feared in the NFL, restoring the tradition started by the Giants in the 1950s.

Suggestions of retirement surfaced by 1988, although Carson still led the Giants in tackles and pass interceptions. Popular with fans and with reporters, the veteran defensive back was named "the soul of the team" by fellow teammates and was noted for game-side antics. In February 1987, he was photographed dumping popcorn over President Ronald Reagan in the wake of the Super Bowl victory. Carson's 13-year career included nine NFL Pro Bowl selections and seven All-NFL awards. After declining an offer from the San Francisco 49ers (NFL) in 1989, Carson retired and pursued sports broadcasting with ABC, and engaged in private business. Carson's autobiography, *Point of Attack*, appeared in 1986.

BIBLIOGRAPHY: "After 13 Giant Years, Carson Ready for Career Change," *Newsday*, December 26, 1988; "Carson and Martin Thrive on Giant Change Following Football," New York *Daily News*, October 22, 1989; "Carson Remembers Giants' Bad Old Days," Chicago (IL) *Tribune*, January 23, 1987, p. 4–4; "Carson, Rock Hard

Linebacker," *NYT Biographical Service* 15 (November 1984), pp. 1435–1437; "Carson's Bad Times Long Gone," *NYT*, January 13, 1987, p. A22; "Ceremonial Dousing," *NYT*, February 14, 1987, p. I47; Iris Cloyd, ed., *Who's Who Among Black Americans, 1990–91*, 6th ed. (Detroit, MI, 1990), p. 212; "The Giants' Keepers of the Flame," *NYT*, August 11, 1986, pp. C1, C3; "Harry Carson Can't Look," *NYT*, December 17, 1984, p. III3; "Jocks," *People Weekly* 26 (January 1987), p. 68; William C. Matney, ed., *Who's Who Among Black Americans, 1985*, 4th ed. (Lake Forest, IL, 1985), p. 139; "New York's Other Linebackers," Los Angeles (CA) *Times*, January 19, 1987, pp. III1, III3.

John L. Godwin

CASEY, Edward Lawrence "Eddie" "Natick Eddie" (b. May 16, 1894, Natick, MA; d. July 25, 1966, Boston, MA), college and professional athlete and coach, was the son of James Francis Casey and Ellen (Ahern) Casey and graduated from Phillips Exeter Academy, where he captained the football team. At Harvard University, he served as captain and center fielder on the freshman baseball team and played halfback on the freshman and varsity football teams. After injuring his shoulder, Casey blocked opponents by "Indianizing" or throwing his body in front of them. When his memorable 72-yard run was called back because of a penalty, the 1916 Harvard Crimson lost to Yale University, 6–3. Walter Camp (FB) selected Casey for his Second All-America Team in 1916 and for his 1917 All-Service team. Casey, a seaman second class in the U.S. Naval Reserve, played at the Boston Navy Yard. He attended officer school and was assigned as an ensign to the U.S.S. *DeKalb* on transport duty.

Upon rejoining the Crimson in 1919, the 5-foot-10-inch, 161-pound "pony-gaited" Casey helped Harvard tie Princeton University, 10–10, with his touchdown and scored the winning touchdown in the 10–3 triumph over Yale. In the 1920 Rose Bowl, Harvard's only postseason intersectional game, Casey caught two passes to help the Crimson defeat the University of Oregon, 7–6. An All-America First Team selectee in 1919, he was selected one of Harvard's all-time halfbacks and a back on Allison Danzig's (OS) all-time specialists list. In 1968, he was elected to the NFF College Football Hall of Fame.

Casey's extracurricular activities included being president of his sophomore class and the Pi Eta Society and belonging to the Institute of 1770—Hasty Pudding Club and Delta Kappa Epsilon. After receiving his Bachelor of Arts degree in January 1920, he played for the Buffalo, NY, All-Americans (NFL) and was employed as a salesman for A. G. Spalding & Brothers in Boston. He also coached football for two years at Mount Union College in Alliance, OH, and from 1922 to 1925 at Tufts College in Medford, MA.

From 1926 to 1934, Casey coached football at Harvard. His record with the freshman squad from 1926 to 1928 was 16–1–1, including an undefeated

1928 season. After being varsity backfield coach in 1929 and 1930, he served as head coach from 1931 to 1934 and compiled a 20–11–1 record. Harvard defeated Yale only once, triumphing 19–6 in 1933, but was shut out by the Elis three years under Casey. His worst season came in 1934 with three wins and five losses. The Crimson suffered a 19–0 shutout by Princeton University, whom Harvard had resumed playing after a seven-year severance. Faced with disagreements among the assistant coaches, the "shy and soft-spoken" Casey resigned. After coaching the Boston Redskins (NFL) to a 2–8–1 record in 1935, he became Massachusetts director of the National Youth Administration from 1935 to 1939. In 1940, he coached the Boston Bears (AFL) to a 5–4–1 mark. He served as a lieutenant commander in the U.S. Naval Reserve in 1944 and 1945 and worked as an Internal Revenue Service agent before becoming principal of Coolidge Junior High School in Natick. Casey married Anna L. Cusick in 1921 and had a daughter, Janice Ann.

BIBLIOGRAPHY: Thomas Bergin, *The Game: The Harvard-Yale Football Rivalry, 1875–1983* (New Haven, CT, and London, England, 1984); John A. Blanchard, ed., *The H Book of Harvard Athletics 1852–1922* (Cambridge, MA, 1923); Clippings on "Edward Lawrence Casey, 1919," quinquennial file, Harvard University Archives, Cambridge, MA; Allison Danzig, *The History of American Football: Its Great Teams, Players, and Coaches* (Englewood Cliffs, NJ, 1956); "Edward Lawrence Casey," biographical sketches in the *Harvard College Class of 1919* albums (Cambridge, MA): senior year album (1919), pp. 91–92, 161; *Fiftieth Anniversary Report* (1969), p. 90; Ralph Hickok, *Who Was Who in American Sports* (New York, 1971); John D. McCallum and Charles H. Pearson, *College Football U.S.A., 1869–1973* (New York, 1973); Geoffrey H. Movius, ed., *The Second H Book of Harvard Athletics 1923–1963* (Cambridge, MA, 1964); *Thirtieth Anniversary Report* (1949), p. 24; *Twenty-fifth Anniversary Report* (1944), p. 128.

Marcia G. Synnott

CHAPMAN, Samuel Blake "Sam" (b. April 11, 1916, Tiburon, CA), college and professional athlete, was the first of two famous University of California (PCC) Golden Bears All-America football players who enjoyed major league baseball careers. The other, Jackie Jensen (S), was named an All-America back from the same campus in 1948. Coach Leonard "Stub" Allison recruited Chapman to play halfback for California from 1935 to 1937. In 1935, the Golden Bears finished 9–1 and shared the PCC title with Stanford University and UCLA, outscoring opponents, 163–22, and ranking fifth nationally in the Dickinson system. Chapman excelled as a blocking back and caught several passes from Vic Bottari. California won the PCC title in 1937 with a 10–0–1 record, outscoring opponents, 314–33, and defeating the University of Alabama 13–0 in the Rose Bowl. In 1937 at the age of 22, Chapman made All-America as a California fullback and punter. George Trevor named Chapman an All-Time blocking back. Chapman received his B.A. degree in May 1938 and then began an 11-year major league career as a regular outfielder with the Philadelphia Athletics (AL, 1938–1941, 1945–1951) and Cleveland Indians (AL, 1951). The six-foot-one-inch 190-pounder enjoyed golf and hunting in his spare time. Chapman honed his baseball skills well in his first four years with a composite .284 average. The 1941 season featured his hitting .322, fifth highest in the major leagues, with 25 home runs and 106 RBIs. In his second major league season, he enjoyed a two-day hit parade against the St. Louis Browns. On May 5–6, 1939, he hit a single, double, triple and 3 home runs in nine at bats in two games. The 1941 season marked a change of careers for him, as Chapman lost four prime years to military service in World War II. Subsequently, Chapman's baseball skills never reached the promise he had shown. In 1949, he hit .278, his highest postwar average. With the perennial second division Philadelphia Athletics under Connie Mack (BB), Chapman never appeared in a World Series. He, however, performed in an All-Star Game in 1946. Chapman's lifetime .266 batting average, 180 home runs, and 773 RBIs indicate what four lost years meant to the career of a major league baseball player.

The power-hitter's career RBIs were almost matched by his 682 strikeouts. Many ranked Chapman among the premier defensive outfielders in the game, noting his speed, strength, and strong arm. He led AL outfielders four times in putouts, once in assists, and three times in errors. In 1941, he also paced the AL in double plays by an outfielder with five. Chapman returned to Tiburon and worked as an industrial inspector for the Bay Area Air Quality District.

BIBLIOGRAPHY: Harold Claassen and Steve Boda, Jr., eds., *Ronald Encyclopedia of Football* (New York, 1960); L. H. Baker, *Football: Facts and Figures* (New York, 1945); Rich Marazzi and Len Fiorito, *Aaron to Zuverink* (New York, 1982); *NYT*, May 6–7, 1939; Mike Shatzkin, ed., *The Ballplayers* (New York, 1990); John Thorn and Pete Palmer, eds., *Total Baseball*, 3rd ed. (New York, 1993); *TSN Official Baseball Register*, 1951.

Lee E. Scanlon

CHERRY, Deron Leigh (b. September 12, 1959, Riverside, NJ), college and professional player, attended Palmyra, NJ, High School, where he played quarterback on the football team and participated in basketball and baseball. The 5-foot-11-inch, 196-pound Cherry, a strong safety and punter at Rutgers University, earned AP All-East honors in 1979 and 1980. Under coach Frank Burns, the Scarlet Knights from 1978 to 1980 compiled a 24–10–0 win–loss record. Following the 1978 season, Rutgers met Arizona State University in the Garden State Bowl and lost to the Sun Devils, 34–18. Cherry earned a bachelor's degree in biology from Rutgers in 1981.

The Kansas City Chiefs (NFL) signed Cherry as a free agent punter in 1981 but switched him to a defensive secondary position during preseason. Cherry, among the most feared NFL defensive backs, played as a reserve for two years before assuming a starting role in 1983. Cherry performed 11 seasons for the Chiefs from 1981 through 1991, appearing in 148 regular season games. He intercepted 50 career passes for 688 return yards and one touchdown and ranked among the Chiefs' leading tacklers. Cherry's 50 career interceptions places him third on the all-time Chiefs' list behind Emmitt Thomas and Johnny Robinson (S), while his 688 interception return yards stand fourth and his 9 interceptions in 1 season share third. Against the Seattle Seahawks on September 29, 1985, Cherry intercepted 4 passes to tie a Chiefs' and NFL record for most interceptions in a single game. His performance matched 15 other NFL players, including former Chiefs Bobby Hunt (1964) and Bobby Ply (1962). Cherry's first professional interception came in 1981 against the Oakland Raiders (NFL). He scored his first NFL touchdown in 1985 against the Pittsburgh Steelers, returning an intercepted pass 47 yards. Subsequently, he led the Chiefs in interceptions 7 seasons (1983–1988, 1991). Cherry in 1986 paced the AFC with 9 interceptions, 1 behind NFL leader Ronnie Lott.* He also returned seven career kickoffs for 145 yards and recovered 14 fumbles, including 6 in 1985. In 1986, Cherry twice recovered blocked punts in the end zone for touchdowns. Cherry's honors included being named the Chiefs' MVP in 1988 and safety on the Chiefs' 25-year all-time defensive team. Besides appearing in six Pro Bowls (1983–1988), he was selected All-AFC five times (1983–1986, 1988) and free safety on the *TSN* All-Pro team twice (1986, 1988).

Cherry participated on the Chiefs Academic Corps, a group of players that worked with inner-city high school students, and donated money to the Cystic Fibrosis Foundation for each tackle he made. Cherry and his wife Faith have a son, Deron II.

BIBLIOGRAPHY: *Kansas City Chiefs Media Guide*, 1986; *Kansas City Chiefs Media Guide*, 1993; *TSN Pro Football Register*, 1992.

John L. Evers

CHRISTENSEN, Todd Jay (b. August 3, 1956, Bellefonte, PA), college and professional player and sportscaster, is the son of Ned Christensen, chairman of the Department of Audiology and Speech Pathology at the University of Oregon, and June Christensen. He attended Sheldon High School in Eugene, OR, where he earned nine letters in basketball, baseball, and football. Christensen, a running back and a defensive lineman in football, garnered All-Conference and All-State honors. He also made All-Conference center fielder in baseball and All-America guard in basketball. For eight- and nine-year-olds, he held world records in the shot put and discus.

Christensen attended Brigham Young University (WAC) between 1974 and 1978, majoring in secondary education and starting four years for the Cougars as a receiver. He led Brigham Young in receiving three consecutive seasons, making 152 career receptions for 1,566 yards and 15 touchdowns. Christensen played in the 1974 Fiesta Bowl and the 1976 Tangerine Bowl, as BYU lost to Oklahoma State University, 16–9 and 49–21, respectively. BYU won 18 games while losing only 5 games in 1977 and 1978 and shared WAC titles both campaigns. Christensen, the Cougars' cocaptain in 1977, caught 10 passes to win MVP honors in the 1977 Blue-Gray game.

The Dallas Cowboys (NFL) selected Christensen as a running back in the second round of the 1978 draft as the fifty-sixth player chosen overall. He spent the entire 1978 season on the injured reserve list and was released by Dallas in 1979. Christensen was claimed by the New York Giants (NFL), where he played 1 game before signing as a free agent with the Oakland Raiders (NFL). The six-foot-three-inch, 230-pound Christensen played tight end for Oakland through 1981 and for the Los Angeles Raiders (NFL) when the franchise was transferred in 1982. In 10 NFL seasons from 1979 through 1988, Christensen caught 461 career passes for 5,872 yards (12.7-yard average) and 41 touchdowns in 137 regular season games. He paced the NFL in pass receptions in 1983 with 92 catches and snared 95 spirals in 1986. Christensen recovered one fumble in the end zone for a touchdown against the San Diego Chargers (NFL) and recorded one safety against the Tampa Bay Buccaneers (NFL) in 1981. His honors included being named to the *TSN* NFL All-Star team in 1983 and 1985 and playing in the Pro Bowl following the 1983 through 1987 seasons. Christensen, an excellent special teams player, excelled as a snapper on punts and captained the Raiders' special teams in 1980. Christensen substituted in Super Bowl XV when Oakland registered a 27–10 triumph over the Philadelphia Eagles and started at tight end for Los Angeles in their 38–9 rout over the Washington Redskins in Super Bowl XVIII, making 4 pass receptions for 32 yards.

Christensen and his wife Kathy have three sons, Toby, Tory, and T. J. Since retiring from professional football as a player, Christensen has served as an NFL television color commentator for NBC.

BIBLIOGRAPHY: *Los Angeles Raiders Media Guide*, 1982; *TSN Pro Football Register*, 1989; Paul Zimmerman, "I Can Catch the Rock," *SI* 67 (August 10, 1987), pp. 74, 76–78, 80, 82–84.

John L. Evers

CLAYTON, Mark Gregory (b. April 8, 1961, Indianapolis, IN), college and professional player, is the son of Clarence Clayton and Gwendolyn Clayton and graduated from Cathedral High School in Indianapolis, where he was selected an All-State football player. He majored in communications at the University of Louisville from 1979 to 1983, setting several Cardinals football records for wide receivers. The Miami Dolphins (NFL) selected Clayton in the eighth round of the 1983 draft. Clayton spent 10 years with the NFL club before becoming a free agent and signing with the Green Bay Packers (NFL) in June 1993. The Packers released him in February 1994.

Clayton starred as a football wide receiver for Louisville, starting three of his four years there. His 2,004 career yards remain a school record for receivers. Clayton also holds several single-season Cardinals records and was named Louisville's MVP in 1982, when his 1,112 yards made him the only receiver in school history to gain over 1,000 yards in a season. He was selected for the All-South Independent team following the 1982 season.

With the Miami Dolphins, Clayton set eight team records as a premier wide receiver. In his second year with the club in 1984, Clayton established a Dolphin and then–NFL record for most touchdown receptions in a season with 18. Following the regular season, the Dolphins played in Super Bowl XIX. Clayton caught 6 passes for 92 yards in the 38–16 loss to the San Francisco 49ers. Clayton, selected to the Pro Bowl squads following the 1984 through 1986 seasons and again after the 1988 and 1991 campaigns, became the Dolphins' all-time pass receiver with 550 catches and also set the team mark for most touchdown receptions with 81. Of those 81 touchdowns with Miami, 79 were thrown by Dan Marino (FB) to make the duo the NFL's career best quarterback-to-receiver scoring combination. During his NFL career through 1993, he has caught 582 passes for 8,974 yards (15.4-yard average) and 84 touchdowns and returned 52 punts for 485 yards and 1 touchdown.

Off the field, Clayton has been involved in several public service organizations, including south Florida's Say No to Drugs campaign and the fight against cystic fibrosis. He also founded Clayton's Kids, which from 1984 to 1986 enabled Miami-area underprivileged children to attend Dolphin games. An avid bowler, Clayton also practices martial arts and enjoys basketball and golf. Clayton, who remains single and has one child, divides his residences between Pembroke Pines, FL, and Indianapolis.

BIBLIOGRAPHY: *Green Bay Packers Media Guide,* 1993; David S. Neft et al., eds., *The Football Encyclopedia,* 2nd ed. (New York, 1994); *TSN Pro Football Register,* 1994.

Brian S. Butler

COOPER, John (b. July 2, 1937, Powell, TN), college player and coach, grew up in Powell, TN, a small community near Knoxville. After graduating from Powell High School and spending two years in the U.S. Army, Cooper enrolled at Iowa State University (BSC, BEC) in 1957. An outstanding football performer at tailback and safety, Cooper captained the Cyclones and was named MVP his senior year. Iowa State compiled 7–2 marks in both 1959 and 1960 and 5–5 in 1961. Cooper remained at Iowa State following his graduation in 1962 as the Cyclones' freshman football coach. In 1963, Cooper joined Tommy Prothro's staff at Oregon State University (PEC). The Beavers won the PEC crown but lost, 34–7, to the University of Michigan in the Rose Bowl. In 1964, Cooper accompanied Prothro to UCLA (PEC), where the Bruins copped the PEC title and upset Michigan State University, 14–12, in the Rose Bowl.

Cooper also served as assistant coach at the University of Kansas (BEC) from 1967 through 1972 and the University of Kentucky (SEC) from 1972 to 1976. From 1977 to 1984, Cooper held the head coaching reins at the University of Tulsa (MVC) and recorded a 57–31 win–loss mark. Cooper's Hurricanes won five straight MVC football titles. Cooper moved to Arizona State University (PTC) as head coach in 1985 and guided the Sun Devils to a 25–9–2 mark, including a PTC championship in 1986, a 22–15 Rose Bowl victory over the University of Michigan in 1987, and recognition as 1986 National Coach of the Year.

Ohio State University (BTC) hired Cooper as head coach in 1988. In Cooper's first 7 years, the Buckeyes have boasted a 54–26–4 mark. He has led the Scarlet and Gray to 6 consecutive post-season appearances, including the Hall of Fame Bowl twice, the Florida Citrus Bowl twice, the Liberty Bowl, and the Holiday Bowl. Ohio State finished the 1993 season with a 9–1–1 tally and narrowly missed going to the Rose Bowl. His 18 years as a head coach have produced a 136–66–6 mark. In Columbus, Cooper partic-ipates in the United Way, Big Brothers/Sisters, Alzheimer's Foundation, Arthur James Cancer Hospital, and Children's Hospital. Cooper and his wife Helen have two children, John, Jr., and Cindy, and reside in the Columbus area.

BIBLIOGRAPHY: Akron (OH) *Beacon Journal*, 1988–1993; Ohio State University Sports Information Department, Columbus, OH.

Allan Hall

COULTER, DeWitt E. "Tex" (b. 1925, Tyler, TX), college and professional player, made consensus All-America as a tackle in 1945 at the U.S. Military Academy and All-Pro in 1951 with the New York Giants (NFL). Coulter starred on two of the greatest U.S. Army teams, as the Cadets in 1944 and 1945 under Coach Earl Blaik (FB) posted two perfect seasons and won unan-imous national championships.

Coulter's father died when he was five years old. His mother moved with her three children to the Masonic Home and School in Fort Worth, TX. Coulter lettered four years in football and track and field at Masonic Home High School, making All-State as a triple threat back and defensive tackle. The Masonic Home won four district football championships, once advanc-ing to the state semifinals. Coulter, who broke the national interscholastic shot put record and excelled at high jumping and throwing the discus, made *Look* magazine's All-America High School Track and Field team.

Coulter joined the U.S. Army after graduating in 1943 and served as a physical education instructor before attending Cornell University to prepare for West Point. He joined Doc Blanchard (FB) and Glenn Davis (FB) in 1944 on the Cadets' alternate team, a unit composed mostly of plebes who started the second and fourth quarters. "Since Blaik had the material," Coul-ter recalled, "he let us play [platoon] football in effect the way it's done right now." Coulter left West Point after failing trigonometry but resumed his studies in the fall of 1945. The Cadets continued to demolish all opponents, including the University of Notre Dame, 48–0, the University of Pennsylvania, 61–0, and Navy, 32–13, outscoring foes, 412–46. Author Henry E. Mattox wrote, "Tex Coulter personified football meanness and aggressiveness. While peaceable off the field, he was a holy terror when playing football." Coulter also boxed, knocking unfortunate opponents around the ring.

The six-foot-three-inch, 250-pound Coulter failed trigonometry a second time and left West Point at the end of the fall semester. He received permission to play with the New York Giants (NFL) in 1946, although his original class had not graduated. The Chicago Cardinals (NFL) drafted Coulter in the first round in 1947 and traded him to the New York Giants. Coulter played six seasons with New York (1946–1949, 1951–1952) and in 1953 with the Montreal Alouettes (CFL) before pursuing a lengthy career as a commercial artist and sports commentator in Canada. He lives in Austin, TX, working full-time with institutionalized mentally retarded men.

BIBLIOGRAPHY: Army-Navy Football Game Program, December 2, 1944; Army-Navy Football Game Program, December 2, 1945; Henry E. Mattox, *Army Football in 1945* (Jefferson, NC, 1990); Ronald L. Mendell and Timothy B. Phares, *Who's Who in Football* (New Rochelle, NY, 1974); Beau Riffenburgh, *The Official NFL Encyclopedia*, 4th ed. (New York, 1986).

James D. Whalen

CRAIG, Roger Timothy (b. July 10, 1960, Preston, MS), college and professional player, attended Central High School in Davenport, IA, where he lettered for three years in football, track and field as a hurdler, and wrestling. A three-year football letterman at the University of Nebraska (BEC), he finished as the fourth-ranking all-time leading rusher among Cornhuskers with 2,446 yards gained as a fullback and tailback and scored 26 touchdowns. As a hurdler, Craig lettered in track and field. After his senior year, Craig played in the Orange Bowl, the East-West Shrine game, and the Hula Bowl. His college major came in criminal justice.

The San Francisco 49ers (NFL) selected the six-foot, 219-pound star in 1983 in the second round of the draft. As a rookie, he set 49er records with 12 touchdowns (8 rushing, 4 receiving) and 72 points scored. Craig's second season featured him leading the 49ers in pass receptions with 71 and setting Super Bowl game records for points (18) and touchdowns (3). In Super Bowl XIX, he accounted for 135 yards in a 38–16 victory over the Miami Dolphins. In his third season with San Francisco, he in 1985 was selected to his first Pro Bowl. His 1,050 yards rushing and 1,016 yards in pass receptions for 2,066 combined yards established an NFL record. No NFL player previously had surpassed 1,000 yards rushing and 1,000 yards receiving in a single season.

During 1986, he led NFL running backs with 81 receptions, paced the

49ers in three rushing categories, and finished the season with 4 consecutive games with more than 100 combined rushing-receiving yards. Craig's honors in 1987 included being selected UPI Second Team All-NFL and earning his second trip to the Pro Bowl. In 1988, Craig was chosen consensus All-Pro and a Pro Bowl starter. That season, he rushed for 1,500 yards and caught 76 passes to enjoy the greatest season by a running back in 25 years. The AP and UPI named him NFL Offensive Player of the Year, as he gained 190 yards in 22 carries against the Los Angeles Rams and 162 yards in 22 carries against the Phoenix Cardinals. *SI* designated Craig its NFL Player of the Year. In postseason play against the Minnesota Vikings, he set an NFL record with an 80-yard run. In Super Bowl XXIII, San Francisco defeated the Cincinnati Bengals, 20–16. The following year, the 49ers pounded the undermanned Denver Broncos, 55–10, in Super Bowl XXIV. In 1990, his last of nine seasons with the 49ers, he started all 16 games. His production diminished, however, with 439 yards rushing and 201 yards receiving. He played 15 games in 1991 with the Los Angeles Raiders (NFL), leading the team in rushing while splitting time with two other backs.

The Minnesota Vikings (NFL) signed Craig in 1992 as a Plan B free agent but injuries handicapped Craig part of the season. Craig rejoined the San Francisco 49ers briefly before retiring in the summer of 1994. In 11 NFL seasons, he caught 566 passes for 4,911 yards and 17 touchdowns and carried 1,991 times for 8,189 yards and 56 touchdowns. The durable, shifty runner with high knee action has earned three Super Bowl rings.

During the off-season, Craig works as a model and part-time actor in HBO series and movies. He also owns and operates a restaurant in Cupertino, CA. He and his wife have four children and live in Portola Valley, CA.

BIBLIOGRAPHY: Dan Barreiro Column, Minneapolis (MN) *Star-Tribune*, December 13, 1992; Roger Craig, letter to Stan Carlson, December 1992; Roger Craig, *Strictly Business* (New York 1992); *Minnesota Vikings Media Guide*, 1993; *San Francisco 49ers Media Guide*, 1992.

Stan W. Carlson

CUFF, Ward Lloyd (b. August 13, 1912, Redwood Falls, MN), college athlete and professional player, graduated from Redwood Falls High School. From 1934 through 1936, the six-foot-one-inch, 192-pound Cuff started at fullback and placekicked for Marquette University in football. He blocked for prolific scoring halfback Art Gueppe; caught passes from All-America back Ray Buivid; and handled extra point, field goal, and punting duties. After compiling a 4–5 mark in 1934, the Marquette football squad boasted marks of 7–1 in 1935 and 7–2 in 1936. Marquette won its first seven games in 1936 to rank among the top 10 nationally but lost the season finale to Duquesne University and the first-ever Cotton Bowl game, 16–6, to TCU. Cuff also lettered in boxing and track and field as a javelin thrower.

The New York Giants (NFL) selected Cuff on the fourth round of the 1937 draft. Besides playing offensive and some defensive back, Cuff led the NFL in field goals in 1938 (5), 1939 (7), 1943 (3), and 1947 (7) to tie Jack Manders of the Chicago Bears for most seasons at the forefront. With the exception of 1939, however, he shared the NFL field goal lead. Cuff remained with the Giants through the 1945 season but scored only 2 touchdowns his final campaign there. Ken Strong (FB) replaced him as regular kicker in 1944. Following the 1945 season, New York traded Cuff to the Chicago Cardinals (NFL). Cuff's fortunes revived with Chicago in 1946, as he scored a career-high 55 points. Chicago sent Cuff to the Green Bay Packers (NFL) in 1947, when he combined with Ted Fritsch to give the club the best NFL kicking duo. Cuff's toe accounted for 51 points, including 30 conversions and a career-best 7 field goals. He retired after the 1947 campaign with 423 career points, including 156 conversions, 43 field goals, and 23 touchdowns. Altogether, Cuff rushed 344 times for 1,851 yards (5.4-yard average) and caught 106 passes for 1,559 yards (14.7-yard average).

Cuff played in three NFL Championship games with the Giants. New York defeated Green Bay, 23–17, in the 1938 contest, but the Packers prevailed over the Giants in the 1939 and 1944 title games. Cuff, who scored a touchdown in the 1944 14–7 championship game loss, played in the Pro Bowl following the 1939, 1940, and 1942 seasons and was voted All-Pro in 1943 and 1944. He and his wife, Doris Ann, have been married 57 years and have three children. Subsequently, Cuff was employed as a teacher and coached football.

BIBLIOGRAPHY: Ward Cuff, letter to Richard Gonsalves, April 1994; Rick Gonsalves, NFL Placekickers' Stat Sheets, Gloucester, MA; *Green Bay Packers Press Guide*, 1946; David Neft et al., eds., *The Football Encyclopedia*, 2nd ed., (New York, 1994); *New York Giants Press Guide*, 1946; James D. Whalen, letter to David L. Porter, March 22, 1994.

Richard Gonsalves

CUNNINGHAM, Randall (b. March 27, 1963, Santa Barbara, CA), college and professional player, is the son of Samuel Cunningham and Mabel Cunningham, graduated from Santa Barbara High School, and attended the University of Nevada—Las Vegas. His older brother, Sam, played fullback with the New England Patriots (NFL) between 1973 and 1982. Cunningham, who set several Rebel records as a quarterback at Nevada—Las Vegas, has quarterbacked nine years with the Philadelphia Eagles (NFL) and proved a potent offensive threat as both a passer and a runner.

Cunningham started at quarterback three seasons from 1982 to 1984 with Nevada—Las Vegas (PCAA), where he majored in recreation and business. He set every Rebel and PCAA passing record, including most pass completions (614), yards passing (8,290), and passing touchdowns (60). He was named All-PCAA as a quarterback and punter from 1982 to 1984 and an

All-America as a punter in 1983. With Cunningham at quarterback, Nevada—Las Vegas had a combined record of 21 wins and 14 losses and defeated the University of Toledo, 30–13, in the 1984 California Bowl.

The Philadelphia Eagles chose Cunningham in the second round of the 1985 draft and made him the team's starting quarterback in 1986. Cunningham directed the Eagles into the NFC playoffs following the 1988, 1989, 1990, and 1992 seasons and leads all NFL quarterbacks in career rushing with 4,072 yards through the 1994 season. He remains the only quarterback in NFL history to lead his team in rushing four consecutive seasons, accomplishing the feat from 1987 to 1990, and has scored 32 rushing touchdowns. Cunningham's best year came in 1990, when his 942 rushing yards placed him second behind Bobby Douglas (968 yards in 1972) for most rushing yards in a season by a quarterback. In 1990, Cunningham also became the only NFL quarterback to rush for over 100 yards and throw 4 touchdown passes in one game in the Eagles' 48–20 win over the New England Patriots. His 91-yard punt against the New York Giants in 1989 marked the third longest in NFL history and set an Eagles' record. In both 1988 and 1990, he received the Bert Bell Award from the Maxwell Football Club as the NFL's top player. He was voted to the Pro Bowl following the 1988 through 1990 seasons and was selected an alternate after the 1987 campaign. Cunningham returned in 1992 after sustaining a season-ending knee injury in his first game in 1991 and was voted the NFL's Comeback Player of the Year by *PFW*. Through the 1994 season, he has completed 1,805 passes in 3,241 attempts (55.7 percent) and 147 touchdowns and has thrown 100 interceptions.

Cunningham keeps busy in community activities, including the United Way and other charitable agencies. He married Felicity de Jager on May 8, 1993, and resides in Moorestown, NJ.

BIBLIOGRAPHY: David S. Neft et al., eds., *The Football Encyclopedia*, 2nd ed. (New York, 1994); *Philadelphia Eagles Media Guide*, 1994; *TSN Pro Football Register*, 1994.

Brian S. Butler

DAVID, James T. "Jim" "The Hatchet" (b. December 2, 1927, Florence, SC), college and professional player and coach, performed as an undistinguished football end and halfback with Colorado A&M College (now Colorado State University) from 1949 to 1951. Colorado A&M (RMC) compiled records of 9–1 in 1949, 6–3 in 1950, and 5–4 in 1951.

The Detroit Lions (NFL) in the early 1950s had enjoyed success with two former Colorado A&M players, defensive tackle Thurman McGraw and defensive back Jack Christiansen (FB), both All-NFL stars. Upon Christiansen's recommendation, the Lions drafted the hard-hitting David in the twenty-second round in 1952 to play defensive back. At training camp, Lions coach Raymond "Buddy" Parker (FB) was unimpressed with David's 5-foot-

11-inch, 178-pound frame and started another rookie at cornerback. After that player was injured, David started at cornerback and missed only six plays the rest of the 1952 season.

The Detroit defensive backfield, nominally led by safety Christiansen, became the NFL's most celebrated of the 1950s. Nicknamed "The Chris Crew," the backfield included safeties Christiansen and Yale Lary (FB) and cornerbacks Jim Smith and David. The quartet received All-NFL honors various seasons, with Christiansen and Lary eventually earning Pro Football Hall of Fame honors. When Smith retired after the 1953 season, Carl Karilivacz, another talented defender, replaced him. In David's rookie year, he intercepted seven passes to help the Lions win their first NFL Championship since 1935. Detroit defeated the Cleveland Browns, 17–7, in the NFL title game. The Lions repeated as champions with a 17–16 victory over Cleveland in 1953, won the Western Division crown in 1954, and took a third NFL championship by routing Cleveland, 59–14, in 1957.

Although intercepting 36 passes during his eight NFL seasons from 1952 to 1959, David won principal acclaim for his ferocious tackling and earned the nickname "The Hatchet." His hits remained clean, but he put every ounce of his strength into them. In 1953, he smashed into Los Angeles Rams stellar end Tom Fears (FB), cracking two of the receiver's vertebrae. A year later, San Francisco 49ers quarterback Y. A. Tittle (FB) broke his jaw because of David's hit.

David, named to the UP All-NFL team in 1954, made the Pro Bowl each of his final six NFL seasons. After retiring as a player, David served as an assistant football coach with the Los Angeles Rams (NFL), San Francisco 49ers (NFL), and Detroit Lions.

BIBLIOGRAPHY: James David file, Pro Football Hall of Fame, Canton, OH; David S. Neft et al., eds., *The Football Encyclopedia*, 2nd ed. (New York, 1994); Beau Riffenburgh, *The Official NFL Encyclopedia*, 4th ed. (New York, 1986).

Robert N. "Bob" Carroll

DAVIS, Anthony "A. D." (b. September 8, 1952, San Fernando, CA), college and professional athlete, is the son of William Davis and Velma Davis and attended San Fernando High School, where he won several honors as a baseball and football athlete. He in 1971 enrolled at the University of Southern California (PEC), succeeding Heisman Trophy winners Mike Garrett (FB) and O. J. Simpson (FB) at tailback. Coach John McKay (FB) used an innovative I-formation offense, featuring precise blocking patterns and elusive ball carriers adept at finding running lanes.

Davis's finest game occurred during his sophomore year in 1972 against a highly regarded University of Notre Dame squad. In a remarkable display of speed and elusiveness, Davis scored 36 points, returned two kickoffs for 97-yard and 96-yard touchdowns, and finished with 368 all-purpose yards.

Southern California won, 45–23, to finish the season with 11 wins and no losses. Notre Dame coach Ara Parseghian (FB) lauded Davis as the best kick returner he had ever coached against. Davis played on the 1972 and 1974 national championship Southern California squads, starred in the 1973 and 1975 Rose Bowl contests, and earned unanimous All-America status in 1974. He finished second to Ohio State University's Archie Griffin (FB) in the 1974 Heisman Trophy balloting. Davis, a tailback, gained over 1,000 yards rushing each of his three varsity seasons and finished his career as the NCAA's second all-time kickoff returner with 37 attempts for 1,299 yards and a 35.1 average yards per return.

The five-foot-nine-inch, 185-pound Davis, an all-around athlete while attending Southern California, was drafted three separate times by professional baseball clubs, including the Baltimore Orioles (AL) in 1971 and 1974 and the Minnesota Twins (AL) in 1975. Davis chose football over baseball, however, and was selected in the 1975 draft by the New York Jets (NFL). He signed instead with the Southern California Suns of the fledgling, but ultimately unsuccessful, WFL. After the Suns breached his contract, he in 1976 played for the Toronto, Canada, Argonauts (CFL) and a year later joined the Tampa Bay Buccaneers (NFL). He began the 1978 season with the Houston Oilers (NFL) but was released following only two games with an injury. The Los Angeles Rams (NFL) immediately signed him. Injuries kept him from playing in 1979 and caused his retirement. During his NFL career, he rushed 98 times for 304 yards (3.1-yard average) and one touchdown and caught eight passes for 91 yards (11.4-yard average). In 1983, he made a brief comeback in the newly established USFL. Subsequently, Davis worked in the property and development business.

BIBLIOGRAPHY: Anthony Davis file, University of Southern California Sports Information Office, Los Angeles, CA; Joe Hoppel et al., *TSN College Football's Twenty-Five Greatest Teams* (St. Louis, MO, 1988); *TSN Football Register*, 1978.

John Hanners

DENT, Richard Lamar (b. December 13, 1960, Atlanta, GA), college and professional player, graduated from Atlanta's Murphy High School and was selected an All-State football player his senior year. Dent starred in football at Tennessee State University (OVC), where he holds the Tigers' record with 39 career sacks. During his four-year career at Tennessee State, he compiled 158 tackles (including 72 solo) and recorded six fumble recoveries. Since the six-foot-five-inch Dent weighed only 235 pounds as a senior, many NFL teams did not want to take a chance on drafting him. Upon graduating in 1983 with a bachelor's degree in commercial art, Dent remained uncertain about his football future.

The Chicago Bears (NFL) selected Dent in the eighth round of the 1983 draft. According to Bill Tobin, the Bears vice president of personnel, "He was the best pure pass rusher in the '83 crop." During his rookie 1983 season, Dent saw limited playing time. The 1984 season saw Dent move into the starting lineup at defensive end, where he became the Bears' all-time sack leader and helped them make the NFC Championship game. Dent set a club record with 17.5 sacks during the regular season and 10.5 sacks during the playoffs. The latter mark established the NFL record for playoff games. The Bears defeated the New England Patriots, 46–10, in Super Bowl XX. Dent's football accomplishments also have earned him trips to the NFL Pro Bowl following the 1984, 1985, 1990, and 1993 seasons. He was voted First Team All-NFC by UPI, *FN*, and *PFW* after the 1990 season. Through the 1994 season, Dent had recorded 126.5 sacks, recovered 13 fumbles, intercepted eight passes, and scored two touchdowns. In June 1994, the San Francisco 49ers (NFL) signed Dent as a free agent. He missed most of the 1994 NFL season with torn right knee ligaments. He reinjured the knee in the playoffs, and did not play in Super Bowl XXIX against the San Diego Chargers. In February 1995, San Francisco released Dent.

Dent's off-the-field activities made him one of the most popular Bears. His many local activities included often traveling to Chicago area hospitals to visit children with serious illnesses and leading a fund-raising drive to collect money for a baby's heart operation. Dent also played for the Chicago Bears traveling basketball team, which donates its off-season time to raising money for high school athletic teams by performing in exhibition games.

Dent's hobbies include racquetball, tennis, swimming, and horseback riding. He and his wife Leslie have one daughter, Mary Frances, and reside in Buffalo Grove, IL.

BIBLIOGRAPHY: *Chicago Bears Media Guide*, 1993; *TSN Pro Football Register*, 1994.

Raymond C. Fetters

DETMER, Ty Hubert (b. October 30, 1967, San Marcos, TX), college and professional player, is the son of Sonny Detmer, a high school football coach, and Betty Detmer and was selected All-America, All-State, and Texas Player of the Year at Southwest High School in San Antonio, TX, where his father coached him. He lettered three times in football, baseball, basketball, and golf and once in track and field and belonged to the National Honor Society. Detmer, who earned a B.S. degree in recreation administration at BYU, married Kim Herbert in July 1991. His younger brother, Koy, quarterbacks at the University of Colorado (BEC).

Numerous major schools recruited Detmer. BYU (WAC) redshirted him in football as a freshman. In 1988, the six-foot, 183-pound quarterback played mostly as a reserve until November. Detmer was named the MVP of the Freedom Bowl after taking BYU from a 14–7 deficit to a 20–17 victory over the University of Colorado. During his freshman season, he completed 83 of 153 passes for 1,252 yards and 13 touchdowns. As a sophomore in 1989, Detmer was selected First Team All-WAC and the Cougars' MVP while setting 11 NCAA records. He completed 265 of 412 passes (64.3 percent) for 4,560 yards and 32 touchdowns that season. Detmer led the nation with a 175.6 passing efficiency rating and ranked second nationally in total offense, averaging 369.4 yards per game. Detmer set NCAA all-time bowl records with 594 yards in total offense and 576 yards passing (42 completions in 59 attempts) in the Cougars' 50–39 loss to Pennsylvania State University in the Holiday Bowl, as he was selected Co-MVP.

In his second game as a junior, Detmer passed for 406 yards while leading BYU to an upset of the top-ranked University of Miami. He set 42 NCAA records and tied five other marks that season, directing BYU to a 10–3–0 record. He completed 361 of 562 passes (64.2 percent) for 5,188 yards and 41 touchdowns, breaking the NCAA season record of 4,699 yards set by Andre Ware.* Detmer established an NCAA season mark with 12 straight 300-yard passing games, becoming the Cougars' all-time leading passer, the first junior to throw for over 10,000 yards in his career, and the first quarterback to enjoy consecutive 4,000-yard seasons. Detmer's honors during the 1990 season included winning the Heisman Trophy, earning All-America, Player of the Year, and All-WAC honors, receiving the Maxwell Trophy and Davey O'Brien Award, and being selected Cougar cocaptain and MVP. He suffered two separated shoulders in the Holiday Bowl, when Texas A&M University outclassed the Cougars, 65–14.

Detmer in 1991 led BYU to an 8–3–1 record, including a 13–13 tie with the University of Iowa in the Holiday Bowl. An All-WAC and repeat All-America selection, he also won the Davey O'Brien Award for the second consecutive year and placed third in the Heisman Trophy voting. Detmer completed 249 of 403 passes (61.8 percent) for 4,031 yards and 35 touchdowns as a senior. He succeeded on 31 of 54 passes for a Cougar record 599 yards and 6 touchdowns in a 52–52 tie with San Diego State University. Detmer holds 59 NCAA records, including career records for most touchdown passes (121), yards passing (15,031), pass completions (958), pass attempts (1,530), offensive plays (1,785), yards total offense (14,665), touchdowns responsible for (135), games with 300 or more yards passing (33), yards gained per game (326.8), and consecutive games throwing a touchdown pass (35).

The Green Bay Packers (NFL) selected Detmer in the ninth round of the 1992 draft as the two hundred and thirtieth pick overall. As a rookie, he backed up quarterbacks Brett Favre and Don Majkowski and did not see action in any of the Packers' contests. In 1993, Detmer completed 3 of 5 passes for 26 yards in 3 games. He did not play in any 1994 contests.

BIBLIOGRAPHY: *Brigham Young University Football Media Guide*, 1991; *Green Bay Packers Media Guide*, 1994; Richard Haffer, "A Ty Vote for the Heisman," *SI* 73 (December 10, 1990), pp. 52–54; Hank Hersch, "Tying One on Miami," *SI* 73 (September 17, 1990), pp. 44–46; *1992 NCAA Football.*

John L. Evers

DILLON, Bobby Dan (b. February 23, 1930, Temple, TX), college and professional player, is the son of Clyde Dillon and Ruby Dillon and spent his first seven years on a farm in central Texas. His father then left farming to become a police officer in nearby Temple, TX. Dillon attended Temple schools and began his football career playing both offensive and defensive back in junior high and high school. Temple High School won its district championship during Dillon's senior year, but the UIL declared it ineligible for postseason play because of an illegal scrimmage against Belton.

Recruited by head coach Blair Cherry, Dillon attended the University of Texas (SWC) and lettered in football from 1949 to 1951. His Longhorn teammates honored his leadership ability by selecting him as team captain in 1951. Dillon played primarily at safety, but the versatile athlete also started several games at offensive halfback in 1950. Although Dillon lost an eye at age 10, a capacity for big plays earned him All-SWC and All-America honors during his senior season. Two of his most remarkable plays as a collegiate included a 50-yard interception return for a touchdown against the University of Oklahoma and an 87-yard touchdown on a punt return against Baylor University. Dillon gained 830 yards on 47 returns for an average of 17.7 per return, ranking among the all-time collegiate leaders.

Dillon contributed largely to the success of the University of Texas. Texas finished third in the SWC in both 1949 and 1951 and won the SWC championship in 1950, earning the right to play the University of Tennessee in the 1951 Cotton Bowl.

The Green Bay Packers (NFL) drafted the six-foot-one-inch, 185-pound Dillon as a number-three pick. Dillon made a quick transition to the professional game. Using his uncanny ability to sense the flight of the ball, he intercepted 52 passes for 976 yards and five touchdowns during his eight-year tenure with the Packers to rank him as their all-time interception leader. For his outstanding defensive play, Dillon made All-NFL safety five times and played in four Pro Bowl games.

After his retirement from professional football in 1959, Dillon received several honors. *TF* magazine named him as the best collegiate pass defender for the era from 1945 to 1965. The University of Texas inducted Dillon into its Hall of Honor in 1972, while the Green Bay Packers likewise honored him with induction in 1974.

Dillon worked in Temple during the off-season and began a career with Wilsonart, a manufacturer of high-pressure decorative laminates. Currently, he presides over the company, which employs approximately 3,000 people.

Dillon married his high school sweetheart, Ann Morgan, on January 27, 1951, and has two children, Karen and Dan.

BIBLIOGRAPHY: Dave Campbell, *The Best of Dave Campbell's Texas Football* (Dallas, TX, 1989); Bill Cromartie, *Annual Madness* (Nashville, TN, 1987); John Hillman, telephone interview with Bobby Dillon, March 23, 1993; Ronald L. Mendell and Timothy B. Phares, *Who's Who in Football* (New Rochelle, NY, 1974); David Neft et al., eds., *The Football Encyclopedia*, 2nd ed. (New York, 1994); Don Schiffer, ed., *1959 Pro Football Handbook* (New York, 1959); Paul Soderberg, ed., *The Big Book of Halls of Fame* (New York, 1977); Kern Tips, *Football—Texas Style* (New York, 1964).

John Hillman

DOBBS, Glenn Jr. (b. July 12, 1922, McKinney, TX), college and professional player, coach, and administrator, is the oldest son of Glenn Dobbs, Sr., a grocery store owner, and Mary Tennie (McGraw) Dobbs and grew up in Texas and in Frederick, OK. Dobbs graduated from Frederick High School, playing basketball and making All-State in football.

Dobbs graduated from the University of Tulsa a Dean's Honor Roll student with a B.A. degree in 1943. The standout passer and punter starred as a single wing tailback from 1940 to 1942, leading Tulsa (MVC) to a 25–5–0 record. In three seasons, the six-foot-three-inch, 195-pound Dobbs completed 138 of 259 pass attempts (53.3 percent) for 1,980 yards, gained 884 yards rushing on 211 attempts (4.2-yard average), and punted 136 times for a 40.1-yard average. Dobbs, a three-time All-MVC selection, was named Tulsa's first All-America player. His younger brother, Bobby Lee, was a teammate and later coached at Tulsa.

In 1942, the triple threat Dobbs sparked Tulsa to a 10–1 record, as he rushed for 361 yards on 72 carries (5.0-yard average). He completed 67 of 107 passes for 1,066 yards, leading the nation with a 62.6 completion percentage. Dobbs also punted 26 times for a 48.3-yard average, making All-America. He starred in the 1942 Sun Bowl against Texas Tech and in the 1943 Sugar Bowl against the University of Tennessee.

Dobbs joined the U.S. Army Air Force and graduated from Officer's Training School with top military, academic, and athletic honors. In 1943, he led Randolph Field to a 10–1 record and to the Cotton Bowl against the University of Texas, being named to the All-Service team. Dobbs, MVP in the 1944 College All-Star Game against the Chicago Bears, played that season with the 2nd Air Force team.

Dobbs excelled in professional football for the Brooklyn Dodgers (AAFC) in 1946 and 1947 and Los Angeles Dons (AAFC) in 1948 and 1949. In 1946, he led the AAFC in total offensive plays (364), total offense (2,094 yards), pass attempts (269), pass completions (135), passing yards (1,886), punts (80), and punting average (47.8 yards). He threw 13 touchdown passes and scored 6 touchdowns, being unanimous choice for AAFC MVP and making All-Pro.

In 1948, Dobbs enjoyed another superlative season, compiling 2,942 total offense yards on 460 plays, completing 185 of 369 pass attempts, and punting 68 times for a phenomenal 49.1-yard punting average, all AAFC-leading marks. The 49.1-yard punting average remains second best ever in professional football history. Dobbs also passed for 2,403 yards, threw 21 touchdown passes, rushed for 539 yards on 91 carries (5.9-yard average), and scored 4 touchdowns. Dobbs retired temporarily after the 1949 season due to injuries. In his four-year AAFC career, he completed 446 passes on 934 attempts for 5,876 yards and threw 45 touchdown passes, rushed for 1,039 yards on 262 carries (3.97-yard average) and 12 touchdowns, and punted 231 times for a 46.1-yard average. Dobbs played for Saskatchewan, Canada (CFL) from 1951 to 1953 and briefly with Hamilton, Canada (CFL) in 1954, being named CFL MVP in 1951.

Dobbs served as athletic director at the University of Tulsa and then director of capital improvements for a year. Tulsa made Dobbs head football coach from 1961 to 1968, succeeding his brother Bobby Lee. Dobbs coached Tulsa to three MVC titles and Bluebonnet Bowl appearances in 1965 and 1966, while compiling a record of 45–37–0. His pro style offense produced five consecutive NCAA passing championships.

Subsequently, Dobbs entered public relations and presided over a gasoline and oil distributorship and the Tulsa, OK, Drillers (TL) baseball team. Dobbs, who married June Manchester in 1942, has two sons, Glenn III and John. Now retired, the Tulsa resident enjoys playing golf and following college and professional sports. Dobbs, whose uniform number 45 was retired by Tulsa, belongs to the Oklahoma Athletic Hall of Fame and in 1980 was elected to the NFF College Football Hall of Fame.

BIBLIOGRAPHY: *AAFC Record Manuals*, 1947, 1948, 1949, 1950; Bob Braunwart and Bob Carroll, "Glenn Dobbs," *TCC* 11 (September 1980); Kyle Crichton, "Pass Master," *Collier's* 118 (November 16, 1946); Glenn Dobbs, letter to Edward J. Pavlick, June 1993; Jim Dynan, "Hurricane Warning," *Sports Review Football: College & Pro* 15 (September 1955); Larry Klein, *NCAA: College Football All-Time Galaxy* (New York, 1970); University of Tulsa Sports Information Office, Tulsa, OK.

Edward J. Pavlick

DONCHESS, Joseph "Joe" (b. March 17, 1905, Youngstown, OH; d. January 29, 1977, Pittsburgh, PA), college player and coach, was named an All-America football end at the University of Pittsburgh in 1928 and 1929. His other honors included induction into the NFF College Football Hall of Fame in 1979 and being named in 1984 as one of eight ends on the All-Time Pittsburgh team.

After dropping out of school in the fifth grade to work in the steel mill, Donchess entered Wyoming Seminary in the northeastern Pennsylvania hard coal region five years later and made up three grades in one year. The six-foot-one-inch 170-pounder matriculated at the University of Pittsburgh in 1926 and started at end for the Panther football squads under coach Dr. John "Jock" Sutherland (FB) from 1927 through 1929. Donchess led Pittsburgh pass receivers in 1928 and 1929, making some All-America First Teams in 1928 and becoming a consensus choice in 1929. The Panthers finished 8–1–1 in 1927, 6–2–1 in 1928, and 9–1 in 1929, garnering the 1929 national championship, then based on only regular season play. Donchess attributed Pittsburgh's success to the genius of Coach Sutherland. "Sutherland," he recalled, "had no superior in choosing football talent and placing an individual player into a team that had trigger precision, sound fundamentals, and was usually a winner." Donchess performed in two Rose Bowl games, a 7–6 loss to Stanford University in 1928 and a 47–14 setback to the University of Southern California in 1930.

After graduating with a bachelor's degree in 1930, Donchess earned an M.D. degree in 1932 from the University of Pittsburgh Medical School and served as an assistant coach in 1930 and 1931. From 1933 to 1937, he did postgraduate work in orthopedic surgery at the Dartmouth College Medical School. Coach Earl "Red" Blaik (FB) recruited Donchess to coach the Dartmouth ends from 1934 to 1936. The pinnacle of Donchess's medical career came from 1943 to 1965 as chief surgeon for the U.S. Steel Corporation works at Gary, IN. He wrote numerous articles for medical publications and remained quite active in civic and University of Pittsburgh organizations. The football training room at Pitt Stadium was dedicated in his name in 1978. His wife Lucille survived him.

BIBLIOGRAPHY: Jim O'Brien, ed., *Hail to Pitt: A Sports History of the University of Pittsburgh* (Pittsburgh, PA, 1982); Harry G. Scott, *Jock Sutherland: Architect of Men* (New York, 1954); *University of Pittsburgh Football Media Guides;* James D. Whalen, letter to David L. Porter, March 21, 1994.

Robert B. Van Atta

DONOGHUE, Michael Joseph Sr. *See* Michael Joseph Donohue, Sr.

DONOHUE, Michael Joseph Sr. "Mike" (b. Michael Donoghue, June 4, 1879, County Kerry, Ireland; d. December 16, 1958, Baton Rouge, LA), college player, coach, and executive, was the son of John Donoghue, a laborer, and Mary Rosalie (Sheehan) Donoghue. His education in Ireland was given by a parish priest in Hedgerows since his class was not permitted in formal schooling. Donohue migrated to the United States at age 14 and graduated with honors from Norich Academy in New Haven, CT. At Yale University, he starred in football, basketball, boxing, track and field, and cross country. He graduated in 1904 with proficiency in English, Greek, Latin, Gaelic, and mathematics. He accepted a coaching position at Auburn University (SC) in 1904, the same year Dan McGugin (FB) began at Vanderbilt University and John Heisman (FB) began at Georgia Tech. The trio created the modern era of southern football. From 1904 to 1922, Donohue's coaching record was 101–37–5. Auburn finished undefeated in 1904, 1908, 1913, and 1914, being unscored on in 1908 and 1914. The Tigers captured the SC championship in 1904, 1908, 1913, and 1914, defeating the Carlisle Indians, 7–0, in 1914 and tying Ohio State University, the WC champions, 0–0, in 1917. Donohue coached at Louisiana State University (SC) from 1923 to 1927 and received a salary of $10,000, the highest paid a southern coach to that time. His record at LSU was 23–19–3. He served as athletic director at Springfield College in Mobile, AL, from 1929 to 1937. He returned to LSU in 1937 as intramural director and golf coach, serving in this capacity until his retirement in 1949.

The innovative coach developed "hiking," the practice of pushing, carrying, or hurtling the ball carrier through or over the opposing line (straps attached to the football pants aided this), and the line divide, gapping the offensive line as in the modern split "T." In the line divide, the gap from center to the next man might be two to three yards with an unbalanced line. From 1913 to 1915, his teams finished 21–0–1 with 14 consecutive shutouts of the opposition. No southern coach used the forward pass until his Auburn team used it against Sewanee (the University of the South) in 1906.

Donohue, one of the first seven coaches inducted into the NFF College Football Hall of Fame in November 1951, became one of the first eight inductees into the Alabama Sports Hall of Fame in 1969, joining "Bear" Bryant (FB), Joe Louis (IS), and Ralph "Shug" Jordan (S).

Donohue married Rosalie Sheehan Boudreaux and had two daughters, Eileen and Rosalie, and three sons, John, Julian, and Michael, Jr. Only Michael, Jr., survives and works as a physician in Baton Rouge.

Michael, Sr., loved to tell of his first contract at Auburn in his first year of coaching. He was paid $80 per week for football, served as professor of Greek and Latin, and was assigned to teach math. Due to a good cotton crop, Auburn enrolled 400 students. Donohue laughed about trying to teach Latin and Greek to farm boys who were wearing their first pair of shoes.

BIBLIOGRAPHY: Alabama Sports Hall of Fame Archives; Auburn University Sports Information Department Records, Auburn, AL; Michael J. Donohue, Jr., interviews with and letters to Robert T. Bowen, Jr., 1993; Elliot Hebert, "He Wanted Coaches Put in the Stands," *Dixie Times-Picayune States Roto Magazine*, September 6, 1953; Zipp Newman, "Mike Donohue . . . Father, Coach," Birmingham (AL) *News*, December 18, 1958.

Robert T. Bowen, Jr.

DRAKE, John W. "Johnny" (b. March 27, 1916, Chicago, IL; d. March 26, 1973, Detroit, MI), college and professional player, excelled as a rugged fullback equally famed for his strong running and bruising blocking. At Purdue University (WC), Drake started three years in football from 1934 through 1936 and combined with future All-Pro passer Cecil Isbell (FB) as the "Touchdown Twins." The Boilermakers finished with marks of 5–3 in 1934, 4–4 in 1935, and 5–2–1 in 1936. He started in the backfield for the Collegians in the annual College All-Star Game at Chicago, IL, in 1937, helping the college players defeat the NFL champions for the first time. With the All-Stars leading Green Bay by 6–0, Drake broke loose late in the game and was prevented from scoring only by a desperation tackle by Don Hutson (FB).

The Cleveland Rams (NFL) selected the six-foot, 215-pound Drake as their first pick in the 1937 NFL draft. The Rams, an expansion team, won only a single game in their first season. Drake led Cleveland in rushing with 333 yards and in scoring with 30 points. Although Cleveland improved somewhat in its second season, a foot injury sidelined Drake part of the year. Under new coach Earl "Dutch" Clark (FB), the Rams finished with a .500 record during their third season. Drake, called "the best player I ever coached" by Clark, rushed for 453 yards and led the NFL in rushing touchdowns with nine.

Drake, who wore number 13 in defiance of superstition, made the Official All-NFL team in 1940, rushing for 480 yards and again leading the NFL with 9 rushing touchdowns. He finished second to Hutson in scoring by one point and second in rushing to Byron "Whizzer" White (FB) of the Detroit Lions. The best game of his NFL career came on November 3, 1940, when he scored a rushing touchdown, threw a touchdown pass, and kicked an extra point in the Rams' 24–0 upset of Detroit. A foot injury again limited him in 1941, his final NFL season. In five NFL years, he rushed for 1,700 yards on 525 attempts for 24 touchdowns and caught 41 passes for 530 yards (12.9-yard average) and 3 touchdowns.

During off-seasons, Drake appeared in Hollywood westerns and worked as a forest ranger, life guard, teacher, policeman, and night watchman. After leaving professional football, he rose to director of personnel for the Michigan Division of TRW, Incorporated. He and his wife Florence had two daughters.

BIBLIOGRAPHY: John Drake file, Pro Football Hall of Fame, Canton, OH; David S. Neft et al., eds., *The Football Encyclopedia*, 2nd ed. (New York, 1994); Beau Riffenburgh, *The Official NFL Encyclopedia*, 4th ed. (New York, 1986).

Robert N. "Bob" Carroll

EDDY, Nicholas M. "Nick" (b. August 25, 1944, Dunsmuir, CA), college and professional player, is the son of Joe Eddy, a welder's foreman, and Angelina Eddy. His father, a rabid University of Notre Dame football enthusiast, especially admired Johnny Lujack (FB) and Johnny Lattner (FB). To no surprise, Eddy, after earning eight letters in track and field, football, baseball, and basketball at Tracy High School, gravitated toward South Bend, IN's golden dome.

Besides sharing his father's appreciation for Lattner, Eddy also idolized younger Notre Dame stars Paul Hornung (FB) and Nick Pietrosante. The six-foot-one-inch, 205-pound Eddy, who possessed 9.9-second speed in the 100-yard dash, was characterized as a bulldozer with breakaway speed. At Notre Dame, Eddy excelled as a football halfback, fullback, and kick returner from 1964 to 1966. Coach Ara Parseghian (FB) classified him as the best open field runner he had ever coached. During his South Bend career, Eddy rushed for 1,625 yards (5.6-yard average), caught 44 passes for 708 yards, returned kickoffs for 404 yards, and scored 140 points. Upon leaving the Fighting Irish in 1966, Eddy ranked ninth on the all-time Notre Dame rushing list behind Lattner. Eddy scored two touchdowns in the 1967 East-West Shrine All-Star Game, one on a pass reception and the other on a run up the middle that saw him break three tackles. The 1966 campaign proved Eddy's personal best year, as he was named consensus All-America, finished third in the Heisman Trophy balloting behind Steve Spurrier (FB) and Bob Griese (FB), and was selected by his teammates as the Fighting Irish's MVP. He earned a B.A. degree from Notre Dame in 1967.

The Detroit Lions (NFL) picked Eddy in the second round of the draft and signed him for a reported $400,000 after a bidding war with the Denver Broncos (AFL). The first time Eddy touched the ball in an NFL game, he returned a punt 75 yards for a touchdown in an exhibition contest against the Buffalo Bills in August 1967. Sadly, Eddy's brief NFL career was marred by knee injuries. Injuries sidelined him for the entire 1967 and 1971 seasons, despite his heroic efforts at rehabilitation. In four years with the Lions from 1968 to 1970 and in 1972, Eddy rushed 152 times for 523 yards, three touchdowns, and a 3.4-yard average. He caught 24 passes for 237 yards, for two touchdowns and a 9.9-yard interception average. Eddy married high school sweetheart Jean Ender in 1965. They have four children, Nicole, Nick, Jr., Alicia, and Angela. Currently, Eddy works as an insurance executive in Modesto, CA.

BIBLIOGRAPHY: Nick Eddy file, Office of Sports Information, University of Notre Dame, Notre Dame, IN; Ronald L. Mendell and Timothy B. Phares, *Who's Who in Football* (New Rochelle, NY, 1974); *NYT*, 1964–1966; *TSN Pro Football Register*, 1973; Jack Ziegler, telephone interview with Nick Eddy, January 5, 1994.

John H. Ziegler

EMERSON, Gover Connor "Ox" (b. December 16, 1907, Douglas, TX), college and professional player, graduated from Orange, TX, prep school in 1927 and entered the University of Texas (SWC) in the fall.

A lanky 5-foot-11-inch, 192-pound guard, he captained the freshman team. Noted for his defensive powers, he won All-SWC honors as a member of the 1930 championship squad. Emerson was also acclaimed the most popular athlete on campus. He was slated to be captain of the 1931 team, but a sportswriter discovered he had played two downs in 1928. Consequently, he lost his last year of eligibility.

After earning his B.A. degree in 1931, he joined the Portsmouth, OH, Spartans of the young NFL in the fall. Although the Spartans were a top team, the small city could not support them. In 1935, the Spartans were shifted to Detroit and became the Lions. Attesting to the quality of their talent, the Lions became the NFL champions in 1936, and Emerson was chosen to the Official NFL All-Star team. Following the 1937 season, he joined the now-extinct Brooklyn Dodgers as a player–coach for his final NFL campaign.

Emerson coached at Wayne University from 1939 to 1941 before entering the U.S. Navy. During his four and a half years in the navy, he attained the rank of lieutenant commander and coached the Corpus Christi Naval Air Station team. Following his release from duty, he returned to coaching for three years at Alice, TX, High School. After spending a year at Delmar JC, he returned as a line coach to the University of Texas from 1951 through 1956. Due to a change in head coaches, he was released and returned to high school coaching until 1974. In a poll taken in 1969, he was voted to the All-Time Pro team of the 1930s.

He is married to Virginia Opie.

BIBLIOGRAPHY: Harold Johnson, *Who's Who in Major League Football* (Chicago, IL, 1935); David S. Neft et al., eds., *The Football Encyclopedia*, 2nd ed. (New York, 1994); Beau Riffenburgh, *The Official NFL Encyclopedia*, 4th ed. (New York, 1986).

                                                                                                Stanley Grosshandler

ERICKSON, Dennis Brian (b. March 24, 1947, Everett, WA), college player and coach, is the son of "Pink" Erickson, a former football coach, and Mary Erickson and graduated from Washington High School in his hometown in 1965. Erickson enrolled at Montana State University (BSAC), starting at quarterback for three years and earning his bachelor's degree in physical education in 1970. His honors included being a two-time BSAC First Team selection and an honorable mention All-America his senior year while establishing several school passing and total offense records.

Subsequently, Erickson served as a football graduate assistant at Montana State in 1969 and at Washington State University (AAWU) for the 1970 spring practice. Erickson became the head football coach at Billings, MT, Central High School in 1970, guiding his team to a 7–2 win–loss record and a second-place state finish. Assignments followed as offensive backfield coach at Montana State from 1971 to 1973 and offensive coordinator at the University of Idaho (BSAC) in 1974 and 1975, Fresno State University (CaCAA) from 1976 to 1978, and San Jose State University from 1979 to 1981. As head football coach at the University of Idaho four seasons from 1982 to 1985, Erickson led the Vandals to a 32–15 record and a berth in the NCAA Division I-AA playoffs in 1982 and 1985. The University of Wyoming (WAC) named him as head football coach in 1986, when the Cowboys posted a 6–6 record and placed second nationally in pass offense. Erickson coached the Washington State University Cougars (PTC) for the next two seasons, earning PTC 1988 Co-Coach of the Year honors. The Cougars in 1988 finished with a 9–3 mark and recorded their first bowl game victory since 1916, a 24–22 triumph over the University of Houston in the Aloha Bowl. Washington State ranked sixteenth nationally, the Cougars' highest rating ever, and accomplished nine victories, the most by any Cougar squad since 1930.

In March 1989, the University of Miami named Erickson head coach, his fourth head coaching job in 8 years. From 1989 through 1994, the Hurricanes won 63 games, lost only 9 contests, and compiled one undefeated season, two national championships, and Orange, Cotton, and Sugar Bowl triumphs. Miami narrowly missed a third national title in 1992, losing to the University of Alabama, 34–13, in the Sugar Bowl. The Hurricanes were shut out, 29–0, by the University of Arizona in the Fiesta Bowl following the 1993 season and lost 24–17 to national champion University of Nebraska in the Orange Bowl following the 1994 season. Erickson guided the Hurricanes to the national crown in his first year at Miami, making him only the second coach in NCAA history to lead a team to the national title in his initial season at a school. Bennie Oosterbaan (FB), the first, accomplished the feat at the University of Michigan (BTC) in 1948. Erickson, selected Coach of the Year by the *FN* and *Street and Smith's* in 1991, became only the second coach in NCAA history to win two national championships in 3 years at one school. Barry Switzer (FB) previously accomplished this feat in 1974 and 1975 at the University of Oklahoma (BEC). Besides being inducted into Montana State's Hall of Fame in 1991, Erickson was named BEaC Coach of the Year in Miami's first year in the league. Erickson's 13 years as head coach from 1982 through 1994 have produced a 113–40–1 record for a .736 winning percentage, ranking him fifth among all active Division I-A coaches. In January 1995 the Seattle Seahawks (NFL) selected him as head coach to replace Tom Flores (FB).

Erickson married Marilyn Selley and has two sons, Bryce and Ryan.

BIBLIOGRAPHY: Bruce Newman, "Just Call It Erickson," *SI* 19 (May 1, 1989), pp. 82–83; *University of Miami Media Guide*, 1993.

John L. Evers

ESIASON, Norman Julius Jr. "Boomer" (b. April 17, 1961, West Islip, NY), college and professional player and sportscaster, is the son of Norman Esiason, Sr., an insurance agent, and grew up with his father following his mother's death in 1966. Esiason, an all-around athlete at East Islip, NY, High School, compiled a 15–0 record as a baseball pitcher his senior season. The University of Maryland (ACC) recruited the six-foot-four-inch, 190-pound southpaw for football and made him the Terrapins' first-string quarterback for three seasons from 1981 through 1983. In 31 games, Esiason led the Terrapins to 20 victories overall and 8 triumphs in each of his last two seasons. His career passing statistics at Maryland included 461 completions in 850 attempts for 6,259 yards, 42 touchdowns, and a .542 completion percentage. He recorded 196.2 total offensive yards per game and 6.0 yards per play. In 1982, Esiason completed 19 of 32 passes for 251 yards and 2 touchdowns in the Aloha Bowl, but the Terrapins lost, 21–20, to the University of Washington. Esiason, who finished tenth in the 1983 Heisman Trophy voting, suffered a second-quarter shoulder separation in the Florida Citrus Bowl 30–23 loss to the University of Tennessee.

The Cincinnati Bengals selected Esiason in the second round as the thirty-eighth pick of the 1984 NFL draft. Esiason started at quarterback for several games his rookie year and took over full-time the following season. By 1988, he led the Bengals into Super Bowl XXIII with the AFC championship and AFC Central Division title. Cincinnati lost in the Super Bowl, 20–16, when the San Francisco 49ers scored a touchdown with 34 seconds remaining. In 1990, the Bengals also captured an AFC Central Division crown. Although Ken Anderson (FB) holds most of the Bengals' individual passing records, Esiason ranks close behind and holds the club mark for most passing yardage in one season (3,959, 1986) and passing yardage in one game (440, 1990). His 400 passing yards against the Los Angeles Rams remains the seventh-best single-game yardage total in NFL history. Esiason played in the 1986 Pro Bowl and was selected for this prestigious game in 1988 and 1989 but was replaced because of injuries. His honors included selection as *TSN* 1988 NFL Player of the Year and quarterback on the NFL All-Pro team. In 11 seasons from 1984 through 1994, Esiason has completed 2,440 of 4,291 passing attempts for 31,874 yards, 207 touchdowns, and 154 interceptions. Following the 1993 season, Esiason ranked tenth with 82.1 rating points on the list of leading lifetime passers. In March 1993, Cincinnati traded Esiason to the New York Jets (NFL).

Esiason served as an analyst for television coverage of the WFL football games for the second year in 1992. The official spokesman for the National Arthritis Foundation, he hosted a golf tournament for the organization in Cincinnati for seven years. Owner of the Waterfront Restaurant in Covington, KY, Esiason and his wife Cheryl have one son, Gunnar.

BIBLIOGRAPHY: Pete Axthelm and Bill Robinson, "Once Reviled, Now Revered, Top Cat Boomer Esiason Sharpens His Claws for the Super Bowl," *PW* 3 (January 23, 1989), pp. 42–43; *Cincinnati Bengals Media Guide*, 1992; *NCAA Football's Finest*, 1990; *TSN Pro Football Register*, 1994.

John L. Evers

EVANS, Ray Richard "Riflin' Ray" (b. September 8, 1922, Kansas City, KS), college athlete and professional football player, ranked among the nation's most illustrious multisport athletes during the 1940s. His brilliant football career at the University of Kansas (BSC) began in 1941 and ended with the 1948 Orange Bowl game. Evans played four varsity seasons in both football and basketball and two years in both sports with the U.S. Army Air Corps. The five-time All-BSC selection helped the Jayhawks win five BSC championships, including three in basketball and two in football. During World

War II, he starred for the Second Air Force Bombers and alternated with Glenn Dobbs,* the former University of Tulsa All-America. In 1945, Evans outgained Dobbs in both passing and rushing yardage while leading the undefeated Bombers.

Evans was born on Strawberry Hill, the youngest of six children. His mother, Susie, had immigrated from Czechoslovakia. His father, Joseph, worked during the day with his wife in their grocery store and also worked as a night watchman. Evans starred in football, basketball, and baseball at Wyandotte High School, graduating in 1940. Evans, who entered the University of Kansas, was best known for his ability on the football field but was also selected on the HAF All-America basketball teams as a guard in 1942 and 1943 under legendary coach Forrest C. "Phog" Allen (IS). By 1948, Evans became one of only six collegiate athletes ever to achieve All-America honors in both basketball and football and the only player west of the Mississippi River to do so. In 1942, the Kansas star led the nation in pass completions with 101. His 1,464 yards total offense in 1942 included 293 rushing and 1,171 passing. His career 3,755 yards total offense covering the 1941, 1942, 1946, and 1947 seasons included 1,431 yards rushing and 2,324 yards passing.

In 1947, he was chosen First Team halfback on the AP All-America team. Evans also was selected to the Grantland Rice (OS) All-America team (*Collier's*), the NAFS team (*Pic Magazine*), and the New York *Sun* All-America team. Evans captained the 1946 Kansas football team and played on the 1947 Jayhawks, losers to Georgia Tech University, 20–14, in the 1948 Orange Bowl. In that losing effort, Evans scored both Jayhawks touchdowns. During his football career, Evans remained a consistent 60-minute performer and also excelled as a defensive halfback. In January 1948, the University of Kansas retired Evans' jersey number 42, marking the first time in the university's history that an athletic number had been retired.

Evans began his banking career in Kansas City, MO, after graduation in 1948 and played professional football in 1948 with the Pittsburgh Steelers (NFL). In February 1949, Evans married Edith Marie Darby, daughter of Kansas City, KS, industrialist Harry Darby. They became the parents of one son and three daughters. Evans served as president of Traders National Bank in Kansas City and was elected to the NFF College Football Hall of Fame in 1964, the Kansas All-Sports Hall of Fame in 1961, and the Orange Bowl Hall of Fame in 1988.

Evans remained a modest hero to Jayhawk fans and balanced his athletic renown with an outstanding career in local, state, and national service. His coach, George Sauer, Sr. (S) described him as "the greatest back I've ever seen."

BIBLIOGRAPHY: Ray Evans file, University Archives, University of Kansas, Lawrence, KS; "Former KU Star to Be Orange Bowl Honoree," Kansas City (MO) *Star*, December 9, 1988; Laura Rollins Hockaday, "The New Man Behind the Royal," Kansas

City (MO) *Star*, November 2, 1987; "Ray Evans to All-America," Lawrence (KS) *Journal-World*, December 3, 1947.

Arthur F. McClure

FERRANTE, Jack Anthony "Blackjack" (b. March 9, 1916, Camden, NJ), professional player, is the youngest of four children of Joseph Ferrante, a salesman, and Florence (Benditti) Ferrante and starred at defensive-offensive end in the late 1940s on the great Earle "Greasy" Neale (FB)–coached and Steve Van Buren (FB)–led Philadelphia Eagles (NFL) teams. Philadelphia won three straight NFL Eastern Division titles (1947–1949) and two consecutive NFL Championships (1948 and 1949).

The Ferrantes moved in 1923 to Philadelphia, where Ferrante quit high school to work full-time. He began playing football in 1934 with a local independent team, the Rockne AtA. In 1935, he signed with the Seymour AC, a semiprofessional sandlot football team from South Philadelphia and EPFC member. He remained with Seymour until 1939, when he tried out with the Philadelphia Eagles. Although not making the team, he joined the Eagles AtA farm club, Wilmington, DE, Clippers. In his first season with the Clippers, Ferrante led the AtA in scoring. The Eagles in 1941 signed Ferrante, who caught two passes for 22 yards in three games. Ferrante returned to Wilmington in 1942 for more seasoning but clashed with the Clipper management in 1943. He was suspended and played just two games with an independent club.

A severe World War II manpower shortage in 1944 promoted Ferrante to the Philadelphia Eagles as a starting offensive-defensive left end. He started with the Eagles in every game except one for the next seven years. The six-foot-one-inch, 205-pound Ferrante played both ways at end until 1947, when two-platoon football led to his use strictly as an offensive end. Ferrante began slowly, catching only 3 passes for 66 yards and one touchdown in 1944. He emerged as Philadelphia's top receiver in 1945, hauling in 21 passes for 474 yards and seven touchdowns. Another good season followed in 1946, as he made 28 receptions, 451 yards, and four touchdowns.

Pete Pihos (FB), a future pro football Hall of Famer, joined Philadelphia in 1947, giving one-eyed quarterback Tommy Thompson (S) another star receiver for his passes. Pihos and Ferrante established perhaps the most formidable NFL offensive end duo, grabbing 256 passes for 3,960 yards and 47 touchdowns the next four years. The duo, matched with a stalwart defensive line and the running of the bruising Van Buren and elusive "Bosh" Pritchard,* assured the Eagles two NFL championships. Backfield injuries, financial problems, and internal dissension dashed the Eagles' hopes for a third straight NFL title in 1950. Ferrante, at age 34, nevertheless, enjoyed one of his best seasons, catching 35 passes for 588 yards and 3 touchdowns. After Ferrante reported to the Eagles' preseason camp in 1951, the Eagles released him. The Detroit Lions (NFL) claimed Ferrante but did not meet his salary demands. Ferrante retired from professional football, having compiled an eight-season NFL mark of 169 receptions, 2,894 yards, and 31 touchdowns.

Ferrante secured a sales position with the Ortlieb Brewing Company in 1949 and remained with the firm until 1977. He also officiated high school football games in the PhCL in 1951 and 1952 and served as football coach at Monsignor Bonner High School from 1953 to 1961, leading the Philadelphia school to City championships in 1959 and 1961. Ferrante, elected to the Pennsylvania Sports Hall of Fame in 1978, married Connie DiMascio in 1940 and has two children, Joseph and Jacqueline.

BIBLIOGRAPHY: Jack C. Braun, telephone interview with Jack Ferrante, June 3, 1993; Jack Ferrante file, Pro Football Hall of Fame, Canton, OH; David S. Neft et al., eds., *The Football Encyclopedia*, 2nd ed. (New York, 1994); Richard Pagano, "Jack Ferrante: Eagles Great," *TCC* 10 (Late Spring 1988), pp. 5–7.

Jack C. Braun

FILCHOCK, Frank (b. 1917, Crucible, PA), college and professional player and coach, led the NFL in passing in 1944 and later became the first head coach of the Denver Broncos (AFL) in 1960–1961. His career was marred because the NFL banned him from 1947 until 1950 for failure to report a rejected bribe attempt to the NFL before the 1946 title game.

The son of Slovak parents in a bituminous coal patch in southwestern Pennsylvania, he lived in Braznell, PA, and starred as a passing and running halfback at Redstone Township High School in Fayette County, PA, and graduated from there in 1934. He earned a B.S. degree in 1938 from Indiana University, where he earned three letters as an outstanding halfback from 1935 through 1937. The Hoosiers compiled records of 4–3–1 in 1935, 5–2–1 in 1936, and 5–3 in 1937.

The Pittsburgh Steelers, then Pirates (NFL), drafted him as their second-round choice after Byron "Whizzer" White (FB) in 1938. He was traded partway through the season to the Washington Redskins (NFL). In October 1939, he completed the first 99-yard touchdown pass play in NFL history to Andy Farkas against his former Pittsburgh teammates. The 5-foot-10½-inch, 185-pound Filchock played for Washington through the 1941 season before entering the U.S. Navy in World War II. In 1942, he played for the Georgia Pre-Flight squad and was named to the UP All-Service team as tailback.

Upon returning to the Redskins for the 1944 season, he nosed out teammate Sammy Baugh (FB) as the NFL's top passer with 84 completions in 147 attempts for 1,139 yards and 13 touchdowns. After being traded to the New York Giants (NFL) in 1946, he signed the first Giant multiyear contract for $35,000 over three years.

In 1946, Filchock won Giant MVP and All-Pro halfback honors, leading

New York to the Eastern Division title and NFL championship game with the Chicago Bears. Just before that game, however, it was learned that Filchock had rejected a bribe effort and had not reported it to the NFL. After being cleared to participate, he played 50 minutes and threw two touchdown passes in a valiant losing effort. Filchock, suspended right after the season by NFL commissioner Bert Bell (FB), went through a divorce problem. He joined the Hamilton, Canada, Tigers (CFL) as playing coach for 1947.

From 1947 through 1950, he coached and played two years each with Hamilton and the Montreal, Canada, Alouettes (CFL). He was named CFL MVP in 1948 and starred in Montreal's Grey Cup win over the Calgary Stampeders in 1949. The NFL reinstated him in 1950. After completing the Canadian season, he joined the Baltimore Colts (NFL) at age 33. In 1951, he became coach–player of the Edmonton, Canada Eskimos and led them to the division title. He remained as head coach at Edmonton but retired as a player after the 1953 season. For the balance of that decade, he served as a CFL head coach with Regina, Sarnia, and Calgary.

When the AFL began play in 1960, the Denver Broncos named him head coach. Denver released him after the 1961 season with a 2-year record of 7–20–1. His professional career spanned 14 years as a player, but his career statistics are not available because of incomplete Canadian records. His 8-year NFL passing statistics included 342 completions in 677 attempts (50.5 percent) for 4,921 yards and 47 touchdowns. Filchock, who also threw 79 NFL interceptions, served 11 years including 9 in Canada, as a head coach.

Off the field, Filchock operated a restaurant and an asphalt company. During his early professional football career, he also played minor league baseball.

BIBLIOGRAPHY: L. H. Baker, *Football: Facts and Figures* (New York, 1945); Bob Braunwart et al., "The Peregrinations of Frankie Filchock," *Second Annual Historical and Statistical Review of the PFRA*, 1981; James D. Whalen, letter to David L. Porter, March 21, 1994.

                                                                        Robert B. Van Atta

FISCHER, Patrick "Pat" "Mouse" (b. January 2, 1940, St. Edward, NE), college and professional player, grew up in Omaha, NE, and starred in football and basketball at Omaha Westside High School. He in 1957 enrolled at the University of Nebraska (BEC) as one of four brothers to play football for the Cornhuskers, lettering in football from 1958 to 1960. In 1961, he received his B.S. degree in business administration. At Nebraska, Fischer enjoyed a productive, if somewhat unspectacular, career as a quarterback and halfback. The five-foot-nine-inch, 170-pound Fischer was considered a poor NFL prospect because of his lack of size and speed. The St. Louis Cardinals (NFL) selected him in the seventeenth round of the 1961 college draft, enabling him to launch one of the longest careers in NFL history.

Fischer's first two NFL years were spent mostly as a punt and kickoff returner, but in 1963 he started at left corner defensive back and led the Cardinals with 8 pass interceptions. The next season, he intercepted 10 passes and returned them for 164 yards and an NFL-leading two touchdowns. Fischer played three more seasons for St. Louis before signing as a free agent with the Washington Redskins (NFL), where he excelled a decade before retiring in 1978. With the Redskins, he played with the "Over the Hill Gang" in the 1972 NFL Championship game and Super Bowl VII against the Miami Dolphins (AFC). These fine aging veterans had been assembled by Coach George Allen (FB). Fischer still performed well as a cagey, experienced defensive back and fearless tackler. In 1976, the 36-year-old intercepted 5 passes to help the Redskins win 10 of 14 games. During his NFL career, Fischer intercepted 56 passes and returned 5 for touchdowns. He also returned 17 punts for 80 yards (4.7-yard average) and 26 kickoffs for 613 yards (24.5-yard average).

Altogether, Fischer played 17 NFL seasons, including 14 as a starter, was named to the *TSN* NFL All-Star team four times (1964–1965, 1968–1969), and played in the NFL Pro Bowl game following the 1964, 1965, and 1969 seasons. Although NFL players increased dramatically in weight, size, strength, and speed, the diminutive Fischer demonstrated that the smaller athlete with exceptional skills, experience, and determination could still contribute to the quality of the game. Subsequently, Fischer settled in Leesburg, VA, and became a highly successful stockbroker.

BIBLIOGRAPHY: George Allen with Ben Olan, *Pro Football's 100 Greatest Players* (Indianapolis, IN, 1982); Pat Fischer file, University of Nebraska Sports Information Office, Lincoln, NE; *1965 Official Pro Football Almanac* (Greenwich, CT, 1965); *TSN Pro Football Register*, 1974; *TSN Pro Football Register*, 1978.

John Hanners

FISHER, Robert Thomas "Bob" (b. December 3, 1888, Boston, MA; d. July 7, 1942, Newton, MA), college player and coach, was the son of Rollin Bradshaw Fisher and Ida C. (Thomas) Fisher. After attending Dorchester, MA, High School, he graduated from Phillips Andover Academy and played football at tackle there. At Harvard University from 1908 to 1912, the 5-foot-11-inch, 193- to 205-pound Fisher played right guard on the freshman and varsity football teams and captained the Crimson his senior year. Yale University defeated the Crimson, 8–0, in 1909 and held them to scoreless ties in 1910 and 1911. In its first game with Princeton University since 1896, Harvard in 1911 lost to the Tigers. Fisher was named a First Team All-America guard in 1910 and 1911 and a Third Team selectee in 1909. The all-time Harvard guard was elected to the NFF College Football Hall of Fame in 1973.

Besides being president of his sophomore class, Fisher also served on the

Student Council and the Governing Board of the Union and was chosen second class marshal. He belonged to the Institute of 1770—Hasty Pudding, Delta Kappa Epsilon fraternity, Digamma Club, and Signet Society. After graduating in 1912, he served as an assistant football coach at Harvard for four years and worked at the C. F. Hovey & Company dry goods store in Boston. Fisher was commissioned a first lieutenant in the supply department of the air service in 1917 and was discharged a captain in 1919.

A disciple of Percy Haughton (FB), Harvard's first paid coach, who had won 71 out of 83 games from 1908 to 1916, Fisher eagerly agreed to serve as Crimson football coach from 1919 to 1925. His teams posted a 43–14–5 record, defeating Yale University four times, losing twice to the Elis on soggy fields, and holding the Bulldogs to one scoreless tie. Fisher's best season came in 1919, when the Crimson shut out seven opponents, defeated Yale, and tied Princeton. Harvard then edged the University of Oregon, 7–6, in the 1920 Rose Bowl game, its only postseason intersectional game. Harvard participated in the contest largely to encourage fund-raising among Far Western alumni.

In 1920, Harvard shut out seven foes, including Yale, and tied Princeton. The 1921 Crimson defeated seven teams, including Yale, tied with Pennsylvania State University, was shut out by Centre College of Kentucky, 6–0, and lost to Princeton. The following year, Harvard again posted four shutouts and seven wins. Although avenging itself against Centre College, 24–10, and defeating Yale, Harvard lost to Princeton and Brown University. In each of Fisher's final three seasons, the Crimson managed only four wins. Moreover, 1924 marked the first year no Crimson player made the All-America First Team. After Fisher retired, subsequent Harvard coaches worked under a director of Athletics. The position was created in 1926 to take athletics from alumni control.

Fisher, a stockbroker at Lee, Higginson & Company from 1921 to 1927, later served as office manager for Harriss & Voss Company and joined Spencer Trask & Company in 1931. He married Louise Alexander Winters in 1919 and had five children, Robert Thomas, Jr., Rollin Bradshaw II, John Winters, William Orne, and Alice Ann Fisher.

BIBLIOGRAPHY: Thomas Bergin, *The Game: The Harvard-Yale Football Rivalry, 1875–1983* (New Haven, CT, and London, England, 1984); John A. Blanchard, ed., *The H Book of Harvard Athletics 1852–1922* (Cambridge, MA, 1923); "Robert T. Fisher," biographical sketches in the *Harvard College Class of 1912: First Report* (April 1913), pp. 34, 35, 64–66, 164; *Twenty-fifth Anniversary Report* (1937), pp. 237–239; *Thirty-fifth Anniversary Report* (1947), pp. 89–90; "Robert T. Fisher, 1912," quinquennial file, Harvard University Archives, Cambridge, MA; John D. McCallum and Charles H. Pearson, *College Football U.S.A., 1869–1973* (New York, 1973); Geoffrey H. Movius, ed., *The Second H Book of Harvard Athletics 1923–1963* (Cambridge, MA, 1964); Rube Samuelsen, *The Rose Bowl Game* (Garden City, NY, 1951).

Marcia G. Synnott

FRALIC, William P. Jr. "Bill" (b. October 31, 1962, Pittsburgh, PA), college and professional player, played football with the University of Pittsburgh, Atlanta Falcons (NFL), and Detroit Lions (NFL), being named All-America as a tackle in high school and college and later an All-Pro.

The son of William P. Fralic, Sr., and Dorothy Fralic, he stood six foot three inches and weighed 235 pounds as an eighth grader. Upon his graduation from Penn Hills High School in suburban Pittsburgh, he already had won four letters in both football and wrestling, had earned *Parade* All-America honors as a tackle, and garnered Dial Male Athlete of the Year accolades, an unusual distinction for a scholastic athlete.

He started his first game as a freshman at the University of Pittsburgh in 1981, achieving some All-America honors as a sophomore and being named a consensus All-America choice his junior and senior years. His devastating blocking skills inspired the sports information staff at Pittsburgh to initiate a "pancake" statistic for Fralic in putting defensive linemen on their backs. The Panthers compiled a 31–14–2 record during his four years there.

Fralic placed extraordinarily high for an offensive lineman in Heisman voting, ranking eighth in 1983 and sixth in 1984. His uniform number 79 became one of four that Pittsburgh has retired. He played with the Panther team in the 1982 Sugar Bowl win over the University of Georgia, the 1983 Cotton Bowl loss to SMU, and the 1984 loss to Ohio State University in the Fiesta Bowl. He also participated in the 1985 Hula Bowl.

The six-foot-five-inch, 280-pound athlete was the first-round draft choice of the Atlanta Falcons (NFL) in 1985 and the second selection overall. He played for Atlanta from 1985 through 1992 as an offensive guard and performed in the 1986, 1987, and 1989 Pro Bowls. He was also selected in 1988 but could not play due to injury. During that period, he was also named to several All-NFL teams. After being granted unconditional free agency by Atlanta in March 1993, he signed the following month with the Detroit Lions (NFL) and played the 1993 season there. In April 1994, the Lions released Fralic.

BIBLIOGRAPHY: *TSN Pro Football Register*, 1994; *University of Pittsburgh Football Media Guides*, 1981–1985.

Robert B. Van Atta

FRANZ, Rodney Thomas (b. February 8, 1925, San Francisco, CA), college player and coach, starred as a football guard from 1946 to 1949 and made three-time All-America at the University of California at Berkeley (PCC). He is the son of Carl Franz, a San Francisco restaurateur, and Ruby (Chatterton) Franz, an accountant, and graduated from Galileo High School in San Francisco. After graduation, he served in the U.S. Army Air Force from March 1943 to April 1946.

Under coaches Frank Wickhorst in 1946 and Lynn "Pappy" Waldorf (FB) from 1947 to 1949, Franz started at right guard on teams that compiled 2–7, 9–1, 10–1, and 10–1 win–loss marks. Franz played in 40 consecutive football games, including two Rose Bowls. His job on offense consisted of opening holes for fine backs Jackie Jensen (S) and Bob Celeri. The six-foot-one-inch, 200-pound Franz also excelled defensively. In one game against the University of Washington, the Golden Bears' defense proved especially stingy in allowing the Huskies only 61 total yards. At one point, Franz exhorted his teammates to tighten up because they had allowed the Huskies to gain a yard on the previous play.

His postseason All-America teams included the 1947 All-America Board First Team, Coaches First Team, Grantland Rice (OS) First Team, 1948 AP First Team, New York *Sun* First Team, 1949 Football Writers (*Look*), New York *Sun*, New York *News*, AP, UP, INS, *Touchdown*, and *Police Gazette*.

After graduating from California, Franz coached Mt. Diablo, CA, High School to a stellar three-year 20–2 win–loss record. In 1956, he coached the University of California—Riverside football squad to a 1–2 mark during the school's abbreviated first season. He served as an assistant football coach at the University of California at Berkeley in 1957 and 1958. Franz worked at U.S. Steel from 1959 to 1967 and at the East Bay, CA, Municipal Utility District from 1967 to 1990, managing legislative affairs. The NFF College Football Hall of Fame enshrined him in 1977. Franz married Lois Richter on January 29, 1949, and has seven children.

BIBLIOGRAPHY: S. Dan Brodie, *66 Years on the California Gridiron* (Berkeley, CA, 1949); *California Football Review*, 1949; Rodney Franz, letter to NFF College Football Hall of Fame, May 31, 1968; Rodney Franz, letter to Robert L. Cannon, December 28, 1992; Rodney Franz, questionnaire completed for the California Athletic Department, 1970.

Robert L. Cannon

GAITHER, Alonzo Smith "Jake" (b. April 11, 1903, Dayton, TN; d. February 18, 1994, Tallahassee, FL), college athlete, coach, and athletic director, guided Florida A&M University's football squads from 1945 to 1969 to an .845 winning percentage, the highest among all coaches with 200 or more victories. His composite career record of 203 wins, 36 losses, and four ties included six national black college championships and 22 SIAA titles. The Rattlers garnered SIAA titles every year from 1945 to 1969 except 1951, 1952, and 1966. Gaither, who guided the Rattlers to three undefeated seasons and 12 one-loss campaigns, produced 36 All-Americas and was the first college coach to win the Triple Crown of football awards. He produced at least 1 All-America player every year except 1949 and sent 42 players to the NFL. In 1970, Florida A&M defeated the University of Tampa, 34–28, in the first college interracial football game in Florida. In 1975, he was elected to the NFF College Football Hall of Fame and received the AFCA's

Amos Alonzo Stagg Award and the Walter Camp Foundation Award for contributions to football and humanitarianism.

Gaither, whose father served as a Zion A.M.E. minister, grew up in Memphis, TN, with his four siblings in a Christian environment and wanted to be a lawyer. During high school in Memphis, he earned extra money digging ditches, shining shoes, and working as a bellhop. Gaither enrolled at Knoxville, TN, College, where he starred in football, basketball, and track and field. He was named All-SIAA end in football and graduated in 1927 with a Bachelor of Science degree. During the next decade, he taught and coached in a high school and served as head football coach at Henderson, NC, Institute and St. Paul Polytechnic Institute at Lawrenceville, VA. In 1937, he earned a master's degree in physical education and health from Ohio State University.

Gaither, an assistant football coach from 1937 to 1944 at Florida A&M under coach William Bell, helped the Rattlers achieve two undefeated seasons. In 1942, Gaither overcame two brain tumors, temporary blindness, and a broken leg. He assumed the football head coaching position in 1945, along with serving as classroom instructor and basketball and track and field coach. He helped to shape the lives of tennis champion Althea Gibson (OS) and John D. Glover, the FBI's first black inspector. His gridiron stars included three-time All-America center Curtis Miranda, wide receiver and track sprint champion Bob Hayes (OS), halfback Willie Galimore,* cornerback Ken Riley, defensive back Major Hazleton, and fullback Hewritt Dixon. In 1963 Gaither authored *The Split Line T Offense of Florida A&M University*, describing his revolutionary, widely imitated offense.

Gaither did not tolerate swearing and insisted that his players graduate. Former Ohio State University coach Woody Hayes (FB) said, "He could sell himself to youngsters, and those players respected him." Gaither married Sadie Robinson, his former Knoxville College classmate who taught English at Florida A&M. He retired from coaching in 1969 but continued as athletic director and professor of physical education until reaching mandatory retirement at age 70 in 1973. Gaither, named 1962 College Division Coach of the Year, was elected to the HAF, NACDA, Tennessee, and Black Athletic Halls of Fame. He also served as FCF president.

BIBLIOGRAPHY: Norris Anderson, "Confidentially," *FN*, November 11, 1986; Alvin Hollins, Florida A&M SID, letter to James D. Whalen, October 1993; Michael Hurd, *Black College Football, 1892–1992* (Virginia Beach, VA, 1993); *The Lincoln Library of Sports Champions*, vol. 5 (Columbus, OH, 1974); *Spalding and NCAA Football Guides*, 1938–1970; John Underwood, "The Desperate Coach, Concessions and Lies," *SI* 31 (September 8, 1969), pp. 28–32, 37–40.

James D. Whalen

GALIMORE, Willie Lee (b. March 30, 1935, St. Augustine, FL; d. July 26, 1964, Rensselaer, IN), college and professional player, was a six-foot-one-inch, 188-pound star halfback at Florida A&M under coach Jake Gaither.* From 1954 to 1956, Galimore led his team to a 23–3–1 won–lost–tied record and three appearances in the postseason Orange Blossom Classic. Jockey Willie Frank recommended Galimore to Phil Handler, assistant coach for the Chicago Bears (NFL).

A fifth-round draft choice of the Bears, Galimore won acclaim as a spectacular breakaway runner reminiscent of former Chicago great George McAfee (FB). As a rookie in 1957, the swift back gained 538 yards rushing, to place second on the team behind Rick Casares (S). The following season, Galimore increased his rushing production to 619 yards while scoring 12 touchdowns. The dangerous return man also averaged 37.6 yards on nine kickoff returns. Galimore consequently played in the 1958 Pro Bowl for the WC. Injuries slowed Galimore in 1959, but he returned the following season to gain 368 yards rushing and average 5.0 yards per carry.

Galimore's best year came in 1961, when he led the Bears with 153 rushing attempts for 707 yards (4.6 yards per carry) and caught 33 passes for 502 yards (15.2 yards per reception). Injuries sidelined Galimore again in 1962, limiting him to only 233 yards on the ground. Healthy again in 1963, he rushed for 321 yards on one of the greatest Chicago squads ever. The 1963 Bears lost only one game during the regular season and defeated the New York Giants, 14–10, in a hard-fought NFL championship game. Galimore started at halfback against the Giants, gaining 12 yards rushing in the defensive struggle.

As the Bears prepared for their title defense in 1964, Galimore and teammate John Farrington died in an automobile accident near Rensselaer, IN. Galimore's career totals included 670 rushing attempts for 2,985 yards and 26 touchdowns; 87 pass receptions for 1,201 yards and 10 touchdowns; and 43 kickoff returns for 1,100 yards (25.6-yard average) and 1 touchdown. He was survived by his wife Audrey and three children. Ron, one son, won the NCAA Long Horse Vault Gymnastics title at Iowa State University in 1980 and 1981.

BIBLIOGRAPHY: Harold Claassen and Steve Boda, Jr., eds., *Ronald Encyclopedia of Football* (New York, 1963); Ralph Hickok, *Who Was Who in American Sports* (New York, 1971); David S. Neft et al., eds., *The Football Encyclopedia*, 2nd ed. (New York, 1994); *NYT*, July 27, 1964; Murray Olderman, *The Running Backs* (Englewood Cliffs, NJ, 1969); Beau Riffenburgh, *The Official NFL Encyclopedia*, 4th ed. (New York, 1986).

                                                                                    Marc S. Maltby

GIBRON, Abraham "Abe" (b. September 22, 1925, Michigan City, IN), college and professional player and coach, excelled at guard for the Cleveland Browns NFL Championship teams of the 1950s. The 5-foot-11-inch 250-pounder proved unusually large and fast for a guard at the time and is often ranked among the three or four best at his position during the decade. Although gruff on the field, he remained a strong family man and took pride in his wife and three children.

Gibron graduated from Michigan City High School and attended Valparaiso University. He graduated from Purdue University (WC), where he played guard for the 1947 5–4 and 1948 3–6 Boilermaker squads. The Buffalo Bills (AAFC) selected the two-year Purdue letterman as their first draft choice in a secret draft held in July 1948 before Gibron's final Purdue season. The AAFC hoped to gain the advantage on the rival NFL in signing college seniors. Gibron was selected on the sixth round in the 1949 NFL draft by the New York Giants, but he signed with Buffalo and immediately started for the Bills. When the AAFC merged with the NFL after the 1949 season, the players from Buffalo and the other defunct AAFC clubs were put into a general pool to be drafted by the remaining NFL teams. The Cleveland Browns had joined the NFL as part of the merger and chose Gibron. Cleveland coach Paul Brown (FB) remembered Gibron "had the fastest and quickest charge I ever saw. He was very spirited and played at 250 pounds."

The roly-poly Gibron, one of the Browns' "messenger guards," alternated in taking each play called by the coach into the quarterback. Eventually, the Browns deemed Gibron too valuable to play part-time and kept him in the lineup while the "other" guards ran messages. Gibron was selected for the Pro Bowl four times from 1952 through 1955 and was named All-NFL by the UP in 1955. Cleveland, meanwhile, played in six consecutive championship games, winning three. The Browns captured NFL titles by defeating the Los Angeles Rams, 30–28, in 1950 and, 38–14, in 1955 and the Detroit Lions, 56–10, in 1954. Gibron was traded to the Philadelphia Eagles (NFL) in the middle of the 1956 campaign and joined the Chicago Bears (NFL) in 1958, retiring after the 1959 season.

Gibron became an assistant football coach with the Washington Redskins (NFL) in 1960 and returned to the Chicago Bears as an assistant in 1965. He served as head coach of the Bears from 1972 to 1974, compiling an 11–30–1 record. The Chicago Wind (WFL) appointed Gibron as head coach for the 1–4 1975 season. From 1976 to 1984, Gibron assisted John McKay (FB) with the Tampa Bay Buccaneers (NFL).

BIBLIOGRAPHY: Abe Gibron, Pro Football Hall of Fame, Canton, OH; David S. Neft et al., eds., *The Football Encyclopedia*, 2nd ed. (New York, 1994); *Official 1984 National Football League Record & Fact Book* (New York, 1984); Beau Riffenburgh, *The Official NFL Encyclopedia*, 4th ed. (New York, 1986).

Robert N. "Bob" Carroll

GILCHRIST, Carlton Chester "Cookie" (b. May 25, 1935, Brackenridge, PA), professional player, excelled as the most awesome runner in AFL history and remains among the few to perform well professionally without benefit of college experience. After starring at Har-Brack High School, he tried out with the Cleveland Browns (NFL) and was the last cut. Gilchrist then traveled to Canada, playing in the Ontario Rugby Football Union for the Sarnia Imperials and the Kitchener club.

Nicknamed "Cookie" because of his love of sweets as a child, the 6-foot-2½-inch, 252-pound Gilchrist starred in the CFL for the Hamilton Tiger-Cats in 1956 and 1957, Saskatchewan Roughriders in 1958, and Toronto Argonauts from 1959 to 1961. After having a dispute with Toronto management, he enjoyed three productive seasons with the Buffalo Bills (AFL).

Gilchrist in 1962 became the first AFL runner to surpass 1,000 yards, pacing the AFL in rushing with 1,096 yards. He averaged 5.1 yards on 214 carries, scored an AFL-leading 13 touchdowns, and caught 24 passes for 319 yards, being named All-AFL and AFL MVP. Injuries hampered Gilchrist the following season, but he still rushed for 979 yards on 232 carries, averaged 4.2 yards per carry, and scored 12 touchdowns. Against the New York Jets, Gilchrist set an AFL record by carrying for 243 yards. His yardage remains the fifth highest game total in professional football history. In 1964, he led the AFL with 981 yards on 230 attempts (4.3-yard average), caught 30 passes for 343 yards, and made All-AFL. During the AFL championship game, Gilchrist gained 122 yards on 16 carries and scored a touchdown to help the Bills defeat the San Diego Chargers, 20–7.

A dispute with coach Lou Saban prompted Buffalo to trade Gilchrist to the Denver Broncos (AFL). Despite running behind a weak line, he in 1965 gained 954 yards rushing on an AFL-record 252 carries, averaged 3.8 yards per carry, and was selected All-AFL. A salary dispute caused Gilchrist to announce his retirement. He joined the Miami Dolphins (AFL) in October 1966 overweight and out of shape, gaining just 262 yards in eight games. Miami sent Gilchrist back to Denver in 1967, but injuries limited him to only one game. His six-year AFL record included 4,293 yards rushing on 1,010 attempts (4.3-yard average) with 37 rushing touchdowns. He caught 110 passes for 1,135 yards and 6 touchdowns and scored 296 points.

The individualistic, colorful, outspoken Gilchrist often clashed with coaches and management but proved a tireless blockbusting runner with deceptive speed, an outstanding pass receiver, and superior blocker. Gilchrist married Gwendolyn Noreen Roan in 1957 and has two sons, Jeffrey and Scott. He resides in southeastern Pennsylvania.

BIBLIOGRAPHY: *Buffalo Bills Press, Radio, TV Guide*, 1964; Murray Olderman, *The Running Backs* (Englewood Cliffs, NJ, 1969); *TSN Pro Football Register*, 1966; Edwin Shrake, "Tough Cookie Marches to His Own Drummer," *SI* 21 (December 14, 1964), pp. 70–80.

                                                                 Edward J. Pavlick

GOLDENBERG, Charles R. "Buckets" (b. March 10, 1911, Odessa, Russia; d. April 16, 1986, Greendale, WI), college and professional athlete, came to the United States at age four with his family and settled in Milwaukee, WI. Goldenberg, an All-City halfback on the 1927 West Division High School city championship football team, enrolled at the University of Wisconsin (WC) and started for three years as a football blocking back from 1930 to 1932. The 1932 Badgers fielded a fine team with a 6–1–1 record, as Goldenberg received some All-America recognition.

In the pre-NFL draft days, the New York Giants (NFL) and Green Bay Packers (NFL) both sought Goldenberg's services. Green Bay's small size, friendliness, and close proximity to Milwaukee influenced him to join the Packers. During his first 3 NFL seasons, Goldenberg played fullback and linebacker behind the legendary Clarke Hinkle (FB). Since the 5-foot-10-inch 225-pounder possessed the build and speed of a guard, the Packers in 1936 moved him there, where Green Bay lacked quality players. Goldenberg remained pivotal in the interior of the Packer offensive and defensive lines until retiring in 1945. During his 13 NFL seasons, Green Bay captured four Western Division championships and three NFL titles. The 1939 Packers, believed the best of the prewar Green Bay teams, crushed the New York Giants, 27–0, in the NFL championship game. The Packers also defeated the Boston Redskins, 21–6, for the 1936 NFL title and the New York Giants, 14–7, for the 1944 NFL crown.

Goldenberg wrestled professionally during the off-season but eventually entered the restaurant business in both Green Bay and Milwaukee so that he would not have to travel. He stayed in the restaurant business following his retirement as an NFL player and served on the Packers' board of directors from 1953 to 1985. He and his wife Marian have two sons, Gary and Don. His honors included being named to the Packers Hall of Fame in 1971, the Packers "Iron Man Era" All-Time team in 1976, and the *Wisconsin State Journal* All-Time Wisconsin football team in 1985. The Green Bay B'nai B'rith Lodge named Goldenberg the "Outstanding Jewish Athlete of All Time" in 1969.

BIBLIOGRAPHY: Harold Claassen and Steve Boda, Jr., eds., *Ronald Encyclopedia of Football* (New York, 1963); Charles "Buckets" Goldenberg, clipping file, Green Bay Packers Hall of Fame, Green Bay, WI; Charles "Buckets" Goldenberg, clipping file, Pro Football Hall of Fame, Canton, OH; *Green Bay Packers Media Guide*, 1942, 1945; Beau Riffenburgh, *The Official NFL Encyclopedia*, 4th ed. (New York, 1986).

C. Robert Barnett

GREEN, John Frederic "Jack" (b. January 15, 1924, Republican Township, Jefferson County, IN; d. August 4, 1981, Nashville, TN), college athlete and football coach, was the son of Dewey Green and May Green in a family of 10 children and spent his childhood on the family farm in Jefferson County. He handled a newspaper route, served as a boy scout, mowed lawns, milked cows, and worked in his father's grocery store. Green, president of his high school class, made All-State in football as a quarterback. At Tulane University (SEC), he studied premedicine and became the first freshman to letter in football for the Green Wave.

The U.S. Military Academy in 1943 recruited Green, who became one of the finest guards to ever play football at West Point and was an outstanding NCAA heavyweight wrestler. The 5-foot-11-inch, 190-pound Green, a powerful lineman, excelled in the use of the head fake and stagger step and frequently knocked opponents off their feet. The outstanding blocker proved strong, quick, and mean on defense but was considered extremely nice off the field. Green played for the 1943 Army team as a plebe under coach Earl "Red" Blaik (FB), helping the Cadets to a 7–2–1 record. Army lost to the U.S. Naval Academy and the University of Notre Dame, tying the University of Pennsylvania. Green excelled both offensively and defensively on the 1944 and 1945 Army teams, ranked by many as the best two teams ever developed by the U.S. Military Academy. Both teams won national championships, being led by the blocking of Green and the running of Glenn Davis (FB) and Felix "Doc" Blanchard (FB). Both teams produced perfect 9–0–0 records, with the 1944 squad scoring 504 points and holding opponents to just five touchdowns. The 1945 team boasted the great backfield of Arnold Tucker (FB), Davis, Blanchard, and Thomas "Shorty" McWilliams. The Cadets, captained by Green, scored 412 points and held the opposition to 80 points. Army routed the University of Notre Dame, 59–0, in 1944 and 48–0 in 1945. Green, a consensus All-America in 1944 and 1945, later was elected to the NFF College Football Hall of Fame.

Following his graduation from West Point, Green remained on the football staff as an offensive or defensive line coach for Coach Blaik from 1947 through 1952. After leaving West Point, Green served as an assistant football coach at Tulane University (SEC) and the University of Florida (SEC). Green twice declined invitations to return to the academy, where he likely would have succeeded Blaik. He accepted the head football coaching position at Vanderbilt University (SEC) in 1963 and encountered little success with the Commodores. In four seasons from 1963 to 1966, his squads compiled a 7–29–4 win–loss record. In 1967, Green left coaching to join AVCO, an aircraft manufacturer in Nashville. In 1980, Green was under serious consideration for the athletic directorship at West Point when he was stricken with a brain tumor and underwent major surgery.

Green and his wife Jeanne had one daughter, Nancy, and two sons, David and Daniel.

BIBLIOGRAPHY: Army-Navy College Football Game Program, December 2, 1944; Army-Navy College Football Game Program, December 1, 1945; Earl H. Blaik, *The Red Blaik Story* (New Rochelle, NY, 1974); Darilynne Hatton, Registrar, Jefferson County, IN, Health Department, letter to John L. Evers, September 8, 1993; Henry E. Mattox, *Army Football in 1945* (Jefferson, NC, 1990); Nashville (TN) *Banner*, August 5, 1981, pp. C7, D1.

John L. Evers

GRIMM, Russell "Russ" (b. May 2, 1959, Scottdale, PA), college and professional player and coach, played in four Super Bowl games and five NFC Championship games as an offensive guard before retiring as an NFL player in 1992.

The son of Charles Grimm and Jane Grimm, he starred as an all-around athlete at Southmoreland High in Alverton, PA, and won three letters each in football, basketball, and track and field. An offensive quarterback and defensive linebacker as a two-way football player, he received All-State recognition for his defensive efforts. Grimm established the school career basketball scoring record and the one-game mark with 41 points. He also earned county scholar-athlete honors and was selected to the National Honor Society.

At the University of Pittsburgh, he lettered for three years from 1978 to 1980 and moved from offensive tackle to center his senior year. Although receiving some All-America Second and Third Team mention, the position change hurt his selection chances. He served as Panther cocaptain and was selected for the East-West Shrine and Japan Bowl games his senior year. He played for Pittsburgh in the loss to North Carolina State University in the 1978 Tangerine Bowl game, the victory over the University of Arizona in the 1979 Fiesta Bowl game, and the triumph over the University of South Carolina in the 1980 Gator Bowl game.

In the 1981 draft, the Washington Redskins (NFL) selected Grimm as their third-round draft choice and the sixty-ninth pick overall. The six-foot-three-inch 275-pounder played in 140 games for the Redskins from 1981 through 1991, being known for his strength and technical excellence. He played in the 1983 and 1986 Pro Bowls and was chosen to the *TSN* and other All-Pro teams in 1985. Grimm performed in the 27–17 victory over the Miami Dolphins in Super Bowl XVII in 1983, the 38–9 loss against the Los Angeles Raiders in Super Bowl XVIII in 1984, the 42–10 triumph over the Denver Broncos in Super Bowl XXII in 1988, and the 37–24 win over the Minnesota Vikings in Super Bowl XXVI in 1992. The Redskins appointed Grimm as assistant coach of tight ends and halfbacks in 1992.

BIBLIOGRAPHY: *TSN Pro Football Register*, 1992; *University of Pittsburgh Football Media Guides*, 1977–1981.

Robert B. Van Atta

HAMPTON, Daniel Oliver "Dan" "Danimal" (b. September 19, 1957, Oklahoma City, OK), college and professional player and sportscaster, moved with his family to Cabot, AR, at an early age and attended Jacksonville, AR, High School. After two years of playing band, Hampton tried out for football. As a junior, he started learning the game and taking it seriously. Hampton became a Prep All-America as a senior and earned a scholarship to the University of Arkansas (SWC).

At Arkansas, Hampton majored in business and earned many honors and awards. His senior accomplishments included being named to the All-America football team and being chosen the SWC's Defensive Player of the Year. A three-year starter, the six-foot-five-inch, 274-pound Hampton played in the Senior, Fiesta, Orange, and Cotton Bowls at Arkansas.

The Chicago Bears (NFL) chose Hampton in the first round of the 1979 draft. Hampton played 12 years for the Bears and received many awards, including being named All-Pro MVP in 1982 by *PFW*. In 1985, he starred as a defensive tackle on the Bears team, which defeated the New England Patriots, 46–10, in Super Bowl XX. The UPI selected him to the 1986 First Team All-NFL. Hampton also played in the NFC championship games following the 1984 and 1988 seasons and in the Pro Bowl after the 1980, 1982, 1984, and 1985 campaigns.

After 10 knee operations, Hampton retired from the Bears in 1990. Hampton, affectionately nicknamed "Danimal," became a color commentator for NBC Sports during the football season and played with a local Chicago band called the "Traffic Jam." A multitalented musician, Hampton plays the bass guitar, classical guitar, drums, saxophone, piano, and organ. He and his wife Terry live in Cabot, AR.

BIBLIOGRAPHY: *Chicago Bears Media Guide*, 1990, pp. 47–48; Richard Whittingham, *Bears in Their Own Words* (Chicago, IL, 1989), pp. 81–92.

Raymond C. Fetters

HARPSTER, Howard (b. May 14, 1907, Akron, OH; d. April 9, 1980, Pittsburgh, PA), college player and coach, starred at quarterback for Carnegie Institute of Technology from 1926 to 1928 and in 1926 helped engineer one of college football's greatest upsets. As a sophomore in 1926 under coach Walter Steffen (FB), the six-foot-one-inch, 160-pound athlete guided Carnegie Tech to a 7–2 overall mark and a stunning 26–0 upset over coach Knute Rockne's (FB) University of Notre Dame team. Rockne had anticipated certain victory and had ordered his assistant coach to start the second team while he scouted the Army-Navy game.

After a lackluster 5–4–1 1927 season, Carnegie Tech rebounded in 1928. As a senior team captain, Harpster made consensus All-America and led the sixth-ranked Tartans to a 7–1 overall mark. Carnegie Tech defeated Notre Dame, 28–0, in the final game played at Cartier Field in South Bend, IN, and upset the University of Pittsburgh. The Tartans' loss to powerful NYU, however, brought Harpster the most attention, as he completed a then-amazing 20 passes. Grantland Rice (OS) wrote, "He completed more passes than I have seen all year [from many major university teams combined]." According to Rice, Harpster "tied up NYU with the speed, deception, and accuracy of his passing game," "ran and kicked exceptionally well," and "intercepted two long passes on defense." Harpster was named to the All-Time

East team after directing his squad in December 1928 to a 20–0 victory in the East-West Shrine game.

Harpster served as head coach at Carnegie Tech from 1933 through 1936, producing a lackluster 12–19–3 record. Under Harpster, the Tartans struggled to 4–3–2 in 1933, 4–5 in 1934, 2–5–1 in 1935, and 2–6 in 1936. Victories over Notre Dame, Temple University, NYU, and Purdue University and ties with Pittsburgh and Michigan State University highlighted his coaching tenure. Harpster was named in 1958 as one of two quarterbacks on Carnegie's All-Time football team and was inducted into both the HAF and NFF College Football Halls of Fame.

BIBLIOGRAPHY: *Carnegie-Mellon University Football Media Guides;* Chet Smith and Marty Wolfson, *Greater Pittsburgh History of Sports* (Pittsburgh, PA, 1969); James D. Whalen, letter to David L. Porter, March 21, 1994.

Robert B. Van Atta

HAYNES, Michael James "Mike" (b. July 1, 1953, Denison, TX), college and professional player, grew up in Los Angeles, CA, where he attended John Marshall High School. Haynes, who lettered in football and track and field, captained the football squad his senior year and was voted Athlete of the Year. He did not attend college immediately following his high school graduation but took a job as a shipping clerk. In 1972, Arizona State University (WAC) gave Haynes a football scholarship. The six-foot-two-inch, 195-pound Haynes was selected an All-America defensive back as a junior and senior. The nation's top defensive back, he played under coach Frank Kush (FB) and earned All-WAC honors as a safety and kick returner three consecutive seasons. Haynes played in the Fiesta Bowl in 1973 and 1975, earning MVP honors in the Sun Devils' 1973 triumph over the University of Pittsburgh, 28–7. In 1975, Arizona State defeated the University of Nebraska, 17–14. Following the 1975 season, Haynes garnered MVP defensive honors in the Japan Bowl. Haynes, the Sun Devils' football captain his senior year, lettered twice in track and field. He captured the WAC championship in the long jump, with a career best leap of 25 feet 7 inches.

The New England Patriots (NFL) selected Haynes in the first round of the 1976 draft as the fifth player overall. A cornerback and kick returner for the Patriots from 1976 through 1982, Haynes established seven new club punt return records his rookie season. He paced the AFC and finished second in the NFL in punt returns with 45 returns for 608 yards (13.5-yard average). Two returns resulted in 89- and 62-yard touchdowns. His rookie season honors included making his first Pro Bowl appearance, winning the Bert Bell Award, and being named the *TSN* AFC Rookie of the Year. Haynes, the Patriots' top interceptor from 1976 through 1978, became the club's all-time punt returner with 111 returns for 1,159 yards (10.44-yard average) and two touchdowns. He became the first player in Patriot history to return a punt for a touchdown with his 89-yard scamper against the Buffalo Bills (NFL) on November 7, 1976.

In 1983, Haynes became a free agent holdout with the Patriots due to a contract dispute. Following a trade that was voided and a suit against the NFL, he signed with the Los Angeles Raiders (NFL) in March 1983 for two high draft choices. Haynes, a cornerback for the Raiders from 1983 until his retirement from football following the 1989 season, helped lead the Raiders to a 38–9 triumph over the Washington Redskins in Super Bowl XVIII. Redskin quarterback Joe Theismann (FB) was frustrated by the strong defensive coverage of Haynes and teammate Lester Hayes. They allowed wide receivers Charlie Brown and Art Monk* only four catches altogether. Haynes paced the NFL in interception return yardage (220 yards) in 1984, making the *TSN* NFL All-Star team in 1984 and 1985. He appeared in the Pro Bowl following the 1976 through 1980, 1982, 1985, and 1986 seasons and made the Pro Bowl team in 1984 but did not play. In 14 NFL seasons between 1976 and 1989, Haynes intercepted 46 passes for 688 yards (15.0-yard average) and two touchdowns and returned 112 punts for 1,168 yards (10.2-yard average) and two touchdowns in 177 regular season games. He also returned a blocked field goal 65 yards for a touchdown. In 1994 a panel of NFL and Pro Football officials, former players, and reporters named him one of four cornerbacks on the NFL All-Time Team.

Haynes received a bachelor's degree in business administration from Arizona in 1982 and has worked in the off-season as an investment analyst. His brother Reggie played tight end for the Washington Redskins (NFL) in 1978. Haynes and his wife Julie were married in 1977 and have three children, Vanessa, Jared, and Aaron.

BIBLIOGRAPHY: *Los Angeles Raiders Media Guide*, 1984; *New England Patriots Media Guide*, 1982; Rick Telander, "He's Got 'Em Cornered," *SI* 61 (September 24, 1984), pp. 38–40ff; *TSN Pro Football Register*, 1990.

John L. Evers

HENNIGAN, Charles Taylor "Charlie" "The Horse" (b. March 19, 1935, Bienville, LA), college and professional player, is the son of Roland Hennigan, a former deputy sheriff of Webster Parish, LA, and Laura (Taylor) Hennigan. Doctors informed Hennigan at age 11 that he would never participate in athletics due to a tubercular condition. This advice gave Hennigan the motivation to excel in his athletic endeavors. He participated in football, basketball, and track and field at Minden, LA, High School, making All-North Louisiana at end in football and twice winning the state 880-yard run title.

Hennigan began his collegiate athletic career in track and field at Louisiana State University (SEC). As a freshman, he ran on LSU's winning mile relay team in the SEC championship meet.

Hennigan transferred to Northwestern State University (GSC) in Natch-itoches, LA. Hennigan played halfback, lettering from 1955 to 1957 and cocaptaining as a senior. Nicknamed "The Horse" or "Hoss," he primarily blocked for future Houston Oiler teammate Charley Tolar. As a senior, however, he scored five rushing touchdowns and caught 12 passes for 143 yards. Northwestern State finished 1957 with a 7–2 record, tying for the GSC championship. The AP and LSWA both named Hennigan to their All-GSC teams.

Hennigan also lettered in track and field, serving as cocaptain in 1957 and 1958. Northwestern State won the GSC track championship in both 1956 and 1957. Hennigan won the 440-yard run in the GSC championship meet three straight years, and fared well in the 100-yard, 220-yard, and 880-yard events; he also anchored the 880-yard and mile relays. Hennigan set GSC records in the 440- (47.2 seconds) and 880- (1:54.2) yard runs and was named All-GSC for three years.

After completing his bachelor's degree in physical education in 1958, Hennigan taught biology at Jonesboro-Hodge High School. "Red" Conkright signed him to a professional contract with the newly formed Houston Oilers (AFL) in 1959. Hennigan possessed great speed, but his sub-par catching ability hampered his efforts to make the Oilers. End coach Mac Speedie (FB) convinced Oiler head coach Lou Rymkus* to keep Hennigan, who caught 44 passes for six touchdowns in 1960 to help the Oilers capture the initial AFL championship.

In 1961, Hennigan caught 82 passes for 12 touchdowns and set a professional record for reception yardage (1,746). The Oilers won their second consecutive AFL championship, with quarterback George Blanda (FB). Hennigan's productivity continued in 1962 and 1963 with 54 and 61 catches, respectively. His greatest AFL season came in 1964. Due to a weak running game, the Oilers relied primarily on passing. Hennigan gathered a record 101 passes for 1,561 yards.

A knee injury limited Hennigan to 41 receptions in 1965 and only 27 in 1966. Houston traded him to the San Diego Chargers (AFL), but he retired instead. In his seven-year AFL career, Hennigan caught 410 passes, gained 6,838 yards receiving, and scored 51 touchdowns. He gained over 100 yards receiving in 26 games and gained over 200 yards in 4 games, making five straight AFL All-Star teams and four All-AFL squads.

His honors include induction into the Louisiana Sports Hall of Fame, the Northwestern Louisiana State Hall of Fame, and the Ark-La-Tex Track and Field Hall of Fame and selection to the Houston Oilers' 30th Anniversary Dream Team.

Hennigan completed a doctorate in education at the University of Houston in 1967 and worked with the Louisiana Department of Education, Mc-Graw-Hill Publishing, and Success Motivation Institute, and taught school in Minden, LA. The Woodlands, TX, resident operates the Hennigan Institute, an educational and treatment center for troubled youth near Houston.

Hennigan married Pamela Kay Lassiter on February 22, 1975, and has seven children, Charles, Jr., Steve, James, Taylor, Jordan, Shalom, and Faith.

BIBLIOGRAPHY: Jerry Byrd, *Louisiana Sports Legends* (Natchitoches, LA, 1992); John Hillman, telephone interview with Charlie Hennigan, May 16, 1993; Northwestern State University, *Potpourri* (Natchitoches, LA, 1956–1958); Edwin Shrake, "The Flanker Who Catches Too Many Passes," *SI* 23 (September 20, 1965), pp. 109–111; Bill Wise, ed., *1965 Official Pro Football Almanac* (Greenwich, CT, 1965).

John Hillman

HIGGINS, Robert A. "Bob" (b. December 24, 1893, Corning, NY; d. June 6, 1969, Bellefonte, PA), college athlete and coach, excelled as an All-America end and football coach at Pennsylvania State University. Several major universities recruited Higgins, a schoolboy star athlete at Peddie School in New Jersey, but he chose instead to go to Penn State, where he participated in baseball, boxing, wrestling, and track and field (the pole vault and the pentathalon) and won most acclaim as a star end in football.

He played football from 1914 to 1916 and was selected by Walter Camp (FB) as a Second Team All-America in 1915. He was chosen captain-elect for 1917 but instead entered the U.S. Army and rose to captain in the infantry. He missed the entire 1918 intercollegiate season but was an All-Star in the American Expeditionary Force football league after the Armistice. In 1919 he returned to Penn State, captaining the football team and being selected an All-America end. In Higgins's four seasons of play, Penn State enjoyed a 28–8–1 record.

Higgins, a strong, wiry Irishman, starred as a hard-charging defensive end, an excellent blocker, and an outstanding punter. He was also a sure-handed pass receiver, possessing the speed to make long runs after catches. He came to the fore in big games such as Penn State's 20–0 upset of traditional rival University of Pittsburgh in 1919.

He received his B.A. degree in liberal arts in 1920 and then coached football at West Virginia Wesleyan later that year. He then played for two seasons with the Canton Bulldogs of the fledgling NFL before returning to coaching at West Virginia Wesleyan from 1922 to 1924. After leading his team to a 9–7 bowl game victory over SMU on January 1, 1925, he coached Washington University of St. Louis to a composite record of 8 wins, 13 defeats and 3 ties from 1925 to 1927 before returning to Penn State as an assistant football coach in 1928 and becoming head coach in 1930.

His teams had losing records in his first seven seasons at Penn State partly because the institution, reacting to the famous 1929 Carnegie report on intercollegiate football problems, eliminated athletic scholarships. Higgins consequently did not have a winning record until 1937 and, to the disgust of alumni and students, lost numerous games to traditional rivals. From 1939 through 1948, however, Higgins's teams achieved an impressive record of 62 wins, 17 losses, and 4 ties and brought Penn State to prominence as a national football power. His overall coaching record from 1920 through 1948 was 123 victories, 80 losses, and 17 ties.

The development of his undefeated 1947 team, which was ranked fourth nationally and tied SMU, led by All-America Doak Walker, in the Cotton Bowl, marked Higgins's greatest achievement. The Cotton Bowl game held added significance because Penn State fielded the first African-American players to compete in that contest. Unable to find hotel accommodations for the African-American players in Dallas, Higgins housed his team in a nearby naval air station. The action displeased some of his players who were World War II veterans, but the game was played without incident. Penn State's 1948 team, which finished with a 7–1–1 win–loss record, did not get a bowl bid. Higgins then gave up coaching in early 1949 because of a long-standing heart ailment.

Strict about his players' decorum on and off the field, the "stately gentleman" Higgins was devoted to his wife Virginia and his three daughters, Mary Ann, Virginia, and Nancy. He was respected by his players as a sound teacher of football. He insisted on employing the older single wing offensive formation and consequently developed numerous outstanding running backs. But he was best known for his teams' rugged defense. In the record-setting 1947 season, Penn State led the nation defensively while allowing a meager 76.8 yards per game. The Nittany Lions also held opponents to the lowest average yards per rush (an amazing 0.64 yards), surrendered an average of only three points per game, allowed the fewest yards per game (17.0), and set a record for permitting the fewest yards in a single game (a *minus* 47 yards against Syracuse University). Several of his players were mentioned for postseason honors, with his greatest being guard Steve Suhey. Suhey, also Higgins's future son-in-law, subsequently was elected to the NFF College Football Hall of Fame. Higgins was elected as a coach to the same Hall of Fame in 1954.

BIBLIOGRAPHY: L. H. Baker, *Football: Facts and Figures* (New York, 1945); John D. McCallum and Charles H. Pearson, *College Football U.S.A., 1869–1973* (New York, 1973); *NYT*, June 7, 1969, p. 35; Tom Perrin, *Football: A College History* (Jefferson, NC, 1987); Ridge Riley, *Road to Number One* (Garden City, NY, 1977); Sports Information and Alumni Offices, Pennsylvania State University, University Park, PA; Alexander M. Weyand, *The Saga of American Football* (New York, 1955).

Daniel R. Gilbert

HILL, Drew (b. October 5, 1956, Newman, GA), college and professional player, retired after the 1993 season as the eleventh all-time leading receiver in NFL history. He made 634 receptions for 9,831 yards, with his 13,337 combined yards ranking him fifteenth on the NFL all-time list. He appeared in 28 games with over 100 yards receiving.

Hill starred in football at Newman High School, just south of Atlanta, GA, and enjoyed an outstanding football career at Georgia Institute of Technology, where he earned a bachelor's degree in industrial management in 1981. At Georgia Tech, the kickoff return specialist led the nation his senior year in 1978 in kickoff return yardage with 570 yards on 19 kickoff returns and two touchdowns. His Georgia Tech career included 84 kickoff returns for 2,361 yards and a 28.1-yard career return average. Georgia Tech finished 4–6–1 in 1976, 6–5–0 in 1977, and 7–5–0 in 1978, losing to Purdue University, 41–21, in the Peach Bowl.

His NFL career spanned from 1979 through 1992. He played 6 seasons with the Los Angeles Rams (NFL), although confined to the injured reserve during the 1983 season. The five-foot-nine-inch, 172-pound Hill then spent 7 seasons with the Houston Oilers (NFL) and the 1992–1993 campaign with the Atlanta Falcons (NFL). His 60 kickoff returns for the Rams in 1981 remains an NFL record. During his 14 NFL seasons, he returned kicks for 3,487 yards and one touchdown. Of his 634 pass receptions, 60 resulted in touchdowns. Hill gained 9,831 yards receiving, averaging 15.5 yards per catch. He played in Super Bowl XIV in 1980 with the Rams against the Pittsburgh Steelers and was named to the Pro Bowl in 1988 and 1990.

BIBLIOGRAPHY: Atlanta Falcons, Sports Information Department, Atlanta, GA; Los Angeles *Times*, 1979–1984; *TSN Pro Football Register*, 1994.

Allan Hall

HILLEBRAND, Arthur Rudolph Thomas "Doc" "Art" (b. March 9, 1877, Freeport, IL; d. December 14, 1941, Corvallis, OR), college athlete and coach, excelled as a two-time football All-America tackle at Princeton University (IvL) and was elected in 1970 to the NFF College Football Hall of Fame. In 1912, sportswriter Jack Kofoed selected Hillebrand on the All-Time All-America team, published in the Philadelphia (PA) *Record*. Hillebrand, who captained the football varsity in 1898, played four seasons from 1896 to 1899 on Tiger elevens, amassing a 43–2–2 composite record. During that span, Princeton finished undefeated twice, humbled Yale University three times, and won or shared three national championships.

Hillebrand's father, surgeon Christian M. Hillebrand, was born in Lippe Detmold, Germany, while his mother, Caroline (Wenzell) Hillebrand, taught piano at Normal College of Missouri. Hillebrand starred in football and baseball at Phillips Andover Preparatory School, graduating in 1896. He enrolled at Princeton the same year and immediately joined the celebrated Tiger line, which included NFF College Football Hall of Famers Garrett Cochran at end and Bill Edwards at guard, plus All-Americas William Church at tackle and center Robert Gailey. Edwards, an 1899 captain who played next to Hillebrand four years, recalled, "He was a fine, supple athlete, as gentle as a lamb but full of fury in a football game." The six-foot, 190-

pound Hillebrand proved a powerful ballcarrier in the tackle back era but also excelled at blocking technique and conversion kicking.

Hillebrand pitched four seasons for the Princeton baseball team, helping the Tigers win Big Three titles in 1897, 1899, and 1900 and once striking out three Yale batters on 10 pitches with the bases loaded. A good hitter, he boasted season batting averages of .305, .250, .364, and .343 and captained the nine his final season. He served as sophomore class president and majored in geology, earning a Bachelor of Arts degree from Princeton in 1900.

Hillebrand coached football in 1901 and 1902 at Penn Charter School, guided the U.S. Naval Academy baseball team one year, and mentored the football and baseball teams at Princeton from 1903 to 1905. The Tiger gridders compiled a combined 27–4–0 record and won the 1903 national championship. Hillebrand, a bachelor, farmed stock near Webster, SD. During a visit to his brother's farm in Oregon, he, his sister-in-law, and nephew died tragically in a house fire. Princeton classmates erected a tablet to his memory in Osborn Field House.

BIBLIOGRAPHY: Allison Danzig, *The History of American Football* (Englewood Cliffs, NJ, 1956); Jay Dunn, *The Tigers of Princeton* (Huntsville, AL, 1977); William H. Edwards, *Football Days* (New York, 1916); Ronald L. Mendell and Timothy B. Phares, *Who's Who in Football* (New Rochelle, NY, 1974); Seeley G. Mudd Manuscript Library, Princeton University, letter to James Whalen, April 3, 1993; Frank Presbrey and James Moffatt, *Athletics at Princeton* (New York, 1901).

James D. Whalen

HITCHCOCK, James Franklin Jr. "Jimmy" (b. June 28, 1911, Inverness, AL; d. June 24, 1959, Montgomery, AL), athlete, coach, and official, was the son of James Franklin Hitchcock, a farmer and circuit court clerk, and Sallie (Davis) Hitchcock and had five brothers and two sisters. One brother, Billy, also played college football and major league baseball and served as SA president in minor league baseball. "Jimmy" attended several high schools in Alabama and Florida, where he starred in football, basketball, and baseball. He graduated in 1933 from Auburn University (SC), earning three letters each in football and baseball and captaining the 1932 football and 1933 baseball teams. The 5-foot-11-inch 170-pounder, a triple threat tailback, led the Southeast in scoring in 1932. Auburn finished 1932 undefeated and outscored its opponents, 274–48. Hitchcock punted 232 times without a kick being blocked and was selected Auburn's first football All-America in 1932. In 1933, he signed a professional baseball contract with the New York Yankees (AL). Hitchcock played infield in the minor leagues for eight years and in 1938 performed with the Boston Braves (NL), batting only .171. He served as an assistant football coach at Auburn from 1933 to 1941 and coached the baseball team in 1941 and 1942.

Hitchcock served in the U.S. Navy from 1942 to 1945, being discharged as a lieutenant senior grade. In 1946, he managed the Opelika, AL, Owls, a

GAL minor league team. Hitchcock was elected to the Alabama Public Service Commission in 1946 and served until his death. He officiated football in the SEC and originated the Dixie Youth Baseball Program in Montgomery, AL. The Jimmy Hitchcock Memorial Award was established in 1961 to recognize the Outstanding Senior High School Student in Montgomery.

Hitchcock married Dorothy Shawkey and had two sons, Bobbie and Jimmy. His honors included induction into the NFF College Football Hall of Fame in 1955 and selection for the Alabama Sports Hall of Fame in 1969.

BIBLIOGRAPHY: Auburn University Sports Information Archives, Auburn, AL; Robert T. Bowen, letters to and interview with Billy Hitchcock, January 10–18, 1993; John D. McCullum, *Southeastern Conference Football* (New York, 1980).

Robert T. Bowen, Jr.

HOERNSCHEMEYER, Robert James "Bob" "Hunchy" (b. September 24, 1925, Cincinnati, OH; d. June 18, 1980, Detroit, MI), college athlete and professional football player, was the son of William A. J. Hoernschemeyer and Emma M. Byrnes (Delaney) Hoernschemeyer. His father operated an Ice, Coal, and Hauling business and died when Bob was attending eighth grade. He graduated from Cincinnati's Elder High School, starring in football, baseball, and basketball.

The husky, 5-foot-11-inch, 192-pound Hoernschemeyer played football and baseball at Indiana University (BNC). As a freshman tailback in 1943 under coach Alvin "Bo" McMillan (FB), he led the nation in total offense with 1,648 yards (1,133 passing and 515 rushing) and was selected to the All-BNC team. Against the University of Nebraska, he set NCAA freshman records with six touchdown passes and 458 total yards. Although handling the ball less in 1944, he still finished sixth nationally with 1,103 total offense yards (722 passing and 291 rushing). He entered the U.S. Navy and played T-formation quarterback in football for the U.S. Naval Academy in 1945.

The versatile Hoernschemeyer starred as a single wing tailback for the Chicago Rockets/Hornets (AAFC) in 1946, 1947, and 1949 and the Brooklyn Dodgers (AAFC) in 1947 and 1948 and served as T-formation halfback for the Detroit Lions (NFL) from 1950 to 1955. In 10 professional seasons, he rushed for 4,548 yards on 1,059 carries (4.3-yard average) and 27 touchdowns, passed 4,302 yards with 319 completions in 714 attempts for 42 touchdowns, caught 109 passes for 1,139 yards and 11 touchdowns, and scored 234 points. His honors included being named *TSN* All-NFL in 1952 and 1953.

Hoernschemeyer's best season passing came in 1946, when he completed 95 of 193 passes (49.2 percent) for 1,266 yards and 14 touchdowns and finished third in the AAFC in total offense with 1,644 yards. In 1947, he gained 705 yards rushing on 152 carries (4.3-yard average) and scored 6 touchdowns. Four years later, he rushed for 678 yards (5.3-yard average) and caught 23 passes for 263 yards. Hoernschemeyer played on NFL championship Detroit teams under coach Raymond "Buddy" Parker (FB) in 1952 and 1953. Against the New York Yanks on November 23, 1950, he ran 96 yards from scrimmage for a touchdown and gained 198 yards rushing.

After a shoulder injury ended his career, Hoernschemeyer opened a bar, the Lion's Den, in Detroit and then worked as a design coordinator for the Ford Motor Company. He married Marybelle Groene of Cincinnati in 1947 and had four children, Robert, Dianne, Mary Ann, and Sue Ann. Hoernschemeyer, a great all-around back, was considered the first option passer halfback from the T-formation and was elected to the Indiana University and Michigan Sports Halls of Fame.

BIBLIOGRAPHY: *AAFC Record Manual*, 1947; Detroit (MI) *News*, June 18, 1980; William J. Hoernschemeyer, letter to Edward J. Pavlick, June 1993; Indiana University Sports Information Office, Bloomington, IN; *NCAA Football Guides*, 1944, 1945; Murray Olderman, *The Running Backs* (Englewood Cliffs, NJ, 1969); *TSN Pro Football Register*, 1966.

Edward J. Pavlick

HORRELL, Edwin Chilion "Babe" (b. September 29, 1902, Jackson, MO), college player and coach, played center on two University of California PCC championship football teams and one second-place club. His Golden Bears amassed a composite 26–0–3 record from 1922 to 1924. Horrell, who received some All-America mention as a junior, captained the 1924 Golden Bears and was selected consensus All-America on coach Andy Smith's (FB) last of five undefeated Wonder Teams. Horrell, a member of the HAF Hall of Fame, was elected to the NFF College Football Hall of Fame in 1969 and was named on the All-Time PCC Second Team, chosen in 1948 by West Coast sports editors.

Horrell, called "Babe" as the youngest of 10 children, grew up in Pasadena, CA, where he graduated from Pasadena High School in 1921. The senior class president captained the football and tennis teams and starred in basketball, track and field, swimming, and water polo. The Pasadena High School Stadium subsequently was named Horrell Field in honor of the four Horrell brothers.

The six-foot-two-inch, 200-pound Horrell in 1923 helped California defeat Stanford University, 9–0, by blocking Ernie Nevers's (FB) punt and carrying it for a touchdown and by downing a Stanford back for a safety. He recovered a blocked University of Washington punt in 1924, enabling California to tie the Huskies, 7–7. He also led the Golden Bears to an historic 20–20 tie against undefeated Stanford and a triumph over undefeated University of Pennsylvania. Horrell, who earned a B.S. degree in business administration from California in 1925, was elected permanent class president. He recovered three fumbles for the West in the 1925 East-West Shrine game, outplaying legendary center Ed Garbisch (FB), and in 1950 was named to the West All-Time Second Team. Coach Smith boasted, "He's the best football center I have ever seen."

Horrell married Winifred Martin, a University of California graduate, in 1926 and had one son and two daughters. He joined a Los Angeles, CA, insurance firm and worked as volunteer football coach at UCLA until 1931, when he was hired as full-time assistant under coach Bill Spaulding. Horrell served as head mentor of the Bruins from 1939 to 1944, compiling a combined 24–31–6 record. He guided UCLA the first season to a PCC cochampionship and seventh-place AP rating and in 1942 to an outright title, thirteenth-place national ranking, and 9–0 Rose Bowl loss to University of Georgia. His players included halfbacks Kenny Washington (FB), Jackie Robinson (BB), and Al Solari, end Woody Strode, and quarterback Bob Waterfield (FB). The dignified, sincere Horrell never smoked or drank and exercised by playing tennis and handball. He owned real estate, remained active in the fruit packing industry, and maintained an interest in two golf courses.

BIBLIOGRAPHY: Dr. L. H. Baker, *Football: Facts and Figures* (New York, 1945); S. Dan Brodie, *66 Years on the California Gridiron* (Oakland, CA, 1949); California–Pennsylvania Football Game Program, Berkeley, CA, January 1, 1925; John D. McCallum and Charles H. Pearson, *College Football U.S.A. 1869–1973* (New York, 1973); Ronald L. Mendell and Timothy B. Phares, *Who's Who in Football* (New Rochelle, NY, 1974); Brick Morse, *California Football History* (Berkeley, CA, 1937); Rose Bowl Football Game Program, Pasadena, CA, January 1, 1943; John Sullivan, *The Big Game* (West Point, NY, 1982); Hendrik Van Leuven, *Touchdown UCLA* (Huntsville, AL, 1982).

James D. Whalen

HOWARD, Desmond Kevin (b. May 15, 1970, Cleveland, OH), college and professional player, is the son of J. D. Howard, a tool and die maker, and Hattie Howard-Dawkins. Desmond's parents divorced when he was age 13, and he lived with his father after that. A two-way player at tailback and safety, Howard led St. Joseph High School in Cleveland to the state football semifinals in both his junior and senior seasons. He received All-State and All-America recognition in football in 1987 and played point guard on the basketball team, which made the state finals his junior year. Howard earned three letters each in football and track and field and one in basketball.

Howard attended the University of Michigan (BTC) from 1988 to 1992, earning a bachelor's degree in communications in 1992. As a freshman, he was redshirted in football and did not see action. During the 1989 season, the five-foot-nine-inch, 170-pound wide receiver, who possessed 4.3-second speed in the 40-yard dash, led the Wolverines in kickoff returns with 295 yards on 13 attempts. He caught nine passes for 136 yards and two touchdowns and rushed five times for 11 yards. The second touchdown reception of his career came from quarterback Elvis Grbac, his high school teammate.

The Wolverines registered a 10–2 record but lost 17–10 to the University of Southern California in the Rose Bowl. Michigan compiled a 9–3 record in 1990 and defeated the University of Mississippi, 35–3, in the Gator Bowl, as Howard enjoyed a phenomenal season. He was named All-BTC, setting a single-season Wolverine record with 504 yards on kickoff returns and establishing a single-game mark with 135 yards against Michigan State University. Howard led the Wolverines in receptions (63), receiving yards (1,025), touchdown catches (11), and all-purpose yardage (1,642) and also paced the BTC with 78.0 yards receiving per game and in kickoff return yards with 29.5 yards per return. His achievements included registering the second-best single-season totals in Michigan football history in receptions, receiving yardage, and touchdown catches. He enjoyed seven games with 75-plus yards receiving, tying the Wolverine single-season record, and finished second in team scoring with 72 points. Howard caught touchdown passes of 63 and 50 yards against Mississippi in the Gator Bowl, eclipsing the Wolverines' single-game bowl record of 141 yards receiving with his 167-yard performance.

In Howard's final season at Michigan in 1991, the Wolverines compiled a 10–2 record and lost, 34–14, in the Rose Bowl to the University of Washington. His incredible season featured winning the Heisman Trophy, Maxwell Award, and All-America, Player of the Year, and All-BTC honors. Howard, the first BTC receiver to lead the BTC in scoring, also led the BTC in punt returns (17.4 yards per return) and receiving (5.5 receptions per game). On the all-time Michigan football list, Howard ranks second in career receptions (134), kick return yards (1,548), touchdowns (37), and punt return average (14.0), third in career receiving yardage (2,146), and first in career kickoff return average (26.9). He remains first in single-season receiving touchdowns (19) and second in career receiving touchdowns (32) in both Michigan and BTC history. He holds the Wolverine single-season scoring record with 138 points, breaking the standard of 117 points set by Tommy Harmon (FB) in 1940. His 23 touchdowns in 1991 marked the most ever by a Wolverine in a single season.

Howard's 93-yard punt return for a touchdown against Ohio State University also broke the Wolverine record. He caught at least 1 touchdown pass in each of the season's first 10 games, tying the NCAA record for most games in a single season with a touchdown catch and the NCAA record for most consecutive contests with at least 1 touchdown reception. Howard remains tied for second on the NCAA single-season touchdown reception list with 19. His 1-yard touchdown pass reception from Grbac against the University of Illinois enabled him to tie the NCAA single-season mark for most touchdown passes for the same passer and receiver (19) and set the NCAA standard for most touchdowns thrown from the same passer to the same receiver in a career (31).

The Washington Redskins selected Howard in the first round as the fourth pick overall in the 1992 NFL draft. He was used primarily as a kick return specialist in 1992, returning 22 kickoffs for 462 yards and six punts for 84 yards and one touchdown. He made three pass receptions for 20 yards and rushed three times for 14 yards. In 1993, Howard caught 23 passes for 286 yards (12.4-yard average) and returned 21 kickoffs for 405 yards (19.3-yard average). The following season, he grabbed 40 aerials for 727 yards and 5 touchdowns. In February 1995, the Jacksonville Jaguars (NFL) selected Howard in the expansion draft.

BIBLIOGRAPHY: Sally Jenkins, "And How!" *SI* 75 (September 23, 1991), pp. 14–19; Sally Jenkins, "In His Grasp," *SI* 75 (December 9, 1991), pp. 90–94; *Michigan Football*, 1992; *1992 NCAA Football*; *TSN Pro Football Register*, 1994.

John L. Evers

HUMBLE, Weldon Gaston "Hum" (b. April 4, 1921, Nixon, TX), college and professional player, is the son of Collie Humble and Lenora Humble and lived on a farm in Gonzales County, TX, until age 13. His father then left farming to work in a San Antonio, TX, furniture store.

Humble did not play organized sports until the move. At San Antonio Brackenridge High School, Humble lettered in football, basketball, swimming, and track and field. The fullback and end received football scholarship offers from the University of Texas, Texas A&M University, Tulane University, and the University of Southern California, but Rice University recruiters persuaded him to sign in 1940.

Humble played one game at end for Rice in 1941 but was moved to offensive guard to replace an injured starter. His guard play earned him All-SWC honors in 1942. The six-foot-two-inch, 208-pound Humble also played some on defense to take advantage of his quickness and intelligence. Rice University compiled winning records in both 1941 and 1942—6–3–1 in 1941 and 7–2–1 in 1942. After the 1942 season, Humble left Rice to enlist in the U.S. Marines. He served in the 2nd Marine Division and participated in the invasion of Okinawa. He was discharged in 1946 with the rank of first lieutenant and returned to Rice to play his senior season of football. Humble's Marine Corps years did not diminish his playing ability, while his added maturity helped him garner All-SWC and All-America honors in 1946. Rice University finished the 1946 season, 8–2, defeating the University of Tennessee, 8–0, in the 1947 Cotton Bowl.

The Baltimore Colts (AAFC) originally drafted Humble and traded him to the Cleveland Browns (AAFC) prior to the 1947 season. An offensive guard and defensive linebacker, he played on three straight AAFC championship squads from 1947 to 1949. The Browns merged with the NFL in 1950 and astonished the professional football world by winning the NFL championship in their first season.

Humble, still a member of the U.S. Marine Corps Reserve, was recalled to active duty in 1951. The Marines stationed Humble at the Quantico, VA,

Training Station, where he played football for its service team. After being named Service Player of the Year in 1951, he was discharged in 1952 with the rank of captain. Cleveland traded Humble to a new NFL franchise, the Dallas Texans, in 1952. The Texans, one of the worst teams in NFL history, triumphed only once in their lone season. Humble retired from professional football after the 1952 season.

Humble's honors include membership in the Texas Sports Hall of Fame and the NFF College Football Hall of Fame. *TF* magazine named Humble as one of three guards on their All-SWC team from 1920 to 1970.

Subsequently, Humble worked as a vice president for First City National Bank in Houston, TX. He also owned and operated an office supply and furniture company and served on the Harris County Tax Review Board. Humble married Lorraine Merritt on November 18, 1944, and has three children, Weldon II, Lorraine, and Jim.

BIBLIOGRAPHY: Dave Campbell, *The Best of Dave Campbell's Texas Football* (Dallas, TX, 1989); Thomas Hopwood, *Great Texans in Sports* (Fort Worth, TX, 1975); Weldon Humble, letter to John Hillman, May 1993; Ronald Mendell and Timothy Phares, *Who's Who in Football* (New Rochelle, NY, 1974); Kern Tips, *Football—Texas Style* (New York, 1964).

John Hillman

JACOBSON, Larry Paul "Jake" (b. December 10, 1949, Sioux Falls, SD), college and professional player, graduated from O'Gorman High School as an All-State football player and enrolled at the University of Nebraska (BEC) in 1971. His Cornhusker football career culminated in 1971, when his squad compiled a 13–0 record and joined football lore as one of the century's greatest collegiate teams.

As a defensive end, the huge six-foot-six-inch, 260-pound Jacobson represented a prototype of the modern pass rusher. Jacobson stood tall enough that passing quarterbacks could not see over him and possessed such quickness that shorter, bulkier linemen had difficulty blocking him. He helped launch an era of college defensive linemen who specialized in confusing, harassing, and tackling for lost yardage quarterbacks attempting pass plays.

The 1971 Nebraska squad, coached by Bob Devaney (FB), overwhelmed 13 opponents with an offense that scored 507 points and averaged 39 points per game and a Jacobson-led defense that allowed a mere 104 points or only 8 points per game. Jacobson and his fellow All-America linemen Willie Harper (S) and Rich Glover (S) arguably formed the best college defensive line of the modern era. Only three opponents scored over one touchdown against the Cornhuskers. Nebraska handed the University of Oklahoma its only season loss, 35–31, before 55 million television viewers, the largest audience for a college football game. In the 1972 Orange Bowl, the Nebraska squad held coach Paul "Bear" Bryant's (FB) University of Alabama Crimson Tide to one touchdown while winning, 38–6, and inflicting the worst defeat ever for a Bryant-coached Alabama team. Nebraska defeated teams ranked second, third, and fourth in the AP poll by an average of 20 points.

Jacobson in 1971 was named All-BEC and consensus All-America and became the first Nebraska player awarded the Outland Trophy as the nation's best lineman. He also was selected a finalist for the prestigious Lombardi Award.

In 1972 the New York Giants (NFL) selected him in the first round of the NFL draft. He played every game during his rookie year, but a broken ankle prematurely ended his NFL career by 1974.

BIBLIOGRAPHY: Joe Hoppel et al., *TSN College Football's Twenty-Five Greatest Teams* (St. Louis, MO, 1988); Larry Jacobson file, University of Nebraska Sports Information Office, Lincoln, NE; *TSN Pro Football Register*, 1973.

John Hanners

JOHNSOS, Luke A. (b. December 6, 1905, Chicago, IL; d. December 10, 1984, Evanston, IL), college and professional player and coach, spent nearly 40 years with the Chicago Bears (NFL) as one of George Halas's (FB) most trusted football assistants. During Johnsos's tenure with the Bears, Chicago won six NFL titles.

Johnsos quarterbacked at Schurz High School in Chicago and played end at Northwestern University (WC). Although Johnsos earned nine varsity letters in football, baseball, and basketball at Northwestern from 1926 through 1928, the Chicago Bears offered him a contract for only $100 a game in 1929 as a condition to their signing Wildcat teammate Walter Holmer. Holmer received a $5,000 bonus but never became a star. Johnsos, however, earned All-NFL honors in 1930, 1931, and 1932. He also signed a professional baseball contract with the Cincinnati Reds (NL) as a shortstop, but poor eyesight ended his diamond aspirations. His vision, though, did not deter him from ranking among the NFL's top pass receivers with teammate Bill Hewitt (FB). Unofficially, Johnsos caught nearly 100 passes in eight active NFL seasons from 1929 to 1936 to rank among the era's NFL reception leaders. The six-foot-two-inch 195-pounder held his own defensively and played for the Bears' 1932 and 1933 NFL championship teams. Chicago defeated the Portsmouth Spartans, 9–0, for the 1932 NFL crown and the New York Giants, 23–21, for the 1933 NFL title. Johnsos, who performed for the 1934 Western Division winners, was voted the Bears' MVP in 1935.

Johnsos retired as an active player after the 1936 season and joined the Bears' coaching staff. When head coach Halas entered the U.S. Navy in 1942, Johnsos, Heartley "Hunk" Anderson (FB), and John "Paddy" Driscoll (FB) shared head coaching responsibilities for the duration of World War II. They piloted Chicago to a 1942 Western Division title and a 1943 NFL championship by defeating the Washington Redskins, 41–21. When Halas returned in 1946, Johnsos resumed his position as assistant coach.

Johnsos specialized in "press-box" coaching, sitting high above the field to spot weaknesses in opposition defenses. In the 1963 NFL Championship game against the New York Giants, his "Ditka special" call helped the Bears triumph. The Giants led, 10–7, in the third quarter, when the Bears confronted a third down and 9-yard situation at the New York 15-yard line. Johnsos called for Bear end Mike Ditka (FB) to run a short pattern over center. Ditka's reception put the ball on the Giants' 1-yard line, where quarterback Bill Wade scored on a sneak for the winning touchdown. A keen football student, Johnsos contributed to the development of the modern T-formation.

During the off-season, he worked as a printing executive with Johnsos and Coppock. He was married and had four daughters and one son.

BIBLIOGRAPHY: *Chicago Bears Media Guide*, 1955; Luke Johnsos file, Pro Football Hall of Fame, Canton, OH; David S. Neft et al., eds., *The Football Encyclopedia*, 2nd ed. (New York, 1994); Beau Riffenburgh, *The Official NFL Encyclopedia*, 4th ed. (New York, 1986); *TSN*, "Obituary," December 1984.

Robert N. "Bob" Carroll

JONES, William A. "Dub" (b. December 29, 1924, Arcadia, LA), college and professional player and coach, is the son of John E. Jones, a farmer, and Bertha G. (Hays) Jones, who kept a boarding house following her husband's death in 1927. Jones lettered in football, basketball, and baseball at Ruston, LA, High School and was named to the 1941 All-State football team. He enrolled at LSU (SEC) and played on the Tigers' 1942 football team before entering the U.S. Navy Submarine Service during World War II. The U.S. Navy sent Jones to Tulane University (SC), where he played halfback and fullback on the 1943 and 1944 Green Wave football teams.

Professional football marked Jones's career pinnacle. After playing as a defensive back for the Miami Seahawks (AAFC) part of the 1946 season, he was traded to the Brooklyn Dodgers (AAFC) and played there the rest of the 1946 and the 1947 campaign. Jones then joined the Cleveland Browns (AAFL, NFL), where he played for eight seasons from 1948 through 1955. The six-foot-four-inch, 205-pound Jones possessed good size for a defensive halfback, but his excellent speed and ability to catch passes caused coach Paul Brown, who possessed an eye for talent and innovation, to use Jones almost exclusively as an offensive "man in motion" or flanker back. Jones, one of the first halfbacks to be used primarily as a receiver, joined the Browns during their golden age. Over the next eight seasons, the Browns won a phenomenal eight division championships and five league (two AAFC, three NFL) titles.

He joined ends Dante Lavelli (FB) and Mac Speedie (FB), forming a corps of outstanding receivers for stellar quarterback Otto Graham (FB). Jones's best season came in 1951, when he led the Browns in rushing (492 yards), caught 30 passes, scored 12 touchdowns, and made the All-Pro team. His finest game came against the Chicago Bears in 1951, when he scored 6 touchdowns and still shares the NFL record with Gale Sayers (FB) and Ernie Nevers (FB). During his AAFC-NFL career, he rushed 541 times for 3,209 yards (4.1-yard average) and 21 touchdowns and caught 171 passes for 2,894 yards, 16.8-yard average, and 20 touchdowns.

The offensive coordinator position lured Jones back to the Cleveland Browns for the 1963 through 1967 seasons. He has worked since 1967 in general contracting business in Ruston, LA. He married Shumpert Barnes and has seven children. One son, Tom, starred at quarterback at the University of Arkansas, while another son, Bert (FB), earned All-America honors as a quarterback with LSU and later enjoyed a fine NFL career with the Baltimore Colts.

BIBLIOGRAPHY: C. Robert Barnett, personal interview with William Jones, January 27, 1994; Paul Brown and Jack Clary, *PB: The Paul Brown Story* (New York, 1979); William "Dub" Jones, clipping file, Pro Football Hall of Fame, Canton, OH; David Neft et al., eds., *The Football Encyclopedia*, 2nd ed. (New York, 1994); Beau Riffenburgh, *The Official NFL Encyclopedia*, 4th ed. (New York, 1986).

                                                                    C. Robert Barnett

JUNIOR, Ester James III "E.J." "The Enforcer" (b. December 8, 1959, Salisbury, NC), college and professional player, attended Maplewood High School in Nashville, TN. His father, Ester J. II, served as vice chancellor at Fort Valley, GA, State College, while his mother worked as a high school principal. As a defensive end and linebacker at the University of Alabama (SEC) under legendary coach Paul "Bear" Bryant, Junior became a dominant force on the Crimson Tide squad. Alabama won the Sugar Bowl, 14–7, against Pennsylvania State University and the 1979 national championship. Named to the strength coaches' All-America team and later voted to Alabama's Team of the Decade, he graduated with a bachelor's degree in public relations.

A first-round pick of the St. Louis Cardinals (NFL) in 1981, Junior moved quickly into the NFL limelight. The 22-year-old middle linebacker was sidetracked in 1982, however, when arrested on charges of drug possession. With encouragement from Coach Bryant and support from the St. Louis Cardinals, Junior soon began rehabilitation that included work with youth groups and other forms of community service. Junior returned to the starting lineup four games into the 1983 season and was chosen for the 1983 Pro Bowl. The Alabama star blitzed in the same class with the NFL best and, by the end of 1984, led the Cardinals with 101 tackles, 31 more than his closest competitor.

After Junior set out to restore his stature in the NFL, his performance remained superlative. Junior, nicknamed "The Enforcer" by fellow teammates, made the Pro Bowl teams from the 1984 through 1986 seasons and piled up an impressive record of quarterback sacks and pass interceptions, with 9.5 sacks in 1984 and five interceptions in 1985. Yet Junior's big moment remained elusive, as the Cardinals failed to capture a season title or a trip to the Super Bowl. In October 1987, Junior crossed a picket line during a player's strike. Thereafter, his status changed alternately from team affiliation with St. Louis to the Phoenix Cardinals in 1988 and the Miami Dolphins from 1989 to 1992. He was released by Miami in August 1992 and split the 1992 season between the Tampa Bay Buccaneers (NFL) and the Seattle Seahawks (NFL). Junior played four games with Seattle in 1993.

BIBLIOGRAPHY: "Cards Linebacker Pleads Not Guilty," *NYT*, August 24, 1982, p. B17; Iris Cloyd, ed., *Who's Who Among Black Americans, 1990–91*, 6th ed. (Detroit, MI, 1990), p. 212; "Dolphins Junior Zips Lips," *USA Today*, December 14, 1989, p. C7; "Junior Thrives in Second Chance," *NYT Biographical Service*, December 15, 1984, pp. 1631–1632; "NFL Suspends Four for Drugs," Chicago (IL) *Tribune*, July 26, 1983, p. 4; "Players Fate Undecided," *NYT*, March 18, 1983, p. A23; "Pro Football, NFL," *TSN*, October 26, 1992, p. 24; "Rozelle Makes Right Call," *NYT*, July 27, 1983, p. II5; "Rozelle Suspends Four for Cocaine Use," *NYT*, July 26, 1983, p. II5; *TSN Pro Football Register*, 1994.

John L. Godwin

KAER, Morton A. "Mort" "Devil May" (b. September 2, 1903, Omaha, NE; d. January 12, 1992, Mount Shasta, CA), college athlete, professional player, and coach, made All-America in football as quarterback at the University of Southern California (PCC) and participated in the Olympic pentathlon. In 1972, he was elected to the NFF College Football Hall of Fame. Kaer starred at Southern California from 1924 to 1926, setting Trojan career records with 36 touchdowns and 216 points. Those marks lasted 42 years until broken by O. J. Simpson (FB). Kaer, Southern California's second All-America, garnered consensus acclaim in 1926 after the Trojans finished 8–2 under coach Howard Jones (FB).

Kaer grew up in Red Bluff, CA, and starred in football and track and field at Red Bluff High School. Following his freshman year at Southern California, he competed in the pentathlon at the 1924 Paris, France, Summer Olympics. He tied for first in the 200-meter dash and placed well in the broad (long) jump, discus, and javelin but faded in the 1,500-meter run to finish fifth overall. The 5-foot-11-inch, 167-pound Kaer set a Trojan single-season football scoring standard in 1925 with 114 points. The Cardinal and Gold eleven amassed the second-highest national point total (465) that season, finishing 11–2.

The Trojans in 1926 placed second to Stanford University in the PCC after losing 13–12 to the Cardinal. Southern California defeated the University of California for the first time in 11 years, as Kaer romped for 36-, 10-, and 48-yard touchdowns at Berkeley before 72,000 patrons. The Cardinal and Gold dropped a one-pointer to the University of Notre Dame in front of 76,000 spectators at the Los Angeles Coliseum. Kaer led the Trojans to a 71-yard touchdown that could have tied the contest, but the conversion was blocked.

Kaer teamed with other Trojan grid luminaries, including Brice Taylor, Morley Drury (FB), Jess Hibbs, and Don Williams. Kaer scored four touchdowns in a single game once, notched three touchdowns in two others, and gained 1,588 career yards rushing (5.65-yard average). He starred on Southern California's 880-yard relay team, which set an NCAA record under legendary track and field coach Dean B. Cromwell (IS), and won the AAU junior 440-yard hurdles title. Kaer returned one punt for a touchdown with the Frankford, PA, Yellow Jackets (NFL) in 1931, the same year the franchise disbanded after posting a 1–6–1 record. He coached football at Weed, CA, High School for 28 years, his clubs winning or sharing 17 championships. He guided Weed to five undefeated seasons and nine single-loss campaigns, compiling a composite 187–47–7 record.

BIBLIOGRAPHY: Cameron Applegate, *Notre Dame vs. USC* (Hollywood, CA, 1977); Braven Dyer, *Ten Top Trojan Football Thrillers* (Los Angeles, CA, 1949); Ronald L. Mendell and Timothy B. Phares, *Who's Who in Football* (New Rochelle, NY, 1974); Don Pierson, *The Trojans, Southern California Football* (Chicago, IL, 1974); Ken Rappoport, *The Trojans* (Huntsville, AL, 1974); Beau Riffenburgh, *The Official NFL Encyclopedia*, 4th ed. (New York, 1986); H. D. Thoreau, ed., *Pacific Coast Conference Record Book* (Los Angeles, CA, 1948); USC-Stanford Football Game Program, October 30, 1926; Alexander M. Weyand, *The Olympic Pageant* (New York, 1952).

                                                                James D. Whalen

KATCAVAGE, James Richard "Jim" "Kat" (b. October 28, 1934, Wilkes-Barre, PA), college and professional player, coach, and scout, made All-Pro three times from 1961 to 1963 as a member of the New York Giants' (NFL) fabled "Fearsome Foursome" defensive football line. Katcavage participated in three Pro Bowls from 1962 to 1964 and played on the Giants' 1956 championship squad. A six-foot-two-inch, 210-pound end for the University of Dayton, he captained the Flyers in 1955 and made the INS All-Midwest and *Police Gazette* All-America squads.

The son of Michael J. Katcavage, a government employee, and Anna (Margolis) Katcavage, he was selected an All-City gridder at Philadelphia, PA's Roman Catholic High School. In 1964, he made the all-time Philadelphia High School All-Star football team. College football scholarship offers dwindled for Katcavage after he injured a shoulder playing high school basketball. Katcavage starred at the University of Dayton under coach Hugh Devore on clubs that compiled a combined 11–16–2 record against mostly major opponents. He played in the East-West Shrine All-Star Game in 1956 and was elected to Dayton's Athletic Hall of Fame. Katcavage earned a B.S. degree in business administration in 1956 at Dayton.

The New York Giants (NFL) made Katcavage a fourth-round draft choice in 1956 after Devore alerted New York's assistant coach Vince Lombardi (FB). Katcavage performed with the Giants from 1956 to 1968, helping them win six Eastern Conference titles. He played in the famous 1958 championship sudden-death, 23–17, overtime loss to the Baltimore Colts, rated by some "the best football game ever played." Nicknamed "Kat" for his agility, he possessed so much quickness that he occasionally overplayed his position. Katcavage eventually learned to control his actions. The Fearsome Foursome, including tackles Dick Modzelewski (FB) and Roosevelt Grier (FB) and end Andy Robustelli (FB), played as a unit six seasons and employed defensive coach Tom Landry's (FB) 4–3 concept.

Katcavage, who tied an NFL career record by causing three safeties, once completed a game with a broken shoulder. Robustelli suggested, "If Katcavage had played on my side, on the right where there rarely was a tight end's block to contend with, he might have had much more recognition." Katcavage, New York's defensive line coach from 1969 to 1973, scouted for the Philadelphia Eagles (NFL) until 1987. He married Cathy Gould of Philadelphia, PA, and has a son and daughter. Katcavage resides in Philadelphia, where he works in the automobile business and evaluates NFL officials.

BIBLIOGRAPHY: Dayton-Villanova Football Game Program, November 27, 1955; Marc Katz, "Where Are They Now?" Dayton (OH) *Daily News*, January 9, 1993; Ronald L. Mendell and Timothy B. Phares, *Who's Who in Football* (New Rochelle, NY, 1974); Norm Miller, "Glory Days," *TCC* 14 (February 1993); Beau Riffenburgh, *The Official NFL Encyclopedia*, 4th ed. (New York, 1986).

James D. Whalen

KELL, Curtis Cliff "Chip" (b. March 10, 1949, Atlanta, GA), college and professional player, is the son of Curtis Kell and Lydia Kell and grew up in Decatur, GA. His father coached high school football for 36 years. Kell, who gained attention at age 13 when he was named to the U.S. Junior Olympic track team, participated in football, track and field, baseball, and basketball at Avondale High School in Decatur. Kell won acclaim as an All-State lineman in football but attracted most attention for an incredible State shot put mark of 66 feet 7 inches. Kell's mark, established in 1966, remains a State record.

The University of Tennessee (SEC) recruited Kell for football and track and field. From 1968 to 1970, Kell's stellar play as an offensive lineman propelled the Volunteers to a three-year 28–5–1 win–loss record. The six-foot-one-inch, 250-pound Kell displayed tremendous strength and explosiveness and bench-pressed over 500 pounds, being recognized as the strongest football player in Tennessee history. Kell's blocking led Tennessee to appearances in the 1969 Cotton Bowl, 1969 Gator Bowl, and 1971 Sugar Bowl.

Kell, an All-SEC center as a sophomore, won consensus All-America honors in 1969 and 1970 while playing guard. He received the coveted Jacobs

Award, signifying the SEC's best blocker, following his junior and senior seasons. In 1970, Kell finished runner-up to Jim Stillwagon* of Ohio State University in balloting for the first annual Lombardi Trophy, honoring the nation's best lineman. Kell won the SEC shot put championship in 1968, 1969, and 1970.

The San Diego Chargers (NFL) selected Kell in the seventeenth round of the 1971 NFL draft, but he opted to play the 1971 and 1972 seasons with the Edmonton, Canada, Eskimos (CFL). Kell then entered coaching, beginning as an assistant at the University of Tennessee—Chattanooga in 1973. He served as a head football coach in Georgia at Calhoun High School in 1975 and Hixon High School from 1976 to 1978, compiling a 15–24–1 win–loss–tie record. His final assignment came as an assistant football coach at Chamblee, GA, High School from 1980 to 1982. Kell married Ann Parham of Chattanooga, TN, and has one son, Dusty, and twin daughters, Annette and Abigail.

Since 1978, Kell has served as owner and president of Kell Strength Equipment, Incorporated. His expertise in the field proved successful, as he has designed weight rooms and equipment for several professional and collegiate teams, including the New York Giants (NFL), the University of Alabama, the University of Miami, and Florida State University.

BIBLIOGRAPHY: Russ Bebb, *The Big Orange: A Story of Tennessee Football* (Huntsville, AL, 1973); Bud Fields and Bob Bertucci, *Big Orange: A Pictorial History of University of Tennessee Football* (West Point, NY, 1982); Chip Kell file, Sports Information Office, University of Tennessee, Knoxville, TN; Mike Siroky and Bob Bertucci, *Orange Lightning: Inside University of Tennessee Football* (West Point, NY, 1982).

Robert T. Epling

KELLY, James Edward "Jim" (b. February 14, 1960, East Brady, PA), college and professional player, attended East Brady High School, where he starred at quarterback on a championship team. He is the fourth son of Joseph Kelly, an amateur boxer who struggled to maintain his family while coaching his sons at football, and Alice Kelly. At the University of Miami, Kelly developed a rifle arm perfect for the passing offense and led the Hurricanes to a high national ranking and a 20–10 Peach Bowl victory over Virginia Tech in 1980. A college All-America, he ranked among leading contenders for the 1982 Heisman Trophy until injured at midseason. In 1982, he graduated with a bachelor's degree in business management.

Kelly in 1983 was drafted first by the Buffalo Bills (NFL) and in the fourteenth round by the Chicago Blitz (USFL), who traded his rights to the Houston Gamblers (USFL). He achieved instant success with Houston, completing 63 percent of his passes for 5,219 yards and 44 touchdowns to establish a record and being named the USFL's MVP for 1984. A superb tactician of the "run and shoot" offense, Kelly in 1985 broke a 34-year-old American professional football single-game record by completing 35 of 54 passes for 574 yards and 5 touchdowns. Although Kelly was named the 1984 USFL Rookie of the Year and made the 1985 *TSN* USFL All-Star team, other quarterbacks overshadowed him. In two USFL seasons, he completed 730 of 1,154 passes for 9,842 yards and 83 touchdowns.

After a brief stint with the New Jersey Generals (USFL), Kelly signed a five-year, $8 million contract with the Buffalo Bills (NFL) to become the then-highest-paid professional football player. Buffalo ticket sales boomed, as the working-class quarterback rescued the New York team from the doldrums. Kelly led the Bills through several AFC playoff and championship games from 1988 to 1993. By 1990, the Bills had become the dominant AFC club.

Kelly was regarded as the number-four passer in NFL history by 1994, being praised as a team leader and play caller. The quarterback on the *TSN* NFL All-Pro team in 1991, he played in the Pro Bowl in 1987, 1988, and 1991 and was invited to the Pro Bowl in 1989 and 1993. Although at times subjected to criticism, the "millionaire athlete" gained stature by organizing business ventures and raising money for charity. Kelly led the Bills to four Super Bowls, which Buffalo lost to the New York Giants, 20–19, in 1991, Washington Redskins, 37–24, in 1992, and Dallas Cowboys, 52–17, in 1993 and 30–13 in 1994. An injured knee sidelined him in the second quarter of the 1993 defeat at the Pasadena, CA, Rose Bowl Stadium. Through 1994, he had completed 2,397 passes in 3,942 attempts for 29,527 yards and 196 touchdowns in the NFL.

BIBLIOGRAPHY: "Cowboys Gun Down Bills with 52–17 Win," Los Angeles (CA) *Times*, February 1, 1993, p. 1; "Feud for Thought," Los Angeles (CA) *Times*, January 21, 1993, p. C1; "Jim Kelly," *CB* (1992), pp. 330–334; "Jim Kelly Tells It as Only He Can," Los Angeles (CA) *Times*, January 7, 1989, p. III1; "Kelly and Bills Find Success with Marchibroda's Help," *NYT*, December 13, 1990, p. D23; "Kelly Becoming Buffalo Ambassador," Buffalo (NY) *News*, May 12, 1989, p. F9; "Kelly Is Happy and Bills Are Happy," Los Angeles (CA) *Times*, August 31, 1986, p. III2; "Kelly Rises from the Shadows," *NYT Biographical Service* 16 (January–June 1985), pp. 408–409; "Life with Lord Jim," *SI* 65 (July 21, 1986), pp. 58–70; "A New Namath, But with Knees," *SI* 65 (September 15, 1986), pp. 40–44; *TSN Pro Football Register*, 1994.

John L. Godwin

KETCHAM, Henry Holman "Hank" "Ketch" (b. June 17, 1891, Englewood, NJ; d. November 1986, Seattle, WA), college athlete, was named a consensus football All-America center in 1911 and 1912 at Yale University (IvL) and captained the Elis at guard in 1913 while making the All-America Second Team. Ketcham, elected in 1968 to the NFF College Football Hall of Fame, played in every game for three seasons to help Yale compile a combined 19–5–5 record.

The son of Henry Belden Ketcham, an attorney, and Sally (Holman) Ketcham, he excelled in football and track and field at Hotchkiss Preparatory School before graduating in 1910. Ketcham joined All-America teammates, including end Douglas Bomeisler, quarterback Arthur Howe, tackle Nelson Talbott, and fullback Harry LeGore, at Yale. The Elis in 1911 held coach Percy Haughton's (FB) Harvard University to a second consecutive scoreless tie but suffered a three-point loss to Princeton University's national championship squad. Yale's stout defense in 1912 allowed only two field goals while winning the first seven games before being tied by Princeton and suffering a 20–0 setback to undefeated Harvard.

The six-foot, 177-pound Ketcham, determining that Yale's antiquated captain-appointed coaching system could no longer compete on even terms with Harvard, called a meeting of former Blue captains and field coaches. The meeting, held before the 1913 season, led to the formation of the Yale Graduate Committee, which hired Howard Jones (FB) as the Elis' first salaried coach. Nevertheless, the diminished quality of the Yale players surfaced, as Jones guided the Elis to a mediocre 5–2–3 finish. In the *1913 Official Football Guide*, Walter Camp (FB) wrote, "So many times he [Ketcham] tackled the runner down the field that he was mistaken for an end, and so many times he stopped a runner as he came through the line that he was mistaken for a secondary defensive man."

Ketcham, a member of Psi Upsilon fraternity, Skull and Bones, and Senior Committee, graduated from Yale in 1914 with a B.S. degree. He served as first lieutenant in the U.S. Army artillery in France during World War I and was hospitalized at Verdun, France, after being gassed. Subsequently, he presided over Henry H. Ketcham Lumber Company in Seattle, WA. Ketcham, who married Katherine Eugenia Peters of Seattle in 1921 and had three sons, served on the board of trustees of the Seattle Trust and Savings Bank and the Episcopal Church Council and enjoyed playing tennis, golf, and bridge.

BIBLIOGRAPHY: L. H. Baker, *Football: Facts and Figures* (New York, 1945); Thomas G. Bergin, *The Game* (New Haven, CT, 1984); Tim Cohane, *The Yale Football Story* (New York, 1951); Ronald L. Mendell and Timothy B. Phares, *Who's Who in Football* (New Rochelle, NY, 1974); Yale-Harvard Football Game Program, New Haven, CT, November 23, 1912; Yale University Library, Manuscripts and Archives, New Haven, CT, letter to James D. Whalen, August 31, 1993.

James D. Whalen

KINER, Steven Albert "Steve" (b. June 12, 1947, Sandstone, MN), college and professional player, is the son of George Kiner and Gertrude Willie Kiner and spent much of his youth traveling. Since his father served in the U.S. Army, the Kiners moved often before settling in Tampa, FL. Kiner first gained recognition on the football field at Hillsborough High School in Tampa, where he starred at several positions between 1964 and 1966.

During his scholastic years, Kiner earned All-City and All-Conference honors and was elected team captain.

In 1966, the University of Tennessee (SEC) signed Kiner to a football scholarship. As a sophomore in 1967, Kiner started at linebacker on a Volunteer team that won nine games and played against the University of Oklahoma in the 1968 Orange Bowl. After that season, Kiner won SEC Sophomore of the Year honors. The six-foot-two-inch, 205-pound quick linebacker led a defense that propelled the Volunteers to a three-year 26–6–1 record. Kiner not only led the Volunteers in tackles in 1968 and 1969 but also intercepted nine passes during his career. Tennessee played against the University of Texas in the 1969 Cotton Bowl, following the 1968 season, and against the University of Florida in the 1969 Gator Bowl.

Kiner earned All-America honors in both 1968 and 1969 and played with an aggressive sideline-to-sideline style, prompting University of Alabama coach "Bear" Bryant to call him the best SEC linebacker to play during this era. Kiner's colorful demeanor sometimes angered foes. Kiner's remarks in 1968 prompted the University of Mississippi to bring a donkey named "Mr. Kiner" to their practices the week they played the Volunteers. The inspired Rebels thrashed Tennessee, 38–0, in a game known as the "Jackson Massacre."

The Dallas Cowboys selected Kiner in the third round of the 1970 NFL draft. He played professionally in the NFL from 1970 to 1978. His NFL career included stints with Dallas in 1970, the New England Patriots in 1971 and 1973, the Washington Redskins in 1972, and the Houston Oilers from 1974 to 1978. Kiner enjoyed his most success at Houston, where he started at middle linebacker for coach "Bum" Phillips's squad. Following his retirement, Kiner pursued private business in Houston, TX, and later in Georgia. In 1980, Kiner married Carol Smith. They have three daughters, Stacey, Hailey, and Chrissy.

BIBLIOGRAPHY: Russ Bebb, *The Big Orange: A Story of Tennessee Football* (Huntsville, AL, 1973); Bud Fields and Bob Bertucci, *Big Orange: A Pictorial History of University of Tennessee Football* (West Point, NY, 1982); Steve Kiner file, Sports Information Office, University of Tennessee, Knoxville, TN; Mike Siroky and Bob Bertucci, *Orange Lightning: Inside University of Tennessee Football* (West Point, NY, 1982).

Robert T. Epling

KOSAR, Bernard Joseph Jr. "Bernie" (b. November 25, 1963, Boardman, OH), college and professional player, is the oldest son of Bernard Joseph, Sr., an industrial engineer, and Geraldine (Krajcirik) Kosar, a registered nurse. He first played football in the seventh grade as a quarterback and linebacker at Byzantine Catholic Central in Boardman. In 1981, he was named the Ohio Back of the Year as a senior quarterback at Boardman High School. The heavily recruited Kosar joined the University of Miami Hurricanes, a perennial power with a pass-oriented offense.

After being redshirted as a freshman, Kosar only played two seasons at Miami. In 1983, he led the Hurricanes to the national championship with a 31–30 victory over the University of Nebraska in the Orange Bowl and was chosen game MVP. The following year, he quarterbacked Miami against UCLA in the Fiesta Bowl. The same season, in one of the most memorable college games ever, he passed for 447 yards against Boston College. Miami, however, lost on quarterback Doug Flutie's (FB) dramatic 65-yard "Hail Mary" pass on the last play of the game. Following his selection as a Second Team AP All-America, he graduated that summer with two years of eligibility remaining and a 3.28 grade-point average in finance. After announcing he wanted to play for Cleveland, whose Brian Sipe–led Kardiac Kids had inspired him in 1980, the Browns (NFL) selected him in the 1985 supplemental draft.

In over eight years with the Browns, the six-foot-five-inch, 215-pound Kosar became the team's second top career performer behind Brian Sipe in passes attempted (3,150), passes completed (1,853), and total yards passing (21,904). He holds the team's career highest passing percentage (58.9) mark and has thrown 116 touchdown passes, 38 less than Sipe. He has thrown only 81 interceptions and leads the NFL with the lowest career interception percentage (2.6). He also holds the NFL season record for passes attempted without an interception (308), breaking Bart Starr's (FB) record of 294. The innumerable Browns' game records he possesses include most consecutive completions (16), the longest pass completion (97 yards), most yards completed (489), most passes attempted (64), and, sharing with Sipe, most passes completed (33). The latter three records came in a double-overtime playoff victory against the New York Jets in January 1987. His best season came in 1987, when Kosar led the AFC in passing with a 95.4 rating, a 62.0 percentage for completions (241 of 389), and 7.8 yards per attempt. He threw for 3,033 yards despite playing in only 12 games. As the second alternate, he played in the Pro Bowl that year.

Kosar's achievements transcend passing statistics. Despite his relative immobility ("scrambles with the grace and speed of a giraffe on Quaaludes") and his lack of a Marino-like arm, he remains an inspiring team leader with an uncanny knack of dissecting defenses, audibilizing, and getting the ball to receivers. He throws sidearm or underhanded, if necessary. His courage remains unquestioned. Against the Miami Dolphins in 1992, he rallied the Browns to a near victory despite playing more than half the game with a broken ankle. He led the Browns to the AFC playoffs, including four Central Division titles, in five of his first eight NFL seasons. With an unstable offensive line, he has suffered several injuries and demonstrated less effectiveness in recent years. After the Cleveland Browns released Kosar in November 1993, the Dallas Cowboys (NFL) signed the veteran as a backup to the injured Troy Aikman. Kosar completed 36 aerials in 63 attempts for 410 yards and three touchdowns and threw one 42-yard touchdown pass to

Alvin Harper in the NFC championship game in January 1994 to help defeat the San Francisco 49ers. Kosar, who married Babette Ferre and has one child, played briefly in the Cowboys' 30–13 victory over the Buffalo Bills in Super Bowl XXVIII. In April 1994, the Miami Dolphins (NFL) signed Kosar to a $1.6 million, two-year contract.

BIBLIOGRAPHY: *Cleveland Browns' Fan and Media Guide*, 1992; James N. Giglio, telephone interview with Bernard Kosar, Sr., May 5, 1993; James N. Giglio, telephone interview with Dino Lucarelli, Player Relations and Media Services for the Cleveland Browns, May 25, 1993; Douglas S. Looney, "There's a Love Feast on Lake Erie," *SI* 63 (August 26, 1985), pp. 38–45.

James N. Giglio

KRAUSE, Paul James (b. February 19, 1942, Flint, MI), college and professional player, is the son of Olin Samuel Krause and Ora Ernestine (Dietzel) Krause and attended Bendle High School in Flint, MI. The versatile athlete enrolled at the University of Iowa (BTC) to play baseball, but a shoulder injury forced him to abandon the sport for football. While in college, Krause married Bette Pamela Henry. They have three children. From 1961 to 1963, Krause played a solid defensive back for mediocre Iowa squads. The Washington Redskins chose Krause in the second round of the NFL draft. In 1964, he played for the College All-Stars in the annual game against the NFL champion Chicago Bears.

As a six-foot-three-inch, 200-pound rookie free safety in 1964, Krause led the NFL with 12 interceptions for the third-highest total in NFL history. Krause set an NFL mark by intercepting passes in seven consecutive games, becoming the only safety to make consensus All-Pro in his first two seasons. Krause intercepted 28 passes in 4 years with Washington. Before the 1968 season, the Redskins traded Krause to the Minnesota Vikings for Marlin McKeever and a draft choice. Krause played 12 years for the Vikings and won consecutive All-NFC honors from 1970 to 1973, helping the Vikings become one of the decade's dominant teams. Krause led the NFL in interceptions with 10, a Viking record, in 1975, while capturing All-NFC and All-Pro recognition.

Krause, who retired from professional football following the 1979 season, holds the NFL's career record for most interceptions (81) and the Vikings' career interception record (53) and ranks third in yards gained from interceptions with 1,185. In 1985, Krause was named to the Minnesota Vikings' All-Time team. Vikings' coach Bud Grant (FB) summarized Krause's playing style, "I would have to say that Paul Krause had the game down to a science. His intuition and instinct for playing the receiver and the football was terrific. His ability to make a big play was almost constant . . . he could turn a game around for us."

Off the field, Krause has been involved in investment banking, land development, cattle ranching, the insurance business, and Minnesota county politics.

BIBLIOGRAPHY: Harold Claassen and Steve Boda, Jr., eds., *Ronald Encyclopedia of Football* (New York, 1963); Ronald L. Mendell and Timothy B. Phares, *Who's Who in Football* (New Rochelle, NY, 1974); David S. Neft et al., eds., *The Football Encyclopedia*, 2nd ed. (New York, 1994); Beau Riffenburgh, *The Official NFL Encyclopedia*, 4th ed. (New York, 1986); *WWA*, 40th ed. (1978–1979), p. 1837; Joe Zagorski, "Paul Krause: Defender," *TCC* 9 (1987), pp. 3–4.

                                                                                                Marc S. Maltby

KWALICK, Thaddeus John Jr. "Ted" (b. April 15, 1947, Pittsburgh, PA), college and professional player, is the son of Thaddeus Kwalick, Sr., and Mary M. Kwalick and grew up in McKees Rock, PA, where he starred in basketball and football at Montour High School. At Pennsylvania State University, he lettered in football from 1966 to 1968 and played an instrumental role in the Nittany Lions' achievement of a three-year record of 23 wins and 7 losses. The undefeated 1968 team finished second in the AP rankings, placed third in the UP poll, and defeated the University of Kansas, 15–14, in the Orange Bowl.

Kwalick, an offensive end on the 1967 AFCA All-America team and the 1968 AP All-East team, was unanimously chosen for All-America in 1968. No Penn State player had achieved that honor previously. He also ranked fourth on the Heisman Trophy balloting that year and subsequently was named to the NFF College Football Hall of Fame.

The six-foot-four-inch, 225-pound Kwalick, the archetypical tight end in the modern football system, possessed strong hands and 4.6-second speed for the 40 yards, making him an excellent pass receiver capable of long runs after catching the ball. He also proved a strong blocker. The legendary coach Tommy Prothro commented, "He was better at his position than anyone I've seen play at any position." In his final collegiate season in 1968, he caught 31 passes for 403 yards and averaged 13.0 yards per catch. He also scored two touchdowns, including one reception and touchdown run of 63 yards.

After Kwalick received his B.S. degree in health and physical education in 1969, the San Francisco 49ers (NFL) selected him in the first round. He starred there from 1969 to 1974, catching 52 passes for 664 yards and five touchdowns in 1971, 40 passes for 751 yards and nine touchdowns in 1972, and 47 passes for 729 yards and five touchdowns in 1973. All three of these seasons he appeared in the All-Star Pro Bowl game. After the 1974 season, he moved to the Philadelphia Bell team of the new WFL. In 1975, he caught 29 passes for 400 yards. Upon the collapse of the WFL later that year, he signed with the Oakland Raiders (NFL) and played in AFC championship games in 1975 and 1977. He retired after the 1977 season and entered business in California. Married while an undergraduate, he has one daughter.

BIBLIOGRAPHY: Frank Bilovsky, *Lion Country; Inside Penn State Football* (West Point, NY, 1982); Joe Hoppel et al., *College Football's Twenty-five Greatest Teams* (St. Louis,

MO, 1988); *1991 NCAA Football* (Overland Park, KS); Joseph Paterno, *Paterno: By the Book* (New York, 1989); Ken Rappoport, *The Nittany Lions* (Huntsville, AL, 1973); Ridge Riley, *Road to Number One: A Personal Chronicle of Penn State Football* (Garden City, NY, 1977); Sports Information Office files, Pennsylvania State University, University Park, PA; *TSN Football Register*, 1978.

Daniel R. Gilbert

LAHR, Warren (b. September 5, 1923, Mt. Zion, PA; d. January 19, 1969, Cleveland, OH), college and professional player, attended West Wyoming High School and served three years in the U.S. Navy during World War II. Lahr resumed his education at Western Reserve University, where he played college football as a back.

In 1948, Lahr married Rowena Scott, a union that produced five daughters. That same year, the Cleveland Browns (AAFC) signed the 5-foot-11-inch, 189-pound Lahr as a free agent. After being injured that season, Lahr was switched from offense to defensive safety in 1949 and intercepted 4 passes for 32 yards. He enjoyed a standout career the next 11 years, retiring after the 1959 season. Lahr then held the Browns' career record with 40 pass interceptions for 530 yards (13.3-yard average) and five touchdowns. Lahr was named to the Browns' all-time All-Star team, the 1951 All-Pro team, and the NFL EC team in 1956.

With the Browns, Lahr played on several championship teams. In 1949, Cleveland defeated the San Francisco 49ers, 21–7, for the AAFC title. Upon joining the NFL the following year, the Browns triumphed over the Los Angeles Rams, 30–28, to gain another championship. Toward the end of the game, Los Angeles quarterback Norm Van Brocklin's (FB) 55-yard pass was intercepted by Lahr to preserve the NFL title. Cleveland earned two subsequent NFL crowns during Lahr's tenure, defeating the Detroit Lions, 56–10, in 1954 and Los Angeles, 38–14, in 1955. Lahr also participated in the 1951, 1952, and 1953 NFL championship games.

Following his retirement from active play, Lahr became a local sports broadcaster and covered Browns' games from 1963 to 1967. In 1968, he handled some games for the CBS-Radio network but then became a manufacturer's agent in industrial sales in the Cleveland area. Shortly thereafter, he suffered a fatal heart attack.

BIBLIOGRAPHY: Chicago (IL) *Tribune*, January 20, 1969, p. II3; Ralph Hickok, *Who Was Who in American Sports* (New York, 1971); Warren Lahr file, Pro Football Hall of Fame, Canton, OH; Roger Treat, *Encyclopedia of Football*, 16th rev. ed. (New York, 1979); *TSN Football Register*, 1969.

Gerald R. Gems

LAURICELLA, Francis Edward "Hank" "Hurrying Hank" (b. October 9, 1930, Harahan, LA), college player, is the son of John Lauricella and Theresa Lauricella, originators of a successful real estate and home building firm in

New Orleans, LA. His first acclaim came at Holy Cross High School of New Orleans, where he led his team to a share of the city football championship in 1947.

The University of Tennessee (SEC) recruited Lauricella for football. Lauricella ran the Volunteers' single-wing offense from the tailback position and also handled punting chores. At 5 feet 11 inches and 165 pounds, Lauricella played with a graceful style that belied his nickname, "Hurrying Hank." During his collegiate career from 1949 to 1951, he rushed for 1,463 yards, passed for 1,105 more, and also punted for a 36.5-yard average. Tennessee fielded tremendous teams during this era, winning 28 games, losing only 4, tying 1, and competing in the 1951 Cotton Bowl against the University of Texas and the 1952 Sugar Bowl against the University of Maryland. The 1951 Volunteers were selected college football's National Champions.

In 1951, Lauricella garnered individual honors as a consensus All-America and finished runner-up in balloting for the prestigious Heisman Trophy to Princeton University's Dick Kazmaier (FB). Perhaps his most memorable feat, a fantastic 75-yard run, came in the 1951 Cotton Bowl victory over Texas. Many Tennessee fans regard Lauricella's weaving run as the greatest in school history.

Lauricella, who earned his bachelor's degree in business administration from the University of Tennessee in 1953, returned to New Orleans and married former Tennessee beauty queen Betty Valker. The couple have five children, Hank, Jr., Louis, Marc, Chris, and Elizabeth. He and his brother John, Jr., continued the family business, Lauricella Land Company. He also ventured into state politics, having served in the Louisiana legislature for well over two decades as a state representative and then a state senator. He played an influential role in having the famous Louisiana Superdome built in New Orleans.

In 1980, Lauricella received the Distinguished American Award from the East Tennessee Chapter of the College Football Hall of Fame. His election into the NFF College Football Hall of Fame quickly followed in 1981. These awards symbolized Lauricella's success both on and off the football field.

BIBLIOGRAPHY: Russ Bebb, *The Big Orange: A Story of Tennessee Football* (Huntsville, AL, 1973); Bud Fields and Bob Bertucci, *Big Orange: A Pictorial History of University of Tennessee Football* (West Point, NY, 1982); Hank Lauricella file, Sports Information Office, University of Tennessee, Knoxville, TN; Tom Siler, *The Volunteers* (Knoxville, TN, 1950); Mike Siroky and Bob Bertucci, *Orange Lightning: Inside University of Tennessee Football* (West Point, NY, 1982).

Robert T. Epling

LeBARON, Edward Wayne Jr. "Eddie" (b. January 7, 1930, San Rafael, CA), college and professional player, sportscaster, and executive, is of French,

Scotch, and Irish descent and the only child of Edward LeBaron, Sr., and Mabel (Sims) LeBaron. His father operated a large dairy farm and moved the family to Valley Home, CA, when LeBaron was 8 years old. After skipping several grades, he enrolled at Oakdale, CA, High School at age 12.

A good high school quarterback, LeBaron began his college career as a 16-year-old single-wing tailback for coach Amos Alonzo Stagg (FB) at the College of the Pacific (PCC) in 1946. His honors included All-PCC from 1946 through 1948, Little All-America honors from 1947 through 1949, and All-America selection by INS and NEA in 1949. He also won the Pop Warner Award in 1949, leading College of the Pacific to an 11–0 record and NCAA scoring mark of 575 points. Over four seasons, LeBaron completed 204 of 430 attempts for 3,841 yards and 49 touchdowns. The two-way player made 10 career interceptions as a defensive back and punted 75 yards against the University of Montana in 1948. The NFF College Football Hall of Fame enshrined him in 1980. Despite LeBaron's small five-foot-seven-inch, 165-pound frame, the Washington Redskins (NFL) selected him in the tenth round of the 1950 draft. LeBaron led the College All-Stars to a 17–7 upset of the Philadelphia Eagles before reporting to training camp.

After playing just two exhibition games, LeBaron joined the U.S. Marine Corps for two years and won two Purple Hearts and a Bronze Star while serving in Korea for nine months. He returned to the Washington Redskins in 1952, splitting time at quarterback with Sammy Baugh (FB) in his last NFL season. LeBaron married Doralee Wilson on June 4, 1954, and has three sons, Edward III, Bill, and Richard.

LeBaron played the 1954 season with the Calgary, Canada, Stampeders (CFL) before returning to the Washington Redskins in 1955. He performed in the 1956 Pro Bowl and led the NFL in passing in 1958. Simultaneously, he attended George Washington University Law School from 1956 to 1958 and earned his law degree.

LeBaron announced his retirement from professional football in 1960 to pursue his law career full-time but changed his mind when the first-year Dallas Cowboys (NFL) traded two draft choices for him. He practiced law while with the Cowboys, retiring following the 1963 season. His NFL career totals included 897 completions in 1,796 attempts for 13,399 yards and 104 touchdowns. He also rushed for 650 yards and punted 171 times for a 40.9-yard average.

LeBaron moved to Reno, NV, in 1964 to continue his law practice and also worked as a football television commentator for several seasons. In 1977, he returned to the NFL as general manager of the Atlanta Falcons. He was named *TSN* Executive of the Year in 1980 and was promoted to executive vice president and chief operating officer in 1982. LeBaron joined an Atlanta law firm after the 1985 season and moved to Sacramento, CA, in 1989 to affiliate with his current firm, Pillsbury, Madison, and Sutro.

BIBLIOGRAPHY: *Atlanta Falcons Media Guide*, 1985; Larry Fox, *Little Men in Sports* (New York, 1968); Jay Langhammer, interview with Edward LeBaron, Jr., January 28, 1993; *University of Pacific Football Media Guide*, 1990.

Jay Langhammer

LETLOW, Willard Russell "Russ" (b. October 5, 1913, Diuba, CA), college and professional player, starred as an NFL football guard. A four-year football letterman at left tackle for the University of San Francisco from 1932 to 1935, he in 1935 made the All-Pacific Coast team and played in the East-West Shrine All-Star Game. The Dons steadily improved, compiling records of 2–6 in 1932, 1–6–1 in 1933, 3–3–1 in 1934, and 5–3 in 1935.

In 1936, the initial year of the NFL player draft, the Green Bay Packers (NFL) made the six-foot, 214-pound Letlow their first draft selection ever. The Packers, coached by Earl "Curly" Lambeau (FB), boasted stellar pass receiver Don Hutson (FB), fullback Clarke Hinkle (FB), and passer Arnie Herber (FB). Green Bay also fielded numerous unusually strong linemen, notably tackles Ernie Smith,* Bill Lee (S), and Buford "Baby" Ray, guards Lon Evans, Charles "Buckets" Goldenberg,* and Pete Tinsley, and centers George Svendsen and Charley Brock.

Letlow, switched to guard, immediately became a mainstay of the Packers' 1936 NFL championship team, a 10–1–1 club that defeated the Boston Redskins, 21–6, for the NFL title. In 1938, Letlow made the NFL Coaches Official All-NFL team and several other All-NFL squads. The 1938 Packers won the NFL Western Division with an 8–3 record but lost the NFL championship game, 23–17, to the New York Giants. Green Bay rebounded in 1939 to post a 9–2 mark and win the NFL title game, 27–0, over the Giants. Following the 1939 and 1940 seasons, Letlow played in Pro Bowl games at Los Angeles, CA. Green Bay lost only one game during the 1941 season, tying the Chicago Bears for the Western Division crown. Chicago defeated the Packers, 33–14, in a postseason playoff and captured the NFL title.

Letlow, who entered the U.S. Navy in 1943, made the All-Service football team in 1943 and 1944. After World War II, he returned to Green Bay in 1946 for one final season with the Packers. The Hall of Fame Selection Committee chose Letlow as a guard on the All-Pro squad of the 1930s, while the Green Bay Packers Hall of Fame enshrined him in 1972.

BIBLIOGRAPHY: *Green Bay Packers Official Media Guide*, 1993; Russ Letlow file, Pro Football Hall of Fame, Canton, OH; David S. Neft et al., eds., *The Football Encyclopedia*, 2nd ed. (New York, 1994); Beau Riffenburgh, *The Official NFL Encyclopedia*, 4th ed. (New York, 1986).

Robert N. "Bob" Carroll

LEVY, Marvin David "Marv" (b. August 3, 1928, Chicago, IL), college and professional player, coach, and sportscaster, is the son of Samuel Levy, a wholesale produce businessman, and Ida Levy and graduated in 1946 from

Chicago's South Shore High School, where he participated in football, basketball, and track and field. A star football running back and a sprinter on the track and field team at Coe College (MWC) in Cedar Rapids, IA, from 1948 to 1950, Levy graduated Phi Beta Kappa in 1950 and earned a master's degree in English history from Harvard University in 1957. Levy and his wife Dorothy reside in Orchard Park, NY.

Levy began his career on the high school level as head football coach at St. Louis, MO, Country Day High School in 1951 and 1952, compiling a 13–0–1 record in two seasons. He returned to Coe College, his alma mater, as an assistant football coach for three seasons from 1953 to 1955. After joining the University of New Mexico (MSAC) staff as an assistant football coach in 1956, Levy served as head football coach for the Lobos in 1958 and 1959. Both squads finished with 7–3 records, as he earned MSAC Coach of the Year honors both seasons. As head coach at the University of California at Berkeley (AAWU) from 1960 to 1963, Levy encountered minimal success with an 8–29 record. Levy's next stop came at the College of William and Mary (SC), where he compiled a 23–25–2 record from 1964 to 1968 and a 1965 SC championship.

Levy began his professional career in 1969 as an assistant football coach with the Philadelphia Eagles (NFL). George Allen (FB) of the Los Angeles Rams (NFL) recruited him as an assistant football coach for the Rams in 1970 and for the Washington Redskins (NFL) the next season. Levy remained with the Redskins through the 1972 season, when Washington lost to the Miami Dolphins in Super Bowl VII. He was named head coach of the Montreal, Canada, Alouettes (CFL) in 1973 and compiled a 50–34–4 record there over five seasons. His Alouette teams appeared in three Grey Cup (CFL championship) games, defeating the Edmonton Eskimoes, 20–7, in 1974 and 41–6 in 1977.

As head coach of the Kansas City Chiefs (NFL) from 1978 to 1982, Levy produced a 31–42 record. After leaving Kansas City following the strike-shortened 1982 season, he worked as a color commentator with NBC and ESPN television and the University of California radio team in 1983 and became head football coach of the Chicago Blitz (USFL) in 1984. His squad recorded a 5–13 record in the Blitz's only year in existence. Levy spent 1985 as director of Football Operations for the Montreal Alouettes and replaced Hank Bullough in November 1986 as head football coach of the Buffalo Bills (NFL). In Levy's 9 seasons there through 1994, the Bills have compiled an 86–54 win–loss record, won five AFC Eastern Division championships, including four consecutive titles (1988–1991, 1993), and appeared in four successive Super Bowls. Buffalo lost to the New York Giants, 20–19, in 1991, Washington Redskins, 37–24, in 1992, and Dallas Cowboys, 52–17, in 1993 and 30–13 in 1994. Levy's career, including 1 USFL season, 5 CFL campaigns, and 13 NFL seasons, has produced a head coaching record of 182–143–4. He was named the 1988 NFL Coach of the Year.

BIBLIOGRAPHY: *Buffalo Bills Media Guide*, 1994; *TSN Pro Football Register*, 1994.
                                                                      John L. Evers

LOCKE, Gordon C. (b. August 3, 1899, Denison, IA; d. November 9, 1969, Kensington, MD), college player and coach, made football All-America in 1922 at fullback and captained the University of Iowa (WC) squad. His honors included membership in the HAF Hall of Fame and election in 1960 to the NFF College Football Hall of Fame. The two-time All-WC fullback played on Iowa's national championship teams of 1921 and 1922, earning the Hawkeyes' WC scholar–athlete Medal of Honor. Hawkeye fans in 1970 named Locke to their All-Time Iowa All-Star team.

Locke graduated in 1919 from Denison High School, starring three seasons on the gridiron. Iowa coach Howard Jones (FB) used two blocking halfbacks and two ballcarriers, including All-America quarterback Aubrey Devine (S) and the 5-foot-10-inch, 180-pound fullback Locke. A triple threat, Locke carried the ball in short yardage situations, exhibited sufficient speed to run around the ends, and possessed powerful knees to plow up the middle. In 1921, Locke rushed over 700 yards and ranked as the WC's second leading scorer. He plunged from the 1-yard line for the Hawkeyes' only touchdown to help terminate the University of Notre Dame's 20-game winning streak and rushed for 202 yards and both touchdowns in a 14–2 triumph over the University of Illinois.

Iowa in 1922 lost to graduation three fourths of its backfield plus All-America tackle Fred "Duke" Slater (FB), but the Hawkeyes duplicated their perfect slate and shared the WC title with the University of Michigan. Locke set a WC five-game scoring record that lasted 21 years with 72 points on 12 touchdowns. He notched the only touchdown in Iowa's 6–0 triumph over Yale University, scored 3 touchdowns to help defeat the University of Minnesota for the fifth straight season, garnered both tallies and gained 126 yards in a 12–0 win over Ohio State University, and posted 4 touchdowns when the Hawkeyes overwhelmed Northwestern University.

Locke carried 430 times for 1,978 yards, averaging 4.6 yards per carry rushing during his career. He tallied 4 touchdowns in a game four times and set Hawkeye career records with 32 touchdowns and 192 points. Legendary coach John Heisman (FB) once wrote, "Powerful is an inadequate adjective to use in describing his strength and ramming talents. He had the legs that gave the drive the momentum of a battle tank."

Locke earned a B.A. degree in 1924 and a J.D. degree in 1925 from Iowa, ranking third in his class. He served as assistant football coach at Iowa and (Case) Western Reserve University and then concentrated on his law practice in Washington, D.C. until retiring in 1965. Locke married Marguerite Pappano and had one child.

BIBLIOGRAPHY: Chuck Bright, *University of Iowa Football* (Huntsville, AL, 1982); Dick Lamb and Bert McGrane, *The Fighting Hawkeyes* (Dubuque, IA, 1964); Ronald

L. Mendell and Timothy B. Phares, *Who's Who in Football* (New Rochelle, NY, 1974); Earl M. Rogers, University of Iowa Archivist, Iowa City, IA, letter to James Whalen, 1993.

James D. Whalen

LONG, Howard M. "Howie" (b. January 6, 1960, Somerville, MA), college and professional player and sportscaster, grew up in the street gang environment of Charleston, MA, a suburb of Boston, and learned to work hard for everything he got. Long attended Milford, MA, High School, where he started as a three-year letterman in football, basketball, and track and field. In track and field, he set State records for the discus and shot put and threw the javelin. His football honors included being named defensive lineman to the Scholastic Coaches All-America team as a senior. For the basketball squad, he started three years at forward.

Long's football achievements earned him a scholarship to Villanova University, where he lettered as a defensive player all four years. During his sophomore year, he led the Wildcats in quarterback sacks. As a senior, he was selected to the All-East Honorable Mention All-America team and appeared in the 1980 Blue-Gray All-Star Game. With the Blue team, he was chosen the MVP of the game. Long graduated from Villanova in 1981 with a Bachelor of Arts degree in communications.

The Oakland Raiders (NFL) selected Long, a six-foot-five-inch, 270-pound defensive end, in the second round of the 1981 draft. In 1982, he earned a starting spot on the defensive line. Two years later, the NFLAA voted him Defensive Lineman of the Year. He garnered the top defensive lineman award from the Raiders' Lineman Club in 1985 and was selected to the NFL Pro Bowl team following the 1982 to 1987, 1989, 1992, and 1993 seasons. In 1986, fans named Long NFL Lineman of the Year. Long recorded 5 quarterback sacks in leading the Raiders to a 38–9 victory over the Washington Redskins in Super Bowl XVIII and also appeared in the AFC championship game in 1990. During the 1987 players' strike, Long crossed the picket line. He retired following the 1993 season, having recorded 84 sacks and intercepted two passes in 179 games. Long, who is married and has three sons, Christopher, Kyle, and Howie, resides in Rolling Hills Estates, CA. In 1994 FBC signed him as a commentator for NFL games.

BIBLIOGRAPHY: Dave Cunningham, "The Defensive End from Central Casting," *Game Day National* (1986), pp. 1–7; Howie Long file, Pro Football Hall of Fame, Canton, OH; *TSN Pro Football Register*, 1994.

Raymond C. Fetters

LOTT, Ronald Mandel "Ronnie" (b. May 8, 1959, Albuquerque, NM), college and professional athlete, is the son of Roy D. Lott, a career Air Force member, and Mary (Carroll) Lott. After residing in Albuquerque and Washington, D.C., Lott in 1969 moved with his family to Rialto, CA. At Eisenhower High School, he lettered three years in football, basketball, and baseball and received All-CiL honors three years in football and basketball and two years in baseball. In 1977, his honors included being named *Parade* Magazine High School All-America in football and earning the Ken Hubbs Memorial Award as the San Bernardino area's outstanding athlete.

Lott entered the University of Southern California (PTC) in 1977 and received his bachelor's degree in public administration in 1981. He lettered one year as a sophomore guard in basketball. As a defensive back in football, Lott achieved All-America and All-PTC honors in his junior and senior years. In 1980, Lott intercepted eight passes to rank second nationally and was chosen team MVP and "Most Inspirational Player." Southern California won the national collegiate football championship in 1978 and ranked number two nationally in 1979, winning Rose Bowl games both seasons.

The San Francisco 49ers (NFL) selected the six-foot, 200-pound defensive back as their first-round choice (eighth overall) of the 1981 NFL draft. During a distinguished 10-year career with San Francisco, the hard-hitting, intense Lott played cornerback from 1981 through 1984 and free safety from 1985 through 1990. He holds 49er records for career interceptions (51), interception yardage returns (643) and interception touchdowns (five). Lott was named All-Pro in 1983, 1986, 1987, and 1989, making the Pro Bowl nine seasons at both cornerback and free safety. The 49ers won four Super Bowl championships, defeating the Cincinnati Bengals, 26–21, in 1982 in Super Bowl XVI, the Miami Dolphins, 38–16, in 1985 in Super Bowl XIX, Cincinnati, 20–6, in 1989 in Super Bowl XXIII, and the Denver Broncos, 55–10, in 1990 in Super Bowl XXIV. In 1991, the New York Giants defeated the 49ers, 15–13, in the NFC championship game. On March 2, 1991, Lott married Karen Collmer. They have one daughter and live in Cupertino, CA. Lott also has a son, Ryan, born in 1979.

Lott, left unprotected by San Francisco, signed for two years as a Plan B free agent with the Los Angeles Raiders (NFL) in March 1991, receiving $800,000 per year and a $100,000 signing bonus. In 1991, Lott led the NFL in interceptions with 8 and was selected as a strong safety, his third position, to his tenth Pro Bowl. The Raiders lost to the Kansas City Chiefs, 10–6, in the AFC Wild Card playoff game. Lott, who received the 1991 Raider "Commitment to Excellence" Award, topped the 7–9 Raiders with 103 tackles the following season but made only 1 interception. Lott's 63 career interceptions rank fifth in NFL history. In March 1993, Lott signed with the New York Jets (NFL) as an unrestricted free agent for two years at $3.6 million, including a $500,000 signing bonus. The following year, a panel of NFL and Pro Football officials, former players, and reporters named him one of three safeties on the NFL All-Time Team. In September 1994, *USA Today* named Lott to its 75th Anniversary Team. In February 1995, the Jets released Lott.

BIBLIOGRAPHY: *Los Angeles Raiders Media Guide*, 1992; Ronnie Lott with Jill Lieber, *Total Impact* (New York, 1991); *NYT*, March 9, 1993; *TSN Pro Football Register*, 1994; Michael W. Tuckman and Jeff Schultz, *The San Francisco 49ers: Team of the Decade* (Rocklin, CA, 1989); *Who's Who Among Black Americans*, 1992–1993.

David Bernstein

LOURIE, Donald Bradford "Don" (b. August 22, 1899, Decatur, AL; d. January 15, 1990, Longwood, FL), college player and referee, was the son of George B. Lourie, manager of Peru, IL, Plow and Wheel Company, and Anna (Crocker) Lourie and had one sister. Lourie attended LaSalle-Peru High School and graduated from Phillips Exeter Academy, where he captained the football team, participated in track and field, and was chosen class and senior council president. He served as a private in the U.S. Army's Central Officers Training Corps before entering Princeton University in 1918. He captained the freshman track and field team. A three-year varsity football player, the 5-foot-11-inch, 158- to 164-pound Lourie exemplified coach William W. Roper's* belief that "any boy can be a football player."

Princeton in 1920 enjoyed its best season since 1896, sharing national honors with the University of California and the University of Notre Dame. Princeton and Harvard University tied each other, while winning six and eight games, respectively. Consequently, the East had no undisputed champion. Lourie scored six touchdowns in five games, making a memorable 50-yard touchdown from a fake placekick in Princeton's 20–0 shutout of Yale University. The First Team All-America quarterback was, wrote Donald Grant Herring, "a superb field general."

Princeton's 4–3 1921 season proved disappointing. Lourie scored three touchdowns before being sidelined by an injury for three games. He returned for the Harvard and Yale games but did not score. A "triple H-Y-P tie" resulted because Princeton defeated Harvard and lost to Yale, while Harvard vanquished Yale. Lourie was selected as a Third Team All-America quarterback. His scholarship, leadership, and athletic prowess also earned him Princeton's Arthur Wheeler* and [John P., Jr.] Poe Cups. He received the Gold Medal Award of the NFF and Hall of Fame in 1964 and was elected to the NFF College Football Hall of Fame in 1974.

Lourie won the broad jump at several track and field competitions, including the July 1920 British Amateur Athletic Association annual championships (22 feet 4 inches), the July 1920 dual Princeton-Oxford University meet (21 feet 6 inches), and the May 1921 Princeton-Yale meet.

Classmates voted Lourie "best all-around athlete" and the one who had "done most for Princeton." His activities included being president of his sophomore and senior classes and of Tiger Inn, an upperclass eating club, and serving on the senior council and on several committees.

After graduating in 1922, Lourie scouted for Princeton and assisted occasionally in coaching before big games. He also refereed games in the Middle West. Lourie declined an offer to play football professionally with the Chicago Bears (NFL) and joined Quaker Oats Company as a trainee. He rose to the Quaker Oats presidency (1947–1962), held the chief executive officer post (1956–1966), chaired the board (1962–1970), and served as a director (1945–1990). He took a leave of absence in 1953–1954 to become President Dwight D. Eisenhower's undersecretary of state for Administration. Lourie was awarded honorary Doctor of Law degrees by Lincoln College in 1956, Cornell University in 1958, Lawrence University in 1965, and the University of Chattanooga in 1965. Both an alumnus and a charter trustee of Princeton, he jointly gave the Lourie-Love Hall with George Hutchinson (Cupe) Love, his Exeter and Princeton roommate. An Episcopalian, Lourie married Mary Edna King in 1923 and had three children, Donald King, Nancy Bradford, and M. Ann Lourie.

BIBLIOGRAPHY: "Donald Lourie, 91, a Retired Chairman of Quaker Oats Co.," *NYT*, January 20, 1990; Jay Dunn, *The Tigers of Princeton: Old Nassau Football* (Huntsville, AL, 1977); Donald Grant Herring, "The Football Season in Review," *Princeton Alumni Weekly* 22 (November 30, 1921), pp. 198–199; Donald Grant Herring, "Football, the Princeton Season Reviewed," *Princeton Alumni Weekly* 21 (November 24, 1920), pp. 173–176; Donald Grant Herring, "Princeton 20 Yale 0," *Princeton Alumni Weekly* 21 (November 17, 1920), pp. 152–157; Donald Grant Herring, "The Track Team's Trip to England," *Princeton Alumni Weekly* 21 (October 6, 1920), pp. 12–17; John D. McCallum and Charles H. Pearson, *College Football U.S.A., 1869–1973* (New York, 1973); Ronald L. Mendell and Timothy B. Phares, *Who's Who in Football* (New Rochelle, NY, 1974); Princeton University, *Class of 1922 After 40 Years* (Princeton, NJ, 1962), pp. 181–182; Princeton University, *Princeton Bric-a-Brac* (Princeton, NJ, 1923); Princeton University, *Princeton Class of 1922, Nassau Herald Class of Nineteen Hundred and Twenty-two* (Princeton, NJ, 1922), pp. 203–204, 437–438; Princeton University, *Quarter Century Class of 1922, Twenty-five Year Record* (Princeton, NJ, 1947), pp. 137–138; William W. Roper, *Football—Today and Tomorrow* (New York, 1927); Jack Weller and Cornelia Weller, *Princeton Football Surviving Letter Men 1916–1942* (Princeton, NJ, 1984); *WWA*, 36th ed. (1970–1971), p. 1396; *WWWA*, vol. 10 (1989–1993), p. 218.

                                                                    Marcia G. Synnott

LOWERY, Nicholas Dominic "Nick" (b. May 27, 1956, Munich, Germany), college and professional player, is the son of Sidney Lowery, a Fulbright scholar, and Hazel Lowery, an honors Oxford University student. Lowery graduated from St. Albans High School in Washington, D.C. and Dartmouth College, where he earned a B.A. degree in government in 1978, won its first President's Award for outstanding leadership and achievement, and placekicked two seasons for the football team. In 1976, he converted all eight field goals, including a 52-yarder, and 35 consecutive extra points for 6–3 Dartmouth (IvL).

After graduation, however, the six-foot-four-inch, 205-pound Lowery found it quite difficult to make the NFL as a placekicker. From 1978 to

1980, he was released 11 times by eight different teams. In his brief stint with the New England Patriots (NFL) in 1978, Lowery managed just 7 extra points and no field goals. He replaced Jan Stenerud (S), the Kansas City Chiefs' (NFL) popular 13-year veteran, in 1980 in a move that stunned the professional football world. Lowery embarked on a tremendous scoring spree, accumulating at least 100 points 11 times in his 15-year career and setting an NFL record for most seasons cracking the centennial mark. During this span, he broke the 100-point barrier 6 consecutive times from 1988 to 1993 to share this unique record with Gino Cappelletti (FB).

Lowery in 1989 became only the fifteenth player in NFL history to reach the 1,000 career point plateau. Following that season, he visited his German birthplace to view the remains of the Berlin Wall after its historic destruction several months earlier. Lowery, an extremely accurate kicker, led the NFL a record six times in field goal average and especially demonstrated precision on distance kicks. In 1989, he set an NFL record with his eighteenth 50-yard-plus career field goal. Lowery made 2 field goals of at least 50 yards in three different games to set another NFL mark. His NFL career distance bests comprised 58-yarders in 1983 and 1985. In 1992, he reached another milestone by becoming just the sixth player in NFL history to collect 300 career field goals.

Through the 1994 season, Lowery has made 349 field goals in 434 attempts and 512 conversions for 1,559 points. In June 1994, the New York Jets (NFL) signed Lowery as a free agent. He ranks third among NFL career scorers in points and field goals and first in field goal average (80 percent), having broken virtually all of Stenerud's Chiefs' team records. Lowery appeared in the Pro Bowl following the 1981, 1990, and 1992 seasons. He remains single and participates in many business ventures concerning the social development of youth. As a former volunteer for the Drug Abuse Police Office in 1987–1988, he became the only active NFL player ever to serve on the White House staff.

BIBLIOGRAPHY: Rick Gonsalves, NFL Placekickers' Stat Sheets, Gloucester, MA; *Kansas City Chiefs Press Guide*, 1993; *TSN Pro Football Register*, 1994.

Richard Gonsalves

LYNCH, James Robert "Jim" (b. August 28, 1945, Lima, OH), college and professional player, played football for Lima Central Catholic High School and entered the University of Notre Dame, where he started as a linebacker for three consecutive years.

Lynch led the Fighting Irish in tackles in both 1965 and 1966, captaining the 1966 national championship team. Coach Ara Parseghian (FB) never picked his finest team, but it may have been the 1966 aggregation that finished 9–0–1.

Ten of Lynch's teammates in 1966 joined him in receiving All-America

mention, including Nick Eddy,* Tom Regner, Alan Page (FB), Pete Dur-
anko, Paul Seller, Kevin Hardy, Jim Seymour, Tom Schoen, George Goed-
deke, and Larry Conjar. Lynch also received the Maxwell Award as the top
College Player of the Year and the Outstanding Lineman Award from the
Washington, D.C. Touchdown Club, being selected to both the East-West
Shrine game and the Coaches All-America game. He captained the College
All-Stars when they played the NFL champion Green Bay Packers.

In 1967, he earned a B.A. degree in sociology and was the second-round
draft choice of the Kansas City Chiefs (AFL). He started at linebacker for
the Chiefs in 142 consecutive games between 1967 and 1977. He played in
both the 1969 AFL All-Star and Championship games and then helped defeat the Minnesota Vikings in the 1970 Super Bowl.

During his professional career, Lynch intercepted 17 passes and recovered
14 fumbles. He was inducted into the Kansas City Chiefs Hall of Fame in
1990 and the NFF College Football Hall of Fame in 1992.

Following his professional career, he served as vice president of a food
brokerage house and became prominent in the civic affairs of Kansas City.

BIBLIOGRAPHY: Richard M. Cohen et al., *Notre Dame Football Scrap Book* (New York,
1977); David Neft et al., eds., *The Football Encyclopedia*, 2nd ed. (New York, 1994);
Gene Schoor, *100 Years of Notre Dame Football* (New York, 1987).

                                                                Stanley Grosshandler

McCLENDON, Charles Youmans "Charlie Mac" (b. October 17, 1923, Lewisville, AR), college player, coach, and executive, is the son of Leigh Alexander McClendon, a farmer, and Susie (Robey) McClendon. He graduated
in 1941 from Lewisville High School but never played football there. After
serving in the U.S. Navy from 1943 to 1946, McClendon attended Magnolia,
AR, JC on a basketball scholarship and performed at running back and defensive end on their football team. McClendon played tight end and defensive end for coach Paul "Bear" Bryant (FB) at the University of Kentucky
(SEC) in 1949 and 1950 and proved instrumental in the Wildcats' defeat of
the University of Oklahoma in the 1951 Sugar Bowl, snapping the Sooners'
31-game winning streak. His teammates included George Blanda (FB), Babe
Parilli (S), and Jerry Claiborne (S). McClendon earned his bachelor's degree
at Kentucky in 1950 and his master's degree in school administration from
there the following year.

McClendon's first assistant football coach assignments came at Kentucky
for two seasons and at Vanderbilt University (SEC) for one season. Upon
joining the Louisiana State University staff, McClendon spent 9 years as an
assistant football coach under Gaynell Tinsley (FB) and Paul Dietzel. As
LSU head coach for 18 years from 1962 to 1979, McClendon compiled a
137–59–7 win–loss record for a .692 winning percentage and a 7–6–0 bowl
game record. His squads triumphed twice in the Cotton (1963, 1966) and

Sugar (1965, 1968) Bowls and once each in the Peach (1968), Sun (1971), and Tangerine (1979) Bowls. McClendon's honors included being named 1970 National AFCA Coach of the Year and SEC Coach of the Year in 1969 and 1970. McClendon, who coached 17 All-Americas and 53 All-SEC players, was named in 1982 to the Louisiana and Arkansas Sports Halls of Fame and in 1986 to the LSU Hall of Distinction and the NFF College Football Hall of Fame. For McClendon's outstanding service in the advancement of the best interests of football, the AFCA in 1992 selected him as the forty-seventh recipient of the Amos Alonzo Stagg Award.

Following his active coaching career, McClendon served two years as executive director of the Tangerine Bowl. In 1982, the AFCA named McClendon its executive director, a position he maintained until his retirement in 1994. During his tenure, AFCA membership doubled to 6,000. McClendon devised a retirement plan, adopted in 1987, expressly for those in the coaching profession and initiated a project giving assistant coaches more job security. In 1986, he played an instrumental role in the establishment of a $500,000 scholarship program, currently underwritten by McDonald's Corporation. McClendon married Dorothy Faye Smart in December 1947 and has two children, Scott and Dee.

BIBLIOGRAPHY: *AFCA Proceedings of the Sixty-ninth Meeting*, 1992; *Louisiana State University Media Guide*, 1992; Russell Rice, *The Wildcats: A Story of Kentucky Football* (Huntsville, AL, 1975); *WWA*, 47th ed. (1992–1993), p. 2241.

John L. Evers

McGOVERN, John Francis "Johnnie" (b. September 15, 1887, Arlington, MN; d. December 14, 1963, LeSueur, MN), college player and coach, was the son of Hugh McGovern and Mary Ann (Mohan) McGovern. His father worked as a police officer. At Arlington High School, he starred at football and baseball. At the University of Minnesota (WC), he lettered in both football and baseball. During McGovern's junior year of varsity football in 1909, authorities considered him the nation's best college quarterback. The small star captained the Golden Gophers and became Minnesota's first All-America selection.

McGovern's principal asset remained his ability to inspire the Golden Gophers by his own courage and determination. Several football tactics attributed to him included zigzagging instead of hitting the line, slanting off tackle and skirting the ends, and faking passes and running and cutting. He led the Gophers to a WC title in 1909, excelling as a brilliant open field runner and scoring many points with his accurate dropkicking.

Late in the 1909 season, McGovern broke his collar bone in a game against the University of Chicago. Games remained with the University of Wisconsin and the University of Michigan. The break was not healed, but McGovern believed that Walter Camp (FB) would not select him to the mythical team if he did not play against Michigan. McGovern convinced coach Henry Williams (FB) to let him play. Michigan coach Fielding Yost (FB), upon hearing of McGovern's plans, told his Wolverine squad to play hard but to be careful not to hurt McGovern further. Michigan won the game, handing the Gophers their only loss. Minnesota's six wins in seven games gave them the WC title. Camp selected McGovern to his 1909 All-America team.

McGovern returned for the 1910 season, which produced another 6–1 record and a loss to Michigan. The Michigan victory led to the return of the Little Brown Jug, a water bottle left in the Minnesota locker room in 1903. A great tradition was established, with the winner of the Minnesota-Michigan game earning the jug.

After graduation from the Minnesota Law School in 1911, McGovern coached Macalester College's football team. He rejected offers to coach the University of Washington (PCC) football team and play professional baseball. He served in the submarine service in World War I and worked for the U.S. Department of Justice, investigating sabotage. He practiced law in Washington, D.C. for a short time and served as president of its Touchdown Club. McGovern worked as sports editor of the Minneapolis (MN) *Journal* in the 1920s and in 1929 began broadcasting Minnesota football games on station KSTP.

McGovern subsequently became a vice president of Green Giant Canning Company and president of the National Canners Association. A gifted master of ceremonies, he remained much in public demand. His University of Minnesota affiliations included memberships in the Grey Friars, Alpha Tau Omega, and Phi Delta Phi fraternities. In 1949, he became national chairman of the Greater University Fund. An enthusiastic hunter, he is enshrined in the NFF College Football and Minnesota Sports Halls of Fame. He married Wade Masterman and had one son, Duff.

BIBLIOGRAPHY: George A. Barton, *My Lifetime in Sports* (Minneapolis, MN, 1957); Stan W. Carlson, *Dr. Henry L. Williams: A Football Biography* (Minneapolis, MN, 1936); Dick Fisher, *Who's Who in Minnesota Athletics* (Minneapolis, MN, 1941); John McGovern file, University of Minnesota Archives, Walter Library, Minneapolis, MN; Ralph Turtinen, ed., *100 Years of Golden Gopher Football* (Minneapolis, MN, 1981); *University of Minnesota Football Media Guide*, 1992.

Stan W. Carlson

MACK, Thomas Lee "Tom" (b. November 1, 1943, Cleveland, OH), college and professional player, is the son of Ray Mack, a professional baseball player, and Jean (Fischer) Mack and starred at offensive guard for the Los Angeles Rams (NFL) from 1966 to 1978. His father played second base for the Cleveland Indians (AL), New York Yankees (AL), and Chicago Cubs (NL) from 1938 to 1947. The younger Mack attended Cleveland Heights

High School, where he played football and baseball and set records in swimming.

Mack played football at the University of Michigan (BTC) under coach Bump Elliott. He started on the 1964 team, which defeated Oregon State University, 34–7, in the Rose Bowl. His honors as a senior included being named an All-America on the UPI and NEA teams and participation in the East-West, Hula Bowl, and College All-Star games. He received his Bachelor of Science degree from Michigan in 1968.

The Los Angeles Rams (NFL) made Mack a first draft choice in 1966 and the second overall pick behind Tommy Nobis (FB). Mack began starting at left guard midway through his rookie season, even though Rams' coach George Allen (FB) rarely used rookies in the starting lineup. The six-foot-three-inch, 250-pound Mack was known for his speed and consistency and never missed a game with the Rams, specializing in blocking for the run.

Mack won numerous honors during his illustrious career, including selection to the *TSN* NFL WC All-Star team in 1969, *TSN* NFC All-Star team in 1970, 1972–1975, and 1977, UPI All-Pro team in 1977, and *PFW* All-Pro team in 1977. Mack, who played in the Pro Bowl following the 1967 through 1975 and 1977 seasons, recovered four fumbles in 1974 and one fumble in 1975, and retired following the 1978 season.

Mack in 1966 married Anne Tollefson, a 1965 Rose Bowl princess. They have three daughters. Since 1979, he has been employed by the Bechtel Corporation as an engineer.

BIBLIOGRAPHY: Steve Bisheff, "Make Room for Tom Who," *Sport* 57 (January 1974), pp. 35–36; *Los Angeles Rams Media Guide*, 1978; Los Angeles Rams Press Release, November 22, 1971; *TSN Pro Football Register*, 1978.

Robert L. Cannon

McNEIL, Freeman (b. April 22, 1959, Jackson, MS), college and professional player, is the son of Freeman McNeil, Jr., who died at age 26 when McNeil was seven, and Gladys McNeil. After his father's death, McNeil withdrew until well into his adult life. McNeil was much influenced by his absent father. An uncle showed him an old photo of Freeman McNeil, Jr., as a running back at a Mississippi JC and inspired him to pursue football. McNeil's mother taught him to cook, sew, and iron and emphasized that few people get a free ride in life. As a tenth grader, McNeil tried out for football at Centennial High School in Compton, CA, but did not make the team. In 1975, McNeil moved to Wilmington, CA, and starred at I-back at Banning High School. McNeil, highly recruited as a senior, rushed for 1,343 yards (8.1-yard average) with 27 touchdowns and was named 1976 Los Angeles City Player of the Year.

Due to his friendship with soft-spoken Bruins assistant football coach Frank Gansz, McNeil chose UCLA and played there behind Theotis Brown and James Owens. By 1979, the Bruins installed an I-formation running attack well suited to McNeil's talents. He rushed for a UCLA record 1,396 yards and gained 1,105 yards in 1980. McNeil made 1980 All-America teams, which included three running backs. Heisman Trophy winner George Rogers (FB) and Herschel Walker (FB) dominated the two back teams.

The New York Jets (NFL) made McNeil the first-round pick in 1981 and third selection overall behind Rogers and Lawrence Taylor (FB). The 5-foot-11-inch, 214-pound McNeil excelled at running back with the Jets for 12 years, becoming their all-time career rushing leader with 8,074 yards (4.5-yard average) and 38 touchdowns. He also caught 295 passes for 2,961 yards (10-yard average) and 12 touchdowns. His football honors included UCLA's MVP in 1979 and 1980, the Mackey Award in 1981, the Jets' MVP from 1981 through 1984, 1,000 yards rushing in 1984 and 1985, and a Pro Bowl selection in 1982, 1984, 1985, and 1986. McNeil led the NFL in rushing in 1982, gaining 786 yards for a 5.2-yard average. In 1990, McNeil and seven other NFL players sued the NFL, charging that the Plan B system constituted an illegal restraint of trade. The case was decided in McNeil's favor in 1992, allowing individual players greater freedom of movement and increased bargaining power. McNeil married his wife, Rosaria, in 1987 and has two children, Luca and Freeman.

BIBLIOGRAPHY: Bruce Newman, "Remorse? Not in the NFL," *SI* 71 (October 16, 1989), p. 112; *NYT*, 1979–1993; *TSN Pro Football Register*, 1993; *Who's Who Among Black Americans, 1994–95* (Detroit, MI, 1994), p. 1008; Paul Zimmer, "The Loneliness of the League's Leading Rusher," *SI* 57 (December 20, 1982), pp. 28–32.

John H. Ziegler

MALLORY, William Guy "Bill" (b. May 30, 1935, Glendale, WV), college player and coach, is the son of Guy Mallory, a teacher, coach, and administrator, and Freda Mallory and graduated in 1953 from Sandusky, OH, High School, where he played football and served as Student Council president.

At Miami University of Ohio (MAC), Mallory played offensive and defensive end three years for Ara Parseghian (FB) and one for John Pont and was twice named to the All-MAC team. Mallory, who cocaptained the Redskins as a senior, earned a bachelor's degree in education from Miami in 1957 and a master's degree from Bowling Green University in 1958.

After serving as head football coach at East Palestine, OH, High School, he worked as an assistant coach at Bowling Green (MAC), Yale University (IvL), and Ohio State University (BTC) under Doyt Perry, Carmen Cozza, and Woody Hayes (FB), respectively. In 1969, Miami named him head football coach. His first four teams each produced 7–3 win–loss records, while his 1973 squad won all 11 contests. The Redskins captured the 1973 MAC championship and defeated the University of Florida, 16–7, in the Tangerine

Bowl, as Mallory was named MAC and District Coach of the Year. Mallory in 1974 was appointed as head coach at the University of Colorado (BEC), where the Buffaloes compiled a five-year 35–21–1 record. His 1975 squad lost to the University of Texas, 38–21, in the Bluebonnet Bowl. His 1976 Buffaloes won the BEC cochampionship, but Ohio State defeated Colorado, 27–10, in the Orange Bowl. Colorado released Mallory following the 1978 season. Mallory returned from a one-year hiatus to head coaching in 1980, guiding Northern Illinois University (MAC) to a 25–19 record in four seasons. His 1983 Huskies compiled a 10–2 record, won the MAC title, and triumphed, 20–13, over Fullerton State University in the California Bowl.

As Indiana University's head football coach 11 seasons from 1984 through 1994, Mallory has garnered a 63–61–3 record and 3 seasons with 8 victories. The Hoosiers have appeared in six postseason bowl games, including a 34–10 triumph in 1988 over the University of South Carolina in the Liberty Bowl and a 24–0 win in 1991 over Baylor University in the Copper Bowl. Mallory, the first BTC mentor voted BTC Coach of the Year consecutive seasons, won the honor in 1986 and 1987. The AFCA selected him Regional Coach of the Year both years. His 63 victories share first place in Hoosier history, equalling only Alvin "Bo" McMillan's (FB) 63 triumphs between 1934 and 1947.

In 25 seasons, Mallory's college teams have compiled a 162–113–4 mark and averaged 6.5 wins per season. Mallory, in 38 years as a collegiate player or coach, has been associated with 30 winning teams, 10 league champions, and two national titlists and has participated in 10 different bowl games. Lou Holtz (S), Earle Bruce,* and Mallory are the only coaches to guide four different schools to bowl games. Mallory in 1980 was enshrined in Miami University's Athletic Hall of Fame.

Mallory and his wife Eleanor have one daughter, Barbara, and three sons, Mike, Doug, and Curt, all of whom excelled defensively in football at the University of Michigan.

BIBLIOGRAPHY: *Indiana University Official Souvenir Magazine* (October 17, 1992), pp. 7–9; Bill Mallory, letter to John L. Evers, March 4, 1993.

John L. Evers

MARINARO, Edward Francis "Ed" "Italian Stallion" (b. March 31, 1950, New York, NY), college and professional player, is the son of Louis J. Marinaro, a sign painter, and Rose (Errico) Marinaro. After graduating in 1968 from New Milford High School in New Jersey, the heavily recruited Marinaro chose Cornell University (IvL) because of a desire for an Ivy League education. In 1972, he received a B.S. degree in hotel management.

In three years of varsity football for the Big Red from 1969 through 1971, the 6-foot-2½-inch, 210-pound Marinaro set 11 national and 12 IvL records and held virtually every team rushing and scoring mark. A slashing tailback with ability to run outside, the workhorse Marinaro rushed for a record-setting 4,715 career yards on 918 carries (174.6 yards per game average) and averaged 209 yards per game as a senior. He rushed for more than 100 yards in 23 out of 27 games and rambled for over 200 yards on 10 occasions. He averaged almost 2 touchdowns a game (2.7 as a senior). In his sophomore year, he set an IvL game mark while rushing for 281 yards against Harvard University. The rushing standard stood until 1980.

Marinaro led Cornell to the IvL cochampionship in his senior year. In over half of those games, he rushed at least 42 times while becoming the first nonpasser to win the IvL total offense title. Only Dartmouth College, the IvL coleader, defeated Cornell that year. A First Team UPI All-America in 1970, Marinaro earned consensus All-America honors his senior year and won the Maxwell Award as College Player of the Year. He finished a close second in the Heisman Trophy balloting to quarterback Pat Sullivan (FB) of Auburn University. Some sportswriters did not vote for Marinaro because they regarded the IvL an inferior conference. In 1981, he made the IvL Silver Anniversary Player of the 1956–1980 Era. A decade later, he entered the NFF College Football Hall of Fame.

In 1972, the Minnesota Vikings (NFL) made Marinaro the fiftieth selection in the second round of the draft. In four seasons for the Vikings, Marinaro rarely carried the ball more than seven times a game. He served as a blocking back for Chuck Foreman (FB), a 1,000-yard-per-season rusher, and also showed his versatility by catching passes out of the backfield, something he rarely had done at Cornell. In one NFL game in 1975, Marinaro snagged 11 receptions. That year, he finished third in the NFC with 54 catches. Supposedly lacking outside speed, the converted fullback was restricted to rushes into the center of the line. After playing out his option, Marinaro joined the New York Jets (NFL) for the 1976 season. After a slow start under coach Lou Holtz (S), he rushed for over 100 yards in two consecutive games. He then suffered a freak foot injury against the New England Patriots, ending his 1976 season. Marinaro played briefly for the Jets the following season and failed in comeback efforts that year with the Seattle Seahawks (NFL) and the Chicago Bears (NFL) in 1978. His career NFL statistics included 1,319 yards rushing for a 3.4-yard average and 246 receptions for 1,176 yards and an 8-yard average. He scored 13 touchdowns.

Jets teammate Joe Namath (FB) introduced the handsome Marinaro to Hollywood, where he emerged as a serious actor in the 1980s. His big breaks came as a regular on the "Laverne and Shirley" TV sitcom and as Policeman Joe Coffey in the critically acclaimed "Hill Street Blues." In the 1990s, he became a regular on another sitcom, "Sisters." Marinaro, a bachelor, resides in Los Angeles, CA.

BIBLIOGRAPHY: Harriet Ink, Administrative Aide, Research and Records Office, Cornell University, letter to James N. Giglio, June 7, 1993; Edward Marinaro, clipping file, Research and Records Office, Cornell University, Ithaca, NY; Edward Marinaro, clipping file, Sports Information Office, Cornell University, Ithaca, NY; *TSN Pro Football Register*, 1978.

James N. Giglio

MARTIN, James Richard "Jim" "Jungle Jim" (b. April 8, 1924, Cleveland, OH), college athlete and professional football player and coach, captained his football and swimming teams at East Technical High School in Cleveland and served four years with the U.S. Marines during World War II, winning a Bronze Star for Southwest Pacific Theater service. After enrolling in 1946 at the University of Notre Dame, he captured the school's 1947 heavyweight boxing championship and starred on four undefeated football teams. Under coach Frank Leahy (FB), the six-foot-two-inch, 238-pound Martin started 36 games at left end from 1946 to 1948 and defensive end and offensive tackle in 1949. Notre Dame compiled records of 8–0–1 in 1946, 9–0 in 1947, 9–0–1 in 1948, and 10–0 in 1949, taking AP national championships in 1946, 1947, and 1949 and ranking second in 1948. Martin, a remarkable tackle and blocker, earned the Herring Medal in 1946 as the Fighting Irish's best blocking end and made *Look* Third Team All-America in 1948. From 1946 to 1948, he caught 31 passes for 305 yards and one touchdown and netted 86 yards and one touchdown on end around plays. Martin cocaptained the 1949 squad with Leon Hart (FB), earning AP, INS, and NEA First Team All-America honors at tackle and ranking fifth in UP Lineman of the Year balloting. In 1950, he started for the East in its 28–6 triumph over the West in the Shrine All-Star Game and for the victorious College All-Stars in their 17–7 conquest of the Philadelphia Eagles.

The Cleveland Browns (NFL) selected Martin as a defensive end in the 1950 draft and dealt him in 1951 to the Detroit Lions (NFL). The Lions primarily used Martin as an offensive guard from 1952 to 1954 and defensive linebacker from 1955 to 1961 and kicker from 1957 onward. The Lions won the 1952–1954 and 1957 WC titles and 1952, 1953, and 1957 NFL championships, defeating the Cleveland Browns each time. In the 1957 title game, Martin tied Lou Groza's (FB) record with 8 conversions and also kicked 1 field goal in the Lions' 59–14 demolition of Cleveland. Martin's stellar play as linebacker and kicker in 1959 earned him Detroit's MVP award, although he made just 7 field goals for 21 points. In 1960, he broke the team record with 13 field goals and made 26 conversions for 65 points. Against the Baltimore Colts, Martin became the first NFL kicker to make 2 field goals of at least 50 yards in the same game. His output in 1961 increased to 70 points on a team-record 15 field goals and 25 extra points. In 1962, the Denver Broncos (AFL) appointed him an assistant football coach.

Martin, who played in one Pro Bowl, came out of retirement in 1963 at age 39 with Baltimore (NFL), finishing second in NFL scoring with 104 points, leading the NFL with 24 field goals, and recording 32 conversions. The total points, field goals, and extra points all marked career highs for

Martin, whose toe provided the winning margin in five of the Colts' eight victories. He kicked 4 field goals against Detroit to extend his consecutive streak to 9, both Baltimore records. Martin's outstanding season earned him NFL Comeback Player of the Year honors. In his final NFL season, Martin kicked for the Washington Redskins (NFL) in 1964. His 14-year NFL career produced 434 points on 92 field goals and 158 extra points. In 1995, the NFF College Football Hall of Fame inducted him. He and his wife Gloria have five children, Susanne, Beverly, Kevin, Lori, and Michael.

BIBLIOGRAPHY: *Baltimore Colts Press Guide*, 1964; *Detroit Lions Press Guide*, 1961; Rick Gonsalves, NFL Placekickers' Stat Sheets, Gloucester, MA; James R. Martin, letter to Richard Gonsalves, April 1994; *TSN Pro Football Register*, 1965; James D. Whalen, letter to David L. Porter, March 22, 1994.

Richard Gonsalves

MATHESON, Riley "Snake" (b. December 6, 1915, Shannon, TX), college and professional player, ranked among the premier NFL defensive football linemen of the World War II era. A rancher in the off-season, the rugged Matheson earned his nickname by being twice bitten by rattlesnakes. Teammates joked that the rattlesnakes died.

Matheson did not play high school football and performed as an undistinguished tackle and end at Texas School of Mines (now the University of Texas at El Paso). The Miners (BC) finished 5–2–1 in 1936, losing to Hardin-Simmons University, 34–6, in the Sun Bowl and compiled a 7–1–2 mark in 1937. Matheson graduated with a bachelor's degree in 1938, but no NFL team drafted him. In 1939, Cleveland Rams (NFL) coach Earl "Dutch" Clark (FB) offered him a $115 per game contract. Matheson reported to the Rams' training camp at Berea, OH, and was tried at guard. Although exhibiting considerable quickness, the inexperienced Matheson fell victim to "mousetraps" and was released after two games. He joined the Columbus, OH, Bullies (AFL) and learned to diagnose plays well.

Upon returning to the Rams in 1940, the six-foot-two-inch, 210-pound Texan verged on excellence. Matheson started for the Rams from 1940 through 1942, played the 1943 campaign with the Detroit Lions (NFL) when the Rams shut down operations for a season, and returned to Cleveland, garnering AP and UP All-NFL team honors in both 1944 and 1945. Despite Matheson's stellar performance, however, the Rams struggled through losing seasons from 1940 to 1942 and in 1944. Matheson played offensive guard and called defensive signals from his linebacker position. His ability to outmaneuver opponents, once a weak point, became one of his strongest assets. Several times, he faded back from his linebacker position to make pass interceptions beyond his own safety. The crowd favorite was given $1,125 and a gold watch on a special Riley Matheson Day ceremony.

The 1945 Rams rebounded to win the NFL championship by edging the Washington Redskins, 15–14. The Rams moved to Los Angeles in 1946, when Matheson made the UP All-NFL squad. Following the 1947 season, he jumped to the San Francisco 49ers of the rival AAFC and played his final professional season there.

BIBLIOGRAPHY: Riley Matheson file, Pro Football Hall of Fame, Canton, OH; David S. Neft, et al., eds., *The Football Encyclopedia, 2nd ed.* (New York, 1994); Beau Riffenburgh, *The Official NFL Encyclopedia*, 4th ed. (New York, 1986); Roger Treat, ed., *The Encyclopedia of Football*, 16th rev. ed. (New York, 1979).

Robert N. "Bob" Carroll

MATTE, Thomas Roland "Tom" (b. June 14, 1939, Pittsburgh, PA), college and professional player, is the son of Roland Joseph Matte, a professional hockey player, and graduated from Shaw High School in East Cleveland, OH, in 1957. He then played football for Ohio State University (BTC) from 1958 to 1960 under coach Woody Hayes (FB), receiving a Bachelor of Science degree in business administration in 1962. As a junior, Matte became the Buckeyes' starting quarterback and led Ohio State with 629 yards in total offense in 1959. Matte enjoyed a stellar senior season, rushing for 833 yards in 161 attempts and completing 50 of 95 passes. The six-foot, 214-pound option threat won All-BTC honors that year and was voted the outstanding back of the postseason East-West Shrine game.

The Baltimore Colts (NFL) selected Matte in the first round of the 1961 draft. Matte served as a reserve halfback during his first two seasons, but an injury to starter Lenny Moore (FB) increased Matte's playing time in 1963. That season, Matte rushed for 541 yards and caught 48 passes. Matte's greatest fame came in 1965, when injuries to Johnny Unitas (FB) and Gary Cuozzo forced him into action at quarterback. With a share of the WC title at stake, Matte gained 99 yards rushing and guided the Colts to a 20–17 victory over the Los Angeles Rams. The victory forced a playoff game for the WC championship against the Green Bay Packers, but the Colts lost, 13–10, despite Matte's determination. Two weeks later, he led the Colts to a Playoff Bowl victory over the Philadelphia Eagles, garnering MVP honors.

In 1967, Matte won the Colts' starting halfback job and led Baltimore in rushing with 636 yards. The following year, Matte again paced the Colts in rushing with 662 yards and scored 3 touchdowns in Baltimore's 34–0 victory over the Cleveland Browns in the NFL Championship game. In Super Bowl III, Matte played an outstanding game against the New York Jets while rushing for 116 yards in a losing effort. Matte enjoyed his finest season in 1969, pacing the Colts in rushing (909 yards) and receiving (43 catches) and the NFL in rushing touchdowns (11) and combined rushing and receiving yardage (1,422). He played in the Pro Bowl for the second consecutive year.

Matte spent most of 1970 on the injured list, as Baltimore won Super Bowl V with a victory over the Dallas Cowboys. The Colts traded Matte to the San Diego Chargers (NFL) after the 1972 season, but he retired before the 1973 campaign.

One of the NFL's most versatile backs during his career, Matte excelled as a runner, blocker, and passer on the halfback option play. His NFL lifetime statistics included 4,646 yards rushing in 1,200 attempts, 249 receptions for 2,869 yards, and 57 touchdowns.

BIBLIOGRAPHY: Doug Brown, "Behind the Tom Matte Miracle," *Sport* 41 (March 1966), pp. 20–22, 90–92; Harold Claassen and Steve Boda, Jr., *Ronald Encyclopedia of Football* (New York, 1963); Jack Clary, *30 Years of Pro Football's Greatest Moments* (New York, 1976); Ronald L. Mendell and Timothy B. Phares, *Who's Who in Football* (New Rochelle, NY, 1974); Paul Michael, *Professional Football's Greatest Games* (Englewood Cliffs, NJ, 1972); David S. Neft et al., eds., *The Football Encyclopedia*, 2nd ed. (New York, 1994); Beau Riffenburgh, *The Official NFL Encyclopedia*, 4th ed. (New York, 1986); Wilbur Snypp, *The Buckeyes: A Story of Ohio State Football* (Huntsville, AL, 1974); *TSN Pro Football Register*, 1969.

Marc S. Maltby

MILLER, Creighton Eugene (b. September 26, 1922, Cleveland, OH), college football player and coach, was the seventh member of his family to play football at the University of Notre Dame between 1906 and 1943. His father, M. Harry "Red" Miller, captained the 1908 team, while his brother Tom preceded him at South Bend by one year. Four of his uncles enjoyed impressive gridiron careers at Notre Dame. Ray substituted for the famed end and coach Knute Rockne (FB) and later became mayor of Cleveland, while Walter was a teammate of the legendary George Gipp (FB). Both tackle Gerry and halfback Don (FB) performed on Rockne's teams from 1922 through 1924, with the latter playing right half in the famous Four Horsemen backfield.

Creighton played football for Wilmington DE's Alexis I DuPont High School, making All-State twice. Altogether, he won 13 letters in football, basketball, baseball, and track and field. Upon entering Notre Dame in the fall of 1940, he stood six feet tall and weighed 185 pounds. During Miller's three varsity seasons at left halfback, the Fighting Irish lost but three games. The 1943 Notre Dame team came within 40 seconds of an undefeated season, losing their final game to Great Lakes Naval Training Station on a last-second pass. Nevertheless, the AP poll proclaimed Notre Dame the nation's number-one team.

Miller enjoyed a spectacular 1943 season, averaging 6.3 yards per carry, gaining 911 yards, and scoring 13 touchdowns. His best game came against the powerful University of Michigan Wolverines, as he scored twice to help the Fighting Irish demolish them, 35–12. Miller received All-America recognition at the end of the 1943 season and finished fourth in the Heisman voting, won by teammate quarterback Angelo Bertelli (FB).

Although a first-draft choice of the New York Giants (NFL), Miller attended Yale Law School. He graduated with a Bachelor of Law degree in 1947, serving as an assistant football coach for the Elis in 1945. He practiced law in Cleveland and helped form the Cleveland Browns (AAFC), working as their legal counsel from 1946 to 1953. In 1956, he became the first legal counsel for the NFLPA. Miller also served as Ohio assistant attorney general in 1949 and 1950.

When Miller was inducted into the NFF College Football Hall of Fame in 1976, his former teammate and fellow Hall of Famer John Lujack (FB) called him the finest ballcarrier he had ever seen.

BIBLIOGRAPHY: Allison Danzig, *The History of American Football* (Englewood Cliffs, NJ, 1956); Bernie McCarty, *All Americans, Vol. 1, 1889–1945* (University Park, IL, 1991); Ronald L. Mendell and Timothy B. Phares, *Who's Who in Football* (New Rochelle, NY, 1974); Gene Schoor, *100 Years of Notre Dame Football* (New York, 1987); Gene Schoor, *A Treasury of Notre Dame Football* (New York, 1962); David S. Neft et al., *The Notre Dame Football Scrap Book* (New York, 1977).

Stanley Grosshandler

MILSTEAD, Century Allen (b. January 1, 1900, Allegheny, PA; d. June 1, 1963, Pleasantville, NY), college and professional player, starred as an All-America football tackle on Yale University's 1923 squad, considered the Bulldogs' finest team. Milstead was named by his father, Lucian, who believed his birth coincided with the start of the twentieth century. His mother, Henrietta, countered unsuccessfully that the new century would not begin until 1901. The Milsteads lived in Pittsburgh, PA, and Denver, CO, before settling in Rock Island, IL. Milstead, large for his age, possessed natural football size at Rock Island High School and played there after overcoming his distaste for the game.

In 1921, Milstead enrolled in Wabash College and excelled at the tackle position. He transferred to Yale University in 1922, sitting out one season. Besides attending classes that year, he practiced with the football reserves, joined the wrestling and track and field teams, and earned money stoking furnaces in a local hotel. In his only season under coach Tad Jones (FB), Milstead joined transfers Mal Stevens, Lyle Richedson, and William "Widdy" Neale to help lead the 1923 Yale squad to an undefeated 8–0 record. The Elis scored 230 points while holding eight opponents to 38 points. Star back Bill Mallory, Milstead, Stevens, Richardson, and center Win Lovejoy were honored on Walter Camp's (FB) All-America team. Left tackle Milstead attracted attention for both his six-foot-four-inch, 220-pound size and his outstanding speed. Sportswriter Grantland Rice (OS) lauded Milstead as "one of the greatest tackles . . . a line in himself."

Milstead married Mildred Bechtel in 1924, violating Yale policy. After an investigation, the Yale faculty committee suspended Milstead from school. The penalty was lightened to allow him to take the final exams to graduate with his class, but he was not permitted to attend class. Milstead finished courses, although not officially graduating with his class. He and his wife had four children, Century, Jr., Millicent, Violet, and Mildred.

Milstead pursued professional football in 1925 with the New York Giants (NFL) and teamed there with several other great linemen, including Joe Alexander (FB), Cal Hubbard (FB), and Steve Owen (FB). In 1926, he jumped to Red Grange's (FB) new AFL with the Philadelphia Quakers. Milstead played tackle, coaching the Quakers to a 7–2 record and the AFL championship. The Quakers lost to the New York Giants, 31–0, in the first-ever interleague playoff. He returned to the Giants the following season and played two more NFL campaigns before retiring from professional football. Subsequently, Milstead worked in personnel, business management, and insurance sales before becoming a manager with the New York–New Jersey Waterfront Commission in 1953.

BIBLIOGRAPHY: *After Twenty-five Years, the Class of 1926* (New Haven, CT, 1951); Tim Cohane, *Great College Football Coaches of the Twenties and Thirties* (New Rochelle, NY, 1990); Tim Cohane, *The Yale Football Story* (New York, 1951); *History of the Class of 1926* (New Haven, CT, 1926); John McCallum, *Ivy League Football Since 1872* (New York, 1977); NYT, February 15, 1925, p. 6; June 3, 1963, p. 29.

Brian L. Laughlin

MONK, James Arthur "Art" (b. December 5, 1957, White Plains, NY), college and professional player, is the second of two children of Arthur Monk, a welder, and Lela Monk. A second cousin of the famous jazz musician Thelonius Monk, Monk excelled musically as a child. He graduated from White Plains High School, where he starred as a football back and performed as a national class high and intermediate hurdler. Monk entered Syracuse University in 1976 and played four seasons for the Orangemen as a halfback and wide receiver, catching 102 passes for 1,644 yards. He also rushed for 1,140 yards and gained 1,105 yards in kick returns.

The Washington Redskins (NFL) made Monk their first-round selection in the 1980 NFL draft. Monk, an immediate star, led Washington with 58 receptions his rookie season. His NFL-leading 106 receptions in 1984 set an NFL record that remained intact until broken in 1992 by Sterling Sharpe of the Green Bay Packers. The following season, Monk's 91 receptions placed him only 1 catch behind NFL leader Roger Craig.* Through the 1994 season, Monk had caught 934 passes for 12,607 yards and 68 touchdowns. He has surpassed the 1,000-yard mark in receptions five seasons and was named to the Pro Bowl team following the 1984, 1985, and 1986 campaigns. In December 1985, he made 13 catches for 230 yards against the Cincinnati Bengals. An All-Pro selection in 1984, he played in the Super Bowl XVIII loss against the Los Angeles Raiders, the Super Bowl XXII triumph over the Denver Broncos, and the Super Bowl XXVI victory over the Buffalo Bills. A broken foot prevented Monk from playing in Super Bowl XVII against the Miami Dolphins. Monk caught a touchdown pass in Super Bowl XXII and pulled in 7 receptions in Super Bowl XXVI.

Monk broke Steve Largent's (FB) NFL career reception record of 819 in the fifth game of the 1992 season and extended his streak of consecutive games with at least 1 reception to 180 through the 1994 season. Monk became a free agent following the 1993 season, signing in June 1994 with the New York Jets (NFL). In February 1995, the Jets released Monk. The soft-spoken Monk, considered a prodigious worker, specializes in the tough third down catch in traffic. Monk and his wife Desiree have three children, James Arthur, Jr., Danielle, and Monica.

BIBLIOGRAPHY: Tom Boswell, "The King of Third and Nine," *Washington Post Magazine*, September 9, 1990; Art Monk file, Sports Information Department, Syracuse University, Syracuse, NY; William Nack, "A Monk's Existence," *SI* 77 (September 7, 1992), pp. 32–40; *USA Today*, December 9, 1994, pp. 16–26; *Washington Redskins Media Guides*, 1980–1992.

Jim L. Sumner

MOON, Harold Warren (b. November 18, 1956, Los Angeles, CA), college and professional player, is the only boy in a family of seven children. Since his father Harold Moon, a laborer, died when Warren was seven, his mother, Pat Moon, a nurse, brought him up. Moon grew up in the Baldwin Hills section of Los Angeles and began playing organized football at age seven. He quarterbacked Hamilton High School as a senior in his hometown, being named the city's MVP, and was selected to the National All-America team. Moon played his freshman season at West Los Angeles JC and was elected to its Hall of Fame. Moon enrolled in 1975 at the University of Washington (PEC), where he majored in communications. Moon's three seasons as quarterback for coach Don James's (FB) Huskies featured 242 completions in 496 passing attempts (48.8 percent) for 3,277 yards and 19 touchdowns and 239 rushes for 429 yards and 9 touchdowns. His honors included being PEC Player of the Year in 1977 and being selected MVP of the 1978 Rose Bowl for guiding the Huskies to a 27–20 upset triumph over the University of Michigan.

The Edmonton, Canada, Eskimoes (CFL) signed Moon as a free agent in March 1978 prior to the NFL draft, while no NFL team selected him. He played six seasons from 1978 through 1983 for the Eskimos, completing 1,369 of 2,832 passes (57.5 percent) for 21,228 yards, 144 touchdowns, and 77 interceptions, and rushed 300 times for 1,700 yards and 17 touchdowns. Under his leadership, Edmonton compiled an 81–21–5 win–loss record. Moon threw for over 5,000 yards in his final two CFL seasons. His 5,648 passing yards and single-game mark of 555 yards in 1983 remain the all-time season high for professional football. Edmonton captured the Grey Cup CFL championship five consecutive seasons from 1978 through 1982 with Moon at the helm. Moon was selected the CFL's MVP in 1983, when he completed 380 of 664 passes in his best CFL season.

The Houston Oilers (NFL) signed Moon as a free agent in February 1984. Moon started all 16 games in 1984 and earned All-NFL Rookie honors. Following 2 average seasons, Moon led the Oilers to seven straight playoff appearances from 1987 through 1993. In 1989, he was named *FN* AFC

Player of the Year and was selected the NFL's Traveler's Insurance Man of the Year for his outstanding community work. Moon played in seven Pro Bowl games between 1988 and 1994 and was named quarterback on the *TSN* NFL All-Pro team in 1990. Moon's 2 best seasons came in 1990 and 1991. The 1990 campaign saw him tie Dan Marino's (FB) NFL record with nine 300-yard games in a season. On December 16, 1990, Moon threw for 527 yards against the Kansas City Chiefs for the second-highest single-game yardage in NFL history. His 4,689 yards that season ranked fifth highest in NFL history. He also led the NFL in attempts (584), completions (362), and touchdown passes (33). Moon in 1991 completed 404 of 655 passing attempts, both NFL records, pacing the NFL in passing yardage (4,690) and touchdown passes (21). In 10 seasons with the Oilers from 1984 through 1993, Moon became the club's all-time leader in completions (2,632), attempts (4,546), passing yards (33,685), and touchdown passes (196). He also has rushed 439 times for 1,541 yards and 21 touchdowns. Moon has thrown for more total yards (54,913) in his 16-year career than any quarterback in professional football history. He surpassed Ron Lancaster's 19-year CFL career record passing yardage (50,535) in 1992 and remains the only player in professional football history to throw for over 20,000 yards in two different leagues. In April 1994, Houston traded Moon to the Minnesota Vikings (NFL). Moon completed 371 of 601 passes for 4,264 yards and 18 touchdowns for Minnesota in 1994.

Moon and his wife Felicia, whom he married on February 8, 1981, reside in Sugar Land, TX. They have two sons, Joshua and Jeffrey, and two daughters, Chelsea and Blair.

BIBLIOGRAPHY: *Houston Oilers Media Guide*, 1993; *TSN Pro Football Register*, 1994; Paul Zimmerman, "The Big Moon Launch," *SI* 73 (November 5, 1990), pp. 68–70, 75.

John L. Evers

MORGAN, Stanley Douglas (b. February 17, 1955, Easley, SC), college and professional player, is the son of Coralee Sutton and grew up in Easley, SC. Morgan began his athletic career at Easley High School, where he starred in various sports from 1971 to 1973. His football exploits brought him All-State and All-America recognition. In 1973, Morgan was honored as the High School Athlete of the Year in the Carolinas.

Morgan earned a football scholarship to the University of Tennessee (SEC) and soon began an outstanding college career. As wingback in the Volunteers' offensive attack, Morgan proved adept at rushing, receiving, and returning kicks and punts. From 1973 to 1976, Morgan accumulated over 4,600 all-purpose yards. He rushed for 1,952 yards (5.5-yard average), caught passes for 1,075 yards (22.4-yard average), and totaled 1,615 combined yards for kickoff and punt returns. Such versatility helped the Volunteers record

28 wins, 17 losses, and 2 ties, including a 1973 Gator Bowl loss to Texas Tech University and a 1974 Liberty Bowl victory over the University of Maryland. At the completion of his college football career in 1976, Morgan ranked as Tennessee's all-time kick return leader and second leading rusher. Morgan's 39 touchdowns placed him second on the Tennessee scoring list. He garnered All-SEC honors in 1974 and 1976.

The New England Patriots made Morgan their first-round choice (twenty-fifth pick overall) in the 1977 NFL draft. The first receiver taken in that year's draft, Morgan joined former Volunteers Willie Gault, Anthony Hancock, and Carl Pickens in starring professionally at the position. From 1977 to 1990, Morgan established himself among the premier receivers in NFL history. He played with the Patriots 13 seasons and finished his career in 1990 with the Indianapolis Colts (NFL). Altogether, Morgan caught 557 passes for 10,716 yards and averaged 19.2 yards per reception. Morgan, who in 1979 became the first Patriot to gain 1,000 yards receiving in a season and in 1983 the club's career receiving leader, earned All-Pro recognition in 1979, 1980, 1986, and 1987. He helped New England make Super Bowl XX, where he caught 7 passes in a 46–10 loss to the Chicago Bears. He ranked among the top 20 in NFL career receptions upon his retirement.

Morgan received a B.S. degree in education from the University of Tennessee in 1979 and returned following the 1990 season to his home in Germantown, TN, where he and his wife Rholedia own and manage a dress shop. They have two daughters, Sanitra Nikole and Monique.

BIBLIOGRAPHY: Bud Fields and Bob Bertucci, *Big Orange: A Pictorial History of University of Tennessee Football* (West Point, NY, 1982); *New England Patriots Media Guide*, 1988, 1989; Mike Siroky and Bob Bertucci, *Orange Lightning: Inside University of Tennessee Football* (West Point, NY, 1982); *TSN Pro Football Register*, 1991, p. 228.

Robert T. Epling

MORRIS, Lawrence C. "Larry" (b. December 10, 1933, Decatur, GA), college and professional player, played fullback and linebacker for the Los Angeles Rams (NFL), Chicago Bears (NFL), and Atlanta Falcons (NFL) from 1955 to 1966. Morris attended Decatur High School, where he played fullback on the undefeated 1949 and 1950 State championship teams.

After graduation in 1951, Morris attended Georgia Tech University. He played linebacker on Bobby Dodd (FB)–coached football teams, which finished 10–0–1 in 1951, 11–0 in 1952, 8–2–1 in 1953, and 7–3 in 1954. He played on the undefeated 1952 Yellow Jackets, which defeated Baylor University in the Orange Bowl, and was named a consensus First Team All-America in 1953.

The Los Angeles Rams (NFL) made Morris a first-round draft choice in 1955. Morris played linebacker and fullback on the WC-winning team. His rushing record in 1955 included 40 carries for 148 yards (3.7-yard average) and one touchdown. After the 1955 season, the six-foot-two-inch, 230-

pound Morris played linebacker exclusively. Los Angeles traded Morris to the Washington Redskins (NFL) for Gene Brito* in 1959 after the linebacker had missed the 1958 season because of a knee injury. He did not reach a contract agreement with George Marshall (FB), owner of the Redskins, and was traded to the Chicago Bears (NFL) before the 1959 season for a second-round draft choice.

Morris joined linebackers Bill George (FB) and Joe Fortunato (FB), serving as the captain and mainstay of the Bears' defense. Morris played with the Bears until 1966, when he signed with the Atlanta Falcons (NFL). His biggest moment came in the 1963 NFL Championship game against the New York Giants, as he harassed quarterback Y. A. Tittle (FB) and intercepted two passes for 83 yards. One of his interceptions involved a 60-yard return to the Giants' 5-yard line, earning him MVP game honors. His NFL career record included eight interceptions for 113 yards.

Morris played the 1966 season with Atlanta and then entered the real estate development business there. He married Katherine Newman Wilder on June 13, 1957, and has four children. In 1992, he was elected to the NFF College Football Hall of Fame.

BIBLIOGRAPHY: Atlanta (GA) *Journal and Constitution*, September 12, 1965; October 23, 1967; *Chicago Bears Media Guide*, 1964; *TSN Pro Football Register*, 1966.

Robert L. Cannon

MOSCRIP, James H. "Monk" (b. September 17, 1913, Adena, OH; d. October 11, 1980, Atherton, CA), college and professional player, was named an All-America football end in 1934 and 1935 at Stanford University (PCC) and was elected in 1985 to the NFF College Football Hall of Fame. The six-foot, 190-pound Moscrip started three years with Stanford's heralded "Vow Boys," who refused to lose to the University of Southern California and won or shared three PCC titles between 1933 and 1935. Coach Claude "Tiny" Thornhill guided the Cardinal to a combined 25–4–2 record and eleventh-, tenth-, and fifth-place national rankings by football authority Frank G. Dickinson. Moscrip, named in 1954 a charter member of the Stanford Hall of Fame, averaged 55 minutes' playing time in three consecutive Rose Bowls. The Cardinal dropped the first two Rose Bowls to Columbia University and the University of Alabama but prevailed in the third against undefeated SMU.

Moscrip had attended Kiski, PA, Prep School, excelling on the gridiron and graduating from there in 1932. Coach Thornhill in 1933 guided Stanford to its first victory over Southern California in seven years, starting the eight sophomore Vow Boys against the Trojans. The Cardinal ended Southern California's 27-game undefeated streak, 13–7, sparked by Moscrip's versatile performance that included a 30-yard end around. The Vow Boys played for fun in practice, with Moscrip being the biggest prankster of all on the practice field, but exhibited seriousness on Saturdays. Besides demonstrating outstanding defensive play and excellent blocking and pass receptions on offense, Moscrip kicked field goals in key situations. In 1935, he booted two field goals to defeat the University of Washington, 6–0, and decisive field goals in 9–6 and 3–0 triumphs over Santa Clara University and Southern California. Moscrip downed a 62-yard quick kick at the SMU 10-yard line in the 1936 Rose Bowl, gaining excellent field position before Stanford's only score. Moscrip, the fastest on the Cardinal squad, joined tackle Bob Reynolds (FB), fullback Bobby Grayson (FB), and halfback Robert "Bones" Hamilton as NFF College Football Hall of Fame members. He was named on the All-Time PCC Second Team chosen in 1948 by West Coast sports editors.

Moscrip, a member of Zeta Psi fraternity, earned a bachelor's degree in political science from Stanford University in 1936. He married Mary Elizabeth Wright, a Stanford graduate, and had two daughters. Moscrip played the 1938–1939 campaigns with the Detroit Lions (NFL), catching 18 passes for 375 yards (20.8-yard average) and three touchdowns and kicking 11 extra points and four field goals. He served as a U.S. Naval lieutenant during World War II, participating in battles at Guadalcanal, Iwo Jima, and Okinawa. The vice president and general manager of the Moscrip Coal Mining Company in Ohio, he overcame an addiction to alcohol and for 25 years managed an alcoholic rehabilitation center in Woodside, CA. Moscrip died of a heart attack.

BIBLIOGRAPHY: L. H. Baker, *Football: Facts and Figures* (New York, 1945); Pete Grothe, ed., *Great Moments in Stanford Sports* (Palo Alto, CA, 1952); John D. McCallum and Charles H. Pearson, *College Football U.S.A., 1869–1972* (New York, 1972); Fred Merrick, *Down on the Farm* (Huntsville, AL, 1975); Rose Bowl Football Game Program, Pasadena, CA, January 1, 1936; Stanford University Libraries, Department of Special Collections, Stanford, CA, letter to James D. Whalen, September 17, 1993; John Sullivan, *The Big Game* (West Point, NY, 1982).

James D. Whalen

MUDD, Howard Edward (b. February 10, 1942, Midland, MI), college and professional player and coach, is the son of Howard Mudd and Vivian (Kelly) Mudd. He began his athletic career at Midland High School and attended Michigan State University for one year. After transferring to Hillsdale College, he played tackle and cocaptained the 1963 team. The six-foot-two-inch, 254-pound Mudd earned Little All-America mention and graduated with a Bachelor of Science degree in biology in 1964. He is a member of the NAIA Hall of Fame.

The San Francisco 49ers (NFL) selected Mudd in the ninth round of the 1964 draft. Mudd, an outstanding offensive guard for the 49ers over six seasons, was selected All-WC in 1967 and 1968 and played in Pro Bowls following the 1966, 1967, and 1968 seasons. He closed out his professional career with the Chicago Bears (NFL) in 1969 and 1970 and was named to the NFL All-Pro squad of the 1960s.

Mudd became an assistant football coach at the University of California at Berkeley in 1972 and moved to the NFL professional ranks in 1974 as offensive line coach for the San Diego Chargers. Following three seasons in San Diego, he served as offensive line coach for the San Francisco 49ers (1977), Seattle Seahawks (1978–1982), Cleveland Browns (1983–1988), and Kansas City Chiefs (1989–1992) and held that position with Seattle in 1993. Mudd was divorced from Jean Marie Sasho in 1992 and has two children, Darren and Ami. He married Shirley Ball on July 4, 1992.

BIBLIOGRAPHY: *Kansas City Chiefs Press Guide*, 1991; *TSN Pro Football Register*, 1970.

Jay Langhammer

MUNOZ, Michael Anthony (b. August 19, 1958, Ontario, CA), college and professional player and sportscaster, attended Chaffey High School in Ontario and the University of Southern California from 1975 to 1980, graduating with a B.S. degree in public administration. In his junior and senior years, Munoz was designated First Team All-America in football as a tackle.

The Cincinnati Bengals (NFL) selected the six-foot-six-inch, 289-pound offensive left tackle in the first round of the NFL draft (third overall) in 1980. Munoz's 13-year career with the Bengals featured his being consensus choice as the NFL premier offensive tackle and best pass blocker. His honors included being named All-Pro from 1981 through 1992, selected unanimously to the NFL Team of the 1980s, and chosen to participate in the Pro Bowl for 11 straight seasons from 1981 through 1991. Munoz, who possesses impeccable footwork, was awarded NFL Offensive Lineman of the Year 1981, 1987, and 1988, NFLPA Offensive Lineman of the Year in 1981, 1985, 1988, and 1989, and NFLAA Offensive Lineman of the Year in 1982, 1987, and 1989. In 1991, Munoz was recognized as the NFL Man of the Year, an award that honors players for their excellence as role models on and off the field. Munoz underwent major surgery for a torn rotator cuff on his right shoulder in 1992.

Munoz played in AFC championship games following the 1981 and 1988 seasons, helping the victorious Bengals each time to the Super Bowl. The San Francisco 49ers defeated Cincinnati, 26–21, in Super Bowl XVI and, 20–16, in Super Bowl XXIII. In his 13-year Bengal career, Munoz caught seven passes on tackle eligible plays for four touchdowns and made six fumble recoveries. He was chosen Cincinnati Bengal Man of the Year five times from 1987 through 1991. Washington Redskins' general manager Charley Casserly asserted, "Munoz is the best in the league," while San Francisco 49er offensive line coach Bob McKittrick added, "He was probably as good as anyone before his injury." Munoz and his wife De De have two children, Michael and Michelle, and reside in Cincinnati, OH. In April 1993, the

Tampa Bay Buccaneers (NFL) signed Munoz as a free agent. FBC named Munoz an NFL analyst in April 1994. A panel of NFL and Pro Football officials, former players, and reporters named him one of three offensive tackles on the NFL All-Time Team.

BIBLIOGRAPHY: *Cincinnati Bengal Media Guide*, 1992; *FD 1991 NFL and College Football Yearbook, Exclusive Player Ratings; TSN Pro Football Register*, 1993.

David Bernstein

NEHLEN, Donald Eugene "Don" (b. January 1, 1936, Canton, OH), college player and coach, is the son of Carl Nehlen, a steel company accountant, and Marge Nehlen and graduated from Canton Lincoln High School in 1954. He and his wife Merry Ann (Chopson) Nehlen have two children, Danny and Vicki. Vicki married Los Angeles Raiders (NFL) quarterback Jeff Hostetler.

Nehlen attended Bowling Green University (MAC), where he quarterbacked the Falcons for three seasons. He led coach Doyt Perry's squads to a 21–2–4 win–loss record and a MAC championship in 1956. Nehlen earned his bachelor's degree from Bowling Green in 1958 and his master's degree from Kent State University. His football coaching career began as an assistant at Mansfield, OH, High School in 1958. He served as head football coach at Canton South High School with a 24–11–2 record from 1959 through 1962 and also coached Canton McKinley High School to a 9–1 mark and a second-place finish in the State playoffs in 1964.

On the collegiate level, Nehlen gained experience as backfield coach under Chuck Studley at the University of Cincinnati in 1963 and as defensive coordinator at Bowling Green from 1965 to 1968. Bowling Green named Nehlen head football coach in 1968. For nine seasons from 1968 through 1976, Nehlen led the Falcons to a 53–35–4 record. His best season came in 1974, when his Falcons finished with an 8–3 mark. Between 1977 and 1979, Nehlen joined the University of Michigan (BTC) as an assistant coach under Glenn "Bo" Schembechler (FB). During Nehlen's three seasons there, the Wolverines played in two Rose Bowls and a Gator Bowl.

Nehlen was named head football coach at West Virginia University in December 1979 and has become the Mountaineers' winningest coach ever. From 1980 through 1994, the Mountaineers have compiled a 110–62–4 record under Nehlen's guidance and appeared in nine bowl games. The Mountaineers, ranked in the Top 20 in 1981, were led by quarterback Oliver Luck and surprised the University of Florida, 26–6, in the Peach Bowl. West Virginia the next season earned a Top 10 ranking for the first time in the Mountaineers' history but lost, 31–12, to Florida State University in the Gator Bowl. The Mountaineers triumphed, 20–16, over the University of Kentucky in the Hall of Fame Bowl in 1983 and over TCU, 31–14, in the Bluebonnet Bowl in 1984. After suffering a 35–33 setback to Oklahoma State

University in the 1987 John Hancock Bowl, West Virginia recorded a perfect 11–0 season mark in 1988 and a berth in the Fiesta Bowl. Sensational sophomore quarterback Major Harris led the Mountaineers, who lost to the University of Notre Dame, 34–21, for the national championship. West Virginia lost, 27–7, the following year to Clemson University in the Gator Bowl. In 1993, West Virginia finished the regular season with an 11–0 mark before losing, 41–7, to the University of Florida in the Sugar Bowl. The University of South Carolina defeated the Mountaineers, 24–21, in the 1994 Carquest Bowl.

During 23 seasons as a head football coach, Nehlen has compiled a 163–97–8 career win–loss record. In 1988, he received the AFCA, Bobby Dodd, Walter Camp, and Scripps Howard Coach of the Year Awards for his outstanding ability. He served as head coach of the East team in the 1984 and 1991 East-West Shrine games and as assistant coach for the East team in the 1983 and 1990 Hula Bowls. Nehlen also chairs the CFA Coaches' Committee and serves on the AFCA board of trustees.

BIBLIOGRAPHY: Sports Information Office, West Virginia University, letter to John L. Evers, October 25, 1992; *West Virginia University Football Media Guide*, 1993.

John L. Evers

OBERLANDER, Andrew James "Jim" "Swede" (b. February 17, 1905, Chelsea, MA; d. January 1, 1968, New Vernon, NJ), college athlete and coach, was selected a unanimous All-America football halfback at Dartmouth College (IvL) while leading the undefeated Big Green in 1925 to a shared national championship. Oberlander, a member of the HAF Hall of Fame, was elected in 1954 to the NFF College Football Hall of Fame. The six-foot 197-pounder starred three years from 1923 to 1925 under coach Jesse Hawley, helping Dartmouth compile a combined 23–1–1 record and boast two Top 10 national ratings.

The son of Andrew Oberlander and Viola (Holman) Oberlander, he attended Everett, MA, High School and excelled there in football, track and field, and wrestling before graduating in 1922. Oberlander started for Dartmouth at tackle his sophomore season and shifted to halfback his last two campaigns, finishing eighth and thirteenth in scoring nationally. A triple threat, he contributed many additional points with his passing and deep punting. Oberlander possessed a strong arm, being capable of passing accurately up to 50 yards. In a 62–13 demolishing of a fine Gil Dobie (FB)–coached Cornell University squad in 1925, Oberlander threw six touchdown passes to help post the highest football score against the Big Red in 36 years. He completed four touchdown passes, as Dartmouth humbled the University of Chicago's defending WC champions, 33–7. "Dartmouth," Grantland Rice (OS) wrote, had "the finest passing attack that any team ever used before, a passing attack that used length, deception and uncanny accuracy."

Oberlander combined with his receivers by using the jingle "Ten thousand Swedes" to time his throws, thus earning the nickname "Swede." He performed with other Dartmouth All-America nominees, including guard Carl Diehl, ends George Tully and Henry Bjorkman, tackle Nate Parker, and quarterback Eddie Dooley. The entire Dartmouth starting eleven made Phi Beta Kappa. The quiet, unassuming, self-effacing Oberlander, who also participated in varsity track and field and wrestling for the Big Green, graduated in 1926 with a Bachelor of Science degree from Dartmouth.

Oberlander took premedical courses from 1926 to 1930 at Ohio State University while serving as assistant football coach there. As head coach at Wesleyan University in Middletown, CT, from 1930 to 1933, he guided the Cardinals to a 17–10–3 overall mark. Simultaneously, he earned an M.D. degree from Yale University Medical School. Oberlander headed the University of New Hampshire infirmary for three years before becoming medical director of the National Life Insurance Company in 1940. A lieutenant commander in the U.S. Navy during World War II, he served as senior medical officer at various bases. From 1953 until his death from a heart attack, he worked as medical director of the Mid-American office of the Prudential Life Insurance Company. Oberlander married Madeline Chase of Everett, MA, in 1927 and had two sons, both Dartmouth graduates.

BIBLIOGRAPHY: L. H. Baker, *Football: Facts and Figures* (New York, 1945); Dartmouth College Library, Archives and Special Collections, Hanover, NH, letter to James D. Whalen, August 10, 1993; Dartmouth-Cornell Football Game Program, Hanover, NH, November 7, 1925; Ralph Hickok, *Who Was Who in American Sports* (New York, 1971); John D. McCallum and Charles H. Pearson, *College Football U.S.A., 1869–1972* (New York, 1972); Bernie McCarty, "Oberlander's 500-Yard Game," *CFHS* 3 (August 1990), pp. 17–18; Ronald L. Mendell and Timothy B. Phares, *Who's Who in Football* (New Rochelle, NY, 1974).

James D. Whalen

O'BRIEN, Christopher "Chris" (b. 1881, Bohmeen, County Meath, Ireland; d. June 3, 1951, Chicago, IL), professional player, executive, and scout, was the son of Patrick O'Brien and Brigid (Clarkin) O'Brien. Brigid tended to their large family in Ireland, while Patrick emigrated to the United States and served with the Seventh Cavalry. Patrick later entered the construction trade, investing his money in real estate and periodically visiting his family. Christopher was baptized on October 4, 1881. At age seven, he and a brother, Patrick, followed their father to Chicago. As members of the Morgan AC on Racine Avenue, the brothers played in the backfield on the Racine Cardinals football team from 1898 until it disbanded in 1906.

O'Brien, who started his own painting business, married Frieda Bencke in 1904 and had one son. By World War I, he also operated the concession stand at Normal Park and resurrected the Cardinals football team. With O'Brien as owner–manager and Marston Smith of the University of Chicago as coach, the Cardinals operated as a semiprofessional organization from 1916 to 1920 and played against numerous independent teams in the Chicago area. The Cardinals allegedly won franchise rights in a showdown match with the Chicago Tigers, when Paddy Driscoll (FB) kicked a field goal for a 6–3 victory. The Chicago Cardinals entered the APFA-NFL as charter members in 1920, changing their name to distinguish themselves from the Racine, WI, team by 1921.

O'Brien rented Comiskey Park but soon faced competition when the Decatur, IL, Staleys franchise moved to Chicago in 1921. The cross-town rivalry lasted nearly 40 years, but both teams found it difficult to make a profit in the early years because they often played against small town teams. In 1925, O'Brien's club won its only NFL championship in a disputed decision. The Pottsville, PA, Maroons claimed the NFL title by virtue of their 10–2 record and a victory over the 9–1–1 Cardinals in the season finale. Pottsville, however, violated the territorial rights of the Frankford Yellow Jackets by playing a postseason exhibition game against College All-Stars in Philadelphia, causing commissioner Joe Carr (FB) to impose punishment. Carr ordered the Cardinals to play two more hastily arranged games against the weak Milwaukee Badgers and Hammond Pros clubs. The resulting Cardinal victories allowed them to supplant Pottsville with an 11–2–1 record.

The handsome, affable O'Brien supported the Cardinals through his painting business and work as a circuit court bailiff but incurred too many losses. O'Brien sold Driscoll, his best player, to the Chicago Bears after the 1925 season and the franchise to David Jones, a Chicago dentist, in July 1929. O'Brien, who became an official NFL scout and a friend of the Bears organization, remained active in labor unions, several Catholic fraternal associations, and the circuit court office until cancer took his life.

BIBLIOGRAPHY: Chicago (IL) *Tribune*, June 4, 1951; Gerald R. Gems, telephone interviews with O'Brien family members, Carol Judge and Patricia Needham, October–December 1992; Gerald R. Gems, telephone interview with Rudy Custer, November 3, 1992; William Gudelunas and Stephen R. Couch, "The Stolen Championship of the Pottsville Maroons: A Case Study in the Emergence of Modern Professional Football," *JSH* 9 (Spring 1982), pp. 53–64; Eddie McGuire, "Cardinals History," *Chicago Cardinals Yearbook*, 1947, pp. 6–7; *Southtown Economist*, June 6, 1951 (care of Joel Steinberg); Richard Whittingham, *The Chicago Bears* (New York, 1986), pp. 19–23.

Gerald R. Gems

PARCELLS, Duane Charles "Bill" (b. August 22, 1941, Englewood, NJ), college and professional player and coach, is the son of Charles "Chubby" Parcells and Ida (Naclerio) Parcells and grew up in several states. Before Parcells had started school, his family had lived in Pennsylvania, Illinois, and New Jersey. Parcells graduated from River Dell High School in Oradell, NJ, where he played football, basketball, and baseball. He attended Colgate University for one year, participating in baseball and football, and then transferred to Wichita State University (MVC). At Wichita State, he was selected All-MVC twice as a football linebacker and performed in the Sun Bowl,

Blue-Gray, and Senior Bowl games as a senior. In 1964, he earned a B.A. degree in education.

The Detroit Lions (NFL) drafted Parcells in the seventh round, but he immediately entered college coaching. His first job came in 1964 as an assistant coach at Hastings, NE (NeCC) College. He returned in 1965 to Wichita State as an assistant defensive coach. From 1966 to 1969, he served as an assistant coach for the U.S. Military Academy at West Point, NY. His next assistant coaching assignments came at Florida State University from 1970 to 1972, Vanderbilt University (SEC) in 1973 and 1974, and Texas Tech University (SWC) from 1975 to 1977. In 1978, Parcells landed his first head coaching job, compiling a 3–8 record at the U.S. Air Force Academy. His initial NFL coaching position came with the New York Giants in 1979 as a defensive coach.

Parcells quit coaching after the 1979 season to pursue private business but joined the New England Patriots (NFL) as a linebacker coach in 1980. After spending one year there, he returned in 1981 to the New York Giants (NFL) in 1981 as defensive coordinator under Ray Perkins.

The Giants appointed Parcells head coach in 1983. As only the twelfth coach in Giants' history, Parcells accumulated a regular season 77–49–1 record from 1983 through 1990. Under Parcells, the Giants finished first in the Eastern Division four times and compiled a 14–2 record in 1986 and 12–4 mark in 1990. His 8–3 playoff record culminated with the Giants' 20–19 victory over the Buffalo Bills in Super Bowl XXV at Tampa, FL. New York also had defeated the Denver Broncos, 39–20, in Super Bowl XXI at Pasadena, CA.

In 1991, Parcells joined NBC as a football analyst on the NFL pregame show "NFL Live." In 1993, Parcells returned to the NFL head coaching ranks with the struggling New England Patriots. Under Parcells, the Patriots improved considerably during the 1993 season and finished with a 5–11 mark. In 1994, New England won its final seven regular season games to make the NFC playoffs with a 10–6 mark. Through the 1994 campaign, Parcells has compiled a 92–66–1 regular season record as an NFL head coach. He, his wife Judy, and daughters Suzy, Jill, and Dallas live in Upper Saddle River, NJ.

BIBLIOGRAPHY: Bill Parcells and Mike Lupica, *The Biggest Giant of Them All* (Canton, OH, 1989), pp. 1–50; *TSN Pro Football Register*, 1994.

                                                                    Raymond C. Fetters

PATTON, James Russel Jr. "Jimmy" (b. September 29, 1933, Greenville, MS; d. December 26, 1972, Villa Rica, GA), college and professional player and coach, was the son of James Russel Patton, Sr., and Josephine Patton and was forced to quit the E. E. Bass High School football team as a 140-pound sophomore because his father feared possible injury. Patton, however, subsequently grew to 158 pounds and quarterbacked the high school team his junior and senior years.

Patton played football as a two-way halfback for legendary coach John Vaught (FB) at the University of Mississippi (SEC). Although only 5 foot 11 inches and 175 pounds, Patton possessed 9.9-second speed in the 100-yard dash. He led "Ole Miss" to three excellent football seasons from 1952 to 1954 and Sugar Bowl appearances against Georgia Tech in 1953 and the U.S. Naval Academy in 1955. He cocaptained the 1954 football team and also lettered in baseball and track and field. Patton, who received his Bachelor of Science degree in education in 1955, married Adonis Bridgers and had four sons.

The New York Giants (NFL) selected Patton in the eighth round of the 1955 draft to play defensive back and safety. He did not break into the starting lineup during his first two seasons because he experienced difficulty adjusting to pass defense and was knocked unconscious on two occasions after tackling much larger opponents. He scored two touchdowns on a 98-yard kickoff return and a 70-yard punt return in a 35–7 defeat of the Washington Redskins his rookie season.

The 1956 season marked the Giants' ascendancy into the first rank of professional teams. In Patton's eight seasons from 1956 to 1963, the New York Giants played in six NFL championship games and triumphed only once. The five NFL title game losses included the now-legendary 1958 23–17 sudden-death contest loss to the Baltimore Colts. During that span, Patton became an excellent safety, made five Pro Bowls, and was named to three All-Pro teams from 1959 to 1961.

Patton led the NFL in interceptions in 1958 with 11 and finished second in 1961 with 8. He had garnered 52 career interceptions, third on the all-time list at his retirement. Patton also served as an assistant coach in 1963 and 1964 with the Giants before retiring in 1966. The intense Patton often roamed the streets of New York all Sunday night with a teammate to release the adrenalin from games.

He worked in public relations for the Phillip Morris Tobacco Company, a firm he joined while still playing with the Giants. Patton died tragically at age 39 in an automobile accident.

BIBLIOGRAPHY: Gerald Eskenazi, *There Were Giants in Those Days* (New York, 1976); David Neft et al., eds., *The Football Encyclopedia*, 2nd ed. (New York, 1994); *The New York Giants Media Guide*, 1964; Jim Patton clipping file, Pro Football Hall of Fame, Canton, OH; Beau Riffenburgh, *The Official NFL Encyclopedia*, 4th ed. (New York, 1986).

C. Robert Barnett

PEABODY, Endicott II "Chub" (b. February 15, 1920, Lawrence, MA), college athlete, was one of five children of Malcolm Endicott Peabody, bishop of the Protestant Episcopal Diocese of Central New York, and Mary Elizabeth (Parkman) Peabody. He attended William Penn Charter School in Philadelphia, PA, and graduated in 1938 from the Groton School in Massachusetts, whose founder and headmaster was his clergyman grandfather Endicott Peabody, for whom he had been named.

After being a reserve on the freshman team at Harvard University, the six-foot Peabody increased his weight by bodybuilding from 175 to 185 pounds. As varsity left guard, he was nicknamed "the Baby-Faced Assassin" by Boston (MA) *Globe* writer Jerry Nason. Although Harvard finished 4–4–0 in 1939 with losses to both Princeton University and Yale University, Peabody contributed a safety and two points to the Crimson's 15–0 victory over the U.S. Military Academy. The Crimson's 3–2–3 1940 squad posted three shutouts, including a 28–0 victory over Yale and ties with Army, Princeton, and the University of Pennsylvania. The Crimson held the U.S. Naval Academy to a scoreless tie in 1941, when Peabody's hard tackle of Bill Busick caused the Navy halfback to fumble. By defeating Princeton, Army, Brown University, and Yale, Harvard finished 5–2–1 and won the "Big Three" championship. Peabody, the first Crimson player in a decade selected as an All-America, was named both outstanding lineman and football player in New England in 1941 and also won the All-America Football Trophy of the City of Boston, the Knute Rockne Memorial Trophy for the outstanding college lineman, and the Bulger-Lowe Trophy. In 1973, he was elected to the NFF College Football Hall of Fame.

A dean's list history major, Peabody played ice hockey and tennis and served on the student council his junior and senior years. After graduation from Harvard in 1942, he was commissioned an ensign. He married Barbara Welch "Toni" Gibbons in 1944 in New York City in a ceremony performed by his father. Two of his patrols in 1945 on the USS *Tirante* submarine resulted in sinking a Japanese ammunition ship and two destroyers in the East China Sea. Lieutenant Peabody led a prisoner-taking action and was awarded a presidential unit citation, the Silver Star, and a commendation ribbon.

After earning his Bachelor of Laws degree from Harvard Law School in 1948, Peabody joined the Boston law firm of Goodwin, Proctor, and Hoar. During the Korean War, he became assistant regional counsel in the Office of Price Stabilization and then regional counsel and assistant to the director of Small Defense Plants Administration. In September 1952, he started his own law office, Peabody, Kaufman & Brewer.

Peabody, a Democrat, won the Massachusetts governorship in 1962 by campaigning statewide in a borrowed compact bus with his wife and three children, Barbara Welch, Endicott, Jr., and Robert Lee. Peabody promoted the constitutional and legal strengthening of gubernatorial powers, the inauguration of the country's first statewide transportation system, and the creation of a Massachusetts domestic peace corps. After failing reelection, he became counsel for Roche & Leen of Boston from 1965 to 1967. In 1969, he was a founding partner in Peabody, Rivlin, Lambert, & Meyers, in Washington, D.C. He ran unsuccessfully for U.S. senator from Massachusetts in 1966 and from New Hampshire in 1986 and unsuccessfully sought the 1972 Democratic vice presidential nomination. He moved to Hollis, NH, in 1982 and practiced law in Nashua, NH. *Partnership in Progress* (1966) and the *Papers of Governor Peabody* (1967) describe his political philosophy and accomplishments.

BIBLIOGRAPHY: Thomas Bergin, *The Game: The Harvard-Yale Football Rivalry, 1875–1983* (New Haven, CT, and London, England, 1984); Geoffrey H. Movius, ed., *The Second H Book of Harvard Athletics 1923–1963* (Cambridge, MA, 1964); "Endicott Peabody," biographical sketches in the *Harvard College Class of 1942* albums (Cambridge, MA): *Harvard Freshman Red Book 1938* (1938), pp. 128, 192, 212, 214–215; senior year album (1942), pp. 120, 171, 178–179; *Sixth Anniversary Report* (June 1948), p. 227; *Twenty-fifth Anniversary Report* (1967), pp. 1009–1011; *Thirty-fifth Anniversary Report* (1977), p. 161; *Forty-fifth Anniversary Report* (1987), p. 137; and *Fiftieth Anniversary Report* (1992), pp. 408–409. "Endicott Peabody, 1942," quinquennial file, Harvard University Archives, Cambridge, MA; Paul A. Theis and Edmund L. Henshaw, Jr., eds., *Who's Who in American Politics*, 4th ed. (1973–1974), p. 824; *WWA*, 39th ed., (1976–1977), p. 2442.

Marcia G. Synnott

PETITBON, Richard Alvin "Richie" (b. April 18, 1938, New Orleans, LA), college and professional player and coach, is the son of John Baptiste Petitbon, a native of France, and attended Jesuit High School in New Orleans. His brother John, considered one of the greatest high school football players ever, played at the University of Notre Dame and in the NFL with the Dallas Cowboys, Cleveland Browns, and Green Bay Packers. Richie attended Loyola University in New Orleans for one year on a track and field scholarship and transferred to Tulane University (SEC), where he became an All-SEC quarterback and defensive halfback during the 1957 and 1958 seasons. In his final season, Petitbon passed for 728 yards and rushed for 188 yards. He holds the Tulane game record for completion percentage (90.9), completing 10 of 11 passes on September 26, 1958, against the University of Texas. Petitbon, second in career kickoff return average (24.3) and a member of the Tulane Football Hall of Fame, graduated with a B.A. degree in business from there in 1960.

A second-round choice of the Chicago Bears (NFL) in the 1959 draft, the six-foot-three-inch, 208-pound Petitbon played defensive back there from 1959 through 1968. He was named to the *TSN* WC All-Star team in 1966 and played in the Pro Bowl following the 1962, 1963, 1966, and 1967 seasons. Besides leading the NFL in interception yardage, Petitbon played a key role on the 1963 Bears' squad that triumphed, 14–10, over the New York Giants in the NFL Championship game. On December 9, 1962, he returned an interception 101 yards for a touchdown against the Los Angeles Rams, the second longest in NFL history. Petitbon ranks second on the Bears' all-time list for interceptions with 37. In May 1969, Chicago traded

Petitbon to the Los Angeles Rams (NFL) for defensive back Lee Calland and two draft choices. Petitbon played under head coach George Allen (FB) for two years with the Rams and from 1971 to 1973 with the Washington Redskins (NFL). Upon retiring following the 1973 season, Petitbon had intercepted 48 passes for 801 yards, averaged 16.7 yards per return, and scored three touchdowns.

Petitbon's football coaching career began as a defensive backfield coach with the Houston Oilers (NFL) in 1974 under Sid Gillman (FB) and the following three seasons under O. A. "Bum" Phillips. He joined the coaching staff of the Washington Redskins in 1978, serving as defensive coordinator and assistant head coach in charge of defense through the 1992 season. He belonged to every Redskin Super Bowl team as either a player (1972) or coach (1982, 1983, 1987, 1991).

In 1993 Petitbon served as the eighteenth head coach in Redskin history, replacing Joe Gibbs (FB). The Redskins struggled to a 4–12 record in Petitbon's only season as head mentor. After 15 years of directing the Redskins' defense, Petitbon had built the longest tenure with the team until released as head coach in January 1994. He and his wife Beverly reside in Vienna, VA, and have three children, Hope, Richie, and Vicki Leigh.

BIBLIOGRAPHY: Ronald L. Mendell and Timothy B. Phares, *Who's Who in Football* (New Rochelle, NY, 1974); *TSN Pro Football Register*, 1993; *Washington Redskins Media Guide*, 1993; Washington *Times*, March 10, 1993, pp. D1, D5.

John L. Evers

PHILBIN, Gerald John "Gerry" (b. July 31, 1941, Pawtucket, RI), college and professional player, graduated from Tolman High School in Pawtucket. Philbin, a six-foot-two-inch, 245-pound tackle, played football at the State University of New York at Buffalo, where he earned a Bachelor of Science degree in sociology in 1967. A four-year performer in football for the Buffalo Bills between 1960 and 1963, Philbin made the All-America Second Team, All-East First Team, and Academic All-America in 1963 and played in the Senior and All-America Bowls in 1964.

Philbin in 1964 was selected in the third round of the AFL draft by the New York Jets and by the Detroit Lions in the NFL draft. New York signed Philbin, who played 110 regular season games during 9 seasons for the Jets, including 6 in the AFL (1964–1969), and 3 in the NFL (1970–1972). Philbin performed in the AFL All-Star Game following the 1968 and 1969 seasons and was elected to the All-Time AFL team by the Pro Football Hall of Fame. He played in the 1968 AFL championship game when the Jets defeated the Oakland Raiders, 27–23, and starred in Super Bowl III, where Jets' quarterback Joe Namath (FB) guaranteed victory. The New York Jets upset the highly favored Baltimore Colts (NFL), 16–7, in Super Bowl III. Numerous injuries slowed Philbin and caused the Jets to trade him to the

Kansas City Chiefs (NFL) in 1973 for running back Mike Adamle. The Chiefs traded the unhappy Philbin with a draft choice to the Philadelphia Eagles (NFL) for defensive tackle Ernie Calloway and defensive back Leroy Keyes (FB). Philbin played in 13 games for the Eagles in 1973 but was released the following year and ended his professional football career in 1974 with the New York Stars (WFL). In 10 AFL-NFL seasons, Philbin returned one punt for 2 yards, intercepted one pass for 18 yards, and recovered seven fumbles in 123 regular season games.

Philbin and his wife Trudy have two sons, John and Douglas. He remains an excellent speaker, whose community involvement helped elevate public relations for professional football. In recognition of his antidrug work, Philbin was invited to Washington, DC to meet with President Richard Nixon concerning the nation's drug abuse problem. His off-season activities included operating the Gerry Philbin Goal Post restaurants, located in East Massapequa, NY, and Pawtucket, RI.

BIBLIOGRAPHY: Ronald L. Mendell and Timothy B. Phares, *Who's Who in Football* (New Rochelle, NY, 1974); *New York Jets Media Guide*, 1972; *TSN Pro Football Register*, 1974.

John L. Evers

PHILLIPS, Loyd Wade (b. May 2, 1945, Fort Worth, TX), college and professional player, is the son of Loyd Faye Phillips, a police officer, and Verna Phillips, a grocery store employee. Phillips played offensive guard, defensive linebacker, and noseguard at Longview, TX, High School, being named All-District in 1961 and 1962 and All-State Super team in 1962. Phillips was selected the MVP of the 1962 Texas High School All-Star football game.

The six-foot-three-inch, 230-pound Phillips rejected a scholarship offer from the University of Oklahoma, signing with coach Frank Broyles (FB) of the University of Arkansas (SWC) in 1963. The first Arkansas player ever selected All-SWC three times, he won the honor at defensive tackle in 1964, 1965, and 1966. Phillips, a consensus All-America in 1965 and 1966, won the Outland Trophy in 1966 as the nation's best defensive lineman. The University of Arkansas enjoyed considerable success during Phillips's tenure, finishing first in the SWC with 10–0 records in both 1964 and 1965 and ranking second nationally with UPI both years. The Razorbacks defeated the University of Nebraska, 10–7, in the 1965 Cotton Bowl and lost to LSU, 14–7, in the 1966 Cotton Bowl. In 1966, a season-ending 21–16 loss to Texas Tech University prevented Arkansas from winning its third straight SWC championship. In three seasons as a starter, Phillips led the Arkansas defense in allowing only 234 points or an average of 7.8 per game. The Razorbacks won 29 games and lost only 3 for a .906 winning percentage, one of the highest in SWC history.

The Chicago Bears (NFL) drafted Phillips as their number-one pick and tenth player overall in 1967. Phillips played three seasons with the Bears at defensive end, taking advantage of his quickness. A knee injury suffered against the New York Giants in 1969 shortened his NFL career. Chicago traded Phillips to the New Orleans Saints (NFL) after the 1969 season. Phillips retired after playing only three exhibition games when phlebitis developed from his knee injury.

Phillips returned to the University of Arkansas and earned his bachelor's degree in 1972. He remained at the University of Arkansas to attend graduate school, completing a master's degree in education in 1973. He served as vice principal at Springdale, AR, High School and now holds the same title at Rogers, AR, Junior High School.

Phillips was selected to the University of Arkansas Sports Hall of Honor in 1991 and the NFF College Football Hall of Fame in 1992. *TF* magazine named Phillips and Bob Lilly (FB) as the starting defensive tackles on the All-SWC team of the 1960s. Phillips married Betsy McNabb on May 18, 1968, and resides on a farm outside of Cape Springs, AR. They have two children, MacKenzie and Jo Anne.

BIBLIOGRAPHY: Dave Campbell, *The Best of Dave Campbell's Texas Football* (Dallas, TX, 1989); John Hillman, telephone interview with Loyd Phillips, April 2, 1993; Ronald Mendell and Timothy Phares, *Who's Who in Football* (New Rochelle, NY, 1974); Beau Riffenburgh, *The Official NFL Encyclopedia*, 4th ed. (New York, 1986); SWC, *Football '77* (Dallas, TX, 1977); *TSN Pro Football Register*, 1969.

John Hillman

PICCOLO, Louis Brian "Pic" (b. October 21, 1943, Pittsfield, MA; d. June 16, 1970, New York, NY), college and professional player, was the son of Joseph Piccolo, a restaurant owner, and Irene Piccolo. He married Joy Murrath on December 26, 1964, and had three daughters, Lori, Traci, and Kristi.

Piccolo's family moved to Ft. Lauderdale, FL, when he was three years old. He attended Central Catholic High School in Ft. Lauderdale, participating in baseball, football, and basketball. Following his graduation, Piccolo majored in speech at Wake Forest University (ACC) and played football. A varsity performer for three seasons from 1962 to 1964, Piccolo enjoyed little success until his senior year. Following two seasons with only one victory, Piccolo's Demon Deacons boosted their record to 5–5 in 1964. Piccolo ran the option series under new coach Bill Tate and joined star quarterback John Mackovic in accounting for Wake Forest's success. Mackovic serves as the head football coach at the University of Texas. During the 1964 season, Piccolo broke the ACC rushing record of 1,010 yards. Wake Forest's Bill Barnes had set the ACC rushing standard in 1956. Piccolo also established an ACC record when he carried the ball 36 times against Duke University. Piccolo gained 1,044 yards rushing to capture the national title, nosing out Jim Grabowski of the University of Illinois, and led the nation in scoring with 111 points, edging Howard Twilley (FB) of the University of Tulsa.

His honors included being named the MVP in the ACC and making several All-America teams. He played in the North-South game but was not selected in the NFL draft.

The Chicago Bears (NFL) signed Piccolo as a free agent. After reporting to the Bears' rookie camp in 1965, Piccolo suffered an injury and was placed on their taxi squad. During the next four seasons, the six-foot, 205-pound running back/fullback enjoyed moderate success. His career statistics included 927 yards rushing on 258 attempts and four touchdowns. Piccolo also gained 537 yards as a pass receiver on 58 catches for one touchdown. His best season came in 1968, when he garnered 450 yards rushing and 291 yards as a receiver.

During the ninth game of the 1969 season against the Atlanta Falcons, Piccolo removed himself from the contest with breathing difficulty. Piccolo, at age 26, died in seven months from embryonal cell carcinoma after struggling to conquer the dreaded cancer. Piccolo's tenacious mental attitude, courage, and bravery inspired many people. He was the subject of a book entitled *Brian Piccolo: A Short Season* and an award-winning television movie, *Brian's Song*. When his close friend, teammate, and roommate Gale Sayers (FB) earned Most Courageous Athlete of the Year honors for his comeback from a serious injury, he dedicated and presented the award to Piccolo.

BIBLIOGRAPHY: Ronald L. Mendell and Timothy B. Phares, *Who's Who in Football* (New Rochelle, NY, 1974); Jeannie Morris, *Brian Piccolo: A Short Season* (Chicago, IL, 1971); David S. Neft et al., eds. *The Football Encyclopedia*, 2nd ed. (New York, 1994).

John L. Evers

POOLE, James Eugene "Jim" "Buster" (b. September 9, 1915, Gloster, MS; d. November 16, 1994, Oxford, MS), college and professional player, was the oldest of three brothers who starred in football at end for the University of Mississippi (SEC) and enjoyed outstanding professional careers. Ray captained Mississippi in 1946 and played six years with the New York Giants (NFL), while Barney (S) was selected an All-America at the U.S. Military Academy during World War II and at Mississippi in 1947 and 1948 and performed six NFL seasons. A cousin, Oliver Poole, also played end for Mississippi and spent three seasons in the professional ranks.

When his father, a Mississippi farmer and saw mill operator, died, Jim became "the man of the family" at age nine. The Poole brothers grew up playing baseball and basketball, but their small town did not have football facilities. The Natchez High School football coach spotted Jim and convinced him to attend high school there so he could play football. Poole won an athletic scholarship to the University of Mississippi, where he started three years in football, basketball, and baseball. In football, Mississippi finished with marks of 4–5–1 in 1934, 9–2 in 1935, and 5–5–2 in 1936. As a junior, Poole scored one of Mississippi's touchdowns in a 20–19 Orange

Bowl loss to Catholic University. He started the next year and received the Norris Trophy, presented to the outstanding "Ole Miss" scholar–athlete.

The New York Giants (NFL) selected the six-foot-three-inch, 218-pound end on the seventh round of the second annual draft in 1937. Poole earned a starting role his first year. Although an adequate pass receiver, Poole proved most valuable to the ground-oriented Giants for his blocking and defense. In 1939, he was named to the All-NFL team while catching 7 passes. His fondest football memory came when blocking a punt that helped New York win the 1938 NFL Championship game against the Green Bay Packers. Poole also played in NFL title games lost to the Green Bay Packers, 27–0, in 1939 and the Chicago Bears, 37–9, in 1941 and, 24–14, in 1946. After the 1941 season, Poole served in the U.S. Navy through 1944. He spent the first part of the 1945 season with the Chicago Cardinals (NFL) and then returned to the New York Giants. In 1946, his final NFL season, he caught a personal-high 23 passes and earned AP All-NFL honors. During his NFL career, Poole caught 65 passes for 895 yards (13.8-yard average) and 13 touchdowns.

When John Vaught (FB) became head football coach at Mississippi in 1947, he hired Poole as his first assistant. Poole held that position until his retirement.

BIBLIOGRAPHY: Ronald L. Mendell and Timothy B. Phares, *Who's Who in Football* (New Rochelle, NY, 1974); David S. Neft et al., eds., *The Football Encyclopedia*, 2nd ed. (New York, 1994); Jim Poole file, Pro Football Hall of Fame, Canton, OH; Beau Riffenburgh, *The Official NFL Encyclopedia*, 4th ed. (New York, 1986); Christy Walsh, *College Football and All-America Review* (Culver City, CA, 1949).

Robert N. "Bob" Carroll

PRITCHARD, Abisha Collins "Bosh" (b. September 10, 1919, Windsor, NC), college and professional player, is the ninth of 10 boys of Octavius Coke Pritchard, a farmer, and Lettie (Collins) Pritchard, a silk mill worker. Pritchard attended Hopewell, VA, High School from 1934 to 1938 and lettered in football, basketball, baseball, and track and field. At VMI between 1938 and 1942 as a premed and then liberal arts major, he again lettered in these sports and excelled particularly in football. The halfback's speed and broken-field running proved instrumental in his selection as All-SC and honorable mention All-America in 1940 and 1941.

The 5-foot-10¾-inch, 165-pound Pritchard began his NFL football career in 1942 with the Cleveland Rams. After Pritchard played only three games, Cleveland released him on waivers. The Philadelphia Eagles (NFL) signed Pritchard for $100, starting him as a defensive-offensive back. Pritchard was named to the 1942 Pro Bowl team. In January 1943, Pritchard joined the U.S. Navy as a chief petty officer (specialist A) and physical fitness instructor in the V-12 program. He served in that capacity during World War II from 1943 to 1945 at Philadelphia, PA (Villanova University), Atlanta, GA (Georgia Institute of Technology), and San Diego, CA. During his military service, he played tailback in 1945 for the professional San Diego Bombers (PCL).

In 1946, Pritchard rejoined the Eagles at right halfback and quickly developed into one of the most feared NFL breakaway runners. The elusive scatback averaged better than 4 yards per carry in 1947 and joined bruising left halfback runner Steve Van Buren (FB) in forming the NFL's best rushing combination and led the Earle "Greasy" Neale (FB)–coached Eagles to the NFL Eastern Division championship. Pritchard rushed for over 500 yards each of the next two seasons, finishing fifth in NFL rushing in 1949 with a 6.0-yard average per carry. Nicknamed "Bosh," Pritchard combined with the NFL's best runner, Van Buren, star passing quarterback Tommy Thompson (S), ends Pete Pihos (FB) and Jack Ferrante,* and stalwart defensive linemen Alex Wojciechowicz (FB), Bucko Kilroy (FB), and Vic Sears (FB). Philadelphia captured two NFL championships in 1948 and 1949, defeating the Chicago Cardinals and Los Angeles Rams. In 1950, Pritchard injured a knee in training camp and did not play that season. After spending three games with the Eagles in 1951, he was released and signed by the New York Giants (NFL) on waivers. He finished the 1951 season with New York and then retired.

A punt return specialist, Pritchard ended his six-year NFL career with 95 returns for 1,072 yards (11.28-yard average) and 2 touchdowns to rank among the lifetime NFL leaders. Pritchard rushed 392 times for 1,730 yards (4.4-yard average) and 11 touchdowns, caught 75 passes for 1,166 yards (15.6-yard average) and 10 touchdowns, and returned 41 kickoffs for 938 yards (22.9-yard average) and 1 touchdown. His honors included election to the All-Time Philadelphia Eagles team in 1965, VMI Sports Hall of Fame in 1972, Virginia Sports Hall of Fame in 1977, and Pennsylvania Sports Hall of Fame in 1981.

During the 1950s, Pritchard served as the vice president and sales manager of Tel Ra Productions, one of the nation's top producers of television sports films, and also worked as a radio and TV sportscaster in the Philadelphia area. Pritchard sold real estate and later was employed as sales manager of a sports complex in the Cherry Hills, NJ, area. From 1970 to 1985, he was executive director of the Canuso Leukemia Foundation. Pritchard married Betty Kidd Solly, his third wife, in 1973 and resides in Ft. Myers, FL. He has two children, Bruce and Vaney, by his second marriage.

BIBLIOGRAPHY: Jack C. Braun, telephone interview with "Bosh" Pritchard, June 17, 1993; Gene Murdock, "The Year Greasy Neale Was Fired," *TCC* 10 (Late Spring 1988), pp. 8–10; David S. Neft et al., eds., *The Football Encyclopedia*, 2nd ed. (New York, 1994); Abisha Pritchard file, Pro Football Hall of Fame, Canton, OH.

                                                                        Jack C. Braun

PUTNAM, Duane (b. September 5, 1928, Pollock, SD), college and professional player and coach, played offensive guard with the Los Angeles Rams (NFL), Dallas Cowboys (NFL), and Cleveland Browns (NFL) between 1952 and 1962. He is the son of Paul Putnam, who worked in the drafting department of U.S. Steel, and Frieda Putnam. At Antioch, CA, High School, he played tackle in football and participated in basketball and track and field. After graduation in 1946, Putnam served with the First Cavalry of the U.S. Army during the occupation of Japan. Upon being discharged from the army in the spring of 1948, Putnam enrolled at the College of the Pacific. As a collegian, Putnam performed as an offensive tackle in football and engaged in the shot put for the track and field team.

After Putnam graduated from the College of the Pacific in June 1952, the Los Angeles Rams (NFL) selected him on the sixth round of the draft. Although small by NFL standards at six-feet, 195 pounds, Putnam started during his rookie season. Putnam grew to 230 pounds during the off-season by lifting weights. He excelled on running plays, comprising the last of the great small NFL guards. One of Putnam's coaches called him the best NFL offensive guard. Putnam's honors included playing in the Pro Bowl four times (1955, 1956, 1958, 1959) and being named to the All-Pro team three times (1957, 1958, 1959).

In 1960, the new Dallas Cowboys (NFL) drafted Putnam for their first campaign. After being released from the Cowboys following the 1960 season, Putnam played for the Cleveland Browns (NFL) in 1961 and returned to the Los Angeles Rams in 1962. Putnam served as an assistant football coach at Los Angeles Valley College from 1963 to 1965 and later for the Atlanta Falcons (NFL), Philadelphia Eagles (NFL), and St. Louis Cardinals (NFL). Putnam married Patty Dease on July 8, 1950, and has two children, Pamela and Steve.

BIBLIOGRAPHY: Robert L. Cannon, interview with Duane Putnam, March 8, 1993; *Los Angeles Rams Media Guide*, 1958, 1959.

Robert L. Cannon

RANDLE, Ulmo Shannon "Sonny" (b. January 6, 1936, Fork Union, VA), college and professional player and coach, graduated from Fork Union Military Academy, where he competed in track and field. Randle played football only his senior season, but a broken collarbone sidelined him after three games. Virginia Military Institute offered Randle a scholarship in 1955, but he transferred to the University of Virginia and played split end for the Cavaliers. After two seasons with run-oriented Virginia squads, Randle starred in 1958 when new coach Dick Voris instituted a passing offense. In 1958, the swift, sure-handed Randle led the nation with a 24.1 yards per punt return average and set a Virginia record with 47 pass receptions.

The Chicago Cardinals (NFL) drafted Randle in 1958 as a future choice in the nineteenth round. The Cardinals moved in 1960 to St. Louis, where Randle emerged as one of the NFL's best receivers. He finished second in the NFL in pass receptions with 62 and led the NFL with 15 touchdowns in 1960, making the NFL's All-Pro squad and participating in the Pro Bowl. Randle regained his top form in 1962, catching 63 aerials for 1,158 yards (18.4 yards per reception) and becoming one of the NFL's most dangerous deep threats. His honors included being named to the EC's Pro Bowl squad for the third straight year. In 1963, Randle again surpassed the 1,000-yard mark in pass receiving yardage. He gained 1,014 yards on 51 receptions, as the Cardinals developed into a playoff contender. An injury hindered his 1964 campaign, but Randle hauled in 51 passes the following year and played in the Pro Bowl for the fourth and final time of his career.

In 1967, St. Louis traded Randle to the San Francisco 49ers (NFL). After the 49ers released him in October 1968, Randle finished the season and his career with the Dallas Cowboys. In 10 NFL seasons, Randle caught 365 passes for 5,996 yards and 65 touchdowns. He holds Cardinal records for career touchdowns (60) and most receptions (16) and most receiving yardage (256) in one game.

Randle served as head football coach at East Carolina University from 1971 to 1973, the University of Virginia from 1974 to 1976, and Marshall University from 1979 to 1983. Altogether, Randle's squads won 39 games, lost 69, and tied 1. He married Judy Bransford in 1959.

BIBLIOGRAPHY: Bob Barnett and Bob Carroll, "Is There Life After Football: Sonny Randle," *TCC* 7 (1985), pp. 5–6; Booton Herndon, "Randle Catches 'Em in the Clutch," *Sport* 32 (November 1961), pp. 24–25, 90–92; Ronald L. Mendell and Timothy B. Phares, *Who's Who in Football* (New Rochelle, NY, 1974); David S. Neft et al., eds., *The Football Encyclopedia*, 2nd ed. (New York, 1994); *TSN Pro Football Register*, 1969.

Marc S. Maltby

REINHARD, Robert R. "Bob" (b. October 17, 1920, Hollywood, CA), college and professional player, was named an All-America football tackle in 1940 and 1941 at the University of California Berkeley (PCC), despite playing for three losing clubs. Reinhard grew up in Montrose, CA, and played football at California, followed by his brother, William. Reinhard quickly assumed line duty and punted for the Golden Bears. The six-foot-four-inch, 225-pound tackle was named to several All-America teams as a junior in 1940 because of his ability to block and handle field goals, placekicking, and punting. As a senior, he was selected by Grantland Rice (OS) to *Collier's* 1941 All-America team for a second year, edging out Dick Wildung (FB) of the national champion University of Minnesota Gophers. His ability to pass, receive, block, and kick gave him the edge for the First Team.

After serving in World War II, Reinhard played tackle four seasons for the Los Angeles Dons (AAFC). The Dons struggled despite having 1943

Heisman Trophy winner Angelo Bertelli (FB) and one of the AAFC's best lines in Bob Nelson, Lee Arote, Bill Radovich, and Reinhard. Reinhard quickly ranked among the AAFC's finest punters, averaging nearly 45 yards a punt for his career. In 1947, Reinhard rushed 41 times for 150 yards, averaging 3.7 yards per carry. For the 1948 and 1949 seasons, Reinhard again teamed with younger brother Bill on the Dons. When the AAFC ceased operations, Reinhard finished his football career in 1950 with the Los Angeles Rams (NFL). During his AAFC-NFL career, he rushed 43 times for 141 yards (3.3-yard average) and caught nine passes for 101 yards (16.2-yard average) and seven touchdowns.

Reinhard was named to the All-Time All-Pacific Coast team in 1969, joining greats O. J. Simpson (FB), Ernie Nevers (FB), and George Wilson.* Reinhard, who majored in engineering at California, later worked for Remco Hydraulics and served as vice president and general manager of Remco until 1981.

BIBLIOGRAPHY: David S. Neft et al., eds., *The Football Encyclopedia*, 2nd ed. (New York, 1994); Grantland Rice, "All-American Football Team," *Collier's* 161 (December 14, 1940), p. 12; Grantland Rice, "The All-American Football Team," *Collier's* 165 (December 13, 1941), p. 10; *Standard and Poor's Register of Corporations, Directors and Executives* (New York, 1980–1981).

Brian L. Laughlin

RENFRO, Raymond "Ray" (b. November 7, 1930, Whitesboro, TX), college and professional player and coach, graduated from Leonard, TX, High School in 1948 and attended North Texas State University, where he played football under head coach Odus Mitchell. The six-foot-one-inch, 192-pound Renfro enjoyed his best collegiate season in 1951. As a senior halfback, Renfro set Eagles records for rushing yardage (950) and points (90). The high-powered Eagles averaged better than 36 points and 400 yards per game in total offense, as Renfro received Little All-America recognition.

The Cleveland Browns (NFL) selected Renfro in the fourth round of the 1952 draft. Used mostly on special teams as a rookie, Renfro returned punts and kickoffs for the Browns. He tied the NFL Championship game record with four punt returns against the Detroit Lions. In 1953, Renfro led the Browns in rushing with 360 yards, averaging 5.9 yards per attempt, and finished second on the club with 39 receptions. Following the season, Renfro played in his first Pro Bowl and scored a touchdown for the victorious EC All-Stars.

The Browns won the NFL Championship in 1954 but lost Renfro for half the season because of injuries. Renfro starred in the NFL title game, however, catching two Otto Graham (FB) touchdown passes in Cleveland's 56–10 thrashing of Detroit. In 1955, head coach Paul Brown (FB) began using Renfro almost exclusively as a wide receiver. Renfro, the Browns' deep threat, led the NFL in average yards per reception in 1955 (20.8) and 1957

(28.0). He played in the Pro Bowl following the 1957 season, scoring the East's only touchdown in a losing effort. A knee injury hobbled Renfro throughout the 1960 season, but he again made the East's Pro Bowl squad. Renfro enjoyed his best season statistically in 1961, when he paced the Browns with 48 receptions for 834 yards and averaged 17.4 yards per catch. The biggest day of his professional career came that season, as he caught seven passes for 166 yards against the New York Giants.

Renfro retired after the 1963 season. His NFL career totals included 682 yards rushing on 137 attempts (5.0 yards per carry), 281 receptions for 5,508 yards (19.6 yards per catch), and 55 touchdowns. Subsequently, Renfro served as an assistant coach for the Detroit Lions (NFL) in 1964 and 1965 and the Washington Redskins in 1966 and 1967 under former teammate Graham. Renfro became the Dallas Cowboys' pass offense coach in 1968 and held the position for five years.

BIBLIOGRAPHY: Harold Claassen and Steve Boda, Jr., *Ronald Encyclopedia of Football* (New York, 1963); Ronald L. Mendell and Timothy B. Phares, *Who's Who in Football* (New Rochelle, NY, 1974); David S. Neft et al., eds., *The Football Encyclopedia*, 2nd ed. (New York, 1994); Beau Riffenburgh, *The Official NFL Encyclopedia*, 4th ed. (New York, 1986); *TSN Pro Football Register*, 1969.

                                                                     Marc S. Maltby

RENTNER, Ernest John "Pug" "The Flying Dutchman" (b. September 18, 1910, Joliet, IL; d. August 24, 1978, Glencoe, IL), college and professional player and coach, was the son of John Rentner and Amalia Rentner, who operated a boarding house. His father died before he entered college. At Joliet Township High School, he won four letters each in football, basketball, and track and field and captained each team his senior year. He played halfback in football and center and guard in basketball and performed the high jump, discus, and shot put in track and field. Rentner's track and field team won the conference title his senior year.

Northwestern University (WC) recruited Rentner to play football. In his first college game against Tulane University in 1930, Rentner scored on a 30-yard run. Rentner's first WC game against Ohio State University saw him throw two touchdown passes and score on a long run. The following week, he threw two more touchdown passes against the University of Illinois and scored another on a 98-yard kickoff return. A shoulder separation sidelined him for the rest of the season.

The 1931 Northwestern University football season featured spectacular play by Rentner. In the opener against the University of Nebraska, he scored on a 60-yard run and recorded another touchdown. He made a 50-yard scoring run against Ohio State University and tallied three touchdowns against Illinois. The University of Minnesota Gophers held a 14–0 lead at halftime the next week. Rentner returned the second-half kickoff for a 95-yard touchdown run, his longest of the season, and later returned a punt 80 yards for a score, sparking the Wildcats to a 32–14 comeback victory. Rentner scored in six of Northwestern's nine games. In 1931, he handled the ball 181 times for 1,554 yards. From scrimmage, he gained 648 yards in 112 carries. He also returned 54 punts for 573 yards, seven kickoffs for 250 yards, and five interceptions for 49 yards and caught three passes for 34 yards. He tallied seven touchdowns on runs ranging from 13 to 95 yards. Grantland Rice (OS) called Rentner "a balanced back—one of the best backs the Western Conference [WC] has ever produced." Besides having the best change of pace since Red Grange (FB), Rentner possessed remarkable drive and led WC passers. Northwestern University won the WC football title in 1930 and 1931.

The 1932 Northwestern football squad was decimated by graduation losses. Rentner scampered for a 65-yard touchdown run against Ohio State and threw a touchdown pass to George Potter to earn a 7–7 tie with Purdue University, depriving the Boilermakers a share of the WC title. In the Notre Dame game, Rentner suffered three broken ribs. Nevertheless, he returned the following week to climax his impressive college career with a touchdown run in a 44–6 rout over the University of Iowa.

Rentner ranked among the top kickoff and punt return leaders in college football history. The six-foot-one-inch 185-pounder was named an All-America selection at halfback and fullback in 1930 and 1931. Rentner graduated in 1933 with a Bachelor of Science degree in the social sciences. His awards included the Purple Key junior honor society and the Deru honorary senior society. He coached the Wildcats freshman football team in 1933 and on January 2, 1933, played in the East-West Shrine football game.

Rentner and his wife Helen had two daughters, Paige and Tracy. Rentner played four NFL seasons, including 1934 through 1936 with the Boston Redskins and 1937 with the Chicago Bears. During his NFL career, Rentner rushed 197 times for 717 yards for a 13.6-yard average and caught 10 passes for 134 yards and two touchdowns. He completed 24 of 89 passes for 346 yards and one touchdown and intercepted 3 passes.

Rentner entered the military service as a lieutenant, junior grade, in naval aviation in October 1942 and initially was stationed at the Fleet Air Wing in New York. In July 1945, he was transferred to the Cleveland, OH, detachment of the Naval Air Transport Service. He reached the rank of lieutenant commander and was stationed in the British Isles, training runners.

In 1970, Rentner was named to the All-Time Northwestern football team, ranking with Otto Graham (FB) and Frank "Moon" Baker as top individual vote-getters. In July 1971, the Chicago NFF College Football Hall of Fame chapter presented him with a distinguished American award for extending the lessons learned on the football field to a lifetime of community service. The NFF College Football Hall of Fame enshrined him in 1979.

Rentner worked mostly as an investment securities banker and then was employed at the H. C. Wienecke Hardware Store in Glencoe.

512   FOOTBALL

BIBLIOGRAPHY: Chicago (IL) *Sun Times*, August 24, 1978; David Condon, "Dutch Loved the Big Games," Chicago (IL) *Tribune*, August 29, 1978; Evanston (IL) *Review*, November 25, 1942; Ernest Rentner as told to Charles Bartlett, "Is Football Worth While?" Chicago (IL) *Tribune*, November 27, 1932; Zag N. Smith, "Suburban Scene," Chicago (IL) *Sun Times*, February 27, 1977; "Wildcat Grid Legend Pug Rentner Dies," Glencoe (IL) *News*, August 31, 1978.

Stan W. Carlson

RHOME, Gerald Byron "Jerry" (b. March 6, 1942, Dallas, TX), college and professional player and coach, is the son of Byron Rhome and Faye Rhome. His father served as head football coach for many years at Sunset High School, winner of the 1950 State championship. Rhome played football, baseball, and basketball at Sunset High School, being named All-City quarterback in 1958 and 1959 and passing for 1,622 yards and 19 touchdowns as a senior. He lettered three years in baseball and was selected an All-City outfielder.

After entering SMU (SWC) in 1960, Rhome became the Mustangs' starting quarterback in 1961 and completed 79 passes in 129 attempts for 683 yards and 5 touchdowns. A change in head coaches caused Rhome to transfer to the University of Tulsa (MVC) and sit out the 1962 season. Rhome started in 1963, completing 150 of 258 attempts for 1,909 yards and 10 touchdowns. He completed a Hurricane record 98-yard pass against Wichita State University and was named to the All-MVC First Team.

As a senior, Rhome finished second in the Heisman Trophy balloting, was chosen All-America and All-MVC, and led the NCAA University Division in passing with a 172.6 efficiency rating. His favorite receiver, Howard Twilley (FB), led the NCAA with 95 receptions for 1,178 yards and 13 touchdowns. Rhome's passing totals that season comprised 224 completions in 326 attempts for 2,870 yards and 32 touchdowns, including a Hurricane record of 7 versus the University of Louisville. Against Oklahoma State University, he recorded 504 total offense and 488 passing yards with 35 completions in 43 attempts. Rhome's other honors included winning the Walter Camp Trophy, being named AP Back of the Year, and garnering Player of the Year awards from the Washington, DC Touchdown Club and Knute Rockne Club. Rhome was elected to the Tulsa Athletic Hall of Fame in 1984.

The Dallas Cowboys (NFL) selected Rhome in the thirteenth round of the 1964 draft and used him as backup quarterback from the 1964 through 1967 seasons. After Rhome spent a season on the taxi squad in 1968, the Cleveland Browns (NFL) acquired him in a 1969 trade and gave him limited playing time. Rhome enjoyed his best professional season with the Houston Oilers (NFL) in 1970, completing 88 of 168 for 1,031 yards and five touchdowns. He spent 1971 with the Los Angeles Rams (NFL), finishing his NFL career with 139 completions in 289 attempts for 1,628 yards and seven touchdowns. He played briefly with the Montreal, Canada, Alouettes (CFL) in 1972 before retiring.

Rhome entered coaching as an assistant at his alma mater from 1973 to 1975 and moved to the NFL as an assistant coach with the Seattle Seahawks in 1976. Seattle promoted him to offensive coordinator in 1978, a post he held until joining the Washington Redskins (NFL) in 1983. After one-season stints with the San Diego Chargers (NFL) in 1988 and Dallas Cowboys in 1989, he served the Phoenix Cardinals (NFL) as offensive coordinator from 1990 to 1993 and the Minnesota Vikings (NFL) as receivers coach in 1994. In January 1995, the Houston Oilers (NFL) hired him as offensive coordinator. Rhome married Gina Burnham on February 12, 1966, and had daughter Shannon before their December 1969 divorce. He married Sharon Eilers on January 29, 1972, and has a daughter, Nicole, and son, Brett.

BIBLIOGRAPHY: *Phoenix Cardinals Media Guide*, 1991; SMU Sports Information files, Dallas, TX; *University of Tulsa Football Media Guide*, 1991.

Jay Langhammer

RICE, Jerry Lee (b. October 13, 1962, Starkville, MS), college and professional player, is the son of Joe Rice, a brick mason, and Eddie B. Rice and competed in football, basketball, and track and field at Crawford, MS, Moor High School. He and his wife Jackie have two children, Jaqui Bonet and Jerry, Jr., and split residences between Atherton, CA, and Crawford, MS.

A consensus football All-America in 1984 at Mississippi Valley State University (SAC), Rice gained 4,693 yards in receptions and set 18 NCAA Division I-A records during his four-year career. He surpassed 100 receptions in his junior and senior seasons, while compiling 1,845 yards and scoring 28 touchdowns in 1984. Rice exceeded 1,000 yards receiving three consecutive years and was selected the MVP in the Blue-Gray game.

The San Francisco 49ers (NFL) selected him in the first round (sixteenth pick overall) of the 1985 NFL draft. Rice has completed ten seasons from 1985 through 1994, ranking as the NFL premier wide receiver. His honors include being selected on the All-Pro team nine consecutive years (1986–1994), *SI*'s NFL Player of the Year in 1986 and 1990, AP NFL Offensive Player of the Year in 1987 and 1993, and the NFL's MVP in 1987. Rice, the Super Bowl XXIII MVP, led the 49ers to a 20–16 triumph over the Cincinnati Bengals. He tied the Super Bowl record with 11 receptions and set a yardage mark with 215. Rice also helped the 49ers defeat the Denver Broncos, 55–10, in Super Bowl XXIV, establishing a record with 3 touchdown receptions. He caught 10 passes for 149 yards and 3 touchdowns, as the 49ers routed the San Diego Chargers 49–26 in Super Bowl XXIX. His career Super Bowl records include most points (42), touchdowns (7), receptions (28), reception yardage (512), touchdown receptions (7) and combined net yardage (527). He twice tied Super Bowl records for most points (18), touchdowns (3), and touchdown receptions (3). Rice's NFL postseason records include most catches (100) and reception yardage (1,539).

Rice led the NFL in reception yardage in 1986, 1989, 1990, 1993, and 1994, his best campaign coming with 1,570 yards in 1986. He paced the NFL six seasons from 1986 through 1993 in touchdown receptions, establishing a single-season record with 22 in 1987. The season mark broke the previous standard of 18, set by Mark Clayton* of the Miami Dolphins in 1984. He finished first in scoring in 1987 with 138 points, becoming the first wide receiver to capture a scoring crown since Elroy "Crazylegs" Hirsch (FB) of the Los Angeles Rams in 1951. In 1990, he became only the fourth player in NFL history to catch at least 100 passes in a season. His distinguished company included Art Monk* of the Washington Redskins with 106 in 1984, Charley Hennigan,* of the Houston Oilers with 101 in 1964, and Lionel Taylor (FB) of the Denver Broncos with 100 in 1984. Rice also holds the NFL record for most consecutive games with 1 or more touchdown receptions (13) and shares the single-game record for most touchdown receptions, making 5 on October 14, 1990, against the Atlanta Falcons. He holds the NFL career record for most seasons (9) with at least 1,000 yards in pass receptions.

In ten NFL seasons, Rice has recorded 820 pass receptions (second on the all-time NFL list) and 13,275 receiving yards (second) and averaged 16.2 yards per catch. His 131 touchdown receptions set an all-time NFL record, eclipsing Steve Largent's (FB) mark of 100. On September 5, 1994, Rice scored three times against the Los Angeles Raiders to surpass Jim Brown (FB) as the NFL career touchdown leader with 127. Rice, who had not scored in his three previous games against the Raiders, broke the record when he outleaped Albert Lewis on a 38-yard touchdown pass from Steve Young (FB) late in the fourth quarter. He holds the 49er club records in pass and touchdown receptions and receiving yardage. Rice's 112 receptions in 1994, 241 reception yards against the Los Angeles Rams on December 9, 1985, and his 13 receptions against the Atlanta Falcons on October 14, 1990, remain his personal bests. He has caught passes in 144 consecutive regular season games. In 1994 a panel of NFL and Pro Football officials, former players, and reporters named him one of four receivers on the NFL All-Time Team. In September 1994, *USA Today* named Rice to its 75th Anniversary Team. The same year, the U.S. Sports Academy named him Professional Male Athlete of the Year.

BIBLIOGRAPHY: *1992 NCAA Football; San Francisco 49ers Media Guide*, 1994; *TSN Pro Football Register*, 1994; Ralph Wiley, "Rice Is a Breed Apart," *SI* 67 (September 28, 1987), pp. 40–43; Ralph Wiley, "A Step Above 'Em All," *SI* 70 (January 30, 1989), pp. 30–31.

John L. Evers

RIGGS, Gerald Antonio (b. November 6, 1960, Tullos, LA), college and professional player, starred in football at Bonanza High School in Las Vegas, NV, winning MVP honors as the best team back. He set Bonanza High records in rushing with 1,517 yards, gaining 236 yards on just eight carries in one game alone his senior year. Riggs also lettered in track and field and basketball at Bonanza High School. After high school graduation in 1978, Riggs attended Arizona State University (PTC) and continually impressed people with his potential. Sun Devil football head coach Darryl Rogers believed Riggs had long been overlooked. "He's a living horse," Rogers beamed. "He runs, blocks and catches the football. He's a complete football player." Arizona State improved during Riggs's tenure, finishing 6–6 in 1979, 7–4 in 1980, and 9–2 in 1981.

Riggs's prowess at Arizona State garnered him a first-round selection by the Atlanta Falcons (NFL) in the 1982 NFL draft as the ninth pick overall. In seven seasons with the Falcons, the six-foot-one-inch, 230-pound Riggs played in 91 games and gained 6,666 yards in 1,587 carries for a 4.12 yard per rush average. He also scored 48 touchdowns for the Falcons and played in three consecutive Pro Bowls from 1985 through 1987.

In April 1989, Atlanta traded Riggs to the Washington Redskins (NFL) with the Falcons' fifth-round pick in the 1990 draft. The Redskins surrendered their second-round pick in the 1989 draft and their first-round selection in the 1990 draft. In three seasons with the Redskins, Riggs appeared in 48 games, scored 21 touchdowns, and amassed 1,557 yards (3.9-yard average) in 402 carries. He played in the NFC championship game against the Detroit Lions in 1991 and the Super Bowl XXVI triumph against the Buffalo Bills. Riggs also enjoyed an outstanding NFL career as a receiver, hauling in 201 passes for 1,516 yards (7.6-yard average) in a decade. The Redskins waived him in August 1992. Altogether, he rushed for 8,188 career yards (4.1-yard average) and 69 touchdowns.

Riggs lives in the Atlanta area and does radio work.

BIBLIOGRAPHY: Arizona State University Sports Information Department, Tempe, AZ; Atlanta Falcons Public Relations Department, Atlanta, GA; Houston (TX) *Chronicle*, January 26, 1992; Los Angeles (CA) *Times*, September 10, 1989; *TSN Pro Football Register*, 1992; Washington Redskins Public Relations Department, Washington, DC.

Allan Hall

RINEHART, Charles Ramsey "Babe" (b. December 31, 1875, Uniontown, NJ; d. October 30, 1933, New York, NY), college athlete, starred in football and track and field at Lafayette College and was named in 1964 to the NFF College Football Hall of Fame. Rinehart, a guard who captained the Leopards's 1897 football team, made Parke H. Davis's All-Time All-America, George Trevor's All-Time East Region team, and the ECAC 50 Year All-Star eleven. Rinehart played on Lafayette's 1896 11–0–1 varsity squad, sharing the national championship with Princeton University.

The son of the Adam Rineharts, he graduated from Phillipsburg, NJ, High School in 1893. He played five seasons from 1893 to 1897 on Lafayette football teams, compiling a combined 35–16–2 record. The Leopards posted a composite 26–4–2 the last three campaigns when talented linemen Bill Worthington and Gus Wiedenmayer, quarterback Charles Best, and fullback Ed Bray joined Rinehart on the varsity. The imposing six-foot-three-inch, 225-pound Rinehart proved a swift ballcarrier, kicked off, dropkicked field goals, led interference on sweep plays, and opened holes in the line.

Lafayette's outstanding 1896 campaign under coach Parke H. Davis featured a 6–4 triumph over the University of Pennsylvania, handing the Quakers their only loss in four seasons, and a scoreless tie with undefeated Princeton. Both opponents boasted nine All-America players, but Rinehart won their respect with his outstanding play. Pennsylvania's coach George Woodruff (S) compared Rinehart to all-time guard greats "Pudge" Heffelfinger (FB) of Yale University and Truxtun Hare (FB) of the Quakers. Hare opined, "Rinehart was better than anyone from Harvard, Michigan, Brown, the Indians, or any other of our opponents sent against us."

Rinehart, who excelled in track and field, threw the hammer and the shot put, served as class president, and belonged to Delta Upsilon fraternity. He graduated in 1899 from Lafayette, earning a bachelor's degree in civil engineering. In 1905, he married Lena Elizabeth Smith of Ithaca, NY. Rinehart worked as a construction engineer for Portland Cement Company before becoming vice president and sales manager of Overman Cushion Tire Company. The Maplewood, NJ, resident died following surgery.

BIBLIOGRAPHY: Archivist, Skillman Library, Lafayette College, Easton, PA, letter to James D. Whalen, 1993; Bernie McCarty, *All-Americans, 1889–1945* (University Park, IL, 1991); Francis A. March, Jr., *Athletics at Lafayette College* (Ithaca, NY, 1926); Walter R. Okeson, ed., *Spalding's Official Football Guide* (New York, 1934); James D. Whalen, *Gridiron Greats Now Gone* (Jefferson, NC, 1991).

James D. Whalen

RODGERS, Ira Errett "Rat" (b. May 26, 1896, Bethany, WV; d. February 22, 1963, Morgantown, WV), college player and coach, was 1 of 11 children born to William Rodgers, a day laborer, and Rosa Rodgers in a small college town. After grade school, Rodgers attended the preparatory part of Bethany College because the town was too small to support a high school. He was allowed to play four years on the college athletic teams and proved an excellent performer. In 1914, Rodgers played an outstanding football game in Bethany's narrow 13–0 loss to West Virginia University.

The following year, Rodgers enrolled at West Virginia University as a college student and joined the Mountaineers athletic programs. Opponents protested that the versatile Rodgers already had played four collegiate years. Rodgers played basketball, baseball, and football for the Mountaineers, captaining each sport his senior year in 1919–1920. He received national recognition in football as a fullback after leading West Virginia to an 8–2 record in 1919, highlighted by a 25–0 triumph over Princeton University. In that game, Rodgers completed 9 of 12 passes for 162 yards and 2 touchdowns. He scored 147 points with 19 touchdowns that season and amassed 313 career points. Walter Camp (FB) named Rodgers to his 1919 All-America team. Rodgers's athletic versatility continued, as he won the 1929 West Virginia Amateur Golf Championship in only his second year performing the sport.

Rodgers graduated with honors in chemistry from West Virginia University in 1920 and coached there for the next 42 years. He served as head football coach for 9 years, guiding the 1920–1925 and 1943–1945 Mountaineer squads to a 44–31–8 composite record. He also coached the baseball team to a 204–210 record from 1921 to 1942 and the golf squad from 1949 until illness forced his retirement in 1961. Rodgers, inducted into the West Virginia Sports Hall of Fame in 1955 and NFF College Football Hall of Fame in 1957, married Marie Thompson and had one son, Ira, Jr.

BIBLIOGRAPHY: Harold Claassen and Steve Boda, Jr., eds., *Ronald Encyclopedia of Football* (New York, 1963); John McCallum and Charles H. Pearson, *College Football USA, 1969–1972* (New York, 1972); "Rat Rodgers, WVU's Greatest Athlete Dies," Wheeling (WV) *Intelligencer*, February 23, 1963; "Rodgers Funeral Will Be Sunday," Charleston (WV) *Daily Mail*, February 23, 1963; C. Robert Barnett, telephone interview with Ira Rodgers, Jr., March 16, 1994; *West Virginia University Football Media Guide*, 1993.

C. Robert Barnett

ROPER, William Winston "Bill" (b. August 22, 1880, Mt. Airy, PA; d. December 10, 1933, Germantown, PA), athlete, football coach, and sportswriter, was one of two sons of Jourdan Wolfolk Roper and Rebecca (Gowen) Roper and played football, basketball, and baseball at both William Penn Charter School and Princeton University. As a substitute left end on Princeton's 1899 championship football team in its game with Yale University, the 5-foot-10-inch, 172-pound Roper smothered a loose ball. The Tigers then defeated Yale, 11–10, with a field goal. Roper, who also captained the 1902 basketball team, belonged to Ivy, an upperclass eating club, and the Episcopalian St. Paul's Society. A rheumatic attack his senior year delayed his degree completion until 1903. He earned a Bachelor of Laws degree from the University of Virginia Law School in 1908, coaching baseball and football. Roper married Elizabeth Binney Haines in 1910 and had two children, Elizabeth and William, Jr. At Philadelphia, Roper practiced law until 1926 and managed the Quaker City Agency of the Prudential Insurance Company of America. President Woodrow Wilson, a Princeton graduate, appointed him port of Philadelphia's appraiser of merchandise. Roper later joined the Republican party and was elected to city council in 1919. He won as an independent city council candidate in 1923, fighting for Sunday blue laws reform to permit sports.

Roper achieved an overall 112–37–19 record as head football coach at Virginia Military Institute in 1903 and 1904, University of the South, Sewanee, TN, in 1905, University of Missouri (MVC) in 1909, Swarthmore College in 1915 and 1916, and Princeton from 1906 to 1908, 1910 to 1911 (director of athletics), and 1919 to 1930. Roper's Missouri squad won the 1909 MVC title with a 7–0–1 record. His 17 Princeton Tiger teams produced an 89–28–16 composite mark. Freely borrowing tactics and technical plays from other teams, Roper left the drills to his assistant coaches. A master in outlining strategy and teaching signals, he encouraged players to pick up and run with fumbled balls until the play was outlawed in 1929. The strict disciplinarian psychologically energized his teams by locker-room talks and instilled the motto, "A team that won't be beat, can't be beat." Roper was called "a damned evangelist" by University of Pennsylvania halfback William M. Hollenback (S) and "the last of the romantic coaches in football" by the *NYT*. Roper's legacy remained his players, over a dozen of whom became All-Americas.

From 1919 to 1930, Princeton split with Yale 6–6 and finished 5–1–2 against Harvard University. The Tigers achieved Big Three championships in 1922, 1925, and 1926. Roper considered the 1925 Princeton team his best because it shut out Harvard, 36–0, and, sparked by quarterback Jake Slagle's 85-yard touchdown run, triumphed, 25–12, over Yale. His undefeated 1922 "Team of Destiny," a 3-to-1 underdog, stunned the University of Chicago with a comeback 21–18 victory. Coach Amos Alonzo Stagg (FB) ruefully observed, "Never before or since has Chicago lost a game which it has tucked away so safely."

In *Winning Football* (1921) and *Football—Today and Tomorrow* (1927), Roper called college football "a democratic game," which developed "initiative, courage and team-play." He in 1926 negotiated with Yale coach Tad (Thomas Albert Dwight) Jones (FB) the first nonscouting agreement. Roper was twice elected to the AIFRC, participating in the successful revolt against Walter Camp's (FB) domination, and served as president of the EASFO. In 1951, he was elected as a coach to the NFF and the HAF College Football Halls of Fame.

Roper, who suffered a nervous breakdown in 1929, posted only an 8–10–4 record during his last three seasons from 1928 to 1930 and died of a two-month streptococcic infection.

BIBLIOGRAPHY: A.C.M. Azoy, "The Magic Worker," *Princeton Alumni Weekly* 31 (November 21, 1930), pp. 219–220; "Bill Roper Is Dead; Noted in Football," *NYT*, December 11, 1933; Tim Cohane, *Great College Football Coaches of the Twenties and Thirties* (New Rochelle, NY, 1973); Allison Danzig, *The History of American Football: Its Great Teams, Players, and Coaches* (Englewood Cliffs, NJ, 1956); Allison Danzig, *Oh, How They Played the Game: The Early Days of Football and the Heroes Who Made It Great* (New York, 1971); Jay Dunn, *The Tigers of Princeton: Old Nassau Football* (Huntsville, AL, 1977); Christian Gauss, "Bill Roper," *Princeton Alumni Weekly* 31

(November 21, 1930), pp. 222–223; Donald Grant Herring, Sr., *Forty Years of Football* (New York, 1940); John D. McCallum and Charles H. Pearson, *College Football U.S.A., 1869–1973* (New York, 1973); Herbert Reed, "The Roper Complex," *New Yorker* 2 (November 13, 1926), pp. 25–27; "Roper to Retire After '30 Season," *Princeton Alumni Weekly* 30 (January 10, 1930), p. 359; William W. Roper files, 1902, Seeley G. Mudd Manuscript Library, Princeton University Archives, Princeton, NJ; Jack Weller and Cornelia Weller, "Princeton Football Surviving Letter Men 1916–1942" (Princeton, NJ, 1984); "William Winston Roper" biographical sketches in the *Princeton Class of 1902* albums (Princeton, NJ): *Nassau Herald Class of 1902 of Princeton University* (1902), pp. 121, 133; *Twenty-fifth Year Record of the Class of 1902* (1927), pp. 25–26, 156; *WWWA*, vol. I (1897–1942), p. 1057.

Marcia G. Synnott

ROTE, Tobin C. (b. January 18, 1928, San Antonio, TX), college and professional player, graduated from Harlandale High School, where he starred in football, and from Rice University with a B.S. degree in physical education in 1950. Rote played quarterback from 1946 to 1949, leading Rice (SWC) to a 28–10–1 record and SWC titles in 1946 and 1949. He guided Rice to a 10–1 record in 1949, including a 27–13 victory over the University of North Carolina in the Cotton Bowl. The same year, he set Owls' season records for pass attempts (141), pass completions (86), and passing yardage (1,020).

Rote played for the Green Bay Packers (NFL) from 1950 to 1956 as an underrated quarterback and outstanding competitor on poor teams. The rugged, six-foot-three-inch 215-pounder, one of the strongest and best running T-formation quarterbacks, gained 523 yards rushing on 76 carries and led the NFL with a 6.9-yard rushing average in 1951. In 1956, Rote completed 146 of 308 passes for 2,203 yards and 18 touchdowns, all NFL-leading marks. He also gained 398 yards rushing on 84 attempts (4.7-yard average) and scored 11 touchdowns, being named All-NFL and playing in the Pro Bowl.

Rote performed for the Detroit Lions (NFL) from 1957 to 1959. He took over for the injured Bobby Layne (FB) in 1957 and directed the Lions to the NFL championship. In a 59–14 title game drubbing of the Cleveland Browns, he scored a touchdown and threw four touchdown passes. Rote starred for Toronto, Canada (CFL) from 1960 to 1962 and spearheaded the Argonauts to CFL titles in 1960 and 1961. He led the CFL in pass attempts, pass completions, and passing yardage all three seasons.

The San Diego Chargers (AFL) signed Rote in 1963. He guided them that season to the AFL championship, completing 170 of 286 pass attempts for 2,510 yards and 20 touchdowns and boasting an AFL-leading 59.4 percent completion rate. Rote garnered AFL MVP and All-AFL honors and played in the AFL All-Star Game. After helping the Chargers win the AFL Western Division title in 1964, he did not play in 1965 and ended his career with the Denver Broncos (AFL) in 1966.

In his 13-year NFL-AFL career, Rote completed 1,329 passes in 2,907 attempts (45.7 percent) for 18,850 yards and 148 touchdowns. He rushed for 3,128 yards in 635 carries (4.9-yard average) and scored 38 touchdowns.

Rote married Betsy Bobo in 1948 and has four children, Tobin, Jr., Robin, Toni, and Rocky. He started two businesses, including a manufacturer's representative concern and an underground conduit sales firm, while still a player and resides in Bloomfield Hills, MI.

BIBLIOGRAPHY: Harold Claassen and Steve Boda, Jr., *Ronald Encyclopedia of Football* (New York, 1963); Evans Kirby, "Quarterback Rote Loved to Run and Run He Did," in *Packers of the Past* (Milwaukee, WI, 1965), p. 28; Murray Olderman, *The Pro Quarterback* (Englewood Cliffs, NJ, 1966); *TSN Pro Football Register*, 1969.

Edward J. Pavlick

RYMKUS, Louis "Lou" "The Battler" (b. November 6, 1919, Royalton, IL), college and professional player, coach, and scout, began an outstanding athletic career at Tilden Technical High School in Chicago, IL. As a football player, Rymkus earned All-City honors three years and made the All-State team in 1938. During his senior year, he captured the City heavyweight wrestling championship and starred for the track and field team as a shot putter. Rymkus continued his winning ways at the University of Notre Dame, capturing the school's 1940 heavyweight boxing championship and playing both offense and defense on the football team. The 1941 Fighting Irish enjoyed an undefeated season. In 1942, Rymkus earned mention on some All-America teams and was honored as Notre Dame's MVP.

The Washington Redskins (NFL) made the six-foot-four-inch, 223-pound tackle their fifth-round draft choice in 1943. Rymkus helped Washington to the Eastern Division title that fall as an offensive and defensive player and was named to the All-Pro team. In 1944, Rymkus joined the U.S. Navy as an athletic instructor. His powerful Bainbridge, MD, Naval Training Station squad enjoyed an undefeated season. Reassignment to Hawaii led him to umpiring baseball games. He later spent two off-seasons as an AAGPBL umpire.

By his discharge in 1946, Rymkus already had a wife, Betty, and twin sons. The Cleveland Browns (AAFC) gave him a more lucrative offer than the Washington Redskins. Rymkus proved equally successful with the Browns in the new AAFC, earning All-Pro honors the next six years and helping the Browns to six Eastern Division and five league (AAFC, 1946–1949; NFL, 1950) titles. Rymkus played both offense and defense until 1948, when his duties were limited to offensive line play. "The Battler's" agility, quick feet, and tenacity made him an outstanding pass blocker until knee injuries forced his retirement in 1951.

Rymkus turned to coaching, but his pride, confidence, and aggressive, outspoken, and sometimes tactless approach produced a well-traveled career. He served as line coach with Indiana University (BTC) in 1952, the Calgary, Canada, Stampeders (CFL) in 1953, the Green Bay Packers (NFL) from

1954 to 1957, and the Los Angeles Rams (NFL) in 1958. Rymkus was selected in 1960 as the head coach of the Houston Oilers (AFL), where he
produced the first AFL championship team and earned AFL Coach of the
Year honors with a 10–4 record. Disagreements with owner Bud Adams led
to Rymkus's firing in 1961 after a 1–3–1 start. In 1965, Rymkus accepted a
high school football coaching position in Many, LA. He returned to the
NFL in 1970 as line coach with the Baltimore Colts and scouted for other
teams during the 1970s before retiring to pursue golf and hunting.

BIBLIOGRAPHY: Bob Carroll, "The Battler," *TCC* 9 (Fall 1987), pp. 1–4; Louis Rymkus file, Pro Football Hall of Fame, Canton, OH.

Gerald R. Gems

SANDERS, Charles Alvin "Charlie" (b. August 25, 1946, Greensboro, NC),
college and professional player, coach, and sportscaster, excelled as a football
and basketball player while attending James B. Dudley High School in
Greensboro. Sanders matriculated at the University of Minnesota (BTC),
where he played football under coach Murray Warmath and basketball under
coach John Kundla (IS). An outstanding blocker and receiver, he completed
his senior season as the Gophers' top pass receiver. Sanders caught 21 passes
for 276 yards (13.1-yard average) and two touchdowns, leading Minnesota to
an 8–2 win–loss record. The Gophers lost only to Purdue University in the
BTC, sharing the 1967 BTC crown with the Boilermakers and Indiana University.

The Detroit Lions (NFL) selected Sanders in the third round of the 1968
AFL-NFL draft. The six-foot-four-inch, 228-pound tight end, known for
making circus catches, possessed good speed and agility and proved an outstanding competitor. Sanders played 10 seasons for the Lions from 1968
through 1977. His best single-game performance came during his rookie
year against the Washington Redskins (NFL) on December 15, 1968, when
he caught 10 passes for 133 yards. Sanders finished second to teammate wide
receiver Earl McCullough for NFL Rookie of the Year honors, the only
rookie selected to appear in the Pro Bowl that season. He paced the Lions
in pass receptions in 1969, 1970, 1973, and 1975 and tied McCullough for
the club lead in 1968 with 40 receptions each. Sanders caught 42 passes in
1974 and enjoyed his best overall season in 1969, when he made 42 receptions for 656 yards and a 15.6-yard average per catch. His honors included
being named to the *TSN* NFL WC All-Star team in 1969, the *TSN* NFC
All-Star team in 1970 and 1971, and the Pro Bowl seven times following the
1968 through 1971 and 1974 through 1976 seasons. During his 10-year
career with the Lions, he caught 336 passes for 4,817 yards (14.3-yard average) and 31 touchdowns. Sanders ranks as the Lions' all-time leading receiver, second in yards gained (behind Gail Cogdill's 5,220 yards), and fourth
in touchdown receptions.

Sanders served as a radio analyst for Lions' broadcasts from 1983 through

1988. In January 1989, Wayne Fontes, head football coach for the Lions, named Sanders tight end coach. Sanders completed his sixth year in that capacity in 1994. In 1990, the Michigan Sports Hall of Fame enshrined him in recognition of his career with the Lions. Sanders and his wife Georgiana have nine children, Mia, Charese, Mary Jo, Georgiana, Charles, Jr., Nathalie, Tallisa, Wayne, and Jordan.

BIBLIOGRAPHY: *Detroit Lions Media Guide*, 1994; Ronald L. Mendell and Timothy B. Phares, *Who's Who in Football* (New Rochelle, NY, 1974); *TSN Pro Football Register*, 1977.

John L. Evers

SANDERS, Orban Eugene "Spec" (b. January 26, 1919, Temple, OK), college and professional player, is the son of Wylie Sanders, a barber, and Hallie (Sporlock) Sanders. He participated in football and track and field at Temple High School and transferred to Cameron JC in Lawton, OK, where he finished his junior and senior years of high school and spent his first two college years. He played four years of JC football, twice making All-Conference, and also participated in track and field.

Sanders played football at the University of Texas (SWC) in 1940 and 1941 as tailback behind All-America Jack Crain. In 1941, he gained 365 yards rushing for a 7.8-yard average, caught 17 passes for 241 yards, and scored 53 points while helping Texas to an 8–1–1 season. Although Sanders did not start at Texas, the Washington Redskins (NFL) drafted him in the first round. Sanders joined the U.S. Navy, playing for the Georgia Pre-Flight squad in 1942 and the North Carolina Pre-Flight team in 1945. His bachelor's degree came in physical education from Oklahoma State University in 1946.

Sanders performed in professional football for the New York Yankees (AAFC) from 1946 to 1948 and New York Yanks (NFL) in 1950. An all-purpose tailback, he excelled on offense and defense. Sanders gained All-AAFC and AP All-Pro (AAFC-NFL) honors in 1946 and 1947 and was named an All-NFL defensive back in 1950. The HAF and *Sport* magazine selected him Pro Football Player–Performer of the Year in 1947.

In 1946, the tough, fast, shifty runner led the AAFC in rushing with 709 yards (5.1-yard average) and touchdowns with 12. Sanders returned a kickoff 103 yards for a touchdown against the Los Angeles Dons. In 1947, Sanders set a professional record with 1,432 yards rushing (6.2-yard average) and scored 19 touchdowns, including 18 by rushing. An October 24 contest against the Chicago Rockets saw Sanders rush for 250 yards, the single-game professional record until broken by O. J. Simpson (FB) in 1976. He played in the AAFC title game in 1946 and 1947 and in the Pro Bowl following the 1950 season. Knee surgery sidelined Sanders the 1949 season, but he returned in 1950 as a defensive safety and punter.

During his professional career, the six-foot-one-inch, 196-pound Sanders rushed for 2,900 yards on 540 carries (5.4-yard average), completed 206 of

421 passes (48.9 percent) for 2,829 yards and 23 touchdowns, punted 192 times for a 40.9-yard average, intercepted 19 passes, and scored 40 touchdowns. Although having a relatively short professional career, he ranks among the greatest runners and all-around backs in gridiron history.

The soft-spoken Sanders married Cletus Madrano of Apache, OK, in 1940 and has one son, Eugene, a Baptist minister. The widower has retired from his dry cleaning business, lives in Lawton, OK, and keeps busy with church-related activities and playing golf. Sanders is enshrined in the Oklahoma Athletic Hall of Fame.

BIBLIOGRAPHY: Blair Cherry, "What Makes Sanders Run?" *SL* (February 1948); Joe King, "Pro League Tough? 'Speck' Sanders Likes That," *TSN: The Quarterback* (October 29, 1947); Orban E. Sanders file, Pro Football Hall of Fame, Canton, OH; Orban E. Sanders, letters to Edward J. Pavlick, June and July 1993; *TSN Pro Football Register*, 1967.

Edward J. Pavlick

SCARBATH, John Carl "Jack" (b. August 12, 1930, Baltimore MD), college and professional player, is the son of Karl Scarbath and has one brother, Dick, and one sister. He graduated from Baltimore Polytechnic High School and attended the University of Maryland (SC) on a Charlie Keller scholarship, usually designated for baseball players. After playing freshman baseball, Scarbath switched to football and lettered from 1950 to 1952. The six-foot-one-inch, 195-pound quarterback, who made All-SC and All-America in the 1952 season, played boldly and skillfully. Under football coach Jim Tatum's (FB) direction, Scarbath became the nation's leading split-T-formation quarterback.

Scarbath guided Maryland to its greatest winning streak, triumphing in 22 consecutive games without defeat. Maryland finished 7–2–1 in 1950 and 9–0 in 1951, outscoring opponents, 353–62. In 1951, Scarbath completed 40 of 76 passes (52.6 percent) for 732 yards and eight touchdowns and rushed 62 times for 273 yards (4.4-yard average) and eight touchdowns. Scarbath spearheaded perhaps Maryland's greatest football victory in the 1952 Sugar Bowl 28–13 upset over top-ranked University of Tennessee, completing his first 6 passes. Although the preseason favorite for the 1952 Heisman Trophy, Scarbath finished second to Billy Vessels (FB) of the University of Oklahoma. Maryland's season-ending losses to the University of Mississippi Rebels and University of Alabama Crimson Tide may have cost Scarbath his prize. Mississippi played in the Sugar Bowl, while Alabama performed in the Orange Bowl.

Scarbath, the fourth leading rusher on the University of Maryland's team in 1952, gained 370 yards on 102 attempts (3.6-yard average) and 3 touchdowns to set season passing records in yards (1,149), attempts (113), and completions (69). His career passing marks of 141 completions in 269 attempts (52.4 percent) for 2,344 yards and 22 touchdowns were not broken until the 1960s. In 1952, he was voted outstanding player of the North-South game. Scarbath also rushed for 915 career yards (3.9-yard average) and 14 touchdowns. Altogether, Scarbath accounted for 36 career touchdowns, an estimable record.

The Washington Redskins (NFL) selected Scarbath in the first round of the 1953 draft. Scarbath shared quarterback duties with Eddie LeBaron* for the 6–5 Redskins in 1953, completing 45 of 129 passes for 862 yards and 9 touchdowns. Washington slipped to 3–9 in 1954, as Scarbath completed 44 of 109 passes for 798 yards and 7 touchdowns. He did not play in the NFL in 1955 and resumed as a backup quarterback for the 5–7 Pittsburgh Steelers in 1956, completing 12 of 41 passes for 208 yards and 2 touchdowns. His three NFL seasons included 101 pass completions in 279 attempts (36.2 percent) for 1,868 yards and 18 touchdowns with 30 interceptions.

In 1986 and 1990, Scarbath, a private businessman and active Maryland alumnus, was considered for his alma mater's athletic director position. Although not selected, Scarbath participates in the Maryland Education Foundation and Terrapin Club. He married Lynn Brown of Rising Sun, MD, has two sons, Tom and Blair, and resides in College Park, MD.

BIBLIOGRAPHY: Paul Attner, *The Terrapins: Maryland Football* (Huntsville, AL, 1975); Morris A. Beale, *Kings of American Football: The Story of Football at Maryland* (Washington, DC, 1952); University of Maryland, Sports Information Office, College Park, MD, telephone calls with Frederick J. Augustyn, Jr., January 26, 1994; February 1, 1994; Washington (DC) *Times*, December 5, 1986; July 13, 1990; *Washington Redskins Official Press, Radio, and Television Guide*, 1953.

                                                                          Frederick J. Augustyn, Jr.

SCHAFRATH, Richard Phillip "Dick" "Schaf" (b. March 21, 1937, Canton, OH), college and professional player, attended Wooster, OH, High School, where he captained the football, basketball, and baseball teams. Schafrath excelled at Ohio State University (BTC) in football, playing offensive lineman for the Buckeyes under coach Woody Hayes (FB). He participated on the 1955 squad that captured the BTC title and starred on the 1957 BTC championship 9–1 team. The Buckeyes, ranked second nationally behind Auburn University that season, triumphed, 10–7, over the University of Oregon in the 1958 Rose Bowl.

The Cleveland Browns (NFL) selected Schafrath in the second round of the 1959 draft. The six-foot-three-inch offensive tackle weighed only 220 pounds as an NFL rookie but added 35 pounds through a strenuous weight-lifting program. Schafrath, who played 13 seasons from 1959 through 1971 for the Browns, started out as a defensive end but became Cleveland's regular left tackle in his second NFL season. Schafrath, an excellent blocker and pass protector, consistently played a principal role in blocking for the Browns' strong running game, spearheaded by fullback Jim Brown (FB). His honors included selection on the All-Pro teams in 1963, 1964, 1965, and

1969 and playing in the Pro Bowl following the 1963, 1964, and 1966 through 1968 seasons. Schafrath started on the Browns' 1964 squad, which defeated the Baltimore Colts, 27–0, for the NFL title. He also played in the NFL championship games in 1965, 1968, and 1969, with Cleveland losing, 23–12 to the Green Bay Packers, 34–0 to Baltimore, and 27–7 to the Minnesota Vikings.

Schafrath married Judith Ann Grimm on July 7, 1968, and has one daughter, Heidi. During the off-season, he worked with International Management Corporation in Cleveland. In 1969, he joined 26 other professional players who visited American troops in Vietnam.

BIBLIOGRAPHY: *Cleveland Browns Media Guide*, 1970; Cleveland Browns News Release, November 12, 1968, p. 2; *TSN Pro Football Register*, 1970.

John L. Evers

SCOTT, Clyde Luther "Smackover" (b. August 29, 1924, Dixie, LA), college athlete and professional football player, is one of five sons and three daughters of Luther Scott, an oil field worker. Scott moved at age eight with his family to Smackover, AR, where he excelled in four sports at Smackover High School. In football, he rushed for 4,301 yards, scored 429 points, and was named All-Southern three times. As a track and field performer, he held two national interscholastic records in the high hurdles and javelin. Scott also averaged 20 points a game in basketball, played baseball, and served as president of his senior class.

After graduation from high school, Scott entered Bullis Preparatory School in 1943 and was chosen All-Prep in football. He attended the U.S. Naval Academy for two years, leading the Middie football team in scoring both seasons and receiving All-America Second Team honors in 1945. He resigned from the U.S. Naval Academy to marry Leslie Hampton, Miss Arkansas of 1945, on August 30, 1946. They have two children, Marsha and Steve. Scott enrolled at the University of Arkansas (SWC) in 1946, earning All-SWC and All-America honors the next three seasons. As a wingback in the single-wing formation, he carried the ball 281 times for 1,463 yards. Arkansas retired his number 12 following his playing career. His honors include induction into the NFF College Football Hall of Fame in 1971 and memberships in the Arkansas Sports Hall of Fame and the University of Arkansas Hall of Fame.

Scott returned to track and field in 1948 and clocked 9.6 seconds in the 100-yard dash, which tied the world record and set a Razorback mark. He won the 1948 NCAA championship in the 110-meter high hurdles in a world record time of 13.7 seconds and earned the Silver Medal in the event at the 1948 London, England, Olympics, barely missing the Gold Medal in a photo finish. After playing in the 1949 College All-Star Game, Scott joined the Philadelphia Eagles (NFL) and helped them win the NFL championship over the Los Angeles Rams. He was hampered by injuries the next three seasons and concluded his NFL career with the 1952 Detroit Lions NFL championship club. During his NFL career, Scott rushed 400 yards on 100 carries (4.0-yard average) for two touchdowns and caught 19 passes for 381 yards (20.1-yard average) and four touchdowns. He joined Union Life Insurance Company of Little Rock, AR, and served as executive vice president for many years, retiring in 1992.

BIBLIOGRAPHY: Orville Henry and Jim Bailey, *The Razorbacks* (Huntsville, AL, 1973); Clyde Scott Day Program, 1971.

Jay Langhammer

SELLERS, Ronald "Ron" "Jingle Joints" (b. February 5, 1947, Jacksonville, FL), college and professional player, is the son of Andrew Sellers and Mary Lee Sellers and attended Paxon High School in Jacksonville, where he excelled in football. Since the stringbean receiver possessed herky-jerky moves, college scouts expressed doubts about his gridiron prospects. Sellers and eight other high school teammates were recruited by Florida State University, then coached by Bill Peterson. During three varsity seasons from 1966 through 1968, Sellers was nicknamed "Jingle Joints" because of his rhythmical moves, jumping ability, knack for catching a pass among a group of defenders, and the spectacular manner of catching most passes. He caught 5 touchdown passes in a game against Wake Forest University on November 23, 1968. Sellers led the Seminoles to a 21–8–1 win–loss record and bowl appearances all three seasons. In 1967, his 1,228 receiving yards led the nation. The following season, his 86 receptions, 1,496 reception yards, and 12 touchdowns paced the nation. In the 1966 Sun Bowl, Sellers caught 6 passes for 170 yards and 2 touchdowns in Florida State's 28–20 loss to the University of Wyoming. He in 1967 set a Gator Bowl record with 14 receptions for 145 yards and 1 touchdown in a 17–17 tie with Pennsylvania State University. His 14 receptions against the Nittany Lions broke the Florida State record, set by Fred Biletnikoff (FB) in the 1967 Gator Bowl. On October 26, 1968, Sellers snared 16 passes against the University of South Carolina to better his mark. The 1968 Peach Bowl saw him catch 8 passes for 76 yards and 2 touchdowns in the Seminoles' 31–27 loss to LSU.

Sellers ranks high on the all-time NCAA Division I career receiving list, placing eighth in receptions (212) and catches per game (7.1), third in reception yardage (3,598), tied for third in average yards per catch (17.0), and tied for eleventh in touchdown receptions (23). Sellers, who remains the NCAA record holder for most games gaining 100 yards or more (16) during a career, holds nearly all the Seminole records for pass receptions, reception yardage, and touchdown catches in one game, one season, and a career. His honors include All-America selections in 1967 and 1968, placing tenth in the 1968 Heisman Trophy voting, and election to the NFF College Football Hall of Fame.

The Boston Patriots selected Sellers in the first round of the 1969 AFL-NFL draft. Sellers, a six-foot-four-inch, 190-pound wide receiver, rated as one of the game's top prospects and potential NFL star. He enjoyed a great rookie year and started in the 1969 AFL All-Star Game. Besides ranking second among all receivers with 26.1 yards per catch, he set a Patriots' record for most yards receiving in 1 game and placed among the top vote getters for AFL Rookie of the Year. Sellers again led the Patriots in receiving during the 1970 season but played in only 10 games in 1971. New England (NFL) traded him to the Dallas Cowboys (NFL) for a draft choice in 1972. Sellers made 31 receptions for 653 yards in 1972 and played in the NFC championship game, which the Cowboys lost to the Washington Redskins, 26–3. The Cowboys traded Sellers with a second-round draft choice to the Miami Dolphins (NFL) for wide receiver Otto Stowe in 1973. Sellers played just 3 games for the Dolphins in 1973 before retiring from professional football. His five-year professional football career included 112 pass receptions, 2,184 reception yards (19.5-yard average), and 18 touchdowns in 52 games.

In 1975, Sellers developed an organization specializing in individual and corporate life and health insurance in Florida. Currently, he serves on the Florida State University Business School's Advisory Board and was a member of their foundation. Additionally, he belongs to the Florida Council on Economic Education and serves as president of the Vincent Draddy Gold Coast Chapter College Football Hall of Fame. Sellers and his wife Kimberly have a daughter, Beverly.

BIBLIOGRAPHY: Bill McGrotha, *Seminoles! The First Forty Years* (Tallahassee, FL, 1987); Herman L. Masin, "Jingle Joints," *Senior Scholastic* 93 (November 8, 1968), p. 28; *NCAA Football's Finest*, 1990; *New England Patriots Media Guide*, 1971; *Official NCAA Football*, 1992; Sports Information Office, Florida State University, Tallahassee, FL, letter to John L. Evers, August 4, 1993; *TSN Pro Football Register*, 1974.

John L. Evers

SHOATE, Roderick "Rod" (b. April 26, 1953, Spiro, OK), college and professional player, is the son of Levester Shoate and Lula (Brown) Shoate and grew up on an eastern Oklahoma farm with four brothers and five sisters. Shoate developed his toughness and aggressiveness playing sandlot football in grade school. He played tackle football without pads and was never afraid to hit anyone.

Shoate played very little organized football, however, until his senior year at Spiro High School. A fullback and linebacker, Shoate impressed few major college scouts due to Spiro's lackluster 5–4–1 record. His principal and coach, L. D. Johnson, however, asked University of Oklahoma (BEC) coaches to view Shoate's football performance on film. Oklahoma defensive coach Larry Lacewell admitted that he drove around the nation for a week with film of one of its best linebacking prospects in his trunk. After viewing the film, head coach Chuck Fairbanks agreed that Shoate should be signed.

Shoate subsequently started every varsity game for Oklahoma upon becoming eligible for competition. Shoate made 420 tackles during his career as a Sooner and 155 as a senior in 1974.

Oklahoma fielded some of its finest teams during Shoate's tenure. In 1972, the Sooners compiled an 11–1 record, including a 14–0 victory over Pennsylvania State University in the Sugar Bowl. The NCAA later changed Oklahoma's season record to 8–4 for using an ineligible player in three games. In 1973 and 1974, the NCAA placed Oklahoma on probation, making it ineligible for postseason play. Despite this handicap, Oklahoma compiled records of 10–0–1 in 1973 and 11–0 in 1974. The AP ranked the Sooners second nationally in 1973 and declared them national champions in 1974. The sports media named the six-foot-one-inch, 215-pound Shoate BEC Sophomore Defensive Player of Year in 1972, All-BEC for three years, and consensus All-America for two years.

The New England Patriots (NFL) drafted Shoate as their number-two pick in 1975, the forty-first player taken overall. Shoate played in four games as a rookie in 1975 but missed the entire 1976 season due to a knee injury. He became a starter in 1977 and played in every game for the Patriots until being traded to the Chicago Bears (NFL) in April 1982. Shoate intercepted five passes in his career, returning one for a touchdown in 1980. Shoate never played in a regular-season game for the Bears, performing instead with the New Jersey Generals (USFL) in 1983 and the Memphis Showboats (USFL) in 1984.

BIBLIOGRAPHY: John Keith, press release, University of Oklahoma Sooner Sports Service, Norman, OK, October 8, 1973; *Outstanding College Athletes of America 1974* (Washington, DC, 1974); *TSN Pro Football Register*, 1982; University of Oklahoma, *Oklahoma Football—1988* (Norman, OK, 1988); Jim Weeks, "Sooner Foes Can't Hide from Shoate," *TSN*, October 5, 1974, pp. 39–40.

John Hillman

SINGTON, Fred William (b. February 24, 1910, Birmingham, AL), college athlete and official, is the son of Max Sington and Hallye (Spiro) Sington. His father sold furniture and established the furniture department in a large retail store in Birmingham. Sington attended high school in Birmingham, lettering in four sports, receiving the Jaffe Trophy as the city's best athlete, serving as vice president of the student body, and belonging to the National Honor Society. At the University of Alabama (SC), he lettered three years in football and baseball. His 1930 team finished undefeated and triumphed over the University of Washington in the Rose Bowl. His honors included being named All-Southern and All-America as a football tackle in 1929 and 1930 and All-America as a baseball catcher in 1931. Sington, who won trophies as best athlete and best scholar–athlete, was elected to Phi Beta Kappa and Blue Key Honor societies, served as vice president of the student body, and was later awarded an Honorary Doctor of Humane Letters degree.

From 1931 to 1934, he served as an assistant football coach at Duke University (SC). He coached the Navy football team at Norman, OK, in 1944 and officiated SEC football games for 15 years, presiding over the association. He was selected to the NFF College Football Hall of Fame in 1955 and the Alabama Sports Hall of Fame in 1961, received the Paul "Bear" Bryant (FB) Athletic Award in 1991, and was named to the Alabama Team of the Century in 1992.

Sington remained involved with his alma mater as president of the National Alumni Association, member of the President's Council, and chairman of the Women's Athletic Committee from 1974 to 1984. Besides being originator and chairman of the All-America Bowl, he held membership on the State Athletic Committee and the board of the Alabama Motor Speedway.

He married Nancy Napier on December 4, 1933, and had three sons. His community activities included being president of the Birmingham Chamber of Commerce and garnering the Junior Achievement Man of the Year and Man of the Year awards. He received honor awards from the City of Hope Hospital in Los Angeles, CA, and the National Federation Hospital in Denver, CO, and the William Booth Award from the Salvation Army.

Sington, who owned sporting goods stores in Birmingham and holds membership in the National Sporting Goods Hall of Fame, still sells sporting goods part-time. He was elected president of his church at age 78 and remains active in many civic organizations.

BIBLIOGRAPHY: Archives of the Alabama Sports Hall of Fame, Birmingham, AL; Robert T. Bowen, letters to and interview with Fred Sington, January 19–February 5, 1993; John D. McCallum, *Southeastern Conference Football* (New York, 1980).

Robert T. Bowen, Jr.

SLATER, Jackie Ray (b. May 27, 1954, Jackson, MS), college and professional player, attended Wingfield High School in Jackson and participated in football, basketball, and track and field there. He attended Jackson State University (SAC) from 1972 to 1976, where he blocked for teammate Walter Payton (FB) in football and lettered in track and field before graduating with a B.A. degree. Slater also studied toward a master's degree in physical education at Livingston University. His honors as a senior included being named All-America by the Pittsburgh (PA) *Courier* and playing in the College All-Star Game. In 1993, Slater was selected by the national media and coaches to the Black College Football Centennial All-Time team.

The Los Angeles Rams (NFL) picked the six-foot-four-inch, 270-pound right offensive tackle in the third round of the draft (eighty-sixth overall) in 1976. Upon completing the 1994 campaign, Slater had set team records for longevity (19 seasons) and games played (262 regular season for thirteenth on the all-time NFL list and 270 including postseason play) and remains the oldest NFL offensive lineman. The durable Slater has missed only parts of two seasons on the injured reserve list.

A Rams' starter since 1979, Slater played in NFC championship games following the 1976, 1978, 1979, 1985, and 1989 seasons and in Super Bowl XIV, a losing effort to the Pittsburgh Steelers in 1980. In 1984, Slater declined a lucrative offer to join the Los Angeles Express of the fledgling USFL. Slater, correctly judging the Express's finances to be shaky, remained with the Rams. A four-time All-Pro selection from 1986 through 1989, Slater was chosen *USA Today* Offensive Lineman of the Year three times (1986, 1987, 1989) and the NFLPA's Lineman of the Year in 1987. He was named to the Pro Bowl squad seven times, including 1983 and 1985 through 1990. After the 1992 season, the SCSBA voted the 38-year-old Slater the Daniel F. Reeves Memorial Award as the Rams' MVP. In September 1994, Slater appeared in his 250th NFL game to tie New York Jets' kicker Pat Leahy for fifth place on the all-time list.

Although neither superstrong nor amazingly agile, Slater demonstrates guile, intelligence, and savvy. New York Jets' general manager Dick Steinberg states, "He's been good for a long time." Slater and his wife Annie have two sons, Matthew and David, and reside in Orange, CA.

BIBLIOGRAPHY: *FD 1991: NFL and College Football Yearbook*; Los Angeles (CA) *Times*, April 3, 1993; *Los Angeles Rams Media Guide*, 1993; Orange County (CA) *Register*, December 29, 1992.

David Bernstein

SMITH, Bruce Bernard (b. June 18, 1963, Norfolk, VA), college and professional player, is the son of George Smith and Annie Smith and played State championship basketball at Booker T. Washington High School. The youngest of five children, Smith was considered too big and too slow for sports. His father boxed as an amateur and worked as a shipping clerk and truck driver, while his mother played basketball in high school competition. Although not recruited to play college football, he played defensive tackle for Virginia Tech University, eventually made All-America, and received the Outland Trophy as the nation's best interior lineman for the 1984 season.

Smith's career soared when he entered the NFL as one of the most widely sought after defensive players. The Buffalo Bills (NFL) made Smith the number-one draft pick in 1985. Smith weighed in at over 300 pounds but was praised for his quickness and agility as a pass stopper, earning Defensive Rookie of the Year honors. With the Bills, Smith became a defensive end and helped Buffalo rise to dominance in the NFL. In 1986, he ranked among the NFL leaders in quarterback sacks with 15. The following year, Smith was named Pro Bowl MVP and Defensive Lineman of the Year. Although temporarily set back by a drug offense and a four-game suspension, Smith improved in outlook and performance when Buffalo became a national contender.

As the Bills prepared for Super Bowl XXV in 1991, the 27-year-old already was considered the dominant defensive player in professional football.

Buffalo lost that Super Bowl to the New York Giants, but Smith finished second in the NFL with 19 sacks and 101 tackles in 1990. Besides being invited to the Pro Bowl for the fourth consecutive time, he was named the 1990 Defensive Player of the Year and earned $1.5 million in average annual salary. Fame added to Smith's thirst for further glory, while a program of weight training and a diet change produced a leaner and quicker player. By 1991, Smith's wife, Carmen, saw her weight-obsessed husband trimmed to 262 pounds. After a slow recovery from knee surgery, he returned with the Bills to Super Bowl XXVI in the 1992 setback against the Washington Redskins. Smith played better than ever in the 1993 Super Bowl, which Buffalo lost decisively to the Dallas Cowboys. Smith was named to the Pro Bowl following the 1992 season but was sidelined with injuries. Smith's play remained at the pinnacle of the NFL, being marked by an explosiveness that dazzled fans and astounded teammates. In 1993, Smith shared second place in AFC sacks with 14.0, was named All-Pro, and was selected for his sixth Pro Bowl. In 1994, Smith played in his fourth consecutive Super Bowl, a 30–13 loss to the Dallas Cowboys. Although the Bills missed the NFC playoffs in 1994, he made All-Pro again, played in his seventh Pro Bowl, and was named NFLPA AFC Defensive Lineman of the Year. Smith ranks as Buffalo's all-time sack leader (123) and the NFL's all-time playoff sack leader (11). He and his wife Carmen have one child, Alston.

BIBLIOGRAPHY: "Bills Hope Third Time Is Charmed," Washington *Post*, January 17, 1993, p. D13; "A Force Grows in Buffalo," *NYT*, December 9, 1990, p. 8; "Forget Taylor, Smith Says He's Best," Washington *Post*, December 22, 1990, p. F1; "Giants-Bills Side Show: Battle of Best Defenders," *NYT*, December 13, 1990, p. D23; "Giants' Taylor, Bills' Smith, 3 Others Reinstated by NFL," Chicago (IL) *Tribune*, September 28, 1988, p. 4; "Lean, Mean Sack Machine," *SI* 75 (September 2, 1991), pp. 28–33; "NFL Benches Smith for Substance Abuse," Buffalo (NY) *News*, September 3, 1988, p. F12; "NFL Draft Turns 50—A Solid 50," Los Angeles (CA) *Times*, April 28, 1985, p. III3; "Smith Strikes Fear in Falcons' Linemen," Atlanta (GA) *Journal & Constitution*, September 21, 1992, p. C3; *USA Today*, November 8, 1994, p. 4C; "Zola Budd Wins First Major Race; Bruce Smith," *Christian Science Monitor*, March 28, 1985, p. 22.

John L. Godwin

SMITH, Ernest F. "Ernie" "Sliphorn" (b. November 26, 1909, Spearfish, SD; d. April 25, 1985, Altadena, CA), college and professional player, graduated from Gardena, CA, High School and excelled as a football tackle for 28–3 University of Southern California (PCC) under legendary coach Howard Jones from 1930 to 1932. The six-foot-two-inch, 220-pound Smith, who wore size 14 shoes and who earned $500 a week playing the trombone for a week of performances, compensated for lack of exceptional physical talent with tremendous desire and courage. During Smith's sophomore 1930 season, the Trojans lost only to Washington State University and the University of Notre Dame en route to an 8–2 mark. Smith teamed with guard Aaron

Rosenberg (FB) in 1931, blocking for running backs Gus Shaver and Erny Pinckert (FB). Southern California overwhelmed opponents 363–52 and finished with a 10–1 record, winning the PCC title, earning the first Knute Rockne Award as national champion, and defeating Tulane University, 21–12, in the Rose Bowl. Smith earned All-America honors in 1932, blocking effectively for diminutive halfback Cotton Warburton (FB). The 10–0 Trojans unleashed devastating defense, blanking eight foes and surrendering just two touchdowns. The PCC titlists vanquished the University of Pittsburgh, 35–0, in the Rose Bowl and were named national champions by the Dunkel and Williamson ratings systems. Richard Whittingham named Smith to his 1930s Second Team All-American squad.

Smith starred at tackle for the Green Bay Packers (NFL) from 1935 to 1937 and in 1939. Under coach Curly Lambeau (FB), Green Bay won the 1935 Western Division crown with an 8–4 mark. Smith handled kicking responsibilities, converting one field goal and 11 of 12 extra point attempts. The 1936 Packers repeated as Western Division titlists with a 10–1–1 record and defeated the Boston Redskins, 21–6, for the NFL championship. Smith earned All-Pro honors, providing pass protection for quarterback Arnie Herber (FB), blocking for fullback Clarke Hinkle (FB), and contributing four field goals and 17 of 18 extra points. Smith shared kicking duties with Hinkle for the 7–4 1937 Packers, recording one field goal and 12 of 14 extra points. He helped Green Bay in 1939 to an impressive 9–2 record and Western Division crown, converting 3 extra points. Smith's interference helped Packer backs lead the NFL in rushing. In the NFL championship game, Green Bay overwhelmed the New York Giants, 27–0. Smith booted a 34-yard field goal in the Packers' 45–28 victory over the College All-Stars in 1940. During four NFL seasons, Smith booted six field goals and 43 of 48 conversions for 61 points.

Smith, who served in the U.S. Army Air Force during World War II, worked 53 years for Occidental Insurance and appeared in around 85 movies, including *A Connecticut Yankee in King Arthur's Court* (1931). He served as commander of the Altadena, CA, American Legion Post, president of the Maestros Music Association and Los Angeles Country Music and Performing Arts Commission, music codirector for the Rancheros Visitadores, and member of the Tournament of Roses Committee. His honors included election to the NFF's College Football Hall of Fame in 1970 and HAF College Football Hall of Fame. He and his wife Ruth had two sons, Ernie and Brad, and one daughter, Vicki. Leukemia caused his death.

BIBLIOGRAPHY: L. H. Baker, *Football: Facts and Figures* (New York, 1945); Jack Clary, *College Football's Great Dynasties: USC* (New York, 1991); David S. Neft et al., eds., *The Football Encyclopedia*, 2nd ed. (New York, 1994); *NFF and College Football Hall of Fame Newsletter*, July–August 1985; Alexander M. Weyand, *The Saga of American Football* (New York, 1955); James D. Whalen, letter to David L. Porter, March 7, 1994; Richard Whittingham, *Saturday Afternoon* (New York, 1985).

David L. Porter

STANFILL, William Thomas "Bill" (b. January 13, 1947, Cairo, GA), college and professional player, is the son of Noah Stanfill, a farmer, and Muriel (Ulm) Stanfill. At Cairo High School, he starred in football, basketball, and track and field. His teams won three regional championships in football and a State title in basketball. Stanfill won the State discus championship three times, establishing a State record, and the State shot put crown once. His honors as a senior included being named Georgia Lineman of the Year in football and MVP in the State Basketball Tournament. He enrolled at the University of Georgia (SEC) in 1965 and earned three letters in football. His teams won two SEC championships and participated in three major bowl games, winning the Cotton Bowl over SMU in 1967 and losing to North Carolina State University in the 1968 Liberty Bowl and the University of Arkansas in the 1969 Sugar Bowl. He was named an All-SEC tackle for three years, Second Team All-America as a junior, and Consensus All-America as a senior. In 1968, he was selected SEC Lineman of the Year, won the Outland Trophy as the nation's best lineman, and was chosen an Academic All-America.

In 1969, the Miami Dolphins (NFL) made Stanfill their first draft choice and also selected his teammate, Jake Scott (FB), who was named MVP in the 1973 Super Bowl. Stanfill, who played for the Dolphins eight years, finished runner-up for Rookie of the Year honors in 1969 and made All-Pro from 1971 to 1974. The Dolphins lost to the Dallas Cowboys in the 1972 Super Bowl but became the first undefeated Super Bowl victors in 1973 with a 17–0 record, defeating the Washington Redskins, 14–7. The Dolphins repeated as Super Bowl champions in 1974 with a win over the Minnesota Vikings. Injuries terminated Stanfill's career following the 1976 season.

Stanfill married Sharon Seller while at Georgia and had two sons, Stan and Jake, before their divorce. Stan followed his father's footsteps as a football player at the University of Georgia. Stanfill later married Gail Dozier. They have a daughter, Kristin, and a son, Scott. Stanfill lives in Albany, GA, where he works as a real estate broker selling farm and timberland. His avocations include farming, fishing, and hunting.

BIBLIOGRAPHY: Higdon Hall, *Pro Football, USA* (New York, 1976); Loran Smith, *Glory, Glory* (Atlanta, GA, 1981); Bill Stanfill, letters to and interviews with Robert T. Bowen, January 21–31, 1993; University of Georgia Sports Information Archives, Athens, GA.

Robert T. Bowen, Jr.

STEFFY, Joseph Benton Jr. "Joe" (b. April 3, 1926, Chattanooga, TN), college player, is the son of Joseph Benton Steffy, Sr., a medical supplies salesman in Knoxville, TN. Steffy graduated from the Baylor School in Chattanooga, where he won 10 cumulative letters by participating in football, track and field, wrestling, and boxing. He captained Baylor's football team as a senior and made the All-City and All-Midsouth teams two seasons. Steffy captured City championships in boxing and wrestling as a heavyweight and won the City shot put and javelin titles in track and field. He also served as regimental commander of the corps at Baylor.

Steffy attended the University of Tennessee (SEC), where he studied liberal arts and played guard on the football team. He participated on the 1944 Volunteer squad, playing in the 1945, 25–0, Rose Bowl loss to the University of Southern California. An incoming plebe at the U.S. Military Academy in 1945, the 5-foot-11-inch, 190-pound lineman developed into one of the best guards in academy history. Although not a starter, Steffy played regularly and lettered on the 1945 national championship team. Guard Jack Green* captained the squad, featuring the unequaled backfield of Arnold Tucker (FB), Glenn Davis (FB), Felix "Doc" Blanchard (FB), and Thomas "Shorty" McWilliams. In 1946, Tucker, Davis, and Blanchard starred in the backfield, while Steffy started at guard for the 9–0–1 Cadets. A scoreless tie with the University of Notre Dame led to the Cadets being ranked second nationally behind the Fighting Irish. With the famed backfield gone in 1947, the Cadets slipped to a 5–2–2 win–loss–tie record. Army lost the fifth game that season, 21–20, to Columbia University, breaking a string of 32 consecutive games without a loss. Steffy, captain of the 1947 team and an All-America guard, won the Outland Trophy. No other player from a service academy won this prestigious honor until Chad Hennings of the Air Force Academy was selected in 1987, the same year Steffy was elected to the NFF College Football Hall of Fame. According to Army coach Earl Blaik (FB), Steffy leveled a Naval Academy end in 1947 with one of the two most vicious blocks in his memory. Herbert O. "Fritz" Crisler (FB), head football coach at the University of Michigan, lauded Steffy as the best lineman he had seen during the 1946 season and claimed that the guard possessed greater alertness and as much drive as Army All-America DeWitt "Tex" Coulter.*

Steffy graduated from the U.S. Military Academy in 1949 and served in combat in the Korean War, earning the Bronze Star and Purple Heart. He resigned his commission to enter his father-in-law's Buick Agency automobile business in Newburgh, NY, and later became the principal owner. Steffy, married and the father of one son, lives on five acres overlooking the Hudson River and the Newburgh Bridge.

BIBLIOGRAPHY: Earl H. Blaik, *The Red Blaik Story* (New Rochelle, NY, 1974); Henry E. Mattox, *Army Football in 1945* (Jefferson, NC, 1990); NFF Football Letter, April 1987; 1945 Army-Navy College Football Game Program, December 1, 1945; 1946 Army-Navy College Football Game Program, November 30, 1946; Al Vanderbush, Athletic Director at the United States Military Academy, letter to John L. Evers, August 23, 1993.

John L. Evers

STEPHENSON, Dwight Eugene (b. November 20, 1957, Murfreesboro, NC), college and professional player, was one of six children from a poor family and was considered "skinny and vulnerable" as a youth. "Even the girls pushed me around," he recalled. Stephenson reportedly developed his six-foot-two-inch, 255-pound frame by working at a local grocery store and using his paycheck to buy discounted groceries. He did not play organized football until his junior year at Hampton, VA, High School but was selected All-State by his senior year.

Stephenson enrolled in 1976 at the University of Alabama (SEC) as a defensive end for coach Paul "Bear" Bryant (FB). Bryant switched Stephenson to offensive center, where he excelled as a punishing blocker. Alabama used a triple option offense, requiring quickness, determination, and intelligence. Bryant termed Stephenson "a man among children" and lauded him as "the greatest center I've ever coached." Stephenson's Alabama squad shared the national championship in 1978 and was chosen unanimously for the 1979 national title, compiling a 12–0 record and decisively defeating the gritty University of Arkansas Razorbacks, 24–9, in the Cotton Bowl. His honors included selection in 1979 to the All-SEC squad and earning the Jacobs Award as the SEC's best blocker. In 1987, he was named to the All-SEC 25-Year 1961–1985 team.

In 1980, the Miami Dolphins (NFL) drafted Stephenson in the second round. Stephenson immediately started every game at center for coach Don Shula (FB) his rookie year. For the next several years, peers generally recognized Stephenson as the finest NFL center. Many considered him among the best NFL centers ever. He combined enormous strength, steady play, and durability with a relentless and aggressive work ethic to perfect both his pass and run blocking techniques. Stephenson, named All-Pro five times from 1983 to 1987, was chosen the 1983 AFC Lineman of the Year. The Dolphins won AFC championships in 1982 and 1984 with a strong defense and an experienced, Stephenson-led offensive line, which made few mistakes and controlled play with extended drives for touchdowns. Stephenson starred in Super Bowls XVII and XIX, although the Dolphins lost both times to NFC teams. At the peak of his NFL career in 1987, he suffered a career-ending knee injury.

BIBLIOGRAPHY: Zander Hollander, ed., *The Complete Handbook of Pro Football, 1984* (New York, 1984); Joe Hoppel et al., *TSN College Football's Twenty-five Greatest Teams* (St. Louis, MO, 1988); Dwight Stephenson file, University of Alabama Sports Information Office, Tuscaloosa, AL; *TSN Pro Football Register*, 1988.

                                                                                        John Hanners

STILLWAGON, James R. "Jim" (b. November 18, 1948, Mount Vernon, OH), college and professional player, is the son of Woody Stillwagon and Anna Stillwagon and attended Mount Vernon High School. After transferring to Augusta Military Academy in Fort Defiance, VA, he won numerous football honors. Upon returning in 1967 to his native state, Stillwagon enrolled at Ohio State University (BTC) and played defensive middle guard and linebacker there for coach Woodrow "Woody" Hayes (FB). Stillwagon lettered in football from 1968 to 1970 and anchored an innovative, complex defensive scheme, confusing opponents with three basic formations and 72 different variations. As a middle guard, the six-foot, 220-pound Stillwagon roamed in pursuit of ballcarriers and passers both left and right on the line of scrimmage. His exceptional quickness, speedy pursuit, and unrelenting pressure on opposing blockers prompted Hayes to laud Stillwagon as the best defensive lineman he had coached in his long college football career.

In Stillwagon's sophomore year, 10–0 Ohio State was selected unanimously as 1968 national champion. The Buckeyes recorded a convincing 50–14 triumph over archrival University of Michigan and a hard-fought 27–16 Rose Bowl victory over PEC champion and previously undefeated University of Southern California. Stillwagon made consensus All-America in 1969, helping the 8–1 Buckeyes share the BTC title with Michigan and rank among the top four nationally. In 1970, he helped Ohio State repeat as BTC champion and compile a 9–0 record. Stanford University defeated the Buckeyes, 27–17, in the Rose Bowl, but Ohio State still finished among the top five in the AP and UPI polls. Following his senior season, Stillwagon was the nation's most honored lineman. The unanimous All-America received the first-ever Vince Lombardi/Rotary Award and the prestigious Outland Trophy, given by the FWAA to the nation's best college lineman.

Stillwagon surprised many observers in 1971 by spurning the NFL to sign with the Toronto, Canada, Argonauts (CFL), where his quickness and pursuit abilities on the longer, wider Canadian playing field made him a star defensive player. He started for the Argonauts from 1971 through 1976, earning All-Pro honors from 1972 through 1974 and the E.C. Schenley Award as Outstanding Player in 1973. Following his CFL career, Stillwagon became a businessman in Hilliard, OH, where he and his wife Effie have three children, Nicole, Angela, and Electra. He in 1978 was inducted into the NFF College Football Hall of Fame.

BIBLIOGRAPHY: Jerry Brondfield, *Woody Hayes and the 100-Yard War* (New York, 1974); Richard M. Cohen et al., *The Ohio State Football Scrapbook* (Indianapolis, IN, 1977); W. Woodrow Hayes, *You Win with People* (Columbus, OH, 1973); Joe Hoppel et al., *TSN College Football's 25 Greatest Teams* (St. Louis, MO, 1988); Robert Ours, *College Football Encyclopedia: The Authentic Guide to 124 Years of College Football* (Rocklin, CA, 1994); James Stillwagon, letters to John Hanners, December 1993; April 1994; James Stillwagon file, Sports Information, Department of Athletics, Ohio State University, Columbus, OH; Robert Vare, *Buckeye* (New York, 1974).

John Hanners

STRZYKALSKI, John "Johnny" "Strike" (b. December 24, 1922, Milwaukee, WI), college and professional player, is the son of John Strzykalski and Teolofia (Bonza) Strzykalski and graduated from Milwaukee's South Division High School, where he starred in football, basketball, and track and field.

He made All-City conference three times in football and twice in basketball, winning the State championship in the shot put.

Strzykalski played single-wing tailback for Marquette University in 1942, sparking the Hilltoppers to a 7–2 record. He gained 579 yards rushing (5.6-yard average) and scored six touchdowns, completed 35 passes for 434 yards and five touchdowns, punted 42 times for a 41.9-yard average and third best nationally, and intercepted 4 passes. He returned kickoffs for touchdowns of 90 yards against Iowa State University and 93 yards against Manhattan College.

Strzykalski joined the U.S. Army Air Force, playing halfback for the Second Air Force team in 1943 and the Fourth Air Force squad in 1944 and 1945. He skipped his remaining two years of eligibility at Marquette and performed in professional football with the San Francisco 49ers (AAFC, 1946 to 1949; NFL, 1950 to 1952) under coach Lawrence T. "Buck" Shaw (FB). The five-foot-nine-inch 190-pounder, a fast, bull-like halfback, excelled on both offense and defense.

In 1947, Strzykalski rushed for 906 yards on 143 carries (6.3-yard average) and five touchdowns. His best season came in 1948, when he rushed for 915 yards, just 49 yards short of AAFC leader Marion Motley (FB), on 141 carries (6.5-yard average) and four touchdowns, caught 26 passes for 485 yards and seven touchdowns, and was selected All-AAFC. He set an AAFC record by scoring in nine consecutive games from August 29, 1948, to October 24, 1948.

In seven pro seasons, Strzykalski gained 3,415 yards on 662 attempts for a 5.2 yard rushing average and 19 touchdowns, caught 93 passes for 1,218 yards and 12 touchdowns, and intercepted eight passes. Strzykalski, who played in the Pro Bowl game following the 1950 season, married Betty Lynn of Los Angeles, CA in 1946 and has two daughters, Dorothy Diane and Deborah. A former automobile salesman, he lives in retirement at Burlingame, CA and serves as a church counselor and volunteer shopper for shut-ins. Strzykalski plans on moving to North Carolina to be closer to his daughters and four grandchildren.

BIBLIOGRAPHY: David S. Neft et al., eds., *The Football Encyclopedia*, 2nd ed. (New York, 1994); Marquette University Sport Information Office, Milwaukee, WI; John Strzykalski, letter to Edward J. Pavlick, September 1993; John Strzykalski File, Pro Football Hall of Fame, Canton, OH.

Edward J. Pavlick

SWINK, James Edward "Jim" "The Rusk Rambler" (b. March 13, 1936, Sacul, TX), college and professional player, is the son of Curtis Swink, a farmer-rancher, and Allie (Bass) Swink. At Rusk, TX, High School, he played football and baseball, participated in track and field, and made All-State in basketball. Swink entered TCU (SWC) in 1953 and played both football and basketball his first two years. As a sophomore halfback in 1954, he led the Horned Frogs football team in rushing 670 yards on 99 attempts and lettered as a guard on the basketball squad.

In 1955, Swink finished second in the Heisman Trophy balloting and made the All-America, Academic All-America, and All-SWC teams in leading the Horned Frogs to a 9–1 win–loss record, number-five ranking, and Cotton Bowl berth. He rushed for 1,283 yards (8.2-yard average), caught 19 passes for 390 yards (20.5-yard average), and scored a still-standing TCU record 125 points. Against the University of Texas, he ran for 235 yards and tallied four touchdowns.

Swink became more of a decoy and blocker his senior year but still earned Academic All-America and All-SWC honors. TCU compiled a 7–3 record and defeated Syracuse University, 28–27, in the Cotton Bowl. Swink rushed for 669 yards on 157 carries and played in the Hula Bowl. The holder of 14 TCU records at one time, he currently ranks third in both career yards rushing (2,618 yards on 413 carries) and scoring (201 points).

The Chicago Bears (NFL) drafted Swink second, but he skipped professional football to study at Southwestern Medical Center in Dallas, TX. When the AFL was founded in 1960, he played briefly with the Dallas Texans while continuing his medical studies. In 1960, he rushed 10 times for 15 yards, caught four passes for 32 yards, and returned one kickoff 36 yards. After graduation from Southwestern in 1961, Swink interned in Sacramento, CA, and practiced three and a half years in Tyler, TX. He served as a captain in the U.S. Army Medical Corps for two years, including one year in Vietnam, and returned to general practice in Temple, TX. In 1971, he moved to Fort Worth, TX. He currently resides there, practicing as an orthopedic surgeon. Swink, divorced from his first wife, married Deborah Deere on August 27, 1982, and has three sons, Jed, Dan, and Charlie.

Swink's honors included election to the Texas Sports Hall of Fame in 1977 and the NFF College Football Hall of Fame in 1982. He was named an NCAA Silver Anniversary honoree in 1982 and a 1989 charter inductee into the GTE Academic Hall of Fame.

BIBLIOGRAPHY: Jay Langhammer, interview with James Swink, January 26, 1993; *Texas Christian University Football Media Guide*, 1992; *Texas Sports Hall of Fame Yearbook* (Grand Prairie, TX, 1981).

Jay Langhammer

TAGLIABUE, Paul John (b. November 24, 1940, Jersey City, NJ), college player and professional commissioner, is the son of Charles Tagliabue, a building contractor, and Mary Tagliabue and graduated from St. Michael's High School in Union City, NJ, where he excelled as an honor student, the State high jump champion, and a basketball player. Tagliabue received an athletic scholarship to Georgetown University, where he majored in government and played basketball for the Hoyas. The six-foot-five-inch Tagliabue captained the 1961–1962 Hoyas, helping them to a 14–9 record. He presided over his senior class, earned Rhodes Scholar finalist accolades, and graduated with honors in 1962. Tagliabue attended New York University Law School on a public service scholarship, editing the law review and graduating with honors in 1965.

Tagliabue began his law career as a clerk in Federal Court in Washington, DC in 1965. In 1966, he worked in the office of the secretary of state as a defense policy analyst on European and North Atlantic affairs. Upon leaving the State Department in 1969, Tagliabue was awarded the Secretary of Defense Meritorious Civilian Service Medal. After joining the law firm of Covington and Burling, he commenced involvement with the NFL concerning television, expansion, legislative affairs, franchise moves, labor, and antitrust cases. His first contact with the NFL came when Commissioner Pete Rozelle (FB) obtained his service during the Joe Namath (FB) Bachelor's III incident. Tagliabue, a member of the New Jersey and District of Columbia Bars, chaired the Sports and Entertainment Committee of the Antitrust Section of the American Bar Association and served as associate professor at the Georgetown University Law School. His memberships include the board of the Pro Football Hall of Fame, board of trustees of the NYU Law School, board of governors of the National United Way, and board of directors of the New American Schools Development Corporation, which strives to improve the public schools. Tagliabue, a senior partner of Covington and Burling, served on the management committee that supervised their 275-lawyer firm.

On October 26, 1989, Tagliabue was elected the seventh NFL commissioner. Tagliabue remained a controversial choice to succeed Rozelle, who had served as commissioner from 1960 to 1989. New Orleans Saints chief executive Jim Finks (S) had failed to get the needed votes. During Tagliabue's tenure, the NFL has secured the largest television contracts in entertainment history, initiated a new regular-season and playoff schedule, adopted tougher policies on steroids and other drugs, and developed plans for the addition of the Carolina Panthers and Jacksonville, FL, Jaguars franchises for the 1995 season.

Tagliabue married Elizabeth Chandler Minter on August 28, 1965, and has two children, Drew and Emily.

BIBLIOGRAPHY: *NFL News*, April 1992; NFL Press Release, July 1992; Rick Telander, "The Force of Sweeping Change," *SI* 73 (September 10, 1990), pp. 39–44.

                                                                         John L. Evers

TIPPETT, Andre Bernard (b. December 27, 1959, Birmingham, AL), college and professional player, was selected All-City and team captain in football, track and field, and wrestling at Barringer High School in Newark, NJ, and belongs to Newark's Sports Hall of Fame. Tippett spent one year at Ellsworth JC in Iowa before transferring to the University of Iowa (BTC). The six-foot-three-inch, 241-pound Tippett played defensive end and linebacker for the Hawkeyes, leading Iowa to a BTC cochampionship his senior year and a 1982 Rose Bowl invitation. The Hawkeyes lost, 28–0, to the University of Washington in the Rose Bowl. In two seasons at Iowa, Tippett recorded 141 tackles and 35 sacks. An All-America selection in 1981, Tippett enjoyed his best single-game performance against Iowa State University while recording 6 solo tackles, three assists, 2 sacks, and four broken passes. In 1980, his 20 tackles for 153 yards in losses paced the BTC. Tippett, who received a B.A. degree in liberal arts from Iowa in 1983, made the Hawkeyes' All-Decade team for the 1980s.

The New England Patriots (NFL) selected Tippett in the second round of the 1982 draft as the forty-first pick overall. Tippett played outside linebacker for the Patriots for 11 seasons from 1982 through 1993, missing the entire 1989 campaign on injured reserve with a shoulder injury. Tippett led the AFC in sacks in 1985 and 1987, with his 100 sacks through the 1993 season ranking the best in franchise history. He set the Patriots' record for sacks in 1 season with 18.5 in 1984, breaking Tony McGee's 1977 mark of 13.5. Tippett, one of the all-time leading tacklers for the Patriots, had recorded 702 total tackles and 406 solo tackles in 135 regular-season games through 1992. He has recovered 19 fumbles, turning 2 into touchdowns, and forced a club high 13 fumbles through 1993. Tippett's 1985 Patriot squad defeated the New York Jets, 26–14, in a wild card game, the Los Angeles Raiders, 27–20, in a second-round playoff game, and the Miami Dolphins, 31–14, in the AFC championship game, before losing to the Chicago Bears, 46–10, in Super Bowl XX. His honors included being selected for the Pro Bowl (1984–1988) and named AFC Defensive Player of the Year (1985), NFL Linebacker of the Year (1987), and linebacker on the *TSN* NFL All-Pro team (1985).

Tippett has studied martial arts for 20 years and has earned black belts in three different styles of karate. Tippett, certified to teach karate, started his own club in Dedham, MA, in 1991 and serves as director of player resources for the New England Patriots. He has two daughters, Janea Lynn and Asia.

BIBLIOGRAPHY: Zander Hollander, ed., *The Complete Handbook of Pro Football* (New York, 1993); *New England Patriots Media Guide*, 1993; *TSN Pro Football Register*, 1994.

John L. Evers

TOWLER, Daniel Lee "Deacon Dan" (b. March 6, 1928, Donora, PA), college and professional player, starred at running back for little Washington and Jefferson College and the Los Angeles Rams (NFL) before he entered the ministry. At Donora High School, he led his team to two western Pennsylvania football championships in 1944 and 1945 and set a conference scoring record his senior year with 24 touchdowns and 8 extra points. His 152-point season total was not surpassed until 1977.

He entered Washington and Jefferson College in the fall of 1946 and immediately attracted attention by running for three touchdowns and passing for another score against Carnegie Tech as a freshman. The following spring, he set the college track and field record in the 100-yard dash. Towler won All-Pennsylvania honors in football from 1946 through 1948 and led the nation in scoring in 1948, garnering Little All-America acclaim. Washington and Jefferson compiled records of 6–2 in 1946, 4–5 in 1947, 5–3 in 1948, and 2–6 in 1949. An excellent student, he graduated cum laude from Washington and Jefferson.

The Los Angeles Rams made Towler their twenty-fifth-round draft choice in 1950. The six-foot-two-inch, 226-pound Towler became starting fullback in 1951, leading the Rams in rushing with 854 yards in 1951 and the NFL in rushing with 894 yards and scoring with 10 touchdowns in 1952. Over a four-year period, Towler finished first, second, third, and fourth in NFL rushing, and led the Rams each year. In 1954, he paced the NFL with a career-high 11 touchdowns in 12 games. In six NFL seasons, Towler amassed 3,493 yards in 672 attempts (5.2-yard average) and scored 264 points on 44 touchdowns, all but 1 rushing. By his retirement, he had gained more yards than any other back in Ram history and held the record for most yards in one season (894) and 1 game (205). Towler, voted the outstanding player of the 1952 Pro Bowl game, gained All-Pro honors from 1951 until 1953. He earned a master's degree in theology from the University of Southern California, retiring from professional football following the 1955 season.

He became pastor of a Methodist congregation at Pasadena, CA, and at the California State University campus at Los Angeles and directed the Wesley Foundation. Active in FCA, he frequently lectured and served as president of the Los Angeles County Board of Education.

BIBLIOGRAPHY: *The Los Angeles Rams Official Press, Radio, and Television Guide*, 1955; Murray Olderman, *The Running Backs* (Englewood Cliffs, NJ, 1969); Beau Riffenburgh, *The Official NFL Encyclopedia*, 4th ed. (New York, 1986); *She Produces All-Americans, Story of Football at W&J* (Washington, PA, 1947).

Robert B. Van Atta

TRYON, J. Edward "Eddie" "Cannonball" (b. July 25, 1900, Medford, MA; d. May 1, 1982, St. Petersburg, FL), college and professional player and coach, starred as a football halfback four seasons from 1922 to 1925 at Colgate University and earned All-America Second Team honors in 1925, leading the Red Raiders to an undefeated season and fourth-place national rating by the Dickinson system. Tryon, who captained the football squad his final year, was selected to the HAF Hall of Fame and in 1963 to the NFF College Football Hall of Fame. He served as head football coach at Hobart College from 1946 to 1962, guiding the Statesmen to a composite 64–54–6 record.

The five-foot-eight-inch, 180-pound Tryon attended Medford High School and Suffield, CT, Prep School, starring in football and basketball. He enrolled at Colgate in 1922 and excelled on the gridiron the next four seasons, helping Red Raider elevens compile a combined 24–9–3 record under head coach Dick Harlow (FB). Tryon, one of the leading scorers in the East, tallied 89 points in 1924 and finished third nationally with 111 points in 1925. As a freshman, he scored five touchdowns against Columbia University with carries ranging between 35 yards and 85 yards. The following season, Tryon notched 65-yard and 25-yard touchdowns against Ohio State University and caught a touchdown pass to help Colgate upset Syracuse University.

The stocky, low-slung, lightning-quick Tryon exhibited excellent balance and performed most of Colgate's punting for four years. Coach Harlow declared Tryon "could do everything and was an excellent boy to handle." Tryon produced winning touchdowns in 1925 against the otherwise undefeated Princeton University and Syracuse squads and sparked the Red Raiders to a come-from-behind, 14–14 deadlock with Brown University. Tryon, a member of Delta Upsilon fraternity, earned a Bachelor of Science degree in 1926 from Colgate. He teamed two professional seasons with Red Grange (FB) of the New York Yankees (AFL, NFL). He rushed for six touchdowns, caught two touchdown passes, kicked two field goals, and converted 12 extra points for the 10–5 Yankees in 1926. In 1927, he tallied two touchdowns via rushing, caught two touchdown passes, and booted 8 extra points for the 7–8–1 Yankees. Tryon served as director of athletics and physical education of Rutherford, NY, Public Schools from 1928 to 1946. His football teams amassed a composite 122–28–13 record, while his basketball teams advanced to the State finals three times and won one championship.

Tryon, who married and had one daughter, coached football at Hobart College from 1946 to 1962. Between 1953 and 1957, his Hobart Statesmen produced two undefeated seasons and compiled a combined 32–3–1 record. Tryon served as a member of the NCAA Rules Committees from 1960 to 1963 and officiated eight years for the AA and NFL.

BIBLIOGRAPHY: L. H. Baker, *Football: Facts and Figures* (New York, 1945); Colgate-Syracuse Football Game Program, Syracuse, NY, November 14, 1925; Dr. Ellery C. Huntington, *Fifty Years of Colgate Football* (Hamilton, NY, 1940); John D. McCallum and Charles H. Pearson, *College Football U.S.A., 1869–1972* (New York, 1972); Ronald L. Mendell and Timothy B. Phares, *Who's Who in Football* (New Rochelle, NY, 1974); Ray Schmidt, "Eddie Tryon," *CFHS* 4 (February 1991), pp. 6–8.

James D. Whalen

WACKER, James Herbert "Jim" (b. April 28, 1937, Detroit, MI), college player and coach, is the son of Bill Wacker, a Lutheran minister, and Eleanor Wacker and graduated from Detroit Lutheran High School. Wacker attended Valparaiso, IN, University, where he lettered three years as an offensive lineman in football and graduated in 1960. He also earned a master's degree from Wayne, NE, State University in 1961 and a doctorate in education from the University of Nebraska in 1970. Wacker authored *The Explosive Veer Offense*. He and his wife, Lillian (Korsmeyer) Wacker, have three sons, Mike, Steve, and Tom.

Wacker began his career as head football coach at Concordia High School in Portland, OR, from 1960 through 1963 and served as an assistant football coach at Concordia, NE, College between 1964 and 1968 and Augustana College in Sioux Falls, SD, from 1968 to 1970. Wacker's first collegiate head football coaching position came at Texas Lutheran College. In five seasons from 1971 to 1975, Wacker led the Bulldogs to a 38–16 win–loss record. His 1974 squad compiled a perfect 11–0 season and captured the NAIA Division II championship with a 42–0 triumph over Missouri Valley College. Wacker's 1975 team lost only 1 of 12 games and repeated as NAIA champion with a 34–8 victory over California Lutheran University. In three seasons at North Dakota State University (NCC) from 1976 to 1978, Wacker guided the Bison to a 24–9–1 record and two NCC championships. Southwest Texas State University (LSC) hired him as head football coach in 1979. Wacker's teams the next four seasons posted a 42–8 record and two NCAA Division II championships. His 1981 Bobcat squad won 13 games while losing only 1 game and registered a 42–13 triumph over North Dakota State for the national title. The Bobcats posted a perfect 14–0 record the following year and again captured the national crown with a 34–9 victory over the University of California at Davis. Wacker was named College Division Coach of the Year.

In November 1982, Wacker accepted the head football coaching position at TCU (SWC). In nine seasons from 1983 to 1991, Wacker led the Horned Frogs to a 40–58–2 win–loss record. Following a 1–8–2 record during Wacker's first year, TCU registered one of the most celebrated comebacks in SWC history by winning 8 of 11 games in the 1984 regular season. The Horned Frogs, however, lost 31–14 to West Virginia University in the Bluebonnet Bowl. Wacker's success during the 1984 season earned him National Coach of the Year honors from *TSN*, UPI, and ESPN and the Bobby Dodd (FB) Coach of the Year Award. In 1985, Wacker uncovered a payment plan to TCU players in violation of NCAA rules. The plan had commenced prior to Wacker's arrival at TCU. Seven players were dismissed from the Horned Frogs, as the violations were reported to the NCAA. Wacker won national acclaim for his actions, but the NCAA stripped 30 football scholarships. Twenty-two losses during the next three seasons and three years of NCAA sanctions resulted from the illegal payments. By 1991, Wacker rebuilt the program with a 7–4 season.

In December 1991, the University of Minnesota (BTC) named Wacker head football coach. The Gophers, facing a rebuilding program, suffered through a 2–9 season in Wacker's first year at the helm, a 4–7 mark in

1993, and a 3–8 mark in 1994. In 24 seasons from 1971 through 1994, Wacker has compiled a 153–115–3 win–loss record. His teams have accomplished two perfect seasons and consecutive conference titles and have appeared in national playoff competition six times, winning four titles.

BIBLIOGRAPHY: *TCU Football Media Guide*, 1991; *University of Minnesota Football Media Guide*, 1994.

John L. Evers

WARD, Robert "Bob" (b. 1927, Elizabeth, NJ), college player and coach, is the son of Jim Ward, a plainclothes detective, and starred as a football guard for the University of Maryland (SC) from 1948 to 1951, becoming the initial Terrapin to make First Team All-America and have his uniform number 28 retired. Jim Tatum (FB), the Terrapin football coach, lauded Ward as "the greatest football player I've ever seen ounce for ounce, and the best I've ever coached." Ward made several All-America teams as a junior on defense in 1950 and Consensus All-America as a senior offensive guard in 1951, the same year that he became Maryland's first SC Player of the Year. The WTC named him 1951 College Lineman of the Year.

Ward enlisted in the U.S. Army as a paratrooper soon after high school and played football at Fort Benning, GA, where his coach recruited him for the University of Alabama Crimson Tide (SEC). Tatum preempted that move by sending one of his assistants to see Ward play and signed him up. Ward entered Maryland in 1947 and graduated with a bachelor's degree in business administration in 1952. The 5-foot-10-inch 180-pounder, the smallest member of the Maryland line, played with special aggressiveness and intensity as a Terrapin letterman and MVP from 1948 through 1952. Maryland compiled a 6–4 record in 1948 and 8–1 mark in 1949, outscoring opponents, 246–75, and ranking fourteenth nationally in the AP poll.

Ward was voted MVP in Maryland's 20–7 1950 Gator Bowl win over the University of Missouri. After starring for the 7–2–1 Terrapins in 1950, he helped Maryland garner a 10–0 record and third-place finish in the AP poll in 1951. The Terrapins, also featuring star linemen Dick Modzelewski (FB) and Ed Modzelewski, shared the SC title with VMI. Ward, senior cocaptain, played in perhaps Maryland's greatest football victory, the 28–13 1952 Sugar Bowl upset over first-ranked University of Tennessee.

Ward served as assistant football coach under Tatum at Maryland from 1952 to 1956, at Iowa State University (BEC) in 1957, 1958, and 1963 through 1965, under Bud Wilkinson (FB) at the University of Oklahoma (BEC) from 1959 to 1962, and at the U.S. Military Academy in 1966. In December 1966, Ward landed the job he had always wanted, signing a five-year, $100,000 contract to replace Lou Saban as head football coach at Maryland. He lasted only two years, however, during perhaps the worst period in Maryland football history. Maryland lost all 9 games in 1967 and won only 2 of 10 contests in 1968. Ward's energy, demanding nature, zest for winning, and triumphs as a player had not prepared him to handle defeat. Some players complained that Ward mistreated them during practice and took away scholarships, denying that they were influenced by the widespread protest mood on campuses across the nation. After meeting with athletic director Jim Kehoe, Ward resigned. Ward and his wife Ellen have three sons, Jim, Chip, and Kelly, and one daughter, Kathy. Ward, who owns a retail liquor business near Annapolis, MD, was elected to the NFF College Football Hall of Fame.

BIBLIOGRAPHY: Paul Attner, *The Terrapins: Maryland Football* (Huntsville, AL, 1975); Morris A. Beale, *Kings of American Football: The Story of Football at Maryland* (Washington, DC, 1952); Harold Claassen and Steve Boda, Jr., eds., *Ronald Encyclopedia of Football* (New York, 1963); *University of Maryland Terrapin Yearbook*, 1952; Zipp Newman, *The Impact of Southern Football* (Montgomery, AL, 1969); *NYT*, December 31, 1966, p. 14; University of Maryland Sports Information Office, College Park, MD, telephone calls with Frederick J. Augustyn, Jr., January 26, 1994; February 1, 1994; James D. Whalen, letter to David L. Porter, March 21, 1994.

                                                                              Frederick J. Augustyn, Jr.

WARE, Andre T. (b. July 31, 1968, Galveston, TX), college and professional player, is the son of Robert Ware, a school teacher, and Joyce (Gentry) Ware, a postal clerk. His parents were divorced when Andre was only three years old. Ware, whose father died at age 30, attended Dickinson, TX, High School and quarterbacked the Gators his junior and senior years to a 15–4–1 win–loss record.

Ware attended Alvin, TX, CC during the first semester of 1986 and entered the University of Houston (SWC) for the second semester. Under coach Jack Pardee, the six-foot-one-inch, 208-pound quarterback engineered Houston's run and shoot offense. In 1987, Ware started three games before suffering a fractured arm. The following year, Pardee named Ware the Cougars' starting quarterback. Houston finished the 1988 season with a 9–3 record, losing, 24–22, to Washington State University in the Aloha Bowl. Ware, the Heisman Trophy winner and a consensus All-America in 1989, quarterbacked the Cougars to nine victories. Houston lost only to Texas A&M University and the University of Arkansas, scoring 589 points. During the 1989 season, Houston recorded 6,874 yards in total offense (624.9 yards per game), 5,624 passing yards (511.3 yards per game), and 55 touchdown passes to set NCAA Division I-A records. Ware led the nation in passing attempts (578), completions (365), yardage (4,699), and touchdowns (46) and total offense plays (628), yardage (4,661), and offense yards per game (423.7). Against Temple University, Ware connected on 7 touchdown passes. By the 1989 season's end, Ware had set 27 NCAA passing and total offense records. Five of his marks remain NCAA records, including most passes completed in four games (144), passing yards gained in one quarter (340), and passing yards made in one half (517). Ware's 4,699 aerial yards surpassed the single-season mark of 4,571 yards set by BYU's Jim McMahon (FB), while his 46 touchdown passes fell 1 short of McMahon's record. The Cougars spent the 1989 season on probation because of NCAA violations and did not appear on national television. Ware became the ninth junior, the first black quarterback, and the first player from a school on probation to win the Heisman Trophy. In his three varsity seasons as the Cougars' quarterback, Ware completed 660 of 1,074 passes (61.5 percent) for 8,202 yards and 75 touchdowns. He compiled 8,058 yards in total offense and 277.9 total offense yards per game.

Ware, who is single, received a B.A. degree from Houston and gave up his senior year of eligibility to enter the 1990 NFL draft. The Detroit Lions (NFL) selected him in the first round as the seventh pick overall. Ware joined running back Barry Sanders (FB) of Oklahoma State University as the second straight Heisman Trophy winner drafted by Detroit. In his first four seasons from 1990 through 1993, he saw limited action as a backup quarterback to Rodney Peete, Bob Gagliano, and Erik Kramer. Due to injuries, Ware started the last three games of the 1992 season and helped the Lions win two of those contests. His four-year record includes 83 completions in 161 passing attempts (51.6 percent) for 1,112 yards and five touchdowns. In May 1994 the Minnesota Vikings (NFL) signed Ware as a free agent. In September 1994 the Vikings released Ware. The following month, Ware joined the expansion Jacksonville, FL, Jaguars (NFL).

BIBLIOGRAPHY: Chicago (IL) *Tribune*, December 21, 1992; "Houston QB Andre Ware Wins '89 Heisman Trophy," *Jet* 77 (December 18, 1989), p. 51; Jill Lieber, "Mom Runs the Ware House," *SI* 72 (April 30, 1990), p. 60; Austin Murphy, "A Lid Lifter in Texas," *SI* 71 (October 23, 1989), pp. 56–58; *NCAA Football's Finest*, 1990; *1992 NCAA Football*; *TSN Pro Football Register*, 1994.

John L. Evers

WASHINGTON, Eugene "Gene" (b. November 23, 1944, LaPorte, TX), college athlete and professional football player, is the son of Henry Washington and Alberta Washington. A superb natural athlete, Washington starred in basketball, baseball, track and field, and football at George Washington Carver High School in Baytown, TX. Washington, one of several great southern African-American players recruited by Duffy Daugherty (FB), the celebrated Michigan State University football coach, enrolled in 1963 and began establishing himself as one of the finest collegiate ends in history during the 1964 season. As a member of Daugherty's greatest Spartan teams in 1965 and 1966, the six-foot-three-inch, 216-pound Washington emerged as the finest receiver in Michigan State history and was selected consensus All-America both campaigns.

The sure-handed Washington, possessing world-class speed, led the Spartans in receptions all three varsity seasons. In 1964, Washington caught 35 passes for 542 yards and 5 touchdowns. He made 40 receptions for 638 yards and 4 touchdowns in 1965. His 1966 figures included 27 passes caught for 677 yards and 7 touchdowns. He averaged an astonishing 25 yards per catch, still a Spartan season record. His career output featured 102 receptions for 1,857 yards and 16 touchdowns. In six collegiate games, Washington gained 100 yards or more in receptions.

Washington contributed significantly in several very important games in collegiate history. In the 1966 Rose Bowl, won 14–12 by UCLA, Washington caught four passes for 81 yards and made a key 42-yard reception from quarterback Steve Juday on the first touchdown drive. Writer Mike Celizik called the legendary 1966, 10–10 tie against the University of Notre Dame the "Biggest Game of Them All." In that contest, Washington caught a crucial 42-yard pass from quarterback Jimmy Raye on the lone Spartan touchdown drive and made five receptions for a superlative 123 yards. One of Washington's greatest games occurred in the 1965 contest against Indiana University, as he caught three touchdown passes while contributing to a 27–13 victory. For his brilliant efforts, which included solid blocking skills, Washington was named to the All-Spartan team in 1969, elected to the NFF College Football Hall of Fame in 1987, and inducted into the Michigan State University Hall of Fame in 1992. Washington also ranked among the finest hurdlers in the nation while lettering for the Spartan indoor and outdoor track and field teams in 1965, 1966, and 1967, serving as cocaptain the latter two seasons. A fine student, Washington received a B.S. degree in physical education and social science in 1967. He returned to Michigan State to work for the Placement Services in the off-season, earning a master's degree in college student personnel administration in 1972.

Washington's professional career proved equally distinguished. The Minnesota Vikings (NFL) selected Washington as a first-round draft choice in 1967. Washington quickly established himself among the NFL's premier ends, playing for the Vikings through the 1972 season and ending his NFL career with the Denver Broncos (NFL) in 1973. During his 7 NFL seasons, Washington caught 182 passes for 3,237 yards, averaged 17.8 yards per reception, and scored 26 touchdowns. One of his greatest professional games occurred in Minnesota's 27–7 victory over the Cleveland Browns for the 1969 NFL championship. Washington caught 3 passes for 160 yards, including a 75-yard reception of a touchdown aerial thrown by quarterback Joe Kapp. In 1970, Washington started in the Super Bowl IV 23–7 upset loss to the Kansas City Chiefs. He was selected for the Pro Bowl in 1969 and 1970. The All-Pro's playing days were cut short by a foot injury.

Washington resides in the Minneapolis–St. Paul, MN, area, where he works as a staffing manager (with college relations as a specialty) for the 3M Company. He married Claudith Goudeau, a 1970 Spartan graduate, and has three daughters, Lisa, Gina, and Maya. In his professional and community activities, Washington has remained a "class act." The articulate, perceptive, and highly intelligent Washington has provided leadership both on and off the field.

BIBLIOGRAPHY: Mike Celizic, *The Biggest Game of Them All: Notre Dame, Michigan State and the Fall of '66* (New York, 1992); Duffy Daugherty with Dave Diles, *Duffy: An Autobiography* (Garden City, NY, 1974); John Devaney, "The Receiver Who Goes Beyond the Line of Duty," *Sport* 49 (March 1970), pp. 46–48, 67; *Michigan State University Football Media Guide*, 1992; Michigan State University Sports Information Office, East Lansing, MI; David Neft et al., eds., *The Football Encyclopedia*, 2nd ed. (New York, 1994); *Official Banquet Program, Inaugural, Michigan State University Athletics Hall of Fame* (East Lansing, MI, 1992); Patrick Scheetz, telephone interview, January 26, 1994; "Spartan Hall of Fame Inducts Class of 30," *MSU Alumni Magazine* 10 (Winter 1993), pp. 22–26; Fred Stabley, *The Spartans: Michigan State Football* (Tomball, TX, 1988); Roger Treat, ed., *The Encyclopedia of Football*, 16th rev. ed. (New York, 1979); *TSN Pro Football Register*, 1974; Gene Washington, telephone interview, January 27, 1994.

Erik S. Lunde

WASHINGTON, Joe Dan, Jr. "Little Joe" "The Crockett Rocket" (b. September 24, 1953, Crockett, TX), college and professional player, is the son of Joe Washington, Sr., a football halfback at Prairie View A&M from 1948 to 1950. His father coached him at Lincoln High School in Port Arthur, TX, where he played quarterback. Washington, who received his B.A. degree in public relations from the University of Oklahoma in 1976, progressed from ninth on the depth chart to become starting running back. For the Sooners (BEC), Washington was noted for his hand-painted silver shoes and heart-stopping punt and kick returns. When Washington left Oklahoma in 1975, he ranked as the all-time leading rusher with 3,995 yards for a 6.1-yard average. Washington gathered numerous honors, including All-BEC from 1973 through 1975, *TSN* All-America as a running back in 1974, Washington, D.C. Touchdown Club NCAA 1974 Player of the Year, and consensus All-America in 1974 and 1975.

The San Diego Chargers (NFL) drafted the speedy, all-purpose back first in 1976, but he missed that year due to a knee injury. After the 1977 season, San Diego dealt him to the Baltimore Colts (NFL). Washington performed for the Colts from 1978 to 1980 and enjoyed his best NFL statistical year in 1978, rushing for 956 yards, catching 45 passes, and averaging 26.6 yards on kickoff returns. In 1979, Washington led the NFL with 82 catches for 750 yards. From 1981 to 1984, he played for the Washington Redskins (NFL). He led the Redskins in both rushing and receiving in 1981, being selected by his teammates as the Redskins' MVP. Washington completed his NFL career with the Atlanta Falcons (NFL) in 1985. In the NFL, Washington rushed 1,195 times for 4,839 career yards and 12 touchdowns. His numerous off-field charity works included Special Olympics, Wednesday's Child, and Vital Organ Donors. Washington, the Washington Redskins' 1983 Man of the Year, owns and operates several successful auto sales franchises.

BIBLIOGRAPHY: *TSN Pro Football Register*, 1985; Joe Washington file, University of Oklahoma, Norman, OK; *Who's Who Among Black Americans, 1994–95* (Detroit, MI, 1994), p. 1525.

John H. Ziegler

WEDEMEYER, Herman John "Wedey" "Squirmin' Herman" (b. May 20, 1924, Hilo, HI), college and professional player, made All-America as a halfback at St. Mary's College of California in 1945 (consensus) and 1946. He placed fourth in 1945 and fifth in 1946 in the Heisman Trophy Award balloting. His honors included being named in 1979 to the NFF College Football Hall of Fame and selected to the St. Mary's and Hawaii Sports Halls of Fame. He played in 1943 and from 1945 to 1947 with the Gaels, compiling 4,061 yards in total offense and being responsible for 40 career touchdowns.

Wedemeyer attended St. Louis College, a high school in Honolulu, twice making the City Interscholastic All-Star football team. He enrolled in 1943 at St. Mary's, performing brilliantly on the Gaels' 2–5 wartime varsity. Wedemeyer served in the U.S. Merchant Marine and U.S. Navy in 1944 before returning to St. Mary's. Coach James Phelan's 1945 squad consisted mainly of players under 19 years of age but posted an amazing 7–1 record and ranked seventh in the AP poll. The Gaels that year defeated the University of California, the PCC champion and eleventh-rated University of Southern California, and the University of Nevada at Reno, which boasted its best record in 26 years. The 5-foot-10-inch, 173-pound Wedemeyer sparked his youthful, free-spirited teammates, who occasionally made up plays in the huddle or improvised during plays.

St. Mary's won seven straight games in 1945 but then was upset by mediocre UCLA and lost to fifth-ranked Oklahoma (State) A&M University, 33–13, in the Sugar Bowl. After trailing Oklahoma A&M by only seven points with five minutes remaining, St. Mary's surrendered two more touchdowns to the superior Cowboys. Nationally, Wedemeyer finished the season third in total offense and fourth in passing and punting. Grantland Rice (OS) wrote, "Wedemeyer was something more than a brilliant ball carrier, passer and defensive star; he was also the spark plug of a group of 17-18-year-old kids."

Wedemeyer led the Gaels in 1946 to a 6–2 finish, including a loss to Georgia Tech in the Oil Bowl. The 1947 Gaels, however, dropped to 3–7 in Wedemeyer's final season. He played twice in the East-West Shrine All-Star Game, garnering All-Time West team honors, and performed in 1948 with the College All-Stars against the Chicago Cardinals (NFL). Wedemeyer earned a B.A. degree from St. Mary's in 1948 and played two AAFC seasons with the Los Angeles Dons and Baltimore Colts. He gained 540 yards in 143 carries (3.8-yard average), caught 46 passes for 442 yards (9.6-yard average) and two touchdowns, and returned kickoffs and punts. He worked in public relations for the Hawaiian travel industry, served on the Honolulu City Council, and was elected to the Hawaii House of Representatives. Wedemeyer played the role of "Duke" for 10 years on the television series "Hawaii Five-O" and served as vice president of Servco Pacific International. He and his wife Carol have a son and a daughter.

BIBLIOGRAPHY: Randy Andrada, *They Did It Everytime* (Piedmont, CA, 1975); Ronald L. Mendell and Timothy B. Phares, *Who's Who in Football* (New Rochelle, NY, 1974); Beau Riffenburgh, *The Official NFL Encyclopedia*, 4th ed. (New York, 1986); St. Mary's College, Library Archives, Moraga, CA, letter to James D. Whalen, 1993; James D. Whalen, *Gridiron Greats Now Gone* (Jefferson, NC, 1991).

James D. Whalen

WELSH, George Thomas (b. August 26, 1933, Coaldale, PA), college athlete and coach, is the son of Thomas Welsh, a coal miner, and Anna Lillian (Lotwick) Welsh. After playing football at Coaldale High School and Wyoming Seminary Prep School, Welsh received an appointment to the U.S. Naval Academy in 1952. As quarterback for Navy between 1953 and 1955, Welsh led the Midshipmen to 18 victories. Navy recorded a 21–0 upset triumph over the heavily favored University of Mississippi in the 1955 Sugar Bowl. An All-America in 1954 and 1955, Welsh finished third in the Heisman Trophy voting his senior year. He led the nation that year with 94 pass completions, a 62.7 completion percentage, 1,319 passing yards, and 1,348 yards of total offense. During his career, Welsh completed 172 of 313 passes (55 percent) for 2,335 yards and 20 touchdowns. Welsh, who also played infield on the baseball team, earned six varsity letters before his 1952 graduation. He was awarded the Thompson Trophy Cup as the midshipman who had done the most to promote athletics at the Naval Academy.

On active duty with the U.S. Navy between 1956 and 1962, Welsh assisted coach Wayne Hardin with the football program at the U.S. Naval Academy in 1960 and 1961. He resigned his commission from the Navy in 1963 and served 10 years as an assistant football coach at Pennsylvania State University under Rip Engle (FB) and Joe Paterno (FB). Navy appointed Welsh head football coach in February 1973. Welsh spent nine seasons there, compiling a 44–46–1 win–loss record. His best season came in 1978, when the Midshipmen completed a 9–3 season with a 23–15 triumph over BYU in the Holiday Bowl. Navy also played in the 1980 Garden State Bowl 35–0 loss to the University of Houston and the 1981 Liberty Bowl 31–28 setback to Ohio State University. Welsh's teams recorded the most wins in Navy history.

In December 1981, the University of Virginia (ACC) named Welsh head football coach. In 13 seasons at Virginia from 1982 through 1994, Welsh has compiled an 89–59–3 win–loss record. His best season came in 1989, when he led the Cavaliers to a 10–3 mark. Virginia shared their first-ever ACC championship and participated in the 1990 Florida Citrus Bowl, which they lost to the University of Illinois, 31–21. Welsh has led Virginia to seven bowl appearances in the last ten years, including victories in the 1984 Peach Bowl, the Cavaliers' initial bowl appearance, over Purdue University, in the 1987 All-American Bowl against BYU, and in the 1994 Independence Bowl against TCU. In 22 seasons from 1973 through 1994, Welsh's teams have recorded a 144–105–4 win–loss record. His honors included being National Coach of the Year in 1989 and 1991 and ACC Coach of the Year four times (1983, 1984, 1989, 1991). Welsh coached Virginia's first unanimous All-America, tackle Jim Dombrowski in 1985. In 1990, Cavalier quarterback Shawn Moore and wide receiver Herman Moore both earned All-America honors.

Welsh married Sandra Hubiscak and has four children, Sally, George, Matt, and Adam.

BIBLIOGRAPHY: Ronald L. Mendell and Timothy B. Phares, *Who's Who in Football* (New Rochelle, NY, 1974); *1994 NCAA Football; University of Virginia Football Media Guide*, 1994; George Welsh's office, letter to John L. Evers, November 11, 1992.

John L. Evers

WHARTON, Charles Marin "Buck" (b. 1873, Magnolia, DE; d. November 14, 1949, Dover, DE), college player and executive, starred as an All-America guard at the University of Pennsylvania from 1893 to 1896. He received a D.D.S. degree in 1896 and an M.D. degree in 1899 from the University of Pennsylvania and also studied at the University of Tennessee Medical School in Sewanee, TN.

Wharton and several other players helped make the University of Pennsylvania (IvL) a dominant intercollegiate football team. During Wharton's playing career, the Quakers won 52 out of 56 games, remained undefeated in both 1894 and 1895, and won recognition as the national champion in 1895. Penn's NFF College Football Hall of Fame coach, George Woodruff (S), an 1889 graduate of Yale University, developed innovative systems on both offense and defense. His "guards back" offensive system provided moving interference for the running backs and allowed the guards occasionally to carry the ball. On defense, Woodruff moved his guards back off the line so they could stop plays up the center or penetrate into the opponent's backfield.

Wharton, an ideal player for these new offensive and defensive systems, stood six foot two inches and weighed over 195 pounds, considered exceptional for that day. The durable, quick, and mobile Wharton proved an outstanding blocker in leading the devastating Penn running offense and a consistent defensive force in breaking through the line to block punts or tackle runners. A Second Team All-America nominee in 1894, he was selected to the First Team in both 1895 and 1896 and was subsequently elected to the NFF College Football Hall of Fame. He also captained the University of Pennsylvania football team in 1896.

Upon completion of his medical training, he practiced briefly in the Philadelphia, PA, and Delaware region, helped coach the Quakers' defense, served as an assistant professor of physical education and the field director of athletics at the University of Pennsylvania from 1919 to 1931, and headed the Physical Education Department at Delaware University (now the University of Delaware) from 1932 to 1936. He participated in Pennsylvania politics, serving as a state senator from 1914 to 1918, the first executive director of that state's Unemployment Compensation Commission, and the unsuccessful Democratic Party candidate for governor in 1928. During World War I, he joined Walter Camp's (FB) program to develop a system of physical training for both the U.S. Army and the U.S. Navy.

BIBLIOGRAPHY: L. H. Baker, *Football Facts and Figures* (New York, 1945); Edward R. Bushnell, *The History of Athletics at Pennsylvania* (Philadelphia, PA, 1909); Allison Danzig, *Oh, How They Played the Game* (New York, 1971); Ralph Hickok, *Who Was Who in American Sports* (New York, 1971); John D. McCallum and Charles H. Pearson, *College Football U.S.A., 1869–1973* (New York, 1973); *1991 NCAA Football; NYT*, November 16, 1949, p. 30; Tom Perrin, *Football: A College History* (Jefferson, NC, 1987); University of Delaware Archives, Newark, DE; University of Pennsylvania Archives, Philadelphia, PA; Alexander M. Weyland, *The Saga of American Football* (New York, 1955).

Daniel R. Gilbert

WHEELER, Arthur Ledlie "Beef" (b. May 12, 1873, Philadelphia, PA; d. December 20, 1917, Philadelphia, PA), athlete, was selected a three-time All-America football guard from 1892 to 1894 at Princeton University (IvL) and was elected in 1969 to the NFF College Football Hall of Fame. Wheeler started four years for the Tigers, who compiled a combined 43–5 record and won the 1893 national championship with 11 consecutive victories.

The son of Andrew Wheeler and Sarah (Carpenter) Wheeler, he entered St. Paul's School, a college preparatory school at Concord, NH, and starred in football and track and field. After graduating in 1891 from St. Paul's, Wheeler enrolled at Princeton. He was elected vice president of the freshman class, assisting legendary football teammate Johnny Poe (FB). The six-foot-one-inch, 207-pound Wheeler, a quick, rugged defender, spearheaded Tiger lines that blanked 38 of 48 opponents over four seasons. He kicked off, booted conversions, and occasionally carried the ball in tough yardage situations. Wheeler in 1893 blocked a University of Pennsylvania punt, setting up Princeton's only touchdown during the Tigers' 4–0 triumph. He tackled several Yale University ballcarriers for losses to help the Tigers defeat the Elis, 6–0, marking Yale's first defeat in 38 games. Wheeler played with several All-Americas, including halfback Samuel Morse, end Thomas

Trenchard (FB), tackle Langdon Lea (FB), and quarterback Phil King (S). Lea and King also made the NFF College Football Hall of Fame.

Wheeler's football career at Princeton coincided with that of Frank Hinkey (FB), the immortal end for the nearly invincible Elis. The Tigers in 1894 lost 24–0 to the Elis and 12–0 to the first of Pennsylvania's four outstanding clubs, which suffered defeat only once during that span. Wheeler also lettered in track and field, scoring points in the shot put and hammer throw at the IC4A and Caledonian Games. He graduated from Princeton in 1895 with a B.S. degree and the next year joined Morris Tasker and Company, Philadelphia bankers and brokers. Four years later, he switched to the banking firm of Winthrop Smith and Company. After being employed as a partner with Butcher, Sherrerd, and Hansell in 1913, he the following year began serving as vice president of J. D. Este and Company manufacturers. Wheeler, a bachelor, died after a lengthy illness. His many friends established two scholarships at Princeton in his memory.

BIBLIOGRAPHY: Allison Danzig, *The History of American Football* (Englewood Cliffs, NJ, 1956); Ralph Hickok, *Who Was Who in American Sports* (New York, 1971); Ronald L. Mendell and Timothy B. Phares, *Who's Who in Football* (New Rochelle, NY, 1974); Frank Presbrey and James Moffatt, *Athletics at Princeton* (New York, 1901); Princeton-Pennsylvania Football Game Program, November 5, 1892; Princeton-Yale Football Game Program, December 1, 1894; Seeley G. Mudd Manuscript Library, Princeton University, letter to James D. Whalen, April 3, 1993.

James D. Whalen

WHITE, Reginald Howard "Reggie" (b. December 19, 1961, Chattanooga, TN), college and professional player, is the son of Charles White and Thelma White and grew up in the housing projects with an alcoholic father. White turned early to sports and religion. At Howard High School, he made All-State in basketball and football and was licensed as a Baptist minister at age 17. At the University of Tennessee (SEC), he was named a 1983 Lombardi Award finalist, made *TSN* College All-America, and was selected SEC Player of the Year. White began his professional football career with the Memphis TN, Showboats (USFL) in 1984, being named to the USFL All-Rookie team in 1984 and USFL Defensive Player of the Year in 1985.

At six feet five inches and 295 pounds, the unstoppable preacher ran the 40-yard dash in 4.6 seconds to rank among the most explosive of defensive players. The Philadelphia Eagles (NFL) signed White as a defensive end in 1985, when he was chosen NFL Rookie of the Year. White made the Pro Bowl every season from 1986 to 1994 and in 1987 achieved a career-high of 21 quarterback sacks, setting an NFC record. White, a complete player, recorded impressive numbers in tackles, assists, and "hurries." Named the best defensive NFL player in a 1989 player poll, White signed a $6.1 million, four-year contract to move among the highest paid figures in sports.

White, dubbed by players and fans as the Eagles' "minister of defense," became the team's spiritual and psychological leader and made *TSN*'s NFL All-Pro team in 1987, 1988, and 1991. By 1992, he led a small group of NFL players in a suit to establish unrestricted free agency and remained the only lineman in NFL history to have more sacks than games played. In April 1993, he signed with the Green Bay Packers (NFL). He shared the NFC lead in quarterback sacks with 13 in 1993, made the *TSN*'s NFL All-Pro team in 1993 and 1994, and was named NFLPA NFC Defensive Lineman of the Year in 1994. Through the 1994 season, he had recorded 145 career NFL sacks. In 1994, a panel of NFL and Pro Football Hall of Fame Officials, former players, and reporters named White one of three defensive ends on the NFL All-Time Team. Off the field, he preached at numerous ches, crusaded against drugs and crime, and conducted a weekly radio talk show. He married Sara Copeland in 1985 and has two children, Jeremy and Jecolia. His book *Reggie White, Minister of Defense* was published in 1991.

BIBLIOGRAPHY: "Bears Gird for Eagles' Holy Terror," Chicago (IL) *Tribune*, October 2, 1989, sec. 3, p. 1; "A Commitment to Winning," *TSN*, January 25, 1993, p. 7; "Eagles' Reggie White Delivers a Message from Field, Pulpit," Los Angeles (CA) *Times*, October 21, 1989, p. C1; "Eagles' White Leads Rush to Free Agency," Washington (DC) *Post*, October 16, 1992, p. B8; "Great Player, Great Person," Baltimore (MD) *Sun*, November 12, 1989, p. C3; "Honor for White Benefits Howard," Chattanooga (TN) *News–Free Press*, March 23, 1989, p. C11; "A Star on the Street Corner," Philadelphia (PA) *Inquirer*, September 29, 1991, p. F13; "Trip to Bountiful," *SI* 78 (March 15, 1993), pp. 20–23; "White Heat," *SI* 71 (November 27, 1989), pp. 65–69; *Who's Who Among Black Americans*, 6th ed. (Detroit, MI, 1990), p. 1341.

                                                                    John L. Godwin

WHITE, Wilford Daniel "Danny" (b. February 9, 1952, Mesa, AZ), college and professional athlete, is the son of Wilford White and Shirley (Merrill) White and attended Westwood High School in Mesa and Arizona State University. "Whizzer," his father, played halfback in football with Arizona State University and the Chicago Bears (NFL) in 1951 and 1952. White, nicknamed "Danny," performed 15 professional seasons as a quarterback. His first 2 seasons were spent with the Memphis, TN, Southmen (WFL), while the remaining 13 came with the Dallas Cowboys (NFL). White holds many collegiate and Cowboy team records for passing. Since his retirement after the 1988 season, White has engaged in business and public service and serves as the general manager and head coach of the Arizona Rattlers (ArFL).

Before leaving Arizona State following his senior year in 1973, White set several Sun Devil and NCAA records as a quarterback. He finished his college career as the most efficient passer in NCAA history with a 148.9 rating, a mark since bettered by Jim McMahon (FB). He still holds NCAA records for yards per completion (17.2) and highest percentage of touchdowns per pass attempts, with 9.09 percent of his passes going for touchdowns. White also retains Arizona State marks for career total offense (6,453 yards), most passing yardage (5,932 yards), and touchdowns (59). He was named All-

America following his senior year. White also played baseball at Arizona State and was drafted as an infielder by the Cleveland Indians (AL) in 1973, Houston Astros (NL) in 1974, and Indians in 1974 and 1975.

The Dallas Cowboys (NFL) selected White in the third round in 1974, but he spent the 1974 and 1975 seasons with the Memphis Southmen (WFL). At Memphis, White completed 183 of 350 pass attempts for 2,635 yards and 22 touchdowns. White signed with the Cowboys when the WFL folded in April 1976 and backed up quarterback Roger Staubach (FB) his first four seasons in Dallas while serving as the Cowboys' punter. In his 13 years with the Cowboys, White set several career and single-season passing marks. White in 1980 established the Dallas record for most touchdown passes (28) in a season and surpassed the mark in 1983 with 29 touchdowns. From 1980 through 1982, White led the Cowboys to consecutive NFC Eastern Division titles and into three NFC championship game losses to the Philadelphia Eagles, San Francisco 49ers, and Washington Redskins. White broke or tied eight Dallas passing records during the strike-shortened 1982 season and made the Pro Bowl. He crossed the picket line to play during the 1987 strike season. White posted club records for most pass completions (1,761), touchdown passes (155), and passing accuracy (59.7 percent).

White has engaged in public service, including the Boy Scouts of America and the United Way, and has varied business interests. As head coach and general manager of the Arizona Rattlers in 1992 and 1993, White has compiled 12 wins and 12 losses with a 1–1 playoff record. White's Rattlers were defeated, 38–34, by the Detroit Drive in the 1993 American Conference championship. He lives with his wife JoLynn and their four children in Gilbert, AZ.

BIBLIOGRAPHY: Arizona Rattlers, Press Release, 1993; *1991 NCAA Football*; David S. Neft et al., eds., *The Football Encyclopedia*, 2nd ed. (New York, 1994); *TSN Pro Football Register*, 1989.

Brian S. Butler

WIETECHA, Raymond Walter "Ray" (b. November 4, 1928, East Chicago, IN), college and professional athlete and coach, participated in basketball and baseball at Roosevelt High School in East Chicago. Wietecha did not make varsity football team until his senior year, when he excelled as an All-State center. Wietecha initially declined scholarship offers to work at Youngstown Sheet and Tube Company, but a few weeks in the mill changed his mind. At Northwestern University (BTC), Wietecha lettered in baseball and football and was selected BTC football center in 1950. The six-foot-one-inch 225-pounder played on Northwestern's 8–2 1949 Rose Bowl team and in the 1950 Blue-Gray Classic. From 1950 to 1953, Wietecha served as an officer in the U.S. Marine Corps and played baseball and football for the Quantico, VA, base team. After being discharged in 1953, Wietecha played half a baseball season as a third baseman with Charlotte, NC (TSL), hit .264

for the Washington Senators' (AL) farm team, and led his team in home runs and RBIs.

In July 1953, Wietecha reported to the New York Giants (NFL) training camp, having been their number-one draft pick in 1950. Wietecha initially played various positions, including special teams, linebacker, cornerback, and offensive end. From 1954 to 1962, Wietecha started at center. He performed in 133 consecutive NFL games, breaking Emlen Tunnell's (FB) previous "iron-man" record of 118 straight games. Wietecha, a superb offensive lineman, excelled at power and finesse blocking. Wietecha performed well at diverting defensive linemen and shooting linebackers from the play, prompting Giants head coach Allie Sherman to laud him as the best NFL center. Wietecha's honors included selection as All-NFL center in 1958 and All-Pro in 1957, 1960, and 1962. With the Giants, Wietecha played on five EC titlists (1956, 1958, 1959, 1961, 1962) and the 1956 NFL championship team. Subsequently, Wietecha served as an assistant coach with the Los Angeles Rams (NFL) in 1963 and 1964, Green Bay Packers (NFL) from 1967 to 1970, New York Giants (NFL) from 1972 to 1976, Buffalo Bills (NFL) in 1977, and Baltimore Colts (NFL) in 1980 and 1981. He scouts college players for the Green Bay Packers (NFL). He married Joan Warren and has four children.

BIBLIOGRAPHY: John H. Ziegler, telephone interview with Bob Carroll, August 23, 1992; *NYT*, 1953–1980; Al Silverman, ed., *The Specialist in Pro Football* (New York, 1965); Ray Wietecha file, Northwestern University, Evanston, IL.

John H. Ziegler

WILSON, George "Wildcat" (b. 1903, Everett, WA; d. December 27, 1963, San Francisco, CA), college and professional athlete, ranked among the first football stars from the Pacific Northwest, being the University of Washington's first All-America and leading the Huskies to the 1924 and 1926 Rose Bowls. Wilson grew up in Everett, WA, where he played high school football for Enoch Bagshaw, and followed Bagshaw to the University of Washington (PCC) in 1922. In three seasons from 1923 to 1925, the 5-foot-11-inch, 200-pound Wilson led Washington to a 28–2–3 football record. The Huskies outscored opponents, 1,435 to 141, as Wilson scored 37 career touchdowns, threw 12 career touchdown passes, and played defense. Wilson, a Second Team All-America in 1924, made First Team All-America in 1925 with Red Grange (FB) of the University of Illinois and Ernie Nevers (FB) of Stanford University.

Wilson guided Washington to the Rose Bowl twice. In 1924, Washington tied the U.S. Naval Academy, 14–14, in the Huskies' first Rose Bowl appearance. In 1926, the Huskies were upset, 20–19, by the University of Alabama. The game, however, may have been Wilson's finest, as he rushed 15 times for 134 yards, completed 5 of 11 passes for 77 yards and two touchdowns, and intercepted a pass to set up a touchdown. Wilson missed the third quarter with an injury, as Alabama rallied for 20 points and held Washington to only 17 yards offense. New York sportswriter Damon Runyon (OS), who witnessed Wilson's Rose Bowl exploits, lauded him as "one of the finest players of this or any time."

Two weeks after the Rose Bowl, Wilson made his NFL debut against Grange's touring club in a Los Angeles, CA, exhibition game. Wilson temporarily knocked Grange out of the contest on the opening kickoff and outgained him, 128 yards to 30 yards. Wilson joined Grange in promoter C. C. Pyle's (OS) AFL in 1926, leading the traveling Los Angeles franchise. The "Wildcats," named for him, posted a 6–6–2 record, with Wilson rushing for 4 touchdowns and passing for four scores. Wilson starred with the Providence Steamrollers (NFL) from 1927 to 1929. Providence captured the 1928 NFL title behind Wilson's 906 yards passing and 412 yards rushing, earning All-NFL laurels. In three NFL seasons, Wilson passed for 2,188 yards and 12 touchdowns, rushed for 1,012 yards (4.7-yard average) and 10 touchdowns, and punted 125 times for nearly a 36-yard average.

Wilson was persuaded to leave football in 1930 by former Dartmouth College star Gus Sonnenberg (IS) and became a professional wrestler in Australia and the United States. Wilson, who did not graduate from college, worked on the docks in Washington State and San Francisco, CA, and as an oil rigger in Texas. He was named to the HAF Hall of Fame in 1957, the NFF College Football Hall of Fame in 1951, and the All-Time Pacific Coast team backfield with Nevers and O. J. Simpson (FB) in 1969.

BIBLIOGRAPHY: Joe Hendrickson, *Tournament of Roses: The First 100 Years* (Los Angeles, CA, 1989); John D. McCallum and Charles H. Pearson, *College Football U.S.A.,* *1867–1972* (New York, 1972); David S. Neft et al., eds., *The Football Encyclopedia,* *2nd ed.* (New York, 1994); Tom Perrin, *Football: A College History* (Jefferson, NC, 1987); *Washington Centennial: Celebrating 100 Years of Husky Football* (Seattle, WA, 1990).

Brian L. Laughlin

WYATT, Bowden (b. November 3, 1917, Loudon, TN; d. January 21, 1969, Sweetwater, TN), college player and coach, was the son of Hugh Wyatt and Julia Wyatt and grew up in Kingston, TN. His father initially captained a steamboat, but later both parents worked with the local school system. Wyatt became a standout football player at Roane County High School, starring as an end, fullback, and kicker from 1932 to 1934.

Wyatt earned a football scholarship at the University of Tennessee (SEC) in 1935, playing under the legendary Robert Neyland (FB). An excellent blocker and defensive player from his end position, he spurred the Volunteers to a 23–5–3 record over three years. In 1938, he captained the Volunteers and led Tennessee to an undefeated season and its first-ever bowl game, a 17–0 victory over the University of Oklahoma in the 1939 Orange

Bowl. Wyatt, a consensus All-America in 1938, won All-SEC honors his junior and senior seasons. He captained the 1939 College All-Stars against the New York Giants.

Wyatt's accomplishments as a football coach perhaps eclipsed his success as a player. Wyatt, who refused an offer from the Chicago Cardinals (NFL) to play professionally, began his football coaching career as an assistant at Mississippi State University (SEC) from 1939 to 1942. He returned to Mississippi State in 1946 after serving in the U.S. Navy from 1943 to 1945. His 15 years as a head football coach included stints at the University of Wyoming (BSAC) from 1947 to 1952, University of Arkansas (SWC) in 1953 and 1954, and University of Tennessee (SEC) from 1955 to 1962. His last assignment came as an assistant coach at Oklahoma State University (BEC) in 1964 and 1965.

A dynamic leader with striking good looks, Wyatt became the first coach in college football history to win championships in three major conferences (BSAC, SWC, SEC). Wyatt's 1950 Wyoming team defended the BSAC title and earned an invitation to the Gator Bowl, where the Cowboys defeated Washington and Lee University, 20–7, in their first-ever postseason contest. Wyatt guided the 1954 Arkansas Razorbacks to eight wins and a Cotton Bowl appearance, a 14–8 loss to Georgia Tech. Wyatt was honored as national Coach of the Year in 1956, when his second-ranked Tennessee Volunteers lost only to Baylor University in the Sugar Bowl. His overall 99–56–5 record suffered because he took over three struggling programs. At the University of Tennessee, his teams compiled a 49–29–4 win–loss record. Tennessee replaced him after a disappointing 1962 season. Wyatt, who died suddenly of viral influenza, was elected in 1969 to the NFF College Football Hall of Fame. Wyatt was married to Molly Miller of Jackson, TN, and had one daughter, Missy.

BIBLIOGRAPHY: Russ Bebb, *The Big Orange: A Story of Tennessee Football* (Huntsville, AL, 1973); Bud Fields and Bob Bertucci, *Big Orange: A Pictorial History of University of Tennessee Football* (West Point, NY, 1982); Tom Siler, *The Volunteers* (Knoxville, TN, 1950); Mike Siroky and Bob Bertucci, *Orange Lightning: Inside University of Tennessee Football* (West Point, NY, 1982); Bowden Wyatt file, Sports Information Office, University of Tennessee, Knoxville, TN.

Robert T. Epling

YOUNG, Andrew Alva (b. December 18, 1881, Hamilton County, IN; d. August 9, 1942, Chicago, IL), athlete, professional owner, and manager, participated in the group founding the NFL. A descendant of Brigham Young's brother, he received his medical degree from the Central College of Physicians in Indianapolis, IN, in 1905 and established a general medical practice at Hammond, IN. During 1917 and 1918, he served in the U.S. Medical Corps at Camp Travis in San Antonio, TX. The athletic Young played semiprofessional baseball and wrestled as a lightweight in his youth. During the

World War I era, he promoted amateur and semiprofessional boxing matches in Hammond. Thoroughbred racing comprised his greatest love, as he owned a stable of horses and founded the A. A. Young Laboratories Company. His firm developed a vitamin-calcium supplement for thoroughbreds.

Young supported professional football and served as team doctor and trainer for the Hammond Clabby A. A. from 1915 to 1917. In 1919, promoter Paul Parduhn established a strong Hammond team to compete for the mythical U.S. professional football championship. Hammond played its home games in Cubs Park (now Wrigley Field) in Chicago, IL, and featured star end George Halas (FB). Young probably owned part of the Hammond club.

On September 17, 1920, Young represented Hammond at a meeting of the nation's leading professional football team managers in Canton, OH, to create a professional league. The APFA, formed at that meeting, became the NFL in 1922. Young's Hammond Pros, a charter NFL member, belonged to the APFA-NFL from 1920 to 1926. Young served on several NFL committees that helped shape the future of professional football, but his Hammond team struggled on the field. Over seven seasons, the Pros compiled a lackluster 5–26–4 record. Since Hammond lacked an adequate stadium, the Pros played nearly all of their games on the road. Hammond usually settled for a visitor's guarantee, severely limiting its ability to pay top salaries. The most important contribution to the NFL by the Hammond Pros may have been Young's willingness, unlike some contemporaries, to employ black players. Several outstanding black stars, notably Fred "Fritz" Pollard (FB), Jay "Inky" Williams, John Shelbourne, and Sol Butler, performed with the Pros during the 1920s. Young's contribution remains especially notable because Indiana was a bastion of the Ku Klux Klan then.

BIBLIOGRAPHY: David S. Neft et al., eds., *The Football Encyclopedia*, 2nd ed. (New York, 1994); Beau Riffenburgh, *The Official NFL Encyclopedia*, 4th ed. (New York, 1986); Andrew A. Young file, Pro Football Hall of Fame, Canton, OH; Dr. Young's son, letter to Bob Carroll, 1988.

Robert N. "Bob" Carroll

YOUNGSTROM, Adolph F. "Swede" (b. May 24, 1897, Waltham, MA; d. August 5, 1968, Boston, MA), college and professional player, was named an All-America football guard at Dartmouth College (IvL) in 1919, blocking nine punts that season, and became one of the greatest punt blockers in professional football history. Youngstrom served in the U.S. Navy during World War I and played football for the Newport, RI, Naval Training Station team in 1917 and 1918. The Newport team, primarily made up of IvL stars, finished 5–4–1 in 1918 and used Youngstrom as both a guard and fullback. The six-foot-one-inch, 181-pound guard-tackle returned to Dartmouth in 1919 and was named a consensus All-America at guard. With future professionals Gus Sonnenberg (IS) and Eddie Lynch, Youngstrom led coach Clarence "Doc" Spears' (FB) Big Green to a 6–1–1 record. He also blocked nine punts, including three against Colgate University and two against Cornell University. Youngstrom's punt blocking prowess attracted so much attention that he made 11 of 14 All-America squads. Walter Camp (FB), one of the All-America selectors, called Youngstrom and Syracuse University star Joe Alexander (FB) "the greatest pair of defensive guards that have ever been seen on the gridiron."

Youngstrom played eight seasons professionally, specializing with blocked punts. He played first with the Buffalo All-Americans (APFA-NFL). Buffalo, led by Youngstrom and quarterback Tommy Hughitt (FB) from the University of Michigan, featured seven former All-Americas and claimed a share of the APFA title after a 7–3 victory over the Canton Bulldogs. Youngstrom blocked a Jim Thorpe (FB) punt and returned it for the game's only touchdown. Youngstrom blocked 11 punts in 1920, helping Buffalo to a 4–1–1 record. The All-Americans finished 9–1–2 in 1921, with Youngstrom blocking 9 punts. Youngstrom played with the All-Americans through 1923, except for a brief stint with the Canton Bulldogs (NFL) in 1921. The Buffalo franchise, which became the Bison in 1924, retained Youngstrom through 1925. He was named to the Green Bay *Press Gazette*'s inaugural All-NFL poll in 1923 and repeated the honor in 1924. In 1926, he joined the Frankford, PA, Yellow Jackets (NFL) as a reserve. Youngstrom scored two touchdowns during the season on blocked punts, helping the Yellow Jackets capture the NFL title.

Youngstrom sold real estate after leaving professional football and eventually worked as a review appraiser for the state of Massachusetts. He suffered from poor health during the 1960s after being treated for stomach ulcers.

BIBLIOGRAPHY: Walter Camp, "The All-American Team," *Collier's* 77 (December 13, 1919), p. 7; Harold Claassen, *History of Professional Football* (Englewood Cliffs, NJ, 1963); Ronald L. Mendell and Timothy B. Phares, *Who's Who in Football* (New Rochelle, NY, 1974); David S. Neft et al., eds., *The Football Encyclopedia*, 2nd ed. (New York, 1994); Tom Perrin, *Football: A College History* (Jefferson, NC, 1987); *Spalding's Official Football Guide, 1919–1920.*

                                                                                    Brian L. Laughlin

GOLF

BAUER, Marlene. *See* Marlene Bauer Hagge.

FINSTERWALD, Dow (b. September 6, 1929, Athens, OH), golfer, is the son of Russell Finsterwald, a lawyer and BTC football official, and seriously began pursuing golf as an Athens High School senior, taking lessons from professional Art Smith. He played golf at Ohio University (MAC), where he served as an ROTC cadet. After shooting a 61 in the 1950 St. Louis, MO, Open, Finsterwald the next year won the Central Ohio Amateur title and was named a Walker team alternate. After graduating from Ohio University with a bachelor's degree, he entered the U.S. Air Force as a second lieutenant. Finsterwald launched his professional golf career while stationed at Shaw Air Force Base in South Carolina and triumphed in the 1954 Carolinas Open.

Shortly after his military discharge, the 5-foot-11-inch, 160-pound Finsterwald in 1955 joined the PGA Tour and prevailed in the Fort Wayne, IN, Invitational. He quickly became a force on the PGA Tour, demonstrating "course management" comparable to Ben Hogan (OS). During his first three years on the PGA Tour, Finsterwald finished among the top ten 50 times and captured three tournaments. He earned the Vardon Trophy for the lowest stroke average in 1957 and garnered the 1958 PGA Championship by two strokes, recording a 276 at Llanerich CoC in Havertown, PA. He ranked among the top ten 18 times and set a record by finishing "in the money" for seventy-two straight tournaments. In 1958, the PGA of America named him Player of the Year.

Although Finsterwald performed well several more years, his very conservative play prevented him from becoming the dominant player that some had expected. By the early 1960s, Arnold Palmer (OS), Gary Player, and Jack Nicklaus (OS) overshadowed him. At Augusta, GA, Finsterwald lost the

1962 Masters to Palmer in a three-way playoff involving Player. He made the 1957, 1959, 1961, and 1963 Ryder Cup teams, recording his eleventh and last tour victory in the 1963 "500" Festival Open Invitation. Although leaving the PGA Tour in 1973, he served as nonplaying captain of the 1977 Ryder Cup team.

The Colorado Springs, CO, resident married his high school sweetheart, Linda Pedigo, in November 1953 and has four children, John, Jane, Dow, and Russell. As one of professional golf's most consistent performers with a short game of metronomic precision, he helped raise golf to sporting prominence. Finsterwald served as PGA vice president from 1976 to 1978 and on the USGA Rules of Golf Committee from 1979 to 1981.

BIBLIOGRAPHY: Peter Alliss, *The Who's Who of Golf* (Englewood Cliffs, NJ, 1983); Al Barkow, *The History of the PGA Tour* (New York, 1989); *The Golf Digest Condensed Almanac*, 1987; Jack Zanger, "Finsterwald Is Always in the Money," *Sport* 24 (September 1957), pp. 36–37.

Luther W. Spoehr

GEIBERGER, Allen Lee "Al" (b. September 1, 1937, Red Bluff, CA), golfer, won the 1954 National Jaycees golf tournament and earned a B.S. degree in business administration in 1959 from the University of Southern California, where he played golf under coach Stan Ward. After turning professional in 1959, he joined the PGA Tour in 1960 and recorded his first victory in the 1962 Ontario Open Invitational. Geiberger's next triumphs came in the 1963 Alamedan Open Invitational and 1965 American Golf Classic. In 1966, he captured his only major championship, the U.S. PGA title, by four strokes at Firestone CoC in Akron, OH. Geiberger, who played on the 1967 and 1975 Ryder Cup teams, shared second place in the 1969 U.S. Open tournament at the Champions GC in Houston, TX. A nervous stomach disorder sharply limited his PGA Tour appearances from 1969 to 1972. At the 1974 Sahara Invitational, Geiberger garnered his first tournament title in eight years. Nevertheless, he finished five times among the top ten and enjoyed his peak years in 1975 and 1976. Geiberger ranked sixth in earnings in 1975 with $175,000 and fifth in 1976 with $194,000. In 1975, he took two near majors, the MONY Tournament of Champions and Tournament Players Championship. Victories followed in 1976 with the Greater Greensboro Open and Western Open, accompanied by a second-place result in the U.S. Open at the Atlanta AC in Duluth, GA.

The six-foot-two-inch, 185-pound Geiberger electrified the sports world on June 10, 1977, by recording a 13-under 59 in the second round of the Danny Thomas Memphis, TN, Classic at the Colonial CoC. He scored 30 on the first nine holes and a 29 on the back nine, making six pars, 11 birdies, and an eagle and needing only 23 putts. A seven-hole stretch in the middle of his round resulted in 8-under par. On the final hole, Geiberger putted eight feet for a birdie. His 59 established a record for lowest one-round score on a full-length course in an officially recognized U.S Tour event. He recorded 72, 72, and 70 on the other three rounds to win his tenth PGA tournament. Geiberger's only other PGA Tour triumph came in the 1979 Colonial National Invitational.

Altogether, he registered 11 PGA Tour victories and earned $1,256,548. His record included 13 second places, 10 third places, and 128 top-10 finishes. Intestinal surgery in 1978 and a knee operation in 1979 sidelined him. After severe abdominal pains struck Geiberger in 1979, doctors disclosed he had developed several large polyps on his colon. In 1980, surgeons took out his colon and operated twice more, removing a growth the size of a football. During the next few years, Geiberger appeared infrequently on the regular PGA Tour. In 1982, the GWAA gave him the Ben Hogan Award for remaining active in golf despite a physical handicap.

Geiberger joined the Senior PGA Tour in 1987, garnering nine victories and $3,028,331 through December 1993. In 1989, he ranked third in Senior PGA Tour earnings with $527,033. His victories included the Las Vegas, NV, Senior Classic, Hilton Head Seniors International, and Vantage Championship in 1987, Arizona Classic in 1988, GTE Northwest Classic in 1989 and 1993, Kroger Senior Classic in 1991, and Infiniti Senior Tournament of Champions in 1992 and 1993. The amount of his 1987 Vantage Championship check was nearly three times larger than his biggest paycheck on the regular PGA Tour. Geiberger married Lynn Butler and has five children, Lee Ann, John, Robby, Brent, and Brian.

BIBLIOGRAPHY: Peter Alliss, *The Who's Who of Golf* (Englewood Cliffs, NJ, 1983); Al Barkow, *The History of the PGA Tour* (New York, 1989); Charles Gillespie, "It Was a Day Unlike Any Other Day," *SI* 46 (June 20, 1977), p. 50; *Golf Almanac*, 1993 (New York, 1993); Dan Jenkins, "Happy Stroll for Golf's Smiling Gei," *SI* 25 (August 1, 1966), pp. 16–19; *WWA*, 41st ed. (1980–1981), p. 1222.

David L. Porter

HAGGE, Marlene Bauer "Grem" (b. February 16, 1934, Eureka, SD), golfer, is the daughter of David Bauer, a golf professional, and Madeline (Eckman) Bauer and a storied veteran of golf, whose lengthy career has resulted in distinctive records for youth and maturity. She began playing at age three under the tutelage of her father and dropped out of high school in the tenth grade. After winning at least five amateur championships in California in the 1940s, she became a charter and founding LPGA member in 1950 and remains the youngest player ever to join the LPGA Tour.

Hagge played on the LPGA Tour for the next 40 years, ranking by 1994 as the LPGA's most senior member. She won 25 titles, ranging between 1952 and 1972. Hagge, at only 18 years old, captured the Sarasota Open in 1952, making her the youngest player ever to take a tour event. Her best year came in 1956, when she triumphed in eight tournaments, including the

LPGA Championship, her only major title. She led LPGA golfers that year with earnings of $21,532. Prize money then was not substantial, as the LPGA Tour awaited the day of widened television coverage and corporate sponsorship of events. When that day finally came in the 1970s, Hagge recalled without lamentation that her victories gave her purses of about $350. Hagge, noted for her full turn and long backswing, was quite accurate off the tee and possessed an excellent wedge game from 30 yards in.

Although her scoring average did not markedly decline in the 1970s and 1980s, remaining around 74 and 75, Hagge was eclipsed by a host of younger players. Nonetheless, her nine-hole record of 29, set at the Buick Open in 1971, stayed the standard until 1984. She and several other players were caught up in the controversy surrounding Jane Blalock (S), whom the LPGA suspended from play for a year in 1972 for allegedly cheating in the spotting of the ball on the green. Defending Blalock, Sandra Palmer* declared that players who had accused her of cheating had "lied." Hagge, who supported the LPGA, and Palmer engaged in a war of "quotes and counterquotes" and initiated lawsuits against each other but finally dropped their actions. In May 1994, she tied for third in the LPGA Sprint Senior Challenge at Daytona Beach, FL. The five-foot-two-inch Hagge has auburn hair, remains a "health nut" who eats "natural" foods, and takes up to 50 vitamin pills a day. Divorced in 1964, she lives in Palm Springs, CA.

BIBLIOGRAPHY: "The Blalock Affair," *Newsweek* 80 (August 28, 1972), pp. 74–76; Marlene Hagge, questionnaire for Carl M. Becker, January 4, 1993; "Lawsuit Dropped by Women Golfers," *NYT*, September 11, 1973; LPGA, *1992 Player Guide* (Daytona Beach, FL, 1992); Barry McDermott, "Bracing for a Rich Breakthrough," *SI* 36 (April 24, 1972), pp. 53–54; Barry McDermott, "Keeping a Close Eye on the Ball," *SI* 36 (June 19, 1972), pp. 21–23.

                                                           Carl M. Becker

INKSTER, Juli Simpson (b. June 24, 1960, Santa Cruz, CA), golfer, is the daughter of Jack Simpson and Carole (Davies) Simpson and began playing golf at age 14 at her parents' encouragement and, by her own admission, as a means of meeting boys. At San Jose State University, she was selected a collegiate All-America for four years from 1979 through 1982 and captured the U.S. Amateur title three consecutive years from 1980 through 1982. *GD* ranked her the best amateur in the nation in 1981 and 1982.

Inkster turned professional in 1983 but failed to win her qualifying LPGA Tour card early in the year. She found herself in "total shock" and "moped around." After sloughing off her failure, she won the Safeco Classic and earned her card later in the year. In 1984, she became the first rookie to capture two major championships, the Dinah Shore and du Maurier Classic tournaments, and was also named Rookie of the Year. Her best year came in 1986, when she posted four victories and placed third in earnings at $285,293. Inkster continues to compete, sharing second with Pat Bradley (S) at the LPGA Ping Welch's Championship in July 1994. Altogether, she has won 16 titles and earned over $2 million. The brown-eyed, five-foot-seven-inch Inkster considers her good short game the key to her success.

Inkster, a resident of Los Altos, CA, created a stir in 1989, when she withdrew from the U.S. Women's Open tournament several days before it began because of suffering from "morning sickness." Her pregnancy, she added, had come during the celebration of her victory in the Crestar Classic. When a USGA official noted that not everybody celebrated a victory that way, she retorted, "How do you know?" Perhaps in consonance with her relaxed view of victory, she has advised young players to "take it slow and not burn yourself out." She is married to Brian Inkster, a golf professional, has a daughter, Hayley, and serves as a *GM* playing editor.

BIBLIOGRAPHY: John Garrity, "A King Is Crowned Queen," *SI* 71 (July 25, 1989), pp. 71–72; Juli Inkster, questionnaire for Carl M. Becker, December 10, 1992; "The Inkster Team Is Honing Skills," *NYT*, July 7, 1986; "Inkster Triumphs After Trailing by 10," *NYT*, August 22, 1989; LPGA, *1992 Player Guide* (Daytona Beach, FL, 1992); Sara Reeder, "Pro Golfer: Juli Inkster," *WSFi* 8 (September 1986), p. 30.

Carl M. Becker

JAMESON, Elizabeth May "Betty" (b. May 19, 1919, Norman, OK), golfer, started playing the game at age 12 and broke 100 within six months. As a teenager, she won several amateur titles in Texas and captured the Southern Golf Championship on her fifteenth birthday. Besides claiming the U.S. Amateur title in 1939 and 1940, she in 1942 became the first player to capture the Western Open and Western Amateur in the same year. Observers called her "the slowest thing on grass," as she usually took a full minute to line up a putt. Jameson, distressed by her opponents' impatience, attempted to speed up her play. After suffering a deterioration in her game, however, she returned to her methodical approach.

Jameson turned professional in 1945 and joined the WPGA Tour. The WPGA had been organized in 1944. She won three WPGA tournaments, including the 1947 U.S. Women's Open, before the WPGA collapsed. She became a founding and charter LPGA member in 1950 and then played for seven years on its tour, taking seven championships. Her scoring average rose from 77 to 80 between 1954 and 1955, but she posted her best record in the latter year by registering three victories. Since purses were relatively small on an LPGA Tour that had little public visibility and that awaited television coverage, her aggregate earnings amounted to only $91,470.

The five-foot-eight-inch Jameson, who presented a striking figure to the gallery and enjoyed a reputation as a "glamor girl," helped create an award for the woman golfer with the best scoring average and in 1952 gave a trophy to the LPGA in the name of Glenna Collett Vare (OS) to honor the winner. She has designed golf clothing for women and written weekly golf columns for newspapers. For relaxation, she played the grand piano and often turned to Beethoven's compositions. In 1951 the LPGA Hall of Fame inducted the Delray Beach, FL, resident.

BIBLIOGRAPHY: LPGA, *1992 Player Guide* (Daytona Beach, FL, 1992); "Putterer," *AmM* 131 (June 1941), p. 78; Benjamin G. Rader, *American Sports: From the Age of Folk Games to the Age of Spectators* (Englewood Cliffs, NJ, 1983).

Carl M. Becker

JANUARY, Don (b. November 20, 1929, Plainview, TX), golfer, attended North Texas State University and joined the PGA Tour in 1955, winning 10 PGA tournaments and placing second and third 18 times each in over two decades. His most notable triumph came in the 1967 PGA Championship at the Columbine CoC in Littleton, CO, where he garnered a 281 score. January, who ranked ninth in earnings in 1963, finished second in the 1961 PGA tournament to Jerry Barber and the 1976 PGA tournament to Dave Stockton.* His other PGA Tour victories included the Dallas, TX, Centennial Open in 1956, Tucson, AZ, Open in 1960 and 1963, St. Paul, MN, Open in 1961, Philadelphia, PA, Golf Classic in 1966, Tournament of Champions in 1968, and Jacksonville, FL, Open in 1970. In 1961, he earned $50,000 for recording a hole in one at Palm Springs, CA. January's erect posture, deep Texas drawl, dry wit, slow golf swing, and deliberate play made him one of the sport's most noticeable figures. In 1972, he left the PGA Tour to work in golf course construction in the Dallas area. Upon returning to the PGA Tour in 1975, he made a dramatic comeback by capturing the San Antonio, TX, Open. The next year, the 46-year-old became the oldest golfer ever to win the Vardon Trophy for lowest stroke average. Besides taking his second MONY Tournament of Champions in 1976, January ended ninth on the money list with his PGA Tour best earnings of $163,622 and became one of the oldest Ryder Cup players. He also had performed on the 1965 Ryder Cup team. His PGA Tour career earnings amounted to $1,140,925.

Since joining the PGA Senior Tour in 1979, the six-foot, 165-pound January has won 22 tournaments and earned over $2.7 million. The first Seniors player to surpass $1 million, he triumphed in the 1979 and 1982 PGA Seniors, the 1982 Legends of Golf with Sam Snead (OS), the 1985 and 1986 Legends of Golf with Gene Littler (OS), and the 1987 Senior Tournament of Champions. January, the circuit's second-leading money winner in 1981 and 1982, led the PGA Senior Tour in earnings the next two years. He played in comparatively few tournaments each year, often leaving the PGA Tour after earning $60,000 in a given year. A serious automobile accident in 1988 sidelined the Dallas, TX, resident for a while, but he subsequently dominated the Vantage Classic Series for players 60 and over. He and his wife Patricia have three children, Timothy, Cherie Lynn, and Richard.

BIBLIOGRAPHY: Peter Alliss, *The Who's Who of Golf* (Englewood Cliffs, NJ, 1983); Al Barkow, *The History of the PGA Tour* (New York, 1989); *Golf Almanac*, 1993 (New

York, 1993); Dan Jenkins, "A Sick Man Gets a Quick Cure," *SI* 28 (April 29, 1968), pp. 66–67; Alfred Wright, "Two Dons in Quest of a Title," *SI* 27 (July 31, 1967), pp. 18–21.

Luther W. Spoehr

KING, Elizabeth "Betsy" (b. August 13, 1955, Reading, PA), golfer, is the daughter of Weir King, a physician, and Helen King and enjoyed a distinguished amateur career presaging success as a professional. She participated on the Furman University golf squad, winners of the 1976 Women's National Collegiate Championship, and placed as the low amateur in the U.S. Women's Open tournament the same year, finishing eighth in the entire field.

But after turning professional in 1977, the five-foot-six-inch King endured the Biblical seven lean years before enjoying seven fat years. She won no LPGA tournaments from 1977 through 1983, with her putting often letting her down. King's game, though, improved after 1980, a pivotal year for her. That year saw her increasingly active in Christian organizations and rekindled her spiritual values. King also took lessons that year from Ed Oldfield, a teaching pro who helped rebuild her swing. Due to King's upright position, her swing required an inside arc to strike the ball squarely and caused excessively low-trajectory shots. Oldfield altered King's take-away so as to permit her to strike the ball squarely with greater ease. At the same time, she improved her putting.

The spiritual and physical improvement helped King begin playing superb golf in 1984. From 1984 through 1993, she won at least two tournaments every year and 29 titles altogether. Tournament victories eluded her in 1994, although she finished sixth at the U.S. Women's Open and fourth in the du Maurier Classic. Her titles included the Nabisco Dinah Shore in 1987 and 1990, the U.S. Women's Open in 1989 and 1990, and the LPGA Championship in 1992. She has earned over $4.5 million on the LPGA circuit to rank second behind Pat Bradley (S). Her scoring average never exceeded 71, and she placed first in earnings to years. The du Maurier Classic remains the only major tournament that she has not won. King's next victory will qualify her for the LPGA Hall of Fame. King barely missed making the LPGA Hall of Fame in September 1994, finishing second in the Cellular One Ping Championship at Portland, OR, and second in the Toray, Japan, Queen's Cup in November. In an *NYT* survey in 1991, King's playing associates ranked her first in the use of midirons and fairway woods, third in the use of the driver and long irons, and third in long putting. She earned a kind of immortality at the JAL Big Apple Classic in 1990, when she hit a fairway wood 240 yards to the final green and sank an eagle putt. King, who holds 29 career titles, has won numerous honors, including *GM* and *GI* Player of the Year in 1987 and *GW* Player of the Year in 1989.

Playing comrades often viewed King as an "ice lady" because of her apparent diffidence in play. One player noted that "nothing fazes Betsy," but she was quite shaken in 1989 when she squandered a four-stroke lead in the third round of the U.S. Women's Open. King, active in the LPGA Christian Fellowship, takes time off each year to work for Habitat for Humanity, assisting carpenters in building homes. Her commitment to Christianity, she believes, gives her the assurance that she is at the "right place" when she plays golf. She resides in Scottsdale, AZ, and spends leisure time at concerts and sporting events.

BIBLIOGRAPHY: "Bradley Is Best, Say L.P.G.A. Peers," *NYT*, July 22, 1991; James Dodson, "The King Nobody Knows," *GM* 33 (July 1991), pp. 54–57; John Garrity, "In a World of Her Own," *SI* 72 (February 12, 1990), pp. 184–186; John Garrity, "Joyless Open," *SI* 73 (July 23, 1990), p. 26; John Garrity, "A King Is Crowned Queen," *SI* 71 (July 24, 1989), pp. 71–72; LPGA, *1992 Player Guide* (Daytona Beach, FL, 1992); Sonia Steptoe, "Good as It Gets," *SI* 73 (August 27, 1990), pp. 32–33.

Carl M. Becker

McSPADEN, Harold "Jug" (b. July 21, 1908, Rosedale, KS), golfer, turned professional in 1927 and earned his first victory in the 1933 Santa Monica, CA, Amateur-Pro Tournament. In 1934, he prevailed in the Pasadena, CA, Open and entered his first Masters tournament. At the 1937 PGA tournament, held at Pittsburgh FC in Aspinwall, PA, McSpaden finished runner-up to Denny Shute (OS). After going 20 holes in his second match, he vanquished young Sam Snead (OS), 3 and 2, in the next round, defeated Henry Picard (OS) in 39 holes in the quarterfinals, and edged Ky Laffoon in the semifinals. During the title match with Shute, McSpaden missed a short birdie putt for a victory on the thirty-sixth hole and lost on the first extra hole. His most prestigious victory came at the Canadian Open in 1939, the same year he shot below 60 in a practice round for the Texas Open. McSpaden also triumphed in the Sacramento, CA, Open and San Francisco, CA, Match Play in 1935, Massachusetts Open in 1936 and 1937, Miami, FL, Open and Houston, TX, Open in 1938, Thomasville, GA, Open in 1941, and All-American Open in 1943. His tour pinnacle came in 1944 and 1945, when asthma exempted him from military service. In 1944, McSpaden won 5 titles, including the Los Angeles, CA, Open, Phoenix, AZ, Open, Gulfport, MS, Open, Chicago, IL, Victory Open, and Minneapolis, MN, Four Ball, accumulated nearly $24,000, and ranked among the top 10 in 19 of 23 tournaments. Byron Nelson (OS), who won 13 titles the same year, and McSpaden earned nearly $62,000 in War Bonds. McSpaden triumphed once and finished second 13 times in 1945, when Nelson captured 17 of 31 tournaments and a record 11 consecutive crowns from March to August. The pair, nicknamed "The Gold Dust Twins," collected nearly $100,000, with McSpaden pocketing over $36,000. They remained good friends, Nelson serving as godfather to McSpaden's son.

Before leaving the tour in 1947, McSpaden won 17 events, placed second 32 times, and finished among the top ten 144 times. He worked as golf professional at Dubs' Dread GC in Piper, KS, an 8,100-yard par 78 course. He competed in senior golf events, including the Senior PGA Championship and 1993 Legends of Golf Over-70 Division at age 84.

BIBLIOGRAPHY: Peter Alliss, *The Who's Who of Golf* (Englewood Cliffs, NJ, 1983); Al Barkow, *The History of the PGA Tour* (New York, 1989); Mark H. McCormack, *The Wonderful World of Professional Golf* (New York, 1973); Herbert Warren Wind, *The Story of American Golf* (New York, 1956).

Luther W. Spoehr

NELSON, Larry Gene (b. September 10, 1947, Fort Payne, AL), golfer, is the son of Vernon Earl Nelson and Rudell (Fant) Nelson and came to his career by a circuitous route. Unlike most professionals, he did not play golf as a child or adolescent. As a teenager, he aspired to become a professional baseball player and played baseball at Southern Tech School. He also attended Kennesaw College before entering the U.S. Army. Nelson returned home in 1968 from Vietnam, where he had served as an artillery observer, and still had visions of balls and strikes. He was employed as an illustrator at an aircraft factory near Acworth, GA, when he hit a bucket of golf balls at a driving range. Nelson, "hooked" by the game, began to play golf, turned professional in 1971, and qualified for the PGA Tour in 1973.

Nelson enjoyed modest success for the next five years, winning $99,000 in his best year (1977) and taking no tournaments. Later, he acknowledged that he was not "ready" to play and needed to become a "more accurate hitter." In 1979, he won the Inverrary Classic and Western Open and finished second in tournament earnings. The next year, he captured the Atlanta Classic. In 1981, he won the Greater Greensboro Open and claimed his first major title, the PGA championship by four strokes with his "workmanlike" job of hitting the fairways. Nelson won the 1983 U.S. Open by one stroke, making a 60-foot birdie on the seventieth hole. After Nelson won the 1984 Walt Disney Classic, his game deteriorated slightly. He contemplated leaving the tour for business but resolved to win "one more" before quitting. The victory came in 1987, when he captured a second PGA title and, for good measure, the Walt Disney-Oldsmobile Classic. Nelson won over $500,000, ranking fourteenth in earnings. In 1988, he captured his last tournament, the Atlanta Classic. After 1989, he entered relatively few tournaments and spent more time on his golf course architecture business. He has won 10 PGA tournaments altogether, played on the Ryder Cup team in 1979, 1981, and 1987, and amassed over $3 million in career earnings.

The five-foot-nine-inch, 150-pound Nelson hits not long off the tee, but his "simple rhythmic" swing gives him consistent accuracy. He possesses "mild manners" and "masterly control" of his emotions on the golf course and enjoys snow skiing. A devout Christian, he often gives inspirational speeches to church groups. He and his wife Gayle have two children, Drew and Josh, and reside in Marietta, GA.

BIBLIOGRAPHY: Peter Alliss, *The Who's Who of Golf* (Englewood Cliffs, NJ, 1983); Carl M. Becker, telephone interview with Rudell Nelson, November 3, 1993; "Golf: Nelson Posts First Victory," *NYT*, March 12, 1979; Dan Jenkins, "A Drive Down Easy Street," *SI* 55 (August 17, 1981), p. 48; "Nelson, on 67–270, Victory by 7 Shots," *NYT*, June 9, 1980; "Nelson Takes P.G.A. Title by 4 Strokes," *NYT*, August 10, 1981; *1993 PGA Tour: Official Media Guide of the PGA Tour* (Ponte Vedra, FL, 1993); Gordon S. White, Jr., "A Champion and His Mild Manners," *NYT*, June 22, 1983; Gordon S. White, Jr., "Nelson Wins P.G.A. in Playoff Against Wadkins," *NYT*, August 10, 1987.

Carl M. Becker

PALMER, Sandra Jean (b. March 10, 1941, Ft. Worth, TX), golfer, started playing golf at age 13 in Maine, where she caddied. She became a leading amateur in Texas in the early 1960s, winning several regional and state titles. In 1961, she finished second in the Women's National Collegiate Championship while attending North Texas State University.

Palmer joined the LPGA Tour in 1964 and, like many other young professionals, did not soon taste success. For seven years, she recorded no victories. Her game gradually improved as she moved from thirty-first to eighth place in earnings from 1964 through 1970. From 1971 through 1977, she won at least two tournaments each year. These included two major events, the Titleholders Championship in 1972 and the U.S. Women's Open in 1974. She led the LPGA golfers in earnings in 1975. Her scoring average through this period remained remarkably consistent, ranging between 72 and 73. From 1977 through the 1980s, Palmer sustained her scoring average at about 73. She enjoyed only occasional success, however, winning but three tournaments and plunging as low as fifty-seventh in earnings. Her playing career stood virtually at an end by 1991, when she ranked one hundred and seventeenth in earnings. Nevertheless, Palmer won the LPGA Sprint Senior Challenge in May 1994 at Daytona Beach, FL. Altogether, she won 21 events on the LPGA Tour.

The 5-foot-1½-inch Palmer possessed a distinctive personality on the course. Observers characterized her as "fiercely competitive," a player with a "fighting instinct," "plucky," and "unflappable in the clutch." Asked whether she possessed a "killer instinct," she replied "Hell, yes! I hate to lose." Her combative nature surfaced in 1972 during the controversy surrounding Jane Blalock (S). The LPGA had suspended Blalock from play for a year for allegedly moving the ball beyond spike marks on the green. Palmer denounced the LPGA and accused one player of lying in reporting Blalock's illegal play. The LPGA still placed Palmer on probation for a year, noting that it was a "violation of ethics to accuse a member of lying and saying one of the affidavits is false." Palmer and Marlene Hagge,* who supported the LPGA's decisions, fought a war of "quotes and counterquotes" and then initiated lawsuits against each other. Finally, though, they settled the issue out of court. The North Texas State graduate, who has been enshrined in the Texas State Golf Hall of Fame and the National Collegiate Hall of Fame, resides in La Quinta, CA.

BIBLIOGRAPHY: "The Blalock Affair," *Newsweek* 80 (August 28, 1972), pp. 74–76; "Lawsuit Dropped by Women Golfers," *NYT*, September 11, 1973; LPGA, *1992 Player Guide* (Daytona Beach, FL, 1992); Barry McDermott, "Keeping a Close Eye on the Ball," *SI* 36 (June 19, 1972), pp. 21–23; "Miss Palmer Captures Open," *NYT*, July 21, 1975; "Miss Palmer Wins by a Stroke," *NYT*, April 21, 1975; "Miss Palmer Wins on a 281 After Losing 5-Stroke Lead," *NYT*, April 18, 1977; "Mrs. Carner Takes Open Golf Title," *NYT*, July 31, 1976; *NYT*, August 4, 1972.

Carl M. Becker

SIMPSON, Juli. *See* Juli Simpson Inkster.

SMITH, Marilynn Louise "Smitty" (b. April 13, 1929, Topeka, KS), golfer, is the daughter of Lynn Smith and Alma (Tillmanns) Smith and helped pioneer women's professional golf. She began taking lessons at age 12 from the professional at the Wichita, KS, CoC. After winning the Kansas State Amateur title for the third consecutive year in 1948 and the National Collegiate Championship in 1949 while playing for the University of Kansas, Smith joined the professional ranks. She became one of the founding LPGA charter members in 1950 and played on the LPGA Tour for over 30 years, winning 22 LPGA tournaments. All of her LPGA victories came from 1954 through 1972. Smith played her best golf through the 1960s when her scoring average ranged from 73 to 75. *Annus mirabilis* for her came in 1963, when she won the Titleholders Championship and 3 other tournaments and finished fourth in earnings at $21,691. From 1962 to 1972, Smith finished 10 times among the top 10 in earnings and placed fourth three times. She, one of the longest hitters on the LPGA Tour in the 1950s, lacked good putting skills. Smith described herself as a "combination swing/hitter." Smith played well at the wrong time. Public awareness of women's golf grew in the 1960s, but substantial television coverage and corporate support of the tour did not develop until the 1970s. Consequently, prize money remained small. As late as 1970, the LPGA Tour divided only $345,000 among 21 tournaments.

Throughout her career, Smith, often known as "Miss Personality," has remained a vibrant voice for women's golf. She has conducted golf demonstrations in all 50 states and 34 countries, becoming an ambassador for the game. In 1973, she became the first woman to serve as a television commentator for a men's golf tournament. In 1987, she founded and organized the Marilynn Smith Founders Classic, the first women's senior professional tournament. Smith's numerous awards for her golf and general community contributions have included the Patty Berg Award in 1979 for distinguished service to women's golf and the *GD* LPGA Founders Cup in 1983 for charitable service off the course. She resides in Richardson, TX.

BIBLIOGRAPHY: LPGA, *1992 Player Guide* (Daytona Beach, FL, 1992); Benjamin G. Rader, *American Sports: From the Age of Folk Games to the Age of Spectators* (Englewood Cliffs, NJ, 1983); Marilynn Smith, questionnaire for Carl M. Becker, January 8, 1993.

Carl M. Becker

STADLER, Craig Robert "The Walrus" (b. June 2, 1953, San Diego, CA), golfer, is the son of David Edwin Stadler and Betty (Adams) Stadler and attended the University of Southern California. In 1973, Stadler served notice that he could become a leading professional golfer by winning the U.S. Amateur tournament. After turning professional in 1975, he played reasonably well on the PGA Tour for four years. Stadler did not win any PGA tournaments, though, until 1980, capturing the Bob Hope Classic and the Greater Greensboro Open. He took the Kemper Open in 1981 and posted the best record of his career in 1982, winning the Masters, Kemper Open, Tucson Open, and World Series of Golf and becoming the top money winner on the PGA Tour. *GM* named Stadler 1982 Player of the Year. The next eight years saw Stadler's play decline, as he won only the Byron Nelson Classic in 1984 and finished anywhere from eighth to fifty-third in earnings. He appeared among the titlists again, winning the 1991 Tour Championship and 1992 NEC World Series of Golf and finishing second in earnings in 1991. He has captured 11 titles, including the PGA Tour Buick Invitation in February 1994, and played on the Walker Cup team in 1975 and the Ryder Cup squad in 1983 and 1985. Stadler struggled in the 1994 PGA Tour, missing the cuts several times.

Early in his career, Stadler acted "short-tempered" and engaged, noted one observer, in a "certain amount of club-throwing" that made him his own worst enemy. Controversy surrounded him in 1987 at the Andy Williams Open. Television viewers noted that Stadler knelt on a towel to play a shot beneath a small tree. Responding to their inquiries, PGA officials disqualified him because he had "built a stance" and then had failed to take a two-stroke penalty on his scorecard. Although losing as much as $37,000, he accepted the disqualification with little complaint.

Stadler, who has always hit long and accurate drives, finished sixth in total driving, including distance and accuracy, in 1991 and nineteenth in 1992. Although Stadler's bunker play and putting have faltered on occasion, Jack Nicklaus (OS) has noted that at times Stadler shows an excellent touch around the greens. Stadler projects a colorful image, partly because of his heavyset, 5-foot-10-inch, 220-pound frame and partly because of his whiskers. In 1980, he was the only player on the PGA Tour with a beard. Stadler, who lives in Rancho Santa Fe, CA, married Susan Barrett in January 1979 and has two sons, Kevin and Christopher. His special interests include skiing and hunting.

BIBLIOGRAPHY: Peter Alliss, *The Who's Who of Golf* (Englewood Cliffs, NJ, 1983); Dave Anderson, "Green Jacket for a Walrus," *NYT*, April 12, 1982; Dave Anderson, "Stop Golf's Tattle-Tales," *NYT*, February 17, 1987; "Burns Wins by 4; Stadler Disqualified," *NYT*, February 16, 1987; *1993 PGA Tour: Official Media Guide of the PGA Tour* (Ponte Vedra, FL, 1993); "Stadler Defeats Pohl in Playoff," *NYT*, April 12, 1982; "Stadler Takes Golf by Stroke," *NYT*, January 15, 1980; *WWA*, 47th ed. (1992–1993), pp. 3201–3202.

Carl M. Becker

STOCKTON, David Knapp "Dave" (b. November 2, 1941, San Bernardino, CA), golfer, is the son of Gail Rufus Stockton, a professional golfer, and Audrey (Knapp) Stockton and earned a B.S. degree in general management from the University of Southern California in 1964. Stockton entered professional golf after suffering chronically from a back injury, incurred when he was only 14 years old. He could not practice regularly and developed his limited power, by guiding his club through the ball, not by snapping through it. Nonetheless, Stockton believed that he possessed the ability to play good golf and turned professional in 1964.

By 1968, Stockton had won three tournaments on the PGA Tour. In 1970, he claimed the PGA title, triumphing in a final round punctuated by numerous bogeys and birdies. He edged Arnold Palmer (OS), who never added the PGA title to his laurels. Stockton nearly won 3 of the 4 Grand Slam titles in the 1970s, finishing runner-up in the 1975 Masters and sharing second place in the 1978 U.S. Open. He garnered a second PGA title in 1976, sinking a 12-foot putt on the eighteenth hole. His most productive year came in 1974, when he captured three tournaments (the Los Angeles, Greater Hartford, and Quad City Opens) and placed sixth in earnings. He earned no PGA Tour titles after 1976, entering fewer tournaments late in the decade. Altogether, he captured 11 titles on the PGA Tour. He represented the United States in the 1970 and 1976 World Cups and 1971 and 1977 Ryder Cups and shared the former record for fewest putts (19) over 18 holes.

Through the 1980s, Stockton frequently played with businessmen in corporate outings. He averaged 90 days of such play a year, becoming known as the "King of the Corporate Outings." After joining the PGA Senior Tour in 1991, he soon won the 1992 Mazda Open tournament. Stockton earned over $600,000 in 1992 for seventh place on the tour and was selected Senior Tour Rookie of the Year. In 1993, he captured five Senior Tour titles and earned over $1 million. The following year, he won three Senior Tour titles and became the first Senior Tour golfer to earn over $1 million two consecutive years. On both the PGA and Senior circuits, he hit relatively short off the tee but putted well and ranked first in putting on the Senior Tour in 1992. He enjoyed his greatest thrill in 1991, captaining the U.S. Ryder Cup squad to victory over the European team for the first time since 1985 at Kiawah Island. Stockton, who married Catherine Fay Hales in February 1965, has two sons, David Bradley and Ronald, and lives in Mentone, CA.

BIBLIOGRAPHY: Peter Alliss, *The Who's Who of Golf* (Englewood Cliffs, NJ, 1983); *1993 Senior PGA Tour: Official Media Guide of the Senior PGA Tour* (Ponte Vedra, FL, 1993); Gordon S. White, Jr., "Stockton Wins P.G.A. Title by Stroke," *NYT*, August 17, 1976; *WWA*, 47th ed. (1992–1993), p. 3245.

Carl M. Becker

WALL, Arthur Jonathon Jr. "Art" (b. November 25, 1923, Honesdale, PA), golfer, is the son of Arthur Wall, Sr., a feed merchant and representative to the Pennsylvania legislature, and Louise (Riefler) Wall and won the Pan-American Open tournament in 1943 as a 19-year-old amateur. After three years in the U.S. Air Force, he attended Duke University from 1946 to 1949 as a business major, participated on the golf team, and roomed with future golf professional Mike Souchak. Upon graduation from Duke and winning the Pennsylvania Amateur title, Wall turned professional. His first PGA victory came at the Fort Wayne Open in 1953. Wall, assisted by fellow-pro Doug Ford (OS), reached his peak during the 1950s. His PGA victories included the Tournament of Champions (1954), Fort Wayne Open (1956), Pensacola Open (1957), Rubber City Open (1958), and five other tour events. By far his greatest accomplishment came in the 1959 Masters at Augusta, GA, where he birdied five of the last six holes in a final round 66 to defeat Cary Middlecoff (OS) by one stroke. In 1959, he was named Player of the Year, winning the Vardon Trophy and finishing first on the money list. Wall's successes led to his participation on the Ryder Cup team in 1957, 1959, and 1961. During the 1960s, the six-foot, 165-pound Wall won 10 titles on the Caribbean Tour and the Canadian Open (1960), San Diego Open (1964), and Insurance City Open (1966). Wall's only PGA victory during the 1970s, the Greater Milwaukee Open (1975), saw him fire rounds of 67, 67, 67, and 70 at age 51.

Wall gravitated to the Senior Tour by the late 1970s, winning the 1978 U.S. National Senior Open, 1980 Legends of Golf (with Tommy Bolt [OS]), and 1982 Energy Capital Classic. In recent years, physical problems have plagued him. Rotator cuff surgery in 1989 limited him to only two tournaments. At the Greater Rapids Open, he won the Super Seniors title by defeating Jack Fleck and Mike Fetchick in a playoff.

The unflappable, modest, and articulate Wall, nicknamed the "master of concentration," possesses a baseball grip that enables him to generate more power and more unwanted hooks. A forte remains his uncanny ability to judge distance. Wall, a superb putter and iron player, has made 45 career holes-in-one, a record he downplays. He crossed out that statistic in the Senior PGA Tour Book copysheet he sent to this author. Wall's PGA career earnings total $1,019,753, with $638,816 from the PGA Tour and $380,937 from the Senior PGA Tour. Wall married his wife, Jean, on April 22, 1950, and has five children, Gregory, Carolyn, Laurie, Valerie, and Douglas.

BIBLIOGRAPHY: Gwilym Brown, "Wall Was Wondrous," *SI* 10 (April 13, 1959), pp. 14–17; *CB* (1959), pp. 470–471; *Senior PGA Tour Book*, 1991; Art Wall, Jr., letters to James N. Giglio, February 25, June 15, 1993; Herbert Warren Wind, "Historic Masters," *SI* 10 (April 20, 1959), pp. 38–46.

James N. Giglio

HORSE RACING

BAEZA, Braulio (b. March 26, 1940, Panama City, Panama), thoroughbred jockey and trainer, grew up in a cultural milieu, where horse racing marked a way of life. Baeza recalled, "I was born across the street from the old Juan Franco Racetrack in Panama. My father was a jockey and trainer, as was my grandfather, and I was always around the barn." Baeza began his American racing career in 1960, when he visited Florida for a holiday. Baeza, like many successful athletes seeking professional advancement within the United States, already had successfully completed a tough apprenticeship as a jockey in his native Panama and had been its champion rider/winner.

Jockeys traditionally enjoy long careers if they can endure and recover from falls and racing spills. During 17 years of thoroughbred racing, Baeza amassed a staggering 3,140 wins. This statistic alone earned induction into the NMR's Hall of Fame in 1976. Eight years earlier, he had received the George Woolf Memorial Jockey Award for his contributions to horse racing.

On five separate occasions, he led the nation's jockeys in earnings. He also won the Belmont Stakes three times, accomplishing the feat aboard Sherluck in 1961, Chateaugay in 1963, and Arts and Letters in 1969. In a major race toward the end of his career, he in July 1975 guided Kentucky Derby winner Foolish Pleasure to victory over Ruffian (OS) in a $350,000 match at Belmont Park. Ruffian pulled up lame in the race and eventually was destroyed. Baeza, mournful about his victory, stated, "I am so sorry to see such a fine filly get hurt. . . . What a shame."

Many jockeys, including Baeza, become trainers on their retirement from the track. According to an NYRA *Media Guide*, Baeza believed "good hands and a good sense of pace" to be the most important qualities in a jockey. As a trainer, he regarded patience as a virtue and considered his greatest pleasure as having a "young horse . . . develop into a good horse." He saddled his first winner as a trainer in 1979 on the Aqueduct Race Track in Jamaica, NY.

Despite knowing little English upon settling in the United States, Baeza became fluent in his new language with one year of watching movies and watching television. At five feet five inches, he was taller than most jockeys. During his racing prime, he kept his weight between 110 and 114 pounds. He and his wife Debra have many sons and daughters.

BIBLIOGRAPHY: *The Lincoln Library of Sports Champions*, vol. 1 (Columbus, OH, 1974); *NYRA Media Guide*, undated, T. G. Gilcoyne Collection, NMR, Saratoga Springs, NY; "Ruffian Destroyed After Injury in Race," *NYT*, July 7, 1975; Ron Smith, *TSN Chronicle of Twentieth Century Sport* (New York, 1992).

Scott A.G.M. Crawford

BARRERA, Lazaro Sosa "Laz" (b. May 8, 1924, Marianao, Cuba; d. April 25, 1991, Downey, CA), thoroughbred trainer, was the son of Crispin Barrera, a quarter horse jockey, and Blanca Fouquet Sosa. The ninth of 12 children, he enjoyed baseball and horses and soon joined his older brothers working at nearby Oriental Park. In 1937, he walked hot horses for Hirsch Jacobs (OS) and met the latter's daughter, Patrice, the future Mrs. Louis Wolfson and co-owner of Affirmed. An aspiring turf writer, he later aided Sergio Verona, Oriental Park's publicity director, and began reporting in 1940 for *El Mundo*.

In 1942, Barrera obtained his trainer's license. Joe Hoskins taught him trainer's skills. After a 1944 hurricane damaged the track, Barrera moved to Mexico and debuted at the Hippodromo de Las Americas in October. Barrera won his first five races before stewards discovered his age and revoked his license. Carlos Oriani hired him as stable adviser and promoted him to head trainer in 1947. For 17 years, Barrera perennially led Hippodromo trainers in earnings. Hal King convinced Barrera to come to the United States. Barrera operated a public stable and on July 23, 1960, saddled his first American winner, Destructor.

Barrera gained national prominence in 1976, training sprinter Bold Forbes to Kentucky Derby and Belmont Stakes victories. He also won three stakes at three tracks on May 8, 1976. Affirmed's (OS) 1978 victories over Alydar (OS), in perhaps the greatest Triple Crown races, helped Barrera break the trainer's single-year earning record with $3,314,564. In 1979, Barrera broke his record by earning $3,608,517 and was elected to the NMR Hall of Fame. Affirmed defeated Spectacular Bid (OS) in a thrilling JoC Gold Cup Stakes. Heart surgeries in 1979 and 1984 curtailed Barrera's training activities. He still saddled seven consecutive winners at Santa Anita Race Track in January 1984 and in 1990 trained Mister Frisky, winner of 16 consecutive races. In 1991, Barrera, D. Wayne Lukas (S), and others were exonerated from a 1989 charge of drugging horses with cocaine. Truesdail Labs could not duplicate their original findings, while several independent labs found no traces of cocaine in the urine samples.

Barrera won 2,268 U.S. races, earned over $50 million in purses, and trained 128 different stakes winners. His National/Eclipse champions included Affirmed, Bold Forbes, It's in the Air, J. O. Tobin, Lemhi Gold, and Tiffany Lass. He tied the record by leading the nation's trainers in money earned from 1977 to 1980 and won four Eclipse Awards as North America's outstanding trainer from 1976 to 1979.

According to Barrera, "You see things in horses that nobody else can see. I see trainers all the time, looking at their stopwatch instead of their horses." He did not believe in long workouts or interval training, keeping his horses sharp to run fast. Joseph Durso characterized Barrera as "brilliant with horses, warm with people."

Barrera married Carmen Miramontes on May 24, 1949, and had three children, Alberto and Lazaro, Jr., both trainers, and Blanchita Uriza. Eight of Barrera's brothers also worked at race tracks. "We believe," Barrera stated, "in taking good care of the horses and hope they will take care of us." Barrera died of cardiopulmonary failure.

BIBLIOGRAPHY: Deirdre B. Biles, "Laz Barrera, 1924–91: A Life with Horses," *TBH* 117 (May 4, 1991), p. 2365; Rick Bozich, "Laz Barrera Had Winning Touch with People, Too," Louisville (KY) *Courier-Journal*, April 26, 1991, pp. E1, E6; *DRF*, April 5, 1965; May 4, 1976; December 23, 1976; October 2, 1979; October 26, 1979; December 12, 1979; December 14, 1979; February 1, 1980; May 27, 1989, p. 7; March 17, 1991; April 28, 1991; Joseph Durso, "Fondness and Grief Run Deep for Laz Barrera," *NYT*, April 30, 1991, p. B12(N); Jay Hovdey, "A True Conquistador," *TTR* 224 (April 1990), pp. 100–105; William Leggett, "Why Isn't This Man Smiling?" *SI* 48 (June 12, 1978), pp. 67–68; Lexington (KY) *Leader*, June 7, 1978; Louisville (KY) *Courier-Journal*, May 14, 1976; March 8, 1979; Mike Marten, "All Charges Against Lukas, Barreras, Others Dropped," *DRF*, June 1, 1989; *NYT*, April 26, 1991, p. D18; Jay Privman, "Training Methods: Laz Barrera," *TTC* 76 (July 1985), pp. 18–22; *PUI* 6 (April 26, 1990), p. 14; Mark Ratzky, "Laz Barrera Dies," *DRF*, April 27, 1991, pp. 5, 13; *TT* 7 (May 3, 1991), pp. 1, 10; *TTR* 228 (October 1988), p. 1240.

Steven P. Savage

BURCH, William Preston (b. 1846, Cheraw, SC; d. July 9, 1926, Saratoga Springs, NY), thoroughbred jockey, trainer, and racing official, began a dynasty of horse trainers. His son Preston, who started his career as his father's stable agent and assistant from 1902 until 1905, and grandson, John Elliot Burch, are both members of the NMR Hall of Fame. His other son, Shelby, became a prominent trainer, and his great grandson, William Elliot Burch, operated a public stable.

As a youngster, William trained and rode quarter horses. He spent his late teens riding a thoroughbred as a scout and courier for General Wade

Hampton in the Confederate States Army. After the Civil War, he became a jockey and rode his last race in 1876 against rookie Jimmy McLaughlin (OS). Burch trained quarter horses and raced in the midwestern and western fair circuits, later forming a partnership with Charles H. Pettengill. He trained many good thoroughbreds, including Judge Murray, Mittle B., Burch, and Governor Sprague for George H. Kernaghan of Augusta, GA, in the 1880s; Dandelion, Devanter, and Rossignol for Francis R. Hitchcock around 1900; Gnome and My Own, which won the 1926 Maryland Handicap and Saratoga Cup, for Rear Admiral Cary T. Grayson; and Spinaway, Biggonet (winner of the Withers Stakes), Grey Griar (a Matron winner), and Telie Doe for General Mart Geary and Wade Hampton. Burch also trained for W. C. Eustis and Samuel Ross and exhibited patience with horses, especially those showing promise. Subsequently, he served as an official at various tracks and was presiding steward at Laurel Park Race Track's first meeting in October 1911.

Besides adeptly judging horses, he judged human character skillfully. In 1879, he saw racing pictures that clerk Andrew Jackson Joyner had hung in the Weldon, NC, Post Office, talked with him, and hired the future NMR Hall of Fame trainer to work for him. His other initial hirees included Gwyn Tompkins, a Senate page, newsman, and eventual great trainer, and George M. Odom (OS), a Burch apprentice in 1896 and later Belmont Stakes winning rider and trainer.

Son Preston lauded William, "I have always considered my father a great horseman and a great trainer of horses, and I have tried in a small way to emulate him. He is said to have had more friends on the race track than any man who ever trained horses. Racing has been my whole life, and like my father, I love my horses." Burch, who believed in the beneficial effects of Saratoga Springs waters, usually arrived there well before the race meeting started and normally rode a saddle horse every morning at Horse Haven. Burch trained horses until his death from a brief illness at age 80. His wife and three children lived in Washington, DC after she grew weary of traveling the race circuit. Her brother, Green B. Morris, a leading owner, trained 1882 Kentucky Derby winner Apollo. In 1955, William was inducted into the NMR Hall of Fame.

BIBLIOGRAPHY: Preston M. Burch, *Training Thoroughbred Horses* (Menasha, WI, 1992); *DRF*, March 11, 1965; June 5, 1990; Don Graham, "Bill Burch Advancing Tradition," *DRF*, July 3, 1980; William Leggett, "Invitation to the Dancer," *SI* 12 (February 22, 1960), p. 51; NTWA, *Members in the National Museum of Racing Hall of Fame* (Saratoga Springs, NY, 1976); *NYT*, July 10, 1926, p. 8; Harry Worcester Smith, "Clippings," *TTR* 104 (August 14, 1926), p. 88; *TTR* 103 (April 24, 1926), p. 505; *TTR* 104 (July 17, 1926), p. 27.

                                                                    Steven P. Savage

CORDERO, Angel Tomas Jr. (b. November 8, 1942, Santurce, PR), thoroughbred jockey and trainer, is the son of Angel T. Cordero, Sr., and Mercedes (Hernandez) Cordero and studied at the Institute of Puerto Rico. Although two years younger than Braulio Baeza,* Cordero shared many similarities with his Panamanian rival. Cordero, like Baeza, grew up in a world dominated by thoroughbred horses and race tracks. His father performed as a thoroughbred jockey and later trained horses at El Commandante Race Track in San Juan, PR. His first job came as grooming racehorses.

He rode his first winner aboard Celador at El Commandante Race Track on June 15, 1960. The 18-year-old embarked on a long thoroughbred racing career, marked by numerous racing highlights but tinged by several horrifying accidents. Toward the end of his career, he still maintained a grueling racing schedule. In 1991, as a 49-year-old, he started 1,341 races with 238 first places, 212 seconds, and 186 thirds and earned $9,383,904. By the end of 1992, he had amassed 7,057 wins in 38,600 racing starts. His career earnings reached phenomenal proportions in an era when some baseball, basketball, football, tennis, and golf stars have become multimillionaires. Cordero's career earnings have amounted to a staggering $164,526,217.

Cordero was inducted into the NMR Hall of Fame on August 11, 1988, one year after becoming the sixth jockey to ride 6,000 winners. He attained this feat while guiding Lost Kitty to a first place at Monmouth Park in Oceanport, NJ. On October 17, 1991, Cordero joined Willie Shoemaker (OS) and Laffit Pincay, Jr.,* as the only thoroughbred jockeys to achieve 7,000 wins. When asked, "Which of your victories has meant the most to you and why?" Cordero replied, "The Kentucky Derby; winning it three times was special. It's everybody's dream." Cordero won aboard Cannonade in 1974, Bold Forbes in 1976, and Spend a Buck in 1985.

On January 12, 1992, Cordero, no stranger to serious injury on the race track, tumbled during a race at the Aqueduct Race Track in Jamaica, NY. He suffered various injuries, including a broken elbow, three smashed ribs, and a damaged spleen, and retired from thoroughbred racing to seek a trainer's license. His first triumph in this role came as trainer of Puchinito on June 13, 1992, at Belmont Park Race Track in Elmont, NY.

He and his first wife, Santa, had two children, Angel Thomas and Merly, before their divorce. He and his present wife, Marjorie, have one son and one daughter. Cordero won acclaim for his fiercely competitive intensity and "daring risk-taking." His numerous honors include earning Eclipse Awards as Jockey of the Year in 1982 and 1983 and leading jockey in earnings for 1976, 1982, and 1983. He remains a folk hero for the New York Puerto Rican community and was featured in the pop song "Cordero y Belmonte" by Latino singer Ismael Rivera.

BIBLIOGRAPHY: *CB* (1975), pp. 91–93; *NYRA Media Guide*, undated, T. G. Gilcoyne Collection, NMR, Saratoga Springs, NY; Ron Smith, *TSN Chronicle of Twentieth Century Sport* (New York, 1992); Michael Watchmaker, "Horse Racing," in *Athletes* (New York, 1985).

Scott A.G.M. Crawford

DAY, Patrick Alan "Pat" (b. October 13, 1953, Brush, CO), thoroughbred jockey, attended high school in Eagle, CO, and won the 98-pound State wrestling championship as a junior. After a short stint as a bull rider on the rodeo circuit, he became an exercise boy at Turf Paradise (now Prescott Downs) in Arizona. He began his career as a thoroughbred jockey in 1973, winning his first race that July. Day's career started slowly in the 1970s because of serious problems with drugs and alcohol. Day's first agent, Jim Read, marriage to his current wife, Sheila, a fashion designer, in 1979, and religious conversion in 1984 all helped him focus his energies on thoroughbred racing. He led the nation's jockeys in winners from 1982 to 1984 and in 1990 and 1991 and earned the Eclipse Award as the nation's outstanding jockey in 1984, 1986, 1987, and 1991. He also earned the 1985 George Woolf Memorial Jockey Award, presented by the JG.

Through September 1994, Day had achieved 6,239 wins in 28,352 starts and ridden mounts winning an aggregate $144,469,546. His many triumphs included a record eight Breeder's Cups, one Kentucky Derby, three Preaknesses, two Belmonts, and three Travers Stakes. Day has enjoyed his greatest success at Churchill Downs in Louisville, KY, but his first Kentucky Derby winner did not come until his tenth try, aboard Lil E. Tee in 1992. His Preakness victories came aboard Tank's Prospect in 1988, Summer Squall in 1990, and Tabasco Cat in 1994, while his Belmont triumphs came aboard Easy Goer in 1989 and Tabasco Cat in 1994. Tabasco Cat finished sixth in 1994 in the Kentucky Derby and third at the Travers Stakes and contended for Horse of the Year honors. On June 20, 1984, he rode seven winners in eight races at Churchill Downs to set a track record. On September 13, 1989, he recorded eight victories and placed in nine races at Arlington International Race Course in Chicago, IL.

The 4-foot-11-inch, 100-pound Day has seldom been involved in race track controversies involving fouls or careless riding. In the 1988 Belmont Stakes, however, his mount, Forty-Niner, trained by Woody Stephens (OS), allegedly bumped Winning Colors. Both horses finished considerably back in the race. Day denied the allegation, claiming he was simply holding his position on the track.

In 1991, Day was inducted into the NMR Hall of Fame. Contemporaries describe Day as a very smart rider with "marvelous" and "gentle" hands, who can "read a race as it progresses" and keep his mount out of trouble. Day, who lives in Crestwood, KY, enjoys fishing, camping, and recreational horseback riding.

BIBLIOGRAPHY: Pat Day clipping file, Churchill Downs Media Relations Office, Louisville, KY; Louisville (KY) *Courier-Journal*, August 9, 1991; May 3, 1992; November 7, 1992; *NYT*, January 6, 1988; May 22, 1988; John Rolfe, "He Works Like a Horse," *Sport* 76 (May 1985), pp. 65–71; J. E. Vader, "Day of Reckoning," *SI* 70 (May 1, 1989), pp. 74–76.

John E. Findling

HEALEY, Thomas J. (b. July 16, 1866, Fordham, NY; d. October 7, 1944, Holmdel, NJ), thoroughbred trainer and track official, was born on his father's dairy farm and worked there as a youngster, becoming interested in horses and life at the Morris Park Race Track. His rapid growth precluded a career as a thoroughbred jockey. As a teenager in 1881, Healey worked in E. A. Clabaugh's stable and was trained there by Jeter Walden. Walden had trained the 1877 Preakness winner. Healey began working for the Lamasney Brothers at the Kansas City, MO, Stable in 1882 and was employed in 1885 by Commodore N. W. Kittson's Erdenheim Farm in Chestnut Hill, PA.

Healey served his apprenticeship under trainer Walter Rollins and, by 1888, was second trainer for Walter Gratz of Philadelphia, PA. Healey's first winner, Pocatello, triumphed at Gravesend Track in Brooklyn, NY, on May 28, 1888. After training for Edward Kelly's Clabaugh Farm, Healey established one of the nation's largest public stables.

From around 1900 until 1921, Healey worked exclusively for Richard T. Wilson, SaA president. His stakes winners included The Parader, victor of the 1901 Lawrence Realization and the Withers; Olambala, Healey's favorite; and Campfire, Olambala's colt, the 1916 leading money-winner. Healey's other stakes winners included Olambala's colts, Pillory, 1922 Preakness and Belmont victor, and Hannibal; and Campfire's offspring, Tall Timber, Wilderness, Ethereal, and Forest Lore.

In 1921, Healey added a client, Walter J. Salmon, and won Stakes races with his Flight of Time, Display, Vigil, Dr. Freeland, Careful, and Step Lightly. When Wilson and James Rowe, Sr. (S), trainer for Harry Payne Whitney, both died in 1929, Whitney hired Healey. After H. P. Whitney died in 1930, Healey continued to train the stable for Cornelius Vanderbilt Whitney. For C. V. Whitney, Healey developed Whichone and Top Flight, the world's leading money-winning filly. In 1933, he trained the five-year-old Equipoise (OS), his best horse. Healey won a record $1,453,868 for C. V. Whitney over a four-year span. C. V. Whitney sold his stable at a dispersal auction in 1937.

Healey retired from training in 1939 to become a New York track official. Laurel Park, MD, hired him in 1941 as steward, a capacity he also filled at Garden State Park in New Jersey, Tropical Park in Miami, FL, the Fair Grounds in New Orleans, LA, and Pimlico Race Track in Baltimore, MD. He was considered among the nation's best stewards.

Healey won over 1,000 races and $3 million as a trainer and captured the Preakness five times with The Parader (1901), Pillory (1922), Vigil (1923), Display (1926), and Dr. Freeland (1929). He maintained horses in fine racing condition while shipping them great distances for important Stakes races. Neil Newman said of him, "There is no more popular man on the racecourse than Mr. Healy [*sic*]. He is universally admired and is a credit to the sport, and a man young trainers might with profit take for a model."

The Healeys had four daughters and one son, John A., Christiana Stable trainer. In 1955, Healey was inducted into the NMR Hall of Fame.

BIBLIOGRAPHY: "Laurel's New Judge, Thomas J. Healey," *TABR* 1 (September 13, 1941), pp. 16–19; Neil Newman, "Thomas Healy," *TNTD* 6 (March 1929), pp. 169, 210; NTWA, *Members in the National Museum of Racing Hall of Fame* (Saratoga Springs, NY, 1976); *NYT*, October 15, 1944, p. 44; *TBH* 42 (October 14, 1944), pp. 491–492; *TTR* 140 (October 14, 1944), p. 373.

                                                                           Steven P. Savage

LAURIN, Lucien (b. March 18, 1912, St. Paulin, Quebec, Canada), thoroughbred jockey and trainer, left school to muck stalls at Delormier and Blue Bonnets Parks in 1927 and worked up to exercise boy. In 1929, the five-foot-four-inch French Canadian rode his first race at Mount Royal Park for Rosaire LaCroix. His best year came in 1935, when he won 35 of 226 races and Quebec's King's Plate on Sir Michael. Altogether, he captured 161 of 1,445 races (11 percent) at tracks in Canada, the United States, and Cuba.

Weight difficulties compelled Laurin to become a trainer in 1942. He began tasting success in 1946, when he saddled 42 winners and earned $127,997. Roger, Laurin's son, left his position as Meadow Stable trainer to work for the Phipps Stable in 1971 and recommended his father as his replacement. Lucien earned the Trainer of the Year award and gained national prominence in 1972, when he trained Riva Ridge, Kentucky Derby and Belmont Stakes winner, and Secretariat (OS), owned by Mrs. Helen C. (Penny) Tweedy Ringquist and the first two-year-old to win Horse of the Year honors. In 1973, Secretariat captured the Triple Crown, setting track records in each race and again earning Horse of the Year honors. Canadian jockey Ron Turcotte rode Secretariat in the Triple Crown victories and his last, the Canadian Turf Championship. Laurin, inducted into the NMR Hall of Fame in 1977, resigned as Meadow Stable trainer in 1976 but still trained and bred horses, using his shares in Secretariat and Riva Ridge. In 1985, Laurin sold his Holly Hills, SC, training center, horses, and Secretariat breeding share to Cornelius N. Ray of Evergreen Farm in Paris, KY, and became his trainer. In 1990, he retired from training and was inducted into the Oriental Park Hall of Fame by the CTC.

Laurin, treating his horses as unique individuals, used no set training formula. He trained numerous other Stakes winners, including Champion Quill, 1958 Two-Year-Old Champion; Amberoid, 1966 Belmont Stakes winner; Capelet; Count Amber; Clansman; Crystal Boot; Dike, 1969 Wood Memorial victor; Drone; Gordan; Jay Ray; Sorceress; Spanish Riddle; and Upper Case, 1972 Florida Derby and Wood Memorial winner. He trained for owners Ben Lister, F. H. Wegener, Joseph Gratton, Reginald Webster for 32 years and Claiborne Farms from 1966 to 1970, Mrs. Horace Davis,

Jean Louis Levesque, and Leon J. Peters, among others. As a trainer, Laurin won 1,156 races and $11,922,407 in North America. Since 1982, Laurin and his wife Juliette have lived in Key Largo, FL, and Hallandale, FL.

BIBLIOGRAPHY: Rich Bozich, "Arazi Worth a Ticket? Put Lucien Laurin in Front Row," Louisville (KY) *Courier-Journal*, March 6, 1992, pp. E1, E7; Teddy Cox, "Laurin Resigns as Meadow Trainer," *DRF*, March 2, 1976; *DRF*, January 16, 1973; October 13, 1983; April 9, 1985; May 29, 1985; March 18, 1987; Don Grisham, "Laurin Back After Giving Retirement 'Best Shot,' " *DRF*, May 30, 1983; Joe Hirsch, "Geriatric Kids Kick Up Their Heels," *DRF*, April 9, 1985; William C. Phillips, "Lucien Laurin, Eb Pons to Hall," *DRF*, September 19, 1990; William C. Phillips, "Lucien Laurin Looks Back with Fondness," *DRF*, April 20, 1990, p. 9; Press Release, "Trainer-Riva Ridge" and "Trainer-Secretariat," May 1973, Keeneland Library, Lexington, KY; Julie Howell Turner, "Lucien Laurin: Reflections of a Triple Crown Trainer," *TFH* 24 (April 1982), pp. 581–582.

Steven P. Savage

LONGDEN, John Eric "Johnny" "The Pumper" (b. February 14, 1907, Wakefield, England), thoroughbred jockey and trainer, is the son of Herb Longden, a coal miner, and Mary Longden, Mormons who had eight children. Although booked on the *Titanic*, the Longdens missed that boat and emigrated instead to Taber, Canada. As a child, Longden rode ponies, read about horse racing, played ice hockey, and herded cattle. He started working at age 13 in the coal mines, where he strengthened his arms and shoulders by driving mules and digging. He rode on the Canadian and Montana County Fair circuit from 1924 to 1927. Longden hopped a freight train to Salt Lake City, UT, where he won his first official thoroughbred race on Hugo K. Asher on October 4, 1927, and returned to Canada to attend school in Toronto.

Longden rode for Fred Johnson from 1928 to 1931, when he decided to freelance. In 1930, he had met owner–trainer Al Tarn and led British Columbian riders in victories. In 1935, Longden began to ride horses for Jim Fitzsimmons (OS) and raced more in the United States, surpassing $100,000 in purses for the first time. After finishing second in wins in 1936, he led the nation in victories in 1938, 1947, and 1948. He compiled the most Stakes wins in 1943 and highest earnings in 1943 and 1945, finished among the top 10 in purses from 1936 to 1957 and in 1961, and amassed over $1 million a year eight times. As a jockey, he won 6,032 (19 percent) of his 32,400 races, placed second in 4,914 races and third in 4,272 races, and earned $24,584,325 in purses.

On May 22–23, 1936, Longden won the Illinois Derby and Latonia Derby aboard Rushaway. He rode John Hertz's Count Fleet (OS) to the Triple Crown and Horse of the Year honors in 1943 and recorded six winners on December 5, 1947, at Bay Meadows. In the 1950 San Juan Capistrano, he defeated Citation (OS) aboard Noor for his greatest racing thrill. He surpassed Sir Gordon Richards's 4,870 lifetime victories on September 3, 1956, and ranked as the world's leading jockey until Willie Shoemaker (OS) broke his record of 6,072 victories in 1970. Longden rode Busher, Silver Spoon, Swaps (OS), Whirlaway (OS), Porterhouse, St. Vincent, T. V. Lark, and Fleet Nasrullah. He suffered numerous injuries and retired at age 59, his last victory coming aboard George Royal in the 1966 San Juan Capistrano. A member of the Canadian Racing Hall of Fame, he was inducted into Pimlico's National Jockeys Hall of Fame in 1956 and NMR's Hall of Fame in 1958. Longden's experience on half-mile tracks helped him think quicker and improve his neck reining in a crowd.

In 1966, Longden began training for Frank McMahon of Calgary, Canada, and prepared Majestic Prince, 1969 Kentucky Derby and Preakness Stakes victor, making him the only rider–trainer to win the Kentucky Derby. Longden often exercised his own horses to gain direct information and developed at least two dozen Stakes winners. His conditioned horses won 443 of 3,330 races, placed second 391 times and third 397 times, and earned $6,038,871. He quit training in 1990, one year after his second wife's death, and moved to Banning, CA. Longden, who served as director of the CTBA in 1964 and Sunland Par, NM, and an adviser to the SDCTC, considers founding the JG as his greatest contribution to racing. Longden married Helen McDonald in 1929 and had one son, Vance, before their 1939 divorce. He married Hazel Tarn, Al's daughter, in 1941 and had two children, Eric and Andrea. After divorcing in 1984, they remarried in 1985. Longden's sons and second wife were licensed trainers.

BIBLIOGRAPHY: Bob Baskett, "Boxcar Payoff," *TTR* 173 (May 6, 1961), p. 15; Gordon Beard, "Longden Learns by Riding Prince," Lexington (KY) *Leader*, May 13, 1969; Brainerd K. Beckwith, *The Longden Legend* (Cranbury, NJ, 1973); Ray Cave, "An Old Man with Two Chances to Win," *SI* 14 (May 1, 1961), pp. 23–25; Stephanie Diaz, "Johnny Longden: A Rider's Reverie," *TB* 32 (April 1993), pp. 44–47, 67; *DRF*, August 28, 1965; February 25, 1971; February 13, 1982; June 21, 1985; Jay Hovdey, "Longden Legend," *Spur* (January–February 1986), pp. 20, 22; Charles H. Johnson, "Johnny Longden," press release, October 28, 1956, Jockeys Hall of Fame, Pimlico Race Course, Baltimore, MD; Lexington (KY) *Leader*, August 17, 1965; Harry Mahan, "Longden Saga Unparalleled in Sports," *DRF*, March 12, 1966, pp. 6, 11; Mike Marten, "Longden Tribute Saturday; Legend Recalls Good Times," *DRF*, February 14, 1987, pp. 10–11; Mike Marten, "Longden Yearns for Call of the Bugle," *DRF*, July 18, 1991; *MT*, December 17, 1964; March 11, 1967; NTWA, *Members in the National Museum of Racing Hall of Fame* (Saratoga Springs, NY, 1976); Maryjean Wall, "Longden Pining for the Roar of the Track," Lexington (KY) *Herald Leader*, March 9, 1993, pp. C1, C5.

Steven P. Savage

PINCAY, Laffit Alegando Jr. (b. December 29, 1946, Panama City, Panama), thoroughbred jockey, is the son of Laffit Pincay, Sr., and Rosario Pincay and ranks among the strongest jockeys of all time. Writer Michael Watchmaker described him as a rider "who can practically pick a tiring horse up and carry him across the finishing line." Pincay, like fellow Panamanians Jorge Luis Velasquez* and Braulio Baeza,* was immersed in the horse-racing subculture from an early age. Pincay stated, "I got a job as a groom and hotwalker [a person who helps a horse to warm down after exercise]. I worked for no pay, just on the chance that somebody would give me the opportunity to ride." Pincay's celebrated strength as a jockey was achieved despite his slight five-foot-1-inch, 117-pound physical frame.

He was elected to the NMR Hall of Fame in 1975 at the relatively young age of 29. Pincay's precocious rise to prominence came from his daily eagerness to ride, love to travel, and stamina with numerous racing "starts" that would have overwhelmed a lesser jockey. He received the Eclipse Award as the nation's leading jockey for 1971, 1973, 1974, 1979, and 1985. Two of Pincay's accomplishments may never be repeated. He won three consecutive Belmont Stakes, triumphing aboard Conquistador Cielo in 1982, Caveat in 1983, and Swale (OS) in 1984. On March 14, 1989, he became the only jockey to have seven wins on a single program at the Santa Anita Race Track in Arcadia, CA.

By the end of the 1992 racing season, Pincay had made 37,473 starts and recorded 7,888 first places, 6,210 second places, and 5,174 third places. In virtually 50 percent of his starts, Pincay placed. He ranks second to Willie Shoemaker (OS) in career victories with 8,055 through 1993. Not surprisingly, Pincay leads jockeys in career earnings with the astronomical amount of $177,071,603. Among many successful years of racing, 1987 and 1989 races remain special for Pincay. He triumphed in the Kentucky Derby on Swale in 1989 and rode Le Glorieux to victory in the Laurel-Washington, D.C. International in 1987.

He and his wife Jeanine have a daughter, Lisa, and a son, Laffit III.

BIBLIOGRAPHY: *NYRA Media Guide*, undated, T. G. Gilcoyne Collection, NMR, Saratoga Springs, NY; Ron Smith, *TSN Chronicle of Twentieth Century Sport* (New York, 1992); Michael Watchmaker, "Horse Racing," in *Athletes* (New York, 1985).

Scott A.G.M. Crawford

VELASQUEZ, Jorge (b. December 28, 1964, Chepo, Panama), thoroughbred jockey, stated, "I always loved horses as a child. I began my first job on the track walking horses in Panama. My small size told me I should be a jockey and that's how the story went." Velasquez's upbringing resembled that of fellow thoroughbred jockeys Braulio Baeza* and Angel Cordero, Jr.* Michael Watchmaker, who described the childhood of the typical jockey, could have been summarizing Velasquez's youth. "Being a jockey . . . takes years of training. Often jockeys are bred, born into families involved in some way with horses. . . . They have an advantage in that they learn 'the beast' at a very early age."

Velasquez has enjoyed an illustrious racing career full of memorable moments. He won 57 Stakes races in 1985, setting a single-year record. Jockey Craig Perret equaled that number in 1990, while Pat Day* ended the 1991 season with 60 victories. Velasquez's life was highlighted by his election to the NMR Hall of Fame in 1990. In 1969, he led the nation's jockeys in money earned with $2,542,315. Four years earlier at the Garden State Park in New Jersey, he won six straight races on six mounts. He was named the New York champion jockey in 1971, 1972, 1974, 1976, and 1978 and still enjoyed much success in the 1980s. At the inaugural meet of the Arlington International Race Course in 1989, the Panama native helped forge a special trans-Atlantic sporting connection. He rode Unknown Quantity II, owned by Queen Elizabeth II, to victory.

Through the 1993 season, Velasquez had recorded 6,611 first places in over 38,600 career starts to rank fourth on the all-time list and earned $122,043,875.

He considers his sense of pace as his strongest asset as a jockey and Alydar as his favorite horse. He and his wife Margarita live in Woodmere, NY, and have three children.

BIBLIOGRAPHY: *NYRA Media Guide*, undated, T. G. Gilcoyne Collection, NMR, Saratoga Springs, NY; Ron Smith, *TSN Chronicle of Twentieth Century Sport* (New York, 1992); Michael Watchmaker, "Horse Racing," in *Athletics* (New York, 1985).

Scott A.G.M. Crawford

ICE HOCKEY

ADAMS, Charles Francis (b. October 18, 1876, Newport, VT; d. October 2, 1947, Boston, MA), professional administrator, played a major role in the expansion of professional ice hockey in the United States. Adams, born of humble parents, started as chore boy at a corner grocery store and rose to chief executive officer of the First National Stores, a major grocery chain store operation. During his business career, he developed an interest in amateur hockey in the Boston area. He traveled to Montreal, Canada, in March 1924 to witness the Stanley Cup finals between the Montreal Canadiens (NHL) and the Calgary Tigers (WCHL). Adams loved the professional game and approached NHL president Frank Calder concerning the possibility of securing an NHL franchise for Boston, MA. The Boston franchise was obtained by midsummer 1924. With the assistance of Art Ross, the Boston Bruins were assembled and played their first game in December. The contest marked the first played by the NHL in the United States.

Boston's initial efforts proved unsuccessful, as the Bruins won only six games. The Bruins improved in 1925–1926, as Adams planned to provide a winner for Boston's demanding fans. The dissolution of the WCHL in 1926 permitted Adams to use his substantial financial resources to obtain stars Eddie Shore, Harry Oliver, Perk Galbraith, Archie Briden, and Harry Meeking. Some 40 WCHL players joined other new NHL franchises. Conn Smythe, the creator of the New York Rangers, obtained Bill Cook and Bun Cook. Dick Irvin, George Hay, and Gord Fraser joined the Chicago Blackhawks, while the Detroit Falcons (Red Wings) purchased Frank Fredrickson, Frank Foyston, Clem Laughlin, and Jack Walker.

With Adams's financial impetus, the NHL developed into a viable international professional league. Baseball nor the fledgling NFL held international status. After Boston acquired the player strength to make the Bruins a serious contender, Adams sought to secure better playing facilities. The

Bruins initially played in the small Boston Arena, but Boston needed an all-purpose venue for all indoor sports. Adams guaranteed $500,000 over a four-year term for the 24 regular-season home games the Bruins would play. This action allowed the construction of a Boston Garden facility, which opened on November 20, 1928. Some 17,000 fans, including those who broke down the doors of the 13,909 capacity arena, watched the Montreal Canadiens defeat the Bruins, 1–0. The Bruins rebounded from the defeat eventually to win the Stanley Cup in a two-game series with the New York Rangers. Adams tasted Stanley Cup victories on two more occasions during his ownership tenure. The Bruins defeated the Toronto Maple Leafs, four games to one, in 1938–1939 and Detroit, four games to none, in 1940–1941.

Two other sports, thoroughbred horse racing and baseball, claimed Adams's interest. Adams played a major role in creating Suffolk Downs Race Track and served as the motivating force behind the passing of the pari-mutuel bill in Massachusetts. He also became a major shareholder in the Boston Braves (NL) baseball club and proved instrumental in the campaign to permit Sunday baseball. Weston, his son, said of his father, "Where he got his interest in sports, I don't know. He studied and worked so hard as a young man he had not the time for them." He was elected to the Hockey Hall of Fame in Toronto, Canada, in 1960.

BIBLIOGRAPHY: Charles T. Adams file, Hockey Hall of Fame, Toronto, Canada; *The NHL Official Guide & Record Book*, 1991–1992.

Roger A. Godin

BROWN, George V. (b. October 21, 1880, Boston, MA; d. October 17, 1937, Boston, MA), amateur and professional administrator, helped pioneer ice hockey in the United States. After the Boston Arena was built in 1910, the Boston AtA hockey team was formed. Brown served as the driving force behind the Boston team, which played top amateur eastern U.S. clubs and leading Canadian and college teams. When the Boston Arena burned down in 1918, Brown formed the corporation constructing the new arena. He then managed the new building and continued the AtA team. Brown's allied interests in track and field and the Olympic games brought about his support for Olympic hockey competition at the Chamonix, France, Winter Games in 1924. The Boston team formed the basis of the 1924 U.S. Olympic team, providing 7 of the 10 members. The United States finished second, losing only to Canada, 6–1, in the finals.

Brown was not involved initially in professional hockey. Once Boston secured the first American NHL franchise, however, he soon entered the professional scene. When the Bruins moved into the new Boston Garden in 1928, Brown helped organize the CAL, a forerunner of the present AHL, and entered the Boston Tigers (AHL). In 1934, Brown became general manager of both the Boston Arena and Boston Garden. His American pioneering role continued, as he constantly boosted ice hockey at all levels. Tom Hines, founder of the Massachusetts State High School Hockey Tournament, recalled Brown's astute foresight regarding the future of high school hockey, "I told George V. Brown ... when he was in charge of the Boston Arena we didn't make very much money in that first go. He said not to worry about it. He felt high school hockey would someday fill Boston Arena. I guess he was right. It's now filling Boston Garden."

Brown, who married Elizabeth Gallagher, retained his positions with the Boston Arena and Boston Garden until his death. His honors included selection as a member of the Hockey Hall of Fame in Toronto, Canada, in 1961 and the U.S. Hockey Hall of Fame in Eveleth, MN, in 1973. His son, Walter A. (IS), succeeded him as general manager of the Boston Arena and Boston Garden in 1937.

BIBLIOGRAPHY: William Collins, Builder Biography, Hockey Hall of Fame, Toronto, Canada; Roger A. Godin, *U.S. Hockey Hall of Fame 1973–1983 Enshrinee Biographies* (Eveleth, MN, 1984).

Roger A. Godin

CHELIOS, Christos "Chris" (b. January 25, 1962, Chicago, IL), college and professional player, was educated at Mt. Carmel, IL, and San Diego, CA, public schools, and the University of Wisconsin (WCHA). Chelios's family moved to San Diego when he was 14 years old. He continued his ice hockey development there prior to entering Wisconsin. The Montreal Canadiens (NHL) drafted him fifth as the fortieth overall selection in the 1981 Entry Draft. An outstanding college player, he performed on the 1982–1983 NCAA Champion Wisconsin Badgers and made the All-Tournament team. A year earlier, he had been named to the WCHA Second All-Star team and helped the Badgers finish second to the Canadian-dominated University of North Dakota in the NCAA Tournament.

After his Wisconsin career, Chelios played for the 1984 U.S. Olympic team and joined future American NHL players Pat LaFontaine (IS), Al Iafrate,* and Ed Olczyk.* He turned professional after the Sarajevo, Yugoslavia, Winter Olympic games and remained a stalwart on the Montreal Canadiens defense through the 1989–1990 season. In his first full season, he made the NHL's 1984–1985 All-Rookie team. The Canadiens won the Stanley Cup against the Calgary Flames in 1985–1986 and reached the Stanley Cup finals in 1988–1989. The latter season featured Chelios winning the James Norris Memorial Trophy as the NHL's best defenseman and be named a First Team All-Star. Chelios reached career highs in goals (20) in 1987–1988, assists (58) in 1988–1989, and points (73) in 1988–1989 with the Canadiens. Hockey observers believed that maturity came late for Chelios, although some noticed it before he won the Norris Trophy.

Chelios returned to his hometown in June 1990, when Montreal traded him and a second-round draft pick to the Chicago Blackhawks (NHL) for Quebec native Denis Savard. The trade of the two superstars was reportedly triggered by long-standing animosities between the respective players and their coaches. The Savard feud with Chicago coach Mike Keenan was well known, but Chelios's differences with then-Montreal coach Pat Burns were less publicized. Since arriving in Chicago, he has continued his high level of play and characteristic belligerency. The 1991–1992 season featured the Blackhawks reach the Stanley Cup finals, as Chelios logged a career-high 245 penalty minutes. An incident in the Stanley Cup finals with Pittsburgh Penguins defenseman Larry Murphy resulted in a costly penalty, assuring Chicago of a crucial loss. He has been involved in controversial off-ice incidents with the U.S. Olympic team and in Madison, WI, in June 1990. In 1992–1993, Chelios tied career highs for assists (58) and points (73).

Through the 1993–1994 season, Chelios has scored 124 goals and 438 assists for 562 points in 719 games. He has participated in 11 Stanley Cup playoffs, logging a career-high 21 points in 1991–1992 on 6 goals and 15 assists. He has played in the 1985, 1990, 1991, 1992, 1993, and 1994 All-Star Games and again was awarded the Norris Trophy for the 1992–1993 season. Internationally, Chelios has played for the United States in the 1984, 1987, and 1991 USCC Tournaments. Chelios and his wife Tracee have two sons, Dean and Jake.

BIBLIOGRAPHY: *Chicago Blackhawks Press Guide*, 1992–1993; "Chris Chelios," in *Hockey Stars* (n.d.); Stan Fischler, "Who's Better, Chris Chelios vs. Scott Stevens?" *HD* 21 (December 1992); Zander Hollander, ed., *The Complete Encyclopedia of Hockey* (Detroit, MI, 1993); *The NHL Official Guide & Record Book 1991–1992*; *USA Today*, April 19, 1994, p. 6C; Mike Zeisberger, "Chelios Tells His Side of the Story," Toronto (Canada) *Star*, August 20, 1990.

Roger A. Godin

HATCHER, Kevin John (b. September 9, 1966, Detroit, MI), professional player, came from an ice hockey–playing family. His father, who played semiprofessional football, guided Hatcher and brothers Mark and Derian in their U.S. ice hockey careers. The second oldest of five children, he began skating at four years old and playing on a team at age five. "While some other kids watched basketball and football, I remember watching hockey when I was real little. I was good for my age and then finally at 16, I got on a good team that won several tournaments," he recalled. The club, the Detroit Compuware, included eventual teammate Al Iafrate.*

Hatcher's selection by the North Bay, Canada, Centennials (OHL) followed. At North Bay, he played one year with his older brother, Mark, as defenseman. They were imposing on the blueline, with Mark being six foot five inches, 205 pounds and Kevin being six foot four inches, 225 pounds. The Washington Capitals (NHL) made Hatcher their first pick and seventeenth overall selection in the 1984 Entry Draft. This draft held significance for American players, as Iafrate, Ed Olczyk,* and David Quinn were also chosen in the first round. Hatcher scored his first NHL goal in his second game with Washington during the 1984–1985 season. He spent almost the entire year with North Bay, however, and was named to the OHL's Second All-Star team. He joined the Capitals permanently for the 1985–1986 season and became a fixture on defense, being initially paired with two-time Norris Trophy winner Rod Langway (IS).

Hatcher's second season saw him paired less frequently with Langway, as he made some glaring mistakes. The 1986–1987 season began with an impressive performance for the United States in the USCC Tournament, but a torn knee cartilage delayed his regular-season start by nine games. Over the subsequent seasons, Hatcher blossomed into the quintessential offensive defenseman. Besides possessing one of the hardest NHL wrist shots, he has developed the necessary instincts to properly judge when to move up and shoot or stay back and defend. After averaging 11 goals a season during his first five years, he recorded 24 tallies in 1990–1991, 17 in 1991–1992, 34 in 1992–1993, and 16 in 1993–1994. The 34 goals represent the eighth highest total by a defenseman in a single season. Through the 1993–1994 season, he had scored 149 goals and 277 assists for 426 points in 685 regular-season games. He recorded his first hat trick on January 13, 1993, against the New York Rangers, the first by a defenseman in the Capitals' history.

When Langway sat out the remainder of the 1992–1993 season, Hatcher was selected as the Capitals' eighth captain in February 1993. In January 1995, Washington traded him to the Dallas Stars (NHL). He also played for the United States in the 1991 USCC Tournament, represented Washington in the 1990 and 1991 NHL All-Star Games, and participated in 10 Stanley Cup playoff seasons.

BIBLIOGRAPHY: *The NHL Official Guide & Record Book 1991–1992; 1992–1993 Washington Capitals Game Program*, January 23, 1993; Dean Schuyler, "Coming of Age in the NHL," *Washington Capitals Fan Club News*, January 1988; *USA Today*, April 19, 1994, p. 6C.

                                                                    Roger A. Godin

IAFRATE, Alberto Anthony Jr. "Al" "Alley Cat" "Drifter" (b. March 21, 1966, Dearborn, MI), professional player, is the son of Alberto Iafrate, Sr., an Italian immigrant, and grew up in the Detroit suburb of Livonia. He played youth ice hockey for the Detroit Compuware team, which Team Illinois upset in the USAH 1982 National Midget Tournament championship game. Iafrate performed an additional midget hockey season and then joined the 1984 U.S. Olympic team. Following the Sarajevo, Yugoslavia, Winter Olympics and Iafrate's brief stint with the Belleville, Canada, Bulls (OHL), the Toronto Maple Leafs (NHL) made him their first choice and fourth overall selection in the 1984 Entry Draft.

Iafrate debuted with the Maple Leafs as an 18-year-old defenseman in the

1984–1985 season. Following a good rookie season with five goals and 16 assists in 68 games, the six-foot-three-inch defenseman reported overweight for his second season. He weighed 241 pounds, 21 pounds above his normal playing weight. The extra pounds gave rise to some unflattering nicknames and incurred the wrath of both coach Dan Maloney and assistant coach John Brophy. The coaches worked him hard, causing Iafrate to leave the Maple Leafs unannounced. He did not remain away long, however, returning to have a reasonably good season with eight goals and 25 assists in 65 games. Inconsistency plagued him. His erratic performance was blamed on immaturity as a teenager turning to adulthood under the pressures of playing in a hockey media capital. Iafrate's subsequent marriage in 1986 to longtime girlfriend Melissa Weber marked a significant turning point in his career.

Iafrate came to training camp for the 1986–1987 season a more self-assured person. He finished his third NHL season with 9 goals and 21 assists in 80 games and recorded his first playoff goal. After declining amidst much criticism to play for the United States in the USCC, he started quickly in the 1987–1988 season. He scored 10 goals in his first 19 games, finishing with a then-career-high 22 goals. The Maple Leafs were quickly eliminated by the Detroit Red Wings in the playoffs, but Iafrate scored 3 goals in the 6-game series. The next two years proved productive for Iafrate, highlighted by a career-high 42 assists in the 1989–1990 season. A knee injury, suffered in a March 24, 1990, game against the Quebec Nordiques, proved instrumental. Iafrate's belief that the Maple Leafs management forced him back into action too quickly at the start of the 1990–1991 season, combined with coach Tom Watt's decision to use him less, made him unhappy in Toronto. Toronto traded him to the Washington Capitals (NHL) in January 1991 for center Peter Zezel and defenseman Bob Rouse. The trade reunited him with midget teammate Kevin Hatcher,* enabling him to attain career highs in goals (25) and points (66) in the 1992–1993 season. His 237 penalty minutes in the 1990–1991 split season with Toronto and Washington remains a career high. In March 1994, Washington traded him to the Boston Bruins (NHL) for winger Joe Juneau.

During his 10-year NHL career, Iafrate has scored 144 goals and 295 assists for 439 points in 740 regular-season games. He also has participated in playoffs seven seasons and in the 1988, 1990, 1993, and 1994 All-Star Games. Internationally, he has played on the 1991 USCC team. His marriage to Melissa Weber ended in divorce.

BIBLIOGRAPHY: Damien Cox, "Relaxed-Looking Iafrate 'Feels Good' with Capitals," Toronto (Canada) *Star*, January 18, 1991; Steve Dryden, "The Drifter and Eddie-O," *IH* (January–February 1988); David Ferry, "Iafrate Gives the Capitals Another Threat on the Blue Line," *Stars and Stripes* 4 (March 2, 1991); *The NHL Guide & Record Book, 1992–1993; Washington Capitals Press Guide*, 1992–1993; *USA Today*, April 19, 1994, p. 6C.

Roger A. Godin

IKOLA, Willard John "Ike" (b. July 28, 1932, Eveleth, MN), college player, high school coach, and scout, is the son of John Ikola, a carpenter, and Sadie (Nara) Ikola and graduated in 1950 from Eveleth High School, where he won three letters each in football, ice hockey, and baseball and served as team captain in all three sports. An All-Range football player in his senior year, he was named All-State goalie in ice hockey three consecutive years, from 1948 to 1950. The Eveleth hockey team won three State tournament championships with undefeated seasons. Ikola played baseball in the high school State tournament in 1949 and was selected outstanding high school athlete of the Iron Range in 1950. The five-foot-eight-inch Ikola weighed 155 pounds.

Ikola, who received a hockey scholarship at the University of Michigan (WCHA) in 1950, played four years of college hockey and participated in freshman baseball. As a sophomore and junior, he starred at goalie on the NCAA championship Michigan squads in 1952 and 1953. The 1954 Wolverines placed third in the NCAA tournament. His honors included being named All-America in 1952, 1953, and 1954 and making the WCHA and NCAA All-Tournament teams those seasons. Sphinx and Michigumo honor societies also invited him. Ikola, who was chosen for Michigan's College Hockey Hall of Fame and Hall of Honor, graduated in June 1954 with a B.S. degree in education and physical education major.

Through the ROTC program, Ikola was commissioned a second lieutenant in the U.S. Air Force. The Detroit Red Wings (NHL) drafted him, but he declined their invitation to fulfill his military commitment. From 1954 to 1958, he served on active duty with the U.S. Air Force and received navigation wings in 1955. He played on the 1956 U.S. Olympic hockey team, which finished second for Silver Medal honors at the Cortina d'Ampezzo, Italy, Winter Games. Ikola, who was named to the All-World Olympic hockey team, played on the 1957 and 1958 U.S. National teams. In 1958, the Chicago Blackhawks (NHL) drafted Ikola, but the latter accepted a high school hockey job instead.

Ikola spent his entire hockey coaching career at Edina, MN, High School in suburban Minneapolis, MN. His coaching career spanned 33 years from October 1958 to June 1991. He also served as assistant football coach for 25 years and taught physical education and health classes. His impressive scholastic coaching record in hockey included 616 wins, 149 losses, and 38 ties, with 22 of his teams winning LC titles. His Edina teams also won 19 sectional titles and eight state tournaments including 1969, 1971, 1974, 1978, 1979, 1982, 1986, and 1988. Two teams finished second for State titles, while 4 teams won consolation honors. Ikola highly regards all 8 of his State title teams, taking special pride in his 1974 undefeated squad.

Ikola married Laurie McLean on December 28, 1954, and has four children, Debbie, Matt, Steve, and Sarah. His numerous honors include being chosen Minnesota High School Coach of the Year eight times, being elected to the MSHSL Hall of Fame, the U.S. Hockey Hall of Fame, and the NHSS Hall of Fame, and receiving the Mariucci Award from American College Coaches.

Ikola's memberships include the MHSCA, MHSHCA, AHCA, and the Minnesota Federation of Teachers. He spent 18 years in the U.S. Army Reserve, retiring with the rank of lieutenant colonel. The Edina, MN, resident, who enjoys camping, fishing, and all sports, scouted part-time for the Minnesota North Stars hockey club (NHL) and conducts youth hockey clinics.

BIBLIOGRAPHY: Willard Ikola, letter to Stan W. Carlson, January 6, 1993; Minnesota High School League Archives, Brooklyn Center, MN.

Stan W. Carlson

LEETCH, Brian Joseph (b. March 3, 1968, Corpus Christi, TX), college and professional player, is the son of John Leetch and Janet Leetch and attended Avon Old Farms School for Boys in Avon, CT, and Boston College (HE). Leetch grew up in Connecticut and proved an outstanding ice hockey player at Avon Old Farms. He collected MVP honors two consecutive seasons, making the All–New England Prep School squad and being selected New England Prep School Player of the Year in 1985–1986. Such achievements persuaded the New York Rangers (NHL) to select him in the first round as the ninth overall choice in the 1986 NHL Entry Draft.

Although playing only one year of college hockey, Leetch left his mark by winning HE Player of the Year and Rookie of the Year awards. He led Boston College to the HE Championship and was named to the All-America and All-HE teams. His honors included being a finalist and first freshman ever nominated for the Hobey Baker Memorial Award, symbolic of college hockey's best player, in 1986–1987. After his freshman year, Leetch played for the U.S. Olympic team and began the pre-Olympic schedule in August 1987. Coach Dave Peterson named him captain in December 1987. In the 80 games leading up to the Calgary, Canada, Winter Olympics in February 1988, he paced the U.S. team with 74 points on 13 goals and 61 assists. The U.S. team played well in the loss to the Soviet Union but finished seventh overall. Leetch, who scored 1 goal and 5 assists in 6 games, quickly appeared in a New York Ranger (NHL) uniform.

Leetch quickly established himself not only as one of the premier American hockey players but as one of the top NHL defensemen. After playing 17 games at the end of the 1987–1988 season, he won the Calder Trophy as the NHL's Rookie of the Year for 1988–1989. His 71 points on 23 goals and 48 points ranked fifth among NHL defensemen, while his 23 goals established an NHL record for a rookie defenseman. The following season, Leetch played in the Rangers' first 71 games before suffering a fractured ankle in March 1990. His 45 assists and 272 shots led New York defensemen.

Leetch represented the Rangers in the All-Star Game. The 1990–1991 season saw Leetch capture the Norris Trophy as the NHL's outstanding defenseman, making him only the third American to win the coveted award. His 88 points on 16 goals and 72 assists placed him fourth among all defensemen, while his assists total ranked sixth highest in the NHL. He finished third in the NHL with 52 power play points and returned to the All-Star Game. Leetch once again won the Norris Trophy in 1991–1992, finishing ninth in the NHL scoring race with 22 goals and 80 assists for 102 points. He appeared again in the All-Star Game and helped the Rangers take the Patrick Division championship for the second time during his career. Leetch's considerable offensive skills have given the Rangers an attacking defenseman in the mold of Bobby Orr and Paul Coffey. In 1993–1994, he tallied 23 goals and 56 assists for 79 points and played in his fourth NHL All-Star Game. In 1994, the New York Rangers won the Stanley Cup for the first time since 1940, defeating the Vancouver Canucks four games to three. Leetch scored 11 goals in the playoffs, being only the fifth defenseman and the first American to win the Conn Smythe MVP award.

Leetch has played for the United States in the 1987 and 1991 USCC Tournaments and the 1987 and 1989 World Tournaments and was named the best player on the 1989 U.S. team. Through the 1993–1994 season, he had scored 103 goals and 343 assists for 446 points in 437 regular-season games and participated in four Stanley Cup playoff seasons.

BIBLIOGRAPHY: Zander Hollander, ed., *The Complete Encyclopedia of Hockey* (Detroit, MI, 1993); *USA Today*, April 19, 1994, p. 6C; *USA Today*, June 15, 1994, pp. 1C, 3C; Austin Murphy, "Oh, You Kids, You," *SI* 70 (January 30, 1989), pp. 67–68; *New York Rangers Press Guide*, 1990–1991.

Roger A. Godin

MILBURY, Michael James "Mike" (b. June 17, 1952, Brighton, MA), college and professional athlete, coach, and administrator, participated in several sports at Walpole, MA, High School and concentrated on ice hockey after receiving a football scholarship to Colgate University. He started in ice hockey at Colgate (ECAC), an institution that featured predominantly Canadian student athletes. After graduating with a B.A. degree in sociology in 1974, Milbury signed as a free agent with the Boston Bruins (NHL) in November 1974. Although a tireless worker, he had previously recognized that his work ethic alone would not be enough to allow him to play regularly in the NHL. He later recalled, "In the winter of 1974, I was invited to fill in for an injured guy with the Bruins' American League Club, then located in Boston. I still remember the embarrassment of my first workout. Guys were whizzing by me, around me. I was on my backside more than my feet. It was horrendous. That's when I realized I'd have to learn to skate if I intended to play in the NHL. Which is what I intended to do, definitely."

Milbury played two seasons for the Rochester, NY, Americans (AHL) before being promoted to the parent Bruins for the 1976–1977 season. In order to improve his skating, he and his wife Debbie arrived at the rink in Rochester, NY, at 6:30 A.M. daily. For the next 90 minutes, he would shoot the puck into the corner of the rink from the blue line, and she would wheel and retrieve it. Don Cherry, then Bruins' coach, for whom Milbury later played, recalled, "I'd arrive about 7:45 and he'd have an hour in already, him and his wife, who was six months pregnant. . . . I told myself right then, with determination like that, this kid was bound to make himself into a big leaguer, come hell or high water. And he was. I put him among the top 10 defensemen in the league [1978]. Yet less than five years ago, his feet would get tangled up and he'd fall down anytime he had to turn."

Before his rookie season with Boston, he played for the United States in the first USCC Tournament in 1976. Once in Boston, he became a fixture on defense for the next 11 years. During those seasons, the Bruins made the NHL playoffs every year but one. In both the 1976–1977 and 1977–1978 campaigns, Boston lost in the Stanley Cup finals to the Montreal Canadiens. Milbury's 47 penalty minutes in the 1976–1977 series marked the high for the playoffs. His best total points production came in 1977–1978 with 8 goals and 30 assists for 38 points. He initially retired after the 1984–1985 season and served as assistant coach for Boston under Butch Goring. Boston's injuries the next season forced Milbury back to active duty from February 1986 through the 1986–1987 season finale. He finished his regular-season NHL career with 49 goals and 189 assists for 238 points and recorded 1,552 penalty minutes.

The 1987–1988 and 1988–1989 seasons found Milbury as both coach and general manager of the Maine Mariners (AHL). The Bruins named him head coach in May 1989. Milbury led Boston in 1989–1990 to the Stanley Cup finals, where they lost to the Edmonton Oilers, four games to one. In the 1990–1991 season, the Bruins were eliminated by the eventual Stanley Cup Champion Pittsburgh Penguins in the PWC finals, four games to two. In May 1991, Milbury stepped down as coach to become the team's assistant general manager. He had contemplated a management move for some time and did not leave coaching because of stress. In April 1994, Boston College appointed Milbury head coach. He resigned this position two months later without coaching a game there and joined ESPN as NHL studio analyst in September 1994. He and his wife Debbie have two sons, Owen and Luke, and two daughters, Allison and Caitlin.

BIBLIOGRAPHY: *Boston Bruins Press Guide*, 1986–1987; "Bruins Name Mike Milbury as Coach," Toronto (Canada) *Star*, May 17, 1989; "Milbury Moves to Assistant GM," Toronto (Canada) *Star*, May 30, 1991; *The NHL Official Guide & Record Book*, 1987–1988; Jim Proudfoot, "Wife Helped Mike Milbury, a Big Leaguer," Toronto (Canada) *Star*, February 15, 1978.

Roger A. Godin

MURRAY, Hugh "Muzz" (b. October 1, 1892, Sault Ste. Marie, MI; d. February 13, 1961, Sault Ste. Marie, MI), amateur and professional player, grew up in the Upper Peninsula of Michigan, an early spawning ground for ice hockey. The world's first professional hockey league, the IPHL, was centered there under the leadership of dental surgeon Dr. J. L. "Doc" Gibson. Native American stars, including Joe Linder (IS), Nick Kahler, "Taffy" Abel (IS), and Murray, learned their ice hockey skills there.

Murray's brilliant play as a cover point (defenseman) with Sault Ste. Marie, MI (AAHA) earned him a professional hockey contract with Sault Ste. Marie (PCL). Between 1912 and 1918, Murray consistently excelled in the Western Division of the AAHA, then the highest level of organized competition in the United States. An early press account noted, " 'Muzz' Murray with his energetic outburst of speed and his remarkable elusive power, starred for the Soo. 'Muzz' proved the effectiveness of his rushes by scoring one of the Soo's goals after bringing the puck the entire length of the rink and passing all the Calumet players." Murray captained the 1914–1915 Sault Ste. Marie team to the Western Division Championship before losing to Cleveland in the finals and was named to the AAHA All-Western team for that season.

Murray, only the second American-developed player to participate in the Stanley Cup finals, played for the Seattle, WA, Metropolitans (PCHA) in the historic 1918–1919 series against the Montreal Canadiens. The series was suspended at 2–2–1 due to an influenza epidemic. Murray, the third leading scorer in the series, subsequently appeared in the 1919–1920 finals against the Ottawa Senators. After playing one more season with Seattle, he closed his career with Calgary, Canada (WCHL) in 1921–1922 and later performed briefly for Tulsa, OK (AAHA).

Murray was known as both a rough and tumble player as well as a scorer. His spirit, fire, and drive made him a team leader. Another early newspaper story recounted, " 'Muzz' Murray took an ugly slide into the boards, striking his face on the side. His nose was injured and also his head. Another time he got a jab in the mouth with a stick, but none of these retarded his playing the least." Murray continued playing local senior amateur hockey until nearly age 60 while serving as Superintendent of Streets for Sault Ste. Marie, MI. He also took an active role in the development of youth hockey in his hometown. In 1987, the U.S. Hockey Hall of Fame in Eveleth, MN, enshrined him.

BIBLIOGRAPHY: Roger A. Godin, *U.S. Hockey Hall of Fame 1987 Enshrinee Biography* (Eveleth, MN, 1987).

Roger A. Godin

NORRIS, James D. Sr. "Big Jim" (b. December 10, 1879, St. Catherines, Ontario, Canada; d. December 4, 1952, Chicago, IL), professional sports administrator, played a significant role in arena ownership in the United States and the development of the Detroit Red Wings as a major NHL power. Norris grew up in Montreal, Canada, and in his grammar school years formed an early love for ice hockey, which permanently remained with him. He regarded ice hockey as the king of sports and later built a skating rink in the backyard of his house in Lake Forest, IL. Potential butlers and chauffeurs allegedly could not qualify unless they could make the house staff ice hockey team. Norris played both ice hockey and lacrosse at McGill University and performed as a defenseman for the Montreal Victorias (AHA) in the ice sport.

Norris moved to the United States in 1898 and eventually controlled or held interests in a business empire worth about $200,000,000. The empire included a railroad, a fleet of 40 freighters on the Great Lakes, the Norris Grain Company, and the Norris Cattle Company, which operated three of the largest U.S. cattle ranches. Since real estate sold at 10 cents on the dollar following the 1929 stock market crash, Norris bought up large acreage in Indiana, numerous grain elevators, a large interest in the Chicago, IL, furniture mart, the bankrupt Olympia Stadium in Detroit, MI, and the facility's NHL hockey team, the Falcons (Red Wings). Eventually, he became one of the largest stockholders in New York's Madison Square Garden. When the $6.5 million Chicago Stadium went bankrupt, he purchased it at a fraction of the original cost. Norris also held large interests in the St. Louis Arena, Omaha Arena, and Indianapolis Arena.

Prior to acquiring the Detroit team, Norris had owned the Chicago Shamrocks and was denied a Chicago NHL franchise. The Chicago Blackhawks (NHL) owner, Major Frederic McLaughlin, had refused to approve Norris's bid for a second NHL team in Chicago, thus setting off a colorful feud between the two owners. After purchasing the Detroit franchise, Norris changed its name to the Red Wings. The Red Wings wore the insignia of the Montreal AmAA, to which he had once belonged. He retained Jack Adams as coach and launched one of the sport's great dynasties. The Red Wings won Stanley Cups in 1935–1936 and 1936–1937 with their first great line of Larry Aurie, Marty Barry, and Herbie Lewis. Sid Howe led another line, while Ebbie Goodfellow excelled on defense. Detroit's "Liniment Line" of Sid Abel, Don Grosso, and Ed Wares helped the Red Wings win the NHL season championship and Stanley Cup in 1942–1943. Before his death, Norris saw Detroit capture two more Stanley Cups in 1949–1950 and 1951–1952. During this era, Jack Adams and Tommy Ivan launched the Red Wings to four straight NHL season championships and the two Stanley Cup victories. All-time great Gordie Howe debuted in the NHL during this era, joined by outstanding players "Red" Kelly, Ted Lindsay, and Marty Pavelich. Since Norris liked hard-hitting players, the Red Wings usually reflected that preference. Goodfellow, Lindsay, Howe, and Jack "Blackjack" Stewart became his favorite players. He also believed that members of his team should always dress like champions and wear a coat and tie with shined shoes for dinner on the road.

Norris exhibited interest in boxing and horse racing, owning a stable. He took over the boxing empire of the ailing Mike Jacobs (IS) in 1949 and formed the IBC, heading it for nine years. Norris promoted numerous championship bouts and ushered in the sport's television era, backed by John Reed Kilpatrick (S), chairman of the Madison Square Garden board. Norris's children, James D., Jr., Bruce A., and Marguerite, inherited his vast fortune. He was elected to the Hockey Hall of Fame in Toronto, Canada, in 1958.

BIBLIOGRAPHY: "Jim Norris, Sr., Noted Figure in Hockey, Dies," Canadian *Press*, December 5, 1952; Robert A. Styer, *The Encyclopedia of Hockey* (Cranbury, NJ, 1970).

Roger A. Godin

OLCZYK, Edward Jr. "Eddie" (b. August 16, 1966, Chicago, IL), professional player, is the oldest son of Edward Olczyk, Sr., and Diane Olczyk and attended public schools in Palos Heights, IL, and Stratford, Ontario. Olczyk excelled in Chicago area youth ice hockey and for Team Illinois, which won the USAH's National Midget Championship over Detroit Compuware. The latter team featured future American NHL players Al Iafrate,* Chris Chelios* and Pat LaFontaine (IS). He subsequently played Junior B ice hockey in Stratford, Ontario, scoring a league-leading 141 points. The hometown Chicago Blackhawks (NHL) made right-wing Olczyk their first choice and third overall pick in the 1984 Entry Draft.

Olczyk spent the 1983–1984 season with the U.S. Olympic team. His play forced coach Lou Vairo's staff to take notice. He performed regularly on the squad, collaborating with LaFontaine and David A. Jensen to form the teenage "Diaper Line." He scored 21 goals and 47 assists in 62 pre-Olympic games. The seventh-place finish at the 1984 Sarajevo, Yugoslavia, Winter Olympic Games proved disappointing after the United States' 1980 Gold Medal victory, but Olczyk retained fond memories of the event.

Olczyk joined the Blackhawks for the 1984–1985 season, achieving instant celebrity and on-ice success. "In my first game I scored a goal and the fans started chanting my name like they used to for Tony Esposito," he recalled. "I'd never felt better in my whole life." He finished his rookie season with 20 goals and 30 assists and scored 6 goals and 5 assists in the playoffs. The following season, he played with center Troy Murray and left-wing Curt Fraser and improved to 29 goals and 50 assists to help Chicago earn first place in the Norris Division. A groin injury and concern over the death of a boyhood friend caused Olczyk to slump badly in the 1986–1987 season with only 16 goals and 35 assists. The hometown fans soon expressed their verbal displeasure, shouting "Eddie No-Check" and hurting the overly sensitive Olczyk. Some teammates protested that he received preferential treatment because of his hometown status.

During the 1987 USCC Tournament, Chicago traded Olyczyk with Al Secord to the Toronto Maple Leafs (NHL) for Rick Vaive, Steve Thomas, and Bob McGill. Olczyk responded with a career-best 42 goals and 33 assists. The 1988–1989 and 1989–1990 seasons proved equally productive, but Olczyk clashed with coach Doug Carpenter. Carpenter had taken over from John Brophy and George Armstrong after the 1988–1989 season. Olczyk was disappointed about not being named team captain and asked to be traded. Linemate Gary Leeman and Olczyk disagreed with Carpenter's systems of play. Toronto traded Olczyk and Mark Osborne to the Winnipeg Jets (NHL) in November 1990 for Dave Ellet and Paul Fenton. Olczyk completed the season in Winnipeg by reaching the 30-goal mark for the fourth time in his career. In December 1992, he was traded to the New York Rangers (NHL) for Tie Domi. During his 10-year NHL career, Olczyk has scored 263 goals and 363 assists for 626 points in 718 regular season games and has participated in six Stanley Cup playoff seasons.

Internationally, Olczyk has played for the United States in the 1987 and 1989 World Tournaments and in the 1987 and 1991 USCC. He married Diane Vickers in 1988, and they have two children.

BIBLIOGRAPHY: Damien Clark, "Olczyk 'Ecstatic' About Joining the Jets," Toronto (Canada) *Star*, November 12, 1990; Steve Dryden, "The Drifter and Eddie-O," *IH* (January–February 1988); Zander Hollander, ed., *The Complete Encyclopedia of Hockey* (Detroit, MI, 1993); *The NHL Official Guide & Record Book*, 1991–1992; *USA Today*, April 19, 1994, p. 6C.

                                                                    Roger A. Godin

OTTO, Joel Stuart (b. October 29, 1961, Elk River, MN), college and professional player, attended Bemidji, MI, State College, where he was selected the top NCAA Division II player in 1983–1984. He was nominated for the Hobey Baker Award, given annually to college hockey's outstanding player by the DeCathalon AC in Bloomington, MN.

The Calgary Flames (NHL) signed Otto as a free agent in September 1984 and sent him most of the 1984–1985 season to Moncton, Canada (AHL). He averaged over a point a game in the AHL, scoring 27 goals and 36 assists in 63 games. He played 17 games with the Calgary Flames in his rookie season, tallying 4 goals and 8 assists. Otto debuted in the NHL on November 23, 1984, against the St. Louis Blues, recording his first point on March 1, 1985, against the Montreal Canadiens and his first goal against the Los Angeles Kings on March 3, 1985.

Bob Johnson (IS), then Calgary's coach, enthusiastically supported Otto, who at six foot four inches and 220 pounds was difficult to move out of the slot. Johnson compared him sizewise to former Philadelphia Flyer forward Tim Kerr, but Otto has never scored at Kerr's level. "He doesn't have to score a lot of goals to be a valuable player for us," commented Johnson.

Otto, through the 1993–1994 season, had scored 159 goals and 248 assists for 407 points in 683 regular-season games. His best offensive production came in 1985–1986, his first complete NHL season, when he scored 25 goals and 59 points. In 1987–1988, he recorded a career-best 39 assists. When Calgary won the Stanley Cup in 1988–1989, he proved particularly productive in the playoffs with 6 goals and 13 assists for 19 points to establish a career playoff high. During the playoffs, he scored the winning goal at 19: 21 of overtime in Game 7 on April 15, 1989, to eliminate the Vancouver Canucks. Otto had finished the 1988–1989 regular season on an 11-game scoring streak (6 goals, 9 assists), the longest of his career. An aggressive player, he has averaged over 165 penalty minutes per season. Opposing teams frequently have coveted him.

Otto has played for the United States at the 1985 and 1990 World Tournaments and at the 1987 and 1991 USCC Tournaments. He captained the 1991 USCC team, centering the checking line and scoring four goals and helping the team make the finals against Canada. Otto married Kari Agar during the 1991 All-Star Game break.

BIBLIOGRAPHY: *Calgary Flames Press Guide*, 1992–1993; Eric Duhatschek, "Future Not Otto-Matic for Big, Bad Joel," *HN*, September 27, 1991; "Flames Let Otto Handle Scoring," Canadian *Press*, November 4, 1986; "Joel Otto," *HN*, February 7, 1986; *USA Today*, April 19, 1994, p. 6C.

Roger A. Godin

SUTER, Gary Lee (b. June 24, 1964, Madison, WI), college and professional player, was educated at Culver, IN, Military Academy and the University of Wisconsin-Madison (WCHA). His brothers, Bob and John, also played at Wisconsin, the former making the 1980 U.S. Olympic team. Suter and his brothers were recruited to Wisconsin by the late Bob Johnson (IS), who later coached him with the Calgary Flames (NHL). After playing two seasons at Wisconsin, Suter joined the Calgary Flames. Calgary made the defenseman a ninth-round pick and one hundred and eightieth overall selection in the 1984 Entry Draft.

Suter's initial 1985–1986 season for the Flames saw him capture the Calder Trophy as the NHL's top rookie, as he scored 18 goals and 50 assists for 68 points. His 6 assists on April 4, 1986, versus the Edmonton Oilers established a club record. The Flames made the Stanley Cup finals against the Montreal Canadiens, losing four games to one. Suter did not participate in the finals, as he suffered a broken leg in a preliminary series with Edmonton. Prior to the injury, he had scored a game-winning goal in an earlier playoff game. Suter played in the 1986 All-Star Game as a rookie and made return visits to the game in 1988, 1989, and 1991. The 1987–1988 season saw him reach career highs in both goals (21) and assists (70). He made the NHL All-Star Second Team and was nominated for the James Norris Trophy as the NHL's top defenseman. Suter suffered a broken jaw on April 11, 1989, versus the Vancouver Canucks, sidelining him for the remainder of the playoffs and once again preventing him from participating in the Stanley

Cup finals. The injury particularly disappointed Suter, as the Flames this time defeated Montreal, four games to two.

The 1989–1990 season saw Suter attain two 5-point games and record 4 points (1 goal, 3 assists) against the Quebec Nordiques in the first period on December 14, 1989, tying a team record for most points in a single period. His four hundredth career point came on an assist against the Los Angeles Kings on February 12, 1991, while his five hundredth NHL game was recorded against the Philadelphia Flyers on March 12, 1992. Suter made at least 40 assists in eight of his nine NHL seasons. An aggressive player, he has averaged 106 penalty minutes per season during his career. His most celebrated moments came during play for the United States in both the 1987 and 1991 USCC Tournaments. In 1987, his high sticking of Andrei Lomakin opened a deep gash on the Soviet's face and resulted in a 10-game suspension. Four years later, his blind side check of Canada's Wayne Gretzky sidelined the legendary star from the tournament. In 1993–1994, he played for Calgary and the Chicago Blackhawks. Through the 1993–1994 season, Suter had scored 130 goals and 440 assists for 570 points in 633 games and participated in eight Stanley Cup playoff seasons. Suter and his wife Cathy have a son, Jacob.

BIBLIOGRAPHY: *Calgary Flames Press Guide*, 1991–1992; Steve Dryden, "Mission Accomplished," *HN*, September 27, 1991; "Suter Number 20," *HS* 3 (December 1986); *USA Today*, April 19, 1994, p. C6.

Roger A. Godin

VANBIESBROUCK, John "Beezer" (b. September 4, 1963, Detroit, MI), professional player, learned to play goal in ice hockey by kicking out a taped-up old sock in his basement against his older brother and friends. He was signed as a free agent by the Sault Ste. Marie, MI, Greyhounds (OHL) after being bypassed in the midget draft as a 16-year-old goalie for the Detroit Little Caesars. Vanbiesbrouck had gone uninvited to the Sault Ste. Marie training camp and made the Greyhounds shortly after his seventeenth birthday. The following spring, the New York Rangers (NHL) made him their fifth choice in the fourth round as the seventy-second overall pick in the 1981 Entry Draft.

Vanbiesbrouck played three years for Sault Ste. Marie, winning the OHL's Dinty Moore Trophy as the rookie goalie with the lowest average in 1980–1981. In 1982–1983, he led OHL goaltenders in games (62), and finished second in wins (39). The Greyhounds' record of 48–21–1 ranked the best in the OHL. Following his junior hockey career, Vanbiesbrouck joined the Rangers' Tulsa Oilers affiliate (CHL), and led them to the CHL Championship in 1983–1984. He compiled a 20–13–2 record during the regular season, boasting the CHL's second-best goals against average (3.46) and finishing 4–0 in the playoffs with a CHL-leading 2.50 goals against mark.

His three shutouts composed almost 50 percent of the total recorded in the CHL that season.

The New York Rangers promoted Vanbiesbrouck near the end of the 1983–1984 season. He had made a spectacular 1-game debut earlier on December 5, 1981, with a 30-save performance in a 2–1 victory over the Colorado Rockies. In his first full season (1984–1985), he stopped at least 40 shots nine times and recorded his first shutout. The 1985–1986 season established Vanbiesbrouck as one of the NHL's premier goaltenders. He won the Vezina Trophy for being the NHL's best goaltender and made the All-Star First Team. Vanbiesbrouck's 31 wins tied for the NHL leadership, while his 3.32 goals against average ranked fifth best in the NHL. The next three seasons saw him play over 50 games per year and achieve two career-high marks. He enjoyed a 7-game unbeaten streak (6–0–1) in 1987–1988 and a 5-game winning streak the following season, allowing only 10 goals. He exceeded his winning streak by one the following year, earning NHL Player of the Month honors. During the streak, he recorded shutouts over the Montreal Canadiens and Quebec Nordiques. Vanbiesbrouck's 2.85 goals against average for 45 games in the 1991–1992 season marked his second-lowest figure. An aggressive goaltender, he has averaged 19 penalty minutes per season and recorded two 5-assist seasons.

On the international level, Vanbiesbrouck has played for the United States in the 1982 and 1983 World Junior Tournaments and the 1985, 1987, 1989, and 1991 World Tournaments. He was named a Second Team All-Star following the 1985 tournament, leading the United States to the medal round for the first time since 1976. He has also represented the United States at the 1984, 1987, and 1991 USCC Tournaments. During his NHL career, Vanbiesbrouck has played in 506 regular-season games and recorded a 3.17 average with 17 shutouts and participated in eight Stanley Cup play-offs. Following the 1992–1993 season, Vanbiesbrouck was traded to the Vancouver Canucks (NHL) and subsequently selected by the Florida Panthers (NHL) in the Expansion Draft. In 1994, he was selected to appear in the NHL All-Star Game and enjoyed his best season, allowing only 2.53 goals per game in 57 games.

BIBLIOGRAPHY: Zander Hollander, ed., *The Complete Encyclopedia of Hockey* (Detroit, MI, 1993); *HS*, December 1986; *New York Rangers Press Guide*, 1991–1992; New York Rangers Press Release, June 12, 1986; Jim Proudfoot, "A Case of Mistaken Identity Among Goaltenders," Toronto (Canada) *Star*, February 11, 1986; *USA Today*, April 19, 1994, p. C6.

Roger A. Godin

WIRTZ, Arthur Michael Sr. (b. January 22, 1901, Chicago, IL; d. July 21, 1983, Chicago, IL), professional executive, was the son of a Chicago policeman. Following his graduation from the University of Michigan in 1922, he initially worked in sales. Wirtz, disappointed with his income, quit and joined two other men in starting the real estate firm of Wirtz, Hubert, and Little with $10,000 capital in 1927. Within a short time, the firm managed nearly 80 buildings with some 3,000 rental units, mostly around Chicago's North Side lakefront.

Wirtz prospered during the depression, becoming an expert in reorganizing failing building corporations to reduce their debts and save them from receivership. He began associating with James Norris, Sr.,* in numerous sports and arena ventures. The projects included Detroit's Olympia Stadium and its ice hockey team, the Detroit Red Wings (NHL), Chicago Stadium, New York's Madison Square Garden, and the Omaha, NE, Arena, Indianapolis, IN, Arena, and St. Louis, MO, Arena. Wirtz also collaborated with Norris in the IBC, which promoted numerous championship bouts in the early 1950s.

Norway's Sonja Henie became the darling of the sports world after her Gold Medal figure skating achievements at the 1928 St. Moritz, Switzerland, 1932 Lake Placid, NY, and 1936 Garmisch-Partenkirchen, Germany, Winter Olympic Games. Wirtz brought Henie to the United States and launched the first major ice show, the highly profitable Hollywood Ice Review, with the young Norwegian as its star. In 1946, Wirtz, assisted by Norris, cleared the way for its subsequent ownership of the Chicago Blackhawks (NHL), providing financing for the franchise's purchase by a third party. When Wirtz took control of the Blackhawks in 1954, attendance had fallen off so badly that the Chicago team was playing some home games at neutral sites. Thomas N. Ivan, who had built a dynasty with the Detroit Red Wings, was hired as general manager and rebuilt the farm system. Wirtz lost $2.5 million between 1954 and 1957 but began turning the franchise around.

In 1957–1958, Chicago secured Glenn Hall, an outstanding goaltender, from the Detroit Red Wings. The Chicago farm system produced Bobby Hull, a muscular left wing, destined to rank among ice hockey's all-time greats. Pierre Pilote, a fine defenseman, had previously joined Chicago in 1955–1956, while Stan Mikita, a scrappy center and inventor of the curved stick, arrived in 1959–1960. The Blackhawks made the NHL playoffs in 1959–1960 and the next season presented Wirtz with a Stanley Cup. Chicago did not win another Stanley Cup during his lifetime, but the Blackhawks remained an NHL contender. The Blackhawks participated in the Stanley Cup finals in the 1961–1962, 1964–1965, 1970–1971, and 1972–1973 seasons, forcing the powerful Montreal Canadiens to seven games in 1964–1965 and 1970–1971.

The Chicago Bulls (NBA) joined the Wirtz holdings in 1972, when he purchased a 25 percent share of the team. At age 77 in 1978, he took over the chairmanship of the bankrupt Chicago Milwaukee Railroad. He also owned prime Chicago real estate, which included the Bismarck Hotel, many lakefront apartment buildings, liquor distributorships, movie theaters, and banks in Chicago and Miami. His sons, William and Arthur, Jr., have continued ownership and management of the Blackhawks. Wirtz was inducted into the Hockey Hall of Fame in Toronto, Canada, in 1971.

BIBLIOGRAPHY: "Arthur Wirtz Dead at 82," Chicago (IL) *Sun Times*, July 23, 1983; *The NHL Official Guide & Record Book*, 1991–1992; Robert A. Styer, *The Encyclopedia of Hockey* (Cranbury, NJ, 1970).

Roger A. Godin

SHOOTING

LANE, Alfred P. "The Boy Wonder" (b. September 26, 1891, New York, NY; d. February 1968, Royalton, IL), shooter, began his shooting career with the MRRA in New York. Nicknamed "The Boy Wonder," he won several USRA Championships in 1911 at age 19. In 1912, the USRA selected the U.S. pistol shooters for the Stockholm, Sweden, Summer Olympics and made Lane their top choice. At Stockholm, Lane competed in four events and captured three Gold Medals. Lane won both of his individual pistol events, the free pistol and the rapid-fire pistol. In team events, Lane helped the United States to the Gold Medal in the military pistol event at 50 meters. In the military pistol team event at 30 meters, Lane led the United States to a fourth-place finish.

After the 1912 Olympics, Lane held the USRA Championship crown for three consecutive years. Lane qualified for the 1920 U.S. Olympic team to compete at the Antwerp, Belgium, Summer Games. This time, tryouts were conducted at the U.S. Marine Corps Base at Quantico, VA. During the trials, Lane finished first in the free pistol event and second in the rapid-fire pistol competition. At the Antwerp Olympic Games, Lane again participated in the free pistol and rapid-fire pistol, both individual and team. He helped the U.S. squads earn Gold Medals in both team events, bringing his career Olympic victories to five Gold Medals. He did not retain either of his individual titles, however, finishing third in the free pistol event and out of the top six in the rapid-fire pistol. Lane later worked in the advertising department of the Remington Company until leaving to head the photographic department for a magazine publisher.

BIBLIOGRAPHY: Colonel Jim Crossman, *Olympic Shooting* (Washington, DC, 1978); Bill Mallon and Ian Buchanan, *Quest for Gold: The Encyclopedia of American Olympians*

(New York, 1984); *Report of the American Olympic Committee: Seventh Olympic Games, Antwerp, Belgium, 1920* (New York, 1921).

Bill Mallon

LEE, Willis Augustus Jr. (b. May 11, 1888, Natlee, KY; d. August 25, 1945, Portland, ME), rifle and pistol marksman, was the son of Willis Lee, Sr., and won five Gold Medals, one Silver Medal, and one Bronze Medal at the 1920 Summer Olympic Games in Antwerp, Belgium. A distant relative of General Robert E. Lee and the great-great-grandson of Charles Lee, the third attorney general of the United States, he graduated from the U.S. Naval Academy in 1908. As a midshipman in 1907, he became the only national champion in both rifle and pistol shooting in the same year. After graduating, he represented the Naval rifle team from 1908 to 1930.

At the 1920 Summer Olympic Games, Lee participated in 14 events and won seven medals. All his medals came in team events, including Golds in the free rifle; military rifle, prone (300 meters); military rifle, prone (600 meters); military rifle, prone (300 and 600 meters); and small bore rifle, standing; a Silver in the military rifle, 300 meters, standing, team; and a Bronze in the running deer, single shot, team. After making his last appearance for the Naval rifle team in 1930, he concentrated on his naval career and rose to become a senior officer. He was appointed Assistant Chief of Staff to the U.S. Fleet Commander-in-Chief in 1941 and later served as Commander of Battleships for the Pacific Fleet. Lee commanded the forces that defeated the Japanese on Guadalcanal in 1942. At the time of his death, he held the rank of vice-admiral.

BIBLIOGRAPHY: Bill Mallon and Ian Buchanan, *Quest for Gold: The Encyclopedia of American Olympians* (New York, 1984).

Ian Buchanan

OSBURN, Carl Townsend (b. November 5, 1884, Jacksonville, OH; d. December 28, 1966, Helena, CA), rifle marksman, was the son of Logan F. Osburn and Mary C. (Tavenner) Osburn and participated on the U.S. Naval Academy shooting team in 1905 and 1906. After graduating in 1906, he participated on the Navy team from 1907 to 1919. A specialist in the military rifle event, he also won championships with the small bore rifle. The Summer Olympic Games of 1912, 1920, and 1924 featured his winning 5 Gold, 4 Silver, and 2 Bronze Medals. Only swimmer Mark Spitz (IS) among U.S. Olympians has equaled Osburn's record of 11 Olympic medals. The Olympic program in Stockholm, Sweden, in 1912 provided for 18 shooting events. Osburn took part in 7 events, winning 2 Silver Medals (military rifle, any position; military rifle, prone) and a Bronze (small bore rifle, prone) in the individual events and a Gold (military rifle) and a Bronze (running deer, single shot) in the team competitions. At Antwerp, Belgium, in 1920, Osburn enjoyed his most successful Olympic Games with 3 Gold Medals (free rifle;

military rifle, 300 meters, prone; military rifle, 300 and 600 meters, prone) and a Bronze in the team events and an individual Gold in the military rifle, standing. His distinguished Olympic career ended at the Paris, France, 1924 Summer Games, when he only took part in one event and won a Silver Medal in the individual free rifle.

In addition to his Olympic successes, Osburn competed in the 1913 Pan-American matches and the 1921, 1922, 1923, and 1924 World Championships. The career naval officer retired with the rank of commander.

BIBLIOGRAPHY: Bill Mallon and Ian Buchanan, *Quest for Gold: The Encyclopedia of American Olympians* (New York, 1984); *Who's Who in American Sports* (Washington, DC, 1928).

Ian Buchanan

SPOONER, Lloyd S. (b. October 6, 1884, Washington, D.C.; d. December 1966, Zephyr Hills, FL), shooter, served as a first lieutenant in the U.S. Army's 47th Infantry when he competed in 12 events at the 1920 Antwerp, Belgium, Summer Olympic Games. No athlete has competed in more events at one Olympics. The slight, mustachioed Spooner won seven medals, which remained the record until Alexander Dityatin of the USSR won eight gymnastics medals at the 1980 Moscow, USSR, Summer Olympic Games. Spooner shares the American record of seven medals with Mark Spitz (IS), who accomplished the feat at the 1972 Olympic Games in Munich. At Antwerp, Spooner won four Gold Medals in team events, including the free rifle team; military rifle, 300 meters, prone, team; military rifle, 600 meters, prone, team; and military rifle, 300 and 600 meters, prone, team. He added two other team medals, a Silver in the military rifle event, standing, and a Bronze in the single shot running deer event. His only individual medal came in the prone 600-meter military rifle event. Spooner, a career army officer, was promoted to captain in 1924.

BIBLIOGRAPHY: Colonel Jim Crossman, *Olympic Shooting* (Washington, DC, 1978); Bill Mallon and Ian Buchanan, *Quest for Gold: The Encyclopedia of American Olympians* (New York, 1984); *Report of the American Olympic Committee: Seventh Olympic Games, Antwerp, Belgium, 1920* (New York, 1921).

Bill Mallon

SKATING

BOSTLEY, Cathy Ann Turner (b. April 10, 1962, Rochester, NY), short-track speed skater, is the daughter of Tim Turner and Nancy (Price) Turner, who subsequently divorced. Turner's father taught her how to win and encouraged her to participate in sports, but they subsequently became estranged. The five-foot-two-inch 116-pounder performed as a long-track skater in the late 1970s and trained with Bonnie Blair (S). Turner, convinced that she would never be a world-class athlete, retired from the sport in 1980. She became a songwriter and singer, touring with a Las Vegas–style barnstorming act from 1981 to 1988.

Turner began short-track skating in August 1988, under coach Jack Mortell. She moved to the U.S. Winter Olympic Training Center at Northern Michigan University, where she refined her skating skills and finished a bachelor's degree in computer programming. During the 1989–1990 season, Turner became the first woman to win every event in the U.S. World Short Track Team Trials. In 1990, she was ranked first in the United States and tenth in the world. Turner placed tenth in the 1991 World Speedskating Championships, set American records in the 500-meter and 1,000-meter short track, and led an international field, finishing first in overall points at Hamar, Norway, in January 1992.

Turner won the 500-meter race for the Gold Medal in 47.04 seconds, edging Yan Li of China by .04 second at the 1992 Albertville, France, Winter Olympic Games at age 29. Turner also garnered a Silver Medal in the 3,000-meter relay at the same games. Subsequently, she scored a co-headlining role with the Ice Capades and appeared in a fitness video, produced by *Shape* magazine. Turner took a break from short-track skating for nearly two years. At the 1994 Lillehammer, Norway, Winter Olympic Games, Turner won a second Gold Medal in the 500-meter event and was disqualified in the 1,000 meters. Her 3,000-meter relay team placed third, capturing a Bronze Medal. Turner ranks third among U.S. Winter Olympians in medals won with four, having earned medals in every event she entered. Short-track skating, competed on a 365-foot circle on a hockey rink, had debuted as an Olympic demonstration sport at the 1988 Calgary, Alberta, Canada, Winter Olympic Games and became a medal sport at the 1992 Games. She married Tim Bostley, a veterinarian, in June 1993 and lives in Hilton, NY.

BIBLIOGRAPHY: Sally Jenkins, "Leader of the Pack," *SI* 76 (February 24, 1992), pp. 34–35; Cathy Turner, "A Parting Word," *Olympian* 18 (April 1992), p. 62; *USA Today*, February 7, 1992, p. E10; February 24, 1992, p. E10; February 24, 1994, p. E5; February 25, 1994, p. E3.

Miriam F. Shelden

JANSEN, Daniel "Dan" (b. June 17, 1965, Milwaukee, WI), speed skater, is the youngest of nine children of Harry Jansen, a police officer, and Gerry Jansen and began skating at age four. Although he played football and baseball at West Allis High School, speed skating remained his real passion. Jansen became the greatest sprinter in speed skating history but met heartbreaking frustration in Olympic competition until his last race. At the Sarajevo, Yugoslavia, 1984 Winter Olympics, the six-foot 195-pounder narrowly missed a Bronze Medal in the 500 meters and ranked sixteenth in the 1,000 meters. He captured the 1986 WoC Championships in both the 500 meters and 1,000 meters and easily won the 1988 World Sprint title before experiencing misfortune at the Calgary, Canada, Winter Olympics. A few hours before his 500-meter race, he learned that Jane Beres, his 27-year-old sister, had died of leukemia. Jansen slipped and fell on the first turn of the 500 meters, finishing a disappointing eighth. Four days later, he fell on the backstretch of the 1,000 meters. A disheartened Jansen received the Olympic Spirit Award. In the 1988 WoC Overall Standings, he ranked first in the 1,000 meters and second in the 500 meters. From 1989 to 1991, Jansen finished fourth three consecutive years at the World Sprint Championships.

U.S. sprint coach Peter Mueller, a 1976 Olympic Gold Medalist, stoked Jansen's competitive fire and taught him how to pace himself in the 1,000 meters. In the 1992 WoC Overall Standings, Jansen finished first in the 500 meters and second at 1,000 meters. Jansen set the world 500-meter record in January 1992, clocking 36.41 seconds at Davos, Switzerland. At the 1992 Albertville, France, Winter Olympics, however, misfortune plagued him. Jansen finished fourth in the 500 meters and slipped on the soft outdoor oval ice in the 1,000 meters, languishing in twenty-sixth place. The 1993 season saw him rank fifth in the World Sprint Championship and win his fifth WoC Overall title in 11 years. At Calgary, Alberta, in March, he lowered Takahiro Hamamachi's short-lived world 500-meter standard with a 36.02-second performance. At a December 1993 WoC race in Hamar, Norway, Jansen shattered the 36-second barrier with a 35.92-second clocking. "To look up and see 35," he acknowledged, "was something I've dreamed of for a long time." The next day, Jansen narrowly missed setting a world 1,000-meter record with a 1 minute 13.01 seconds time. In January 1994, he lowered the 500-meter world standard to 35.76 seconds. Authorities expected Jansen to win a Gold Medal in the 500 meters at the 1994 Lille-hammer, Norway, Winter Olympics. Jansen skated more aggressively but lost control of his left skate on the last turn. His left hand grazed the ice, costing him one-half second for an eighth-place finish in the 500 meters. In his final Olympic race four days later, Jansen almost fell twice on the back turn of the 1,000 meters. He stayed afloat to win the Gold Medal, crossing the finish line at 1:12:43 and breaking the world record by .11 second. Before a wildly cheering throng, Jansen saw his time and thrust his arms toward the heavens. His wife Robin burst into tears. With a single spotlight shining down, the smiling Jansen cradled his nine-month-old daughter, Jane, while circling the dark arena on a victory lap. At the medals ceremony, he offered a small salute skyward to his deceased sister. His record includes over 30 WoC titles, over 50 WoC medals, and over 20 World Championship med-als. The USOC named the Sullivan Award nominee 1994 Male Speedskater of the year.

Jansen married Robin Wicker of Charlotte, NC, in April 1990 and resides in Greenfield, WI. Besides giving motivational speeches for Maxwell House Coffee, he works part-time in marketing for the Miller Brewing Company and in the Olympic Job Opportunities Program. Jansen coauthored an au-tobiography, *Full Circle* (1994), and is planning an autobiographical film.

BIBLIOGRAPHY: Dan Jansen with Jack McCallum, *Full Circle* (New York, 1994); Sally Jenkins, "Glory and Gloom," *SI* 76 (February 24, 1992), pp. 18–19; *NYT*, February 15, 1988, sec. 3, pp. 1, 6; December 22, 1991, sec. 8, p. 4; February 2, 1992, sec. 8, p. 15; February 15, 1992, sec. 1, p. 31; W. Plummer, "After the Fall," *PW* 37 (January 13, 1992), pp. 32–35; Rick Reilly, "Felled by a Heart," *SI* 68 (February 22, 1988), pp. 24–26, 47; *TSN*, February 28, 1994, pp. 10–11; *USA Today*, February 7, 1992, p. E10; February 11, 1994, p. E11; Alexander Wolff, "Fourth Down," *SI* 80 (Feb-ruary 21, 1994), pp. 28–29; Alexander Wolff, "Whooosh!" *SI* 80 (February 28, 1994), pp. 18–23.

David L. Porter

KERRIGAN, Nancy (b. October 13, 1969, Woburn, MA), figure skater, is the daughter of Daniel Kerrigan, a welder, and Brenda Kerrigan, who is legally blind, and grew up in a tight-knit family with two brothers, Mark and Mi-chael. Kerrigan started skating at age 6 and immediately won local and re-gional championships. A strong jumper, she routinely performed difficult jumps and leaps as a novice and trained at the Skating Club of Boston as a teenager. Kerrigan, coached by Evy and Mary Scotvold, placed third in the 1987 New England Juniors and captured the 1988 NCAA Championships. She also won the 1990 Olympic Festival in Minneapolis, MN, and the Bronze Medal at the 1991 World Championships at Munich, Germany. By

1991, she delivered elegant performances and joined the small circle of elite skaters.

In 1992, Kerrigan placed second at the U.S. Nationals in Orlando, FL, garnered the Bronze Medal at the Albertville, France, Winter Olympics, and earned a Silver Medal at the World Championships. She won the 1993 U.S. Championships at Phoenix, AZ, and was ranked best in the world but struggled to a fifth-place finish at the World Championships. Kerrigan trained hard for the Olympics, winning the Piruettan competition in October 1993 at Lillehammer, Norway. After finishing a practice in January 1994 for the U.S. Figure Skating Championships in Detroit, MI, she was attacked and hit above the right knee with a police baton. Kerrigan did not compete in the U.S. Figure Skating Championships, but the USFSAIC named Tonya Harding and her to the U.S. Figure Skating team. The Plymouth, MA, resident won the Silver Medal at the 1994 Lillehammer, Norway, Winter Olympic Games, being edged by Oksana Baiul of the Ukraine for the Gold. She signed a lucrative deal with Disney involving a made-for-television movie, skating specials, a children's book, skating video, and assorted appearances. Her other endorsements include Campbell's Soup, Reebok Shoes, and Seiko. The USOC named the Sullivan Award nominee 1994 Female Figure Skater of the Year.

BIBLIOGRAPHY: S. Avery Brown, "Fancy Nancy," *People* 37 (February 3, 1992), pp. 34–35; Wayne Coffey and Filip Bondy, *Dreams of Gold: The Nancy Kerrigan Story* (New York, 1994); Randi Reisfield, *The Kerrigan Courage: Nancy's Story* (New York, 1994); E. M. Swift, "Stirring," *SI* 76 (March 2, 1992), pp. 16–21; Mark Starr, "I'm So Scared," *Newsweek* 123 (January 17, 1994), pp. 41–43; *TSN*, March 7, 1994, pp. 12–14; *USA Today*, January 22, 1993, pp. S1, S2; February 23, 1994, p. E6; February 24, 1994, p. E1; February 25–27, 1994, pp. A1, A2.

                                                                                    Miriam F. Shelden

MUELLER, Leah Jean Poulos (b. October 5, 1951, Berwyn, IL), speed skater, married Peter Mueller, one of the nation's top men's speed skaters, in September 1979. Her speed skating career initially included both distance races and sprints competition. Since pure sprinting marked her forte, she focused on the shorter distances. During her early career, she was coached by her father and three-time World Champion John Werket. She won the World Sprint Championship in 1974 and 1979, placing second in 1976 and 1977. As a participant on the 1976 U.S. Olympic team, she earned the Silver Medal in the 1,000-meter distance at the Innsbruck, Austria, Winter Games. With the 1980 U.S. Olympic team, she again captured Silver Medals at the 1,000-meter distance and the 500-meter event at the Lake Placid, NY, Winter Olympic Games. Mueller's second Silver Medal at the 1980 Winter Olympics came at age 28 years, 135 days, making her the oldest speed skating medalist. She also had participated on the 1972 U.S. Olympic team at the Sapporo, Japan, Winter Olympic Games.

Mueller originally retired from competitive speed skating in 1978 to travel with Peter, her speed skating husband, but she became restless without the competition and came out of retirement in 1979. Mueller's husband and Peter Schotting coached her in preparation for the 1980 Winter Olympics.

BIBLIOGRAPHY: Bill Mallon and Ian Buchanan, *Quest for Gold: The Encyclopedia of American Olympians* (New York, 1984).

Miriam F. Shelden

POULOS, Leah Jean. *See* Leah Jean Poulos Mueller.

TURNER, Cathy Ann. *See* Cathy Ann Turner Bostley.

WYLIE, Paul (b. October 28, 1964, Dallas, TX), figure skater and sportscaster, has been coached since 1985 by Evy and Mary Scotvold. Wylie's career has spanned much longer than most amateur skaters, including 11 years of major competitions. The slightly built Wylie won the World Junior Championship in 1981 and competed on the Senior level from 1982 to 1992. Wylie, a friendly, engaging personality, skated with an emotional, lyrical style and beautiful artistry. Not a powerful jumper, he often did not perform well technically in competitions. When Todd Eldridge withdrew from the U.S. National Competition with a sore back in January 1992, the USFSAIC named Wylie to the U.S. Olympic team.

Wylie skated in the 1988 Winter Olympics at Calgary, Alberta, Canada, finishing tenth in the Men's Singles. He earned a Silver or Bronze Medal in every U.S. Championship from 1988 to 1992 but placed tenth in the 1990 World Championships and eleventh in the 1991 World Championships. The 1992 Winter Olympic Games in Albertville, France, marked Wylie's finest performance, as he finished second and earned the Silver Medal. He made a nearly flawless performance and completed five triple jumps in the free skate program, trailing just Viktor Petrenko of the Unified Team. Wylie, who had finished second in the U.S. Nationals the month before, has skated professionally since 1992.

Wylie participated on the USOC policy-making as an AAC member and won both the U.S. Olympic Spirit Award in 1992 and the Clairol Personal Best Award. He graduated from Harvard University in 1991 cum laude with a bachelor's degree in political science and applied to several law schools. Wylie, a bachelor, has been accepted at Harvard Law School but has delayed entry to continue his professional skating career. In 1992, his victories included the U.S. Open Professional Figure Skating Championship, the World Challenge of Champions, and the Pro-Am Figure Skating Challenge. Wylie joined CBS-Sports as a commentator and analyst in 1993 and covered the Lillehammer, Norway, 1994 Winter Olympic Games. He won the 1994 World Professional Figure Skating Championship and placed second in 1995.

BIBLIOGRAPHY: *Olympian* 18 (April 1992), p. 8; E. M. Swift, "Silver Lining," *SI* 76 (February 24, 1992), pp. 14–17; *USA Today*, February 7, 1992, p. E9; February 13, 1992, p. E2; February 17, 1992, pp. E1, E2; *WWA*, 48th ed. (1994), p. 3745.

Miriam F. Shelden

YAMAGUCHI, Kristi Tsuya (b. July 12, 1971, Hayward, CA), figure skater, is the daughter of Jim Yamaguchi, a dentist, and Carol Yamaguchi, a medical secretary. She grew up in Fremont, another community in the San Francisco Bay area, and has two siblings, Lori and Brett. Yamaguchi was born with club feet, but the condition was easily treated with corrective shoes. She began skating lessons at age five and entered her first figure skating competition at age eight. Christy Kjarsgaard-Ness has coached Yamaguchi in singles since around 1979.

In 1983, Yamaguchi began skating with Rudi Galindo in the pairs competition under coach Jim Hulick. Their pairs accomplishments included fifth in the U.S. National Junior Championships in 1985, first in the same competition in 1986, and first in the 1988 World Junior Pairs Championships. In 1989, they captured the U.S. National Senior Pairs crown. The pair placed fifth in the 1989 and 1990 World Pairs Championships. In December 1989, Coach Hulick died. Yamaguchi withdrew from pairs competition in May 1990 to concentrate solely on singles competition.

Yamaguchi's singles fortune followed close behind. She finished fourth in the 1986 U.S. National Junior Singles Championships and first in the 1988 World Junior Singles Championships. The same year, the WSkF named her the Up-and-Coming Artistic Athlete of the Year. In 1989, she won the Silver Medal in the U.S. National Women's Singles Championships. Veteran singles coach Christy Kjarsgaard-Ness moved to Edmonton, Alberta, Canada in the spring of 1989. Yamaguchi moved there the day after high school graduation. In 1990, she finished second again in the U.S. Nationals and fourth in the World Singles Competition.

In July 1990, the compulsory figures were eliminated from all major competitions. The compulsory figures had been difficult for Yamaguchi, who often lagged behind before the free skate portion of the competitions. She placed first at the 1990 Goodwill Games, the Nations Cup, and Skate America and again finished second in the 1991 U.S. Nationals but captured the Singles Competition at the Worlds. In 1992, she won the U.S. Nationals just prior to capturing a Gold Medal at the Albertville, France, Winter Olympic Games. Yamaguchi, who also won her second World Championships the month after the 1992 Olympics, has skated professionally since. She captured the 1993 and 1995 World Professional Figure Skating Championships and placed second in 1994.

BIBLIOGRAPHY: *CB* (1992), pp. 616–619; E. M. Swift, "Silver Lining," *SI* 76 (February 24, 1992), pp. 14–17; *WWA*, 48th ed. (1994), p. 3748; *Young and Modern* 40 (December 1992), p. 58.

Miriam F. Shelden

SKIING

McKINNEY, Tamara (b. October 16, 1962, Lexington, KY), skier, was the youngest of seven children in an athletic Kentucky family. Her great-great-great-great uncle, Elisha Warfield, bred the outstanding thoroughbred sire Lexington (OS) and gained renown as the Father of Kentucky Turf. Her father, Rigan, an accomplished steeplechase jockey, was inducted into the NMR Hall of Fame in 1968, while her mother, Frances, worked as a ski instructor and horse trainer. Tamara began skiing at the age of nine months and working with a coach when she was five years old.

McKinney first competed nationally at age 12 and finished seventh in the National Slalom Championships in 1977 when she was 14. Between 1978 and 1989, she won 18 WoC titles for the most crowns ever by an American skier. These triumphs came despite McKinney's several serious injuries and family tragedies. In 1983, she became the first American to win the overall WOC Championship. McKinney placed fourth in the giant slalom in the 1984 Sarajevo, Yugoslavia, Winter Olympics for the highest finish by an American competitor. She medaled in the World Championship combined event in 1985 and 1987 and won the Gold Medal in that event in 1989.

A broken right hand, caused by a collision with an Italian television crewman on a ski course in December 1981, sidelined McKinney for most of the 1982 season. A broken leg, the result of a training accident in November 1987, prevented her from performing well in the 1988 Calgary, Canada, Winter Olympics. Her mother, with whom she had always been very close, died in 1988, the same year a brother committed suicide and another brother was critically injured in a helicopter accident.

During her career, the five-foot-four-inch, 115-pound McKinney developed a skiing technique that was described as a combination of "daintiness and speed." Observers noted how she almost "seeme[d] to skip" down the slopes in an "extremely economical" manner. In November 1990, McKinney retired from competition to become a spokesperson for a Colorado-based organization that raises money to fight multiple sclerosis.

BIBLIOGRAPHY: Denver (CO) *Post*, February 3, 1989; William O. Johnson, "A Flight So Fancy," *SI* 70 (February 13, 1989), pp. 14–21; William O. Johnson, "To Her, Speed Thrills," *SI* 58 (February 7, 1983), pp. 40–41; G. Kramer, "On Top of the World," *WS* 6 (February 1984), pp. 40–43; Lexington (KY) *Herald-Leader*, November 28, 1990; Louisville (KY) *Courier-Journal*, November 28, 1990; *NYT*, March 19, 1983; March 27, 1983; December 18, 1983; January 23, 1984; January 30, 1987; November 14, 1987; February 3, 1989.

John E. Findling

MOE, Thomas Sven Jr. "Tommy" (b. February 17, 1970, Anaconda, MT), skier, is the son of Thomas S. Moe, Sr., a contractor and outdoorsman of Norwegian descent, and grew up in Anaconda, where his father taught him to ski. After the Moes divorced when he was only two, he lived with his paternal grandmother, Valerie Tomlinson. Moe's father eventually constructed buildings in remote areas of Alaska. Dynastar Skis signed Moe to an endorsement contract at age 13. He mingled with the wrong crowd as an adolescent and was banned in 1984 from junior ski competition in the Idaho-Montana region for smoking marijuana and drinking alcohol at a Helena, MT, ski race.

Moe's father summoned him to Alaska, where he began skiing well and finished sixth in the 1985 U.S. National Alpine Championships at Copper Mountain, CO. In 1986, Moe was removed again from the U.S. junior squad for drinking and smoking marijuana. Moe's father assigned his son to a construction crew at an isolated outpost in the Aleutian Islands. Moe labored from 12 to 16 hours a day for a month, a hellish experience that renewed his appreciation for skiing. At the World Junior Championships, he earned a Silver Medal in the downhill in 1987 and finished fourth the following year. The 1989 World Junior Championships were held at Mount Alyeska in his home state. After a disappointing fifth place in the downhill, the 5-foot-10-inch, 191-pound Moe rallied to win Gold Medals in the Super G and combined events.

Moe joined the WoC circuit in 1990, finishing among the top 15 in three consecutive 1991 downhill races. Moe's father pushed him very hard, but he finished a disappointing twentieth in the downhill, twenty-eighth in the Super G, and eighteenth in the combined at the 1992 Albertville, France, Winter Olympics. After struggling part of the 1992–1993 WoC season, Moe improved markedly and replaced A. J. Kitt as the top American downhill skier. He finished fifth in the downhill at the February 1993 FIS World Championships in Japan and recorded his best WoC race the following month, placing second at Whistler Mountain near Vancouver, Canada.

During the pre-Olympic 1993–1994 WoC season, Moe garnered thirds in the downhill and Super G and compiled five other top-10 finishes. U.S. Olympic skier Megan Gerity, his girlfriend from Anchorage, Alaska, counseled him before the men's downhill competition at the 1994 Lillehammer, Norway, Winter Olympic games to "just go for it." Kjetil Aamodt of Norway, the Gold Medal favorite and overall WoC racing circuit leader, led the downhill by .3 seconds when Moe began his run. Moe flew from top to bottom in a beautifully controlled, technically perfect run. He flashed across the finish line .04 of a second faster than Aamodt to take the Gold Medal, bringing self-redemption after years of unfulfilled promise. With his elfin smile, the popular Moe joined Bill Johnson (OS) as the only U.S. Olympic men's downhill champions. "It's a lifetime dream," Moe observed, "being on top in a big race like this." On his twenty-fourth birthday four days later, he captured a Silver Medal in the shorter, Super G event. Markus Wasmeier of Germany edged Moe by .08 seconds, as the latter lost time on a turn near the bottom of the course. "I am in a zone right now," Moe told reporters, "where I almost can't stop myself from skiing fast." He finished fifth in the men's combined competition after ranking third in the downhill portion. Moe etched his name in the annals of Winter Olympic history. He gave the U.S. men their first WoC race win since 1991 by capturing the Super G at Whistler Mountain in March 1994. At the U.S. Alpine Championships, held in March 1994 at Winter Park, CO, Moe won the Super G event. The USOC named the Sullivan Award nominee its Male Skier of the Year.

BIBLIOGRAPHY: William Oscar Johnson, "The Son Finally Rises," *SI* 80 (February 21, 1994), pp. 20–24, 27; William Oscar Johnson, "Zone of Their Own," *SI* 80 (February 28, 1994), pp. 24–26, 31; Daniel Pederson, "An American Dream on the Slopes," *Newsweek* 123 (February 28, 1994), pp. 51, 53; *USA Today*, February 7, 1992, p. E8; February 14, 1994, pp. C1–C2.

David L. Porter

ROFFE, Diann. *See* Diann Roffe-Steinrotter.

ROFFE-STEINROTTER, Diann (b. March 24, 1967, Warsaw, NY), skier, is the daughter of thoroughbred horse breeders in Williamson, NY, and began skiing at age two on the Brantling Ski Slopes near Rochester, NY. Roffe first attracted international attention at the 1984 World Alpine Junior Championships, earning a Silver Medal in the giant slalom. No American had ever won a medal at the World Alpine Junior Championships. In 1985, the 17-year-old surprised the world by becoming the first American to capture the giant slalom World Championship in Burmio, Italy. She added another WoC victory that year in the giant slalom, her best event, at Lake Placid, NY. Only one younger skier had captured a world or Olympic title. Two severe left knee injuries interrupted Roffe's career, keeping her from the WoC victory stand. She tore her patellar tendon in January 1986 and left knee ligaments in 1991, both requiring surgery. Her best year prior to the second injury came in 1990, when she finished fourth in the WoC giant slalom and tenth overall.

Roffe competed in the 1988 Calgary, Canada, 1992 Albertville, France, and 1994 Lillehammer, Norway, Winter Olympics. In 1988, she finished fifteenth in the slalom and twelfth in the giant slalom. Four years later, Roffe-Steinrotter failed to finish the Super G in 1992 and trailed in ninth place after the first giant slalom run. She blitzed nearly everyone on the second run, winning the Silver Medal. Between 1992 and 1994, she did not finish higher than thirteenth in the giant slalom and ranked thirty-sixth in the Super G competition. At the 1994 Winter Olympics, Roffe-Steinrotter failed to qualify for the second giant slalom run. On February 15, however, she unexpectedly took the Gold Medal in the Super G competition. Roffe-Steinrotter, who led off the competition, relied on her instincts and experience in a gutsy skiing performance. She negotiated the tricky, turning course in 1 minute 22.15 seconds and waited over an hour for the final race outcome. No American woman had won an Olympic Alpine ski race in a decade. Paul Major, U.S. ski coach, called her victory "the most amazing thing I have ever seen in sports." Her international career ended with a flourish when Roffe-Steinrotter captured the WoC Super G Finals at Vail, CO, in March 1994. USOC named her its 1994 Female Skier of the Year.

Roffe-Steinrotter, a contemplative, mature, bright, daring, and competitive skier noted for her upright stance and immaculate racing style, achieves her best results on hard snow. Since her five-foot-three-inch, 132-pound frame is quite small for a world-class ski racer, she lifted weights to strengthen her. She married Austrian Willi Steinrotter, a soccer and skiing coach at Clarkson University, in 1991 and resides in Potsdam, NY. Roffe-Steinrotter enjoys riding horses at her family farm and dreams of making the U.S. Olympic equestrian team. She left skiing competition after the 1994 season and plans to complete her undergraduate degree.

BIBLIOGRAPHY: ABC-TV Research Information for the XV Olympic Winter Games; Margot Hornblower, "SchuuuUSss!" *Time* 143 (February 28, 1994), pp. 58–59; Nicholas Howe, "Diann & Kristi," *Skiing* 43 (October 1990), pp. 206–208; Nicholas Howe, "Small Is Beautiful," *Skiing* 38 (November 1985), pp. 113–114; William Oscar Johnson, "Zone of Their Own," *SI* 80 (February 28, 1994), pp. 24–26, 31; *NYT*, February 20, 1992, pp. B7, B9; *TSN*, February 28, 1994, p. 14; *USA Today*, February 12, 1992, p. E10; February 20, 1992, p. E5; February 16, 1994, p. E12; *U.S. Olympic Committee Media Guide*, 1988, 1992, 1994; *U.S. Skiing Media Biography*.

Bill Mallon

WEINBRECHT, Donna (b. April 23, 1965, West Milford, NJ), freestyle skier, remains the greatest female freestyle performer in U.S. history. She is the daughter of Jim Weinbrecht, a semiprofessional football player and builder, and Caroline Weinbrecht and has one older brother, Jim, and one younger sister, Joy. Weinbrecht grew up in West Milford, where her father encouraged her to participate in sailing, surfing, windsurfing, skating, and skateboarding. When a neighbor started a ski club at Hidden Valley, she and her family began skiing. Weinbrecht's father built a second home in Killington,

VT, enabling her to ski regularly and meet U.S. freestyle team members. Following graduation from West Milford High School, she attended an art and design school for one year and contemplated a fashion design career. The art and design school, however, went bankrupt after her first year. Weinbrecht moved to Killington, where she waited tables at a pasta restaurant and spent her free time on the ski slopes. She did not pursue skiing seriously, however, until being prodded by her parents and did not have a coach until making the U.S. freestyle mogul team in 1987.

The offbeat Weinbrecht, who found traditional slalom events too confining, loved the challenge and creativity of weaving through a mogul field. Weinbrecht joined international moguls competition in 1988, being named WoC Rookie of the Year for the 1988–1989 season. She attained a new skiing level, winning five consecutive U.S. Moguls Championships from 1988 to 1992. In 1989, Weinbrecht triumphed in two WoC mogul events and finished the year second overall, losing the title by one point to France's Raphaelle Monod. From 1990 to 1992, she dominated the moguls tour en route to capturing the overall WoC Moguls Championship three consecutive years. In 1990, the USSA named her Skier of the Year. Weinbrecht has taken 30 WoC mogul events, including 8 in 1990, 7 in 1991, 8 in 1992, and 6 in 1994, and won the 1991 World Championship. No woman had performed a double aerial maneuver in competition until she accomplished the feat at Calgary, Canada, in 1990. Moguls were first held as an Olympic full-medal sport in 1992. Weinbrecht earned the initial Olympic Gold Medal in the sport at the 1992 Albertville, France, Winter Games. A torn anterior cruciate ligament in her knee, suffered during practice on a difficult aerial maneuver at Breckenridge, CO, in November 1992, sidelined her from competition for several months in 1993. Weinbrecht resumed training in June 1993 and won six of seven WoC pre-Olympic competitions. In the middle of her training run at the 1994 Lillehammer, Norway, Winter Olympic Games, however, she almost fell on the landing of a jump and lost her confidence. Weinbrecht finished a disappointing seventh in the finals, lacking her usual verve, spark, inspiration, dramatic aerials, and boldness. "I was lacking the winning edge," she explained.

BIBLIOGRAPHY: "From Ski Bum to Gold Medalist," *USA Weekend*, February 11–13, 1994, p. 16; *NYT*, February 14, 1992; *USA Today*, February 12, 1992, p. E10; February 17, 1994, p. E10; *U.S. Olympic Committee Media Guide*, 1988, 1992, 1994.

Bill Mallon

SWIMMING

BARROWMAN, Michael "Mike" (b. December 4, 1968, Asunción, Paraguay), swimmer, is the son of Ray Barrowman, a U.S. Army cartographer, and Donna Barrowman and comes from a swimming family. His grandmother, Jean Albert, a Red Cross swimming instructor, began taking him at six months to suburban Maryland pools. His younger sister, Sophia, swam on the American University team. The 5-foot-11-inch, 160-pound Barrowman, a Potomac, MD, resident, trained compulsively under coach Jon Urbanchek at the University of Michigan, where he majored in English and journalism, and under coach Joszef Nagy at American University and the Curl-Burke SwC. Barrowman fuels up on fast food, especially hamburgers, before racing.

Coach Nagy, who had come to the United States from Hungary because of his wife's job offer at the International Monetary Fund, taught Barrowman a new breaststroke technique. This technique, the topic of Nagy's thesis at the University of Budapest, used more of Barrowman's arms than his legs, imitating the action of waves, and was based on the running movement of the cheetah. Barrowman perfected this method, bringing new efficiency to the slowest of all swimming strokes. Barrowman qualified third in the 200-meter breaststroke at the Seoul, South Korea, 1988 Summer Olympics in 2 minutes 15.85 seconds, although he thought that he should have done better. In the 1988 200-meter breaststroke finals, his fourth-place time was 2 minutes 15.45 seconds. Joszef Szabo of Hungary, who won the 1988 Gold Medal, also had trained under Nagy.

Barrowman spent four years being driven by bad memories of his fourth-place finish in his specialty, the 200-meter breaststroke. Barrowman had trained by July 1993 for nine years, "fanatically" so for six. He took off the fall 1990 semester from Michigan to train full-time. He arrived at the 1992 Barcelona, Spain, Summer Olympics as arguably the world's most consistently excellent swimmer. Barrowman had earned U.S. Swimmer of the Year honors three times, finished as a finalist for the Sullivan Award, and lowered the world men's 200-meter breaststroke record five times. He had won 16 of 17 races at the distance since the 1988 Summer Olympic Games, his only loss being at the March 1992 Olympic trials. Barrowman claimed that his slower, but still qualifying, time was calculated to relieve the pressure of high expectations. It may have also been influenced by the illness of his father, who died two weeks later.

Barrowman's Barcelona results were impressive. He won the Gold Medal in the 200-meter breaststroke heat in 2 minutes 10.16 seconds, breaking his own world record by .44 of a second. The soft-spoken, but intense, Barrowman planned to stop pushing himself so hard after the 1992 Summer Olympics. After travel and some coaching to give something back to the sport of swimming, Barrowman hoped to resume a regular life. He planned to skip the 1996 Atlanta, GA, Summer Olympic Games because of the financial drain that intensive training put on his family.

Instead of returning to competitive swimming and his previous, rigorous training schedule, Barrowman engaged in other activities immediately after Barcelona. In the fall of 1992, he delivered talks to businessmen on a mini tour and then returned to the University of Michigan to continue work on his bachelor's degree. From May through August 1993, he made a "Gold Wave Tour," a paid speaking engagement through 45 U.S. cities in 20 states. He distributed t-shirts and gave pep talks to young people. He did not get exorbitantly rich but earned some money to help pay for his schooling.

BIBLIOGRAPHY: Mike Meserole, ed., *The 1993 Information Please Sports Almanac* (Boston, MA, 1993); *NYT*, March 28, 1991; July 30, 1992; University of Michigan, Athletic Public Relations Office, Ann Arbor, MI, telephone call with Frederick J. Augustyn, Jr., January 26, 1993; Washington (DC) *Post*, August 26, 1988; September 23, 1988; September 24, 1988; January 12, 1991; February 20, 1991; March 5, 1992; July 22, 1992; July 30, 1992; August 8, 1993; Washington (DC) *Times*, August 21, 1989; July 30, 1992.

Frederick J. Augustyn, Jr.

HAISLETT, Nicole (b. December 16, 1972, St. Petersburg, FL), swimmer, is the daughter of Ben Haislett and won acclaim for her three Gold Medal victories at the 1992 Barcelona, Spain, Summer Olympics. At these Olympics, she triumphed in the 200-meter freestyle (1 minute 57.90 seconds), 400-meter freestyle, and 400-meter relay. Despite historical eras when the Germans and the Australians have performed well, the United States usually has been the dominating force in women's swimming. Haislett's victory in the 1992 Olympics 400-meter relay echoed the 1964 400-meter relay medal success of fellow American Donna de Varona (IS) with one major exception. After enjoying Olympic victories in 1964 as a 17-year-old, de Varona retired. Haislett, on the other hand, achieved her triple medals at age 20 and epitomized a sport featuring longer swimmer careers and Olympians competing through their midtwenties. Haislett owes much to the constant encouragement of her father, Ben.

At the beginning of the 1990s, a renaissance occurred in American women's swimming. The successes of Janet Evans (S) at the 1988 Seoul, Korea, Summer Olympics and the relative decline of German swimming following the dissolution of East Germany and deemphasis of that nation's elite sports system impacted the renaissance. Haislett, a "New Kid on the Block," was given significant coverage in high-circulation publications such as *TSN* and *SI*. Her celebrity status was shaped at the 1990 Goodwill Games in Seattle, WA, where she won the 100-meter freestyle. This marked the first time since the 1972 Munich, Germany, Summer Olympics that an American bested an East German in this event. Haislett, who reigned as a five-time U.S. Open champion and a four-time NCAA champion, was awarded Florida's first Tracy Caulkins Super Scholarship and remains the fastest female in high school history over the 100-yard freestyle. In 1993, she avoided any career letdowns by remaining focused and committed to a demanding training regimen. At the 1993 NCAA Championships, she finished first in the 200-yard individual medley and 200-yard freestyle and second in the 100-yard freestyle. The 1993 U.S. National Outdoor Championships at Austin, TX, featured her victory in the 200-meter freestyle. During the 1994 St. Petersburg, Russia, Goodwill Games, she placed second in the 200-meter medley, third in the 100-meter freestyle, and fourth in the 200-meter freestyle. At the 1994 U.S. National Outdoor Championships in Bloomington, IN, Haislett finished second in the 200-meter freestyle and 200-meter medley and tied for second in the 100-meter freestyle. At the World Aquatic Championships in Rome, Italy, Haislett finished second in the 4 × 100-meter freestyle relay, third in the 4 × 200-meter freestyle relay, and fifth in the 200-meter freestyle. Although not as slight as Janet Evans nor as powerful as Jenny Thompson,* the five-foot-eight-inch 140-pounder possesses an ideal build for the demands imposed by her sprint swimming.

Haislett's performances highlight the quality of contemporary women's swimming. Her 1992 Olympic winning time of 1 minute 57.90 seconds in the 200-meter freestyle would have made her the male world record holder until August 1, 1964, when America's Don Schollander (IS) swam the distance in 1 minute 57.6 seconds.

BIBLIOGRAPHY: Pat Besford, *Encyclopedia of Swimming*, 1st ed. (New York, 1971); Biographical profile, undated, courtesy of Jill Cooper, U.S. Swimming, Colorado Springs, CO.

                                                        Scott A.G.M. Crawford

HAWKINS, Jan Margo Henne (b. August 11, 1947, Oakland, CA), swimmer, is the daughter of Paul Henne and Giselle (Craven) Henne and won four Olympic medals at the 1968 Mexico City, Mexico, Summer Olympic Games.

A double Gold Medalist for the 100-meter individual freestyle and the 400-meter freestyle relay with teammates Jane Barkman, Linda Gustavson, and Sue Pedersen, she recalled, "It was surprising because I was swimming in my second stroke. I swam the breaststroke until the summer of '68, when George [Haines] switched me to freestyle at a swim meet in Santa Clara. I trusted him." The trust was well placed. Henne also won a Silver Medal, placing behind Debbie Meyer (IS) in the 200-meter freestyle. Henne's Bronze Medal was awarded for the 200-meter individual medley.

Henne grew up amid a family of swimmers in Menlo Park, CA, as her mother, sister, and brother all swam competitively. Henne graduated from Menlo Atherton High School in 1965 and attended San Mateo JC, where she stayed an extra year to continue swimming with the Santa Clara SwC. She won numerous AAU titles and set several U.S. records in the breaststroke. As a 21-year-old, she swam at the Mexico City Olympics in the presence of her family. "Truthfully in 1968, most of my competition was from my own teammates," she admitted.

After the Olympic Games, Henne traveled the globe to participate in swimming exhibitions and competitions. Arizona State University offered her a swimming scholHenne graduated from there with a bachelor's degree in physical education.

In 1972, Henne married Paul Hawkins, a former high school athlete and manager of a parts and service center of Sears Roebuck and Company. They reside in Tucson, AZ, with their two children, Jennifer and Jeffrey. She graduated from a two-year nursing program at Mesa, AZ, CC in 1985. Her nursing specialities include chemical dependency and eating disorders. She currently works with adolescents at Palo Verde Hospital and brings personal experience to her professional qualifications. "I had an eating disorder," she confided, "from which I've recovered."

BIBLIOGRAPHY: AP, *The Olympic Story: Pursuit of Excellence* (New York, 1979); June Wuest Becht, *America's Golden Girls* (unpublished); June Wuest Becht, personal interview with Jan Hawkins, February 10, 1993; Bill Mallon and Ian Buchanan, *Quest for Gold: The Encyclopedia of American Olympians* (New York, 1984); David Wallechinsky, *The Complete Book of the Olympics*, rev. ed. (New York, 1988).

June Wuest Becht

HENNE, Jan Margo. *See* Jan Margo Henne Hawkins.

HICKCOX, Charles Buchanan (b. February 6, 1947, Phoenix, AZ), swimmer, coach, and sportscaster, enjoyed an outstanding record in the individual medley and backstroke at every level of competition. After an exceptional swimming career as an age-group and high school swimmer in Phoenix, Hickcox enrolled at Indiana University in 1965. Hickcox eventually won seven individual NCAA titles, swimming on the winning medley relay team for Indiana in 1969 and leading Indiana to two NCAA team championships.

His individual titles included the 100-yard backstroke (1967–1968), 200-yard backstroke (1967–1969), and 200-yard individual medley (1968–1969). His three individual titles in 1968 equaled an NCAA record. Hickcox also won eight national AAU Championships, among them the 100-meter backstroke (1966–1967), 200-meter backstroke (1966–1967), 100-yard indoor backstroke (1968), 200-yard indoor backstroke (1966, 1968), and the 200-yard indoor individual medley (1968).

Hickcox debuted internationally in 1967 at the Pan-American Games in Winnipeg, Canada, winning two individual medleys, a Gold in the 100-meter backstroke, a Silver in the 200-meter backstroke, and another Gold on the 4 × 200-meter freestyle relay. Later that year, he added two individual Golds at the World University Games in both backstroke events and another Gold on the 4 × 100-meter medley relay team. Hickcox achieved his greatest moments in swimming at the 1968 Mexico City Summer Olympics Games. There he won Gold Medals in both the 200- and 400-meter individual medley, took a Silver Medal in the 100-meter backstroke, and earned a third Gold in the 4 × 100-meter medley relay. Hickcox already had won all three individual events at the 1968 Olympic Trials. For his efforts, Hickcox was named *SW* Swimmer of the Year in 1968, and was world ranked first in both individual medleys. *SW* had ranked Hickcox first in 1966 for the 100-meter backstroke and in 1967 for the 200-meter backstroke. Hickcox set four individual long-course world records, including two in the 100-meter backstroke at the 1967 World University Games and in both individual medley events at the 1968 Olympic Trials. He also participated in two medley relay world records at the 1967 World University Games and the 1968 Olympics.

Hickcox, who later spent some time as a coach and television announcer, graduated from Indiana University in 1970 with a bachelor's degree in business management and earned a law degree in 1976. He married U.S. Olympic diver Lesley Bush, a Gold Medalist in the platform event at the 1964 Tokyo, Japan, Summer Olympics, but they later divorced.

BIBLIOGRAPHY: Pat Besford, *Encyclopedia of Swimming*, 2nd ed. (London, England, 1976); Bill Mallon and Ian Buchanan, *Quest for Gold: The Encyclopedia of American Olympians* (New York, 1984); *The Official Book of Swimming Records: American Swimmer*, 2nd ed. (Los Angeles, CA, 1976).

Bill Mallon

MONTGOMERY, James Paul "Jim" (b. January 24, 1955, Madison, WI), swimmer, was the first male to swim the 100-meter freestyle in less than 50 seconds, accomplishing the feat in 49.99 seconds on July 25, 1976. His accomplishment remains one of those athletic "barrier-breaking" moments on a par with the running of the mile in under 4 minutes, breaking 13 minutes for the three-mile track run, eclipsing the 8- and 20-foot barriers in the high jump and pole vault, respectively, and tossing the javelin 300 feet.

At the 1976 Montreal, Canada, Summer Olympics, Montgomery showed that Mark Spitz's (IS) incredible, seemingly invincible 1972 collection of seven Olympic medals could be threatened. Montgomery won three Gold Medals (100-meter freestyle, 4 × 200-meter freestyle relay, 4 × 100-meter freestyle relay) and one Bronze Medal (200-meter freestyle). His relay leg of 49.57 seconds was nearly half a second faster than his 100-meter record of 49.99 seconds, set at the Montreal Olympics. The *NYT* observed, "The major reason for the success of the American men is the strong swimming programs in the Amateur Athletic Union and the National Collegiate Athletic Association."

At the 1972 Munich, Germany Summer Olympics, Spitz benefited from his swimming training at Indiana University under coaching maestro Doc Counsilman (IS). Similarly, Montgomery profited from that successful combination. He also enjoyed the keen mentoring of Counsilman, who served as the 1976 U.S. Olympic swimming coach. Montgomery drew on his remarkable successes at the 1973 World Championships in Yugoslavia, taking Gold Medals in two individual events and three relays. At Indiana University, he won the NCAA Championship in the 200-yard freestyle and participated on five world record-breaking relay teams between 1973 and 1976. He also captured four first places at the 1975 and 1978 World Championships, held at Cali, Colombia, and Berlin, Germany, respectively.

Montgomery has continued to enjoy aquatic challenges. In the mid-1980s, he won the 2.4-mile Waikiki, HI, Roughwater Ocean Swim. An Indiana honors business graduate, he returned to swimming all that the sport gave him. He coached the Lone Star Masters team, guiding his squad the first year to the Masters National Team Championship. The Wisconsin native exemplified the talented athlete who attached great importance to "concentration and goal setting."

BIBLIOGRAPHY: "Better Training Is Key to Swim Records," *NYT*, July 24, 1976; Biographical profile, undated, courtesy of Jill Cooper, U.S. Swimming, Colorado Springs, CO; Bill Mallon and Ian Buchanan, *Quest for Gold: The Encyclopedia of American Olympians* (New York, 1984).

                                                                                          Scott A.G.M. Crawford

MORALES, Pablo (b. December 5, 1964, Santa Clara, CA), swimmer, is the son of Pedro Morales and Bianca Morales and in 1992 was voted the USOC Sportsman of the Year and a finalist for the Sullivan Memorial Award.

The time span of competitive careers varies considerably in different sports. Top European and American thoroughbred jockeys often enjoy success into their fifties, competing much longer than swimmers. Successive Olympic games, by contrast, normally see the arrival of new swimming champions. In this context, Morales remains a unique swimmer and extraordinary athlete. At the 1984 Los Angeles, CA, Summer Olympics, he won a

Gold Medal in the 4 × 100-meter medley relay. Four years later at the U.S. Olympic Trials, he placed third in the 100-meter and 200-meter butterfly events. Anguish and despair followed because he was not selected as an American Olympian and retired from swimming. This seemingly marked the end of an already distinguished swimming career, but the final chapter remained to be written.

In August 1991, the 27-year-old started on the comeback trail as a fit, relatively old swimmer. He harnessed all of his energies for one event, the 100-meter butterfly. This event may be the single-most explosive activity in the gamut of sport, entailing a vigorous thrashing and flailing of arms and legs. The stroke is not as fast through the water as the freestyle reach-push-pull action, but the demands are extreme even on a trained body. Morales's long layoff may have been a blessing in disguise because he showed no hint of staleness or mental fatigue in 1992. At the 1992 Barcelona, Spain, Summer Olympics, he earned a Gold Medal in the 100-meter butterfly and swam the butterfly leg on the world record–setting 4 × 100-meter medley relay.

Morales swam at Stanford and graduated with a bachelor's degree in 1987. Six years later, he completed law studies at Cornell University. Morales, the only butterfly swimmer to have dipped under 53 seconds in the 100-meter dash, has dominated butterfly sprint swimming like Mark Spitz (IS) did in the early 1970s. The six-foot-two-inch, 165-pound Morales was brought up by Cuban emigre parents. His 11 NCAA Championships established a record that could endure into the twenty-first century. His mother, Bianca, died of cancer just weeks after Morales began his Olympic training in 1991. At the 1992 Summer Olympics, his father, Pedro, kept Bianca's photograph at the poolside while watching Pablo's race to victory. *USA Today* reported Morales senior exclaiming, "Way to go, my son!"

BIBLIOGRAPHY: Biographical profile, undated, courtesy of Jill Cooper, U.S. Swimming, Colorado Springs, CO; Tom Weir, "Tragedy Often Dilutes Joyful Olympic Tears," *USA Today*, July 1992.

                                      Scott A.G.M. Crawford

ROSS, Norman DeMille "Uncle Normie" "The Big Moose" (b. May 2, 1896, Portland, OR; d. June 19, 1953, Evanston, IL), swimmer, won three Gold Medals at the 1920 Summer Olympic Games in Antwerp, Belgium. Ross began swimming at the Hill Military Academy in Portland and then studied at Stanford University but left Palo Alto, CA, in 1917 to enlist in the U.S. Army during World War I. During that conflict, he became a military flyer and an aerial acrobatic instructor and was decorated by General John Pershing. Ross knew fellow flying cadet Jimmy Doolittle, who later became a famous general. After the war, the 6-foot-2½-inch, 240-pound Ross won five swimming events at the Inter-Allied Games in Paris, France, in 1919. At the 1920 Olympics, he won Gold Medals in the 400-meter freestyle,

1,500-meter freestyle, and on the U.S. 4 × 200-meter freestyle relay team. Ross set 12 world records at international distances and won 18 AAU Championships. At various distances, he has been credited with as many as 60 American swimming records. After World War I, he swam for the San Francisco OlC and the Illinois AC.

During a swim meet in Honolulu, HI, Ross met a Hawaiian princess, Beatrice. They later married and had two children, Norman, Jr., and Betty Jean. After retiring from swimming competition, he earned a law degree from Northwestern University and became a sportswriter at the Chicago *Daily Journal*. During a baseball World Series assignment for the newspaper in 1931, Ross was asked to provide radio commentary. He entered the radio business to handle sports events and serve as a news commentator and became the nation's first classical disc jockey, known to millions as "Uncle Normie." His son, Norman, Jr., followed him on the airwaves, becoming a familiar radio and television voice in the Chicago, IL, area. Norman, Sr., joined NBC in 1933 and conducted five morning shows. During World War II, Ross again served in the U.S. military. The Evanston, IL, resident reached the rank of lieutenant colonel and served as aide to his old friend General Jimmy Doolittle.

BIBLIOGRAPHY: Pat Besford, *Encyclopedia of Swimming*, 2nd ed. (London, England, 1976); Bill Mallon and Ian Buchanan, *Quest for Gold: The Encyclopedia of American Olympians* (New York, 1984); *NYT*, June 20, 1953; David Wallechinsky, *The Complete Book of the Olympics*, 3rd ed. (London, England, 1992).

Bill Mallon

SANDERS, Summer Elisabeth (b. October 13, 1972, Roseville, CA), swimmer, won four medals and set two American records at the 1992 Barcelona, Spain, Summer Olympics. When her parents, Bob, a dentist, and Barbara, an airline attendant, installed a pool in their backyard, they were concerned over water safety and enrolled their children, Trevor and Summer, in swimming lessons. Summer's aquatic talent manifested itself early. By age four, she competed with a local swim team against children up to three years older.

The steadily improving Sanders showed great promise at the 1988 U.S. Olympic Trials. Although 15 years old, Sanders finished third in the 200-meter individual medley and missed a spot on the Olympic team by only .27 of a second. She built on this success with victories at the 1989 U.S. Short Course Nationals in the 200-yard butterfly, the 1990 U.S. Short Course Nationals in the 200-yard butterfly and 400-yard individual medley, and the 1990 U.S. Long Course Nationals in the 200-meter individual medley.

Prior to entering Stanford University, she again surprised the swimming world at the 1990 Goodwill Games in Seattle, WA. Sanders captured Gold Medals in the 200-meter individual medley, 200-meter butterfly, and 400-meter individual medley. Her biggest headlines came while upsetting Janet

Evans (S) in the 400-meter individual medley. Sanders broke Evans's four-year-old winning streak and recorded the eighth-fastest time ever in the event.

As a freshman at Stanford University, she teamed with Evans in leading the Cardinal to second place in the NCAA Championships. She was named Swimmer of the Year in 1991, setting NCAA marks in the 200-yard butterfly and 400-yard individual medley and an American record of 1 minute 57.02 seconds in the 200-yard individual medley. Sanders's sophomore year saw her pace Stanford to the 1992 NCAA crown by winning three events. She established an American record in the 200 butterfly and the NCAA mark in the 400-yard individual medley, repeating as Swimmer of the Year. After the 1992 season, she relinquished her college eligibility to pursue endorsement opportunities.

Sanders's star shone again at the 1992 U.S. Olympic Trials and Barcelona, Spain, Summer Olympic Games. At the trials, she won three events and qualified in four events and the medley relay. Consequently, she became only the third U.S. woman to qualify for five Olympic swimming events. At the Olympics, Sanders captured four medals and set two American records. Her two Gold Medals came in the 200-meter butterfly and 400-meter medley relay. She also garnered a Silver Medal and record of 2 minutes 11.91 seconds in the 200-meter individual medley and a Bronze Medal and record of 4 minutes 37.58 seconds in the 400-meter individual medley. She also placed sixth in the 100-meter butterfly. Sanders won the 100-meter butterfly at the U.S. Indoor Championships in March 1993. Despite relinquishing her college eligibility, Sanders still attends Stanford.

BIBLIOGRAPHY: "A Bigger Splash," *Time* 140 (July 27, 1992), p. 66; "The Butterfly Queen," *Newsweek* 120 (July 27, 1992), p. 48; "Happy Trials to You," *SI* 76 (March 16, 1992), p. 36; Mike Meserole, ed., *The 1993 Information Please Sports Almanac* (Boston, MA, 1993); "Stunning Strokes," *SI* 73 (July 30, 1990), p. 40; "Summer Heat Wave," *SI* 74 (April 1, 1991), p. 44; "Summer Time," *SI* 76 (June 1, 1992), p. 46.

Brian L. Laughlin

STEWART, Melvin "Mel" (b. November 18, 1968, Gastonia, NC), swimmer, is a six-foot-two-inch, 182-pound Charlotte, NC, resident and two-time Olympian. Stewart is the son of the athletic director for the now-notorious "Heritage USA" Theme Park, created by the formerly united evangelists Jim and Tammy Baker.

Stewart first impacted international swimming with his 1986 victory at the Goodwill Games in Moscow, Russia, in the 200-meter butterfly. In his third year of top-level swimming, he survived the 1988 U.S. Olympic Trials. At the Seoul, South Korea, Summer Olympics, however, he only placed fifth in the 200-meter butterfly. The year 1991 marked Stewart's move to the highest level of elite swimming. He won the Pan Pacific 200-meter butterfly title at Edmonton, Canada, breaking the 1 minute 56 second barrier for that event. He also defeated formidable Michael Gross of Germany in the 200-meter butterfly handsomely, by more than a second. Stewart's ultimate achievement may have been his dethroning of legendary champion Gross. Gross, nicknamed the "Albatross" because of his incredible arm span, body height, and reach, seemed to fly through the water. He had dominated swimming in the 1980s.

The 1992 Barcelona, Spain, Summer Olympic Games pitted Gross against Stewart in the 200-meter butterfly. On the starting blocks, the towering German dwarfed Stewart. But Stewart defeated the legendary Gross, won a Gold Medal in the 400-meter medley relay and a Bronze Medal in the 800-meter relay, and placed fifth in the 100-meter butterfly. At the 1993 U.S. National Outdoor Championships in Austin, TX, Stewart captured the 200-meter butterfly. He won the 200-meter butterfly and finished third in the 100-meter butterfly at the 1994 St. Petersburg, Russia, Goodwill Games. A tonsillectomy forced him to miss the 1994 U.S. National Outdoor Championships at Bloomington, IN. Stewart's underwater swimming technique enabled him to set American records of 1 minute 54.76 seconds in the 200-meter butterfly and of 52.78 seconds in the 100-meter butterfly at the 1994 U.S. Open Swimming Championships in Buffalo, NY. The University of Tennessee student, a world and Olympic champion, achieved these successes on a campus where traditional champions have been forged on the football field and in track and field.

BIBLIOGRAPHY: Biographical profile, undated, courtesy of Jill Cooper, U.S. Swimming, Colorado Springs, CO.

                                                                          Scott A.G.M. Crawford

THOMPSON, Jennifer "Jenny" (b. February 26, 1973, Danvers, MA), swimmer, is a 5-foot-10-inch, 155-pound swimmer not built along the same lines as the powerful East Germans of the 1980s. Nevertheless, she became the greatest American sprint swimmer with her 1992 world record in the 100-meter freestyle. Thompson's 54.48-second clocking made her the first U.S. female swimmer to hold the 100-meter freestyle world record since the 1930s. Dawn Fraser of Australia dominated the event from 1956 to 1964, while the East German women reigned supreme in the post–1973 era.

Thompson owes much of her success to her mother, Margrid, who brought up Jenny and her three older brothers. At age 13, Thompson moved to Dover, NH. At the Dover SeC, she trained under coach Mike Parratto. Parratto took Thompson on a two-day trip to Tuscaloosa, AL, so that she could participate in the 50-yard national championship. Until race time, Thompson remained a typical, fun-loving 12-year-old. Parratto recalled, "But about five minutes before her race she [Thompson] changed. She became a competitor. She focused. Then five minutes after the race she was a 12 year old again." Thompson attends Stanford University and plans to graduate in 1995. Stanford and U.S. Olympic swimming coach Richard Quick lauded Thompson's competitive fire, "She is willing to train, to dream and to live at the level it takes every day. She was intense from the first day she came. She wants to be challenged, to anchor every relay. She's like the basketball player who wants to take the last shot in every game."

Thompson won the 1987 Pan-American Championships in the 50-meter freestyle. Three years later, she was ranked fourth in the world in the 100-meter freestyle and fifth in the 50-meter freestyle. She exhibited exciting glimpses of her true potential in 1991, winning Gold Medals at the Pan-Pacific Championships. At the 1991 World Championships in Perth, Australia, she anchored the Gold Medal–winning American record–breaking 400-meter freestyle relay.

For Thompson, 1992 marked a bittersweet year. Although setting a world record in the 100-meter freestyle with a 54.48-second clocking at the Barcelona, Spain, Summer Olympics, she won a Silver Medal rather than the Gold. Compensations came in two relays, as she garnered Gold Medals in the 400-meter freestyle and 400-meter medley. She continues her excellent swimming for the Dover SeC. At the U.S. National Indoor Championships at Nashville, TN, Thompson placed first in the 500-meter freestyle, the 1000-meter freestyle, and the 100-meter backstroke. That same year, she earned the Kiphuth Award at the U.S. National Outdoor Championships in Austin, TX, following her victories in the 50-meter freestyle, 100-meter freestyle, and 100-meter backstroke. The same year, *USS* honored Thompson as Swimmer of the Year following her incredible six Gold Medals at the Kobe, Japan, Pan-Pacific Championships. Her titles included the 50-meter freestyle, 100-meter freestyle, and 100-meter butterfly. In March 1994, she secured victories in both the 100-yard freestyle and butterfly and anchored two winning relays at the NCAA Championships at Bloomington, IN, for defending titlist Stanford. Despite a broken left arm suffered in a water slide accident, Thompson still triumphed in the 100-meter freestyle and the 100-meter butterfly and placed third in the 50-meter freestyle and the 200-meter freestyle at the 1994 U.S. National Outdoor Championships in Bloomington, IN. At the 1994 World Aquatic Championships in Rome, Italy, Thompson finished second in the 4 × 100-meter freestyle relay, second in the 4 × 100-meter medley relay, and third in the 4 × 200-meter freestyle relay.

BIBLIOGRAPHY: Karen Allen, "Thompson Talks Good Game, Swims Better," *USA Today*, July 1992; Biographical profile, undated, courtesy of Jill Cooper, U.S. Swimming, Colorado Springs, CO; Scott Crawford, telephone interview with Mike Parratto, October 5, 1993.

Scott A.G.M. Crawford

TENNIS AND OTHER
RACQUET SPORTS

AGASSI, Andre Kirk (b. April 29, 1970, Las Vegas, NV), tennis player, is the son of Emmanuel "Mike" Agassi and Elizabeth Agassi. After demonstrating extraordinary tennis skills under the tutelage of his father, Agassi, at age 13, enrolled in the famous Nick Bollettieri Tennis Academy in Bradenton, FL, and joined the professional tour at age 16 in 1986. Bollettieri remained Agassi's coach until 1993, when tennis great Pancho Segura replaced him. Much was expected of Agassi because of his luminous talents, but the 5-foot-10-inch, 155-pound right-hander did not fully "cash in" on his initial promise until the early 1990s. He became a finalist in three of the Grand Slam tournaments, only to lose in each one. In 1990, he was defeated in the French Open by Andres Gomez, 6–3, 2–6, 6–4, 6–4. The same year, he lost the U.S. Open to Pete Sampras* in straight sets, 6–4, 6–3, 6–2. In 1991, he again tasted defeat in the French Open in a tough match with Jim Courier,* 3–6, 6–4, 2–6, 6–1, 6–4.

After these disappointments, Agassi achieved the greatest triumph of his career in the 1992 Wimbledon finals, defeating Goran Ivanisevic, 6–7, 6–4, 6–4, 1–6, 6–4. This "breakthrough" victory proved doubly sweet because Agassi had shunned Wimbledon in 1988, 1989, and 1990, presumably due to some uncertainty over how he could adapt his classic baseline game to a grass surface. In recent years, Agassi has served as a vital member of the U.S. Davis Cup team. His two most productive tour victory seasons came in 1988, when he won six tournaments, and 1994, when he triumphed five times. In February 1994 Agassi made a triumphant comeback from a wrist injury by taking the Nu-Veen Championships at Scottsdale, AZ. He also won the Canadian Open tournament in Toronto in July. Although unseeded at the 1994 U.S. National Open tournament, Agassi defeated five seeded players to win his second major title. In the finals, he triumphed over fourth seed Michael Stich, 6–1, 7–6 (7–5), 7–5. Agassi dropped to his knees, raised his arms to the skies, and shared his joy with the adoring crowd. He became only the third unseeded player to take the crown, jumping from 20th to 9th in the world rankings. Following the match, J. Howard Frazer, president of the USTA, declared, "He is the most popular tennis player in the entire world." Agassi, who has 24 career victories, completed the 1994 season with triumphs at the CA Trophy Tournament in October and the Paris Open Tournament in November. At the 1995 Australian Open, Agassi did not lose a set until the finals. He captured his second consecutive Grand Slam title by defeating top-ranked Sampras, 4–6, 6–1, 7–6 (8–6), 6–4, to close in on the Number One ranking. Agassi exhibits brilliant ground strokes, achieved with a powerful forehand and a two-handed backhand, and possesses the greatest "return of serve" since Jimmy Connors (OS). Agassi's telegenic good looks and flair for showmanship have landed him in numerous television commercials endorsing various products. Although still single, Agassi remains prominently linked with Brooke Shields, Amy Moss, and Wendy Stewart. The highly intelligent, articulate Agassi, a devout Christian, finished his high school education by enrolling in correspondence courses. Due to Agassi's relative youth, most observers predict that his greatest achievements are yet to come.

BIBLIOGRAPHY: Andre Agassi, "Diary of a Rookie on Tour," *WT* 35 (December 1987), pp. 32–36, 50; Peter Bodo, "Image Isn't Everything," *Tennis* 28 (February 1993), pp. 34–39; *CB* (1989), pp. 10–14; Mike Davis, "Agassi Hogs Wimbledon Headlines," Lansing (MI) *State Journal*, July 1, 1993; Robin Finn, "On Wimbledon's Grass, Agassi Hits Pay Dirt," *NYT*, July 5, 1992; David Higdon, "Breakfast with Andre," *Tennis* 29 (July 1993), pp. 79–80; David Higdon, "On the Road with Mac & Andre," *Tennis* 29 (September 1993), pp. 46–52; Curry Kirkpatrick, "Born to Serve," *SI* 70 (March 13, 1989), pp. 63–74; Tony Trabert, "Great Shots: Agassi's Ripping Return," *Tennis* 29 (July 1993), p. 85; *WWA*, 47th ed. (1992–1993), p. 26.

                                                                                    Erik S. Lunde

BARGER, Maud. *See* Maud Barger Wallach.

CLARK, Grace Roosevelt. *See* Grace Walton Roosevelt Clark under Ellen Crosby Roosevelt.

COURIER, James "Jim" (b. August 17, 1970, Sanford, FL), tennis player, is the son of James Courier and Linda Courier. The six-foot-one-inch, 175-pound right-hander, ranked second behind Michael Chang among the U.S. 18-year-olds in 1987, entered the top 50 in the 1988 ATP computer rankings, finishing forty-third in the world and sixteenth nationally. After placing twenty-fourth in the world in 1989, he ranked twenty-fifth in the world and seventh nationally in 1990. In 1991, he rose to first nationally and second in the world behind Stefan Edberg of Sweden. The next year, Courier attained first in the world, highest of any American since John McEnroe (OS) in 1984.

     Courier, victorious in the 1986 and 1987 Orange Bowl tournaments, turned professional in 1988. His early tournament triumphs included the

Basel in 1989 and the Indian Wells and Key Biscayne in 1991. He captured his first Grand Slam tournament in 1991, winning the French Open over fellow-American Andre Agassi,* and finished second to Edberg in the U.S. Open. Courier began 1992 by taking the Australian Open, defeating Edberg, 6–3, 3–6, 6–4, 6–2. He won his third Grand Slam tournament, besting Petr Korda in the 1992 French Open. In 1993, Courier successfully defended his Australian Open crown, defeating Edberg, 6–2, 6–1, 2–6, 7–5, and finished second in both the French Open, losing to Sergei Bruguera of Spain, and at Wimbledon, falling to fellow-American Pete Sampras,* 7–6, 7–6, 3–6, 6–3. His other 1993 tournament victories included the Kroger/St. Jude International, the Newsweek Champions Cup, the Italian Open, and the RCA/U.S. Hardcourts. Sampras also ousted Courier in the semifinals of the 1994 Australian Open, while Bruguera ousted him in the semifinals of the 1994 French Open. Tournament victories eluded Courier in 1994, as he suffered elimination in the second round of the U.S. Open. In January 1995, Courier won the Australian Hardcourt Championship at Adelaide, Australia, and lost in five sets to Sampras in the quarterfinals of the Australian Open.

Courier played on the U.S. Davis Cup team, victorious over Switzerland in December 1992. He also participated on the 1994 and other Davis Cup teams and on the U.S. Olympic team in the 1992 Barcelona, Spain, Summer Games, reaching the finals of the doubles competition with Sampras.

BIBLIOGRAPHY: *NYT*, June 8, 1992, p. C1; January 28, 1994, p. B9; *The Official USTA Yearbook* (Lynn, MA, 1992); *Wall Street Journal*, November 21, 1992, p. D2; January 31, 1993, p. D1; June 7, 1993, p. A1; Washington *Post*, November 21, 1992, p. D2; *WWA*, 47th ed. (1992–1993), p. 716.

Miriam F. Shelden

DEVLIN, Judy. *See* Judy Devlin Hashman.

FALKENBURG, Robert "Bob" (b. January 29, 1926, New York, NY), tennis player, is the son of Eugene L. Falkenburg, a mining engineer, and Marguerite "Mickey" (Crooks) Falkenburg and lived in Brazil and Chile until the mid-1930s, when the Falkenburgs settled at Los Angeles, CA. The Falkenburg children, Jinx (originally Eugenia), Tom, and Bob, became ranking California tennis players. At Fairfax High School, the brothers won the U.S. Interscholastic doubles title and Robert the singles championship. Robert captured the 1940 and 1941 U.S. Boys (under age 15) singles and doubles titles, the 1942 and 1943 U.S. Junior (under age 18) doubles, and 1943 singles before playing the adult Eastern tournament circuit and ranking seventh nationally. He then enlisted in the U.S. Air Force but still competed sufficiently in 1944 to defend his U.S. Junior titles successfully, rank sixth nationally, and win the U.S. doubles championship with Don McNiell (S).

After serving as flight engineer on a B-29 Super Fortress to the end of World War II, he attended the University of Southern California on a tennis scholarship for two years and won the 1946 U.S. Intercollegiate crowns in singles and in doubles with brother Tom. On a South American tennis tour, he met Lourdes Machado, a Brazilian, and married her in early 1947. Their children are Roberto and Claudia Jean.

Falkenburg ranked eighth, seventh, and fifth in the United States from 1946 through 1948, but his best success came at Wimbledon. The gangling six-foot-three-inch, 175-pound right-hander, who developed exceptionally swift flat first serves, fiery smashes, and deadly volleys, exhibited only mediocre ground strokes. Frequently, his vigorous serve-and-volley style exhausted him prematurely during hard matches. He won the 1947 Wimbledon doubles with Jack Kramer (IS), but a cramp in his right hand caused his loss to Dinny Pails in a singles quarterfinal. In 1948, however, he won the prestigious All-England crown, defeating Frank Sedgman, Gardnar Mulloy (S), and in the final, John Bromwich, after coolly surviving three fifth-set match points against him. Versus Mulloy and Bromwich, he incurred crowd displeasure by repeatedly taking extra time to arise after his many lunging falls to the turf. He faced Bromwich again in a 1949 quarterfinal. After winning two sets, the exhausted Falkenburg lost the next three.

Falkenburg in 1950 moved his family to Rio de Janeiro, Brazil, where he operated an ice cream business profitably and played on the 1954 and 1955 Brazilian Davis Cup teams. After spending 22 years in Brazil, he sold out and retired to southern California. He was elected in 1974 to the International (then National Lawn) Tennis Hall of Fame.

BIBLIOGRAPHY: J. P. Allen, "Bob Falkenburg Joins Army," New York *Sun*, February 15, 1944; Maurice Brady, *The Centre Court Story* (London, England, 1957); *CB* (1953), pp. 392–395; Bud Collins and Zander Hollander, eds., *Bud Collins' Modern Encyclopedia of Tennis*, 2nd ed. (Detroit, MI, 1993); Stan Hart, *Once a Champion: Legendary Tennis Stars Revisited* (New York, 1985).

                                                                Frank V. Phelps

FREEMAN, David Guthrie "Dave" (b. September 6, 1920, Pasadena, CA), badminton and tennis player, is the son of Robert Freeman, a Presbyterian minister, and Margery (Fulton) Freeman, Occidental College professor of religion. He won the Pasadena City Table Tennis championship at age 13 and ranked sixth among southern California boy tennis players at age 14. In 1938, he graduated from Pasadena JC, reached the U.S. Badminton championship semifinals, won the U.S. Junior tennis singles and doubles titles, and made the final of the USPP tennis championship.

Freeman graduated in 1942 from Pomona College with a B.A. degree but competed only on the golf and cross-country teams there. Off campus, he dominated American badminton. After Ted Pollock defeated him at the 1939 New England badminton championship, Freeman never again lost a tournament singles match. He won the U.S. singles badminton titles from 1939 through 1942 and doubles and mixed doubles crowns from 1940 through 1942. He conquered Ted Schroeder (OS) and Jack Crawford in tennis in

1939, earning national rankings of twenty-second in singles and, with Schroeder, fourth in doubles.

Freeman married Dolly Rees in 1942 and studied at Harvard Medical School from 1942 to 1945. He played sufficient tennis in 1943 to rank sixteenth nationally in singles and, with Bill Talbert (OS), third in doubles following a second-place finish in the U.S. doubles championship. After obtaining his M.D. degree, he spent a U.S. Army duty tour as a medical officer at Gorgas Hospital in the Canal Zone. When the U.S. Badminton championships resumed after World War II, he captured the 1947 and 1948 singles and doubles titles while on 10-day leaves. Upon completion of his tour duty, the blond right-hander led the first U.S. Thomas Cup team to an 8–1 victory over Canada in the winter of 1948–1949. The United States lost to Malaya, 6–3, in the next round, at Glasgow, Scotland, although Freeman triumphed over great international badminton players Wong Peng Soon and Ooi Teik Hock. He vanquished both twice more, adding the All-England and Danish singles championships to his record.

A four-year residency in neurosurgery at the University of Michigan curtailed his sports activity until 1953. After one warm-up tournament, he won his last U.S. Badminton singles crown and then retired permanently. The Freemans have three children, Rees Guthrie, David Frederick, and Diana Mae, and settled in San Diego, CA, where the doctor established and still maintains his practice as a neurosurgeon.

The 5-foot-11-inch, 150-pound Freeman's tennis style featured sure volleys and severe overheads. At badminton, his expressive enjoyment, agility, and miraculous low saves attracted attention. English critic Betty Uber particularly noted Freeman's almost perfect footwork, infinite patience, and "ability to play attacking and constructive games for an unlimited time with practically no mistakes." He was elected to the USBA Hall of Fame as a charter member in 1956.

BIBLIOGRAPHY: John E. Garrod, ed., *The Official Badminton Guide . . . 1947* (New York, 1947), pp. 54–82; Ted Jarrett, "Freeman the Fabulous," *TRq* (March 1953), pp. 11, 22, 27; E. C. Potter and Robert C. Hynson, "Leaning on the Fence," *ALT* 33 (September 20, 1939), p. 38; Charles and Jack Shelton, "This Champion Doesn't Practice," *SEP* 213 (March 22, 1941), pp. 27, 47, 49; Betty Uber, *That Badminton Racket* (London, England, 1950).

Frank V. Phelps

GOULD, Jay (b. September 1, 1888, Mamaroneck, NY; d. January 26, 1935, Margaretville, NY), court tennis player, was a grandson of Jay Gould, a financial and railroad magnate, and a son of George Jay Gould, a railroad tycoon and sportsman, and Edith (Kingdon) Gould. His father installed a real tennis court at his Georgian Court Lakewood, NJ, estate and in 1900 hired Frank Forester, an experienced coach of racket sports, to teach racquets and court tennis to Jay and his brother Kingdon. Jay, a right-hander, quickly mastered all the mechanics and strategies of this difficult, intricate indoor game, known variously as tennis, royal tennis, and court tennis. At age 17, he reached the finals of the Tuxedo, NY, Gold Racquet tournament before losing to Charles E. Sands.

He won the Gold Racquet in 1906, besting Pierre Lorillard, Jr., in the final. In his first U.S. amateur championship, in 1906, he recorded narrow brilliant victories over J. J. Cairnes, Joshua Crane, and in the challenge round, Sands. Accompanied by Forester to Great Britain, he reached the challenge round of the English championship before falling to defending champion Eustace Miles. A year later, he overcame Miles to take the British title.

After his 1906 loss to Miles, he remained undefeated until Edgar Baerlein bested him, 4–8, 8–5, 8–4, in the 1923 Bathhurst Cup final. In 1923, Great Britain vanquished the U.S. team, 3–2. Gould won the U.S. amateur singles crown 18 times from 1906 through 1925, losing only one game to Crane in 1909. He captured the U.S. doubles crown 19 times from 1909 through 1932, performing variously with Tevis Huhn, Joe Wear, and William Wright. Gould also won the Tuxedo Gold Racquet three times and triumphed against professionals in the 1919 and 1921 U.S. Open singles. He prevailed over Fred Covey in 1916 to become World Open Champion but resigned the title without defending it. Gould retired from singles competition in 1925 and ceased competition completely in 1932 due to failing health.

Gould, who attended Columbia University, married Annie Douglass Graham in April 1911 and had three children, Eleanor, Anne, and Jay, Jr. He shared in management of the vast Gould estate and eventually engaged in realty business in New York City. His residence on an entire floor of 444 East Fifty-seventh Street included a court tennis dedans. A hemorrhage of the esophagus caused his death.

BIBLIOGRAPHY: Lord Aberdare, *The Willis Faber Book of Tennis & Rackets* (London, England, 1980); *ALT* 29 (February 20, 1935), p. 36; Allison Danzig, *The Racquet Game* (New York, NY, 1930); Allison Danzig, *The Winning Gallery* (Philadelphia, PA, 1985); *NYT*, May 7, 1923, pp. 1, 6; January 28, 1935, p. 15; Thomas D. Richter, "Champion of Champions, Jay Gould," *SpL* (April 22, 1916), p. 22.

Frank V. Phelps

HASHMAN, Judy Devlin (b. October 22, 1935, Winnipeg, Canada), badminton player, is the daughter of J. Frank Devlin, a badminton player, and married Dick Hashman, another badminton player. After moving to the United States with her family, she began playing badminton at age 7. Hashman was coached by her father, Frank, an All-England badminton champion six times between 1925 and 1931. At age 13, she won the singles, doubles, and mixed doubles at the U.S. Junior National Badminton Championships and defended her titles successfully at the U.S. Junior Nationals six years in singles, five years in doubles, and three years in mixed doubles.

Hashman, who captured her first U.S. National women's singles championship in 1954, garnered the title 11 more times. She won 31 U.S. Badminton Championship titles and seven Canadian Open titles, including three singles, three doubles, and one mixed doubles crown. Her first All-England singles title came in 1954. She retired from singles competition following her tenth singles crown in the 1967 All-England championships. Hashman, the holder of seven doubles titles, was elected to the HAF Badminton Hall of Fame in 1963.

Hashman, an All-America lacrosse player at Goucher College in 1954, 1955, 1957, and 1958, became an American citizen in 1956 and a British citizen in 1970.

BIBLIOGRAPHY: *The Lincoln Library of Sports Champions*, vol. 6 (Columbus, OH, 1974), pp. 31–32.

Miriam F. Shelden

HOVEY, Frederick Howard (b. October 7, 1868, Newton Centre, MA; d. October 18, 1945, Palm Beach, FL), athlete, was the son of Alvah Hovey, a Baptist minister and president of Andover-Newton Theological Seminary, and Augusta Maria (Rice) Hovey and graduated from Brown University in 1890 with a B.A. degree and from Harvard University in 1893 with an LL.B. degree. He performed in four intercollegiate tennis championships for Brown, enjoying little success, and two for Harvard, winning the 1890 and 1891 singles titles and the 1891 doubles crown with Bob Wrenn (OS). He also played shortstop for the Harvard baseball team in 1891, 1892, and 1893.

At Newport, RI, in 1891, he battled through four five-set matches and two others to reach the U.S. All-Comers final. The exhausted Hovey, however, lost a five-set final to Clarence Hobart. After winning the prestigious Longwood title and four other 1892 tournaments, he triumphed in the U.S. All-Comers event. He lost in the challenge round to Ollie Campbell (OS), whom he had defeated in the 1890 intercollegiate tournament. After successfully defending the Longwood Bowl in 1893, Hovey teamed with Hobart to capture the U.S. doubles crown. He again reached the All-Comers final at Newport, vanquishing Eddie Hall, Val Hall, and Hobart. In that final, Wrenn thwarted Hovey's strong net game by lobbing incessantly and defeated him, 6–4, 3–6, 6–4, 6–4. Hovey and Hobart retained their doubles title in 1894, but Hovey lost to Bill Larned (OS) at Longwood and to Manliffe Goodbody of Ireland in the second round at Newport.

Despite losing the U.S. doubles championship in 1895, Hovey experienced his best year. After recapturing the Longwood Bowl, he again won the national All-Comers tournament and successfully challenged Wrenn, 6–3, 6–2, 6–4. Hovey eliminated Wrenn's prime weapon, the lob, by staying backcourt and frequently passing the net-rushing Wrenn.

Hovey married Sara Hayes Sanborn in April 1896 and had a daughter, Margaret, and a son, Frederick, Jr. Hovey seldom competed after his marriage and finished his lawn tennis career in 1896, losing to Wrenn first at Longwood and then in the U.S. singles challenge round. Subsequently, he left the practice of law and became a stockbroker. He moved during the early 1900s from Newton Centre to Montclair, NJ, and later retired to Palm Beach, FL. The five-foot-eight-inch, 170-pound right-hander, who excelled at volleying and smashing, possessed less effective ground strokes, particularly his backhand. Hovey, who ranked among the top five American players each season from 1891 through 1896, became enshrined in the International Tennis Hall of Fame in 1974.

BIBLIOGRAPHY: *ALT* 35 (April 20, 1931), p. 13; *ALT* 49 (December 1945), p. 37; *ALT* 49 (January 1946), p. 37; Bill Talbert with Pete Axthelm, *Tennis Observed* (Barre, MA, 1967); USLTA, *Fifty Years of Lawn Tennis in the United States* (New York, 1931); *Wright and Ditson Official Lawn Tennis Guide*, 1890–1897 (Boston, MA, 1890–1897).
                                                                          Frank V. Phelps

HUNTER, Francis Townsend "Frank" (b. June 28, 1894, New Rochelle, NY; d. December 2, 1981, Palm Beach, FL), athlete, played tennis when lissome stroke players reigned supreme. Hunter, a rugged former captain of the Cornell University ice hockey team, starred on the tennis court with a formidable forehand stroke. Hunter was eliminated from the tennis singles in the third round at the 1924 Paris, France, Summer Olympic Games. In the doubles, he and Vinnie Richards (OS) won a five-set match in the semifinal against Jean Borotra and René Lacoste of France and in the finals against Jacques Brugnon and Henri Cochet of France to take the Olympic title.

Hunter, a burly, aggressive player, achieved success mostly as a doubles player. Hunter combined with Richards to win the Wimbledon doubles in 1924 and with the great Bill Tilden (OS), who considered Hunter his best friend, to win in 1927. Hunter and Tilden also captured the U.S. doubles title in 1927 and played together in the Davis Cup competition in 1927 and 1928. As Tilden's partner, Hunter made the semifinals at Wimbledon in both 1928 and 1929. Hunter triumphed in the mixed doubles at Wimbledon in 1927 with Helen Wills (OS) and 1929 with Elizabeth Ryan (OS) before turning professional in 1931. In 1928, he and Wills lost semifinals of the Wimbledon mixed doubles. In singles competition, Hunter enjoyed his greatest success at the U.S. championships. He never won the singles title, being unable to defeat the great Tilden or France's "Four Musketeers." He lost in the 1927 semifinals to Tilden, 1928 finals to France's Henri Cochet, and 1929 finals to Tilden.

Hunter graduated from Cornell University in 1916 and served in World War I as a lieutenant commander in the U.S. Navy. He was assigned to Admiral David Beatty's flagship when the German fleet surrendered and later wrote a book about his naval experience of serving under Beatty. Hunter ultimately prospered in the business world, owning a chain of newspapers in the Westchester County, NY, area in the 1920s and 1930s. He in 1933 founded "21" Brands Incorporated, and later "21" Brands Distillers, both importers and distillers of wines and liquors, serving as president of both corporations until 1963. Hunter, who operated three coal mines in West Virginia and also owned and controlled a fleet of cargo ships, was enshrined in the International Tennis Hall of Fame in 1961.

BIBLIOGRAPHY: Maurice Brady, *The Encyclopaedia of Lawn Tennis* (London, England, 1958); Frank Deford, *Big Bill Tilden: The Triumphs and the Tragedy* (New York, 1976); Bill Mallon and Ian Buchanan, *Quest for Gold: The Encyclopedia of American Olympians* (New York, 1984); *NYT*, December 4, 1981.

Bill Mallon

MAKO, Constantine Gene (b. January 24, 1916, Budapest, Hungary), tennis player, is the son of Bertalan Mako, a painter, sculptor, and architectural engineer, and Georgina (Farkas) Mako and moved with his parents to Buenos Aires, Argentina, and then Glendale, California. A natural athlete, he soon excelled at handball, basketball, baseball, table tennis, and tennis. Mako graduated from Glendale, CA, High School and attended the University of Southern California but left before graduating. He won the 1934 national intercollegiate tennis singles and doubles for Southern California.

Mako, who started playing tennis in 1927, captured four successive U.S. Junior doubles crowns with different partners. These titles included the 1931 Boys (under age 15) and 1932, 1933, and 1934 Juniors (under age 18) crowns. He also won the U.S. Junior singles finals in 1932 and 1934 by defeating Frank Parker (OS) and Don Budge (OS) but lost the 1933 finals to Budge. He and Budge formed a doubles team, which ranked nationally third for 1934, second for 1935, and first for 1936, 1937, and 1938. The duo represented the United States in Davis Cup matches from 1935 through 1938, scoring a 6–2 win-loss record and losing only to John Bromwich and Adrian Quist in the 1937 and 1938 challenge rounds. They won the 1937 and 1938 championships at Wimbledon and reached the U.S. final round four times, winning in 1936 and 1938 and losing in 1935 and 1937. Mako, although not as successful in singles, reached his high point during the 1938 U.S. championships. The unseeded Mako upset Frank Kovacs, Franjo Puncec, Gil Hunt, and Bromwich before dropping a four-set final to his close friend Budge, who thus completed his "Grand Slam" sweep of the world's top tournaments. The performance earned Mako a number-three ranking, his best in singles, but he slipped to fourteenth in 1939, his last year of serious competition.

Mako featured explosive serves and smashes as a junior until arm and shoulder injuries weakened his power. A net specialist, he compensated by quickness, volleying expertise, mastery of angles and pace, steadiness, and keen strategy. The husky, broad-shouldered, six-foot, 170-pound right-hander played the deuce court when paired with Budge.

Mako, who married Laura Mae Church in November 1941, had no children. After serving in the U.S. Navy during World War II, he briefly played professional tennis. At Los Angeles CA, Mako has worked as a designer and builder of tennis courts and as an art dealer specializing in nineteenth-century subjects. He in 1973 was elected to the International (then National Lawn) Tennis Hall of Fame.

BIBLIOGRAPHY: *ALT* 32 (April 20, 1938), p. 13; Bud Collins and Zander Hollander, eds., *Bud Collins' Modern Encyclopedia of Tennis* (Detroit, MI, 1993); Stan Hart, *Once a Champion: Legendary Tennis Stars Revisited* (New York, 1985); John McDiarmid, "Our Three Hopefuls," *ALT* 28 (October 20, 1934), pp. 11, 33.

                                                                                    Frank V. Phelps

MARTIN, Alastair Bradley (b. March 11, 1915, New York, NY), court and lawn tennis player and administrator, is the son of Bradley Martin, a capitalist, and Helen (Phipps) Martin, a socialite, and lived at Guennol, the family Westbury, NY, estate. After attending Deane School in Santa Barbara, CA, he in 1938 graduated from Princeton University with a B.A. degree and married Edith Park. They have a son, Robin, and a daughter, Dorothy. Martin's business involved ownership, development, and management of six FM radio stations in the East and Midwest. His nonathletic hobbies included the collection of medieval, folk, and pre-Colombian paintings and artifacts. The Martins' Guennol Collection was exhibited at the Metropolitan Museum of Art in New York in 1969.

A fine lawn tennis player, he ranked nationally in Class A (from thirty-second through forty-fifth places) in 1951. Court tennis earned him recognition as a truly great all-time competitor. Punch Fairs, famous English champion and coach, taught him a style of vigorous, unceasing attack. Mastery of mechanics and tactics, a superb railroad service, foot speed, stroke accuracy, exceptional stamina, and constant maintenance of top physical condition enabled Martin to enjoy competing successfully for over 30 years. The blond, 5-foot-11-inch, 170-pound right-hander, a thorough sportsman who never took unfair advantage of an opponent, off court remained a quiet, modest, reserved, but friendly man.

From 1940 through 1966, his many important tournament championships included eight U.S. amateur singles, 11 U.S. amateur doubles, one U.S. Open singles, one U.S. Open doubles, 10 Tuxedo Gold Racquet singles, one United Kingdom singles, and one United Kingdom doubles. In 1950 and 1952, he challenged Pierre Etchebaster unsuccessfully for the World Open championship. Martin combined with Norty Knox in 1958 to defeat a British team at Queens Club in London, England, to win the Bathhurst Cup for the United States. Martin, a member of the prestigious New York RTC, scored a remarkable record by winning the club doubles title 20 consecutive years from 1949 through 1968. His 10 different doubles partners included twin brother Esmond Bradley Martin, first cousin Ogden Phipps, a noted court tennis champion, basketball player Bud Palmer, and tennis players Frank Shields (OS) and Bill Talbert (OS).

When the USCTA was founded in 1955, Martin served as its first secretary-treasurer. Martin, USLTA vice president in 1966, 1967, and 1968 and USLTA president in 1969 and 1970, was enshrined in the International Tennis Hall of Fame in 1973. The same year, the 58-year-old Martin reached the final of the U.S. court tennis amateur doubles championship.

BIBLIOGRAPHY: Lord Aberdare, *The Willis Faber Book of Tennis & Rackets* (London, England, 1980); *ALT* 27 (March 20, 1934), p. 42; Allison Danzig, *The Winning Gallery: Court Tennis Matches and Memories* (Philadelphia, PA, 1985); *NYT*, January 19, 1969, sec. 5, p. 1; November 8, 1969, p. 26; *WWWA*, vol. 4 (1961–1969), p. 615.

Frank V. Phelps

MILES, Richard "Dick" (b. June 12, 1925, New York, NY), table tennis player, is the son of Emmanuel Miles, a journalist, and Ivy (Adler) Miles and grew up in Manhattan. After learning table tennis on a toy set, he honed his skills at New York parlors against star players and made the sport a career instead of music or journalism. Miles assiduously devoted time to practice and competition, dropping out of DeWitt Clinton High School. After attaining championship status, however, he earned his high school diploma and attended New York University four years without graduating. Subsequently, he studied at Hunter College and Columbia University.

Miles won his first U.S. Open table tennis championship in 1945 by overwhelming defending titleholder John Somael and repeated as champion, winning the finals against veteran Sol Schiff in 1946 and 1947 and Marty Reisman in 1948 and 1949. He again triumphed over Reisman in the 1951 final, lost the 1952 tournament to Lou Pagliaro, took the 1953 and 1954 finals against Somael, and prevailed in the 1955 tournament against Richard Bergmann, four-time world champion. He captured his tenth and last U.S. Open singles crown in 1962, vanquishing Norbert Van Dewalle in the final round. Miles won the U.S. Open doubles four times, combining with Schiff in 1953, Somael in 1955, Reisman in 1958, and Van Dewalle in 1962. He prevailed in the mixed doubles twice, teaming with Betty Blackbourn in 1947 and Mildred Shahian in 1955.

Czechs, Hungarians, Japanese, and Chinese dominated international competition, denying Miles any World championships. He came closest to a World title in 1959, when he narrowly lost to Jung Kuo-tuan, the tournament winner. He secured the World 1948 mixed doubles crown with Thelma Thall and led the 1947 U.S. team to the Swaythling Cup final, which it lost to Czechoslovakia in the best post–World War II American showing. As a nonplaying member, he accompanied a U.S. team into the People's Republic of China during April 1971. This historic "Ping Pong Diplomacy" incident ended the impasse that had existed between the United States and the People's Republic of China since 1949.

The 5-foot-7½-inch, 118-pound right-hander exhibited a well-rounded, mechanically perfect style without weakness. He played a consistent attacking game, featuring a formidable "Windmill" forehand, bolstered by a solid defense. The introduction of the sponge rubber bat in 1952 radically altered competitive methods, but Miles, unlike many, adjusted appropriately. As his playing career decelerated, Miles worked as a freelance journalist and wrote about table tennis and other sports for *SI*. His book, *The Game of Table Tennis*, remains a thorough, finely detailed instruction manual. From 1974 until retirement in 1991, Miles conducted a business involving the import of table tennis equipment principally from the Far East. Miles, who resides in Manhattan and enjoys classical music, was one of the first players inducted into the USTT Hall of Fame when it was established in 1966.

BIBLIOGRAPHY: *The Lincoln Library of Sports Champions*, vol. 9 (Columbus, OH, 1974); Dick Miles, "Exterminating a Ping Pong Pest," *SI* 30 (June 28, 1971), pp. 30–35; Dick Miles, *The Game of Table Tennis* (New York, 1968); Dick Miles, "Spongers Seldom Chisel," *SI* 23 (November 15, 1965), pp. 102–122; Dick Miles, *Sports Illustrated Table Tennis* (New York, 1974); Frank Phelps, telephone interview with Dick Miles, November 15, 1993; Marty Reisman, *The Money Player* (New York, 1974).

                                                                                          Frank V. Phelps

PELL, Clarence Cecil (b. July 29, 1885, Newport, RI; d. November 3, 1964, Westbury, NY), athlete, was the son of Herbert Claiborne Pell, a founder of the elite Tuxedo Park, NY, community, and Katherine Lorillard (Kernochan) Pell and graduated from Pomfret, CT, School and from Harvard University in 1908 with a B.A. degree. At Harvard, he played four years on the ice hockey team and captained it during his senior year. The Crimson's four-year win–loss–tie ice hockey record was 29–4–1. He in May 1910 married Madeline Boreland, by whom he had three children, Clarence, John, and Katherine. After Madeline's death in 1949, he later wed Susan Wesselhoeft. During World War I, he served in the U.S. Army Signal Corps as a flying instructor in Texas and Louisiana and finally reached France three days before the Armistice. Subsequently, he became a partner with stock brokerage firms on Wall Street in New York until his retirement in 1929.

Family affluence and prestige afforded Pell the opportunity to participate freely in the exclusive, skillful racket-and-ball sports, which fascinated him. As a boy, he learned rackets (sometimes called "racquets") and court tennis technique and strategy from Robert Moore, imported from England to serve as the professional at the Tuxedo Club. A well-coordinated natural athlete with a broad-shouldered, deep-chested, sturdy physique, he possessed stamina, quickness, alertness, and competitive instinct. The right-hander became one of the truly great amateur racket players of all time by combining extremely hard hitting with consummate placing and a service delivery unexcelled in length, pace, and cut, considered worth five aces per game. From 1914 through 1933, he won the U.S. singles championship 12 times, Canadian title 8 times, English crown in 1925, and the prestigious Tuxedo Gold Racquet tournament 11 times. With Stanley Mortimer, his Tuxedo teammate and chief singles rival, he from 1915 through 1931 captured the U.S. doubles titles 9 times and Canadian championship 3 times. He also took the Canadian tournament with Alan Corey twice.

Pell excelled at other racket sports also. The USLTA ranked him four times in singles, putting him fifty-seventh in 1907, forty-fourth in 1909, Class 2 (twenty-first through thirtieth) in 1915, and Class 5 (fifty-first through sixtieth) in 1916. He held the Tuxedo Club court tennis championship in 1909 and won the New York RTC 1913 Class A handicap squash tennis tournament.

Clarence, Jr., nicknamed "Clarry," followed his father's athletic trail by playing three years on the Harvard ice hockey team. Clarence, Jr., later became a first-class rackets competitor, winning the U.S. amateur rackets title in 1958 and the doubles crown seven times from 1937 to 1950.

BIBLIOGRAPHY: Lord Aberdare, *The Willis Faber Book of Tennis & Rackets* (London, England, 1980); Allison Danzig, *The Racquet Game* (New York, 1930); *Harvard College Class of 1908 Twenty-fifth Anniversary Report* (Cambridge, MA, 1933), pp. 550–551; *NYT*, February 28, 1926, p. 28; November 4, 1964, p. 39.

Frank V. Phelps

ROOSEVELT, Ellen Crosby (b. August 20, 1868, Hyde Park, NY; d. September 26, 1954, Hyde Park, NY) and **Grace Walton Roosevelt CLARK** (b. June 3, 1867, Hyde Park, NY; d. November 29, 1945, Hyde Park, NY), tennis players, were first cousins of Franklin Delano Roosevelt and daughters of John Aspinwall Roosevelt, a wealthy estate proprietor, and Ellen Murray (Crosby) Roosevelt. They were born and died at "Rosedale," the Roosevelt mansion. Ellen, who remained single, lived there, while Grace married lawyer Appleton LeSure Clark in 1895, resided at New Brighton, Staten Island, NY, and had two sons, Russell and Roosevelt. After her husband died in 1930, Grace returned to Rosedale.

John Roosevelt installed a turf tennis court at Rosedale in 1879. The self-taught girls became expert players, both being right-handed, short, slender, and weighing about 95 pounds. Grace was fair and blonde, while Ellen was darker and brunette. They performed best at doubles, with Grace playing at net and Ellen in the backcourt in the approved style of the period. The duo served underhand, stroked accurately with consistency, and lobbed effectively. The Roosevelts lost only twice in doubles, first to Adeline Robinson (S) and Kitty Smith in 1887 at Hastings-on-the-Hudson, NY, and then to Mabel Cahill (OS) and Emma Morgan in the 1891 U.S. final. They won seven major tournaments from 1887 through 1892. The 1888 Philadelphia, PA, CrC Open, which did not become a U.S. championship until 1889, saw them defeat the best of Philadelphia and New York duos, including Ellen Hansell (OS) and Laura Knight and Robinson and Vi Ward. In 1890, they captured the U.S. crown, downing Cahill and Lida Voorhees and Bertha Townsend (OS) and Margarette Ballard, the initial 1889 titleholders.

Ellen, the sounder baseliner and better singles player, lost four times during 1887 and 1888 to Robinson. After Robinson retired, she won six important tournaments. The 1890 national championship featured her successively defeating Cahill, Voorhees, and Townsend. The win over Cahill proved indecisive, however, because leg cramps forced the Irish lady to default during the final close set. Seeking redress, Cahill then invaded Roosevelt territory by entering and winning the Hudson River Championship. The victory remained hollow because defending champion Ellen refused to play and defaulted her title.

Grace played her best singles to reach the 1891 national final, where she lost a spirited 6–4, 7–5 struggle to Cahill. Cahill then wrested her crown from Ellen in a four-set challenge match. The Roosevelts concluded their tournament career in 1892 at the prestigious SILCOS Invitation. The pair won the doubles crown, while Ellen took the singles from fields of excellent opponents in both events. Ellen in 1975 was enshrined in the International Tennis Hall of Fame.

BIBLIOGRAPHY: *ALT* 39 (February 1946), p. 11; New York *World Telegram*, September 27, 1954; *NYT*, June 12, 1930, p. 25; November 30, 1945, p. 23; September 27, 1954, p. 2; Poughkeepsie (NY) *Sunday Courier*, October 6, 1940.

Frank V. Phelps

SAMPRAS, Peter "Pete" (b. August 12, 1971, Washington, DC), tennis player, is the son of Samuel Sampras and Georgia Sampras and grew up in California. The six-foot, 170-pound right-hander, who lives in Florida, was ranked sixth nationally as a junior player in 1987 and turned professional in 1988. In 1990, the 19-year-old won the U.S. Open championship, defeating fellow-American Andre Agassi* to become that tournament's youngest male victor and the lowest seed (twelfth) to capture that title since professionals began competing in 1968. The ATP computer ranked him twenty-third in the world in 1988, sixteenth in 1989, and second in 1990 and 1991. Sampras won the inaugural Grand Slam Cup at Munich, Germany, in December 1990 and IBM/ATP Tour World Championship crown at Frankfurt, Germany, in December 1991. His other tournament victories included the U.S. Pro Indoor at Philadelphia, PA, and Manchester, England, Open in 1990 and Volvo/Los Angeles, CA, U.S. Hardcourt in Indianapolis, IN, and Lyon, France, Grand Prix in 1991.

Sampras captured the ATP Championship and U.S. Hardcourt in Indianapolis, IN, in August 1992 and finished second at the 1992 U.S. Open championship, losing the finals to Stefan Edberg of Sweden. He won his second U.S. Open tournament in 1993, defeating Cedric Pioline of France in three straight sets. The victory marked Sampras's second consecutive 1993 Grand Slam victory, as he had prevailed in the Wimbledon finals over fellow-American Jim Courier,* 7–6, 7–6, 3–6, 6–3. The triumph made Sampras the youngest American male Wimbledon champion. His other 1993 wins included the New South Wales Open in Sydney, Australia, Lipton Championships in Key Biscayne, FL, Japan Open in Tokyo, Japan, Salem Open in Hong Kong, and Lyon Grand Prix. Sampras finished 1993 as the world's top ATP computer–ranked player and retained that ranking with his 1994 Australian Open victory over Todd Martin, 7–6, 6–4, 6–4. Sampras captured six other tournaments in the first half of 1994. After being idle for six weeks because of an ankle injury (and missing the hardcourt circuit because of it), Sampras lacked stamina at the 1994 U.S. Open tournament and was eliminated by Jaime Yzaga of Peru in the fourth round. He won the 1994 Wimbledon, defeating Goran Ivanisevic of Croatia, 7–6, 7–6, 6–0. In November 1994, he won the European Community Championship at Antwerp, Belgium and the IBM/ATP World Championship at Frankfurt, Germany. Altogether, Sampras captured 10 tournaments and earned a tour record of $3,607,812 in 1994. The USOC named him its 1994 Male Tennis Player of the Year. Sampras reached the finals of the 1995 Australian Open before losing to Agassi in four sets.

Sampras competed on the U.S. Davis Cup teams in 1991, 1992, and 1994. Guy Forget defeated him in the 1991 singles, giving France its first Davis Cup title since 1932. In 1992, Sampras played singles and combined with John McEnroe (OS) in doubles.

BIBLIOGRAPHY: *NYT*, September 13, 1993, p. C1; *The Official USTA Yearbook* (Lynn, MA, 1992); *USA Today*, September 1, 1994, p. 3C; *Wall Street Journal*, January 30, 1994, p. D1; Washington *Post*, August 24, 1992, p. C8; *WWA*, 47th ed. (1992–1993), p. 2945.

Miriam F. Shelden

WALLACH, Maud Barger (b. June 15, 1870, New York, NY; d. April 1, 1954, Baltimore, MD), tennis player, was the daughter of Samuel F. Barger, a lawyer, director of the New York Central Railroad and associate of Cornelius Vanderbilt, and Edna Jenie (LaFavor) Barger and lived in New York City and at "Edna Villa," the family Newport, RI, summer residence. Affluence enabled Maud and her sister Edna to enjoy leisure, sports, and elite society throughout their lives. Maud married sportsman Richard Wallach in June 1890. They had a daughter, Jean, but divorced within the decade. Publicly, she then became "Mrs. Barger Wallach," frequently written with a hyphen interposed.

An adept figure skater and fox hunter, Wallach began playing tennis when about 30 years old. She won a mixed doubles tournament two years later and improved her skills progressively during the next few summers. She entered the U.S. Women's championships in 1906 at the Philadelphia, PA CrC, advancing to the final before losing to Helen Homans. Cramps contributed to her close, three-set, third-round loss to Carrie Neely the next year. Wallach won the 1908 national championship, downing Marie Wagner (OS) in the final and Evelyn Sears in the challenge round. At age 38, she became the oldest woman titleholder ever. The following year, not fully recovered from an appendicitis attack, she lost her crown to Hazel Hotchkiss (OS). Although never again faring as well in the nationals, she continued to play amazingly fine tennis at advanced ages. She ranked fifth among American women at age 46 in 1915 and tenth in 1916. At age 57, she bowed out of the 1926 U.S. championships by winning two games from fourth-seeded Mary K. Browne (OS) in her first-round loss.

A baseliner and scrambler, the right-handed Wallach featured accurate, consistent, soft forehands and compensated for her weak backhands by running around them, if possible. When pressed severely, she lobbed effectively to remote backcourt corners. Her underhand serve, low and strategically placed, frequently confused opponents. Wallach's unique, unorthodox style worked because of her accurate placements, intelligence, determination, and will to run down every ball. She especially enjoyed mixed doubles, particularly with partner Craig Biddle.

She chaired the committee that prepared the first American women's national ranking in 1913. Wallach, who worked repeatedly on tournament committees at Newport and helped generously on occasion as a patron of the sport, was enshrined in the National Lawn Tennis (later International Tennis) Hall of Fame in 1958.

BIBLIOGRAPHY: *ALT* 2 (July 1, 1908), pp. 89–94; Maud Barger-Wallach, "Recollections of Newport," in USLTA, *Fifty Years of Lawn Tennis in the United States* (New York, 1931); Newport (RI) *News*, April 1, 1954; April 2, 1954; *NYT*, June 15, 1890, p. 13; April 2, 1954, p. 15; *Wright & Ditson Official Lawn Tennis Guide*, 1905–1927 (Boston, MA, 1905–1927).

Frank V. Phelps

TRACK AND FIELD

BURRELL, Leroy Russell (b. February 21, 1967, Philadelphia, PA), athlete, is the son of Leroy Burrell, a barber, and Delores Burrell and ranks among history's fastest humans. He won the 100 meters, 200 meters, long jump, and triple jump to steer Penn Wood High School in Landsdowne, PA, to the 1985 State High School Championship and was named the 1985 Eastern Track Athlete of the Year. Burrell graduated from Penn Wood High School and entered the University of Houston (SWC). Although a serious knee injury sidelined him through 1987, he placed fifth in the 100 meters and seventh in the long jump in the 1988 NCAA Championship and qualified for the semifinals in the 100 meters at the 1988 Summer Olympic Trials.

In 1989, Burrell emerged as one of the world's premier sprinters. Despite a fifth-place performance in the NCAA Championship 100 meters, he captured the TAC Championship 100 meters in 9.94 seconds and finished second in the WoC 100 meters to Great Britain's Linford Christie. At the 1990 SWC Championships, Burrell captured the 100 meters in 9.94 seconds and 200 meters in 19.61 seconds. Although both races were wind-aided, the latter was history's fastest furlong under any conditions. Later, he garnered the 1990 NCAA Championship 100 meters in another wind-assisted performance of 9.94 seconds and captured the 100 meters at the Seattle, WA, Goodwill Games, a race in which he defeated teammate and rival Carl Lewis (OS).

Burrell, who established an indoor world record of 6.48 seconds for 60 meters, captured the 1991 TAC Championship 100 meters in a world record of 9.90 seconds. In the latter, he once again defeated Lewis, who finished second in 9.93 seconds, one tenth slower than his former world record. Prior to the World Championships that year, Burrell ran on two U.S. 4 × 100-meter relay teams. The quartet first tied the world record of 37.79 seconds, set by France in 1990, and then established a new world record of 37.67 seconds. Although he improved his time to 9.88 seconds in the World

Championships, it only accounted for second place. Lewis won the race in a world record of 9.86 seconds. Burrell, however, garnered a World Championship Gold Medal on the U.S. 4 × 100-meter relay team, which lowered the world record to 37.50 seconds.

In 1992, Burrell began the track season with a world record of 1 minute 19.11 seconds in the 4 × 200-meter relay at the Penn Relays. Despite finishing a disappointing fifth in the 100 meters in the 1992 Summer Olympic Games at Barcelona, Spain, he won a Gold Medal on the 4 × 100-meter relay team, which established a world record of 37.40 seconds. In 1993, Burrell finished fifth in the 100 meters in the USTF Championships and later upset Christie and Lewis at Zurich, Switzerland. At the 1993 World Championships in Stuttgart, Germany, Burrell anchored the victorious 4 × 100-meter team in equaling the world record.

Burrell set a world record in the 100 meters on July 7, 1994, clocking 9.85 seconds at the Lausanne, Switzerland, Athletissima Grand Prix. At the St. Petersburg, Russia, 1994 Goodwill Games, he finished second in the 100 meters and participated on the victorious 4 × 100-meter relay team. He was nominated for the Sullivan Award in 1994.

BIBLIOGRAPHY: Scott Davis, "Lewis Reclaims WR," *TFN* 44 (November 1991), p. 9; Scott Davis, "WR: 9.90 for Burrell," *TFN* 44 (August 1991), p. 5; Jim Dunaway, "Lewis & Co. Flying Again," *TFN* 45 (June 1992), p. 19; Jim Dunaway, "100: CR 9.94 for Burrell," *TFN* 42 (August 1989), p. 4; Jon Hendershott, "Burrell Has 'The Attitude,'" *TFN* 42 (August 1989), p. 8; Jon Hendershott, "Burrell Preaches Goodwill," *TFN* 43 (October 1990), p. 5; Jon Hendershott, "Windy, But Still a 19.61," *TFN* 43 (July 1990), p. 5; Jeff Hollobaugh, "T&FN Interview: Leroy Burrell," *TFN* 44 (April 1991), pp. 56–57; Sieg Lindstrom, "Burrell Burns: WR 9.90," *TFN* 44 (August 1991), p. 6; Bill Mallon, "Burrell in a Breeze," *TFN* 43 (August 1990), p. 5; Walt Murphy, "U.S. Runs WR 37.40," *TFN* 45 (October 1992), p. 36; Walt Murphy, "U.S. Smashes WR," *TFN* 44 (November 1991), p. 24; Shawn Price, "U.S. Ties WR, Wins," *TFN* 46 (November 1991), p. 24.

Adam R. Hornbuckle

CLARK, Ellery Harding Sr. (b. March 13, 1874, West Roxbury, MA; d. July 27, 1949, Boston, MA), athlete, coach, and author, is the son of Benjamin Cutler Clark and Adeline (Weld) Clark and grew up in New England. He earned a Bachelor of Arts degree from Harvard University in 1896 and a Bachelor of Laws degree in 1899. During his undergraduate days, he participated in the 1896 Athens, Greece, Summer Olympic Games as a member of the Boston AtA and won Gold Medals in the high jump (1.675 meters) and the long jump (6.35 meters). Clark's victorious long jump was made on his last attempt, following two fouls, and helped American jumpers sweep all three medals in the event.

Clark seriously injured his knee during a high jump exhibition on Prince Edward Island, Canada, in 1897 and remained out of major competition until 1903. At the 1904 St. Louis, MO, Summer Olympic Games, he finished fifth (out of six competitors) in the grueling "all-around event." This event, a forerunner of the modern decathlon, featured participants competing in 10 different events in a single day and earning performance points based on percentage tables drawn up in 1892. He captured the U.S. All-Around Athletic Championship in 1897 and 1903 and the New England Championship in 1896–1897 and 1909–1910. In 1930, at age 56, he won the one-mile Eleanora Sears (OS) Trophy walk in Boston.

Clark practiced law in Boston after 1900 and served on the Boston School Committee from 1902 to 1904, chairing the subcommittee on hygiene and physical training. Clark, who was elected to Boston's Board of Aldermen in 1908, coached the Harvard track and field team for four years and was employed as physical director of the Brown and Nichols School in Cambridge, MA, from 1918 to 1928. He served as secretary for 40 years of the Massachusetts Humane Society. He married Victoria Maddelena in 1904 and had one son, Ellery H., Jr., a naval officer and historian of the Boston Red Sox (AL) baseball team. Clark died of a heart attack while riding a train near Boston in 1949.

Clark wrote prolifically. His works include his memoirs, *Reminiscences of an Athlete: Twenty Years on Track and Field* (Boston, 1911); *Practical Track and Field Athletics* (with John Graham, Boston, 1904); *Track Athletics Up-to-Date* (Boston, 1920); and many works of law, fiction, and poetry.

BIBLIOGRAPHY: Barry J. Hugman and Peter Arnold, *The Olympic Games: Complete Track and Field Results, 1896–1988* (New York, 1988); Richard D. Mandell, *The First Modern Olympics* (Berkeley, CA, 1976); *NYT*, January 20, 1904; July 28, 1949; *WWWA*, vol. 2 (1943–1950), p. 116.

John E. Findling

CONLEY, Michael Alex "Mike" (b. October 5, 1962, Chicago, IL), athlete, excelled as a two-time Olympic medalist and is considered the finest combination long/triple jumper in history. He is the second of three children born to Alex Conley and Ora Conley. His father manages a rental car garage, while his mother worked as a computer analyst. At Chicago's Luther South High School, Conley starred in basketball and track and field and won four titles in a single State track and field meet. During his first year at the University of Arkansas (SWC), he competed in both sports.

A world-class performer in the long and triple jumps by his junior year, Conley won the triple jump at the 1984 U.S. Olympic Trials. At the Los Angeles, CA, Summer Olympic Games, he finished second to Al Joyner, a teammate and close friend. Four years later, Conley was favored to make the Olympic team in both events. He failed to qualify, however, placing fourth in the long jump and fifth in the triple jump.

Conley again tried to double at the 1992 Olympic Trials. He finished a nonqualifying fourth in the long jump but made the team in the triple jump.

In the Barcelona, Spain, Summer Olympic Games, Conley jumped 59 feet 7½ inches on his fourth attempt. The jump surpassed the seven-year-old world record of 58 feet 11½ inches, but a barely aiding wind of 2.1 meters per second (.1 meters per second over the allowable) nullified the performance for record consideration. But the mark stood up, as Conley won the Olympic Gold.

Conley's major triple jump titles include the 1981 U.S. Junior, 1984–1985 NCAA, 1984 Olympic Trials, 1984, 1987–1989, 1993–1994 USA/Mobil, 1986 Olympic Festival, 1987 Pan-American Games, 1989 World Cup, 1992 Olympic Games, and 1993 World Championships. Indoors, Conley owns two NCAA crowns and five USA/Mobil crowns. He won world indoor titles in 1987 and 1989. Conley's top long jump wins came at the 1984–1985 NCAA, 1985 USA/Mobil, 1985 Olympic Festival, and 1985 World Cup meets. *TFN* ranked Conley the world's top triple jumper in 1984, 1986, 1989, 1992, and 1993. In the summer of 1994, he finished second in the triple jump at the St. Petersburg, Russia, Goodwill Games and at the Pan-Africa-USA Meet at Durham, NC. In the final 1994 Outdoor European Grand Prix standings, Conley finished first in the triple jump with a 59 foot, 9¾ inch distance and ranked third among all competitors.

With Al Joyner as his best man, Conley married Renae Corbin on October 26, 1985. They have two sons, Michael and Jordon. Conley serves as a part-time assistant track and field coach at Arkansas.

BIBLIOGRAPHY: Dave Johnson, "Conley's Super Decade," *TFN* 45 (October 1992), p. 45; Ruth Laney, "Conley Goes Out with a Bang," *TFN* 38 (July 1985), p. 8; Ruth Laney, "Conley Over 28 and Near 59," *TFN* 40 (August 1987), p. 15; *NBC Olympic Track & Field Research Manual: USA Men's T&F Biographies*—"Mike Conley" (New York, 1992), pp. 509–510; 1993 *USA Indoor Track* (Indianapolis, IN, 1993); *1992 American Athletics Annual* (Indianapolis, IN, 1992); *University of Arkansas Track & Field Media Guide*, 1992.

Peter Cava

DAVIS, Harold "Hal" (b. January 5, 1921, Salinas, CA), athlete, was deprived of almost certain Olympic sprint honors in 1940 and 1944 by World War II. The Morgan Hill, CA, High School graduate enrolled at Salinas, CA, JC and as a freshman won both sprints at the 1940 AAU Championships and finished only one tenth of a second behind the world record in both the 100 and 200 meters. A poor start cost him his AAU 100-meter title in 1941, but he successfully defended his 200-meters crown. He transferred to the University of California (PCC), winning the sprint doubles at both the NCAA and AAU Championships in 1942 and 1943. After leaving high school, he remained undefeated in the furlong. His only important 100-yards/100-meters loss came at the 1941 AAU Championships. In addition to his unrivaled record at major championships, Davis also proved his greatness when his abilities were measured against the stopwatch. He equaled the world 100-meter record of 10.2 seconds in 1941 and the world 100-yard record of 9.4 seconds in 1942. His last major 200-meter race came at the 1943 NCAA Championships, where his winning time of 20.2 seconds was one tenth inside the world record. He missed official recognition, however, because the following wind was slightly over the permitted limit. A notoriously poor starter, he possessed an exceptional finishing burst and won many of his races by making up seemingly impossible deficits in the closing stages of a race.

Following his graduation from California in June 1943, Davis enlisted in the U.S. Marine Corps. He did not compete again seriously until 1947, when he made a comeback and hoped to make the 1948 Olympic team. After winning his first race, however, he was plagued by a recurring muscle injury and announced his retirement.

BIBLIOGRAPHY: Cordner Nelson, *Track's Greatest Champions* (Los Altos, CA, 1986); D. H. Potts, "The World's Fastest Humans," *TFN* 2 (June 1949), p. 6.

Ian Buchanan

DELLINGER, William Solon "Bill" (b. March 23, 1934, Grant's Pass, OR), athlete and coach, is the son of Averil Joyce Dellinger and Shirley (Davis) Dellinger, a retired employee of Shell Oil Company. Dellinger, who discovered his penchant for distance running in a freshman physical education class at Springfield, OR, High School, won the 1949 State cross-country crown as a sophomore and the 1952 State mile and half-mile titles as a senior. As a University of Oregon (PCC) trackman under the regimen of Bill Bowerman (OS), he captured NCAA titles in the mile in 1954 and the 5,000 meters in 1956.

After graduating from Oregon in 1956, Dellinger continued to compete in the middle distances. He took the 5,000 meters at the 1956 Olympic Trials in an American record of 14 minutes 26 seconds, a time that he lowered by 9.6 seconds before the Summer Olympic Games at Melbourne, Australia. In 1958, he established an American record of 3 minutes 41.5 seconds for 1,500 meters. Dellinger, who garnered indoor world records of 8 minutes 49.9 seconds for two miles and 13 minutes 45 seconds for three miles, won the 5,000-meter outdoors at both the AAU Championships and the Pan-American Games in 1959. The next year witnessed him establish outdoor American records of 8 minutes 48 seconds for two miles and 14 minutes 3 seconds for 5,000 meters and compete in the 5,000 meters in the Summer Olympic Games at Rome, Italy. Dellinger won the Bronze Medal in the 5,000 meters in the 1964 Summer Olympic Games at Tokyo, Japan.

Dellinger, who completed three years of service in the U.S. Air Force in 1959, earned an M.S. degree in education in 1961 and coached cross-country and track and field at Thurston High School, Springfield, OR, until 1966. After teaching physical education at Lane CC for a year, he became head cross-country and assistant track and field coach at the University of Oregon (PTC) in 1967. Under Dellinger, the Ducks have garnered 12 PTC and 4 NCAA cross-country titles. In 1973, he succeeded Bowerman as head track and field coach and has steered his alma mater to four PTC crowns and one NCAA Championship. Dellinger, one of three individuals to have won NCAA Championships both as an athlete and a coach, served as an assistant coach for men's distance running for the 1984 U.S. Olympic team.

BIBLIOGRAPHY: William Dellinger, letter to Adam R. Hornbuckle, November 1992; *University of Oregon Track and Field Media Guide*, 1992; David Wallechinsky, *The Complete Book of the Olympics*, rev. ed. (New York, 1988).

Adam R. Hornbuckle

DEVERS, Yolanda Gail (b. November 19, 1966, Seattle, WA), athlete, won an Olympic title. Devers, the fastest combination sprinter/hurdler in history whose career was jeopardized by serious illness, grew up in San Diego, CA, as the second and last child of Larry Devers and Alabe Devers. Her father served as a Baptist minister, while her mother worked as a teacher's aide.

Devers began competing as a distance runner for Sweetwater High School in National City, CA, but excelled after switching to the sprint events. She graduated in 1984 and received a track and field scholarship to UCLA (PTC), where she majored in sociology. Bobby Kersee coached Devers, who in 1987 won 100-meter titles at the U.S. Olympic Festival and the Pan-American Games. In 1988 as a senior, Devers lowered the American record for the 100-meter hurdles to 12.61 seconds. She captured 100-meter titles at the NCAA Championships and at the U.S. Olympic Trials, qualifying for the U.S. team in the 100-meter hurdles. At the Seoul, South Korea, Summer Olympic Games, she reached the semifinal round.

Just before the Seoul Olympics, Devers began having migraine headaches. Later, she suffered from insomnia, temporary blindness, weight fluctuation, fits of shaking, bulging eyes, and nearly constant menstrual bleeding. Doctors diagnosed her ailments in September 1990 as Graves' disease, a thyroid disorder. She underwent radiation treatment, but soon her feet began to swell and became infected. Devers faced possible double amputation when doctors changed her therapy.

After a 30-month layoff, Devers resumed partial workouts in March 1991. She claimed her first U.S. title just three months later, winning the 100-meter hurdles to qualify for the World Championships. At the world meet, Devers placed second. The next month, she lowered the U.S. record for the 100-meter hurdles to 12.48 seconds. During 1991, Devers's brief marriage to Ron Roberts, a former UCLA miler, ended in divorce.

In 1992, Devers made the U.S. team, winning the 100-meter hurdles and placing second in the 100 meters at the Olympic Trials. At the Barcelona, Spain, Summer Olympic Games, she hoped to become the first athlete since

1948 to win both the sprint and hurdle events. After winning the 100 meters, Devers led in the hurdles race before tripping over the final barrier and finishing fifth.

In 1993, the Palmdale, CA, resident broke the U.S. 60-meter indoor record three times and ran a 6.95-second time in winning the World indoor title. She also posted the fastest 50-meter time by an American, clocking 6.10 seconds. At the 1993 World Championships in Stuttgart, Germany, Devers prevailed in both the 100 meters and 100-meter hurdles. No female had accomplished the rare double since Fannie Blankers-Koen in 1948. Her 10.82-second 100-meter clocking barely edged Jamaican Merlene Ottey. Devers set an American record in the 100-meter hurdles in 12.46 seconds and anchored the U.S. team to a silver medal in the 4 × 100-meter relay with an American record of 41.49 seconds. In 1993, she earned the Jesse Owens Award as the year's top track and field athlete. *TFN* named her 1993 U.S. Female Athlete of the Year. Devers also captured the 100 meters at the 1994 U.S. National Outdoor Championships in Knoxville, TN.

BIBLIOGRAPHY: Dave Johnson, "A Truly Amazing Comeback," *TFN* 44 (December 1991), p. 11; Ruth Laney, "Devers Won Wrong Race," *TFN* 45 (October 1992), p. 53; Sieg Lindstrom, "A Long Medical Chart," *TFN* 44 (August 1991), p. 24; Kenny Moore, "Gail Force," *SI* 78 (May 10, 1993), pp. 41–43; *NBC Olympic Track & Field Research Manual: USA Women's T&F Biographies*—"Gail Devers" (New York, 1992), pp. 656–658; *1993 American Athletics Annual* (Indianapolis, IN, 1993); Dick Patrick, "Devers Seeks Gold Medal After Clearing Huge Hurdle," *USA Today*, January 7, 1992, p. C5; Dick Patrick, "Illness Makes Devers Determined," *USA Today*, July 14, 1992, p. C14; Bert Rosenthal, "On the Road to Barcelona: Gail Devers," *American Athletics* (Winter 1991), pp. 34–36.

Peter Cava

DOHERTY, John Kenneth (b. May 16, 1905, Detroit, MI), athlete, coach, and author, is the son of Corbett W. Doherty, a laborer, and Elizabeth Doherty and began participating in track and field at Detroit's Western High School. He graduated from Western High School in 1923 and entered Detroit CiC (now Wayne State University), where he excelled in the high hurdles, javelin throw, pole vault, and shot put. Doherty achieved national athletic acclaim by winning the AAU decathlon championship and the Bronze Medal in the 1928 Summer Olympic Games at Amsterdam, The Netherlands. Doherty defended his national decathlon title in 1929, establishing an American record of 7,784 points.

Doherty, who earned master's and doctorate degrees in education from the University of Michigan in 1933 and 1948, respectively, enjoyed a long successful career as a track and field coach. He started coaching track and field in 1928 at Detroit's Southwestern High School, where he also taught mathematics. Doherty then assumed an assistant track and field coaching position at Princeton University in 1929 and the University of Michigan

(BTC) in 1930. He became the head track and field coach at Michigan in 1939 and led the Wolverines to seven BTC championships. Doherty held the head track and field coach position at the University of Pennsylvania (IvL) from 1948 until 1959. He served as president of the NTFCA in 1956 and the vice president of the ITCA in 1960. Doherty also became a fellow and trustee of the American College of Sports Medicine in 1957.

After retiring from coaching in 1959, he directed several important track and field meets. Doherty, a U.S. State Department specialist in track and field in India and Finland, directed the inaugural U.S.-USSR dual meet in Philadelphia, PA, in 1959. He administered the Penn Relays, the nation's oldest and largest relay carnival, and the Philadelphia *Inquirer* Games from 1959 to 1969 and also coordinated the 1961 NCAA Track and Field Championships in Philadelphia. Doherty's lasting impact on track and field came as an author. His initial coaching text, *Modern Track and Field*, was first published in 1953. *Track and Field Movies on Paper* appeared next in 1954, with second and third editions made in 1961 and 1967, respectively. In 1964, Doherty published *Modern Training for Running*. His *Track and Field Omnibook*, which is regarded as one of the most authoritative books on track and field technique and psychology, is currently in its fourth edition. Doherty, who was elected to the NTF Hall of Fame in 1976, married Lucile Mason and has two sons, Lynn and Robert.

BIBLIOGRAPHY: John Kenneth Doherty, letter to Adam R. Hornbuckle, January 1993; University of Michigan Sports Information, Ann Arbor, MI, letter to Adam R. Hornbuckle, January 1993; University of Pennsylvania Sports Information, Philadelphia, PA, letter to Adam R. Hornbuckle, January 1993; Wayne State University Alumni Association, Detroit, MI, letter to Adam R. Hornbuckle, January 1993.

                                                          Adam R. Hornbuckle

EASTON, Millard Elsworth "Bill" (b. September 13, 1904, Stinesville, IN), athlete and coach, is the son of Perry Herschel Easton, a real estate salesman, small businessman, farmer, and Indiana state senator, and Fannie (Culross) Easton. Easton, who earned the nickname "Bill" to avoid confusion with his grandfather, competed in basketball and track and field at Sandborn, IN, High School. After graduating from high school in 1922, he entered Indiana University (WC). Billy Hayes coached the versatile track and field performer, who competed in the quarter mile, half mile, mile, 220-yard low hurdles, high jump, and long jump. Easton's best event proved the quarter mile, which he ran in about 50 seconds. Easton also played basketball through his junior year at Indiana.

Easton, who graduated from Indiana University with bachelor degrees in political science and business in 1927, worked one year for the Indiana Sanitary Commission before settling on a high school coaching career. He coached basketball at Ellettsville, IN, High School in 1928 and 1929, basketball and track and field at Lowell, IN, High School in 1929 and 1930, basketball at Hobart, IN, High School from 1930 to 1932, and cross-country and track and field at Hammond, IN, High School from 1932 to 1940. Easton returned to Indiana University, earning a bachelor's degree in physical education in 1932 and a master's degree in education in 1935. His collegiate coaching career began in 1940, when he became the head track and field coach at Drake University (MVC) and director of the Drake Relays. Easton led Drake to three consecutive NCAA cross-country titles between 1944 and 1946. In 1947, he became the head cross-country and track and field coach at the University of Kansas (BEC) and director of the Kansas Relays. Kansas dominated the BEC under Easton, winning 16 cross-country, 11 indoor track and field, and 12 outdoor track and field titles. The Jayhawks also won the NCAA cross-country championship in 1953 and the NCAA outdoor track and field championship in 1959 and 1960. The 1957 Kansas Relays saw Easton's four-mile relay quartet become the first collegiate team to break 17 minutes with a clocking of 16 minutes 57.8 seconds. Easton also coached Jayhawk notables Bill Nieder (S) in the shot put, Al Oerter (OS) in the discus throw, Billy Mills (OS) in the 10,000 meters, and Wes Santee* in the mile.

Easton, who retired from the University of Kansas in 1965, worked as a U.S. State Department Educational specialist and coached track and field in Malaysia in 1959 and 1962. He led the Malaysian track and field team to one Gold, two Silver, and five Bronze Medals in the 1962 Asian Games. Easton also coached the Mexican Olympic team in 1968 and conducted track and field clinics in Paraguay in 1973. He served as the president of the USTFCA in 1966 and was elected to the NTF Hall of Fame in 1976. Easton married Adamarie Scharbach of Hobart, IN, in 1932. They have a son, Richard, and a daughter, Lindsey.

BIBLIOGRAPHY: Adamarie Easton, letter to Adam R. Hornbuckle, February 1993; James E. Gunn, "Second Isn't Good Enough: A Day in the Life of Bill Easton," *University of Kansas Alumni Magazine* 57 (May 1959), pp. 4–6, 32; NTF Hall of Fame, letter to Adam R. Hornbuckle, November 1992; University of Kansas Sports Information, Lawrence, KS, letter to Adam R. Hornbuckle, February 1993.

Adam R. Hornbuckle

ELLIOT, James Francis "Jumbo" (b. July 8, 1914, Philadelphia, PA; d. March 22, 1981, Juno Beach, FL), athlete and coach, ranks among the twentieth century's most successful track and field coaches. Elliot, a lifelong Philadelphian, graduated from West Catholic High School and entered Villanova University in 1931. He went undefeated in dual meet competition as a collegiate quarter-miler, but an untimely injury spoiled his opportunity to qualify for the 1936 Summer Olympic team. Elliot, who graduated from Villanova in 1935, remained at the university as a volunteer track and field and golf coach. He soon dropped the duties as golf coach, however, concentrating solely on track and field. In the meantime, he established Elliot

& Franz, Incorporated, a construction equipment leasing firm. The firm made him a multimillionaire and enabled him to devote his spare time to coaching track and field.

Elliot coached at Villanova until his death from cardiac arrest in 1981. His teams dominated the IC4A from 1955 to 1980, winning nine cross-country championships and 17 indoor and 13 outdoor track and field titles. His athletes won 377 individual IC4A titles. Elliot led Villanova to eight NCAA Championships, including four in cross-country, three in indoor track and field, and one in outdoor track and field. Sixty-six individual NCAA champions, including 1 in cross-country, 29 in indoor, and 36 in outdoor track and field, performed under Elliot. He enjoyed great success with runners competing in the 800 through the 5,000 meters. Sixteen of Elliot's mile specialists bettered four minutes for the distance. His middle-distance corps, comprising dozens of relay quartets, established national and world records and dominated the Penn Relays. Since 1955, Villanova had captured 75 events at the Penn Relays. His most noteworthy middle-distance runners included Mark Belger, Dick Buerkle, Eamon Coghlan, John Harnett, Marty Liquori (OS), Sidney Maree, and Don Paige. Elliot produced five Olympic champions, including Ron Delany in the 1,500 meters in 1956, Charlie Jenkins (OS) in the 400 meters and 4 × 400-meter relay in 1956, Don Bragg (S) in the pole vault in 1960, Paul Drayton in the 4 × 100-meter relay in 1964, and Larry James in the 4 × 400-meter relay in 1968.

As implied by the title of his autobiography, Elliot produced both milers and men. From Elliot, young men gained self-confidence in their abilities and pride in themselves. His message to them was, according to Liquori, "Look like a champion and act like a champion, because you are." In 1976, Elliot's fellow IC4A coaches honored him as the Coach of the Century. In 1977, Villanova bestowed an honorary doctorate on him. He also was inducted into the Pennsylvania Sports Hall of Fame in 1977. Elliot, who earned the nickname "Jumbo" because of his likeness to Philadelphia Phillies (NL) pitcher James "Jumbo" Elliot, also belongs to the NTF Hall of Fame.

BIBLIOGRAPHY: Neil Amdur, "Jumbo!" *TFN* 32 (September 1979), pp. 48–49; Ira Berkow, "Elliot Is Given Final Tributes," *NYT*, March 27, 1981, p. A19; James F. Elliot and Theodore J. Berry, *Jumbo Elliot: Maker of Milers; Maker of Men* (New York, 1982); Bob Hersh, "Jumbo Elliot (1914–1981)," *TFN* 34 (April 1981), p. 27; NTF Hall of Fame, letter to Adam R. Hornbuckle, November 1992; Thomas Rogers, "Jumbo Elliot of Villanova Is Dead; Long an Outstanding Track Coach," *NYT*, March 23, 1981, p. B14; Villanova University Sports Information, letter to Adam R. Hornbuckle, January 1993.

Adam R. Hornbuckle

FOSTER, Gregory "Greg" (b. August 4, 1958, Chicago, IL), athlete, ranks among history's most enduring high hurdlers. As a junior at Proviso High School in Maywood, IL, in 1975, Foster equaled the national high school record of 6.8 seconds for the 60-yard low hurdles. During his senior year, he won the 1976 State High School championship in the 120-yard high hurdles. His winning time was 13.9 seconds, but he clocked 13.3 seconds in the qualifying heats for the third-fastest time in prep history. Foster, who graduated from UCLA in 1980, won three consecutive PTC titles in the 110-meter high hurdles from 1978 to 1980 and the 200-meter crown in 1979. He captured two NCAA championships in the 110-meter high hurdles in 1978 and 1980, along with the 200 meters in 1979. His first-place time of 13.22 seconds in the 1978 championship race marked an American record and history's second fastest by one-hundredth of a second.

Foster, nevertheless, ran in the shadow of Renaldo Nehemiah (OS), the world's premier high hurdler from 1979 to 1981. Foster, who finished runner-up to Nehemiah in the latter's 12.93-second world record performance in 1981, clocked 13.03 seconds for history's second-fastest performance. Later that year, he captured the WoC title in the 110-meter high hurdles. Foster, who was ranked first globally in 1982 and 1983, captured his specialty in the 1983 World Championship. Although heavily favored to win the Gold Medal in the 1984 Los Angeles, CA, Summer Olympic Games, he stumbled over the last hurdle and finished second to Roger Kingdom (S). Foster ranked second in the world to Kingdom in 1984 and 1985 and regained the premier position in 1986, establishing an indoor world record of 7.36 seconds for the 60-meter high hurdles. In 1987, he captured a second World Championship.

Two weeks before the 1988 Olympic Trials, Foster fell in practice and broke his left forearm. Despite wearing a 24-inch cast, he qualified for the semifinals in the Olympic Trials and was forced to drop out of the race after striking the seventh hurdle. Foster, who had been ranked globally for 11 years, was not rated in 1988 and received fifth- and fourth-place recognition in 1989 and 1990, respectively. In 1991, he won a fifth TAC title and third straight World Championship. The world's premier high hurdler lost the chance to compete for another Olympic medal, however, as he placed fourth in the 1992 Olympic Trials. Foster continued to compete in the 110-meter hurdles, finishing fourth in the St. Petersburg, Russia, 1994 Goodwill Games and placing on the 1994 European Grand Prix circuit.

BIBLIOGRAPHY: Jim Dunaway, "Foster Outleans Pierce," *TFN* 44 (October 1991), p. 19; Jon Hendershott, "Age No Barrier to Foster," *TFN* 44 (August 1991), pp. 4–5; Jon Hendershott, "Foster's Power Saves the Day," *TFN* 36 (September 1983), p. 17; Jon Hendershott, "T&FN Interview: Greg Foster," *TFN* 31 (August 1978), pp. 16–18; Jon Hendershott, "T&FN Interview: Greg Foster," *TFN* 36 (March 1983), pp. 48–49; Dave Johnson, "Foster Turns Back Time," *TFN* 43 (October 1990), p. 15; Harv Rentschler, "110H: Foster Best Vet," *TFN* 44 (August 1991), pp. 12–13; David Wallechinsky, *The Complete Book of the Olympics*, rev. ed. (New York, 1988).

Adam R. Hornbuckle

GALLAGHER, Kimberly Ann "Kim" (b. June 11, 1964, Philadelphia, PA), athlete, remains one of only two American women to win Olympic medals in the 800-meter event. Gallagher, the daughter of John Gallagher and Barbara Gallagher, grew up in the Philadelphia suburb of Ambler, PA. Her father, a car salesman, is of Irish descent, while her mother, a factory supervisor, is African-American. Gallagher began running competitively at age seven and the next year set a national age group record for the mile. Gallagher first trained under Larry Wilson of the Ambler OlC and her older brother Bart.

During her sophomore year at Upper Dublin High School in Fort Washington, PA, she placed eighth in the 800-meter final at the 1980 U.S. Olympic Trials. Two years later, she won the U.S. Olympic Festival 800-meter event in 2 minutes .07 seconds to set an American Junior (under 20 years of age) record. Gallagher attended the University of Arizona but left after one cross-country season. In hopes of qualifying for the Olympics, she began working with Los Angeles TrC coach Chuck DeBus in 1983.

In 1984, Gallagher won the U.S. 800- and 1500-meter titles. She captured the 800-meter event at the Olympic Trials to qualify for the U.S. team. Gallagher placed second at the Los Angeles, CA, Summer Olympic Games, joining 1968 champion Madeline Manning (OS) as the only American women to win medals in the Olympic 800 meters. *TFN* ranked Gallagher first among American 800-meter runners for the year.

Prior to the 1984 season, Gallagher experienced abnormal uterine bleeding. When the problem worsened after the Olympics, doctors found that she had developed polycystic ovaries. For the next three years, Gallagher did not compete in any major events. Her health improved after surgery in 1987.

At the 1988 Olympic Trials, Gallagher qualified in the 800- and 1,500-meter events. At the Seoul, South Korea, Summer Olympic Games, she placed eleventh in the 1,500 meters and earned a Bronze Medal in the 800 meters. For a second time, *TFN* ranked Gallagher the nation's top female 800-meter runner.

Gallagher rarely competed after the Seoul Olympics but reached the 800-meter semifinals at the 1992 U.S. Olympic Trials. Gallagher, who is unmarried, has one daughter, Jessica.

BIBLIOGRAPHY: Peter Cava, phone conversation with Kim Gallagher, July 16, 1993; Sieg Lindstrom, "Gallagher Rides Again," *TFN* 41 (December 1988), p. 10; *NBC Olympic Track & Field Research Manual: USA Women's T&F Biographies*—"Kim Gallagher" (New York, 1988), pp. 600–601; *1993 American Athletics Annual* (Indianapolis, IN, 1993).

                                                                    Peter Cava

GARRETT, Robert (b. June 24, 1875, Baltimore, MD; d. April 25, 1961, Baltimore, MD), athlete, was the son of Thomas Harrison Garrett and Alice Dickinson (Whitridge) Garrett and attended Princeton University. In 1896, he joined three other Princetonians participating in the track and field events at the first Modern Summer Olympic Games at Athens, Greece, in 1896, competing in the high jump, long jump, shot put, and discus throw. The discus had not yet been introduced into the track and field program in the United States. Garrett's knowledge of the discus event was consequently restricted to his reading of the Greek classics. An implement was specially made in accordance with the specifications of the discus used in Ancient Greece, but Garrett found that it was far too unwieldy to handle and abandoned the idea of taking part in the event at the Olympic Games. Upon his arrival in Athens, Garrett found that the Olympic discus weighed some 15 pounds less than the experimental model fashioned at home. He decided to enter the discus and defeated the highly favored Greek champion by eight inches. The discus remains on display at the Dillon Gymnasium on the Princeton campus. The day after his victory in the discus, Garrett earned first place in the shot put and second places in the high jump and long jump to become the most successful track and field athlete at the first Modern Olympic Games.

At the 1900 Summer Olympics in Paris, France, Garrett managed only seventh place in the discus and captured Bronze Medals in the shot put and the standing triple jump. Garrett, who married Katherine Barker Johnson in 1907, came from a wealthy Baltimore banking family and agreed to underwrite the expenses of the Princeton delegation to Athens. He later joined the family bank in Baltimore and remained a strong supporter of the Olympic movement and of Princeton, where the track in Jadwin is named after him.

BIBLIOGRAPHY: Bill Mallon and Ian Buchanan, *Quest for Gold: The Encyclopedia of American Olympians* (New York, 1984); Charles B. Saunders, Jr., "Olympic Princetonians," *Princeton Alumni Weekly* (December 7, 1956).

Ian Buchanan

JOHNSON, Michael Duane (b. September 13, 1967, Dallas, TX), athlete, is the son of Paul L. Johnson, a truckdriver, and Ruby Johnson, a teacher. Johnson, who joined the track and field team at Skyline High School in Dallas as a sophomore, finished second in the 1986 State High School championship 200 meters as a senior. A number of injuries befell him as a Baylor University (SWC) freshman, but he still clocked 20.41 seconds for 200 meters. In 1988, Johnson finished second in the SWC Championship 200 meters in 20.07 seconds. A cracked fibula, which occurred in the NCAA Championship furlong, prevented him from finishing the race. Indoors, he placed second in the 400 meters at the 1989 TAC Championship and first in the 200 meters at the NCAA Championship, setting an American record of 20.59 seconds. An injury, suffered in the 1989 SWC Championship, however, kept him out of the outdoors NCAA Championship. In 1990, Johnson defended his NCAA 200-meter title and garnered the indoor TAC 400-meter crown. Despite losing to Leroy Burrell* in the SWC Championship furlong, he remained undefeated at 200 meters outdoors and claimed major victories in the NCAA and TAC Championships and Seattle, WA, Goodwill Games. That year, Johnson clocked personal records of 19.85 seconds and 44.21 seconds for the 200 meters and the 400 meters, respectively.

As the world's premier performer at both 200 and 400 meters, Johnson was recognized by *TFN* as the 1990 Athlete of the Year. In 1991, he lowered the indoor 200-meter world record to 20.55 seconds and raced undefeated at the distance outdoors, with major triumphs in the TAC and World Championships. During the final fortnight of the 1991 season, Johnson enjoyed an unprecedented four consecutive 200-meter performances under 20 seconds. He also performed an undefeated season at twice the distance, recording a personal best of 44.17 seconds for 400 meters. Johnson, who repeated as the world's premier 200-meter and 400-meter dashman in 1991, won the 200 meters in the 1992 Olympic Trials in 19.79 seconds. Johnson, however, failed to qualify for the 200-meter finals of the Olympic Games at Barcelona, Spain. Although weak from an illness prior to the Olympics, he recovered well enough to garner a Gold Medal in the 4 × 400-meter relay. The United States set a world record of 2 minutes 55.74 seconds for the event. Before the Olympic Games, Johnson improved his 400-meter best to 43.98 seconds in becoming the first dashman to break 20 seconds for the 200 meters and 44 seconds for the 400 meters.

In 1993, he captured the 400 meters at the USTF Championships in 43.74 seconds while defeating "Butch" Reynolds* and Quincy Watts.* At the World Championship that year in Stuttgart, Germany, Johnson won the 400 meters in 43.65 seconds and anchored the victorious U.S. 4 × 400-meter relay to a world record of 2 minutes 54.29 seconds. His final 400 meters of 42.94 seconds marked the fastest relay leg of all time. At the St. Petersburg, Russia, 1994 Goodwill Games, Johnson recorded victories in the 200 meters at 20.1 seconds and the 400-meter relay. Later that summer, he prevailed in the 200 meters at the Zurich, Switzerland, Grand Prix and the Brussels, Belgium, Grand Prix and the 400 meters at the Pan-Africa-USA Meet at Durham, NC, and the Berlin, Germany, Grand Prix. In the 1994 Outdoor European Grand Prix standings, Johnson recorded the best 400-meter time with 44.32 seconds and the second best 200-meter time with 19.97 seconds. His 44.04-second clocking in Berlin marked the fastest 1994 time in the 400 meters. The USOC selected the Sullivan Award nominee its 1994 Male Track and Field Athlete of the Year.

BIBLIOGRAPHY: Roy Conrad, "Johnson Dashes 20.55," *TFN* 44 (March 1991), p. 24; Scott Davis, "200: Johnson Joins Elite," *TFN* 41 (August 1990), p. 19; Jon Hendershott, "19.85 & 44.21," *TFN* 43 (November 1990), pp. 40–42; Dave Johnson, "Another WR for US," *TFN* 45 (October 1992), p. 37; Dave Johnson, "Johnson

Cracks 44," *TFN* 45 (September 1992), p. 16; Dave Johnson, "U.S. Stomps WR," *TFN* 46 (November 1993), p. 26; Sieg Lindstrom, "Johnson Makes Euro Impact," *TFN* 43 (September 1990), p. 21; Sieg Lindstrom, "Johnson: 2 + 4 = No. 1," *TFN* 44 (January 1991), pp. 4–5; Bill Mallon, "200: Johnson Holds On," *TFN* 41 (August 1990), p. 5; Don Potts, "Johnson Up to Snuff," *TFN* 44 (November 1991), p. 10; Betsy Reed, "Johnson Whips Burrell," *TFN* 44 (August 1991), p. 5.

Adam R. Hornbuckle

LARRABEE, Michael Denny "Iron Mike" (b. December 2, 1933, Los Angeles, CA), athlete, is the son of Denson Larrabee, a wholesale beer distributor, and Enid Larrabee, a bookkeeper. Larrabee, who started running because he "was faster than the rest of the kids," starred in the sprinting events at Ventura, CA, High School. He posted personal records of 21.5 seconds for 220 yards and 51.2 seconds for 440 yards and placed third in the 220-yard dash at the 1952 California State Championship. After graduating from high school that year, he entered the University of Southern California (PCC). Larrabee did not win an NCAA track title but triumphed in the quarter mile at the PCC Championships in 1955 and 1956. At Southern California, he lowered his time for 220 yards to 21.0 seconds and 440 yards to 46.1 seconds.

Larrabee graduated from Southern California with a B.S. degree in geology and began teaching math at Monroe High School in Sepulveda, CA, in 1957. He continued to run competitively as a member of the Southern California Striders TrC and contended for a position on the 1960 Olympic team until an injury dashed his hopes. His greatest year as a quarter-miler came in 1964, when he won the AAU title in 46.0 seconds and defeated the Soviets in the U.S.-USSR dual meet. At Oslo, Norway, he lowered his time to 45.9 seconds. Larrabee won the 400 meters at the U.S. Olympic Trials, equaling the world record of 44.9 seconds. At age 30, he became the oldest Olympic performer to capture the Gold Medal in the 400 meters. His feat was accomplished at the 1964 Summer Olympic Games in Tokyo, Japan. Larrabee won a second Gold Medal with the victorious U.S. 4 × 400-meter relay team, which established a world record of 3 minutes 0.7 seconds.

Larrabee later worked as a regional distributor for the Coors Company and now shares ownership of Larrabee Brothers Distributing Company in Santa Maria, CA. He and his wife Margaret have three children, Tracy, a college professor, Lisa, a dental hygienist, and Mike, a businessman.

BIBLIOGRAPHY: Michael Denny Larrabee, Santa Maria, CA, letter to Adam R. Hornbuckle, September 1993; Bill Mallon and Ian Buchanan, *The Quest for Gold: The Encyclopedia of American Olympians* (New York, 1984); Frank G. Menke, *The Encyclopedia of Sports*, 4th rev. ed. (New York, 1969); University of Southern California Sports Information, Los Angeles, CA, letter to Adam R. Hornbuckle, February 1993; David Wallechinsky, *The Complete Book of the Olympics*, rev. ed. (New York, 1988).

Adam R. Hornbuckle

LARRIEU, Frances. *See* Frances Anne Lutz "Francie" Larrieu-Smith.

LARRIEU-SMITH, Frances Anne Lutz "Francie" (b. November 23, 1952, Palo Alto, CA), athlete, remains one of history's most enduring distance runners. In an athletic career spanning nearly a quarter of a century, Larrieu-Smith has developed from a world-class miler to marathoner. Older brother Ron, a 10,000-meter finalist in the 1964 Summer Olympic Games at Tokyo, Japan, inspired Larrieu-Smith, who equaled the American record of 4 minutes 16.8 seconds for 1,500 meters at age 16. After graduating from Fremont High School in Sunnyvale, CA, in 1970, Larrieu-Smith won the first of seven AAU/TAC 1,500 championships. Subsequent 1,500-meter titles followed in 1972, 1973, 1976, 1977, 1979, and 1980. She won the 1,500 meters at the 1972 U.S. Olympic Trials, garnering the American record of 4 minutes, 10.4 seconds. The 1972 Summer Olympic Games at Munich, Germany, however, witnessed Larrieu-Smith's elimination from the 1,500 meters in the semifinals.

Although Larrieu-Smith dominated women's middle-distance running through the 1970s, younger runners outpaced her in the early 1980s. After graduating from De Anza CC in 1973, she competed for UCLA (PCC) and won AIAW titles in the 800, 1,500, and 3,000 meters in 1974. By the end of 1975, her indoor American records included 2 minutes 40.2 seconds for 1,000 meters, 4 minutes 9.8 seconds for 1,500 meters, 4 minutes 28.5 seconds for one mile, 9 minutes 2.4 seconds for 3,000 meters, and 9 minutes 39.4 seconds for two miles. She also held the outdoor American record of 4 minutes 8.5 seconds for 1,500 meters and lowered it to 4 minutes 7.2 seconds in the 1,500-meter qualifying heats of the 1976 Summer Olympic Games at Montreal, Canada. Although Larrieu-Smith captured TAC titles in the 3,000 meters in 1979 and 1982, younger runners Mary Decker (OS), Julie Brown, and Leanne Warren dethroned her as the queen of the 1,500 meters and relegated her to fourth place in the 1980 Summer Olympic Trials. In the 1984 Summer Olympic Trials, she placed fifth in the 3,000 meters.

Since the late 1980s, Larrieu-Smith has found renewed running success at longer distances. She captured the 10,000 meters at the TAC Championship in 1985 and completed her first marathon in 2 hours 33 minutes 36 seconds at Houston, TX, in 1991. The fifth-place finisher in the 10,000 meters in the 1988 Summer Olympic Games at Seoul, South Korea, clocked 31 minutes 35.52 seconds, missing the American record by three tenths of a second. She garnered the American record for 10,000 meters with a 31-minute 28.92-second performance at the 1991 Texas Relays. Larrieu-Smith, whose best time for the marathon is 2 hours 27 minutes 35 seconds, placed twelfth in the 26.2-mile footrace in the 1992 Summer Olympic Games at Barcelona, Spain. A 1977 graduate of California State University, Long Beach, she married sprinter Mark Lutz the previous year. After their divorce in 1978, she married Jimmy Smith, an exercise physiologist, cyclist, and son of former Baylor University track coach "Catfish" Smith, in 1980.

BIBLIOGRAPHY: Jim Dunaway, "Francie Larrieu-Smith," TAC/TAFWA Biography Data Sheet, 1992; Jon Hendershott, "Running Is Francie's Way of Life," *TFN* 42 (March 1989), p. 40; Don Kardong, "Fabulous Francie," *RW* 26 (October 1991), pp. 82–87; Larry Story, "10K AR for Larrieu-Smith," *TFN* 44 (May 1991), pp. 14–15; Jack Welch, "Francie Born to Run," *TFN* 43 (July 1990), p. 42.

Adam R. Hornbuckle

LASH, Donald Ray "Don" (b. August 15, 1912, Bluffton, IN; d. September 19, 1994, Terre Haute, IN), athlete, was the son of Brandon R. Lash, a foundry molder, and Pearl (Landis) Lash and became one of America's finest distance runners. He began running on his grandfather's farm as a boy by chasing small rabbits, many of which he caught, caged, and fattened for food. Lash, who won State championships in the mile and half-mile events, graduated from Auburn, IN, High School in 1933 and entered Indiana University (WC).

Lash captured seven consecutive AAU national cross-country titles from 1934 to 1940. His winning streak stood as a record until Pat Porter garnered an eighth consecutive TAC cross-country crown in 1984. In 1936, Lash won the NCAA 5,000-meter championship and the AAU 5,000- and 10,000-meter titles. The latter resulted in American records of 30 minutes 9.0 seconds for six miles and 31 minutes 6.9 seconds for 10,000 meters. The 1936 Berlin, Germany, Summer Olympic Games saw Lash finish thirteenth in the 5,000 meters and eighth in the 10,000 meters. He also established an outdoor world record of 8 minutes 58.3 seconds for two miles in 1936, becoming the first American to finish under 9 minutes for the distance. Besides clocking an indoor world record of 8 minutes 58 seconds for two miles in 1937, he anchored the Indiana University four-mile relay team to a world record of 17 minutes 16.1 seconds at the 1937 Penn Relays. He reigned as the AAU indoor champion at three miles in 1938 and 1939 and the AAU outdoor champion at 10,000 meters in 1940. Lash, who received the James E. Sullivan Award as the nation's premier amateur athlete in 1938, participated in the scientific study of exercise at the Harvard Fatigue Laboratory and Indiana University.

Lash graduated from Indiana University with a bachelor's degree in education in 1938 and with a master's degree in police science in 1939. He then worked for the Indiana State Police for 3 years before joining the Federal Bureau of Investigation (FBI) as a special agent. Lash, who retired from the FBI after 21 years of service, worked on many important cases during and after World War II and found that his running ability enabled him to apprehend criminals who fled on foot. The former FBI agent spent the next decade as a state representative in the Indiana General Assembly. Lash also devoted 10 years to the Fellowship of Christian Athletes and established its National Conference Center at Camp Wapello near Turkey Run State Park in Indiana. In 1963, he and his wife, Margaret (Mendenhall) Lash, started the Don Lash Real Estate Company in Rockville, IN, which is now operated by their son David. Lash, a former trustee of Indiana University, was selected to the Indiana University Sports Hall of Fame in 1984.

BIBLIOGRAPHY: Indiana University Alumni Association, letter to Adam R. Hornbuckle, November 1992; Donald Ray Lash, letter to Adam R. Hornbuckle, January 1993; Frank G. Menke, *The Encyclopedia of Sports*, 6th rev. ed. (New York, 1977); David Wallechinsky, *The Complete Book of the Olympics*, rev. ed. (New York, 1988).

Adam R. Hornbuckle

LUTZ, Frances. *See* Frances Anne Lutz Larrieu-Smith.

MARSH, Michael L. "Mike" (b. August 4, 1967, Los Angeles, CA), athlete, is the son of Jonnie Brown, a certified public accountant, and stepson of Thomas Brown, a real estate agent, and ranks among the fastest 100- and 200-meter dashmen of all time. Marsh, who graduated from Hawthorne High School in Los Angeles in 1985, captured the State High School championship in the 200 meters as a senior and recorded personal best times of 10.6 seconds for 100 meters and 20.82 seconds for 200 meters. Marsh entered UCLA (PTC), where coaches focused his talent on the shorter distance. Marsh claimed only one major 100-meter title as a Bruin, winning the 1989 Olympic Festival. He also finished third in both the 1986 TAC Junior Championships and the 1987 NCAA Championships, sixth in the 1988 Olympic Trials, and ninth in the 1989 NCAA Championships. In the 200 meters, he ended third in the 1986 TAC Junior Championships and seventh in the 1989 NCAA Championships. Marsh graduated from UCLA in 1989, having posted personal records of 10.07 seconds in the 100 meters and 20.35 seconds in the 200 meters.

Following graduation, Marsh moved to Houston, TX, to join the Santa Monica TrC. Under the tutelage of Tom Tellez, the coach of Carl Lewis (OS) and Leroy Burrell,* Marsh realized his promise as a world-class sprinter. In the 100 meters, he garnered fourth place in the 1990 TAC Championships and second place in the New York Games. After winning the 100 meters at the Mt. SAC Relays, he placed seventh in the 100 meters and fifth in the 200 meters at the TAC Championships in 1991. The 1991 campaign featured Marsh's participation on the U.S. 4 × 100-meter relay team, which initially tied the world record of 37.79 seconds set by France at the 1990 European Championships and later established a new world mark of 37.67 seconds. Marsh finished third in the 60 meters at the indoor 1992 TAC Championships and then joined the Santa Monica TrC 4 × 200-meter relay team, which set a world record of 1 minute 19.11 seconds at the Penn Relays. In May 1992, he recorded personal bests of 9.93 seconds in the 100 meters and 19.94 seconds in the 200 meters. At the 1992 Olympic Trials, Marsh ended fourth in the 100 meters, qualified for the 4 × 100-meter relay team, and placed second in the 200 meters in 19.86 seconds. In the semifinals of the 200 meters in the Summer Olympic Games at Barcelona, Spain, he clocked 19.73 seconds for an Olympic and American record and history's fastest sea-level time. Marsh won Gold Medals in the 200 meters and the 4 × 100-meter relay, in which the United States set a world record of 37.40 seconds. In 1993, Marsh captured the 200 meters at the USTF Championships in the wind-aided time of 19.97 seconds and finished fourth in the World Championships. At the 1994 St. Petersburg, Russia, Goodwill Games, he finished fourth in the 200 meters and participated on the victorious 4 × 100-meter relay team.

BIBLIOGRAPHY: Roy Conrad, "U.S. Sticks It to France," *TFN* 44 (October 1991), pp. 4–5; Jim Dunaway, "Lewis & Co. Flying Again," *TFN* 45 (June 1992), p. 19; Bob Hersh, "Marsh Sets AR Early," *TFN* 45 (October 1992), pp. 14, 16; Jeff Hollobaugh, "Marsh More Than a Relayer," *TFN* 45 (June 1992), p. 7; Dave Johnson, "Move Was Key for Marsh," *TFN* 45 (October 1992), p. 17; Walt Murphy, "U.S. Runs WR 37.40," *TFN* 45 (October 1992), p. 36.

Adam R. Hornbuckle

MATTHEWS, Vincent Edward "Vince" (b. December 16, 1947, New York, NY), athlete and coach, ranked among the world's leading quarter-milers in the late 1960s and early 1970s. His father immigrated from the Virgin Islands to Harlem as a youngster and worked as a cutter for a Manhattan clothier. Vincent and his younger sister, Celia, grew up in run-down apartments and public housing projects in Brooklyn until the family moved into a small, six-room house in suburban Queens during the early 1950s.

Matthews joined the Andrew Jackson High School track and field team in 1963 and specialized in the 440-yard dash. Although academic problems prevented him from participating extensively as a sophomore and junior, Matthews captured the PSAL 440-yard dash title in 48.0 seconds as a senior. He graduated from high school and received an athletic scholarship to Johnson C. Smith College, a small predominantly black institution in Charlotte, NC, in 1965. Under coach Kenneth Powell, the freshman history major lowered his 440-yard dash time to 45.5 seconds in 1966. Matthews challenged for national supremacy in the 400 meters in 1967, finishing second to Lee Evans (OS) of San Jose State University in both the AAU Championships and the Pan-American Games. In the latter, he improved his 400-meter time to 45.1 seconds and captured a Gold Medal in the 4 × 400-meter relay. In the 1968 AAU Championship, Evans narrowly defeated Matthews in the 400 meters by three one-hundredths of a second.

Before the 1968 Olympic Trials, Matthews sprinted 400 meters in 44.4 seconds to eclipse Tommie Smith's (OS) 1967 world record by one-tenth of a second. The IAAF refused to recognize the time, however, because Matthews wore shoes, newly developed for artificial running surfaces, with 68 tiny brush spikes instead of the standard 6. Matthews, who finished fourth in the 400 meters at the 1968 Olympic Trials, ran the opening leg of the 4

× 400-meter relay in the 1968 Summer Olympic Games at Mexico City, Mexico. The U.S. quartet of Matthews, Evans, Larry James, and Ron Freeman captured the Gold Medal in the stunning world record time of 2 minutes 56.1 seconds. Matthews retired from track and field and joined the Johnson C. Smith College football team as a wide receiver during his senior year.

After graduating in 1969, Matthews tried out with the Washington Redskins (NFL) football club. Matthews returned to New York, where he married and began working for the Neighborhood Youth Corps as a payroll clerk. In 1971, he staged a successful comeback in the 400 meters with a 44.8-second clocking. Matthews finished third in the 400 meters in the 1972 Olympic Trials and captured the Gold Medal in the 1972 Summer Olympic Games at Munich, Germany. He lost the chance for an almost certain second Gold Medal in the 4 × 400-meter relay, after the IOC banished Matthews and teammate Wayne Collett, the Silver Medalist, from future Olympic competition for their indignant behavior during the awards ceremony. Matthews and Collett talked and refused to stand at attention during the national anthem. Matthews whirled his Gold Medal around his finger and implied erroneously that the prize meant nothing to him. He told an *NYT* reporter that the medal meant "I was the best quarter-miler in the world that day. If you don't think that's important, you don't know what's inside an athlete's soul." Matthews, who competed on the short-lived professional ITA circuit after the 1972 Olympic Games, coached track and field in Nigeria and resumed a career in social work in New York.

BIBLIOGRAPHY: Neil Amdur, "Matthews Wins in 400; Munich Fans Boo Him," *NYT*, September 8, 1972, p. 21; Bill Mallon and Ian Buchanan, *The Quest for Gold: The Encyclopedia of American Olympians* (New York, 1984); "Matthews Breaks World 400 Record," *NYT*, September 1, 1967, sec. 5, pp. 1, 5; Vincent Matthews (with Neil Amdur), *My Race Be Won* (New York, 1974); Roberto L. Quercetani, *Athletics: A History of Modern Track and Field Athletics, 1860–1990* (Milan, Italy, 1990); David Wallechinsky, *The Complete Book of the Olympics*, rev. ed. (New York, 1988).

                                                                    Adam R. Hornbuckle

O'BRIEN, Daniel Dion "Dan" (b. July 18, 1966, Portland, OR), athlete, is the adoptive son of Jim O'Brien and Virginia O'Brien, excelled as an All-State football and basketball player, starred as a four-time State track and field champion, and captured the TAC Junior Decathlon Championship as a senior at Henley High School in Klamath Falls, OR, in 1984. Although graduating from the University of Idaho (BSAC) in 1989, he missed track and field competition from 1985 through 1987 due to academic ineligibility. At Spokane CC for a year to improve his grades, O'Brien raised his decathlon score to 7,891 points and qualified for the 1988 Olympic Trials. He withdrew from the trials, however, because of an injury sustained in the long jump. In 1989, O'Brien improved his decathlon best to 7,987 points and was poised to win the NCAA Championships before an injury sustained at the BSAC Championships ended his season.

O'Brien, who first exceeded 8,000 points (8,267) at Washington State University's Cougar Invitational in 1990, scored a wind-aided 8,483 points to finish second in the TAC Championships. In the long jump, he eclipsed Daley Thompson's decathlon world record of 26 feet 3½ inches by 1 inch. Moreover, his first-day total of 4,656 points produced an American record and exceeded Bill Toomey's (OS) 4,526 points from 1968. O'Brien scored 8,358 points and finished second in the Seattle, WA, Goodwill Games, despite leading the competition up to the 1,500 meters, the final event. Dave Johnson, the TAC champion, defeated O'Brien in the "metric mile" by less than 10 seconds. O'Brien captured the 1991 TAC Championships in a wind-aided total of 8,844 points. Despite the wind, O'Brien's tally represented history's second-highest score to Thompson's world record of 8,847 points. O'Brien captured the 1991 World Championship with an American record of 8,812 points, which surpassed Bruce Jenner's (OS) 1976 standard by 178 points.

In 1992, he surprised the athletic world by failing to qualify for the U.S. Olympic team. A first-day world record of 4,698 points notwithstanding, O'Brien failed to clear any height in the pole vault and placed eleventh in the Olympic Trials. Nevertheless, he completed 1992 with a world record of 8,891 points at Talence, France, a performance that included a decathlon world record long jump of 26 feet 6¼ inches and a first-day world record total of 4,720 points. In 1993, O'Brien captured the heptathlon at the indoor World Championships at Toronto, Canada, in a world record of 6,476 points. Later that year, he won the decathlon at both the USTF Outdoor Championships in Eugene, OR, and the outdoor World Championships in Stuttgart, Germany. O'Brien also prevailed in the decathlon at the 1994 Outdoor Championships in Knoxville, TN, and the 1994 St. Petersburg, Russia, Goodwill Games, where his 8,176 points fell just 176 points short of his world record. O'Brien's 5 minute, 10.94 second clocking in the final 1,500-meter event was 30 seconds slower than he needed to break the standard. At the World Cup in Talence, France, in September 1994, O'Brien solidified his standing as top decathlete and finished with 8,710 points.

BIBLIOGRAPHY: Jon Hendershott, "Difficult Questions to Ask," *TFN* 45 (August 1991), p. 26; Jon Hendershott, "O'Brien Fires Up Decathlon," *TFN* 44 (August 1991), p. 19; Jon Hendershott, "Respectable Once Again," *TFN* 43 (December 1990), pp. 4–6; Bob Hersh, "Don't Sell O'Brien Short," *TFN* 44 (November 1991), p. 19; Jeff Hollobaugh, "Forget Barcelona," *TFN* 45 (November 1992), pp. 4–5; Glen McMicken, "Dec: Goodbye Dan, Hi Dave," *TFN* 45 (August 1992), pp. 26–27; Dick Patrick, "O'Brien Sets Course for 'Greatest' Tag," *USA Today*, August 4, 1992.

Adam R. Hornbuckle

POWELL, Michael Anthony "Mike" (b. November 10, 1963, Philadelphia, PA), athlete, ranks among history's greatest long jumpers. On August 30, 1991, he bounded 29 feet 4½ inches to win the World Championship at Tokyo, Japan, and surpass by 2 inches the venerable standard established by Bob Beamon (OS) in the 1968 Mexico City, Mexico, Summer Olympic Games. Moreover, Powell defeated Carl Lewis (OS), who had won 65 consecutive long jump finals since 1982.

Powell, whose family moved to California when he was 11 years old, excelled in basketball at Edgewood High School in West Covina, CA. After graduating from high school in 1981, he received a basketball scholarship to the University of California at Irvine. Powell also broad-jumped at Edgewood, reaching 21 feet 11 inches as a junior and 23 feet 7 inches as a senior. At California—Irvine, he improved his long jump best to 26 feet 5¼ inches in 1983 and finished second in the TAC Championships and sixth in the Olympic Trials in 1984. Before 1984, Powell already had quit playing basketball to concentrate solely on long jumping. He left California—Irvine in 1985, finishing third in the TAC Championships, improving his best to 26 feet 9¾ inches, and ranking tenth in the world in the long jump. Powell, who competed for UCLA (PTC) in 1986, neither performed well in any major meets nor improved his personal best.

Throughout Powell's long-jumping career, a tendency to foul out of competition hampered his success. Coach Randy Huntington in 1987 helped Powell develop a more controlled approach, enabling him to reach 27 feet 1¾ inches and attain sixth ranking in the world. Powell, who then represented the Stars and Stripes TrC, finished third in the 1988 Olympic Trials and second to Lewis in the Summer Olympic Games at Seoul, South Korea. Powell's Silver Medal performance measured 27 feet 10¼ inches. After being ranked third globally in both 1988 and 1989, he won the 1990 TAC Championships and garnered the premier world ranking. Despite a second-place finish to Lewis at the 1991 TAC Championships, Powell defeated him in the World Championship and remained number one in the world. Powell bested Lewis at the 1992 Olympic Trials but finished second to him at the Barcelona, Spain, Summer Olympic Games. Lewis won an unprecedented third Olympic long jump title there. In 1993, however, Powell captured the long jump in both the USTF Championships in Eugene, OR, and the World Championships in Stuttgart, Germany. The following year, he prevailed in the long jump at the USTF Championships and at the St. Petersburg, Russia, Goodwill Games. Powell matched his world record with a wind-aided 29 foot 4½ inch leap at Sestriere, Italy, on July 31 and also finished first at the Pan-Africa-USA Meet at Durham, NC. In August 1994, he split a jackpot of $315,000 with British hurdler Colin Jackson by winning the long jump at the IAAF Grand Prix Meets. In the final 1994 Outdoor European Grand Prix Standings, Powell ranked first in the long jump.

BIBLIOGRAPHY: Gene Cherry, "LJ: Powell Gets First," *TFN* 41 (August 1990), p. 24; Roy Conrad, "Powell's Longest Jump," *TFN* 44 (October 1991), p. 7; Jon Hendershott, "Powell Fears No One," *TFN* 44 (September 1991), p. 5; Garry Hill, "Lewis Edges Powell," *TFN* 45 (October 1992), p. 42; Jeff Hollobaugh, "Powell Had Better Jumps," *TFN* 43 (September 1990), p. 15; Ruth Laney, "Powell's Dream Jump," *TFN* 44 (November 1991), p. 31; Sieg Lindstrom, "The Coach Behind Powell," *TFN* 45 (March 1992), pp. 56–57; Sieg Lindstrom, "LJ: Powell over Lewis," *TFN* 24 (August 1992), p. 22; Sieg Lindstrom, "Next Stop 10 Yard," *TFN* 45 (March 1992), pp. 52–54; Sieg Lindstrom, "Things Less Foul for Powell," *TFN* 41 (December 1988), p. 34; Dick Patrick, "Powell's Long Chase for Gold at Hand," *USA Today*, August 5, 1992, pp. C1–C2; Don Potts, "Powell Ends Lewis Streak," *TFN* 44 (November 1991), p. 30.

Adam R. Hornbuckle

REYNOLDS, Harry Lee "Butch" (b. June 8, 1964, Akron, OH), athlete, is the son of Harry Lee Reynolds and Catherine Reynolds and remains history's fastest 400-meter dashman. The outstanding football player, basketball player, and long jumper did not compete in the 400 meters until a senior at Archbishop Hoban High School in Akron, OH, in 1983. Reynolds declined a basketball scholarship from West Virginia University and football scholarships from the University of Akron (MAC) and Miami University of Ohio (MAC) and instead attended Butler County CC in El Dorado, KS, where he honed his 400-meter dash skills. In 1984, Reynolds reached the semifinals of the 400 meters at the U.S. Olympic Trials. He transferred to Ohio State University (BTC) in 1985 and, within two years, eclipsed Buckeye records held by Jesse Owens (OS) in the 200 meters and Glenn Davis (OS) in the 400 meters. In 1987, Reynolds clocked 44.13 seconds to secure the NCAA Championship and 44.46 seconds to capture the TAC Championship in the 400 meters. The 1987 World Championships saw Reynolds win a Bronze Medal in the 400 meters and a Gold Medal in the 4 × 400-meter relay.

During the late 1980s, Reynolds and several other 400-meter specialists possessed both the speed and stamina to surpass the world record of 43.86 seconds, held by Lee Evans (OS) since the 1968 Summer Olympic Games at Mexico City, Mexico. Reynolds won the 1988 U.S. Olympic Trials in 43.93 seconds, with UCLA's Danny Everett closely following him in 43.97 seconds. On August 17, 1988, prior to the Summer Olympic Games at Seoul, South Korea, Reynolds clocked 43.29 seconds for the 400 meters to eclipse Evans's venerable global standard. He failed, however, to capture the Olympic title. Teammate Steve Lewis won the 400 meters in a Junior world record of 43.87 seconds. Reynolds garnered an Olympic Gold Medal in the 4 × 400-meter relay in which the U.S. foursome equaled the world record of 2 minutes 56.16 seconds set by the United States at the 1968 Summer Olympic Games.

TFN ranked Reynolds first globally in the 400 meters in 1988 and 1989.

Reynolds lost his premier position in 1990 to Michael Johnson,* who defeated him handily in their only 400-meter race that year. In 1990, Reynolds supposedly tested positive for nandrolone, a banned steroid, and received a two-year suspension from the IAAF. Two years of decisions by TAC and IAAF officials and rulings by federal judges and Supreme Court justices followed before he was permitted to participate in the 1992 U.S. Olympic Trials. Reynolds qualified for the U.S. Olympic team as an alternate on the 4 × 400-meter relay team, but the IAAF clung to its original decision and did not permit him to compete in the Summer Olympic Games at Barcelona, Spain, under any conditions. Reynolds, who eventually sued the IAAF for $34 million in lost income and punitive damages, was awarded $27 million by a federal judge in December 1992. In May 1994, an appeals court reversed the federal judge's decision.

In 1993, Reynolds returned to competition in the 400 meters and won the indoor World Championship at Toronto, Ontario. Outdoors, he finished second to Johnson at both the USTF Championships and the World Championships at Stuttgart, Germany. At the latter, he also performed on the triumphant U.S. 4 × 400-meter relay team, which established a world record of 2 minutes 54.29 seconds.

BIBLIOGRAPHY: "Big Names Accused," *TFN* 44 (January 1991), p. 72; Roy Conrad, "Reynolds Kills Target," *TFN* 41 (October 1988), p. 7; Ed Gordon, "Reynolds Slashes WR to 43.29," *TFN* 41 (October 1988), pp. 24–26; Bob Hersh, "Mexico Mark Matched," *TFN* 41 (November 1988), p. 35; "How Reynolds Ran," *TFN* 45 (August 1992), p. 72; Ohio State University Sports Information, letter to Adam R. Hornbuckle, January 1993; Keith Peters, "Youthful Lewis Prevails," *TFN* 41 (November 1988), p. 14; "Reynolds a Step Closer," *TFN* 44 (December 1991), p. 48; "Reynolds Ban Extended," *TFN* 45 (October 1992), p. 80; "Reynolds Wins Suit," *TFN* 46 (January 1993), p. 76.

                                                                 Adam R. Hornbuckle

SANTEE, David Wesley "Wes" (b. March 25, 1932, Ashland, KS), athlete, ranked among the top milers of the 1950s and was the first of three children born to David Samuel Santee and Ethel May (Benton) Santee, both farmers. As with great American milers Glenn Cunningham (OS) and Jim Ryun (OS), Santee grew up in Kansas and ran for the University of Kansas (BSC).

In 1951, Santee as a freshman placed second in the AAU 5,000-meter event. He developed into the nation's top mile prospect within a year, winning both the NCAA 5,000-meter and the AAU 1,500-meter titles in 1952. Santee qualified for the Olympics in the 5,000 meters but was eliminated after one round at the Helsinki, Finland, Summer Olympic Games.

Santee won the NCAA and AAU outdoor mile titles in 1953 and set American records for both the 1,500 meters (3 minutes 44.2 seconds) and the mile (4 minutes 2.4 seconds). That fall, he led Kansas to an NCAA title with a first-place finish at the cross-country nationals. *TFN* ranked Santee first among American milers and second internationally to Australia's John

Landy. Landy, Santee, and Great Britain's Roger Bannister were considered the top candidates for the first sub-4-minute mile.

Santee appeared ready in February 1954, setting an indoor world best mile mark of 4 minutes 4.9 seconds. Three months later, however, Bannister made history with a 3 minute 59.4 second performance in Great Britain. On June 4 at the Compton, CA, Relays, Santee set a 1,500-meter world record of 3 minutes 42.8 seconds. In 1954, he was ranked third in the world for the mile behind Bannister and Landy.

On active duty as a U.S. Marine Corps officer for the 1955 season, Santee won the AAU indoor mile title and set indoor world bests for both the mile (4 minutes 3.8 seconds) and the 1,500 meters (3 minutes 48.3 seconds). Upon switching to outdoor competition in March 1955, Santee won a Silver Medal in the 1,500 meters at the Pan-American Games in Mexico City, Mexico. On April 2, he set his fourth American mile record with a time of 4 minutes .5 seconds at the Texas Relays. He was ranked America's best miler for 1955 but later was charged with accepting excessive amounts of expense money and was declared ineligible in 1956.

Santee, who was married three times, has three children, Edward, Robert, and Susan. After leaving active military service in 1957, he settled in Lawrence, KS, and worked in the insurance business until 1982. He retired from the U.S. Marine Corps Reserves in 1985 with the rank of colonel. In 1992, Santee was appointed to the board of trustees of the Kansas Sports Hall of Fame.

BIBLIOGRAPHY: AAU Convention Minutes for 1955, p. 22; Hal Bateman, *America's Best: A Compilation of U.S. Olympic and International Track and Field Stars, 1896–1987* (Indianapolis, IN, 1988); Hal Bateman, "The Greatest Mile Runners," *Track Newsletter*, August 24, 1960; Peter Cava, telephone interview with Wesley Santee, September 8, 1994; Wally Donovan, *A History of Indoor Track & Field* (El Cajon, CA, 1976); Bill Mallon and Ian Buchanan, *The United States' National Championships in Track and Field Athletics* (Indianapolis, IN, 1986); Cordner Nelson, "Track Talk," *TFN* 8 (February 1956), p. 9; Cordner Nelson and Roberto Quercetani, *The Milers* (Los Altos, CA, 1985); *3rd IAAF World Indoor Championships in Athletics Statistics Handbook* (London, England, 1991); *1993 American Athletics Annual* (Indianapolis, IN, 1993); *1993 USA Indoor Track* (Indianapolis, IN, 1993); *1992–1993 U.S. Cross Country Handbook* (Indianapolis, 1992); D. H. Potts and Scott Davis, *The United States National Record Progression from 1877* (Goleta, CA, 1983); University of Kansas Sports Information Department, file for Wes Santee, Lawrence, KS; Ekkehard zur Megede and Richard Hymans, *Progression of World Best Performances and IAAF Approved World Records* (London, England, 1991).

Peter Cava

SNYDER, Laurence Nelson "Larry" (b. August 9, 1896, Canton, OH; d. September 25, 1982, Columbus, OH), athlete and coach, is the son of William H. Snyder and Susan (Crolius) Snyder. His older brothers encouraged him to develop his skills in baseball, football, and ice hockey as a child. He played ice hockey so well that a Cleveland, OH, professional team offered him a contract when he graduated from Canton High School. Snyder rejected the offer, however, because he wanted to go to college. He also concentrated more upon track and field, becoming a State champion high hurdler and high jumper. Snyder, who attended Dartmouth College for a semester, joined the U.S. Army Air Corps in December 1917 and enrolled in flight school at Ohio State University (WC). During World War I, he served as a flight instructor at Fort Sill, OK, and Fort Worth, TX. Snyder married Mibs M. Moser in 1918 and had a daughter, Betsy. Snyder barnstormed the nation as an aviator following his discharge in 1919, carrying passengers and performing stunt exhibitions. As a Los Angeles, CA, resident in 1921 and 1922, he managed a Piggly Wiggly grocery store. Snyder returned to Ohio State University, where he graduated in 1925 with a B.S. degree in business administration. Snyder, who played as a halfback on the football team in 1923 and captained the track and field squad in 1924 and 1925, performed in the 120-yard high hurdles, 220-yard low hurdles, one-mile relay team, high jump, and broad jump.

Snyder, recipient of the WC Scholarship medal for combined excellence in academics and athletics, was hired as an assistant track and field coach at Ohio State University in 1925. In 1932, he replaced his former mentor, Dr. Frank Castleman, as head track and field coach. Snyder coached numerous Olympic and world record performers, including George Simpson in the 100 and 200 meters, Jack Keller in the 110-meter high hurdles, Jesse Owens (OS) in the 100 and 200 meters, 4 × 100-meter relay, and long jump, David Albritton (S) in the high jump, Mal Whitfield (OS) in the 800 meters, Gene Cole in the 400 meters, and Glenn Davis (OS) in the 400-meter hurdles. Snyder, who presided over the NCTCA in 1941, led Ohio State to the BTC indoor championships in 1942, 1948, 1950, and 1952 and outdoor crowns in 1942 and 1948. Besides accompanying Owens and Albritton to the 1936 Summer Olympic Games at Berlin, Germany, Snyder later served as an assistant track and field coach for the 1952 U.S. Olympic team and as head track and field coach for the 1960 U.S. Olympic team. In 1965, he retired as head track and field coach at Ohio State. His honors include memberships in the U.S. Track and Field Hall of Fame, NTF Hall of Fame, and Ohio State University Sports Hall of Fame.

BIBLIOGRAPHY: William J. Baker, *Jesse Owens: An American Life* (New York, 1986); Reid M. Hanley, *Who's Who in Track and Field* (New Rochelle, NY, 1973); Laurence N. Snyder, biographical file, Ohio State University Archives, Columbus, OH.

Adam R. Hornbuckle

STONES, Dwight Edwin (b. December 6, 1953, Los Angeles, CA), athlete and sportscaster, is the son of Richard Stones, a general contractor, and

Sandra Godfrey, a child care worker. Stones, who dreamt of becoming a major league baseball player, started high jumping after watching the televised world record performance of Valeri Brummel from the Soviet Union in the high jump during the 1963 U.S.-USSR track and field meet. Before entering high school, he captured the Glendale, CA, City Championships in the Class "F" Division in 1967 and Class "E" Division in 1968 of the high jump. As a Glendale High School student, Stones won the FOL Class "C" Championship in 1969 and the FOL Varsity Championship in 1970 and 1971. He enjoyed an undefeated season in 1971, claiming high jump titles in the California State Championships, the All-American High School Meet, and the Golden West Invitational. Stones, who also established a national high school record of 7 feet ½ inch in the high jump in 1971, placed tenth in the senior AAU Championships that year.

After graduating from high school in 1971, Stones developed into one of the world's leading high jumpers. As a UCLA freshman in 1972, he won the PEC title, placed third in the NCAA Championship, and captured the U.S. Summer Olympic Trials with a high jump performance of 7 feet 3 inches to establish a world record for 18-year-olds. Stones, who won the Bronze Medal in the high jump in the 1972 Summer Olympic Games at Munich, Germany, left UCLA after the Olympics and competed for the PaCC through 1975 and California State University, Long Beach, in 1976, winning six indoor and eight outdoor national titles. He established indoor world records of 7 feet 4 inches in 1974; 7 feet 5 inches, 7 feet 5¼ inches, 7 feet 5½ inches (twice), and 7 feet 5¾ inches in 1975; 7 feet 6¼ inches and 7 feet 6½ inches in 1976; as well as outdoor world records of 7 feet 6½ inches in 1973 and 7 feet 7 inches and 7 feet 7¼ inches in 1976. Stones, who finished second in the 1976 U.S. Summer Olympic Trials, captured a second Bronze Medal in the Summer Olympic Games at Montreal, Canada. From 1973 to 1976, *TFN* ranked him first globally in the high jump.

Stones remained the nation's top high jumper through the early 1980s, but his global dominance steadily declined. He won both the indoor and outdoor AAU titles in 1977 and the outdoor AAU Championship in 1978. The AAU, however, suspended Stones for the 1979 season for diverting his winnings from the 1978 ABC's "Superstars" competition to his track club. In 1980, he placed third in the outdoor AAU Championship and tenth in the U.S. Summer Olympic Trials. Stones, who took the indoor TAC crown in 1982 and outdoor TAC title in 1983, placed sixth in the 1983 World Championships at Helsinki, Finland. In 1984, he won the U.S. Summer Olympic Trials in an outdoor American record of 7 feet 8 inches and placed fourth in the Summer Olympic Games at Los Angeles, CA. After failing to qualify for the high jump finals of the 1988 U.S. Summer Olympic Trials, Stones retired quietly from track and field. His honors include induction into the California State Long Beach 49'er Sports Hall of Fame in 1988 and Orange County Sports Hall of Fame in 1991. Stones frequently provides commentary for televised track and field events and owns Dwight Stones Enterprises in Irvine, CA. Married since 1981, he has a son and a daughter.

BIBLIOGRAPHY: Bill Mallon and Ian Buchanan, *The Quest for Gold: The Encyclopedia of American Olympians* (New York, 1984); Dwight Stones, letter to Adam R. Hornbuckle, April 1993; David Wallechinsky, *The Complete Book of the Olympics*, rev. ed. (New York, 1988).

Adam R. Hornbuckle

TEMPLETON, Robert Lyman "Dink" "The Boy Coach" "Ol' Mr. Gravel Voice" (b. May 27, 1897, Helena, MT; d. August 7, 1962, Palo Alto, CA), athlete, coach, sportscaster, and sportswriter, the son of Joseph C. Templeton, a businessman, was one of the twentieth century's most successful track and field coaches. Templeton, whose athletic career began in the shadow of older brother Rick, entered Stanford University in 1914. The outbreak of World War I, however, caused him to leave Stanford and become an aviator in France. Templeton returned to Stanford (PCC) after the war and gained fame as a football player and track and field athlete. The five-time Stanford letterman achieved acclaim for opening the 1919 football game against the University of California, Berkeley, with a 52-yard dropkick. After being disqualified for diving over the bar in the high jump at the 1920 Olympic Trials, Templeton entered the long jump and qualified for the U.S. team. In the 1920 Summer Olympic Games at Antwerp, Belgium, he placed fourth in the long jump. He also won a Gold Medal in rugby, leading the United States to an 8–0 rout of France. Once again, Templeton demonstrated his potent dropkick, booting one 55 yards against the French.

In 1921, Templeton graduated from Stanford and informally began coaching the track and field team. He took over the position officially the following year, becoming at age 25 one of the youngest mentors to hold such a position at a major American university. Templeton, nicknamed "The Boy Coach," led the Indians (then the Stanford mascot) to four IC4A (1927–1929, 1934) and three NCAA (1925, 1928, 1934) track and field championships. Stanford also finished second in the IC4A five times (1926, 1930–1933) and NCAA four times under his leadership. In his 19-year career, Templeton coached 19 individual NCAA titlists, 24 world record holders, and nine Olympic medalists. The most notable of the Templeton elite, Ben Eastman (OS), established world records of 46.4 seconds for 440 yards in 1932 and 1 minute 49.8 seconds for 880 yards in 1934. Templeton, who served as the U.S. Olympic weight event coach in 1924 and 1928, emphasized finesse over strength in the discus throw and the shot put. At Stanford, he coached world record holders Glen Hartranft (157 feet 1⅝ inches, 1925) and Eric Krenz (167 feet 5⅜ inches, 1930) in the discus throw and Harlow Rothert (52 feet 1⅝ inches, 1930) and John Lyman (54 feet 1 inch, 1930) in the shot put. He revolutionized track and field coaching by insisting on year-round preparation, then a controversial concept for coaches believing such a regimen would "burn out" athletes.

Templeton retired from Stanford in 1939 and coached part-time for the San Francisco OlC. Later he became a radio announcer, being nicknamed "Ol' Mr. Gravel Voice," and a sports columnist for the Palo Alto (CA) *Times*. Templeton, who also earned a law degree from Stanford in 1924, died of a heart attack following a bout with pneumonia. His death came four days after that of coaching rival Dean Cromwell (OS) of the University of Southern California. Brutus Hamilton (S), track and field coach at the University of California, Berkeley, lauded Templeton as "the only one among us with the touch of genius."

BIBLIOGRAPHY: Bob Brachman, "Track Coach Dink Templeton Dies," San Francisco (CA) *Examiner*, August 8, 1962, pp. 53, 55; "Dink Templeton, Former Coach of Track at Stanford, 65, Dies," *NYT*, August 8, 1962; Art Rosenbaum, "The Man They Called 'Genius,'" San Francisco (CA) *Chronicle*, August 8, 1962, p. 46; Bud Spenser, *High Above the Olympians* (Palo Alto, CA, 1966); Stanford University Alumni Association, Palo Alto, CA, Letter to Adam R. Hornbuckle, July 1993.

Adam R. Hornbuckle

TRUEX, Max (b. November 4, 1935, Warsaw, IN; d. March 24, 1991, Milton, MA), athlete, was one of the nation's premier distance runners during the 1950s. Truex, whose first race was a half-mile timed in 2 minutes 37.8 seconds at age 12, established a national high school record of 4 minutes 20.4 seconds for the mile as a senior at Warsaw High School in 1954. At the 1954 AAU Championships, he clocked 4 minutes 18.5 seconds for the mile. The time, however, could not be listed as a national interscholastic standard since Truex had graduated from high school. He entered the University of Southern California (PEC), becoming one of the Trojan's finest distance runners. Truex set freshman class records of 4 minutes 16.2 seconds for the mile and 9 minutes 15.5 seconds for the two-mile in 1955. As a sophomore, he qualified for the 1956 U.S. Summer Olympic team in both the 5,000 and 10,000 meters, winning the latter in 30 minutes 52.0 seconds at the Olympic Trials. A painful hip injury during the 1956 Summer Olympic Games at Melbourne, Australia, however, forced the Trojan distance ace to bypass the 5,000 meters and drop out of 10,000 meters. In 1957, Truex established a collegiate two-mile record of 8 minutes 55.0 seconds and an American record of 14 minutes 4.2 seconds for the 5,000 meters and won the PEC and NCAA cross-country championships. Truex finished sixth in the 10,000 meters in the 1960 Summer Olympic Games at Rome, Italy, clocking an American record of 28 minutes 50.2 seconds.

Truex attended Southern California on an academic scholarship and graduated with a bachelor's degree in accounting in 1959. After completing a three-year stint in the U.S. Air Force, he returned to Southern California to study law. Truex graduated from the Southern California School of Law in 1965 and practiced as a successful trial attorney for Los Angeles County, specializing in real estate litigation. In 1979, he was diagnosed with Parkinson's disease. The chronic, progressive disease of the nervous system, marked by tremor and weakness of the muscles, is caused by the inadequate production of dopamine in the brain. Truex's condition deteriorated so badly that he retired from practicing law in 1981. He and his wife Catherine, sons Gene and John, and daughter Mindy moved to Milton, MA, in 1988 so that he could live near a clinic specializing in the treatment of the disease. Truex traveled to China in 1989 to have experimental surgery to transplant brain tissue necessary for the production of dopamine, an operation that was forbidden in the United States because the federal government prohibited the use of aborted fetal tissue. His condition improved dramatically immediately following the operation, but the seizures gradually returned within six months. Before his death, Truex advocated reform of the nation's policy toward experimental treatments for Parkinson's disease.

BIBLIOGRAPHY: *TFN* 44 (May 1991), p. 29; University of Southern California Sports Information, Los Angeles, CA, letter to Adam R. Hornbuckle, February 1993; David Wallechinsky, *The Complete Book of the Olympics*, rev. ed. (New York, 1988).

Adam R. Hornbuckle

VIRGIN, Craig Steven (b. August 2, 1955, Belleville, IL), athlete, is the son of Vernon C. Virgin, a farmer and agricultural businessman, and Lorna (Lee) Virgin, a retired teacher and agricultural businesswoman. He began distance running as a Lebanon, IL Community High School freshman, immediately breaking national age group and high school class records from 3,000 to 5,000 meters. Virgin captured Illinois State High School Championships in the mile in 1972 and cross-country and two-miles in 1972 and 1973. He placed second in the 5,000 meters at the 1972 AAU Junior National Championships and won the race in 1973, both times qualifying him for the AAU Junior National team. *TFN* selected Virgin, who established a national high school record of 8 minutes 40.9 seconds for two miles, as the 1973 High School Athlete of the Year.

Virgin, who graduated from the University of Illinois in 1977, won nine BTC Championships in cross-country and indoor and outdoor track. His only NCAA Championship came in cross-country in 1975. The Illinois trackman, however, placed second in the 10,000-meter outdoors in 1976 and 1977 and the two-mile indoors in 1976 and third in the six-mile outdoors in 1975 and the three-mile indoors in 1976 and 1977. The 10,000 meters was Virgin's best track event. At that distance, he won three AAU/TAC Championships in 1978, 1979, and 1982 and qualified for three consecutive Olympic teams in 1976, 1980, and 1984. Virgin's accomplishments included establishing a collegiate record of 27 minutes 59.4 seconds for the distance in 1976 and an American record of 27 minutes 39.4 seconds in 1979. He garnered a Silver Medal in the 1979 WoC but did not compete for an Olympic medal in 1980 because of the U.S.-led boycott of the Moscow, USSR, Summer Olympic Games. Nevertheless, he recorded the fastest time in the world that year for 10,000 meters. His clocking of 27 minutes 29.2 seconds marked an American record and history's second-fastest time.

In 1980, Virgin became the first American ever to capture the IAAF World Cross-Country Championship. He defended the title in 1981. As one of the leading long-distance runners of the 1980s, he established national road-race records of 22 minutes 46.9 seconds for 8,000 meters and 28 minutes 4 seconds for 10,000 meters. The 1981 Boston Marathon featured Virgin defeating Bill Rogers (OS) and finishing second to Toshiko Seko of Japan. To support himself as an amateur athlete, he founded Front Runner, Incorporated, a sports marketing, promotion, and consulting firm, in 1980. Virgin, who retired from competitive running and campaigned unsuccessfully for the Illinois State Senate in 1992, is married and the stepfather of a son and daughter.

BIBLIOGRAPHY: Roy Conrad, "Virgin Wins International Cross Country," *TFN* 33 (April 1980), pp. 6–7; Tom Jordan, "Craig Virgin," *TFN* 33 (May 1980), pp. 50–51, 53; Tom Jordan, "Notes on an American Champion," *TFN* 30 (August 1977), pp. 10–11; Don Kopriva, "Virgin Authors Own Script," *TFN* 28 (December 1975), p. 4; Craig Virgin, letter to Adam R. Hornbuckle, December 1992; "Virgin Defends XC Title," *TFN* 34 (May 1981), p. 46; "Virgin Is the Star," *TFN* 26 (January 1974), p. 59.

Adam R. Hornbuckle

WATTS, Quincy Dushawn (b. June 19, 1970, Detroit, MI), athlete, is the son of Rufus Watts, a retired post office employee, and Allitah Hunt and is the fastest 400-meter runner in Olympic history. Watts lived with his mother in Detroit until age 13, when she sent him to Los Angeles, CA, to live with his father, as she was concerned that her son was getting involved with the wrong crowd in Detroit. The elder Watts recognized his son's potential as a runner and introduced him to John Smith, the sprint coach at UCLA and one of the finest 400-meter runners of the 1970s, who since has coached Watts.

Watts, a graduate of Taft High School in Woodland Hills, CA, in 1988, won State High School championships in the 100 meters in 1987 and the 200 meters in 1986 and 1987 before concentrating on the 400 meters in 1988. Nagging hamstring injuries befell Watts that year, but he still recorded 20.67 seconds for 200 meters and 46.67 seconds for 400 meters. Watts graduated from the University of Southern California (PTC) with a bachelor's degree in communications in 1992 but was hindered by injuries as a freshman and as a sophomore. A healthy Watts demonstrated his potential as a 400-meter specialist in 1991 by taking second place in both the NCAA Championships and the USOC Olympic Festival, third in the TAC Championships, and fourth in the Pan-American Games. His best time that year, a 44.98-second clocking, came in the TAC Championships. The U.S. 4 × 400-meter team won the Silver Medal in the 1991 World Championships, as Watts was timed in 43.4 seconds for one of history's fastest 400-meter relay legs.

In 1992, Watts accomplished everything in the 400-meter dash except setting the world record. After winning both the PTC and NCAA titles, he finished third in the Olympic Trials in 43.97 seconds and then won the Gold Medal at the Summer Olympic Games at Barcelona, Spain. His winning time of 43.50 seconds, the second-fastest 400 meters of all time, marked an Olympic record. Watts, however, first eclipsed the Olympic record of 43.86 seconds, set by Lee Evans (OS) in the 1968 Mexico City, Mexico, Summer Olympic Games, with a 43.71-second performance in the semifinals. Watts, whose relay leg of 43.1 seconds ranks as history's fastest, collected another Gold Medal in the 4 × 400-meter relay. In this race, the U.S. 4 × 400-meter corps established a world record of 2 minutes 55.74 seconds. This clocking erased the standard of 2 minutes 56.16 seconds, first set by the United States in the 1968 Summer Olympic Games and tied by the United States in the 1988 Summer Olympic Games at Seoul, South Korea. In 1993, he finished third in the 400 meters behind Michael Johnson* and Butch Reynolds* at the USTF Championships and fourth in the World Championships at Stuttgart, Germany. At the latter, he teamed with Johnson, Reynolds, and Andrew Valmon in the 4 × 400-meter relay to establish a world record of 2 minutes 54.29 seconds. Watts prevailed in the 400 meters with a 45.21-second clocking at the 1994 St. Petersburg, Russia, Goodwill Games, and competed on the 1994 European Grand Prix Circuit.

BIBLIOGRAPHY: Jon Hendershott, "Britain Stuns U.S.," *TFN* 44 (November 1991), p. 25; Jon Hendershott, "The Man Called 'Q,'" *TFN* 46 (March–April 1992), pp. 52–54; Jeff Hollobaugh, "Watts Breaks OR Twice," *TFN* 45 (October 1992), p. 18; Dave Johnson, "Another WR for U.S.," *TFN* 45 (October 1992), p. 37; Ruth Laney, "Watts Nabs a Pair of Golds," *TFN* 45 (October 1992), p. 19; Sieg Lindstrom, "Watts Steps Up—and Out," *TFN* 45 (July 1992), p. 20; TAC Press Information, letter to Adam R. Hornbuckle, November 1992; University of Southern California Sports Information, letter to Adam R. Hornbuckle, November 1992.

                                                                          Adam R. Hornbuckle

YOUNG, Kevin Curtis (b. September 16, 1966, Los Angeles, CA), athlete, ranks among history's fastest 400-meter intermediate hurdlers and is the son of William Young, a counselor, and Betty Champion, a hospital administrator. His stepfather, Arthur Champion, serves as a minister. Young, who clocked 14.23 seconds for the 110-meter high hurdles and 37.54 seconds for the 300-meter intermediate hurdles, graduated from Jordan High School in Los Angeles in 1984 and entered UCLA. John Smith, one of history's finest 400-meter dashmen, coached Young, who quickly adapted to the longer hurdle race. In 1986, Young improved to 48.77 seconds and garnered second place in the NCAA Championships and third place in both the TAC Championships and USOC Olympic Festival. Young captured the NCAA Championship in 1987 and defended the title in 1988. The 1988 Summer Olympic Trials witnessed the UCLA hurdler record a personal best time of 47.72 seconds, as he edged out David Patrick and Danny Harris. The trio finished within four hundredths of a second of each other, for third place and a position on the Olympic team. Despite coming in fourth in the 1988 Summer Olympic Games at Seoul, South Korea, he was ranked third globally in the 400-meter intermediate hurdles that year.

Young, who ran in the shadow of Edwin Moses (OS) and Andre Phillips while at UCLA, surpassed his rivals in 1989 by posting the year's fastest time of 47.86 seconds. *TFN* recognized Young as the world's premier 400-meter intermediate hurdler. His dominance over the 400-meter intermediate hurdles was short-lived, however, as Harris and Zambia's Samuel Matete ranked first globally in 1990 and 1991, respectively. Besides placing second in the TAC Championships in 1990 and 1991, Young finished third in the Seattle, WA, Goodwill Games in 1990 and fourth in the World Championships in 1991. He reaffirmed his premier global standing in 1992 by completing the season undefeated in the 400-meter intermediate hurdles and claiming the Summer Olympic title at Barcelona, Spain, in a shocking world record of 46.78 seconds. His time eclipsed the standard of 47.02 seconds held by Moses since 1983. Young triumphed in the 400-meter hurdles in both the USTF Championships and the World Championships at Stuttgart, Germany, in 1993.

BIBLIOGRAPHY: Jed Brickner, "Phillips Rings Moses' Bell," *TFN* 41 (November 1988), p. 28; Ed Gordon, "Young Gets First Sub-48," *TFN* 42 (October 1989), p. 24; Jon Hendershott, "400H: Young in New Wave," *TFN* 45 (August 1992), p. 20; Jon Hendershott, "The Man Who Passed Moses," *TFN* 46 (January 1993), p. 5; Jon Hendershott, "T&FN Interview: Kevin Young," *TFN* 45 (September 1992), pp. 14–15; Jon Hendershott, "WR 46.78 for Young," *TFN* 45 (October 1992), p. 32; Jon Hendershott, "Young Beats Prediction," *TFN* 45 (October 1992), p. 33; Sieg Lindstrom, "Kevin Young: A Hurdler for the '90s?" *TFN* 42 (December 1989), pp. 14–15; "Kevin Young," Games of the XXV Olympiad, Barcelona, Spain, NBC-Sports Research Information, vol. 8 (1992), pp. 573–574.

Adam R. Hornbuckle

WRESTLING

BAUMGARTNER, Bruce (b. August 31, 1962, Haledon, NJ), college wrestler and coach, is the second son of Bob Baumgartner, a diesel mechanic, and Lois Baumgartner and was by his own admission a mediocre athlete as a teenager. At Manchester Regional High School, he played some football and finished third at the NJ State Wrestling Tournament as a senior. Baumgartner wrestled at Indiana State University, finishing second in both the 1980 and 1981 NCAA Tournaments. As a senior, he won his last 44 matches and captured top honors in the superheavyweight division. Academically, he earned an excellent 3.77 grade-point average.

Baumgartner, like smaller Olympic teammate John Smith,* improved even further in the tough international circuit. Between 1981 and 1985, Soviet wrestlers had won every World and European championship in the super-heavyweight 286-pound class. Almost single-handedly, Baumgartner broke this monopoly. After finishing second in the 1982 and 1983 WoC Tournaments, he won the crown three times. At the World Championships, Baumgartner gained his first title in 1986 and earned Silver or Bronze Medals four other times. He has performed his best in Olympic competition, becoming the first American in any weight class to take home three medals. After overwhelmingly winning a Gold Medal at the 1984 Los Angeles, CA, Summer Olympic Games, he finished second at the 1988 Seoul, South Korea, Summer Olympic games and brilliantly regained the title at the 1992 Barcelona, Spain, Summer Olympic Games. The second Gold Medal proved especially sweet because Baumgartner had appeared to lose his wrestling desire while finishing seventh in the 1991 World Championships. His other important wrestling titles included the 1987 World University Games and 1987 Pan-American Games. He earned his eleventh U.S. National Freestyle Championship, including 10 consecutive, in 1992 and has not suffered defeat to an American in over a decade. The USWF, the sport's governing body, voted him 1986 Wrestling Athlete of the Year. In April 1994, Baumgartner defeated Tom Erikson for the U.S. Freestyle National Open heavyweight title. The Sullivan Award nominee also claimed his seventh WoC gold medal and was selected USOC 1994 Wrestler of the Year. At the 1994 World Freestyle Wrestling Championships in Istanbul, Turkey, Mahmut Demir of Turkey upset Baumgartner.

The massive six-foot-two-inch, 270-pound Baumgartner has 18-inch biceps and a 52-inch chest. On the mat, he combines great strength with surprising quickness and remains very agile for such a large man. He lives with his wife Linda and son Brian in a farmhouse near Cambridge Springs, PA. After serving several years as an assistant wrestling coach at nearby Edinboro University, he assumed the head coaching position in 1990.

BIBLIOGRAPHY: Mike Chapman, "Best," *WUSA* 22 (March 15, 1987), pp. 10–12; Barry McDermott, "A Guy You Do Not Fool With," *SI* 65 (October 20, 1988), p. 78; Rich O'Brien, "Golden Oldies," *SI* 77 (August 17, 1982), p. 58.

Frank P. Bowles

MONDAY, Kenny "Puma" (b. November 25, 1961, Tulsa, OK), college wrestler, is the son of Fred Monday and won four State wrestling championships at Washington High School in Tulsa, boasting an amazing 140–0–1 record. After entering Oklahoma State University (BEC), he rapidly became a key member of the team his freshman year. During his sophomore and junior seasons in 1982 and 1983, Monday reached the NCAA 150-pound finals before losing to Nate Carr of Iowa State University both times. In 1984, he captured the 158-pound crown.

After graduating with a bachelor's degree, Monday began practicing international wrestling techniques that differed markedly from his college freestyle methods. He won the 1985 U.S. National Championships, the first of his three national crowns. His initial major international victory came with his Gold Medal WoC performance. The 1988 campaign boded especially well for the 5-foot-10-inch, 163-pound Monday, as he upset Adlan Varaev of the Soviet Union to capture the Gold Medal at the Seoul, South Korea, Summer Olympic Games. He also won the 1988 Tbilisi Championship, which most contestants consider far tougher than the Olympics. The same year, he captured his second U.S. National title and finished second in the WoC to earn Man of the Year honors. In 1989, he garnered his first World Championship by defeating Arsen Fadzaev, another outstanding Soviet wrestler, in the final match.

Since 1988, Monday has ranked among the best wrestlers in the world. In the very formidable 163-pound division, he has competed against talented American Dave Schultz (IS) and many impressive Eastern bloc grapplers. His important 1991 tournament victories included the U.S. National crown and Pan-American title. In 1989 and 1990, he garnered Grand Masters Champion and Outstanding Wrestler accolades. The 1992 Barcelona, Spain,

Summer Olympic Games brought Monday disappointment. He lost his final match, 1–0, to Park Jang-Soong of South Korea after shutting out all previous competitors. In April 1994, Royce Alger edged Monday in the 180.5-pound semifinals of the U.S. Freestyle National Open.

Monday personifies grace and fully lives up to his nickname "Puma," given him by foreign rivals. The extremely strong, very quick grappler exhibits no known weakness and employs almost perfect defense. Monday recently married and lives in Tulsa, OK, where he has pursued several business ventures. The 33-year-old may seek a third Olympic medal at the 1996 Atlanta, GA, Summer Olympic Games.

BIBLIOGRAPHY: National Wrestling Hall of Fame, letter to Frank P. Bowles, 1994; Craig Neff, "Mighty Tough Cowboys," *SI* 69 (October 10, 1988), p. 102; *WUSA* 28 (December 15, 1992), p. 19.

Frank P. Bowles

RODERICK, Myron (b. February 15, 1934, Attica, KS), college wrestler, coach, and administrator, is the son of Boyd Roderick and Julia Roderick and starred in wrestling at Winfield, KS, High School. At Oklahoma State University (BEC), he quickly established himself as a dynamic grappler. In three varsity wrestling campaigns for the Cowboys from 1954 through 1956, he won 42 of 44 matches and captured three NCAA titles. The stocky, 5-foot-5½-inch Roderick earned his first title at 137 pounds and his final two crowns at 130 pounds. He qualified for the 1956 U.S. Olympic team and finished fourth at the Melbourne, Australia, Summer Games, losing a split decision to the eventual champion.

Roderick, a fierce mat competitor, transferred his fighting spirit to his wrestlers as an Oklahoma State coach. After succeeding Art Griffiths in 1957, he led the Cowboys to the 1958 NCAA Championship at age 23 and became the youngest mentor ever to capture a national title in any sport. Roderick, a "hands-on" coach, wrestled with his charges while combining his abilities as a teacher and motivator. Under his tenure, Oklahoma State captured seven NCAA crowns in a 13-year span. The noted takedown artist imbued his wrestlers with his aggressive take-them-down, let-them-up style. Between 1957 and 1969, his Cowboys recorded 140 dual meet wins with just 10 losses and seven ties. Oklahoma State compiled an 84-match winning streak during the early 1960s. Roderick, who produced 20 individual NCAA champions and four Olympic Gold Medalists, coached the U.S. wrestling squad at the 1963 World University Games and served as assistant mentor of the 1964 wrestling team at the 1964 Tokyo, Japan, Summer Olympic Games. Roderick, a strong recruiter voted Coach of the Year in 1959, 1962, and 1966, brought numerous promising wrestlers to Stillwater, OK, and may have been the first college wrestling coach to look abroad for talent. Consequently, Yojiro Uetake and other superb international wrestlers helped maintain Oklahoma State's dominance.

After the 1969 season, Roderick sought new challenges and retired from the collegiate coaching ranks. He served as USWF executive director and from 1983 to 1989 as athletic director at his alma mater. An excellent racquetball player, Roderick presided over the IRA. He currently works as president of the National Wrestling Hall of Fame, an honorary body that enshrined him in 1976. He lives in Stillwater with his wife JoAnn and has two children, Tara and Ty.

BIBLIOGRAPHY: Mike Chapman, *Encyclopedia of American Wrestling* (Champaign, IL, 1990), pp. 518–519; Charles Coe, "Crunch for Coach Roderick," *Life* 66 (February 14, 1966), p. 75; National Wrestling Hall of Fame, letter to Frank P. Bowles, 1994.

Frank P. Bowles

SMITH, John (b. August 9, 1965, Del City, OK), wrestler, is the seventh of 10 children of Lee Roy Smith and Madalene Smith and grew up in wrestling-intense Oklahoma, where he and his three brothers pursued the sport naturally. After being an outstanding high school wrestler, he starred at Oklahoma State University (BEC). The rangy five-foot-seven-inch lightweight realized that he could not match many opponents in physical strength and became very innovative. Although not inventing new moves, Smith used established ones in new ways with flawless technique. After finishing second at the 1985 NCAA Tournament, he captured NCAA 136.5-pound division titles in 1987 and 1988. Smith was chosen Outstanding Wrestler at the 1987 NCAA Tournament and finished his collegiate career with 90 consecutive wins, graduating with a bachelor's degree.

His college heroics served as a prelude to an outstanding international career, during which Smith has reached a level fully comparable to the great Dan Gable (IS). In his initial year of international wrestling, he in 1987 won the first of his six World Championships and earned *AWN* Man of the Year accolades. Smith captured the 137-pound freestyle Gold Medal at the 1988 Seoul, South Korea, Summer Olympic Games and dominated his weight division internationally for five years. He dropped a 4–2 decision to John Fisher at the 1992 U.S. Olympic Trials, his first setback since 1990 and first loss to an American in four years. Smith, however, defeated Fisher in the next two matches to make the U.S. Olympic team. He won a second straight Gold Medal at the 1992 Barcelona, Spain, Summer Olympic Games, making him only the second American to win consecutive Olympic championships. Two most prestigious honors were bestowed on Smith during this period. In 1991, he became the first wrestler to garner the Sullivan Award as the year's best American amateur athlete. The following year, FILA, the international wrestling organization, named him Wrestler of the Year. His success centered around "Smith's Low Single," a move in which the limber, agile Smith wrestles effectively at a lower angle than his opponent and reaches either of his opponent's lower legs to record a takedown. Smith's rivals know what to expect but rarely can block his move. His takedowns, dedication to victory, and alert intelligence make the 29-year-old virtually unstoppable.

Oklahoma State named Smith an assistant wrestling coach in 1991 and promoted him to head coach the next year following the departure of Joe Seay. Smith guided the Cowboys to the 1994 NCAA crown, terminating the three-year domination by Gable's University of Iowa wrestlers. Lee Roy, his older brother, won the 1980 NCAA title at 136.5 pounds and earned a Silver Medal at the World Championships. In March 1994, Pat, his 158-pound younger brother, became the first wrestler to win four NCAA crowns. Mark, his youngest brother, demonstrated remarkable talent as a high school wrestler and wrestles for Oklahoma State.

BIBLIOGRAPHY: Shannon Brownless, "How Low Can You Get?" *SI* 68 (March 14, 1988), p. 52; "Grappling with Obscurity," *AH* 11 (July–August 1992), pp. 58–59; Craig Neff, "Mighty Tough Cowboys," *SI* 69 (October 10, 1988), p. 102.

Frank P. Bowles

MISCELLANEOUS SPORTS

DOWNING, Burton Cecil (b. February 5, 1885, San Jose, CA; d. January 1, 1929, Red Bank, NJ), cyclist, was the son of Lorenzo Downing and spent his boyhood on his father's ranch. He learned to bicycle as a young boy in California, but little is known of his early record. Downing, not well known by the eastern riders, surprised many observers by consistently defeating Teddy Billington in races. He competed at the 1904 St. Louis, MO, Summer Olympic Games while traveling east to begin his career as a contractor. Downing's first Olympic event came on August 2, when he finished third behind Marcus Hurley and Billington in the ½-mile race. On August 3, he took a Silver Medal behind Hurley in the ¼-mile race and won his first Gold Medal in the 2-mile race. Two days later, he finished his Olympic and cycling career with another Gold Medal in the 25-mile race and Silvers in the 1-mile and ⅓-mile races. His six medals at the 1904 Olympics have been surpassed by only three Americans at one competition. He never again raced after the Olympics or won a national championship, but his Olympic performance alone merits his recognition as a great cyclist.

Downing was accompanied on his trip east by his older brother, Hardy, another renowned cyclist. After settling in Salt Lake City, UT, Hardy later became a well-known professional cyclist on the velodrome in that city from 1904 to 1914 and a promoter for Jack Dempsey (IS), a great heavyweight boxing champion.

Burton settled in New York City in 1904 and joined a contracting firm, the George B. Spearin Company. Upon Spearin's death in 1909, he became the president of that firm. During World War I, Downing administered his company's construction of the Army base in Brooklyn, NY. He later served as president of the New York Contracting Dock Builders Association and as vice president of the Redbank Hotel Company, which built the Molly

Pitcher Hotel on the site of Downing's former home. Downing married May Vought and had two daughters, Dorothy and Virginia.

BIBLIOGRAPHY: Bill Mallon and Ian Buchanan, *Quest for Gold: The Encyclopedia of American Olympians* (New York, 1984); Peter Nye, *Hearts of Lions: The Story of American Bicycle Racing* (New York, 1988); *NYT*, January 2, 1929.

Bill Mallon

MILLER, Shannon Lee (b. March 10, 1977, Rolla, MO), gymnast, is the daughter of Ron Miller, who teaches physics at the University of Central Oklahoma, and Claudia Miller, a bank vice president. Shannon, who has an older sister, Tessa, and a younger brother, Troy, is coached by Steve Nunno and Peggy Liddick at Dynamo Gymnastics. Miller attends Edmond, OK, North High School, where she maintains a 4.0 grade-point average and belongs to the Oklahoma and National Honor Societies.

Miller began gymnastics at age 6. In 1988, the 11-year-old won the U.S. Classic and took second at the American Classic. Since 1988, she has ranked among top U.S. contenders, having competed in 13 national championship meets and earned 23 medals (13 Gold, 7 Silver, and 3 Bronze) in all four events and the all-around. In 1992, she captured the all-around at the Olympic Trials in Baltimore, MD.

Miller also entered her first international gymnastic competition in 1988, the Junior Pan-American Games in Puerto Rico, and placed second in the all-around and third on the uneven bars. From 1988 to 1993, Miller represented the United States in 21 international competitions. These included the McDonald's American Cup (1990–1993), USA against Romania (1991), the World Championships (1991, 1993), and 1992 Barcelona, Spain, Summer Olympics. In international competition, she has won 37 medals (20 Gold, 7 Silver, and 10 Bronze). Miller was the only American to qualify for all four individual event finals at the 1991 (Indianapolis, IN) and 1993 (Birmingham, Great Britain) World Championships and the 1992 Olympic Games.

Miller starred on the first U.S. Women's Gymnastics team to win a medal in a nonboycotted Olympic Games in 1992 at Barcelona, Spain. She gained worldwide recognition by earning the Silver Medal in the all-around, the highest finish by an American gymnast. Her five medals, including two Silver and three Bronze, represented the most medals won by an American athlete. At the 1993 World Championships in Birmingham, England, she won the all-around, uneven bars, and floor exercise events. Previously, only one American had ever won a World Champion title. At the 1993 U.S. National Championships in Salt Lake City, UT, Miller took her first all-around title and won the uneven bars and floor exercise. In April 1994, she retained her all-around title at the World Gymnastic Championship in Brisbane, Australia, for the second consecutive year. Her remarkable performance, which included two spectacular vaults, came after missing two weeks of training due to a stomach muscle injury. The 1994 St. Petersburg, Russia, Goodwill

Games saw her place first in the floor exercise and balance beam and second in the all-around, uneven bars, and vault. In the August 1994 U.S. National Championships at Nashville, TN, she finished second in the all-around, vault, uneven bars, balance beam, and floor exercise. Injuries forced her to withdraw from the 1994 World Team Championships in Dortmund, Germany, but the U.S. team earned a gold medal.

Her several awards have included the WSF's "1991 Up & Coming" Award, the New York Downtown AC's 1992 Steve Reeves Fitness Award as the first female recipient, and the 1993 Female Athlete of the Year. She also earned the 1992 Nuprin Comeback Award, given for her tremendous comeback after surgery for a dislocated elbow. In 1994 Miller was named USA Gymnastic Athlete of the Year and Dial Award recipient. The USOC selected the Sullivan Award nominee its Female Gymnast of the Year.

BIBLIOGRAPHY: *NYT*, July 19, 1992, p. SO6; August 2, 1992, sec. 8, p. 5; *USAG* 21 (November–December 1992), pp. 25–27; USA Gymnastics (USGF) Bio Sheet on Shannon Miller, June 21, 1993.

                                                                Susan J. Rayl

PLUMB, John Michael "Mike" (b. March 28, 1940, Islip, NY), equestrian, is the son of Charles Plumb and Meems Plumb and remains one of the most storied of American equestrians. He has competed in seven Summer Olympic Games (1960–1976, 1984, 1992) and made eight Olympic teams (1960–1984, 1992), missing the 1988 Olympic Trials due to injury. His father, a steward at the Yonkers and Roosevelt harness tracks in New York, served as huntsman for the Meadowbrook Hounds, a fox hunting club near Syosset, NY. "Mike" and his mother served as "whippers-in" for the club, keeping straggling hounds up with the pack. He played football at Millbrook School and the University of Delaware and began competing on horses in the three-day event in 1958.

Plumb first participated internationally at the 1959 Pan-American Games in Chicago, IL, where he won team and individual Silver Medals. He later earned a team Gold at 1963 Pan-American Games and team and individual Gold Medals at 1967 Pan-American Games in the three-day event. Plumb has won six Olympic medals, including two Golds in the 1976 and 1984 team three-day event and four Silvers. His Silvers came in the 1964, 1968, and 1972 team three-day event and 1976 individual three-day event. Plumb has also garnered four medals at the world championships, including the 1974 individual Silver and team Gold on Good Mixture, 1978 team Bronze on Laurenson, and 1982 team Bronze on Blue Stone. He has been voted U.S. Combined Training Association Rider of the Year 10 times, among them 1965–1967, 1970–1971, 1973–1974, 1976–1977, and 1979.

Plumb has remained at 5 feet 11¾ inches, 165 pounds throughout his career by eating only one meal per day. His son, Charlie, also competes in three-day events, having narrowly missed making the 1992 U.S. Olympic team. Mike, his father, and son all have won the USET Gladstone Trophy, emblematic of the USET Fall Three-Day Event Championship. He now farms in Maryland, where he lives with his wife, Donnan (Sharp) Plumb, a well-known equestrienne.

BIBLIOGRAPHY: Bill Mallon and Ian Buchanan, *Quest for Gold: The Encyclopedia of American Olympians* (New York, 1984; USET, press release, June 1993; *USOC Media Guides*, 1960, 1964, 1968, 1972, 1976, 1980, 1984, 1992.

Bill Mallon

VANDERBILT, Harold Stirling (b. July 6, 1884, Oakdale, NY; d. July 4, 1970, Newport, RI), yachtsman, was the son of William Kissam Vanderbilt I and Alva Erskine (Smith) Vanderbilt. After graduating from Harvard University with a B.A. degree in 1907, he attended Harvard Law School from 1907 to 1910. Vanderbilt served as a lieutenant in the U.S. Navy in 1917 and 1918 aboard a submarine chaser detachment based in Ireland. His family amassed a huge fortune in the railway pioneering days, giving him ample funds to indulge his passion for sailing. The greatest yachtsman of his generation, he defended the AMC in 1930, 1934, and 1937 and remains the only yachtsman to skipper and steer in three successive defenses in three different yachts. In 1930, he sailed *Enterprise* to victory in four straight races against the British challenger, *Edward Heard*. Although losing the first two races in 1934, he won the next four with *Rainbow* to overcome another British challenge from *Tommy Sopwith*. *Tommy Sopwith* challenged again in 1937, but Vanderbilt sailed *Ranger* to triumph in four straight races and retained the AMC for the third successive time.

Although much of his time was devoted to yachting, Vanderbilt kept active in the business world and chaired the executive committee of the New York Central Railroad. He was the last Vanderbilt to play a role in the railroad, which his family had founded in 1853. He also served as commodore of the NYYC and as a major benefactor and chairman of the board of trustees of Vanderbilt University. Vanderbilt also invented contract bridge, devising the game on a cruise in 1925. The game soon swept the world, replacing the popular auction version. In 1933, Vanderbilt married Gertrude L. Conaway of Philadelphia. They had no children.

BIBLIOGRAPHY: K. Adlard Coles and Terence L. Stocken, eds., *The Yachtsman's Annual and Who's Who* (London, UK, 1938); Jerry E. Patterson, *The Vanderbilts* (New York, 1989).

Ian Buchanan

ZIMMERMAN, Arthur August "Zimmy" "Zim" (b. June 11, 1870, Camden, NJ; d. October 20, 1936, Atlanta, GA), cyclist, was the son of Theodore A. Zimmerman, a hotel proprietor and real estate broker, and Anna Zimmerman. He grew up at Manasquan, NJ, and attended a military school, where he excelled in track and field as a high, long, and triple jumper. Subsequently, he entered a law office, but soon decided not to make the legal profession his career.

He began bicycle racing in 1887 at a Freehold, NJ, meet and won his first prize as a wheelman in late 1888 in a novice sprint at Queens, NY, riding an "ordinary" (i.e., high-wheel) cycle. Zimmerman quickly became an accomplished sprinter, defeating Willie Windle, American sprint champion, and Alfred Lumsden in 1-mile and 10-mile events at Peoria, IL, in September 1890. Like others, he switched from his ordinary to a "safety" bicycle but without diminishing his performance results. By British invitation, Zimmerman rode through the 1892 English racing season as a representative of the New York AC and won the NCU's 1-, 10-, and 50-mile championships. Although inexperienced at the longest distance, the superbly conditioned Zimmerman wore down the opposition and sprinted by Frank Shorland, the English favorite, at the finish. Zimmerman returned in 1893, but British officials barred him and charged professionalism because Raleigh bicycle advertisements featured him. Not banned elsewhere, he raced in Ireland and France, where "le Yankee volant" was admired greatly. At Chicago, IL, he won the first amateur world 1-mile and 10-kilometer championships. As 1893 ended, he turned professional.

Zimmerman contracted to ride Raleigh bicycles and in 1894 dominated competition in Europe and then Australia. Mediocre performances in Europe during 1895 and 1896 followed. The constant strains of travel and racing had worn down his competitive instincts and physical skills. Although no longer a big winner, he still drew large crowds, especially in Paris, France. Zimmerman, who retired from racing in 1903, purchased a hotel at Point Pleasant Beach, NJ, and operated it for 18 years. He and his wife Grace, whom he married in 1904 or 1905, moved to Asbury Park, NJ, in 1928 and lived there until his death. He died of a heart attack while visiting his only child, Mrs. Ella (Zimmerman) Toll.

Zimmerman, a 5-foot-11-inch, 160-pounder, consistently observed strict training routines, diet control, and avoidance of alcohol and tobacco. He set few record times on the track because he normally trailed his competition until the final stages, when his long legs generated the amazing speed that swept him to victory. Allegedly, he won more than 1,400 races, including heats. Zimmerman's superiority at his peak stimulated both attendance and the quality of competition, as he "carried the sport to a new level of popularity and prominence." He also wrote one of the first cycling instruction texts, *Zimmerman on Training*, published in Leicester, England, in 1893.

BIBLIOGRAPHY: Asbury Park (NJ) *Evening Press*, October 21, 1936, pp. 1, 3; Victor Breyer, "Arthur Zimmerman—Greatest Pedaller of All Time," *CW* (April 30, 1947), pp. 336–337; New York *Clipper*, February 7, 1891, p. 761; Peter Nye, *Hearts of Lions: The History of American Bicycle Racing* (New York, 1988); *NYT*, October 11, 1936; Andrew Ritchie, *Major Taylor: The Extraordinary Career of a Champion Bicycle Racer* (Mill Valley, CA, 1988).

Frank V. Phelps

Appendix 1

Alphabetical Listing of Entries with Sport

The following lists the entries in alphabetical order with sport. The entries with asterisks appear in the Miscellaneous Sports section.

Jesse Peter "The Book" Abramson—communications

Donna Adamek—bowling

Charles Francis Adams—ice hockey

Andre Kirk Agassi—tennis

Marvin Philip "Marv" Albert—communications

Felipe (Rojas) Alou—baseball

Mateo (Rojas) "Matty" Alou—baseball

Lyle Martin Alzado—football

Knowlton Lyman "Snake" Ames—football

Lewis Peter "Lew" Andreas—basketball

Elmer Joseph "Bud" Angsman, Jr.—football

John August Antonelli—baseball

Gordon Scott Appleton—football

Jon Dwayne "Jaguar Jon" Arnett—football

Mike Aulby—bowling

Roberto Francisco "Bobby" Avila—baseball

Braulio Baeza—horse racing

Elzie Wylie "Buck" Baker, Sr.—stock car racing

Francis Carter "Banny" Bancroft—baseball

David "Davey" "Flash" "Fatty" "Pretzel" Banks—basketball

Don Angelo Barksdale—basketball

David "Dave" "Impo" "Skinny" Barnhill—baseball

Nathan "Nate" Barragar—football

Lazaro Sosa "Laz" Barrera—horse racing

Charles "Chuck" Barrett—football

Michael "Mike" Barrowman—swimming

Jimmy "Chicago's Little Tiger" Barry—boxing

Henry Albert "Hank" Bauer—baseball

Bruce Baumgartner—wrestling

Hubert "Hub" Bechtol—football

Glenn Alfred "Bruno" Beckert—baseball

Russell K. "Bull" "Bully" Behman—football

David Russell "Gus" Bell—baseball

George Antonio Mathey Bell—baseball

Ricky Lynn Bell—football

Wilfred "The Dragon" Benitez—boxing

Cornelius O'Landa "Biscuit" Bennett—football

Christopher "Chris" "Boomer" Berman—communications

Lester "Les" Bingaman—football
Max Frederick "Tilly" "Camera Eye" Bishop—baseball
Rolando Antonio "Ro" Blackman—basketball
Ewell "The Whip" Blackwell—baseball
Wade Anthony Boggs—baseball
Barry Lamar Bonds—baseball
Ernest Edward "Ernie" "Tiny" Bonham—baseball
Roberto Antonio "Bobby" "Bobby Bo" Bonilla, Jr.—baseball
Raymond Otis "Ray" "Ike" Boone—baseball
Ronald Bruce "Ron" Boone—basketball
Vincent Joseph "Vince" Boryla—basketball
Cathy Ann Turner Bostley—speed skating
Brian Keith "The Boz" Bosworth—football
Richard J. "Dick" Boushka—basketball
Max Ray Boydston—football
William Joseph "Bill" Bradley—baseball
Raymond Robert "Ray" "Muscles" Bray, Sr.—football
Chester Arthur "Chet" Brewer—baseball
Frank Sands "Flash" "Frankie" Brian—basketball
Gene Herman Brito—football
George Haycock Brooke—football
James Robert Brooks—football
Thomas J. "Tom" Brookshier—football
David Steven "Dave" Brown—football
George V. Brown—ice hockey
Hardy "Butcher Boy" "The Hump" "Thumper" Brown—football
Johnny Mack "Dothan Antelope" Brown—football
Raymond "Ray" Brown—baseball
Earle Dunseth Bruce, Jr.—football
John Tomlinson Brush, Jr.—baseball
Victor Albert "Vic" Bubas—basketball
Edward Leon "Ed" Budde—football
William Preston Burch—horse racing
Simon "Si" Burick—communications
Adrian Matthew Burk—football

Leroy Russell Burrell—track and field
Owen Joseph "Donie" Bush—baseball
Earnest Alexander Byner—football
William "Bill" "Daddy" Byrd—baseball
George "Bad News" Cafego—football
Samuel Howard "Howie" Camnitz—baseball
Dagoberto Blanco "Bert" Campaneris—baseball
Jimmy Cannon—communications
Jose Canseco, Jr.—baseball
John Peerless Carmichael—communications
Gordon "Shorty" Carpenter—basketball
Clay Palmer "Hawk" Carroll—baseball
Harry Donald Carson—football
Joseph Cris "Joe" Carter, Jr.—baseball
Ricardo Adolfo Jacobo "Rico" Carty—baseball
George Washington Case, Jr.—baseball
Edward Lawrence "Eddie" "Natick Eddie" Casey—football
David "Dave" Cash, Jr.—baseball
Elton P. "Icebox" Chamberlain—baseball
Thomas Doane "Tom" Chambers—basketball
Wilmer Dean Chance—baseball
Samuel Blake "Sam" Chapman—football
Christos "Chris" Chelios—ice hockey
Deron Leigh Cherry—football
Louis Joseph Chevrolet—auto racing
Todd Jay Christensen—football
Ellery Harding Clark, Sr.—track and field
Grace Walton Roosevelt Clark—tennis
William Nuschler "Will" "The Thrill" Clark, Jr.—baseball
Mark Gregory Clayton—football
William Roger "Rocket" Clemens—baseball
John J. "Jack" Clements—baseball
Timothy Sylvester "Tim" Cohane—communications
James Anthony "Ripper" Collins—baseball

Frank Filchock—football

Dow Finsterwald—golf

Patrick "Pat" "Mouse" Fischer—football

Robert Thomas "Bob" Fisher—football

Lowell Cotton Fitzsimmons—basketball

Julius Timothy "Tim" Flock—stock car racing

Theodore "The Georgia Deacon" "Tiger" Flowers—boxing

Russell William "Russ" Ford—baseball

Robert Herbert "Bob" "Forschie" Forsch—baseball

Fulvio Chester "Chet" "Chet the Jet" Forte, Jr.—basketball

Gregory "Greg" Foster—track and field

William P. "Bill" Fralic, Jr.—football

William Henry Getty "Bill" France, Sr.—stock car racing

Clarence "Bevo" Francis—basketball

Julio Cesar Franco—baseball

Rodney Thomas Franz—football

World B. Free—basketball

David Guthrie "Dave" Freeman—badminton and tennis

John Frank "Buck" "Bucky" Freeman—baseball

Linus Reinhard "Lonny" "Junior" Frey—baseball

Gary Joseph Gaetti—baseball

Alonzo Smith "Jake" Gaither—football

Willie Lee Galimore—football

Kimberly Ann "Kim" Gallagher—track and field

Robert Garrett—track and field

Ned Franklin Garver—baseball

Allen Lee "Al" Geiberger—golf

Abraham "Abe" Gibron—football

Carlton Chester "Cookie" Gilchrist—football

James William "Junior" "Jim" Gilliam—baseball

Martin "Marty" Glickman—communications

Charles R. "Buckets" Goldenberg—football

Dwight Eugene "Doc" "Doctor K" Gooden—baseball

Jay Gould—court tennis

William "Billy" Graham—boxing

John Frederic "Jack" Green—football

Michael Lewis "Mike" Greenwell—baseball

Darrell Steven "Griff" "Golden Griff" "Dr. Dunkenstein" Griffith—basketball

Russell "Russ" Grimm—football

Pedro "Pete" Guerrero—baseball

Anthony Keith "Tony" Gwynn—baseball

Marlene Bauer "Grem" Hagge—golf

Nicole Haislett—swimming

Burdette Eliele "Burdie" Haldorson—basketball

Daniel Oliver "Dan" "Danimal" Hampton—football

Samuel "Sam" Hanks, Jr.—auto racing

Merle Reid Harmon, Sr.—communications

Howard Harpster—football

Raymond "The Little Professor" "The Bedouin" Harroun—auto racing

Judy Devlin Hashman—badminton

Donald Lee "Don" "The Bear" "H" Haskins—basketball

Kevin John Hatcher—ice hockey

Jan Margo Henne Hawkins—swimming

Frank Whitman "Blimp" Hayes—baseball

Michael James "Mike" Haynes—football

Thomas J. Healey—horse racing

John Geoffrey "Jeff" Heath—baseball

Charles Taylor "Charlie" "The Horse" Hennigan—football

Orel Leonard "Bulldog" Hershiser IV—baseball

Charles Buchanan Hickcox—swimming

Robert A. "Bob" Higgins—football

Drew Hill—football

Arthur Rudolph Thomas "Doc" "Art" Hillebrand—football

John Frederick Hiller—baseball

Larry Eugene Hisle—baseball

James Franklin "Jimmy" Hitchcock, Jr.—football

Charles Richard "Charlie" Lau—base-
ball
Francis Edward "Hank" "Hurrying
Hank" Lauricella—football
Lucien Laurin—horse racing
Vernon Sanders "Vern" "Deacon"
Law—baseball
Edward Wayne "Eddie" LeBaron, Jr.—
football
Thornton Starr "Lefty" Lee—baseball
Willis Augustus Lee, Jr.—shooting
Brian Joseph Leetch—ice hockey
Chester Earl "Chet" Lemon—baseball
A. E. "Abe" Lemons, Jr.—basketball
Christopher Michael "Archie" "Chick"
"The Dog" "Chris" Leonard—bas-
ketball
Hubert Benjamin "Hub" "Dutch"
Leonard—baseball
Willard Russell "Russ" Letlow—football
Marvin David "Marv" Levy—football
John Kelly "Buddy" Lewis, Jr.—baseball
James Richard "Jim" Leyland—baseball
Gordon C. Locke—football
John Theodore "Johnny" "Yachta" Lo-
gan, Jr.—baseball
Howard M. "Howie" Long—football
John Eric "Johnny" "The Pumper"
Longden—horse racing
Ronald Mandel "Ronnie" Lott—football
Donald Bradford "Don" Lourie—foot-
ball
Nicholas Dominic "Nick" Lowery—
football
Frank John Lubin—basketball
Henry Van Noye Lucas—baseball
Frederick William "Fred" "Ludy" Lu-
derus—baseball
James Robert "Jim" Lynch—football
James Dickson "Dick" McBride—base-
ball
Charles Louis "Clem" McCarthy—com-
munications
Charles Youmans "Charlie Mac" Mc-
Clendon—football
Gilbert James "Gil" "Smash" Mc-
Dougald—baseball

Patrick Francis "Packy" McFarland—
boxing
Willie Dean McGee—baseball
John Francis "Johnnie" McGovern—
football
Frederick Stanley "Fred" McGriff—
baseball
Mark David McGwire—baseball
Thomas Lee "Tom" Mack—football
Horace Albert "Bones" McKinney—
basketball
Tamara McKinney—skiing
Freeman McNeil—football
Harold "Jug" McSpaden—golf
Garry Lee Maddox—baseball
Constantine Gene Mako—tennis
William Guy "Bill" Mallory—football
Karl Anthony "The Mailman" Ma-
lone—basketball
Raymond Michael "Ray" "Boom Boom"
Mancini—boxing
Edward Francis "Ed" "Italian Stallion"
Marinaro—football
Michael L. "Mike" Marsh—track and
field
Alastair Bradley Martin—court and lawn
tennis
James Richard "Jim" "Jungle Jim" Mar-
tin—football
Riley "Snake" Matheson—football
Thomas Roland "Tom" Matte—football
Vincent Edward "Vince" Matthews—
track and field
Donald Arthur "Don" Mattingly—base-
ball
Thomas William "Tom" Meany—com-
munications
Ramon B. "Ray" Mears—basketball
Sabath Anthony "Sam" Mele—baseball
Frederick Charles "Fred" Merkle—
baseball
Michael James "Mike" Milbury—ice
hockey
Richard "Dick" Miles—table tennis
Creighton Eugene Miller—football
*Shannon Lee Miller—gymnastics
Abraham Gilbert "The Bismarck of
Baseball" Mills—baseball

Century Allen Milstead—football
Kevin Darrell Mitchell—baseball
Loren Dale Mitchell—baseball
Thomas Sven "Tommy" Moe, Jr.—skiing
John Moir—basketball
Kenny "Puma" Monday—wrestling
Donald Wayne "Don" Money—baseball
James Arthur "Art" Monk—football
James Paul "Jim" Montgomery—swimming
Harold Warren Moon—football
Wallace Wade "Wally" Moon—baseball
Davey Moore—boxing
Walter "Dobie" Moore—baseball
Pablo Morales—swimming
Stanley Douglas Morgan—football
Edward "Cannonball" Morris—baseball
Lawrence C. "Larry" Morris—football
James H. "Monk" Moscrip—football
John Anthony "Johnny" "Bananas" Mostil—baseball
Howard Edward Mudd—football
Leah Jean Poulos Mueller—speed skating
Van Lingle Mungo—baseball
Michael Anthony Munoz—football
Daniel Francis "Danny" "Old Reliable" Murphy—baseball
Jack Raymond Murphy, Jr.—communications
Hugh "Muzz" Murray—ice hockey
Donald Eugene "Don" Nehlen—football
Larry Gene Nelson—golf
James D. "Big Jim" Norris, Sr.—ice hockey
Joseph John "Joe" Norris—bowling
Kenneth Howard "Ken" Norton, Sr.—boxing
Andrew James "Jim" "Swede" Oberlander—football
Christopher "Chris" O'Brien—football
Daniel Dion "Dan" O'Brien—track and field
John Thomas "Johnny" O'Brien—basketball

Hakeem Abdul "The Dream" Olajuwon—basketball
Edward "Eddie" Olczyk, Jr.—ice hockey
Shaquille Rashaun "Shaq" O'Neal—basketball
John Jordan "Buck" O'Neil, Jr.—baseball
James Edward "Tip" O'Neill—baseball
Carl Townsend Osburn—shooting
Joel Stuart Otto—ice hockey
Stephen Michael "Stevie" "Steve" Palermo—baseball
Sandra Jean Palmer—golf
Duane Charles "Bill" Parcells—football
Robert Lee "Chief" Parish—basketball
Daniel Francis "Dan" Parker—communications
Lance Michael Parrish—baseball
John "Johnnie" Parsons—auto racing
Camilo Alberto y Lus "Little Potato" Pascual—baseball
James Russel "Jimmy" Patton, Jr.—football
Endicott "Chub" Peabody II—football
Clarence Cecil Pell—court tennis
Antonio Francisco "Tony" Peña—baseball
Terry Lee Pendleton—baseball
Gary Charles Peters—baseball
Richard Alvin "Richie" Petitbon—football
Americo Peter "Rico" Petrocelli—baseball
Lee Arnold Petty—stock car racing
Edward Joseph "Jeff" "Hassen" Pfeffer—baseball
Gerald John "Gerry" Philbin—football
Loyd Wade Phillips—football
Louis Brian "Pic" Piccolo—football
James Anthony "Jimmy" Piersall—baseball
Laffit Alegando Pincay, Jr.—horse racing
Ralph Arthur "Babe" "The Soft Thumb" Pinelli—baseball
Walter Clement "Wally" Pipp—baseball
Richard "Rick" Pitino—basketball

*John Michael "Mike" Plumb—equestrian

Howard Joseph "Howie" Pollet—baseball

James Eugene "Jim" "Buster" Poole—football

Darrell Ray Porter—baseball

Shirley Lewis Povich—communications

Michael Anthony "Mike" Powell—track and field

Abisha Collins "Bosh" Pritchard—football

Kirby Puckett—baseball

Duane Putnam—football

Ernest Cosmas "Ernie" Quigley—basketball

Alexander "Alec" Radcliffe—baseball

Theodore Roosevelt "Ted" "Double Duty" Radcliffe—baseball

Ulmo Shannon "Sonny" Randle—football

William Larry "Willie" Randolph, Jr.—baseball

Jeffrey James "Jeff" "The Terminator" Reardon—baseball

Joseph "Joe" Reiff—basketball

Robert R. "Bob" Reinhard—football

Harold Patrick "Pete" "Pistol Pete" Reiser—baseball

Raymond "Ray" Renfro—football

Laurence Henry "Dutch" Rennert, Jr.—baseball

Ernest John "Pug" "The Flying Dutchman" Rentner—football

Harry Lee "Butch" Reynolds—track and field

Richard Alan "Rick" Rhoden—baseball

Gerald Byron "Jerry" Rhome—football

Jerry Lee Rice—football

Nolan Richardson, Jr.—basketball

Robert Clinton "Bobby" Richardson, Jr.—baseball

J. Lee Richmond—baseball

Francis Charles "Frank" Richter—communications

Gerald Antonio Riggs—football

Charles Ramsey "Babe" Rinehart—football

Calvin Edwin "Cal" Ripken, Jr.—baseball

Arnold Denny "Arnie" "Stilts" Risen—basketball

Claude Cassius "Little All Right" Ritchey—baseball

Myron Roderick—wrestling

Ira Errett "Rat" Rodgers—football

Diann Roffe-Steinrotter—skiing

Stephen Douglas "Steve" Rogers—baseball

Ellen Crosby Roosevelt—tennis

William Winston "Bill" Roper—football

Norman DeMille "Uncle Normie" "The Big Moose" Ross—swimming

Tobin C. Rote—football

Clarence Henry "Pants" Rowland—baseball

George Napoleon "Nap" Rucker—baseball

Louis "Lou" "The Battler" Rymkus—football

Bret William Saberhagen—baseball

Edward A. "Big Ed" Sadowski—basketball

Kenneth Lloyd "Kenny" Sailors—basketball

Eyre "Ayers" "Bruiser" Saitch—basketball

Carmen Mario "Spook" Salvino—bowling

Peter "Pete" Sampras—tennis

Ryne Dee "Ryno" Sandberg—baseball

Charles Alvin "Charlie" Sanders—football

Orban Eugene "Spec" Sanders—football

Summer Elisabeth Sanders—swimming

David Wesley "Wes" Santee—track and field

John Carl "Jack" Scarbath—football

Richard Phillip "Dick" "Schaf" Schafrath—football

Christopher Eugene "Chris" Schenkel—communications

Clyde Luther "Smackover" Scott—football

Raymond "Ray" Scott—communications

Ronald "Ron" "Jingle Joints" Sellers—football

James Luther "Luke" Sewell—baseball

Ralph Orlando "Socks" Seybold—baseball

Paul Norman Seymour—basketball

Roderick "Rod" Shoate—football

Wilfred Charles "Sonny" Siebert III—baseball

James Shores "Jim" Simpson—communications

Fred William Sington—football

Jackie Ray Slater—football

Bruce Bernard Smith—football

Elmer Ellsworth "Mike" Smith—baseball

Ernest F. "Ernie" "Sliphorn" Smith—football

John Smith—wrestling

Marilynn Louise "Smitty" Smith—golf

William T. "Wee Willie" "Slim Green" Smith—basketball

Laurence Nelson "Larry" Snyder—track and field

Arthur Henry Soden—baseball

Stanley Orvil "Stan" Spence—baseball

Lloyd S. Spooner—shooting

Craig Robert "The Walrus" Stadler—golf

Charles Sylvester "Chick" Stahl—baseball

William Thomas "Bill" Stanfill—football

Joseph Benton "Joe" Steffy, Jr.—football

George Michael Steinbrenner III—baseball

Dwight Eugene Stephenson—football

David Keith Stewart—baseball

Melvin "Mel" Stewart—swimming

James R. "Jim" Stillwagon—football

David Knapp "Dave" Stockton—golf

Dick Stockton—communications

John Houston Stockton III—basketball

Maurice "Mo" Stokes—basketball

Dwight Edwin Stones—track and field

George Washington Stovey—baseball

Darryl Eugene "Straw" Strawberry—baseball

C. Vivian Stoner Stringer—basketball

T. R. "Ted" Strong—baseball

John "Johnny" "Strike" Strzykalski—football

William Reed "Bill" Summers—baseball

Gary Suter—ice hockey

Eddie Sutton—basketball

Ezra Ballou Sutton—baseball

James Edward "Jim" "The Rusk Rambler" Swink—football

Paul John Tagliabue—football

John W. "Jack" Taylor—baseball

George Robert "Bird" "Birdie" Tebbetts—baseball

Robert Lyman "Dink" "The Boy Coach" "Ol' Mr. Gravel Voice" Templeton—track and field

Herbert Watson "Herb" Thomas—stock car racing

Jennifer "Jenny" Thompson—swimming

Andre "Andy" "Thor" "Thunder" Thornton—baseball

Andre Bernard Tippett—football

Clifford Earl "The Earl of Snohomish" Torgeson—baseball

Daniel Lee "Deacon Dan" Towler—football

Theodore "Ted" "Highpockets" "Big Florida" Trent—baseball

Quincy Thomas Trouppe—baseball

Max Truex—track and field

J. Edward "Eddie" "Cannonball" Tryon—football

Thomas Joseph "Tommy" "Foghorn" "Noisy Tom" Tucker—baseball

John Thomas "Tute" Tudor—baseball

James Riley "Jim" "Milkman Jim" Turner—baseball

Fernando (Anguamea) Valenzuela—baseball

Willem Hendrick "Bill" "Butch" Van Breda Kolff—basketball

Andrew James "Andy" "Slick" Van Slyke—baseball

John "Beezer" Vanbiesbrouck—ice hockey

*Harold Stirling Vanderbilt—yachting

William Kissam Vanderbilt—auto racing
Andrew "Andy" Varipapa—bowling
Robert Andrew "Bob" Veale, Jr.—baseball
Jorge Velasquez—horse racing
Francis Thomas "Fay" Vincent, Jr.—baseball
Frank John Viola, Jr.—baseball
Craig Steven Virgin—track and field
James Herbert "Jim" Wacker—football
Lisa Rathgeber Wagner—bowling
Arthur Jonathon "Art" Wall, Jr.—golf
Maud Barger Wallach—tennis
Robert "Bob" Ward—football
Andre T. Ware—football
Eugene "Gene" Washington—football
Joe Dan "Little Joe" "The Crockett Rocket" Washington, Jr.—football
Quincy Dushawn Watts—track and field
Herman John "Wedey" "Squirmin' Herman" Wedemeyer—football
Donna Weinbrecht—skiing
Robert Lynn "Bob" Welch—baseball
George Thomas Welsh—football
Charles Marin "Buck" Wharton—football
Arthur Ledlie "Beef" Wheeler—football
Reginald Howard "Reggie" White—football
Roy Hilton White—baseball
Wilford Daniel "Danny" White—football
Arthur Carter "Pinky" Whitney—baseball
James Evans "Grasshopper Jim" Whitney—baseball
Frank "Red Ant" Wickware—baseball

Raymond Walter "Ray" Wietecha—football
Howard "Handsome Howdy" Wilcox—auto racing
Glenn Newton Wilkes—basketball
James Thomas "Jimmy" "Buttons" "Home Run" Williams—baseball
Edward Nagle "Ned" Williamson—baseball
Arthur Lee "Artie" Wilson—baseball
George "Wildcat" Wilson—football
Herbert Warren Wind—communications
Arthur Michael Wirtz, Sr.—ice hockey
Harry Wismer—communications
Eugene Richard "Gene" "Old Faithful" Woodling—baseball
Rufus Stanley "Stan" Woodward—communications
Philipp D. "Phil" "The Thin Man of the Hilltop" Woolpert—basketball
Burnis "Bill" "Wild Bill" Wright—baseball
Bowden Wyatt—football
John Whitlow "Whit" Wyatt—baseball
Paul Wylie—figure skating
Kristi Tsuya Yamaguchi—figure skating
Andrew Alva Young—football
Kevin Curtis Young—track and field
Adolph F. "Swede" Youngstrom—football
Jonathan Thompson Walton "Tom" "Ol' Tom" Zachary—baseball
Charles Louis "Chief" Zimmer—baseball
*Arthur August "Zimmy" "Zim" Zimmerman—cycling
Richard Walter "Richie" Zisk—baseball

Appendix 2
Entries by Major Sport

The following lists the entries included in the book by major sport.

AUTO AND STOCK CAR RACING (14)

Elzie Wylie "Buck" Baker, Sr.
Louis Joseph Chevrolet
Mark Donohue
Julius Timothy "Tim" Flock
William Henry Getty "Bill"France, Sr.
Samuel "Sam" Hanks, Jr.
Raymond "The Little Professor" "The Bedouin" Harroun
Ned Miller Jarrett
Robert Glenn "Junior" Johnson, Jr.
John "Johnnie" Parsons
Lee Arnold Petty
Herbert Watson "Herb" Thomas
William Kissam Vanderbilt
Howard "Handsome Howdy" Wilcox

BASEBALL (202)

Felipe (Rojas) Alou
Mateo (Rojas) "Matty" Alou
John August Antonelli
Roberto Francisco "Bobby" Avila
Francis Carter "Banny" Bancroft
David "Dave" "Impo" "Skinny" Barnhill
Henry Albert "Hank" Bauer
Glenn Alfred "Bruno" Beckert
David Russell "Gus" Bell
George Antonio Mathey Bell
Max Frederick "Tilly" "Camera Eye" Bishop
Ewell "The Whip" Blackwell
Wade Anthony Boggs
Barry Lamar Bonds
Ernest Edward "Ernie" "Tiny" Bonham
Roberto Antonio "Bobby" "Bobby Bo" Bonilla, Jr.
Raymond Otis "Ray" "Ike" Boone
William Joseph "Bill" Bradley
Chester Arthur "Chet" Brewer
Raymond "Ray" Brown
John Tomlinson Brush, Jr.
Owen Joseph "Donie" Bush
William "Bill" "Daddy" Byrd
Samuel Howard "Howie" Camnitz
Dagoberto Blanco "Bert" Campaneris
Jose Canseco, Jr.
Clay Palmer "Hawk" Carroll
Joseph Cris "Joe" Carter, Jr.
Ricardo Adolfo Jacobo "Rico" Carty
George Washington Case, Jr.
David "Dave" Cash, Jr.
Elton P. "Icebox" Chamberlain
Wilmer Dean Chance
William Nuschler "Will" "The Thrill" Clark, Jr.

William Roger "Rocket" Clemens
John J. "Jack" Clements
James Anthony "Ripper" Collins
David Ismael (Benitiz) Concepcion
Robert Joe "Bobby" Cox
Delmar Wesley "Del" Crandall
James Otis "Doc" Crandall
Frank Peter Joseph "Frankie" "The Crow" Crosetti
Anthony Francis "Tony" "Chick" Cuccinello
Roy Joseph Cullenbine
Thomas Peter "Tom" "Tido" Daly
Curtis Benton "Curt" "Coonskin" Davis
Eric Keith Davis
John B. Day
Arthur McArthur "Art" Devlin
James Alexander "Jim" Devlin
William "Dizzy" Dismukes
August Joseph "Augie" Donatelli
John Joseph "Dirty Jack" Doyle
Edwin Hawley "Eddie" Dyer
Howard Easterling
Charles Andrew "Duke" Farrell
Donald Martin Fehr
Robert V. "Bob" "Death to Flying Things" Ferguson
Cecil Grant "The Big Man" Fielder
Russell William "Russ" Ford
Robert Herbert "Bob" "Forschie" Forsch
Julio Cesar Franco
John Frank "Buck" "Bucky" Freeman
Linus Reinhard "Lonny" "Junior" Frey
Gary Joseph Gaetti
Ned Franklin Garver
James William "Junior" "Jim" Gilliam
Dwight Eugene "Doc" "Doctor K" Gooden
Michael Lewis "Mike" Greenwell
Pedro "Pete" Guerrero
Anthony Keith "Tony" Gwynn
Frank Whitman "Blimp" Hayes
John Geoffrey "Jeff" Heath
Orel Leonard "Bulldog" Hershiser IV
John Frederick Hiller
Larry Eugene Hisle
James Wear "Bug" Holliday

Richard Dalton "Dick" Howser
Kent Alan Hrbek
Cecil Carleton "Tex" Hughson
Bruce Vee Hurst
Frederick Charles "Fred" "Big Bear" "Hutch" Hutchinson
William Forrest "Wild Bill" Hutchinson
Lawrence Joseph "Larry" Jansen
Howard Michael "Hojo" Johnson
William Frederick "Billy" Jurges
Benjamin Michael "Benny" Kauff
Jay Thomas "Tom" Kelly
Donald Eulon "Don" "Kess" Kessinger
Frank Bissell Killen
Ellis Raymond "Old Folks" Kinder
George John "Whitey" Kurowski
Ferdinand Cole "F.C." Lane
Hubert Max Lanier
Carney Ray Lansford
Henry E. "Ted" Larkin
Don James "Gooneybird" Larsen
Frank Strong "Mule" "Yankee Killer" Lary
Walter Arlington "Arlie" "The Freshest Man on Earth" Latham
Charles Richard "Charlie" Lau
Vernon Sanders "Vern" "Deacon" Law
Thornton Starr "Lefty" Lee
Chester Earl "Chet" Lemon
Hubert Benjamin "Hub" "Dutch" Leonard
John Kelly "Buddy" Lewis, Jr.
James Richard "Jim" Leyland
John Theodore "Johnny" "Yachta" Logan, Jr.
Henry Van Noye Lucas
Frederick William "Fred" "Ludy" Luderus
James Dickson "Dick" McBride
Gilbert James "Gil" "Smash" McDougald
Willie Dean McGee
Frederick Stanley "Fred" McGriff
Mark David McGwire
Garry Lee Maddox
Donald Arthur "Don" Mattingly
Sabath Anthony "Sam" Mele
Frederick Charles "Fred" Merkle

Abraham Gilbert "The Bismarck of Baseball" Mills

Kevin Darrell Mitchell

Loren Dale Mitchell

Donald Wayne "Don" Money

Wallace Wade "Wally" Moon

Walter "Dobie" Moore

Edward "Cannonball" Morris

John Anthony "Johnny" "Bananas" Mostil

Van Lingle Mungo

Daniel Francis "Danny" "Old Reliable" Murphy

John Jordan "Buck" O'Neil, Jr.

James Edward "Tip" O'Neill

Stephen Michael "Stevie" "Steve" Palermo

Lance Michael Parrish

Camilo Alberto y Lus "Little Potato" Pascual

Antonio Francisco "Tony" Peña

Terry Lee Pendleton

Gary Charles Peters

Americo Peter "Rico" Petrocelli

Edward Joseph "Jeff" "Hassen" Pfeffer

James Anthony "Jimmy" Piersall

Ralph Arthur "Babe" "The Soft Thumb" Pinelli

Walter Clement "Wally" Pipp

Howard Joseph "Howie" Pollet

Darrell Ray Porter

Kirby Puckett

Alexander "Alec" Radcliffe

Theodore Roosevelt "Ted" "Double Duty" Radcliffe

William Larry "Willie" Randolph, Jr.

Jeffrey James "Jeff" "The Terminator" Reardon

Harold Patrick "Pete" "Pistol Pete" Reiser

Laurence Henry "Dutch" Rennert, Jr.

Richard Alan "Rick" Rhoden

Robert Clinton "Bobby" Richardson, Jr.

J. Lee Richmond

Calvin Edwin "Cal" Ripken, Jr.

Claude Cassius "Little All Right" Ritchey

Stephen Douglas "Steve" Rogers

Clarence Henry "Pants" Rowland

George Napoleon "Nap" Rucker

Bret William Saberhagen

Ryne Dee "Ryno" Sandberg

James Luther "Luke" Sewell

Ralph Orlando "Socks" Seybold

Wilfred Charles "Sonny" Siebert III

Elmer Ellsworth "Mike" Smith

Arthur Henry Soden

Stanley Orvil "Stan" Spence

Charles Sylvester "Chick" Stahl

George Michael Steinbrenner III

David Keith Stewart

George Washington Stovey

Darryl Eugene "Straw" Strawberry

T. R. "Ted" Strong

William Reed "Bill" Summers

Ezra Ballou Sutton

John W. "Jack" Taylor

George Robert "Bird" "Birdie" Tebbetts

Andre "Andy" "Thor" "Thunder" Thornton

Clifford Earl "The Earl of Snohomish" Torgeson

Theodore "Ted" "Highpockets" "Big Florida" Trent

Quincy Thomas Trouppe

Thomas Joseph "Tommy" "Foghorn" "Noisy Tom" Tucker

John Thomas "Tute" Tudor

James Riley "Jim" "Milkman Jim" Turner

Fernando (Anguamea) Valenzuela

Andrew James "Andy" "Slick" Van Slyke

Robert Andrew "Bob" Veale, Jr.

Francis Thomas "Fay" Vincent, Jr.

Frank John Viola, Jr.

Robert Lynn "Bob" Welch

Roy Hilton White

Arthur Carter "Pinky" Whitney

James Evans "Grasshopper Jim" Whitney

Frank "Red Ant" Wickware

James Thomas "Jimmy" "Buttons" "Home Run" Williams

Edward Nagle "Ned" Williamson

Arthur Lee "Artie" Wilson
Eugene Richard "Gene" "Old Faithful" Woodling
Burnis "Bill" "Wild Bill" Wright
John Whitlow "Whit" Wyatt
Jonathan Thompson Walton "Tom" "Ol' Tom" Zachary
Charles Louis "Chief" Zimmer
Richard Walter "Richie" Zisk

BASKETBALL (58)

Lewis Peter "Lew" Andreas
David "Davey" "Flash" "Fatty" "Pretzel" Banks
Don Angelo Barksdale
Rolando Antonio "Ro" Blackman
Ronald Bruce "Ron" Boone
Vincent Joseph "Vince" Boryla
Richard J. "Dick" Boushka
Frank Sands "Flash" "Frankie" Brian
Victor Albert "Vic" Bubas
Gordon "Shorty" Carpenter
Thomas Doane "Tom" Chambers
Jody Conradt
Charles Joseph "Chuck" Daly
Charles Robinson "Chick" Davies
John F. "Johnny" Dee
Clyde Austin Drexler
Walter Dukes
Wayne Richard Embry
Robert Joseph "Bob" Feerick
Lowell Cotton Fitzsimmons
Fulvio Chester "Chet" "Chet the Jet" Forte, Jr.
Clarence "Bevo" Francis
World B. Free
Darrell Steven "Griff" "Golden Griff" "Dr. Dunkenstein" Griffith
Burdette Eliele "Burdie" Haldorson
Donald Lee "Don" "The Bear" "H" Haskins
Rodney Clark "Hot Rod" Hundley
Kevin Maurice Johnson
George A. "The Golden Greek" Kaftan
Christian Donald Laettner
A. E. "Abe" Lemons, Jr.

Christopher Michael "Archie" "Chick" "The Dog" "Chris" Leonard
Frank John Lubin
Horace Albert "Bones" McKinney
Karl Anthony "The Mailman" Malone
Ramon B. "Ray" Mears
John Moir
John T. Thomas "Johnny" O'Brien
Hakeem Abdul "The Dream" Olajuwon
Shaquille Rashaun "Shaq" O'Neal
Robert Lee "Chief" Parish
Richard "Rick" Pitino
Ernest Cosmas "Ernie" Quigley
Joseph "Joe" Reiff
Nolan Richardson, Jr.
Arnold Denny "Arnie" "Stilts" Risen
Edward A. "Big Ed" Sadowski
Kenneth Lloyd "Kenny" Sailors
Eyre "Ayers" "Bruiser" Saitch
Paul Norman Seymour
William T. "Wee Willie" "Slim Green" Smith
John Houston Stockton III
Maurice "Mo" Stokes
C. Vivian Stoner Stringer
Eddie Sutton
Willem Hendrick "Bill" "Butch" Van Breda Kolff
Glenn Newton Wilkes
Philipp D. "Phil" "The Thin Man of the Hilltop" Woolpert

BOWLING (8)

Donna Adamek
Mike Aulby
Patty Costello
Marshall "The Medford Meteor" Holman
Joseph John "Joe" Norris
Carmen Mario "Spook" Salvino
Andrew "Andy" Varipapa
Lisa Rathgeber Wagner

BOXING (10)

Jimmy "Chicago's Little Tiger" Barry
Wilfred "The Dragon" Benitez

James "Buster" Douglas
Theodore "The Georgia Deacon" "Tiger" Flowers
William "Billy" Graham
Evander Holyfield
Patrick Francis "Packy" McFarland
Raymond Michael "Ray" "Boom Boom" Mancini
Davey Moore
Kenneth Howard "Ken" Norton, Sr.

COMMUNICATIONS (26)

Jesse Peter "The Book" Abramson
Marvin Philip "Marv" Albert
Christopher "Chris" "Boomer" Berman
Simon "Si" Burick
Jimmy Cannon
John Peerless Carmichael
Timothy Sylvester "Tim" Cohane
Robert Bernard "Bob" Considine
Robert Quinlan "Bob" Costas
John Henry "Jack" Drees
Irwin "Win" Elliot
Martin "Marty" Glickman
Merle Reid Harmon, Sr.
Charles Louis "Clem" McCarthy
Thomas William "Tom" Meany
Jack Raymond Murphy, Jr.
Daniel Francis "Dan" Parker
Shirley Lewis Povich
Francis Charles "Frank" Richter
Christopher Eugene "Chris" Schenkel
Raymond "Ray" Scott
James Shores "Jim" Simpson
Dick Stockton
Herbert Warren Wind
Harry Wismer
Rufus Stanley "Stan" Woodward

FOOTBALL (181)

Lyle Martin Alzado
Knowlton Lyman "Snake" Ames
Elmer Joseph "Bud" Angsman, Jr.
Gordon Scott Appleton
Jon Dwayne "Jaguar Jon" Arnett

Nathan "Nate" Barragar
Charles "Chuck" Barrett
Hubert "Hub" Bechtol
Russell K. "Bull" "Bully" Behman
Ricky Lynn Bell
Cornelius O'Landa "Biscuit" Bennett
Lester "Les" Bingaman
Brian Keith "The Boz" Bosworth
Max Ray Boydston
Raymond Robert "Ray" "Muscles" Bray, Sr.
Gene Herman Brito
George Haycock Brooke
James Robert Brooks
Thomas J. "Tom" Brookshier
David Steven "Dave" Brown
Hardy "Butcher Boy" "The Hump" "Thumper" Brown
Johnny Mack "Dothan Antelope" Brown
Earle Dunseth Bruce, Jr.
Edward Leon "Ed" Budde
Adrian Matthew Burk
Earnest Alexander Byner
George "Bad News" Cafego
Harry Donald Carson
Edward Lawrence "Eddie" "Natick Eddie" Casey
Samuel Blake "Sam" Chapman
Deron Leigh Cherry
Todd Jay Christensen
Mark Gregory Clayton
John Cooper
DeWitt E. "Tex" Coulter
Roger Timothy Craig
Ward Lloyd Cuff
Randall Cunningham
James T. "Jim" "The Hatchet" David
Anthony "A.D." Davis
Richard Lamar Dent
Ty Hubert Detmer
Bobby Dan Dillon
Glenn Dobbs, Jr.
Joseph "Joe" Donchess
Michael Joseph "Mike" Donohue, Sr.
John W. "Johnny" Drake
Nicholas M. "Nick" Eddy
Gover Connor "Ox" Emerson
Dennis Brian Erickson

Norman Julius "Boomer" Esiason, Jr.
Ray Richard "Riflin' Ray" Evans
Jack Anthony "Blackjack" Ferrante
Frank Filchock
Patrick "Pat" "Mouse" Fischer
Robert Thomas "Bob" Fisher
William P. "Bill" Fralic, Jr.
Rodney Thomas Franz
Alonzo Smith "Jake" Gaither
Willie Lee Galimore
Abraham "Abe" Gibron
Carlton Chester "Cookie" Gilchrist
Charles R. "Buckets" Goldenberg
John Frederic "Jack" Green
Russell "Russ" Grimm
Daniel Oliver "Dan" "Danimal" Hampton
Howard Harpster
Michael James "Mike" Haynes
Charles Taylor "Charlie" "The Horse" Hennigan
Robert A. "Bob" Higgins
Drew Hill
Arthur Rudolph Thomas "Doc" "Art" Hillebrand
James Franklin "Jimmy" Hitchcock, Jr.
Robert James "Bob" "Hunchy" Hoernschemeyer
Edwin Chilion "Babe" Horrell
Desmond Kevin Howard
Weldon Gaston "Hum" Humble
Larry Paul "Jake" Jacobson
Luke A. Johnsos
William A. "Dub" Jones
Ester James "E.J." "The Enforcer" Junior III
Morton A. "Mort" "Devil May" Kaer
James Richard "Jim" "Kat" Katcavage
Curtis Cliff "Chip" Kell
James Edward "Jim" Kelly
Henry Holman "Hank" "Ketch" Ketcham
Steven Albert "Steve" Kiner
Bernard Joseph "Bernie" Kosar, Jr.
Paul James Krause
Thaddeus John "Ted" Kwalick, Jr.
Warren Lahr

Francis Edward "Hank" "Hurrying Hank" Lauricella
Edward Wayne "Eddie" LeBaron, Jr.
Willard Russell "Russ" Letlow
Marvin David "Marv" Levy
Gordon C. Locke
Howard M. "Howie" Long
Ronald Mandel "Lonnie" Lott
Donald Bradford "Don" Lourie
Nicholas Dominic "Nick" Lowery
James Robert "Jim" Lynch
Charles Youmans "Charlie Mac" McClendon
John Francis "Johnnie" McGovern
Thomas Lee "Tom" Mack
Freeman McNeil
William Guy "Bill" Mallory
Edward Francis "Ed" "Italian Stallion" Marinaro
James Richard "Jim" "Jungle Jim" Martin
Riley "Snake" Matheson
Thomas Roland "Tom" Matte
Creighton Eugene Miller
Century Allen Milstead
James Arthur "Art" Monk
Harold Warren Moon
Stanley Douglas Morgan
Lawrence C. "Larry" Morris
James H. "Monk" Moscrip
Howard Edward Mudd
Michael Anthony Munoz
Donald Eugene "Don" Nehlen
Andrew James "Jim" "Swede" Oberlander
Christopher "Chris" O'Brien
Duane Charles "Bill" Parcells
James Russel "Jimmy" Patton, Jr.
Endicott "Chub" Peabody II
Richard Alvin "Richie" Petitbon
Gerald John "Gerry" Philbin
Loyd Wade Phillips
Louis Brian "Pic" Piccolo
James Eugene "Jim" "Buster" Poole
Abisha Collins "Bosh" Pritchard
Duane Putnam
Ulmo Shannon "Sonny" Randle
Robert R. "Bob" Reinhard

Raymond "Ray" Renfro
Ernest John "Pug" "The Flying Dutch-
  man" Rentner
Gerald Byron "Jerry" Rhome
Jerry Lee Rice
Gerald Antonio Riggs
Charles Ramsey "Babe" Rinehart
Ira Errett "Rat" Rodgers
William Winston "Bill" Roper
Tobin C. Rote
Louis "Lou" "The Battler" Rymkus
Charles Alvin "Charlie" Sanders
Orban Eugene "Spec" Sanders
John Carl "Jack" Scarbath
Richard Phillip "Dick" "Schaf" Schaf-
  rath
Clyde Luther "Smackover" Scott
Ronald "Ron" "Jingle Joints" Sellers
Roderick "Rod" Shoate
Fred William Sington
Jackie Ray Slater
Bruce Bernard Smith
Ernest F. "Ernie" "Sliphorn" Smith
William Thomas "Bill" Stanfill
Joseph Benton "Joe" Steffy, Jr.
Dwight Eugene Stephenson
James R. "Jim" Stillwagon
John "Johnny" "Strike" Strzykalski
James Edward "Jim" "The Rusk Ram-
  bler" Swink
Paul John Tagliabue
Andre Bernard Tippett
Daniel Lee "Deacon Dan" Towler
J. Edward "Eddie" "Cannonball" Tryon
James Herbert "Jim" Wacker
Robert "Bob" Ward
Andre T. Ware
Eugene "Gene" Washington
Joe Dan "Little Joe" "The Crockett
  Rocket" Washington, Jr.
Herman John "Wedey" "Squirmin'
  Herman" Wedemeyer
George Thomas Welsh
Charles Marin "Buck" Wharton
Arthur Ledlie "Beef" Wheeler
Reginald Howard "Reggie" White
Wilford Daniel "Danny" White
Raymond Walter "Ray" Wietecha

George "Wildcat" Wilson
Bowden Wyatt
Andrew Alva Young
Adolph F. "Swede" Youngstrom

GOLF (14)

Dow Finsterwald
Allen Lee "Al" Geiberger
Marlene Bauer "Grem" Hagge
Juli Simpson Inkster
Elizabeth May "Betty" Jameson
Don January
Elizabeth "Betsy" King
Harold "Jug" McSpaden
Larry Gene Nelson
Sandra Jean Palmer
Marilynn Louise "Smitty" Smith
Craig Robert "The Walrus" Stadler
David Knapp "Dave" Stockton
Arthur Jonathon "Art" Wall, Jr.

HORSE RACING (10)

Braulio Baeza
Lazaro Sosa "Laz" Barrera
William Preston Burch
Angel Tomas Cordero, Jr.
Patrick Alan "Pat" Day
Thomas J. Healey
Lucien Laurin
John Eric "Johnny" "The Pumper"
  Longden
Laffit Alegando Pincay, Jr.
Jorge Velasquez

ICE HOCKEY (15)

Charles Francis Adams
George V. Brown
Christos "Chris" Chelios
Kevin John Hatcher
Alberto Anthony "Al" "Alley Cat"
  "Drifter" Iafrate, Jr.
Willard John "Ike" Ikola
Brian Joseph Leetch
Michael James "Mike" Milbury

Hugh "Muzz" Murray
James D. "Big Jim" Norris, Sr.
Edward "Eddie" Olczyk, Jr.
Joel Stuart Otto
Gary Suter
John "Beezer" Vanbiesbrouck
Arthur Michael Wirtz, Sr.

SHOOTING (4)

Alfred P. "The Boy Wonder" Lane
Willis Augustus Lee, Jr.
Carl Townsend Osburn
Lloyd S. Spooner

SKATING (6)

Cathy Ann Turner Bostley
Daniel "Dan" Jansen
Nancy Kerrigan
Leah Jean Poulos Mueller
Paul Wylie
Kristi Tsuya Yamaguchi

SKIING (4)

Tamara McKinney
Thomas Sven "Tommy" Moe, Jr.
Diann Roffe-Steinrotter
Donna Weinbrecht

SWIMMING (10)

Michael "Mike" Barrowman
Nicole Haislett
Jan Margo Henne Hawkins
Charles Buchanan Hickcox
James Paul "Jim" Montgomery
Pablo Morales
Norman DeMille "Uncle Normie" "The Big Moose" Ross
Summer Elisabeth Sanders
Melvin "Mel" Stewart
Jennifer "Jenny" Thompson

TENNIS AND OTHER RACQUET SPORTS (16)

Andre Kirk Agassi
Grace Walton Roosevelt Clark
James "Jim" Courier
Robert "Bob" Falkenburg
David Guthrie "Dave" Freeman
Jay Gould
Judy Devlin Hashman
Frederick Howard Hovey
Francis Townsend "Frank" Hunter
Constantine Gene Mako
Alastair Bradley Martin
Richard "Dick" Miles
Clarence Cecil Pell
Ellen Crosby Roosevelt
Peter "Pete" Sampras
Maud Barger Wallach

TRACK AND FIELD (29)

Leroy Russell Burrell
Ellery Harding Clark, Sr.
Michael Alex "Mike" Conley
Harold "Hal" Davis
William Solon "Bill" Dellinger
Yolanda Gail Devers
John Kenneth Doherty
Millard Elsworth "Bill" Easton
James Francis "Jumbo" Elliot
Gregory "Greg" Foster
Kimberly Ann "Kim" Gallagher
Robert Garrett
Michael Duane Johnson
Michael Denny "Iron Mike" Larrabee
Frances Anne Lutz "Francie" Larrieu-Smith
Donald Ray "Don" Lash
Michael L. "Mike" Marsh
Vincent Edward "Vince" Matthews
Daniel Dion "Dan" O'Brien
Michael Anthony "Mike" Powell
Harry Lee "Butch" Reynolds
David Wesley "Wes" Santee
Laurence Nelson "Larry" Snyder
Dwight Edwin Stones

Robert Lyman "Dink" "The Boy Coach" "Ol' Mr. Gravel Voice" Templeton

Max Truex

Craig Steven Virgin

Quincy Dushawn Watts

Kevin Curtis Young

WRESTLING (4)

Bruce Baumgartner

Kenny "Puma" Monday

Myron Roderick

John Smith

MISCELLANEOUS SPORTS (5)

Burton Cecil Downing

Shannon Lee Miller

John Michael "Mike" Plumb

Harold Stirling Vanderbilt

Arthur August "Zimmy" "Zim" Zimmerman

Appendix 3
Entries by Place of Birth

The following lists the entries alphabetically by their state or, in a few instances, American territory or foreign nation of birth.

ALABAMA (19)

Cornelius O'Landa "Biscuit" Bennett
Johnny Mack "Dothan Antelope" Brown
Clay Palmer "Hawk" Carroll
William "Dizzy" Dismukes
Julius Timothy "Tim" Flock
James Franklin "Jimmy" Hitchcock, Jr.
Evander Holyfield
Frank Strong "Mule" "Yankee Killer" Lary
Donald Bradford "Don" Lourie
Larry Gene Nelson
Alexander "Alec" Radcliffe
Theodore Roosevelt "Ted" "Double Duty" Radcliffe
James Luther "Luke" Sewell
Fred William Sington
William T. "Wee Willie" "Slim Green" Smith
Andre "Andy" "Thor" "Thunder" Thornton
Andre Bernard Tippett
Robert Andrew "Bob" Veale, Jr.
Arthur Lee "Artie" Wilson

ARIZONA (2)

Charles Buchanan Hickcox
Wilford Daniel "Danny" White

ARKANSAS (5)

Gordon "Shorty" Carpenter
Donald Eulon "Don" "Kess" Kessinger
Ellis Raymond "Old Folks" Kinder
Charles Youmans "Charlie Mac" Mc-Clendon
Wallace Wade "Wally" Moon

CALIFORNIA (56)

Donna Adamek
Jon Dwayne "Jaguar Jon" Arnett
Don Angelo Barksdale
Ewell "The Whip" Blackwell
Barry Lamar Bonds
Ernest Edward "Ernie" "Tiny" Bonham
Raymond Otis "Ray" "Ike" Boone
Gene Herman Brito
Samuel Blake "Sam" Chapman
Delmar Wesley "Del" Crandall

Frank Peter Joseph "Frankie" "The Crow" Crosetti
Randall Cunningham
Anthony "A.D." Davis
Eric Keith Davis
Harold "Hal" Davis
Burton Downing
Nicholas M. "Nick" Eddy
Robert Joseph "Bob" Feerick
Cecil Grant "The Big Man" Fielder
Robert Herbert "Bob" "Forschie" Forsch
Rodney Thomas Franz
David Guthrie "Dave" Freeman
Allen Lee "Al" Geiberger
Anthony Keith "Tony" Gwynn
Jan Margo Henne Hawkins
Marshall "The Medford Meteor" Holman
Juli Simpson Inkster
Kevin Maurice Johnson
Carney Ray Lansford
Michael Denny "Iron Mike" Larrabee
Frances Anne Lutz "Francie" Larrieu-Smith
Edward Wayne "Eddie" LeBaron, Jr.
Thornton Starr "Lefty" Lee
Willard Russell "Russ" Letlow
Frank John Lubin
Gilbert James "Gil" "Smash" McDougald
Willie Dean McGee
Mark David McGwire
Michael L. "Mike" Marsh
Kevin Darrell Mitchell
Harold Warren Moon
Pablo Morales
Michael Anthony Munoz
John "Johnnie" Parsons
Terry Lee Pendleton
Ralph Arthur "Babe" "The Soft Thumb" Pinelli
Robert R. "Bob" Reinhard
Summer Elisabeth Sanders
Craig Robert "The Walrus" Stadler
David Keith Stewart
David Knapp "Dave" Stockton
Dwight Edwin Stones
Darryl Eugene "Straw" Strawberry
Roy Hilton White
Kristi Tsuya Yamaguchi
Kevin Curtis Young

COLORADO (1)

Patrick Alan "Pat" Day

CONNECTICUT (5)

Timothy Sylvester "Tim" Cohane
William Forrest "Wild Bill" Hutchinson
Daniel Francis "Dan" Parker
James Anthony "Jimmy" Piersall
Francis Thomas "Fay" Vincent, Jr.

DELAWARE (1)

Charles Marin "Buck" Wharton

DISTRICT OF COLUMBIA (7)

Robert Bernard "Bob" Considine
Arthur McArthur "Art" Devlin
William Henry Getty "Bill" France, Sr.
Donald Wayne "Don" Money
Peter "Pete" Sampras
James Shores "Jim" Simpson
Lloyd S. Spooner

FLORIDA (12)

James "Jim" Courier
Willie Lee Galimore
Dwight Eugene "Doc" "Doctor K" Gooden
Nicole Haislett
Richard Dalton "Dick" Howser
Howard Michael "Hojo" Johnson
Frederick Stanley "Fred" McGriff
John Jordan "Buck" O'Neil, Jr.
Richard Alan "Rick" Rhoden
Ronald "Ron" "Jingle Joints" Sellers
Theodore "Ted" "Highpockets" "Big Florida" Trent
Lisa Rathgeber Wagner

GEORGIA (15)

James Robert Brooks
Earnest Alexander Byner
William "Bill" "Daddy" Byrd
Richard Lamar Dent
Theodore "The Georgia Deacon" "Tiger" Flowers
World B. Free
Drew Hill
Curtis Cliff "Chip" Kell
Walter "Dobie" Moore
Lawrence C. "Larry" Morris
George Napoleon "Nap" Rucker
William Thomas "Bill" Stanfill
Quincy Thomas Trouppe
Glenn Newton Wilkes
John Whitlow "Whit" Wyatt

HAWAII (1)

Herman John "Wedey" "Squirmin' Herman" Wedemeyer

IDAHO (1)

Vernon Sanders "Vern" "Deacon" Law

ILLINOIS (30)

Knowlton Lyman "Snake" Ames
Lewis Peter "Lew" Andreas
Elmer Joseph "Bud" Angsman, Jr.
Henry Albert "Hank" Bauer
Jimmy "Chicago's Little Tiger" Barry
Christos "Chris" Chelios
Michael Alex "Mike" Conley
John W. "Johnny" Drake
John Henry "Jack" Drees
Gregory "Greg" Foster
Gary Joseph Gaetti
Merle Reid Harmon, Sr.
Arthur Rudolph Thomas "Doc" "Art" Hillebrand
Luke A. Johnsos
Marvin David "Marv" Levy
Patrick Francis "Packy" McFarland

John Anthony "Johnny" "Bananas" Mostil
Leah Jean Poulos Mueller
Joseph John "Joe" Norris
Kenneth Howard "Ken" Norton, Sr.
Edward "Eddie" Olczyk, Jr.
Edward Joseph "Jeff" "Hassen" Pfeffer
Walter Clement "Wally" Pipp
Kirby Puckett
Ernest John "Pug" "The Flying Dutchman" Rentner
Louis "Lou" "The Battler" Rymkus
Bret William Saberhagen
Carmen Mario "Spook" Salvino
Craig Steven Virgin
Arthur Michael Wirtz, Sr.

INDIANA (20)

Mike Aulby
Vincent Joseph "Vince" Boryla
Victor Albert "Vic" Bubas
Owen Joseph "Donie" Bush
Mark Gregory Clayton
James Otis "Doc" Crandall
Millard Elsworth "Bill" Easton
Donald Martin Fehr
Abraham "Abe" Gibron
John Frederic "Jack" Green
Don James "Gooneybird" Larsen
Donald Ray "Don" Lash
Donald Arthur "Don" Mattingly
Christopher Eugene "Chris" Schenkel
Charles Sylvester "Chick" Stahl
T. R. "Ted" Strong
Max Truex
Raymond Walter "Ray" Wietecha
Howard "Handsome Howdy" Wilcox
Andrew Alva Young

IOWA (2)

John F. "Johnny" Dee
Gordon C. Locke

KANSAS (9)

Nathan "Nate" Barragar
Chester Arthur "Chet" Brewer

Ray Richard "Riflin' Ray" Evans
Harold "Jug" McSpaden
Myron Roderick
David Wesley "Wes" Santee
Marilynn Louise "Smitty" Smith
Eddie Sutton
Frank "Red Ant" Wickware

KENTUCKY (10)

David Russell "Gus" Bell
Samuel Howard "Howie" Camnitz
Michael Lewis "Mike" Greenwell
Darrell Steven "Griff" "Golden Griff"
    "Dr. Dunkenstein" Griffith
Willis Augustus Lee, Jr.
Tamara McKinney
Davey Moore
Arnold Denny "Arnie" "Stilts" Risen
Stanley Orvil "Stan" Spence
Philipp D. "Phil" "The Thin Man of the
    Hilltop" Woolpert

LOUISIANA (13)

Frank Sands "Flash" "Frankie" Brian
William Nuschler "Will" "The Thrill"
    Clark, Jr.
Clyde Austin Drexler
Edwin Hawley "Eddie" Dyer
Charles Taylor "Charlie" "The Horse"
    Hennigan
William A. "Dub" Jones
Francis Edward "Hank" "Hurrying
    Hank" Lauricella
Karl Anthony "The Mailman" Malone
Robert Lee "Chief" Parish
Richard Alvin "Richie" Petitbon
Howard Joseph "Howie" Pollet
Gerald Antonio Riggs
Clyde Luther "Smackover" Scott

MAINE (1)

Shirley Lewis Povich

MARYLAND (4)

George Haycock Brooke
Robert Garrett
Calvin Edwin "Cal" Ripken, Jr.
John Carl "Jack" Scarbath

MASSACHUSETTS (23)

Francis Carter "Banny" Bancroft
George V. Brown
Edward Lawrence "Eddie" "Natick
    Eddie" Casey
Ellery Harding Clark, Sr.
Erwin "Win" Elliot
Charles Andrew "Duke" Farrell
Robert Thomas "Bob" Fisher
Frederick Howard Hovey
Nancy Kerrigan
Howard M. "Howie" Long
Michael James "Mike" Milbury
Andrew James "Jim" "Swede" Oberlan-
    der
Stephen Michael "Stevie" "Steve" Pa-
    lermo
Endicott "Chub" Peabody II
Louis Brian "Pic" Piccolo
Jeffrey James "Jeff" "The Terminator"
    Reardon
Arthur Henry Soden
Jennifer "Jenny" Thompson
J. Edward "Eddie" "Cannonball" Tryon
Thomas Joseph "Tommy" "Foghorn"
    "Noisy Tom" Tucker
Herbert Warren Wind
Rufus Stanley "Stan" Woodward
Adolph F. "Swede" Youngstrom

MICHIGAN (14)

Raymond Robert "Ray" "Muscles" Bray,
    Sr.
Edward Leon "Ed" Budde
John Kenneth Doherty
Kevin John Hatcher
Alberto Anthony "Al" "Alley Cat"
    "Drifter" Iafrate, Jr.

Paul James Krause
Charles Richard "Charlie" Lau
Howard Edward Mudd
Hugh "Muzz" Murray
John "Beezer" Vanbiesbrouck
James Herbert "Jim" Wacker
Quincy Dushawn Watts
Robert Lynn "Bob" Welch
Harry Wismer

MINNESOTA (9)

Ward Lloyd Cuff
Burdette Eliele "Burdie" Haldorson
Kent Alan Hrbek
Willard John "Ike" Ikola
Jay Thomas "Tom" Kelly
Steven Albert "Steve" Kiner
Ferdinand Cole "F.C." Lane
John Francis "Johnnie" McGovern
Joel Stuart Otto

MISSISSIPPI (8)

Roger Timothy Craig
Howard Easterling
Chester Earl "Chet" Lemon
Freeman McNeil
James Russel "Jimmy" Patton, Jr.
James Eugene "Jim" "Buster" Poole
Jerry Lee Rice
Jackie Ray Slater

MISSOURI (13)

Richard J. "Dick" Boushka
Curtis Benton "Curt" "Coonskin" Davis
Lowell Cotton Fitzsimmons
Linus Reinhard "Lonny" "Junior" Frey
James Wear "Bug" Holliday
Edwin Chilion "Babe" Horrell
Henry Van Noye Lucas
Shannon Lee Miller
Darrell Ray Porter
Harold Patrick "Pete" "Pistol Pete"
   Reiser
Stephen Douglas "Steve" Rogers

Wilfred Charles "Sonny" Siebert III
James Thomas "Jimmy" "Buttons"
   "Home Run" Williams

MONTANA (2)

Thomas Sven "Tommy" Moe, Jr.
Robert Lyman "Dink" "The Boy
   Coach" "Ol' Mr. Gravel Voice" Tem-
   pleton

NEBRASKA (4)

Wade Anthony Boggs
Patrick "Pat" "Mouse" Fischer
Morton A. "Mort" "Devil May" Kaer
Kenneth Lloyd "Kenny" Sailors

NEVADA (1)

Andre Kirk Agassi

NEW HAMPSHIRE (1)

Walter Arlington "Arlie" "The Freshest
   Man on Earth" Latham

NEW JERSEY (18)

Bruce Baumgartner
George Washington Case, Jr.
Deron Leigh Cherry
Mark Donohue
Jack Anthony "Blackjack" Ferrante
Fulvio Chester "Chet" "Chet the Jet"
   Forte, Jr.
Frank Whitman "Blimp" Hayes
Henry Holman "Hank" "Ketch" Ket-
   cham
John Thomas "Johnny" O'Brien
Shaquille Rashaun "Shaq" O'Neal
Duane Charles "Bill" Parcells
Charles Ramsey "Babe" Rinehart
William Reed "Bill" Summers
Paul John Tagliabue
Willem Hendrick "Bill" "Butch" Van
   Breda Kolff
Robert "Bob" Ward

Donna Weinbrecht
Arthur August "Zimmy" "Zim" Zimmerman

NEW MEXICO (2)

Thomas J. "Tom" Brookshier
Ronald Mandel "Ronnie" Lott

NEW YORK (57)

Jesse Peter "The Book" Abramson
Marvin Philip "Marv" Albert
Lyle Martin Alzado
John August Antonelli
David "Davey" "Flash" "Fatty" "Pretzel" Banks
Wilfred "The Dragon" Benitez
Christopher "Chris" "Boomer" Berman
Roberto Antonio "Bobby" "Bobby Bo" Bonilla, Jr.
Cathy Ann Turner Bostley
John Tomlinson Brush, Jr.
Jimmy Cannon
David "Dave" Cash, Jr.
Elton P. "Icebox" Chamberlain
Grace Walton Roosevelt Clark
Robert Quinlan "Bob" Costas
Anthony Francis "Tony" "Chick" Cuccinello
Norman Julius "Boomer" Esiason, Jr.
Robert "Bob" Falkenburg
Robert V. "Bob" "Death to Flying Things" Ferguson
Martin "Marty" Glickman
Jay Gould
William "Billy" Graham
Thomas J. Healey
Orel Leonard "Bulldog" Hershiser IV
Robert A. "Bob" Higgins
Francis Townsend "Frank" Hunter
William Frederick "Billy" Jurges
George A. "The Golden Greek" Kaftan
Christian Donald Laettner
Alfred P. "The Boy Wonder" Lane
Christopher Michael "Archie" "Chick" "The Dog" "Chris" Leonard
John Theodore "Johnny" "Yachta" Logan, Jr.
Charles Louis "Clem" McCarthy

Edward Francis "Ed" "Italian Stallion" Marinaro
Alastair Bradley Martin
Vincent Edward "Vince" Matthews
Thomas William "Tom" Meany
Sabath Anthony "Sam" Mele
Richard "Dick" Miles
Abraham Gilbert "The Bismarck of Baseball" Mills
James Arthur "Art" Monk
Edward "Cannonball" Morris
Americo Peter "Rico" Petrocelli
Richard "Rick" Pitino
John Michael "Mike" Plumb
Diann Roffe-Steinrotter
Ellen Crosby Roosevelt
Eyre "Ayers" "Bruiser" Saitch
Ezra Ballou Sutton
John Thomas "Tute" Tudor
Harold Stirling Vanderbilt
William Kissam Vanderbilt
Andrew James "Andy" "Slick" Van Slyke
Frank John Viola, Jr.
Maud Barger Wallach
James Evans "Grasshopper Jim" Whitney
Richard Walter "Richie" Zisk

NORTH CAROLINA (14)

David "Dave" "Impo" "Skinny" Barnhill
Ned Miller Jarrett
Robert Glenn "Junior" Johnson, Jr.
Ester James "E.J." "The Enforcer" Junior III
Hubert Max Lanier
John Kelly "Buddy" Lewis, Jr.
Horace Albert "Bones" McKinney
Lee Arnold Petty
Abisha Collins "Bosh" Pritchard
Charles Alvin "Charlie" Sanders
Dwight Eugene Stephenson
Melvin "Mel" Stewart
Herbert Watson "Herb" Thomas
Jonathan Thompson Walton "Tom" "Ol' Tom" Zachary

OHIO (43)

William Joseph "Bill" Bradley
David Steven "Dave" Brown
Raymond "Ray" Brown
Simon "Si" Burick
Wilmer Dean Chance
William Roger "Rocket" Clemens
Joseph "Joe" Donchess
James "Buster" Douglas
Walter Dukes
Wayne Richard Embry
Dow Finsterwald
Clarence "Bevo" Francis
Ned Franklin Garver
Samuel "Sam" Hanks, Jr.
Howard Harpster
Larry Eugene Hisle
Robert James "Bob" "Hunchy" Hoernschemeyer
Desmond Kevin Howard
Benjamin Michael "Benny" Kauff
Bernard Joseph "Bernie" Kosar, Jr.
Hubert Benjamin "Hub" "Dutch" Leonard
James Richard "Jim" Leyland
James Robert "Jim" Lynch
Thomas Lee "Tom" Mack
Garry Lee Maddox
Raymond Michael "Ray" "Boom Boom" Mancini
James Richard "Jim" "Jungle Jim" Martin
Ramon B. "Ray" Mears
Creighton Eugene Miller
James H. "Monk" Moscrip
Donald Eugene "Don" Nehlen
Carl Townsend Osburn
Harry Lee "Butch" Reynolds
J. Lee Richmond
Richard Phillip "Dick" "Schaf" Schafrath
Ralph Orlando "Socks" Seybold
Paul Norman Seymour
Laurence Nelson "Larry" Snyder
George Michael Steinbrenner III
James R. "Jim" Stillwagon

John W. "Jack" Taylor
Eugene Richard "Gene" "Old Faithful" Woodling
Charles Louis "Chief" Zimmer

OKLAHOMA (16)

Ronald Bruce "Ron" Boone
Brian Keith "The Boz" Bosworth
Max Ray Boydston
Joseph Cris "Joe" Carter, Jr.
Robert Joe "Bobby" Cox
Daniel Oliver "Dan" "Danimal" Hampton
Donald Lee "Don" "The Bear" "H" Haskins
Elizabeth May "Betty" Jameson
A. E. "Abe" Lemons
Loren Dale Mitchell
Kenny "Puma" Monday
Jack Raymond Murphy, Jr.
Joseph "Joe" Reiff
Orban Eugene "Spec" Sanders
Roderick "Rod" Shoate
John Smith

OREGON (4)

William Solon "Bill" Dellinger
Lawrence Joseph "Larry" Jansen
Daniel Dion "Dan" O'Brien
Norman DeMille "Uncle Normie" "The Big Moose" Ross

PENNSYLVANIA (53)

Charles "Chuck" Barrett
Glenn Alfred "Bruno" Beckert
Russell K. "Bull" "Bully" Behman
Max Frederick "Tilly" "Camera Eye" Bishop
Earle Dunseth Bruce, Jr.
Leroy Russell Burrell
Todd Jay Christensen
John J. "Jack" Clements
James Anthony "Ripper" Collins
Patty Costello

Charles Joseph "Chuck" Daly
Thomas Peter "Tom" "Tido" Daly
Charles Robinson "Chick" Davies
James Alexander "Jim" Devlin
August Joseph "Augie" Donatelli
James Francis "Jumbo" Elliot
Frank Filchock
William P. "Bill" Fralic, Jr.
John Frank "Buck" "Bucky" Freeman
Kimberly Ann "Kim" Gallagher
Carlton Chester "Cookie" Gilchrist
Russell "Russ" Grimm
Raymond "The Little Professor" "The
    Bedouin" Harroun
James Richard "Jim" "Kat" Katcavage
James Edward "Jim" Kelly
Frank Bissell Killen
Elizabeth "Betsy" King
George John "Whitey" Kurowski
Thaddeus John "Ted" Kwalick, Jr.
Warren Lahr
Henry E. "Ted" Larkin
James Dickson "Dick" McBride
Thomas Roland "Tom" Matte
Century Allen Milstead
Daniel Francis "Danny" "Old Reliable"
    Murphy
Lance Michael Parrish
Gary Charles Peters
Michael Anthony "Mike" Powell
Francis Charles "Frank" Richter
Claude Cassius "Little All Right"
    Ritchey
William Winston "Bill" Roper
Edward A. "Big Ed" Sadowski
Raymond "Ray" Scott
Elmer Ellsworth "Mike" Smith
Dick Stockton
Maurice "Mo" Stokes
George Washington Stovey
C. Vivian Stoner Stringer
Daniel Lee "Deacon Dan" Towler
Arthur Jonathan "Art" Wall, Jr.
George Thomas Welsh
Arthur Ledlie "Beef" Wheeler
Edward Nagle "Ned" Williamson

RHODE ISLAND (2)

Clarence Cecil Pell
Gerald John "Gerry" Philbin

SOUTH CAROLINA (8)

Elzie Wylie "Buck" Baker, Sr.
William Preston Burch
Harry Donald Carson
James T. "Jim" "The Hatchet" David
Stanley Douglas Morgan
Van Lingle Mungo
William Larry "Willie" Randolph, Jr.
Robert Clinton "Bobby" Richardson, Jr.

SOUTH DAKOTA (4)

Marlene Bauer "Grem" Hagge
Larry Paul "Jake" Jacobson
Duane Putnam
Ernest F. "Ernie" "Sliphorn" Smith

TENNESSEE (10)

Lester "Les" Bingaman
John Cooper
Roy Joseph Cullenbine
Alonzo Smith "Jake" Gaither
James William "Junior" "Jim" Gilliam
Joseph Benton "Joe" Steffy, Jr.
James Riley "Jim" "Milkman Jim"
    Turner
Reginald Howard "Reggie" White
Burnis "Bill" "Wild Bill" Wright
Bowden Wyatt

TEXAS (30)

Gordon Scott Appleton
Hubert "Hub" Bechtol
Ricky Lynn Bell
Hardy "Butcher Boy" "The Hump"
    "Thumper" Brown
Adrian Matthew Burk
Jody Conradt

DeWitt E. "Tex" Coulter
Ty Hubert Detmer
Bobby Dan Dillon
Glenn Dobbs, Jr.
Gover Connor "Ox" Emerson
Michael James "Mike" Haynes
Cecil Carleton "Tex" Hughson
Weldon Gaston "Hum" Humble
Don January
Michael Duane Johnson
Brian Joseph Leetch
Riley "Snake" Matheson
Sandra Jean Palmer
Loyd Wade Phillips
Raymond "Ray" Renfro
Gerald Byron "Jerry" Rhome
Nolan Richardson, Jr.
Tobin C. Rote
James Edward "Jim" "The Rusk Rambler" Swink
Andre T. Ware
Eugene "Gene" Washington
Joe Dan "Little Joe" "The Crockett Rocket" Washington, Jr.
Arthur Carter "Pinky" Whitney
Paul Wylie

UTAH (2)

Thomas Doane "Tom" Chambers
Bruce Vee Hurst

VERMONT (2)

Charles Francis Adams
George Robert "Bird" "Birdie" Tebbetts

VIRGINIA (2)

Ulmo Shannon "Sonny" Randle
Bruce Bernard Smith

WASHINGTON (7)

Yolanda Gail Devers
Dennis Brian Erickson

Frederick Charles "Fred" "Big Bear" "Hutch" Hutchinson
Ryne Dee "Ryno" Sandberg
John Houston Stockton III
Clifford Earl "The Earl of Snohomish" Torgeson
George "Wildcat" Wilson

WEST VIRGINIA (4)

George "Bad News" Cafego
Rodney Clark "Hot Rod" Hundley
William Guy "Bill" Mallory
Ira Errett "Rat" Rodgers

WISCONSIN (9)

John Peerless Carmichael
Daniel "Dan" Jansen
Frederick William "Fred" "Ludy" Luderus
Frederick Charles "Fred" Merkle
James Paul "Jim" Montgomery
Laurence Henry "Dutch" Rennert, Jr.
Clarence Henry "Pants" Rowland
John "Johnny" "Strike" Strzykalski
Gary Suter

AMERICAN TERRITORIES

Puerto Rico (1)

Angel Tomas Cordero, Jr.

FOREIGN NATIONS (38)

Canada (8)

Russell William "Russ" Ford
Judy Devlin Hashman
John Geoffrey "Jeff" Heath
John Frederick Hiller
Lucien Laurin
James D. "Big Jim" Norris, Sr.
James Edward "Tip" O'Neill
Ernest Cosmas "Ernie" Quigley

Cuba (4)

Lazaro Sosa "Laz" Barrera
Dagoberto Blanco "Bert" Campaneris
Jose Canseco, Jr.
Camilo Alberto y Lus "Little Potato"
   Pascual

Dominican Republic (7)

Felipe (Rojas) Alou
Mateo (Rojas) "Matty" Alou
George Antonio Mathey Bell
Ricardo Adolfo Jacobo "Rico" Carty
Julio Cesar Franco
Pedro "Pete" Guerrero
Antonio Francisco "Tony" Peña

England (1)

John Eric "Johnny" "The Pumper"
   Longden

Germany (1)

Nicholas Dominic "Nick" Lowery

Hungary (1)

Constantine Gene Mako

Ireland (3)

Michael Joseph "Mike" Donohue, Sr.
John Joseph "Dirty Jack" Doyle
Christopher "Chris" O'Brien

Italy (1)

Andrew "Andy" Varipapa

Mexico (2)

Roberto Francisco "Bobby" Avila
Fernando (Anguamea) Valenzuela

Nigeria (1)

Hakeem Abdul "The Dream" Olajuwon

Panama (4)

Braulio Baeza
Rolando Antonio "Ro" Blackman
Laffit Alegando Pincay, Jr.
Jorge Velasquez

Paraguay (1)

Michael "Mike" Barrowman

Russia (1)

Charles R. "Buckets" Goldenberg

Scotland (1)

John Moir

Switzerland (1)

Louis Joseph Chevrolet

Venezuela (1)

David Ismael (Benitiz) Concepcion

UNKNOWN (1)

John B. Day

Appendix 4
Women Athletes by Sport

The following lists the sport of each woman athlete.

BASKETBALL (2)

Jody Conradt
C. Vivian Stoner Stringer

BOWLING (3)

Donna Adamek
Patty Costello
Lisa Rathgeber Wagner

GOLF (6)

Marlene Bauer "Grem" Hagge
Juli Simpson Inkster
Elizabeth May "Betsy" Jameson
Elizabeth "Betsy" King
Sandra Jean Palmer
Marilynn Louise "Smitty" Smith

SKATING (4)

Cathy Ann Turner Bostley
Nancy Kerrigan
Leah Jean Poulos Mueller
Kristi Tsuya Yamaguchi

SKIING (3)

Tamara McKinney

Diann Roffe-Steinrotter
Donna Weinbrecht

SWIMMING (4)

Nicole Haislett
Jan Margo Henne Hawkins
Summer Elisabeth Sanders
Jennifer "Jenny" Thompson

**TENNIS AND OTHER RACQUET
SPORTS (4)**

Grace Walton Roosevelt Clark
Judy Devlin Hashman
Ellen Crosby Roosevelt
Maud Barger Wallach

TRACK AND FIELD (3)

Yolanda Gail Devers
Kimberly Ann "Kim" Gallagher
Frances Anne Lutz "Francie" Larrieu-
  Smith

MISCELLANEOUS SPORTS (1)

Shannon Lee Miller

Appendix 5
Cross-References for Married Women Athletes

The following lists the maiden and married names of the women athletes.

Maiden Name	How Woman Athlete Listed
Maud Barger	Maud Barger Wallach
Marlene Bauer	Marlene Bauer "Grem" Hagge
Judy Devlin	Judy Devlin Hashman
Jan Henne	Jan Margo Henne Hawkins
Frances Larrieu	Frances Anne Lutz "Francie" Larrieu-Smith
Leah Poulos	Leah Jean Poulos Mueller
Lisa Rathgeber	Lisa Rathgeber Wagner
Diann Roffe	Diann Roffe-Steinrotter
Grace Roosevelt	Grace Walton Roosevelt Clark
Juli Simpson	Juli Simpson Inkster
C. Vivian Stoner	C. Vivian Stoner Stringer
Cathy Turner	Cathy Ann Turner Bostley

Appendix 6

Major U.S. Sports Halls of Fame

The following lists major U.S. Sports Halls of Fame pertaining to sports covered in this volume.

Hall of Fame (H of F)	Location
American Bowling Congress (AmBC) H of F	Greendale, WI
American Sportscasters Association (ASA) H of F	New York, NY
Helms Athletic Foundation (HAF, Citizens Savings Bank) H of F	Los Angeles, CA
Indianapolis Motor Speedway (IMS) H of F	Indianapolis, IN
International Boxing H of F	Canastota, NY
International Motorsports H of F	Talledega, AL
International Swimming H of F	Fort Lauderdale, FL
International (formerly National Lawn) Tennis H of F	Newport, RI
International Women's Sports (formerly Women's Sport Foundation) H of F	New York, NY
Jockey's H of F	Baltimore, MD
Ladies Professional Golfers Association (LPGA) H of F	Sugar Land, TX
Motorsports H of F of America	Novi, MI
Naismith Memorial Basketball H of F	Springfield, MA
National Baseball H of F and Museum	Cooperstown, NY
National Bowling H of F	St. Louis, MO
National Football Foundation (NFF College) Football H of F and Museum	South Bend, IN
National Museum of Racing (NMR) H of F	Saratoga Springs, NY
National Sportscasters and Sportswriters (NASS) H of F	Salisbury, NC
National Track and Field (NTF) H of F	Indianapolis, IN
National Wrestling H of F	Colorado Springs, CO
Professional Bowlers Association (PBA) H of F	Akron, OH
Pro Football H of F	Canton, OH

Professional Golfers Association (PGA, World Golf) H of F	Pinehurst, NC
U.S. Figure Skating H of F	Colorado Springs, CO
U.S. Hockey H of F	Eveleth, MN
U.S. Olympic H of F	Colorado Springs, CO
U.S. Speed Skating H of F	Newburgh, NY
U.S. Track and Field H of F	Angola, IN
Women's International Bowling Congress (WIBC) H of F	Greendale, WI

Appendix 7
Sites of Olympic Games

The following lists the sites of the modern Olympic Games.

SUMMER OLYMPIC GAMES THROUGH 1992

Year	Location
1896	Athens, Greece
1900	Paris, France
1904	St. Louis, MO, U.S.
1906*	Athens, Greece
1908	London, England
1912	Stockholm, Sweden
1920	Antwerp, Belgium
1924	Paris, France
1928	Amsterdam, The Netherlands
1932	Los Angeles, CA, U.S.
1936	Berlin, Germany
1948	London, England
1952	Helsinki, Finland
1956	Melbourne, Australia
1960	Rome, Italy
1964	Tokyo, Japan

*The 1906 games were not recognized by the International Olympic Committee. The 1916, 1940, and 1944 games were not held. The 1980 Summer Games were boycotted by 62 nations, including the United States. The 1984 Summer Games were boycotted by the USSR and most Eastern Bloc nations.

1968	Mexico City, Mexico
1972	Munich, Germany
1976	Montreal, Canada
1980	Moscow, USSR
1984	Los Angeles, CA, U.S.
1988	Seoul, South Korea
1992	Barcelona, Spain

WINTER OLYMPIC GAMES THROUGH 1994

Year	Location
1924	Chamonix, France
1928	St. Moritz, Switzerland
1932	Lake Placid, NY, U.S.
1936*	Garmisch-Partenkirchen, Germany
1948	St. Moritz, Switzerland
1952	Oslo, Norway
1956	Cortina d'Ampezzo, Italy
1960	Squaw Valley, CA, U.S.
1964	Innsbruck, Austria
1968	Grenoble, France
1972	Sapporo, Japan
1976	Innsbruck, Austria
1980	Lake Placid, NY, U.S.
1984	Sarajevo, Yugoslavia
1988	Calgary, Canada
1992	Albertville, France
1994	Lillehammer, Norway

*The 1940 and 1944 games were not held.

Index

Note: The locations of main entries in the dictionary are indicated in the index by *italic* page numbers.

Contributors

Charlene E. Agne-Traub, Assistant Professor of Physical Education, Howard University, Washington, DC.

William E. Akin, Professor of History and Dean, Ursinus College, Collegeville, PA.

Sheldon L. Appleton, Professor of Political Science, Oakland University, Rochester, MI.

Frederick J. Augustyn, Jr., Subject Cataloger of Economics and Political Science, Library of Congress, Washington, DC.

C. Robert Barnett, Professor of Physical Education, Marshall University, Huntington, WV.

June Wuest Becht, freelance writer, resides in St. Louis, MO.

Carl M. Becker, Professor of History, Wright State University, Dayton, OH.

Gaymon L. Bennett, Professor and Chairman, Department of English, Northwest Nazarene College, Nampa, ID.

David Bernstein, Professor of History, California State University, Long Beach, CA.

Lowell L. Blaisdell, Professor Emeritus of History, Texas Tech University, lives in Denton, TX.

William A. Borst, freelance writer, radio host, and Adjunct Professor, Webster University, resides in St. Louis, MO.

Robert T. Bowen, Jr., Professor Emeritus of Physical Education, University of Georgia, lives in Athens, GA.

Frank P. Bowles, retired Associate Professor of English, University of Northern Colorado, Greeley, CO.

Jack C. Braun, Associate Professor of History, Edinboro University, Edinboro, PA.

Robert J. Brown, Associate Professor of History and Political Science, Rochester Institute of Technology, Rochester, NY.

Ian Buchanan, director of a reinsurance company, President, International Society for Olympic Historians, and freelance writer, lives in Norfolk, England.

Brian S. Butler, Department of History, University of Nebraska, Lincoln, NE.

Robert L. Cannon, freelance writer, resides in Santa Monica, CA.

Stan W. Carlson, freelance writer, editor, and publisher, lives in Minneapolis, MN.

Robert N. "Bob" Carroll, freelance writer and Editor, *Coffin Corner*, resides in North Huntingdon, PA.

Peter Cava, Press Information Director, USA Track & Field, Indianapolis, IN.

Dennis S. Clark, Instructor, Alternative Secondary Program, Lane Community College, Eugene, OR, and Ph.D. candidate, Educational Policy and Management, University of Oregon, Eugene, OR.

Scott A.G.M. Crawford, Associate Professor of Physical Education, Eastern Illinois University, Charleston, IL.

L. Robert Davids, retired federal government public affairs officer and founder, Society for American Baseball Research, lives in Washington, DC.

Bruce J. Dierenfield, Associate Professor of History, Canisius College, Buffalo, NY.

Robert T. Epling, graduate student, Department of Human Performance and Sport Studies, University of Tennessee, Knoxville, TN.

John L. Evers, retired high school teacher and administrator, resides in Carmi, IL.

Raymond C. Fetters, graduate student, U.S. Sports Academy, lives in Naperville, IL.

John E. Findling, Professor of History, Indiana University Southeast, New Albany, IN.

Gerald R. Gems, Chair, Department of Health and Physical Education, North Central College, Naperville, IL.

Larry R. Gerlach, Professor of History, University of Utah, Salt Lake City, UT, Associate Editor, *American National Biography*, and freelance writer.

James N. Giglio, Professor of History, Southwest Missouri State University, Springfield, MO, and freelance writer.

Daniel R. Gilbert, Professor Emeritus of History, Archivist, Moravian College, Bethlehem, PA.

Horace R. Givens, Professor of Business Administration, University of Maine, Orono, ME.

Roger A. Godin, Curator, U.S. Army Ordnance Museum, Aberdeen Proving Ground, resides in Bel Air, MD.

John L. Godwin, Instructor of History, Wingate College, Wingate, NC.

Richard Gonsalves, freelance writer, lives in Gloucester, MA.

Ralph S. Graber, retired Professor of English, Muhlenberg College, Allentown, PA.

Lloyd J. Graybar, Professor of History, Eastern Kentucky University, Richmond, KY.

Stanley Grosshandler, physician and freelance writer, resides in Raleigh, NC.

Adolph H. Grundman, Professor of History, Metropolitan State College, Denver, CO.

Allan Hall, Athletic Director, Department of Athletics, Ashland College, Ashland, OH.

John Hanners, Professor, Chair, Department of Communication and Theatre, East Texas State University, Commerce, TX.

James W. Harper, Associate Professor of History, Texas Tech University, Lubbock, TX.

John Hillman, certified public accountant and lecturer, Department of Accounting, Southwest Texas State University, lives in Waco, TX.

George W. Hilton, Professor Emeritus of Economics, University of California, Los Angeles, resides in Columbia, MD.

Adam R. Hornbuckle, researcher, History Associates Incorporated, The Historical Montrose School, Rockville, MD, and freelance writer, lives in Alexandria, VA.

Louis E. Hunsinger, Jr., freelance writer, resides in Williamsport, PA.

John R. Husman, maintenance manager, lives in Sylvania, OH.

Frederick Ivor-Campbell, freelance writer and historian, resides in Warren, RI.

Merl F. Kleinknecht, U.S. Postal Service employee, lives in Galion, OH.

Raymond D. Kush, software documentation supervisor, resides in Minneapolis, MN.

Jay Langhammer, Sales Manager, Freeman Exhibit Company, freelance writer, and sports editor of fraternity magazines, lives in Fort Worth, TX.

Brian L. Laughlin, student, Creighton University Law School, resides in Omaha, NE.

Larry Lester, historian and freelance writer, lives in Kansas City, MO.

Erik S. Lunde, Professor of American Thought and Language, Michigan State University, East Lansing, MI.

Arthur F. McClure, Professor, Chairman, Department of History and Anthropology, Central Missouri State University, Warrensburg, MO.

Bill Mallon, physician, Secretary General, International Society of Olympic Historians, and freelance writer, resides in Durham, NC.

Marc S. Maltby, Associate Professor of History, Owensboro Community College, Owensboro, KY.

Curtice R. Mang, insurance underwriter, lives in Phoenix, AZ.

David S. Matz, Associate Professor of Humanities, University of Pittsburgh at Bradford, Bradford, PA.

William J. Miller, retired Associate Professor of History, St. Louis University, St. Louis, MO.

Douglas A. Noverr, Professor of American Thought and Language, Michigan State University, East Lansing, MI.

Frank J. Olmsted, Theology teacher, De Smet Jesuit High School, St. Louis, MO.

Edward J. Pavlick, freelance writer, resides in Milwaukee, WI.

Frank V. Phelps, freelance writer, resides in King of Prussia, PA.

David L. Porter, Shangle Professor of History, William Penn College, Oskaloosa, IA, Associate Editor, *American National Biography*, and freelance writer.

Susan J. Rayl, Instructor of Physical Education, Iowa State University, Ames, IA.

Samuel O. Regalado, Associate Professor of History, California State University, Stanislaus, Turlock, CA.

James A. Riley, teacher and freelance writer, lives in Rockledge, FL.

John Robertson, freelance writer and member, International Boxing Research Organization, resides in Cambridge, Canada.

John P. Rossi, Professor of History, LaSalle University, Philadelphia, PA.

Steven P. Savage, Professor, Department of Anthropology, Sociology, and Social Work, Eastern Kentucky University, Richmond, KY.

Lee E. Scanlon, Associate Professor, Department of Communicative Arts and Sciences, Eastern New Mexico University, Portales, NM, sports announcer, and freelance writer.

Miriam F. Shelden, Professor of Physical Education, University of South Carolina at Spartanburg, Spartanburg, SC.

William M. Simons, Associate Professor of History, State University College, Oneonta, NY.

Duane A. Smith, Professor of History, Fort Lewis College, Durango, CO, and freelance writer.

Luther W. Spoehr, history teacher, Lincoln School, and freelance writer, resides in Barrington, RI.

A. D. Suehsdorf, freelance writer and retired editor, lives in Sonoma, CA.

Jim L. Sumner, Historian, North Carolina State Historical Preservation Office, Raleigh, NC.

Marcia G. Synnott, Associate Professor of History, University of South Carolina, Columbia, SC.

Frank W. Thackeray, Professor of History, Indiana University Southeast, New Albany, IN.

Robert B. Van Atta, freelance writer and history editor, Greensburg *Tribune Review*, resides in Greensburg, PA.

David Quentin Voigt, freelance writer and Professor of Sociology and Anthropology, Albright College, Reading, PA.

James E. Welch, Associate Professor of Business Administration, Human Resource Management, and Industrial Relations, Kentucky Wesleyan College, Owensboro, KY.

James D. Whalen, freelance writer, lives in Dayton, OH.

Thomas P. Wolf, Dean of Social Sciences and Professor of Political Science, Indiana University Southeast, New Albany, IN.

John H. Ziegler, Professor, English, Film, and Humanities, Cochise College, Sierra Vista, AZ, and freelance writer.

ISBN 0-313-28431-8

90000>

HARDCOVER BAR CODE